THE BOOK OF AMERICA

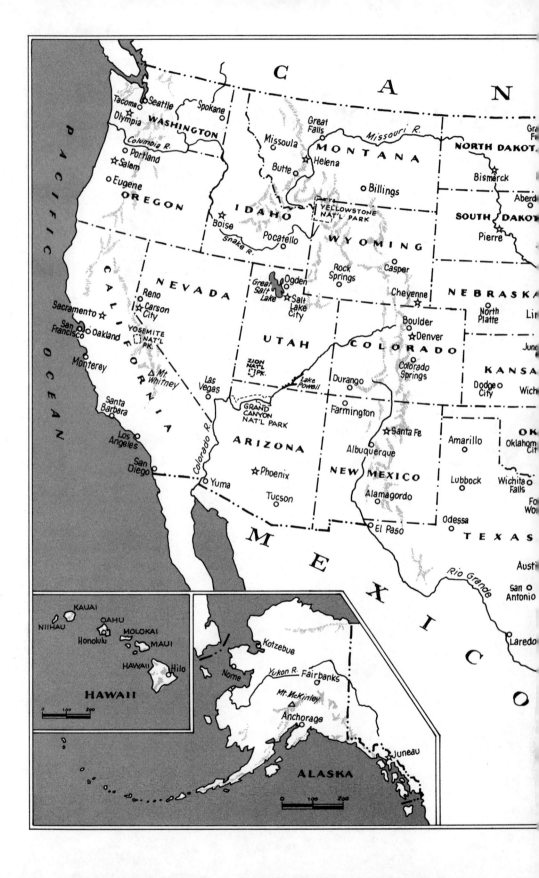

THE UNITED STATES
OF AMERICA

0   100   200   300

MILES

THE BOOK OF
AMERICA
Inside 50 States Today

NEAL R. PEIRCE

AND

JERRY HAGSTROM

W·W·NORTON & COMPANY

New York·London

COPYRIGHT © 1983 BY NEAL R. PEIRCE AND JERRY HAGSTROM
ALL RIGHTS RESERVED.
PUBLISHED SIMULTANEOUSLY IN CANADA BY GEORGE J. MCLEOD LIMITED, TORONTO.
PRINTED IN THE UNITED STATES OF AMERICA.

THE TEXT OF THIS BOOK IS COMPOSED IN 10/12 POINT JANSON ALTERNATE, WITH DISPLAY TYPE
SET IN BEMBO. COMPOSITION AND MANUFACTURING BY THE HADDON CRAFTSMEN, INC.
BOOK DESIGN BY MARGARET M. WAGNER. CARTOGRAPHY BY JACQUES CHAZAUD

LIBRARY OF CONGRESS CATALOGING IN PUBLICATION DATA

PEIRCE, NEAL R.
THE BOOK OF AMERICA.

BIBLIOGRAPHY: P.
INCLUDES INDEX.
I. UNITED STATES—SOCIAL CONDITIONS—1970-
2. UNITED STATES—ECONOMIC CONDITIONS—1971-
3. UNITED STATES—POLITICS AND GOVERNMENT—1981-
I. HAGSTROM, JERRY. II. TITLE.
HN59.2.P44 1983   973.92   82-24642

ISBN 0-393-01639-0

W. W. NORTON & COMPANY, INC.,
500 FIFTH AVENUE, NEW YORK, N.Y. 10110
W. W. NORTON & COMPANY LTD.,
37 GREAT RUSSELL STREET, LONDON WCIB 3NU

5 6 7 8 9 0

For our editor and friend,
Evan W. Thomas II,
Whose will made this book be

Contents

A regional map appears at the beginning of each section. City maps are located as follows: New York City, p. 49; Washington, D.C., p. 147; and Los Angeles, p. 801. State maps are included for Alaska, p. 853, and Hawaii, p. 863.

STATES IN ALPHABETICAL ORDER

CONTENTS

Foreword

THIS BOOK OF AMERICA grew out of years of travels through the 50 states of the United States, to all of the great cities of the land, to suburbs and villages beyond numbering. In it we view the nation, its states and regions, from the perspective of the early 1980s, a decade in which the states, the cities, towns, and neighborhoods of the nation have become the turf from which significant renewal of American society must come.

The roots of this project go back much further, however, to the late 1960s and the idea that the time was ripe for a modern-day sequel to John Gunther's *Inside U.S.A.*, researched during World War II and published in 1947. Before Gunther died, he was consulted about a new book, recognized its need, and gave us, as he put it, his "good luck signal." There followed not just one book but nine, reflecting our fascination with the infinite variety of modern-day America, in every field from politics to ethnic complexion, from great city dynamics to small-town life to questions of the economy and the environment. Those books, to which the reader interested in greater detail and especially historical and political detail may wish to turn, began in 1972 with *The Megastates of America*, treating the 10 most heavily populated states, and then continued up through 1980 with eight regional volumes: *The Pacific States of America*, *The Mountain States of America*, *The Great Plains States of America*, *The Deep South States of America*, *The Border South States*, *The New England States*, *The Mid-Atlantic States of America*, and *The Great Lakes States of America*. In the latter two books, Michael Barone and John Keefe, respectively, joined Neal Peirce as co-authors.

To prepare *The Book of America*, Peirce and co-author Jerry Hagstrom, his longtime associate and *National Journal* colleague, again traversed the United States to take the pulse of the states and cities in the '80s. Many others helped in the enterprise. In addition to the work of Michael Barone and John Keefe, reflected in many of these pages, there was substantial editorial assistance from Carol Steinbach, Robert Guskind, Jane Denison, George Horvath, Stephen Farber, Alice Porter, Steven Forrester, Brian Sullam, Fred Jordan, William Anderson, and Martin Kohout. Reporter-researchers included George Hatch, Roger Fillion, Erin Ann MacLellan, Jay Hamilton, Calvin Troup, Patricia Leitner, Wade Atkinson, and Peter Choharis. Several *National Journal* colleagues, among them Richard Cohen, Linda Fowlie, and James Morse, offered invaluable assistance.

Without the caring and dogged insistence of senior editor Evan W. Thomas, of W.W. Norton, and his associate, Rose Franco, whose unflagging support covered no less than a decade and a half, this book would never have come to fruition. We also extend our thanks to Star Lawrence, our editor after Evan Thomas' retirement.

Beyond all of these, there are the literally thousands of Americans, in 50 states and the District of Columbia, who offered their time and wisdom to this book—in every way from casual conversations to lengthy interviews to reading and criticizing our state manuscripts. To great degree, it is through these Americans' eyes that we viewed the United States in our times. Our debt to them is beyond measure.

NEAL R. PEIRCE
JERRY HAGSTROM

THE BOOK OF AMERICA

Introduction

COMMONPLACE IT IS TO VIEW all of the United States as a monolith—one culture, one citizenry, one mass market. The homogenizing forces in American life—evidenced on every front from standardized television to eroded regional accents, from national banking to the appalling sameness of cookie-cutter Holiday Inns and McDonald stands—have brought us to that point.

This book asserts a contrary theme, that however real the nationalizing and leveling power of mass communications, of centralized government and corporate power, each of the 50 states remains a unique blend of history and peoples and economy and politics and natural environment, unduplicated on this continent or anywhere in the world. To experience the world of Massachusetts or Texas, of Vermont or Arizona, of Florida or Oregon, is to live and move in strikingly different places. We have traveled to each of these states, some many times, to inquire of their growth over time, the geography, the ethnic and racial groups, the factories and farming and universities, the worlds of business, labor, the arts and communications. Everywhere we have sought to determine which people and groups hold the reins of power, what forces set the tone of politics and public life. Our constant search has been for those threads of individuality that set this state (or great city or great region) apart from the rest of America. This book is an account, as frank and honest as we could render, of what we discovered in these incredibly diverse United States of America.

Before we proceed to our fine-line drawing of the states, we propose some broad brush strokes as backdrop. We found this a nation that inspires—even in times of economic reversal, even as its international spheres of influence are challenged—little less than awe. The "greatness of America" so often extolled by politicians is not altogether myth. The inquisitive traveler will find it in the sweep and drama of natural America, in the energy that surges through the country's labyrinthine economic machine, and above all in the people in their infinite variety of ethnic backgrounds, their openness and freshness of spirit.

A Post-Federal Era

We concluded our 50-state odyssey sensing a vital turn by Americans to resources close at home, in their own communities, including state and local governments, for the solution of problems. Americans' faith in national government action had been deeply shaken. Few people doubted that a boldly assertive national government had rescued the nation from the Great Depression of the 1930s, had led to victory in World War II, had indeed been central to the country's gigantic steps toward a society at once more affluent, more socially equitable, better educated, more mobile.

Plagued by inflation, increased international competition, and the need to incorporate a huge, postwar "baby boom" generation into the work force, Washington policymakers found it impossible to maintain the full employment and rising standard of living to which most Americans had become accustomed since World War II. After the U.S. government financed much of its involvement in the disastrous Vietnam War by borrowing money rather than raising taxes, inflation seemed insoluble—until it shattered on the rocks of a deep national recession in the early 1980s.

On social policy, the federal government's plate was too full. It had taken on not just the bill for a welfare state of proportions scarcely dreamed of in prior times, ranging from Social Security and food stamps to medical care for the aged and needy, but also gargantuan obligations for national defense and paying the interest on a fast-mounting national debt. A "do-good" Congress had thrust Washington into such wildly disparate and appropriately local matters as rural fire protection, carpool demonstrations, remedial reading programs, and jellyfish control in the Chesapeake Bay. Although on specific issues—environmental protection, for example, or maintaining Social Security—Americans remained committed to a strong national role, the sheer weight of the federal presence was taking its toll in public patience. More and more people questioned whether federal programs (however noble their intentions) could possibly apply well in tens of thousands of communities of a continent-sized, highly variegated nation. They were sensing a disturbing loss of control over their own lives and communal fortunes. A strong counter-reaction to national dominance was building well before the political advent of the president who seemed to symbolize a new, post-federal era in American life—Ronald Reagan.

But if Americans in the '80s were to turn to their state and local governments for answers to economic and social problems, would those governments be able to do the job? Could the states and localities play a serious role in an increasingly international economy in which capital, goods, and services moved quickly about the world? Would the grassroots governments now move to meet social needs as they had refused to, or been fiscally incapable of doing, in earlier times (thus propelling the federal government into many service areas in the first instance)? The questions, however acute, did not have ready answers. We found the state and local governments of the early '80s to be a very mixed bag: some dull and quiescent, some progressive, some highly capable, others of mediocre capacity, some impeccably honest, others wracked by patterns of corruption rooted deeply in their historic development. Yet in the aggregate, we think it fair to say that America's "subnational" governments, on every front from professional competence to broad-based revenue-raising capacity, had progressed by light years in the generation since World War II. And it was precisely in economic strategizing—encouraging growth industries, tapping such new capital sources as pension funds, fostering small business start-ups, and reaching out to new international markets—that states from New York to North Carolina to California were making their most dramatic advances.

Against that, several negatives were operating: the trend toward "nationalized" banking siphoning capital into money funds and reducing investment funds available in regional and local banks, the onslaught of national chain stores and voracious shopping malls imperiling Main Streets and even the most efficient local retailers. Simultaneously came the broad economic revolution accompanying the introduction of high technology. Entire industries (and by proxy the areas in which they operate) were facing massive changes as production lines became "robotized," elementary manufacturing migrated overseas, and offices were transformed by the personal computer. The percentage of the U.S. work force in manufacturing, 22 percent in the early '80s, was projected to drop to less than 10 percent by the mid-1990s. We saw the regions of America reacting quite differently to radically changed economic futures, depending on their particular cultures. High technology, for example, was literally born in such states as California and Massachusetts, where great institutions of learning incubated it; then it spread into surrounding states—New Hampshire in the Massachusetts orbit, for instance. But high-tech has also bounced to the New York City suburbs, North Carolina, Colorado, Texas, Arizona, Minnesota, and Florida—all places where a fine school of engineering (often state-related) allows professionals to keep up with changes in their fields and provides a ready source of graduates. Other drawing cards—all in the control of state and local officials—are the level of personal taxes (preferably low, of course), good schools, high culture, and protection of the natural environment. As entire industries faced "robotization" of their production lines in order to keep product prices competitive with those made in other countries, and high technology promised to develop products literally unknown a few years earlier, the states would hold enormous power to affect company location decisions and modernize the curricula of universities and elementary and secondary schools. Sadly the most resistant to change were the Midwestern states, where even in the depression of the '80s many leaders in both management and labor seemed to imagine they could continue their old adversarial ways and regain their lost prosperity without fundamental readjustments.

At the same time, the nation seemed to be moving into a new period of entrepreneurship as the "baby boom" generation of the '40s to '60s found the path up the corporate ladder blocked by older people and too much competition from their own peers. Once again, this seemed an area in which state and local governments could have dramatic effect on the rate of small-business formation through their regulatory and tax policies, and by the degree they encouraged local financial institutions to foster creativity and risk taking.

On the social side, the question appeared to be, if Washington was to play a dramatically reduced role, would the voters allow their state and local governments to pick up the slack? The revolt against high taxation and spending had not been limited to the national level. From the mid-1970s onward a blistering backlash developed against the escalating state and local budgets that had expanded along with—and often been propelled by—the explosion of federal programs. For year after year, state and local government had been the fastest-expanding segment of the national economy. The first warning bell came with New York City's fiscal collapse and near-bankruptcy in 1975, a sure sign—as New York's Governor Hugh Carey put it at that time —that "the days of wine and roses" were over. Then, in 1978, came an even greater tidal wave in state and local affairs: California's passage of its fiercely restrictive Proposition 13. But that vote was not alone. In all, 23 states enacted some form of budget cap or taxing limitation during the 1970s. The 1980 vote passing Massachusetts' tough-as-nails Proposition 2 1/2, cutting the heart out of the property tax in a state so traditionally free spending it had been dubbed "Taxachusetts," was a sure sign that the taxpayers' revolt would remain a vibrant force in the '80s. In one sense, the election of Ronald Reagan and of a Republican Senate simply ratified nationally the cutback revolution already abundantly clear in state and local government.

The 1982 congressional and gubernatorial elections gave more power to the Democrats. But not even a Democratic president in the '80s would necessarily signal a return to the big government growth period of the postwar decades.

States, Cities, Governors, Mayors

Clear through the 1940s, the states of the American Union were burdened with antique constitutions, fragmented executive structures in which governors were often figureheads, and grossly malapportioned and unprofessional legislatures. Then, reaching its zenith in the '60s and '70s, came the dramatic federal court orders forcing "one man, one vote" representation, ending the centuries-old domination of state governments by rural interests, and the "quiet revolution," centered on new constitutions, wider authority for governors, cabinet-style executive branch organizations, and professionally staffed state legislatures. By the early '80s most states had highly professional bureaucracies. Nor were the states fiscal weak sisters any more. The taxpayer revolts notwithstanding, virtually all had enacted high-yielding, broad-based taxes on sales and/or individuals' incomes.

Power had shifted, too: no longer was Maine in the palm of the hand of pulp and paper interests, Montana the wholly owned subsidiary of Anacadona Copper, Florida controlled by a regressive and narrow-minded "pork chop gang" of rural legislators, Pennsylvania a manipulated satrapy of U.S. Steel and the Pennsylvania Railroad. The "Barnwell Ring" of Low Country rural legislators Edgar Brown and Solomon Blatt, who for 30 years controlled the South Carolina legislature for the benefit of planters, textile firms, utilities, and banks, was no longer. Even perennially colonized West Virginia had begun to shake the total control of the coal companies. In most states, power came to be dispersed among a host of hotly competing private lobbies, town and city interests, teachers, and in some states, environmental and public interest lobbies. In some states vestiges of reaction were hard to shake. In 1982 Florida House Speaker Ralph Haben could comment with impunity: "The poor don't represent an active constituency. It's easier to cut social services. That same year, the Mississippi Legislature established public school kindergartens for the first time in the state's history. But it financed them by a sales tax boost rather than raising taxes on a powerful minerals industry.

The new political dynamic of the '80s made it unlikely, however, that such attitudes would persist, in unmitigated form, through the decade. There were bands of progressives in every legislature. As state legislatures gained control over more and more federally initiated programs during the '80s, it was likely that lobbies for blacks, Hispanics, the poor and disadvantaged would transfer more and more of their efforts there and away from the fiscally paralyzed national government. And women were coming on strong in the state legislatures. They tripled their number, from 4.5 percent of all seats in 1972 to 13 percent a decade later, and were still growing—even while the number of women in Congress (4.3 percent of combined Senate and House membership) showed virtually zero progress. With their chief power base in state and local government, women might well have more substantive power under New Federalism than a highly centralized system. Some women, such as Cleta Deatherage, youthful chairman of the Oklahoma House appropriations and budget committees, had risen to posts of substantive power. And while women legislators normally split along partisan lines, they tended—perhaps because of their special concern for families, education, health, and children —to be more progressive on human service issues.

As for the governors, there had been a distinct fading of the breed so aptly depicted as "good-time Charlies" by political scientist Larry Sabato. The glad-handing, intellectually vacuous, administratively inept breed that populated governors' conferences until the late '60s faded in favor of generally younger, more incisive, better educated, manager-type executives. Among the more outstanding of them in the 1970s and early '80s were Dan Evans of Washington (first man to galvanize the nation's governors into an effective force on federal system questions), William Milliken of Michigan, Jerry Brown of California, Reubin Askew of Florida, Dick Thornburgh of Pennsylvania, Michael Dukakis of Massachusetts, Richard Snelling of Vermont, George Busbee of Georgia, Scott Matheson of Utah, Richard Lamm of Colorado, Tom McCall of Oregon, Cecil Andrus of Idaho, Hugh Carey of New York, and Bruce Babbitt of Arizona. Occasionally some turkeys cropped up on the gubernatorial farm, the ilk of James Rhodes, the listless leader but canny politician elected no less than four times as governor of Ohio, or Dolph Briscoe, the remote, imperious, do-nothing chief executive of Texas during the '70s. A few governors eventually became residents, rather than supervisors, of prisons—for example, Tennessee's Ray Blanton, suspected of selling paroles and initially convicted of selling liquor licenses. Ironically, one of the best individual governors of the last decades, Marvin Mandel of Maryland, ended up in prison—led astray by the corrupt political ways of a state he otherwise served with considerable distinction.

In the great cities, the glamorous John Lindsay variety of "hero mayor" of the '60s was a forgotten commodity by the '80s. Gone too was the strong-arm model of Mayor Richard Daley of Chicago. (Boston's Kevin White started to emulate Daley's patronage tactics in the late '70's—only to find his once-clean image tarnished in the process.) Perhaps the last hero mayor had been Neil Goldschmidt of Portland, who used federal aid—and a superb sense of timing and priorities—to make his West Coast city one of America's most progressive during the '70s. There were some colorful personalities on the mayoral scene—the likes of New York's Edward Koch and Milwaukee's perennial leader, Henry Maier. But management and entrepreneurial talent were the prime requisites of the '80s. With the great growth era of federal aid a matter of history and the cities fighting to stem off ever-deeper national aid cuts, the focus turned to cool and capable "cutback" skills and a capacity to achieve "more with less." Among the more popular methods were rigorous and ongoing review of expenditures, enlisting the private sector to lend executive talent and join in development partnerships, tough negotiations with the public employee unions (which no longer looked ten feet tall in the altered political climate of the '80s), and selective contracting out of services previously performed by civil service bureaucracies. The big city mayors proving most adept at the requisite new skills were of all parties, sexes, and races, among them George Voinovich of Cleveland, Coleman Young of Detroit, Dutch Morial of New Orleans, William Donald Schaeffer of Baltimore, Dianne Feinstein of San Francisco, Tom Moody of Columbus, and William Hudnut of Indianapolis. Strategies to attract high-technology industry moved onto mayors' agendas, with San Antonio's Henry Cisneros setting a model others would likely emulate.

Cities, Suburbs, and the Return to the Country

America's cities faced a fearsome set of problems at the dawn of the 1980s. Most, over the course of the two preceding decades, had become dangerously dependent on Washington: "federal aid junkies," as it were. The early '80s saw cities suffering intense withdrawal pains as the tourniquet was tightened to stop their mainline aid. Since the late '70s, many had experienced a precipitous drop in their bond ratings—followed by sharply increased borrowing costs. Many were dangerously delaying their outlays for essential maintenance of their physical infrastructure, from streets and bridges to prisons and water systems. Most major transit systems were years behind in their maintenance schedules, many burdened with grossly overgenerous labor agreements. To all of that one could add the generally gloomy condition of the urban schools, plus an alarming rise of illegitimacies and single-parent families, especially among minorities, virtually assuring higher rates of school failure, juvenile delinquency, and general social disintegration in years to come. Most cities were already afflicted by high crime rates and appallingly high rates of unemployment among youths, with all the human waste and societal tension that stems from idle and poverty-afflicted young lives.

Paradoxically, a strong urban revival had already been underway in America since the mid-1970s. The center city in the early '80s was a substantially more hopeful place than it had been in the early '70s. Exhibit No. 1 was a phenomenal nationwide center-city office boom, catering to corporate offices and specialized services ranging from law to financial houses. There was talk of a totally decentralized future, in which employees remained in their homes working at computer terminals and rarely darkening an office door—yet it would be, if ever, a future still quite a ways in the offing. Exhibit No. 2 lay in revived neighborhoods, blue and white collar alike. For many young professionals, the city feared and fled in the early '70s had become the "chic" place to be a decade later. Not just the restoration of old center-city homes, but construction of major downtown residential neighborhoods was booming. And smaller, more affluent, longer-single and sooner-divorced households seemed likely to provide cities with an ample share of population for years to come. We found some hyperbole in the prediction of developer James Rouse that "the forces now favorable to the inner city are as massive in number and content and power as those that forced the suburban explosion of the '50s and '60s." But Rouse had proven many a cynic wrong before with the surprise successes of his "festival marketplaces" in Boston, Baltimore, Philadelphia, and Milwaukee. The cities doing best were those advertising themselves not as welfare reservations but rather as places of revival, growth, and immense promise, the linchpins of their states' economies, centers of high finance, the beacons of tourism and conventions and port trade, as centers of the lively arts and sports and good eating and just enough sin to be fun.

Nor was it any accident that so many cities—even in the face of immense disabilities—were refusing to become the disaster zones many "experts" had predicted would be their fate. In Baltimore, in Chicago, in Philadelphia and Denver and San Francisco, in Niagara Falls, N.Y., Roanoke, Va., Dallas, San Diego, Pittsburgh, and literally hundreds of communities large and small, the business community had upgraded the extent and quality of its involvement with city governments, both in management counseling and in helping to plan, finance, and execute large developments, both public and commercial (and often a mix of the two). In Denver, the business community contracted to "manage" the retail-commercial-street area around the new downtown transit mall, and, on its own, to promote inner-city housing and historic preservation and cooperative ties (rather than the familiar tensions) with close-in neighborhoods. Going to bat for embattled Detroit and Cleveland, major corporations lobbied on their behalf before indifferent state legislatures, winning crucial financial concessions. By the early '80s, led by the insurance and oil industries, a number of corporations were moving community relations to the mainstream of corporate strategic planning.

A strong renewal of corporate interest in cities was not only welcome but long overdue. When John Gunther surveyed America for his *Inside U.S.A.* at the end of World War II, he was often able to identify one or at most a handful of great family-owned corporate powers dominating a given city. Three decades later, we found power far more dispersed—among business groups, pension portfolio managers, varying political camps, even neighborhood organizations. Democracy was the winner, most vividly so in cities such as Columbus, Ohio, where a single family's dominance had been deeply oppressive. Cities paid a heavy price, however, when a large number of their home-grown, home-developed firms were sold off to conglomerates. All too often, such sell-outs were just a first step toward disastrous job losses or total plant shutdowns. Just as serious, cities lost vital civic leadership, be it for United Funds, downtown renewals, museums and civic centers, manpower programs for the disadvantaged, or practically any project requiring broad community leadership. Branch plant managers, urbanologist Norton Long commented, often show no more concern for the cities in which they operate "than a United Fruit Company representative in a banana republic." But cities jealously guarding their major corporations against outside takeover—Minneapolis-St. Paul, for example—have exhibited extraordinary civic resilience.

Another peril for cities was "megastructure blight": huge new office or hotel monoliths of concrete and glass and steel, cold and repelling to pedestrians at street level, soaring skyward on a scale hostile to the city's existing tone and architectural texture. In cities such as Atlanta, megastructures so inflated the price of nearby land parcels that they created a ghostly (and dangerous) strip of parking lots and porno shops about them. A welcome countertrend did set in during the '70s—a burst of sensitivity to issues of historic preservation and a newborn consciousness about the plazas, streets, buildings, and neighborhoods of the American city. Not for a century and a half, for instance, had the nation's city waterfronts—so long abused with factories and tenements, abandoned railway lines and rotting piers—been the subject of such thoughtful and sustained attention. By the early '80s there was a degree of waterfront revival—in handsome new retailing and restaurant complexes, in civic centers, marinas, waterfront parks, and walkways—that would have been considered a pipedream a decade before. Among premier cities in waterfront revival were such far-flung places as Memphis and Boston, Seattle and Savannah, Portland (Maine) and Portland (Oregon).

Another urban "plus" has been the self-help movement sweeping through city neighborhoods since the early '70s. In such places as St. Louis' black Jeff Vanderlou area, the Portuguese Ironbound section of Newark, Chicago's Woodlawn area, Baltimore's SECO (South East Community Organization) section, in Cincinnati's Mt. Auburn and Cleveland's Buckeye and Memphis' Greenlaw area and even the devastated South Bronx, a new message came through: that neighborhoods organized through cooperative self-help can significantly affect the security, the housing, the employment, the health, and the self-respect of their inhabitants. Community development corporations, neighborhood citizen security patrols, sweat equity housing, and gardening and energy conservation experiments, all have flourished beyond expectation.

Some benefitted from federal grants and were imperiled when those funds sloughed off in the early '80s. But the strongest groups found ways to make valuable new alliances—with business, church, university, and historic preservation groups, for example—and prosper anyway.

It was easy to despair that there were not "enough" strong self-help organizations. An apparent *sine qua non* of such groups was strong leadership, and not every neighborhood was so lucky. But we found the self-help movement assuredly growing, well beyond the ken of the national media, across the U.S. cityscape and to lesser but discernible degree in suburban and rural areas as well. It represented a welcome antidote to the enervating politics of selfishness and entitlement psychology—the "it's owed to me" syndrome—that had spread rapidly and dangerously through America in the years of its comfortable postwar affluence. In times of fiscal stringency, of a shrinking rather than growing public wealth, of potential economic breakdown or dire energy shortages, the self-help movement represented not only one hope but a potential salvation for American society. Its direct counterpart and ally was found in citywide or statewide energy conservation plans (Minneapolis-St. Paul, Portland, Seattle, and the state of California were leading examples) and in the concept that local government leaders must be entrepreneurial and tough managers in times of scarce resources and citizen-forced tax cuts.

Nothing neighborhoods or cities might try to do for themselves could dim the reality of the tough conditions they faced. The 1980 Census found, for the first time, more poverty-stricken people in cities than in rural areas. Middle-class families, blue and white collar, began to flee the cities in the 1940s. Thirty years later, even middle-class black families were heading for the same suburban refuges. In the '70s alone, the population of New York declined by 10 percent; Cleveland, 24 percent; Philadelphia, 13 percent; Chicago, 11 percent. St. Louis lost 27 percent of its people in the '70s, shrinking to its population level of 1890. Cleveland and Detroit were slipping toward their World War I levels. While many Sunbelt cities grew through the '70s, those with restricted borders—Atlanta, Birmingham, San Francisco, Oakland, Seattle, and New Orleans, for example—declined in the manner of their Northeastern and Midwestern counterparts, albeit not as precipitously.

It was possible to envision a late-20th-century American city restricted to pockets of plenty beside pockets of poverty, the middle class evaporated into some suburban or exurban mist. There was concern that cities, always the great ports of entry and processing points for immigrant Americans and others at the bottom and striving to find a way up, might be so disabled by the flight of their tax-paying public, beset by such problems as broken down transit or even civil disorders, that they could no longer perform their historic function. Yet America's cities, their every problem notwithstanding, remained *the* places that the crucial decisions in the society were made, from academic to cultural to economic to political. The figure of speech of the glowing city on the hill disregarded what great cities always have been: not some embodiment of achieved perfection, but rather places of striving, growing, tension, defeat, recovery, the stages on which the heights and depths of the human condition are thrown into most vivid relief.

By most statistical measures, America's suburbs were places of grand success through the 1970s. They grew by 17 percent in that decade, perhaps a comedown from their phenomenal 27 percent growth in the '60s but still impressive enough. The average income of suburbanites—compared to city folk—continued to climb. By 1970 suburban growth had accelerated to such a degree that the typical resident of a metropolitan area didn't live in a center city; he or she was a suburbanite instead. Then, in 1975, came news that the typical suburbanite no longer depended on the center city for employment, that a majority of working suburbanites also worked in the suburbs. Around virtually every city in America, one could witness the incredible suburban growth of the last decades: not just infinities of tract housing, but office centers, strip development *ad nauseum*, and shopping centers by the thousands. Suburbia U.S.A. had not become a monolith, however: it ranged from settled close-in suburbs such as Chicago's Evanston or Los Angeles' Pasadena, dating back to World War I or earlier, to rough-and-ready subdivisions miles distant from center city. Super-heated real estate prices in California were forcing some workers to commute 100 miles or more a day. By the '80s, however, harsh economic reality was catching up with the American dream of the big free-standing single house, as it had a bit earlier with Detroit's gas guzzlers. Row houses, condominiums, and garden-style apartments were becoming the order of the day. And mobile homes—suddenly mutated into "manufactured housing"—accounted for an astounding 36 percent of all housing starts in America by 1981.

Nor was it difficult to foresee a more difficult future for Suburbia U.S.A. Many of the nation's older inner-ring suburbs were already experiencing the phenomena cities had faced for years: stagnant or declining populations, more low income, single and elderly residents, and municipal fiscal crises to match. The remainder of the century promised a marked "graying" of the suburbs, as the post–World War II suburban pioneers aged in place. The rising question became: would the suburbs be prepared to transport, feed, and care for the infirm among their aging population?

But what of rural America—all the farmlands and little towns and cities out beyond the metropolitan areas? From the beginning of the 20th century they had been declining in relative population as the nation's people deserted them for city life. But in the early '70s, an historic shift was suddenly noted. More people were moving *out* of metropolitan areas than *into* them. In time it was found that this was not simply a spillover of metropolitan population into counties just outside the metropolitan ring. The greatest growth was in the truly rural counties, far removed from metropolitan centers. They declined by 4 percent in the 1960s, but increased by 14 percent in the '70s. America had taken a fascinating turn: away from its great metropolitan migration of the century, back to the rural roots of its early history.

What impelled the change? Perhaps Americans' innate preference—revealed in polls for many years—for rural life. Many of the age-old scourges of rural life—mud roads and pellagra, isolation and brackish wells and grinding poverty—had disappeared. In their place came all-weather roads and access to interstates, adequate health services, electricity, telephones, radio, and television. Land was cheaper for starting new factories (an amazing 56 percent of all new manufacturing jobs in the '70s came in rural areas). A heady search began for energy in rural areas of Appalachia and the Mountain states, attracting new population. Retirees, made mobile by Social Security and private pensions, often headed for bucolic spots. And demographers discovered that the fastest-growing counties of America tended to be those with good climate, recreational opportunities, and attractive scenery.

Who were the new ruralites? A mixed bunch, without doubt. They included affluent part-time commuters, young professionals willing to take salary cuts for the attraction of country life, mining engineers, resort managers, artisans, unemployed idealists, and returning natives—even Southern-born blacks—deciding they'd prefer life at home to that in the city. One could find them everywhere, from the Ozarks of Missouri to Michigan's Upper Peninsula, from sun-drenched desert locations in New Mexico to little villages of northern New England.

What the new wave of rural folk was not was farmers, except for a few hobbyists said to have one foot in the manure pile and the other in the money market. In 1980, 2.7 percent of Americans lived on farms—down from 15.3 percent in 1950 and 30.1 percent in 1920. The rural areas were receiving people often quite urban—or at least suburban—in their lifestyles. One could see them from coast to coast, spreading out along country roads, causing a sprawly suburbanization that threatened to ruin the charm of many rural places. Nor was this, primarily, a romantic return to small-town life. Much of it seemed to be Americans seeking not so much community as the good life for one's self and immediate family by escaping the strains and hardships of modern society. The trend was so strong that it continued into the 1980s even as the pace of economic development slowed in already populous places.

North and East to West and South

Even more dramatic than the movement from city to suburb to quiet rural reaches was that fantastic interregional migration that seemed to have reached —but may not have—its apex in the 1970s. In that decade, just three states— Florida, Texas, and California—accounted for almost half (42 percent) of the United States' entire population gain of 23 million people. The South as a whole grew by 21 percent, the West by 24 percent, even while the Northeast squeaked through with a 0.5 percent increase, and the Midwest barely inched forward at 4 percent. New York and Rhode Island actually lost people. A number of entire metropolitan regions (not just center cities) lost population during the '70s, among them New York, Cleveland, Pittsburgh, St. Louis, and Boston. In contrast, Nevada grew by an extraordinary 63 percent (on top of 71 percent in the '60s), Arizona by 53 percent, Florida by 43 percent, Utah by

38 percent, Alaska by 32 percent, Colorado by 31 percent, Texas by 27 percent, South Carolina by 20 percent.

Political power flowed inexorably to match these shifts. Eastern and Midwestern states lost 35 seats in the U.S. House (and an equal number of presidential electoral votes) between 1950 and 1982, even while the South and West gained proportionately. A strong rightward tilt accompanied the shift, as the areas gaining population (and thus more congressional seats) proved to be those that voted most strongly for Republicans and conservatives, even while those growing the most slowly for the most part supported Democrats and liberals.

Not surprisingly, the storm flags of present loss and future peril were flying all across America's traditional Northeastern and Midwestern industrial heartland at the start of the '80s. A drumbeat of newspaper headlines drove home the message: "South Leads, Northeast Lags in New Living Standard Measure," "Energy to Foster Boom in the West," "Ohio Governor Urges New Taxes to Prevent 'Economic Disaster.' " And behind the headlines, equally grim trends were reported. During the '70s some million manufacturing jobs had been lost in the region stretching from the chemical plants of Wilmington and the factories of Baltimore to the steel mills of Pittsburgh and Youngstown, the rubber plants of Akron, and the auto plants of Dayton, Pontiac, and Flint. Aged plants, high union wages, decaying physical infrastructure, and bitter winters were all said to be part of the Frostbelt's dilemma. Many Northern cities were teetering on the edge of a financial abyss. Accelerating decontrol of oil and gas prices flooded the treasuries of such states as Texas, Alaska, Oklahoma and Louisiana with billions of dollars in severance taxes and royalty payments—a sum likely, by some estimates, to reach $120 billion during the 1980s. As a result, energy-rich states could transfer huge portions of their state and local tax burden to consumers in the energy-poor states. In 1980, for example, Alaska abolished its income tax and ordered $1,000 payments to all its citizens out of oil taxes and royalties. And all this was occurring even while service cutbacks and budget emergencies were the order of the day from the Atlantic to the Great Lakes.

During the 1970s the regional political debate in America had been between "Frostbelt" and "Sunbelt" (neither ever exactly defined). The Northeast and Midwest complained bitterly about the inequitably heavy weight of defense contracts and military bases going to the South and West, causing multibillion-dollar flows of wealth out of their region. At the start of the '80s, the debate began to fall into East-versus-West terms. And among the Eastern alarmists, fears were mounting that the 1980s could be an era of two Americas: one thriving, one hemorrhaging at every pore; one reaching new levels of growth and prosperity, one headed down a steep slope of decline. This was the grim specter raised by Felix Rohatyn, chairman of New York's Municipal Assistance Corporation, when he warned of "half the country nearly bankrupt, many of its major cities pools of unemployment and unrest, and the other half swimming in oil, industry and wealth." Moreover, said Rohatyn, national security would be ill served by letting such basic industries as steel, autos, and rubber, all centered in the industrial heartland, fold up shop and drift overseas.

The deep recession of the early '80s tended to mute the interregional issue as virtually every area of the country suffered severe unemployment—as did even the once-inviolate California, not to mention the Pacific Northwest, which was plunged into a depression so deep it seemed to match the woes of Michigan and other auto-dependent Midwestern states. That did not mean vast interregional disparities could or would disappear, however. The 1980 Census showed the West enjoying vast advantages in the average level of residents' education, in proportions of young people, and in the numbers of families with high incomes. It was estimated that in the first 15 months following the 1980 Census, 54 percent of all U.S. population growth was in the triumvirate of California, Florida, and Texas, and indeed that five states, all in the Midwest, seemed to be suffering absolute population losses: Michigan, Indiana, Ohio, Iowa, and South Dakota.

No region of the country, however, was monolithic in population change or economic progress. While Florida and Texas expanded rapidly, for example, sluggish growth figures at best were noted in traditional Dixie "Black Belt" areas of Mississippi, Arkansas, Alabama, Georgia, and Tennessee. New England, in the flowering of its high-technology industries, achieved a latter-day economic renaissance that was the envy of many other areas—among them the hard-pressed Great Lakes States and Pacific Northwest.

And if one talked with Westerners—especially leaders in the Mountain States, a region that experienced a surge of energy development on every front from coal to synthetic fuels—one found deep agonizing about the problems of growth, and fear for the future. High energy-based taxes are an absolute necessity, one heard there, to finance energy-related public facilities and special services in socially explosive "boom towns," to encourage diversification to minimize the classic boom-and-bust pattern of minerals exploitation, and finally to provide for environmental cleanup in an area of America so arid and ecologically delicate that one can still see the tracks of the Oregon Trail laid down by wagon trains over a century ago. In Montana a visitor is constantly reminded of how the Butte copper mine, once known as the richest hill on earth, ended up as a humongous hole in the ground that devoured half the city before Anaconda pulled out, leaving a city in economic travail as dire as any deserted New England mill town has ever known. State Sen. David Towe, author of the 30 percent severance tax on Montana coal—the tax that triggered Eastern criticism of Westerners being "blue-eyed Arabs"—tells one how the copper kings came and raped Montana, leaving nothing behind and how "We are determined to leave future generations something more than unknown environmental problems and a depressed economy."

But such points, however compelling, failed to answer the question of *how much* energy taxation by the energy-rich states might be fair. Nor did they, understandably, quell fears among Midwestern and Eastern leaders about their immense competitive disadvantage in attracting and retaining industry and jobs when their "friendly competitors" to the South and West could offer rock-bottom (or nonexistent) taxes and all other manner of special induce-ments. In the final analysis, the regions of the United States were all so deeply interdependent that any one region's unmitigated sectionalism and profiteer-ing off another would likely return to haunt it. For all their problems, North-eastern and Midwestern states and cities accounted for roughly half of Amer-ica's people and a vast portion of its manufacturing and financial strength.

The Great Regional Advances

In our travels for this book, we found virtually every American region offer-ing some special qualities worthy of admiration—or emulation. New Eng-landers were demonstrating, through their high-technology-based economic success, their region's historic capacity, whenever the tides of economic change seemed to turn against it, to adapt and rise again as a phoenix from the ashes.

From the Mid-Atlantic states came the model developed by New York City after its brush with bankruptcy: taking the harsh medicine of honest book-keeping, for a change, together with mutual sacrifices by government bureau-cracies, labor union members, pension funds, and citizens long accustomed to generous benefits from the public treasury. The entire United States, Felix Rohatyn suggested perceptively, had caught a version of New York City–style economic flu (unbalanced budgets, wages driving industry elsewhere, high income taxes, low productivity) and would eventually have to swallow similar medicine to survive. A companion model came from New York State, where the largely unheralded governor from 1975 through 1982, Hugh Carey, developed a kind of "supply side economics with a head *and* a heart." Carey first cut back on all major state expenditures, supported stimulative tax cuts only when the state budget was safely in balance, targeted business induce-ments to hard-pressed cities and firms adding new workers, and concentrated heavily on small-business start-ups and expansions—where the real job payoff lies.

It was during the 1960s that the South made its magnificent forward historic leap, achieving in the civil rights revolution a second and permanent Recon-struction. Most of the years since then have been used to solidify those gains, garnering the economic benefits that became possible when a third of the region's people were no longer denied the most fundamental liberties and opportunities. The scourge of Southern poverty is not yet eradicated, but it is a shadow of its former self.

The Great Lakes States, long past their creative early decades and seem-ingly preoccupied with heavy industry and materialistic goals, never pre-sented a very attractive spectacle—even while their luck held out. General Motors, one of the great economic engines of all time, proved shockingly negligent over its history in providing innovative leadership, either in techno-logical or in social and political fields. Now, in adversity, the Great Lakes region may provide a more attractive model, starting with survival pacts between auto managements and unions and moving on to collective efforts to formulate long-term economic revival strategies, including a bid to snare high-technology industries. Ironically, many Great Lakes cities have begun to show class and originality—troubled Ohio cities such as Toledo and Akron are examples—at the very moment their economic base is most threatened by destruction.

The Great Plains States, physically still an immense swath through America, constitute our most static region: serving primarily agriculture, not terribly rich, not terribly poor, changing only under extraordinary stress, such as the poor farm prices that led Nebraska in 1982 to ban additional corporate farming years after other states had taken such action. These states are in a way a comforting presence—a reminder of a simpler America that not only was, but lives on. But Minnesota, on the northeast corner of this region, continues to throw off fresh social and governmental ideas like a Fourth of July sparkler. Texas and Oklahoma, on the Great Plains' southern anchor, have been too busy with their oil and gas industries to offer models helpful elsewhere. Yet their entrepreneurial spirit is precisely what economically troubled areas like the Midwest and Northwest need to survive in the '80s.

The Mountain States are refreshingly youthful, boisterous, and confident of themselves. Through their crop of highly articulate governors they have been sought to take their fate into their own hands, negotiating effectively with the federal government, as a unified block, on such issues as energy development. Providing the Mountain States proceed with some restraint in taxing the rest of America for access to their great treasure trove of energy, they should be able to gain steadily in stature, influencing broad areas of national policy, their leaders among the formidable presidential contenders of the '80s and '90s.

In the Pacific Northwest, Oregon distinguished itself by producing the best plan yet for preservation of a state's open spaces and agricultural land—a task to which all states would eventually have to turn, or failing to do so, bequeath a degraded environment to generations to come.

California provided another generation of fresh governmental ideas under and especially because of the mercurial Jerry Brown. Examples: a full-scale state energy plan, including heavy use of conservation and alternative sources; the California Conservation Corps (giving young people a sense of purpose and achievement through "hard work, low pay, miserable conditions"); and efforts to turn massive pension funds to socially constructive investment in the state's own future.

American Dilemmas

As one viewed American regions from the perspective of the early 1980s, the most perplexing problem of all seemed that of the industrially musclebound Midwest, losing markets to Sunbelt and foreign competition, caught without a clear economic alternative at the start of a post-industrial age. Yet the

Midwest has had great universities, a skilled labor force, some of the world's greatest reserves of fresh water in the Great Lakes. Late 20th-century obstacles just as great, we concluded, might surround the hot *growth* syndrome of the Sunbelt/Western states. Nowhere on the American continent were the limits to nature being pushed in such reckless fashion: the constant draining of Louisiana's richly fertile coastal wetlands (800 square miles lost since the 1950s), Florida's building of tens of thousands of homes and motels and mobile homes on exposed coastal stretches all but sure to be ravaged by hurricane one day, the arid West's rapid use of subsurface aquifers and ever-rising consumption of scarce surface water.

And even if natural limits to rapid population growth could somehow be overcome, what of the social spinoffs? Not only have American citizens rushed, lemminglike, to the South and West, but these are the areas of the nation most affected by immigration. During the 1970s, the Census reported, the number of Hispanics in the United States rose to almost 15 million. California's in 1980 was the highest with 4.5 million, Texas second with 3 million. Two-thirds of America's Hispanics were concentrated in those two states, plus Arizona, New Mexico, Colorado, and Florida. A new Cuba-in-America had arisen in South Florida. Across the continent, California was becoming the foremost melting pot of modern America: the great vessel into which thousands upon thousands of refugees and other immigrants, legal and illegal, were pouring. From every nation south of the border (Mexico to Argentina), from Southeast Asia and Taiwan and Samoa and Korea and Cuba they came. The number of Californians of Asian or Pacific Island ancestry ballooned by 140 percent, to 1.25 million, in the '70s, even while the proportion of "Anglo" California residents dropped from 89 to 76 percent. Some suggested California had become the Ellis Island of the '80s, replacing New York as America's great immigrant magnet. By some estimates, the U.S. immigrant stream—legal and illegal immigrants combined—had risen to 1 million a year or more by the early '80s, a trend that if continued could more than double the population the country might otherwise expect by the late 21st century. The mounting pressures on the nation's supplies of food, energy, land, and water—most particularly in the Sunbelt states, which accepted the lion's share of fresh settlement and growth—could reach degrees of magnitude hard to imagine.

Through all of their history, Americans—and the constant streams of newcomers arriving to share their destiny—were a restless, contentious brand of folk, refusing to settle into predictable patterns, sublimely confident that this spacious and incredibly rich continent would provide sustenance and opportunity into a future so distant as to be indiscernible. Almost a century ago, in his famed essay *The Significance of the Frontier in American History*, Frederick Jackson Turner declared the end of "the first period of American history" because the United States' internal frontier had virtually disappeared. But in an important sense, the American frontier never closed. Generations found it in the glittering opportunities of city life, where the industries were. Then they began our strange outward trek from the centers of population—from center city to suburbia, from suburbia to exurbia, then outward to the most remote areas again beginning in the 1970s. Concurrently came the natural, historic movement to America's beckoning South and West, a movement that did not, as one might expect, moderate in time, but instead became an ever-greater torrent.

If there was a problem in these great movements, especially in the last decades of the 20th century, it was in their sheer velocity. At each step of their great migrations following World War II—from city to suburbia or Frostbelt to Sunbelt—Americans seemed to have abandoned the places whence they came, leaving behind them semi-vacant towns and neighborhoods, the tax obligations of a mature society, deserted factories, underused schools and roads and waterworks. Had the movements proceeded somewhat more slowly, the areas being left would have had time to make more reasonable, orderly adjustments—both physical and social. And the places receiving population would have had time to develop their own institutions, their own public facilities, indeed their own culture, with more thought and care and quality. What that meant for the 1980s was abandonment of existing plants, schools, roads, and sewer systems in the depopulating areas, and the necessity to rebuild them—at a time of severe capital shortages, and at incredibly high cost—in suburbs or Sunbelt areas already reeling under the impact of suburban sprawl, poor and energy-wasteful transportation, growing crime, high immigrant flows from the Hispanic world, and ever-more-worrisome water scarcities.

In times past, the problems of rapid economic change and population shift could be overlooked because all areas were somehow progressing—even if differentially. By the late 1970s, however, overall growth in America had slowed dramatically. The limits of capital finance, deep problems in international economics, the maturing of the nation's economy and population, all these foreclosed the familiar and easy solutions of past times. Unbeknownst to itself, the United States had passed from adolescence and faced the realities of adulthood. An era of tradeoffs, of hard choices, was dawning. In bedraggled and unimaginative cities and towns, in state cultures still tolerating high degrees of corruption and exploitation of people and the land, in places practicing the most narrow "beggar thy neighbor" economic development policies, we found much to dishearten. Yet in the fire-in-the-ashes renewal of many older cities, in the neighborhood and self-help movements cropping up in community after community, in the new wave of public-private partnerships, in more careful and resource-conscious public leadership, we found the potential ingredients of an American society both mature and adaptive. America, as it had always been, was in a state of becoming. But which future would triumph, no one could yet know.

THE
MID-ATLANTIC
STATES

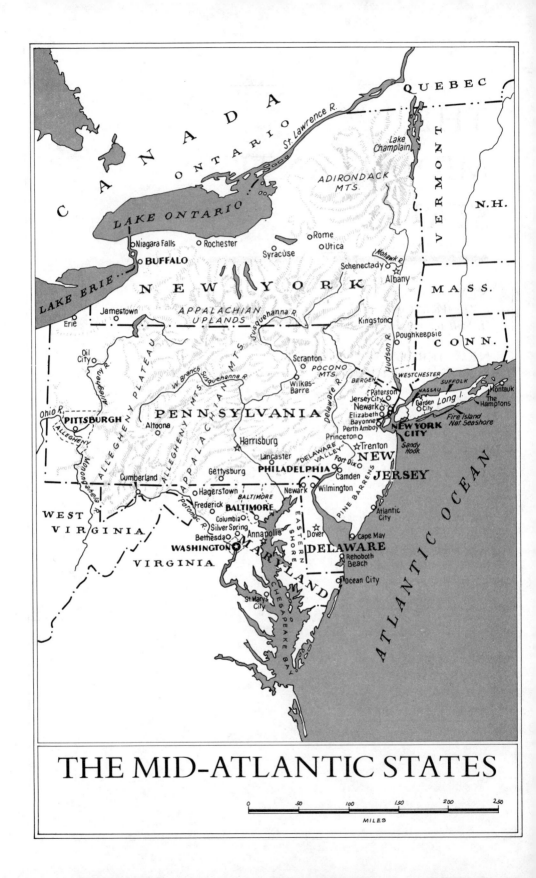

THE MID-ATLANTIC STATES

NEW YORK

I. The World City

IF NEW YORK CITY HAS A HEART, it may well be found in the famed
Rainbow Room high on the 65th floor of Rockefeller Center. To tourists, the
Rainbow Room's Art Deco, mirrored interior is a symbol of nostalgia, a place
to go for wedding anniversary dinners or to experience the 1930s of Ginger
Rogers and Fred Astaire. But to New York's high and mighty, the Rainbow
Room means lunch, and it is quite a different affair—a gathering of the
brethren in a private club to discuss decisions affecting the nation and the
world. Lunch in the Rainbow Room captures in real life that famous Saul
Steinberg *New Yorker* cartoon in which New York is at the center of the
world while the landmarks of the rest of America and the world are scattered
haphazardly across the horizon. All around you is a density of skyscrapers
unparalleled in the world, in front of you the whole of the American continent and at your back Long Island and the Atlantic Ocean. It seems downright logical that the world below is there to be ruled and that the people in
the Rainbow Room and other skytop dining clubs should be in charge.

When we went to lunch in the Rainbow Room in preparation for this book,
it was with some irony we recalled that we were there to discuss the unthinkable: the near bankruptcy of New York City. But our hosts, the financial
wizards of the global investment banking company of Lazard Freres, were
optimistic; they had worked out a financial plan to save New York—at least
temporarily—and were applying the same expertise to other cities.

What kind of city is this New York where people meet high in the sky to
discuss its possible financial demise? Troubled? Yes. Decadent? Sometimes.
Less supreme than in the past? Surely. Beaten down? No. For all its pains,
for all its sorrows, New York is still the world's most brilliant and creative
city, a match and more for such metropolises as London, Paris, Moscow, and
Tokyo. Outside of government, New York is the capital of America. And
what transpires in this center of finance and communications, of art and
theater and fashion and intellect, not only sets the pace for the United States
but sways the world. Boston may offer more academic distinction, Houston
and Dallas more new oil-fired wealth. California is still the nation's most
advanced social laboratory, spinning off lifestyles that others scramble to
copy. In recent decades regional economic capitals in America have gained
—as it was inevitable, given the spread of our national population, they one
day would—increased roles as centers of finance and distribution.

Yet even when you have counted all of New York's losses, its reversals, its
close calls with bankruptcy and civil anarchy, this goliath of a city remains the

controlling and creative center of a nation. And as befits a nation of no small materialism, that role starts with money. New York still has more corporate headquarters than any other city—73 of the companies on Fortune's list of the largest 500 industrial firms, and another 28 on the second 500. No matter that New York has lost corporate headquarters (67 in the last two decades). It is still, without real rival, the financial capital of national and global preeminence. And New York doesn't just have money; it infuses its money with strength and imagination. Even distant firms turn to it for the financing for truly gigantic projects. Jacob Javits, then U.S. Senator, once described New York as "an open market for ideas, and courageous enough to back them." "And this," he noted, "has been its role for a century and more."

And not just spirit, but a mighty headstart and adaptive capacity maintain New York's role in finance. The New York Stock Exchange and its junior partner, the American Stock Exchange, are here. Only the large New York investment banking houses, we were told by Michael Johnston, president of Blyth, Eastman, Paine, Webber, Inc., have the international networks of hundreds of thousands of individual and institutional investors who can collectively come up with $100 million or more for a choice deal. New York also leads America, Johnston said, in the use of high-technology information services for financial decision making, in the invention of creative new financial instruments, and in such Byzantine processes as putting together international deals in several currencies to combat inflation and take advantage of currency fluctuations. This near monopoly has turned Wall Street into a boom town employing 500,000 people and growing.

Most large corporations also have relationships with New York commercial banks. Six of the seven largest commercial banks of the nation—Citicorp, Chase Manhattan Bank, Manufacturers Hanover, J.P. Morgan, Chemical Bank, and Bankers Trust—are located in the city. Insurance money is another source of capital, and New York competes with Hartford for the title of insurance capital of America, accommodating three of the five largest insurance companies in the nation: Metropolitan Life, Equitable Life, and New York Life, plus Prudential in nearby Newark. There is also an unparalleled concentration of commodity exchanges: the Produce Exchange (wheat and other grains), Cotton Exchange (cotton and wool), Coffee and Sugar Exchange, Commodity Exchange (hides, silk, rubber, metals), Cocoa Exchange, and Mercantile Exchange (butter, eggs, and many other farm products). New York is also the chief municipal bond market for the nation. Only after a rating by the New York firms of Standard and Poors or Moody's Investor Services, can states, localities, and school districts sell bonds to build highways, schools, and other capital projects.

Then there are the myriad specialized services in which the city excels. Here are the biggest and best firms specializing in market research, advertising, public relations, management consultation, engineering, and custom brokerage. And then the lawyers: when any state or locality across the country decides to issue a bond for a new or unusual purpose, for instance, the odds are strong that it will turn for advice to a Wall Street law firm employing lawyers so expert that their opinions are trusted by investors even when the issue sets new legal precedents.

New York was made by its port, which still sustains the city. The harbor is one of the largest and best in the world. It is virtually fog and ice free; it is calm and protected; its shores are easily accessible. The Port Authority of New York and New Jersey has built modern container port facilities, mostly in the New Jersey portion of the metropolitan area. Kennedy International Airport handles over 35 percent of the country's overseas air travel and almost 50 percent of the nation's import-export air cargo. About 76.8 million people —35.6 percent of the entire U.S. population—live within one day's delivery of the city. Nearly 20 million people—7.5 million households—live within a 60-mile radius. Not surprisingly, New York then remains a distribution center of local, regional, national, and even international scope. And this largest market in the Americas sustains New York's role as a prime manufacturing center, even if a declining one. Nearly one-half million New Yorkers still make everything from clothes to chemicals to bread. Only the Los Angeles, Chicago, and Detroit regions have more manufacturing jobs. Even when production moves to lower-cost locations, New York remains the decision-making center. For all the losses in the garment trade, New York is still the trend-setting place where the buyers from across the country congregate, the receiving port for the choicest hides and skins, and the home of America's best fashion libraries and textile and costume collections. Ten of the largest retailing companies of America have their headquarters in New York. In all the world there is no shopping town on a par with New York.

Likewise, even though most books are printed elsewhere, New York remains the capital of book publishing, a title it has held since the 19th century. New York television, radio, newspapers, magazines, books, and fashions mold and influence American thought year-in, year-out, as no other force in the land. Sometimes the country reacts *with* New York, sometimes *against* it, but always *to* New York. The major networks (CBS, NBC, ABC) all have their headquarters in the city and determine the news and entertainment diet of a nation (though most entertainment programming is produced in California, and cable television produced on a dispersed basis may dim the influence of the networks in the '80s and '90s). The *New York Times*, despite competition from the *Washington Post*, the *Los Angeles Times*, and Gannett's *U.S.A. Today*, is the country's only national newspaper of record, in that it is read by government, business, and other opinion leaders from one coast to the other; with satellite printing, the influence of the *Times* (as, indeed, that of the *Wall Street Journal*, another Manhattan-based newspaper of national stature) has grown ever greater. (The *Times* is not the largest circulation paper; that honor belongs to the tabloid *New York Daily News*, which speaks with a more conservative voice and caters to less sophisticated and less affluent New Yorkers. The *News* prints 1.5 million copies daily, almost double the *Times*, but the *News* has suffered from the declining working-class population in New York, and in 1981 its owners, the *Chicago Tribune*, announced the paper was losing so much money they wanted to sell it. The only evening paper,

the *Post*, owned by Australian newspaper lord Rupert Murdoch, prints 640,-
000 papers.) The two leading national newsweeklies—*Time* and *Newsweek*—
emanate from New York as does almost every other national magazine from
Sports Illustrated to *Fortune* to *People* to *Rolling Stone*, which moved from San
Francisco when publisher Jann Wenner decided he had to try the Big Apple.

Foundations and charities abound on the island of Manhattan, making it the
center of America's "Philanthropic Industrial Complex." New York foundations usually lead the nation in their inventiveness and willingness to take up
a new cause. By far and away the largest is the Ford Foundation, which has
assets of about $3 billion and distributes about $120 million annually. The
headquarters of mainstream organized religion are located in New York, as
is the National Council of Churches. It was from New York that the churches
organized their important campaigns in favor of civil rights and against the
Vietnam War.

In the performing arts, New York seems ever to be the premier city of the
land. Despite the growth of a strong regional theater in America since World
War II, no play is considered a true success until it has undergone baptism
by fire of the critics and audiences of Manhattan. A classical concert artist may
receive warm receptions in Los Angeles or Cleveland, but not be counted a
full success until New York joins in the accolades. New York remains the
cultural center of the nation because it has the huge, sophisticated audience
concentrated in one great metropolitan center, and because the required
money—lots of it—is there to launch productions. New York theater producers launched forty to sixty productions per year in the early '80s, while
attendance figures were between 10 and 11 million. No other American city
can begin to compete with New York in the quality and regularity of opera
or ballet.

New York is also the art nexus of the continent, and one of global importance; as American artists operating largely out of New York made their mark
internationally in the years after World War II, the English critic Lawrence
Alloway said that New York in our times is "what Paris was to the early 20th
century; it is the center of western art." The Abstract Expressionism of our
time—photography, sculpture, allied graphic arts, pop art—is centered in the
city. And there are hundreds of distinguished private galleries and great
public museums.

New York, in short, is America's imperial city. The people who live there
often exhibit a pride that is offensive to all other Americans. John Leonard,
of the *New York Times*, once described a friend of his this way: "On the whole,
he preferred never leaving New York. And if he had to leave New York, he
wanted to go to some other imperial city, Paris or Rome or Baghdad, where
the citizens knew that they were at the center of things."

Yet for all its eminence, New York is a frightening Oz to many Americans.
Across the country, in hundreds of interviews, we found people who avoid
New York, who find it too brash, too uncivil, too anonymous—as well as
scarily influential. The 1980 Census showed that fewer Americans were now
drawn to the Big Apple, and that many New Yorkers had found the traumas

of city life greater than the pleasures, and left. In the 1970s, the city lost 824,533 people, a staggering 10.4 percent of its population, bringing the total down to 7,071,030—the lowest since 1930. The change in the city's demography was all the more striking in view of the illegal immigrant count—said to exceed 1 million by 1980—and a tumbling proportion of youths in the population (from 21 percent in 1970 to 18 percent a decade later) as parents decided they wanted to raise their children elsewhere. Nor did the decline indicators stop at the city's border. The entire New York–New Jersey metropolitan region lost 8.5 percent of its population, bringing the total down to 9,119,737. Most of the loss was in New York City, and companies reported they were finding it increasingly difficult to get young executives to move to New York. The commuting, the high taxes, the crime, and the incivility were just not worth it, they said.

It is true that turmoil, brashness, and a feeling of loneliness amid the millions have always marked life in the city. Walk down the streets and look into people's eyes, and you can all too often see the emptiness, the shell of self-defense built up around each cell of the human organism. The wellsprings of hostility are so continually close to the surface that New Yorkers congratulate themselves for taking a brief interest in each other whenever a real New York–scale crisis occurs, such as the telephone system ceasing to function, a blackout, one of the many public employee strikes, or the city's financial difficulties. Even then, predators remain ready to pounce on any letdown in the façade of law and order. It was reported that $150 million in property was stolen or destroyed within 30 minutes of the great 1977 power failure. As the *Chicago Tribune* commented, "Has anarchy ever worked faster?"

New Yorkers do find a way to handle, with some equanimity, the everyday roster of afflictions—traffic jams, the terrifying, graffiti-splattered subway system, the filthy streets, the high crime—which seem to have grown steadily worse since the fiscal crisis of the mid-1970s. The public services in which New York once took special pride—its schools, its libraries, its housing standards—have declined alarmingly. The tensions can be seen in human relations. Pushy subway riders, predatory motorists, abusive cab drivers, arrogant city workers, surly sales clerks and waiters, argumentative customers, all seem to have adopted the attitude: "If no one knows who I am, what difference does it make what I do?" As the city's traditional homogeneous ethnic neighborhoods have broken up and people's sense of turf has been threatened, the incivility has increased.

The same combination of a gigantic population and accompanying anonymity has produced in New York a system of politics and government that is at once a monument to idealism and a model of the worst bloated municipal inefficiency. The sheer number of people who live in the city has made it possible for almost any group to organize to improve its lot. But because there were so many needs and so many people who considered themselves needy, a system of demand developed. Everybody had to have his piece *now*. Confrontation, not compromise and reconciliation, became the prevailing model. For many years New Yorkers of every stripe and interest demanded everything, and because the city was rich and wanted to preserve the social peace, demands—outrageous or not—were met. From the era of the great fires in the early 1900s to the Great Society of the 1960s and early 1970s, New York pioneered in programs to make vast improvements in the life of common people and the poor. In 1958, New York was one of the first cities to grant collective bargaining rights to the city employees. Over the years their wage and benefit demands—as well as their militancy and willingness to strike—skyrocketed.

From its earliest times, it is worth remembering, New York was a place of remarkable ethnic, cultural, and racial differences. Most of the colonial population was Dutch, but there were many Englishmen as well as Brazilians, French, Finns, Portuguese, and Swedes. There were blacks, most of them from Brazil, some of them slaves, whose rebellions led to the deaths of both blacks and whites. In the early 19th century, as New York made its rise to prominence, displacing Philadelphia as the population center of America and Boston as the cultural center, immigrants began to pour in from Europe. Ethnic hatreds were pronounced, and men gathered into gangs to protect themselves, their neighborhoods, and their property from other gangs. During the Civil War the draft was deeply resented, and between 50,000 and 70,000 Irish Catholics, who blamed blacks for the war and the draft, rampaged through the city and left a wake of death and destruction, torturing and hanging blacks and burning and looting houses. Before order was restored, at least 1,000 people had been killed—a far worse situation than the racial disturbances of the 1960s in which death was rare.

During the half-century following the Civil War, New York was the fulcrum of fantastic growth generated by free-wheeling capital and the industrial revolution. Lords of finance such as Cornelius Vanderbilt, Jay Gould, John D. Rockefeller, and J.P. Morgan masterminded the building of great empires of rail, steel, and oil. In this era some of New York's most famous structures went up: the first Madison Square Garden, St. Patrick's Cathedral, the Metropolitan Museum of Art, the Brooklyn Bridge, the first Metropolitan Opera House, the Statue of Liberty, the first Waldorf-Astoria Hotel, the 13-story Tower building (the first skyscraper), and the still unfinished Cathedral of St. John the Divine, which held its first service in 1899. But in this same era politics was dominated first by the infamous Tweed Ring, and then by a series of lesser Tammany Hall thieves. In 1898, a new city charter effected the consolidation of Manhattan with Brooklyn, Queens, the Bronx, and Staten Island, making a city of 3.3 million people, covering 320 square miles of territory. But immigration continued, and working conditions for the average man and woman were abysmal.

As the U.S. entered World War I, New York was torn by anti-German sentiment, and anything German was removed. In the 1920s, New York was a hyperactive swinging town as its investment bankers increasingly took over world financing. It all came to a roaring end on October 24, 1929, when the stock market crashed. The Depression saw New Yorkers by the thousands standing in bread lines or queuing up at the soup kitchens. Professional men slept in subways or on park benches. It really took World War II to revive New York again. The late 1940s and the 1950s are now viewed as New York's most peaceful age, a time when the bridges, streets, and subways were in good repair and social tension was less acute, a time when New York was leading the nation in building a better society. But almost unrecognized the flight of the stable middle-class citizenry had begun, the manufacturing economy was already beginning its decline, and in the bus stations and airports were arriving millions of poor southern blacks and Puerto Ricans looking for a better life. Their expectations would prove in the 1960s and 1970s to be some of the most difficult for New York to meet.

In its various eras, New York has been run by a series of colorful and sometimes brilliant mayors. The job is considered the ultimate prize a political figure can win in Municipal Politics, U.S.A. No matter how hard the job might be, whoever wins the office is the biggest man in the biggest town, surrounded by trappings of power: a beautiful City Hall from which to reign, an historic private residence (Gracie Mansion), a high salary, private limousine always available with chauffeurs, aides, and police bodyguards. He is the representative of urban America, sought out by the great from America and abroad.

One of the mayors remembered from earlier years is Jimmy Walker (1926–32), who brought back fraud, favor, and mistresses reminiscent of the Tweed days and established the first citywide sanitation system, hospitals department, and tunnels for many subways. His corrupt practices were uncovered by Governor Franklin D. Roosevelt, and he resigned, sailing the next day for Europe and oblivion. Fiorello H. LaGuardia (1934–45) is widely regarded as the best mayor New York ever had. He ran for office at various times as a Republican, a Socialist, and a Progressive, and with independent Democratic backing, inventing the "fusion" model of candidacy. He also cracked down on crime and brought aviation to the city. Mayor Robert F. Wagner, Jr. (1954–65) inherited a social consciousness from his Senator father, negotiated among the city's growing conflicting interests, but ended up covering city deficits through bonding, a practice that would pave the way for financial disaster in the 1970s. "I do not propose to permit our fiscal problems to set the limits of our commitments to meet the essential needs of the people of the city" were Wagner's now-infamous words. John V. Lindsay (1966–73) personally strode the streets as the great ghettos seethed with racial tension in the 1960s, bringing by his very presence a message of concern and respect unknown before. Lindsay, a good-looking, photogenic aristocrat, successfully convinced rich Manhattan whites and poor blacks and Puerto Ricans that he cared about them, but the great white middle class—the traditional backbone of the city—never felt he cared much about them.

Lindsay was succeeded by Abraham Beame, a former city controller who became the first Jewish mayor of New York City, something almost incredible to believe since the city then contained some 20 percent of the Jews in the world. (The figure has since fallen to 13 percent.) Before Beame's service was half complete, the great New York City fiscal crisis of 1975 had intervened, an event that left Beame's reputation—in matters both financial and political—in tatters. Beame had told his constituents that the budget was balanced when it wasn't, borrowed money at high interest rates rather than cut the budget, and falsely certified to investors that city revenues matched expenditures.

Underwriters began to turn a sharp eye toward New York City fiscal practices in the wake of the mid-1970s default of the New York State Urban Development Corporation. Bankers and investors began to realize that for many years the city had been spending beyond its means, paying its employees the world's highest municipal wages to provide an unmatched array of social services to a population that could no longer pay for so many luxuries —if indeed it ever could. We shall not attempt a blow-by-blow account of that crisis here. But it is important to understand the factors that converged in something very close to financial *Götterdämmerung*. Mayor Wagner began, in 1965, his last year in office, to borrow against tax revenues on the grounds that it was better to borrow now and pay later to work on the war against crime, narcotics addiction, and ghetto problems. Lindsay, faced with labor demands from his first day in office, bought off the unions with concessions that startled even union leaders. Since the city's charter forbids the adoption of an unbalanced budget, Wagner and Lindsay learned to play intricate games with the budget, placing various types of spending in inappropriate categories, counting anticipated revenues from the state and federal government in one fiscal year while actually receiving them in later years, dramatically overestimating anticipated revenues while clearly underestimating expenses (predicting a decline in welfare rolls was a favorite maneuver). From 1964 onward, the state also allowed the city to use the capital budget to borrow money for current expenses. During these same years, manufacturing concerns were leaving the city; the increase in "service jobs" was mostly in the city government, which forced increased taxes, depressing the economy and driving away private business. The problems worsened as the city lost its middle-class tax base and gained dependent citizens. As New York's growing black and Hispanic population found too few places for themselves in the declining economy, the welfare and unemployment burdens increased. No effective force worked against union demands. Finally, New York tried to provide an incredible range of services, including as many as 19 public hospitals, the most extensive fire protection service of any U.S. urban area, low transit fares (as long as possible), public housing aid for the middle class as well as the poor, municipal radio and television stations, and free tuition at the city university (a practice finally abandoned in 1976). New York also performed functions for New York State such as care for long-term prisoners and bore a high proportion of state court system costs. The city also claimed the unique burden of being the country's principal port of entry, responsible for every service from police protection for the United Nations to aid for illegal aliens. (Critics viewed the range of New York's foreign residents, however, as ultimately benefiting the city on every front from increased trade to cheap labor.)

When, in 1975, the state and city leaders finally absorbed the fact that *this time* the combination of spending, inflation, and a changed economic base could not be ignored, the state took control of city finances, programs were cut, and city taxes raised. Eventually the federal government guaranteed some bonds issued to restructure the city's debt. The Municipal Assistance Corporation for the City of New York (Big Mac) was created by the state to issue debt benefiting the city, but at arms length from the city itself. The state placed the city's financial planning under the supervision of a Financial Control Board, which had the ultimate power to file for bankruptcy without the permission of city officials. Felix Rohatyn, a senior partner in the global investment banking company of Lazard Freres, was named chairman of Big Mac and a member of the Financial Control Board.

What could one fairly make of this venture to the financial precipice by the nation's premier city? The combination of the city's errors added up to a gigantic failure for American liberalism. The liberals' ideological commitment to redistribution of wealth, their view that profits were somehow wicked, the contention that businesses that moved out of New York City were somehow "immoral," and the assumption that better services came from more money, not better management, were ultimately proven contrary to the American way of doing things, Ken Auletta wrote in *The Streets Were Paved with Gold*. "New York City's fiscal crisis," Auletta concluded, "is liberalism's Vietnam. Liberals' traditional firepower—more money, more programs, more taxes, more borrowing—didn't work here, just as more troops, more bombs, more interdiction, more pacification didn't work there."

After the state and federal governments had to help bail out the city, New Yorkers sobered up from their spending spree and elected a mayor, Edward I. Koch, who courted business and made a point of standing up for the middle class, which had been abandoning the city. Koch turned his back on nine years of liberal votes as an East Side Manhattan congressman and ran as a "liberal with sanity," attacking unions and many of the city's workers he said "didn't give a full day's work for a full day's pay." He endorsed the death penalty. In office he even called himself "Mayor Culpa" and apologized for voting in Congress for a maze of federally imposed education, labor, handicapped, and clean air and water directives that were now proving extraordinarily expensive for the city to implement.

No mayor so personified ethnic, upwardly mobile New York City since Fiorello LaGuardia, whose desk Koch used. Born in the Bronx to Polish Jewish immigrant parents, he grew up in New York City except for a period during the Depression when the family was forced to move in with relatives in Newark, N.J. Koch worked as a shoe salesman to make his way through City College, served in World War II, returned to New York University Law School, and settled down in Greenwich Village. He was a reformer in city politics and a Stevensonian Democrat in the 1950s before winning five terms in Congress and then the mayor's office. A bachelor, Koch was a full-time public servant.

What charmed New Yorkers most about Koch was his outspokeness, his one-liners, his very "New York–ness." A collection of his sayings titled *How'm I doing? 'The Wit and Wisdom of Ed Koch'* contained gems such as

> You know how I always ask everybody how am I doing? Well, today, I asked myself, and the answer was "tarrific."

> The labor unions make contributions to everybody. They don't care if you're Attila the Hun as long as you do what they want.

> I am the sort of person who will never get ulcers. Why? Because I say exactly what I think. But I am the sort of person who might give other people ulcers.

> Never forget, rarely forgive.

Koch won the highest popularity ratings of any mayor in New York history, and was reelected in 1981 as the first mayor ever to have both the Democratic and Republican designations. But Koch's stories could also be mean and occasionally bordered on racism, and the real message of the 1981 primary, *New York Times* columnist Sydney H. Schanberg contended, was "racial polarization." Blacks and Hispanics, who by 1980 made up 45 percent of the city's population, both rejected Koch, the blacks by more than 2 to 1 due to anger over Koch's closing hospitals in their neighborhoods. The liberals also denounced Koch. Labor mediator Ted Kheel claimed that Koch had won his Irish-Italian-Jewish middle-class support by appealing "to peoples' emotions on race relations." If that was Koch's main strategy it seemed to wear out by 1982 when he ran for the Democratic nomination for governor and was defeated. Koch's loss was partly due to his rejection by upstate New Yorkers who were offended by a *Playboy* interview in which Koch derided rural and suburban life. He won the city, but opponent Mario Cuomo managed to attract many black, Hispanic, and liberal voters, as well as Italian-Americans proud to nominate their first gubernatorial candidate.

There were also questions about how well the budget balancing had been handled. The number of city employees had been reduced from 284,000 in 1974 to 210,000 in 1982. The number of cops alone was cut from 30,779 in 1972 to 22,472. The city also lost 5,537 teachers and 2,000 street sweepers. Crime rose even on Staten Island, the number of potholes had increased, and the subway was near collapse—although the state, in 1981, did enact an ambitious $7.9 billion "Marshall Plan" for a total capital renovation of the transit system. Koch was also faulted for failing to institute sorely needed training and guidance for New York City's small army of middle managers. At times it seemed as if Koch's bravado was being substituted for the tough, day-by-day management that might one day make New York into a strong, resilient municipality again. The hard fact was that while Koch had restored the mayoralty to center stage, and managed to present to the world a view of a city struggling to cope with its problems, even its fiscal recovery was fragile in the extreme. Six years after the initial crisis, Moody's Investor Services still termed the city's bonds a speculative investment. The city had made improvements and thus received a slightly higher bond rating, but Moody's said the city still faced tough problems in managing its employees, was too dependent on federal and state aid, which might be cut off, and needed badly to rebuild its transit system and repair other poorly maintained physical structures. Moody's, predictably, did not credit New York for its remarkable outpouring of citizen self-help efforts to save Gotham in its time of need. Some 14,000 block associations developed throughout the boroughs, assisting with crime prevention, clean up (one group called itself the SweepCorps), tree and flower planting, garbage collection, and recreation. Through the block clubs, many socially isolated New Yorkers were also discovering the satisfaction and sense of security that comes from knowing one's neighbors.

At the same time, New Yorkers were engaged in an even deeper and more emotional debate over the city's past and future manufacturing base. Though never the city's economic mainstay, manufacturing played a central role in the city's political, philosophical, and psychological life. Factory jobs provided entry-level, relatively highly paid employment to millions of unskilled and semi-skilled people, making possible one of the most cherished promises of the city: upward mobility. Manufacturing was also the wellspring of the trade union movement. For the city's unskilled and new generation of migrants, it helped little that a precipitous overall job decline in the city was reversed by addition of 167,000 jobs between 1977 and 1981. Almost all those jobs were in Manhattan in such service fields as law, finance, advertising, and communications. The high-paying jobs in these service industries required college and often professional degrees for entry; the low-skilled jobs in these fields were poorly paid, non-union, and offered no upward track. So the problem remained: how could New York integrate its millions of poor, black, and Hispanic people into the mainstream economic fabric of the city? Although the migration of poor blacks from the South and Puerto Ricans had declined sharply, New York was still receiving the immigrant poor—Asian refugees, Russian Jews, South Americans (often illegal aliens)—for whom any job, housing, health care, and training were an improvement but who eventually expected the same upward mobility as previous generations. The most obvious answer was improved education, but the New York school system had fallen on hard times. Said Frank J. Macchiarola, shortly after becoming the city's school superintendent in 1978, "Too many of those who should have been serving our children—supervisors, principals, and teachers —are only serving themselves. We have not only tolerated mediocrity, we have developed, congratulated, and promoted it." From public unions rose howls of protest, but all knew there was much truth to the charge. Yet demographers could predict that the city as well as the schools would become increasingly black and Hispanic, and that if those groups were relegated permanently to low-paying jobs or welfare, the city would become poorer.

Manhattan's phenomenal economic boom of the late '70s and early '80s was accompanied by job growth, office construction, and housing rehabilitation. But charges arose that New York was turning into two cities: rich Manhattan and the poor outer boroughs. Although Manhattan's overall population declined and the black percentage actually dropped in the 1970s, the island was attracting new residents: young professionals, both single and married but childless, with high disposable incomes, and wealthy foreigners, many fleeing political instability in Italy and South America. At the same time, the outer boroughs languished, losing jobs. New York officials, several analysts argued, aided and abetted this process. The most often-cited examples were the continued neglect and deterioration of the subway system, which takes millions of New Yorkers to their jobs every day, while Koch and governors Carey and Cuomo decided to back the construction of Westway, a billion-dollar highway that would run from 42nd Street to the Battery, give Westchester commuters easy automobile access to Wall Street, and open up the Hudson River shore to development even as other boroughs languished. Environmentalists and community activists stopped Westway in the courts, but the political, business, and labor establishment's battle to get it built promised to continue. Plans for refurbishing subway stations and buying new equipment were proceeding, but obviously on a much slower track than if the federal highway money were diverted (as was legally possible) to the subways.

The high tempers with which some New Yorkers viewed the alleged preference for Manhattan and the affluent was mirrored in a *New York* magazine article that charged that "A super rich mercantile class is arising at the expense of the disadvantaged. New York, after a hundred or so years as the melting pot, has entered the age of the Uncommon Man. The common man has virtually no future in the brave new city. White-collar, high-technology jobs are of no help to the unskilled poor. . . . If nothing is done, though, Manhattan will continue its metamorphosis into a 1980s version of Shanghai in 1937, an international settlement and paradise for the wealthy. For New York, the reality is that it is becoming a smaller, smarter city."

The Worlds of New York

And now for a view of the fantastic city in its constituent parts, though we will be obliged, for reasons of space, to omit many interesting communities. The raw statistics are:

BOROUGHS	POPULATION 1980	% POPULATION SHIFT (1970–80)	BLACK %	HISPANIC %
Manhattan	1,427,533	−7	21.7	23.5
Brooklyn	2,230,936	−14.3	32.3	17.6
Queens	1,891,325	−4.8	18.7	13.9
Bronx	1,169,115	−20.6	31.8	33.9
Richmond (Staten Island)	352,121	+19.2	7.2	5.4
Total	7,071,030	−10.4	25.2	19.9

Manhattan. To travelers and even many New Yorkers Manhattan is "the city," the densest concentration of business and creative activity on the face of the earth. It is also an unequaled romantic vision and one seen best, like a beautiful woman, at night. As Le Corbusier wrote,

> Beneath the immaculate office on the 57th floor the vast nocturnal festival of New York spreads out. No one can imagine it who has not seen it. It is a titanic mineral display, prismatic stratification shot through with an infinite number of lights, from top to bottom, in depth, in a violent silhouette like a fever chart beside a sick bed. A diamond, incalculable diamonds.

In years past, Manhattan was a diversified city in itself, the first American home of many immigrants, a center of manufacturing. But today Manhattan real estate is so highly valued for its office space and homes for highly paid professionals, mostly white, that manufacturers and low-income immigrants can rarely afford it. "Manhattan has become the golden ghetto," Virginia Dajani, editor of *The Livable City*, told us. "The melting pot has crossed the East River."

We will view some of Manhattan's chief districts and neighborhoods from south to north. We begin with Lower Manhattan, home of Battery Park. Within a handful of blocks north and west of the park are the canyons of Wall Street, the greatest concentration of financial power in the world. Millions of feet of office space have been constructed here since World War II.* The building boom has not ended, but the most dominant and oppressive is the World Trade Center, two 110-story, 1,350-foot towers put up by the Port Authority with tax-exempt dollars. Massive and graceless, the buildings have been rightfully condemned as hulking examples of the America that has relentlessly sought profit and "progress" at the expense of human values, examples of the worst of public sector adventurism. Greater hopes were nurtured in the early '80s for quality in Battery Park City, a self-contained community of apartments, offices, schools, shops, and parks to be located off a one-mile section of previously decaying waterfront. Paul Goldberger, the *Times*'s architecture critic, wrote that the project could be "the finest grouping of skyscrapers since Rockefeller Center . . . a dramatic counterpoint to that impossible neighbor, the World Trade Center." Battery Park City's 1,809 housing units would create the first substantial residential area near the financial district and create—it was hoped—lively round-the-clock activity. An International Hilton Hotel opened, the first in decades, and the nearby South Street Seaport, a Rouse Company "festival marketplace" based on the concept

---

*The true princes of New York City, according to Nicholas Pileggi of *New York* magazine, are the owners of commercial and residential real estate. "They are the recipients of the city's most highly sought invitations, and, somehow there is always a table waiting for them, at standing-room-only hangouts such as Elaine's, P.J. Clarke's, and '21,' " Pileggi wrote. "They are fussed over by brain surgeons and judges in need of apartments and by mayors, governors, and presidents in need of campaign funds."

of Quincy Market in Boston, was expected to provide the financial district with a "Main Street." In fact Lower Manhattan became so popular that the journal of the Municipal Art Society, an organization concerned with New York's physical well-being, expressed fears that the demand for space would threaten institutions such as the wholesale Fulton Street Fish Market and the few remaining and unduplicable low-scale 18th- and 19th-century streets near the South Street Seaport Museum. Also now strangely, but increasingly attached to the financial district are the neighborhoods of "SoHo" (south of Houston Street), "NoHo" (North of Houston Street), and "TriBeCa" ("Triangle Below Canal"). The loft buildings in these areas were once used by small manufacturers, but then lived in illegally by artists looking for cheap, inexpensive living and work space. Eventually the conversions were legalized, but by then loft living had become so popular with stockbrokers, lawyers, and other professionals that small manufacturers were being pushed out and artists could no longer afford the space.

As Broadway starts boldly up the middle of Manhattan, north of the financial district, it passes the Civic Center—elegant old City Hall surrounded by government office buildings and the courts—city, state, and federal—plus the Brooklyn Bridge. Chinatown, an area along Mott Street, has swelled with Asian refugees; its "victim" is Little Italy and the elderly of that section, since most young Italians have left for other parts of the city or suburbs. New York still has its legendary Lower East Side of bustling streets filled with shops and street vendors and fruit carts. The area is still Jewish, housing many refugees from Nazi Germany, but the Irish and Italians have been replaced by Hispanics (mostly Puerto Ricans) and Asians. There is much desperate poverty on the Lower East Side, but even here Manhattan young-professional affluence can be felt. Just before Midtown one finds chic, bohemian Greenwich Village, a low-scale respite amid the skyscrapers (due in part, we are told, to geologic difficulty in constructing massive buildings there—plus urban critic Jane Jacob's campaigns to save the neighborhood in the '50s). New Yorkers considered only the west side of lower Manhattan to be the Village until the 1960s when both rents and house prices became increasingly expensive, and hippies of middle-class background began to move east toward St. Marks Place. So developed the terms "West Village," a relatively quiet neighborhood, and "East Village," a bastion of hippies and punk rockers in the early '70s and young professionals toward the end of the decade. Although higher housing prices have made both Villages increasingly middle class and concerned about crime, Greenwich Villagers still retain their traditional *laissez-faire* attitude about deviant lifestyles. Greenwich Village was also the birth place of the national gay liberation movement, in 1969, when gay men reversed their previous meekness by fighting police in a raid on a gay bar; it remains the spiritual, if not actual home of New York's gay community, which is believed to be the largest in the nation, though it is politically impotent compared to its counterparts in San Francisco, Houston, and Washington, D.C.

The Bowery, traditional hangout of drunks and derelicts, only a few blocks from the eastern fringe of Greenwich Village, remains the mixture of com-

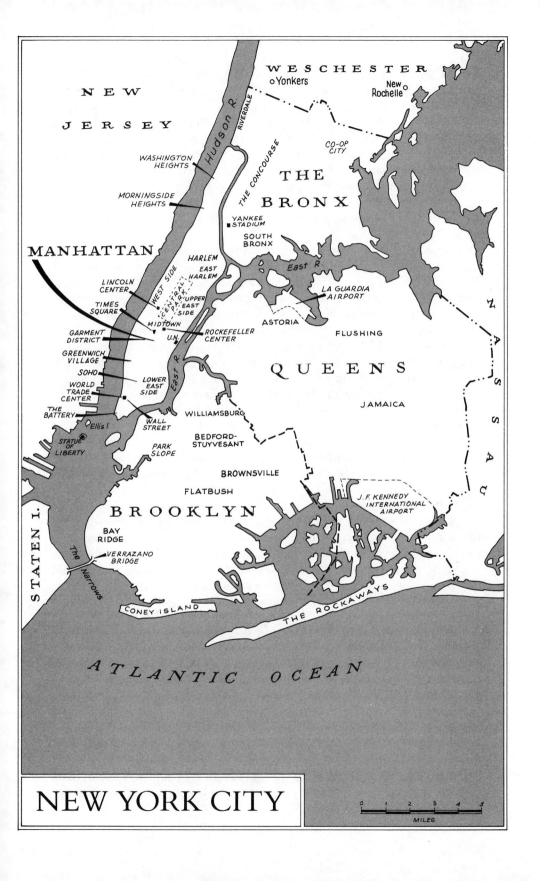

NEW YORK CITY

mercial activity and human squalor it has been for a century. In the affluent postwar years, the Bowery's population of Depression-era unemployed went way down, but in the 1970s it sadly began to rise again. The largest group of newcomers were mental patients who had been dumped into the city in the spirit of "deinstitutionalization." Others who migrated to the Bowery were black and Hispanic men in their 20s and 30s, as their youth-unemployment problem became one of adult unemployment. There were also a surprising number of young, white men unable to cope with the stresses of modern society. The problem of the homeless has spread throughout the city, and the total number of homeless people on the streets of New York has been estimated at 36,000.

Midtown begins at 14th Street, extends to 59th, and may be divided into three sections: the area along the Hudson River on the west, the long strip of the island on the East River, and the glittering heart of Manhattan between. The highly variegated area along the Hudson is mixed industrial-residential, the distinctive communities of Chelsea (location of both the General Theological Seminary and the belly-dancing center of the Western Hemisphere), Clinton (the old Hell's Kitchen, east of 10th Avenue), the garment district (from 34th to 40th Streets), the Lincoln Tunnel, the Port Authority Bus Terminal, Madison Square Garden, and Penn Station, now underground. Midtown-East begins with the massive and deadening brick high rises of Metropolitan Life's Stuyvesant Town and Peter Cooper Village, moves on to Union Square (meeting place of speakers and hecklers, radicals and agitators and resting place for addicts and the homeless), the private Gramercy Park, a cluster of medical institutions, and finally the United Nations Headquarters, built in 1946 on six city blocks, former site of slaughterhouses, along the East River. There are 32,000 diplomatic personnel in New York, including families of delegates and 5,000 U.N. staff members. Their consulates add an exotic touch, underscoring New York's status as *the* world city. In between these riverside districts are 234 square blocks throbbing with people, packed with soaring skyscrapers, the business-entertainment center of the nation and the world. So much is concentrated in Midtown that a mere cataloguing could take pages, but the street and place names alone are evocative: Fifth Avenue, Park Avenue, Madison Avenue, Broadway, 42nd Street, Grand Central, Times Square, Empire State Building, Rockefeller Center. No "economic development" plan is needed here, but the pressure to put up ever-bigger office buildings bringing more and more workers into the area is so intense that the city has sought, through zoning regulations, to shift development from the East Side to the West Side. Immense additional density may be coming. Over 150,000 more office workers were expected to work in Midtown by the end of the 1980s. There was great danger the massive new office buildings might blot out the last islands of sunlight, zoning reform or not. Many Midtown streets, lined with cold bank and airline ticket offices rather than small and interesting shops, have ended up barren of human-scale activities, mere pedestals for the skyscrapers that in turn are built either as corporate symbols, or to maximize every potential rentable square foot of space—or both. The city, moreover, has failed to create significant pedestrian-only areas or to redesign streets such as Fifth Avenue for their pedestrians rather than the maddening oceans of traffic. In a very real sense, Midtown Manhattan today is too successful for its own good.

From an aesthetic standpoint, Midtown has another blight: the sleaze of Times Square, at 42nd and Broadway. Times Square jumps 24 hours per day with the best theater in the land, top-flight movie houses, actors' hangouts— and porno shops, sex movies, and marauding prostitutes. There are perennial campaigns to clean up Times Square, and the latest consensus is that a massive rebuilding may be necessary—together with real danger that architectural distinction may be stamped out by "megastructure" redevelopment, including a 2,020-room hotel the city promoted, to be developed by Atlanta architect-builder John Portman. Demolition of two aging theaters, the Morosco and the Helen Hayes, sparked protests from the theatrical community. Protesters had to be hauled away in police vans. And even if rebuilding erases the atmosphere supportive of crime and vice, we wonder where the sleaze will go. Will it be dispersed around the city, as some hope and others fear, or simply take over another neighborhood?

Midtown's corporate architecture is the most closely observed and trendsetting in the United States. Two architectural "events" of recent years have had nationwide repercussions. The first was the 1978 Supreme Court decision that New York City could prohibit construction of a proposed 53-story office building above Grand Central Terminal because it would significantly alter the terminal's historic landmark status. The case has been cited again and again to save other buildings. The second was the construction of American Telephone and Telegraph's new headquarters at 540 Madison Avenue. AT&T broke with the 20th-century American corporate tradition of modernist "glass box" flat-topped buildings to put up a new headquarters sporting arches, huge windows, and unquestionably decorative elements all the way up to what looks like a Chippendale pediment at the very top. The significance here is not so much the building, but once again New York's *power*. Postmodern architects and smaller companies had tried alternative building styles, but the fact that the designers of this building were Philip Johnson, the dean of the modern school, and his partner John Burgee, and the client was AT&T, was expected to influence corporate buildings across America.

At 59th Street begins Central Park, one of America's grandest municipal parks, 840 sylvan acres, filled with sunken roads (revolutionary when the park was laid out in the 1850s), miles of paths, bridges, gates, lawns, statues, the zoo, and skating rinks. Central Park has fallen into disrepair due to the pressure on the city first to spend money on the dependent poor and then to cut the budget. But improvements—some financed by private industry—are slowly being made. The Upper East Side from the southern end of Central Park up the East River to 96th Street (where the subway comes out of the ground and East Harlem begins) is the choicest residential area in the city. This is the New York of rows of ornate old apartment buildings, exclusive clubs of the rich, art galleries, museums, cultural and scientific academies, expensive cafés and restaurants, town houses, and great hospitals. The pressure to turn many of the East Side's town houses and small apartment buildings into huge towers became so intense that much of the area has been designated an historic district. The northern part of the Upper East Side is known as Yorkville, an intown suburb of office buildings and apartment houses and stores that replaced an old German community. The West Side has moved from the condition of deteriorated slumhood that characterized it at the end of World War II to near luxury but it retains a looser, funkier atmosphere than the staid East Side; the Upper West Side is one of the most racially mixed areas of the city. Many famous Broadway stars live on the West Side; the most prestigious apartment building is the Dakota, home of Lauren Bacall and the late John Lennon and so named because its West 72nd Street location was considered far from city life at the time of construction. But the Upper West Side was slated to receive much of Manhatten's explosive high-density development in the '80s, a pressure that could ruin its traditional character.

Harlem dominates Manhattan above Central Park from 116th Street to 155th Street. Long gone are the days of such flamboyant politicians as Marcus Garvey early in the century and later, Adam Clayton Powell, Jr., of Harlem, Renaissance writers such as Langston Hughes, and the great black nightspots (the Sugar Cane, the Savoy, the Cotton Club). A few great institutions such as the Theater of Harlem have come as latter-day developments. Harlem has maintained a certain middle-class population, and there has been not only some rehabilitation of brownstones by young black professionals but even fear that whites would try to buy up the buildings with the best architecture. Churches and community groups have used federal funds to rehabilitate buildings and put up new subsidized housing.

But Harlem as a community has been a victim of black progress. As housing opened up throughout New York City and in the suburbs, the blacks who could afford better moved. In the 1970s Harlem lost one-third of its population, declining to 81,000. The result is a loss of concentrated black political power. The strongest institutions remain the many churches, but the congregations are often composed of the elderly who now live elsewhere and travel many miles to church on Sunday. "I only wish I could deliver the vote," the Rev. David Jones of All Souls Episcopal Church, told us. "But my parishioners live elsewhere." What the upwardly mobile blacks have left behind is a world of poverty and easy drug dealing, a very real part of the Harlem scene and a business that has begun to attract 13- and 14-year-old entrepreneurs.

An uneasy neighbor in the Harlem community is Morningside Heights, along the Hudson River, the site of Columbia University, a great academic institution whose land-aggrandizing policies have caused community relations problems over the years—most vividly in the 1960s.

Washington Heights–Inwood at the northern tip of Manhattan is one of the most hopeful stories in the city. This neighborhood has long been a haven for people escaping tenement life. Moving into its many apartment buildings were first the Irish, followed by Greeks and Armenians, and in the 1930s and

'40s by many European Jews (including Henry Kissinger's family) fleeing the Hitler regime. Blacks moved in from nearby Harlem after World War II, and they have been joined by Puerto Ricans, Dominicans, Haitians, Cubans, and most recently, Central and South Americans and Koreans. The neighborhood is one of the most densely populated in the city. But residents have managed —just barely—to stave off decline. A coalition of business and community leaders has sought economic development and in the late '70s obtained government money to rehabilitate 5,000 of the area's 72,000 housing units.

The important landmarks of this "land's end" of Manhattan are the George Washington Bridge (one of the world's greatest in both engineering and aesthetics), Yeshiva University, the great Columbia-Presbyterian Medical Center, the Cloisters, and the Morris Jumel Mansion.

Outer Boroughs. Manhattan may be the center of power, jobs, and world prominence for New York City, but only 20 percent of the city's population lives there. The vast majority of the city's people live in The Bronx, Queens, Brooklyn, and Staten Island. None of these boroughs enjoys anything approaching Manhattan's prestige—some Manhattanites refer to *all* residents of other boroughs as "the bridge and tunnel people." But many outer borough areas offer nice residential accommodations, certainly more spacious homes and grounds. Important institutions are scattered throughout them. There are also sections of terrible poverty.

The Bronx achieved new status in the 1960s as the first majority black and Hispanic borough in New York City's history. Yet at its northern end it includes the community of Riverdale, an echo of the East Side, a white suburbia within the city, where public, political, and professional people live in colonial, Tudor, and Georgian homes in rustic elegance. The Bronx moves quickly, however, to middle- and lower-middle class neighborhoods, the homes of office workers, teachers, minor bureaucrats, and the elite of the blue-collar class. These areas are becoming increasingly elderly. Children have mostly gone to college and moved to the suburbs. The old folks are stuck where they started.

Then we come to the South Bronx, which became *the* symbol of American urban poverty when President Jimmy Carter visited it in 1977. The South Bronx was never an urban jewel, but it had a proud tradition providing homes for immigrants escaping the five-story walk-ups of Manhattan. Then in the 1960s the arrival of blacks and Puerto Ricans coincided with the decline of New York's manufacturing jobs. "By 1968, the place was beyond description," wrote Adele Chatfield-Taylor of the New York Landmarks Preservation Commission. "Wild dogs roamed the streets, tearing in and out of buildings and through the trash that covered sidewalks and streets. Persons scarcely recognizable as human were prey and predator to one another. Fires burned everywhere—in cans on the corner, in empty lots, in all kinds of buildings." By the time Carter arrived, the South Bronx had settled down somewhat, but the sight was very grim. Carter visited Charlotte Street, where empty lots were strewn with rubble, garbage, and old tires. In the background, densely occupied old walk-ups stood like scattered islands amidst the shells of burned-out apartment buildings.

Contrary to the image presented by the photographs taken of Carter's visit, parts of the South Bronx—the territory south of Fordham Road—remain densely occupied to this day. The population is estimated at 600,000 in 13,000 acres or 20 square miles—about the same number as in the entire city of Boston's 50 square miles. The poverty statistics by 1980 were astounding. One-third of the population was dependent on welfare, and even though the South Bronx had lost at least 20 percent of its population since 1970, it had lost only 3 percent of its welfare cases. At least 20,000 to 25,000 people were believed to lack any job skills.

The aftermath of the Carter visit was a mixture of a little hope and much despair. The federal government offered money to sponsor a housing project on Charlotte Street, but the city government, faced with demands from leaders from other boroughs for part of the money and fearing that the housing project would be the beginning and end of South Bronx development, rejected the plan. The city did appoint Edward J. Logue, former president of the Urban Development Corporation and famed developer of New Haven and Boston, to coordinate the South Bronx revival efforts, a job he approached with a care and caution he and his colleagues rarely exhibited in the old urban renewal days. In the absence of federal or city money for massive redevelopment, the South Bronx became a major experiment station for the latest theories in urban renewal: pragmatic, incremental plans that emphasize economic development, local determination, "self-help," "sweat equity," home ownership for low income people, urban agriculture, public- and private-sector partnerships, and low-cost. The gritty determination of many of the South Bronx's indigenous groups—to build a more decent environment for themselves in the face of every conceivable obstacle, and even while some Manhattan-based urban "experts" preached a gospel of "planned shrinkage" to terminate city services to the South Bronx—was perhaps the most exciting, heartening story we found in America's devastated city areas in recent years. There were, for example, such neighborhood groups as the Banana Kelly Community Improvement Association, a hearty band of remaining residents who began to refurbish individual structures and then a whole block of apartment buildings. But the continuing problem was the South Bronx's relationship to the mainstream economy. When newly trained neighborhood youth finished rehabilitating houses, for example, they still found entry into construction unions blocked. By late 1982, there had been some success in attracting private industry into the South Bronx.

Despite the South Bronx's overwhelmingly negative outside image, just a little time spent there suggests what an outrage it would be to abandon it. Subway connections into Manhattan are excellent. Much usable infrastructure is still in place. And amidst its poverty the South Bronx still harbors Yankee Stadium; a "Little Italy" on the northern fringe of the distressed area; the Grand Concourse, a truly handsome boulevard of Art Deco buildings; the

Mott Haven Historic District; a large railroad yard; the Hunts' Point Market, where much of the agricultural produce for the mid-Atlantic states is processed; and finally human capital in incredibly energetic social workers, neighborhood leaders, and social activists.

In sharp contrast to the South Bronx is Queens, the most well-to-do of New York's four major boroughs, the most spacious, and the stablest in population, which totaled 1,891,325 in 1980, only 4.8 percent less than a decade earlier. Queens is also the whitest borough, but it added 96,000 blacks in the '70s, and Elmhurst in Queens is believed to be the most ethnically diverse neighborhood in the city, with 20,000 immigrants from more than 110 countries. The many communities within Queens have stronger identities than the borough itself; instead of saying they are from Queens, people say they are from Flushing, Jamaica, or Astoria. (Astoria is said to have the largest concentration of Greeks outside of Greece.) Queens is mostly homes, homes, homes— typically sturdy, small single-family homes, on small lots in early suburban style. There are some factories; the borough has also succeeded in attracting some office complexes, which accounted for most of an 8,000 job increase in the late '70s. At Queens Plaza, a declining railroad and industrial area, young professionals driven out of Manhattan by high prices are fixing up loft residences, and a retail market has proven popular.

Brooklyn (also officially Kings County) is first of all a massive fact: despite a 14.3 percent population loss in the 1970s, it still has 2.2 million people, enough to make it, if it were independent, the fourth-largest city in the United States. Second, Brooklyn is a legend. Do you remember when the Dodgers came from Brooklyn; when Coney Island, massed throngs and all, still stood for summertime fun; and when all America thought warmly of *A Tree Grows in Brooklyn?* Why, the place even had its own patois and a fierce local nationalism practically no other American community could match.

Third, Brooklyn is a place in trouble—deep trouble. The borough still employed 365,800 people in 1980, but its manufacturing industries were declining and it lost 3,000 jobs in the 1970s. Its waterfront has largely lost out to New Jersey, although there is some talk of revival. Brooklyn harbors two of the largest, worst ghettos in the world: Brownsville and Bedford-Stuyvesant. Fourth, Brooklyn has islands of growth and renewal. The best examples are Brooklyn Heights and nearby Park Slope, both of which began as the first suburbs of Manhattan's well-to-do, declined during the Depression years, and since World War II have been slowly revived.

The great bulk of Brooklyn, however, is a case study of what happens when a city begins to decay, its more stable citizens leave, and only the old and weak and poor are left. Consider the problems: neighbors who speak different languages and have differing religious customs (ultraorthodox Yiddish-speaking Jews living check-by-jowl with untutored, Spanish-speaking Puerto Ricans, for example); communities bitterly divided over whether land should be used for housing or schools; absentee landlords and a steady downward slide in services; real estate blockbusters playing on the fears of homeowners; and, overriding all other considerations, racial conflict.

The decay of the northern half of Brooklyn gives credence to the argument that New York City is simply too big to govern itself properly. Both the city and the private economy gave up in Brooklyn. To the extent that it's possible, private neighborhood organizations have tried to step in. These smaller local organizations have at least met with more success than the city did. The most famous is the Bedford-Stuyvesant Restoration Corp., started by the late Sen. Robert Kennedy after a walking tour in February 1966 and financed by the Ford Foundation and other private and government donors. Bed-Stuy created a new recreational area, renovated brownstones, and brought in an IBM plant and a supermarket. It also provided a model for many other organizations, which, with even fewer resources, have managed to cope with an incredible variety of problems. The Sunset Park Redevelopment Committee forced the city to make a new wholesale meat market compatible with the neighborhood and went on to renovate abandoned homes and sell them to low- and moderate-income people. The Southern Brooklyn Community Organization, founded to help Orthodox Jews, and the Sunset Park group have tried to alleviate conflicts between the two groups. The Flatbush Development Corp., at the very center of Brooklyn, has tried to keep the area middle class by refurbishing Flatbush Avenue and providing management assistance to absentee owners of apartment buildings to keep them from giving up the buildings for taxes.

Staten Island (the borough of Richmond) is the most un–New Yorkish of the five city boroughs. Staten Islanders often complain that their island is "the forgotten borough" and "the dumping ground of New York City" because of its chemical and sludge dumps.

Staten Island's lack of land connection to the other New York City boroughs is certainly responsible for its historically rural, leisurely pace. Despite closer ties now, this borough still has some of the safest public schools in New York City and probably the best teachers since they fight hard for assignments there. Crime rose in the 1970s, but the rate remained New York's lowest by far. Staten Island is the last remaining borough to support its own newspaper, the Newhouse-owned *Advance*.

But the most un–New Yorkish thing about Staten Island was that it continued to grow in population (mostly Italians and Jews fleeing other boroughs) and jobs. A drive through Staten Island in the early 1980s was more like touring Long Island or a Sunbelt city than anywhere else in New York; new roads, houses, shopping centers, and fast-food restaurants were under construction. The land speculation and development began with the completion in 1964 of the lovely, soaring Verrazano Narrows Bridge, providing easy vehicular access to Brooklyn. The pace and quality of the developments have not always pleased longtime Staten Islanders; "very little was done to plan for what the bridge would mean to the community," Terry Benbow, a Staten Island resident and Wall Street attorney, told us.

We were sad to learn that many Staten Island executives now prefer buses over the Verrazano bridge to the ferry service, which has existed since 1712. From the ferry, the view of New York Harbor is stupendous. But two sights are food for thought: the Statue of Liberty and Ellis Island. In a way, they speak of times past—when the floodgates of immigration were open and Ellis Island accepted 20 million new Americans, when America really meant what Emma Lazarus wrote for the state's pedestal: "Give me your tired, your poor,/ Your huddled masses yearning to breathe free . . ./Send these, the homeless, tempest-tossed, to me:/I lift my lamp beside the golden door." The closing of Ellis Island to immigrants in 1954 (in 1976 it was reopened as an historic relic) underscored the end of all that. But did it? In the 1950s and 1960s New York continued to be the port of entry and point of sojourn for the tired and the poor of the American Southland and Puerto Rico. In the 1970s New York became the destination of Russian Jews, Asian refugees, and Central and South Americans, who defied the immigration laws to reach the land—and city—of opportunity illegally. New York never had an easy time with its immigrants, and does not today. But still they come. Even with the decline of manufacturing the city still offers hope, the chance to get a minimum-wage job, the possibility of opening a restaurant or a little food store, the first rung on the ladder of success. It brings to mind what New York City's former economic development administrator, Kenneth Patton, told us: "It's an outrage that the country looks at New York and other cities as down and out. They are the only thing that holds the country together."

II. Still the Empire State?

BEFITTING ITS SOBRIQUET OF EMPIRE STATE, New York is a place of many civilizations.

It is New York City, that perpetually fascinating, pain-plagued Colossus-on-the-Hudson whose distinction, pain, and paralysis we have just examined.

It is the state of industrious, obscure, and sometimes troubled upstate cities: Buffalo, Rochester, Syracuse, Albany, Schnectady, et al.

It is a state of natural grandeur: the beautiful valley of the Hudson, Adirondack, and Catskill mountains, of millions of acres of placid farmland, woods, and lakes.

It is the home of Westchester, America's senior suburb, and of Long Island, where a slapdash civilization superimposed upon an ancient vacation retreat and farming-fishing economy is starting to gray and fray as it barely reaches its adolescence.

It is a state that was ruled—and that word is not too strong—for 15 years by Nelson A. Rockefeller, a man who for all his false starts and foibles and unquestionable extravagances left as indelible a mark on New York as any chief executive of a state in American history.

It is a state that long pioneered, in area after area, in innovative methods of government.

It is a state that long spent and lived beyond its means—and has only started back toward fiscal sanity in recent years.

It is the state where greed and selfishness of self-centered groups has threatened to undermine the community of consent by which free peoples live.

It is a state that fell strangely into the shadows in the 1970s, doubted and mistrusted by the rest of the nation.

But it is a state that by the early '80s had quietly begun a transformation into a high-technology, information-based economy. It remained a state and a power in American life to be reckoned with.

Geography almost ordained that it would be so. Fifty million years ago the Hudson gnawed its way from the Great Lakes across the highlands of upper New York State to the sea. Forty million years later it carved a gigantic gorge and its water cascaded for 36 miles down off the coastal plain into the great valley of the Atlantic basin. The ice came some 20,000 to 25,000 years ago, shaping and smoothing the hills of Manhattan, making it the island we know today. And the ice, as it melted, filled and flattened the land and the great gorge of the river. It made the Hudson an estuary, subject to tidal action, as far as Albany, 150 miles upstream. Man could hardly have planned a more superb harbor than the one at the Hudson's mouth. And as European explorers came on the scene, they found an excellent means of access to the hinterland along the Hudson Valley, on its line northward past Albany and into the Adirondacks, and the connection near Albany to the Mohawk River Valley, and then the flatlands of the Lake Ontario Plain all the way out to Buffalo and Lake Erie—the chief natural highway into the interior of the continent. This incomparable "water level route" was exploited first by boat and barge, then by rail and highway connections, to capitalize on New York's unique status as the only American state that faces both the Atlantic Ocean and the Great Lakes.

In 1784, after a tour of the state's harbors, waterways, and fertile countryside, George Washington ventured the prediction that it would become the "seat of empire." To become truly dominant, however, New York needed inexpensive access to the farm products and raw materials of the interior. The obvious answer was water transportation, and after 15 years of political struggle and an unprecedented $7 million investment, the 363-mile Erie Canal was built to make possible barge transportation from the Hudson to Lake Erie. In 1825 the feat was completed and Governor De Witt Clinton boarded a barge in Buffalo and traveled all the way to New York City by water, emptying a barrel of fresh water from Lake Erie into the Atlantic Ocean as a symbolic joining of the waters. Instantly the cost of shipping a ton of freight from Buffalo to Albany dropped from $100 to $10. Within a few years, the little villages along the canal's route—Buffalo, Rochester, Syracuse, Rome, and Utica—had become important cities. To this day, the population of upper New York state remains thickly clustered along the Hudson Valley up to Albany, and then the Mohawk Valley westward toward Buffalo. Railroads took to the same route, and the New York State Thruway (also known as the Gov. Thomas E. Dewey Thruway) parallels the Erie Canal.

Up to 1820, most of New York's population was of English or Dutch extraction. Then commenced the great floods of European immigration, bringing five million into America, most of them by way of New York, between 1820 and 1860. The dominant groups were Irish, fleeing famine in their homeland, and Germans, seeking escape from political upheaval at home, or religious freedom, or both. A majority of the immigrants passed through, but many remained. Later in the century, the flood of Germans and Irish continued, complemented by many English, Scots, and Welsh. Millions of Italian peasants, uprooted from the land, joined the immigrant flow starting in the 1880s; by 1917, there were over 700,000 first- and second-generation Italian immigrants in New York City alone. Hundreds of thousands of Jews were driven out of Russia and Eastern Europe by persecution; collectively, they made New York the most Jewish state of the Union, which it remains today with a 12.2 percent Jewish population. (New York is also one of the nation's most heavily Roman Catholic states, with 1.8 million Catholic residents—10 percent of the state population.)

By 1940, European immigration had largely ended. But not other flows. Between 1940 and 1970, there was a net immigration of 917,000 blacks into New York, and hundreds of thousands of Puerto Ricans came, too. New York simultaneously became an exporter of population, especially white people. As *Congressional Quarterly* has noted, "the state has now become the 'old country' for tens of thousands of emigrants searching for a better life elsewhere." The 1980 Census figures showed just how dramatic the change had become. In a single decade, New York had lost 3.8 percent of its population, dropping to 17,557,288. From 1790 until California overtook it in 1963, New York had had more people than any other state. In the 1940s, New York had held 45 seats in the U.S. House of Representatives, California only 23. In the 1980s, the figures had switched dramatically: 45 for California, only 34 for New York.

Consider the political implications. Over the course of American history, New York supplied the country with five presidents—Van Buren, Fillmore, Cleveland, both Roosevelts—and a sixth man, Tilden, who won the popular vote but lost in the electoral college. Between 1900 and 1948, 11 of the 26 major party nominations went to New Yorkers. But since then, only one New Yorker—William E. Miller, Barry Goldwater's running mate in 1964—has appeared on a national ticket. Miller's candidacy was taken seriously by few people (least of all himself).

But New York's drop in population during the 1970s—thrown into bold relief as southern blacks and Puerto Ricans stemmed their immigration to New York, and in some cases even returned to the South or Caribbean—did not mean New York had lost its role, national or international. Despite the state's troubles, for example, it offered more opportunity than quantities of nations in Latin America, Africa, and Asia; and the people kept coming, legally and illegally. In recent years New York has drawn an increasing number of wealthy refugees who bring their money along to invest in what they regard as the more stable United States.

Assessing modern-day New York brings one inevitably to the dilemma, is the glass half empty, or half full? On the "empty" side, for instance, there's the fact that per capita income in this erstwhile Empire state has sunken to 11th among the 50 states—not a particularly strong position, considering the state's notoriously high cost of living. New York state manufacturing has declined, especially when one measures total factory jobs (down 29 percent between 1967 and 1982). Finally, the state that once blazed the trail for governmental innovation in America can no longer afford that luxury.

But on the half-full side of the ledger, the glass is not an insignificant one. New York remains second place in population among the 50 states, and is likely to remain there for the foreseeable future. Its 17.5 million people make up an extraordinary market and a creative force in themselves. New Yorkers' total personal income was $180 billion in 1980, second-highest in the nation. According to a study by the U.S. Trust Company, New York still has the largest number of millionaires in America—some 36,000. In several manufacturing fields, New York is still so strong that comparisons are often made between this single state and the entire Southeast region. And New York's position has actually grown stronger as a *world* capital of financial decision making, the arts, and shopping.

The Political Tradition

Politics and economics intertwine inextricably to explain New York's years of triumph and defeat. In the years of the Gilded Age following the Civil War, for instance, the city and to a great degree the state was dominated by bosses, corruption, and favors for special interests. The infamous Tammany Hall leader in New York City, William Marcy Tweed, known to his contemporaries and history simply as "Boss Tweed," capitalized on the naïveté of the unlettered Irish to build an invincible political machine. The Tweed Ring pilfered as much as $75 million from the city government and with the help of blatant vote stealing even placed an ally in the governor's chair in Albany. It was smashed in the early 1870s by Samuel J. Tilden, who in turn became a respectable reform governor of the state. But neither Tilden nor Grover Cleveland, the other prominent Democratic governor of the late 19th century, undertook any fundamental changes in the weak and generally ineffective format of state government.

It was only in the Progressive Era, begun with Theodore Roosevelt's inauguration as governor in 1899 and climaxed in the administration of Charles Evans Hughes a few years later, that the tables were turned and New York government began to place public interest ahead of selfish private interests. The outstanding legislation of that era included laws to curb the excesses of utilities, regulate public service corporations, unify and improve the civil service system, guarantee certain basic rights to industrial workers, and create the nation's first workmen's compensation law.

In 1918, Alfred E. Smith, a native son of Manhattan's Lower East Side and product of a close-knit Irish neighborhood, the Roman Catholic Church, and Tammany Hall, was elected governor of New York. Smith's inauguration marked the start of a continuous stream of governors of the highest character and ability that no other American state has even begun to match.

Al Smith set the pattern for what was to follow. His political acumen was demonstrated by the fact that he never broke with Tammany Hall, but was able to demand and get increased independence from it. In the administrative realm, Smith first got the legislature to approve and then the people to ratify the consolidation of 187 boards and commissions into 19 departments, the executive of each appointed by the governor and serving at his pleasure. Sixty years later some states have still to take this fundamental step toward effective gubernatorial control. The second major reform was the institution of the executive budget system, placing on the governor responsibility for reviewing the needs of all branches of state government and then preparing an overall state budget, listing expenditures and tax sources, for submission to the legislature. Throughout Smith's regime of the 1920s, New York stood out as a liberal island in a conservative nation. Under goading from Smith, the legislature vastly increased state aid to local schools and through an accompanying equalization program saw to it that poor districts got commensurately greater aid. Consolidation of rural school districts was begun, the 48-hour maximum work week adopted for labor, many park and other public works projects initiated, and an income tax (that would eventually become the mainstay of state government financing) approved.

Smith, we may note parenthetically, also brought to power Robert Moses, the master builder, who in the words of New York Times architecture critic Paul Goldberger "played a larger role in shaping the physical environment of New York State than any other figure in the 20th century." Holding a variety of posts between 1924 and 1968, Moses built the Triborough Bridge, the Jones Beach State Park on Long Island, the Verrazano-Narrows Bridge, the West Side Highway, the Long Island parkway system, the Niagara and St. Lawrence power projects, Lincoln Center, the huge Co-op City housing project; he played a role in selecting the United Nations site and increased the size of the state's parklands to over 2 million acres. His vision of a city of highways and towers—rather than neighborhoods and brownstones—became a model for the nation until a younger generation of planners discredited it as dehumanizing.

In 1928, Al Smith went off to make his unsuccessful bid for the presidency, 30 years ahead of the time the country was willing to accept a Roman Catholic as its leader. Franklin D. Roosevelt, scion of an aristocratic Dutch-descended family from Dutchess County, ran in his place for governor and was elected. FDR was not as distinguished a state chief executive as he would prove to be a president, perhaps because he viewed Albany chiefly as a stepping-stone to Washington. Nor was Roosevelt during his Albany years forceful about taking stands on controversial issues. But as the Depression deepened, he moved decisively to prevent bankruptcy of municipalities and starvation among New Yorkers by providing imaginative measures for public relief, including establishment of a temporary emergency relief administration. Thus the formula was developed in New York for the New Deal programs that would effect America's recovery from the severest economic reversal it had ever known. Herbert Lehman, the son of an immigrant Jewish family from Germany and founder of the successful banking firm of Lehman Brothers, succeeded FDR as governor from 1932 to 1943. Lehman was totally lacking in the charisma of his political mentors, Smith and Roosevelt, but he pushed forward myriad Depression relief measures, converted an inherited budget deficit into a surplus, was a great champion of the civil service, and pushed through a series of labor laws that were more progressive than either the federal laws or those of any other state at the time.

For sheer administrative talent, it is difficult to think of a 20th-century governor who has excelled Thomas E. Dewey. A native of the little city of Owosso, Michigan, Dewey went to New York City in 1923 to study music and law and became the fabulously successful prosecutor of mobster Lucky Luciano and countless other racketeers in the trucking, restaurant, poultry, and baking businesses. Dewey served from 1943 to 1955 and was the father of the tradition of progressive Republicanism, which thrived in New York State as nowhere else. Like his contemporary (and 1948 vice-presidential running mate) Earl Warren in California, he refused to lower tax rates while the state experienced wartime budget surpluses. The result was a $450 million fund that could be expended for delayed public works projects after the war. Hundreds of thousands of New York youngsters owe Dewey thanks for his leadership in creating a state university, which New York had lacked up to that time. A vigorous health-department program virtually eradicated tuberculosis in New York, highway building was pushed forward, and the state's mental hygiene program was thoroughly reorganized. And in response to Dewey's initiative, the legislature in 1945 passed a proclamation of economic emancipation for New York's minority groups—the nation's first fair-employment practices law. Dewey ran twice unsuccessfully for the presidency. The loss of the 1944 presidential campaign against FDR, a popular wartime president, was predictable enough. But his 1948 defeat at the hands of Harry Truman, after he had been declared the winner by the *Chicago Tribune*, must have been excruciating. The consensus was that the Democrats' down-to-earth pocketbook promises had more appeal. Dewey "retired" to a Wall Street law practice in which he became a multimillionaire; President Nixon offered to appoint him Chief Justice of the United States, but Dewey declined due to age.*

Dewey's successor, Averell Harriman, the only Democrat to have broken the solid 30-year wall of Republican control in Albany, was a real disappointment in the job—a man of great renown in foreign affairs but unfortunately

---

*New York has been a breeding ground of great jurists, including the likes of Charles Evans Hughes, Benjamin Cardozo, Harlan Fiske Stone, John Marshall Harlan, Harold Medina, and Learned Hand.

preoccupied with the possibility that he might run for president in 1960. Harriman did set up the nation's first office of consumer affairs. The governorship obviously meant a great deal to Harriman; when he finally retired from public life at an advanced age, he chose to be addressed as "Governor" rather than any of his other many titles.

Harriman was defeated by Nelson Rockefeller, a man who was to build the most complex, fascinating, and socially activist state government in U.S. history. To the job of governor, Rockefeller brought an unusual background, even for New York. His paternal grandfather, John D. Rockefeller, in the best robber-baron tradition had manipulated his Standard Oil empire into monopolistic control of the U.S. oil industry—and then just as industriously, began to give away part of his fortune. Rockefeller's family continued the tradition, and Nelson's political involvement was only one aspect of his generation's commitment to public service through which their influence permeated New York State socially and physically on a scale that defies measurement. John D. III headed the Rockefeller Foundation and the Lincoln Center; Laurence managed the family's business interests and was an activist in conservation; Winthrop became a cattle breeder and twice Arkansas governor; David became president of the Chase Manhattan Bank and promoted the physical rebuilding of lower Manhattan; their sister, Abby, gave away money on a quieter basis. With the exception of Winthrop, the generation was New York–based, clearly the premier family of the city and state. The political tradition of activism and big-spending campaigns was carried on with the 1976 and 1980 elections of John D. Rockefeller IV, or "Jay" as he is popularly known, as Democratic governor of West Virginia.

Nelson entered electoral politics after he became disenchanted with the role of political appointee he had held under Roosevelt and later Eisenhower. In 1958, he waged an astounding, high-impact campaign as the New York gubernatorial nominee. He mingled with the masses, gulped down blintzes and bagels and pizza, kissed babies, and assailed Democratic "bossism." The public responded; Rockefeller beat a thoroughly outclassed Averell Harriman by more than a half-million votes.

Rockefeller was hot news from 1958 onward. Much coverage surrounded his abortive bids for the 1960, 1964, and 1968 Republican presidential nominations, presidential politics apparently being the one area in which the fabled Rockefeller expertise came to naught. The whole country watched with fascination, sometimes with opprobrium, as he divorced his wife of 32 years and in 1963 married Margaretta Fitler Murphy, the just-divorced mother of four. Appropriately, the press rode him hard for preaching frugal "pay-as-you-go" fiscal policies in his first year in office and later incurring fantastic debts through questionable bonding practices. In December 1973, Rockefeller resigned after 15 years as governor, planning another presidential bid; several months later, it turned out, he would reach Washington a different way, accepting the vice presidency on the nomination of Gerald Ford. The public scrutiny continued even after his death on Jan. 26, 1979. The Rockefeller family spokesman announced that Rockefeller had died of a heart attack at his

Rockefeller Center office, but it was later revealed that Rockefeller had died in his private office in a town house at 13 West 54th Street, in the company of his young female assistant, Megan Marshack.

Eclipsed by this personal history were the vast programs of Nelson Rockefeller, who was an absolutely irrepressible builder-manager-operator. Despite his reputation as a liberal Republican, Rockefeller was ideological only to the extent that he was a *doer*, rather than a *thinker*, a total pragmatist. Rockefeller, in the words of one writer, "changed the physical face of New York more than any governor since De Witt Clinton built the Erie Canal," and in many ways he succeeded in changing the way New Yorkers live. He built so many highways—the Long Island, Southern Tier, Adirondack, and Interstate 81 among them—that his campaign commercials could boast his roads would "stretch all the way to Hawaii—and back." Rockefeller turned the decade-old State University of New York, which had 38,000 students, into the largest public university system under one control.

To increase low-income housing, Rockefeller in 1968 created the Urban Development Corporation, a trailblazer state agency in that it had power to do whatever might be required—condemn property, override local zoning, or create just about any conceivable form of financing—to get development accomplished.* In 1975, after the Nixon administration cut off federal housing subsidies, UDC defaulted on $100 million worth of bond anticipation notes and had to be bailed out by the legislature. (Later the UDC switched to assisting commercial development such as Battery Park City, the South Street Seaport in Manhattan, and the Syracuse Stadium, the first domed football stadium in the Northeast.) Rockefeller also inserted state government into mass transit on an absolutely unprecedented scale when he set up the Metropolitan Transportation Authority, which took over the Long Island Railroad, all New York City subways, buses, the Triborough and other bridges, the New York share of the New Haven Railroad, and the Penn Central line running through Westchester. A multibillion-dollar modernization and expansion program resulted in better train service, but the subways just got worse.

Rockefeller's worst failure, so he admitted when we pressed him, was his attempt to curb drug abuse—first with progressive programs and later with the nation's toughest narcotics law. But history will probably note a much more grievous Rockefeller error: his handling of the Attica prison revolt (30 miles east of Buffalo) in 1971 during which 32 prisoners and 9 hostage guards lost their lives; Rockefeller refused to visit the riot scene personally.

Rockefeller critics were fond of accusing him of having an "edifice complex." He built things most of his adult life, playing a hand in Rockefeller

---

*UDC's power to override local interests offended many people, but it had a great success: the transformation of Welfare Island in the East River into Roosevelt Island, a "new town" only 3½ minutes by cable car from Bloomingdale's department store in Manhattan. When *Los Angeles Times* reporter John Goldman visited Roosevelt Island in 1981, residents boasted their "Little Apple" had the cleanest streets, the lowest crime rates (some residents didn't even lock their doors), and some of the best public schools in New York.

Center, Colonial Williamsburg, the United Nations headquarters, Lincoln Center, the World Trade Center, and the building of 17 new university and college campuses in New York State. Where many critics believed he really went overboard was the grandiose Albany South Mall project, which he conceived in 1959 to make the decaying old city of Albany into "the most spectacularly beautiful seat of government in the world"—or what *Fortune* called "a modern imperial enclave." At $2 billion, it was the most expensive project ever undertaken by any state government.

And it is the misuse of money for which many now most remember Rockefeller and his years of power. The state budget grew almost geometrically—from $2.04 billion in 1959–60, Rockefeller's first year in office, to $8.8 billion in 1973–74, even while the state's private economy languished and declined. But even more distasteful in the long run was the "backdoor" municipal bond financing for capital construction. The financing was perfected by none other than John Mitchell, later Nixon's attorney general and Watergate felon, who at the time was a senior partner in the Nixon law firm of Mudge and Rose and one of the nation's leading experts in the municipal bond field. Because Rockefeller wanted to avoid the constitutional requirement of placing bond issues before the voters, and thereby risking rejection, he created appendages to state government to issue the bonds. These bonds bore higher interest rates than if they had been issued directly by the state.

Rockfeller also drove up other costs. He supported the highest minimum wage in the country at the time ($1.85); his vast construction programs delighted the building trades by driving up wages; and he started the pensions spiral that later came to plague state and local governments around the country. In 1963, just after he won reelection with first-time support from New York City police and firefighters unions, Rockefeller asked the legislature to establish the principle that firemen's and patrolmen's pensions after 20 years on the job would be computed on the basis of the individual's salary during his last year. The legislation was passed in 1967, and the same budget-busting principle later spread to transit police, sanitationmen, housing police, and corrections officers.

To Rockefeller's credit, it must be said that he had deep civil rights convictions, and that he sincerely believed he was doing what was right for New York State and its future. Had he been a man of less principle, he might have bowed to Republican party conservatives on racial and social policies and won a presidential nomination. Nevertheless, Rockefeller was a spendthrift governor—and would likely have been a spendthrift president, on every issue from welfare to defense spending. Perhaps his greatest weakness, in his home state, was trying to do too much too fast. By describing Rockefeller as "the Last Colonialist," John Lindsay captured the essence of Rockefeller's elitism, his indifference to community control or participation, and his lack of belief in the common sense of ordinary people. He relied on experts he could afford to hire personally (and who were never likely to say "no" to any of his ideas). He disregarded repeated warnings of State Comptroller Arthur Levitt, who opposed the shaky and expansive bond measures and warned Rockefeller that the state economy was declining. Ultimately, it was Rockefeller's money—the habit of unlimited money that was his birthright, the coincidence of being governor when public money seemed too easy to obtain—that gave him excessive control and sowed bitter seeds for others to reap later.

The inevitable fiscal retrenchment of New York began in 1971, two years before Rockefeller's departure, when a rebellious (for a change) Republican legislature cut $760 million from the gubernatorial budget. But it was Hugh Carey, elected in 1974, the first Democrat elected to that office in 20 years and a man with a 14-year record of liberal votes in the U.S. House, who had to issue the harsh call for economy, frugality, and retrenchment. "All around us in this capital are symbols of splendor, monuments of glass and marble," said Carey in his inaugural speech, in the shadow of the nearly finished Albany Mall. "They stand as living embodiments of an idea of government as an ever-expanding institution, to be paid from the ever-expanding riches of tomorrow. To the citizens of New York, I say: Tomorrow is here. We have learned that every resource of this earth is finite, so is the resource by which the government sustains itself: the earnings of the people."

In his first year in office, Carey won a $600 million package of new taxes on business and banks to cope with the city and state financial crisis. But noting that the state and local tax burden on households and firms had reached 60 percent above the national average, Carey and the legislature finally began reducing taxes. Between 1977 and 1981 New York reduced personal income taxes, increased personal exemptions, phased out several business taxes, exempted manufacturing supplies and equipment from the state sales tax, and reduced income and estate taxes for farmers.* It must be noted, however, that Carey and Rockefeller shared a love of building things even when the financing had to be in a backhand manner. In 1978, Carey renamed the Albany Mall the Nelson A. Rockefeller Empire State Plaza. Carey fully supported the questionable Westway project in New York City and continued using oddly constructed and expensive bond financing to pacify the pro-development interests of the building trades unions and bankers.

Historians will most certainly remember Carey for his role in helping New York City avoid fiscal disaster. As he noted when he announced his retirement in 1982, he did have other accomplishments, including an $8 billion subway-improvement program and financing of major economic development projects in many communities of the state. Carey would also be remembered for staving off conservatives trying to reinstate the death penalty and gut New York's liberal abortion laws. Carey also went out on a limb to improve the tax situation for small, growing high-technology firms—even though his own political constituency saw little value in such a move.

---

*Though often unnoticed, New York agriculture is still a $2.6 billion industry—and once again a growing one. The number of acres under cultivation increased by 500,000 in the 1970s, and farm income rose at better than twice the rate of inflation. Much of the new production was in fruits and vegetables, and the demand for them was believed to indicate a change in consumer buying habits toward fresh, rather than frozen, foods.

The Democratic hold on the New York governorship continued with the 1982 election of Mario Cuomo, lieutenant governor under Carey. Cuomo won only after a tough primary race against Mayor Koch and then multimillionaire Republican businessman Lewis Lehrman, an apostle of supply-side economics. A man of high erudition and intelligence, Cuomo ran as a traditional Democratic liberal and was aided by support of Italian-Americans who enthusiastically grasped the opportunity to elect—for the first time—one of their number to New York's highest office. But Cuomo faced the excrutiating problem of trying to appease his friends in organized labor—who were instrumental in turning out the vote for his election—in a season of severe fiscal stringency for the state government.

By the dawn of the 1980s New York's overall tax burden still remained a significant 41 percent above the national average. But the state's economy did appear to have recovered to the point that it could weather national recessions fairly well. One sign was the unemployment rate, which remained below the national average during the recession of the early '80s (although New York City's rate, reflecting the large numbers of poor and untrained residents, rose above most of the rest of the country). Roger Vaughan, an economist and former adviser to Carey, told us that New York may have passed through its worst economic storms. New York, Vaughan said, had once again led the nation in a fundamental transformation of the economy, this time moving from an economy based "on the capacity to process materials to growth based on the capacity to process information."

The results have been dramatic. New York City reached an historic milestone in 1982 when jobs in finance, insurance and real estate surpassed those in manufacturing. And in 1982, for the first time ever, the majority of the state's 1.5 million manufacturing jobs directly involved high technology products and services.

There was another, quite real danger, however: that the new information-based economy might sow the seeds of social discord since most of the high-paying jobs go to people with high levels of training, leaving crumbs (if any employment at all) for low-skilled people and factory workers with outdated skills. New York also faced the need to spend $80 to $100 billion to repair its declining roads, bridges, and other physical structures before the end of the century. The lingering question was whether New York could keep its taxes sufficiently high to satisfy its social needs and yet low enough to avoid another era of business flight.

A word might be added here about the forces that control New York's legislature. On the Republican side, leaders have often been of the mold of Warren M. Anderson, a colorless, austere Republican state senate leader from Binghamton. It might be said that Anderson's Republicanism was more akin to the Midwestern Taft variety than the New York Dewey-Rockefeller tradition. Yet Anderson and his Republican colleagues worked tirelessly to avert a New York City bankruptcy. Democratic leaders have generally been of quite a different brand, typified by the Democratic Speaker from Brooklyn, Stanley Fink. Here is leadership from the world of the regular Democratic clubhouse, the lawyers, appraisers, insurance agents, and unions that provide the lifeblood of old-style New York urban politics.

The budget and powers of New York State government are so colossal that Albany draws lobbyists as flowers attract bees. They are a sophisticated group, representing virtually every interest in the state, and a far cry from the old stereotype of the cigar-chomping, vote-buying influence peddler. By general consensus, the teachers' lobby (except in years of extreme fiscal stringency) is the biggest and most powerful on the Albany scene. A major power here is the New York State United Teachers, headed by New York teacher union boss Albert Shanker. The teachers' union pension fund was one of the major buyers of the city bonds that helped New York City avoid bankruptcy—and gave Shanker the leverage he did not fail to use. Among other major players on the Albany scene are the Associated Industries of New York and Empire State Chamber of Commerce, banking interests, organized labor, and the big, highly efficient New York City lobby.

Multistate, Multiparty New York

New York politics have two great divisions: of geography, and of party. The geographic division centers around New York City versus its suburbs and the rest of the state. And here the story is simply told: while the city's share of the state population has fallen sharply from 55 percent in 1930 to 40 percent in 1980, its loss of political power has been even more precipitous. Right after World War II, the city was still casting 51.5 percent of the statewide vote; by 1980, that figure was down to 31 percent. Since the city has traditionally registered massive Democratic majorities, while the growing suburbs and upstate areas have on the whole tended toward the Republican party, it is not hard to divine why New York politics were ripe (at least as soon as Nelson Rockefeller cleared the scene) for a strong move to the right.

It was, of course, not Nelson Rockefeller but Thomas Dewey who inaugurated the great 20th-century era of liberal New York Republicanism on which the curtain has only recently been drawn. Dewey, with his crime-busting image and agility at co-opting Democratic policies, was able to cut down the New York City Democratic majorities that had so often decimated Republican candidates. Rockefeller, also nurturing a centrist, near-liberal image, continued to improve the Republicans' position in the city until in his fourth-term race in 1970 he lost there by a minuscule 16,541 votes, a startling achievement for a Republican.

By force of personality, and even more concretely the vast amounts of money he was willing to expend on the exercise, Rockefeller dominated the New York Republican Party thoroughly—and for a while, it seemed permanently. But like so many dominant figures, he left no direct political heirs. In fact, there had long been suppressed, conservative forces within the Republican party waiting for Rockefeller to exit the scene. When he did, they went to work with a vengeance, and great effectiveness. Without the Rockefeller subsidies, Republican fundraisers had to pay more attention to conservative donors. Without Rockefeller's domination, the centralized authority of the state Republican party fell apart, to be replaced by a series of geographic fiefdoms. Among the most powerful of these, it turned out, were the conservative Republican organizations of Long Island and Westchester County, where Italian-Americans (ex-city residents or the sons and daughters of same) had forsaken the Democratic for the Republican party as they gained affluence and became increasingly disenchanted with liberal Democratic social policy on such issues as racial integration and freedom of choice on abortion. The 1970s found Italian-Americans heading the Republican organizations in vote-heavy Nassau, Suffolk, and Westchester counties. The Nassau GOP, run by Joseph Margiotta, was probably the strongest old-style machine in New York —perhaps in the entire nation—with more of the trappings of patronage and contracts for which urban Democratic organizations are so often criticized. (Margiotta was in such firm control that even after a 1981 conviction for arranging an elaborate political kickback scheme, his power eroded only slowly.)

The conservative shift was exemplified by the 1980 Republican Senate primary in which Senator Jacob Javits, an incumbent since 1956, was defeated by Alfonse D'Amato, a little-known conservative town supervisor from Long Island. Javits lost partly due to his age (76) and ill health. (He persisted in running in the general election as a Liberal, and he and Rep. Elizabeth Holtzman of Brooklyn split the vote to elect D'Amato.) Though both were Republicans, there could not be a stronger difference between Javits and D'Amato. Javits, the son of immigrant Jewish parents on New York's Lower East Side, was a leading exemplar of liberal Republicanism even before Rockefeller. Among the bills for which he could take a major share of the credit were the student college loan program, major civil rights laws between 1957 and 1965 (he served first in the House), Medicare, major housing acts, the Pension Reform Act of 1973, and the War Powers Act. Like Rockefeller, Javits was also arrogant; his fellow Republicans in Washington respected him more than they loved him. D'Amato, by contrast, started out with the endorsements of the Conservative and Right-to-Life parties before he challenged Javits.

On the New York Democratic side, one finds as quarrelsome a group of politicians as American politics offers. Back in the "Golden Age" of Smith, Roosevelt, and Lehman, the party's core of New York City ethnic groups did forge a coalition that was the prototype of the national New Deal coalition. But ethnic rivalries boiled to the top, and in 1949 the Italians, led by Carmine De Sapio of New York City, finally wrested control of Tammany Hall (the regular Democratic Manhattan organization) from the Irish. De Sapio looked mildly reformist when he came to power, but eventually he was corrupted and went to prison for conspiring to bribe Mayor Lindsay's water commissioner and for extorting contracts. In 1949 the first glimmerings of the largely Jewish modern reform movement in New York Democratic politics emerged on Manhattan Island, politics that would dominate the 1950s and '60s. The reformers elected "anti-boss" candidates to Congress and as state chairman and in 1967 replaced New York's noisy convention system of nominating statewide candidates (it was prone to boss control and essentially undemocratic, they charged) with a primary. Instead of shifting to a simple primary, New York opted for a hybrid system. The state committee of each party meets in the spring and designates its preferred candidate, but candidates who receive 25 percent of the committee vote and others who collect 10,000 signatures from party members spread throughout the state can also get on the ballot. This hybrid committee-primary system pleases political scientists who want to see "the party" have a major voice in the nomination process, but in practice it has provided Republican orators with an opportunity to berate the Democrats' "boss handpicked candidate."

New York Democrats have a particularly vexsome problem: the inordinately strong voice that Jewish voters have in their primaries. Voting far out of proportion to their numbers, Jews can and do swing key primaries. In the 1976 Democratic presidential primary, they were instrumental in giving their friend on the Israel issue, Washington State's Henry M. Jackson, a clear plurality in New York. They provided the winning margin in 1980 for Massachusetts' Edward M. Kennedy because they were disgruntled with a Carter administration vote in the United Nations the week before. Neither man was able to repeat his performance in later state primaries in which the Jewish vote was not nearly so important.

And what has happened to the old Democratic "bosses"? There are still a few around, but none has a fraction of the power De Sapio exercised. The "machine's" mainstay these days is probably judicial patronage. Judges in New York City are nominated by county party conventions, which the oldtimers still control (except in Manhattan). The hundreds of judges so nominated never have to face a Democratic primary, and they are routinely elected in November; the judges in turn appoint law secretaries who appoint appraisers, executors, administrators, and trustees. Aside from that, the machine Democrats do very little in this media age except get quoted by reporters, who assume they possess a commodity called power. Even the reporters, however, began to question the importance of the clubhouse after former member of Congress and Senate candidate Elizabeth Holtzman beat the last stronghold, the Brooklyn regulars, to capture the nomination for district attorney in that borough in 1981. The real power in determining who wins elections has shifted to pollsters such as Patrick Caddell, to television advertising and media specialists like David Garth, and in 1982 to the labor unions, which organized Cuomo's get-out-the-vote drives.

Even with the old-style bosses dethroned, the political concerns of white ethnic, middle-class New Yorkers were winning renewed attention in the Democratic party by the 1970s. Reformers and members of the "New Left" faced an ever-steeper political road. Koch's mayoralty victories proved that. So did the 1976 election of Daniel Patrick Moynihan to the U.S. Senate. Moynihan's backers engineered votes at the convention so that three of the "left"—former Attorney General Ramsey Clark, state party leader and city council member Paul O'Dwyer, and Rep. Bella Abzug—qualified in addition to Moynihan for primary ballot spots. The strategy worked: Moynihan was the composite candidate who could appeal to blue-collar, Catholic, Jewish, and liberal voters. An Irish wit who was born in Oklahoma and raised in New York City's Hell's Kitchen, Moynihan had been teaching at Harvard and had little connection with the state in later years except as the combative and quotable U.S. ambassador to the United Nations for the Ford administration. During his campaign, Moynihan did not object to being described as both a "decent liberal" and a "neoconservative." But Moynihan also defended Franklin Roosevelt's New Deal and fondly recalled the sense of community and hope in the New York City of his youth. Once in the Senate, Moynihan turned out to be a strong defender of all the federal domestic spending programs on which the Northeast had become so dependent. He complained lustily about shortchanging of New York in federal spending programs. And despite his neoconservative label, he turned out to be a critic of the Reagan administration, especially on foreign policy.

New York's history of significant "third" parties goes all the way back to 1829, when disgruntled laborers in New York City formed their own Working-Men's party and upset the powers-that-were by electing several candidates to office. The minor-party tradition has been carried a lot further in this century, aided and abetted by New York laws that permit a candidate to run on the ticket of more than one party.

For many years the most famous and powerful of the minor parties was the Liberal party. It started as an off-shoot of the American Labor party, founded in 1936 by a group of socialist-type union leaders to give New Deal supporters who were unwilling to vote Democratic because of their opposition to Tammany Hall an opportunity to vote for Roosevelt. One of its important goals was to keep the Democratic party in the city and state left of center. The organizational core of the Liberals was of first-generation central European Jews who worked in the needle trades and belonged to the sponsoring unions. But on election day, the Liberal party line was a favorite haven of independent voters who were Democratic at heart but fervently anti-Tammany. In the 1970s the Liberals faded rapidly. Their organization, many noted, was less a crusading force than an encrusted organization of elderly Jews.

Into the vacuum came the New York Conservative party. The idea for its formation was hatched one day at lunch by two young Manhattan lawyers who happened to be brothers-in-law, Kieran O'Doherty and J. Daniel Mahoney. The Conservative party has registered a smashing success in achieving its goal to shift the spectrum of New York politics to the right by putting pressure on the Republicans. The Conservatives started off by running unsuccessful obscure candidates and then, as a well-publicized lark, William F. Buckley, the publisher, for mayor of New York City in 1965. By edging the Liberals in 1966, the Conservatives got the coveted third line on the New York voting machines. In 1970, the Conservative party nominee, James L. Buckley, was elected to the U.S. Senate over Democrat Richard Ottinger and Republican-Liberal Charles Goodell. Buckley's 1976 defeat at the hands of Patrick Moynihan suggested strongly that his earlier victory had been a fluke, but in

1980 the Conservatives pulled off another coup when their candidate, Alfonse D'Amato, defeated veteran Jacob Javits to win the Republican nomination and went on to win election to the Senate. With D'Amato in the Senate, their candidate Reagan in the White House, and the party's founder O'Doherty in Washington, the Conservative leadership wondered whether success would spoil the "joy of being right." "They'll kill me for saying this," said Thomas A. Bolan, a party member with close ties to Reagan, "but I think the party is very close to having achieved its goal." In hard fact, however, no Conservative had yet won a two-person race in New York State.

D'Amato, we might add, was also endorsed by New York's newest "third party," the Right-to-Life party. Boasting only 15,000 members statewide, it nevertheless achieved distinction when it outpolled the Liberals in the 1978 gubernatorial race. The Right-to-Lifers oppose abortion in any situation, even rape, incest, or to save the mother's life. The party found Ronald Reagan too liberal on abortion and ran its own candidate for president.

Republicans, Conservatives, and Right-to-Lifers have all given their endorsements to the latter-day star of the New York congressional delegation, Jack F. Kemp of Buffalo. Kemp came from one of the most depressed regions of New York State, although his own district was mostly middle- to upper-class suburban with a few residential areas suffering from the decline of industry in adjoining Buffalo. He won election, initially in 1970, by breaking from the New York tradition of advocating government job programs and business bailouts. Kemp preached that problems could be solved "through the private enterprise system, the greatest engine of social welfare that we have in a free society." He became *the* congressional advocate for "supply-side economics" and the "Laffer curve" theory that tax cuts would lead to economic expansion, which would eventually increase federal revenues. The handsome, All-American Kemp's political life started as a result of his football career with the Buffalo Bills. During his many speeches to promote the Reagan administration's economic policies and himself, Kemp invited comparisons with John F. Kennedy when he quoted Kennedy's remark that "a rising tide lifts all boats." Even some conservative economists faulted Kemp for overoptimism. ("A rising tide," noted Herbert Stein, chairman of Richard Nixon's Council of Economic Advisers, "does not lift the boats that are underwater.")

Other notable New York Republican members of Congress include William Green of Manhattan's East Side "Silk Stocking District" (an advocate for women's rights and public housing); Hamilton Fish, Jr., of Millbrook (member of a distinguished family that has sent a member to Washington from each generation since his great-grandfather's time, an immigration expert, environmentalist, and nuclear-power critic); Frank Horton of Rochester (founder and co-chairman of the Northeast-Midwest Congressional Coalition); and Barber Conable, Jr., of Rochester (ranking Republican member of the Ways and Means Committee and one of the more thoughtful economic experts in Congress).

But New York is even more noted for its liberal Democratic members of

Congress, many of whom have become national household names or at least experts in their fields. Among the most accomplished in the early 1980s were Thomas J. Downey of Long Island (first elected at age 25 in 1974, arms limitation advocate); Joseph P. Addabbo of Queens (Pentagon critic); Benjamin Rosenthal of Queens (consumer protectionist, until his death in early 1983); Mario Biaggi of the Bronx (leading congressional advocate for Catholic militants in Northern Ireland); Shirley Chisholm of Brooklyn (author of the minimum-wage law for domestic workers, 1972 presidential candidate, and retired from Congress in 1982); Stephen Solarz of Brooklyn (foreign policy expert, a defender of Israel); Charles Rangel of Harlem (described by *Congressional Quarterly* as "the least ideological of the senior black members of Congress"); Ted Weiss of the West Side of Manhattan (crusader for liberal causes); Robert Garcia of the Bronx (co-author with Kemp of the "enterprise zone" proposal, which would provide deregulation and tax breaks for business in poor neighborhoods); Geraldine Ferraro of Queens (mass transportation advocate); and Richard L. Ottinger of Westchester County (environmentalist). A conservative Democrat deserving mention is Sam Stratton of Schenectady, who ranks high on the House Armed Services Committee and was a strong defense advocate even through the Vietnam War years.

Geographic New York

New York is a state of remarkable diversity. It is a Great Lakes and Canadian border state along its northern reaches, a New England state on the east, a Pennsylvania Appalachian state along its Southern Tier, an Atlantic state around New York Harbor and out Long Island. We move around the state in a clockwise direction, starting with the Catskills and leaving for last the New York City suburban ring.

The Catskills. These lovely and gently rounded hills emerge from the Hudson's wooded west banks, where Rip Van Winkle once slept, and include the famous borscht belt in Sullivan and Ulster counties, where New Yorkers have headed for a bucolic interlude and sometimes gaudy entertainment at hotels such as Grossinger's and the Concord. Fires, some caused by arson, have plagued the area in recent years, symbolizing the decline of the Catskills as a resort area. Woodstock, a Catskills haven for painters, musicians, and artists of all types, became famous for the 1969 three-day rock festival that was the event of a generation. The affair was actually held at Max Yasgur's farm near Bethel, 50 miles away.

The Southern Tier. This section of deeply wooded hills and valleys, part of the Appalachian Highlands shared with Pennsylvania, runs along two-thirds of the state's width and is cut by strong rivers such as the Delaware, the Susquehanna, and the Allegheny. The Southern Tier is sparsely populated by Eastern standards, the only cities of appreciable size being Binghamton

(55,860), Elmira (35,327), Jamestown (35,775), and Ithaca (28,732), home of Cornell University. All except Ithaca have lost population in recent years. Near Binghamton is a high-paying IBM plant. Jamestown, home of famous factories for furniture and voting machines, has become nationally distinguished for its unusual level of labor-management cooperation in the face of industrial decline. The Southern Tier also has the Corning Glass Company, which produces the world-famous Steuben glassware and gigantic telescope mirrors. Both tourism and agriculture (including grape production) are mainstays of the local economy. A big Indian reservation is home for the last of the proud Senecas. Near Lake Erie is Chautauqua Lake, home base of the famed Chatauqua Circuit that once brought culture, including orator William Jennings Bryan, to crossroads and hamlets of the nation. It has survived as a musical and philosophical center that blends traditional speakers with such modernists as Buckminster Fuller and Masters and Johnson, the sex therapists. The delightful old Victorian-era Hotel Athenaeum, replete with high-ceilinged rooms and porches, galleries, and immense fireplaces, is a remembrance of the leisure of times gone by.

Set between the Southern and Northern Tiers are the slender Finger Lakes: Canandaigua, Keuka, Seneca, Cayuga, Owasco, and Skaneateles, a summer refuge for New Yorkers.

Upstate cities. Now our focus shifts to the urban corridor along the Great Lakes coastal plains, and then the Mohawk Valley, from Buffalo to Albany.

Buffalo (357,870), with its metropolitan area (1,254,573), is New York's second-largest city. Buffalo is a classic example of a Northeastern city suffering as companies close up old and inefficient plants and move to what the industrialists view as greener pastures. The center city lost over 22 percent of its population in the 1970s, and the metro area almost 8 percent. Buffalo has lost much of what once made it great. It had a superb location: both the eastern terminus of the Great Lakes shipping lanes and the western terminus of New York's low-level water route from the east. With the construction of the St. Lawrence Seaway, ocean-going ships began to sail directly inland. Buffalo's great grain elevators are now largely automated. Thousands of steelworkers have lost their jobs—permanently. Even before these economic difficulties, Buffalo had a celebrated inferiority complex due to equal parts bad weather ("a snow-covered Pittsburgh"), grimy industry (the steel plants, foundries, and auto factories), and a sinewy blue-collarism more inclined to sports than the arts. In the downtown, many old buildings are empty or under-used; after the immense population loss of the '70s, one local writer moaned that "Main Street north of downtown aches with the loss."

Yet amid all these cries of despair, there has also been a forward-looking and doggedly optimistic Buffalo. The State University there is the center for New York State–sponsored graduate education. The city obtained federal aid to build a light rail line to the university. Some distinguished old downtown buildings have been recycled rather than bulldozed. The city has built a new convention center and hotel, invested federal aid funds in local business ventures, and emphasized waterfront development and even the role of the arts downtown. The mayor strongly credited for many of these new departures was James D. Griffin, a maverick Democrat who was reelected in 1981 with the endorsement of the Republican, Conservative, and Right-to-Life parties. Since Democratic rules prohibit multiparty endorsements, Griffin ended Buffalo's reputation as forever following the Democratic party line. Neighborhood leaders complained that too much city money was going into downtown ventures, but Griffin prevailed, winning the title of the "Ed Koch of Western New York" for his multiple endorsements and his poor relations with the city's 26.5 percent black population. Indeed, if you want to find a city that still personifies raw, muscular ethnic politics, Buffalo is your place. Divided into rather homogeneous nationality pockets are contingents of Italians, Poles, Hungarians, Czechs, Irish, Jews, American Indians, Puerto Ricans, and the big black community.

Buffalo's most famous suburb is Niagara Falls (71,834), where the world-famous cataract draws millions a year to a sight that hasn't changed much since Father Louis Hennepin first viewed this natural wonder in 1678. The use of hydroelectric power on the American continent was pioneered here. The city of Niagara Falls, physically so dreary in comparison to its Canadian twin, has tried to dress itself up with a convention center and a truly elegant Winter Garden, a glittering, glass-windowed structure featuring charming and intimate gardens. Volunteer business aid rescued the city government from fiscal disaster in the mid-1970s. But the city has been plagued with troubles, the worst being the discovery in 1978 that toxic chemical wastes, dumped at Love Canal by the Hooker Chemical Co. during the 1940s and 1950s, were leaching out of the landfill into the basements of area homes. The term "Love Canal" became in fact a catchword for the grim, growing national problem of chemical waste dumping.

Rochester, once described as "quiet, conservative, contented, and Kodak," is indeed a center for the optical business and other precision instrumentation. Eastman Kodak employes 1 of every 11 people, but the city is also home to Bausch and Lomb and birthplace of the Xerox copier. These expanding industries made the city (241,741) and metropolitan area (971,879) the shining exception to upstate New York's economic problems in the '70s. The city proper saw its image decline for years following a 1964 race riot. Later, though, downtown facelifting went forward. A cultural district was formed surrounding the famed Eastman School of Music, which had thankfully resisted the outward push to the suburban University of Rochester campus. One problem was that the city became heavily dependent on federal aid. Rochester is the corporate headquarters of the robustly expanding Gannett newspaper chain, although much of Gannett's national news operations have moved to the Washington, D.C., area. Rochester and Monroe County have shared some functions since the 1960s, and municipal experts have suggested they may need to share more taxes to survive in the future.

Syracuse (170,105) and its metropolitan area (642,375) are regarded as the real capital of upstate conservatism, thanks in part to the rightward tilt of the local press. But Syracuse is not a closed, narrow-minded community. It has been a crossroads from the days of the Indian trails to the great canals to the superhighways. (The city is famed for truck terminals and rail yards.) Syracuse workers turn out a variety of products; in contrast to Rochester, no single industry dominates. There are many ethnic groups; again, no single one dominates. Local government is competent and honest. And there is the benign influence of Syracuse University, whose Maxwell Graduate School of Citizenship and Public Affairs has trained some of the country's most able civil servants at local, state, and federal levels. Syracuse's chief drawback is undoubtedly snow: an average of 108 inches a year, more than any other American city.

We now pass into mountainous territory, cut by the handsome, historic Mohawk Valley. All the significant settlement is crammed into the rather narrow river valley; the two principal cities are Utica and Rome, whose combined metropolitan area lost 5.9 percent in the 1970s, bringing the total down to 320,180. Industrially, this is tired, aged territory with little dynamism. In Utica, one finds a splendid center of community life, the Munson-Williams-Proctor Institute; its design by Philip Johnson has made it the most elegant structure in the entire upstate area. A few miles to the south is picturesque Cooperstown, where baseball was supposedly invented in 1839 and where the Baseball Hall of Fame now stands.

The Albany-Schnectady-Troy metropolitan area (795,019) is heavy with state offices, federal regional offices, and factories. Albany (101,727) in the '70s finally began to show some signs of life, not only around the South Mall—the state-government office building, discussed earlier—but in the neighborhoods. The State Capitol itself was spruced up. One thing that never seems to change in Albany is the political machine in charge. "Uncle" Daniel P. O'Connell, who ran it for *half a century*, died in 1977, but his mayor, Erastus Corning II, in office *since 1942*, maintained his position. Albany is notorious for its low city taxes and easy-going snow removal. (Some reporters believe the only removal methods are solar heat and spring.) The irony has not been lost that Albany, the city with the highest proportion of public employees in the state, consistently supports a municipal administration that delivers a relatively low level of public services and is notoriously resistant to public employee unionization.

The North Country. Here is distant and truly "uncivilized" New York State, known to comparatively few Americans. In the northwest is Lake Ontario and the region of the Thousand Islands (there are actually some 1,700), and then a long stretch of the St. Lawrence River. On the state's northernmost extremity are 60 miles of border with Quebec. On the east one comes upon the beautiful Champlain Valley, centered on 107-mile long Lake Champlain (across from Vermont), which connects with Lake George to form the great north-south waterway that was the path of empire through several wars. Making a living is an acute problem; the chief industries are tourism, mining for iron ores, lead and zinc, lumbering and paper mills, all characterized by seasonal job fluctuations. The Adirondack Mountains and their Park, decreed by the New York legislature in 1892, fill the great land bulk of the North Country. The beautiful Adirondacks have suffered from environmental problems for generations. Garish strip development has plagued tourist havens; the air and water have been contaminated by industrial activity; and, most recently, acid rain from the Middle West valley has threatened trees and animals.

The Adirondacks' most famous community is Lake Placid, site of two world Winter Olympic meets.

The Hudson River. Among the great rivers of America, the Hudson is one of the shortest. From its point of birth—jewel-like Lake Tear of the Clouds, a two-acre pond below the summit of Mt. Marcy in the high Adirondacks—it flows only 315 miles until it enters the Atlantic at New York Harbor. Yet its role in the story of New York State—geologic, aesthetic, ecologic—is a major one.

Three hundred years ago, Dutch explorers rhapsodized about the handsome forests and mountains that line the Hudson's banks, and later Winslow Homer did some of his finest paintings of the river. The upper Hudson is a fast-flowing trout stream, but below the Adirondack Forest Preserve, paper company, municipal and industrial waste intrude. A great suspense story of the late 20th century is whether the state and federal pure-waters programs will be sufficient to restore the Hudson to something approaching its cleanliness of times past.

The mid-Hudson Valley—from the capital district southward to the Westchester County line—has some grand turn-of-the-century mansions along its banks and smaller retreats for New York Cityites but is still relatively undeveloped. The U.S. Military Academy at West Point, FDR's ancestral home at Hyde Park, and his presidential library have long added luster to the region and stimulated the local economy. Agriculture, especially apple growing and dairy farming, is strong. But light industry and relative proximity to New York City spurred these Hudson Valley counties to strong growth rates in the 1970s—a dramatic exception to the state's general population loss. Dutchess County's population went up 10.2 percent to 245,055, Orange County 17.1 percent to 259,603, little Putnam County 36.2 percent to 77,193, Rockland County, opposite Westchester on the widest part of the Hudson, 12.9 percent to 259,530.

Classic Suburbia. To understand New York City's suburban sphere, one would have to include northern New Jersey and southern Connecticut, but here we will limit ourselves to the instate suburbs of Westchester County and Long Island, some of the nation's most famous.

Westchester, the *New York Times* once commented, "is the ultimate suburban myth. Surely all Westchester must be one big Scarsdale, the myth goes, one chain of fine Colonial Homes and Tudor-style grocery stores stretching from Hudson to [Long Island] Sound." In reality, Westchester is many worlds. America's greatest concentration of highly paid corporate executives and their families do live in clipped, groomed, and lovely places such as Larchmont, Rye, Bronxville, Mount Kisco, Pound Ridge, Bedford, Irvington, and Scarsdale itself. But for many years Westchester has also had tens of thousands of people on welfare. Nor is Westchester lily white; more and more blacks have moved to the county in recent years, reaching 104,815, or 12 percent of the county's people, in 1980. The numbers take on greater significance when one notes that the overall Westchester population declined 3.1 percent to 866,599, as the children of the baby boom moved out of their parents' homes. The city of Mt. Vernon is 49 percent black. Westchester's greatest future challenge may lie in providing services to its increasingly elderly population. Contrary to popular impression, most of these retirees will not move to the Sunbelt, and their living arrangements in large, single-family dwellings spread out over the countryside make it expensive to provide health services and transportation for them. One solution would be zoning changes to allow construction of apartments, but many Westchester residents are still afraid anything but single-family dwellings will bring *them* in.

Westchester is not just residences. Several corporations abandoned Manhattan and set up headquarters in parklike settings in Westchester: IBM in Armonk, General Foods in White Plains, Pepsico in Purchase, and others. Many smaller industries began or expanded operations in the county, and almost as many people commute *into* Westchester as out to jobs in New York City and elsewhere. Industrialization has added to the diversity. In northern Westchester, the scene is still an idyllic one of rolling farmland, lush forests, and pristine villages; by contrast, the city of Yonkers (the state's third-largest —195,351 in 1980) is really just an extension of the Bronx and has suffered severe New York City–style financial stress. The county seat of White Plains underwent substantial urban renewal and has become a major office center. New Rochelle (70,794) is home of theater celebrities, corporate executives, and upwardly mobile working-class families, but its business district reached such a state of decay in the late 1970s that federal community development funds were used to put new façades and signs on the buildings. The unemployment rate was high enough to qualify for a federal action grant to build an industrial park.

Westchester has been a commuting suburb since the arrival of the railroad before the turn of the century. In contrast, Long Island is largely a World War II phenomenon. In 1940 Long Island was still a series of quiet little villages, each with a Main Street, some shops, a movie house, and a soda parlor, with the land of the farmer at the back doorstep. After Pearl Harbor aviation plants (which had opened up on the island before the crash of 1929) suddenly received multimillion-dollar government contracts. A great job boom ensued. After the war, New York's returning GIs were desperate for new housing, and in 1947 entrepreneur-builder William Levitt and his brother began building the first of thousands of inexpensive Cape Cod–style homes on a potato field in the center of Nassau County. The result was the first Levittown: 17,544 homes in all. There were many predictions that the Levitts' basementless houses, with their inexpensive construction, would be the "slums of the future." The homes have stood up fairly well, but the same cannot be said for miles of Long Island's ugly commercial strips of shops, stores, pizza parlors, and gas stations, all of which have come to look the worse for wear. As Nassau County's land filled up with houses, the population pressure shifted to Suffolk County, and one need only check the latest home-builders' ads in the newspapers to see how far east the movement has pro-gressed at any moment in time. Like many suburban communities across the country, Nassau County lost population in the 1970s (7.5 percent, down to a total of 1,321,582, even as Suffolk County, still on the cutting edge of growth, gained 13.9 percent for a new total of 1,284,231). Urban decay crept into Nassau County, most noticeably in the town of Hempstead, once Long Island's business hub but since the 1960s a victim of steady commercial decline and white flight. The urban decline did spark revival efforts, including a new district courthouse, office buildings, and a performing arts center.

In the postwar era Nassau County provided improved living conditions for hundreds of thousands of people who fled crowded New York City, but its child-oriented culture sadly did not create a very strong sense of belonging among its youth. Syndicated columnist Maxwell Glen, who grew up in Syosset in the early 1960s, told us he sometimes has to think twice to remem-ber living there. *Newsday*, Long Island's newspaper owned by the Los An-geles Times and Mirror Co., warned in the late '70s that three-fourths of the post–World War II generation was leaving and that the island could be headed "down the path of decay recently trodden by New York City." Long Island, *Newsday* reported, "has no effective central power structure, in either its government or its business and cultural communities. Its residents have strikingly little awareness that many problems of individual communities— problems of high taxation or polluted groundwater, for example—call for regional response. It has no comprehensive library, no important concert hall or museum, no public zoo or aquarium. Long Island does not have a slogan, a song or even a symbol that indicates pride of place."

There are questions about how uniquely suburban—in the sense of exclu-sively single-family homes—Long Island will remain. The housing crunch, stemming from the coming of age of the post–World War II baby boom, has led to a rash of dividing up houses into two or even three separate units, often in violation of local zoning laws. And nowhere have reports of such doubling-and tripling-up been more prevalent than Long Island. Ironically, this shift to suburban density can occur even while overall population drops. Mom and dad and four children, for instance, represent a household of six; a decade later, with the children gone and two illegal renters moved in, the house will hold just four people.

Nassau and Suffolk's middle-class suburbs are not the beginning or the end of Long Island. Geographically, Long Island has the shape of a fish. It actually includes the New York boroughs of Queens and Brooklyn on its western end. Long Island is no longer preeminently a bedroom area for New York City. Fully two-thirds of the Nassau and 86 percent of the Suffolk labor pools now work on the island, and they depend first and foremost on the military-industrial complex. The biggest contractor is Grumman Aircraft, which employed 20,000 workers in 1982. Defense provided the initial impetus for a high-technology community, which by the early 1980s included so many small, owner-run telecommunications defense-related and computer businesses that Chemical Bank economist Jerome Gilbert said Long Island has "the entrepeneurial spirit that used to make New York City great." Long Island lacked the great universities near Massachusetts' Route 128 and California's Silicon Valley, but entrepreneurs were attracted by land, construction, and labor costs lower than those in New York City, while maintaining access to the city's markets and transportation facilities. The result was a thriving, growing economy.

Suffolk remained one of the top counties in New York State in value of agricultural produce (potato and cauliflower farms, vineyards), but had a hard time competing with the distribution systems of Florida and California growers. Both farmers and their neighbors who loved the "farmscape" worried that its days were numbered as owners contemplated the fantastic amounts of money that could be made from subdividing compared to the ups and downs of agriculture. The county instituted a program of outright purchase of farmland and development rights, but it proved luxurious and hard to justify in a time of tightened local budgets.

At the end of the island, just before Montauk Point, are the illustrious Hamptons (South-, East-, West-, and Bridge-), popular with high society but now ever so slightly tainted by publicity and crowds. Indeed, one might say of the Hamptons what one says of all of New York State: classy, interesting, an object of envy for many. But not quite what it used to be.

NEW JERSEY

In the Shadows of a Megalopolis

NEW JERSEY HAS A PROBLEM WITH ITS IMAGE. Suspended between the great urbs of New York and Philadelphia, it still fits the description applied in colonial times—a cask tapped at both ends. There are several places in America, such as Oakland and East St. Louis, that suffer from what is known as "second city" syndrome; only New Jersey could be said to have a second- (or perhaps third-) state syndrome. New Jersey lacks a single city of distinction. The very names of New Jersey's leading cities—Newark, Jersey City, Atlantic City, Paterson, Camden, Trenton, Elizabeth, Bayonne, Hoboken—conjur up visions of alarming decay, an image often grossly inaccurate but still well-nigh universal. New Jersey has a greater percentage of people living in suburbs than does any other state, even though many of its suburban places rightfully belong in the influence realm of metropolises outside its borders. So the upper- and middle-income executives who live in the state find their civic time split between the affairs of New Jersey and the jurisdictions where in fact they spend their working hours.

Then there is the problem of the media. New Jersey did not have a single commercial television station until 1982 when the Federal Communications Commission authorized the movement of the license of New York's WOR across the Hudson River to Secaucus. The press situation is only a little less serious. Somehow the *New York Times* and *Daily News* steal the thunder of the last remaining big Jersey paper, the *Newark Star-Ledger*. The *Philadelphia Inquirer* circulates heavily in southern New Jersey. On the other hand, there are strong local papers—among them the *Bergen Record, Camden Courier-Post, Asbury Park Press, Passaic Herald-News*, as well as the *Trenton Times*—which have their individual territories so well in hand that papers of statewide scope cannot penetrate.

The overall result is a state of low public consciousness. Organized crime in New Jersey, more than any other state of the Union, has been able to take over whole city governments and even infiltrate to high levels in the state government. The history of New Jersey governance is a constant switching back and forth between revelations of corruption, promises of reform, and then a few years later, new revelations of corruption. The illegalities reached one of their most celebrated levels with the convictions of Senator Harrison Williams and Rep. Frank Thompson in the FBI's "Abscam" operation, in which several members of Congress were videotaped accepting bribes from agents posing as Arabs desiring citizenship or help in obtaining government contracts. The "Abscam" sting also uncovered New Jerseyans willing to accept bribes for help in obtaining casino gambling licenses, a clear tipoff to the fetid atmosphere that moved across the Jersey flats after the 1976 decision to create a Vegas East in Atlantic City.

As if this reputation were not bad enough, New Jerseyans must be constantly aware of the air and water pollution that beset the state. Part of the problem is one of image. The impression most outsiders have of New Jersey is confined to the dreary view of belching factories, oil refineries, railroad sidings, and auto graveyards along the Philadelphia–New York highways and railroad tracks. But New Jersey, in fact, has one of the highest incidences of cancer in the nation, and many New Jerseyans must wonder daily about their own risk of exposure to dangerous chemicals in their air and water. New Jersey has made great progress in the environmental area, but the long history of thoughtless dumping has left such a residue in this heart of megalopolis that cleanup will last well into the next century, with grave perils along the way.

New Jersey is not without natural, economic, and human resources to improve itself. The per capita income, $10,924 in 1980, ranks fourth in the nation. With its superb location on the East Coast, New Jersey has long been a favorite site for plants. Today it is much less a colony of New York and Pennsylvania than in the early part of this century. In fact New Jersey has on occasion been accused of "stealing" jobs and population away from New York and Pennsylvania through the aggressive industrial recruitment and advertising that tries to lure prospects through allegedly lower costs and taxes. Nineteen Fortune 500 corporations have their headquarters in New Jersey. The postwar suburban growth brought hundreds of thousands of New York and Philadelphia executives and their families to the state, adding a new element of wealth and leadership talent. There are plenty of brains at Princeton and Rutgers Universities and in the research and development arms of the corporations.

Physically, New Jersey is vest-pocket size: only 7,532 square miles, 46th among the 50 states. But there is a lot more to New Jersey than the congested cityscape and industrial wastelands one sees from a car on the New Jersey Turnpike, or from the window of a through train. Despite the constant inroads of suburbia, there are forests, farms, small towns, and the unspoiled beauty of the Appalachian foothills in the northwestern part of the state and the Atlantic Coast.

It's also possible to overaccentuate the negative in New Jersey, true as all we have said may be. A 1977 poll by the Eagleton Institute of Politics at Rutgers, the state university of New Jersey, showed that 62 percent of New Jerseyans rated their state excellent or good as a place to live. Among the happiest New Jerseyans by far were ex–New Yorkers, who settled in the state in large numbers during the 1950s and 1960s and found relief from the pressures of big-city life. New Jersey has not suffered the same population loss as New York or quite the same degree of stagnation as Pennsylvania. The 1980 Census found 7.4 million people in New Jersey, a modest 2.7 percent gain over 1970. Within those stable figures, however, was the shift within the state, away from established cities and suburbs near New York and Philadelphia and toward even more distant suburbs and rural western and southern areas. "In the last ten years, 75 percent of the new jobs in New Jersey have located in our own Sun Belt, consisting of Morris, Somerset and Middlesex Counties," said George Sternlieb, director of the Center for Urban Policy Research at Rutgers. "The work force that has left the cities has leapfrogged the second ring of expensive suburbs that are zoned against inexpensive housing, to the third ring, the undeveloped rural counties where they can still find housing they can afford," he added. Perhaps away from the dominance of New York and Philadelphia these young people will eventually develop a strong consciousness as New Jerseyans. New Jersey faces, however, preplexing problems trying to keep its young and talented people. We have interviewed countless young professionals around the country who have sheepishly admitted they were raised in New Jersey but sought somewhere else to live.

New Jersey's difficult role as an economic hinterland of New York, yet separated governmentally from the metropolis, dates from 1664 when the English took over the New York area from the Dutch. The Duke of York, given a vast tract of land on the eastern seaboard, unwisely severed the territory between the Hudson and Delaware Rivers from the natural capital in New York and assigned it to two of his court favorites. Unfortunately the duke's representative had already made land grants in Jersey, and a century of court battles ensued between the new lord's proprietors and the grantees. William Penn gained control of the entire present state of New Jersey but presumably became discouraged with the interminable disputes over land ownership and petitioned Charles II for a patent to what is now Pennsylvania. Thus Philadelphia, the great Quaker city, rose on the west bank of the Delaware River, instead of in New Jersey.

Due to its strategic location, New Jersey was the scene of nearly 100 battles and skirmishes in the Revolutionary War. The state's future role began to appear in 1791 when Alexander Hamilton founded the Society for Establishing Useful Manufactures and chose the falls of the Passaic River for the industrial town of Paterson. The 19th century witnessed rapid growth of canals, railways, and manufacturing in such cities as Jersey City, Newark, Paterson, and Camden. Ownership either began in, or inevitably gravitated toward, New York or Philadelphia. Likewise, the chief market for Jersey's farm goods was in the big cities on its borders. From the 1840s to the 1870s the railroads dominated economic and political life in the state. Liberal incorporation laws passed in the 1870s would lead to a charge by Lincoln Steffens that New Jersey was the "traitor state," where corporations fleeced the poor.

New Jersey has always been a melting pot of nationalities. Dutch, British, Finns, and Swedes were all there in ample numbers before the Revolution. There were Quakers, Baptists from Long Island and New England, and later Irish, Germans, Poles, Hungarians, and Russian Jews. Today New Jersey has 437,000 Jews, or 5.9 percent of its population. Only New York has a higher percentage. (Jersey's Jews, however, have shown fewer leadership qualities

than their counterparts across the Hudson.) Italian-Americans, by some estimates, make up 35 percent of the population, blacks 12 percent, and Hispanics,
from both Puerto Rico and Latin America, 6 percent.

New Jersey's modern economy rests on several pillars: manufacturing,
research, corporate headquarters, farming, commuting, and transportation.
Ninety percent of all types of manufacturing are represented, with chemicals
especially prominent. New Jersey has long been a state of inventions, starting
with Thomas Edison's electric light bulb. The state is still a national leader
in pure and applied research. It also has substantial white-collar employment.
A leader is the Newark-based Prudential Life Insurance Co., the country's
largest insurance company, with $60 billion in assets. The diversity of New
Jersey industry is illustrated by the names of some Fortune 500 industrials:
Allied Chemical, Johnson and Johnson, CPC International, Warner-Lambert,
American Cyanamid, Nabisco, Campbell Soup, Thomas J. Lipton, and Me-
tromedia. But significantly, not a single New Jersey bank is on the list of the
50 largest U.S. banks. Since the mid-1970s, there has been a vague uneasiness
about New Jersey's industrial economy, a fear that it has taken on the characteristics of a stagnant "mature" economy. Manufacturing jobs declined from
900,000 in 1969 to 700,000 in 1975 and came back to 770,000 by 1980, but no
economist expected a full recovery. Like many Northeastern states, New
Jersey suffered from a low birth rate of new, small firms with growth potential. But in the recession of the early 1980s, New Jersey's unemployment rate
did remain a couple percentage points below the national average due to the
state's large service industries, stable pharmaceutical companies, and growing
high-technology sector, especially telecommunications. New Jersey's largest
employer was American Telephone and Telegraph, and even after the divesti-
ture of regional companies, employment was expected to expand due to the
continued presence of Bell's long-distance operations and Bell Laboratories.
Tourism at resorts, historic sites, and conventions is a vitally important part
of the economy.

New Jersey still has important agriculture—large dairy herds in the Appalachian valleys of the northwest, truck farming for vegetables on the rich
soil of central and southwestern Jersey, peaches and apples on the sandy
coastal plain, cranberries and blueberries in the marshy bogs of the Pine
Barrens. Farmland conversion to housing and industrial use has threatened
New Jersey agriculture for many years, but the rate of conversion has been
slowed slightly by a lower tax rate on land kept in farm production and more
by rising housing costs. New Jersey farming has a "small is beautiful" quality
to it, and its vegetable products are popular at farmers' markets in many cities.

Politics in "Joisey"

New Jersey has always engaged in close, competitive two-party politics.
Now, like the prototype suburban state it is, it has developed prototypal

suburban politics. New Jersey is more than anything else the home of the independent voters who live in their mortgaged houses, expect high quality government services (especially for their children's education), but fret about higher taxes. They shun party identification, and their contact with the candidates is overwhelmingly through television. (New Jersey candidates must pay gargantuan bills for television political advertising since air time must be purchased on New York City and Philadelphia stations. That was one rationale given when the state passed public financing of campaigns for all candidates for governor who raise $50,000.)

Though the suburbs, with their independent voters and media advertising, dominate the politics of modern New Jersey, no story of public life in "Joisey"—to use the slightly derisive local patois—would be complete without a mention of the mighty county party bosses of yore. The entry into politics of the most illustrious Jersey resident of all time, Woodrow Wilson, was in fact sponsored by Democratic bosses who had made fortunes auctioning off the state to the burgeoning railroads and utilities in exchange for stock options and side deals. Wilson repudiated them, thus asserting his independence and beginning his climb to national and global fame.

The bosses were many, but we will restrain ourselves to the tale of Frank ("I Am the Law") Hague, the Democratic boss of Hudson County and mayor of Jersey City from 1917 to the late 1940s. Hague was a perfect example of his breed: born of immigrant parents and raised in the teeming Horsheshoe slum of Jersey City, a devout and almost puritanical Roman Catholic who rose to power first on the issue of "reform," an intractable opponent whose enemies would often end up in jail—or the hospital—and an almost totally uneducated man with a taste for personal violence. Yet Hague's immigrant, often illiterate supporters were rewarded with Christmas food baskets, summertime boat rides and picnics, a great free medical center, and the highest city tax rates in America. Hague himself earned only $7,500 a year as mayor, but by his own secret admission a few years before his death, he ended up worth at least $8 million. He said his wealth came from stocks and lucky investments; the more probable truth was that he was paid by city vendors and the gamblers who operated off-track betting and numbers games throughout his reign. (On the other hand, he drove out organized prostitution and was intolerant of mobsters.) His greatest prestige came when he delivered Hudson County for FDR, who embraced him. He also controlled the governorship for most of the 1920s and 1930s since Hudson County at that time was large enough to control a statewide Democratic primary and usually a general election. At the end of his life, Hague became a virtual exile from Jersey City, living in a Park Avenue apartment but fearing to enter Jersey because a subpoena was always awaiting him in connection with a $15 million suit filed against him by city employees trying to regain tribute money they had been forced to contribute to his campaigns. Hague returned to Jersey for his funeral. A sparse crowd of Jersey Cityites turned out, one of them an elderly woman standing in the street holding an American flag and a hand-lettered sign reading

"God have mercy on his sinful, greedy soul."

Hague's removal did not end bossism, which continued into the 1970s. The sins of the bosses appeared relatively minor, however, compared to the mafia corruption that has plagued New Jersey. In the 1960s, the U.S. Justice Department put not only many of Jersey's hoodlums behind bars, but also literally dozens of congressmen, state officials, and mayors of both parties. The arrests have continued sporadically ever since.

Why is it, one may ask, that there seems to be no end to scandal and debasement of public life in New Jersey? There is the historical background. A hospitable climate for the Mafia was originally created because New Jersey voters turned out in such low numbers for primary elections that the county political bosses held almost unlimited power. And there is geography. Organized crime first moved into the state during Prohibition, using the cove-dotted coastline for rum-running. During the 1930s when Thomas E. Dewey made New York too uncomfortable for racketeers, many moved across the Hudson. But the continuing question is why New Jersey has never been able to clean up organized crime or governmental corruption, even after it became a largely suburban state of generally well-educated, middle-class people who would theoretically be repelled by official thuggery.

This is not to say that New Jerseyans do not revere honesty. They have elected governors of such impeccable personal integrity as Republican Alfred Driscoll (1947–54) and Democrat Richard Hughes (1962–70). Embarrassed by the widespread corruption turned up by federal prosecutors in the '70s, Jerseyans finally gave the state attorney general broad powers to seek indictments and take over cases from slow-to-act county prosecutors. The attorney general broadened his activities into such areas as white collar crime, casino gambling, and Medicaid fraud. The corruption issue made the political career of Democrat Governor Brendan Byrne (1974–82). When federal prosecutors in 1970 made public wiretapped conversations with a local racketeer, Angelo "Gyp" DeCarlo, he was recorded as saying, "It's Byrne, we can't make him" —a way of saying Byrne could not be bribed. In the 1973 race, Byrne's lack of charisma and wooden speaking style didn't seem to matter to voters. What was relevant was his slogan: "One honest man can make a difference."

Byrne ran an ostensibly honest administration, but his greatest contribution to New Jersey public life was pushing a long-overdue income tax through an extraordinarily reluctant state legislature. New Jerseyans have traditionally not objected to high taxes, but by excessively relying on the local government property tax, the estate owners and suburbanites were able to keep the money close to home, rather than sharing it with those less fortunate. New Jerseyans also tried to "gimmick" their way out of fundamental tax reform through such measures as a state lottery, which passed in 1970. It was not until 1966, in fact, that New Jersey even passed a sales tax. The income tax was approved only after the state supreme court closed the public schools, curbing a summer session, on the grounds that school finance was so grossly unequal that it violated the state constitution. Yet the income tax did not solve Jersey's fiscal problems.

In 1981, after multiple-candidate primaries in both parties, Republican Thomas Kean beat Democrat James Florio to win the governorship.* A man so mild, decent, and thoughtful he almost seemed out of place in Jersey politics, Kean was quickly plunged into bitter battles with the Democratic-controlled legislature over grim state budget shortfalls. But he did come forward with the ingenious idea of a state "infrastructure bank" that would pool federal sewer and water grants and state bond issues into a revolving fund. It would issue infrastructure loans to localities, permit New Jersey to meet its $2.4 billion clean water bill in 10 years rather than 20, and conceivably make New Jersey independent of all federal water grants by the late '80s.

New Jersey's model state constitution, drafted to replace an inferior older version in 1947, narrowed statewide elective posts to the governor and in turn gave him sweeping powers of appointment and a strong veto power. The legislature was authorized to finance capital improvements without going directly to the voters (very important to higher education). Finally, the document decreed a simplified and more unified court system. So admired was New Jersey's 1947 constitution that when Alaska joined the union in 1959, it copied its basic charter quite closely on the New Jersey model.

Other New Jersey "firsts" include election of the first black presiding officer in an American legislative body (Howard Woodson, a black minister from Trenton in 1974), creation of the cabinet-level position of public advocate (described by a supporter as "the gadfly in government that stings the bureaucratic beast whenever it sits on the people"), and passage of one of the country's first divorce laws permitting "no-fault" decrees. Indeed, Jersey government by the early '80s bore little resemblance to its low-service, low-tax, county-dominated profile of yesteryear. Propelled in part by federal grants, the payroll grew from 36,000 employees to over 66,000 in 15 years. The total state budget has been $323 million in 1957; in 1982 the figure was $900 million for Medicaid alone. Mirroring the fantastic growth of state governments across the nation, New Jersey found itself deeply involved in such disparate fields as energy conservation and drug abuse, consumer protection and subsidized housing, bilingual education and hazardous waste, a women's hotline, daycare, a utility "lifeline" program for the poor elderly, mosquito control, affirmative action, and technical assistance for displaced homemakers. And not only did the bureaucracy grow; a once haphazard legislature had acquired a full, expert staff to help it consider some 6,000 bills a year.

One of New Jersey's continuing and excruciating problems is getting hundreds of thousands of workers across the Hudson to New York every day and back home at night with relative ease and comfort. New Jersey joined with New York in the Port Authority of New York and New Jersey in 1921,

*Governors in New Jersey are elected for four-year terms with elections in odd-numbered years, coinciding neither with presidential nor congressional elections. Only four other states—Kentucky, Louisiana, Mississippi, and Virginia—have an analagous pattern of "off-season" contests. Florio and Kean emerged from a primary of 8 Republicans and 15 Democrats. The reasons for this almost bizarre number of candidates, NBC News political analyst Roan Conrad told us, were the regionalism of New Jersey politics and the availability of public financing.

but until recent years it often got short shrift. There are the many superhighways, of course, all demanding constant improvements and repair. It was a major advance when New Jersey demanded that the authority take over and operate the old Hudson and Manhattan Railroad. The PATH—Port Authority Trans-Hudson system—is the most modern, efficient, and clean mass transit in the New York City area. In 1981 New Jersey Transit took over the ailing private bus system and some commuter trains.

New Jersey has propelled few important leaders onto the national stage since the days of Woodrow Wilson (a born Virginian). The state's best candidate for national distinction in recent years has been Senator Bill Bradley, best known as a basketball star with Princeton and the New York Knicks, but also a Rhodes Scholar. Elected in 1978, Bradley did not star in legislative debate (he has limited public speaking ability). But he showed a broad grasp of issues and was selected by fellow Democrats in 1981 to chair a party anti-Reagan economic task force. The Abscam-scarred Senator Harrison Williams, who resigned in 1982 to avoid expulsion, was a sponsor or co-sponsor of many liberal social program bills early in his career and became (along with Jersey's U.S. Rep. James Howard) a leading proponent of mass transit.

The most famous member of the New Jersey House delegation has undoubtedly been Peter W. Rodino, Jr., an unknown until 1974 when he distinguished himself by his scrupulously fair chairmanship of the House Judiciary Committee during the impeachment hearings on Richard Nixon. Though Rodino did little of note afterward, Watergate assured him of lifelong fame. A special note of class was lent the House delegation from 1974 until 1982, by Millicent Fenwick, a Republican representing mostly wealthy estate counties. Fenwick, a former model and Vogue editor, became famous for smoking her pipe and achieved comic-strip fame when "Doonesbury" cartoonist Garry Trudeau used her as the model for Rep. Lacey Davenport. Fenwick's pet causes were those of the liberal Republicans: feminism, human rights, honest government. New Jerseyans declined to send the iconoclastic Fenwick to the Senate in 1982, however, and chose liberal Democrat Frank Lautenberg, a man of high reputation but more conventional political style.

New Jersey has a presidential primary, though one unlikely to register much national impact as long as it's held on the same day as California's.

North Jersey, South Jersey

Just under five million people, or 67 percent of the entire population of New Jersey, live in a ring of eight counties that extend 40 to 50 miles north, west, and south of Manhattan Island. They divide rather neatly into three groups.

First comes the part of New Jersey that is really part of the New York City core area: Jersey City, Hoboken, Union City, Bayonne, West New York, *et al.*, at the other end of the Lincoln and Holland Tunnels. All are in Hudson County, a boom area at the turn of the century best described as dilapidated in our time. The population held virtually steady from 1920 to 1970 and then fell 8.4 percent, to 556,972, in the 1980 Census. The thought of Hudson County conjures up images of endless miles of low, dingy slums, crumbling waterfront, grime-caked bridges, oil tanks, and fetid marshlands. But in Hoboken and Jersey City, middle-class young adults have moved in to fix up Victorian houses. There is also a string of high-rise apartments along the Palisades, which attract some middle-income New Yorkers who find the location convenient and say it's better to live in New Jersey and look at Manhattan rather than vice versa. The migrants from Manhattan resent the look of amazement on the faces of Upper East Siders when they find out where they live. "I will no longer suffer in silence insults to Hoboken, land of my mortgage," wrote Rita Christopher, New York correspondent for the Canadian Maclean's magazine. "Hoboken, in fact, not only looks like the 1940s, but in some respects preserves the best of those years," she observed. Unfortunately for these North Jersey cities, housing may be their greatest asset. In 1982, Governor Kean announced plans for a $500 million private housing and hotel development on abandoned piers in Hoboken, and developers made a wide range of proposals to develop various parts of the Hudson Shore. But derelict ports, railroad lines, and factories were still so pervasive that a palpable transformation of this much abused parcel of real estate U.S.A. remained hard to imagine.

Close to the place where the Hackensack River reaches Newark Bay are the Meadowlands, a giant marsh of 18,000 acres, stretching 15 miles from Hackensack to Harrison—and the most valuable piece of undeveloped land in the world. For generations Jerseyans used the Meadowlands quite literally as a dumping ground and fought over how to develop it. Finally in 1968, the legislature set up a powerful, unified Hackensack Meadowlands Commission. The biggest piece of development has been a developers' and politicians' dream, the Meadowlands Sports Center in East Rutherford. It opened in 1976 with harness racing and football starring the Giants—who, despite their suburbanization, were still identified as a New York team. Later, basketball and hockey were added. More than 100 office and warehouse buildings, including the international headquarters for Rolls-Royce, the national headquarters of Panasonic, and a Hilton hotel, have sprouted on the Meadowlands.

A quick tour of the north Jersey inner ring of suburban counties, moving from north to south: Bergen (population 845,385), after two decades of hectic growth, finally thinned out by 5.8 percent in the 1970s as the baby-boom generation left home. Bergen's southern parts are primarily blue-collar, middle-class industrial and ethnic in complexion, while farther north, the county blossoms into middle-class and high-income suburbs such as Tenafly, Old Tappan, Haworth, and Alpine. Passaic County (447,585) is a mixture of close-in, older cities such as Paterson (137,970) and Passaic (52,463), dingy, polluted, and trying to come to terms with black and increasingly Hispanic populations. Patersonians have made a valiant effort to revitalize their city, starting with a fight to stop a highway that would have gutted the town. Once the silk capital of the world, this colonial-era city has been trying to attract tourists to such scenes as the Great Falls of the Passaic and perhaps even to draw artists from Manhattan with the lure of studio space in old mills refurbished with federal funds. But on a visit we found Paterson lacked even one decent hotel (we were directed to a chain establishment on the interstate), and the only restaurants downtown were sausage stands and Latin American shops offering the basics. Anomalously tucked into Passaic County is Clifton (74,388), a staid and stable old middle- to upper-class community.

Essex County (850,451) is split between its great and problem-ridden city of Newark (329,248) and its suburban hinterlands. Newark has become a generic term for the pauperized, ghetto-ridden American city, deserted by its upper and middle classes and filled with poor blacks and problems far beyond its own capacity to solve. Newark suffered terrible riots in 1967 and lost 13.8 percent of its population in the 1970s. Those who remained suffered alarmingly high unemployment rates. Arson continued to scourge parts of the city, and an incredibly high one-third of the people were on some form of public assistance.

There are good reasons, however, why Newark should *not* be a dying city. Settled in 1666, its founding postdates only Boston and New York among the major cities of America. The city's heart is still the "Four Corners" intersection selected by the first Connecticut Puritan settlers. Its ethnic history is a microcosm of America, ranging from Yankee Protestants through German, Irish, Jewish, and Italian ascendancies to the black majority (58 percent) today. Even in tough times Newark has formidable assets. It has always been, and remains, New Jersey's most heavily populated city and the state's business and financial center. It remains the connecting point between the nation's most heavily trafficked highway, rail, and air routes and its largest harbor (New York). Newark is both a corporate headquarters and factory town, as well as an educational center (New Jersey University of Medicine and Dentistry, New Jersey Institute of Technology, and a branch of Rutgers), a port, and one of the country's best (though underutilized) airport terminals.

A Newark driving tour reveals no garden city, but a much better looking place than outsiders expect. Downtown still has the Prudential and Mutual Benefit life insurance company headquarters, a Public Service Electric and Gas Company headquarters completed in 1980s, New Jersey Bell and Western Electric, plus two other multistory office complexes of recent vintage, Gateway I and II. Despite such advances, the economic atmosphere at the start of the '80s was still marked by considerable nervousness. The city lost 53 percent of its factory jobs between 1960 and 1981, although some individual new plants were attracted.

Perhaps the most significant sign of Newark's comeback was that thousands of Newark working-class people had invested life savings and taken out substantial loans to rehabilitate their homes, rather than fleeing. Newark's neighborhood rebirth has been a 100 percent blue-collar, black and ethnic, lower-income affair. The most vivid example of all has been offered by the Portuguese, now the majority group of the old Ironbound neighborhood of tightly crowded little houses, shops, and factories close to the center city. The Portuguese, with the pull-yourself-up-by-your-bootstraps attitude of recently arrived immigrants, have redone their houses without government subsidy.

Kenneth Gibson, elected in 1970 as the city's first black mayor, earned credit for starting the city's modest turnabout. A man of palpable goodwill, he struck a refreshingly constructive note. (His predecessor, Hugh Addonizio, was so corrupt that common citizens knew city favors were for sale—a tone in public life that helped create the atmosphere for the 1967 riots. Addonizio later went to prison for plundering the public treasury.) Gibson was sometimes been criticized for sloppy administrative practices and for turning Newark into a federal- and state-aid "junkie." The critics, however, never said how *they* would keep a city of dependent people, cut off from the surrounding pools of suburban wealth, fiscally afloat. Gibson could point out that two-thirds of Newark's property, including the universities, airport, and port, were tax-exempt under state law. Under his administration, Newark's bond rating improved, the crime rate finally leveled off, and public health measures cut down the city's venereal disease and infant mortality rates from what had been some of the highest in the western world. Gibson was reelected to a fourth term in 1982, even while awaiting trial for conspiracy to create a no-show job for a former city councilman, a charge on which he was acquitted, and for official misconduct, a charge dismissed in a mistrial.

The advent of a black mayor did not erase Newark's deep-seated racial antagonisms. But Gibson did forge alliances with groups furthering multiracial cooperation, such as Stephen Adubato's North Ward Educational and Cultural Center ("a kind of white NAACP," as Adubato described it, formed to encourage Italian-Americans to stick it out in Newark's physically comfortable working-class neighborhoods). Mercifully, black poet Amiri Baraka, who had been active in Newark, gave up his ideas of black nationalism. And white councilman Anthony "I represent your fears" Imperiale lost his council seat. (Ironically, the North Ward's biggest ethnic group by the early '80s was not Italian but refugees from the deserted farms and crowded barrios of Puerto Rico.)

The most serious test for Newark remained its overwhelmingly black Central Ward, blasted by the 1967 riots and still plagued by deep poverty, arson, and despair. Yet even there, one could find hope. On a wintry day we climbed over a construction site where the Pilgrim Baptist Church was spearheading development of a 100-acre site with 305 handsome town houses. Several hundred yards away we could see the hulks of public housing high rises, where three young girls had recently been mutilated and thrown off the roof. Such structures, Pilgrim Baptist Pastor Arthur Jones told us, "ought to be dynamited like they were in St. Louis." But his town houses, Jones said, were being built with quality, on a human scale. "Come here in 10 years, and I guarantee you that this complex will not be vandalized," he said. "It will be like a good cancer that spreads."

Essex County's suburbs themselves are a very mixed bag. Some, such as

West Orange and Maplewood, are upper-middle to high income; South Orange and Essex Fells are among the most beautiful residential places in the state. A step below in wealth are Bloomfield, Belleville, and Nutley, all heavily Italian-American. Several towns have become havens for blacks fleeing big-city life. By 1980, Irvington (61,493) was 38 percent black, Montclair (38,321) 27 percent black, and Orange (31,136) 57 percent black. The city of East Orange in the 1970s went from 53.1 to 83 percent black, but its population actually grew (to 77,025). It was a haven for middle class blacks, and when dilapidation started to show up Mayor Thomas Cooke hesitated not to declare war on "the slumlords and slum tenants" wrecking things for the majority. Modern government swept into Essex County in 1978 with the passage of a strong executive form of government and the election of a remarkable county executive, 26-year-old Peter Shapiro. Shapiro's youth and connections with the Washington-based Conference on Alternative State and Local Public Policies gave him a radical national reputation. But at home he labored to cut the tax rate, improve governmental efficiency, and attract jobs for Essex's large reservoir of poor and minority peoples.

Union County (504,094) runs the gamut from depressed cities, such as oil-refining and chemical-producing Elizabeth (106,201), to middle-class commuting territory and "clean" research-oriented industries, including Bell Laboratories. Best known is Plainfield (45,555), which is over half black. Middlesex County (595,893) is a suburban ethnic melting pot. One of the most interesting towns is New Brunswick (41,442), which claims not only Rutgers University but the headquarters of Johnson and Johnson (the medical products company and a strong political force in town and state), as well as Jersey's largest concentration of Hungarian-Americans and a sizable black community. Middlesex has an old industrial heartland around Perth Amboy (38,951), a town with charming waterfront and Victorian homes scarcely known to outsiders. But the county's real economic strength is in research centers, publishing houses, chemical firms, and assorted light industries grouped along the New Jersey Turnpike and Garden State Parkway.

The outer-ring counties have received a massive influx of people in the last 30 years but nonetheless retain large strips of undeveloped, rural territory. The counties of Morris (407,630), and Somerset (230,129), Hunterdon (87,361), Warren (84,429), and Sussex (116,119) west of the metropolitan core, evoke images of lush, rolling hills where the affluent ride to their hounds. Morris County is site of the Great Swamp, a preserve of meadowlands and marsh, visited by dozens of species of birds and animals. Finally, the outer ring encompasses Monmouth County with its beach towns and mostly middle-income communities.

The Philadelphia Orbit, Trenton, Atlantic City, Princeton

More than one million Jerseyans live in the three-county ring of Camden, Burlington, and Gloucester across the Delaware from Philadelphia. The core city is Camden (84,910), separated from Philadelphia by the 1.81 miles of the Benjamin Franklin Bridge. But it might as well be 1.81 light years away. Camden's population dropped 17.2 percent in the 1970s (to 84,910). The city is physically repulsive, an unordered melange of ancient boxlike factories (RCA and Campbell Soup, for example), dingy row houses, a blighted waterfront, and barren, empty fields. But in the early '80s, after Mayor Angelo Errichetti was convicted in the Abscam scandal, Melvin Primas was elected Camden's first black mayor. He instilled tough and honest management, and there were, *mirabile dictu*, first reports of gentrification and incipient waterfront redevelopment.

The rest of Camden County (471,650) is broken up into small boroughs and townships, one of which—Cherry Hill—rose from zero population in 1960 to 68,785 in 1980. To the south lies Gloucester County, which registered a Sunbelt-style growth rate of 15.8 percent in the 1970s, up to 199,917 souls. North and east of Camden County is Burlington, another '70s growth area (up 12.2 percent, to 362,542). Burlington is also the home of two big military complexes, Fort Dix and McGuire Air Force Base.

New Jersey has a capital city. Its name is Trenton; it is located on the Delaware River about halfway between New York and Philadelphia. Trenton has a grand Revolutionary era history, the State House, some gleaming new government buildings, acres of dreary row houses and vacant land, and lost 12 percent of its people in the '70s (down to 92,124). Trenton would also be a strong contender for America's least-attractive capital. Its local politics find blacks and Italian-Americans in dominant roles.

New Jersey also had a vibrant, exciting resort city. Its name was Atlantic City. It had waterfront hotels of the grand 19th-century manner; it was the first sizable American town devoted exclusively to amusement, the birthplace of the boardwalk, saltwater taffy, the rolling chair, and the picture postcard. From the 1930s to 1970s, however, Atlantic City's course was steadily downhill —downhill in the class and affluence of the tourists, downhill in the quality of attractions (the annual Miss America extravaganza notwithstanding), and downhill in its residents' standard of living. New Jersey voters were hoping for a rebirth in Atlantic City (and some painlessly earned new state revenues) when they approved, by a 300,000-vote margin in 1976, a referendum to legalize casino gambling there. Six years later, gaudy new casinos were grossing over $1 billion, and Atlantic City had already overtaken Las Vegas as America's gambling mecca (19 million versus 12 million visitors annually). Some 30,000 new jobs had been created; state tax coffers were being enriched by $112 million annually. But Governor Kean noted that "casino gambling doesn't help our state's image." And indeed, New Jersey—and Atlantic City in particular—were paying a heavy price for the easy money. Irregularities in the state commission regulating the casinos caused a wave of early embarrassment and a medium-level scandal by Jersey standards. Casino patrons ignored the downtown commercial core, where sales plummetted by 20 percent and many stores closed. Crime soared by 171 percent with an influx of muggers, drug dealers, pickpockets, and prostitutes—the latter such an infestation that the chief of police suggested throwing in the towel and legalizing sex for sale. Three-fourths of the casino workers lived outside the city. Unemployment among Atlantic City's largely poor and black and Hispanic people ranged around 20 percent. A housing blight attacked the city as hundreds of elderly people saw their rental units demolished—or as the New Jersey Public Advocate charged, "torched to make way for profitable development." Alleged Republican state assemblyman Chuck Hardwick: "Atlantic City has been taken over by casino market forces, its residents forced out as if victims of a heartless coup."

Gambling did not keep Atlantic City's population from dropping 16 percent in the 1970s (to 40,199), but it did help to spark population growth in other parts of southern New Jersey. The nearby old resort town of Cape May (where Lincoln and other presidents vacationed and now a historic district) grew 10.5 percent in the 1970s to 4,853. In Ocean County, where the population zoomed 66 percent to 346,038, the largest immigration was of that newly mobile class in our society, the elderly. Gambling may have something to do with growth pressures on the land adjacent to New Jersey's Pine Barrens— a vast 3,000-square mile tract of sandy soils, swamplands, pine and blueberry and cranberry stands that lies just inland from the South Jersey shore. At the heart of the Barrens is a pure-water aquifer including a unique pygmy forest, now under federal and state protection. Major planning of recent years has been devoted to the Pine Barrens; ultimately the preservation of this largest ecologically undisturbed area along the Boston-Washington corridor will be a living statement of New Jersey's attitude toward the environment.

Finally, we conclude with New Jersey's preeminent university town: Princeton (12,035), which F. Scott Fitzgerald once described as "rising, a green Phoenix, out of the ugliest country in the world." Despite its relatively small size, Princeton remains one of America's finest universities in terms of faculty-student ratio and high-quality graduate schools. Princeton's strength is that its faculty members, even men of national repute, are expected to teach both graduate and undergraduate courses in addition to their own scholarly activities. In addition to the university, Princeton harbors the Institute for Advanced Study, a place for pure, unharried scholarship. Just outside the town is the Educational Testing Service, whose college and professional-school tests have great (and some say excessive) power in admissions procedures around the nation.

Princeton has one of most sophisticated groups of commuters in the world: high-ranking officials of investment and publishing houses, advertising agencies, banks, and insurance companies who ride the train to New York every day but then return to a town that is uniquely cosmopolitan and cultured. The

Princetonians, both at the university and in the town, often express feelings of superiority and remove themselves from the affairs of state. The university's Woodrow Wilson School of Public and International Affairs tries seriously to compensate for this shortcoming. But most of Princeton's great reservoir of skill and talent, both "town" and "gown," is not available to the host state. Thus we have another reminder of the central dilemma of New Jersey life: too many people taking too much from the state and contributing too little.

PENNSYLVANIA

State of Magnificent Decline

ON MARCH 28, 1979, the biggest news in a generation came from Pennsylvania. And it was bad. The electricity-producing nuclear reactor on Three Mile Island, in the middle of the Susquehanna River near Middletown, was out of control. Machinery had failed, operators had made mistakes, and the reactor had lost much of the water needed to cool its heat-producing radioactive core. Radioactive waters and gases had been released. One hundred forty-four thousand people fled their homes.

The repercussions of the Three Mile Island accident were national and international. Although only minimal radiation was released, and—as the nuclear power industry said time and time again—no one was killed, the accident resulted in a loss of public and investor confidence, first in the federal Nuclear Regulatory Commission, second (and more vitally) in nuclear power in general. Around the world, opponents began arguing more persuasively against new nuclear plants.

For Pennsylvania the accident was particularly tragic. Most of the 144,000 people soon returned, and state and federal investigations showed no ill effects to children born to women who were pregnant when the accident occurred. But several years later, cleanup of the tons of deadly radioactive material and the million gallons of radioactive water still inside the closed generating station proved costly and technically difficult. Pennsylvania was obliged to beg the federal government for financial help to repair the damage. And worst of all for Pennsylvania, the Three Mile incident became yet another link in a long chain of negative economic developments besetting the Keystone State ever since its heyday in World War I. The reasons were not hard to divine. This had been the banner industrial state of the 19th century, but its manufacturing plant had aged. Too much of the economy was geared to steel and coal and rails, even as those industries headed into a long decline in employment. The rate of new capital expenditures by Pennsylvania industries was lagging behind that of the other major industrial states, and there had been far too little investment in modern intelligence-related industries. Between 1970 and 1980, employment in Pennsylvania grew by only 8.4 percent, compared with a national rate of 28.3 percent. Manufacturing, once heart and soul of the Pennsylvania economy, lost 215,000 jobs in the '70s, a 14.1 percent decline and a loss exceeded only by New York and Missouri. All regions lose jobs as economic conditions change and individual businesses close. But Pennsylvania was also registering a low rate of formation of new businesses, which provide a majority of new jobs.

The predictable result: a state of stagnant population. The growth rate during the 1970s was a miniscule 0.5 percent; in 1980 no other state had such a large percentage of residents both born in and still residents of the state. Pennsylvania lost another two House seats after the 1980 Census, making a total of 13 lost House seats since 1910. Early in the '70s, the state slipped behind Texas in population to become the nation's fourth- rather than third-largest.

Yet even in decline, Pennsylvania was not to be ignored. The 1980 Census count was 11,866,728 persons. Any national politician or business planner who ignored Pennsylvania did so at his peril. The state's presidential primary remained important nationally (it gave a great boost to Jimmy Carter's candidacy in 1976). And it was also far too soon to write off the old commonwealth as an economic disaster area. True to its old nickname of Keystone State, Pennsylvania still lay dead astride the great transportation routes that connect the Great Lakes and the Midwest with the major markets and seaports of the East. Its rail service was suffering, but at the same time a network of east-west and north-south interstate roads had opened up previously inaccessible parts of Pennsylvania and put most of the state within quick, easy trucking range of both the East Coast and Great Lakes.

And though the overall picture was one of decline, there were also signs of hope in Pennsylvania. A series of revival efforts, including community-based labor-management committees, were launched throughout the state. Electronics firms grew in the Philadelphia orbit, food and other distribution facilities flowed into the state, and industrial parks sprouted up along the major arteries. Gregg E. Robertson, executive director of the Milrite Council, an economic development group, also pointed out to us that Pennsylvania's reputation as a high tax, high wage state might be outdated. By 1980, he noted, 17 other states had higher tax burdens, and 18 higher manufacturing wage scales. Pennsylvania in recent years has also increased dramatically its support of state university and technical schools, laying the groundwork for a future work force trained for more modern, less outmoded industries. After a 1983 Gallatin Institute study found that Pennsylvania was not taking advantage of its vast supply of native capital, the Milrite Council began encouraging public and private pension funds to invest in neglected sectors of the state economy: commercialization of scientific advances at schools such as Carnegie Mellon and expansion of mid-sized companies short of long-term, fixed-rate debt.

In some ways, Pennsylvania has become a better society than it was at its industrial zenith, when a group of narrow-minded business interests, allied with often-corrupt Republican political bosses, ruled with scant opposition. The Republican machines (and indeed their big-city Democratic counterparts) have faded away; big business domination has become an historic footnote. Though blight and decline have persisted in the mill towns, the extreme environmental degradation that the Industrial Revolution brought to Penn's Woods has now faded. The two great cities, Philadelphia and Pittsburgh, have continued to lose population, yet both have experienced exciting renewal, and some of America's most promising self-help projects have emanated from Pennsylvania.

A Historic Perspective

Pennsylvania has elements of history both idealistic and industrious. William Penn, the remarkable Quaker founder, worked out with his colonists a great law so progressive as to be radical for its time. It included broad guarantees of religious freedom and of suffrage to males who could meet modest property requirements, an assurance of education for all young children, and stipulation that all laws would be made "With the Consent and Approbation of the Freemen in General Assembly met." This mandate for permissive popular government would become a pillar of the U.S. Constitution. Real power in colonial Pennsylvania did, of course, rest with an oligarchy of Quaker leaders, not a broad popular mass. Still, the founder's promises of religious and political freedom were enough to draw great numbers of colonists: Welsh Quakers, Scotch-Irish Presbyterians, Lutherans, Swedes, French Huguenots, and the Pietist Germans who settled in Lancaster and became the Pennsylvania Dutch.

With a Quaker's penchant for wise business, Penn located Philadelphia at the tidewater confluence of two great rivers: the Delaware and the Schuylkill. Along their banks, back into the interior, lay tens of millions of acres of forest with a seemingly endless supply of prime white oak. In the river openings and under the forests lay prime farmland, which would make Pennsylvania the foremost food producer among the colonies.

By the time of the Revolution, Pennsylvania was the third-largest colony, with 275,000 people, and Philadelphia had forged ahead of Boston to become the metropolis of colonial America and in many respects its culturally most prominent city. The colony's most illustrious citizen was Boston-born Benjamin Franklin—author, publisher, scientist, politician, diplomat, and investor of world repute. While Boston was an earlier scene of revolutionary agitation, it was in Philadelphia that the first two Continental Congresses met and adopted the Declaration of Independence, chose George Washington as commander in chief, and first unfurled the American flag. In the Revolutionary War, Pennsylvania was a major scene of action, including the battles of Brandywine, Paoli, and Germantown. It was at Valley Forge that Washington and his troops spent the cruel winter of 1777–78. In the war, Pennsylvania's fledgling ironworks turned out weapons, and its rich farmlands supplied grain, fodder, cattle, sheep, and hogs to feed the army. And it was a decade later, in 1787, that the Constitutional Convention met—again, in Philadelphia. Pennsylvania sent the largest delegation, which fought hard for a strong national government. Then Philadelphia became, for 10 years, the first capital of the United States.

In the six decades stretching from the end of the Civil War and the advent of the Gilded Age through the Great Depression, the life of Pennsylvania was less characterized by idealism than by an incredible forward surge of great industry, led by steel. Western Pennsylvania was rich in bituminous coal; iron ore could easily be imported across the Great Lakes; limestone was plenteous. So were the tycoons: Henry Clay Frick, who became the largest producer of coal and coke in the world; Andrew Carnegie, who brought the Bessemer steelmaking process to America and became the world's richest man by selling out his massive steelworks for $492 million; J.P. Morgan, the great financier who dared to create U.S. Steel; Charles M. Schwab, sometimes called "the world's greatest salesman," who midwifed the creation of U.S. Steel and then built rival Bethlehem Steel; Thomas Mellon, son of a poor Scotch-Irish farming family, who became Pittsburgh's greatest financier and real estate dealer and set the foundations of the great banking and coal combine that would prosper under his sons, Andrew and Richard B. and their heirs. The world's first spouting oil well was driven in 1859 near Titusville in the western part of the state. Pennsylvania's petroleum reserves were later eclipsed by those of the Southwest, but Pennsylvania's Joseph N. Pew did build Sun Oil into a mighty producer and refiner of oil, while the Mellons launched another giant, Gulf Oil. As for railroads, the Philadelphia-based Pennsylvania Railroad was the greatest of all, employing 250,000 men.

Starting around 1890, reformist elements began an outcry about the power of big steel and big rail interests. But strategically placed Pennsylvanians blithely continued to block antitrust, freight regulation, or child labor legislation that might have harmed U.S. Steel and its friends. The year U.S. Steel was formed, the attorney general of the U.S. was Philander C. Knox, a close friend of Frick and Mellon. Elihu Root, a member of both the McKinley and Theodore Roosevelt cabinets, had been an attorney for the old Carnegie Steel Company. The ultimate example was Andrew Mellon's position as Secretary of the Treasury during the Harding, Coolidge, and Hoover administrations.

Economic diversity lagged, however. Steel began declining when the prime steel customers—the railroads—reached the full extent of their routes in the 1920s. And Pennsylvania did not get a major automobile assembly plant until 1976 (a Volkswagen facility in New Stanton), and then only with concessions that critics said amounted to a subsidy. Big steel's problems continued to deepen. Even though U.S. Steel is based in Pittsburgh, production facilities in Pennsylvania are some of the industry's oldest and during the '70s came under government orders to reduce the literally deadly combinations of gases and vapors that pose health problems for both workers and those who live nearby. By the '80s the issue for American steel was simple: survival. The industry was plagued by a flood of imports (some at below-cost prices), hobbled by rising labor costs (an astounding average $23 per hour for wages, benefits and employment taxes in 1982), and seriously lagging productivity. Shipments were down to Depression levels and states like Pennsylvania saw entire steel communities paralyzed by layoffs or permanent plant shutdowns.

For the railroads, the other traditional lifeline of Keystone State commerce, freight service (not to mention passenger service) shrank in territory and declined in reliability over most of the post–World War II period. The problems of the railroads culminated in the 1970 crash of the Penn Central, the biggest commercial bankruptcy in American history, a blow to the pride and prosperity of Philadelphia, and one of the most sordid cases of business mismanagement in the history of American capitalism. Penn Central's owners had not only allowed equipment and roadbeds to deteriorate but kept on paying dividends when the company's cash position had become desperate. Then they saved themselves thousands of dollars by dumping personal stock before the railroad's troubles became public knowledge.

Pennsylvania sits on 35 billion tons of coal, technically enough to satisfy the nation's energy needs for 350 years. But fewer than 40,000 men worked in Pennsylvania coal mines by the early 1980s—a catastrophic decline from the 210,000 who worked there in 1940, and the 387,000 in 1910. Production in the anthracite fields of northeastern Pennsylvania had declined to a mere trickle. The story has differed in western Pennsylvania fields, where the low-sulphur, metallurgical-quality bituminous coal is prized by the big steel companies. Around Johnstown and Altoona, beds of medium-sulphur coal are mined and immediately fed into huge mine-mouth electric generating plants. Strip mining has become the wave of the present and prospective future in western Pennsylvania, but the state fortuitously has one of the nation's better strip mine control laws.

Pennsylvania's industrial development was accompanied by massive immigration in the century preceding World War I. The population soared from 810,091 in 1810 to 7,665,111 in 1910. New Yorkers, New Englanders, and waves of Irish and European immigrants came to work in the factories. Blacks from the South were attracted by Pennsylvania's strong abolitionist views. The conditions under which the newcomers worked and lived in the early factory towns are one of the darkest chapters in American history. Men were obliged to work 12 hours a day, seven days a week, for wages as small as $350 a year —and often that pittance came in company-issued scrip, which could only be spent at inflated prices in the company store or for rent of the shacks or tiny wooden frame houses owned by the company. Children as young as eight years of age were put to work separating slate from coal and at other tasks deep in the mine shafts, at wages of 25 cents a day. The toll in miners' lives was appalling: 43,000 Pennsylvania miners lost their lives between 1880 and 1936. Thousands died in the steel mills, too; there one of the greatest dangers was white-hot metal gushing out of giant ladles that frequently slipped off cranes.

The factory owners and industrial moguls ferociously fought labor unions, but slowly they began to form: the American Federation of Labor (succeeding the old Knights of Labor) in 1881, the United Mine Workers in 1890, the Amalgamated Association of Iron, Steel and Tin Workers in 1878, and finally the Congress of Industrial Organizations in 1935 and the United Steelworkers that same year. The United Mine Workers called successful strikes in 1900 and 1902 that led to an eight-to-nine-hour working day. In the 1920s appeared the powerful and often dictatorial figure of John L. Lewis, who came into his own with the New Deal, and in the 1930s legislation guaranteeing workers the right to organize and bargain collectively through "representatives of their own choosing." Unionization of basic industries was not complete, however, until General Motors capitulated to the CIO in 1937 and U.S. Steel quietly succumbed shortly thereafter.

The Steelworkers won praise in the '70s for sound leadership and democratic operating procedure, plus a unique "experimental negotiating agreement" with management, which provided an industrial guarantee of a substantial wage settlement in exchange for a promise not to call a national strike. What the agreement really meant was higher wages and lack of a competitive position in world markets. By 1982, with 160,000 steelworkers laid off and the industry plunging into red ink, the talk was not of wage increases but rather givebacks or asking the companies to offer workers stock ownership in lieu of higher wages. It was finally becoming clear that in a fiercely competitive world, unprecedented labor-management cooperation—rather than adversarial confrontation—was the only road to survival for workers and steel firms alike.

The United Mine Workers made history after World War II when Lewis won agreement by owners to finance, by means of a royalty on each ton of coal produced, a welfare and retirement fund that in turn made UMW workers eligible for job pensions and free medical care. Times of trouble came when Lewis retired in 1960 and the UMW presidency was taken over by W.A. (Tony) Boyle, his hand-picked successor. As the UMW benefited from every ton of coal dug, Boyle became cozier with the mine operators than individual miners. The UMW did not even defend members of local safety committees from reprisals by mine owners until the Farmington, West Virginia, disaster of 1968. Boyle barely won reelection in 1969, and the situation became a tragic scandal when his challenger Joseph A. (Jock) Yablonski and his wife and young daughter were found shot to death in their Clarksville, Pennsylvania, home. In a rematch mandated tardily by the U.S. Labor Department, Boyle lost and spent years trying to stay out of prison. His successors, Arnold Miller and Sam Church, brought democracy to the union but also faced continual board problems. In 1982, union members were hopeful they also had ushered in a new progressive era by electing 33-yeard Richard Trumka, a miner's son who had worked in the mines himself only while financing his accounting and legal education. Mining company owners at first viewed Trumka as a dangerous radical but were later surprised to find him talking of increasing exports and improving the image of mining. Trumka faced a tough job, however. Since the union had proven unable to organize many new or expanding mines in the West, the union's share of U.S. production had shrunk from 70 percent in 1974 to 44 percent in 1982, and membership had dropped from 400,000 in 1922 to 230,000 in 1982.

Keystone Politics

Pennsylvania Republicans were riding high at the start of the 1980s, with partly stalwarts John Heinz and Arlen Specter in the U.S. Senate and Richard Thornburgh in the governor's chair. Pennsylvania Republicans held additional power in Washington through Reagan Administration Health and Human Services Secretary Richard Schweiker, a former U.S. Senator, and

Transportation Secretary Drew Lewis, former party chairman and unsuccessful gubernatorial candidate. The 1982 elections were sobering to the Republicans, who barely retained the governorship, lost control of one house of the state legislature, and saw the makeup of the U.S. House delegation become 13 Democrats to 10 Republicans.

Any modern-day Republican hegemony was minor league compared with the 70 years between the Civil War and the New Deal, when the Republicans held an extraordinarily durable hammer lock on Pennsylvania's body politic. For this one finds several explanations, beginning with the protective tariff, which helped turn the state for Lincoln in 1860. Pennsylvania was the Union's preeminent manufacturing, rather than commercial or trading, state; thus the tariff, together with other policies to benefit big business, made the Grand Old Party the natural ally of steel, coal, oil, and textile interests—interests that in turn repaid the favor with ample campaign financing. Second, there was the memory of the Civil War. Pennsylvania *had* been invaded, Gettysburg had given the people a great fright, and the bloody shirt could be waved for a generation afterward. Third, no ethnic grouping rose up to fight the ruling classes as the Irish did in Boston. Protestant, Catholic, Jewish, German, Irish, black—everyone was Republican. Finally, a succession of Republican bosses, men of shrewdness and power rarely seen in America, sprang from Pennsylvania soil. The trilogy of Simon Cameron (1865–67), Matthew S. Quay (1887–1904), and Boies Penrose (1904–21) ruled over an Organization whose power extended from the sooty mill towns to the dogwooded suburbs of Philadelphia and Pittsburgh, from the ward clubhouse to the U.S. Senate; it was rarely thwarted.* The Republicans scored an astounding chain of presidential and gubernatorial victories, almost unbroken from 1860 through 1932.

The Depression changed all that. In 1934 the first Democratic governor and U.S. Senator of the 20th century were elected. FDR carried Pennsylvania in 1936, 1940, and 1944. The state has been closely competitive ever since—for Eisenhower twice, Kennedy in 1960, Humphrey in 1968, Carter in 1976, and Reagan in 1980.

The Republican party might have slipped into perennial minority status in the postwar years if it had not been for a succession of moderate-liberals who

---

*About Penrose, whom John Gunther described in *Inside U.S.A.* as a man "who ate himself to death," Nathaniel Burt wrote in *The Perennial Philadelphians*: "As absolute ruler of Pennsylvania, and therefore dominant figure in the Republican party nationally, Penrose was in the early years of the 20th century one of the most powerful men in the country. . . . He disdained the People, the democratic process and other politicians. . . . He was the Old Philadelphia figure of the Iron Age in politics. . . . He swore, he drank, he whored, and he didn't care who knew it. . . . He was a giant in size and strength, six feet four and powerful. . . . He grew immensely fat, almost 300 pounds, but till the very end he never lost his dignity, presence or appetite. . . . There are awed accounts of his breakfasts—a dozen fried eggs, a half-inch slice of bacon, a dozen rolls, a quart of coffee. . . . Penrose could absorb immense quantities of liquor without showing it, but made no pretense of hiding either his occasional drunkenness or continued lecheries. 'I do what I damn please,' said Big Grizzly. 'The masses like that.' " One of Penrose's last acts, according to legend, was to order the nomination of Warren Harding for president from his deathbed in 1920.

took on the conservative Old Guard faction allied with the Pennsylvania Manufacturers' Association. One of the most distinguished of these was William Scranton, governor of the '6os who actually made a bid for the Republican presidential nomination (a battle for which he showed scarce stomach) against Barry Goldwater in 1964. Scranton's calm and reasoned leadership set a standard that his successors had difficulty matching. One of these was maverick Democrat Milton Shapp, an ambitious and hopeful businessman-politician who served two terms in the '70s but found his administration plagued by scandal.

A true class performance was turned in by ex-federal and state prosecutor Richard Thornburgh, who assumed the governorship in 1979 and soon distinguished himself by cool-headed decisions on the life-and-death decisions of the Three Mile Island accident. In the style of Dwight Eisenhower (whom he sought to emulate), Thornburgh concentrated on setting a high moral tone of leadership and "steady-as-you-go" management rather than bold new adventures. He showed unusual understanding of Pennsylvania's economic needs—not hard-to-catch big factories but rather a multiplicity of small business starts and a concerted effort to diversify Pennsylvania's economy into such fields as robotics, computers, biotechnology, energy efficiency and telecommunications. He also mounted a community conservation program, aimed at bolstering small towns as well as larger cities, promulgated popular welfare reform and anti-crime programs and started efforts to repair Pennsylvania's roads, bridges, ports, and water systems while other states still waited to do that job. In 1982, a tough year for Republican gubernatorial candidates, he was reelected with 52 percent of the vote.

Pennsylvania has rarely sent to Washington men who have achieved distinction befitting such a large and economically powerful state. Pennsylvania's last president was the easily forgotten James Buchanan. Hugh Scott (1959–77), by winning election as Republican leader of the Senate in 1969, became the first man in his state to hold a major leadership role in Congress since Frederick Augustus Muhlenberg was Speaker of the House in the First and Third Congresses. Senator Heinz spent $2.6 million of his ketchup fortune to win his seat and, as chairman of the Senate Republican Campaign Committee, skillfully aided candidates in need, helping the GOP win the Senate in 1980. The Pennsylvania House delegation has been remarkably unaccomplished. Two Democratic exceptions were first elected in the 1970s. One was Robert W. Edgar, a former Methodist minister chosen by a Philadelphia suburban district in the 1974 Watergate class of Democrats, who demonstrated an unusual ability to hang on to a seat in a Republican district. Edgar distinguished himself as an environmentalist by publicly criticizing dams and other public works projects he considered a waste of money, and as chairman of the Northeast-Midwest Congressional Coalition, which represented Frostbelt interests in fights over regional divisions of federal expenditures. A second outstanding House Pennsylvanian was William H. Gray III of Philadelphia, first elected in 1978. A Baptist minister who continued to preach each Sunday, Gray won substantial respect of his fellow members and served on the prestigious Budget and Appropriations Committees. Some of Pennsylvania's other House members were proven to be not only undistinguished but dishonest in the 1980 Abscam scandal in which the FBI tempted the Members of Congress with bribes from Arab sheiks. In front of hidden television cameras, Rep. Ozzie Myers, Democrat of Philadelphia, took the money and declared his five-word summary of Philadelphia politics: "Money talks and bullshit walks." After he became the first congressman expelled from the House since the Civil War, Myers explained: "I took money because I like money, because I got greedy and also because I'm poor. I feel I didn't do anything wrong, and if someone were to give me $25,000 this afternoon, I'd take it." Myers and Rep. Raymond F. Lederer were given three-year prison terms and $20,000 fines. Several other Pennsylvania politicians—including the president of the Philadelphia city council—were convicted as well.

Sad to relate, Abscam was not an aberration: corruption seems deeply ingrained in Pennsylvanian public mores, no matter how seriously some of the more outstanding public servants seek to uproot it. There is a word in the Pennsylvanian vocabulary you will search in vain to find in a dictionary: macing. Broadly, it refers to shakedowns of government employees for political contributions. And though prohibited by law now, the spirit of macing continues through such mechanisms as suspect political dinner "invitations." The best job security is to remember to give to the party in power. Business interests remain the mainstay of GOP financing, even though the most overt supergifts to "buy" politicians have declined. Pennsylvania Republican families such as the Pews and Mellons have given millions to Republican campaigns over the generations.

Though seldom an innovator, Pennsylvania government spent the '60s and '70s rushing to catch up with the times, rapidly expanding its services, taking higher public education seriously for the first time, trying to assist local communities' economic development efforts, and finally (under Gov. Shapp in 1971) passing an income tax to cope with its severe, recurrent fiscal headaches. Nevertheless, in 1978 the Philadelphia *Inquirer* could describe the legislature as a "cesspool of self-serving misuse of public funds and public power." Even while the state suffered under severe financial strains, the paper found, legislators were continuing to live well on expense accounts and rewarding political operators with patronage jobs (even though many, in fact, where "ghosts" in the public jobs for which they got paid).

Philadelphia and Beyond

The city of Philadelphia, as its social historian Nathaniel Burt has written, is "a fine vintage, warm, rich, flavorful; but there's a drop of bitterness in the bottom of the glass." It has had three great flowerings, each followed by an era of decay. The first flowering came with birth as William Penn's City of Brotherly Love, building for a century to the crescendo of the Golden Age of Revolution, the Age of Franklin, when in government, finance, commerce, and letters, Philadelphia was the preeminent city of the New World. Then, early in the 19th century, the federal government went to Washington; the state government was transferred to Harrisburg; supremacy in commerce went to the great deep-water port of New York; and financial and cultural dominance transferred to New York too. Philadelphia has lived ever since in the shadow of the great world city to the north.

A second flowering, industrial in nature, rose through the Civil War and was signaled by the Centennial Exposition of 1876, attended by 10 million visitors and one of the grandest shows of technology the world has ever seen. These were the heydays of the Pennsylvania Railroad; the Curtis Publishing Company, owner of the *Saturday Evening Post,* dominated magazine publishing in America; and the great Philadelphia Orchestra began. For the prosperity of its Iron Age, Philadelphia paid in ugly political corruption (this was the era of the sinister bosses, culminating in Penrose) and physical blight in the form of the Pennsylvania Railroad. The railroad built a great brick castle station at the city's very heart, opposite City Hall; then, to connect with its main lines, it erected a massive stone causeway out to West Philadelphia, a block wide (so it could hold 16 parallel tracks) and appropriately called the Chinese Wall. The wall was penetrated by gloomy, dripping tunnels for cross streets and effectively blighted development in a large part of the city's heart. Simultaneously, the railroad built up sumptuous suburbs—some to rank among the most beautiful in America—along its commuting routes, one westward along the Main Line, another northwesterly to Germantown and Chestnut Hill. Thus began the process of suburbanization of Philadelphia's aristocracy that would deprive the city of wealth and leadership.

Down from the Gilded Age, straight through the New Deal and World War II, Philadelphia's politics were unflinchingly Republican, in the grip of one of the most corrupt and unsavory political machines America has ever nourished.

Reform efforts by good government types began in the 1880s, but did not succeed until after World War II under the leadership of two bright, aggressive Democratic attorneys from Republican families: Richardson Dilworth and Joseph Clark. Both eventually became mayor. The Augean stables at City Hall were cleansed, and Philadelphia embarked upon a decade of remarkable political and physical renaissance. As Clark took office in 1951, a new charter strengthening the mayor's executive role, upgrading civil service, and putting city planning on a long-range basis went into effect. Independence Hall, long surrounded by gringy slum buildings, was freed from its yoke of urban blight as one of the most needed urban renewal projects of all time transpired around it, opening up to public view long-hidden treasures such as Carpenter's Hall (site of the First Continental Congress) and Todd House (the home of Dolly Madison). Brick-walled gardens and walkways filled the gaps between the colonial-era structures. Soon nearby Society Hill, the site of historic mansions including the president's home when Philadelphia was the national capital, was restored and reborn as a fashionable inner-city residential area. The ugly old Broad Street Station was finally torn down in 1952, and where the Chinese

Wall once stood rose the massive buildings and walkways of the Penn Center, centerpiece of the downtown renewal effected under a skilled and strong-headed master of urban renewal, Edmund Bacon.

Clark and Dilworth brought to City Hall a high sense of dedication and belief in Philadelphia's future, but the regular organization types in the Democratic party were not pleased when Clark appointed young reformers and talented Old Philadelphians to key posts in his administration, spurning the clamor for Democratic patronage after the long famine of the Republican century. The conflict endured through the Clark-Dilworth era, and Dilworth's successor, James Tate, found it impossible to keep the reform movement even half alive.

Philadelphia's politics had turned Democratic, but the system of machines and ward politics lived on like a page out of yesteryear. For the ward and precinct committeemen, the reward was usually patronage, though the number of city jobs available was reduced. In 1971, this dated political system produced as mayor Frank Lazzaro Rizzo, who would lead the city into eight years of brawling, headline-making infamy. Rizzo, like his immigrant father, was a policeman. He had a reputation as a fearless and colorful cop whose technique of knocking heads first and asking questions later endeared him to Philadelphia's middle-class white homeowners, who had become fearful of blacks and crime. As police commissioner, he beefed up patrols and kept confidential dossiers on thousands of political dissidents and black activists. His two terms as mayor were so stormy that a recall petition was launched against him. The first signer was former Mayor and Senator Joseph Clark, who called Rizzo "Philadelphia's Mussolini." Rizzo survived the recall through judicial maneuvering, but he failed in a 1978 attempt to change the city charter to allow him to run for a third consecutive term.

Rizzo's successor was former Congressman William Green, who had to cope with the huge deficit built up during the spendthrift Rizzo years. Green courageously resisted inflationary demands of powerful public employee unions and battled to get the Philadelphia Federation of Teachers, unquestionably one of America's greediest and least responsible unions, to agree to terms the city could afford and stop its pattern of long strikes depriving Philadelphia children of their schooling. A man of intelligence and high standards, Green appointed a highly competent black city managing director, W. Wilson Goode, eliminated waste and excessive patronage, and ran the cleanest government in years. But Green never really relished the job of mayor and announced he would retire after one term, setting the stage for a highly symbolic contest between Rizzo and Goode.

Downtown Philadelphia's physical renaissance continued to flower into the 1980s with a whole plethora of new hotels and reopening of the elegant old Bellevue-Stratford Hotel (closed after Legionnaire's Disease struck in the '70s), completion of new office buildings (notably the Philadelphia Stock Exchange, which specialized in options trading), and construction on long-decaying East Market Street, the city's traditional retail heart, of the Rouse Company's Gallery I and II (glass, steel, and cream-colored shopping malls that drew an impressive cross-section of Philadelphia races, cityites, and suburbanites), plus digging of a new commuter-railroad tunnel and converting an old railway terminal into a market. Sparked by the Bicentennial in 1976, the city experienced a long-overdue restaurant boom: 375 new ones by 1982, many of high quality, plus ever-increasing tourism. Scoffing at crime dangers, urban pioneers continued to flow back, even into abandoned loft buildings in such heart-of-the-city neighborhoods as Olde City, a SoHo-variety district housing artists and architects. And Philadelphia remained a strong "city of neighborhoods"—109 by one count—many extraordinarily cohesive in character, a number enjoying latter-day renewal. The city's self-esteem was also improved when the Philadelphia Phillies won the World Series in 1980, and the "Rocky" movies put the city on the nation's mental map.

Beneath the glitter, however, loomed deep and possibly permanent economic decay. The eight-county Philadelphia metropolitan area lost over 100,-000 jobs, representing 17 percent of its manufacturing base, during the 1970s. The population of the city proper declined 13.4 percent in the '70s, to a total of 1.69 million; in 1981 Philadelphia slipped behind Houston to become America's fifth- rather than fourth-largest city. More serious than simple population loss was the erosion of middle-class residents and wealth. The Census found the number of Philadelphia households headed by elderly people doubled in the '70s, to almost a quarter. It also showed that Philadelphia's Hispanic population was only 3.8 percent—a much smaller share than most major cities, suggesting even immigrants do not look to Philadelphia for opportunity. The loss of factory jobs was the central problem, but not the only one. The number of *Fortune* 500 companies with Philadelphia headquarters was down to seven in 1980. The city had become, primarily, a branch-office town. And not only, as the *Inquirer* noted, were "the so-called movers and shakers of the local corporate board rooms moving little and shaking less," but little was being done to aid small business or provide venture capital for new ones. An adventuresome "Philadelphia Past, Present and Future" program, launched by University of Pennsylvania professor Theodore Hershberg in connection with the city's 300th anniversary, spotlighted small business creation and growth as key to the city and regional future. The project's citizen-business-academic task forces created an ingenious portfolio of new ideas—from local venture capital funds and an entrepreneurial clearinghouse to an information-referral system for potential investors. The ideas received official state and city blessing, but it was uncertain whether the activist leadership networks necessary to achieve concrete results would actually come into being, and then prove a durable, effective force.

It was, in fact, not easy to be optimistic about the Philadelphia of the early '80s. Against such clear positives as a thriving pharmaceutical industry, some high-technology firms, and increasingly strong universities, the city had (in Hershberg's words) become a "catchment area of poverty" with lagging income levels and "staggering" illiteracy problems. An adversarial social and racial tone made cooperation—within the city, or with its suburbs—excruciatingly difficult. The Delaware Valley ports of Pennsylvania, New Jersey, and

Delaware lacked coordinated leadership and were losing out to more aggressive competitors. Philadelphia's major banks had fallen under constant threat
of takeover by larger New York or Pittsburgh banks with more of a world
view. And Philadelphia's growth in service sector jobs was only half the
national average in the '70s, suggesting that Philadelphia accounting, law,
banking, and the like were stagnant if not in fact declining.

Part of the blame for Philadelphia's long decline must be placed on the
Establishment that John Gunther called "an oligarchy more compact and
more entrenched than any in the United States." That aristocracy of Biddles,
Ingersolls, Morrises, Robertses, Wisters, Scotts, Lippincotts, Peppers, Pews,
their in-laws and friends, lives on, maintaining and fostering its clubs. But
only a few reside in central Philadelphia today. This disengagement as a class
is underscored by the aristocracy's surprisingly small financial stake in Phila-
delphia-related enterprises—nothing even faintly resembling the Mellons'
stake in Pittsburgh, for instance. Philadelphia has long lacked dynamic
growth-oriented business leadership.

The lack of leadership among the aristocracy in Philadelphia may go back
to the Quaker founding of the city, according to E. Digby Baltzell, the
University of Pennsylvania's historian of elites and aristocracy. In *Puritan
Boston and Quaker Philadelphia,* Baltzell noted that such distinguished Boston
families as the Adamses, Cabots, Lowells, and Peabodys produced many
contributors for state and national educational, intellectual, and political life,
while their Philadelphia counterparts had produced few. "While Puritans
placed great value on the 'calling' or devotion of one's chosen vocation,"
Baltzell wrote, "Quakers have always placed more emphasis on being a good
person than on being a good judge or statesman; the Puritans were a thinking,
the Quakers a feeling people." Even though many of the famous Quaker
families long ago converted to Episcopalianism, Philadelphia still presents a
Quaker façade to the world, one that Nathaniel Burt has described as "subdued, careful, moderate, puritanical but never ascetic, honest but shrewd,
modest but firm." Yet along with these virtues come the Quakers' defects—
"conformism, anti-intellectualism, materialism, and lack of enthusiasm."

Philadelphia is still the national headquarters of the Society of Friends and
of its very effective adjuncts, the American Friends Service Committee and
National Friends Legislative Committee. And in their activities, the Quaker
conscience, vivid to America since the Friends became foes of slavery two
centuries ago, lives on. The Quakers were especially effective in opposing the
Vietnam war, as they had opposed all wars before it.

Philadelphia also has the oldest Episcopal church diocese in the country.
It went from being the handmaiden of Privilege to one of the most socially
liberal, starting many programs to correct ghetto conditions and to explore
the role of women's liberation in the church, and returning to a more introspective and traditional tone in recent years. In numbers the real church
power in Philadelphia is in the Roman Catholic Diocese, operator of a huge
parochial school system. The leadership exercised by John Cardinal Krol was
close to the most conservative and authoritarian of any Catholic diocese in

North America; Krol's Polish ancestry also gave him special status after the election of Polish Pope John Paul II.

Philadelphia may be known as home of the Establishment and ethnics, but it has had a black community for three centuries. The first expression against the slave trade occurred in Philadelphia, as did the first abolitionist organization, the first legislation to end slavery, the first attempt at black education, and the first black convention. But as each generation of Philadelphia blacks began to establish itself socially and economically, a new wave of less educated blacks arrived, triggering social tensions and vicious new discrimination. Blacks also endured fierce and often losing competition for jobs with successive waves of immigrants arriving from Europe.

Black professional and business opportunities have multiplied in Philadelphia, and the city has produced black leaders ranging from former Secretary of Transportation William Coleman to journalist Chuck Stone (who has negotiated a number of times between prisoners and officials during riots). Many black professionals have moved from the Philadelphia ghettos to better city neighborhoods and the suburbs, leaving behind a troubled underclass. Philadelphia blacks suffered terribly under Rizzo both because he would not hire black police officers and because he used the police department to repress black unrest (a situation quickly and decisively altered under Green—so much that killings by police declined from 19 in 1979 to 4 in 1981). Yet the ghettoes of Philadelphia have also given birth to some of America's most constructive self-help projects. One thinks, for instance, of the Rev. Leon Sullivan, the black preacher who came to Philadelphia in the '50s, started an economic boycott against giant firms (Sun Oil, Gulf Oil, Coca-Cola, and others) that would not open up jobs to blacks, and then formed the Opportunities Industrialization Center (OIC) to train ill-educated blacks for the jobs made available to them for the first time. An amazing and multifaceted man whose worlds embraced the rural South (he was compelled by his grandmother's deathbed directive to "help your people") and high finance (in 1971 he was invited to join the General Motors board of directors), Sullivan found his efforts endorsed by successive presidents of the United States. Sullivan operated in North Philadelphia, a fetid slum that "beat Harlem in housing decay." Perhaps even more abhorrent conditions existed in West Philadelphia, where a black housewife, Sister Falaka Fattah, feared that her son might join one of Philadelphia's numerous and vicious teenage gangs. Sister Fattah decided it was time to call a halt to the gang wars that were senselessly killing more than 40 youths a year on the streets of the city of brotherly love. She and her husband, David, established, in their own home, "the House of Umoja." They invited gang members, if they'd accept quite strict family discipline, to move in with them. They negotiated treaties among the warring gangs, and gang killings practically disappeared. By the early '80s the Fattahs were on to such projects as America's first inner-city "Boystown," a project involving renovation of 23 abandoned West Philadelphia buildings as a residential-educational-economic development center for black youth.

Worries about the future of black Philadelphia were perhaps greater than ever as the 1980s dawned. Official unemployment figures for teenage blacks were 40 percent in 1982, and in reality probably much higher. Even the most sincere young blacks found themselves searching vainly for work month after month. In part their problem was lack of skill—the fruit of a callous, indifferent public school system. But there was another grim fact: the factories and warehouses where they might have found work a generation ago had mostly closed their doors. All of which obviously bore the seeds of deep social discord, and that in a city where fascist rhetoric (both black and white) was as vivid and frightening as we have witnessed anywhere in the nation. Yet there was one hopeful note: Philadelphia blacks did feel much more a part of city life in Philadelphia than in many large cities. This was demonstrated when a North Philadelphia black was killed by a white policeman in the summer of 1980. The streets were tense, but no one was killed and only 15 people were injured. The reasons, outside reporters observed, lay in the strength and political importance of the black community and the mainstream black political leadership coming from such men as State Rep. Milton Street and his brother, City Councilman John Street, who convinced young demonstrators not to turn the confrontation with the police into a riot. The same week, racial tension in Miami resulted in 18 dead and 400 injured.

A strong voice of reason is offered by the *Philadelphia Inquirer,* one of only two dailies left in the city since the January 1982 death of a once-splendid *Evening Bulletin.* The *Inquirer* has undergone an illustrious rebirth since the Knight Newspapers in 1969 purchased it from conservative publisher Walter Annenberg, who had used the paper for personal whims and vendettas and blacked out news about persons or institutions he disliked. Even after the sale, Annenberg remained a communications mogul, with *TV Guide* his biggest property. He did well as a personal friend of Ronald Reagan and Richard Nixon, who indeed appointed him ambassador to the Court of St. James. The death of the *Evening Bulletin* also led to the birth of the *National Leader,* a national newspaper aimed at the black middle class, edited by former *Bulletin* columnist Claude Lewis and published by Ragan A. Henry, a millionaire owner of eight radio stations.

Physically Philadelphia's chief magic remains in its central precincts. There, at the center of it all, rises the craggy, ostentatious City Hall, home to generations of politicians of often dubious integrity, unmistakably a product of the Gilded Age, and topped off by William Penn's statue, the city's highest structure. Around City Hall lies the massive Penn Center business and government complex. Within a block or two on South Broad Street are offices of the major law firms (where honor and profit are still to be gleaned from being a Philadelphia lawyer), the big banks, the doughty old Union League in its General Grant red-mansarded building, the Bellevue-Stratford, the Academy of Music, and Locust and Shubert Theaters. Privilege, Quality, Continuity—all live on along South Broad. Nearby is the elegant Walnut and Chestnut Streets shopping area and Rittenhouse Square, and to the northwest, the grand tree-lined Benjamin Franklin Parkway, the splendid Philadelphia

Museum of Art, the modern development of Franklin Town, the splendid far reaches of Fairmont Park, the infinitely pleasing sight of sculling on the Schuylkill River past gingerbready old boathouses, and much more. Penn's Landing, on the Delaware, has immense (and still only partially fulfilled) potential as a tourist attraction, grand promenade, and entertainment place for all Philadelphians.

Most of Philadelphia, however, seems an immense, groaning metropolis of too many railroad yards and factories and oil tanks and grimy docks, many now derelict. Many of the region's roads are pothole studded. The regional transit system suffered from perennial fiscal crises and deteriorating equipment until 1979 (when a new management, blessed by Gov. Thornburgh and Mayor Green, took hold and started to turn things around—a proof that positive leadership *can* make a difference). One finds a particular Philadelphia trademark in the endless miles of homes, most of them in less than inspiring row-house style.

Outside of Penn's original city, seven major sections may be discerned. South Philadelphia, starting at South Street, is ethnic Philadelphia in earnest, home of its Little Italy, but increasingly black. This is the original home turf of Frank Rizzo, but also gave the world Mario Lanza, Eddie Fisher, Chubby Checker, Toots Shor, and Angelo Bruno (longtime alleged Mafia chief). South Philadelphia was the city's black ghetto in the 1830s, and there were race riots before a single Son of Italy set foot there. Nor is South Philadelphia's black history without luster, for this was the birthplace, too, of Marian Anderson.

West Philadelphia, beginning at the Schuylkill River, offers the University of Pennsylvania, Drexel University, Philadelphia's major hospitals, and the city's civic and convention center and a joint University City Science Center. The University of Pennsylvania dates back to the 18th century and has a rich heritage; it is officially Ivy League and has sought to overcome its bland image through a series of activist presidents and superb graduate schools (law, medicine, and architecture, for example), not to mention the famed Wharton School of Finance (considered with Harvard and Stanford one of the nation's three top business schools). Most of West Philadelphia on the north side of Market is now a black ghetto, as depressing a slum as one might find—mile after mile of unredeemed row houses where grafitti covers the walls, trash spills out onto the streets, toughs lounge in doorways, children play wherever they can. Thousands of houses are vacant, hundreds of stores boarded up and abandoned. Despite the sodden hopelessness that overlies most of North Philadelphia, there are islands of exception such as Yorktown, where the country's first urban renewal project, begun in 1947, eventually led to quite attractive public housing, plus OIC's federally subsidized Zion Gardens and Progress Plaza shopping center. Temple University, now a state-related institution with one of the highest black enrollments among predominantly white universities, is set somewhat incongruously in North Philadelphia. There was hope for a while in the late '60s that the federal Model Cities program might save North Philadelphia from its squalor. But the hopes came to little, and the big black ghetto continued into the 1980s—waiting for some distant day of redemption, and rotting.

Kensington, a factory enclave set between the Delaware River and North Philadelphia ghetto, remains pretty much as author Peter Binzen described it in a 1970 book: "home for 100,000 proud, irascible, tough, narrow-minded, down-to-earth, old-fashioned, hostile, flag-waving, family-oriented ethnic whites." The visitor is warmly welcomed, hears proudly how this was "Rocky's" neighborhood, and is told of bootstrap housing projects aborning. Many times larger but much duller is Northeast Philadelphia, primarily a phenomenon of the postwar years, a great spilling out of middle-class Catholic and Jewish families from the crowded inner-city wards into a green, sprawling, semi-suburban setting. Germantown, sold by William Penn to Daniel Pastorius and a group of Dutch and German Quakers in 1638, was once one of Philadelphia's most fashionable neighborhoods, became a step upward for blacks wanting to escape the North Philadelphia ghetto, and by the '80s was feeling some middle-class "gentrification" pressure. Chestnut Hill is Establishment Philadelphia, spacious and heavily wooded, filled with fine homes and mansions, still heavily WASP-ish in complexion.

Pennsylvania grew in concentric arcs ranging outward from Philadelphia. In the first arc are four suburban counties, heavily populated with Philadelphia commuters. Bucks County (1980 population 479,211) grew 15 percent in the 1970s. The gentle hills, early stone houses, and colorful barns of Bucks make it one of eastern America's most beautiful areas, and for years it has attracted prominent artists and writers. But Bucks' lower end has a steel works (afflicted by massive layoffs) and box houses. Here, indeed, is the classic Levittown, hailed as a model and condemned as ticky-tacky and monotonous when built in the 1950s. Now it is a place with civic pride but dangerously auto dependent (the first gas riot in U.S. history occurred there in the 1979 energy crisis) and troubled by such emerging suburban problems as vandalism, drugs, and a "graying" population.

Montgomery County (643,621) is Pennsylvania's wealthiest and most sophisticated county, suburban and especially rich, close to Philadelphia, with German farm territory farther out. Delaware County (555,007) has two distinct faces, generally classified as east and west of Media. East of Media the county is overbuilt, close to Philadelphia's industrial underbelly, and the site of grimy, unlovable shipbuilding Chester. West of Media, Delaware is more rural, with open and beautiful countryside. The county was the home of the infamous Republican political machine known as the "War Board," whose decline was finally signaled by the election of Rep. Robert Edgar in 1974. Chester County (316,660) is where the Main Line ends at Paoli. Here one finds Valley Forge and the Brandywine Battlefield, the ultra-ultra Radnor Hunt and Devon Horse Show, Longwood Gardens, covered bridges, no large cities, and lots of rolling peaceful farm land.

The second arc out from Philadelphia swings from fruit-growing Adams County and Gettysburg near the Maryland border to the industrial Lehigh

Valley cities near the Delaware opposite New Jersey. This arc contains a high proportion of those remarkable people, the Pennsylvania Dutch, who with pride and simplicity have preserved their 17th-century culture clear into the cybernetic age. The greatest number are found still in Lancaster County, where their ancestors were lured by Penn's promises of religious freedom and limestone soil rich beyond compare. Lancaster is still one of the preeminent farm counties of America; in 1980 it produced $424 million in farm products —more than all of New Jersey! Nothing is more fun for city people jaded by prepackaged supermarket life than to go through the traditional farm markets in cities like Lancaster and York, where families that have kept the same stalls for generations offer their marvelous array of fresh fruits and vegetables and specialties such as scrapple and Lebanon bolognas, Schmier-kase and Swiss cheese, and homemade bread. Despite the rich soil and hard work and financial success, these farms and the rural life are endangered by urbanization gobbling up thousands of acres of farmland per year. Amos Funk, a Millersville, Pa., fruit farmer, has been waging a lonely fight for growth management plans and farmland retention.

Commercialism has damaged the beauty of the Pennsylvania Dutch Country, but it is far more concentrated at Gettysburg, now dominated by profit-hungry motels and quick eateries to snag the millions of people who come each year to see the spot where the contending armies in blue and gray met in the great and tragic battle of July 1863. Moving northeasterly, we come to a series of settlements in the Gettysburg-to-Easton arc: York, Reading, Lancaster, Allentown, Bethlehem, all declining in population. Amidst them is Harrisburg, the state capital set dramatically on the banks of the Susquehanna River (central Pennsylvania's main waterway) and perenially troubled financially through state neglect. Harrisburg is plagued by Pennsylvania's highest rate of serious crimes, reports half its birth are illegitimate, suffers a dreary and declining downtown retail district, and didn't even begin to get some attention from the governor's office until the Thornburgh administration. There is so little confidence in Harrisburg that its population declined 22 percent in the 1970s.

Northeastern Pennsylvania and the "T-Zone"

The early Pennsylvania Dutch stopped their penetration of Pennsylvania when the farmlands gave out—namely, at the Blue Mountains, the front of Appalachian Highlands. North of the Blue Mountains the first settlers found a densely wooded region of high open hills and mountains, running up to the New York State border. Much of that territory is still sylvan and charming today. But at an early point, some of the world's greatest beds of anthracite coal were discovered, and thereby hung the area's damnation. There was a time when more than 100 million tons a year were mined. Today, the anthracite industry is nearly dead, leaving a bitter legacy of smoking heaps of slate and discarded coal, permanent underground fires, and scorched earth ready to cave in. "The landscape looks spooky, like a TV science-fiction planet," wrote John Fischer. Millions of gallons of water, tainted with sulphuric acid, have seeped out of abandoned mines, turning the sweet streams and rivers a brownish yellow and killing fish.

Northeast Pennsylvania has had to pick itself up by the bootstraps in an effort to develop replacement jobs for those lost in mining. So cities such as Scranton and Wilkes-Barre bought large tracts of land on their outskirts, cleared away the culm dumps, brought in utilities, and offered 100 percent plant financing. Soon many plants were moving in, including printing and warehousing for major publishers. All of this, however, was not enough to stem a continuing outflow of the region's young people, seeking greater opportunity elsewhere. One part of the northeast that is developing nicely is the Pocono Mountains, that group of pretty, not very lofty ridges close to the Delaware Water Gap. Summer vacations, winter skiing, and construction of second homes for vacation and retirement have enlivened the area.

North of the anthracite region and then stretching far out to western Pennsylvania is the Appalachian "T-zone," a far-flung region of forests and streams and mountains, mountains, mountains. The top of the "T" covers the northern tiers of counties, almost 300 miles across, with their Lake Country, the Endless Mountains and the Black Forest, the Seneca Highlands, Buckland State Park, and the big Allegheny National Forest in the northwest. With remarkable foresight, the Pennsylvania state government—its forests and waters, fish and game commissions—bought up vast amounts of land here. The lower portion of the "T-zone" is the main body of the Appalachians between Harrisburg and Pittsburgh. This was the great barrier of the past—first for the wagon trains, then for the railroads, then for automobiles. The final conquest was the completion of the Pennsylvania Turnpike in 1940, the first all-weather limited-access superhighway in the country and a model of all that were to follow. Two cities sit astride the Appalachians in south central Pennsylvania: Altoona (62,900), which grew and then declined with the Pennsylvania Railroad, and Johnstown (35,496), which suffered another of its legendary and terrible floods in 1977, not to mention major steel mill and coal mine closings and an unemployment rate reaching 15 percent by 1982. But with all the adversity, Johnstown began to adjust its expectations downward without much bitterness. A visiting reporter discovered extended family life growing, divorces declining, and church attendance rising—a hint, perhaps, of the future for much of America.

Pittsburgh and Beyond

Pittsburgh is one of just three places in America—New York and San Francisco are the other two—where geography demanded a city. Here, the Ohio River, America's historic water life line to the West, is born at the place that the Allegheny River, flowing southward from New York, meets the Monongahela, flowing northward from West Virginia. A 21-year-old major named

George Washington observed the site in 1753 and described it as "extremely well situated for a Fort, as it has the absolute Command of both Rivers." Here, in 1758, Fort Pitt (named after William Pitt, the English prime minister) was built at the juncture of the rivers.

From the heights of Mount Washington, immediately to the south across the Monongahela, the city of Pittsburgh sparkles of a nighttime with a million lights like a little Manhattan. Off to the left (or west) one can see the spot where the rivers meet, with the new Three Rivers Stadium, home of the Pittsburgh Pirates and Steelers, glowing white on the Allegheny's far bank. At the tip of the "Golden Triangle," Pittsburgh's downtown and business district, lies 36-acre State Park, a grassy front lawn that was created out of a dreary melange of warehouses and railroad tracks. Immediately east of the park stand the jewels of Pittsburgh's postwar renaissance, the Gateway Center with the towering office and apartment high rises, and beyond that, still within the Golden Triangle, the corporate behemoths of Pittsburgh: U.S. Steel, Gulf Oil, Koppers, Alcoa, and others. Pittsburgh also has its black ghetto, the Hill District; Polish Hill, which is white and depressed; the Oakland area, which includes the University of Pittsburgh, Carnegie Mellon University, a fine research institute, and the city's medical center; the nearby Shadyside neighborhood, Pittsburgh's answer to Washington's Georgetown with an architectural style dubbed "Gilded Age High-Ceilinged"; the big Schenley and Frick parks; and Squirrel Hill and East End, the Jewish neighborhoods.

Downtown Pittsburgh was likely to look even better during the 1980s as the city and business community embarked on Renaissance II, the second major building and improvement program since World War II. Traffic-jamming trolleys were scheduled to be replaced by a 1.1 mile downtown subway linked to a surface transit line running 9.5 miles into the southern suburbs. Great new skyscrapers were springing up all around the downtown; the most dramatic was PPG Place, designed by Philip Johnson in the post-modernist style and including a 40-story tower of mirrored, pleated glass, topped by finials. And Pittsburgh was learning the value of restoration of distinguished old buildings. During the 1970s a neighborhood-based historic preservation group—The Pittsburgh History and Landmarks Foundation—seized on the idea of taking a 40-acre site across the Monongahela from the Golden Triangle, including the 1901-vintage terminal of the Pittsburgh and Lake Erie Railroad (P&LE), and turning it into a multi-purpose restaurant, shopping mall, luxury office, riverfront marina, and outdoor museum and hotel site. The plan worked under the name of Station Square, including one of the world's most splendid historic building recyclings, the new Grand Concourse restaurant in the P&LE Edwardian lobby.

Pittsburgh, revamped and revitalized, is America's premier example of a city transformed from blue-collar industry to white-collar professions and services. No one would have expected it at the end of World War II when even Pittsburgh's mayor described the city as "the dirtiest slag pile in the United States." Indeed, dirty, smoky Pittsburgh seemed to represent the most exploitive excesses of the industrial revolution. Pittsburgh's rebirth hinged on the coming together of two very different men whose alliance would create the now-legendary postwar renaissance of the city. The first was Richard King Mellon, who in 1934 became the active head of the celebrated family of bankers which had built its wealth by lending money to promising ventures and taking ownership interests in what became Gulf Oil, Koppers, Alcoa, and other corporate giants. The value of the Mellon interests was estimated in 1979 to be $5 billion. Mellon was deeply influenced by his father, Richard B., who counseled him to "live where you work, work where you live, and stay behind your home town." Home on leave during World War II, Mellon like many other Pittsburghers found the city choked with smoke from the war-busy mills and unbelievably drab and depressing. Not long after, in June 1943, associates of Mellon took a leading role in organizing what would become the Allegheny Conference on Community Development. It would be the moving force to mobilize Pittsburgh's business elite to back smoke abatement, downtown renewal, and virtually every other major civic program in the succeeding generation. The political cooperation of the Democrats who controlled Pittsburgh and Allegheny County politics was needed, and David Lawrence, the second key figure of the Pittsburgh renaissance, entered the scene. Lawrence, a major Democratic power broker, ran for mayor and astounded the city by pledging that he would work with the Republican-dominated Conference to improve Pittsburgh and that he would enforce a strong smoke abatement ordinance. Lawrence was elected, and before long he and Mellon had formed their remarkable alliance. "The only two things that the two had in common were their generally cold personalities and their enlightened self-interest," wrote David E. Koskoff in *The Mellons.* But the monuments of their union—clean air, fine buildings, highways, and dams to prevent flooding—are a legacy few leaders have ever left their home cities.

In retrospect, it is clear that the Pittsburgh renaissance, for all its accomplishments, was an elitist phenomenon in which the wealthy business and strong government leaders made rather unilateral decisions on what would be best for Pittsburgh. If the planning was at the expense of the well-being and self-esteem of a lot of small businesses and neighborhoods in Pittsburgh, that was simply a price that had to be paid. But in the Renaissance II of the 1980s, the urban redevelopment authority was shocked to find that when it sought to use the city's power of eminent domain to condemn four small shops to build a 42-story office building, it was dragged into court, and the new owner—PPG (the diversified successor to the Pittsburgh Plate Glass Company)—was obliged to pay an estimated $2 million for the so-called "blighted property." And that was not an isolated instance: it was an example of how dramatically citizen activism and neighborhood environmental and historic preservationist activism had expanded their power base.

The Allegheny Conference also came up with an inner-city housing construction and rehabilitation program that has been called the best conceived and most comprehensive attack on slum housing in America, even though it fell far short of solving Pittsburgh's alarming shortage of decent lower- and middle-class housing. Starting in the 1960s, the Pittsburgh History and Landmarks Foundation, under Arthur P. Ziegler, began to encourage preservation of the many historically and architecturally significant buildings endangered by the wrecker's ball. But the Pittsburgh group differed from other preservation organizations in its breakthrough efforts to refurbish houses for their poor residents, not just an imported middle class. With government and foundation aid, Ziegler's group renovated houses in 15 poor neighborhoods (starting with one colorfully known as the Mexican War Streets), helping many poor families stay while luring affluent young professionals into vacant units.

Its two renaissances notwithstanding, Pittsburgh has suffered continuous economic problems and population losses. The number of jobs in steel and other manufacturing declined to the point that the number of people working in corporate headquarters in Pittsburgh outnumbered actual production workers. The number of Pittsburgh-headquartered corporations on Fortune's top 500 list dropped from 23 in 1965 to 16 in 1980. There were reports that the management of some of these might leave were it not for the Mellons' ownership interests and influence, which could become a very real problem since many of the Mellon heirs were taking less interest in business affairs and lived away from Pittsburgh. There was some movement of new and diversified industries into industrial parks in the area, together with a growth in scientific laboratories, but not nearly enough to offset the loss in basic metals. The city of Pittsburgh lost 37 percent of its population between 1950 and 1980, down to 423,938. The Pittsburgh metro area began losing people in the 1960s and in the '70s slipped by 5.7 percent, bringing the total population down to 2.3 million. Pittsburgh boosters have tried to ignore or make light of the population loss. "Population growth for the sake of population growth is absolute folly," said the leader of one industry-hunting organization. But several studies have shown there is a distinct loss of faith in Pittsburgh's future, especially among younger people.

The renaissances have never done much to change Pittsburgh's picture as the ultimate company town, where women, incidentally, find it especially hard to break into executive ranks. "What gives Pittsburgh its own unique juice and flavor is not how it plays but how it works," writer Jack Markowitz has observed. "This is what underlies the joyless, grimy image people have of the place: all work and no play." Even "socially and physically," he wrote, "business holds the dominant role in town—its massed skyscrapers resembling nothing so much as the superstructure of a vast ship plowing relentlessly forward." Within that milieu the arts have not been strong, though there are glowing exceptions such as the Pittsburgh Symphony, housed in the magnificently restored Heinz Hall, which hired Andre Previn as its music director.*

*No one could say that Pittsburgh has not tried to change its gritty image. When the city opened its new convention center in 1981, named for David Lawrence, it invited 21 Nobel laureates, the first such gathering since a 1962 meeting at the White House. At the same gala an art show representing 22 countries was assembled. One visiting reporter couldn't help but note, however, that the heart of Pittsburgh was in the elaborate corporate displays. H.J. Heinz, for example, built a robot that talked, shook hands and was shaped like a ketchup bottle.

A successful Pittsburgh businessman can have a real feeling of *belonging*. His day, as Markowitz put it, is "a progress of conferences that *do* reach decisions, of meetings in paneled rooms, guarded by worshipful receptionists, and of a noon-day ritual enjoyed by the top brass: the stately processions to the Duquesne Club, where chauffered Cadillacs line up as they do after Friday afternoon concerts at Philadelphia's Academy of Music." (The Duquesne Club, we should add, is a grim old fortress of blackened stone, sitting directly opposite two equally blackened old and prestigious churches, one Episcopalian and the other Presbyterian. Luxuriously decorated within and offering a superb cuisine, the club is literally packed with private meeting rooms where many a business deal and corporate merger have been effected. After a long battle, the club decided to accept women members, but to oldtimers' delight only a few have been found to be of sufficiently high corporate rank to warrant inclusion.)

The first renaissance also did nothing to change Pittsburgh's politics. Mayor Lawrence, for all his fame as a city rebuilder, was no reformer when it came to the old clubhouse way of practicing politics. Governor Thornburgh, when he was U.S. Attorney in Pittsburgh in 1971, told us that "the mystique of Lawrence as a Second Coming is just not true. He and his successor gave free reign to Mellon and the Allegheny Conference just as long as they were left free to hold on to their own political power, clout, and patronage." Syndicate operators in Allegheny County established their foothold in the '40s and '50s through the cooperation of the Democrats, Thornburgh said, and continued to finance the Democratic party throughout the Lawrence years. The area, he alleged, was afflicted by a "politico-racket complex."

Change did come, however, in the form of Peter F. Flaherty, a North Side city councilman who broke with the organization to win election in 1969 as a "man against the machine." Flaherty promised to be a mayor without strong ties or debts to big business, big labor, or the old political alliances—"nobody's boy," as he boasted. Once installed in office, Flaherty brazenly broke the rules of the political game by firing hundreds of superfluous city workers, breaking a jurisdictional strike by the Teamsters-controlled city garbage collectors, and starting to pare down the city bureaucracy to match the city's declining population and preserve fiscal solvency. Flaherty's successor as mayor, Richard Caliguiri, enjoyed much better relations with the business community and became a leading promoter of Renaissance II.

Beyond the Triangle and such immediate adjuncts as Oakland, Shadyside, and the South Side's Mount Washington and Duquesne Heights (where incline railways left over from Victorian times go up to the classy restaurants), the Pittsburgh geography is simply one of hills, hills, hills, and community isolation. Three quarters of the region's people live outside Pittsburgh proper, in three general types of communities: suburbs for the *very* privileged such as Ligonier, Westmoreland County (domicile of the Mellons), Sewickley Heights, or Fox Chapel; middle-class suburbs such as Mt. Lebanon, Penn Hills, and Monroeville; and in Allegheny County blue-shirted steel mill towns crowded into their narrow valleys—places such as Homestead, Braddock, Duquesne, McKeesport, Clairton, Donora, Ambridge, and Aliquippa. Here —except when dreaded closures have struck—the massive blast furnaces and coke ovens, rolling mills and coal breakers of Big Steel belch out their fumes over the landscape; and people fear clean air as a sign of bad times. The story is much the same in outlying cities such as Sharon, New Castle, Washington, and Jeannette. All these are declining cities, losing population and business at a rapid clip. The raison d'être for these towns is that they lie atop the great bituminous coal fields off which the steel mills feed. Coal moves up and down the Monongahela River, known locally as the "Mon," but most of the locks and dams were built more than 50 years ago and desperately need a repair job. Western Pennsylvania is a combination of the grimmest Appalachian poverty. But it does have a modern interstate road system and other occasional hopeful signs. Indiana County grew an astounding 16 percent in the 1970s, mostly due to the presence of Indiana State University, a thriving state institution. In the Laurel Highlands, skiing and other tourism have grown. The small petroleum industry continues to prosper around Oil City, where the U.S. oil industry got its start in the heady days after the Civil War.

Our Keystone state saga ends with a place that hardly considers itself part of Pennsylvania at all—Erie, in the far northwest corner, a Great Lakes city of 119,123 (third-largest in the state). Erie is much closer to Buffalo and Cleveland than to Pittsburgh or Harrisburg, and trade and travel have always tended to go up and down along Lake Erie. It has never developed much political clout, and few Pennsylvanians visit it. Erie has enjoyed a good business climate, with large General Electric and Hammermill Paper payrolls and a lot of small industries in diversified fields, such as precision tools and plastics. But its politics are unexciting, and racketeering is reportedly run as a branch town operation by the big-time gangsters from Buffalo. It is a long way from Penn's Woods.

DELAWARE

Diminutive State of the Diverse du Ponts

WHY, ONE IS TEMPTED TO ASK, is Delaware a state at all? A modern planner would scarcely conceive of it. And even as a vestige of the disorder of colonial rule, it is singular: a tiny strip of land 110 miles long and no more than 35 miles wide, the 47th state in population, and the 49th in area. With 2,056 square miles, Delaware is half the size of Los Angeles County; with 595,225 people in 1980, it was little more than a third the size of nearby Philadelphia.

Yet there it is, a state with sovereign powers, with its own set of laws, with two United States Senators and three electoral votes. There is even a Delaware accent, which sounds like a cross between the Philadelphia dialect (not the Main Liner's, but the Philadelphian's) and the unintelligible patois of Maryland's Eastern Shore. Next come the Great Economic Facts of Delaware: the E.I. du Pont de Nemours Company (1982 assets $23.8 billion, sales $22.8 billion, the nation's 12th-largest corporation) with headquarters in Wilmington, and the du Pont family, of influence seemingly broad and unending in this diminutive state, and of course well beyond its borders as well. Delaware's liberal incorporation laws and pro-corporate court decisions have led over half of the *Fortune* 500 corporations and thousands of smaller ones to make this their legal home. Finally, there was a 1981 Delaware law letting lenders charge whatever they pleased for credit-card loans, a statute that drew in such giants as Chase Manhattan and Citibank and gave Delaware a headstart in the emerging era of interstate banking.

Even the founding of tiny Delaware was unusual. Unlike most of the 13 colonies, it was not founded by a relatively cohesive group or as part of a purposive enterprise. Henry Hudson, the first white man to set foot on what is now the state, gave his name to quite another place. The man whose name the state bears never saw it. In 1610, a captain sailing past the point where the Delaware River empties into the ocean named the bay and later the river after Sir Thomas West, Lord de la Warre, governor of Virginia. The first white settlers were the Dutch in 1631; later this was the site of New Sweden. William Penn tried to lay claim to it for his Quaker settlement, but his title was clouded, and in 1704 Delaware became a colony of the crown, separate from both Pennsylvania and Maryland.

One of the reasons Delaware retained this separate political identity is that no one coveted it. It produced no tobacco or rice, it had no thriving port, and at the time of the Revolution only 37,000 settlers. It was the first colony to call itself a "state," and it even had its own "presidents" during the Revolutionary War. On December 7, 1787, it became the first state—as its license plates testify—to ratify the Constitution of the United States.

Delaware's later history hinges in major fashion on its identity as a border state. It stayed with the Union during the Civil War but supported white supremacy by voting Democratic for several decades thereafter. For most of its history, Delaware was an economic backwater, a state of small and not particularly prosperous farms that sent its children west in search of more fertile lands. But the du Ponts and liberal incorporation laws would change all that.

The du Ponts have dominated Delaware longer than any single company or family has dominated any other state. Yet the du Ponts' association with Delaware began almost accidentally. Pierre Samuel du Pont was a minor French nobleman who arrived in this country with his family on New Year's Day 1800. In 1802 he acquiesced to his son Eleuthere Irenee's prosaic plan to set up a gunpowder mill. The younger du Pont scouted the East Coast from New York to Washington before he chanced on a likely site on the Brandy-wine Creek in Delaware, 12 miles from the then tiny village of Wilmington. Irenee had a certain hard-headed practicality, illustrated by his decision to put up not one big building but several small ones, generously separated so that fires or explosions would be less likely to spread in a chain reaction. Even with all these precautions there was always the possibility that the entire enterprise would literally go up in smoke. There were some fires, but the du Ponts profited from the War of 1812, the Civil War, the Spanish-American War, various European conflicts, and World War I. Their monopoly on gunpowder was broken by a federal antitrust suit launched in 1907, but only techni-cally—since the two new companies created to compete with du Pont, Atlas and Hercules, were owned largely by du Ponts.

The real founder of the du Pont empire as we know it today was a Pierre du Pont, who after a family battle won control of the company while World War I was raging in Europe. Pierre insisted on 50 percent cash up front from the Allies, grossed $1 billion during the war, and made a profit of $237 million, which he used to diversify widely into chemicals, paints, plastics—and General Motors, of which he gained control in 1920. At both du Pont and General Motors, Pierre hired nonfamily professional managers, a bold move that most of American business would eventually follow. The du Pont corporation that emerged was one of the more innovative of the major American companies. Besides introducing into the United States foreign-developed products such as rubber, cellophane, lucite, and polyethylene, du Pont developed by itself artificial rubber, nylon, teflon, orlon, dacron, and mylar polyester film. But it was not until 1974 that du Pont would finally quit making dynamite, the traditional base of the company's business, substituting a du Pont–invented synthetic. The company's major business in recent years has been not in explosives but in mundane products such as textile fibers and fabrics.

The du Pont family continued to run their expansive corporation for almost 170 years or seven generations, a record few, if any, other American founding families could match. By the early 1970s the family had grown so large that a family firm was no longer practical. In 1974, the board selected for the first time a chairman with no family connections. He was Irving S. Shapiro, a lawyer, a Democrat, and a Jew. By 1979 only three du Ponts worked for the company in full-time positions, none above the middle-management level.

This brings us to the complicated question of how much the du Ponts—company, family, and individuals—control Delaware. Until recent years, the company and the family were truly one, and there was simply no equivalent to this one-family, one-company dominance in any state of America. The classic account of this period, *The Company State,* written by a group of Ralph Nader's "raiders" in 1973, quantified the degree of du Pont control, calculating that the du Pont company generated 21 percent of the gross state product. There were du Pont relatives, spouses, and employees in the legislature. The du Ponts owned the Wilmington newspapers, and much of Delaware's most valuable commercial real estate, and had a major share of control in the state's leading banks. The du Ponts, the "raiders" charged, had done their best to keep out competition and unionization and to see to it that their properties were underassessed.

Given their wealth and business interests, it was inevitable that the du Ponts would have an enormous effect on public and social policy in Delaware. The history of the family's involvement reflects a mixture of open-handed generosity and creative philanthropy alternated with tight-fisted crabbiness and reactionary attempts at thought control. Back in the 1920s, for example, Pierre du Pont commissioned a study of the state's educational system and, while the legislature dawdled over his recommendations, personally paid for more than 100 new school buildings (including many for blacks) at an ultimate cost of $4 million. Another du Pont personally paid for the first paved highway.

Delaware's state government has been surprisingly progressive, given the inevitable du Pont influence and the deep-seated conservatism of so many members of the family. But sometimes the progressivism comes about for strange reasons. The du Ponts have put enormous sums into the University of Delaware, for example, but sometimes with strings attached. *Science* magazine has said the University of Delaware "comes close to being a du Pont-directed enterprise." Much of the money the du Ponts have poured into the university has helped develop a strong chemistry department, which of course was of some help to the company. But university researchers also spent time analyzing baseball swings with sensors at the request of Robert R. M. Carpenter, Jr., a family member and then-owner of the Philadelphia Phillies.

In the 1970s, the newspapers were sold (eventually to be acquired by the Gannett chain). Future du Pont family muscle-flexing—either for economic or social benefit—became more difficult. No one, incidentally, is quite sure just how many du Ponts there are; estimates range up to 2,000, and there are perhaps 400 living in Delaware. This is a different way of saying that this is a much more numerous, and inevitably much more variegated clan than the Rockefellers or the (Henry) Fords. The du Ponts love to tell reporters that on New Year's Day, when du Pont males traditionally "call" and give candy, flowers, and other gifts to women of the family, name tags are now needed. Friends of the du Pont family point out that for years du Ponts have opposed or competed with each other on various social, political, and business issues. There have been both Republican and Democratic du Ponts. What the du Ponts still have in common is their wealth, which ranges from comfortable to extraordinary. Even in the early 1980s, du Pont family members still owned a total of 35 percent of the corporation's stock.

The policies of the du Pont company, still by far the largest economic force in the state, reinforce this rule by the wealthy. Nader's researchers found that du Pont was very generous in allowing executives time off to serve in the legislature, on county boards, and even in the governor's chair, yet refused to apply the same policy to blue-collar employees.

That the du Pont name and money still carry magic in Delaware was evident with the election of Pierre "Pete" du Pont, to the U.S. House in 1971 and to the governor's office in 1976. "Pete" du Pont became an exception to Delaware political tradition when he won his governorship by big margins (57 percent in 1976 and 71 percent in 1980), along the way developing a pioneering state program to train high school students for the world of work and channel them into gainful employment immediately after graduation. But his political actions revealed how complicated it is to be a du Pont in Delaware today. By the mid-1970s, the state income tax promoted by his warring ancestors had risen to 19.8 percent on income over $100,000, giving the state of the du Ponts an antibusiness reputation. So at Governor du Pont's urging the legislature reduced the income tax to a top of 13.8 percent. General economies were ordered, and by 1982 Delaware was spending less in "real" (i.e., noninflated) dollars than it had in 1976, partly because of reduced short-term debt, and thus sharply reduced interest costs. The state was also sharply outperforming national averages in new jobs gained. Governor du Pont did not endorse, however, the business community's moves to repeal the state's model law to protect its fragile coastline. The various alliances that arose over this issue told a lot about Delaware politics and power. Among the leaders of the fights for repeal were the AFL-CIO and Irving Shapiro, the chairman of du Pont (the company had been quite neutral on the 1971 act). Arrayed against repeal were various members of the du Pont family, including Pete du Pont, both as a congressman and governor. So much for the theory that du Pont is some kind of monolith imposing its will on little Delaware.

The Coastal Zone Act and the modern organization of the Delaware state government were shining monuments to Russell Peterson, a former du Pont chemist who served one term as governor (1969 to 1973) before Delawareans tired of his liberalism and tax increases. Peterson later became chairman of the federal Council on Environmental Quality. Under Peterson's reorganization, the 140 separate commissions that had run the Delaware government were abolished in favor of 10 cabinet-level departments.

Perhaps because of the heavily corporate atmosphere with so many transplanted executives and chemical workers, Delaware is unusual among Eastern states in its willingness to elect non-natives to high office. Republican William

V. Roth, Jr., elected to the House in 1966 and the Senate in 1970, was born in Montana and educated at the University of Oregon and Harvard Law School before coming to Delaware to work for a chemical firm. Roth gained national attention for co-authoring, with Rep. Jack Kemp of New York, the Kemp-Roth bill for radical reduction of federal income taxes on the theory that it would stimulate the national economy. Delaware's junior senator, Joseph R. Biden, Jr., a Democrat and Pennsylvania native, won election in an upset in 1972, just short of his 30th birthday, after a campaign dependent on a small campaign war chest and many volunteers. Known for his brash personality and presidential ambitions, Biden also proved an able power broker. After 10 years in the Senate and still under 40, he had become the ranking Democrat on the Senate Judiciary Committee, number two on Foreign Relations, and number three on both Budget and Select Intelligence.

A Quick Tour of a Tiny State

Wilmington owes its existence as a city to the du Ponts; before Eleuthere Irenee set up his powder mill on Brandywine Creek, it was just a tiny village. At the center of Wilmington—and it is really the center of all Delaware, too —is Rodney Square, a pleasant block-wide park. Facing it are the du Pont offices (referred to locally as "the Building"), the Hotel du Pont (referred to locally as "the Hotel"), the Playhouse (Delaware's only legitimate theater), the state's leading banks, and most of Delaware's major law firms; within a block or two are the city and county governments and the Delmarva Power Company. About the only thing lacking to make this the focus of all power in Delaware is the state capitol. (For that one must visit the placid little colonial-era city of Dover—population 23,512—several miles to the south.)

No one could resist noting the contrast between the neat but scarcely gaudy prosperity of Rodney Square and the condition of most of the rest of Wilmington: sad to say, much of the state's only large city is an undistinguished slum. Wilmington's problems are not much different from those of so many of the nation's central cities: tightly confined within borders established years ago, Wilmington is only 15 square miles in size and has been losing population, especially affluent population, to the suburbs beyond. In 1980 Wilmington had 70,195 citizens, 15 percent of Delaware's population; by way of comparison, in 1940 the city had a population of 112,540, 42 percent of the state's total. By 1980 just over half of Wilmington's citizens were black.

In 1973 the city inaugurated the nation's first urban homestead act, under which people took possession of dilapidated and abandoned houses for nominal sums and fixed them up. The idea was later adopted by the federal government. The city also was the first in the East to use mortgage revenue bond financing to enable low- and moderate-income families to buy homes at reduced interest rates and to develop a lease-purchase housing program for young families. The man who started the housing initiatives was Thomas Maloney, just 30 years old when he was elected mayor in 1972. Maloney went on to slash the patronage-heavy city bureaucracy, which won him praise from "good government" groups and conservatives and the label "union buster." He later paid for his efficiency campaign when labor leaders proved only lukewarm during his unsuccessful bid to unseat Senator Roth in 1976. (Maloney became a regional HUD administrator during the Carter administration, a post in which he devised some ingenious ways to clear obstacles in the meshing of gears between federal, state, and local bureaucracies. Maloney also developed an uncanny ability to mimic Jimmy Carter's sing-song voice, staging a series of hilarious practical jokes at the expense of big cheeses who thought it really *was* the President of the United States on the phone.)

Wilmington's downtown has also gotten a facelift in recent years. After a great many starts and setbacks, the city's 1871 Grand Opera House, which had deteriorated into a second-rate movie theater, was restored as Delaware's showcase for the performing arts. A new hotel and headquarters for two of the major employers, Hercules and the Wilmington Trust Company, have laid a strong base for revitalization of the business district. The key to new construction, Mayor William T. McLaughlin, Maloney's sucessor, told us, was public-private partnership in the development effort, including heavy lobbying for federal grants. Without a $16.1 million federal urban action grant to cover the added costs of building in the old city, Hercules and its new $100 million headquarters "would have probably left our region and moved to the Southwest," McLaughlin said.

Beyond Wilmington are its suburbs—stretching northeast toward the circular Pennsylvania border and southwest from the city toward the Maryland line and the town of Newark, where the University of Delaware is situated. The most distinctive part of the suburban ring around Wilmington is the least densely populated, aptly named Chateau Country, northwest of the city. One will find no traces of the petrochemical vapors of lower Wilmington here, just the rolling green hills, the manicured pasturelands, and the giant homes of the du Ponts and some of their wealthy friends. Some of these are now museums, notably the lovely 1,000 acre, 195-room Winterthur.

Most of the rest of Delaware, south of metropolitan Wilmington, bears little resemblance to either the central city or the Chateau Country. In the place of carefully tended forests, downstate Delaware tends to have billboards advertising scrapple; instead of du Pont mansions, it has the huge chicken coops of a thriving broiler industry. This Delaware remains predominantly rural and essentially Southern. Some industry has invaded, and Sussex and Kent Counties had growth rates of 22 and 19.9 percent, respectively, in the 1970s. One area of heavy growth was around the pleasant seaside resort of Rehoboth Beach, a favorite of Washingtonians who arrive each summer to relax in varieties of interesting rooming arrangements. But for the most part, southern Delaware is still what Megalopolis can well use: a quiet cul-de-sac away from the grime, the lifestyles, the affluence, and the rush of modern life.

MARYLAND

The Superimposed Civilizations

MARYLAND FITS ONLY RELUCTANTLY into a single portrait. What, after all, does the blue-collar port city of Baltimore, 55 percent black, have in common with the Washington, D.C., suburb of Montgomery County, which has among the highest family incomes in the nation? What do the watermen of the somnolent Eastern Shore have in common with the residents of mountain-locked Cumberland? What do the people who live in the almost continuous string of middle-class suburbs from Washington to Baltimore, in Prince Georges and Anne Arundel and Baltimore Counties, have in common with the others?* Not very much, except that they all live within Maryland's convoluted boundaries. The lines were drawn in the days when water provided the chief mode of transportation, and so the state spans Chesapeake Bay and includes great swaths of the Potomac River Valley.

This is one of the smallest states in area (ranking 42nd), yet to drive from its easternmost point, Ocean City on the Atlantic, to its westernmost in Garrett County, high in the Appalachians, is at least 350 miles. Its northern boundary is the famous Mason-Dixon line, the traditional boundary between slave and free territory. It is a state with Southern ancestry, yet inhabited mainly by Yankees today. As a colony, it was founded as a refuge for Catholics. Yet in the 1980s it was still only 17 percent Catholic. Maryland has always been mainly Protestant, though here one finds one of the highest Jewish percentages of any state (4.4 percent). Some of its residents live in extreme poverty, both in Baltimore ghettos and rural backwaters. There are also a few concentrations of great wealth, but modern Maryland is most of all a state of salaried people whose pay is very high due to the nearness of the federal capital at Washington, D.C.

Ideology takes a backseat in Maryland politics. Strong conservative instincts occasionally prevail at the local and congressional district levels, but party tradition favors the Democrats—oftentimes with a 3 to 1 edge in registration. Maryland was one of only six states carried by Jimmy Carter in the 1980 presidential election. Even after its Democratic Governor Marvin Mandel was sent to prison, Maryland elected still another Democratic governor in 1978. Quirky primary results seem to underscore Maryland Democrats' lack of ideology: the winner of the state's 1972 Democratic presidential primary was

---

*The city of Baltimore is not part of any county and is often referred to as Baltimore City, to distinguish it from entirely suburban Baltimore County. It was Baltimore County that Spiro Agnew once served as County Executive.

Alabama Gov. George Wallace, the social conservative, and in 1976, California Gov. Jerry Brown, the futurist. In general elections, however, a middle-of-the-roadism has prevailed. For years, Maryland's most distinguished delegate to Washington has been Senator Charles "Mac" Mathias, a liberal Republican.

Scarcely existent ideology, fused with a constant need to reach regional accommodation, has produced a political culture that is tolerant of political shenanigans. After Vice President Spiro Agnew, Governor Mandel, and several suburban county executives were all found guilty of taking kickbacks (or in Agnew's case pleaded nolo contendere), Maryland achieved the reputation of second most corrupt state in the nation, after New Jersey. The reputation may be as much due to the fact that a series of fine United States attorneys caught more of the rascals here than in other states, but the tradition of tolerance is well ingrained and even something of a matter of pride. Several writers have had fun with this aspect of Maryland life. Its distinguished if irascible native son H.L. Mencken once called Maryland the most average of states even in "the percentage of its lawyers sent to prison yearly for felony." After Agnew's resignation, Russell Baker of the *New York Times*, formerly a Baltimore reporter, was moved to write that "Baltimore is permissiveness. The pleasures of the flesh, the table, the bottle, and the purse are tolerated with a civilized understanding of the subtleties of moral questions that would have been perfectly comprehensible to Edwardian Londoners. Gross and overt indulgence, however, is frowned upon. The gunned corpses that litter New Jersey are not part of Baltimore life. That sort of thing is vice. Vice leads to cruelty and suffering, and what's more, is in bad taste. Sin is something else. Baltimore tolerates sin." Still it is possible to see how easily the line can be crossed. Consider the reaction of former Baltimore City State Senator Joseph Staszak when he was asked whether it was a conflict of interest for him to vote on a liquor bill when he made much of his living off a liquor license. Not at all, Staszak replied. There was no conflict because his interests and what the bill would do coincided exactly.*

Modern Maryland is best understood by focusing on the differences between the Old Maryland and the New Maryland and the process of growth that has divided the two. Between 1940 and 1980, Maryland's population more than tripled (to 4,216,446—17th-largest among the states), but the older, earlier populated places—Baltimore City and the rural counties of the Eastern shore and the mountains—grew scarcely at all. In the Old Maryland of 1940, half the people lived in Baltimore, creating a kind of city-state, with another third

---

*In terms of responsiveness, equality of representation, the quality of staff and professional services, the Maryland legislature has advanced light years in the past generation. Some of its leaders have ranked among the best in state legislatures across the nation. Oftentimes, however, the moral tone still leaves much to be desired. It is as if the delegates and senators were sent to Annapolis by rival and antagonistic duchies, to make—and dissolve—entangling alliances in accordance with their county's interest or perhaps just for the Byzantine pleasure. All this takes place in the oldest U.S. state capitol still in use. Built in 1772, it is one of the nation's loveliest public buildings, set in a little city packed with splendid colonial-era structures (many saved from the wrecker's ball by an indomitable preservation group, Historic Annapolis).

in rural counties and only 22 percent in the suburbs. Then came the mush-
roomlike growth of the federal government, and a New Maryland sprang up
in what once was quiet southern countryside, right next to the old. In 1980,
54 percent of Marylanders lived in the four suburban counties surrounding
Washington and Baltimore. By the 1970s the suburbs close to the two major
cities were becoming "expensive and saturated" and suburbia was sprawling
farther and farther out. Even such traditional southern Maryland counties as
Charles, St. Marys, and Calvert, as well as mountainous and hitherto remote
western mountain counties began to swell with new people and jobs in the
late 1970s. This growth has brought the "rural areas" renewed political
strength, but has also raised serious questions about the future of the land and
conflict between the well-educated, highly paid newcomers, the poorly educated laborers, and the aristocracy that has long dominated those places. Only
Baltimore City failed to grow.

Thus the story of Maryland is in two parts: the traditional history of the
Old Maryland, from its founding to the growth of Baltimore as a major port
and manufacturing center; and the World War II and postwar explosive
growth of the New Maryland, with its economic wealth and startling political
and cultural contrasts with the Old.

The crucial date of Maryland's settlement was 1632, when the English King
Charles I granted to Cecil Calvert, the second Lord Baltimore, a charter to
what is now called the Delmarva Peninsula and the land west of the Chesapeake Bay from the Potomac River north to the 40th parallel. Baltimore
tactfully left the name of the colony blank on the document, and King Charles
wrote in "Maryland" in honor of his queen, Henrietta Maria.

In 1633 Baltimore's brother, Leonard Calvert, led an expedition to Maryland
and established St. Marys City as its first capital. Maryland patriots rarely fail
to note that this was the first colony to allow freedom of religion, though in
fact that seems to have been a result more of prudence than of any affection
for the principle of toleration: the Catholic Calverts, after all, held the land
at the sufferance of a Protestant King and Parliament, and in all other respects
the Calverts ran the colony as autocratically as they could. Curiously, Catholics, despite their key role, were apparently never a majority among the settlers, and Lord Baltimore, after whom Maryland's chief city is named, never
even crossed the Atlantic.

Tobacco was the great crop of colonial Maryland, but by the time of the
Revolution much of the Tidewater soil had been exhausted. Though the state
had many rich landholders, it seems also to have supported the Revolution
enthusiastically. Maryland was the only one of the original states invaded by
the British in the War of 1812; in an event that would become legendary to
elementary school children for generations to come, Francis Scott Key wrote
"The Star Spangled Banner" when the British were repulsed from Baltimore
by the guns of Fort McHenry in 1814.

Maryland was a slave state, but it was never dominated by big plantations.
There were almost as many free Negroes counted in the 1860 Census as slaves,
and there was a fierce division of sympathies during the Civil War. If Mary-

land had seceded, Washington would have been cut off from the rest of the Union, so Abraham Lincoln placed the state under military control. It was the scene of much bloody fighting, including the Battle of Antietam in 1862.

The real story of Maryland in the 19th century is an economic one. Maryland was a natural avenue for commerce. The first federally financed highway, the National Road, was completed from Baltimore to Wheeling and the Ohio River in 1818. Maryland also excelled in railroads. In 1830, the first stretch of the Baltimore and Ohio was built—America's first railroad. Before the Civil War, the great B&O connected Baltimore to cities as far west as Cincinnati and St. Louis. The rails insured that Baltimore would be one of the nation's major ports and commercial centers, a status it retains today.

This growth of a large metropolis in an otherwise rural state made for an unusually heterogeneous mix. The rural cultures themselves were always divided between those above and below the "fall line," the imaginary line marking the drop in land level formulated by connecting the waterfalls of rivers (and determining, incidentally, the navigability of rivers). In Maryland, the fall line passes through Washington and up past Baltimore. East of the fall line, on the Chesapeake Bay, one found an English corn culture, generally Southern in its sympathies and Democratic in its politics. West of the fall line, almost as an extension of the Pennsylvania Dutch region, was a German wheat culture, sympathetic to the North in the Civil War and for years after Republican. Add to that the watermen of the Eastern Shore and the immigrants of Baltimore, where the Irish and Polish tended to vote Democratic and the Italians and blacks Republican, and one had—long before anyone dreamed of the suburban New Maryland—as heterogeneous a state as any.

Politically, this produced strange consequences. Maryland voted for a "white supremacy" ticket in 1903, but less than 10 years later a public service commission and child-labor law were passed. Maryland segregated its school children by race, but unlike its Southern neighbors it opposed Prohibition, it licensed race tracks, and even—until the 1960s—allowed slot machines in a few of its counties. By all accounts, the pre–World War II Old Maryland had a basically honest, if cautious, political system. It would take the explosive growth after World War II to place the old system of accommodation under strains it could not handle.

A good place to look for the New Maryland is on the boundary of the District of Columbia and Montgomery County, at the corner of Western and Wisconsin Avenues. There one finds 25-story high-rise apartments (built just outside the District's strict height limitations) next to shops such as Saks Fifth Avenue, Lord and Taylor, and Woodward and Lothrop. Directly across the street on the District side, a block-long white marble edifice called Mazza Gallerie houses the famous Texas department store of Neiman-Marcus, F.A.O. Schwarz, and other chic boutiques and stores.

The mushrooming federal presence was the engine behind this momentous growth. The number of federal employees in the Washington metropolitan area increased by more than 40 percent in the two decades following President Kennedy's inauguration in 1961. By 1980, more Marylanders worked for the federal government than did the residents of any other state except the megastates of California, Texas, and New York, and nearby Virginia. With 118,271 Marylanders working for the federal government, it was by far the single largest employer in the state. Most of Maryland's civil servants were concentrated in Montgomery and Prince Georges Counties, working either in the capital itself or in the many federal offices located in the Maryland suburbs: the National Institutes of Health, the Census Bureau, the National Aeronautics and Space Administration, the National Oceanic and Atmospheric Administration, the National Bureau of Standards, the Food and Drug Administration, to name a few. There was substantial federal employment in Baltimore, too, most notably the huge Social Security headquarters there. Even Maryland's smaller counties have been the beneficiary of the federal presence. The Army's Aberdeen Proving Ground is located in Harford County, 20 miles north of Baltimore, and in long-isolated St. Marys County, 50 miles south of Annapolis, the Patuxent Naval Air Station. In Annapolis, of course, there's the Naval Academy.

Federal salaries skyrocketed, even beyond the federal job totals, in the 1960s and '70s; cumulatively, the infusion of federal dollars had made Maryland one of America's richest states. Its per capita income rose from 17th among the states in 1950 to 8th in 1980. Postwar immigration did bring new and difficult problems, as undereducated, unskilled blacks from the lowlands of the Carolinas, whites from the hills of the Appalachians, and uneducated Hispanics without English language skills poured into the cities. Baltimore experienced some of this, as did Washington.* But to a large extent, Maryland's new arrivals were the cream of the crop: highly educated, well-to-do, upwardly mobile people from all over America who came to work for the government or some enterprise—lobby, trade, or consulting—that depended on the federal presence. Not surprisingly then, the state ranked first among the 50 in 1980 in the number of active physicians per 100,000 population (thanks of course in part to generous federal employees' health insurance plans), fourth in the number of scientists with doctorate degrees, and eleventh in the number of engineers.

The suburbs that grew up around Baltimore developed somewhat differently from Washington's, attracting a lesser share of highly paid people, more Catholics, and more Southerners. Yet they also drew a substantial number of federal employees, and in general one would have to depict both cities' outskirts as part of the same middle-class suburban culture.

One would like to be able to report that all those highly educated, well-paid immigrants from other states propelled Maryland toward an era of good government and clean politics. In fact, the opposite is true. The stench of modern Maryland politics has arisen directly from the growth of the Mary-

---

*Officials from Prince Georges County, across the District line, have complained that the county has had to absorb more than its share of poor people, mostly black, spilling over from Washington. But in reality most of the blacks who have moved to Prince Georges are those who have entered the middle class.

land suburbs and their peculiar populations. The Maryland suburbs fulfilled a dictum of Lincoln Steffens that corruption will be found where local government has the power to confer lucrative benefits on certain people. In Steffens' time, just after the turn of the century, that kind of money flowed mostly in big cities; in Maryland since World War II, such plums as the contracts to build new streets and sewers and the zoning authorization for new housing tracts and industrial plants and office buildings have been the very keys to suburban growth. Agnew, for example, got his start as a member of the Baltimore County Board of Zoning Appeals. Supposedly he complained to friends that his rise in politics was so rapid—from zoning board to Baltimore County executive to governor and vice president—that he never had time to make the money to afford the lifestyle to which he thought he was entitled. Some of those friends were contractors, architects, and engineers, who did much of their business with Baltimore County and the state of Maryland. Some began giving kickbacks—percentages of their public contracts—to Agnew in exchange for his "help" in winning contract awards. Even as he was making speeches sternly denouncing supposedly lawless peace demonstrators, Spiro Agnew was on the take. The immigrants' role in this corruption has been one of political neglect; many Maryland suburbanites, especially in the Washington, D.C., area, simply ignore state and local politics, frying bigger fish on the federal scene or maintaining ties with their home states (and sometimes even voting there).

Of the scandals that have come from Maryland the most disheartening were the revelations that Gov. Marvin Mandel had accepted $350,000 in gifts and business interests in exchange for manipulating the state legislature to increase the value of a race track his friends secretly owned. There is still some truth to the theory that, corruption aside, Mandel was Maryland's finest chief executive. Raised in the Jewish section of Northwest Baltimore and bearing a Baltimore accent and diminutive stature, Mandel overcame considerable odds to become an unbeatable governor. A former state house speaker highly skilled in dealing with the legislature and more interested in control than ideology (as befitted the state), Mandel managed to reorganize the state government from a hopeless hodge-podge of 247 agencies to 11 consolidated, cabinet-level departments. Highways, mass transit, airports, and the port of Baltimore, for instance, were placed under a unified department of transportation. Under Mandel, the state assumed responsibility for all public school construction, thus relieving reliance on the local property tax. He pushed difficult handgun control and land use legislation through the legislature, created the nation's first state-owned insurance company, and developed an innovative emergency health program that, with helicopters and ambulances, put anyone in Maryland within 18 minutes of a fully staffed emergency medical facility. Perhaps this legacy was part of the reason Maryland politicians of all stripes banded together to seek a presidential pardon that got Mandel out of a federal prison camp in late 1981 after serving 20 months of a three-year sentence.

The corruption appeared to be limited to the state and local levels and not to have tainted Maryland's quite distinguished congressional delegations. Despite the fact that nearly half the voters are not natives, Maryland still tends to elect people with pedigree and long-term ties to high office. Mathias, first elected in 1968, came from a distinguished Maryland political family and kept up the dwindling Eastern liberal Establishment Republican tradition in the Senate. Mathias was a Vietnam "dove" and voted against President Nixon on so many issues that he qualified for the White House "enemies" list; later he gave Ronald Reagan only a lukewarm endorsement. Non-WASPs with credentials can make it, however. Senator Paul Sarbanes came from a Greek immigrant family that settled in Salisbury on the Eastern Shore; he studied at Princeton and as a Rhodes Scholar before rising through the hurly-burly of Baltimore Democratic politics to serve three terms in the House and then defeat another blueblood Republican Senator, J. Glenn Beall, Jr., in 1976. Sarbanes quietly established a liberal voting record, which came under heavy fire from the National Conservative Political Action Committee (NCPAC), which sought—ultimately unsuccessfully—to unseat him in a virulent media campaign beginning two years before the 1982 elections.

Maryland's eight-member congressional delegation, reflecting the state's diversity, has become as politically, racially, and sexually representative as any in the nation. The Baltimore suburbs sent the senior congressman, Democrat Clarence Long, a former Johns Hopkins University economics professor who developed impressive foreign policy expertise. From Baltimore came Democrat Barbara Mikulski, a voluble street politician who managed to combine the concerns of her blue-collar constituents with her own commitments to women's rights and other liberal concerns, and Parren Mitchell, a member of a distinguished black family (his brother, Clarence Mitchell, for example, was for many years the skilled lobbyist in Washington for the NAACP). From the Washington suburbs there was Michael Barnes, elected in 1981 as chairman of the increasingly important House Foreign Affairs Subcommittee on Inter-American Affairs. Suburban Prince Georges and Anne Arundel counties sent Marjorie Holt, a conservative Republican who became a budget expert. Key losses in 1980 were Republican Rep. Robert Bauman, of the Eastern Shore, a social conservative and master parliamentarian who had been making life miserable for House Democrats until he was charged with soliciting sex from a 16-year-old boy, and Gladys Spellman, a veteran Prince Georges County Democrat and defender of federal employees who while campaigning suffered a heart attack that left her comatose.

Baltimore: Maryland's Spiritual Capital

The spiritual capital of the Old Maryland is not Annapolis, where suburban legislators make deals in the old State House and bureaucrats run the state government in 1960s replicas of Georgian homes. Rather, it is in Baltimore, the great port town at the head of the Chesapeake Bay once described by its native son H.L. Mencken as "the ruins of a once-great medieval city."

Always one of America's largest urban centers but left behind by the suburban rush of the '50s and '60s, Baltimore seemed the epitome of the fading old eastern city, burdened with a blue-collar, workaday image and an ample share of the poverty and racial problems that outsiders say doom older metropolises. But in the early 1980s, Baltimore suddenly emerged as a glittering example of what can be achieved in urban rejuvenation. The city's fabulously successful waterfront renovation, including the Rouse Company's festival marketplace, Harborplace, won national attention—even a *Time* cover story featuring developer James Rouse. Tourists, suburbanites, and its own residents poured into Baltimore's downtown once again. In 1980, just before Harborplace opened, Rouse told us that "Baltimore in two years will be recognized as the most dazzling center city in America." We scoffed a bit at the claim. But in 1982 it did not seem so preposterous at all.

Baltimore's renewal, however, did not begin or end with the opening of Harborplace in 1980. It was the businessmen who became alarmed about the city's progressive deterioration in the '50s and then formed the Greater Baltimore Committee, which in turn drew up the two great plans that "saved" the inner city. The first was for Charles Center, a huge 15-building office-and-apartment development in the center of downtown, and the second for the Inner Harbor, which came to include (in addition to Harborplace) a fabulous aquarium, a 30-story World Trade Center, and a science center and marina —the berth of the 1797-vintage U.S. Frigate Constellation, the first commissioned warship of the U.S. Navy. On the government side, Baltimore has been fortunate to have a "strong mayor" form of government and a string of able mayors. Mayor William Donald Schaefer, elected in 1971, became a near hero for his indefatigable dedication to city renewal. A bachelor who lived with his mother in the neighborhood where he grew up (now almost all black), Schaefer threw himself into his job with a set of skills described by one magazine as "gall, soft soap, hard nose, demonic energy, and the kind of showmanship Baltimore has not seen since the death of vaudeville."

On the substantive side, Baltimore wisely focused all housing and urban renewal powers through a single housing and community development authority, led for several years by Robert Embry, later U.S. assistant secretary for housing and urban development. Employing "homesteading" and other innovative housing programs, Embry and his successors stimulated new construction or rehabilitation for thousands of families of all income groups. Baltimore also proved phenomenally successful at federal grantsmanship, drawing in literally hundreds of millions of dollars. President Carter once called Schaefer his "favorite mayor," yet when Ronald Reagan defeated Carter, Schaefer started lobbying him immediately, garnering invitations to the White House to make razzle-dazzle presentations of Baltimore's wonders.

In many and major respects, Baltimore still works, like cities used to. Its tax rate is not entirely out of control like Boston's or Newark's, and its government provides services with some efficiency. It is lucky enough to receive substantial aid from Maryland state government, even if its suburbs care little for its fate. It is not a city, like St. Louis or Detroit, where abandonment is rampant. Many reformers have criticized the fact that the distribution of "walk around money" and local bosses still play important roles in Baltimore elections. But on the plus side one must note that this is not a city in which neighborhood, ethnic, racial, and business-labor conflicts have reached unnegotiable levels.

Baltimore enjoys a diversified economy and strong business leadership. The core of Baltimore's economy is, of course, the port, and visitors to the commercial waterfront miss the miles of "real" port facilities farther out in the harbor. In tonnage, Baltimore is the nation's eighth-largest port and has achieved this rank without reliance on a single local commodity, such as Norfolk has with coal. Baltimore manufactures a multitude of goods from steel to spices and is the home of several large insurance companies and of the Black and Decker power tool firm. There are also a major copper refinery and a larger-than-average federal government presence.

The fabric of the city's life is its neighborhoods—237 of them, by popular count, many with colorful histories and offering such descriptive names as Ridgely's Delight, Old Otterbein, Butchers Hill, Chinquapin Hollow, and Violetville. There are Italians in Little Italy (a 12-block area of East Baltimore close to the Inner Harbor and famed for its restaurants), Lithuanians and other East Europeans in Highlandtown, Greeks and Hispanics and Poles in Fells Point, Jews in Northwest Baltimore, and blacks (now Baltimore's majority population) concentrated in East and West Baltimore along a strip emanating from the central city, plus other areas. Baltimore celebrates its varied ethnicity each September at the multisplendored City Fair, held at the Inner Harbor. Over 100 ethnic and neighborhood gropus set up booths where they describe their unique qualities and projects. The smell of kielbasa, calzone, stuffed cabbage, chittlings, and souvelaki is sometimes overwhelming. There are free concerts each evening, offerings ranging from country music to Fats Domino to the Baltimore Symphony Orchestra. There is scarcely another American city where ethnicity and history are so treasured. A grassroots theatrical group, Baltimore Voices, created a sparkling drama based on thousands of oral histories taken from citizens: the play traced the experience of six composite Baltimoreans from 1880 to the 1970s as they coped with such events as the flu epidemic of 1918, the boom of the '20s, the Great Depression, World War II, and the technological age.

Self-help measures abound in Baltimore neighborhoods. The South East Community Organization (SECO), for example, is composed of more than 70 civic associations, senior citizen and church groups, and block clubs representing 94,000 residents in low-income neighborhoods of the classic Baltimorean row houses (often still with their gleaming white marble steps). SECO's projects have run the gamut from a summer job corps to commercial revitalization programs including a supermarket, from work with juvenile criminals to a highly successful Neighborhood Housing Services program.

Even as Baltimore was developing a national reputation for urban redevelopment and ethnic neighborhoods, the city was becoming smaller and blacker. Baltimore dropped from seventh- to tenth-largest of the nation's cities in 1980 when the Census showed it had only 786,755 people, some 72,345 fewer than in 1940. A state legislator representing one of the famed ethnic neighborhoods told us that most of his constituents are elderly whites and blacks while the reunions of his old Roman Catholic high school are held where the graduates live—in the suburbs. The 1980 Census also showed that 55 percent of Baltimoreans are black. Blacks had not achieved a position in politics appropriate to their numbers, but in 1982 there was a breakthrough when Kurt Schmoke, a 32-year-old black attorney who had graduated from Harvard Law School and joined Piper and Marbury, a prominent downtown firm, defeated almost 2 to 1 the longtime white incumbent city prosecutor, William A. Swisher, a favorite son of the old-line blue-collar political clubs. Chicken George, a black-oriented fast-food outlet, and the improvement association of a public housing project had offered free meals to registered voters; black businesses and churches donated 75 vans and trucks to transport voters to the polls. The turnout in black precincts was as high as 50 percent, an unprecedented figure in nonpresidential years. Equalizing the positions of black and white is a tough job in Baltimore. But progress there is. When the city council chairman resigned in 1982, for example, the council chose a black member, Clarence Du Burns, as chairman.

Despite a reasonably balanced economy, unemployment is so high among blacks that when the Social Security Administration announced the availability of 75 entry-level jobs in September 1980, some 26,250 individuals showed up. "Gentrification" has forced poor blacks out of some inner-city neighborhoods. Baltimore has other problems too. The riots in 1968 were among the worst in the nation, and an outbreak during a city sanitation strike in 1974 had to be quelled by state police. Although some promising development plans were announced in 1981, the city was still awaiting substantive renewal of its decayed old retail center at Lexington and Howard Streets. The crime rate is high.

Still, by the early 1980s Baltimore had finally thrown off its lurking fears of being a second city to Washington. And if the nation's capital could boast more continental cuisine restaurants, Baltimore had its incomparable Lexington Market and remained the national center of succulent Chesapeake Bay crabs and oysters—and how to cook them. It also had its beloved Baltimore Orioles baseball team, while Washington remained teamless.

Our review of Baltimore life would be incomplete without reference to three fine Baltimore institutions: Johns Hopkins University, Johns Hopkins Hospital, and the *Baltimore Sun*. Hopkins is the birthplace of the Ph.D. in America. Its medical school is rated second in the nation, behind Harvard, and it has many other fine departments. The *Sun* is one of the best daily newspapers in America, has an excellent Washington bureau, and is one of the few regional papers to still maintain overseas bureaus as scattered as Moscow, London, Bonn, Peking, Jerusalem, New Delhi, and Johannesburg.

The Rest of Maryland

Though the New Maryland suburbs, where the majority of the state's people now live, lack culture and historic roots, they are not one indistinguishable mass. The Washington, D.C., suburbs of Montgomery County (579,053) are really an extension of the well-to-do sections of Northwest Washington. By 1980, houses on the winding side streets and cul-de-sacs of Bethesda and Chevy Chase cost $150,000 and up, and in Potomac, where the grocery stores sell horse feed, sometimes $1 million. Rockville, however, has its own small black ghetto, Wheaton is a solidly middle-class suburb, and Silver Spring has a large Jewish community and an increasing number of blacks, Hispanics, and Asians. East of Silver Spring is Takoma Park—an old suburb laid out in 1890 but a favorite among young black and white professionals who wish to take advantage of the lower housing costs, the Montomgery County schools, and a subway link to Washington.

Takoma Park also straddles the Montgomery–Prince Georges County line, about which some Washingtonians make strong distinctions. Montgomery is known as the white-collar suburb and Prince Georges the blue-, but by national standards, Prince Georges is very white collar. The residents of P.G., as it is locally called, do tend to have lower incomes and less education. Prince Georges (665,071) is the largest jurisdiction in the Washington area (including the District of Columbia itself). The size of P.G. County remained stable in the 1970s, but it went from 15 percent black to 41 percent black, as 156,000 blacks moved in and many whites left due to school busing. The fastest growing parts of Montgomery County are to the west and north, in Gaithersburg, Poolesville, Wheaton, and unincorporated areas. Prince Georges is dominated by such middle-class suburbs as Langley Park, Oxon Hill, Bowie, and Laurel. It is also home of the University of Maryland's main campus, which is less distinguished than it should be, considering the wealth of the state and its proximity to the nation's capital.

In far northeastern Prince Georges, the Baltimore television stations start coming in better than the Washington ones, and for a while we are in a no-man's land where Baltimore and Washington compete for influence. In nearby Howard County is Columbia, the "new town" built by James Rouse in the late 1960s. Rouse's visionary dream for Columbia was a "style of living distinctly its own," not a suburb but a city with its own employment base, racially and economically integrated. Columbia achieved a population of 52,518 by 1980, 15 percent of whom were blacks but mostly middle to upper income. Though many of its residents commuted to Baltimore and Washington, Columbia had become a major employment center of its own. There were some who criticized Columbia's ultra-perfect planning; one outside real estate developer said he expected to find "behind every bush, a tag marking its proper place." But the overall effect was a very pleasing one. Columbia's soul was unquestionably suburban, but the taste light years ahead of the mish-mash of the typical American suburb. Rouse, while retaining his own residence in Columbia, shifted his attention to the inner cities and scored immense successes with such projects as the Boston Faneuil Hall Marketplace and Baltimore's Harborplace. While remaining as board chairman, Rouse in 1982 stepped down as chief executive officer of the Rouse Company, the firm he had founded 40 years before and steered into $2 billion in projects (including operation of 53 shopping centers around the nation). A deeply religious man, he had become interested in refurbishing housing for "the poorest of the poor," using volunteers and corporate expertise, and launched a national organization to further that goal.

The Baltimore suburbs start at the Chesapeake Bay, south of the city, in Anne Arundel County (370,755), where blue-collar workers live in housing subdivisions such as Severna Park and Glen Burnie. Baltimore City is surrounded on the east and west, and then northerly all the way to the Pennsylvania border, by the overwhelmingly suburban Baltimore County (665,615): including, for example, Catonsville (a comfortable, middle-class Catholic town that antedates Baltimore, but gained fame when the Berrigan brothers poured blood on the local draft board's files during the Vietnam protest days); Pikesville and Randallstown, predominantly Jewish extensions of northwest Baltimore's Jewish section; Towson, Baltimore's upper income WASP suburb, an extension of Protestant neighborhoods near Johns Hopkins; Italian-American Parkville; and heavily Polish Dundalk.

Suburbanization—or more accurately sprawl development—seems to be encroaching everywhere in Maryland. Nowhere did the phenomenon seem more evident in the 1970s than in three small counties south of Annapolis and Washington on the western shore of Chesapeake Bay. Calvert County grew 67 percent to 34,638, Charles County 52.6 percent to 72,751, and St. Marys County 26.4 percent to 59,895. Growth, at least of the suburban stripe, does stop, however, at the Chesapeake Bay, the great body that separates Maryland into two unequal parts: the major portion of the state and the Eastern Shore. The bay itself has created an incredibly irregular 3,600-mile shoreline, with hundreds of wide bays that narrow quickly into small rivers. One example is the Patapsco, wide and deep enough at its mouth to lead into Baltimore Harbor, but just a few miles farther up a narrow stream. Descendants of the white men who settled Maryland still make their livings off the richness of the bay's marine life. The crabs, especially the soft-shell crabs caught in late spring and early summer, are the finest in the nation. Pollution in the bay has occasionally been a problem, but less so than in other parts of the nation. Many of the watermen live on the Eastern Shore, a profoundly conservative land in both politics and lifestyle. The Eastern Shore is the northernmost extension of the Old South. There were plantations here, and 20 percent of the population is black. In the 1960s there were civil rights demonstrations and riots in Cambridge, which is now 40 percent black, but most of the Eastern Shore is anything but turbulent. Easton and St. Michaels in Talbot County have become retirement and vacation havens for celebrities, politicians, and the just plain rich. The exception to this placid Eastern Shore life is Ocean City, a narrow strip of land not more than a mile wide and a dozen miles long, with a year-round population of 4,000 and 250,000 in the summer. It is a favorite, said one young Washington woman, "with the crowd that parks their brains at the bridge." A splendid, unspoiled stretch of beach to the south has been preserved as the Assateague National Seashore.

Several cultures away across the fertile Maryland Piedmont we come to the Catoctin Mountains, the northern extension of Virginia's Blue Ridge. Nestled among them is the presidential retreat, Camp David. Beyond is the valley in which sits Hagerstown, the economically depressed industrial hub of western Maryland. Beyond that the mountains become almost continuous, extending far west of the Maryland border. This is the forgotten part of Maryland, where the accent is closer to West Virginia than Baltimore. The largest city is Cumberland (25,993), which has been losing population since World War II. But in the 1970s Garrett County grew 23 percent to 26,498. Looking west over these hills, one can almost imagine how the early settlers here must have felt. The hills themselves beckon, but they also hide the mysteries of a continent beyond. The 22-year-old George Washington, fresh from his family's lands on the lower Potomac, blazed a trail for General Braddock and his ill-fated redcoats when this territory was French and Indian country in 1760. Braddock's army was the first large body of English-speaking white men to cross the Appalachian ridges. Their route became a familiar one. The National Road (now U.S. 40 and in places Interstate 70) still follows much the same path.

WASHINGTON, D.C.

World Capital, Divided City

W ASHINGTON, D.C.,* WORLD CAPITAL, city of monuments, symbol of nationhood, seat of power brokers, workplace of bureaucrats, loved and reviled by its countrymen, is in many ways the polar opposite of the nation of which it is the governmental center.

In the most obvious way such a difference was intended; the Constitution called for a "federal district" separate from the states to serve as the capital. But the founding fathers could not have anticipated how radically unrepresentative—both socially and politically—Washington would become from the nation at large. In 1980, more than 83 percent of the nation's citizens were white, but 70 percent of Washington's residents were black. The United States had developed a strong tradition of two-party politics, but Washington invariably voted Democratic. Washington had one of the nation's higher percentages of people on welfare: 14 percent in 1980. Yet it had achieved a per capita income higher than any state save Alaska: $12,039.

The crowning paradox, however, was that a nation dedicated to representative government had frequently forbidden the residents of its capital the control over their own affairs. For 100 years, from 1874 to 1974, Washingtonians were not allowed to elect their own local officials. Even with the passage of limited home rule, a perennial, agonizing debate continued over Washingtonians' self-government. Only since 1964 have Washingtonians been able to vote for president. In Congress, they are limited to nonvoting representation in the House and none at all in the Senate.

These are, of course, simply the peculiarities of the city of Washington. A giant metropolitan area spreads far beyond the District line into Virginia and Maryland. Only one-fifth of the people who consider themselves Washingtonians actually live within the District of Columbia borders—635,185 in the city in 1980 compared with 3,060,240 in the metropolitan area.

Washington has been called the world's largest company town, and that company is, of course, the United States government. The continuing increase in government spending and government-dependent business made Washington a continual boom town from the early 1930s through the 1960s and into the 1970s. (At least until the advent of the conservative Reagan regime, this was as true in Republican administrations as Democratic; not

---

*Few people who have been in Washington more than a week ever utter the cumbersome syllables "District of Columbia." The capital is referred to as "Washington," or to distinguish it from the suburbs, "the District," or even "D.C."

until 1982 did unemployment mount high enough to suggest Washington was finally losing its recession-proof status.) At the start of the '80s, fully 21 percent of the region's workers were employed directly by the federal government, and the majority were government-dependent; some 83 percent of the jobs were white collar. The Washington metropolitan area could boast the highest educational and income levels of any metro area in the country.

As the government and the city grew, so did federal salaries. Washington became an increasingly sophisticated place to live. What the city and its suburbs lacked in ethnic diversity, they made up for in the truly cosmopolitan nature of the people drawn from the 50 states and from almost every country in the world. The bureaucracy did provide high pay with dull and secure jobs, but Washington has also served as a magnet for some of the nation's most talented men and women hoping for work of consequence—and power over the nation and the world. These are the politicians, aides, lawyers, lobbyists, and journalists for whom workaholism is the fabled social problem and Potomac Fever—the unwillingness to live elsewhere even when out of office or a job—a seemingly incurable disease. Another of Washington's peculiarities is that these hard-working, usually salaried people, rather than than those of distinguished family background or wealth, hold the highest social status. The very highest rank belongs to elected and appointed national officials, however short-lived may be their power.

Beyond the attraction of exciting employment, the Washington area has become increasingly recognized for its high quality of life. *Places Rated Almanac*, a Rand McNally survey of 277 metropolitan areas in the United States, published in 1981, ranked the Washington metropolitan area among the most pleasant places to live in the United States. *Places Rated* praised Washington for its good health care, its parks, its gleaming multibillion-dollar new subway system, its museums, the arts and high-quality public schools in the suburbs and private schools in the city—attributes all dependent, of course, on direct federal subsidy or the high salaries of federal workers.

Washington also has one of the best newspapers in America, the *Washington Post* (circulation 584,500). Since Watergate, when its aggressive reporting led to the forced resignation of a president, the *Post* has become as much a national institution as the branches of government its reporters so assiduously cover. Like all institutions great and powerful, it sometimes trips over its ambition and hubris. The *Post* has taken seriously its obligations as a local newspaper, a reputation albeit damaged in 1981 when one of its reporters fabricated a heart-wrenching story about an 8-year-old heroin addict; the story ran on the front pages and subsequently won a Pulitzer Prize, which the paper was forced to return when the deception was uncovered.*

*Washington has one of the highest rates of newspaper readership in the nation, but in 1981 lost the distinguished *Washington Star* which folded after 128 years of publication. Like evening newspapers in other cities, the *Star*, owned at the end by Time-Life Inc., could not compete with television nor gain a significant share of local newspaper advertising dollars. A new daily, the *Washington Times*, owned by the Rev. Sun Myung Moon's controversial Unification Church, started up in 1982 with a staff of professional journalists.

Even before the Civil War Washington became a haven for free blacks from nearby slave states. By 1960 Washington had become the nation's first majority black city precisely because the federal government offered equal employment opportunities, including professional positions, years before private industry in other cities, and because the District of Columbia had open housing laws years before the Washington suburbs. The cumulative effect of these policies, British journalist Henry Fairlie has written, is that "in no other great city in America are the blacks so evidently and so vividly a part of its whole life," including along the most fashionable streets.

The great irony for the city of Washington, however, is that as open housing laws made it illegal for suburbs to discriminate against blacks, the black middle class began deserting the city in favor of newer houses and better suburban schools. The 1980 Census revealed that, like many central cities, Washington lost people (15.7 percent) in the 1970s. But unlike other cities, the black percentage actually dropped, from 71 to 70 percent. The black population in Washington's suburbs doubled in the 1970s, to a total (404,814) almost equal the number in the city (448,229).

This is not to say that Washington was deserted. In fact, housing remained tight as young professionals bought up properties, even along the riot corridors of the '60s, and Washington became a leader in the "back to the city" movement. And Washington remained a haven for people seeking opportunity and freedom from discrimination. In the 1970s the federal Civil Service extended its equal opportunity rules first to women and later to homosexual men and women. Many women continued their careers after they married, and they and their husbands and small families found that city life worked better for them than the great distances and car commuting in the suburbs. Gay men and women too found the city more hospitable than the suburbs; many held substantial professional and political jobs. During these same years, Washington's Hispanic population, which dates in any significant numbers to the Cuban revolution of 1959, expanded to include many migrants (legal and illegal) from Mexico and Central America. By 1980 the Census recorded 17,652 Hispanics in Washington, or 2.7 percent of the population, a small figure for most cities, but the first real ethnic flavor Washington had ever had.

Washington's population mix is one of the reasons the national capital has never developed efficient government services. To the white liberals, many blacks, the gays, and the Hispanics, some form of liberation has always been a higher priority than management quality in the District Building (Washington's city hall). The liberals have been able to buy themselves out of such problems as the city's notoriously bad school system and concentrate on such problems as saving historic buildings. (Washington's "Don't Tear It Down" is one of the country's most powerful historic preservation organizations.) Poor blacks are most concerned with jobs. The black middle class has partially receded from politics, its numbers diluted by the movement to the suburbs, its anger appeased by high federal salaries. Real estate developers, the only real local economic force in Washington, usually live in the suburbs and focus their attention on the city government's policies toward downtown.

Washington's most serious local political problems, however, stem from its 100 years of poor colonial rule by Congress. Powerful members of Congress often used the city bureaucracy as a dumping ground for federal employees and aides who could not make the grade; even after home rule went into effect in 1974, the District's elected officials still had to cope with less-than-stellar public workers protected by civil service. An even worse colonial legacy was the lack of a political tradition. Either beset by apathy or convinced Congress will make the final decisions anyway, fewer than 40 percent of Washingtonians participate in most elections, the lowest turnout of any major U.S. city. The result: a long-inferior school system and lethargic municipal services.

Washington does elect a mayor and city council who have authority to pass laws and draw up a budget. But for District self-government advocates, the new system of government has been less than full victory. Congress retained full veto power over the D.C. budget (later revised to give District officials more but not total power) and jurisdiction over a substantial amount of federal property. The District has remained dependent on Congress for a federal payment in lieu of taxes on federal property. Congress has also refused to grant the District the right to levy a commuter tax on suburbanites. (If anyone had any doubts that Congress could still interfere in the District's affairs, in 1981 the full House overruled passage of a liberal sexual reform act—apparently only because the Rev. Jerry Falwell, leader of the Moral Majority, threatened to campaign against any House members who supported it.) The drive for more extensive self-government has continued, especially among the more intellectually minded District politicians. In 1978, Congress enacted a proposed Constitutional amendment that would provide full representation in Congress for the District—two Senators and at least one Representative. By 1981, only 9 of the 38 required states had approved the measure, however, and District politicians began seeking true statehood through the means used by all but the original 13 colonies: writing a state charter by constitutional convention, to be submitted to District voters for approval and then to Congress and the president for the last word.

In 1974, in their first mayoral and city council elections in 100 years, Washingtonians chose as mayor Walter Washington, a leading figure in moving the city from colonial status to self-government. Sadly for Walter Washington, his finest moment seemed to come in containing the 1968 riots following Martin Luther King, Jr.'s, assassination. He also made great strides in reforming the police department (as late as the mid-'60s, a police commissioner had refused to order patrolmen to stop calling black men "boy") but was unable to make much progress in rebuilding the riot corridor, reforming the city's jails and juvenile institutions. Some of his appointments were abominable.

In 1978, Washington was defeated in a three-way primary—the significant election in this Democratic city—by a very different sort of politician, Marion Barry, a Southerner and erstwhile militant founder of the Student Nonviolent Coordinating Committee. Barry had moved into mainstream politics, winning election to the Washington school board and the city council. He was heavily promoted by the editorial page of the *Washington Post*, but his victory stunned the city's political powers, including the black ministers, labor unions, and the campaign bankrollers in the white-run Board of Trade. Barry won with less than 30 percent of the black vote, his winning coalition including young white professionals, gays, Hispanics, and those whites—affluent liberals and retirees—who never joined the flight to suburbia.

Once in office, Barry found himself faced with grim '80s-style fiscal problems. He hired the New York investment banking house of Lazard Freres (which had worked out New York City's financial plan) and instituted a controller's office and daily reports on the city cash flow, reduced the work force somewhat, and speeded up collection of business taxes. The fear of municipal financial doom continued, however. Despite several able administrators Barry placed at the helm of his departments, residents still complained that they could not get their incorrect water bills refigured. A sign of the continuing inefficiency came in 1981 when Barry sent letters to members of Congress asking them to contact a special office if they had problems with city government. Even the supportive *Washington Post* pointed out that the real problem was not aiding members of Congress but solving the inefficiencies for all the residents of the city. Not until his victorious 1982 reelection campaign did Barry finally appear to gain the confidence of Washington's black middle class, who originally considered him an arriviste and outsider, or to start thinking seriously about major budget economies and more farsighted economic development strategies.

From Colony to Self-Governing City

The city of Washington was founded, appropriately, as the result of a political compromise. One summer night in 1790, over dinner in New York, Secretary of State Thomas Jefferson agreed to deliver crucial Virginia votes for assumption of the debts of the states while Secretary of the Treasury Alexander Hamilton agreed to deliver Northern votes for a Southern capital. The compromise allowed the president to designate a 10-mile-square site along the Potomac River, and George Washington selected land convenient to his own landholdings at Mount Vernon. Maryland and Virginia obliged by ceding the territory to the federal government, including the then-thriving small ports of Alexandria on the Virginia side and Georgetown on the Maryland side. (Congress, however, gave the portion of the District south of the Potomac back to Virginia in 1846.)

The site was often criticized later for its low and marshy land and hot, humid climate, conditions that in those days were exceedingly conducive to disease. But a site farther up the Potomac would have precluded the possibility of navigation, and the founders, who traveled mainly by water, had hopes that the federal city would become a great emporium of trade and dominant urban center in the nation. As it turned out, New York, Philadelphia, Boston, and even Baltimore had too much of a head start, and Washington's focus never extended beyond government to manufacturing and commerce.

Yet if the founders' dreams of another London or Paris were never realized, the physical layout for the capital still resembles what they planned. In 1791, Major Pierre Charles L'Enfant was commissioned to draw a plan for the federal city. The result was a series of grid streets (with letter and number names) and rather elegant diagonal avenues, squares, and circles. L'Enfant designed extraordinarily broad streets, examined topography carefully, and planned for long vistas down the avenues; he chose the site for the Capitol and the White House. But he was not appreciated much at the time, especially by some of the big land speculators whose plans he tried to thwart. After less than a year on the job, he was fired and died penniless. His initial sketches were reconstructed by a surveyor named Benjamin Banneker, a free Negro —the first of many black Americans who would play a major role in Washington's history.

Situated below the Mason-Dixon line, Washington was slave territory before the Civil War. Nevertheless, so close to the Deep South and yet controlled by legislators mainly from free states, it became a haven for free blacks. By 1867 fully 30 percent of the District's residents were black, and during Reconstruction Washington became a laboratory for civil rights measures. The radical Republicans set up the Freedmen's Bureau in the 1870s, and among its lasting accomplishments were Freedmen's Hospital and Howard University. Up through the Civil War, Washington had had an elective city government (as had Georgetown, then still a separate city within the District). But the Republican Congress had suspected Washington's white majority of Confederate sympathies during the War, and set up in 1871 an elected territorial government whose officials included blacks. In 1874, Congress became disgruntled with the District's handling of its finances and abolished the territorial government, replacing it with a system of three commissioners, appointed by the president and confirmed by the Senate. The termination of territorial rule coincided with the end of Reconstruction—and the end of any hope for equal treatment of Washington's black minority.

As in most of the South, Jim Crow laws did not follow immediately. The highwater mark of segregation in Washington, ironically, occurred when President Woodrow Wilson personally endorsed the practice of segregating black workers. When the Lincoln Memorial was dedicated in 1922, a separate stand was set up, aside from all the others, for Negro dignitaries. Blacks were not allowed in white restaurants and theaters; the only integration in Washington was on trolleys and buses, at Griffith Stadium (but not on the baseball field itself, of course), and in libraries. As Washington grew the black percentage in the city actually declined to a low of 25 percent in 1920, but rose again when blacks made up about one-third of the massive migration to Washington during the New Deal and World War II years. Despite the problems of segregation, Washington was still a relatively hospitable place for blacks, and the black middle class grew into one of the strongest in the country. The District's Dunbar High School, the first black high school in America, graduated such leaders as Benjamin David, the first black general in the army, Charles Drew, the discoverer of blood plasma, and Edward Brooke, the first black U.S. Senator since Reconstruction. But as Washington spread out beyond the District line, blacks were unable to buy houses or rent in most suburbs; consequently nearly all the black population growth occurred within the District lines. Desegregation of public schools, beginning in 1954, doubtless accelerated white flight.

Agitation for self-government grew, especially since the District was usually ruled by Southern congressmen who viewed the area—and its residents —as their personal plantation. Conversely, as Washington's future as a black majority city became more and more certain, opposition to home rule hardened in Congress. In an almost unbroken reign from 1948 to 1972, the House District of Columbia Committee was chaired by John McMillan of South Carolina, leader of a group of hostile Southerners and Republicans. In the 1960s the Senate regularly passed home rule bills, and in 1969 the District was finally allowed to elect a nonvoting Delegate to Congress, a position won by Walter Fauntroy, a well-spoken black minister. But only in 1973, with McMillan defeated and black Detroiter Charles Diggs in command of a large pro– home rule majority on the House District Committee, did home rule reach the floor of the House and pass.

A Tour of the District

L'Enfant divided Washington into four quadrants radiating from the Capitol —Northeast, Northwest, Southeast, Southwest. But the center of the city is really the Mall. This greensward, planned by L'Enfant and laid out in much its current form by the 1902 McMillan Commission, runs west from the Capitol, past the Smithsonian and to the Washington Monument, between the Jefferson Memorial and the White House, and across the Reflecting Pool to the Lincoln Memorial. From early April to late fall the Mall is thronged with tourists, but it has also been the stage for many of our national dramas. It was here in the shadow of the Lincoln Memorial that Martin Luther King proclaimed his noble dream before 200,000 civil rights marchers in 1963 and here that thousands of antiwar marchers gathered during the Vietnam War. The Mall also became the town square of the nation and home to much of the nation's highest culture in the National Gallery of Art and the splendid museums of the Smithsonian Institution.

North of the mall is Pennsylvania Avenue, through elegant new street design and intensive construction activity finally on the way to becoming a grand world boulevard two decades and more after President Kennedy expressed horror at the seedy business slums along the inaugural route from the Capitol to the White House. North of Pennsylvania Avenue is Washington's old downtown, which by the 1980s, with intensive new office-retail-hotel building and a new convention center, was slowly catching up with the newer office district north and west of the White House, along K Street and Connecticut Avenue. The Connecticut-K corridor area gleams (albeit not always so tastefully) with latter-day buildings housing many of the satellite industries of the federal government: 3,000 news-gathering organizations, more than 2,500 trade associations (900 coming to Washington during the 1970s alone), and 33,000 lawyers. The World Bank, the International Monetary Fund, the Inter-American Development Bank, and such magnificently profitable non-profit institutions as the *National Geographic*, are also there. While a height limitation (nothing, in effect, higher than the Washington Monument) has kept Washington commercial architecture monotonous, it has also kept the city at a reasonably human scale, avoiding the dwarfing of historic old structures that has occurred in other world capitals. Sadly distanced from Washington's downtown, on a Potomac River site really too small for it, sits the John F. Kennedy Center for the Performing Arts, a smash success in artistic terms and symbol of big-time culture come to the national capital.

The closest residential area to downtown is DuPont Circle (named for an admiral, not the chemical family), just eight blocks northwest of the White House, the focus of Washington's grandest mansions at the turn of the century and of the student protests in the '60s, and more recently home to affluent singles. West from the Circle, Massachusetts Avenue becomes "embassy row," where Arab and African ambassadors work and live in Victorian mansions built by the railroad or silver millionaires who had bought themselves seats in the Senate. Embassies abound in posh Kalorama, just north of Massachusetts Avenue. Connecticut Avenue, all the way to the Maryland border, is lined with apartment buildings whose population has grown younger as the buildings have been converted to condominiums. Across from Kalorama, on the east side of Connecticut Avenue is Adams-Morgan, center of Washington's Hispanic community and the closest thing Washington has to the mixture of cultures, incomes, and classes found in most great cities.

Just west of Rock Creek, set on high ground north of the Potomac, is Georgetown, Washington's most famous neighborhood. On Georgetown's edge is the Roman Catholic university of the same name founded as a seminary in 1789. Georgetown began as a river port, antedates Washington, and was a slum in the 1920s before New Dealers bought houses for a song and renovated them. Its mostly tiny lots comprise some of the most expensive residential real estate in the world. Other neighborhoods with bigger houses actually have higher incomes, but Georgetowners think of their official historic district as special, and a citizens' association vigorously uses all means to preserve not only the buildings, but the atmosphere, even if it means selfishly refusing to allow a subway stop or opposing waterfront development. Nevertheless, Georgetown's M Street and Wisconsin Avenue throb with some of the continent's most vibrant night life, and new retail-entertainment-restaurant-hotel development seemed on a nonstop trajectory in the early '80s. Lesser-known but distinguished neighborhoods in upper Northwest include Cleveland Park, with clapboard houses particularly fashionable during the Kennedy administration, Spring Valley, and Palisades. This entire area west of Rock Creek Park is heavily white, yet more liberal and affluent than a typical cross-section of white America.

East of the park is mostly—but not all—black Washington. Upper 16th

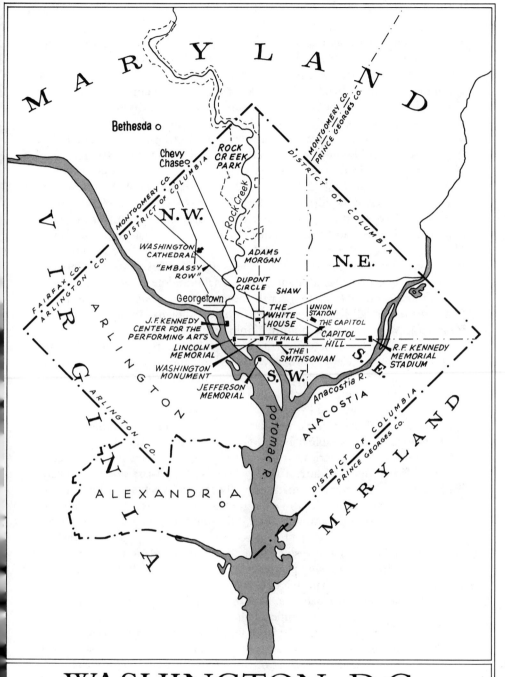

MARYLAND

Bethesda o

Chevy Chase o

ROCK CREEK PARK

Rock Creek

Montgomery Co.
DISTRICT OF COLUMBIA

Montgomery Co.
Prince Georges Co.

DISTRICT OF COLUMBIA

N.W.

WASHINGTON CATHEDRAL

"EMBASSY ROW"

Georgetown

J.F. KENNEDY CENTER FOR THE PERFORMING ARTS

LINCOLN MEMORIAL

WASHINGTON MONUMENT

JEFFERSON MEMORIAL

ADAMS MORGAN

DUPONT CIRCLE

SHAW

THE WHITE HOUSE

THE MALL

THE SMITHSONIAN

N.E.

UNION STATION

THE CAPITOL

CAPITOL HILL

R.F. KENNEDY MEMORIAL STADIUM

S.W.

S.E.

Anacostia R.

ANACOSTIA

DISTRICT OF COLUMBIA
Prince Georges Co.

VIRGINIA

FAIRFAX CO.
ARLINGTON CO.

ARLINGTON

ARLINGTON CO.

ALEXANDRIA o

Potomac R.

MARYLAND

WASHINGTON, D.C.

0   1   2   3   4

MILES

Street is at the extreme northern tip of the District with the areas called the Gold Coast and Shepherd Park; here one finds the tranquil streets of what was once a predominantly Jewish neighborhood. Now most of the people who live here are affluent blacks who work for the government or law firms and send their children to the same private schools as the nearby whites. Toward downtown, however, the black middle-class neighborhoods eventually give way to a maze of unrenovated apartment buildings, a mix of single-family dwellings, and public-housing projects accompanied by very little feeling of community organization and a lot of crime and drug trafficking.

The neighborhood of the nation's Capitol—sections of Northeast and Southeast immediately adjacent to East Capitol Street—is filled with town houses that have been renovated since the 1950s by congressional aides, journalists, and lawyers and their families. Each year the renovation of Capitol Hill moved outward until it reached the Robert F. Kennedy Stadium and land's end at the Anacostia River. The renovation has moved in bits and pieces, however, so that affluent professionals, middle-class blacks, singles who often must double up to meet the rent, and poor people living in public housing projects all live close to each other, somewhat testily. Farther out Northeast Washington is a mixture of middle-class black areas such as Brookland, home of the Catholic University of America and its noted drama department. In Southeast, Capitol Hill row houses end abruptly at the point where I-95 breaks up the neighborhood; beyond the highway sit Washington's most massive public housing projects and warehouses.

South of the Capitol and the federal office buildings is Southwest, in the 1940s the scene of many pictures that showed filthy alley dwellings with the Capitol dome clearly visible behind. Starting in the 1950s the area was almost totally bulldozed in America's most massive single urban renewal project. It became a community of attractive town houses, high-rise apartments, and condominiums. Restaurants, marinas, sailboats, and yachts on the Potomac add color to the scene. Southwest's greatest attractions are its location—within easy reach of downtown or the Hill—and its integration. Southwest was about 64 percent black and 36 percent white in 1980, but sadly there is little contact between the residents of the high-priced new buildings and adjacent low-income housing projects; the area, moreover, lacks the seasoned character of an older urban neighborhood.

Finally, we come to Anacostia, almost a complete mystery to most white Washingtonians. Anacostia is officially a part of the Southeast quadrant, but conveniently forgotten because it is so out of sight; one must take an expressway bridge to get there. Yet it is a major part of the city and has nearly twice as many residents as the area west of Rock Creek Park. Anacostia is known for its poverty and problems, but that is not the whole story. Frederick Douglass chose to move here from Capitol Hill in the 19th century, and there are still very pleasant residential areas. But many of the District's worst problems have been dumped here. Anacostia is home to St. Elizabeth's, the District's mental hospital. Crime rates are high, supermarkets are few, and public services often neglected. It is also believed that many of the poor

Washingtonians displaced by "gentrification" in Capitol Hill and other fashionable neighborhoods are living in overcrowded quarters out of sight in Anacostia.

Mayor Barry bought a house in Anacostia to improve his relationship with less affluent black Washingtonians and to bring attention to the neighborhood. Anacostia surely needs attention: in spirit and appearance, it is a place worlds removed from the seat of western power in the White House a few miles distant.

THE
NEW ENGLAND
STATES

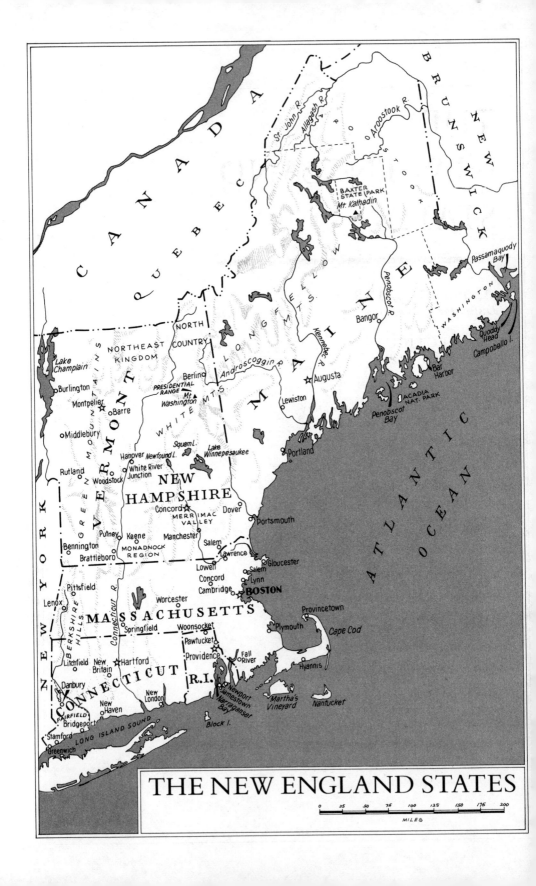

THE NEW ENGLAND STATES

MILES

0   25   50   75   100   125   150   175   200

MASSACHUSETTS

Distinction in Adversity

Not just once, but twice in the last generation, Massachusetts has effected a miraculous recovery from what seemed overwhelmingly negative circumstances. One of our very oldest, it has emerged as one of America's most resilient states.

Remember Massachusetts' plight at the end of World War II. Its cities and its industries were obsolescent, its politics ethnic-oriented and patronage-ridden, its leadership tired and unimaginative. Only its universities continued to show some of the vitality that had made Boston the Athens of America in the 18th and 19th centuries, and even they seemed cut off from the public life of the state. A patina of the historic preciousness, of proper Bostonianism contraposed to Irish sentimentality, lay over Massachusetts.

But while the nation was looking westward and away, remarkable things occurred in the old Bay State. Its people began to discard the ancient enmities between Protestant and Catholic, Yankee and Irish, that had corroded public life for a century. The universities in Cambridge became vital and advanced intellectual centers, not only on the national scene, but in the political life of the state. The economy survived the flight of textiles to the South, and Massachusetts evolved into a preeminent state in electronics and industry based on imaginative scientific research. The state legislature began to pioneer in field after field of social legislation. Great strides were made in purging corruption from government. And finally, Massachusetts furnished a president who could fire the ideals of a nation.

By the early 1970s, however, this flowering had run its course, and Massachusetts faced another period of trouble. The slowdown in the space race and research in new weaponry took the bloom off the science-based industries. The Massachusetts commitment to social programs had grown so costly that its government was plunged into one of the severest financial crises ever to confront an American state. State and local taxes skyrocketed into what one business group called "a separate orbit." Increasing energy costs reinforced business firms' tendency to relocate or open branch plants outside cold, high-wage "Taxachusetts." By 1977, unemployment had reached 13 percent, one of the highest rates in the entire United States.

But once again, Massachusetts recovered. The savior was a new, intensified wave of high technology, ranging from personal computers to medical testing equipment to technical objects and services that defy quick explanation. Traditional manufacturing also stabilized, and high-grade services such as finance, law, architecture, and business consulting, long Massachusetts specialties, grew even faster than "high tech." In 1982, when the unemployment rate nationwide soared to the highest level since the Great Depression, Massachusetts' remained significantly lower.

The "high-techers," as they referred to themselves, did more than just create jobs. They renewed the spirit of entrepreneurism that had once flowered among the Bay State's old Yankees but been largely forgotten by a modern-day establishment of aristocratic business owners and labor union bosses. Genteel, liberal Massachusetts was not paradise on earth, the high-tech entrepreneurs began saying; young engineers, they complained, were either refusing to move to the state or leaving for other states where the climate was warmer, the taxes lower, and the politics at least in appearance less corrupt.

The high-techers also touched off a Bay State political revolution. They found traditional business executives so uninterested in their concerns that in 1977 they formed their own Massachusetts High Technology Council. In 1980 the council successfully promoted Proposition 2½, a ballot initiative measure that put Massachusetts property taxes—which had soared to truly astronomical heights—on a reduction schedule down to a modest 2.5 percent of market value. Most established business leaders stayed out of the fray, while liberal politicians and unions fought the proposal bitterly. But 2½ captured the favor of an electorate deeply resentful of ever-increasing property taxes.

Proposition 2½ was a slap in the face to the Massachusetts liberal establishment. Public sector unions were horrified at the loss of 40,000 public jobs in less than two years, the elimination of binding arbitration, the dispute resolution mechanism that had brought hefty wage increases to police and firefighters, and the loss of autonomy of school committees that had to learn to fight with other municipal agencies over scarce dollars. Liberals complained that the broad brush cuts caused terrible hardships for innocent people. But even many opponents conceded that this bold move had begun to address the problem of overreliance on the property tax and forced municipalities to rethink their cozy relations with unionized public employees.

Despite its economic recovery, Massachusetts is not an expansionary state. In the 1970s, its population grew only 0.8 percent, and Massachusetts lost its "megastate" position as the nation's 10th largest to North Carolina. The congressional delegation shrank from 12 to 11. While the economy in general flourished, many old mill towns had yet to recover from the loss of their great factories. And the state still had serious social problems. Though the 1980 Census found that only 3.85 percent of the Bay State's 5,737,037 people were black, Boston (by 1980 22.4 percent black) was afflicted by a cruel and divisive racism. The New England Commission on Higher Education in 1982 warned that the educational superiority of Massachusetts and New England was in danger; the public secondary school system had deteriorated measurably, the commission said, and the region's great universities would face increasing competition from Sunbelt institutions able to tap energy resources for money to expand.

Overcoming Ethnic Politics

"The modern history of politics in Massachusetts," political scientist Murray B. Levin once wrote, "begins with the great Irish potato famine of 1845." In five years, an estimated million Irish died of starvation and another 1.6 million left their native land, many to settle in New England and especially Massachusetts. By 1860, 61 percent of the population of Boston was foreign born, and the percentage was not far different in cities such as Lowell, Lawrence, and Fall River. Starting in the 1880s, large numbers of Italians, Poles, Lithuanians, Portuguese, Scandinavians, and Germans began to follow the Irish. By 1920, more than two-thirds of the people of Massachusetts were either foreign born or of foreign parents. Boston elected its first Irish-born mayor in 1885, Massachusetts its first Irish Catholic governor in 1918.

The Irish and their fellow immigrants did not enter a political vacuum. For more than 200 years, a homogenous Yankee Protestant population had held sway on the shores of Massachusetts Bay. The story of that civilization, begun on the November day of 1620 when the hardy Pilgrims first touched the bleak shore at Provincetown and "fell upon their knees and blessed ye God of heaven, who had brought them over ye vast and furious ocean," is of course deeply embedded in American legend. In those two centuries Massachusetts had grown from one of the strictest theocracies the world had ever known to a seedbed of sedition in the days of John Adams, John Hancock, and Paul Revere. It had been the site of the Boston Tea Party, the Boston Massacre, and the shots from Lexington and Concord "heard 'round the world." From a colony of hardscrabble farming and modest cottage industries, it had grown in eminence as an Atlantic fishing center and as the home port of prosperous seaborne commerce in the West Indian trade (including rum and slaves). It then gained even greater profits in the China and East India trade and the brief, colorful era of the Yankee clippers racing at full sail across the world's oceans. The great New England insurance industry had arisen from a pooling of maritime shipping risks in the late 18th century, and the textile industry from a pirating of secret English mill techniques around 1800. Transcendentalism, America's first major intellectual movement, had begun to flower in Massachusetts, expounded by writers such as Bronson Alcott, Ralph Waldo Emerson, and Henry David Thoreau. And this was the leading American state in the move to abolish slavery under the American flag. In every part of life, Massachusetts deserved the region's title of "New England"; as Yale President Timothy Dwight wrote of the Bostonians in 1796: "They are all descendants of Englishmen and, of course, are united by all the great bonds of society—language, religion, government, manners and interest."

The clash between old Yankee and Catholic immigrant was predictable, bitter, and lasting. Both sides abhorred the other's religion. The Puritan settlers of early New England had gained their name because their sect wanted to "purify" the Anglican Church of all vestiges of popery, and they had persecuted and driven from Massachusetts nonconformers to their narrow way, including Baptists and Quakers. The Roman Catholic Irish viewed

all Protestantism as apostasy; writer Joe McCarthy quotes one of their spokesmen as saying that "a Christian Protestant . . . is a contradiction in terms."
The Yankees were proud of their British ancestry; the Irish, remembering
centuries of English exploitation of their homeland, despised everything British. The Yankees were reform-minded, fond of causes such as abolition,
women's rights, and improving conditions in the prison; their philosophy was
one of the perfectibility of man. The Irish Catholics viewed true salvation as
an occurrence of life after death; they feared job competition from blacks and
were proslavery; they believed in hierarchy, authority, and a politics based on
personal loyalties rather than abstract philosophies.

The old Yankees stopped at nothing to subjugate the Irish immigrants. An
unskilled workman would earn a mere $4.50 to $5.50 a week, a woman
working as a domestic as little as $1.75 a week, of which 75 cents was taken
for board. The Irish were crowded into the mudflats of the cities and waterfront slums; five to 15 might live in a single basement. But with the professions
and economic advancement closed to them, the Irish turned to their favorite
avocation—politics—and made a grand success of it. Because the Yankees
were Republicans after the Civil War, the Irish were automatically Democrats. As the Irish and their fellow immigrants began to outnumber the
Yankees, they gained offices. The ward political organizations provided loyal
voters with jobs, licenses, street lights, emergency welfare aid. The system
flourished right up through two World Wars and into the 1950s. James Michael Curley was a symbol of it, a kind of Robin Hood whose stealing from
the rich was tolerated because he "took care" of his own.

By the 1920s the Irish controlled Boston and much statewide politics as well.
After voting Republican in every presidential election from the Civil War
(except the three-way race of 1912), Massachusetts cast a final sentimental vote
for its own Calvin Coolidge in 1924 and then switched to Al Smith and the
Democrats in 1928, to remain in the Democratic column, except for the
Eisenhower and Reagan elections. Curley served not only four terms as
mayor of Boston, but one as governor of Massachusetts (1935–37). Yet the
success of the Irish outside of politics—especially in business—was severely
limited.

The rise of the Kennedy family as Green Brahmins and the climactic
election in 1960 of John Kennedy to the presidency, the first Roman Catholic
ever to hold that post, were grand symbols of what was happening more
quietly and more importantly for the civilization of Massachusetts. Thousands
of young Irishmen took advantage of the GI Bill after World War II; they
emerged as talented professionals, pragmatists, able to communicate and work
with the Yankee aristocracy as equals. And while the Irish and Yankees were
coming to new terms, the fierce inter-ethnic rivalries between Irish, Italian,
Jewish, Polish, and other groups were beginning to wane. It should be
remembered that when the Irish became dominant in the 19th century, they
turned as cold a shoulder on the Italians and Poles and other ethnic groups
as the chilly Yankees had turned on them. A key factor in the change was the
high amount of intermarriage following World War II between Irish and

Italians. Concurrently came the postwar suburban housing boom. Today, the settled, generations-old ethnic communities still exist in Boston and other cities, but their residents are aging. More and more of the immigrants' descendants live in homogenized suburbia where ethnic loyalties, like straight ticket voting, are out of style.

The overall Protestant-Catholic animosities of Massachusetts were tremendously lightened by the changes within the Roman Catholic Church, especially the Archdiocese of Boston. At the end of World War II, Richard Cardinal Cushing began a tireless effort to build bridges of understanding between Catholics, Protestants, and Jews. "We are told there is no salvation outside the church—nonsense! Nobody can tell me Christ died on Calvary for any select group," said Cushing. Most Americans, of course, remember Cushing delivering the invocation at President Kennedy's inauguration in 1961 and his voice cracking with grief at the funeral, as he called on the angels to carry his "dear Jack" to Paradise.

Cushing retired after 26 years in 1975 and died two months later; Rome's choice for a new archbishop (later to become cardinal) was Humberto Sousa Medeiros, a native of the Portuguese Azores. For the first time in 124 years, Boston had a non-Irish Catholic leader. Medeiros had grown up in Fall River, where he once swept floors at 62 cents a day. His selection was a sign of the changing times, since Boston has experienced a heavy influx of Spanish-speaking Puerto Ricans and Cubans. Medeiros was counted a friend of the poor but no flaming liberal; he actively encouraged, for instance, "right-to-life" groups, which successfully lobbied the Massachusetts legislature for anti-abortion legislation.*

The conflict between ideological liberals and social conservatives gives real vibrancy—and a certain suspense—to Massachusetts Democratic politics. The fact that Massachusetts was the only state of all 50 to vote for George McGovern for president in 1972, the national liberalism of Senator Edward M. Kennedy, political rebuffs for the church, and the 1970s elections of key antiwar congressmen—Michael Harrington and the Rev. Robert F. Drinan —led some to call Massachusetts the nation's "most liberal" state. That analysis was, however, always open to argument. Senator Kennedy doubtless carried many Massachusetts Democrats further to the left than their own predilections. Opposition to the Vietnam War, which mobilized Massachusetts' thousands of students, was destined to be a fleeting issue. And the Bay State's ethnic and religious ties militate against doctrinaire liberalism. Massachusetts is second only to Rhode Island in the percentage of its population with foreign-born parents (24.6 percent in 1980); likewise, after Rhode Island

---

*While the Roman Catholics get the most attention, other religious groups continue to prosper in Massachusetts. The Mother Church of the Christian Scientists is there, and that group's newspaper, the *Christian Science Monitor*, is one of the finest in America—an organ with more influence outside of Boston than within it. The Yankee-dominated Episcopal Diocese of Massachusetts made a change as momentous as the Catholics' shift to a non-Irish bishop when in 1970 it chose the Rt. Rev. John M. Burgess, son of a dining-car porter, to be the first black man to head an Episcopal diocese in the United States.

it is America's most heavily Catholic state. Moreover, the image of Massachusetts as the most liberal state had become dated by the early '80s. Harrington, for instance, had quit Congress, and Drinan was forced by Pope John Paul II to quit.

And then there was the matter of Edward J. King, the Democrat elected governor in 1978. An old style politician, King got most of his money from business circles (especially high-tech) but campaigned on so many conservative social positions—anti-abortion, anti-gun control, pro-capital punishment—that an aide remarked he won by putting all the hate groups in a pot and letting them boil. And it was not just anybody whom King defeated. He won the Democratic primary by unseating Massachusetts' nationally recognized governor, Michael S. Dukakis. The son of Greek immigrants who had risen to power as a cool-headed, tenacious state legislator undaunted by trial lawyers and other special interest lobbies, Dukakis had won election in 1974 on promises of reform in fiscal management of state affairs, criminal justice, mental health, and a promise to eliminate the patronage system in Massachusetts, "lock, stock and barrel." As governor, he pioneered in the use of state regulatory and investment powers to fashion America's first clear state urban policy, favoring redevelopment of downtown areas and urban neighborhoods and opposing the "scatterization" of housing and business development to the countryside. Business leaders, however, charged that Dukakis was too concerned with directing growth, rather than creating it. They were horrified by a 1975 tax increase he pushed to rescue the state from its fearsome fiscal crisis in that year. Doctrinaire Bay State liberals, by contrast, faulted Dukakis for trimming social welfare benefits (among the country's highest) to keep the state solvent. Dukakis was also hurt by his personal manner, his disdain for patronage and political niceties.

By 1982, however, liberals had regained the upper hand. After four years of King's generally inept and scandal-ridden administration, the Democrats gave the gubernatorial nomination to Dukakis, who went on to win the general election with ease—and once again face another fiscal crisis. An even more dramatic liberal victory was the reelection of colorful, outspoken U.S. Rep. Barney Frank. The conservative Democratic legislators, who had long been offended by Frank's maverick ways, used the redistricting process after the 1980 Census to pit him against the long-popular Republican Rep. Margaret Heckler. But Frank, as he put it, became "the poster child for liberalism in 1982," raised $1.5 million to Heckler's $1 million, and won, to the consternation of both Republican and Democratic pols.

In a state of more even partisan balance, this conflict among Democrats would be suicidal. But in Massachusetts it is healthy because of the prolonged quiescence of the state Republican party. The presence in high Massachusetts offices, at least up to the mid-1970s, of Republicans such as Leverett Saltonstall, Christian Herter, Edward Brooke, John Volpe, Elliott Richardson, and Francis Sargent gave outsiders the impression the Bay State was a two-party state. But without overwhelming support among independents, Republicans have little chance. (The 1982 registration figures, for example: Democratic 45.5

percent, Republican 14.5 percent, independent 39.9 percent.) Only two Republican Members of Congress have been elected in recent years, the long popular Silvio Conte from western Massachusetts, the state's only remaining rural district, and Margaret Heckler, from the Boston suburbs, finally defeated following 1982 redistricting. The Republicans' anemia is so dire that it has been almost 30 years since they had a plurality in the legislature. Their occasional statewide victories might not be possible at all if it were not for the "Massachusetts ballot," adopted years ago and now a model for several other states. Under it, there is no single party column or voting machine lever, and the voter is obliged to make an individual choice for each office.

The wild cards of Massachusetts politics are the managers and technocrats of the new postwar society: highly educated and professional administrators, teachers, lawyers, clergymen, scientists, technicians, advertising, and communications specialists. They earn well, but do not have the social status, reserves of wealth, or corporate power of the patricians. They are highly independent in politics, the proverbial ticket splitters. The extraordinary success of their fast-growing industry has led them to hold conservative free market, but also free trade economic views. On social issues they are liberals. They coalesced with the students to form the core of Massachusetts' strong anti–Vietnam War peace movement. Rep. James Shannon, a young congressman who represents a heavily high-tech district, told us their votes were crucial when he faced a difficult 1980 primary challenge when Cardinal Medeiros asked Catholics to vote against candidates who refused to take the church position on "right-to-life." This combination of economic conservatism and social liberalism seems likely to grow as the high-tech companies expand.

A Leadership Roundup

No name is so synonymous with modern Massachusetts as that of Kennedy —and no family so encompasses the contradictions within Bay State Democratic politics today. Joseph P. Kennedy, father of former President John F. Kennedy, son of Patrick J. Kennedy (an East Boston Democratic leader, owner of three saloons), and grandson of Patrick Kennedy (native of County Wexford, Ireland, who arrived penniless in Boston in 1848), was the first Irishman to break into the Yankee-held State Street banking and financing community. He was the first of his clan to attend once-hated Harvard (class of 1912). Two years later, he was a bank president; in the 1920s, he became phenomenally successful in the stock market and moving pictures and acquired the famous Kennedy fortune; in the 1930s President Roosevelt made him first chairman of the Securities and Exchange Commission, and later, ambassador to Great Britain. Still Kennedy never was socially accepted in Boston. But he did see his sons attend elite Protestant prep schools and Harvard—and, of course, enter politics on a grand scale.

The retrospective analyses of John F. Kennedy's presidency have gone from the romantic, sentimental, and self-serving odes written by former aides to impassioned charges that his family-related drive for power and his charismatic style led America into the Cuban missile crisis and the tragedy of Vietnam. The most important fact about his career may still be that an Irish Catholic could seek and win the nation's highest office against embedded religious and class prejudices, thus encouraging a similar drive by Americans of multiple religious and ethnic backgrounds—and indeed many peoples around the world.

The Kennedy name has acquired a more liberal hue than history justifies. Careful historians note that John Kennedy was slow to support what would become the crucial social movement of the 1960s: civil rights for blacks. It was John Kennedy's brothers, Robert, the senator from New York assassinated in Los Angeles in 1968, and Edward, the senator from Massachusetts, who became enemies of the Vietnam War and defenders of just about every minority group and liberal cause in the nation. Edward Kennedy, has, by most accounts, established a stronger record as a senator than either of his brothers, fighting successfully for liberal immigration laws and airline deregulation. His long-sought goal of national health-care insurance remained elusive, even as in the early '80s he switched his major attention to the issue of nuclear disarmament. Edward Kennedy's combination of assets—record as a Senate stalwart for liberal issues, impressive rhetorical skill, and the magic name—made him the all-but-certain presidential candidate of his party before the death of his auto companion, the late Robert Kennedy's pretty secretary, Mary Jo Kopechne, at the bridge at Chappaquiddick Island in 1969. His failed 1980 bid to wrest the presidential nomination from a politically weakened Jimmy Carter suggested that the Kennedy name, and the programmatic liberalism with which it had become associated, were losing political currency in America. Teddy Kennedy, however, may also have time on his side. Even in the campaign year 2000, he would be only 68 years old, younger than Ronald Reagan when he took office.

Massachusetts' other senator, Democrat Paul Tsongas of Lowell, has made something of a mark espousing a revisionist attitude toward a number of conventional liberal beliefs. He won his Senate seat in a bitter 1978 battle against Edward Brooke, the first black to win a Senate seat since Reconstruction and embodiment of the Massachusetts liberal Republican tradition. Brooke was a calm, articulate legislator who chose not to become a national leader of black people but still worked quietly with some apparent effectiveness for black goals. Financial problems associated with a messy divorce were his downfall.

Modern-day Massachusetts has contributed three prominent Speakers of the U.S. House: John W. McCormack (1962–1970), Joseph W. Martin, Jr., during the Republican 80th Congress (1947–48); and Thomas P. O'Neill, Jr., since 1977. O'Neill is a big (six-foot-two, 260-pound), bluff Irishman, gregarious and knowledgeable, at once a page out of *The Last Hurrah* and an issue-oriented congressman. O'Neill's constituency include Irish and Italian working people by the thousands. The component populations range from Portuguese in Somerville and East Cambridge to blacks in East Boston housing projects, Armenians in Watertown, the remnants of Back Bay and Beacon Hill Protestant elite, the young professionals who are "gentrifying" parts of Boston, and the cerebral Democrats of the Harvard and M.I.T. communities. O'Neill had great success as a Speaker from 1977 to 1980 when he had a 2-to-1 majority in the House. A cigar-chomping, old-style politician, O'Neill found it a not-always-easy job to compete with President Reagan, "The Great Communicator," especially during Reagan's first two years in the White House.

State Government: Glory and Travail

Through most of the 20th century, Massachusetts' state government has struggled with the competing forces of tradition, extraordinary progressivism, and corruption.

As a legacy from colonial times and distrust of the Crown, the state was left with a form of government deliberately designed to restrict the governor's authority. The governor had to work with an independently elected governor's council that could reject any appointment he made and pass on every state contract—an invitation to partisan maneuver and graft, both of which were indeed palpable in the council's chambers. After a series of scandals in the 1960s, the council's powers were finally made mostly ceremonial. Today official corruption is less of a problem than it used to be in Massachusetts, but it is by no means expunged. Charges of improper behavior continued to abound in the 1970s, the comparatively high moral tone of the Dukakis administration notwithstanding, and they reerupted under Governor King in the early 1980s. The state government does appear to be better coordinated than in past years. In the early 1970s the state's 300 agencies were grouped into ten cabinet-level departments each with its own secretary appointed by the governor and serving at his pleasure.

The Massachusetts legislature, familiarly known by the bombastic name of the Great and General Court of Massachusetts, is dominated by big-city ethnics and small-town businessmen who sometimes combine to defeat the will of reform-minded governors. The house membership, an unwieldly 240 since 1857, was finally reduced to 160 in 1977 after a tough initiative campaign by the reform-minded Massachusetts League of Women Voters.

The General Court is characterized by an unusual constitutional right of free petition by all citizens, together with the custom of giving all the petitions a hearing before a legislative committee. The bills filed by common citizens have ranged from a few excellent ideas to many that are, in the words of one legislative leader, "pretty flaky" proposals such as heating all sidewalks or impeaching every judge on the Massachusetts bench.

Back in the fiscal salad days of the '60s and early '70s, Massachusetts often led other states in progressive legislation. It passed the nation's first "no-fault" insurance law, a "bill of rights" for consumers, an "environmental bill of rights," tough campaign spending laws and reporting requirements, gun controls hailed as the nation's toughest, and a pioneering public-school racial imbalance law that gave communities a 15 percent state school construction aid if they placed new schools in locations to relieve segregation. Massachusetts has also led the way in progressive prison reforms, mental health efforts, and civil liberties (the latter including a local option "bill of rights" for high school students, guaranteeing freedom of speech and assembly).

After 1980 and the passage of Proposition 2½, the legislature shifted its focus from social legislation to partial fiscal bailouts for localities whose property tax base had been decimated. None of Massachusetts' powers approached the challenge of 2½ in a very thoughtful, orderly, or caring way, however.

Some cities saw their budgets plunge precipitously—in Quincy, for example, from $103 million to $67 million in a single year. But as MIT urban planning professor Lawrence Suskind commented in spring 1982: "All we've seen are coping strategies aimed at avoiding eliminating anything. First the cities banded together to go after the legislature, and they got $265 million, about half the budget gap. Next they convinced the state to allow them to raise their assessments so they could collect 2.5% of a higher base. Then they instituted higher user fees and charges, for water and sewer charges, for example. Then they put off capital expenditures rather than fire anybody."

Liberal laws and high taxes have led many Massachusetts businessmen to claim they have little power in the state. But powerful statewide lobbies such as the Associated Industries of Massachusetts, the more recently formed Massachusetts High Technology Council, and individual lobbyists for established corporations have often succeeded in getting tax benefits and advantageous arrangements from the Democratic legislators. Government employee unions are a potent force and were authorized to bargain collectively with the state in 1974. The power of the labor unions intensified the problems of the Massachusetts civil service, which many national experts consider the most ossified and unresponsive in America, plagued by meaningless job placement tests and incredibly cumbersome procedures to fire incompetent workers. The result: a state government rife with excess jobs and incompetent people at the lower rungs.

Collegia Massachusettensis and the Economy

Massachusetts has educational resources rivaled only by California's, and no state has a larger number of prestigious, nationally influential colleges and universities. The state boasts 117 institutions of higher learning, including 15 that grant Ph.D. or equivalent degrees. It attracts more students from out of state than any other state.

Harvard and the Massachusetts Institute of Technology, both in Cambridge, stand at the apex of the pyramid and represent what many regard as the most powerful educational nexus in America. Harvard (16,027 students in 1982) is in many people's view not only the oldest of all American universities, but also the greatest. Its law, medical, and government schools continue foremost in their fields, and the business school competes vigorously with Stanford University for No. 1 in educational quality. Listing the Harvard faculty who have achieved international reputation or contributed importantly to American government would take pages.

Harvard College—admission to which remains for many the unparalleled prize in academic competition—has a student body that has shifted from a preponderance of private prep school graduates to a broad cross-section of the U.S.A. Of those admitted for the Class of 1985, 69 percent had graduated from public high schools. Among 6500 undergraduates in the early '80s, 37 percent were women, 400 blacks, 300 Asians, 250 Hispanics. The university has a $1.6 billion endowment, still the nation's largest, although the University of Texas' oil and gas holdings keep edging closer. Graduates of Harvard College and the professional schools unquestionably occupy more positions of power and prestige than those of any other single university.

The Massachusetts Institute of Technology (9,475 students in 1982) remains the preeminent engineering school in America. Its physical science and economics departments are also outstanding. MIT has made distinct national contributions in a multitude of fields, including computers of all types, and has occupied a more significant place in Massachusetts' postwar heavily technological economic development than has Harvard. MIT has made a strong effort to supplement its basic science and engineering pursuits with a major emphasis on the humanities and the arts. "A person is much less of a human being if he thinks of himself only as a technocrat," said James B. Wiesner, the former science adviser to President Kennedy who became MIT's president in 1971. "Society needs the cognitive reaction of a poet as well as a technologist." The politics within MIT are highly complex. The university has long had a deep involvement in war-related research while its departments of architecture and urban studies are among the most leftist in mainstream institutions.

Among the other well-known academic institutions in the Boston area are Northeastern University, the nation's largest private university; Boston University, the fourth-largest, with a brilliant, driving, highly controversial president, John Silber; Boston College, a Jesuit institution that has shown a strong commitment to improving the Boston community and ethnic relations in the state; Brandeis University, a Jewish-sponsored but officially nonsectarian institution, well known for its radicalism in the '60s and widely respected for its academic excellence; Tufts University, known chiefly for its Fletcher School of Law and Diplomacy; and Wellesley College, a high-quality women's residential college. Western Massachusetts has a set of distinguished small colleges where the emphasis is strictly on good teaching: Williams, Mount Holyoke, Amherst, and Smith.

Since 1960 the state has been attempting to transform the University of Massachusetts, long the proverbial stepchild of higher education in the commonwealth, into a university in the tradition of the great public institutions of the Midwest and West. Enrollment is divided between the campus at Amherst, a medical school at Worcester, and the Boston campus, a branch primarily dedicated to serving students from the low-income neighborhoods of the Boston area.

In the 1940s, the great preponderance of Massachusetts wealth, built up in the days of the China trade and textile-mill ventures along the rivers, was tied up in restrictive "Boston trusts" that limited heirs' ability to do much that was constructive with their fortunes. Safety was the key factor, and a four-percent return on capital was considered adequate, one banker told us. At the end of World War II, the first serious efforts were made to utilize New England's remarkable university-based scientific brain power for promising, innovative economic enterprises. Ralph Flanders (later U.S. Senator from Vermont) persuaded a few Boston capitalists to put some of their dusty money into a new firm called American Research and Development, which was founded to invest in (but not control) promising new enterprises. The initial customer was Tracerlab, then a capital-starved enterprise begun by three young Harvard students but destined (through its timely loan) to be the first of Boston's postwar science-based industries.

In the years that followed, hundreds of electronics and highly technical research and development companies sprang up in or near Cambridge, drawing on the scientific talents of MIT, Northeastern University, Worcester Polytechnic, and other institutions. Route 128, a new circumferential expressway built in the 1950s to divert through traffic from Boston's streets, became a foremost world center of space-missile-electronics technology. Thus was reconfirmed the amazing pattern that has permitted Massachusetts (and New England as a whole) to recover again and again from economic slumps that might have been fatal at the time. One can trace the pattern back to the flowering of New England's agriculture, only to be eclipsed with farming's mid-19th-century move westward to less rocky soils; to the growth of New England as a great maritime power, only to be eclipsed by New York and, later, Baltimore; to the early rise in New England of insurance and banking, only to be overshadowed once more, at least in part, by Gotham; and of course the momentous New England industrial boom in textiles and shoes, only to lose out again, after decades of prosperity, to the American Southland and inexpensive foreign competition.

Yet on each occasion, like a Phoenix rising from the ashes, the region has staged a comeback, its location at the corner of a nation, its harsh climate and lack of valuable fuels or minerals notwithstanding. It has done this by a remarkable combination of pluck, luck, the China trade and clipper ships, technological innovation, products at the cutting edge of their time, cheap immigrant labor, tariffs, smart financing, wartime stimuli, and most vital of all, the momentum built on two fantastic bases—the region's headstart in the Industrial Revolution, and its preeminent universities.

Each wave of development has brought new social values, and not least of all the latest. High-tech companies have proven extraordinarily innovative in social thinking and management relations—and ferociously anti-union. Perhaps because the competition for engineers and qualified support staff is so great, they have offered campuslike workplaces, recreational facilities, stock options, flexitime, and sabbatical leaves. Ray Stata, chairman of Analog Devices, suggested to us that the entrepreneurs behind many high-tech firms have rejected "the whole authority syndrome" of western culture in favor of eastern cultural values and a "more holistic, organic concept" of management. Such views directly contradict Massachusetts' traditional separation between management and labor and make some liberals worry that the workers would not be represented in the case of a conflict.

Massachusetts is a national center for sophisticated technical services. Boston is one of the great medical centers of the western world; patients from from all over the country and other nations are drawn to institutions such as the Harvard Medical School, Peter Bent Brigham Hospital, Boston City Hospital, the Children's Hospital Medical Center, and the Lahey Clinic. Boston is second only to New York as a center of capital allocation in the nation. By the early 1980s Boston-based financial institutions such as the First National Bank of Boston, the State Street Bank, and insurance companies controlled an estimated $125 to $150 billion dollars in investment capital. There was spirited debate about whether an appropriate or fair share of those funds were being reinvested within New England.

After years of alarming decline, Massachusetts' traditional manufacturing industries—ranging across such fields as fabricated metals to textiles, chemicals, and paper—have stabilized and produced $10.6 billion in products in 1980. Massachusetts' agriculture production is not significant compared with western states (for sheer volume it's hard to compare Cape Cod cranberries with Kansas wheat!). But a movement to preserve the fast-vanishing agricultural land and make the state less desperately dependent on outside food supplies has begun to flower. Massachusetts' fishing industry, after years of problems with foreign competition, incursions of Russian and Canadian ships on the Georges Bank, and the fragmented condition of the industry, took off again after the 1976 passage of federal legislation which established a 200-mile limit from U.S. coasts and claimed the right to limit the haul of foreign ships. In New Bedford, modern-day fishing is so successful that there is competition with tourism interests that promote the historic nature of the waterfront. The port of Boston, its illustrious history notwithstanding, has limped from crisis to crisis in recent times, and many of its dock facilities are in disrepair or disuse. Fortunately Logan International Airport is an international transportation nexus that allows Boston-Cambridge-Route 128 academicians, scientists, businessmen, and governmental experts an easy commute to Washington, New York, other U.S. cities, and abroad.

Boston and Environs

By the early 1980s Boston provided two diametrically opposed images to the world. One was of an historic relic, almost endearingly European, a city that had nevertheless moved through physical and spiritual renewal to become one of the most livable and exciting cities of America, a mecca for young professionals seeking exciting careers and a sophisticated lifestyle. The other image, equally true, was one of stubbornly persistent ethnic and racial conflict, continuous financial problems nearing bankruptcy, declining schools and services, and political impasses that paralyzed rational decision making.

Boston's old charm lingers on. You find it first on Beacon Hill, topped by the lovely State House with its gold dome, begun from designs by Charles Bulfinch in 1795, surrounded by lovely old red brick homes and such gems as perfectly preserved Louisburg Square. Sweeping down from Beacon Hill is the pleasant expanse of the Boston Common, where pirates, witches, and Quakers were once hung from an elm near the Frog Pond. Nearby is the Old Granary Burying Ground with the graves of John Hancock, Samuel Adams, and Paul Revere; the Boston Athenaeum, the literary sanctum sanctorum of old Boston; the Old State House and scene of the Boston Massacre; the Old South Meeting House, where Bostonians met to protest the British tea tax before staging their famous Tea Party; Faneuil Hall, where Sam Adams and James Otis delivered the fiery speeches that led to the Revolution; the Old North Church, immortalized by Longfellow's poem about Revere's midnight ride ("One if by land, two if by sea"). Add to all this Bunker Hill, the Charlestown Navy Yard, where the old frigate *Constitution* rests and old buildings have been converted to stores and homes; Back Bay; the Public Garden; and Lexington and Concord not far distant—well, there can be only one Boston, and America needs one.

Life in Boston is superbly enhanced by such preeminent cultural institutions as the Boston Museum of Fine Arts and the Boston Symphony Orchestra, the latter still regarded as one of the world's best orchestras. Culture comes to the masses through the celebrated Boston Pops concerts, played on the Esplanade beside the Charles River Basin, and two magnificent museums: the Museum of Science, with its Charles Hayden Planetarium at Science Park, and the New England Aquarium. For political buffs, there is the new John F. Kennedy Library.

Boston and Cambridge make up one of America's most sophisticated urban melanges. There are private art galleries, shops to please the most discriminating and off-beat customers. Alternative newspapers, FM radio stations for every taste, and WGBH-TV, the public station that originates programming broadcast nationwide, add to the cultural life. Boston is one of America's most creative and competitive commercial television news markets; *Chronicle*, WCVB's pioneering local newsmagazine, has sparked copies around the country. Boston has also become a center of experimental documentary filmmaking second only to Hollywood and New York. In sports, the city no longer has a National League team, but it can boast the Red Sox, the Bruins of the National Hockey League, the Celtics in basketball, and the Patriots in football. And other cities can only try to copy the annual Boston Marathon foot race.

The *Boston Globe* has spurted toward excellence since the 1960s, hiring aggressive reporters willing to dig up scandals in government and write frank coverage about city problems. On public issues such as race and community relations, the *Globe* has become as "sensitive" or "to the left" as any major city daily in the U.S. While pro-civil rights in tone, it has tried to give fair coverage to the city's ethnic neighborhoods and to respond to criticism from antibusing forces and others who have challenged its coverage of their concerns. The other Boston paper, the thoroughly unspectacular *Herald-American*, was sold to publisher Rupert Murdoch in 1982. Outside of Boston, mediocrity often reigns in Massachusetts papers, but there are some bright exceptions, among them the *Berkshire Eagle* (Pittsfield), the *Quincy Patriot-Ledger*, and the improving *Springfield Union*.

If comparisons are at all warranted, Boston is most similar to San Francisco. Both have water on three sides, strikingly similar skylines, almost equal land areas (Boston's 45 square miles, San Francisco's 47), and similar populations (Boston's 562,994, and San Francisco's 678,974). Neither city, points out Ian Menzies of the *Boston Globe*, overawes one in the manner of a New York, Chicago, or Los Angeles. "They are walkable cities, centralized, physically compact, friendly." Of the two cities, San Francisco is of course the more raucous, while Boston reveres tradition. And there is one final difference. San Francisco is not a capital, Boston is. Boston is ultimately more important to Massachusetts than San Francisco is to California. "We are virtually alone among the states," Martin Linsky of Harvard's Kennedy School of Government notes, "in that our capital city is also our most significant city in terms of culture, sports, population, sin, food and fun."

The vital turnaround from the "old" to the "new" Boston appears to have occurred during the reign of John F. Collins, mayor from 1960 to 1967. In the 25 years before Collins became mayor, Boston had lost $500 million worth of assessed valuation. As long as James Michael Curley and his likes ruled, there was no chance that the Brahmin-dominated business community would invest in downtown Boston. As mayor, Collins bridged the traditional walls of distrust between City Hall, State Street, and the Cambridge academia. Collins hired Ed Logue, then the urban renewal director for the nationally acclaimed effort in New Haven. Logue's presence in Boston helped to stir up investors' interest and draw federal dollars. Collins and Logue helped persuade the legislature to enact the so-called Prudential Law, slashing the effective tax rate for new buildings. Prudential promptly erected a 52-story tower complex in the Back Bay area with plazas and arcades on the scale of New York's Rockefeller Center; subsequently the new tax law encouraged many new structures. Collins and Logue are equally remembered for the massive and dramatic Government Center built on 60 acres of land in the heart of the city, where scabrous old Scollay Square once stood. Architect I.M. Pei was commissioned to draw up the overall area plan, replacing 22 old streets with 6 new ones, 2 of them broad thoroughfares leading to a vast new central plaza, an ideal place for civic gatherings, before the new City Hall. That structure, completed in 1969, is architecturally the most exciting city hall in America and certainly one of the most successful public buildings of our times—on a par, perhaps, with a few other modern achievements such as the St. Louis Archway and the Hawaii Capitol. Nine stories high, it has a free-form exterior and many interior elements of simple rough concrete, supplemented within by red New England brick. Ada Louise Huxtable wrote in the *New York Times* that the building "is a tough and complex building for a tough and complex age, a structure of dignity, humanism and power. It mixes strengths with subtleties. It will outlast the last hurrah."

Government Center (with 30 buildings in all) occupies a crucial location, bordering the State Street financial center, Beacon Hill, Faneuil Hall, and the waterfront. With the completion of the Quincy Market-Faneuil Hall festival marketplace, several Pei towers, hotels, a nautical museum, and a new aquarium, Bostonians found they had created an elegant "walkway to the sea" in place of pervasive decay. The attractiveness of this pedestrian link to the waterfront is marred, however, by the elevated Fitzgerald Expressway, which separates both the waterfront and the North End from downtown, an ugly reminder of the 1950s when the highway planners were rampant.

The Collins era, focused on physical renewal and city administration, ended in 1967. The new mayor was Kevin H. White, then 38 years of age, Ivy League graduate, Irish Catholic, and the son of a veteran city councilman. White's first years in office were tough and great ones for big city mayors as racial disturbances were followed by the massive federal Great Society and urban renewal programs. White, alone with Henry Maier of Milwaukee, survived in office clear into the 1980s. Early on, he tried to turn the focus of the city toward the neighborhoods, establishing a series of neighborhood-based "little city halls" and undertaking a tremendous amount of new school, fire house and police station construction. But after White nearly lost an election, he established a political machine consciously modeled on that of Chicago's Richard Daley. By the early 1980s, the once-reformist White was mired in corruption charges typical of strong-arm political organizations. His political success lay in making common cause with hard-pressed ethnic communities, building a unique alliance of blacks, WASPS, Italians, and South Boston Irish. So dominant was the White personality that few dared defy him —at least to his face.

White's mayoralty turned into a spectacular extension of Collins' rejuvenation of downtown Boston. The showpiece was the transformation of old, unused Faneuil Hall and the Quincy wholesale meat market into a festival marketplace of sophisticated shops, restaurants, and offices. Designed by Cambridge architects Benjamin and Jane Thompson and developed by James Rouse, the complex initially encountered immense difficulty in attracting Boston capital. Once opened, however, it quickly drew both great crowds and critical acclaim and became *the* national model for profitable recycling of decayed old center city areas. It also proved an irresistible attraction to hundreds of thousands of suburbanites who rarely ventured into the city and led Boston's two major department stores, Filene's and Jordan Marsh, to support plans for a downtown pedestrian mall, Downtown Crossing. Billions of dollars worth of new buildings were on the drawing boards for the '80s.

White was obliged to cope with the violent political emotions—and on occasion actual violence—generated by implementation of city-wide school busing. But by far his most persistent and vexing problem was Boston's financial situation. The real estate tax doubled in his first four years in office, escalating to the highest rate of any large American city. As early as 1971, White switched to an "austerity" budget, forbidding new hirings and attempting to institute some economies and productivity measures. They were sorely needed: a U.S. Census survey in 1972 showed that Boston's average number of municipal government employees for each 10,000 inhabitants was 213, 76 *percent* above the national average. Later, White came under especially bitter criticism for alleged padding of city payrolls with his patronage appointees; his relations with the city council were also abysmal. Gross abuses of the pension system brought state and federal investigations. Boston's problems were further exacerbated by Proposition 2½, which severely limited its only (and much abused) major source of revenue, the property tax. In 1981 Moody's Investor Services first suspended Boston's bond rating and then revised it to a low "Ba" rating, making it excruciatingly difficult for the city to borrow. Despite the seriousness of the fiscal crises, White once admitted to the press that the continuous financial drama was due in part to his love of the politics of it.

Boston's government problems hark back to the first part of this century, when the Yankees, "retreating to Beacon Hill" in the face of the Irish onslaught, tried to limit the city government by setting up a Boston finance commission, appointed by the governor, to be a watchdog over city expenditures, as well as a state-controlled Boston liquor-licensing agency and a state civil service commission with power over the qualifications for city employees. A Boston home-rule commission, appointed by White shortly after he took office in 1967, said that such bodies, plus separate boards for housing and urban renewal set up in later years, tended to dilute the authority of the mayor and the city council. Eliminating them, or indeed any form of charter reform, has proven politically impossible. By the early 1980s, the Boston public housing authority was in such dire trouble that it went into court receivership.

Boston's public schools, under the control of a totally separate and often politically irresponsible school board, spent much of the 1970s embroiled in bitter school-busing disputes, bribery scandals, overspending, and mismanagement. By the early 1980s, the student body had become 67 percent minority (blacks, Hispanics, and Asians), half the city's high school students were dropping out before graduation, and of those who did finish, only half got jobs or went on to college. There had been seven superintendents in nine years. Then some rays of hope appeared. The anti-busing forces faded and responsible moderates took control of the school board. In 1981, the school committee reached outside the system, for the first time in a century, to hire a professional administrator, Robert Spillane. A tough, outspoken manager, Spillane cut spending, fired half the high-school principals, made the others accountable for performance in their schools, and emphasized basic reading, writing, and computation skills. In 1982, Boston's top business figures, organized in a shadowy coordinating committee informally known as "the Vault," concluded a compact with the schools virtually unprecedented in America. The corporate community promised to recruit 200 local firms to give Boston high school graduates a priority shot at entry-level jobs; the school system, in return, promised to reduce dropouts by 5 percent and guarantee that all graduates would meet minimum reading and math competency standards by 1986. The business leaders' reasons for getting involved were not just altruistic: they wanted a reliable supply of office workers and calculated that educated and employed youth would be less likely to mug office workers on their way home. The compact was a watershed, however, because the public schools, true orphans in modern-day city politics, had acquired (1) a measure of realistic accountability and (2) their first formidable political allies since the flight of the white middle class.

Some of Boston's problems are unique, at least in degree, to the city. Between the universities, churches, libraries, hospitals, and museums, 60 percent of the property in Boston is not on the tax rolls at all. The universities have expanded by leaps and bounds in the postwar era, appropriating huge chunks of formerly commercial real estate.

Boston is also the classic case of 100 suburbs around a small center city, obliged to finance fire, police, and other services for a "9-to-5" population. By 1980, the city's population (562,994) was only 20 percent of the Boston metropolitan area count (2,763,357). Population loss in the 1970s was not, however, limited to the center city. While Boston lost 12.2 percent of its population (mostly whites), the suburbs declined by 2.6 percent. Traditional hostilities— between city and suburb, Catholics and Yankees, and now blacks and whites —keep the parts from cooperating. Oddly enough, in a rudimentary way, Boston began metropolitan planning before any region of America. The start was 1889, when the Metropolitan Sewage Commission was created as an independent state agency to serve Boston and nearby towns. A series of autonomous agencies regulate water supplies, preservation of publicly owned parklands, air pollution, transportation, the port, and Logan Airport. Each is a whipping boy for local officials who criticize their independence.

An area of particularly perplexing problems, despite effective regionalization, is the mass transit system. Boston had the first subway in the U.S. (1897) and with its narrow streets and confined land area proved an ideal city for rapid transit. But the postwar patterns of suburban settlement and work locale, plus more universal car ownership, made mass transit less and less viable. Some farsighted planning and federally funded improvements have gone into the Massachusetts Bay Transportation Authority, but one could sometimes wonder to what avail. Not all, but certainly a high portion of the MBTA's equipment is old. The most perplexing problems have been strikes and the outrageous salary demands and featherbedding of the unionized workers. Riders, frustrated by irregular MBTA service and preferring their own autos, tended to use the system less and less.

Despite Boston's population loss, its neighborhoods have not lost their identities. The WASPs are concentrated in high-cost, historic Beacon Hill and the Back Bay, although these tend to be younger, less class-minded people, often the children of Boston aristocrats who fled to the suburbs when that was fashionable. The creation of the Back Bay is a story in itself. Old Boston was built on a diminutive 783-acre peninsula, connected to the mainland by a narrow neck of land. Big chunks of present-day Boston are built on land created by 19th-century landfill operations. The greatest of these was the reclaiming of the dark and evil-smelling tidal reaches of some 450 acres west of Beacon Hill, creating the Back Bay and what was to become a landmark in American city planning, the central concepts those of Frederick Law Olmsted, the designer of New York's Central Park. Commonwealth Avenue, with its central pedestrian mall, was the first American boulevard. Around Copley Square, the center of the Back Bay, some of the architectural gems of the past century, including the classic revival Public Library and Romanesque Trinity Church, were built. Here too, the Conservatory of Music, the Boston Symphony Hall, the Mother Church of the Christian Scientists, the Prudential Center, and the John Hancock tower sought a home.* Today's Back Bay harbors many fine shops and the handsome old Copley Plaza Hotel, not to mention the luxurious Ritz-Carlton, where the Kennedys and other celebrities always stay when they visit Boston and every suite has a wood-burning fireplace stocked with birch logs.

Boston's white flight and overall population loss has not diminished the "Irishness" of some pockets, of which South Boston may be the most famous. That area is sharply divided from the rest of the city by railroad tracks and an expressway, but its "separateness" is chiefly psychological. When someone is sick, or his house burns, or there is tragedy in the family, the outpouring of neighborly help is astounding. The other side of the close-community coin is the parochialism, the fierce suspicion of outsiders one finds in "Southie." In retrospect, it seems little wonder that some of the ugliest clashes over school desegregation erupted when South Boston and overwhelmingly black Roxbury became the focal point of initial federal busing orders in 1974.

Boston blacks, despite occasional election to a spot on the city council or school board, lack substantive political power. Race-related assaults, stone-throwing and murders, though not commonplace, do occur from time to time in both black and white neighborhoods, a cause of deep concern for political and religious leaders alike. Even in the 1980s blacks have told reporters they dare not go into certain playgrounds and neighborhoods, stay away from Red Sox games, and attend Celtics games cautiously. Poor neighborhoods have also been plagued by arson.

Bostonians of Italian descent are most visibly concentrated in the North End, a congested and sometimes seedy neighborhood of colorful fruit stands and restaurants and of mamas leaning out of second-story windows to social-

---

*The architects of the Hancock Tower created a breathtakingly dramatic effect when they sheathed the building in mirror-glass, to reflect adjacent Trinity Church and other Copley Square surroundings. But the edifice, through the mysterious shattering of its mirror-glass panels, turned into one of the most celebrated snafus in the history of skyscraper construction. Replacements cost millions of dollars and sparked monumental legal action between the owner, architect, glass company, and contractor expected to line lawyers' pockets for long years to come.

ize with neighbors. We have witnessed there some of the most superb ethnic festivals known to this continent. As young Italians have moved to the suburbs, however, students and young professionals have moved in, and there are fears the North End may one day be left with just a "veneer" of Italian eating spots and coffee bars while the actual residents are professionals choosing the neighborhood for its nearness to downtown. Another major concentration of Italian-Americans is in East Boston, where they have fought a desperate battle against being engulfed by Logan International Airport.

An ethnic tour of Boston should not omit Jews, oftentimes very old or young and single, concentrated around the Back Bay; working-class Brighton, and Mattapan; the city's Asian community, which includes many poor, elderly Chinese or recent immigrants from Indochina in the downtown Chinatown; and finally the city's estimated 36,000 people of Spanish origin (mostly Puerto Ricans), the most recent immigrants. The Hispanics do not really have their own neighborhood, but are concentrated in the South End, where Inquilinos Boricuas en Acción (IBA—Puerto Rican Tenants in Action) has built Villa Victoria, one of the best housing projects we have seen.

Suburban Boston begins with Brookline (55,062), geographically but not politically part of the city; it is a place of many lovely residential streets, including one where the birthplace of John F. Kennedy stands. Both Brookline and nearby Newton are towns of affluence and social consciousness where liberal Jews and WASPs dominate the politics.

Famed Cambridge, we should note, is more than distinguished universities; it is a geographic place of 95,322 people, with busy factories and old-style ethnic politicians who are frequently at odds with the Harvard and MIT liberals. Major urban redevelopment projects are afoot in Cambridge, but the most phenomenal place there (and perhaps in all of New England) is Harvard Square. Since the late '60s the square has drawn students of all types, even if they don't attend school in Cambridge. There are always enough long-haired musicians, pot-smoking youths, and student demonstrators to make one believe that the '60s, at least in isolated spots on this continent, live on.

Immediately north and west of Boston lies a belt of industrial-residential cities that have functioned primarily as support towns for two centuries—places such as Chelsea, Revere, Somerville, Everett, Medford, Malden, Watertown, and Arlington. Most have been losing population in recent years; the people either work in local factories or commute to jobs in Boston or on Route 128. Some, such as Chelsea, have been the scene of brave "bootstraps" urban renewal projects. On the state's North Shore, Salem and Beverly, with their rich lore of witchcraft and the merchant princes and shipmasters in the West Indies and China trade, still have a special kind of magic. Beverly is surrounded by towns such as Wenham, Topsfield, and Manchester, with large estates and the homes of some of Massachusetts' richest families. Gloucester, still an important fishing port, has become surrounded by choice summer resorts.

Lowell, which had the reputation of being a model industrial community between 1825 and 1860 and went into a long slump (along with the southerly flight of textiles) early in this century, has achieved a new lease on life. Having escaped the federal bulldozer, a substantial portion of the old city was turned into a national historical park featuring restored textile mills, indoor and outdoor museums with artifacts from the Industrial Revolution, and recreational walkways along the 5.6 miles of canals originally built in the early 19th century to harness the power of the Merrimack River for the textile mills. But at least as exciting as the appreciation of these relics is Lowell's new computer economy based on the presence of Wang Laboratories. Wang moved its headquarters from nearby Tewkesbury to Lowell in 1978 and by 1981 had added a $75 million payroll and $500,000 in property taxes to the city economy. Other cities along Route 128 and Route 495 (an outer belt) have also prospered from the electronics boom. In historic Lexington, with its lovely Green, the Minuteman statue still stands guard. Concord, town of the "shot heard 'round the world," still reveres its Emerson, Thoreau, and Walden Pond and its position as the birthplace of American intellectual life. But both Lexington and Concord received so many Route 128ers and Boston executives during the '70s that the atmosphere became essentially 20th-century suburbia.

Massachusetts' most tragic recent story is that of Lynn, an old shoe and leather town close to Boston. Lynn had suffered terribly from a loss of factories and jobs and was near the final phase of a $194 million urban renewal project when a 1981 fire engulfed the downtown area, leaping from building to building, devastating four city blocks, including 37 businesses employing 1,500 people. The cause was believed to be arson. The city officials promised a rebirth based on federal disaster relief.

The South Shore, stretching from Boston to Plymouth, has never had the social distinction of the North Shore, even though the seashore is just as attractive. Instead of receiving the Boston elite, little bayside communities such as Cohasset, Scituate, and Duxbury are the goals of one-day excursions of Dorchesterites and less-pretentious Bostonians.

If any place in America might be expected to be a Yankee Protestant stronghold, it is Plymouth, where the hardy Pilgrims landed. But, in fact, the town is now heavily populated by Portuguese, Italian, German, and Irish descendants of another century of immigration.

The Other Worlds of Massachusetts

Now the time has come to review the geological variety of Massachusetts, a state small in physical size (only 45th among the 50) but pleasing to the eye for all its recorded history. The eastern third, including all of the Boston orbit, the North Shore, South Shore, New Bedford area, and Cape Cod, belongs to a coastal lowland that was once submerged beneath the sea. The North Shore has a rugged, picturesque character; to the south, the shores are sandy and more level. The unique hook shape of Cape Cod was created by glaciers that swept down from the north 10,000 to 30,000 years ago, halting at the line of what is now the Cape and depositing "terminal moraines," which the wind and waves would later reshape.

The Cape in modern times has received a handsome National Seashore while national attention has periodically focused on Hyannis Port, where the Kennedys repair in times of triumph and tragedy. The Cape has also been subjected to incredible growth pressures, not just for summer vacationers, but for permanent residents, especially retirees, as well. The visitor who drives along the Cape's major road is greeted by a tawdry jumble of motels and neon lights in a show of commercialism as unnecessary as it is tasteless. Yet, as Edward Garside has written:

> Beneath the recent overlay of vulgarity the Cape's ancient nature lives on . . . the land is small, subdued; its colors are low in key. The salt marshes, the low houses at their margins, the woods beyond, the hidden ponds, the suddenly revealed harbors have a comforting dimension. But look outward and there is always the sea, a great presence fraught with sublimity.

And out in that ocean lie the two picturesque islands, Nantucket and Martha's Vineyard, beset in recent times by onslaughts of autos (arriving by ferry), hikers, gawking tourists, and intensive real estate development, which both islanders and the state government have sought to stem. Of quite another world are the southeastern Massachusetts cities of New Bedford (98,478) and Fall River (92,574), for years rated among New England's most depressed towns. The best news of recent times has unquestionably been New Bedford's fishing revival.

Moving westward across the state, one finds that around Worcester the land becomes hillier—an upland region that is actually a southerly extension of the White Mountains of New Hampshire. Further west, the Connecticut River flows from north to south across Massachusetts. It has created a broad plain with deep, alluvial soil. The Connecticut Valley offers a rich harvest of tobacco, onions, and potatoes and is heavily settled in places such as Springfield, Holyoke, Northampton, and Greenfield.

West of the valley rise the Berkshire Hills, a continuation of Vermont's Green Mountains. These rugged hills were long a barrier to easy commerce; today they are favorite summer vacation places, interspersed with small upland farms. Still farther west the land dips again into the pleasant Housatonic River Valley. Finally, Massachusetts ends with the Taconic Range along the New York border, reaching a high elevation point of 3,491 feet in the northwest corner.

The first thing to know about Worcester (161,799), second only to Boston in Bay State population, is that the name is pronounced WOO-ster. The second is that its design and tone have led many people to liken it more to a Midwestern town than an Eastern city. The overwhelming impression is industrial; there are also a number of institutions of higher learning.

Springfield, Massachusetts' third-largest city (152,319), is the trading center of the generally prosperous Connecticut Valley metropolitan area, the home of more than half a million people. Since George Washington decided in 1794 to put an armory in Springfield to provide small-arms manufacturing for his army, it has been primarily an industrial city. In recent years the local power structure has gotten its act together and immense efforts have been devoted to renewal of downtown Springfield. The city also has some model neighborhood revival projects. Nearby Holyoke, the prototype of the deteriorating Bay State mill town, finally achieved some new life in the early '80s with the arrival of a Wang Laboratories assembly plant.

The placid life of an earlier time goes on in the Berkshires, including little "hill towns" such as Florida and Peru, known for their beauty and cool year-round weather. The small towns remain heavily Yankee, but the cities, especially Pittsfield and North Adams, have the same strongly ethnic complexion of the rest of urban Massachusetts. In the late 1970s, Pittsfield was the site of a bitter confrontation with developers over whether a regional shopping mall should be built in nearby Lenox (an option blocked by Governor Dukakis) or in the center of this quite lovely small city, the governmental and economic center of the Berkshires.

Lenox is one of the most charming old Berkshire resorts and for four decades has been host to the Boston Symphony for a summertime of concerts at the famed Tanglewood estate. Quite deservedly, Tanglewood has been dubbed the "pastoral music capital of the United States." And on that high note our story of Massachusetts, a remarkable civilization at once dying and being born anew, is finished.

CONNECTICUT

State of Steady Habits

CONNECTICUT, graciously referred to as a "worthy little state" by John Gunther in his *Inside U.S.A.*, has many assets. The question is: Does this proud and historic little state really measure up to its potential?

Among the states, Connecticut is at or near the top in per capita income and average federal income tax payments. It boasts high educational levels, high teacher salaries, and high numbers of citizens in *Who's Who*. It harbors huge reserves of capital in the insurance companies of Hartford and immense reserves of private wealth in Fairfield County, its affluent suburban appendage in the New York City orbit. Here is a state that was a seedbed of public education in America, led most others in urban renewal, and prides itself on clean government. "We are surrounded by evil on every side except the water," says one of Connecticut's top political reporters. Here is the state of America's oldest continually published newspaper (*The Hartford Courant*), and the first state to elect a woman as governor based simply on her merits.

Look back over history and you will find a storehouse of Connecticut accomplishments. During the Revolutionary War, Connecticut was called "the Nation's Arsenal" because of the industry that sprang up from Samuel Colt's start there in gun making (and to this day still fourth among all states in defense contracts). Colt, along with cotton-gin inventor Seth Thomas and clock man Eli Terry—also Connecticut men—pioneered the development of interchangeable parts, a mainstay of the industrial revolution and an important part of Connecticut's economy to this day.

Connecticut gave us Nathan Hale, the schoolteacher who was hanged as a spy by the British in the Revolution; Benedict Arnold; Harriet Beecher Stowe, author of *Uncle Tom's Cabin*; Mark Twain, who settled in Hartford and wrote *Huckleberry Finn* there; John Brown, the abolitionist; J.P. Morgan, the great financier; and P.T. Barnum, the circus impresario.

And when it comes to counting Connecticut "firsts," the list seems never to end. Here was the first American public school (1640), the first turnpike, the first warship (the 16-gun *Oliver Cromwell*), the first use of anesthetic, the first American Ph.D. degree (at Yale), the first telephone switchboard, the first football tackling dummy (invented by Amos Alonzo Stagg at Yale), the first fish hook, meat grinder, steamboat, lollipop, and hamburger.

So Connecticut has a lot going for it. Indeed, John Naisbitt, in his fascinating book *Megatrends*, written in 1982, identified Connecticut (along with California, Florida, Washington, and Colorado) as a bellwether state for social innovation in our time. He cited Ella Grasso's gubernatorial election, Connecticut's lead in requiring competency standards for high school graduates, elimination of monthly minimum charges for poverty-level customers, the nation's first "right to know" law for workers potentially exposed to carcinogens, and finally a Connecticut Supreme Court decision that "whistle blowers"—employees complaining about violations of law or public hazards created by their bosses—can't be fired. We found all those examples impressive but still conclude that when one adds the pieces together, Connecticut is far more "the land of steady habits," as it has long been known, and less the brilliant innovator or risk taker that it could easily be, if it would only tap its deep wells of affluence and talent. Connecticut has so much that more should be expected of it. Search out *the* salient value of political life in Connecticut and you will find that it has been a negative—opposition to a state personal income tax as if it were a form of the bubonic plague. No governor—not even the likes of Abraham Ribicoff or Ella Grasso, who presented themselves to the world as progressive Democrats—had the courage to back an income tax, even though study after study has demonstrated the regressive nature of Connecticut's existing tax system, which by virtue of high sales and property taxes, places a much heavier burden on poor people than wealthy ones. The policy does benefit some people: Fairfield County executives, for instance, who enjoy their safe haven from New York taxes. Apologists argue the no-income-tax policy has created economic wealth in Connecticut by drawing corporate offices into Fairfield County from New York City. But how much that has benefited low-income Connecticut folk is uncertain. And even if true, the question arises: How noble has it been for affluent, advanced Connecticut to pursue the beggar-thy-neighbor economic policy of trying to draw corporate headquarters from troubled New York? And as if that were not parasitic enough, what is one to say of a state among the first (in 1971) to rush into a state lottery system because it lacked an adequate tax system? (During the '70s, also seeking revenue, Connecticut legalized jai alai games and ran into some unsavory scandals.)

Yankees and Ethnic Bosses

The contradictions in Connecticut's political character—clean government versus antiquated financing and cautious leadership—trace back to the state's colonial history and ethnic diversity. From the earliest days, the progressive forces have been countered, either by the paradoxically parallel influence of the Congregationalists and the Roman Catholic Church, or by the banking and insurance industries, or some combination of all four.

The territory was settled in the 1630s by the Reverend Thomas Hooker— his motives split between land hunger and passion to escape the autocratic and theocratic government of Massachusetts. Connecticut would come to be known as the "Constitution State" because the Fundamental Orders, drafted in 1638 from a Hooker sermon as a governmental framework for three Hartford Colony towns, represented the first constitution drafted in the New

World. In 1661 the colonists received from King Charles II a charter ratifying the Orders; 25 years later, when a Crown-appointed government demanded return of the charter at a meeting in a Hartford tavern, legend says the lights were blown out and the treasured charter hidden in the trunk of a great oak tree nearby.* The colony remained stable under the Fundamental Orders, which decreed a government with close ties to the Congregational Church, for the better part of two centuries. Along with the rocky soil, the Puritan temperament, and the traditional independence of each of 169 towns, all this helped to forge Connecticut's stability and conservatism. Religious freedom came with a new constitution in 1918, but even then the conservative Yankees for years still maintained property ownership as a prerequisite for voting, thereby keeping political power among themselves.

The Yankee hegemony could not, of course, last forever. As the Yankees left Connecticut's flinty land to seek their fortunes in the better farmland of the West, their place was taken by successive, overlapping (and eventually feuding) layers of ethnics. First were the Irish, fleeing the potato famine of 1846, later the Germans, Scandinavians, Italians, Poles, Lithuanians, and Czechoslovakians. The first great wave of blacks came to work on the tobacco farms of the Connecticut Valley around 1870; today they number 7.8 percent of Connecticut's population. Jews have been present in the state since the Revolutionary War and today number 3.3 percent. During World War II, thousands of French Canadians moved to Connecticut to work in factories, and there are about 125,000 Puerto Ricans, most of whom arrived after 1960.

It took nearly a century for the ethnic groups, primarily Catholic in allegiance, to wrest political control from the old Yankees. In the 72 years between 1858 and 1930 the Republican party dominated Connecticut politics, partly due to the state's ingrained conservatism, bolstered by a distrust of the Democrats from the Civil War. Republican rule was reinforced by malapportionment of the state legislature, which favored the Yankee small towns over the immigrant, Democratic cities. The manufacturing interests also preferred the Republican party because of its protectionist stance, a position shared by the workers almost as much as the owners.

From 1912 until 1937, Connecticut Republicans were led—"bossed" is a better term—by J. Henry Roraback, lawyer and utility president, one of the great political bosses of this century, a man whose benevolent dictatorship has been likened to that of the Byrds in Virginia. As for the Democrats, the presidential candidacy of Al Smith in 1928 organized the Catholic urban ethnics as never before, and the political upheaval caused by the Great Depression was to have as marked an effect on Connecticut as on any state. In 1930 Democrat Wilbur "Uncle Toby" Cross, a retired dean of the graduate school

*This great act of resistance came in later years to be celebrated by gavels, chairs, and others objects from the tree. Mark Twain noted he had seen a "walking-stick, dog collar, needle-case, three-legged stool, bootjack, dinner table, tenpin alley, toothpick, and enough Charter Oak to build a plank road from Hartford to Salt Lake City." Hartfordite Twain understood that for all its religious virtue, Connecticut had its share of sharp-eyed Yankee peddlers and traders. The nickname "Nutmeg State" came from the practice of selling wooden nutmegs to the unwary.

at Yale, was elected governor; with his Yankee horsetrader's sense he worked out compromises with Roraback on legislation and turned the governor's office into something other than a ceremonial post.*

Cross was defeated by a Republican in 1938, but that year a couple of upcoming young Democrats, John Moran Bailey and Abraham Alexander Ribicoff, began making their presence felt. Bailey became state Democratic chairman in 1946 and served until he died in 1975, the longest tenure of any state chairman of either party in Connecticut's history. Under his leadership the Democrats completed their long climb from a distant second to the dominant political party of Connecticut while remaining relatively free of the scandals the Democrats had caused in other states.

Bailey was a Harvard graduate who acted as though he wanted to hide the fact and looked like the stereotypical Irish political boss. He struck for national political power by becoming the first state chairman outside Massachusetts to come out for John F. Kennedy for president. In 1956 Bailey circulated the famous "Bailey Memorandum," which was written by Kennedy's aide, Ted Sorensen. The memorandum flew in the face of then conventional political wisdom by pragmatically arguing that a Catholic would be more of an asset than a liability on the national ticket. As president, Kennedy returned the favor by making Bailey national chairman of the Democratic party. Bailey kept the only promise he made to Kennedy: "I won't get you into trouble."

With few exceptions, Bailey's candidates were better than the average public servant of the times: Senators Brien McMahon, William Benton, and Abraham Ribicoff; Governors Chester Bowles, Ribicoff, John Dempsey, and Grasso.

Bice Clemow, the West Hartford editor, expressed a more jaundiced view. "We've never had a candidate for president. Connecticut exports power brokers. When you're a power broker you can't get trapped with ideologies. You have to go with the guy you can move with. The reason John Bailey made John Kennedy had nothing to do with how he felt about Jack's 'liberalism.' It had to do with his salability." Consider Ribicoff's statement concerning Chester Bowles, one of the most liberal men of 20th-century politics: "Chet believes too hard." Clemow concluded: "That's the trick in Connecticut. Don't believe too hard. . . . This never was a state of passionate beliefs except those rooted in the Catholic hierarchical domination."

Abraham Ribicoff, the figure to be remembered as Bailey's most enduring contribution to the Connecticut political scene, was a pragmatist—and usually a very cautious man. A onetime Secretary of Health, Education and Welfare, Ribicoff had to wait until the very end of his Senate career (1980) to see a major piece of legislation he authored become law; it was the creation of the U.S. Department of Education.

By 1968, with anti-Vietnam War supporters of Sen. Eugene McCarthy in

---

*The governor's office was just a room in the prestigious Yankee Hartford Club. This was also where the inaugural parades used to start, until the election of Abraham Ribicoff, a Jew, necessitated "other arrangements."

revolt against the old regulars, Bailey began to lose control of the party. Two of the leaders of that insurrection were Anne Wexler, a Westport housewife, and Joseph Duffey, a Congregationalist minister, who ran unsuccessfully for the Senate. Wexler and Duffey later married. While Jimmy Carter was president, Duffy headed the National Endowment for the Humanities while Wexler became a top White House aide, trying to teach the Georgians how to stay in the good graces of Democrats around the country. But Bailey had his swan song: the election of one of his most loyal party politicians, Ella Grasso, the first woman governor of any state elected in her own right and the first Italian governor of Connecticut. Grasso, the daughter of an immigrant baker who worked 14-hour days to send her to Mt. Holyoke, loved the state as much as any Yankee and surprised many politicians by acting much more "no-nonsense" and conservative than was expected of a woman politician. Grasso offended liberals with her opposition to the income tax and outraged feminists with her refusal to allow Medicaid funds to be used for abortions for poor women. But near the end of the campaign Bella Abzug, then the bombastic congresswoman from New York, persuaded the Connecticut Women's Political Caucus to forgive Grasso her "one mistake" on abortion and endorse her. Suffering from cancer, Grasso resigned at the end of December 1980 and died shortly thereafter.

The election of 1980 restored statewide respectability to another famous name in Connecticut politics: Dodd. Christopher Dodd, a thoughtful and intelligent young congressman, was elected to the U.S. Senate. His father, Thomas Dodd, was a prominent senator (1959–71) and supporter of gun control legislation, but was censured by the Senate for misusing government and campaign funds.

Connecticut's senior senator, Lowell Weicker, became a testament to the health of Connecticut's Republican party and the old independent Yankee political tradition. Weicker, an heir to the Squibb drug fortune, rose to be the dominant figure in the state Republican party and a commanding figure in Connecticut politics generally because of his vehement criticism of the Nixon administration and its Watergate scandals. As a member of the Senate Watergate committee, Weicker rejected the argument that dirty politics, wiretapping, big campaign contributions, and other corruptions were justifiable because everyone else, including Democrats, had done the same thing. "I don't want to hear that everybody does it. Believe me, everybody does not do it. This country is a decent place, peopled by honest, decent men, and that includes politicians." Angry as this made some Republicans, Weicker got standing ovations on his trips home after the committee hearings and substantial independent and Democratic support. By the time Ronald Reagan reached the presidency in 1981, Weicker positioned himself clearly to the party's left, a strategy which clearly helped Connecticut voters decide to reelect him in 1982 over outspoken Democratic Rep. Toby Moffett.

In many ways the Connecticut Republican party is as liberal as the Democratic, if not more so—a fruit of the state's tradition of direct, participatory, small-town democracy. Frederick K. Biebel, elected Republican chairman in

1975, appeared to be taking the place of John Bailey as the state's political kingmaker. He could never hold the same candle power as Bailey since the straight party lever had been made optional in Connecticut's voting booths. But he managed to pay off the party debt and double the number of Republicans in the state legislature.

Geographic, Economic, and Academic Connecticut

The Connecticut coastline is typically New England, rock-bound and rugged with sandy beaches and salt meadows backed by a mildly rolling upland. In the western highlands of the Berkshire Hills one finds the private school center of America and some of the wildest and most spectacular scenery of the eastern U.S.; the gorge of the Mianus River near the New York state line is one of the most primitive areas near New York City.

The country east of the Connecticut River Valley is less rugged than in the west; but it is sparsely populated, and airline pilots note it as one of the few dark spots at night on the urbanized Eastern seaboard corridor from Washington, D.C., to Boston. The rich bottomlands of the Connecticut River Valley itself and the hillier farms with their stone walls and barns make Connecticut farmland some of the most pleasing to behold in America. Thus, it is sad to report that total farm acreage in Connecticut has dropped—from 721,315 in 1960, to only 501,419 in 1980. At the same time the value per acre climbed from $560 to $2,231, one of the highest per acre values for farmland in the country. Priced far above their productive capacity, Connecticut farms do more to provide a pleasing backdrop to the wooded areas and bring natural old New England charm to the center of East Coast megalopolis than they do to produce food. Most of the agricultural revenues come from poultry and dairy products. Despite its cold, northern climate, Connecticut is also a tobacco state—although production dropped almost by half in the 1970s as land prices rose. Work in the tobacco fields was the original lure for Connecticut's Southern black, West Indian, and Puerto Rican populations; they used to turn to the cities in the off-season for apartments, schools, social, and health services; but increasingly, they move there seeking employment.

The geographic and economic spine of Connecticut is the urban corridor that runs from north to south down the center of the state, roughly along the Connecticut River Valley (home of many private secondary schools) from Windsor Locks and Hartford, through New Britain, Middletown, and Meriden to New Haven. The corridor then extends from New Haven along the Long Island Sound through Bridgeport, Fairfield, Norwalk, and Darien to Stamford and Greenwich. By 1980, Hartford, Fairfield, and New Haven counties combined had almost 77 percent of Connecticut's population. Many of the corridor cities are old milling and manufacturing towns that have experienced economic decline, the flight of the white middle class, and the influx of blacks and other generally poor and uneducated minorities. Urban Connecticut, however, has not experienced the degree of urban core rot that has afflicted many East Coast Revolutionary-era cities (particularly in New Jersey). One reason was that many Connecticut cities embarked on urban renewal projects during the 1960s. The urban renewal leader not only of Connecticut but most of the nation was New Haven under its dynamic and persistent mayor, Richard Charles Lee, who served from 1954 to 1970.

Lee and his urban renewal chief, a young lawyer named Edward Logue, with the help of Mitchell Sviridoff, then-president of the Connecticut AFL-CIO, built new housing projects, encouraged downtown shopping (Macy's moved in), and renewed neighborhoods according to a master plan that envisioned New Haven as a traffic center with the renewal planned around the Connecticut Turnpike (Interstate 95) and other new highways. Critics later said the Lee programs succeeded better at constructing new buildings than improving people's lives, but Lee remained fond of the era and bitter over the later deemphasis on federal urban programs. In 1980, the U.S. Conference of Mayors gave Lee its distinguished public service award for his pioneering work. "By God, I am proud of that era," Lee said at the ceremony in far-off Seattle. "We would dream, and we did, and when we succeeded, we succeeded sometimes beyond our fondest expectations." Lee's accomplishments were threatened once again in the early 1980s when a shopping center developer began plans for a huge mall in suburban North Haven. The developer contended that suburbanites so preferred to shop in a mall that they were driving as far as 50 miles to find one. But New Haven officials still saw a vital downtown retail sector, and vowed to use little-known federal environmental laws and the courts, if necessary, to block the shopping center.

Logue, of course, went on to mastermind Boston's urban renewal and later, not so masterfully, the New York State Urban Development Corporation and the redevelopment of the South Bronx. Sviridoff became vice president for national affairs of the Ford Foundation; in the "post-federal," "self-help" era of the '80s he founded the Local Initiatives Support Corporation to corral foundation and corporate dollars to fund crucial loans to low-income community economic development groups.

New Haven (pop. 126,109) is best known as the home of Yale, one of the best and most famous of the nation's universities. Its law school may be second only to Harvard, and its other professional and graduate schools are among the nation's finest. Yale's undergraduate school traditionally has been somewhat more conservative and social than some of the other Ivy League universities, but students (now including 41.7 percent women) get a superior education. As in all university towns, there is town-gown conflict. Many among New Haven's large Italian-American population have class resentments against the Yalies. New Haven residents were offended when former Yale President Kingman Brewster said he was skeptical that Black Panther Bobby Seale could get a fair trial on the murder charges against him. The city actually demonstrated more thoughtfulness than Brewster expected; Seale was acquitted by a calm, judicious, predominantly white jury in 1971.

Yale–New Haven relations have much improved since Brewster was succeeded in 1978 by A. Bartlett Giamatti, the grandson of an Italian immigrant who came to New Haven when he was 13. New Haven's city hall, by the later 1970s, was also Italian-led. The mayor was Biagio "Ben" DiLieto, the city's former police chief, who defeated incumbent Mayor Frank F. Logue, Ed Logue's brother, in a race that featured personalities and ethnic rivalries far more than substantive issues. Yale and New Haven were able to resolve their perennial conflict with the townspeople over tax payments by private educational institutions by jointly lobbying the state legislature to win passage of a bill under which the state compensates cities with large amounts of tax-exempt property for the taxes they would otherwise receive.

Hartford is a famed insurance, banking, and state capital, but also bears over 40 percent of Connecticut's welfare case load and has extraordinarily high poverty levels and high unemployment rates. Over half of Hartford's 1960 residents, mostly whites, had moved out by 1980; the city's population had dropped from 162,178 in 1960 to 136,392 in 1980, and 54 percent of the 1980 residents were black and Puerto Ricans. In the 1970s, Hartford was run by Nicholas R. Carbone, the majority leader of the Hartford City Council. Carbone totally eclipsed a figurehead mayor, controlled the local Democratic party, and enjoyed strong political ties that reached all the way to the Carter White House. Carbone was a younger breed of political boss, however, not only interested in power itself, but determined to fight for the survival of beleaguered Hartford and its poor white ethnic, black, and Puerto Rican population.

Carbone attacked head on the economic disparity between Hartford's densely packed 17.2 square miles and its affluent suburbs. It was a fight worth making since urbanologist Richard Nathan had found the economic disparity between Hartford and its suburbs—measured in unemployment, poverty, education, and crowded housing—third worst in the nation, behind only Newark and Cleveland. Carbone and his city council colleagues shocked Connecticut's comfortable establishment with a law suit that blocked seven Hartford suburbs from receiving $4.4 million in federal community development block grant funds. The suburbs, the city argued, had gone against Congress' wishes when they used the money for roads, sewers, and parks instead of programs for the benefit of low- and moderate-income families. The issue became moot when the Carter administration's Housing and Urban Development Secretary Patricia Roberts Harris strengthened enforcement of the regulations, but Carbone had made his point. Carbone went on to try to correct unfairnesses to the city in unemployment programs, electricity rates, and transportation. He enjoyed surprisingly good relations with Hartford's many corporations on development projects. But those corporate associations and Carbone's own unwillingness to include others in decision making eventually alienated many white ethnic and black voters. In a 1979 attempt to change the city charter and become mayor in title, Carbone was overwhelmingly defeated. In 1981 Hartford became the first New England city to popularly elect a black mayor, Thirman L. Milner.

Hartford's largest single employer is the industrial United Technologies Corp., but its private sector leadership is strongly dominated by insurance company chief executive officers, known locally as "the bishops" or "the gods." Hartford has been able to undertake construction projects more speedily than most cities because its insurance companies and banks can commit their corporations' resources and cash. The big three—Connecticut General, Travelers, and Aetna—dominate private decision making, and it's worth noting that a fourth company just about as large, Hartford Insurance Group, plays a smaller role primarily because it is a part of ITT and not locally controlled. In the late 1960s a number of Hartford's corporations formed the Greater Hartford Process, Inc., to deal with urban blight and sprawl. The Process had plans for an $800 million, 15-year plan to renovate the city, but the combination of recession, inflation, and what became known as the "Puerto Rican memo" has led the corporations to act on their own in development projects and relations with community groups. The memo, which used inappropriate language to discuss how the city might be divided up ethnically in the years to come, created a distrust of the corporations and belief in conspiracy that still exist in Hartford's neighborhoods. The corporations persist in community activities—"almost like they are trying to do penance," noted Jill Diskan, executive director of Riverfront Recapture, Inc., and formerly of the Connecticut Housing Investment Fund. Of all U.S. board chairmen seeking to push their organizations into advanced social activity in the late '70s and early '80s, few if any could equal the record of Aetna's John Filer. The insurance companies did cause some anxiety in Hartford in the early '80s, however, when they began locating their secondary operations such as data processing in cheaper suburban space. There were no immediate indications that the companies would abandon Hartford as a headquarters, but social activists worried that it would be even tougher for poor people in Hartford to find jobs.

Hartford was about 10 years behind New Haven in downtown renewal, but it landed running with projects that demonstrated some of the best of urban renewal—and the worst in thoughtless removal of black and poor white ethnic families. The showpiece development was Constitution Plaza, a hotel-office-broadcasting center complex, bankrolled by the insurance industry, which replaced a decaying downtown section of small businesses, pawn shops, and tenements. There followed a handsome downtown civic center including a coliseum whose roof collapsed during a 1978 snowstorm—providentially, after some 5,000 fans attending a college basketball game had gone home. Strong building pressure continued in Hartford into the 1980s, along with a rebirth of the city's once near-extinct night life. Among the city's charms are the exquisite (and carefully restored) Old State House, the "new" State House (a domed Victorian structure some call a "Gothic Taj Mahal"), and lovely Old Bushnell Park, which a citizens group was seeking to preserve and refurbish in the early '80s. The richest of Hartford's suburbs is West Hartford, which has so many amenities (including back-door garbage collection) that many of its residents who moved in with young children after World War II have resisted giving up their big houses even in retirement.

While New Haven and Hartford claim more fame, Bridgeport (142,546) is

Connecticut's largest city, its 8.9 percent population loss in the '70s notwith-standing. A blue-collar town, the butt of jokes since Mark Twain poked fun at it in *A Connecticut Yankee in King Arthur's Court,* Bridgeport underwent disastrous urban renewal in the '60s and paralyzing industrial loss in the '70s. The '60s demolition cleared away thousands of tenements and small stores, replacing them with a few barren housing projects, mediocre shopping plazas, high-rise office structures—and acre upon acre of emptiness. The parks, Bridgeport's onetime pride, had broad swaths bulldozed through them to funnel business into an ever-less-desirable downtown. The '70s saw such major employers as Singer, Dictaphone, and Bridgeport Brass close their doors; just a smattering of high-tech firms came to replace them. But even a time of particularly unsavory politics did not prevent the city from sinking most of its community development funds into housing. By 1980, a strong revitalization push, including a Neighborhood Housing Services project lead-ing to creation of an historic district in the Washington Park and South End neighborhoods, was underway. Despite an arson problem, many property values were turning around. A major effort to build up the East Main Street retail area had begun. And Bridgeport had joined those many cities paradoxi-cally exhibiting vigor even while their traditional economies lay in tatters.

The winds of change may be ever so subtly felt in Fairfield County, Connecticut's "Gold Coast," or to use Wilbert Snow's memorable phrase—its "Alsace-Lorraine." Fairfield's luxurious enclaves such as Greenwich, Darien, Westport, and Fairfield have remained mostly idyllic settings for homes of New York executives in Brooks Brothers suits commuting to their jobs. But these days many of the executives work close to home, having succeeded in moving the national offices of their corporations to Connecticut. Stamford, Fairfield, and Darien together have become home of 25 of the *Fortune* 500 corporations, and the assets of corporations in Fairfield County total $100 billion. Stamford has been transformed from a sleepy, decaying manufacturing city to the corporate/urban center of the county and a show-case for the corporate architecture of such firms as General Telephone & Electronics, Schweppes U.S.A., American Thread, and Xerox. Many of the corporations that first moved to Fairfield County chose campuslike settings, but the shortage of land and rising construction costs have forced later arrivals into the cities where traffic problems (because of Connecticut's abysmal public transit) and office equipment burglaries have tainted the corporate utopia.

And utopia was what Fairfield County seemed to be in the early 1980s. In the face of a fierce recession, the Stamford area's unemployment rate was one-third the national average, the lowest in the nation. This golden image belied the fact that housing prices had risen so high that lower-level workers were commuting from as far away as New Haven and New Jersey, and if they were unemployed, showed up in the statistics in their home towns. Despite pressures from the Suburban Action Institute and other civil rights groups to build low- and middle-income housing, Fairfield had become ever more high-priced, albeit in patterns reflecting the times. Condominiums and smaller houses, for example, were selling better than executive-style homes. One reason was that the "baby boom" generation was growing up and leaving, to the extent that the excellent Greenwich Public Schools in 1981 advertised that they would accept students from outside the district at $4,000 per year. But another reason was divorce. The Westport Unitarian Singles Group boasted 2,700 members; singles bars—several featuring male strippers—had opened; and politicians began to take note of demands for increased day and after-school care for children. The divorced suburbanites complained that the long distances they had to travel to meet each other conflicted with a single life-style, but they seemed firmly committed to staying in Fairfield County for its fine schools and high status.

The strong ties of such a wealthy, influential area of Connecticut to New York, however, are symptomatic of Connecticut's basic problem of outside domination. Connecticut's media also suffers from the same problem. Except for the Hartford area, opinion leaders are likely to rely as heavily on New York or Massachusetts papers as any printed locally. The only exceptions are the fine *Hartford Courant* newspaper, now owned by the Los Angeles Times And Mirror Company, and television station WSFB-TV in Hartford, owned by the Washington Post Company. Still when all is said and done, Connecticut remains a civilization that has yet to learn enough of itself, and the shortcomings in its own public life, to reach the distinction among American states that should be its birthright and role.

RHODE ISLAND

"City State" and Ethnic Laboratory

"LITTLE RHODY" IS A UNIQUE WORLD. Only 48 miles from north to south, and an even more modest 37 miles from east to west, it is America's smallest state. It has by far and away the highest proportion of Roman Catholics of any state (65 percent) and can safely be called the "most ethnic." Finally, it is the most consistently Democratic state in its voting habits.

For three centuries Rhode Island's political culture has been dominated by the religious toleration and resistance to tyranny established by its founder Roger Williams, who had fled the oppressive Puritanism of the Massachusetts Bay Colony. Only Maryland, among the colonies in the 17th century, rivaled Rhode Island as a society open to free thinkers, nonconformists, and religions of every sort. In 1638 the first Baptist Church in America was established by dissenters from the Puritan Church in Massachusetts. Soon Congregationalists, Quakers, Methodists, and Jews followed. Only later, around the time of the American Revolution, did the first significant numbers of Roman Catholics, who were destined to become the dominant religious group of modern Rhode Island, receive their welcome into the state's religious polyglot.

Williams' spirit of revolt against oppression has also reappeared, time and again, throughout Rhode Island's history. Rhode Islanders like to remember that they were never subjected to the authority of royal governors and that they declared their independence from Great Britain two months before the assembled colonies' joint declaration in July of 1776. The independent Yankee tradition ruled Rhode Island through the 19th century and into the 20th. The state's common people—the Irish, French Canadians, Italians, Poles, Portuguese—found themselves under the control of a narrow WASP elite and powerful mercantile interests, which tried to remain in power by denying the right to vote to persons without property and later to the foreign born.

From the Civil War down to the 1930s, a boss-ridden and often corrupt Republican party, fronting for the mill owners and representing what John Gunther called Rhode Island's "glacially aristocratic families," controlled Rhode Island, buying and stealing elections and rigging state law to ensure its own dominance. The prototype Republican was Charles R. Brayton, a corpulent, affable, almost blind Civil War general who proved that a ruthless, efficient regime could be built on a rural base as well as in a city. Brayton had an alliance with Nelson Aldrich, one of the most powerful Republican senators of the late 19th and early 20th centuries, but in matters internal to Rhode Island, Brayton's rule was supreme. He bought small-town voters, controlled legislators, and played off the growing immigrant groups against each other while helping the corporations that financed him increase their profits.

In the long run, however, the Republican strategy of divide and conquer was to prove untenable. Few are the states in which there was such rancor between a capitalist class centered in one religion and a working class based in another. The presidential election of 1928 and the candidacy of Alfred Smith, a Catholic from the streets of New York, galvanized the state's Catholic ethnic groups into a cohesive Democratic voting bloc. The Great Depression and the rise of a powerful labor movement of heavily Catholic-ethnic composition cemented the relationship. At the state level, Rhode Island had a liberator on the same fundamental scale as Louisiana's volcanic and dictatorial Huey Peirce Long; Rhode Island's was a mild-mannered Yankee Democrat, Governor Theodore Francis Green, who led a "bloodless revolution" that broke the back of the old order. The Democrats tampered with election returns to give themselves control of the eternally Republican state senate, purged the all-Republican supreme court; and in a 15-minute flurry of action on New Year's Day, 1935, reorganized the state government from stem to stern, cleaning out the Republicans. Since then, a heavily ethnic, labor-dominated Democratic party has been the leading political force of Rhode Island. Few other states offer a comparable record of blind one-party loyalty. Rhode Island was one of only six states to vote for Jimmy Carter in 1980, and even the losing Democratic presidential candidate George McGovern, whose views were anathema to old-line Democratic politicians, received an impressive 46.8 percent of the vote in 1972. Rhode Island has elected only one Republican U.S. Senator—popular former Gov. John Chafee—since 1930. It sent no Republican to the U.S. House from 1938 until the 1980 election of Claudine Schneider, an environmentalist whose election helped to reinvigorate the Eastern liberal Republican tradition.

The dominant Democrats of recent times have been standard liberals on issues such as workers' benefits but ideological conservatives on social issues. Though Rhode Island has had a small black population, it took seven years of effort in the 1960s before a fair housing bill could win approval. Rhode Island fought tooth and nail against relaxing its ban on abortions, even after the U.S. Supreme Court decision upholding a woman's right to choose.

The Democrats' secret of success has been a careful ethnic balancing of their statewide ticket among four groups: the Irish, Italian, French-Canadian, and Yankees. Among these "equals," there has consistently been one group more preferred than the others: the Irish. The proclivity of the Irish for political success—even if the Italians have now outstripped them numerically —is one of the wonders of American politics. One explanation is that the Irish spoke English when they arrived in this country and got into politics first; but the luck of the Irish would have dimmed without the exceptional political talent that turned the making of compromises into an art. Among the under-represented with great potential for the future are the latest arrivals, the Portuguese, whose anti-welfare, hard-working ways are providing new life to many of Rhode Island's cities. The Yankees, through their wealth and educational advantages, still make their influence felt in Rhode Island affairs. As

Democratic politician Lawrence McGarry told us from the Irish perspective, "There's an old WASP power structure—the Metcalfs, the Sharpes, the Browns, the Chafees. It's the Rhode Island Hospital Trust National Bank, the *Providence Journal*, the Rhode Island Hospital board of directors." He might also have added Ivy League Brown University in Providence.

The strongest living proof of Yankee influence is Rhode Island's two blueblood senators; Democrat Claiborne Pell and Republican John Chafee. Pell, whose father was a congressman from New York, dabbled in Rhode Island politics, without any elective office, until 1960 when he beat two scandal-tinged machine Democrats to win the nomination for the seat vacated by Theodore Francis Green, the grand old man of Rhode Island Democratic politics, and the oldest man ever to serve in Congress. (Green finally retired at 93.) Typically, Pell has taken on an issue long before it has risen to much public notice and then worked on it, year after year, until he succeeded. He quietly, but firmly, opposed the Vietnam War from 1966 onward, fathered the national endowments for the arts and humanities, was the first senator to take a deep interest in rapid rail transportation in the Northeast corridor, was the person really responsible for a treaty among 85 nations to ban placing "nuclear and other weapons of mass destruction" on the ocean floor, and originated federal direct aid to college students.

Chafee, who inaugurated an unusual GOP winning streak in Rhode Island when he was elected governor in 1962, actually lost his first bid for the Senate, when he ran against Pell in 1972. Chafee's winning 1976 campaign, for the seat vacated by retiring 26-year Senator John Pastore, was marked by high spending. In the Senate, Chafee has tended to side with liberal Republicans and has fought strongly for Northeastern interests.

The state government of Rhode Island is quite average in rates of taxation and levels of service. The legislature is dominated by labor, which has more power in Rhode Island than practically anywhere else in the country, even Michigan. Alone with New York, for instance, Rhode Island has a law permitting workers out on strike to draw unemployment compensation benefits—from a fund set up by taxes on their employers in the first instance! As manufacturing has declined, public labor unions have assumed the former's power; by the early 1980s, 32 members of the 150-member legislature were school teachers, and the state was in danger of becoming a vassal to its public servants. Restrictions of the Hatch Act type had been repealed, and state civil servants could now run for local public office. Public employees had also taken to striking despite a state anti-strike law. Rhode Island legislators are still old fashioned enough to be among the most subservient to leadership —despite the fact that these same leaders are among the politicians, racetrack, and jai alai operators who are often charged with corruption and taking kickbacks on state contracts. (The politicians' peccadilloes, however, pale in comparison with the sins of Rhode Island's Mafia, for which Providence's Federal Hill is the New England headquarters.)

Rhode Island's economy has a colorful history, reaching back to the China trade and legendary whale catches, to its justified claim as the birthplace of the American factory system. Rhode Island remains the most heavily industrialized state, with 31.5 percent of its jobholders (in 1981) working in factories. For years Rhode Island has shown consistently lower hourly manufacturing wages, higher unemployment rates, and more severe reactions to recession than other New England states or the nation. There has been continual soul searching over what can be done to modernize and improve the industrial mix and diversify the economy in general. Rhode Island calls itself the "costume jewelry center of the world," and more than 6 percent of Rhode Island workers make jewelry and silverware. This should be a bright spot for the future, especially as the self-absorbed adults of America's "baby boom" generation gain the affluence to be major customers. The structure of the jewelry and silver industries, however, demonstrates the state's economic problems. There are a few large plants (including Gorham, the world's largest producer of sterling silver products), but most work is done in hundreds of small family-owned firms. These small businessmen continually complain that their market has been hurt by competition from imports and that they will have a hard time complying with federal Environmental Protection Agency guidelines to remove metal wastes from the electroplating process before discharging those wastes into public sewers.

Economic concern turned into crisis in 1974 when the U.S. Navy, then Rhode Island's largest employer, announced it would close almost all operations in the state. Some 6,000 jobs and a payroll of $344 million a year sailed away. Philip W. Noel, governor in the mid-1970s, made economic development the central thrust of his administration. Tax reform legislation passed in 1974 has attracted new industrial plants and expansions, including some high technology. A submarine assembly plant employing more than 4,000 people opened on the former Quonset Point naval base site. Rhode Island's unemployment no longer looks quite as bad in comparison with New England and the rest of the nation. But there have been reports of older workers with outdated skills turning to fishing for clams in Narragansett Bay to eke out a living. Ambitious young people still tend to leave the state.

Rhode Island also has a smattering of powerful national corporations and aggressive banking institutions, including Raytheon, North American Phillips, the conglomerate Textron, and the Fleet Financial Group of Providence, which has nearly 50 percent of the state's banking assets.

Providence, Newport, and Rhode Island's Other Worlds

James Bryce, the British historian and onetime ambassador to the United States, once suggested that Rhode Island might become the first American "city state." Socially, the description fits. Many of the Rhode Islanders with whom we spoke described their home as a communal, tight-knit little state where everyone seems to know everyone; in fact one young professional we interviewed complained about a lack of privacy. Geographically, the city-state theme is borne out by the fact that except for the residents of Block Island, no Rhode Islander is more than 45 minutes by automobile from Providence. Despite its industrialized and urbanized image, the state actually seems fairly spacious. Lovely Narragansett Bay, intruding 28 miles from the sea and cutting the state into two uneven parts, contributes to the open feeling, as do the woodlands (64 percent of the state's land surface) and crop and pasture land.

Rhode Island has failed to capitalize on its unique compactness by becoming a city-state in fact. Though its population (947,154) is only that of a good-sized urban center, it insists on maintaining 39 cities and towns, each with a complete government. There are no county governments to serve as hindrances to efficient administration, but except in a very few minor attempts at consolidation, there is the confusion—and cost—of so many governments in a geographically limited space.

The city of Providence, where Rhode Island began and the nexus of the state's successive stages as an agricultural, shipping, and industrial civilization, is New England's second-largest urban center. But the city's 1980 population count of 156,804 was a long ways down from the peak of 253,504 recorded just before World War II. The population drain notwithstanding, Providence has begun a downtown renewal based on its architectural heritage, which somehow survived the 1960s destruction that spoiled so many older cities. The Providence Preservation Society first sparked a renaissance on College Hill, once the home of the famous Brown brothers and other merchants who had become rich from the rum-slave-molasses trade. Across the street from city hall, the Biltmore Plaza hotel, which was boarded up for many years, was reopened as a luxury establishment. New restaurants also started up and a Greek Revival Arcade, built in 1828, reopened as a small-scale version of Boston's Quincy Market. Much of the credit for the revival is given to Mayor Vincent A. Cianci, Jr., one of the city's rare Republican officeholders, who was first elected in 1974. Cianci doled out federal urban development money in small chunks for merchants to renovate their buildings. He failed, however, to pay as much attention to the city's deteriorating residential neighborhoods, the loss of jobs, or the city's financial conditions, which reached such a state in the early 1980s that taxes had to be increased to avoid bankruptcy and the municipal bond rating was lowered.

Historic old Newport (pop. 22,259) has recovered quite nicely from the Navy draw-down. Higher energy costs have enhanced Newport as a tourist destination from the many Northeastern cities within easy distance, and more tourists than ever have come to enjoy the magnificent seascape, the mild climate, the deep-water harbors, and the America's Cup races and other sports events. A major attraction is Newport's beautifully preserved architectural heritage, both the colonial structures and the "summer cottages" built in the Gilded Age following the Civil War by such unfettered capitalists and conspicuous consumers as the Vanderbilts, Astors, Belmonts, Wideners, Burdens, Dukes, and Goelets. It was at Mrs. William Astor's "cottage," where the ballroom held only 400, that the legend of the Four Hundred at the very peak of the social pyramid was born. A visit to one of these ostentatious mansions, the size of a European palace, is a good lesson for anyone who wonders why it was necessary to institute the income tax in America. For all its glamour, Newport has long been and remains a predominantly blue-collar, Catholic town, and for all the talk of recovery, many apparently had to find jobs elsewhere. A full 15 percent of Newport's population left in the 1970s. The Navy, with the War College and numerous training schools, still adds greatly to Newport's nautical flavor.

Several other little-known worlds are tucked into corners of this Lilliputian state. Woonsocket on the Massachusetts border is reputed to have more French-Canadians than any other city south of Montreal; between Woonsocket and Pawtucket, where the famed Slater Mill has been restored, lies the Blackstone Valley, a heavily industrialized and declining suburban corridor. Northwestern Rhode Island is lightly populated and attractive to the eye with many lakes, streams, forests, parks, and farmlands. East Providence is an industrial suburb where tasteful little parks and tree rows hide oil tanks facing onto Narragansett Bay. At Barrington there are miles and miles of lovely eastern bayshore estates and *the* Rhode Island Country Club. Bristol, where legend says the Vikings visited as early as the year 1000, is a quiet, tree-lined old town of much grace, filled with many lovingly preserved examples of colonial and early 19th-century architecture; and it hosts annually one of the country's biggest 4th of July parades—a patriotic extravaganza dating back to the original Independence Day and attracting hundreds of thousands of spectators. Finally there is Block Island, a pear-shaped piece of rolling land, moorlike in character with seemingly countless salt-water and fresh-water ponds. Block Island, which has only a few hundred permanent residents— many of them descendants of the first settlers from Massachusetts in the 17th century—is filled with old Victorian hotels, white beaches, and towering bluffs bespeaking a refreshing timelessness and solitude that densely packed little Rhode Island would do well to preserve for all time to come.

VERMONT

The Beloved State

VERMONTERS LOVE VERMONT, and with good reason.

The state's physical charm is beyond dispute. Vermont is a pastoral place, with a marvelous juxtaposition of meadow and forest land. The mountains are rounded, friendly, and quiet; as a former governor told us, "man is welcome on our mountainsides." And there are village greens, with their white-spired churches and sturdy little meetinghouses and an architecture as graceful as this nation has ever produced; the barns in red or white; the maples, ready for their yield of sap in spring and flaming red in autumn; stands of white birches and forests of evergreen; dazzling arrays of wildflowers; and beckoning lakes, large and small.

Then there is the image—some say the myth—of the Vermont Yankee: hardy, spare, independent, factual, thrifty, shrewd, self-reliant. That character did not come about by accident; as Bernard DeVoto noted back in the 1930s, it developed from Vermont's ancestral religion of Calvinism: "Its philosophy, that life is an endless struggle against evil and necessarily a losing one, exactly agrees with the experience of a people who settled on a thin, boulder-sown soil in a ferocious climate, where mere survival was success."

There are those who say, and have been saying for years, that those noble Vermonters are a virtually extinct species, and that all the talk about them, together with the promotion of dubious antiques, maple syrup, Calvin Coolidge, covered bridges, and patchwork quilts, is one great tourist trap. Perhaps so, but the melody of the real Vermont, like the melody of Puritanism in America at large, lingers on. One can still say, with conviction, that there are values that set Vermont apart in America: pride and independence, stemming from the pioneer heritage; tolerance, which grew out of respect for others' privacy; conservatism, usually in the best sense—to conserve a way of life that let the individual be what he would, for good or ill, since, as Dorothy Canfield Fisher once wrote, "nobody can help him do his breathing; it is an intrusion to try"; a preference for gradualism over hectic or drastic change; and a deep love and respect for the precious land. The latter, as we shall see, has been translated into the most dramatic political controversy of Vermont in our times.

Vermonters, of course, are only human, and they have their prejudices. Those feelings welled up in the past century as the dilution of the native stock set in. First were the Irish, who came in the wake of the horrifying potato famine in their native land; they built the railroads and then settled. Later there arrived several thousands each of Italians, Poles, Finns, and Slavs, and, in the greatest numbers of all, the French-speaking from neighboring Quebec. But never were more than 15 percent of Vermont's people foreign born, and if the newcomers were at first viewed with leery eye (especially for their Roman Catholicism in this very Congregationalist state), it was not long before those who wanted to be were accepted as true Vermonters. The assimilative process has worked more smoothly in Vermont than in any other state, even though there are clear-cut geographic divisions—the countryside remaining primarily Yankee, the cities with their markedly Catholic-ethnic concentrations. There have been isolated instances of ugly prejudice against blacks, though with a near-invisible two-tenths of 1 percent of the state population, they are scarcely the central social issue. The most important Vermont prejudice is against the affluent out-of-staters who have moved in to buy up (and outrageously drive up the price of) Vermonters' own land.

Geography and History

Vermont is rather neatly delineated by the Connecticut River, which flows along its entire eastern border, and lovely Lake Champlain, which serves as its western border for 112 miles. But it is the ancient Green Mountains that are Vermont's salient physical feature; they stretch from south to north, from the Massachusetts border to Quebec, thus dividing Vermont into eastern and western portions with a high mountain pass between. For generations there was an unwritten "mountain rule" in politics decreeing that governors must come alternately from the eastern and western sides. Today eastern and western Vermont are much alike; the important distinction is between southern and northern Vermont. Southern Vermont is booming because of its thriving ski areas and easy access to megalopolis. Northern Vermont, except for the Burlington and Barre-Mountpelier areas and ski resorts near Stowe and Sugarbush, is relatively poor and remote though there has been some "boom town" style development in recent years as Canadians, fearful of secession in Quebec, have crossed the border to invest their money. In the 1970s the three-county area along the Canadian and New Hampshire borders, known as the "Northeast Kingdom" since George Aiken gave them that name in the 1930s, recovered from decades of population loss and grew by about 15 percent—the same as the state average.

The exception for Burlington, in particular, is a vital one, however. In the surrounding area, one finds 202,715 people, 40 percent of the state total, the major retail center of the state, and its greatest concentrations of wealth, higher education, hospitals, and new-generation industries such as IBM and Digital Equipment Corporation. Set on picturesque heights overlooking Lake Champlain, Burlington registered 37,712 people in the '80 Census, the only Vermont city with more than 20,000 souls. Burlington has long had a progressive reputation, but it was still a shock to Vermonters when fiery socialist Bernard Sanders defeated the five-term incumbent mayor in 1981, and when three of his followers won election to the board of aldermen in 1982, wresting majority control away from the conservative Democrats who with business backing had run the town for three decades.

Among Vermont towns, none is more justly famous than Woodstock, between Rutland to the west and White River Junction on the Connecticut River. The heart of Woodstock, pristine and graceful, is its Green, bordered by lovingly preserved homes of black-and-white clapboard dating back as far as the late 1700s. That placid scene, however, belies Woodstock's fundamental change from a farm trading center to what the *Vermont Times* called "a suburban town for the tourist and the very wealthy." The ski culture is one reason for that; an even more important catalyst was Laurence Rockefeller, the town's largest employer and a man intent on preserving Woodstock as a New England Williamsburg. The other justly famous town is Middlebury, in west-central Vermont, which boasts a world-famous summer language school and the illustrious Breadloaf Writers' Conference. Vermont has produced few artists and writers itself, but has attracted many as summer residents, including Robert Frost, Pearl Buck, John Gunther, Sinclair Lewis, economists Arthur Burns, Milton Friedman, and John Kenneth Galbraith, and painter Norman Rockwell.

Vermont's history began in 1609, 11 years before the Mayflower arrived in Plymouth, when the French explorer Samuel de Champlain became the first white man to see Vermont. But his interest was fleeting, and for another 60 years the white man left Vermont alone. The early settlement of the area proceeded slowly because most of the first arrivals were trappers, not farmers. In the mid 18th century, however, a craftsman-agrarian society began to take hold.

To sense the peaceful dynamic of present-day Vermont political life, one must look back in time to the colonial-era disputes between New Hampshire and Vermont for its lands. In the years before the American Revolution, a number of settlers in the disputed area decided that they alone had the rightful claim and hired a colorful, brash 27-year-old native of Connecticut, Ethan Allen, to be the colonel-commandant of a military company to defend their interests. Allen became one of the leaders of the Green Mountain Boys, which later scored a stunning success in the Revolutionary War by capturing Fort Ticonderoga. New Hampshire dropped its claim on Vermont during the war, but New York refused, and the indignant Vermonters proclaimed themselves a republic. Vermont's constitution, written by Allen and his followers, was heavily influenced by the liberal views of William Penn and included two provisions then unique in America: a complete prohibition of slavery and universal manhood suffrage without property or taxpaying requirements. In 1790, Vermont settled its dispute with New York and the next year petitioned for admission as the 14th state.

In the Civil War Vermonters were to prove that their dedication to the antislavery cause was more than talk. Half of the men of military age—a total of some 35,000—joined the army, and one out of every seven lost his life. The state also appropriated $8 million for the war effort, a huge proportion of its native wealth.

The effects of the Civil War were to be felt for long, hard years. As William Moran has written, "the effort in men and money made Vermont's people tired." After the war, the West opened up, farms were abandoned, and young people left. A certain amount of industry—lumber, paper mills, marble quarrying, asbestos and talc mines, woolen mills—did come to Vermont. But Vermont remained distant from the main railroad mines and centers of commerce and continued to depend on agriculture during the century when the United States as a whole was rushing headlong into industrialization. And what a perplexingly difficult agriculture it was. The soil was rocky, distances to market long. The percent of Vermont's land face in farming plummeted from 75 percent in 1850 to 25 percent in 1970. After World War II, an astounding number of Vermont's smaller farmers sold out to their bigger competitors and to housing developers and summer residents. Between 1850 and 1960, Vermont's total population grew by an average of only 2 percent per decade. Had it not been for the excess of births over deaths, the population in that period would have sunk seriously.

The New Economy . . . and Vermont's Epochal Act 250

In the early 1960s, a remarkable transformation occurred. Vermont became a net importer of Americans from other states. The 1970 Census showed a 14 percent population gain, and the 1980 Census another 15 percent.

What was happening? The reasons were several but could be boiled down to three chief factors: a rise in factory jobs, especially in sophisticated new industries such as electronics; a rapid increase in the ski and summer resort business; and, perhaps most important of all, a heady influx of people from the eastern megalopolis building summer and retirement homes in the Green Mountain State.

For a neat illustration of the forces behind Vermont's new economy—a mix of state/local boosterism and the area's sheer natural attractiveness—one need look only to the arrival of a new IBM plant in Burlington in 1957-58. One Vermonter aptly described this to us "as the most dramatic event in Vermont's economy in half a century." First, there were the jobs: 4,000 immediately, over 7,000 by 1980. And second, the plant's mission: design and production of computer memories, one of the most capital-intensive, high-technology industrial undertakings anywhere. All of this might not have come to pass if an affiliate of the Greater Burlington Industrial Corporation hadn't decided to build a 32,000-square-foot plant on speculation—the facility IBM decided to occupy. But there was the other "intangible" factor, too: IBM chief Thomas Watson was said to be strongly drawn to the location because he loved to ski!

And so the new economic wave continued to gain momentum in the '60s, partly under the leadership of Philip H. Hoff, Vermont's first Democratic governor since the Civil War. New recreational facilities were encouraged. Dozens of light industrial firms constructed plants, more than offsetting the earlier loss of Vermont's few textile plants to the South. The state even launched an advertising campaign in out-of-state newspapers under the tag line, "Calling All Vermonters Wherever You Are"—a pitch to return home for the renewed economic opportunities. Many did just that.

Some observers lamented the high degree of out-of-state ownership of Vermont's leading industries and recreational complexes. Lee Webb, for a period professor at Goddard College and later head of the progressive Conference on Alternative State and Local Public Policies, issued a report charging that Vermont was a "colony" owned by big businesses that had forced poor farmers off the land, paid young housewives wages below the national and New England averages, and then siphoned away the profits for investment elsewhere. But among Vermonters there was little talk of exploitation. In Burlington, the transient professionals from firms such as IBM were said to have become active in civic affairs, their fresh blood energizing bank boards and influential community organizations across the state.

Most Vermonters may not have minded their "colony" status, but they were moved to action in the 1960s by the likelihood that the influx of people, housing, and ski developments would turn their bucolic and isolated home into "Sprawl City, U.S.A." Tourism had existed in Vermont as early as the summer hotels of the 1860s; in 1934 the installation at Woodstock of America's first rope tow for skiers had started a new industry. But those tourists were wealthy and few in number compared to the urbanites who started to inundate Vermont in the 1960s. The interstate highway system and jet air travel, coupled with the sharp rise in Americans' discretionary income and leisure time, had made the state easily accessible to people from Springfield, Albany, Boston, Hartford, and New York City. "Vermont today is a suburb," Governor Hoff told us.

Escalating land prices forced native Vermont families to turn to mobile homes as housing; the high taxes needed to pay for increased road maintenance, police, fire protection, and garbage disposal drove many established farmers out of business. Few towns had zoning laws, and developers even undermined the traditional town meetings with people who would front for them.

By 1969 these concerns resulted in a state environmental control commission and in 1970 the passage by overwhelming margins of Act 250, Vermont's basic land use law. Billboard and bottle bans followed. Act 250 paradoxically established the bedrock principle of late-20th-century Vermont: that the state would not sell its priceless environmental heritage for a mess of developmental porridge, even while the act impinged on the cherished Yankee tradition of a man's right to do whatever he pleased with his land. The statute set up criteria for large-scale real estate or housing developments and established local and statewide citizen review boards that could approve or reject new developments. Vermont legislatures of the early '70s never went the additional step envisioned at the start of the decade—to a detailed statewide land use plan. But Act 250, on its own, accomplished much. For example, the city of Burlington invoked it with success to block a proposed huge regional shopping mall six miles outside of town. The mall was being pushed by New York State developers anxious to make a fast buck and apparently willing to eviscerate the retail heart of one of America's most appealing small cities. The Vermonters did care; the regional Act 250 board said the potential economic hardship to be visited on Burlington would constitute a negative, dangerous impact on Vermont's environment.

In 1980 a statewide conference on Act 250 concluded the measure had worked well in protecting communities from the costs of rapid development and had protected air and water quality and wildlife. It had not been quite so effective in preserving prime agricultural land, ground water, or the effects of some tacky tourist attractions. The overall judgment, however, was clearly positive. As a member of one local review board commented to us, Vermont's 15 percent population growth in the '60s had seemed a state crisis, but a similar growth in the '70s took place far more smoothly. In Act 250, Vermont had created a model of effective state control of its future that too few other states were willing to emulate.

Politics and Government: From "Do-Nothing" to Activism

Much is known of the fabled Republicanism of Vermont, which denied the hapless Democrats a single victory for president, governor, or congressman for more than a century. As an early governor noted, "hostility to slavery is an instinct" with Vermonters, and the people translated their sacrifices in the Civil War conflict into incredibly steadfast Republicanism thereafter. Moreover, rural Vermont had few cities where the Democratic working class could take hold. The Republican machine, led oddly enough by industrialists, elected as governors generations of presidents of railroads and then associates of the Proctor marble company dynasty. "Most Proctor-faction governors," political scientist Duane Lockard wrote, were "conservatives of the 'do-nothing' school." They kept the costs of government low, but the quality of public education was poor, state homes for the mentally ill and retarded were approved only grudgingly and provided anemic funds, and the poor had to depend on the dubious charity of "overseers" in each town.

The only successful challenges to Proctor rule came in the Progressive period (1910–15), and later in the person of George Aiken, a quiet, unassuming, prematurely white-haired nurseryman elected to the governorship (1936–40) and later to the U.S. Senate. Aiken became a kind of living national embodiment of the simple Vermont virtues of honesty, decency, and independence of mind. When he retired in 1974 at age 82 to his "unfinished work" among the orchards and wildflowers of Putney, he was the dean of the Senate, the oldest senator, and the ranking Republican on both the Agriculture and

Foreign Relations Committees. He had also been an unpublicized adviser to presidents from Franklin Roosevelt to Lyndon Johnson.

In the last four decades, however, Vermont has developed a true progressive tradition and often led other states in social programs and election reforms. The progressive era began in the late 1940s under the governorship of Ernest W. Gibson, Jr., a Republican who challenged the Proctor dynasty. And it has continued to this day, under governors such as Republican Richard Snelling, the thoughtful Vermont leader of the late '70s and early '80s, who rose to be chairman of the National Governors Association and the respected leader of the states in a set of historically unprecedented White House-gubernatorial negotiations on "New Federalism" and divisions of responsibility between national and state governments. Viewed as somewhat conservative within Vermont, governors such as Snelling all seemed, to the outside world, to be moderate, thoughtful, careful men. They permitted Vermont's combined state and local taxes to remain near the top for all states, and indeed absolute top in some years, providing in return rather competent full-service government. And not one forgot environmental priorities. Snelling, for instance issued a state economic development policy keyed to encouragement of small business, protection of Vermont's prime farmlands, and energy efficiency—a far cry from most states' strategies of indiscriminately chasing all kinds of factories.

Then there has been the Democratic renaissance, which got underway in the '50s and first surfaced, to national amazement, with the 1958 election of a Democratic congressman (William H. Meyer, a forester and "peace" candidate, who would survive but one term). The real arrival of two-party politics came in the '60s as new voters migrated into Vermont from elsewhere and the Democrats produced a remarkably attractive candidate in Philip H. Hoff. Hoff's years as governor coincided with Lyndon Johnson's Great Society programs, and federal money began to pour into the state to upset the old low-service, high-unemployment communal Vermont. Hoff's performance in later years was pedestrian, but he is still remembered as one of the region's best governors.

Vermont's congressional delegation has continued to be mostly Republican. The senior senator, Robert T. Stafford, has served in public office since 1954 and is known as a bland "moderate-liberal." The state's only representative, Republican progressive James Jeffords, became a national leader in farmland preservation, a field of intense interest in Vermont. In 1974, Vermonters also elected their first Democratic senator in 120 years, Patrick J. Leahy, who was born in 1940, the same year George Aiken went to Washington. Leahy built a progressive record in Washington, and was re-elected in 1980.

Even in this age of political cynicism and tax revolts, one finds in Vermonters a remarkable faith in their government, indeed often real admiration of their leaders. It is a phenomenon found in few other states—Minnesota, Wisconsin, Oregon, and Hawaii would be the salient examples. Is there a common thread? Perhaps. In each, one finds the tradition of English common law operating in a setting where the people in times past have thrown off grave oppressions and then used government as their instrument to create a preferred society. The reader may wonder how we can equate such states as Vermont and Hawaii—yet even that fits if one remembers the strong New England influence on the early settlement of the island state.

Grassroots democracy still lives in Vermont. Town-meeting day still comes the first Tuesday of every March, when the tax rate is set, officials elected, and local issues decided—and indeed some not so local. (The adoption of nuclear weapons U.S.–Soviet bilateral freeze resolutions in some 100 Vermont town meetings in 1981 helped to propel the movement forward on a national basis.) One can disparage town meetings: after all, only 10 to 20 percent of a town's people typically attend, and how can one solve complex issues in a single yearly meeting? But still, Vermonters treasure their town meetings. As indeed, quite uniquely in our time, they seem to treasure their own state with a special brand of quiet fervor.

NEW HAMPSHIRE

Majestic Disappointment

NEW HAMPSHIRE! The words evoke the majesty of Mount Washington and the Presidential Range, lovely Chocorua, the Grand Monadnock. They speak of rivers running headstrong and clean over their rock-strewn beds, of deep pine forests, of the radiance of a clear October day when the red maples and yellow birches, framed in evergreen, create a scene of such loveliness that one would like to make time stop and live forever in the perfection of the moment. Since earliest childhood days, those magical words have also meant for one of us a lake clear and deep, ringed by mountains, and a bright cottage by the water that will always be more home than any other place on earth.

The granite character of New Hampshire—and by inference, the New Hampshireman—is legendary. As Daniel Webster wrote, "Up in the mountains of New Hampshire, God Almighty has hung out a sign to show that there He makes men." But perhaps Webster was a little carried away by his own New Hampshire birth when he penned those lines. For it can be argued that Ralph Waldo Emerson was far more correct when he remarked that "the God who made New Hampshire taunted the lofty mountains with little men." The judgment cannot, of course, be extended to all of the state's leaders, past and present. But compared to most of the other 13 original states, New Hampshire offers a strikingly undistinguished history and tradition. One reads and rereads the state's history in search of great leaders and finds embarrassingly few; one looks for an important tradition in literature, the arts, or public policy and finds practically none; one tries to detect a sense of historic mission and is disappointed again.

Consider these New Hampshire phenomena:

In this state of professed granite character, the chief pillars of state government have been sin taxes: the take on "booze and butts" sold at discount prices to out-of-staters and the nation's first modern-day state-run sweepstakes lottery. Collectively, New Hampshire's tax structure adds up to a tawdry effort (1) to fleece visitors to pay for internal functions, and (2) to trick the state's citizens into thinking they have a good deal because New Hampshire stands alone in having no broad-based state tax (sales or income). As a result, local property taxes are at an almost confiscatory level, and a poor New Hampshire citizen pays twice as high a percentage of his total income in taxes as does a rich one. Mediocre public services are another result of the meager tax base. On a per capita basis, counting the expenditures of both state and local governments, New Hampshire spends less than any other New England state on local schools, has no state-supported junior colleges, and must charge inordinately high tuitions for attending the University of New Hampshire. Public kindergartens, vocational education, and special education classes for the retarded and the handicapped lag far beind those of the remainder of the region. Welfare spending is also low.

The mediocre character of public life in modern New Hampshire is rooted in the state's geophysical and historical backgrounds and the state's unusual ethnic composition. The granite-strewn land was endowed with a thin soil —no match for Vermont's fertile valleys or the plentiful harvest to be taken from the sea along Maine's coast. Agriculture was a losing battle so New Hampshire became an early recruit to the Industrial Revolution as one after another mill sprang up beside the rivers racing down their tight little valleys. The great Amoskeag Mill at Manchester was to become by the early 1920s the world's largest textile manufacturing plant. (Most of this erstwhile colossus of the textile world, once filled with thousands of workers and 700,000 spindles and 23,000 looms, still stands beside the Merrimack River today, a ghostly reminder of past industrial glory in New Hampshire's largest city.) But the factory culture of New Hampshire's cities was also marked by child labor, meager wages, and ferocious opposition to unions by the mill owners.

At first displaced Yankees from the farms provided the manpower for the mills, but soon that labor source became too scarce—or as the mill owners saw it, too high priced—and thousands upon thousands of foreign workers, principally French-Canadians, were imported. As a result, New Hampshire has northern New England's largest concentration of non–Anglo Saxon people. Their descendants still constitute distinct population groups that play a vital role in New Hampshire public life. The Irish, Poles, Scandinavians, Italians, and other immigrant groups managed by sheer perseverance to carve out a comfortable niche for themselves in the Puritan environment. But the French-Canadians, a close-knit inward-looking people who learned to hate the English and their tax in Canada, did not assimilate. Even today this largest concentration of French-Canadians in the United States is still clannish (though less so in recent years), and their resentment of anyone who seeks by taxation to take away from their meager, hard-earned incomes exerts a powerful, conservative influence on New Hampshire politics.

New Hampshire's colonial history also generated among the people a deep suspicion of government. The original grantee to the territory was a London merchant, Captain John Mason, who in 1629 named the colony New Hampshire in honor of the English countryside of Hampshire where he had lived. Interested in establishing a semifeudal domain based on the fur trade, Mason issued a welter of land grants with confusing and overlapping boundaries that caused land claims and litigation clear down to 1787. Mason's land grants were one reason New Hampshire filled so slowly with population that a strong New Hampshire society did not develop until the mid-1700s. New Hampshiremen did, however, serve long and with distinction in the American Revolution—a "fighting" tradition (the state motto is "Live Free or Die") that has recurred in every war the nation has since faced.

What New Hampshire has lacked has been outstanding native leaders.

There were some "middling-great" New Hampshire men in the early days of the republic. But the modern era has scarcely any names to match Maine's Edmund Muskie or Vermont's George Aiken. New Hampshire does claim great men, but they have had to leave New Hampshire to make their success. The most illustrious native son of New Hampshire was Daniel Webster, the great orator and legislative craftsman who contributed greatly to solidifying American nationalism. Yet the fact is that after two terms in Congress, early in his life, New Hampshire refused to reelect Webster, and he moved to Massachusetts, which elected him to his great career in the United States Senate. Of New Hampshire's only president, Franklin Pierce, it is enough to say that his memory is kept alive by a society whose motto is "To rescue him from the obscurity he so richly deserves."

One looks to the era since the Civil War for great New Hampshire leaders and again finds few. The Republican party came to rule supreme, and one can divide its leaders into three general groups: those of the Gilded Age, so corrupt that they virtually sold New Hampshire to the railroad interests; a group of the reformers from the 1910s onward who cleaned up the worst of the corruption, enacted some progressive laws, but failed to grace the national scene with figures of exceptional stature; and finally the snarling conservatives and the radical "New Right" obsessed with Communist witch-hunting and fighting progressive taxation as though it were a plague.

Underlying New Hampshire's dreary public performance—and cited by many as a major reason for it—has been the dominant statewide newspaper, the *Manchester Union Leader*. It was acquired at the end of World War II by William Loeb, an extremist publisher who never became a resident of New Hampshire (his legal domicile was in Nevada, his home in Pride's Crossing, Massachusetts). But his diatribes frightened many decent people from speaking their minds or entering public life at all. Loeb's poison pen wrote of John F. Kennedy as "the Number One Threat to America," Eleanor Roosevelt as "Ellie and her belly-crawling liberal friends," Henry Kissinger as "Kissinger the Kike?; Tool of the Communist Conspiracy." He called Gerald Ford "a Jerk" and once suggested, "Shoot Jane Fonda."

Yet for New Hampshire the saddest fact of Loeb's power was that it need not have happened at all. The paper had belonged to Frank Knox, Franklin Roosevelt's wartime secretary of the Navy, who died in 1944. When Knox's family decided to sell the paper after the war, a group of New Hampshire leaders wanted to buy it; but in one of the most fateful failures of indigenous leadership in any state's history, New Hampshire business leaders refused to provide the necessary financial backing. The paper went to outsider Loeb.

The *Union Leader*'s influence over elections began to dwindle in the late 1970s. The most symbolic event was the 1978 defeat of Loeb's handpicked governor, Meldrim Thomson, Jr., whose tumultuous six years in office— marked by political flag lowerings and pillorying of dissenting bureaucrats— were a cross between the macabre and the surreal. The governor who followed Thomson, Democrat Hugh Gallen, was a modern Democrat who made a real contribution by lowering the political decibel level and starting to return reasoned discourse to New Hampshire's public life. In September 1981, Loeb died, willing all the *Union Leader*'s voting stock to his wife, Nackey Scripps Loeb, to be transferred at her death to nine present or former employees, the youngest of whom was in his 30s. Mrs. Loeb maintained the same conservative editorial policies, but toned down the paper's personal invective because "it makes a woman shrill and ugly to try to do the same thing."

The last gubernatorial candidate Loeb endorsed before his death did not get the Republican nomination, and many New Hampshirites pondered whether influence was moving to the state's fine smaller dailies, including the *Concord Monitor*, published in the state's pleasing capital city. But as afternoon papers, they were not in a position to compete with the *Union Leader*. New Hampshirites pondered whether the growing circulation of the *Boston Globe* or a new degree of dynamism shown by television station WMUR might change the tone of political discourse in the state. Candidates, seeking undistorted exposure to the voters, were increasingly paying the high bill for time on Boston television stations that reach heavily populated southern New Hampshire.

The 1982 elections, however, indicated that while New Hampshirites might not elect the *Union Leader* preferred candidate, they were still unwilling to admit that the Granite State's revenue base was inadequate. State budget crises had become so severe that in 1981 the National Guard had to be called in to provide basic services at the state mental hospitals and youth corrections institution when 80 percent of the state employees called in sick to protest meager wage increases. The squeeze worsened into 1982, compounded by the Reagan administration's cuts in federal funds. Rating services downgraded the state's bonds twice in nine months. Localities complained bitterly after the state dumped millions of previously state-funded functions into their laps. So Governor Gallen, seeking reelection, courageously reversed his prior position and refused to follow the path of all recent gubernatorial candidates—Democrat or Republican—of "taking the pledge" of no broad-based taxes. For that apostasy, New Hampshirites threw Gallen, an otherwise popular governor, out of office. The winner, Republican John H. Sununu, a Tufts University engineering professor, promised to attract new industry and somehow balance the state budget without new taxes.

Perhaps no situation better illustrated New Hampshire's political nature than the protracted controversy over the plans of Public Service Company of New Hampshire to build a nuclear power plant at Seabrook on the state's lovely but brief (18 mile) window to the sea. The Clamshell Alliance, a New England–wide environmental coalition, tried years of law suits, civil disobedience, and even damaging of property to arouse public alarm about the dangers of nuclear power and the cause of seacoast preservation. But the issue was a great bore to most New Hampshirites until it turned fiscal—when the utility, plagued by massive cost overruns, got the state to let it bill electric consumers for "construction work in progress." This expense became such a cardinal issue that it figured heavily in Thomson's 1978 defeat (he had fronted for the utility and nuclear power all along). But as soon as the New Hampshire legislature outlawed the charges and Public Service sold part interest in

Seabrook to a consortium of 27 other power companies, public interest faded until other financial concerns arose.

The Perverse Primary

Every four years New Hampshire emerges from the shadows to command national attention in the presidential sweepstakes. In come the candidates and their entourages, the pollsters, and newspaper and television correspondents for the "first-in-the-nation" presidential primary. A kind of national legend has developed about the hardy Yankees of the north country giving the country down-to-earth advice on the best next man to sit in the White House. And the primary's role must be acknowledged: sometimes New Hampshire voters do provide an early warning to the nation about the personal or electoral weaknesses of a prospective candidate, or the potential of some new movement in national politics. Rarely is a man elected president who failed to win the New Hampshire primary.

Yet making New Hampshire a weathervane of the national pulse, as the national media is wont, is a risky business. Why should the country give particular credence to the counsel of the state that permitted America's most bizarre and self-centered political environment to flourish? Nor, ethnically, is New Hampshire at all representative of the country at large—if for no other reason than because of the extraordinarily high percentage of French-Canadians and small percentages of blacks and Hispanics.

By the 1980s the Granite State primary was, in fact, no longer the very first event of the presidential election year; well-publicized caucuses in Iowa and a primary in Puerto Rico preceded it. Yet it appeared that New Hampshire would continue to carry unusual weight as the earliest regular state primary. The state, indeed, had a law automatically setting its primary date a week before *any* other state's.

The briefest glimpse back over the years confirms the significant impact of the New Hampshire contest. In 1952, President Harry Truman withdrew only three weeks after Estes Kefauver defeated him in New Hampshire; the same year, Dwight D. Eisenhower's 50 percent vote, compared to only 39 percent for Senator Robert A. Taft, proved what would become the former general's legendary vote-getting power. In 1964, Barry Goldwater's later general-election fate was prepared by his own ill-advised campaign statements and by the vivid campaign that Nelson Rockefeller ran against him in New Hampshire.

In 1968, New Hampshire paved the way for Richard Nixon's political comeback and on the Democratic side proved fatal to President Lyndon Johnson's reelection campaign as LBJ, following a blitz by the student anti-war activists supporting Minnesota Senator Eugene McCarthy, received an embarrassingly low 49 percent of the vote. In 1972, after front-runner Edmund Muskie's aides and the press announced that the Maine senator would have "lost" in New Hampshire if he had failed to receive 50 percent of the vote,

Muskie "lost" by garnering only 47 percent of the preference vote, compared to 38 percent for George McGovern, his nearest rival and the eventual Democratic nominee.

In 1976 President Gerald Ford was able to beat Ronald Reagan in New Hampshire—but by such a narrow margin that Reagan received the momentum he needed to win several later primaries and shatter the incumbent's natural command of party allegiance. Ex-Georgia Governor Jimmy Carter, the same year, seemed to come out of nowhere to win a plurality over the other contenders—a victory of only a few thousand votes, but enough to put Carter on the covers of *Newsweek* and *Time* and propel him toward the Democratic nomination. And in 1980, the Granite State primary outcomes clearly positioned Ronald Reagan and Jimmy Carter as the men to beat in their own party's nomination contests. One result, as Dom Bonafede wrote in *National Journal,* was to reduce "Sen. Edward M. Kennedy to a pitiful figure wandering aimlessly on the campaign trail in search of an issue."

The Bright Economy . . . and Saving Natural New Hampshire

New Hampshire still enjoys a robust tourist economy—out-of-staters coming to enjoy the picturesque Monadnock region in the southwest corner, to visit old Portsmouth with its exquisitely preserved Strawbery Banke historic area, its colorful harbor and specialty shops, its restaurants and famed Theatre by the Sea, to spend vacations beside the sparkling waters of Winnipesaukee, Newfound, Squam, and other gems of the Lakes District, or to head—for hiking or skiing—into the heart of the White Mountains with their lovely Sandwich Range and dramatic Presidential Range. Westerners sometimes belittle Eastern mountains, but mighty Washington, at 6,288 feet Northeast America's highest peak, has fiercely arctic weather on its upper slopes and on April 12, 1934, registered the strongest wind ever recorded by man: 231 miles an hour. Far to the north, centered around the rough little city of Berlin, are New Hampshire's chief timber lands.

Tourism and lumber, however, have little to do with New Hampshire's spectacular economic growth since the '50s. Population increase, in the doldrums since the Civil War, heated up to a phenomenal 22 percent between 1960 and 1970 and 25 percent in the '70s. Many of the immigrants were young folk, just starting their productive work years. The gross state product jumped from $1.6 billion in 1960 to $7.8 billion in 1979. The only depression was in the unemployment rate—often far below New England averages. An economic transformation from textiles and shoes to high technology explained this phenomenal good luck. The state's "Golden Triangle" from Manchester to Nashua to Portsmouth joined Massachusetts' Route 128 "Golden Horseshoe" as the industrial growth center of New England. New Hampshire attracted (some would say pirated) dozens of large and small Route 128 companies in the past two decades. Some of the growth was inevitable spillover, but New Hampshire leaders claimed that their low tax, low spending, anti-union, pro-business climate complete with gimmicks such as state-guaranteed loans had a lot to do with it. The growth rate slowed by the early '80s, after Massachusetts tried harder to keep industry in the state and other New England states began recruiting business more aggressively. But the high-tech base was still the envy of many other states. Peterborough, a southern New Hampshire town of 5,000 people 25 miles from any major highway, had become a center of high-technology magazine publishing and mail order industries.

All of the growth, however, exacted a heavy price. A narrow band of territory in southmost New Hampshire—an hour's drive or less from Boston—absorbed four-fifths of the state's population increase and become one huge suburb of new subdivisions, shopping centers, industries, and garish strip development. Once-placid New England towns such as Salem and Exeter became plastered with McDonald's, Burger Kings, Pizza Huts, flashing neon, auto dealerships, and forests of signs. "I drive along some of the roads in southern New Hampshire and I can't see the signs for the signs," Governor Gallen said in 1980. "The growth will destroy our quality of life if we don't do something about it."

Growth controls were hotly debated at New Hampshire town meetings and planning boards in the late 1970s, and some communities, despite legal obstacles, tried to put a lid on new homes and factories.

The growth issue abated in the slowdown of the early 1980s, but if another boom should occur, the prevailing ethos has remained strongly in favor of total town and city "home rule" and against the kind of state guidance that has benefited neighboring Vermont so greatly. Statewide, the scorecard of the early '80s showed no land use regulatory policy, no flood plain control legislation, no regulation of wilderness areas, and an open season for billboard interests. Dedicated environmental groups, such as the Society for the Protection of New Hampshire Forests, have been battling gallantly for decades to stop the loss of natural New Hampshire. There was occasional progress, impressive on some fronts, including cleaned up rivers and lakes and public acquisition of parcels of precious lands. Yet viewing the overall record, one could only read with bittersweet apprehension the quotation from Thoreau, so often cited by the state's conservationists:

> I long for wilderness . . . woods where the woodthrush forever sings, where the hours are early morning ones, and there is dew on the grass, and the day is forever unproven . . . a New Hampshire everlasting and unfallen.

MAINE

The Tides Quicken

THE STATE OF MAINE, set beside the "Down East" tides on America's northeastern extremity, is America's first place to greet the rays of the rising sun each day, most months of the year on the tip of that mighty granite monarch, Mt. Katahdin. So great is the United States' territorial reach that it will be another six hours before the sun filters through Pacific skies to Hawaii, a quarter of the way around the globe.

Maine offers other wondrous characteristics, natural and human. Few shorelines of the world have been more written about or painted than the Maine coast with its quaint, historic fishing and vacation towns hugging the granite-legged shoreline and a galaxy of 2,000 odd islands—tips of the preglacial mountains that were the closest to the sea. This may be the world's most irregular, rugged coastline. As the crow flies, the distance from Kittery, on the New Hampshire border, to Eastport, beside New Brunswick, is only 228 miles. But if one were to follow each bay and cove and inlet, one would see a shoreline of more than 3,500 miles. From York Village to Old Orchard Beach to island-studded Casco Bay beside Portland, from Boothbay Harbor to Rockport and Camden and Penobscot Bay, from Seale Harbor to Bar Harbor clear all the way eastward to Campobello Island, there is a beauty and romance to Maine's coast practically no other shoreline of America can equal.

A kind of continental cul-de-sac, Maine is the only one of the 48 coterminus states that borders on only one other (New Hampshire). By New England standards, Maine is a fantastically large—and diverse—state. Put together, the other five states of the region are only a shade larger, in total area, than Maine's 33,215 square miles. By road, the distance from New York City to Kittery is 268 miles, but from Kittery north to Aroostook County near the Canadian border, the distance is a full 400 miles.

Until the advent of modern transportation, Maine seemed to exist in splendid isolation. Aroostook County covers 22 percent of Maine's land area and is larger than Connecticut and Rhode Island combined. Aroostook was Maine's—and New England's—last frontier; people from southern Maine still say that Aroostook is like a totally different state, as representative of the rest of Maine or New England as an Alaskan wilderness would be if appended to Ohio or Indiana. Aroostook is also home of the Maine potato, which prospers in the red glacial soil, growing free of parasites and diseases because of the cold deep winters and short summers.* Despite its potato reputation, only a seventh of Aroostook is farmed. The rest is forest and wilderness, which brings us to the dominant feature of the state. Ninety percent of Maine's land surface is covered by woods, and to this day, some 50 to 60 percent of Maine consists of "wild lands," or "unorganized territories" largely outside the jurisdiction of any municipal government and mostly owned by huge paper companies, which are semi-sovereignties within the great sovereignty of Maine. Close to 150,000 acres are controlled by the Penobscot Indians, who along with Maine's other tribe, the Passamaquoddys, were awarded $81.5 million in government monies to purchase up to 300,000 acres. The Indians had laid claim to nearly two-thirds of Maine.

The only section of the state feeling hard-to-handle population pressures is York County, on the state's southernmost flank. This is the true end of East Coast megalopolis, a county that rapid rail commuter service could put within 45 minutes of Boston. Maine has only one city that makes a pass at being a metropolis. It is Portland (61,572), New England's most important financial, trade, and cultural center north of Boston. It is a delightful little city that has attracted young professionals from across America, rebuilt its main commercial artery (Congress Street) into one of the country's most attractive, started to refurbish its waterfront and under-utilized port facilities, and developed hundreds of small, charming restaurants and shops.

Until the last few decades, the great majority of Maine people lived in isolated small towns having scant contact with the outside world. Just as in part of Appalachia and the Ozarks, clear representations of Elizabethan English could be heard in places such as Washington County's Beals Island. To this day hundreds of thousands still suffer from peculiar types of isolation. Rural postal service has deteriorated; phone rates are high, with toll charges even for calls from town to town within a single county. There is an appalling dearth of public transportation. While the small town has its appeal, Maine residents have long suffered from inadequate medical facilities, provincial schools, and lack of contact with the outside world. Maine's location at the "end of the line" of railroad and highway building has resulted in relatively little industrial development and a poverty kept out of sight by the backwoods and the state's self-reliant culture.

Out of all this isolation developed the fabled Down Easter character, so devoid of the hail-fellow-well-met exuberance of many Americans. Little affection is shown unless there's a disaster; then if one's house burned down or his traps stolen or broken in a storm, Maine's neighbors are there to help —and one would never have reason to expect otherwise. This defensive

---

*The economic future of Maine's white, round potato has been debated for some years. Competition is stiff from the western russet, which gourmets say tastes better baked and is longer and easier to make into french fries. Growing conditions vary wildly, and the number of farmers willing to undertake the millionaire-vs.-bankruptcy gamble has declined in recent years. Some growers and brokers believe, however, that the development of a new potato and the rising cost of transportation from western states will give Maine potatoes a significant advantage in the huge Boston-to-Washington market.

character developed, wrote Louise Dickinson Rich in *State O'Maine*, because ever since they came to the Maine coast, Down Easters "have necessarily been on guard against unexpected attacks from Indians, the weather, the wrath of God, and smooth-talking, out-of-state salesmen."

That very wariness and disinclination to commit oneself was complemented by the character attributes of Maine's principal "ethnic" group, the French-Canadians, who were drawn to Maine first as lumberjacks and then to man the low-wage textile mills in the last half of the 19th century. The French (some now call themselves Franco-Americans) have felt themselves linguistically and religiously separate from the rest of Maine, though the most educated of recent generations have entered the mainstream of the state's life. Television and intermarriage also are breaking down some of their isolation.

Maine was once known for its rock-ribbed, change-me-not attitudes, but since the 1960s its politics have been marked by lively public debate and unusual levels of participation in local government. Maine has always had a minority of well-traveled and literate professionals (including Buckminster Fuller, the Fords of auto fame, the Rockefellers, the late Rachel Carson, E.B. White) for whom Maine has been only a window on a wider world. But in recent years, as environmental issues became more and more important, people who used to vacation in Maine have found themselves more drawn into its public life. Even more important on the permanent Maine scene than the celebrities have been the many artists, writers, physicians, business executives, intellectuals, and other sensitive people who began to question the urban civilization of modern America in the years following World War II and turned Down East to find a safe harbor, a touchstone with a more basic civilization they felt missing in the heart of megalopolis.

Maine's early political development was dominated by the difficulty of establishing itself. The early history of what is now Maine is one of constant discovery and rediscovery, starting most probably with the Viking expeditions in the early years of the 11th century, skipping almost 400 years to the exploration of the coastline by England's John Cabot and his sons in 1496, permanent English settlements in the 1620s, and a long unhappy status as a colony of Massachusetts. Early Maine was a relatively classless frontier where, as the authors of the WPA guide of Maine noted, "there was little law or respect for law" and "rum was the common beverage, and spirits were consumed on all occasions," a setting strikingly similar to old-time, and not-so-old-time Appalachia. The relationship with Massachusetts never worked very well since the seat of government and protective troops were so distant, but Maine did gain from Massachusetts an early public school system and basic respect for learning, a benefit Appalachia never had. The spread of Congregationalism and the Puritan movement also supplied Maine with some stern laws—prosecution of religious "heresy," limited suffrage, and hidebound conventional morality—plus the abolitionist movement and virulent anti-Roman Catholicism.

Until the early 1950s, Maine's political reputation was as the state second only to Vermont in Republicanism. For a full century, a Republican "machine" dominated by banks, railroads, lumber, and manufacturing interests had controlled the state, and Democrats won only a few isolated races. During the last half of the 19th century, the Republicans sent to Washington three men of immense national stature: Hannibal Hamlin, who left the Democratic party over the slavery issue; James Blaine, who was Secretary of State under Presidents Garfield and Harrison and fathered the Pan-American Union; and Thomas B. Reed, a master of parliamentary law who raised the office of speaker of the House, which he occupied for three terms, to a position second only to that of the president of the United States. No Maine Republican, from Reed's departure to this day, has had an impact on the national scene comparable to that of the giants of the last century. History will, however, remember Margaret Chase Smith as the senator who stood up at the height of the McCarthy anti-Communist hysteria and delivered her "declaration of conscience" in which she assailed "certain elements of the Republican party" for "selfish, political exploitation of fear, bigotry, ignorance and intolerance." The remarks came at a time when many illustrious Democratic Senate liberals were fearfully maintaining silence on McCarthy.

Today Maine is one of the nation's most intensely competitive states in partisan politics. But that does not mean that Maine voters consider party an affiliation particularly important. The candidates who win Maine elections, according to John Day, Washington correspondent for the *Bangor Daily News*, are those who "sell themselves as unaligned." The Democratic renaissance started in Maine in the early 1950s when the Republican "machine" began to lose steam. But the real credit goes to Edmund S. Muskie, lawyer and son of a Polish-born tailor named Stephen Marciszewski. Muskie was a party builder in Maine, just as Hubert Humphrey was in Minnesota, George McGovern in South Dakota, and G. Mennen Williams in Michigan. First elected to the state legislature in 1947, he went on to become governor, U.S. senator, unsuccessful candidate for vice president (1968) and president (1972), and finally Secretary of State during Jimmy Carter's last year as president. Among Muskie's notable accomplishments: raising environmental air- and water-pollution issues long before they were fashionable (though not, we must note, when they conflicted with economic development in Maine); mastering the dull but important issues of revenue sharing and the complex interrelationships of the layers of government within the U.S. system; eloquent opposition to the Vietnam War; and remaining open enough to new ideas that in the 1970s he helped establish the congressional budget process and chaired the Senate Budget Committee, from which he opposed new Democratic liberal spending programs that, he said, would "break" the budget. Some of Muskie's character traits—aloofness, a towering temper and a desire to study issues too long, a lack of burning ambition—probably kept him from becoming president as much as the systematic sabotage of the Nixon campaigners. He was a superb senator.

Senator William S. Cohen, the state's star Republican, began his career as mayor of Bangor and undertook a 500-mile trek across the Second Congressional District to win election to Congress in 1972. Cohen established a reputation in Washington for his eloquence and as a member of the House Judiciary Committee, supporting the impeachment of Richard Nixon. In the late 1970s, Cohen and Republican Congresswoman Olympia Snowe broke with Maine political tradition to oppose the Dickey-Lincoln project, which would construct a hydro-electric complex on the St. John River. At one time, such public works projects were welcomed by all Maine residents, but the political momentum appeared to have swung toward the environmentalists, who noted the river's uniqueness as the longest wilderness river in the Northeast with some of the best white-water canoeing.

A Down East taciturnity has marked many recent Maine governors. But not the ebullient James B. Longley, the self-made insurance millionaire who came out of the proverbial political "nowhere" to win election in 1974 as the first independent governor of any state since William Langer in North Dakota 38 years before. How did he do it? Because both major parties had lackluster nominees, because it was the year of Watergate and voters were turned off to establishment politicians, and because Longley anticipated the tax revolt of the latter '70s. He had been chairman of a state government efficiency survey; he charged not enough of its recommendations were enacted and won election with a whimsical assurance that he could bring Maine folk efficient state government, lower taxes, and adequate if not improved state services at the same time. The reality of Longley's term in office was standard fiscal conservatism, a strong dose of anti-intellectualism, and holding up settlement claims by the Penobscot and Passamaquoddy Indians. He retired in 1979 and died a year later of cancer; his shortcomings notwithstanding, one remembers him with affection for his beguiling innocence. Longley's successor was a Kennedy-style Democrat, Joseph Brennan.

The Low-Wage, Hard Work State and the Debate on Maine's Future

In the early 1980s, after several generations of high unemployment, low incomes, and loss of talented youth, Down Easters were amazed to discover that even during a severe recession the state's unemployment rate was lower than the national average. As one examined the map of Maine, however, it was clear that the economic improvement was largely in the state's southern portion into which the Massachusetts high-technology boom had spread. Shipbuilding also picked up when the Portland-based Bath Iron Works combined Japanese industrial technology, the Yankee work ethic, and large, controversial doses of city and state bond monies to achieve its greatest levels of production and employment since World War II.

Large sections of Maine and its population remained dependent on low-wage, high-polluting industries: leather (shoes), paper, lumber and wood products, food processing and textiles. Tourism, often hailed as a "clean" alternative to industrial development, also paid low wages. Much Maine labor —clam digging and lumbering, for example—was hard and demanding. The per capita income remained only 80 percent of the national average. Tar paper shacks reminiscent of Appalachia could still be spotted all over the state, and more than half the housing starts were mobile homes.

Thus it was not surprising that Maine politicians from the Muskie era onward had made political capital out of the call for increased economic development. Over the years, much of the proposed Maine development became mired in controversy, however. One flamboyant entrepreneur set up potato and sugar beet plants, enlarged with federal loans, only to pollute the land and water so badly that fish died; Canadians built a temporary dam to keep the water from coming into their country. The oil industry was not totally foreign to Maine; Portland, although it cannot handle the new super-tankers, is already the third-largest oil port on the East Coast, after the Delaware Bay ports and New York. But furor over increased oil development on the exposed coast contributed significantly to the passage in 1970 of a law to make the spiller of oil absolutely liable for any cleanup costs and damage to fishermen or shorefront property owners. The environmental legislation of the early '70s also gave state government agencies veto power over any proposed industrial or residential project of more than 20 acres anywhere in the state and required municipalities to adopt subdivision and zoning controls for all areas within 250 feet of the coast or any "navigable" pond. But these laws have been unevenly applied, and because Maine never adopted a compre-hensive land use law stating where development *could* take place, private companies have cited the state's burdensome and expensive regulation process as a reason for not locating facilities in the state.

Many of Maine's young people, back-to-the-earthers, immigrants, academ-ics, and the strongly environmental *Maine Times,* contend that Maine can lead the way (in the words of the *Maine Times*'s John Cole) "from a high energy, centralized system to a low energy, decentralized system" based on cottage industries, self-sufficient agriculture, renewable energy sources, fewer roads, fewer big recreational developments, and community control of people's lives. To some degree this view has prevailed. By the late 1970s, there was mounting opposition to major hydro-electric public works projects such as Dickey-Lincoln and the Passamaquoddy tidal plant, which had first been proposed in 1919 (and was a favored project of Franklin D. Roosevelt). In 1980, Maine voters faced the most extreme anti-nuclear initiative ever to appear on an American ballot—one that would not just have forbidden future plants, but forced immediate closing of the one operating in the state. The initiative received a 59 percent negative vote statewide. But residents of the three counties surrounding the plant voted in favor of the turn-off, apparently convincing power company officials that further nuclear construction in Maine would not be worth the strong local opposition. A 1982 antinuke referendum also lost, but the vote was even closer. By the early '80s it also appeared that water pollution from sawmills and paper plants had lessened, not only because of state anti-pollution laws (some dating back to 1945), but because the high cost of oil had encouraged the paper companies to burn their waste products and save money. Environmentalists, who had promoted wood-burning stoves, suddenly found themselves worrying that the big paper companies had begun such extensive distribution of firewood that hardwood was being cut down in a one-time harvest.

We can happily report that the architecture of Maine's small towns, saved due to *lack* of economic activity, has been rediscovered by Down-easters and newcomers alike. But the social equation is not quite as bright. For all its appearances of stability, Maine is not immune from the social problems of broken families, alcoholism, drugs, unwanted pregnancy, and suicide that afflict the nation at large. Hidden, rural poverty only makes them worse. High technology may have started Maine on the road to a way of life that is both prosperous and environmentally undamaging, but as long as poverty persists in its vast northern reaches, the image of Maine as a place of stability and repose will continue to be challenged.

THE
GREAT LAKES
STATES

THE GREAT
LAKES STATES

0   50   100   150   200   250

MILES

ILLINOIS

I. Chicago: The Mighty Lakeside City

CHICAGO. CHICAGO. How can one adequately describe it? The heart of the heartland, or as a visiting Sarah Bernhardt said at the turn of the century, "the pulse of America," this lusty, brawny, beauty- and terror-filled metropolis remains the archetype of all our cities. It throbs with life and energy, it worships Mammon without qualm, it attracts and repels, it is perennially young yet perennially decaying. It is the one place on the continent where the exercise of power—raw, unfettered, physical, economic, and political power—has been brought to its apex. Chicago is the glory and damnation of America all rolled up into one. Not to know Chicago is not to know America.

Thus our story of Illinois must begin with this mighty lake city, for in its shadow every other aspect of Lincoln's prairie state slides toward afterthought. A native son, John Gunther, sets the stage:

> Being a Chicagoan born and bred I can recall much. . . . The icy wind screaming down snow-clogged boulevards; the sunny haunch of Lincoln Park near the yacht moorings in torrid summers; the angry whistles of angry traffic cops and the automobilelike horns of the Illinois Central suburban trains; the steady lift of bridges, bridges, bridges; holes, bumps and yawning pits in the streets; the marvelous smooth lift of the Palmolive Building and how the automobiles seem to butt each other forward like long streams of beetles; the tremendous heavy trains of the North Shore slipping like iron snakes through the quivering wooden suburban stations; the acrid smell from the stockyards when the wind blew that way, and the red flush of the steel mills in black skies—all this is easy to remember.

The feel of Chicago remains true to the Guntherian image, but some of the specifics are transformed. The stockyards, victims of decentralization of the packing-house business, are now an industrial park, no longer filled with thousands of animals awaiting in terror their moment of dissection. The Palmolive Building stands, but now overwhelmed in a great crush of higher buildings and its name, indignity of indignities, actually changed to the Playboy Building, symbol of the first (now passe) postwar breakthrough in sexual liberation. The North Shore line is gone, and one's eyes are easily diverted to the screaming jets landing and taking off in an incessant stream from O'Hare. More steel and machinery are still fabricated in the Chicago area than anywhere in the world, but worries have mounted about the decline in production of American steel, which is to the Chicago of broad shoulders what autos are to Detroit. Industrial jobs have hemorrhaged rapidly in Chicago, and indeed throughout the entire Midwest region, of which it has long been the economic capital.

By the 1980 Census, Chicago, with 3,005,072 people, was close to losing its second-city status to Los Angeles. Chicago had lost some 100,000 people a decade from the 1940s through the 1960s, but during the 1970s the population dropped 364,285 or a troubling 10.8 percent. The mighty white ethnic bastion was rapidly becoming a black and Hispanic city.

We sensed a deep uncertainty among Chicagoans about the city's position in the country and its economic future. Even while Chicago remained the nation's second most populous city, many people would debate whether it was *really* the nation's second most important city or whether that title properly belonged to Los Angeles or Washington, D.C. Upon the death of the great political boss and leader Richard Daley questions rose about the city's fiscal stability, and the city's political machine lost some of its gritty glamor. The nation's new and growing industries, especially in high-technology, seemed to be developing in other cities in other regions. Illinois, with a large share of its work force in manufacturing, was stung deeply by the recession of the early '80s, registering one of the nation's highest unemployment rates. Belatedly, Chicago and Illinois business leaders began shedding their smugness and complacency, beginning an aggressive search for the initiatives demanded by the ferociously competitive national/international economies of the 1980s and '90s.

They surely had a strong base on which to work. Few American metropolitan areas can match the diversity of "Chicagoland" economy, solidly based in finance and transportation as well as manufacturing. By one estimate of the '70s, the Chicago area was contributing 4.6 percent of the gross national product with just 3.2 percent of the U.S. population. The city and its environs are headquarters for 43 of the 500 largest industrials listed by *Fortune*, and a favorite branch office location. Food processing remains a multibillion-dollar business. Chicago is also the nation's biggest wholesaling center, its traditional mail order headquarters (Sears and Montgomery Ward), and through its Board of Trade and Mercantile Exchange, the world's busiest commodity market and trader in livestock futures. Few cities compete with it as a convention center. Chicago is one of the five largest financial centers of the U.S.A.; of course it has the Federal Reserve Bank for its region. The city has long been the world's greatest railhead. O'Hare Airport is the busiest commercial field in the world. Chicago also boasts having a "Fourth Seacoast" because of its capacity for global freight shipments through the St. Lawrence Seaway; the city is the busiest Great Lakes port and eighth-largest in the nation, even though the business on the Seaway has not lived up to early expectations.

But Chicago is more than just a raw interchange of man and machine. Behind the headlines about colorful politics and declining manufacturing, Chicago has all the elements of a thinking, modern city. The place itself is a jewel, with magnificent architecture and a beautiful and unspoiled shoreline, off which white sails sparkle on a summer day. It has fine universities, most notably the University of Chicago, bastion of free market economic theory in modern America and, a generation ago, the place where Dr. Enrico Fermi accomplished the first sustained controlled production of atomic energy in human history. The University of Chicago Press terms itself the largest academic press in the nation, and there are also many commercial publishing and printing houses. Even in decline, the Chicago story makes best-selling fiction, as proven by Saul Bellow's *The Dean's December,* and Eugene Kennedy's fictionalized account of Mayor Jane Byrne, *The Queen Bee.* More than 75 movies have used Chicago as a location since 1975. Its symphony is one of the nation's best. ABC News has anchored part of its domestic news operation in this capital of the heartland, which is also the base of broadcaster Phil Donahue. Clearly, if Chicago cannot lay clear claim to the title of second city, it is still far more than a regional capital.

The Architectural Lodestone of Chicago

Power, or as it is often said here, "clout"—a peculiarly brutal, raw kind of power—is the essence of Chicago. It springs first to meet the eye, for this city of the Big Shoulders has good reason to regard itself as the capital of modern architecture. The gigantic structures of steel and glass and concrete that thrust at the Chicago skyline represent a symphony of might and mass—and excellence—with which few world cities can compete.

The first great era of Chicago architecture began when Chicago rebounded from its disastrous Great Fire of 1871 to give birth to the skyscraper. Here the masters of the Chicago School built classic high buildings that rejected Victorian gingerbreadism in favor of a simplicity in which "form follows function." Many relics of that age still stand, making the Loop (Chicago's mercantile and financial center, named after the elevated tracks that encircle it) a kind of outdoor architectural museum. A second golden era was inaugurated in the 1950s under the guiding genius of the late Ludwig Mies van der Rohe, who fled Hitler's Germany, settled in Chicago, and became an acknowledged dean of world architecture. Mies designed modern classics of structural clarity, stripped of adornment; one of the finest examples is his four "glass house" apartment towers on Lake Shore Drive, their black-coated metal and shimmering glass mirroring the clouds and the lakefront. Another prime example of the Miesian "skin and bones" principle is the 1966 Chicago Civic Center, designed by Jacques Brownson, a pupil of Mies who became a master himself. The steel skeleton is close to being one with the deep-bronze alloy of the exterior. To grace the plaza before the center, Pablo Picasso designed a great five-story-high steel sculpture. (The abstract Picasso design triggered great controversy among those who saw in it everything from Picasso's dog to a baboon to a great dragon fly; Picasso settled the dispute by saying it was a woman's head.)

Mies and his school designed dozens of other buildings that transformed the Chicago skyline—among them the Time-Life Building with tinted mirrored glass that reflects a bright orange to the outside world; the twin tubelike towers of Marina City on the Chicago River front; and the First National Bank Building, soaring 844 feet over the Loop, sheathed in glistening white granite and shaped like a long, thin stick of butter that has begun to melt at the bottom. As one drives along Lake Shore Drive and glances inland, three of the world's tallest buildings loom into view. To the north, along the "magnificent mile" on North Michigan Avenue, stands the tapered design of the John Hancock Building, a 1,107-foot structure of such mass and height that it dwarfs all near it. Journalist/architectural critic W. M. Newman likened it to "some large horned animal, gazing serenely along the rim of the world." (He also described it as a symbol of the dangers of "giantism"—the "hard, impersonal power of overwhelming technology, the dwarfing of man, the dehumanizing of the city.") Just south of the Chicago River, Standard Oil of Indiana threw up its white marble headquarters, nine feet taller than "Big John," making it the fourth-highest building in the world. The accolade as the "most Chicagoan" building of them all, however, is left for the Sears Tower, at 100 stories and 1,454 feet the tallest in the world.

Sad to report, many of the historic structures of the late 1800s have fallen before the wrecker's ball as Chicago developers, in their incessant search for profit, tore down buildings of masters such as Louis Sullivan in favor of dull new office buildings and parking garages. Yet the architectural creativity of Chicago seems irrepressible. A Postmodernist school sprang up in the 1970s, rejecting the unadorned metal boxes of Mies' "International Style" as joyless, boring, and oppressive. Chicago's hottest architect by the early '80s was the German-born Helmut Jahn, whose bold designs included curved exterior walls, prismatic effects, bright colors, vast atriums, and some of the flavor of 1920s Art Deco. *Chicago Tribune* architectural critic Paul Gapp described Jahn's State of Illinois Center, a gigantic yet delicate wedge clad in variously transparent and opaque glass, as "the most visually startling building in the Loop since the first skyscraper went up in 1884."

Behind the glittering skyscrapers of downtown Chicago lies an exemplary "heritage of involvement" among Chicago's business, government, and civic group movers and shakers, determined to keep the Loop and its environs a vibrant center of Chicago area life and economy. From 1910 to World War II they worked to implement Daniel Burnham's "Monumental City Beautiful" plan, which led to such achievements as the lakefront belt of continuous parks and a green belt of forest preserves encircling the metropolitan area. Respecting planning and detecting incipient postwar deterioration of the city's great State Street retailing center, they banded together as the Chicago Central Area Committee to revitalize the city's central core through such projects as Near North Side renewal, development of Lincoln Park, the University of Illinois Chicago Circle Campus, and the federal office complex in the Loop. The monumental building and headquarters plans of such firms as Sears, Montgomery Ward, and Standard Oil came out of that same process. In the '70s, again fearing central core decline, the same class of leaders formulated a "Chicago 21" plan, intended to lead to some $15 billion of inner-core renewal, including thousands of residential units in Dearborn Park—a high-density new town to be built on abandoned rail yards directly south of the Loop. There it was, for example, that architect Bertrand Goldberg formulated imaginative plans for "River City," a complex of buildings up to 15 stories that would offer an extraordinarily wide variety of services needed by two wage-earner households. State Street was transformed from a traffic-clogged six-lane street into the world's largest shopping mall, with widened sidewalks and tree plantings.* Plans for a $2 billion to $3 billion residential-office-hotel development were announced for the "Streeterville" area, a prime site on the north bank of the Chicago River between Michigan Avenue and Lake Michigan. Finally, Chicago was struggling to launch a $1 billion North Loop redevelopment project on several blocks of vacant or underutilized land between State Street and the Chicago River. The goal was to build a web of shops, hotels, theaters, and rooftop parks that would create a lively atmosphere to entice some of the estimated 450,000 downtown workers not to desert the Loop by night.

The Machine and the Leaders

"Organization, not machine. Get that. Organization, not machine," Mayor Richard J. Daley insisted when the subject came to the Cook County Democratic organization. But this antique and high-powered juggernaut, enduring robust and active years after the atrophy of its counterparts in such cities as New York, Philadelphia, Kansas City, and Jersey City, was a political *machine* if ever there were one. And from his ascendance to power in 1955 until his death in 1976, Daley symbolized it as truly as any political boss in the annals of the American republic.

Chicago, said onetime alderman Leon M. Despres, "is governed by a firmly run, businesslike organization of about 35,000 persons who live off politics. . . . Indeed, it is really a business. It controls the mayoralty, 38 of the 50 members of the city council, the school board, the park board, the library board, the public housing authority, the transit authority, two-thirds of the county board, nearly all the county offices, many suburban governments, the judiciary." Governors, Members of Congress, and federal judges have owed their political lives to it—and upon occasions, even presidents.

Under this authoritarian, hierarchical organization, some 500 patronage jobs are allotted to each ward. Virtually every precinct captain has a city job; the public, in effect, subsidizes the system by salaries paid to patronage workers, who in turn are under tremendous pressures to contribute and work on

*Despite the emergence of almost 150 shopping centers in the Chicago area over the past 30 years, State Street maintained 100 percent occupancy and hundreds of millions in annual sales—at least until 1982, when major retail abandonments surfaced. For years, State Street has faced severe competition from the Magnificent Mile, a 14-block complex of high-fashion stores, luxury hotels, elegant restaurants, stylish theaters, and expensive condominiums along North Michigan Avenue. Even Marshall Field's opened a "branch store" in Water Tower Place, the 74-story showpiece of the district.

election day. For the ambitious Cook County Democrat, a seat in the U.S. House or the general assembly in Springfield, as juicy a political plum as each might appear, is but a stepping stone to higher (more lucrative) things at the local level. Ethnic and racial groups, according to their own ability to deliver votes, queue up for the rewards of power—Irish foremost, Poles and Jews, Italians, blacks. Adlai Stevenson III once called it "a feudal system that rewards mediocrity or worse, with jobs for the blind party faithful, special favors for business, and ineffectual civil service." But its power is so great that he, like his father before him, made his peace with it.

Richard Daley's heavy-set looks and jowls and sometimes awesome temper set the image of a strong-armed boss from the smoke-filled rooms. His malapropisms were easy to make fun of.*

But this was no hack politician. Daley had a thorough grasp of Chicago government; he was a master of finance; he was a keen judge of the level of performance and influence of thousands of Chicagoans in and out of government. When new power bases arose, Daley found ways to incorporate them —or if their holders declined his muscular embrace, to freeze them out. He was extremely hard working and strong willed, a man whose personal honesty was never seriously questioned. He succeeded in curbing the bolder thieves in his organization. Yet, despite all, this master of political weight balancing remained a product of and resident of the simple Irish neighborhood of Bridgeport. A good family man, Daley returned to his modest bungalow there almost every evening for dinner at home with his wife and children. Every day he attended Mass, though, as writer David Halberstam pointed out, his religion was pre-Ecumenical, pre-Pope John XXIII, where there was individual sin but little social sin. He could tolerate small and petty graft, excuse an occasional roaring drunk, but could not excuse adultery nor understand or tolerate a man who fathers a family and then deserts it.

One key to Daley's success was his dual roles: mayor of Chicago and chairman of the Cook County Democratic Central Committee. Holding those two jobs was a bit like being premier of the U.S.S.R. and first secretary of the Communist party at the same time. The vast power of the two offices permitted Daley, with his well-developed political skills, to become an authoritarian ruler of his city, a Buddha-like figure whose slightest word was law, whose machine could produce staggering election-day pluralities for its chosen candidates. Never was a potentially beneficial coalition overlooked. Daley perfected such a close working alliance with Chicago's big businesses that the central business district was superbly serviced in physical facilities and police

---

*Some of the more wondrous examples:

"I resent the insinuendos."—*Chicago Daily News,* May 15, 1965.

"Together we must rise to ever higher and higher platitudes."—*Newsweek,* March 13, 1967.

". . . for the enlightenment and edification and hallucination of the alderman from the 50th ward."—*Life,* February 8, 1960.

"They have vilified me, they have crucified me, yes they have even criticized me."—*Harper's,* August 1968.

protection even when many neighborhoods atrophied; in return, business provided Daley with business campaign contributions and a friendly media, at least until his last five years in office, when the press became critical. The machine's ties with organized labor were so close one could well say that in Chicago the Democratic party was not in the hip pocket of organized labor, but rather that labor was in the pocket of the Democratic party.

When this last of the powerful American machine mayors, an anachronism yet a dominating figure of his time, died at 74, a fitting epitaph came from Mike Royko, newspaper columnist, persistent critic, and biographer of His Honor in a book called *Boss:*

> In some ways, he was Chicago at its best—strong, hard-driving, working fever-ishly, pushing, building, driven by ambitions so big they seemed Texas-boastful. In other ways, he was this city at its worst—arrogant, crude, conniving, ruthless, suspicious, intolerant. He wasn't graceful, suave, witty or smooth. But then, this is not Paris or San Francisco. He was raucous, sentimental, hot-tempered, practical, simple, devious, big and powerful. This is, after all, Chicago.

In 1979, 26 months after Daley's death, Chicago voters handed the machine a stinging rebuke by rejecting its choice as Daley's successor, interim Mayor Michael Bilandic. Instead they chose Jane Byrne, a feisty, apparent independent who had in fact been a long-time Daley protégé and had broken with Bilandic (and been fired from her post as commissioner of consumer sales for the city) after she accused him of greasing fare increases for taxi companies. Byrne's campaign against Bilandic and what she called his "cabal of evil men" might well have failed had it not been for the great Chicago snowstorm of January 1979. Seven feet of snow inundated the city and garbage went uncollected for weeks. The Chicago transit system ground to a halt at many locations. Then the *Chicago Tribune* revealed that a machine stalwart had received two nonbid contracts totaling $90,000 to plan snow and ice removal from Chicago streets. An angry public turned out Bilandic and installed Byrne, who received an overwhelming 67 percent of the once closely controlled black vote.

Byrne's victory was not quite the revolution it first appeared. She did appoint a transition committee heavy with reformers and independents. But then she said her quarrel had not been with the machine per se but with the corrupt ends to which it was allegedly put under Bilandic. By these contradictory moves, Samuel Gove and Louis Masotti later noted in their book *After Daley,* "Byrne demonstrated her capacity to confuse and confound." The tough, angry style of Byrne's campaign carried over into her mayoralty. Many competent city administrators were fired. A mixture of incompetents and able replacements were appointed, yet regardless of their skill, many found themselves on the street if they showed anything short of total fealty to *her.* In two years Byrne ran through four police chiefs, three budget directors, five press secretaries. Political opponents were subjected to catlike attacks. Byrne did show, on occasion, an appealing side—moving, for example, for a few weeks into the bloody, vermin-packed Cabrini-Green public housing project, in an effort to get it cleaned up.

In a hotly contested 1983 mayoral primary, Byrne faced Richard M. Daley, the son of the late mayor who had overcome a Byrne-backed candidate to win election as chief Cook County prosecutor two years before, and Harold Washington, a Southside black congressman who had broken decisively with the Democratic machine that had given him his start in political life. Articulate and riding the tide of a fervid registration drive that had boosted black voter rolls by 150,000 in a single year, Washington emerged the surprise winner with 36.3 percent of the vote. Byrne was second with 33.5 percent while Daley, who turned out to be a lightweight compared to his late father, got 29.8 percent. Even though a split white vote helped explain Washington's victory, there was a feeling that Chicago politics would never be the same again.

Fiscal storm clouds gathered darkly over post-Daley Chicago. The city was faced by a series of crises all-too-familiar to other older American cities: school and transit systems deep in debt, public strikes, lowering of credit ratings. Chicago patronage-style administration swelled costs far beyond reason. The schools carried the extra burden of a system still largely segregated and cursed by gang outbreaks and debilitating cynicism; the transit unions, for purposes of political appeasement, had won by contract the highest wages of their kind in the U.S.A.

There was much good in school and transit systems alike. Through dedicated leadership, and against all odds, some schools pioneered in early childhood education and were turning out adequate-to-high achieving black graduates. The transit system carried 900,000 riders a day, including 80 percent of downtown Chicago's work force—one of the highest percentages in any city. Chicago has long boasted of having "the finest commuter railroad service in the world," including several rail lines to the suburbs and its elevated railway, a beloved clattertrap built at the turn of the century.*

By the 1980s, however, both schools and transit were in deep, deep trouble. Bedeviled by high labor costs and inefficiencies, the school system almost went bankrupt in 1980 and averted a closedown only through city and state loans and a $573 million bond issue of a newly created School Finance Authority. Afterward, its credit rating was nil and it faced huge annual deficits—and the grim fact that the political base was simply not at hand to save an unwieldy system serving an overwhelmingly black-Latino constituency. In transit, both the Chicago Transit Authority and 1973-vintage Regional Transit Authority were dogged by the destructive spiral of increased fares and decreased services on the one hand and ferocious political antagonisms between center-city and

---

*Stand beneath the El's girders as the trains roar overhead, their wheels screeching on the corners, "and you will swear you are back in the days of Studs Lonigan and Al Capone," Tom Huth noted appropriately in *Historic Preservation* magazine. Indeed, the historic preservationists helped lead the fight to prevent dismantling of the Loop El in favor of a centralized subway system.

suburban interests on the other. Added to that was the desperate need for state fiscal aid, which Chicago was finding it ever-more difficult to get as population drain depleted its clout in Springfield. (At one point Chicago had more than half Illinois' population and could get most of what it wanted from the state; by 1980 it had just 26 percent of Illinois' 11,418,461 people, compared to the suburbs' 36 percent and downstate's 38 percent.) Illinois' sectional rivalries are extraordinarily intense, as Abraham Lincoln learned in 1860 when he got 70 percent of the northern Illinois vote and only 20 percent downstate. Sometimes the city has been its own worst enemy—as in the 1981 transit fiscal crisis, when Mike Royko wrote a column suggesting Chicago secede to become a separate state to free itself of control from "downstate hayseeds and polyester-leisure suit suburbanites."

Even the new Cook County Democratic chief and former Daley stalwart, Alderman Edward Vrdolyak (pronounced ver-DOH-lee-ack), proclaimed to the city council: "The city that worked was for 20 years the city that juggled its books." Byrne sowed seeds of even more bitter harvest when she took a confrontational stance vis-à-vis state government and put the city's limited financial resources on the line to bail out the school and transit systems. A city once light on per capita debt was using up its debt capacity to cover immediate operating expenses. No one knew where the money would be found for the city's planned $3.3 billion capital program to maintain its streets, bridges, and water system. An influential banker said: "We're terribly concerned that Chicago is becoming an island, isolating itself from sources of state revenue."

For long years under Daley, and afterward, reformers worked to undermine the power of the Chicago machine. Oftentimes reform aldermen were elected—though never a majority, of course. In the '70s they started agitating against the patronage system; eventually they won a major federal court victory in a decision forbidding city and county officials from dismissing workers for refusing to help organization candidates in elections. But it took Harold Washington's 1983 victory, confirming the shift in Chicago's power base from the various white ethnic wards to the black wards of the South and West sides, to topple finally *l'ancien régime.* Did that mean the organization was dead for good? Not necessarily, said Chicago political historian Milton Racove. The machine, he noted, was "wounded, but the machine transcends things. They had to live with Byrne; they'll live with Harold Washington. They'd live with Hitler if they had to."

What, then, would become of those other ancient machine mainstays: unadulterated vote stealing and ties to the Mafia? Nowhere in America was vote theft practiced on so grandiose a scale. The importance of this was graphically demonstrated in the 1960 presidential election, when John Kennedy carried Illinois by a razor-thin plurality of 8,858 votes in a close national contest; most likely, an honest count would have given Nixon the state's 27 electoral votes. Illegal registrations, coercion of voters by Democratic precinct captains, and intimidation of Republican poll watchers (who in many wards became a wholly owned subsidiary of the Democratic party) have all been part of the Chicago pattern. Since 1960, the energetic efforts of Chicago's Better Government Association and a nonpartisan anti-fraud group called Project LEAP (Legal Elections in All Precincts) have reduced vote stealing significantly. Yet in the tight, hotly contested 1982 gubernatorial election, in which incumbent James Thompson edged Adlai Stevenson III by a mere 5,074 votes, the ghosts of all the past abuses—ballot and voting machine tampering, voting "no shows" or the dead, harassing polling officials and forging election judges' signatures—were promptly resurrected.

The Better Government Association is the only one of its kind in the country—a privately sponsored, unofficial watchdog agency to ferret out malfeasance in government. Nevertheless, it has worked effectively to reveal scores of scandals in city, suburban, and state government and save Illinois taxpayers millions of dollars. BGA's standard operating method is to select one of Chicago's fiercely competitive newspapers or television stations to work with it on an investigation or to cooperate with reporters from one of the papers when they turn up first leads on a potential scandal.

In substantial measures, Chicago has put behind it the days when the syndicate mobsters terrorized and virtually ruled the city, the era of wide-open red-light districts, Prohibition bootleg profiteering, Al Capone, and murder in the streets. But the Mafia still has a Chicago branch that Ovid Demaris in his book *Captive City* described as "the most politically insulated and police-pampered 'family' this side of Sicily." Demaris charged that tens of thousands of Chicagoans were involved in organized crime, a vast army of "burglars, hijackers, fences, counterfeiters, moonshiners, panderers, prostitutes, B-girls, cab-drivers, bartenders, extortionists, narcotics peddlers, juice-men, collectors, torturers, assassins, (corrupt) cops, venal judges and politicians, union and business fronts, plus an array of gamblers including bookies, steerers and policy runners." There is a seemingly endless web of interconnection between the Chicago mob and Chicago politicians. The prime example is the First Ward, a downtown area including the Loop, the banks, City Hall, museums and luxury hotels, a powerful old Italian community, slum homes of derelicts, newly arrived immigrants, and the dispossessed. For years, the First was the heart of Chicago gangsterism and corrupt politics; here flourished such figures as "Bathhouse" John Coughlin; Hinky Dink Kenna, the ward committeeman for 50 years (1895–1944) who ran a flourishing red-light district and fostered countless hoods; and Roland ("Libby") Libonati, a personal friend of Capone who served in the legislature for 22 years blocking anticrime legislation and then went to Congress, where to the horror of some of his more scrupulous colleagues he was placed on the Judiciary Committee. Daley's reasons for professed ignorance of pervasive and frequently documented corruption was not hard to divine: the First Ward turned in stupendous election-day margins for organization candidates.

Corruption had been as endemic to the Chicago police force as patronage to its political system. For decades, policemen were on the take—accepting penny-ante payoffs for minor infractions—or, at the highest levels of the department, senior commanders accepting bribes to let the mob carry on its work of numbers games, prostitution, and extortion, unmolested by honest cops. By the 1980s, however, Richard Brzeczek, a former lawyer and cop and the fourth police superintendent appointed by Mayor Byrne, was waging a diligent war against police corruption, strengthening internal controls and surrounding himself with top quality deputies. In 1982, 10 officers were convicted for protecting multimillion-dollar heroin operations in exchange for cash, guns, sex, and microwave ovens. Not until 1975 did the department shut down its "Red Squad," which spied on hundreds of organizations that had at one time or another been critical of Mayor Daley or the police themselves.

In 1968, infuriated by black rioting following the assassination of Martin Luther King, Jr., Daley gave a celebrated—though quickly withdrawn—"shoot to kill" order against arsonists or looters. Only four months later, the Democratic National Convention opened in Chicago, and with it came thousands of youthful demonstrators bent on protest against the Vietnam War and discrediting the President Lyndon Johnson's party. Into the city streamed a motley band of hippies, yippies, and SDSers in search of confrontation—but also thousands of McCarthy-style liberals who abhorred any kind of violence, and thousands of innocent bystanders swept up in the demonstrations. There followed repeated and escalated street clashes between protesters and police, tear-gassing, and the senseless nighttime curfew at Lincoln Park, the bludgeoning of the curfew-breakers by police in the dark, the cruel violence perpetrated before television cameras, obscene provocation on the one side, and brutal police attacks on the other. "It left a scar on the city of Chicago," *Newsweek* commented, "that may become as indelible a part of its violent history as the Haymarket Riot and the St. Valentine's Day Massacre."

Church, Yards, and the Black Nation

Sharing the same heavily Irish, Polish, and Italian constituencies, the Roman Catholic Archdiocese of Chicago and the Cook County Democratic organization have long been closely allied. Leader of the Catholic flock from 1966 to his death in 1982 was John Cardinal Cody, an authoritarian figure similar to Mayor Daley; in fact, the two men had a close working relationship. "In Chicago," Cody once said, "I am the church." And there was a lot of church to embody: the largest archdiocese in America, with 2.5 million members, $1.4 billion in church property, an annual budget of $18.5 million, and almost 1,000 priests celebrating the mass in 22 languages.

No American diocese was more ready for the Vatican II reforms; indeed Chicago anticipated many of them, including a vernacular clergy and more active role for the laity. With few exceptions, Cody quashed all that activity, centralizing and ruling in an autocratic manner that caused deep resentment. Dozens of Chicago area priests left the priesthood. And then, in the last year of Cody's reign, came the incredible news broken by the *Chicago Sun Times:* Cody was under federal investigation for having diverted some $1 million in church funds to a lifelong female friend. Chicagoans held high hopes for

Cody's successor, former Cincinnati Archbishop Joseph Bernardin, a man known for his personal informality and openness to debate while remaining loyal to Vatican policy. Bernardin led U.S. bishops in opposition to nuclear weapons and in early 1983 became a Cardinal.

Chicago also gave birth to the modern community organization techniques of confrontation, sit-ins, boycotts, and militancy. The man most responsible was Saul Alinsky, a sharp-witted nonconformist who died at 63 in 1972. Alinsky traveled all over the U.S.A. helping numerous community organizations get their start, among them The Woodlawn Organization on Chicago's south side and the FIGHT organization to mobilize blacks to deal with Eastman Kodak in Rochester. He also inspired Cesar Chavez to start the organization of California grape pickers.

The test tube for Alinsky's method was the sprawling steeple-and-smokestack neighborhood of stockyard workers in back (to the west) of the famous Chicago Stockyards. A Back of the Yards Council was formed to tackle problems of poverty, juvenile delinquency, housing, and unemployment, but most importantly seething hostilities among the area's 24 nationality groups. Workers, small merchants, and Catholic parishes of every identity from Irish to Lithuanian joined the effort. The community was drawn together and major accomplishments ticked off year by year: first labor organization to get living wages for the packinghouse workers and to make sure men from the neighborhood got the available stockyard jobs, then a broad school lunch program, an infant-care clinic, water fluoridation, employment counseling for workers, sustained efforts to control street gangs and help out youngsters in their first brush with the law.

Alinsky in 1969 founded the Industrial Areas Foundation to train community organizers from across America, an effort that has proceeded—and flourished—despite his death. Major organizations were set up in 11 cities, perhaps the most successful of all among Hispanics in San Antonio and Los Angeles. Almost always there was church cooperation; government grants were never accepted; local establishments were forced to heed demands through ingeniously staged confrontations. In 1975 Alinsky's followers reached a new level of success with the passage of the federal legislation to end "redlining"— bankers' vicious practice of refusing to grant mortgages in inner-city neighborhoods. The force behind the new law was Gale Cincotta, the first woman to lead an Alinsky-style group, the widow of a service station manager and mother of six sons, veteran of fights to stop real estate blockbusting in her West Side neighborhood in the late '60s, and founder of America's first nationwide neighborhood-based policy lobby—National People's Action (NPA). After getting the Community Reinvestment Act passed, the group persuaded such massive insurance companies as Allstate and Aetna to commit millions to housing projects in NPA-organized neighborhoods. Cincotta, a big, blonde, and sometimes bombastic figure, reveled in colorful Alinsky-style tactics—marching into stockholders' meetings to demand community investment by major corporations or protest big oil's tax breaks, for example. In the early '80s she launched major rallies and marches to protest what tight money policies and "Reaganomics" were doing to low-income communities.

And then there is black Chicago: 1.2 million people in the 1980 Census, 40 percent of Chicago's population, up from 8 percent in 1940, 33 percent in 1970. Black Chicago was populated by immigration from the South, as the cars of the Illinois Central Railroad carried vast numbers up the Mississippi River Valley, from Louisiana and Mississippi, Arkansas and Tennessee, into the city of Chicago. During the 1970s the great northward trek slowed to a trickle, but blacks became ever-more dominant as whites fled to the suburbs.

The black civilization of Chicago is incredibly multifaceted: it embraces the great national black newspaper *The Defender*, the popular black magazines *Ebony* and *Jet*, the longtime headquarters of the Black Muslims, Jesse Jackson and his operations, famous neighborhood organizations, squalid public housing projects—and much more. Until the 1970s when blacks began to move into a number of formerly all-white North Side neighborhoods, it was possible to say this city was America's most rigidly segregated (Cleveland perhaps excepted). In the 1950s and 1960s, whites would flee like locusts whenever a black family moved onto the block. Whites sometimes organized to stem the black expansion; certain streets on the Southwest Side stretched like great Chinese Walls of Segregation, and certain parks remained sanctified holy lands for the ethnics, areas blacks could transgress only at their peril.

Two great black-population concentrations emerged: the first, and by far the largest, on the South Side. Many of its neighborhoods—Woodlawn, Kenwood, and the like—have been black for decades now. Only a handful, most notably Hyde Park, have witnessed successful and durable integration.

In the violent 1960s, the raw, volatile ghetto of the city was in Lawndale and other West Side sections—Jewish communities until the '50s or the '60s which then experienced a lightning transformation into all-black islands. As Chicago's overall black immigration slowed in the '70s, the West Side became more stable; still when West Side blacks began to make some money, the most frequent pattern was to escape to better-to-do sections of the South Side.

Under the Daley machine, the Chicago Housing Authority was guilty of the most gross discrimination in choosing building sites and assigning tenants. The real villain was the city council, where white aldermen would invariably veto any proposed public housing in their areas. Today, Chicago harbors some of the most desperate black-filled housing projects anywhere. (The 150,000 tenants in Chicago public housing, if grouped together, would form the state's second-largest city.) There is Cabrini-Green, rows of cheaply built high-rise towers on the near North Side, made nationally famous (or infamous) through Mayor Byrne's brief residency. Just before she moved in, there had been a wave of 11 murders, at least 130 shootings, and hundreds of rapes, robberies, and assaults. The 13,500 residents were constantly terrorized by gang violence. The crime, in slightly muted form, returned as soon as the mayor and her security guards departed. South of the Loop stands the nation's largest public housing project: the Robert Taylor Homes, 28 identical 16-story towers, supposedly home to 20,000 people, a huge proportion of them youths. The residents, according to a Chicago newspaper reporter, are "all poor, grappling with violence and vandalism, fear and suspicion, teen-age terror and adult chaos, rage, resentment, official regimenting. They're second-class citizens living in a second-class world, and they know it, and hate it."

The Democratic machine had a long history of neutralizing effective political opposition in the ghettos and indeed making the black vote a mainstay of its power. For almost 30 years, the principal agent of machine power in the black wards was Georgia-born Congressman William L. Dawson, who built what writer Chuck Stone called "a black political machine that was as efficient and vicious as the city-wide Democratic machine." (As a lawyer before his election to Congress, Dawson had specialized in defense of black gamblers; as boss, he permitted the numbers racket, organized prostitution, and illegal bookmaking to flourish in exchange for support of his organization.) Dawson died in 1970 at 84; with his passing, his machine disintegrated.

Chicago's black nation has produced two nonpolitical models for black self-assertion: The Woodlawn Organization (TWO), the first and arguably best community organization in any city ghetto, and the efforts of the Rev. Jesse Jackson. Woodlawn, located just south of the University of Chicago, by the 1950s had become a neighborhood of absentee landlords, decaying buildings, and boarded up shops. Here in 1959, in a unique ecumenical effort, one Roman Catholic and three Protestant pastors combined forces to start a community organization, which in succeeding years mounted an Alinsky-style program of issue confrontation and action on an amazingly broad scale. Early efforts included America's first rent strike to force absentee white landlords to make necessary repairs to buildings, and a crucial battle with the gigantic University of Chicago to make it compromise on monstrous urban renewal plans. Alinsky used to glow with pleasure over some of TWO's tactics: "TWO got Mayor Daley to deal with them after they threatened to tie up all the restrooms at O'Hare—keeping all the booths occupied. Another time TWO people piled rats on the steps of City Hall. Daley got that message too." TWO did get into some dangerously high-risk situations—working, for example, with such street gangs as the Blackstone Rangers and Devil's Disciples, thus sparking a congressional inquiry. As it matured, the organization encountered occasional scandal but persevered less as a flamboyant protest group than as a solid economic developer, its projects including a supermarket and some of the most proudly maintained low-income housing to be found anywhere.

Chicago's gift to national black leadership has been Jesse Louis Jackson, Baptist preacher, son of South Carolinian poverty, disciple of Martin Luther King, Jr., organizer of economic boycotts, fiery battler for black rights, politician, and prophet. In the 1960s Operation Breadbasket, which Jackson nurtured in Chicago, established itself as one of the most impressive demonstrations in America of black economic power and self-determination. In the mid-1970s, Jackson began a new national campaign to rid black Americans of the welfare mentality and the assumption that racism is the sole reason for their low status in society. "Blacks must buckle down and apply to academic studies the same formula which they have used so successfully in athletics: sacrifice, discipline, and perseverance," Jackson told both parents and youths. At the same time, Jackson organized new boycotts of the products of major corporations to force them to increase advertising in black-audience publications, buy from black suppliers, put money in black-owned banks and award black franchises to blacks; he won major concessions from Coke, Heublein and Kentucky Fried Chicken. It must be added, however, that the mercurial nature of Jackson's approach never impressed Chicago politicians. For them, all that counts is votes. Jackson never showed great power in that area, but he did help the registration drive that led to Washington's victory.*

The predominantly black South Shore district was also aided by another unique institution, the South Shore National Bank, the nation's first bank committed to preserve a neighborhood. The South Shore went from 99 percent white in the 1950s to 85 percent black in 1979, and as the blacks moved in, the businesses moved out. The South Shore bank began to cut its services, made investments in other neighborhoods, and planned to close. After obtaining $4 million in financing from foundations and other philanthropic groups, Ronald Gryzwinski and three partners took over the bank with the avowed intent of "greenlining" a neighborhood that other banks were "redlining." The bank plowed money back into the community, helping rehabilitate houses, apartments, and commercial buildings, supporting neighborhood crime prevention efforts, child care, senior citizen centers, providing up-to-date banking services—and making a profit. By the early '80s the South Shore was being "rediscovered"—even by middle-class whites—as a place to live. Indeed, "gentrification" was being reported in innumerable Chicago neighborhoods once thought irrevocably lost to blight.

Chicago Miscellany and the Suburbs

Television, former Gov. Richard Ogilvie once reminded us, makes Chicago news and personalities dominant in Illinois; the territory within the 65-mile viewing radius of the Chicago stations embraces 70 percent of Illinoisans. Yet, despite the failure of the *Chicago Daily News*, Chicago has not lost distinction and a sharp competitive edge in print journalism. The contenders today are

---

*By the votes standard, the city's Hispanics—422,000 people, or 14 percent of the city population by 1980—are Chicago's weakest group. Starting in the 1950s, wave after wave of Latinos arrived: first Puerto Ricans, then Mexicans, then Cubans and Central and South Americans, quite literally changing the language of the streets and threatening the blacks' claim to be the most underprivileged and disenfranchised. Unlike other U.S. cities, Chicago did not receive one dominant Hispanic group (as Mexicans in Los Angeles or Puerto Ricans in New York). The multiple nationality strands were often mistrustful of each other and unable to create any kind of a unified political front. A 1978 report on Hispanics in Chicago was entitled *Aquí Estamos* (*We Are Here*) because, author Isidro Lucas said, it was "a statement of presence and demand for recognition." In one sense the Hispanics have been fortunate: they have been able to integrate into Chicago neighborhoods with far less controversy or opposition than blacks.

the scrappy *Chicago Sun-Times*, the nemesis of cardinals and crooked cops alike, and the venerable *Chicago Tribune*. Colonel Robert R. McCormick, the grand, domineering, ferocious ruler of the *Tribune* empire for 45 years, went to his grave in 1955, and not long after the days of rampaging anti-New Deal, anti-British, anti-Russian editorials disappeared too. The latter-day *Tribune* has provided quality coverage, won several Pulitzer prizes, and made its way onto most critics' list of the best U.S. papers. But its business managers have confused the world by buying the Chicago Cubs baseball team and proving highly erratic owners of another great institution, the *New York Daily News*.

Chicago harbors 30 colleges and universities and with its 5 medical schools trains a goodly share of America's physicians. One of the nation's outstanding inner-city university branches is the magnificently designed Chicago Circle campus of the University of Illinois, which opened its doors in 1965. Other outstanding institutions include Northwestern University at Evanston and the Catholic institutions of Loyola and DePaul.

But the University of Chicago, founded in 1890 through the largesse of John D. Rockefeller, remains the greatest of all. Since its founding, the institution has had more than 30 Nobel Prize winners on its faculty; such presidents as Robert Maynard Hutchins (1929–51) and Edward Levi (1968–75) hold firm places in the history of 20th-century education. From the social sciences to mathematics and education, many Chicago departments rank among the very best in the nation—even though, on the financial side, President Hanna Gray has found the sledding very hard in recent years. The university deserves high marks for the accommodations it eventually reached with blacks in the Hyde Park-Kenwood neighborhood, which surrounds it. A stable integrated community was achieved; hundreds of new town houses and high-rise apartment buildings have gone up and many old ones have been renovated; there are restaurants of wide gastronomic variety, coffee houses, and theaters. And the university's spacious Midway strip is a little architectural showplace all on its own, with buildings by Frank Lloyd Wright, Mies van der Rohe, Eero Saarinen, and Edward Durrell Stone.

Chicago has a bewildering variety of suburbs, in both Cook County and the five so-called collar counties that make up metropolitan Chicago. Oldest and most settled in their ways are the North Shore "establishment" suburbs—cities and villages such as Evanston (population 73,706), Wilmette, Glencoe, Highland Park, and Lake Forest, many of them places of stately trees lining streets of gracious older homes. In the more outlying areas one comes on quantities of high-grade postwar residential developments, both low and high rise, sharing with the towns top national ranking of income and educational levels. Of late the North Shore's overwhelming white Protestantism has been leveled by some Jews; Evanston also has a substantial black community.

At the opposite geographic and ethnic pole are the industrialized middle- and lower-income suburbs to the south of Chicago, places such as Oak Lawn and Calumet City, peopled with white laborers and their families who have "made it" through diligent saving and are mainly concerned with escaping the problems of the inner city. The population is mostly white ethnic: Polish, Italian, Slavic, though with occasional pockets of blacks. Here is classic cheap postwar tract housing, literally coming apart at the seams with normal use.

From the southwest to northwest of Cook County lie Will, McHenry, and DuPage Counties, places of rapid growth through the '70s as subdivisions each year consumed thousands of acres of prairie. With the exception of a few major towns such as Joliet (77,956), a decaying industrial center and home of the decrepit state prison, the rest of the area epitomizes urban sprawl.

Finally, there are the three close-in westside suburbs, Cicero, Berwyn, and Oak Park. Cicero and Berwyn are aging bastions of the middle- and lower-class ethnic—Bohemian, Polish, and other Slavic—where business streets are dingy but lawns immaculate. Cicero has a notorious heritage as hangout of Al Capone and the crime syndicate and still harbors some vice and gambling despite periodic raids. Blacks have pressed in on many of these older suburbs, arousing every response from exclusionary zoning to the creative efforts of Oak Park—a showplace suburb with 300 architecturally or historically significant buildings—to integrate with calm and dignity.

II. Statewide and Downstate

Politics of Spoil, Government of Limits

"Under primary, under convention, under despotism or under a pure democracy, Illinois would be corrupt and crooked. . . . It is in the blood of the people," William Allen White opined over 50 years ago. The judgment was harsh and categorical, but amply sustainable—then and now. No true reform movement has come to Illinois government in this century, primarily because Democratic big-city and Republican downstate organizations remain in perpetual conflict, each hungry for the spoils of power. A high proportion of Illinois state officers and state legislators are in politics for profit or patronage and show minimal interest in issues of public service. In California in the '70s, the governor had 120 patronage positions to fill, in Oregon 12, in Iowa 35, in Wisconsin 26. But in Illinois the governor and other cabinet officials controlled 15,000 patronage positions. There were at least twice that many patronage jobs in Cook County, and thousands more in county courthouses where Republican-sponsored venality had proven just as egregious as the venality of the big-city Democrats. Federal court decisions finding patronage systems unconstitutional threaten all this. But the system is so deeply ingrained one best waits to see change before believing it.

A number of postwar Illinois politicians have come acropper of the law, including former Gov. Otto Kerner,* some legislators, and one former House Speaker charged with taking $30,000 in bribes to pass a bill increasing load limits for cement trucks. Republican State Auditor Orville E. Hodge in 1956 was sentenced to 20 years in prison for embezzling at least $2,612,639 in state funds to pay for his own lush living. In 1980, Attorney General William Scott was sentenced to a year in jail for income tax evasion. Later, the director of public health was forced to resign over alleged misuse of $3 million. But relatively few Illinois politicians actually go to jail for corrupt practices simply because prosecutors' offices and the courts are so often compromised.

The classic example of all time has to be that of House Speaker Paul Powell, the self-styled "country boy" from impoverished southern Illinois who died in 1970 leaving an estate of $3.1 million—even though his lifetime earnings, all in 36 years of public service, had come to less than $300,000. In death, Powell's body lay on the same catafalque that once bore Lincoln. A thousand officeholders and politicians crowded the crepe-draped rotunda of the State Capitol to honor the most powerful of all downstate Democrats. Only two and a half months later was the public suddenly told that $750,000 in cold cash had been found crammed into an old shoe box and other containers in the closet of Powell's Springfield hotel room. Then all the sordid details of Powell's way of operating came spilling out, with a flurry of talk (fruitless, it later turned out) about stiff new financial disclosure requirements for public officials.

Of course the politicians had known all along what Powell was up to. The late Adlai Stevenson once said of Powell that he could have been one of the great political figures of American history "if only he didn't believe that the shortest distance between two points is a curve." How did Powell's constituents react to his shenanigans? "He was always a hero to the downstate voter," John Gardner, editor of the *Southern Illinosian* at Carbondale, was quoted as saying. "He was the guy who outslicked the city slickers."

The important point about Powell was that he was no bizarre aberration, but simply a master practitioner of a familiar game. In 1964 state senator Paul Simon (later to be a member of Congress) wrote in a *Harper's* article that about a third of Illinois legislators took payoffs—some in the form of payments for legal services, public relations work, or as campaign contributions, and a smaller number in the shape of outright bribes.

Of course there have been and are men and women of great personal integrity in Illinois state government. But when we asked veteran state political reporters to name the high state officials of the postwar period they were convinced were absolutely honest, the list was embarrassingly short.

The inevitable result of a politics of patronage and payoff is a low level of service for the people. The state's per capita income has hovered around

---

*Kerner's name got national notice when he chaired the presidential commission to study race problems following the great urban riots of 1967. In Springfield, Kerner did essentially what Mayor Daley told him to—no more, no less.

eighth-highest in the United States. But Illinois has spent less than the national per capita average for higher education, for local government aid, for public welfare, and for health and hospitals. The adoption of an income tax in 1969 made available more revenue than ever before, but over most of its history Illinois has been a rich state that chose not to do more for its people.

Two postwar Illinois governors have served with unusual distinction. The first was Adlai Stevenson II, who though he served just a single four-year term (1949–53) was able to double state aid to school districts, place the state police under a merit system, and effect a big increase in gasoline tax and truck license fees to expedite highway construction. But Stevenson's more important contribution was to bring a fresh breeze of integrity and a higher quality of official service into the musty corridors of the state capitol at Springfield; for many, he restored a belief in the viability and purpose of government. Even in defeat, he made a similar contribution to the nation through his eloquence and leadership in two unsuccessful campaigns for the presidency. Stevenson's distinguished public service, running through the years he served as U.S. Ambassador to the United Nations before his death in 1965, has won him a secure place in history.

Richard B. Ogilvie, another one-term governor (1969–73), lacked the Stevensonian charisma or many politicians' physical glamour. A stocky, stolid man, he spoke with a hoarse voice and reminded many people of a small-town banker. As a tank commander in World War II, he was struck by shell fragments that ripped into the left side of his face; plastic surgery left him with a grim, set expression that proved a special liability on television. But few recent American governors demonstrated natural executive skill equal to Ogilvie's. His approach to problems was pragmatic, businesslike, and low-keyed. And he was a gutsy man, willing to undergo stiff criticism if he thought he was right. His great promise was cut short not by any scandal (so characteristic in Illinois); on the contrary, he dared to place the commonweal above political expediency. He supported—strenuously—the state's first income tax. "I knew damn well then it was probably signing my political death warrant as governor," Ogilvie recollected to us later. "But everything I had in mind doing was contingent on our having additional revenues—school needs, social service requirements. The question was, 'Did I want to be a mediocre eight-year governor or a really good four-year governor?'"

Ogilvie was defeated and succeeded by maverick Democrat Daniel Walker, elected narrowly after a 1,197-mile walk from the tip of southern Illinois to the Wisconsin border preaching an evangelistic, antimachine, populist message. Self-righteous and forever yearning for a headline or a fight, Walker accomplished little in office. (Later he would confess that he and his advisers "developed a kind of 'circle the wagons' mentality," repelling outside counsel.) Walker took pleasure in bearding Daley; in 1976 Daley got his revenge by upsetting Walker in the Democratic primary. But the autumn winner was a Republican, James R. Thompson, ex-U.S. attorney of fabled Chicago crime-busting achievements (he obtained a 97 percent conviction rate of more than 350 officials and cronies, including Otto Kerner and Daley's right-hand man as city council finance chairman, Thomas Keane). A personally charming man, Thompson turned out as governor to be more of a compromiser than a crusader. His program included a tight budget, construction of two big new prisons,* increasing subsidies for Chicago-area transit, and what he hoped would be his proudest achievement—providing an administration above reproach on ethical grounds. Revelation that Thompson, albeit legally, had accepted gifts worth hundreds of dollars from appointees and people doing business with the state scarred the "Mr. Clean" image. But he could point with pride to the state's balanced budget and triple A credit rating.

Thompson was challenged for reelection in 1982 by Adlai Stevenson III, who had served a full decade (1971–81) in the U.S. Senate before he decided he could not stand members' lack of substantive power, or the oxenlike pace of reform there. "God, I don't know how they [senators] stand it," he said later. In 1980 Stevenson had actually suggested formation of a third party, only to confound his followers by refusing to lead it himself. The Thompson-Stevenson race degenerated into one of name-calling, negativism, and mud-slinging—an outcome unworthy of either man. Thompson emerged the winner by the slimmest of margins. Soon thereafter his fellow Republican governors placed him in line to become chairman of the National Governors Association.

We have heard such words as "very average," "thoroughly mediocre," and "very corrupt" applied to the Illinois legislature, and one could fill volumes with the wheelings, dealings, and conflicts between Cook County machine Democrats, reformers in both parties, conservative downstate Republicans, the downstate Democratic contingent, and sometimes crime syndicate elements in both parties. Illinois did begin to elect a somewhat different breed of legislators in the '60s and '70s, however. "Each crop of freshman legislators," Charlie Wheeler of the Chicago Sun-Times commented, "has a greater percentage willing to do their homework, willing to find out about issues, not so steeped in one philosophy that they can't compromise." Sessions became annual and the number of full-time legislators increased—even though some of the best qualities of a "citizen" legislature were lost. From 1870 onward, Illinois had a one-of-its kind system of cumulative voting and multimember districts, designed to assure minority representation in a state so thoroughly polarized sectionally and politically. The system, however, was decisively rejected by Illinois voters in a 1980 initiative amendment to their constitution (which itself had been thoroughly, and well, rewritten in 1970). At the same time, the state House was cut back from 177 representatives to 118, suggesting a much put-upon populace had decided "the less, the better."

Reapportionment cut down the once mighty clout of the Farm Bureau

---

*Illinois continues to have some of the nation's toughest, meanest, overcrowded prisons, including the century-old institution at Pontiac, where five hours of prisoner rage in 1978 cost three guards their lives. The state's maximum security prison at Joliet has been described as "a tinderbox ready to explode." As if all that weren't enough, the federal government moved the most rebellious, assaultive, murderous inmates of its prison system to its pen at Marion, Ill.—quite literally the new Alcatraz.

lobby. Lobbies of most influence today include the Illinois Manufacturers Association and Illinois Chamber of Commerce, coal operators, insurance companies, the Illinois Education Association, and the Illinois Medical Society, AFL-CIO unions (especially the Steelworkers), retail merchants, and the racetracks—the latter a key source of patronage with many legislators owning racetrack stock. Many special interests now exert influence in Springfield by getting their own employees or operatives elected to legislative seats. And the chambers are packed with lawyers, real estate, and insurance people who often find the special interests throwing business their way, making them more and more beholden.

Few innovations or accomplishments are associated with Illinois state government, with an exception in higher education. Surveys have placed the University of Illinois system among the country's finest in many disciplines.

Illinois in Washington

Illinois' outstanding national legislators of the past generation have reflected the state's many images: the intellectual community, symbolized by Senator Paul Douglas; the rural and small-city Illinois, by Senator Everett Dirksen and House Republican Leader Robert Michel; and the suburban and new industrial Illinois, by Senator Charles Percy.

The outstanding members of the House delegation have been even more of a microcosm: Dan Rostenkowski, a keen big-city spokesman and erstwhile Daley spokesman who took over the chairmanship of the tax-writing House Ways and Means in 1981; Abner J. Mikva, brilliant but sole representative of the Democratic reform contingent of the Chicago area delegation until he resigned to accept a federal judgeship; Edward J. Derwinski, proud Polish-American and high-ranking Republican on the Foreign Affairs Committee until he lost his seat from southwest Cook County through redistricting; Henry Hyde, Congress' most single-minded—and effective—abortion opponent, representing Cicero and like-minded Chicago suburbs; Melvin Price, the East St. Louis lawmaker who emerged from 34 years of near obscurity to become chairman of the powerful Armed Services Committee; Paul Simon, the bright, affable downstater who retained his reform inclinations after years of frustration as a legislator, lieutenant governor, and Daley's gubernatorial candidate in 1972; Philip Crane, the good-looking and dogmatic Mount Prospect Congressman and president of the American Conservative Union who ran for president in 1980. John B. Anderson, veteran House member from the Rockford area northwest of Chicago, leaped into the 1980 presidential race—first as a Republican, then as an independent. A self-described "onetime conservative who has been steadily jogging leftward," Anderson had been chairman of the House Republican Conference before his decision to run for president. Sharing the fate of many independent candidates before him, he ended up with a disappointing 7 percent of the vote on the day that Ronald

Reagan (born in Tampico, Illinois, on Feb. 6, 1911) was elected president of the United States.

Bob Michel, unobtrusive and congenial congressman from Peoria, was rewarded for 26 years of Republican team playing with election as minority leader in 1980. Michel used his extensive knowledge of the legislative process, a willingness to hear all viewpoints and qualities of "gentle persuasion" to unite potentially quarrelsome House Republicans in the historic conservative budget and tax votes in the first year of the Reagan administration.

Senator Charles H. Percy first hit the national prints as the youthful business genius who propelled the Bell and Howell camera firm into a sparkling success story. In 1966 he defeated the venerable Senator Paul Douglas, then faced years of disappointment as his hopes of a Republican presidential nomination faded—partly through circumstances, partly because the national party was not ready for a candidate of Percy's moderation. In 1978 he was almost defeated for reelection. But fortune smiled on Percy again when Republicans won control of the Senate in the 1980 elections and he was suddenly catapulted into chairmanship of the Foreign Relations Committee, a position of national —and international—influence.

Paul Douglas, U.S. Senator starting in 1949, finally fell victim to old age and the swirling new tides of suburban politics that propelled Percy, his onetime student, into his seat. But Douglas merits a word of note before the tides of history obscure the contributions of a brave, proud, and sometimes self-righteous Quaker who was wounded in combat as a Marine in World War II and later demonstrated extraordinary skill and partisan wit in national office. Douglas was at once an author of such liberal measures as the landmark 1949 Housing Act and a prime opponent of "pork barrel" federal public works spending; he pioneered in consumer protection legislation (especially "truth in lending") and was a long-time battler of the congressional seniority system.

Everett McKinley Dirksen was a personification of the Senate inner circle and though a Republican perhaps the most powerful senator of the Democratic '60s. In 33 years in Congress, Dirksen was variously regarded as an isolationist and an internationalist, a New Dealer and a conservative, a friend and foe of civil rights. Though opposed to Dwight Eisenhower's nomination in 1952, for instance, he became his valued lieutenant when elected minority leader in 1959. "I am a man of principle, and one of my first principles is flexibility," he once said. It was Dirksen's personal change of position that shifted enough conservative Republican Senators to make possible passage of numerous Kennedy-Johnson measures, including the Nuclear Test Ban Treaty and the Civil Rights Act of 1964. Yet he was a defender of Senator Joseph McCarthy, nominated Barry Goldwater for president in 1964, and was the leading figure in a failing effort to turn back the clock on the Supreme Court's reapportionment and school prayer decisions. *Time* writer Neil MacNeil concluded that Dirksen was a man "who played the game of politics for the zest of the game itself, for its fascination, for its exhilaration."

Prairie, City, Farm, and Factory

First there was the prairie, its grasses stretching to far horizons; then there was the cornbelt, one of the world's most productive agricultural areas. To this day, Illinois vies with Iowa for number one position in corn and trails only Iowa in hog production; the state also ranks high in beef production, meatpacking, and soybean crops. In the northern reaches, one comes on Wisconsin-like dairylands. For all of Illinois' industrial might, farming remains its biggest single industry. Rich black glacial soil that goes as deep as 75 feet— called gumbo by early settlers, who had difficulty plowing it—covers all of Illinois except the southern counties; even with urban pressures, no less than 80 percent of the state is still in farmland.

So the rural culture is not gone, even if the number of farms (and opportunities for young farmers) have diminished radically, and even if suburbanization and erosion alike have consumed vast areas of once productive land. In the "downstate" Illinois of plowed fields in spring and rows of drying corn in autumn, there still flourishes a conservative yet concerned way of life, a pride in self, soil, and workmanship, an entrenched independence harkening back to American roots. The naturalist-writer and Illinois native Donald Culross Peattie a few years ago proclaimed that "Illinois is the best state precisely because it is so American. More, it is heartland. As Castile is of Spain, as the plain of Beauce is the granary of France, or Tuscany of Italy, so Illinois is core America. . . ."

Outside of the Chicago metropolis, Illinois remains essentially rural; in the 381 miles of her length, the top north of Boston, the bottom south of Louisville, there are only a handful of significant cities. The largest of these is Rockford (1980 population 139,712—less than a twentieth of the Chicago figure), a quintessential blue-collar town set in the forests and low hills of the Rock River valley of north central Illinois. The flavor is strongly Scandinavian and conservative; the city once struggled with its political conscience before finally accepting urban renewal funds to help rebuild its center city. Rockford is the American Foundry personified: 43 percent of the work force in manufacturing, compared to 23 percent nationwide. Nearly 800 firms produce a range of specialized tools, dies, nuts, screws, and bolts used in farm machinery, autos, heavy equipment, and housing. Once a source of prosperity and stability, the manufacturing turned to nightmare in 1982, producing what was then the highest unemployment rate—over 19 percent—of any American city.

Peoria (124,160), set in the midst of central Illinois' endless cornfields, used to be so renowned for municipal corruption, whiskey bootlegging, and unsolved murders that John Gunther called it "one of the toughest towns on earth." The past two decades have brought an infusion of reform politicians and a constant fight to renovate a decaying central city dealt body blows by such events as new suburban malls. But Caterpillar Tractor, largest Peoria employer with a local payroll of some 33,000, moved its national headquarters into the city proper, and the businesslike young Republican mayor, Richard Carver, predicted an eventual $1 billion in downtown redevelopment. All that, however, was before the national recession and Caterpillar's sudden and grievous loss of foreign markets in 1982. The Reagan administration's decision to bar U.S. companies from providing materials for the Soviet gas pipeline cost Caterpillar a $90 million contract, and even worse, led the U.S.S.R. to shift the vast majority of its tractor-bulldozer-earth moving equipment business from Caterpillar to Komatsu of Japan. Caterpillar laid off 8,000 workers and let thousands more jobs go by attrition. Pabst and Hiram Walker breweries closed down. Depression hit the surrounding farm territory. Representative Michel barely kept his House seat in the 1982 elections. Peoria, a stable island of prosperity through the '70s, agonized about its future.

The major business of Springfield (99,637) is politics and state government. As a state capital with considerable tradition, the city has a social strata of sorts; there are still many names that were prominent in Lincoln's days. Many blacks live in isolated public housing projects. Like most other Illinois cities, Springfield has agonized over the decay of its downtown, but it has capitalized on the Lincoln name and undertaken the renovation of the old Capitol, constructed a mall area around Lincoln's home, and developed a new convention center and hotels.

Diversified industry and dull politics typify most of Illinois' other downstate cities in the 40,000 to 90,000 population bracket—Decatur, self-proclaimed "soybean capital of the world"; Moline, home of John Deere and "farm implement capital of America"; Rock Island, site of the government's largest military arsenal; Champaign and neighboring Urbana, host communities to the University of Illinois; Elgin; Aurora; Quincy, an old river town on the Mississippi; and the like.

Outside of Chicago, the principal industrial activity is along the Illinois Waterway, a combination of the Cal-Sag Canal and the Des Plaines and Illinois rivers stretching 300 miles from Chicago to Joliet, Peoria, and then into the Mississippi River north of St. Louis. A major industrial corridor has developed along the Waterway, which can deliver every heavy commodity from coal to chemicals by cheap barge transportation.

Egypt and Its Cairo; East St. Louis

Far from Chicago's lofty towers, ranging southward from the rich glacier-tilled prairie of central Illinois, lies a 31-county region of hilltop and bottom country wedged between the Ohio, Wabash, and Mississippi rivers that looks like, thinks like, and acts like the American Southland. Perhaps because of its similarity to the deltalands of the Nile, the region has long been known as Egypt (or Little Egypt) and comes complete with towns named Cairo, Karnak, Thebes, and Dongola. It is not only a land of levees and overflowing rivers, but of the Illinois Ozarks with their valleys and hills where the first settlers hacked farmsteads out of the magnificent hardwood forests.

Egypt lies south of prosperity and indeed has been in a spiraling economic decline for several decades. Income levels are abysmally low, the average

education still stops halfway through high school, and high unemployment
is perpetual. Since the 1890s, coal has been a major industry of the region, and
the state still has enough coal to supply the world for almost a century. But
even though Illinois ranks fourth in the nation in coal production (behind
West Virginia, Pennsylvania, and Kentucky), the coal is cursed by its high
sulfur content. What's more, the coal industry has successfully lobbied against
a coal severance tax, so that few of the profits remain to help the coal counties
climb out of poverty and plan a brighter economic future.

Those who know the region have written of Southern Illinois as an "intemperate land" of "great and bitter passions." It was in Williamson County that
one of the most gruesome episodes in American labor history took place in
1922, when 500 striking miners massacred 19 strikebreakers. More recently,
other kinds of terror have stalked across Southern Illinois, centered in the
town of Cairo and the city of East St. Louis.

Cairo (pronounced Kerro), perhaps the only walled city in the U.S.A., is
a squat, drab river town set behind 60-foot levees at the very point of confluence of the Ohio's gray waters and the Mississippi's yellow tide. In its heyday,
this was a great port of call for river crews, trading and cotton production
center, crossroads for seven railroads, and county seat where close to 20,000
people lived. It was also a wide open town, wet during Prohibition, where
riverboat crews could always find women and gambling. The economy spiraled downward a generation ago; by 1980 the town had just 5,931 people.
Bitter racial conflicts tore Cairo apart in the '60s and early '70s, based on
grossly discriminatory practices of ruling whites and blacks' sometimes violent retort. Fires destroyed over $1 million of business property in 1969 alone.
Only under federal court-ordered council districting in 1980 could blacks elect
their first town officials.

East St. Louis, a town of 55,200 people on the Mississippi opposite St. Louis,
has a raucous and violent history that dates back to 1885 when the first mayor
was assassinated by a disgruntled city employee. Up to World War I the town
was largely white, but then the industries (railroads and big meatpackers)
imported Southern blacks as strikebreakers; the result in 1917 was the worst
race riot of the first half of the 20th century, in which 39 blacks and 9 whites
were killed in three days of mob rule. The rise of trucking, departure of the
meatpackers, black immigration, and white suburbanization decimated East
St. Louis after World War II. Terror-ridden crime waves ensued. In the late
'60s an antique, patronage-ridden Democratic machine was ousted, but the
black leaders who took over—despite many good intentions—suffered alternatively from overreliance on federal poverty funds and old-fashioned corruption. Special hope seemed, however, to attend the reform administration of
Carl Officer, elected (at age 27) as mayor in 1979; announcing "East St. Louis
has been living on federal welfare for 10 years," he immediately cut City Hall
employees to 300 from 549. Officer entertained great hopes for a Mississippi
riverfront project of shopping malls, parks, and a marina on 20 acres of land
freed by consolidation of 30 railyards. But that project, too, needed federal
assistance, and the Reagan administration put it on ice. East St. Louis entered

the 1980s with a 96 percent black population, half of its people on public assistance, at least a quarter jobless.

Illinois Municipal League officials reminded us that all of southwestern Illinois is not East St. Louis, that this area contains many comfortable middle-class communities and several thriving industrial towns. Nevertheless, the continued presence of an East St. Louis, with its overwhelming burden of distress, confuses and confounds the visitor. Why, in a state of such affluence and industrial, agricultural, and financial might, must such conditions persist? The conclusion is inescapable: Illinois state government, constitutionally and morally responsible for the cities and counties within its borders, chooses to ignore the festering social sore. A society that makes such decisions must be judged accordingly.

MICHIGAN

An Industrial Behemoth Falls on Hard Times

MICHIGAN, HER WEALTH, HER TRAVAILS, AND HER FATE, often seem synonymous with America at large. Here was the mighty producer of timber, iron, and copper for a growing young America. This was the state that beyond all others could be called the "Arsenal of Democracy" during World War II. In industrial marvels of the 20th century, no other state could outshine her: Michigan put America on wheels and revolutionized transportation around the world. Her great universities were a model of the best a nation could produce, her cities both pioneering and prototypal.

Yet as we wrote these lines in the early 1980s, Michigan was in dire trouble. It had endured seven sharp recessions within 35 years and its situation by 1982 was excruciatingly severe. Early 1983 unemployment stood at 17.2 percent, far beyond the national average, and in many manufacturing cities was in excess of 25 percent. One out of every nine Michiganders was receiving some sort of welfare; thousands of families were added to relief rolls each month; in just 15 months (April 1980–July 1981) 156 percent more people moved out of Michigan than had left during all the 1970s. Within just two years, the Big Three auto makers posted combined losses of $5.5 billion. Business and professional bankruptcies tripled. As tax revenues slumped, road maintenance fell dangerously behind and parks, libraries and other public services were closing or cut back; police, firefighters, and even tenured professors were being laid off. The credit rating on Michigan's short-term notes and long-term bonds fell to the lowest in the nation, and the state government had to express pleasure when five banks from its industrial competitor, Japan, advanced it a "good will" letter of credit supporting its short-term borrowing. Caught between plunging tax revenues and soaring welfare costs, the state government was struggling with multihundred-million-dollar deficits. A "rainy-day fund," thoughtfully established in 1977 to set aside funds in fat years to see the state through lean ones, was unequal to the new blow.

A land of vivid contrasts was this Michigan of the 1980s—grim ghettoes and breathtaking natural beauty; abject poverty and, among the autoworld's privileged classes, vast (on occasion ostentatious) wealth; a world-class symphony orchestra and backwoods shot-and-a-beer bars; a once self-confident and dominant state thrown off balance, struggling to find a new identity in a time it could scarcely comprehend.

For even while Michigan suffered what its governor called "depression conditions," there were bright spots. Already among the top ten oil- and gas-producing states, new discoveries of reserves in northern Lower Michigan, with estimated worth in the billions of dollars, were drawing Michiganders and Texans alike to the sparsely populated north woods. (Reserves in the Pigeon River Country State Forest alone were estimated at $3 billion.) Lumber still contributed about a quarter billion dollars a year to the state economy, and agriculture billions more (this is one of America's leading fruit states, from cherries to strawberries, and is also rich in grains, livestock, and dairy products). Michigan remained (after California) the second-leading exporting state in the nation, shipping $15 billion in manufactured goods and $740 million in farm products abroad yearly. The Detroit River was still the busiest waterway in the world.

Outsiders easily overlooked this state's natural beauty. Limited to one national park (remote Isle Royale on Lake Superior), it nevertheless had two of America's national lakeshores (Pictured Rocks on Lake Superior, Sleeping Bear Dune on Lake Michigan) and millions of acres in public parks, forests, and beaches. One of the jewels was Mackinac Island, famed for its Grand Hotel (nearly 100 years old with the longest front porch in the world).

By the 1980s Michigan seemed safely past some of its severe environmental crises—the massive contamination of livestock feed by a fire retardant called polybrominated biphenyl (PBB), which killed millions of animals and made many humans ill during the 1970s (and indeed was said to have left traces of its poison in the bodies of 90 percent of Michiganders), and the industrial compound polychlorinated biphenyl (PCB), which found its way into Great Lakes waters and necessitated hundreds of millions of public and private dollars to clean up.

Detroit delighted in polishing its tarnished image (and sagging tourist trade) by hosting the 1980 Republican National Convention; the 1982 National Football League Superbowl; and another first—the Renaissance Grand Prix world-class auto race of Formula One cars through downtown Detroit. The state's second-largest city, Grand Rapids, long-time home and power base of President Gerald R. Ford, in 1981 dedicated its Ford Museum and for the second time in 20 years won the coveted All-America City designation from the National Municipal League. Battle Creek wrote a new chapter in the history of American corporate-town relations in 1982 by voting—at the insistence of the Kellogg Co., its biggest employer, which was otherwise prepared to leave town—to merge its quarreling city and suburban township governments and thus pave the way for common economic development strategies. With all those "good things" about, it was easy to sympathize with Chrysler Board Chairman Lee A. Iaccoca when he said: "The trick is to make sure you don't die before prosperity gets here."

Parsing Michigan

Michigan is the keystone of the Great Lakes. Washed by the waters of lakes Michigan, Superior, Huron, and Erie, her coastline runs 3,121 miles (longer than that of any other state). Thus enveloped, pocked with 11,037 inland lakes and streaked with thousands of miles of rivers and streams, Michigan is singularly blessed with one-fifth of the nation's fresh water supply. The Straits of Mackinac (like the island situated there, pronounced "Mack-i-naw") separate Lake Huron and Lake Michigan and split the state in two geographically, another distinctive feature but a mixed blessing at best. Michigan's sheer physical size is remarkable: It is farther from Ironwood in the western Upper Peninsula (U.P. for short) to Detroit, for example—595 miles—than from Detroit to New York.

Those who live "above the Straits" are a fiercely proud, rugged, and independent lot who periodically turn their feelings of isolation and neglect by downstate power centers into agitation for creation of a new State of Superior. But it is not the division of Michigan into two peninsulas—linked since 1957 by the graceful five-mile span of the Mackinac Bridge, fourth-longest suspension span in the world—that really divides the state. Like Caesar's Gaul, Michigan is in three parts:

•Across the whole of the Upper Peninsula and the northern half of the Lower Peninsula is a vast expanse of hills (even mountains in the western U.P.), woods, and water that comprise what has been described as one of the largest areas of unspoiled beauty east of the Mississippi. Though shorn of its stands of virgin white pine by the lumber barons and forest fires of yesteryear, fully half of Michigan's land area today is reforested. This is a land of depleted mines and poor soil, with more deer, bear, and elk than people. With a quarter of the state's land mass, the U.P.'s 320,000 residents account for just 3.5 percent of its population. Roughly twice that number live in the northern Lower Peninsula, which had a population explosion of sorts in the 1970s, with 26 of the 31 counties growing faster than 20 percent and 10 of them by more than 40 percent.

•Spread throughout the southern half of the Lower Peninsula—below an imaginary line from Muskegon on Lake Michigan in the west to Bay City on Saginaw Bay in the east—are the rich farms and quiet towns whose frame houses and steepled churches evoke the spirit of the New England and New York pioneers who made the trek down the Erie Canal to settle in the Michigan wilderness. Here, too, are all of Michigan's "second cities": industrial centers, such as Flint, Lansing, and Grand Rapids, and household names like Battle Creek and Kalamazoo. Ninety percent of Michigan's population lives south of the Muskegon–Bay City line, equally split between 34 outstate counties stretching shore to shore and the 3 teeming counties knotted at the base of Michigan's "Thumb" that comprise metropolitan Detroit.

•Finally, there is the brawny Detroit area itself—bustling, materialistic, seat of one of the greatest industrial and labor empires ever developed but by the 1980s threatened by overseas competition and global energy intrigues. Though decimated by center-city population losses of 20.5 percent in the 1970s, the Tri-county area (Wayne, third-largest in the country, home of Detroit; and Oakland and Macomb, the primary suburbs) in 1980 accounted for 43.7 percent of the state's 9,258,344 population. With six more counties abutting the metropolitan area added in, 56.2 percent of Michigan's people—

as well as 15 of her 20 biggest cities—were concentrated in this southeastern region. Here too are the wealth, power, and the principal troubles of the state. Industrial Michigan and its great hallmarks—the automotive behemoths, the sinewy and socially conscious United Auto Workers, and "programmatic," issue-oriented politics—are the essential Michigan story.

One might add that Michigan is so far-flung geographically and cosmopolitan in its ethnic strains that a common personality is often hard to discern. The early New England settlers were followed by Germans into the Saginaw and Ann Arbor areas. The Dutch came to western Michigan (Holland still exults in its annual tulip festival), the Irish to the rolling green territory they named the Irish Hills, the Scandinavians to the lumber camps and mines. From 1910 onward, East Europeans poured in, drawn by Detroit factory jobs. Then there was the black influx—from 0.6 percent in 1910 to 12.9 percent. But the blacks were highly concentrated in the Detroit area; look for the primary racial minority in Michigan's 83 counties and you find that in 44 it is American Indians. Twenty counties have fewer than 20 black residents; not coincidentally, perhaps, all are in northern areas where spectacular population growth was reported in the 1970s.

Early Michigan

In 1618, two years before the pilgrims reached Plymouth, the first Europeans reached Michigan. These were not English separatists, but rather French *voyageurs,* expanding the horizons of New France and seeking the legendary Northwest Passage to the Orient. Explorers, missionaries, and trappers with fabled names like Brule, Marquette, Jolliet, and LaSalle were the vanguard of French domination that lasted for generations.

The Detroit River, for example, is not a river at all, but literally what the French named it—*Le Detroit,* the strait or narrows connecting Lake St. Clair and Lake Erie. Grosse Pointe, now a posh Detroit suburb, geographically is a huge bulge in the Lake St. Clair shoreline around which the *coureurs de bois* had to paddle to enter *Le Detroit.* It was here on July 24, 1701, that a French soldier who had made a fortune in the fur trade, Antoine de la Mothe Cadillac, began building Fort Ponchartrain—a settlement that would grow one day into one of the world's great cities.

Throughout the 18th century, Michigan was the focus of the titanic struggles for North America. Its strategic location—particularly the Straits of Mackinac, the gateway to the Northwest—made it a prize of tremendous commercial and military significance. The British finally wrested control of the area from the French in 1760, securing their gains under the Peace of Paris ending the French and Indian War in 1763, only to lose it 20 years later to the Americans at the close of the Revolution. But the British, undaunted, refused to leave, and by act of Parliament actually administered the area as part of Canada. When American Col. John Francis Hamtramck finally "liberated" Detroit in 1796, he found 500 inhabitants—still mostly French.

The initial American administration of Michigan was under various Congressional carvings-up of the Northwest Territory. Michigan became a territory in its own right in 1805 and (after a brief British reconquest during the War of 1812) a state in 1837. Statehood was delayed partly because of a fierce and lengthy border squabble with Ohio. This comic-opera war—militias marching in the night, a stabbing in a tavern—was finally ended by Congress, which imposed a "compromise." Ohio would get the disputed narrow strip of land, 468 square miles including Toledo, and Michigan would be awarded the western two-thirds of the Upper Peninsula it had not before controlled. This made nobody in Michigan happy—the legislature viewed the consolation prize as "a sterile region . . . destined by soil and climate to remain forever a wilderness," and the U.P. residents even then wanted their own state—but it got Michigan into the Union. (Even today, the U.P.'s reputation is of "ten months of winter and two of poor sledding.")

These were boom times. In the 1830s, Michigan was both the most popular destination of pioneers seeking natural riches and the fastest-growing area in the country. The bulk of its new settlers coming from New England, it was the most "Yankee" state in the West—setting a political heritage that helps explain the state's progressive political development, the polyglot nature of its later ethnic mix notwithstanding. By the 1840s, there was a strong abolition movement that coalesced into the organization of the Republican party at Jackson in 1854; Michigan became a major terminus of the "underground railroad" that moved escaped slaves to freedom.

Michigan's vast, virtually untapped natural resources—at first, the easily seen timber and farmland—were the primary draw for settlers. But discovery of copper lodes in the western U.P. in 1844 touched off America's first mining boom, and for the next 40 years Michigan was the nation's leading copper producer. Iron, too, was found in vast quantities.

Moving these valuable ores to the industrial East was a problem. Lake Superior is 22 feet above Lake Huron, joined by the rugged rapids of the St. Mary's River (again, named literally by the French Sault Ste. Marie). The solution: a ship canal, dug in just two years' time and opened in 1855. By the mid-20th century, the "Soo" Locks were a major link in the 2,347-mile St. Lawrence Seaway system, moving twice as much tonnage in a nine-month season (being ice-bound the other three) than the Panama Canal in a full year.

Simultaneous with the U.P. mining boom in the latter half of the 19th century was a lumber boom in the Lower Peninsula, centered in the fabled Saginaw Country, "home" of Paul Bunyan. It was the heyday of the lumber barons; millions of dollars were made as billions of board feet were stripped from Michigan's vast stands of hardwood and pine. What the lumber barons didn't claim, fire did. Sparks allegedly blown by gale winds across Lake Michigan from the great Chicago Fire of 1871 torched a conflagration that swept across the state; 20 years later, fire raced through the "Thumb" area, killing 125 people and prompting the first disaster relief effort of the Red Cross.

At the dawn of the 20th century, a subtle shift began in Michigan's economy: from extracting to processing, from agricultural to industrial, from farms to cities. Huge numbers of foreign immigrants and migrants from the American South caused an equally subtle shift in the state's personality.

But the most wrenching changes of all—that no one could have foreseen —were being wrought in obscure machine shops in Lansing and Detroit by the tinkerings of two men whom history would not forget. Their names were Ransom Eli Olds and Henry Ford.

On Come the Autos

Working independently, Olds and Ford each had perfected a gasoline-powered automobile in 1896. Four years later, R.E. Olds was selling 1,400 of his little curved-dash cars for $650 each; production of the "merry Oldsmobile" jumped to 4,000 in 1904. Ford, plagued by business problems (finally forming his own Ford Motor Company in 1903), tinkered with his design through Models A, B, F, K, and N before coming up with perhaps the most popular car ever made: the Model T. Between 1908 and 1927, 15 million of these "Tin Lizzies" were built. The price steadily declined from $950 to $350, reflecting economies in production Ford realized by creating a moving assembly line at his Highland Park plant. When it fell into full swing in 1913, assembly time for a new Ford plunged from 14 hours to just 93 minutes. Further revolutionizing the infant industry, Ford announced on January 5, 1914, that he would pay his employees $5 for an eight-hour day—double the then-going rate for factory jobs. Ten thousand men showed up seeking Ford jobs the next day. Detroit—and Michigan—were never the same again.

The history of the auto industry is littered with the wrecks of the 2,000-odd makes—Duryea, Mercer, Hudson, LaSalle, Pierce Arrow, and Stanley Steamer among them—eventually doomed to extinction in one of the world's most fiercely competitive industries. By the 1980s, two of the remaining four American auto companies—American Motors and Chrysler—were forced to go, hats in hand, to the federal government for aid to avoid similar fates and even Ford was being kept alive solely by the strength of its foreign operations. The auto industry found itself confronted, and to a degree confounded, by forces seemingly beyond its control. The turn of events was profoundly disturbing for this giant of industries, accustomed by its size and influence to unchallenged mastery in the world of commerce.

General Motors, for instance, is one of the mightiest industrial combines the world has ever seen. In 1977, when it posted record sales, it had 850,000 workers on its global payroll; there were 121 plants in 21 states and more than 60 cities in the United States. Its sales were almost $55 billion, its tax bill $4.7 billion, and its profits $3.3 billion—more than any industrial corporation. GM's gross was twice as large as the budget of any of the states, and its profit larger than the total budget of three-fifths of the states. Aside from producing about half of the passenger cars in the United States, GM formed gigantic divisions producing trucks, buses, refrigeration equipment, diesel motors, marine and aircraft engines, earth-moving equipment, inertial navigation systems, and space-travel components.

But for a corporation with such immense national and international power, GM has been shockingly negligent over most of its history in providing innovative leadership either in technology or in social and political concerns. Smugness and complacency were long its hallmarks—typified by GM President Charles E. Wilson, who at his Senate confirmation hearing on becoming President Eisenhower's Secretary of Defense, uttered his famous line: "What is good for the country is good for General Motors, and what's good for General Motors is good for the country."

Throughout its long glory years, there were no leaders at GM looking ahead to evaluate and prepare for the impact of the auto industry on a changing world in terms of safety, energy conservation, or environmental effects. The problems of auto safety, for example, were known long before Ralph Nader barged onto the scene in the 1960s. But any proposed innovations were dismissed with a shrug that "this safety stuff won't sell."

Indicative of GM's *modus operandi* is that it dispenses virtually no charitable contributions on a national scale, but only locally in communities where its plants are located—and then only when asked. Breaking with this noninitiative policy in 1978, GM unveiled a $20 million proposal to rehabilitate homes, apartments, and businesses in the shabby neighborhood just north of its Detroit headquarters. Skeptics observed that GM's share would be only $1.2 million, that the plan didn't come until 11 years after Detroit's grim riots, and that the firm had never recognized its civic responsibilities before. But others saw it as a hopeful sign of GM's commitment to Detroit.

In partisan politics, GM traditionally pressured its senior executives to contribute to the Michigan Republican party, and they poured between $100,000 and $200,000 yearly into GOP coffers. According to Stuart Hertzberg, treasurer of the Michigan Democratic party, "GM had no bipartisan contribution program until 1968, when we talked them into it"; and even then, contributions came to only a paltry $2,000 a year. GM's top brass could afford to give. Board Chairman Thomas A. Murphy, for example, drew $996,000 in salary, bonuses, and fees in the record 1977 year.

That did not make him the top-paid auto magnate by any means. That distinction fell to Henry Ford II, whose compensation topped $1 million the same year. But then, it's all in the family. Long the third-largest industrial corporation, with annual sales approaching $40 billion, until 1956 Ford Motor Company was tightly held by Fords. Even afterward, despite the millions of shares owned by outside investors, the Ford family retained effective control.

When "Young Henry" took control of Ford from his aging grandfather in the 1940s, the company was losing $10 million a month. Through sound fiscal management and good relations with the UAW, he guided the company to its phenomenal postwar success. But he ruled with an iron hand. In 1978, for example, he fired the oft-flamboyant Lee Iacocca as company president (after a 32-year Ford career) with the curt explanation: "I just don't like you." Ford vetoed Iacocca's ambitious plan to push the company to the top of the small-car market—a decision Iacocca later called "the greatest strategic error in 50 years" at Ford. The result was near-disaster: an estimated $1 billion 1979 loss in Ford's North American division for want of the right products to meet foreign competition. Then there were quality problems: Ford led the industry with mandatory recalls in 1978. It was charged with (but finally acquitted of) reckless homicide with regard to its Pinto. It acceded to federal demands in 1980 to warn consumers that 6 million Fords had engine defects.

Insuring family continuity in leadership, Ford carved out a policy post for his younger brother, William Clay Ford—whose prime business experience had been ownership of the Detroit Lions—and shepherded his own son, Edsel B. Ford II, through management apprenticeship. Subsequently "retired," Henry Ford II was far from forgotten either by his company or Detroit. Long a civic leader, particularly in revitalization of the city following the 1967 riots, he was one of the most influential men in the metropolitan area and the power broker and financial force behind the $350 million riverfront Renaissance Center complex that became the symbol of the city's resurgence.

With Ford headquartered in Dearborn and GM towering remotely in the "New Center," away from downtown, it is Chrysler that long has been viewed affectionately as Detroit's home-town car. It has 21 facilities in the metropolitan area, 15 of them in Detroit. It is the city's second-largest employer, even though it was forced to slash half its work force between 1978 and 1980. Chrysler's Detroit payroll runs roughly $1.5 billion, and area suppliers do close to $2 billion yearly in business with the corporation. Its $800 million payroll to black workers represents 1 percent of the nation's black economy.

The youngest (formed in 1925) and smallest of the Big Three, Chrysler's history has been one of catch-up. Without the vast capital needed to field extensive product lines as could GM and Ford, Chrysler was forced to concentrate its efforts. It found a solid base in the compact-car market and stalled on entering the subcompact fray for fear of undercutting itself. The result: Chrysler got whipsawed in the wild market gyrations of the late 1970s and suffered a staggering $1.097 billion loss in 1979 and another $1.7 billion in 1980. Congress finally approved a $3.5 billion bail-out package in May 1980, including $1.5 billion in federal loan guarantees melded with a complex melange of private aid, and forced Chrysler in return to shape up its operations. The company responded by closing plants, streamlining its product line, laying off 35,000 workers, imposing salary reductions on its management, and winning $1 billion in wage-and-benefit concessions from the UAW. Yet there were many who wondered if Chrysler ever could recover fully—and some who were entertaining similar doubts about Ford. The industry's last good year was 1978, when 9.3 million cars were sold. Higher prices (up an average of 39 percent between 1978 and 1981), record interest rates, and recession combined to depress sales to 6.2 million in 1981, the lowest level in 20 years. In 1982, sales slid further to 5.7 million.

The dramas of the late '70s and '80s merely added to the Motor City's saga of triumphs and failures. Those stories—of flashy fins, of Chrysler's ups and downs, of scrappy little American Motors and of myriad other tales—could well fill chapters. Beyond the colorful specifics lies the obvious: that the stream of automobiles pouring out of Detroit and its satellites has had an impact on Americans' everyday life second to no other modern invention save electricity. The dividends in mobility and convenience are stupendous, and the industry has given birth to others themselves giants of the modern economy —petroleum, tires, road and superhighway construction, tourism. Without the automobile, we might well have remained an essentially rural nation.

But there is bane mixed with the blessings wrought by Detroit. Cars created problems as well as opportunities. Two of them:

•Safety. Between 1950 and 1981, some 1.4 million Americans met their deaths in auto accidents, carnage far exceeding the battlefield casualties of all the wars the nation has ever fought (636,000 through Vietnam). Yet as recently as 1965, the official Detroit attitude was that the driver was the culprit, not his car. Ralph Nader's *Unsafe At Any Speed* focused public attention on auto safety issues, and soon the federal government began requiring scores of safety modifications, ranging from seat belts to tire standards. Tens of millions of cars were subjected to recalls for repairs.

•Pollution. Late in the 1960s, it was discovered that at least 60 percent of the pollutants in the atmosphere came from the internal combustion engine. A decade later, the federal Clean Air Act required Detroit to achieve a 90 percent reduction in auto pollutants by 1975. The cry from the Motor City was "impossible," but with only a year's extension, the impossible was all but achieved. But not without cost: Federal safety and pollution regulations added $700 to the average cost of a new car and were expected to cause another $1,000 price hike by 1985—the prime reason the auto industry and the United Auto Workers joined forces to get the federal regulations reduced.

An Industry in Peril

Since the birth of their industry, nothing has so unsettled the auto magnates as the twin challenges from across the oceans—the energy crisis that began in 1973–74 with the Arab oil embargo, and the Japanese and German encroachment on the American car makers' share of the U.S. market. As recently as 1960, imports accounted for only 7.5 percent of car sales in America; by 1970 the figure was 15 percent; by 1980 it had see-sawed upward to more than 25 percent. The Japanese alone registered an astounding 22 percent market share in 1981.

All of this was a profound shock to what the world calls "Detroit," though in fact the rippling impact of market loss and decline was widely shared. By the late 1970s less than a third of U.S. car and truck production was rolling off Michigan assembly lines. American Motors, the industry's feeble fourth "giant," no longer produced any vehicles in Michigan at all. The industry had spread its plants across the nation after World War II, so that the major "auto states" came to include Delaware, Missouri, Georgia, Illinois, New Jersey, Oklahoma, Wisconsin, and California. Across the industrial Midwest, and to a lesser extent in all regions, plants manufacturing glass and tires and parts for autos represented a mainstay of the economy. One in every five jobs in the United States was said to be somehow auto related. Despite all that, with all the auto firms' headquarters in or near the Motor City, "Detroit" remained synonymous with the industry—and was found to suffer most when it ailed.

One can say the auto makers should have anticipated what awaited them in the 1970s. For years there had been voices in the wilderness warning that oil prices might one day escalate wildly. And it should not have required high genius for multibillion-dollar corporations to figure out that a foreign competitor like the Japanese, with lower wages, modern production methods and aggressive marketing, could one day provide fierce competition—especially in smaller, fuel-efficient cars. But marketing-marketing-marketing was forever the order of the day, looking at next year's sales vis-à-vis domestic competitors, not the changing world beyond our shores. Excessive restyling, from fins to fenders, resulted. And there were perverse market incentives, too. For 25 years GM could build a Cadillac for about $300 more than it could make a Chevrolet—and then sell it for as much as $4,000 more. So why dally in the small-car field, with miniprofits to match?

A reasonable apologia for the auto makers' conduct can, however, be constructed. As early as 1959, Detroit began introducing compact cars, which sold reasonably well, and the first "subcompacts"—such as Ford's Pinto and GM's Chevrolet Vega—successfully countered foreign competition in the early '70s. The Arab oil embargo, imposed in late 1973, spurred a heavy demand for little cars, both domestic and foreign, for a six-month period. But then human nature took over: American motorists, their energy supplies once more assured, again lusted for luxury cars, large sedans and wagons that slurped gasoline at alarming rates. The Big Three were stuck with a glut of little cars no one wanted and invented rebate programs to clear dealer lots and make room for the cars again in demand. Sales of imports also nosedived.

Helping to fuel this demand was the artificially low price of gasoline, which was the last commodity remaining under price controls imposed by President Nixon in 1971. President Ford tried to decontrol oil prices in 1975 to let them rise to world levels, but Congress responded instead by *rolling back* oil prices still further. Having "taken care" of consumers, Congress tacitly acknowledged conservationists by attaching a rider mandating strict fuel-efficiency standards for American-built cars—requiring a "fleet average" of 27.5 miles per gallon by 1985. The perverse result under this 1975 Energy Policy and Conservation Act: oil imports went from an already staggering 6 million barrels per day to 8.3 million barrels daily in 1978.

As Neil Goldschmidt, President Carter's Secretary of Transportation, later evaluated the situation: "Because the political courage to deregulate the price of oil was not present in 1975, the U.S. government allowed the nation to go from importing one-third of its oil to nearly half, and the opportunity to make a gradual shift of the nation's automotive fleet from larger to smaller cars was lost." The result was predictable: an orgy of big-car buying. It was not until gasoline prices started to skyrocket in 1979 (along with inflation and interest rates) that consumers suddenly "rediscovered" small, high-mileage cars. Everyone—foreign competition included—was caught short. There weren't enough little cars to go around.

But the Japanese, it appeared, could build them better, cheaper, and faster. Consumers beat a steady path to Honda, Datsun, and Toyota showrooms and the once-mighty U.S. auto industry was wrestled to its knees—due in no small part to its staggering labor costs that put it at an average $1,500 disadvantage per car. The Big Three fell deeply in the red; even GM, which only once before had posted a loss since its 1908 founding, finished 1980 $763 million in the hole and had to cut dividends 48 percent. In just two years, auto production plunged by 30 percent in the U.S. and by 40 percent in Michigan. When a modest turnaround in profits began in 1982, it was chiefly by virtue of 270,000 worker layoffs—not increased sales.

So the industry would retool, would think small, would think high-mileage. It would be a slow process, since it takes three or four years to bring a new car from the drawing board to the highway. And the grim fact in Michigan was that no one expected the auto industry ever to return to its past employment levels. Symbolic of this was the Michigan legislature's decision to establish a nonprofit Industrial Technology Institute in Ann Arbor. The institute's specialty would be a strategy guaranteeing fewer, not more, auto industry jobs: robots. In place of UAW workers, one could foresee future assembly lines manned by the versatile automated machines that perform repetitive and complicated tasks such as welding and painting—24 hours a day, never asking for paid vacations or pension guarantees.

Rise and Retreat of the Auto Workers

The UAW is the most powerful of Michigan's powerful labor movement. At the start of the 1980s one out of every 17 U.S. unionists lived in Michigan—nearly 1.3 million in all; and they had been so successful that the state's weekly manufacturing wage ($424 in 1981) averaged one-third above the national figure.

Born out of the Great Depression, when auto workers were earning an average of only $20 per week, the United Automobile Workers (with not a few Communist organizers involved) became the survivors of a chaotic campaign for unionization battled by industrialists with murder, mayhem, and relentless intimidation. The National Labor Relations Act of 1935 required employers to bargain collectively, but the auto industry resisted. Not until the UAW staged its great Flint sit-down strike in 1937 did General Motors grant the union recognition. Later that year, a similar sit-down broke Chrysler's resistance, and by the end of 1937 the UAW had contracts with 400 companies. But old Henry Ford dug in; there was a bloody confrontation at the mammoth River Rouge complex in 1937 and not until 1941 did Ford capitulate.

Then, he granted the UAW the industry's first union shop and dues checkoff.

Among those brutally beaten by Ford's thugs was Walter Reuther, the central figure in UAW history and the most influential single trade unionist of the American postwar era. Son of a German Socialist brewery worker, Reuther became an expert tool-and-die man, worked his way through college, was fired by Ford for his union activity, and made a 33-month world tour with his brother Victor to study union movements. Enemies later cited their stay in the Soviet Union as "evidence" of Marxist leanings; but Reuther always was a Socialist, never a Communist, and in fact won the UAW presidency in 1946 after a decisive battle with Communist elements in the union.

A pugnacious redhead, Reuther took the UAW from zero to 1.6 million members and pioneered such innovations as profit-sharing, cost-of-living escalator clauses, a guaranteed annual wage, and early retirement. The contract he won with GM in 1948 remained into the '80s the model followed with the Big Three in triennial negotiations; auto talks eventually became so routine the companies would present identical offers (one year even repeating typographical errors), and the UAW would pick one of the three as a strike "target." But the gains won were so enormous (the average weekly wage in the industry reaching $488 in 1981) that in the 1980s the UAW was forced to re-open its contracts and concede billions of dollars in benefits to help the industry survive and members keep their jobs.

Reuther's horizons extended beyond traditional union concerns to broad social issues and politics. Following his 1970 death in an airplane accident, the *Washington Post* editorialized that Reuther "left his imprint upon the social and economic life of the United States more indelibly, perhaps, than any political figure in his time, Franklin Roosevelt excepted. He was part labor leader, part social reformer, part evangelist."

The union was headed into contract negotiations when Reuther died, and his successor, Leonard Woodcock, promptly struck GM (the first strike in 15 years). It won enormous gains—including an immediate 51-cents-per-hour raise. The UAW victory pattern was repeated in brief strikes against Chrysler in 1973 and Ford in 1976.

In a sense, the UAW became a victim of its own success. UAW members came to average more than twice as much in hourly wages as other American production workers. Total compensation averaged out to $20 per hour, as compared with $12 per hour at Japanese auto factories.

When Woodcock retired, Scottish-born Douglas Fraser took over the UAW. In 1979, he shrewdly seized on Chrysler's troubles to bring home one of the most radical ideas from the European labor movement: in exchange for the union's support of federal aid for Chrysler, he won himself a seat on the company's board of directors. In 1982, with hundreds of thousands of autoworkers nationwide out of work, its membership shrunken to below 1958 recession levels, losing $1 million a month in evaporated dues, the UAW reopened its contracts and gave up billions of dollars in benefits. In return for this, it received pledges of job security and moratoriums on plant closings. Rank-and-file workers ratified the contracts.

Fraser was the last of the UAW chiefs to be drawn from the Reuther inner circle, and he and other labor activists feared that the union would lose its progressive tradition. But Owen Bieber, the vice president for the GM division chosen to succeed Fraser in 1983, had been a UAW staffer in Reuther days and vowed to continue his predecessors' policies.

Political Michigan

For 80 years after its founding under the oaks at Jackson in 1854, the Republican party had an iron hold on the state's elective—and hence, patronage—offices. But a series of events in the New Deal '30s and wartime years created conditions that led to fundamental change. The rise of militant trade unionism—principally, the UAW—together with passage of a strict civil service law in 1941 led the way. Democrats began making inroads, but even in 1947 only nine of them sat in the then-132-member legislature.

A series of conferences in 1947–48 changed not only the shape of the Democratic party but that of Michigan's future as well. Liberal intellectuals and labor leaders coalesced, took over party machinery, and picked as their candidate for governor G. Mennen Williams, 37-year-old heir to a soap fortune who had become an ardent New Deal convert. An effervescent politician in a perennial white polka-dotted green bow tie, "Soapy" Williams won a squeaker election thanks in part to GOP conservatives who sat on their hands. He went on to serve a then-record 12 years.

Republicans constantly attacked Williams either as a "phony" or as a CIO stooge and "a captive of Walter Reuther." He was able to build stature on his own and sometimes made decisions against labor's will. Yet in area after area—civil rights, compulsory health insurance, public recreation, education—Williams and Reuther sought to make Michigan a laboratory for social democracy. They took advanced stands and permanently altered the political complexion of the state. But the politics were precarious. Continually warring with the rural- and business-dominated Republican legislature, Williams let things get out of hand in 1959 by skipping a couple of paydays for state workers when legislators refused to buy his tax proposals to finance a record budget after the 1958 recession. The tactic backfired. Michigan's government became a national laughing-stock (there was a joke that year about a drink called "Michigan on the rocks") and suffered severe financial repercussions.

By 1957, the Democrats held all the elective statewide posts in Lansing. The Democrats and labor had, in fact, succeeded in painting the GOP as the kept creature of big business. And the Republicans had succeeded in casting Williams and the Democrats as the handmaidens of big labor. Thus Michigan entered the 1960s in a political stalemate. The man who proved capable of resolving the stalemate was George Romney, whose contribution looms as large in Republican history as Williams' does in the Democrats'. Romney had made his mark in the 1950s as head of American Motors Corporation, evangelizing for his little Rambler against the "gas-guzzling dinosaurs" of the Big

Three. Handsome, charismatic, and independent, he responded to the "pay-less paydays" crisis of 1959 by founding Citizens for Michigan, which with such allies as the League of Women Voters secured voter approval for a constitutional convention. Elected in 1961 as a Republican delegate, Romney helped shape the model document and then in 1962 challenged and beat for the governorship Williams' lackluster successor, John B. Swainson.

Michigan made a quantum leap forward in the six years that Romney served as governor, a record in no way diminished by the fact that a booming national economy bolstered the auto industry and went a long way toward solving the budget crisis left behind by the Democrats. Romney restored confidence in Michigan government, won approval of the excellent new constitution, set the state's finances in order through enactment of the first income tax in its history, and finally revived and reinvigorated the Michigan Republican party and left it an even match for the still powerful Democratic-labor machine.

By 1966, Romney was invincible. He won reelection with 60.5 percent of the vote (larger than even Soapy Williams had won in his salad days); his coattails carried the GOP to control of the legislature and to victory in five marginal congressional districts. Even interim U.S. Sen. Robert P. Griffin, whom Romney had appointed in April to fill a vacancy, surged to victory over none other than Soapy Williams himself. All this made Romney, overnight, the leading contender for the 1968 GOP presidential nomination. But Romney—sincere, honest, moral, the evangelistic Mormon—stumbled in his campaign for the White House. Not long after he confessed to having been "brainwashed" during a fact-finding trip to Vietnam, he was laughed out of the race, winding up a year later in Richard Nixon's Cabinet.

Romney's lieutenant governor and successor, William G. Milliken, was to transform Michigan politics for the third time—weaving a pattern of biparti-sanship that left some Republicans shaking their heads and many Democrats eager to shake his hand and embrace him. "You have to look at him as a political craftsman," Detroit Free Press political reporter Remer Tyson said after Milliken had been in office nearly a decade. "He's so good, he comes off as a nonpolitician. At first, people thought he was a nice guy but not tough enough. He's kept the soft image, but he acts tough." Among the hallmarks of the Milliken approach, as Tyson ticked them off, were an aura of compe-tence and integrity leading to high credibility; a willingness to admit mistakes; the maintenance of an image of "a guy who will try to do the right thing"; a sensitivity to major problems needing attention.

First and foremost on Milliken's list were the cities (he developed one of the nation's first state urban policies), followed by the environment, transpor-tation, equitable school financing, and land use. Milliken's unflagging com-mitment to the salvaging of Detroit earned him the respect and even tacit political support of Democratic Mayor Coleman Young. Such an alliance would never have been possible had Milliken not supported his rhetoric with responses that pumped hundreds of millions of dollars in aid into the central city. The policy was not without opposition, especially from rural Republicans. But Milliken's superb sense of coalition building repeatedly carried the day. "Failure to deal with the cities where the people are now really means we're abandoning the whole country," he told us in a 1977 interview. "Our investment is there, and I think we have to save our investment."

Progressive government has deep Michigan roots. This state created, for example, a state board of labor in 1883; enacted a 10-hour-day law in 1885 and a child labor law in 1887. The state is unrivaled in its support of education. Every constitution since the first has declared: "Schools and the means of education shall forever be encouraged." Consequently, the state had the nation's first constitutional superintendent of public instruction, the first school aid fund, the first normal school for teacher training west of the Alleghenies, and was the first to provide free high school education.

Michigan's system of public higher education, however, is its even more distinctive achievement, and many regard its public university complex (12 full degree-granting institutions and 29 community colleges with enrollments nearing a half million) as second only to California's in quality. Enrolling about 115,000 students, the major universities—Michigan State at East Lansing, the University of Michigan at Ann Arbor, and Wayne State in Detroit —in 1977 ranked 3rd, 10th, and 15th in the nation, respectively. The oldest (its charter dating to 1817) and for many years the intellectual leader of the group, the University of Michigan draws a politically active intelligentsia that caused a loss of support among legislators, taxpayers, alumni, and the business community in the wake of anti-Vietnam and pro-civil rights activism including a 10 percent black enrollment goal. Even more serious for this flagship of public higher education in America was the toll taken by the deep Michigan recession of the early 1980s. Its funds cut back, it began to have difficulty attracting or holding top faculty. The situation was made worse by skepticism among potential staff or students about the state's future.

Michigan State, founded in 1855 as the world's first center for college-level instruction in agriculture, became the model for America's unique land-grant system and after World War II mushroomed into a major university. Though derided by some as a "cow college" or as "Moo U," MSU under the 27-year tutelage of President John A. Hannah by the 1970s had a 5,000-acre campus itself classified as a botanic garden, more than 40,000 students, a budget in excess of $100 million, and more National Merit Scholars than any university in the country. Wayne became part of the state university system in 1956 but still strove to serve primarily Detroit's urban poor. Nearly one-quarter of its students were black, making Wayne State's the highest minority student body of any "white" U.S. college. Primarily a commuter school, 75 percent of its 33,000 students held down outside jobs while pursuing studies in such fields as the arts, law, social work, or medicine.

Support of education and other public services does not come cheaply. In 1979, this eighth-largest state was fifth in the nation in total revenues and fourth in total spending; it had the fourth-highest property tax rate in the nation and paid its state workers one-fifth more than the national average; it ranked among the top four states in spending on education, health, highways, welfare, and public safety.

And then severe recession hit. Saddled with shrinking population and higher joblessness than during the Great Depression, Michigan was losing both its tax base and federal aid—a loss of $600 million from Washington in fiscal 1982 alone. Compounding the problem was the so-called Headlee amendment to the constitution, adopted by the voters in 1978, which placed on it one of the tightest fiscal lids on any state government. Milliken and the legislature had no choice but to cut, repeatedly and ever more deeply, into the budget. In fiscal 1981, more than $1 billion was slashed; by fiscal 1982, the state was spending (in inflation-adjusted dollars) less than it had 10 years before. Eventually, all this took its toll on Milliken, who chose to retire at the end of 1982. One of Milliken's last acts was to delcare a "human emergency" in his state and launch an unprecedented 40-point plan to aid the homeless and hungry. The Romney-Milliken era was at an end. Perhaps dying with it was those two men's brand of invigorating progressive Republicanism, lost in the polarization of the Reagan "revolution." Yet it was difficult to see how a revival of the Democratic/UAW free-spending, high-wage formula could succeed, notwithstanding the 1982 election of a governor from that political camp, Democrat James J. Blanchard, a 40-year-old congressman from suburban Detroit. (The Republican nominee whom Blanchard defeated was, ironically, none other than insuranceman Richard Headlee, author of the 1978 tax-cut voter initiative.)

Desperate Times for Detroit

Twentieth-century Detroit has had every reason to be a great city. Sixth-largest in the nation in population (indeed fifth until Houston overtook it in the late '70s), it has a convergence of resources—financial, managerial, and in transportation—that should have made it a bulwark of strength for Michigan and the Midwest. Yet repeatedly in the postwar era, the mighty Motor City found itself a metropolis in pain, suffering from repeated recessions, the only U.S. city to suffer directly from the energy crisis (because of its overreliance on a gas-guzzling auto industry), wracked by racial divisions, and at odds with its suburbs and "outstate" hinterland.

In the early '80s, as Michigan seemed headed for trouble, Detroit was a city in desperate straits. Unemployment in summer 1982 was pegged officially at 20.5 percent and by Christmas, the mayor's office claimed 25 percent, the same rate as in 1933. One-third of the auto dealerships closed in two years; some 6,800 area firms had gone bankrupt. Detroit's murder rate, once the shame of the nation but tamed in the '70s, was climbing again. Literally one-third of the city's people were on welfare. The city faced a two-year budget deficit not far short of $300 million and potential bankruptcy.

To that one could add other problems: a perilous city budget that had become far too dependent on heavy federal aid; few public parks (except for the magnificient 985-acre Belle Isle in the Detroit River); public employee unions that had driven police and fire wages up to the highest in the nation; badly deteriorated schools; scores of dilapidated neighborhoods; rampant joblessness; and fearsome crime levels.

Many were tempted to write off the great Motor City as a terminal case of industrial obsolescence, situated in the wrong time and place for any significant revival. The city's immense scale worked against it: at 140 square miles, filled with endless tracts of worker housing, it seemed impractically large and was undoubtedly more expensive for municipal government to service than the remaining population justified. Yet as a frequent return visitor to Detroit, one had to be impressed by its resuscitative qualities, its remarkable spirit, the public and private leadership that seemed to increase in quality and depth even as the problems grew more severe.

Detroit's economic woes, one had to remember, were preceded by others. In this city, into which so many thousand Southern blacks had poured in search of opportunity, the most destructive race riot of U.S. history broke out in 1967. Forty-three persons were killed, 7,000 arrested, and damage of some $50 million inflicted—worse than Watts or Newark or even the 1943 Detroit riot, when 34 died and the Army had to restore order. The race problem prompted a surge of white flight. At some unchronicled moment in the early 1970s, Detroit became a black-majority city—indeed, the largest such in the U.S. The black population figure had risen from 29 percent in 1960 to 44 percent in 1970; by 1980 it would be more than 63 percent. In time, the problem would also become one of class as much as race, as the initial white flight to the suburbs was followed by black flight as middle-class blacks deserted the city, leaving it to the poorest and most desperate.

A burning question was what brand of black leadership—moderate or extremist—would take political control of the city. In 1973 that question was answered with the election of Coleman A. Young as mayor. An Alabama native who had been labeled a radical (even a Communist) in his younger days as a UAW organizer, as mayor Young acted firmly, pragmatically, and with fierce determination to make the city succeed. He proved equally sensitive to the needs of his black brethren and the remaining whites.

The Detroit that Young took over was dreary. The downtown skyline was dominated by high brick office buildings of forbidding '20s and '30s architecture; except for government offices and banks, not a single major new building had risen downtown since World War II. There was a magnificent $100 million Civic Center on the riverfront, but not enough hotel rooms to draw convention business. To correct all this, Young determined to enlist the support of Detroit's economic powers, including those of the auto industry —and he succeeded. The seminal event in the city's physical rebirth occurred in 1977 with the opening of the $350 million Renaissance Center, including a 73-story hotel surrounded by high office towers, touted as the sign of the rebirth of Detroit. Not insignificantly, it was Henry Ford II, pledging the fiscal support of his corporation, who acted as the financial catalyst for the venture involving 51 corporations. It was easy (and appropriate) to criticize the overwhelming "megastructure" architecture of the RenCen, including its moatlike walls at street level. But Detroit may have needed this kind of massive statement to the world that it still lived. Soon the dramatically changed Detroit skyline (breathtaking when seen from Windsor, Ontario, across the river) saw more changes, as the RenCen touched off more than $600 million in construction or renovation of other buildings. The colorful "Greektown" and other downtown restaurant areas also showed fresh life.

Unfortunately, by 1982 some of the blush on Detroit's new downtown had faded. Owners of the RenCen, once the city's symbol of hope, defaulted on their mortgage payments in early 1983. Downtown Detroit suffered another blow: J. L. Hudson's closed its 71-year-old "Big Store," as it was known, at a height of 28 stories and with two million square feet of floor space, once a competitor with New York's Macy's as the world's biggest and grandest. Hudson's, which pioneered the suburban shopping mall by crossing Detroit's northern boundary at Eight Mile Road to build dazzling Northland in the 1950s, did keep its multi-branch suburban empire.

Young's breezy, disarming style proved central in the transition from white to black Detroit. (Example: In his inaugural, the mayor said, "I issue a forward warning now to all those pushers, all rip-off artists, to all muggers. I don't give a damn whether they are black or white, or if they wear Superfly suits or blue uniforms with silver badges—hit Eight Mile Road.") By a decade after the 1967 riots, the city also had a black school superintendent, a black police chief, a black county sheriff, and black majorities on the city council and school board. The way was greatly smoothed by a host of civic groups bent on keeping the city together—notably New Detroit, Inc., formed by leading blacks and whites after the 1967 riot.

Slowly, auto industry investment began to return. Chrysler spent some $100 million to renovate and re-open its Jefferson Avenue plant to produce its K-cars. And Detroit itself, taking advantage of a new Michigan law allowing a city to acquire land for private enterprise, spent $200 million (in federal, state, and borrowed funds) to obtain the old Dodge Main plant and its surrounding "Poletown" neighborhood for a new job-producing GM facility.*

By the late '70s, Detroit's revenue drain from lost population and bankrupt business was proving almost insurmountable, especially when coupled with

---

*Chrysler's Dodge Main, which had once been the world's largest auto factory, with 5 million square feet of space and 20,000 jobs, shut down in January 1980. The scheduled new GM complex was to quadruple the 103-acre site straddling the Hamtramck border. The land taking provoked some furious (albeit eventually fruitless) local opposition because 1,300 homes, businesses, schools, and churches had to be demolished. Some 3,800 people had to be relocated, many of them elderly poor whose lives had been spent in the neighborhood. But so desperate was Young for the potential 10,000 new jobs that he accepted the political flack—and even offered GM a handsome tax abatement on its new plant.

the wildly out-of-sync wages for city employees. The Motor City had lost 310,724 people, or one-fifth of its population, in the 1970s, with a corresponding loss in per capita federal aid of nearly $100 million in 1981–82 alone. At 1,203,339, Detroit was down a half million since its peak in 1950.

Even though its tax rates were four times higher than any other Michigan city, Detroit all but hit bottom in 1981. A blue-ribbon panel appointed by Young predicted bankruptcy; Felix Rohatyn, author of New York City's financial salvation, bluntly warned the mayor: "Your choices are between extreme pain and agony." Rather than a quixotic search for federal or state aid, Young chose to "bite the bullet." He laid off 4,000 city workers (including 1,000 police, the vast majority of them the most recently hired blacks and women), slashed public services, fired those whose unions balked at wage cuts or freezes, and won $90 million in concessions from other public employee unions. Enlisting the support of his influential corporate allies, he then sold the legislature and eventually Detroit voters on a hefty income tax increase —a 50 percent boost (to 3 percent) for city residents and 200 percent (to 1.5 percent) on Detroit's 250,000 commuters. The package won astonishing 64 percent approval after a campaign with clear racist overtones—four out of five blacks voting "yes" after not-so-veiled hints from Young that a hostile white-dominated legislature might take over "their" city. Detroit whites were against the plan by a two-to-one margin. But its passage, together with the sale of $125 million in bonds, generated $8 million a month and pulled Detroit back once more from its seemingly endless string of fiscal crises.

Beyond Detroit

Michigan's world outside of Detroit actually begins within it—the enclave suburbs of Highland Park (population 27,909) and Hamtramck (21,300), tenuously linked like Siamese twins. Highland Park, birthplace of Henry Ford's assembly line, is now 84 percent black; Hamtramck (pronounced Ham-TRAM-ick), citadel of poor Poles and Ukranians who worked in the Ford and Chrysler plants, is 82 percent white. South of the city sprawl the "downriver suburbs," lower-middle-class white factory towns such as Southgate, Wyandotte, Allen Park, and Trenton. To the west, still in Wayne County, are more of the same: notably Dearborn, home to Ford's world headquarters, which for nearly 40 years was one of the last bastions of lily-whitism under Mayor Orville Hubbard. With 90,660 residents, Dearborn's population has slipped by nearly one-fifth since 1960.

Curving along the shore of Lake St. Clair northeast of the city in a compact strip of privilege are the Grosse Pointes, five locales (total population 52,099) for the crème de la crème of Detroit society. Home to the "autostracy" and other "old money" families, the Pointes in recent years have opened the door enough to admit lesser corporate executives along with younger professional families.

North of Motor City lie the huge suburban counties of Macomb (694,660) and Oakland (1,011,793), each of which grew 11 percent in the 1970s. Every one of their older, close-in communities *lost* population, virtually all in excess of 10 percent, while growth was explosive in out-county areas, reaching as high as 100–200 percent in the farthest reaches from Detroit. Warren's story is typical of Macomb County. In 1950, only 727 people lived there; in 1970, there were 179,260 as white factory workers flocked to escape the grime, crime, and blacks of the inner city. The federal Department of Housing and Urban Development under George Romney tried—but failed—to force integration in 1970. By 1980, there were still only 297 blacks living in Warren among its 161,134 residents.

While Macomb County has been a blue-collar haven, Oakland County directly to its west has drawn Detroit's "new money" to towns such as Bloomfield Hills, Birmingham, and Troy. This is a favorite territory of young auto and advertising executives and many of metropolitan Detroit's up-and-coming civic leaders. There are also, just over the Eight Mile "barrier," a string of older working-class suburbs, such as Royal Oak, Oak Park, and Ferndale, and a heavy concentration of Detroit's Jewish community.

Farther north lies the troubled city of Pontiac (76,715), one of GM's principal outposts, a grimy city with a combustible mix of Southern whites, blacks (37 percent by 1980), and Mexican-Americans. In 1971 a school busing plan was imposed on Detroit and its suburbs, and violence erupted in Pontiac—including the dynamiting of 10 empty school buses, a crime officially blamed on the Ku Klux Klan. The political uproar spread to neighboring suburbs, calmed only when the Supreme Court overturned the plan three years later.

Racism/white flight/irrationally rapid dispersion of population afflicted Detroit perhaps more severely than any other American city. In the mid-1970s the Southeast Michigan Council of Governments (SEMCOG) drew up a grim scenario for the region in the year 2000. Though some of the suburban growth trends detected then were subsequently slowed by economic slump, the SEMCOG computer study projected that by the end of the century, Detroit and its older, more established suburbs would lose more than a third of their population—the growth shifting to outlying suburbs. As a result, there would be an additional million cars on the region's roads, driving 40 million miles more a day, and wiping out every gallon of gasoline savings projected from lighter, more energy-efficient autos. As many as 466 square miles of southeastern Michigan farmland would be lost to highways, subdivisions, shopping centers, and industries. At least $2.4 billion worth of existing school space would be abandoned in the city and its older suburbs—while $1.3 billion for new schools on the urban fringe would be required. Yet the study concluded that with appropriate infill development all 700,000 anticipated new households up to 2000 in the Detroit area could be accommodated within the network of already sewered city and suburban areas.

The sharp disparity between Detroit and its suburbs is reflected, as always, in dollars. Bloomfield Hills, for instance, has a per capita income about six and one-half times that of Detroit. Deep-seated antagonisms remain between Detroit and its suburbs. Part of this can be attributed to suburban smugness and prejudice, but part, too, to the implied racism of pronouncements by Coleman Young and his colleagues. The city has been far too slow in forming political coalitions with its poor, close-in, sometimes black suburbs—not to mention the outstate cities that were beginning to suffer many Detroit-style problems, from population flight and housing deterioration to poor schools and retail decline. Both the suburban and outstate cities to a startling degree harbor microcosms of Detroit's black-white dilemma and inner-city decay. Fully half of the Detroit suburban cities and virtually all those outstate lost population in the 1970s; the only ones showing growth were distant suburbs.

Least of the "losers" was Lansing (130,414, down 0.8 percent), 90 miles northwest of Detroit and Michigan's capital since 1847. Home of Oldsmobile and Fisher Body, its blue-collar mix of blacks and Southern whites is balanced by its abutting professional and intellectual neighbor, East Lansing (48,309), home of Michigan State and until the 1960s a strictly white community. Another hour's drive northwest lies Grand Rapids (181,843), once a placid Dutch stronghold touted as the "furniture capital of the world." But the high cost of skilled labor drove most of the furniture business to the South; Poles and blacks poured in to man varied new industries, and the city has escaped the worst of recent crushing unemployment levels.

Stretching directly west from Detroit along I-94 (first cut as the Territorial Road through the 1830s wilderness) are a string of lesser cities. Ann Arbor (107,316) is the first and least typical of the lot. It actually increased in population (up 7.3 percent) during the '70s and has some hard industry but primarily is home to the University of Michigan and spin-off research firms—and a growing number of Detroit commuters. Then come Jackson (39,739); Battle Creek (35,724), the breakfast-cereal capital; and Kalamazoo (79,722), a college and pharmaceutical town. Northward, nestled near Saginaw Bay, are two run-of-the-mill GM cities, Saginaw (77,508) and Bay City (41,593). Nearby Midland (37,250) is the home of Dow Chemical Company, 24th-largest industrial corporation in the U.S. and target of several environmental controversies.

Finally, we come to Flint (159,611, down 17.4 percent in a decade), the blue-collar lunch-bucket city and General Motors town *par excellence*. Until 1980, 60 percent of its workers were employed at GM plants; no city in the U.S.A. had a higher average workingman's wage. But the other side of that economic sword sliced with a vengeance during recession: in 1982, one out of five able-bodied adult Flint residents was out of work.

With large numbers of blacks (41 percent in 1980) and Southern rednecks, Flint has an often tense racial situation. In 1967, for example, it had both its first black mayor, Floyd McCree, and a Ku Klux Klan bold enough to march down the main street. But Flint does have one unique asset—the Mott Foundation, created by GM pioneer and local patriarch C.S. Mott, one of the richest men in America when he died in 1973 at the age of 97. His foundation, one of the nation's ten largest, has poured hundreds of millions of dollars into social, educational, and recreational projects in Flint—most recently seed money for sparkling Riverbank Park and majority funding for Autoworld, a

Disneyland-like exposition of the auto industry.* Flint, indeed, had the audacity to believe it could become a Midwestern convention city.

Michigan in the U.S.A.

Michigan has made repeated contributions to American political life, not the least of which came after the wrenching Watergate trauma climaxed in the resignation of President Richard Nixon. On August 9, 1974, Gerald R. Ford of Grand Rapids—a man who had longed to become Speaker of the House but instead became Vice President and then President without being elected to either job—took over the Oval Office, assuring Americans that their "long national nightmare" was over. An unspectacular but upright and honest leader, Ford reestablished in the presidency and federal government a sense of integrity, so sorely needed in the post-Nixon days. He was a bare loser to Jimmy Carter in 1976 (in large part due to his prompt pardon of Nixon). Then Ford's love of Michigan proved to have its limits: he retired to Palm Springs, Calif., not to the Grand Rapids he had represented for 25 years in Congress.

Until Jerry Ford made his mark, Grand Rapids' most famous son had been Republican Arthur Vandenberg—the isolationist-turned-internationalist who helped write the United Nations charter in 1945 and chaired the Senate Foreign Relations Committee when many of the pioneer postwar international programs were being molded. With his belief that "politics stops at the water's edge," Vandenberg was the architect of bipartisan foreign policy.

A special word must be said about the late Philip A. Hart, the gentle Democratic senator from Michigan who died of cancer only a few days before his planned retirement in 1976. Called the "conscience of the Senate" and widely respected for his work on civil rights and consumer issues, Hart served three terms and in later years wore the only modern-day Senate beard (the result of an election bet with his children). Though a favorite of the UAW and a leading liberal, Hart's genteel manner gave the GOP a feeling he was one of them; somehow they couldn't believe that a man with a home on Mackinac Island and an heiress wife could be so dangerous. From opposite sides of the political spectrum, Hart and Senator Robert Griffin (co-author as a young congressman of the landmark 1959 Landrum-Griffin labor reform law, a close Ford ally, and later assistant Republican leader in the Senate) played a role of greater national significance than any Michiganders in Congress since Vandenberg. Donald W. Riegle Jr., a Republican congressman-turned-Democrat, was elected to the Senate in 1976 and turned from brash criticism of the House to passionate advocacy for his state in its time of trouble. Holding the other Senate seat was Carl Levin, a former Detroit city councilman.

Among Michiganders in the U.S. House in recent times, two black Demo-

*The Mott Foundation has also branched out into innovative urban projects, many of them neighborhood-related, in cities across the U.S.

crats, two Democratic leaders, and three key Republicans spring to mind. Detroit's Rep. John Conyers, Jr., first elected in 1964, became a star in the black caucus. His fellow Detroiter, Charles Diggs, Jr., was convicted in 1978 of 29 charges stemming from a kickback scheme in his office, won reelection, then shrugged off a 414–0 House censure vote (the first since 1921), finally resigned, and then went to jail.

Rep. John Dingell, representing southwestern Detroit and adjacent suburbs, was a pioneering congressional environmentalist but turned parochial when he led a drive to weaken the Clean Air Act. Former Rep. Martha Griffiths of Detroit masterminded congressional approval of the Equal Rights Amendment and was the first woman to sit on the powerful Ways and Means Committee; she was elected lieutenant governor in 1982. Guy Vander Jagt, representative of the cherry and tulip producing section along Lake Michigan, won national prominence as chairman of the Republican congressional campaign committee; critics said his legislative acumen was a faint shadow of his oratorical skills. David Stockman, who left his southwestern Michigan House seat to become director of the Office of Management and Budget and *enfant terrible* of the Reagan administration, doubtless had one of the keenest minds (albeit less in political judgment) than all but a handful of public servants. One might finally mention Carl D. Pursell, of Ann Arbor, who became leader of a group of some three dozen liberal-moderate Republican House members from the Northeast and Midwest—the so-called gypsy moths who wrung from Stockman and the Reagan White House concessions for federal programs sustaining their beleaguered region.

A Michigan Postscript

For years it seemed that Michigan, when all was said and done, was something less than the sum of its parts. The auto industry, with wealth and resources almost unequaled on earth, could and should have been a pacesetter for American business and life. Instead, it waited for Ralph Nader and the Detroit riots, and later for OPEC, to spur it to action. The UAW was for years an innovative force in American life, but it blindly let inflationary wage increases and sloppiness on the assembly line paint it—and the entire U.S. auto industry —into such a corner that foreign imports could devour American jobs.

With its riches and opportunities, Michigan should never have let Detroit "happen," or for that matter let Lansing or Flint happen quite like the way they did. In race, housing, regional governance, Michigan is a disappointment. For too long, men of much wealth but little sensitivity held the ultimate power in Michigan. They lacked foresight and left it to the 1980s for all Michiganders to suffer the bitter consequences.

Perversely, Michigan may provide a more inspiring model in adversity than it did in prosperity. The first hints of that came from Coleman Young's impressive outreach to find allies, within and without, to help rescue Detroit in its time of testing. The state's nascent efforts to formulate long-term economic revival strategies, based on new technologies, together with the hitherto unprecedented mutual survival pacts between auto managements and unions in the early 1980s, were another. Michigan State established an Urban Experimental Research Institute with a federal grant to become to the troubled cities what the Cooperative Extension Service has been to generations of farmers: a source of research, expertise, and technical assistance. Battle Creek achieved its remarkable governmental merger, under prodding from Kellogg—a hint that abolition of costly, overlapping governmental jurisdictions might be one path to economic survival. In Detroit's Virginia Park neighborhood, worst-hit during the 1967 riots, a public-private partnership enabled construction of a large shopping plaza and a $5 million community center next door. A new Economic Alliance for Michigan was launched by 70 influential business and labor leaders—politicians were deliberately excluded—to recommend strategies for job creation, resource development, and economic diversification.

In times past, nature and luck had endowed Michigan with sufficient riches to prosper as a world model of the adversarial economic system, a system brought to a fine science in the tensions of UAW-auto company negotiations. The test of the future would be whether Michigan's leaders could cooperate as well for survival as they had previously clashed to see who would be richest. Should the new cooperative model succeed, there was even a chance, albeit one only hazily glimpsed from the vantage point of the early 1980s, that this state could one day be *more* than the sum of its parts.

WISCONSIN

Tradition, Mavericks, and Good Government

LIKE A BRIGHT METEOR sailing through a midnight sky, Wisconsin in the early 20th century showed what one state can do to enhance the life of its people. The trailblazer was Robert Marion La Follette; the tradition he created was called Progressivism.

But there is far more to Wisconsin than La Follette or Progressivism. The state bred not only La Follette and his political descendants (by bloodline or ideology or both), but Joseph R. McCarthy, the man whose Hitler-like red-baiting eventually made its way into dictionaries as *sui generis*. In fact, Wisconsin is an amalgam of strong political traditions and self-perpetuating political myths, of high government expectations and taxes to prove it, of economic diversity in the extreme (cows to heavy machinery), and a distinctive quality of life found in few of its sister states.

Wisconsin's strain of Progressive politics—born when the people revolted against hard times around 1900 and ousted the corporate magnates and corrupt political bosses they blamed for their misfortunes—runs exceedingly deep, reflected both in an activist government and extraordinarily clean politics. While other states expect (and thus often get) bribery and corruption from their public officials, the people of Wisconsin will make a major issue of incidents customarily shrugged off elsewhere.

In 1978, for example, press and public were outraged when three legislators were charged with sticking the state with $1,700 worth of personal long-distance calls; two of the dial-happy members were promptly dumped from office by offended voters, and the legislature crimped its calling habits.

Wisconsin pays a price for the quality of government it demands. Its individual state and local tax burden is consistently among the highest in the nation. Despite some recent easing in the top brackets and introduction of indexing, personal income taxes tripled in the 1970s, ending up fifth-highest in the nation. Local property taxes doubled in the 1972–82 decade. For those high taxes, Wisconsinites get service to match: A pioneer in revenue sharing, the state shunts close to three-fifths of its general tax revenues back to localities. Even excluding generous school aid, this support of local government was roughly double the rate in bordering Minnesota, triple that in neighboring Michigan, and five times the national average. The state also spends generously on education (both higher and lower); conservation (one-seventh of Wisconsin's 56,154 square miles are devoted to public parks and forests); and health (one of America's more generous Medicaid programs*). "I've given up complaining about taxes, because I believe the people want them," Paul Hassett, president of the Wisconsin Association of Manufacturers and Commerce, told us. "It's part of the sense of a progressive society."

All of this government service does not mean there is no resistance to "progress" in the state. In 1976 a farmer named Ed Klessig and his family moved part of their dairy herd to the lawn of the state capitol, where they set up tents for a month to protest the construction of an interstate road from Sheboygan to Green Bay, which would slice off a few acres of their dairy farms. In the finest tradition of Robert La Follette himself, Klessig railed against the "county boards, the chamber of commerce, the state highway commission, the steel and cement people, [and] the labor unions," who he said were "all determined to lay their hands on so-called free federal trust fund money and build the biggest damn thing they could." (We later spent a day with Klessig at his lovely dairy farm; we found a man who could not only rail against the establishment but had a deep love of the land and a fear of its desecration for needless highway building across all of Wisconsin.)

By contemporary national standards, Wisconsin is not as liberal as many have assumed. Its progressivism is a mutation of old-fashioned individualism and traditional values by a humanistic recognition of the needs of the downtrodden—all stirred together with a fervent insistence that public officials be responsive to the people. As often as not it produces conservatism. Such contradictions may seem incomprehensible to outsiders, but not to the descendants of the rugged and fiercely freedom-loving settlers who four times in early Wisconsin history rejected statehood for fear it would lead to stronger government and higher taxes.

The Land and the People

The congested urban southeast of modern Wisconsin gives way to the flat and sandy central plains that in turn are crowned by the rugged Northwoods, pocked with most of the state's 8,800 lakes and ponds, which were carved by glaciers and then filled by their melting ice. Despite the 785-mile shoreline along lakes Michigan and Superior, two-thirds of the state waters drain into the Mississippi basin through an extensive network of rivers. These rivers were avenues first for the trappers and missionaries of New France and later for lumbermen. As in Michigan, Minnesota, and other timber-rich states, 19th-century lumber barons cut wide swaths of Wisconsin, leaving debris to kindle forest fires—fires that in turn consumed more timber than ever was harvested. It was at Peshtigo, in northeastern Wisconsin, that the nation's most deadly holocaust was touched off in 1871, eventually claiming 1,182 lives.

---

*Wisconsin has a bad deal in its "balance of payments" with the federal government. In one year of the late '70s, for example, Wisconsinites sent $9.3 billion to Washington and received back only $6.8 billion in total federal expenditures.

It was out of the history of exploitation that Wisconsin's determination to protect its natural resources developed. The tradition was also perpetuated by the likes of John Muir, who grew up in and fell in love with "that glorious Wisconsin wilderness," as he called it, and later became the father of the national park system and founder of the Sierra Club.* In the 1960s, however, that significant environmental progress was shown. Then-Gov. Gaylord Nelson won approval of landmark legislation to acquire and develop prime scenic land, for which $50 million was set aside in 1961. Twice since then, under governors of both parties, the program has been expanded. Birth of the department of natural resources (consolidated from earlier agencies) gave the state the enforcement impetus to go after the polluters of lakes and streams: the paper mills, the cheese factories, some farm operations, and the city sewage treatment plants. By the dawn of the 1980s, most Wisconsin waters once more were fit for its citizens to take pride in and enjoy.

The 1980 Census, confirming a pattern of many decades, found a third of Wisconsin's 4,705,335 people living in just four counties nestled in the southeastern corner of the state, encompassing Milwaukee, Waukesha, Racine, and Kenosha. Fully two-thirds were to be found on a somewhat wider 18-county southeastern quadrant stretching west to Beloit, Janesville, and Madison and north to Green Bay. And even though it has been eight decades since the rush of European immigrants into Wisconsin passed its peak, there are vestiges of Wisconsonites' cultural heritage. Witness the beer and bratwurst of the Germans in Milwaukee, Sheboygan, and other Lake Michigan communities; the periodic feasts of Norwegian *lutefisk* and musical *sangerfests* in Stoughton; the Cornish pasties in Mineral Point, and the Swiss cheese in New Glarus. There are Swedish meatballs and coffee *klatschen* in the St. Croix Valley; Danish *kringle* in Racine; square-logged homes (with the sauna out back) of the Finns around Superior; sausage, *sokols* (physical development centers), and three-day wedding ceremonies of the Poles in Stevens Point and Milwaukee. Pockets of French Canadians, Belgians, Russians, Czechs, and Italians scattered around the state add to the cultural stew. So heavy was the latter-day immigration that the first settlers—the Yankees from New York and New England —almost became a cultural minority themselves. At the turn of the century, four out of every ten Wisconsinites had been born abroad; Milwaukee Socialists in 1910 had to print their circulars in 12 languages. By 1980 the foreign born were rare and 77.2 percent of Wisconsinites were born in the state, one of the highest percentages among all the states.

Blacks never found Wisconsin quite the lure of other industrial centers; although in 1980 they were the state's biggest minority (182,593), they remained the least assimilated: four-fifths lived in Milwaukee and most of the rest were

---

*The diversity of Wisconsin is reflected in the achievements of her notable people: In the military (Gen. Douglas MacArthur); history (Frederick Jackson Turner); economics (Thorstein Veblen); architecture (Frank Lloyd Wright); jazz (Woody Herman) literature (Zona Gala); drama (Spencer Tracy). And, of course, in Golda Meir, the Russian immigrant who became prime minister of Israel.

in Madison, Kenosha, Racine, and Beloit; 30 counties had fewer than 20 black residents. In fact, blacks were the primary minority in only 7 of the state's 72 counties—Indians were the largest nonwhite group in 30 counties, and a fast-growing Hispanic population the largest minority in the remaining 35. Hispanics—many of them former migrant farm workers—by 1980 totaled 62,981 and actually outnumbered blacks in all but 9 counties.

Wisconsin's Indians, despite their shared and sad history of tribal wars, exploitation, and relocation, have survived to number nearly 30,000 in six separate tribes. They have 11 reservations in northern and western Wisconsin; the Menominees, the largest tribe, were a county unto themselves until 1980 when they reverted to reservation status.

Progressivism: Birth and Aftermath

Wisconsin's independent, maverick, polyglot nature was firmly established by 1848, the year it became a state. That same year the University of Wisconsin was chartered, an institution destined not only to become an academic leader but to shape Wisconsin's political, social, and economic life for generations. "The boundaries of the campus are the boundaries of the state," is the university's long-heeded dictum. That concept of public service became embodied in the "Wisconsin Idea"—the precept of utilizing university resources to turn theory into practice for the good of the people. Robert La Follette and his band of Progressive Republicans seized on these ideas and rode the surge for reform that followed the Panic of 1893 to win the governorship in 1900. What La Follette and his Progressive successor, Francis McGovern, did was to draw on the energies and ideas of the new social scientists and convert them into practical legislation: the Wisconsin civil service act of 1905; the nation's first state workmen's compensation law in 1911; the first state direct primary in 1903; a minimum wage law in 1913. While La Follette reformed the political structure, it was McGovern who extended the Progressive philosophy into the economic and industrial realm—winning enactment of the first state income tax (progressively graduated), a state life insurance fund, and factory safety legislation, among many landmarks.

Wisconsin has lived largely on its laurels for more than half a century. The state has maintained the honesty, openness, and responsiveness of the political system, to be sure. But with the exception of its pioneering unemployment compensation law in 1932 (three years before any other state), Gov. Gaylord Nelson's outdoor recreation land acquisition program in 1961, a farmland preservation law in 1977, and the creation of a citizens' utility board in 1979, the nationally significant innovations have been woefully thin. This is not a state to which our futurist friends would have one look for signs of incipient national trends.

"Fightin' Bob" La Follette went to the U.S. Senate in 1906, and for the next 19 years was a crusader for isolationism, corporate regulation, and trust-busting; heading a Progressive presidential ticket in 1924, he rallied dissident

Republicans and Democrats and garnered 17 percent of the vote. In Wisconsin, where Progressivism remained an essentially Republican movement, La Follette left a double legacy: the *Progressive Magazine* (which he founded in 1909 and has a circulation in the neighborhood of 40,000 even in the early 1980s) and his two sons, Robert, Jr., and Philip.

Following his father's death in 1925, "Young Bob" took the Senate seat and Philip was elected governor in 1930 as a Republican. Together, they formed a separate Progressive party that quickly won majorities. Though Philip was ousted in the 1932 FDR landslide, he subsequently won two more terms as a Progressive before his final defeat in 1938. By then, the party was withering. It was finally disbanded in 1946 when "Young Bob" returned to the GOP fold —only to be beaten in the primary by a relatively unknown county judge from Appleton named Joseph R. McCarthy.*

McCarthy, from the time he was elected to the Senate in 1946 until he sought reelection six years later, compiled an unmemorable record notable for its lack of legislative accomplishment. Many have said his crusade against Communism was simply an effort to generate a campaign issue. If so, it succeeded. Once McCarthy in 1952 declared that he had in his hand "a list of 205 that were known to the Secretary of State as being members of the Communist party and who, nevertheless, are still working and shaping policy in the State Department," the issue was to snowball and engrave itself in American political history. How could a state such as Wisconsin elect a man such as McCarthy? Communism raised the specter of political control, an anathema to Wisconsinites. They also have a staunch isolationist streak. McCarthy usually managed to contrast atheistic Communism with God-fearing Christians protecting democracy, another theme that struck a responsive chord. The reaction was emotional. He was reelected and soared to national heights with his red-baiting crusade, only to be shot down by his excesses and a 67–22 Senate censure vote in 1954. McCarthy finally died a broken and bitter man in 1957, yet to this day true believers still make pilgrimages to his grave on a bluff overlooking the Fox River, where Marquette and Jolliet once walked.

The Progressive party disbanded after World War II and during the McCarthy years the GOP once again dominated Wisconsin politics. But a stunning Democratic comeback began in a Green Bay hotel room in 1949, when a group of young liberals of the La Follette tradition—including two who later would be governor, John Reynolds and Patrick Lucey—laid the foundations of the state's modern Democratic party. Just eight years later, they elected William Proxmire to the U.S. Senate, replacing the deceased McCarthy; from then until 1980, Democrats won every U.S. Senate election, seven in all. In 1958, the year after Proxmire's upset win, Democrats unseated the incumbent Republican governor and took control of the lower house in

---

*The latter-day La Follette heir was Bronson C. La Follette, son and grandson of Wisconsin's famous senators—but a Democrat. He served as state attorney general (1965–69), lost a gubernatorial bid in 1968, and was reelected attorney general in 1974, 1978 and 1982.

the legislature for only the second time since 1893. Wisconsin, in the latter half of the 20th century, finally had become a two-party state.

At the national level, Wisconsin's representatives have more often than not reflected the liberal aspects of Progressivism. But at the state and local level, a more complex division has been common: usually liberal on political process issues, often progressive on social issues, and frequently out-and-out conservative on economic issues. The results can perplex non-Wisconsinites. But, without any contradiction in their minds, Wisconsinites can give a majority to a McCarthy or a Richard Nixon while almost in the same breath mobilize around the anti-war sentiments of the Vietnam era or vote 3 to 1 on a nuclear freeze referendum (as they did in September 1982 in the nation's first referendum on the issue). La Follette's campaign against the bosses and rigged party conventions left Wisconsin's official party organizations largely impotent. Statutory parties are only a shell, existing to meet legal requirements, while major political functions (recruitment, fund-raising, and organization) are left to candidate organizations. The flip side of that La Follette legacy is that few states, if any, so jealously guard the public's right to know about and participate in policymaking. Lobbyists remain suspect and subject to rigid reporting laws; campaign expenditures are rigidly monitored; municipal and judicial elections are not only nonpartisan but held in the spring to remove partisanship.

The crown jewel of Wisconsin's good-government diadem has been its presidential primary—a major testing ground for White House hopefuls. The triumphs of John Kennedy, Eugene McCarthy, and George McGovern in Wisconsin reinforced the state's liberal image; but maverick Wisconsinites turned around in each of those years and gave Richard Nixon majorities in November. What made Wisconsin's primary different was its openness. Any voter could participate, regardless of party affiliation, and cross-over voting became notorious. The "open primary" was the vehicle that La Follette championed to destroy brokered nominating conventions and to guarantee the people the right to choose their candidates; Wisconsin children have been reared on the idea that the open primary is as much a right as the vote itself. But the Democratic National Committee thought otherwise, and after a lengthy tussle with Wisconsin Democrats, finally refused to seat their delegation at the 1980 Democratic Convention. When the Wisconsin Supreme Court ordered the lawfully chosen delegation seated, the DNC turned to the federal courts, and in February 1981 the Supreme Court of the United States sided with the national party in a 6–3 decision. After nearly 80 years, one of the keystones of Progressivism had crumbled.

Wisconsin traditionally has had a strong legislature, but the Gaylord Nelson and John Reynolds gubernatorial administrations (1959–65) precipitated a lasting struggle between the legislative and executive branches. Out of the rivalry came a better-staffed, better-paid, and better-educated legislature, confronting a better-organized and better-staffed executive. Annual sessions were required constitutionally in 1971, forcing many part-time lawmakers to quit. Pay ballooned tenfold in 25 years (from $2,400 in 1957 to $25,966 in 1983) and staffing tripled so that the Wisconsin legislature resembled a mini-Congress.

By the time Democrat Patrick J. Lucey reached the governor's chair in 1971, a mood of retrenchment had settled in; the progressive Lucey guided a quasi-conservative administration that stressed consolidation and redistribution of state dollars. The first governor to enjoy a four-year term since that constitutional change was made in 1967, he produced the greatest plethora of initiatives since 1911: university merger; broadscale redistribution of state revenues to cities and schools; increased property tax relief coupled with easing of onerous business taxes; and a host of political reform legislation. A master politician, Lucey was accused by some of politicizing his office; but for the most part he succeeded, sometimes adroitly, sometimes crudely, in making state government more responsive to the governor's will. He left Wisconsin unquestionably a more *governable* state when he resigned in 1977 to become U.S. Ambassador to Mexico. Three years later, he reemerged as John Anderson's running mate on the independent "National Unity Ticket" opposing both Jimmy Carter and Ronald Reagan.

Lucey was a tough act to follow for Lt. Gov. Martin Schreiber, who merely warmed the governor's chair until Lee Sherman Dreyfus charged onto the scene in 1978. Wisconsinites loved college professor Dreyfus' ever-present red vest, his glib repartee, his railing against the bureaucracy, and his very maverickness. He roared into office, took one look at the $1 billion surplus he inherited, and promptly (with the support of the Democratic legislature) rebated $946 million of it to delighted taxpayers. But his inexperience and tendency to hasty decisions—coupled with a national economy turning sour—turned the tables such that by 1983 Wisconsin was staring at a potential cumulative deficit of $2.5 billion by 1985. Dreyfus was forced to slash spending and propose new taxes. Depressed by it all (and the incessant demands on a governor's time), Dreyfus abruptly decided to stop with one term.

Winner of the gubernatorial hotseat in the 1982 elections was Democrat Anthony S. Earl, erstwhile secretary of natural resources in Lucey's cabinet. Though only in his 40s, Earl campaigned as an old-school liberal—ticking off to us a host of Wisconsin programs, from its magnificent university to its road system, which he said must be preserved "if we are ever to return to our level of pre-eminence." While backing such economic-development inducements as an investment capital pool and a jobs tax credit, Earl was not shy in proposing tax boosts to bridge the budget gap and keep Wisconsin services up to snuff. He scoffed at the idea that reduced taxes or services would make Wisconsin more competitive with Sunbelt competitors like Texas—thus setting himself up as a national test of the viability of traditional liberalism in the budget-conscious, cutback era of the '80s.

When Wisconsin Goes to Washington

William Proxmire, five times elected to the U.S. Senate, is such a maverick that as a freshman he had the audacity to stand on the Senate floor and chastise

Majority Leader Lyndon B. Johnson. He became the most popular vote-getter in Wisconsin history, and also one of the cheapest candidates anywhere— spending, for example, exactly $145.10 on his overwhelmingly victorious 1982 reelection bid. Proxmire's penny pinching extended far beyond his campaign; in Washington, his reputation was of an economizer *par excellence*. Whether for the defense budget or a corporate bail-out, his nay-saying became legendary, especially his monthly "Golden Fleece" award bestowed via press release on whatever federal agency he found guilty of the "biggest, most ridiculous or most ironic waste of the taxpayers' money." Behind the parsimoniousness lurked a social liberal, a blend well understood in Wisconsin but still a mystery to many in Washington, where Proxmire, after 25 years, was still seen as a loner, an eccentric (who ran to work, was personally frugal but indulged in the vanity of hair transplants), and a bit of a gadfly. He became chairman of the Banking, Housing and Urban Affairs Committee and of the congressional Joint Economic Committee—only to be forced into a back-bench role when Republicans took control of the Senate in 1981.

Gaylord Nelson, who moved from the governor's office to the Senate in 1963, became a popular member of the Senate inner "club" and staked out the environment as his area of expertise long before it was a trendy issue. Nelson's impeccable liberal credentials finally did him in. Riding the Reagan conservative tide and harping on what he called the "Nelson Gap" between his liberal voting record in Washington and conservative rhetoric at home, Republican Bob Kasten toppled the seemingly invincible Nelson in 1980. Though described as feeling it an affront to himself and to Wisconsin that anyone could take Kasten seriously, Nelson took defeat gracefully after 32 years in public life and remained in Washington as head of the Wilderness Society. Kasten's performance was little respected in Washington; an image of dubious integrity dogged him at home; within 15 months of succeeding straight-arrow Nelson, Kasten was in trouble with state and federal tax authorities for failing to file back returns and had been sued by the state for securities violations.

Two Wisconsin Democrats were long in the fore in the House: Henry Reuss, chairman of Banking, Finance and Urban Affairs, and Clement Zablocki, chairman of Foreign Affairs. Both hailed from Milwaukee, but the similarity ended there. Reuss was an aristocratic, intellectual liberal and a highly skilled legislator with expertise in areas ranging from international finance to the environment. He finally retired in 1982. Zablocki, first elected in 1948, was a low-key moderate who although a Vietnam War hawk became House sponsor of the 1973 War Powers Act, which circumscribed presidential authority to dispatch troops to foreign combat without congressional approval. Up-and-coming young liberals in the Wisconsin delegation of the early '80s included Racine's Les Aspin, an economics Ph.D. who built his reputation fighting fat Pentagon appropriations, and Wausau's David Obey, a hardworking reformer who early caught the Democratic leadership's eye.

Where the Cow Is Queen and Beer Was King

Wisconsin's license plates proclaim it to the world: This is "America's Dairyland." The state's 1.8 million dairy cows are indeed the largest herd in the country. Largely because of this, Wisconsin ranked ninth in the nation in agricultural production in the 1970s, with 60 percent of its $3.5 billion farm income derived from its Holsteins, Jerseys, Guernseys, Brown Swiss, and other dairy cows. Since World War I, Wisconsin has made a major share of the nation's cheese—not only the "standard" Swiss, Cheddars, and Muensters but Wisconsin's own creation, Colby. Today, 200 kinds of cheese are produced in Wisconsin—some 40 percent of the national output. But the abundance of dairy products—while a boon for Wisconsin farmers—is a bane for American taxpayers. A system of milk price supports, originally designed to protect farmers from possibly disastrous swings in the market, produced a glut. The federal government, committed to buy up surplus supplies, faced annual outlays in the billions and discovered dairy interests just as politically formidable in Washington in preventing price-support cutbacks as they had been in Madison against encroachment by oleomargarine. (It was not until 1967 that the legislature finally lifted an extraordinary tax on oleo and allowed it to be sold in colored form.) Finally Congress 1982 imposed a fee—outraged farmers called it a "milk tax." It would offset the swollen cost of the price support program yet likely drain over $100 million a year from the Wisconsin economy.

Wisconsin is also one of the top dozen industrial states in the Union. Widely diversified manufacturing (beer, paper, heavy machinery, automobiles, food processing) adds up to 40 percent of the state's income; tourism and recreation are the third leg of the economy, adding $2.5 billion yearly. Of all the above, one thinks justifiably first of beer. German settlers brought the brewers' art to Wisconsin, and it was beer that made Milwaukee famous, particularly after the Great Fire wiped out Chicago's breweries in 1871 and Milwaukee grabbed the business. By the turn of the century, there were a dozen major brewers in Milwaukee; by 1980, the king had been dethroned and only 1 percent of the city's work force was in the industry. Miller, Wisconsin's biggest brewer, was bought out by Philip Morris in 1973; Schlitz, "the beer that made Milwaukee famous," slipped badly after changing its brew in the mid-70s and was forced to close its Milwaukee plant in 1981 before being taken over by Stroh's of Detroit a year later; Pabst, plagued with complacency and slumping sales, fell into the hands of a competitor in 1982.

So rampant were corporate takeovers in the Wisconsin of the early 1980s that the state suffered under the nation's highest rate of out-of-state takeovers. The phenomenon was not to be taken lightly: it meant not just dramatic job losses but loss of decision making capacity—economic and civic—to outside powers.

Three of Wisconsin's top five publicly held companies—Schlitz, Oscar Mayer, and Clark Oil—were bought out by absentee owners, on top of the three dozen firms taken over by out-of-staters between 1968 and 1980. Another leader, Congoleum Corp., packed up and moved to New Hampshire. The takeover phenomenon so angered Gov. Earl that he vowed to find in-state capital to stem the losses. In part, they could be attributed to Wisconsin's lingering business image problem: too-high taxes, seemingly too-liberal politics, expensive labor, and miserable winters.* But Wisconsin survived the economic tribulations of the 1970s quite well when compared with her neighbors: the population grew 6.5 percent and the number of manufacturing jobs actually crept up between 1970 and 1977 (the rest of the Midwest lost 7.3 percent of theirs). In some amazement, the *Wall Street Journal* in 1977 dubbed Wisconsin the "star of the Snowbelt" and attributed its success in large part to the package of business tax cuts—totaling some $155 million—passed under Lucey in 1973. By 1982, state analysts concluded that Wisconsin's business taxes were virtually the lowest of 16 Midwest, industrial, and Sunbelt states studied for typical corporations involved in the types of industry (ranging from paper products to food processing) that constitute the backbone of the Wisconsin economy. Yet Earl and other Wisconsin officials seemed oblivious to the strong disincentive the state's high personal income tax rate posed for engineers and other footloose "high-techers."

Industrial plants are concentrated geographically, mostly in the Milwaukee area and the Fox River Valley (which has the world's greatest aggregation of paper mills), a prime reason Wisconsin could rank so high in manufacturing and still be perceived as an agricultural and recreation state. The largest private employer is American Motors, which has all its domestic car production plants in Kenosha and Milwaukee (though to survive, it, too, had to turn outside for help and found an eager partner in France's Renault).

Wisconsin workers are heavily unionized and quite well paid, but Wisconsin employers feel they get what they pay for in excellent workmanship. While there have been labor-management clashes over the years (notably an eight-year strike against the Kohler Co., maker of bathroom fixtures), labor and industry work together on many issues—workmen's and unemployment compensation revision, taxation and energy among them—in what has been dubbed the "unholy alliance." While the '70s treated Wisconsin well, the '80s began gloomily. With an economy anchored in industries hardest-hit by the nation's deepening recession, Wisconsin's woes mounted. In 1981, for the first time ever, the state's unemployment rate edged above national levels. Close to 300,000 Wisconsinites were jobless; the case load of aid to families with dependent children jumped by 400 percent. Economists agreed Wisconsin's industries would have to pursue the high-tech path into radical modernization —even though many thousands of jobs could be lost in the process. Suddenly, "the star of the Snowbelt" faced years—perhaps a generation—of painful adjustment.

---

*In the winter of 1978–79, for example, Milwaukee recorded 80 inches of snow and a record 52 straight days of below-freezing temperatures.

Milwaukee and Its Orbit

While not the European ethnic bastion it once was, Milwaukee remains a city where the values of its sturdy German settlers—civic responsibility, public order, frugality, and pride in property—remain firmly rooted. Caught geographically between the two great trade and transportation centers of Chicago and Minneapolis, the city never developed into a regional capital, and opening of the St. Lawrence Seaway never produced the expected port traffic. Rather, Milwaukee remained a hard-working factory town even after the decline of its famous breweries.

Milwaukee may not have the elegance of Boston or New Orleans nor the cosmopolitanism of New York or San Francisco. But it does have culture: its own symphony and burgeoning ballet, and a modern white stone Performing Arts Center as well as the Milwaukee Exposition and Convention Center and Arena (MECCA) downtown, not far from the magnificently refurbished turn-of-the-century Pabst Theater. Beside Lake Michigan (and Milwaukee does have some sections of magnificent lakefront, akin to Chicago's) stands the modernistic Milwaukee Art Center, housing contemporary and primitive art from Europe and the United States.

For the vast majority of Milwaukeeans, however, culture is to be found cheering their beloved baseball Brewers and basketball Bucks and Marquette Warriors or in the conviviality of some 1,650 taverns and 2,600 area bowling alleys. This is a blue-collar town (an exceptionally high 28 percent of workers in Milwaukee County are unionized), where recessions take an early, deep, and lasting toll. With 636,210 citizens in 1980, Milwaukee had just 13 percent of the state's population—but 60 percent of the minority population and 30 percent of the poverty. The white ethnic melange remains to this day: great doses of German and Polish, smaller but important groups of Italian and Irish, and a thousand and one lesser strands. Every year comes Summerfest, a 10-day celebration of cultural heritage. Blacks are now a huge minority, and Latins too. A South Side priest was quoted as saying in 1980: "My funerals are all Polish. My weddings and baptisms are all Latino."

Milwaukee's Socialist party, which controlled the mayor's office for more than 40 years earlier in this century, preached not left-of-liberal socialism but a frugal brand of municipal management—dubbed "sewer socialism" for its stress on practical, basic, and efficient city services. Emil Seidel, the first elected Socialist mayor, rode into office in 1910 on the crest of citizen revolt against the corruption of both Republicans and Democrats of the day. Socialists promised good government, and they produced; with the exception of a hiatus during the 1940s, they held office until 1960. Among the forces leading to the Socialists' demise was the wave of poor blacks from the South—their number jumping from 9,000 in 1940 to 60,000 by 1970 and 146,940 in 1980. To this day, blacks are rare residents in the heavily Polish South Side, though many work there; confined to inner-city ghettoes, blacks have not been welcome south of the Menomonee Valley.

The valley is the heart of Milwaukee's manufacturing might, a congested 4.5 square miles where 30,000 people work in heavy industry. Also described as Milwaukee's Mason-Dixon Line, it was the site of 200 days of sometimes-violent civil rights marches led by Father James Groppi in 1967. That same summer, Mayor Henry Maier moved with Prussian-like efficiency to quell a racial mini-riot and head off any repeat of Detroit or Watts, calling out the National Guard and slapping on a curfew. Racial tensions persisted afterwards, in rigid housing segregation, in school busing disputes, and in relations with the police, which by 1982 had only 129 black officers on the 2,000-person force, none above the rank of sergeant. Charges of police brutality and even murder abounded in the black community; most were ignored by the department or dismissed by the Fire and Police Commission. Responsiveness from the police high command was hardly to be expected. Chief Harold Breier—sometimes known as "Milwaukee's Führer"—was the latest in a line of police heads appointed *for life*, a practice dating back to 1885.

Mayor Henry Maier entered the '80s with nearly a quarter century in office under his belt, the longest-serving big city mayor in America. Ostensibly, Milwaukee has a weak-mayor-and-strong-city-council system; in reality, it is the reverse. Over the years, Maier's raging temper tantrums became legendary as he struck out ferociously at the Milwaukee Journal Co., the state government, the suburbs, or federal agencies—virtually anyone who dared question him or his policies. But no one could deny Maier's total commitment to his city, including insistence on sound planning and tough management, factors that kept Milwaukee healthier (and its bond ratings in better shape) than many other decaying older cities. Another notable force was the Greater Milwaukee Committee, formed in 1939 by the business elite and including leaders from labor, education, and the professions. It was a prime mover in redevelopment (such projects as the Art Center and expansion of the excellent zoo) and in 1973 spawned the Milwaukee Redevelopment Corp. to spur private-sector improvements of the deteriorating downtown retail center. By the early '80s downtown Milwaukee was enjoying a rebirth of sorts. There was a new Hyatt hotel, a 50-story Federal Office Building, and Grand Avenue, an ambitious $60 million shopping complex providing a climate-controlled pedestrian walkway through the heart of the major department stores and speciality shops. The project was opened in August, 1982 by the Rouse Company, a firm whose golden touch had already enriched many U.S. downtown areas.

Milwaukee's affluent migrated decades ago to such Republican enclaves as Shorewood, River Hills, Fox Point, and Whitefish Bay along the North Shore. To the west of Milwaukee lies Waukesha County (280,326), Wisconsin's fastest-growing area for the last two decades and a place combining stereotypical colorless suburbia and breathless panoramas of unfolding hills and nearby lakes. Within Milwaukee County itself, west of the city, lies West Allis (63,982), a heavily industrialized suburb and home of the state fair. To the south are heavily Polish Catholic, conservative, and blue-collar communities such as St. Francis, Cudahy, and South Milwaukee. Further south, near the Illinois border, is Racine (85,725), another industrial city with the highest concentration of blacks—15 percent—outside Milwaukee; and Kenosha (77,685), home to a sizable Italian community, the main plant of American Motors, and the largest UAW local in the state.

Continued growth of the Milwaukee area was severely threatened in the early 1980s by the sorry condition of the area sewer system, so outmoded and overloaded that raw sewage often spilled into Lake Michigan. Milwaukee found itself faced with court orders to clean up its act at an estimated $1.6 million.

From Madison to the Northwoods

Madison, some 70 miles west of Milwaukee, is matched by few if any state capitals: a city of lake-studded beauty, enriched immeasurably by the University of Wisconsin's intellectual stimulation, enjoying white-collar economic vigor, blessed with strong neighborhood traditions. The 1980 population was 170,616. Madison is set in Dane County, the cradle of Progressivism (La Follette was born on a farm near Primrose). The area remains the most liberal in Wisconsin, thanks in part to the influence of the *Capital Times*, a crusading newspaper of the old school. Madison was a hotbed of antiwar agitation in the '60s; in 1982, Dane county had the state's worst rate of compliance with the new draft registration law. Madison elected a "radical boy-mayor" in 1973, Paul Soglin, a former student antiwar activist. Conservative doom-sayers portrayed the 28-year-old Soglin as a radical intent on destroying Madison for the "decent people"; but when he left office in 1979, he had revitalized the city's bus system, pushed through a major mall along State Street (the one-mile thoroughfare linking the capitol with the UW campus), and ended a 25-year stalemate over where to build a downtown civic auditorium.

Other than Milwaukee and Madison, Wisconsin's heaviest population and strongest economic growth are found in the Lake Michigan cities and the Fox and Wisconsin River valleys. In addition to Kenosha and Racine on the lake one might mention Sheboygan (48,085), famous for its tangy bratwursts, and Manitowoc (32,547), a significant shipbuilding center—all ethnic polyglots and overwhelmingly Democratic. In the Fox River Valley in northeastern Wisconsin lie the "Fox Cities," a collection of communities anchored by Green Bay (87,899), home of a dozen papermills and the National Football League Packers, and Appleton (59,032), another papermill town with a first-class liberal arts university, Lawrence. Nearby is Oshkosh (49,678), an old-fashioned town and like others in the region, distinctly German, Catholic, and decidedly conservative. Counties in the Wisconsin River Valley of Central Wisconsin had significant growth in the '70s—11 to 21 percent—although their major cities remained static. Paper mills abound here, too, but give way to dairy and vegetable farms. Over in the western part of the state are the Mississippi River towns of La Crosse (48,347), probably the most rigidly conservative large city in Wisconsin, and Eau Claire (51,509), almost as Democratic as La Crosse is Republican.

North of a line from Green Bay to Hudson on the St. Croix River lie the Northwoods of Wisconsin, a region geographically, politically, and economically distinct. Here the first French trappers and explorers trekked through the majestic wilderness; here remain most of the state's 450,000 acres of forests and two national preserves—a major draw for campers, fishermen, and hunters. Rough-and-tumble politics dominate the region, notorious for sending mavericks to Madison and Washington. Like their neighbors in Michigan's Upper Peninsula, Northwoods natives long have felt neglected by downstate. The post–World War II economic decline of the Northwoods only added to the feelings of isolation.

A stunning turnaround began in the mid-1970s. Mirroring a Michigan trend, thousands of Wisconsites were moving north. In the 1970s, one Northwoods county, Vilas, grew more than 50 percent, 9 others grew 20 percent or more, and three others grew by 15 percent. William Bechtel, federal co-chairman of the Upper Great Lakes Regional Commission and a former Nelson aide, described the situation to us as "an antimetropolitan move." It was almost solely a white flight since fast-growing Vilas County had only four black residents in 1980, and the other dozen averaged just 33 each.

The movement to the Northwoods astonished demographers and traditional economists who wondered what the people would do for a living. Many of the first to move up were retirees living on Social Security and other income earned outside the area. But the Northwoods also attracted manufacturing businesses, many of which shipped products by air. These businesses often controlled their stocks by computers which "interfaced" with computers in more populous areas, and some economic development specialists predicted that computers will make it easier for small businesses to locate in the Northwoods and other isolated spots where their owners can be close to the outdoor life they love. Some 80,000 new jobs were created in the region during the '70s, and manufacturing payrolls swelled by 63 percent. Also raising hopes in the Northwoods for the future was the discovery of immense copper and zinc deposits in Forest County.

The largest city in the Northwoods is Superior (29,571), perched on the westernmost point of Lake Superior; it boasts the largest grain elevator in the world, and its port facilities, combined with those of Duluth, Minn., across the St. Louis River, are second only to Chicago on the Great Lakes.

The Last Word

When every major aspect of Wisconsin's life has passed in review, one remains impressed—almost overwhelmed—by her insistence that government and politics can and should mirror that elusive reality, the "public good." But does the bedrock belief of Wisconsinites that their state is superior to most others hold up?

We have traveled throughout those other states and found in some of them thriving concepts similar to the "Wisconsin Idea." But few others—Minnesota, Vermont, Washington, and Oregon spring to mind as possible competitors—so often *realize* their high expectations. The test of the late 20th century may be whether the industrial economy declines so precipitously that Wisconsin can no longer afford its magnificent Progressivism.

Yet if Wisconsin is to enjoy a 21st-century renaissance, the key could well be the one that unlocked the floodgates of progress in the 19th: the university. The noble "Wisconsin Idea," melding academic theory and public policy, lifted the state to greatness. And even though legislative appropriations for the University of Wisconsin sagged dramatically in the 1970s, the university contribution could again be central. A group known as Wisconsin for Research began in the early '80s to promote closer ties between industry and academia for the high-tech age. The 13-campus university, true to its traditions, was eager to turn its scientific expertise to the revitalization of Wisconsin's economy, even keying its $1.1 billion budget request for 1983–85 to that premise. Yet there was both campus and capitol resistance, keyed to the myriad ethical questions posed by a mutual-benefit alliance between the university and industry. One wondered if the doubters understood the depth of Wisconsin's economic quandary. Indeed, had such hesitance abounded at the turn of the 20th century, progress—and Progressivism—might well have passed Wisconsin by.

A bright sign of the times was formation of Competitive Wisconsin, Inc., an amalgam of business, labor, education, and farm leaders that started out in 1981 as a cheerleader for promoting state business interests but within a year launched an abitious drive to raise a $10 million fund of venture capital to underwrite new and expanded business ventures.

Part of Wisconsin's future, like that of her Great Lakes neighbors, may lie in her natural resources: soil, timber, and especially the vast water resources on which the region first developed. The Great Lakes are truly a wonder, representing one-fifth of all the surface fresh water in the entire world and fully 95 percent of that available in the United States. Thus it was hardly surprising that water-parched Sunbelt states, their own meager resources strained by heavy development and rampant growth, began casting covetous eyes on that natural reservoir. Nor was it surprising that the eight states bordering the Great Lakes took a dim view of sharing their vast lake and underground watery wealth with states that already had drained away population and industry. "Water Belt" governors began meeting in earnest as the '80s dawned to devise defensive strategy.

INDIANA

The Politicians' State

IN THE LAST SPRING of his life, as he criss-crossed Indiana in search of votes in the 1968 presidential primary, Robert F. Kennedy could not withstand the temptation to charter a campaign train retracing the route of the fabled Wabash Cannonball. And in a way, the very name of Indiana, a place where people called "Hoosiers"* live, raises an image of settled Midwestern typicality, of vast cornfields, small villages, and factory cities, of value placed on things familiar.

Indiana is in many ways a microcosm of what America once was. Here one finds people clannish, patriotic, protective of property, suspicious of government. Hoosiers take perverse pride in letting someone else be first. They view with skepticism outsiders' newfangled ideas infiltrating their heart of the heartland.

Yet Indiana, in significant measure, has in recent years begun to shed (or at least modify) the political, social, cultural ideals that served it so long. The result is a civilization of incongruous contrasts. No state had more venal patronage politics, but court decisions and legislation have shriveled the spoils system, all but eliminating that veritable Indiana trademark, the infamous "2 percent club" of public employees whose very jobs depended on kicking back 2 percent of their paychecks to party coffers. Few legislatures have resisted reforms as stringently as Indiana's, yet in 1969 it took a step no other Northern legislature had been willing to take to resolve urban problems: creating a county-wide, consolidated government for the state's capital and premier city, Indianapolis.

Indiana, through the first half of this century, had a history of bigotry unequaled north of the Mason-Dixon line. The Ku Klux Klan openly flourished and laid legitimate claims to controlling the governor, legislature, and many courts and local governments through the late 1920s. Until the 1950s, Indiana state laws deliberately subverted the intent of the Constitution's 14th

---

*There are many theories on the genesis of the term. The most credible is the account of William E. Wilson in his book *Indiana, A History*, that the word originated with the men working for Ohio Canal builder Samuel Hoosier in the 1820s, supposedly the hardest-working and most reliable laborers. As the term spread in Indiana, it took on the connotation of anyone of great virtue and virility. To some outsiders, however, it came to conjur up a country-bumpkin image.

Amendment and subordinated blacks. Yet Indianapolis was the only Northern city of its size (pop. 700,807 in 1980) to escape major racial disturbances in the late 1960s, and it later remained calm through the trauma of a major school busing case. Anti-Catholicism also was a potent force, due in large part to the Klan, and contributed to John F. Kennedy's defeat in Indiana. Still, a disparaging word about Notre Dame, America's best-known Catholic University, at South Bend, can elicit the ire of more than just the Irish in Indiana.

Indiana is the home of the American Legion and the Pulliam publishing family's once ultra-conservative *Indianapolis News* and *Star* (significantly more moderate in recent years), as well as birthplace of the truculent John Birch Society. Yet for 14 years, from 1962 to 1976, Indiana was represented in the U.S. Senate by two liberal Democrats, Vance Hartke and Birch Bayh.

Shortly after World War II, Indiana's legislators cast a suspicious eye toward Washington, passing a vehement resolution declaring federal aid tainted: "We proposed henceforward to tax ourselves and take care of ourselves." By 1979, however, federal aid to Indiana totaled nearly $8 billion and had been a major factor in the 1,134 miles of Interstate highways slicing through Indiana's fields and cities, more than any other state of its size. While highways and certain other aids became acceptable, those for welfare mothers and cities remained suspect.

A strain of insecurity also seems woven into the Hoosier lifestyle. Eugene McCarthy picked up the sentiment during his 1968 quest for the Democratic presidential nomination. "There seemed to be a rather generalized defensiveness in Indiana against outsiders," McCarthy later wrote in his book, *The Year of the People.* "In northern Indiana, especially Gary, people seemed worried about the prospects of being taken over by Chicago. In the south, they were threatened by Kentucky, in the west by Illinois, and in the east, by Ohio. It was as though in Indiana they have to think Indiana for fear that if they do not, it will be absorbed by the outside world."

No single issue, no single city can capture the totality of the metamorphosis in latter-day Indiana. But a glimpse at the people of Muncie (pop. 77,216) shows Indiana has squirmed free of its cocoon. Muncie became famous in the 1920s for its ordinariness, known for the classic sociological study by Robert S. and Helen Merrell Lynd. The Lynds called Muncie "Middletown" because it represented the typical American city. In the late 1970s, another research team moved into Muncie and repeated the questions the Lynds had asked. In *Middletown III*, they found the same beliefs: Half the Muncians interviewed said the Bible was a "sufficient guide to all problems of modern life"; three-quarters believed the U.S.A. to be the "best country in the world"; and 47 percent—the same share the Lynds found—agreed it was "entirely the fault of a man himself if he does not succeed." But it was a new era: Students enjoyed both bubblegum and pot, church-going and pornography. Said one 16-year-old: "Yeah, we smoke dope all over, in our cars, walking around before class, any time, but that doesn't mean we don't believe in God or that we'll let anybody put God down. That can get you in a fight."*

Muncie reflects another changing fact of economic life in Indiana: more and more, its home-grown industry is falling under absentee ownership. Like so many other Hoosier cities, Muncie existed for decades under the patriarchal leadership of the Ball brothers, who went there in 1886 with the promise of free natural gas and free land to make their fruit jars. Their legacy is more than just the company that bears their name—so do the university, hospital, churches, and other civic projects endowed by the brothers' philanthropic foundation. The Ball Corporation, though, is now a diversified, multinational concern, its major operations moved elsewhere. The Ball family is dispersed, its influence in Muncie a shadow of years past. That story—even more commonly, the direct sale of a local corporation to a national or multinational firm, leaving only branch managers to participate in civic affairs—is repeated in countless cities up and down Indiana.

A Look at Hoosierland

Indiana calls itself "the crossroads of America," a motto justly deserved, although with ironic overtones. The state has access to both of the great waterways of the Midwest: the Great Lakes, through Burns Harbor on Lake Michigan, and the Mississippi, through the 1,100-acre Southwind Maritime Center near Evansville on the Ohio River. Rail lines and Interstate highways, none too far from major markets, criss-cross the state. But while access to Indiana is easy, so too is egress: many of its sons and daughters left to find their fortunes elsewhere, leaving behind an increasingly inbred, unwavering, WASP culture short on imagination or innovation.

The Civil War doubtless played a major role in Hoosier provincialism. A potent Copperhead movement sympathetic to the slave-owning South flourished, especially in counties near the Ohio River (an area still more Southern than Midwestern). At the same time, a radical Republican governor sent almost 200,000 Indiana men into battle for the Union, 25,000 of them never to return home alive. The wartime rivalries lingered for generations, with veteran, son, and grandchild reliving the bitterness and voting by rote either Union (Republican) or Copperhead (Democrat). Such unthinking, fixed attitudes only reinforced the innate suspicions and fierce individualism that already existed.

The first Indiana settlements were French (a fort was erected on the Wabash River at Vincennes in 1732); decades of war involving the French, Indians, British, and Americans followed, and Indiana wound up as part of the Northwest Territory in 1787. It achieved territorial status in 1800 and state-

---

*In 1981, a *cinéma vérité* team moved into Muncie to tape hundreds of hours in the lives of Muncie residents. Edited without narration into a multipart series, "Middletown U.S.A.," it ran to critical acclaim on public television (though the final segment was never aired because of controversy surrounding coarse and sexually explicit talk by teenagers).

hood in 1816 as a Northern free state. Yet its first significant number of settlers arrived not from the North but the South: Virginia, the Carolinas, Kentucky. Through the Cumberland Gap and across the Ohio they came, bringing with them all their cultural, political, religious, and social heritage. To this day, no Northern state has such a large share of Southern white stock. These Southerners also brought with them Jacksonian democracy, embedding the spoils system as a cornerstone of Indiana politics.

Indiana had its own Mason-Dixon line, dividing the state—and its politics and accents—roughly in half along the course of the old National Road, now U.S. 40 (paralleled by Interstate 70). The Southerners who came to settle the lands below the illusory line failed to pick a very promising area: it was territory of low-lying hills and barren clay soil, permitting subsistence farming at best. Coal mining later flourished in southwestern counties and, indeed, continues today—with the ready cash benefits for the few and general depression for the many that is typical of extractive industries.

The immigrants who settled Indiana north of the National Road came from New England, New York, and Pennsylvania or, in many cases, directly from northern Europe. They settled first on the flat, black, rich soil north of Indianapolis. Later, Eastern European immigrants came to endure the heat and grime of the mills in the Gary-Hammond-East Chicago industrial complex; many of their heirs voted for George Wallace during his presidential forays of 1964, 1968, and 1972, a delayed reaction, it appeared, to the influx of Southern blacks after World War II. Still, by 1980, blacks numbered only 414,732, or 7.6 percent of Indiana's population—two-thirds of them in just two counties, Marion (Indianapolis) and Lake (Gary/East Chicago).

Marion and Lake counties are Indiana's two great industrial centers. The larger revolves around Indianapolis and its ring of satellite cities (Richmond, Anderson, and Muncie to the east, Kokomo and Marion to the north, Lafayette and Terre Haute to the west, and Columbus to the south). Within these cities and environs, a third of Indiana's 5,490,179 people live, producing everything from cars to telephones, furniture to fruit jars. Unlike most other Northern states, Republicans thrive in most of these cities.

To the north, congregated in Lake County, where Illinois, Indiana, and Lake Michigan meet, is the state's second great industrial center. Its cities, Gary, East Chicago, Hammond, and tiny Whiting, are industrial and political cesspools compared with the rest of urban Indiana. Rough and raw, Gary and environs are more akin to Chicago. The European ethnics have retreated in the face of the influx of Southern blacks, leaving Gary with a 70 percent black majority. In this tiny corner of Indiana, the acrid pollution is not quite as bad as it was as recently as 1970, but it still can turn day into dusk.

For all its industry, Indiana has retained a rural character with close to three-quarters of its land devoted to agriculture. Since 1960 the number of farms has dropped precipitously, but farm acreage slumped only 7 percent—evidence of the trend toward ever-larger farms and some corporate management converting family-run farms into agribusiness. Indiana ranks consistently among the top 10 states in cash receipts from agriculture, running more than $3 billion yearly in the '70s. Nearly three-fifths of that came from crops —chiefly grains and hay.

Fueling the citification of Indiana has been an expanding, remarkably diversified manufacturing and service economy. About a tenth of Indiana's 8,000 manufacturers have foreign markets (many shipping through the St. Lawrence Seaway); by the mid-1970s, Indiana's export trade came to $4 billion yearly. So diversified had the state's manufacturing base grown that 299 of *Fortune's* 500 top corporations were operating in the state. But vehicle manufacturing remained dominant, accounting for nearly a third of Indiana's work force—or out-of-work force, as the case was in the early 1980s.

Despite the 1947 legislative resolution eschewing federal aid, Indiana's view of Washington has mellowed so that Hoosiers came to see it less as an alien and more as a partner. All this began when President Eisenhower launched the Interstate highway system, pledging $9 in federal funds for every $1 states put up. As one observer put it, "Hoosiers may be stubborn, but they're not stupid." Large chunks of highway funds and other federal aid soon began flowing to the land of the Wabash and the Tippecanoe. Mayors soon learned to love urban assistance money, and military contracts were most welcome (the Army Finance Center at Fort Benjamin Harrison in Indianapolis is the largest U.S. military building other than the Pentagon). One politico confided to us: "It's not a Hoosier state in the old sense. And by Hoosier, I mean hard-working, friendly, somewhat conservative, commonsense, sort of a pragmatist, little bit suspicious of government, 'I'll do it my own way.' . . ." There was more than a trace of lamentation in his voice.

Indiana's constitution has always provided for free public education—even though what one historian called "political primitivism" delayed the promise well into the 20th century. At the higher education level, such privately endowed institutions as Notre Dame (Roman Catholic), DePauw (Methodist), and Earlham (Quaker) filled the gap for many decades. The state's premier tax-supported institutions—Indiana University at Bloomington and Purdue at West Lafayette—struggled with meager public support until the World War II era. It was then that Herman B. Wells came to the helm of IU and Frederick L. Hovde to Purdue, and each began transforming his university from a mediocre, isolated school to a prestigious institution. In 1969, IU and Purdue consolidated their satellite campuses at Indianapolis and pooled their resources.

For a state with a reputation for insularity, Indiana nonetheless has produced more than its share of authors, poets, and artists. For a half-century, starting in the 1880s, Indiana writers were in the forefront of America's popular literature. Lew Wallace, of Crawfordville, published *Ben Hur* in 1880. Later came Terre Haute's Theodore Dreiser, one of the early realistic novelists, with his *Sister Carrie* and *An American Tragedy* (his brother, Paul Dresser, wrote what was to become the official state song, "On the Banks of the Wabash"); the dean of Indiana letters, Booth Tarkington of Indianapolis; and in a more contemporary vein, Kurt Vonnegut, also of Indianapolis. Probably the favorite Hoosier writer was the poet James Whitcomb Riley, of Greenfield, whose homespun verses ("When the Frost Is on the Punkin' "; "Little Orphan Annie") captured the speech, mannerisms, and culture of the Indiana —and much of the American heartland—of his time. Other noteworthy Indiana artists included composers Hoagy Carmichael, of Bloomington, and Cole Porter, of Peru (on the banks—where else?—of the Wabash).

A Political Panorama

Indiana developed not a few politicians of such flag waving and nativist prejudice that they would have been dismissed as petty despots or crackpots almost anywhere else. A foremost master of invective was William Jenner, the fire-eating right-wing U.S. Senator who called that great American leader General George C. Marshall a "front man for traitors." Irving Leibowitz in his delightful book *My Indiana* picked Jenner as the "perfect symbol" of what Indiana was before the forces of change spread statewide:

> And what a symbol. He pounds the desk. He cusses. He dramatizes. He shouts. He whispers. He can be warm and gregarious. He can be ice cold. He can turn his emotions on and off. Jenner has been described variously as a Southern Indiana hillbilly, a demagogue, a wild and woolly vigilante, a witch-hunter, a grand inquisitor and a fascist firebrand.

After two impassioned terms in the Senate, Jenner quit in 1958. That autumn, when the Republican campaign faltered in the cities, Jenner caustically advised a closed GOP planning session: "Draw a circle around every single one and don't set foot in them. Forget 'em. Concentrate on the farms and the towns. If we can't win in Indiana, we can't win anywhere. We've got the most conservative press and the most conservative people in America, from Lake Michigan to the Ohio River. Pour it on."

Paul McNutt was another classic character in the annals of Indiana politics. Indiana's Democratic governor during the New Deal, he was a former national commander of the American Legion, a sure-fire ticket to electoral success at the time. McNutt instituted major economic reforms, but he probably is better remembered as the perfecter of the infamous "2 percent club," which required all state government employees patronage to contribute 2 percent of their salaries. He nurtured aspirations for national office, hoping, as one observer put it, to "march into the White House behind a Legion drum and bugle corps." The only Hoosier who did march into the White House was Benjamin Harrison—and even he was born in Ohio, moving to Indianapolis as a young man.

The Grand Exceptionary Indiana Republican of modern times was Wendell Willkie. A small-town boy from Elwood, Willkie made good, not in Indiana, but in New York City as president of the big electric utility, Commonwealth and Southern. At the time of his nomination as the 1940 Republican presidential candidate, and to this day, Old Guard Republicans in Indiana swear Willkie was not one of them, but rather an apostate who had rejected his roots. The *New York Times,* upon Willkie's death, in 1944, said he was "as American as the countryside of his native Indiana."

Strangely enough, Indiana was also the home of the famed Socialist, Eugene Debs, who came out of the Brotherhood of Locomotive Engineers in Terre Haute. In 1900, he received the first of four straight Socialist nominations for president; in 1912, he received more than a million votes. Debs surely was a rarity in Indiana politics—a champion of change.

The last of the Old Guard Republicans to hold major office in Indiana were Homer Capehart and Charles Halleck. Capehart was a down-home industrialist (his firm made Capehart and Zenith radios) who went to the U.S. Senate in 1944 and served 18 years. No Hoosier of recent years moved in such lofty GOP circles as Charles Abraham Halleck, who came to be regarded as the quintessential Midwest Republican during his 34 years in the House, six of them as Republican leader. It was in that role that he found stardom as the sidekick of Senate Republican Leader Everett Dirksen in the "Ev and Charlie Show," the unintentionally entertaining televised GOP critique of the Kennedy and Johnson administrations. But the man Eisenhower described as a "political genius" wasn't always so: in 1965 he was deposed as minority leader by an eager band of Young Turks. The new chief: a congressman from Michigan named Gerald R. Ford. Halleck retired three years later.

Halleck's seat was won by Earl Landgrebe, a zany right-winger dubbed by the *Indianapolis Star* as the worst state legislator just the year before he got elected to Congress. The day before Richard Nixon's resignation, Landgrebe was still hanging tough: "Don't confuse me with the facts," he blurted to reporters. "I've got a closed mind. I will not vote for impeachment. I'm going to stick with my President even if he and I have to be taken out of this building and shot." Voters retired Landgrebe that November.

Partisan politics is a deadly serious and very bitter business in Indiana. Basically conservative in philosophical approach, both Republicans and Democrats honed powerful organizations that were machines in the classic sense of the word, fed by patronage and held in check by old-fashioned bosses who tightly controlled nominating conventions, jobs, and contract disbursement. "Honest graft," or what they called "clean money," fattened the party. At its zenith, the "2 percent club" was worth up to $700,000 a year to the party in power—and that at the state level alone. More than $100,000 a year in commissions on state insurance policies also ended up in partisan coffers, not to mention thousands more in kickbacks from companies doing business with the state. Then, in the 1970s, curbs on corporate campaign giving were enacted; firms began refusing to participate in kickback schemes; the proportion of patronage employees sagged to a quarter of the state payroll.

But vestiges of the old spoils system remained into the '80s. Even with the 2 percent club dead, patronage employees were still "encouraged" to chip in 1 percent of their pay to the party in power. And the governing party, through its county chairmen, still collected 50 cents on every license plate sold, every driver's license issued, and every vehicle title transferred, a 50-year-old tradition netting millions of dollars yearly for party coffers.* Few found it odd. As former Governor Matthew Welsh (an honest executive himself) told us, license plate sales through party operatives "warrant only passing criticism by the political purist."

The hold of the political professionals has weakened in many other ways. Hoosiers now pick their gubernatorial candidates by direct primary (a concession to direct democracy Indiana belatedly made in 1976).

Every Republican presidential hopeful since the end of World War II has run stronger in Indiana than his national average. And yet, this is not a rock-ribbed Republican state—or a Democratic one. Indiana's political map is colored schizophrenic. In any given election, as many as 300,000 Indiana voters split their tickets, leaving the professional pols shivering. The mercurial quality of Hoosier sentiments showed up in George Wallace's presidential campaigns, in which he received 30 to 41 percent of the vote in Democratic primaries but only 12 percent of the 1968 general election vote. In the 1970s, Indiana was still the strongest Ku Klux Klan state in the North. Not many years before, some small Indiana towns posted prominent signs reading: "Nigger, don't let the sun set on you here." It was not until 1949 that Indiana repealed its laws favoring school segregation and not until 1964 that laws forbidding interracial marriage were struck from the books.

Conservative coloration was long lent to Indiana political life by the *Indianapolis Star* and *News*, controlled for a quarter century by Eugene C. Pulliam. The Pulliam papers had some outstanding individual reporters but still editorialized in news columns, ran front-page political cartoons, and openly plugged pet candidates. Pulliam did become more moderate over the years. Despite his blatant slanting of news coverage against Robert Kennedy in the 1968 Democratic presidential primary, for example, Pulliam backed Dwight D. Eisenhower over the "Old Guard" forces of Robert Taft for the 1952 GOP presidential nomination and refused to support Barry Goldwater for president in 1964. When he died, at 86 in 1975, his son Eugene S. took over the empire (not just the Indianapolis papers, but also those in Muncie, Vincennes, and distant Phoenix, Arizona) and began to shift them all toward much higher journalistic standards—and balance.

In 1980, Dan Quayle, grandson of old Eugene Pulliam, defeated three-term incumbent Birch Bayh, riding to the U.S. Senate on the Reagan groundswell.

Bayh, from Terre Haute, had been Quayle's age in 1962, when he dethroned Homer Capehart—using the "18 years is long enough" slogan that Quayle, ironically, would turn on him. Bayh's "aw-shucks" charm and careful attention to constituents lulled conservative Hoosiers into thrice overlooking his liberalism. Despite his natural political gifts, Bayh's two forays into presiden-

*In 1978, the legislature decreed that the $40 fee for each set of personalized "vanity" license plates would be split thusly: $15 to the Republican party, $15 to the Democratic party, $3 to the license branch office (the local party), and $7 to the state treasury. The bipartisan split was no gesture of brotherly love: the legislature was politically divided, and Democrats said they would support the proposed Republican scam only if they got part of the action.

tial politics were short lived. Yet he was a legislator of immense skill and he left an unprecedented legacy in the form of two amendments to the Constitution of the United States, both fashioned in the Judiciary subcommittee he chaired—the 25th, establishing a new procedure for handling presidential disability, and the 26th, reducing the minimum voting age to 18. A third was nearly ratified—the Equal Rights Amendment. Bayh will also go down in history as a strong battler for abolishing the electoral college in favor of a direct vote of the people.

Another liberal who captured Hoosier fancy enough to win three Senate terms was Vance Hartke of Evansville. First elected in 1958, Hartke won a reputation in Washington of taking better care of special interests than the public interest—giving rise to the wisecrack that Indiana's two senators were named Bayh and Bought.

A very untypical Indiana Republican took Hartke's Senate seat: Richard Lugar, Indianapolis native but erstwhile Rhodes Scholar, an intellectual with a sophisticated vocabulary and manner of speech rare among politicians anywhere. Devoid of charisma and dogged by the description of being "Richard Nixon's favorite mayor," Lugar nonetheless parlayed diligence and keen intelligence into an amazing political career. He won the Indianapolis mayor's office in 1967 and within two years sold the idea of wedding Indianapolis and Marion County into an omnibus governmental unit called Unigov. Overnight, the city jumped from the nation's 26th-largest city to the 11th. Some have called Unigov "the suburban takeover of a major city." But advocates rightly noted that Unigov had another potential impact—to save Indianapolis from becoming, like so many other cities, a doughnut, with a suburban circle surrounding a hollow urban core.

As a senator, Lugar voted a moderately conservative line and soon won wide respect on both sides of the aisle; he easily won reelection in 1982. Putting pragmatism over ideology, he fashioned the compromise aid packages to rescue failing New York City in 1978 and to save the Chrysler Corporation in 1980; he flouted President Reagan in 1982 by leading the charge to shore up the recession-plagued housing industry. Lugar nonetheless had full White House support in winning chairmanship of the powerful, fund-dispensing National Republican Senatorial Committee in a secret ballot by Republican senators in December 1982.

As Lugar's star was on the rise, South Bend's Democrat Rep. John Brademas saw his 22-year House career truncated in 1980 by a youthful, scarcely known Republican challenger, John Hiler. Brademas had reached the number three slot in the House Democratic leadership and through his committee post exercised immense power over federal education policy. Client groups (in vocational rehabilitation, for example) counted Brademas their closest Capitol Hill ally; state governments accused him of unwarranted dictation on programs, violating basic precepts of American federalism. Rejected in Indiana, he went off to become president of New York University. In the neighboring Gary-centered district, Rep. Adam Benjamin, Jr., was making quite a name for himself. In just three terms he had risen high in House Democratic councils and was chairman of the Congressional Steel Caucus. But he was stricken by a heart attack in 1982. His successor was Mississippi-born Katie Hall, the first black woman ever sent to Congress from Indiana.

Governors, Legislators, and Lobbies

Despite (or perhaps because of) its "honest graft" tradition, Indiana's state government has been remarkably free from scandal. Governors until recently were permitted only one term, making it difficult for potential scoundrels to become entrenched. The first governor to take advantage of a constitutional change permitting two consecutive terms was Otis "Doc" Bowen (1973–81), so popular he probably could have been elected indefinitely. A country doctor carefully cultivating that kindly image, Bowen delivered on a promised property tax cutback and freeze and promoted "people programs"—tripling spending for education, upgrading parks and prisons, and substantially boosting support for health and welfare. It was a tough act for Bowen's successor, Robert D. Orr, to follow. With some 350,000 Hoosiers out of work, unemployment hitting 20 percent in some auto-industry towns, and tax revenues sagging accordingly, Orr in 1982 was faced with immense shortfalls in both general and property tax relief funds. His attempted recovery strategy: slash state spending, slap on a hiring freeze, stall construction, and seek new taxes.

Left to grapple with these difficult problems was Indiana's antiquated legislature, the hotbed of bitter Hoosier partisanship. Fluctuating majorities and high turnover have plagued both houses. For 43 years before the 1964 "one man, one vote" edict of the U.S. Supreme Court, Indiana failed to reapportion its legislative seats, causing grave urban under-representation. But when equally apportioned districts finally came, Democratic strength increased only slightly because of the strong Republican foothold in Hoosier cities. Reapportionment did dilute the once-formidable influence of the farm lobby and gave new clout to labor. During World War II, Indianapolis was headquarters to 11 major international unions; by 1980, Indiana was still one of the country's most heavily unionized states—some 6 percent higher than the national average. But Indiana's labor ideology was more in tune with Hoosier conservatism than with some labor leader's programmatic liberalism.

Indianapolis, Gary, and Fort Wayne

Indianapolis, Indiana's premier city, and Gary, its third-largest, are so diametrically opposed that it is hard to believe they are in the same state. Indianapolis, conservative but pragmatic, epitomizes Indiana's homogeneity; Gary, liberal and corrupt, is the exception proving the rule. Indianapolis was carved from the wilderness in 1824 as the state's new capital; Gary was born in 1906, sired by U.S. Steel and named for its president. Early Indianapolis was settled by Southern whites with a sprinkling of Easterners; Gary was peopled by

foreign stock (a total of 57 ethnic strains, primarily Slavs and Southern Europeans, were once counted) and later by Southern blacks, all imported to man
the massive, belching mills. Indianapolis has a widely diversified economy,
ranging from auto, pharmaceutical, and electronic manufacturing to food,
service, and financial industries; Gary is full of heavy industry, with the
concomitant fouling of air and water. Indianapolis has culture, recreation, and
entertainment; Gary is sin city squared.

As late as the mid-1960s, Irving Leibowitz could write that Indianapolis
"continues to attract every last-ditch reactionary and screwball in the country." But no longer. Richard Lugar was a major catalyst of change, setting
in motion a revival with rippling political and economic impact. Today, there
is much more to Indianapolis than glowering war memorials, good-ole-boy
Indy 500 fanatics, and American Legion headquarters.

As his springboard to office, Lugar used the Greater Indianapolis Progress
Committee (GIPC), a business-government alliance forged in the '60s that he
transformed from a benign advisory group into an instrument of political
change. Under Lugar and his hand-picked heir, Mayor William H. Hudnut
III, once somnolent Indianapolis seemed to explode with activity.

Besides sprucing up its downtown Monument Circle and environs with
classy brick pavement, restoring inner-city Victorian neighborhoods such as
Lockerbie Square, constructing an arena for the Indiana Pacers basketball
team, renovating the nostalgic century-old City Market area, enticing new
Hilton and Hyatt Regency hotels, and launching a major downtown mall,
Indianapolis scanned the economic horizon in 1978 and took an entirely new
tack. To end its heavy reliance on recession-prone auto manufacturing, the
city designed a new economic tripod: warehousing and distribution (six major
U.S. highways converge on Indianapolis, and the city is within a day's drive
of half the U.S. population); sophisticated medical services (building on the
Indiana University Medical Center); and major convention and exposition
business. It then shrewdly set out to become the amateur sports capital of the
world, hosting championship tourneys in swimming, golf, track, and field,
judo, basketball, and figure skating; it built a 13-acre, $7 million tennis complex
to become the permanent home of the U.S. Clay Court Championships, a $21.5
million natatorium (largest in the nation), a $5.9 million track stadium with
20,000 seats, and a 5,000-seat velodrome for bicycle racing and speed skating.
The crowning glory was a $77 million, 60,000-seat domed stadium planned
to double the city's convention and exhibition space and act as bait for the
professional football or major league baseball franchises Indianapolis yearned
for but still lacked.

Little or none of this, it is worth noting, would have happened without the
Lilly Endowment, which poured millions of dollars into various projects and
then pledged $35 million toward the domed stadium, an unprecedented gift,
even in the rarified world of philanthropy. (The Krannert Charitable Trust
chipped in another $5 million, and the balance was to come from a bond issue,
financed by a 1 percent surtax on food and drink.) Established in 1937 by heirs
of the giant Eli Lilly pharmaceutical firm, the endowment—in the words of

one local official—has "done more for the city than the city itself," in some years topping the $12 million to $14 million received in federal revenue sharing. The endowment has close to $800 million in assets, making it the nation's sixth-largest private foundation; of its $32 million in 1980 grants, three-fifths went for community projects, many of them in home-town Indianapolis.

Until the stadium project came along, the Lilly Endowment's biggest gift to Indianapolis had been $5 million in seed money toward an ambitious Tivoli Gardens-style park, featuring water recreation and amateur athletics, planned for the city's deteriorated White River waterfront. The park was also expected to be a showcase for Indiana history, a 250-acre beginning to a planned 145-mile-long swath of state parkland from Muncie to Martinsville.

For all its renaissance (the revival efforts helped win Indianapolis an All-American City designation in 1982), Indianapolis was still plagued with the kinds of problems found in most Frostbelt cities: budget shortfalls exacerbated by declining federal aid and a state-imposed cap on property tax revenues, declining infrastructure, unfunded liabilities for public employee pensions, and cuts in transit, police, and recreation programs. In the 1970s, far-out suburbs beyond "Unigov's" boundaries grew, while Indianapolis itself lost population.

Not all Indianapolis groups endorsed the effort to draw young professionals, "empty nesters," and university folk into new downtown housing, and to attract travelers. Some neighborhood groups—and they are a strong civic presence in Indianapolis—complained that investment in downtown meant disinvestment in their areas, that public dollars were being used to subsidize playgrounds for the affluent, while ten community centers were closed. Lugar, however, had sought to build some bridges between the mayor's office and the poor and black of Indianapolis, an effort continued and expanded under Hudnut. A third-generation Presbyterian minister, Hudnut had served one term in Congress before following Lugar into the mayoralty. Showing both the dedication appropriate for a man of the cloth and a vivid sense of humor, he was reelected in a 1979 landslide and served with distinction as president of the National League of Cities in 1980–81. The huge margins that Lugar and Hudnut rolled up after enactment of Unigov proved what the Democrats and disadvantaged had feared: that annexation of out-county areas guaranteed Republicans an indefinite lock on governing Indianapolis and effectively diluted the voting power of the city's blacks (22 percent of the city population by 1980).*

In Gary, so starkly the antithesis of Indianapolis, it is the whites who total just 25 percent of the population. From a 1960 peak of 178,320, Gary sagged in numbers to 151,953 in 1980, thus relinquishing to Fort Wayne its status as Indiana's second-largest city. Grim, grimy Gary is still very much the steel town it was built to be. U.S. Steel's $1 billion complex hulks just a few blocks

---

*It should also be noted that Unigov did not merge school districts, which might have meant busing of blacks from central city to suburban schools, or vice versa. Separate city and suburban police departments were also retained.

north of City Hall, simultaneously the city's biggest employer, biggest tax-payer, biggest polluter, and least concerned corporate citizen.

Into Gary's cauldron of crime, corruption, and racial tension stepped the black political leader Richard Hatcher, elected mayor in 1967 over the bitter opposition of the white Democratic machine. Immediately vaulted into national prominence, Hatcher was enormously successful in garnering some $500 million in federal aid for Gary during his first dozen years in office. But remaining whites—put off by Hatcher's confrontational style and by black-power rhetoric emanating from city hall—never felt comfortable with him. The federal money was funneled primarily into showcase edifices along the main downtown business strip, but also into building 13,000 low- and middle-income housing units and a flashy new civic center. Not a dime of state money went into this new Genesis Center—proof, Hatcher bitterly claimed, that the legislature wouldn't even acknowledge Gary, let alone help solve its problems. But could money alone help Gary? "All of that federal money should have had a substantial impact, but it hasn't," said Thomas Crump, a black city councilman opposed to Hatcher. "Hatcher's been antibusiness," he continued. "He hasn't done anything to create a partnership between the city and the business community." Gary's prospects in the early '80s were indeed grim. Massive steel layoffs hit the town. And street crime, gambling, and prostitution, set back during the early Hatcher years, had reestablished their grip.

Gary's black-run city hall certainly was no more corrupt than that of its predecessors or its neighbors. Kickbacks, swindles, fraud, embezzlement, all have been part of the Lake County political landscape for generations and have made it probably the most corrupt urban county in the country.

Fort Wayne (pop. 172,196), 120 miles northwest of Indianapolis, was one of the white man's first settlements in Indiana. For generations, Fort Wayne thrived from the fruits of the rich farmland surrounding it. By the 1970s, it was smugly complacent—boasting of a healthy economy, civic spirit, good restaurants, and burgeoning fine arts. Then the bottom fell out. A bitter 1979–80 strike (followed—perhaps inevitably—by permanent closing in 1983) at the city's biggest employer, International Harvester, coupled with heavy auto-industry layoffs, sent unemployment soaring. Racial tensions, always simmering just under the surface, erupted with overt Klan activity and then the attempted murder in 1980 of Vernon E. Jordan, Jr., president of the National Urban League. To top it off, devastating spring floods poured through Fort Wayne in 1982, causing millions of dollars in damage and leaving thousands temporarily homeless. Civic leaders realized how little cooperative effort had been invested in their city and set about to change it, establishing a public-private partnership for development of the kind Indianapolis had launched years earlier. This won the city an All-American City award in 1983. Then, with the hefty aid package ($31.5 million in loans and guarantees) raised locally in the frantic but fruitless effort to forestall International Harvester's departure, the city set out to attract new business. Fort Wayne—birthplace of night baseball and burial place of Johnny Appleseed—could only hope it wasn't too late.

The Lesser Hoosier Cities

For a state of rural reputation, Indiana harbors a surprising number of substantial cities. The story of South Bend, near the state's historically disputed border with Michigan, is essentially the saga of the Studebaker brothers, who began building wagons in 1852; when horseless carriages came along, Studebaker took the plunge into the new technology, producing the most successful of some 375 makes of cars that have been built in Indiana. But markets began failing after World War II, and the last Studebaker (remember its torpedo shape?) rolled off the South Bend assembly line in 1963. Almost two decades later, the old Studebaker plant stood like a ghostly sentinel—and precursor of what was about to happen to much of the Midwest's auto industry. South Bend itself, however, remained a strong industrial center, a pleasant and neat community, with few serious crimes and even less slum housing. Its blue-collar populace (109,727, down nearly 13 percent in the 1970s) formed a Democratic island in a surrounding Republican sea.

There used to be an old and staid Roman Catholic university in South Bend known as Notre Dame, founded in 1842, home of football legends beyond compare. But since Father Theodore Hesburgh became its president in 1952, South Bend has been home of a new, *avant garde* Notre Dame: an advocate of change (women were admitted beginning in 1972); of increasing academic excellence (the American Council of Education has ranked it among the top 30 private schools in the country); and of openness to modern ideas (a birth-control conference was held on campus and non-Catholics were recruited for its theological faculty). Hesburgh, called by some America's "most influential cleric," stimulated increased social consciousness on campus and off and served for 15 years as member and chairman of the U.S. Civil Rights Commission. And through it all, the Fighting Irish continued to play football as enthusiastically as every Indiana high school throws itself into Indiana's most irrepressible passion: the game of basketball.

Seventy miles southwest of Indianapolis lies Terre Haute (pop. 61,125), on the one-time line of the real Wabash Cannonball. The fancy French name notwithstanding, Terre Haute is a rundown Wabash River city with a spicy past. With coal, industry, breweries, and distilleries, Terre Haute early in the century was poised to become the "Pittsburgh of the West." But in the 1920s, Terre Haute stopped growing, afflicted by coal strikes, Prohibition, floods, and chronic lack of civic leadership. About all that survived from the earlier boom era were flourishing brothels. Shamed by national "sin city" publicity, Terre Haute finally shut down the houses—much to the dismay of former mayor Leland Larrison. "Instead we've got some very high class massage parlors," he said. "Now they're in the motels. It's a rich man's game now. It costs you $50 to $75 . . . ten bucks was the going price when I was in there. The average salesman, he can't sneak $50 onto the expense account."

Evansville (pop. 130,496) did what Terre Haute failed to do: stop the outward flow of industry and rebuild the city. When in the 1950s this Ohio River city saw unemployment skyrocket as several major employers moved out, businessmen and politicians quickly coalesced to form "Evansville's Future, Inc." The dingy old waterfront was cleaned up, new construction begun, transportation upgraded, and substantial new industries enticed to the city. The same assertive spirit cropped up in 1981 when the city budget had to be cut but work still needed doing: Mayor Michael Vandeveer sent out a call for volunteers, and within a year Evansville residents had donated 89,000 hours of time, saving taxpayers $290,000. Evansville was settled early by German Catholics and was strong Copperhead country. Its politics are traditionally rough-and-tumble, reminiscent of riverboat days. But it is the kind of city that tries hard to keep its inner core alive and places high value on historic preservation.

Most travelers would drive through Columbus, some 50 miles southeast of Indianapolis, only on their way to somewhere else—if it weren't for one man. J. Irwin Miller, former board chairman of the dominant Cummins Engine Company, is to Columbus what Cosimo de Medici was to renaissance Florence: patriarch, patron, and social conscience. The reason people stop in this city of 30,292 is its architectural splendor: more than 40 public and private buildings designed by world-famous architects, their fees paid by the Cummins Engine Foundation created by Miller. He also sought out and attracted top-level black executives for the firm. Throughout, Miller kept in the background, becoming, for example, the guiding force (and financier) behind a drive to attract overseas investors to Columbus which by 1982 had born fruit with six foreign companies established there. In 1967, *Esquire,* in a cover story on Miller, suggested he had better qualifications than any other living American to be president. But of course Miller was no politician, and Indiana is a politician's state. Only one Wendell Willkie a century, please.

OHIO

The Middle-Class Society

OHIO, HUNG UP about its own identity (East to Westerners, West to Easterners), and the epitome of the middle-class society, is the least distinctive of the great industrial states of the U.S.A. Ohioans have been described as embodying "the homely virtues of honesty, thrift, steadiness, caution, and distrust of government." But in recent times the "wonderful world of Ohio," as it was so often called by James Rhodes, the hucksterish governor four times elected in the 1960s and '70s, has seemed chiefly interested in *money*. As Rhodes repeated *ad nauseum*, "Profit is not a dirty word in Ohio." The problem, and the tragedy, was that from the late 1960s onward, Ohio, musclebound to heavy industry, was suffering from deep economic malaise as the centers of economic activity turned to new frontiers of services and high technology for which the state was sadly but singularly unprepared. One could not help but wonder what Ohio would do to get out of its mess. Unlike many troubled industrial states, Ohio could hardly prove its friendliness to business by cutting back government and cutting taxes. On the contrary, it could be argued that Ohio had already done too much of that. For years Ohio had bragged to the outside world of its rock-bottom tax levels even as its expenditures per capita for education, health, welfare, mental care, and environmental control placed it near the bottom of the 50 states and in the absolute cellar among the great industrial states (Texas excepted). The failure of this approach showed up not only in economic problems and high unemployment rates, but in population figures as well: a 1.3 percent growth rate in the '70s, and indications of an actual drop in population thereafter.

Even in the most prosperous years after World War II, there was little color, verve, or great culture to relieve the monotony of this state's life. Ohio just plowed through history, turning out immense amounts of manufactured goods, paying among the nation's highest wages to its factory workers but shortchanging others less fortunate, practicing a politics of indifference.

Let us not overstate the case: All along, of course, Ohio has had its redeeming graces, its imaginative and dedicated men and women, and some innovative institutions. Doughty Cincinnati, decades past her prime, still has a certain Old World charm and is in the midst of a graceful renewal; Cleveland since 1979 has achieved dramatic civic revitalization; there are several outstanding small colleges of exemplary quality, including Antioch, Oberlin, Kenyon, and Ohio Wesleyan. A coterie of conscientious, public-spirited, and progressive business leaders—many deeply concerned about the state's future —has been growing. There was some hope that Richard Celeste, the young

Democrat chosen governor in 1982, might provide the leadership Ohio had so long—and disastrously—been denied.

First, a quick tour of geographic Ohio. The state's fertile plains are studded with no fewer than seven cities having more than 100,000 people, 17 metropolitan areas, and some 150 cities with 10,000 or more inhabitants in a state of 10,797,419 people. One can't be on a highway headed in any direction in Ohio for an hour and not hit a medium-sized city—a Steubenville, a Warren, Niles, Sandusky or Freemont.

Most of Ohio's borders are wet—Lake Erie to the north and the Ohio River stretching 436 miles along the east and south. There are, however, some arbitrary cartographer's lines along the Pennsylvania, Michigan, and Indiana borders, so that the overall impression is more or less square. The geographers identify three regions of Ohio. To the southeast lies the Appalachian Allegheny Plateau spilling over from Pennsylvania and West Virginia; along the shores of Lake Erie from Cleveland to the northwest corner is a strip known as the Lake Plains; and all the rest of Ohio, representing its great land bulk, is a central Plains area, with gently rolling land similar to America's Western plains.

The rugged, hilly country of the southeastern Allegheny Plateau, a mixture of sylvan wood and land ravaged by strip coal mining, harbors few cities of any note and much rural poverty; along the Ohio River are some heavy industries including steel companies run out of Wheeling and Pittsburgh. Many of these counties are poor in the extreme, with subquality schools and poor public facilities. The original settlers were mostly Virginia and Kentucky woodsmen.

Northeastern Ohio is highly industrialized and heavily populated, a smokestack-studded industrial complex including the cities of Youngstown, Warren, Canton, Akron, Cleveland, and, somewhat farther west, Toledo. These cities, many now in deep economic trouble, are actually part of an identifiable megalopolis called Chi-Pitts, anchored by Pittsburgh on the east, Chicago (or possibly Milwaukee) on the west. Once a haven for New England settlers, this region is now heavily peopled by the children and grandchildren of European workers—Italians, Slovenians, Hungarians, Poles—who were imported to man the heavy steel and rubber industries earlier in this century. Following them came hundreds of thousands of blacks from the American Southland.

Finally, in central and western Ohio, one comes on the easterly terminus of the great Midwestern farm belt. It is, however, also strong manufacturing territory and site of cities great and small, among them Columbus at center state, Dayton and Cincinnati at the southwesterly corner. Here are the descendants of the Scots, Irish, Pennsylvania German, and assorted Civil War veterans. The German flavor is especially strong in southern Ohio and equals conservatism. Many of the overwhelmingly Republican counties of the U.S.A. are in these central and western regions, but interestingly there are still a handful of counties that have been voting Democratic ever since the Civil War.

An Economy of Heavy Industry

It was probably inevitable that heavy manufacturing would come to dominate the economy of this state strategically located between the iron ore deposits of Minnesota and the coal mines of Appalachia, the St. Lawrence Seaway to the north and the Ohio River to the south. Her manufacturing output ranks third among the states, reflecting steel, broad varieties of machinery production, and the onetime blessing that has become the great decline industry of the '80s: auto assembling and auto parts manufacture. The state's promoters point to many other industries—from business machines to coffins, buckets to Bibles—but all are lightweights in comparison to steel and autos. There's also coal, lime, and some oil and gas mining. Ohio has diversified agriculture (chiefly dairy products, cattle, corn, and hogs) with a total farm income that ranks 11th among the states.

By the 1970s, the percentage of Ohioans employed in manufacturing was 30 percent higher than the national average. But the dangers of this heavy dependence on traditional manufacturing could be seen in the scars of eroded and sometimes abandoned plants that blighted the cityscapes of Cleveland, Toledo, Akron and Youngstown, and the serious problems of obsolesence in plants that were still operating. Yet Ohio leaders failed to understand that centers of high-technology and encouragement of entrepreneurial activity would be the key to the future. Instead, Governor Rhodes set out on one of the greatest smokestack-chasing hunts of American history. Rhodes' industrial "Raiders" undertook scores of industry-hunting tours around the U.S.A. and several foreign trade missions. Prospective advertisers were reminded that Ohio had the lowest state and local tax rates in the country and the lowest proportion of government employees.

The heavy promotional campaign did attract several thousand new industrial jobs during the 1960s and '70s. But with the ever-broadening waves of automation and the aging of facilities in such heavy industries as steel, actual manufacturing jobs in Ohio registered only modest gains in the '60s and declined in the 1970s. Of the actual new factory jobs attracted to the state, most were concentrated in heavy manufacturing such as rolling mills and assembly plants and relatively few in the more exotic, electronic age industries. Ohio was adding significant numbers of new positions, but the lion's share came in "service" jobs—nonmanufacturing jobs such as mining, transportation, utilities, wholesale and retail trade, food stores, department stores, banking, insurance, and government service. Little of this stemmed from the state's job promotion efforts, which were concentrated heavily on industry.

To attract new firms or expansions, Ohio in the '70s went heavily into the tax abatement game, allowing some businesses to avoid up to 100 percent of their property taxes for up to 20 years. First authorized for economically lagging cities in 1973, the tax exemption was widened to virtually all areas of the state—urban, suburban, or small town—in 1977. Economic development officials in the state government and several localities claimed that the exemptions were proving highly successful in luring new firms. And they could point to some big firms that took advantage of the abatements: the Japanese auto maker Honda in building its first U.S. assembly plant near Marysville, expansion of General Motors' huge Lordstown assembly plant near Youngstown, a $412 million Miller Brewing Plant in southwestern Ohio, for instance. But there was solid evidence, developed by the Ohio Public Interest Campaign and others, that many of the firms would have selected Ohio locations in any event. Moreover, each tax abatement reduced local property tax yields essential for funding the schools and other public services, thus reducing the state's general attractiveness as a place to live.

Ohio's state economic development officials were also peculiarly inept in assisting small entrepreneurs in getting new businesses off the ground, in aiding Ohio businesses in trouble. A sure sign of trouble was that Ohio's level of new business incorporations, the breeding ground of new job opportunities, was almost the lowest in the nation.

Neglectful State Government: From Lausche to Rhodes

When Frank J. Lausche was first elected governor of Ohio, in 1944, he bore all the marks of a true American folk hero: son of a Slovenian-born steelworker, outstanding city judge, respected mayor of his home city of Cleveland, disdainer of old-line machine politics, a Democratic candidate who could appeal across all party lines. But in Ohio today, it is hard to find a knowledgeable observer with a kind word for Frank Lausche. For this frugal and conservative Slovenian imposed such a parsimonious, strict pay-as-you-go philosophy in Ohio, akin to the low-spending Byrd regime in Virginia, that the state has yet to regain the position among the states in services to people—in education, welfare, criminology, or mental care—that it held before he took office. Lausche believed in spending money only on highways, always a source of political patronage jobs, campaign contributions from contractors, and visible achievement.

After Lausche, Rhodes was the most influential man in postwar Ohio history; he was governor from 1963 to 1971 and again from 1975 until 1983, ending up, at 73, as America's oldest governor. The Rhodesian mark will be felt in Ohio for years to come. A sturdily built man whose personal manner ranges from hearty back-slapping to cold discourtesy, he was born into rather poor circumstances, his father a coal mine manager. As governor, he avoided press conferences and confrontations with opponents and delegated the details of administration to a generally competent but nonintellectual staff. In more than three decades of office-holding, Rhodes revealed himself as a robust type, a man's man, fond of golf and poker, given to ribald jokes and macho statements* and for the most part, a superbly successful politician.

*At one governors' conference, while Michigan's George Romney was rambling at the speaker's stand, Rhodes slipped a note to fellow Governor Roger Branigan of Indiana. It read: "This guy couldn't sell pussy on a troopship."

What the public wanted, Rhodes determined, was no new taxes. So he promised, "There'll be no new or additional taxes as long as I'm governor of Ohio." It was a promise that, in time, simply had to be broken, and it was—but not substantially. The net impact of the Rhodes regimes was to continue the Lauschian fiscal policy of status quo. As a percentage of personal income, the state's combined state and local taxes were 48th in America in 1953 and 50th in the late 1970s. This made it possible, of course, for the state government's industrial promoters to place ads in the *Wall Street Journal* proclaiming: "OHIO'S STATE AND LOCAL TAXES ARE THE LOWEST IN THE NATION! . . . Ohio makes dollars go farther without loss in essential services."

Where Rhodes made his strongest mark on Ohio—and differentiated himself clearly from the old Lausche approach—was in selling the people, during his first two terms as governor, on massive bond issues (totaling some $2 billion in all) for highways, higher education facilities, and other physical improvements. For years under Rhodes, the bonds in effect substituted for new taxes. Half of them went for highways. "We get the most political credit for another mile of superhighway," Rhodes' finance director, Howard L. Collier, told us in 1969. This was scarcely a prudent policy of careful infrastructure maintenance, however. "Don't put anything under the ground," said Rhodes. "You never get credit for it."

In none of this, of course, was Rhodes doing more than appealing to deeply held Buckeye views about government and its role. Per capita state spending has been below the national average through most of the 20th century. State and local government bureaucracies are thin by national standards. In the 1970s, for instance, only Pennsylvania and Kentucky had fewer public workers in relation to population. Technical capacities of state government are low; small work forces and inexperience in many departments are exacerbated by high turnover. Environmental protection is weak in a state with fearsome air and water pollution problems, some of which Ohio exports. Emissions from the high-sulfur coal burned by its utilities are a major source of "acid rain" falling on New York State, New England, and adjacent Canadian provinces.

A strong point of Ohio government is its jealously guarded (and constitutionally assured) home rule tradition, which has helped the hard-pressed cities survive through their power to impose payroll taxes on all workers, suburban commuters included. The downside is that state government is reluctant to do anything that might ever so slightly infringe on local privileges. A case in point was the total failure of a late 1970s effort to write land use policies to protect farmlands and other areas of critical environmental concern. By the same token, when states such as Massachusetts and California were enacting urban policies to aid hard-pressed cities in the late '70s, Ohio did virtually nothing.

Perhaps the most telling indicator of Ohio's neglect of its fundamental public responsibilities has been the treatment of its public schools. From the late '60s through the '70s, Ohio had the dubious distinction of leading the nation in school closings. Schools in Ohio are far more dependent than in most states on local property taxes, and there are statutory requirements that any increase in local school tax levies be approved by a vote of the people, and that inflation-related increases in property values cannot produce additional tax revenue. By the late '70s the situation became even more acute as schools became a whipping child not just of recalcitrant taxpayers but also of opponents of court-ordered busing to achieve desegregation in several of the state's largest cities, including Cleveland, Columbus, and Dayton. In 1978–79, 10 school districts were forced into state receivership; two years later 35 districts, including Cleveland's, ran out of money. Both governor and legislature seemed paralyzed when it came to devising a decent, long-term solution to the school finance problem—despite the grave dangers that closed or subquality schools implied for Ohio's future. Nor could Ohio citizens themselves be absolved of responsibility. It was they who were voting "no" on local school levies. And it was they who were electing malfeasant state legislators and governors of the quality represented by James Rhodes.

Ohioans' continued support of Rhodes occasionally raised questions about their values deeper than the economic. It remains difficult to forget Rhodes' words about campus antiwar demonstrators at a spring 1970 news conference. The demonstrators, Rhodes said, were "the worst type of people we harbor in America, . . . worse than brown shirts and the Communist element." Two days later came the fatal National Guard shootings at Ohio's Kent State University. The President's Commission on Campus Disorders later reported that the deaths were "unnecessary, unwarranted, and inexcusable."

There were breaks in the Lausche-Rhodes type of regime, personified by two single-term governors. The first was Michael V. DiSalle, the genial, roly-poly former mayor of Toledo and wartime chief of the Office of Price Administration elected in the Democratic sweep of 1958. Twelve years later came John J. Gilligan, Notre Dame graduate and erstwhile teacher of literature at Xavier University in Cincinnati, a man about as unlike Rhodes as one could imagine.

The Gilligan record in four years as governor was exemplary. Gilligan won enactment of the first income tax in Ohio's history, applicable to both corporations and individuals. In addition to sharply increased appropriations for schools and human services, he fought for and won a tough strip mine reclamation law, instituted a consumer protection program, and weakened the hold of middle-aged white males on state boards and commissions by setting out consciously to include more representatives of organized labor, blacks, and women. Where Gilligan failed was as a personal leader. Often charming and personally generous, he also illustrated at times a brashness and low "boiling point" that got him into political hot water. And when he ran for reelection in 1974 he found himself outmaneuvered and outfoxed by none other than backslapping, garrulous James Rhodes, returning to the political wars in a bid for a third term. Rhodes scored political points by attacking the "Gilligan gougers" for taxing "everything in Ohio that walks, crawls, or flies" and promising more roads, more bridges, a $1,000-a-year raise for all teachers —and no new taxes.

Four years later, in 1978, Ohioans had another opportunity to vote for a liberal Democrat in place of James Rhodes, and again they chose Rhodes. The Democrats' nominee was a formidable candidate: Richard Celeste, 40, the state's lieutenant governor. Celeste had Cleveland-area ethnic roots, a record as a Yale honor graduate, Rhodes Scholar, and Peace Corps veteran. But he was thoroughly out-campaigned by Rhodes, who wrapped himself in the American flag in a skillful final television commercial blitz, suggested Celeste would somehow double the income tax, got crucial help from the Ohio Right to Life Committee, and ended up winning his fourth term.

By the early '80s, Ohio faced fearsome reality in the form of massive state deficits. Again and again the legislature had to meet to cover deficits by slashing expenditures for universities, mental health, and already rock-bottom welfare levels, and by doing the unthinkable that had suddenly become mandatory: raising taxes. All agreed that Ohio's dependence on autos and steel was chiefly responsible for the bind. Yet as Democratic State Rep. Patrick Sweeney of Cleveland noted, the legislature wasn't "guiltless": the aggressive tax abatement and property tax rollbacks it had sanctioned, he noted, had all contributed to the fiscal crisis.

Celeste had a second shot at the governorship in the deep recession year of 1982 and emerged victorious over Republican Rep. Clarence Brown, Jr. In his campaign Celeste struck a troubling protectionist note (in response, doubtless, to his backing from organized labor). He did propose an "action agenda" to shore up the economy of Ohio and the Great Lakes states, including an economic summit meeting of Great Lakes state governors, a "capital pool" for small businesses, and "SWAT" teams of economic development specialists to help firms modernize or to intervene when companies plan to close plants. It was also time, said Celeste, to invest some of the state's massive pension funds in entrepreneurial activities, protecting the funds by having the state government insure them against risk.

All were sound ideas. The real question would be the skill of Celeste and other Ohio leaders in forming a body of concerned Ohio industrialists and union leaders, financiers and high-technology experts, to transform the spirit and thus the economic future of Ohio in her times of deep trouble.

Issueless Politics

Packed with cities, heavily industrialized and unionized, harboring large populations of East and South Europeans and blacks, Ohio has had every reason to be a liberal Democratic state. Polls of basic party preference almost invariably show more Ohioans identifying with the Democrats than with the Republicans. Yet a Republican aristocracy of industrialists and small-city conservatives, an alliance that began with the great bosses Mark Hanna of Cleveland and George Cox of Cincinnati in the 1880s and in a sense culminated when Hanna sent his protégé, William McKinley of Canton, to the White House in 1896, has dominated Ohio through most of the past century. Democratic presidential victories (as in three of FDR's four elections, or 1948,

1964, and 1976) were exceptions to the rule; so were the occasions on which Democrats won the governorship or legislature.

Although the 1970s brought signs that Republican-conservative hegemony was starting to deteriorate (the Democrats, for instance, won state legislative control on several occasions), one must still ask what accounts for the long-standing dichotomy between the Democratic demography and Republican electoral performance.

Geography is perhaps the most important factor. Ohio has no single dominating city akin to Detroit in Michigan, Chicago in Illinois, or New York City in its state. Cleveland, Ohio's largest city, casts only 7 percent of the statewide vote. Split assunder into many camps, the normally Democratic groups—labor unions, ethnic coalitions, blacks, intellectuals—lacked a single population center in which they could coalesce and begin a bid for statewide dominance. Of the large cities, Columbus and Cincinnati had strong Republican traditions and only Cleveland was dependably Democratic. The Republican business-elite, at least until the 1970s, monopolized the press and public forums in most parts of the state. All but a handful of the smaller cities were Republican bastions and formed the backbone of GOP voting strength in Ohio.

For decades, the fragmented condition of organized labor also led to Democratic weakness. Unlike Michigan's UAW, Ohio had no single dominant union; there were scores of unions across the state whose leaders often preferred to make their own arrangements with political candidates, rather than to work in concert. Only when the interests of all of organized labor seemed in peril—as in 1958, when "right to work" was on the ballot, or in the Goldwater race of 1964—did all elements of organized labor pull together in a concerted campaign. (They won on both occasions.)

Starting in the late 1960s, however, the state AFL-CIO began to take on more of the coloration of its counterparts in other heavily industrialized states. The profound irony is that Ohio unions might be a generation late, learning the skills of modern politics at just the moment labor membership, and concurrently big city population and voting power, were heading into what might well be terminal decline.*

The chief architect of postwar Republican organizational strength in Ohio was Ray C. Bliss, a man whose modest demeanor (that of a small-town banker, or the Akron insurance broker that he was) belied unusual intensity when it came to political matters. Scrupulously careful organization, year-round fund-raising, never leaving a detail unattended—those were the secrets of the Bliss formula. The one thing Bliss never, never did as a party chairman was to talk in public about issues. He was essentially a technician, to whom issues were a propaganda tool, not an end. His ideological neutrality assured him longev-

*Ohio's most powerful unions include the Teamsters, Machinists, and Communications Workers, the Ohio Education Association (its 80,000 teacher members are considered by many Ohio's most politically powerful single union), the American Federation of State, County and Municipal Employees (which organized, among others, the bulk of state employees), the United Auto Workers (most numerous in Toledo, Cleveland, Cincinnati, and Columbus), and the Steelworkers (in Youngstown, Canton, Cleveland, Lorain, and other towns).

ity on the job in Columbus and made him the natural choice (especially with behind-the-scenes backing from former President Eisenhower) to be chosen Republican National Chairman after the Goldwater debacle of 1964.

Since Bliss' departure, Ohio Republicans have suffered intermittent scandals and infighting (Democratic manager Mark Shields once joked about "civil war in the leper colony"). But the powers in the legislature, where the final Ohio decisions get made, have not altered radically. As correspondents Richard Zimmerman and Robert Burdock reported in 1969 in the *Cleveland Plain Dealer*:

> Gone are the days when lobbyists openly paid off legislators in cash in the halls of the Statehouse after they had cast a "right" vote. Gone are the days when "Boss" Hanna arrogantly sat in his Neil House suite and pulled the strings of power, perverting the legislative process as drunken legislators reeled among brass spittoons.
>
> But not gone is the tremendous power of the special interest lobbyists who lurk in the legislative halls. Many if not most of the more complex omnibus bills come directly from Columbus-based legislators representing trade, business and professional associations. The insurance industry, for example, practically dictates the laws that are supposed to control the industry. The same can be said of the banking industry and the utilities.

Combating the power of the Ohio Manufacturers Association, the retail merchants, the bankers, and the exceedingly powerful public utilities, the late '70s and early '80s found organized labor struggling hard along side a number of public interest groups—Common Cause, the League of Women Voters, the Ohio Public Interest Campaign, the Citizens League of Greater Cleveland, for example. But when the public interest groups came up against business or organized labor, they rarely if ever prevailed. And so it was, even when direct appeal was made to the voters. In 1980, for example, the Ohio Public Interest Campaign was able to qualify for the ballot a stem-to-stern reorganization of Ohio taxes, outlawing abatements and shifting the burden from lower income folk to affluent individuals and corporations. Business organized a heavily bankrolled campaign in opposition, and the voters ended up defeating the upstart measure by an overwhelming margin.

The Congressional Contingent

No Ohioan of modern times has enjoyed national prominence akin to that of Senator Robert A. Taft; but for the sudden political emergence of Dwight Eisenhower, Taft would most probably have won the 1952 Republican presidential nomination and possibly the presidency. Taft would have been the eighth Ohio president, following in the footsteps of Grant, Harrison, Hayes, Garfield, McKinley, his own father William Howard Taft, and Warren G. Harding. Despite his general conservatism, Taft had a progressive record on such issues as aid to education and housing, and no one ever doubted the honesty and integrity of this scion of the aristocratic Cincinnati family.

Snowy-haired Senator (and onetime governor) John Bricker of Ohio was once considered a major national figure and actually was selected by Thomas E. Dewey as his vice presidential running mate in 1944. Compared to Taft, however, Bricker was the shallowest of politicians.

Some interesting characters have filled the Senate seats since Taft and Bricker. There was Stephen Young, the aging, irascible Populist-style Democrat who delighted in replying to constituents' insulting letters in kind. Young's colleague for a while was William Saxbe, a shrewd country "squire" picked by a desperate President Nixon as attorney general though he had earlier called Vice President Agnew a "witch hunter" and uttered that unforgettable line about Nixon's professed ignorance of Watergate: "He reminds me of the fellow who played the piano in a brothel for 20 years and insisted he didn't know what was going on upstairs." Then came two senators who were old rivals in Democratic primary battles—John Glenn, the marine who was the first American to orbit the earth in his spaceship *Friendship 7* in 1962, and wealthy Cleveland businessman Howard Metzenbaum, a bread-and-butter liberal Democrat and nemesis of special interests in search of federal tax breaks. Of these two, Glenn is indubitably the more ambitious: a genial, decent, dependable—some liken him to Eisenhower—he stands slightly to the left on domestic issues but has substantially more concern than many liberals about defense and national security. In 1980 Glenn beat his obscure Republican opponent with a remarkable 69 percent of the vote—the same day Ronald Reagan was besting Jimmy Carter in Ohio, 52 to 41 percent. Not long afterward, he began to plan his run for the 1984 Democratic presidential nomination.

Through wily redistricting and able candidate recruitment, Republicans maintained clear control of Ohio's U.S. House seats clear into the 1980s. The delegation has harbored a goodly share of mediocrities, but also some skilled power brokers, such as Michael J. Kirwan, the blunt old Irishman from Youngstown who parlayed his two positions—as chairman of both the pork-dispensing Appropriations Subcommittee on Public Works and the Democratic Congressional Campaign Committee, apportioning election funds to Democratic congressmen—into a position of almost unparalleled power on Capitol Hill before his death in 1970.

Of all the power brokers (and abusers), few if any rivaled Wayne Hays, representative of a poor southeast Ohio district for 30 years, who rose to twin pinnacles of power: chairman of the House Administration Committee and the House Democratic Campaign Committee. Hays wheeled, dealed, placed other congressmen in his political debt, bullied opponents, fought election reform, and as the press finally revealed in 1976, placed a mistress (Elizabeth Ray) on his committee payroll.

Other Ohio congressmen of note include Louis Stokes, brother of former Cleveland Mayor Carl Stokes, first black member of the Appropriations Committee, so respected he was chosen chairman of the House Ethics Committee following the 1980 Abscam scandal. Akron's John Seiberling was on the Judiciary Committee majority that voted to impeach Richard Nixon; in recent years he has been chief sponsor of key environmental laws, including the Alaskan lands bill and control of the strip mining of coal. Delbert Latta, an angry conservative, rose to be senior Republican on the House Budget Committee and the man who got his name on the Reagan-endorsed budget resolutions, marking a profound switch in national policy in the early '80s. Even further to the right among Ohio Republicans, John Ashbrook had a 21-year congressional career that Michael Barone aptly summarized as "a continuing triumph of idealism over practicality, of principle over effectiveness." In 1982 Ashbrook hoped to win election to the U.S. Senate but suddenly collapsed and died during the primary campaign.

Cleveland, Now

If any great American city was obliged to labor heroically and against all odds from the 1960s into the 1980s, that city was Cleveland. In a brawny city whose very soul and livelihood seemed to depend on heavy industry, factory jobs hit a peak in 1950 and by the 1970s were evaporating at a fearsome rate. The city population declined from 914,808 in 1950 to 573,822 in 1980—down 23.6 percent in the '70s alone. The bitter aftertaste of 1960s race riots seemed never to wear off as ethnic whites and blacks continued their thinly disguised, ongoing confrontation—a clash only exacerbated by school busing that began in 1979.* At the same time, a fifth of all families were receiving some income under the AFDC welfare program. Per capita income was well below the state and national average. Retailing was oozing out to the suburbs. Finally, a decade of fiscal sleight-of-hand topped by a roaring political dispute between an often aloof and selfish suburban-based power establishment and a pugnacious young mayor from the ethnic wards made Cleveland the first major city to legally default on its fiscal obligations since the Great Depression. Visitors knew how to be cruel indeed: a *Washington Post* reporter in 1981 described Cleveland as "this grim industrial city, a cheerless vista of abandoned factories, shuttered shops, decaying neighborhoods."

But it was no accident when, in 1982, Cleveland received the coveted All-America Cities Award and comedians suddenly found it out of vogue to make Cleveland the butt of their jokes. Sometimes it takes a roaring crisis to jolt a city out of its complacency, and Dennis Kucinich, the peppery little Populist under whom the default had occurred, provided just that. By his denunciations of all opponents, he smoked out the business elite, who had long since moved to glades of suburban affluence, leaving the center city with its polyglot minorities to cope for itself. "Kucinich did Cleveland a great

---

*Hundreds of thousands of whites have fled Cleveland, to be replaced by blacks, who were 44 percent of the city population by 1980. Yet in the '70s the black population also declined slightly as blacks (including a number of black community leaders) moved to the suburbs.

favor. He woke up the Union Club. He scared the hell out of them," Homer Wadsworth, president of the highly respected Cleveland Foundation, told us.

George Voinovich, the Republican who defeated Kucinich in 1979, found businessmen willing to do practically anything he asked, and Voinovich, a genial, low-keyed but plain-speaking politician, was not shy to ask. The day after his election he had a volunteer task force, including many of Cleveland's top accountants, at work on a long-overdue review of the city's tangled books.

He persuaded nearly 90 business executives to conduct a full-time, 12-week study of potential city management efficiencies. The task force came up with 650 recommendations, most of which were subsequently implemented. Then came plans to end the city's default (accomplished in November 1980), to pay off the accumulated deficit, and to develop a schedule and financing package to rebuild Cleveland's seriously deteriorated bridges, streets, sewers, and water systems.

Voinovich received help not just from business but also from civic organizations, labor, academics, Cleveland's foundations, and the major newspapers. That coalition helped achieve 63 percent voter support for a $35 million payroll tax increase in February 1981 (a bill of which suburbanites would pay some three-quarters). Then, joined by senior citizens and neighborhood-based groups, the coalition waged a successful initiative campaign to extend terms of the mayors and councilmen from two to four years so they wouldn't start campaigning six months into their terms. Next came voter approval of an initiative to reduce the size of Cleveland's city council (one of the world's most notoriously parochial and quarrelsome) from 33 to 21 members.

Voinovich also enlisted business and foundation support to address education, housing and entry-level job problems, to cope with federal and state human service cutbacks, to clean up industrial properties, and to study the difficult prospects for Cleveland's economy (the latter through a rather ingenious base-line study, forming the basis for ongoing monitoring, produced by the Rand Corporation and paid for by the Cleveland Foundation). But Voinovich did not appear to kowtow to business; indeed he firmly refused tax abatements for plants and offices—a rip-off that Kucinich had appropriately brought into open debate. So stellar and independent was the Voinovich record that he (1) got himself placed on an "unfavorites" list of the Reagan White House and (2) was placed in line for the presidency of the National League of Cities.

No one was pretending that all was suddenly well in Cleveland. The schools were still disastrously underfunded, mismanaged and involved in courts suits over busing. The city had a legacy of poor labor-management relations and a weak technology-and-knowledge base. Plant closings or drastic job reductions continued, especially in such bedrock industries as autos and machine tools. Dependency levels remained alarmingly high. Cleveland, some remembered, had had its "highs" before, perhaps the last in the late '60s when the Carl Stokes served as the city's black "hero mayor" and symbolized for a time a potential for urban renaissance in a multiracial setting. But the business establishment's assumption—for the first time in living memory—of responsibility to *do* something for Cleveland, rather than simply milk it for private profit, was surely a seminal event.

Even at the height of Cleveland's troubles, the city had more strengths than its wretched national image conveyed. From its factories, even in times of recession, pour formidable quantities of iron and steel, machine tools, industrial equipment, and motor vehicles. Cleveland still refines vast quantities of oil and is deep into petrochemicals; it is a global leader in iron ore management and supply. Even in the face of general industrial decline, some of its manufacturing areas—among them fabricated metals and measurement and control devices—added 30 percent or more to their work force in the '70s.

By stretching to include the rubber company headquarters in Akron, 35 miles away, the city can claim to be home of 39 of the top U.S. 1,000 corporations, including such heavies as TRW, Republic Steel, Standard Oil (Ohio), Eaton and Hanna Mining. Only New York and Chicago have more corporate headquarters. Downtown Cleveland, in fact, had a bigger 1980 work force than at any time in its history because of the corporate offices and the ancillary services they demanded, ranging from law, accounting, engineering, and finance to research and computer centers.

While the very thought of Cleveland conjures up for many vistas of dingy mills and smokestacks, the city does offer other amenities: an "emerald necklace" of fine parks, which circles the city (though in contrast to county-run parks, many of the city's own are in a sad state of disrepair); a beautiful, prestigious, and richly endowed art museum, considered one of the nation's finest; the world-famous Cleveland Orchestra; a public library system, blessed with its own special taxing district, more heavily used than almost any other in America; professional opera and ballet companies; a renewed and thriving theater district in the Art Deco buildings of Playhouse Square; and top professional sports teams. The city has a prestigious university, Case Western University, which resulted from the merger of Case (known for its scientific disciplines) and Western Reserve (liberal arts, medicine, engineering, and law).

First to settle Cleveland were New Englanders, then Irish to build the railroads, then more Easterners, and from the 1870s onward, a flood of Germans, Irish, Welsh, French, Scots, Bohemians, Jews, Poles, Slovenes, Lithuanians, Hungarians, Rumanians, Italians, Czechs, and Russians to man the hearths, refine the oil, and build, build, build the city. At one time three-quarters of Cleveland's people were foreign born; the descendants of these people, called the "cosmos," still fill almost every block of Cleveland's West Side with well-defined little ghettos, each preserving its own customs, languages, religions, foods, and costumes. No less than 63 separate ethnic groups have been identified. Except for a couple of black enclaves of many decades' standing, the West Side is all white (and determined to stay that way); block after block of the old wood frame houses and narrow yards march on in what seems to an outsider dreary procession, the monotony relieved only by corner stores and markets, churches of a hundred faiths, and a few dismal old fortress-like schools. There is intense local pride in many of these communities, however. The West Side also harbors Ohio City, in recent years the scene of substantial resurgence by young families (many of them professionals) buying late-19th-century Victorian, Colonial, and Greek revival homes.

The great preponderance of residential neighborhoods on Cleveland's East Side are as black as those on the West Side are white. Between the two there is the natural barrier of the Cuyahoga River, twisting through center city and lined by warehouses, terminals, and railroad tracks. The great black influx began with World War I and continued until the late 1960s. Gradually the blacks forced the cosmos out of old neighborhoods such as Hough (scene of a cataclysmic riot in 1966) and Glenville (where black militants and police staged a celebrated shoot-out in 1968). The visitor to Hough today sees hundreds of deserted buildings, refuse-strewn lawns, streetfront churches, metal grills on store windows, and evidence of the revival in the wake of the 1966 upheaval: community development centers, health and day-care centers, and one of the Great Society's revival efforts—the $3.4 million Martin Luther King Plaza, with stores (some boarded up) and apartments on the upper floors.

Cleveland has few pockets of true racial integration. One exception is on the East Side: Buckeye, once known as the largest Hungarian settlement outside of Budapest. Heavy black incursions led to ugly confrontations in the late '60s, including abductions, shootings, and bombings of homes. But in 1970 the Buckeye Area Development Corporation emerged out of the old Hungarian Tradesmen's Club and persuaded the police to establish an outreach center, which nipped vigilantes and created a skills center for the unemployed. Buckeye was selected for the house-to-house rehabilitation program of the Neighborhood Housing Service. Merchants along Buckeye Road, long famed for its Hungarian meat markets, pastry shops, and restaurants, began to restore to Old World charm their dilapidated red brick buildings, many with architecturally interesting turrets and balconies. The political ferment for constructive change was kept alive by an integrated, militant organization, the Buckeye-Woodland Community Congress.

A chief irony of Cleveland geography is that the swank suburbs lie to the east of the city; the well-to-do white commuters to center Cleveland must pass through the black population belt on their way to downtown and back home each day. Shaker Heights remains the most famous of Cleveland's upper crust suburbs, though in fact it has accepted, with remarkable success, a significant minority of Jews and blacks in recent years.

Cleveland's center remains its Public Square, dominated by the grim old 52-story Terminal Tower. The square harbors a ghastly war memorial and is the hub from which the great avenues—Euclid, Superior, and Ontario—spoke out to all directions save north, a course that would soon land one in Lake Erie. For more than a generation, center city atrophied; then in the 1960s came the architecturally sterile Erieview urban renewal project—"long on desolate, overscaled spaces, defiantly antihuman," wrote one critic—between the Public Square and the lake. The '70s brought a multimillion-dollar revitalization of Public Square, and by the early '80s the Sohio oil company was preparing to invest $200 million in a new headquarters-office-shopping complex on the square, the largest single construction project in Cleveland history. Through the '70s and into the next decade a construction boom proceeded along Superior and Euclid Avenues and other sites in or near the city's core, adding banks and corporate headquarters, Cleveland State University expansion, hotels, medical facilities, luxury apartments and government buildings. A kind of Bohemia—renovated lofts and warehouses, antique and ethnic arts and crafts shops, waterfront restaurants and taverns—sprang up in the Flats, an old industrial district beside the river.

Few world cities ever so despoiled their natural environment, or moved so close to choking on their own pollutants, as Cleveland. The symbol of this was the slimy, chocolate-brown Cuyahoga River, bubbling with subsurface gases, filled with phenols, oils, and acids from the steel mills and refineries along its banks. The Cuyahoga, indeed, was the only river of the U.S.A. to be officially declared a fire hazard; one June day in 1969, its oil-slicked waters burst into flames and burned with such intensity that two railroad bridges that span it were nearly destroyed. A federal report declared that "the lower Cuyahoga has no visible life, not even low forms such as leeches and sludge worms that usually thrive on wastes." Yet by the early '80s, under the gun of federal and local anti-pollution rules, the steel firms and other industries had installed relatively effective water treatment plants; the oil slicks had disappeared and some species of fish were even returning, and miracle of miracles, it was again legal to swim in Lake Erie not far from the river's mouth. There were also reports of notable improvement in Cleveland's air quality, fifth-worst in the U.S. in the late '60s as a result of the cumulative assault of steel mills, power plants, building furnaces, and automobiles.

The state of Ohio agreed to construct a handsome lakefront park, repairing the planning horror by which Cleveland had allowed its window to Erie to become an ugly industrial no-man's land dotted with powerplants and junk-strewn empty lots. Mass transit did better in Cleveland than many cities: the country's first new postwar rapid transit line was opened there in 1955. An airport extension in 1968 made Cleveland the first U.S. city to provide a direct rapid transit line for its airport travelers. Unfortunately the right-of-way was one of the ugliest known to man: it became a "castaway alley" of garbage, tires, unkempt backyards, an industrial no-man's land. In 1976, however, a citizens' cleanup campaign, "Rapid Recovery," was formed to survey the entire right-of-way, engage the aid of artists and landscape architects for beautification projects, paint gigantic wall murals, get homeowners and businesses to clean up their backyards and in some instances landscape the sections of their property visible to transit riders. The project became a national model of transit right-of-way beautification and citizen cooperation.

The laughingstock reputation Cleveland garnered in the '70s sprang in part from its mayors, starting with Republican Ralph Perk (1971–77), a figure still remembered for the day his hair caught on fire while visiting a factory. Perk was the penultimate ethnic mayor; as one reporter noted, "Perk can speak Czech, dance Slovak, sing Polish and pray Bohemian." He also passed on

habits of fiscal sleight-of-hand to his Democratic successor, the incredible
Dennis Kucinich. Just 31 when he was elected, Kucinich (bearing a striking
resemblance to *Mad Magazine* cover boy Alfred Neuman) was a product of
the West Side (Croatian-American truck-driver father and Irish-American
mother) and a young man of supreme self-confidence, determination, and
visceral pugnaciousness. Every public issue was subjected to hysterical treatment with pejorative words for opponents—especially the Cleveland business
community. Kucinich's verbal venom and transparent paranoia aside, he also
espoused a provocative "new urban populism" under which power would be
transferred "to poor and working Clevelanders" and out of the hands of "the
major corporate interests, the banks, the utilities, the real estate trusts." Many
of Kucinich's appointees were exceedingly young, ignorant, and abrasive; he
eventually fired his best appointee, police chief (and former San Francisco
sheriff) Richard Hongisto, on live television.

Cleveland's celebrated default of 1978, on $15.5 million in notes owed six
Cleveland banks, was not due to Kucinch's policies, but the fruit of incredibly
low city taxes and Perk's use of bond funds to cover operating expenses. But
it was proof of the bitter emnity between Kucinich and the business community that the banks deliberately refused to "roll over" (i.e., renew) the loans
to the city. Said Cleveland Trust Chairman Brock Weir: "We had been kicked
in the teeth. We decided to kick back." Amazingly, Kucinich's feud with the
business establishment was even less vitriolic than his companion fight against
the black city council president, George Forbes, a leader of an effort to recall
Kucinich that failed by the paper-thin margin of 236 votes.

No review of the Cleveland scene should omit that of the *Cleveland Plain
Dealer*, a Newhouse paper aggressively led by Thomas Vail. Then there is the
Cleveland Foundation, the country's oldest (founded in 1914) and largest
community foundation (assets of well over $200 million). The foundation
contributes over $10 million annually to a wide variety of programs in such
fields as health, family planning, care of children and the aged, scholarships,
university development, and culture. Its hand is found in practically every
innovative and forward-looking Cleveland activity, from neighborhood
group revitalization projects to downtown planning and Playhouse Square.
Under strong leaders, including, since the early '70s, Homer Wadsworth, it
has rarely backed away from controversial issues. Predictably, the foundation's board was often regarded as the soul of the Cleveland establishment; by
the late '70s, however, it included two blacks and two women.

Columbus: Complacent and Prospering

Well-scrubbed, provincial, and complacent, Columbus is a spacious plains
city whose spirit is entirely Midwestern and logical: set almost dead center
in Ohio because it is the state capital, laid out on an orderly grid system, with
the inevitable central square at its very center, and in the middle of that square,
the State House. Columbus, according to Mayor Tom Moody, is quite con-

tent to be characterized as the "largest small town in America."

It is hard to believe that Columbus now has more than half a million people (564,871, with 1,401,403 in the metropolitan area); somehow the cowtown flavor lingers on, even if the image is now more of a farmer's market grown fat and sleek. There is also ample *lebensraum* (shared, significantly, with another Midwest city doing quite well, Indianapolis). The Columbus land area was vastly expanded—from 40 square miles in 1950 to 184 in 1980—to make it Ohio's biggest city geographically and in fact one of the largest in the U.S. Columbus is less black than other big Ohio cities (22 percent in 1980); except for an influx of Germans in the 1840s it has always been peopled chiefly by Appalachian immigrants. No great smoke-belching industries grew up here. Instead there is a finely balanced economy: government, trade, banking, warehousing, manufacturing, education (Ohio State University has over 50,-000 students, most of any single American campus), research (including the Battelle Memorial Institute, advertised as the world's largest nonprofit research organization), and insurance (47 companies, ranking third behind Hartford and Boston).

A small-town banker and merchant perspective has always held sway in Columbus. That is turning out as a latter-day blessing, since it is local entrepreneurs, with a personal stake, who hold sway in the city, not professional managers appointed from afar.

Maynard E. Sensenbrenner, Columbus mayor during the '50s and '60s, was a Democrat, a conservative, a deep believer in brotherhood, and an aggressive patriot who wore an inch-square rhinestone-encrusted American flag in his lapel. He inaugurated the aggressive annexation drive from which the city still benefits so strongly. Tom Moody, the thoughtful, pipe-smoking Republican who defeated Sensenbrenner in 1971 and then remained mayor into the 1980s, was less colorful but a far more thoughtful man who led urban conservation work for the National League of Cities. Moody ran a highly efficient city government, with excellent local services on Ohio's lowest big city tax rate.

Downtown Columbus became a fulcrum of urban development from the 1960s onward, with a sea of office towers, shopping "gallerias," luxury hotels, and other investments moving toward $1 billion in value. In the early 1980s came plans to build a transit mall on dull old High Street, tied to a pedestrian-oriented redesign of Capitol Square. In the neighborhoods, the 19th-century German Village, just south of city center, was so well preserved that prices for its seemingly modest houses shot up into the six-figure category.

For a touch of Columbus' old power relationships, one had only to walk into the building of the *Columbus Dispatch*, a few yards from the State House and topped with a great red neon sign proclaiming the *Dispatch* "Ohio's Greatest Home Newspaper." Inside the foyer hang two of the grimmest portraits of *homo sapiens* we have ever seen: the cold, arrogant, calculating faces of Robert Frederick Wolfe and Harry Preston Wolfe, founders of what grew to be the most powerful and ruthless single-city-based communications and economic establishment of the United States. The Wolfe brothers made their first fortune by manufacturing shoes, then got control of the *Dispatch*

THE BOOK OF AMERICA   314

early in this century, and went on to bank acquisitions, leading to formation of Banc-Ohio, a far-flung holding firm. Huge farmland and downtown real-estate holdings, a large municipal bond underwriting firm, and finally Columbus radio and television stations WBNS (the call letters stand for Wolfe Banks Newspapers and Shoes) rounded out the holdings of this single family. Practically no one dared cross the Wolfes; for many years the only significant counterforce was the prestigious Lazarus family, owner of Columbus' leading department store (and the Federated Department Stores chain). The Lazarus clan showed little taste for an open power struggle with the Wolfes. By the late 1970s, however, the sheer diversification of Columbus made the Wolfes less decisive in the city's affairs; moreover the latest generations of family leaders were far more moderate men than many of their ancestors.

Ohio State University football games remain Columbus' premier social event; studies have shown local loyalty so high that people are "not free" to say if they're indifferent to the OSU team. Academically, OSU, despite low funding, has mounted an uphill battle against mediocrity.

Cincinnati: Soft Charm in a Heartland City

Before Chicago even existed, and while Cleveland struggled out of village-hood, Cincinnati was one of America's great cities. Set fortuitously on America's early mainline to the West, the Ohio River, Cincinnati prospered as a port city, an early industrial center, a place of culture in the early 19th century, winning from many the sobriquet of Queen City. Her list of illustrious residents included John James Audubon, the artist-naturalist; Stephen Foster, the great songwriter; and William Homes McGuffey, author of the first children's readers. Harriet Beecher Stowe lived here and gathered material for *Uncle Tom's Cabin* when Cincinnati was a key station on the Underground Railway. In 1843, Charles Dickens passed through and described Cincinnati as "a beautiful city, cheerful, thriving, animated." For decades, she was the largest American city west of the Alleghenies and north of New Orleans; in 1860, she was one of three American cities with more than 100,000 people.

After the Civil War, the Ohio River was eclipsed as a main route to the West, and Cincinnati began a long decline in relative population and importance. (By 1980 her population was just 385,457, down from a 1950 peak of 503,998, due to suburban migration and—especially in the '70s—shrinking household sizes.) But her charm and grace, what Gunther called "a certain stately and also sleepy quality, a flavor of detachment, soundness," lingers on in this most untypical of all heartland cities. It is a city, its friends say, of extraordinary "root-edness" and, in its natural beauty, "one of America's best-kept secrets."

Geography and ethnic strains combine to give Cincinnati its unique flavor. The setting is not unlike a giant amphitheatre, with the legendary seven hills surrounding a lower central Basin along the grand curving sweep of the Ohio River. Heights and water combine to give drama and excitement to the scene;

one of the grandest urban vistas we have seen in America was from the blufftop home of Governor Gilligan, just east of the city: the twisting golden cord of the river in the late afternoon sun, the constant commerce of boat and barge along the great waterway, the riverside city, enveloped in the haze of a dying day.

Cincinnati received wave after wave of immigrants in her early years: Virginians, Welsh Quakers, New Englanders, Germans, Irish, Jews, blacks. Of these, the most fascinating may be the Germans, who came in a great rush from the 1850s onward, a liberty-loving, cultured but inherently conservative lot who gave the city much of its latter-day character, including an expectation of clean government and resistance to rapid change. Summertime festivals are a way of life to this day, with quantities of beer, bratwurst, and Limburger cheese. And the city still has some fine old German restaurants (the only group of really excellent restaurants in Ohio).

While middle- and upper-class people pushed first up to the hilltops once covered with vineyards, and then into outlying suburbia, the Basin became the receptacle of the city's poor: blacks and poor, sometimes exploited, Southern Baptist whites from Appalachia. On the eastern outskirts are the wealthiest suburbs, places such as Hyde Park and Indian Hill, home of the aristocratic Tafts (a Cincinnati feature since 1839) and such other families of privilege as the Gambles and the Lazarus clan. These families have traditionally formed a rigid caste system with clubs restrictive in race and religion alike.

Cincinnati has long been said to have the most honest and efficient government of any large American city. It was not always so. From the 1880s until 1925, a corrupt Republican machine held sway. The leader for almost 30 years was a former saloonkeeper named George B. Cox, who became a bank president and millionaire but never lost his touch for predatory politics, keeping a card file on the personal lives and arrests of citizens, dispensing city jobs to ward heelers and many incompetents. Permanent change did not come until the 1920s when influential and dedicated rebels, mainly Republicans, persuaded Cincinnati's long-abused citizens to approve a home-rule charter including the city manager form of government. Outstanding city managers have served Cincinnati: E. Robert Turner, leader in downtown development and an influential figure with the power establishment; William V. Donaldson, who brought a touch of humor and unconventionality—along with a penchant for management innovation—into the staid city; and Sylvester Murray, a talented black who took over when Donaldson departed (to head the Philadelphia Zoo!) in 1979. In 1980 the Urban Institute reported that Cincinnati had done a better job than practically any other older city in keeping its capital infrastructure—streets, sewers, waterworks, bridges—in good repair. Credit for the achievement was given to an earmarked tax base for capital projects, stressing both preservation over flashy new projects and the city manager tradition of city government professionalism. A negative oddity of Cincinnati politics, however, is that the mayor is chosen from among his fellow council members for but a year at a time. Thus some outstanding mayors—for example, Kenneth Blackwell, an insightful black, or David

Mann, who tried to spur the city to futuristic thinking—never had a chance to launch long-term programs.

Cincinnati has an incredibly complex political history of Charterites *vs.* Republicans *vs.* Democrats, and while the Charterites have faded of late, they must be credited with one of the most successful citizen reform efforts of American history. A Charterite from the start and doubtless the most distinguished Cincinnati citizen of the past half century was Charles P. Taft, a warm-hearted and public-spirited man with enduring interest in liberal Republicanism, philanthropies, and national church work. Had he not been such a devoted nonpartisan reformer, Taft might have enjoyed a notable career in national politics. He was elected a Charter council member in election after election, until he finally stepped down in the 1970s at the age of 80, following 31 years in the office. When we last interviewed Taft in 1976, he said he was still enjoying his job despite two metal hips and two bad knees. "I'm not up to Clemenceau yet," he quipped, then drove off in an old car with a 12-foot gold-colored canoe with a 'Charlie Taft for City Council' bumper strip on it. A bitter footnote about the Tafts: Charles' brother Robert stuck with the regular Republican organization for life and never lost a chance to disparage or oppose the reform program in his home town.

Cincinnati excels in strong neighborhood identity, a natural social outgrowth of the sharp line of demarcation provided by a setting of deep ravines between plateaus. Since the 1960s the city government has related extraordinarily well to the neighborhoods, the result of a series of crises in such areas as zoning, freeways, schools, and recreation that motivated new community councils to organize and older civic organizations to renew themselves. Modern Cincinnati history is crowded with stories of remarkable neighborhood revival, from preservation of the architectural salad of federal and Victorian structures on Mt. Adams to the bootstraps-revival of poor but once elegant Mt. Auburn (the latter effort led by a bearded master of street language and historic preservation, Carl Westmoreland). By the 1980s progressive Cincinnatians were at work trying to revive Over-the-Rhine, a once cohesive German working-class neighborhood close to the central business district fallen into decay and torn by social discord.

Race relations remain a serious problem in this 34 percent black city with a high number of single-parent families. Voicing her concern for the schools in particular, Sister Jean Patrice Harrington, president of Mt. St. Joseph College, commented in 1981: "There is a seething antagonism and racism in this city. Unless the danger and frustration is ventilated we are going to have serious racial problems in the next decade."

Cincinnati has labored mightily to preserve its center city. In 1962, at businessmen's urging, Cincinnati voted $150 million toward partial or complete demolition and replacement of eight major downtown blocks. A $10 million convention exhibition hall rose, along with new high-rise office buildings, overhead pedestrian walkways, an underground garage beneath Fountain Square, a new Contemporary Arts Center, and a $40 million sports stadium for the Cincinnati Reds baseball team and the Bengals football team.

Downtown emerged elegantly refurbished, a place of shape and character. All development, as envisioned 30 years before, still fell away from Fountain Square, the highest point (and a particularly charming one with its ornamental bronze-and-porphyry monument brought from Munich in 1871). A downtown covered skywalk passed *through* the Convention Center, banks, restaurants, and department stores; practically the only criticism one could make was that Fountain Square in particular had too much of an office-lobby atmosphere at street level, and too few inviting little shops.

The grip of the old elite Republican families on Cincinnati affairs weakened as the Catholic Church and the neighborhoods reached for a share of power. But there remained power aplenty in that industrial Goliath, Proctor and Gamble, in the headquarters staffs of the Federated Department Stores and the Kroger Company, not to mention the financial houses and hundreds of specialized smaller industries.

The lusty, busy Ohio River coursing 981 miles from Pittsburgh (where the Allegheny and Monongahela rivers meet) to Cairo, Illinois (where the mighty Mississippi awaits), makes Cincinnatti Ohio's chief port city, even as the day of the side-wheelers and stern-wheelers recedes further into history. Today the Ohio carries twice the freight tonnage of the Panama Canal, and it is practically all great bulk stuff in huge tows of as many as 20 steel barges loaded with 20,000 pounds each—coal, iron ore, oil, chemicals, metals, salt, sand, gravel. Coal is the greatest freight item, much of it from West Virginia, Indiana, Kentucky, and eastern Ohio fields and destined for huge steam generating plants along the river. Other coal barges will be destined for Ohio towns such as Steubenville, a place that breathes smoke and fire and exhales great slabs of hot searing steel for the industrial machine of the heartland. Cincinnati watches the industrial flotilla pass her doorstep but prefers for herself, if you please, a less gross way to make money.

A Constellation of Ohio Towns

Brawny industry, much of it in deep trouble . . . downtown decay and the glimpse of renewal . . . ring on ring of suburbia . . . shopping centers with their parking lots eating up the green earth . . . the world of the interstate road . . . and somehow, an incessant insularity, even in the age of instant communications—these are the hallmarks of Ohio's middle-ranked cities, down the population ladder from Toledo (354,635) to Springfield (72,563). A quick tour:

Set at the westernmost point of Lake Erie, not far from Detroit, Toledo is a port of no mean proportions that receives thousands of ships each year, many from distant points of the globe. Nevertheless, as one observer quips, "Few youngsters running away to sea head to Toledo." In the early 1980s, the city was wracked by simultaneous pain and progress. The pain centered around fearsome layoffs and unemployment (especially in the auto industry), the economic problems of grim, melancholy east side neighborhoods, and severe cutbacks in government services. Said the city manager in 1981, "Nothing's cut, nothing's trimmed, nothing's cleaned up, nothing's going on."

But downtown Toledo was in transformation from down-at-the-heels to modern steel-and-glass renewal, led by the dramatic new 32-story, $100 million world headquarters of Owens-Illinois and a new Toledo Trust headquarters building, both beside a new Promenade Park in the so-called Sea Gate project. Several impressive renovations of historic preservation buildings were underway, including one of our favorite in the entire U.S., the exquisitely designed Fort Industry Square block. Downtown was not problem free: there seemed too much distance between individual projects to create the desirable density for retailing and a vibrant street scene. But Toledo leaders were trying, as hard as any in modern times. Toledo's art museum and zoo were still among America's finest. And in the Warren-Sherman neighborhood, with 90 percent black population and excruciatingly high unemployment, Toledo Trust took an active, constructive role, and Control Data Corporation was persuaded to open one of its business and technology centers for new small firms.

For generations the rubber center of the universe, Akron (pop. 237,177), was made by, sustained by, and totally dominated by that single product. It was the home of four of the five great rubber makers, all in the $1 billion a year and up category—Firestone, Goodyear, General Tire, and Goodrich. The great rubber names were everywhere—on schools, banks, country clubs, and residential sections. When the winds were unfavorable, the piercing smell of concentrated rubber chemicals pervaded the town. But they were a sweet smell for Akron, because rubber meant profits and jobs.

But starting in the 1970s, an Akron nightmare came true. One by one, the rubber giants closed the factories. In autumn 1982, the lights flickered out in the 67-year-old General Tire plant, leaving it, as writer Ashley Halsey noted, "to join the hulking brick relics that once housed Goodyear, Goodrich and Firestone, now like a ghostly mothballed navy." While corporate headquarters remained in Akron, production there had been killed off by a combination of foreign competition, efficient radial tires, high labor costs, the strike-proneness of the United Rubber Workers, and the lure (to managements) of nonunionized, Sunbelt plants. The closings left Akron with a huge reservoir of low-skilled laborers—many erstwhile Appalachian immigrants—for whom, because of their age, there might never be another job.

Center-city Akron has suffered every indignity, from retail abandonment (suburban malls were the gainers) to a vicious urban renewal binge destroying a major part of the downtown. But the 1970s brought substantial rebuilding, including imaginative recycling of the old Quaker Oats mill into the new Quaker Square Hilton hotel and convention center. The sensational receptacles of this development were 36 old grain silos, each 120 feet high and 24 feet in diamater. Shops and restaurants thrived in the adjacent Quaker Square Mall. Placed on the National Register of Historic Places, Quaker Square began to draw people into downtown Akron on a scale not seen since the 1940s. Akron moved into the '80s with a master plan for core city revival and had a major governmental achievement to its credit—overwhelming 1979 voter approval of the first county home rule charter in Ohio. A broad-based citizens' coalition campaigned for the charter, complaining that Summit County was plagued by an archaic county structure, fiscal mismanagement, and too much government behind closed doors.

Set in a rich agricultural valley of southwestern Ohio, Dayton (pop. 203,588) is a clean, well-governed town with great civic pride. The good government tradition goes back to 1913, when Dayton became the first major American city to adopt the commissioner-manager form of government—an indication of reformers' early hope to "remove politics from government." As in so many cities, the '60s and '70s brought to Dayton suburban migration, fierce competition from outlying malls, black population rise, and losses of tens of thousands of industrial jobs. A poisonous controversy divided downtown and the suburbs, blacks and whites, on the issue of whether a proposed federal interstate highway link would help suburbs but suck economic activity out of the inner city. Dayton has battled to counter its losses with substantial downtown rebuilding and the refurbishing/refinancing of the splendid old 1904 Arcade —a multi-use complex of stores and restaurants that had been reduced to a bar, a pawn shop, and a wig store before its successful renovation was financed by millions of private, city, and federal funds. But such major Dayton employers as National Cash Register, a corporate native, cut their payrolls drastically. The downtown renaissance of expanding white-collar jobs provided cold comfort for out-of-work blue-collar workers and their families.

Youngstown (pop. 115,436) and Canton (pop. 94,730) form with Akron a smoky, clanging triangle of heavy-industry towns southeast of Cleveland, the quintessence of "The Foundry" described by Joel Garreau in his *Nine Nations of North America*. Youngstown was famous for steel and gangsters—until, in 1977, a conglomerate owner suddenly closed the Youngstown Sheet Tube's Campbell Works. Close to 5,000 workers suddenly lost their jobs, and Youngstown became a national symbol of industrial distress. Not long after came closure of U.S. Steel's Ohio Works and then its McDonald Works. Altogether, over 10,000 steelworkers—men who had enjoyed high-paying, high-status jobs—were discharged, throwing the Mahoning Valley into deep depression. The area had seen its first blast furnace in 1803, and heavy metal manufacturing was woven into its very character: a culture of massive steel mills flanked by churches, union halls, bars, and workers' homes. In immense numbers they had come to man the steel mills, passing the work down through generations—Germans, Poles, Slovakians, Hungarians, Italians. Yet in a few short months, all began to crumble.

Labor strife, including killings, plus all sorts of vice and crooked dealings in city and county government were long the order of the day in Youngstown. The city is a strong contender for the title of ugliest in the U.S.A. Youngstown is one of those places where voters delight in turning down school tax increases and where both public employee and private sector unions alike are strong (and strike prone). In early 1980 when Mayor George Vukovich resisted a police and firefighters' wage increase the city would not be able to pay for, the public workers struck for six days. Vukovich sadly told a visiting reporter, "There is no solution for Youngstown. I shouldn't be saying this. I love this place, but if I were looking for a future I wouldn't look for it here."

Not far from Youngstown is General Motors' highly automated plant at Lordstown, which achieved some notoriety in the '70s as a symbol of the young, militant auto worker just as ready to strike as to put up with repetitive, tedious work. A decade later, many of the rebellious workers, now middle-aged with families to support, were saying they would accept pay cuts to protect their jobs in a newly perilous economy.

Canton is a workingman's town with a strong Catholic element (Polish, Rumanian, Italian, Hispanic), plus a formidable bloc of black voters. Once vice-ridden, with widespread gambling and prostitution, Canton cleaned it-self up some years ago. Revival came to center city, with distinctive urban renewal projects. The biggest employers are Republic Steel and Timken Roller Bearings. The *Canton Repository* has traditionally stood somewhere to the right of Canton's most illustrious past citizen, President William McKin-ley, whose remains are forever encased in a Canton mausoleum almost 100 feet tall. Another architectural monstrosity in Canton is the 1963-vintage National Football Hall of Fame, which is topped by a 52-foot dome shaped like a football.

Some say that the heart of Ohio, and its typicality, may well lie not in the great cities that we have been discussing, but in the vast numbers of smaller cities that account for so much of its population and so much of its conserva-tism—places such as Springfield, Lima, Middletown, Marion, Zanesville, Lancaster, Portsmouth, Kent, Athens, Alliance, Chillicothe, Ashtabula. Yet if that be so, then one would be hard-pressed to be an Ohio optimist in the '80s. Springfield, for example, may retain its rich cultural tradition (home of Wittenberg University, a place German, Lutheran, and conservative in flavor), yet the fact is it has been in sad eclipse ever since its chief employer, Crowell-Collier Publishing, folded in the '50s. Lima has watched its major employers—Ford, Teledyne, Clark Equipment, Dana Corporation—all close plants or scale back operations.

Mansfield has seen its local industries bought out, then drift off to the Sunbelt. Downtown stores have folded or slipped away to the ravenous suburban malls. Like so many Ohioan places, Mansfield has special touches of history: it was at a political gathering there that Abraham Lincoln's name was first mentioned in regard to the presidency; Senator John Sherman, of Antitrust Act fame, came from Mansfield; here was the birthplace of author Louis Bromfield, who turned his famed Malabar Farm there into a conserva-tion showcase and gathering place for writers and entertainers. Malabar was the site of the 1945 marriage of Humphrey Bogart and Lauren Bacall; take a tour and you can still see their nuptial bed. But it has been a long time since Bogart and Bacall bedded down at Malabar, and one may well ask: Is Mans-field's sun—and the suns of all those other Ohio towns and cities that once seemed to encapsulate the spirit of America—on an irreversible downward course?

THE
BORDER SOUTH
STATES

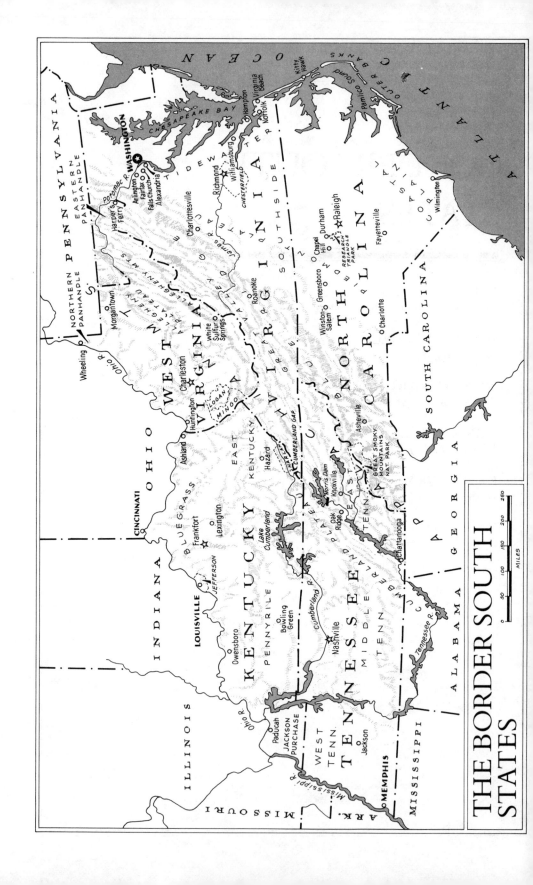

THE BORDER SOUTH STATES

VIRGINIA

The Old Dominion Grows Young

ONE CANNOT APPROACH VIRGINIA, this state in which the roots of American nationhood (and Southernhood) go so deep, the state of Washington and Jefferson and Madison and Patrick Henry, without a certain measure of reverence. Yet just as surely, it is not ancient history but the speed and immensity of change that sets the modern-day story of this state into such bold relief.

Consider, for instance, the words with which Douglas Southall Freeman could still describe the Old Dominion in the Virginia volume of the American Guide Series (WPA) in 1940. In the Virginia of his time, Freeman wrote, life itself had a different tempo from the nervous *accelerando* of the Northeast:

> Life is more leisured. . . . Human relations are somewhat more intimate. . . . Everywhere the dark laughter of the Negro is to be heard. Old houses outnumber modern. . . . The elders seldom talk fifteen minutes without some reference to the War Between the States. There is a deliberate cult of the past. . . . All eastern Virginians are Shintoists under the skin. Genealogy makes history personal to them in terms of family. Kinship to the eighth degree usually is recognized. There are classes within castes. . . .
>
> Many rural communities are depressed. Virginia farmers by tens of thousands still seek pathetically to eke out a living from eroded or starved land. . . .
>
> Politically, the ominous conditions in Virginia are the gradual atrophy of local self-government, the failure of well-educated, unselfish men and women to participate actively in public service, and the abstentions of tens of thousands from the exercise of the franchise.

Had Freeman returned to Virginia four decades later, he would have been amazed indeed by the transformation of the social, political, and economic landscape. The New Deal and World War II had set in motion a chain of events that would urbanize Virginia in a few short years, bring in hundreds of thousands of immigrants from other states, shift the commonwealth from controlled to chaotic politics, and undermine the authority of the old families.

Gone, Freeman would have discovered, were the powerful county courthouse politicians, the hoary Virginia "gentlemen" who ruled the commonwealth with an iron fist, building a political machine that effectively stifled all opposition for half a century. Gone were the poll tax, the literacy test, and virtually every other overt vestige of Jim Crow. Gone were the rural-based economy, the cotton fields, and the incredible hold of a single industry—tobacco.

Gone finally were the psychological walls of isolation that Virginia had thrown up about itself at the end of Reconstruction. Now in fact, as well as in law, Virginia had rejoined the Union.

In its place was a new Virginia, more youthful, more dynamic, more open and affluent than at any time since the late 18th century, when it was the wellspring of the nation. The new Virginia had a larger population, a diversified economy, and a two-party political system. Virginia had grown steadily since World War II, some 17.2 percent in the 1960s and 14.6 percent in the 1970s until the population reached 5.3 million in 1980, placing it 14th among the 50 states. But virtually all the new residents settled in the state's metropolitan areas. Two-thirds of Virginians lived in cities and suburbs in 1980, compared to only 36 percent in 1940. Virginia had become a major manufacturing center, making textiles, apparel, transportation equipment, chemicals, electrical machinery, furniture, printing books, magazines and newspapers, and processing food. With the jobs in such plants—plus huge federal payrolls— the per capita income had risen from 62 percent of the national average in 1929 and 79 percent in 1948 to 99 percent in 1980.

The growth of the cities and suburbs, combined with federal court decisions and national civil rights acts, had altered the face of Virginia politics just as dramatically. In 1981 Virginia completed its political transformation by electing Charles Robb, the son-in-law of Lyndon B. Johnson, to the governor's office. Robb was surely not a liberal Democrat, but he otherwise broke many Virginia political traditions. He was not a native Virginian; he lived in the northern Virginia suburbs of Washington, D.C. (an area deeply distrusted by many other Virginians for its growing power and supposed liberal influence); and to many he was better known as LBJ's son-in-law than as a Virginia leader. Finally, Robb relied heavily on the black vote to win election. Whatever governmental policies Robb developed, his use of modern campaign techniques and coalitions set him light years apart from the *ancien régime* that V. O. Key, Jr., had descibed as a "political museum piece," in his 1949 classic, *Southern Politics.*

With all these transformations, the commonwealth came to share America's common problems, including environmental degradation, declining inner cities, and suburbs cannibalizing the land on which they grew. Yet despite all the changes, some things remained constant in Virginia. To be a *born* Virginian remained a special badge of honor in the Old Dominion. Reverence for the past and for ancestors lived on, albeit in less cloying doses. And one still found that unflappable dedication to conservatism, regardless of party label in Virginia.

The Seamless Fabric of Virginia Roots and Politics

In population, in economic power, and most vitally, as the generator of the ideas of independence and human rights and nationhood, Virginia was preeminent in America from the moment of its settlement at Jamestown in 1607 until well into the 19th century.

The early histories relate how Virginia's first settlers found four major rivers flowing into the Chesapeake Bay in broad estuaries—the Potomac, the York, the James, and the Rappahannock. They cut the new colony's coastal plains into three strips, or "necks," and it was along these that the first settlements and the start of the Old Dominion's great plantations took place. Hunger, disease, and Indian raids took an incredible toll of the first colonists, in part because they had in their number so many gentlemen and noblemen of distinguished families who lacked the practical skills of the artisan or a capacity to work by the sweat of their brow. Before long the immigrant ships contained great quantities of practical working men of more humble origins, many of them indentured servants. But the flow of the "finer folk"—the gentry of the new colony—continued for many years, and set an indelible mark on Virginia. The founding patriarchal dynasties of Lee, Carter, Randolph, Byrd, Harrison, Page, Fitzhugh, and Beverly still dot the Virginia legislature and the top of the social registers.

Blacks were important to Virginia almost from its founding. A Dutch man-of-war in 1619 discharged the first black men, 20 in number, who came as indentured servants. Slavery was legalized in the colony 42 years later. Ironically, the same year blacks touched Virginia soil the colony inaugurated its grand experiment with representative democracy, convening the House of Burgesses, the first democratically elected legislative body of the New World.

In 1700 Virginia began her golden century, the time when her sons would produce some of the most vital statements of human liberty ever written by man—the Declaration of Independence and the Virginia Statute for Religious Freedom, both from the hand of Thomas Jefferson, and Patrick Henry's "give me liberty or give me death" speech. It was the time that her George Washington would lead the American Revolution and become the first of an illustrious line of Virginian presidents. It was the century of the Constitution of the United States, to which so many Virginians contributed, in particular James Madison. And it was the century in which restless and land-hungry Virginians would people the opening of the American West, in Tennessee, Kentucky, the Northwest Territories, and beyond.

Once the Revolution was won, these fabulous men differed markedly in their chosen direction for Virginia and America. Patrick Henry, for example, was against the new constitution because it began "We the 'people,'" instead of the 'states.' Henry foresaw (quite correctly, as time would show) that a constitution so written would come to supersede state laws. Another Virginian, George Mason, refused to sign the constitution until it was enriched with specific guarantees for individual rights. The first ten amendments, the Bill of Rights, were added, and would create the precedent for the later right-granting amendments, the 14th in particular, which would revolutionize the life of Virginia and all the Southland in the 20th century.

Yet even in 1700, Virginia had already established a mode of living that would influence its life straight down to the 1950s and in later years diminish its importance in the country. For while the settlers of New England and other colonies in the North were establishing towns and cities of substantial importance, Virginia had opted for a pattern of widely scattered settlements, consonant with a plantation economy. The consequences of this were many. The plantation had a life of its own, its master wielding unchallenged authority in his own domain. This fostered an aristocratic society, rather than the more democratic mode of New Englanders in their towns and cities. It discouraged education for the masses, because people lived too far apart for many to attend schools, and the plantation owners could afford private tutors for their own offspring. Education, except for the favored few, would remain a poor stepchild in Virginia until well into the 20th century.

In the 19th century Virginia began its long decline. While other states were expanding trade and increasing in wealth and population, Virginia's elite continued their gracious plantation lives, exhausting their soil, quite unable to come to grips with the issue of slavery. Emancipation had been favored by almost all the great Revolutionary period leaders, including Washington, Jefferson, Madison, Mason, and Henry. But the manpower needs of the plantations, as well as the vastly profitable sale of Virginia slaves to the growing cotton states, worked against any ideas of manumission. White Virginians tried to pay as little heed as possible to slave revolts, such as Gabriel's Insurrection at Richmond in 1800 and Nat Turner's bloody insurrection in the southeastern corner of the state in 1831. As the 1860s approached, Virginia tried to take a moderate course, deploring the extremism of the Southern fire-eaters on the one hand while trying to hold the Union together with the other. But the die for secession was cast when President Lincoln, after the bombardment of Fort Sumter, called for 75,000 volunteers to put down the rebellion. Virginia was not willing to coerce a sister state, and a convention at Richmond voted to secede. Robert E. Lee, who only a few years earlier wrote to his son, "I can anticipate no greater calamity for the country than a dissolution of the Union," turned down the command of the United States Army and reluctantly decided his chief obligation was to Virginia.

The destruction of the territory of Virginia was frightful, chiefly because of its geographical position as the advanced front of the Confederacy and its proximity to Washington. In no other part of the South were the campaigns so long, so frequent, and so decisive. Some 15,000 of the 170,000 Virginian men who fought would lie beneath the sod at Manassas, Fredericksburg, Chancellorsville, Petersburg, Richmond, and the many other battle sites within and without the state. Much of the lovely Shenandoah Valley lay in utter desolation.

For five years Virginia had to wait for readmission to the Union, existing under the ignominious title of Military District Number One. The Reconstruction period brought carpetbaggers and scalawags, northern- and black-dominated government and fierce white resistance (the White League, Ku Klux Klan) typical of the rest of the Confederacy, even though the excesses on both sides were less in Virginia than in the Deep South. The Reconstruction era constitution did effect one great breakthrough for Virginians by requiring a statewide system of public schools, available to whites and blacks on an equal basis. But financing schools at even the national average would have to wait until the 1960s. Virginia still had a lingering elitist approach to education, and in the Reconstruction years, grim financial problems. Mired in poverty and her economy in ruins as a result of the war, Virginia was ill equipped to deal with a massive debt incurred to finance canals, railroads, and turnpikes in the prewar years. By 1870 the annual interest payments alone amounted to more than the total state budget in many prewar years. The Conservatives (former Democrats and Whigs, soon to become known as Bourbons, who replaced the radical Republican control of state government in 1869) believed that debt repayment must come first to maintain the unsullied honor and essential credit of Virginia—even if the repayment required drastic underfinancing of the schools and other state functions to satisfy the demands of out-of-state creditors. The heavy burden of the repayment gave rise to a Readjuster party of Republicans, blacks, and impoverished farmers who took control of the state for a few years in the 1880s and voted a downward readjustment of the debt and increased school expenditures and the taxes on corporations.

The Conservatives, who had adopted the Democratic party as their vehicle, used the race issue to return to power in the mid-1880s. By 1900 their position was firmly entrenched, and they set about rewriting the state constitution, undoing most of the gains made by blacks during Reconstruction. The 1902 constitution effectively disenfranchised blacks by instituting a poll tax and literacy test. The number of registered blacks plummeted from 147,000 to 21,000, and thousands of poorly educated whites, many of them Republicans in the state's western mountains, were also deprived of their right to vote. The sharply curtailed electorate, open to easy control by the Democratic organization, would remain a fixture of Virginia politics for six decades.

It was with the name of Harry F. Byrd that the organization would become synonymous. Byrd, a young Shenandoah Valley apple grower and state senator, was elected governor in 1926. Byrd had been an important name in Virginia since the first William Byrd's arrival in the colony in 1670. Harry Byrd's father, Richard Evelyn Byrd, was a successful newspaper publisher in Winchester and speaker of the House of Delegates. Harry Byrd's brother, Rear Admiral Richard Evelyn Byrd, Jr., achieved world renown for his explorations of the Arctic and Antarctica. The Byrd apple orchard business around Winchester would eventually become the largest one-family apple growing, packing, and processing operation in the world. But the financial hardships of the Byrd family paralleled those of Virginia during the years that it was laboring to free itself from the staggering Civil War debt. From this came an abhorrence of public debt that started Byrd's political career (a campaign against a $50 million bond issue for the construction of highways) and would rule much of his political decision making.

Friend and foe agreed that Harry F. Byrd was the most outstanding governor Virginia had had—or was to have—for many years. Byrd consolidated a rambling structure of almost 100 bureaus, boards, and departments, largely independent of the governor, into 14 departments headed by his appointees and responsible to him. As a staunch fiscal conservative, he adopted a "pay as you go" approach that managed to convert a $1 million state deficit into a generous surplus by the time he left office in 1930. Yet the same policy would penalize Virginia in the long run, leading to a drastic underfunding of essential services. Byrd also promoted rural electrification, conservation, and the tourist trade, and sponsored the first law in any state to make all members of a lynch mob subject to murder charges. His regime as governor was virtually free of corruption, an unblemished record that would endure for the five decades of the organization's rule.

The long dominion of the Byrd organization was made possible through control of the state compensation board, which fixed the salaries and office budgets for the principal county officials and circuit judges who appointed the persons running local elections. Byrd also wielded considerable power from his seat in the U.S. Senate, where for 32 years he was of the great Southern patriarchs of that era of Dixie dominance when one could speak of Congress as "the only place in the country where the South did not lose the war." Byrd was chairman of the Senate Finance Committee from 1955 until 1965. During the same era, fellow Virginian Howard Smith took charge of the House Rules Committee, and another Byrd loyalist, A. Willis Robertson, chaired the Senate Banking and Currency Committee. Among them, the triumvirate exercised collective authority over almost all taxation, currency, social security, banking, and housing measures before Congress.

Arm-twisting and the brute use of patronage power were not the secret of the Byrd machine's success. "What has been overlooked," Byrd biographer Harvie Wilkinson wrote, "was the remarkable similarity of viewpoint among organization members which, in the long run, unified them far more effectively and fundamentally than any pressure of patronage tactics ever could have." That philosophy included a love for balanced budgets, loyalty to the cause of states' rights, an aversion to "wild federal spending," a dedication to rural dominance, and a determination among the white organization cadres to maintain the racial status quo in the Old Dominion.

A concomitant of the organization's strength was the incredibly small number of people who actually voted. The winning Byrd organization candidate for governor triumphed in the decisive primaries with the votes of no more than 11.2 percent of the adult population between 1925 and 1945, and one year the figure was a miniscule 2.6 percent. The poll tax and restrictive registration were in part responsible. But much more was involved. Virginia's one-party system had effectively isolated it from the stimulation of national campaigns. Apathy and general indifference became a way of life because the "better people" ran the government and the mass of people saw no reason to distrust them, especially in a state so steeped in tradition.

In time, Virginia was drawn back into the mainstream of American life, making political change inevitable. The contributing developments, all closely related, included the broadening effects of World War II, the national civil rights acts, the growth of cities and suburbs, population-based reapportionment, a broadened franchise for blacks and whites alike, emerging Republicanism, a greater strength in organized labor, and finally a hardening of the Byrd organization's arteries as its leaders grew old and less flexible. The assaults on the Byrd machine began in the late 1940s and early 1950s, but in the nick of time an issue intervened that quickly made it possible for the organization to survive. The issue was school integration, occasioned by the Supreme Court's May 1954 decision in *Brown* v. *Board of Education*. The Byrd organization's answer—in a phrase coined by the senator himself—was "massive resistance." The Virginia legislature, in a special 1956 session, enacted a full massive resistance program, including a requirement that the governor close any schools directed by the courts to integrate or, alternately, cut off state funds for schools in districts that broke the color line. Several schools were closed, but the Virginia Supreme Court of Appeals ruled that the closing laws violated the state constitution, and a federal court in Norfolk found massive resistance in violation of the U.S. Constitution's 14th Amendment. On February 2, 1959, the first school integration in Virginia's history took place in Norfolk and Arlington.

The 1960s brought a rush of events—all beyond the control of the state's politicians or government—that would forever alter the face of Virginia politics. The Supreme Court's "one man, one vote" reapportionment decisions shifted power away from the rural-based Byrd machine to the cities. In 1964, the 24th Amendment to the Constitution took effect, outlawing the use of the poll tax in federal elections and thus knocking out the final prop from beneath the Byrd organization. The impact on the size of the electorate was immediate and dramatic, just as the poll tax's institution in 1902 had been. More than a million Virginians voted for President in 1964, a rise of 35 percent over the 1960 level. By 1972, the state's total vote for President was almost twice the 1960 level. Gains in the black vote were equally impressive: the number of registered blacks in Virginia leapt from 100,000 in 1960 to 250,000 in the latter part of the decade.

Ironically it was blacks (still wary of Republicanism) who helped elect the last of the Byrd machine governors, Mills E. Godwin, Jr., in 1965. Godwin proved to be exceptionally progressive. The rural crowd in the legislature trusted him enough to go along with enactment of a sales tax, which made it possible for Virginia to at least begin catching up with her sister states in financing public services. Godwin won approval of an $81 million bond issue to finance capital outlays for mental hospitals and higher education, thus jettisoning Harry Byrd's sacrosanct pay-as-you-go policy. Godwin also laid the groundwork for a sounder Virginia government through a new state constitution, which guaranteed civil rights, recognized the goal of a decent environment, included the first consumer protection clause in any state constitution, and decreed annual sessions of the legislature. At no time since the 1920s had Virginia government taken such broad steps forward. Indeed one might say that the finest hours of the Byrd organization were its first and last —Byrd's term as governor in the 1920s and Godwin's in the 1960s.

The dual forces of modern change and the Byrdites' superannuation converged in an historic 1966 defeat for the organization. The old senator himself, sick with a brain tumor, had resigned in 1965 and died in 1966. With his passing all the restraints seemed to vanish. Harry Byrd, Jr., had been appointed to his father's vacant seat, but he did not command the devoted organization support his father had and only narrowly survived a primary challenge. (The younger Byrd would leave the Democrats in 1970 to become an independent, but remain in office until 1982 when he retired, thus ending 48 consecutive years of Byrd father-son Senate tenure.) In the 1966 primaries, two great oaks in the Byrd forest, 79-year-old Senator Robertson and 83-year-old veteran Congressman Smith, both lost their bids for renomination. By the end of Godwin's term in 1969, the once potent Virginia Democratic party had split into three factions: the old organization men; the ideological liberals, labor, and blacks; and a varied crowd of moderates sitting uneasily in the middle. In 1969 the Democrats fought such a divisive primary battle that they lost the state governorship for the first time in the 20th century. In 1973, after the death of the very popular Lt. Gov. J. Sargeant Reynolds, a wealthy scion of the Reynolds Aluminum Company, the Democrats did not even offer a candidate.

The Republicans, meanwhile, were returning to their long-abandoned field of battle. The first Republican governor of the century, Linwood Holton, made racial history when he declared in his 1970 inaugural address, "The era of defiance is behind us." As his first official act as governor, Holton issued an exceedingly tough executive order on racial discrimination in state employment. He was also able to exert subtle but effective pressure on private business to open employment opportunities to blacks, and he let himself be pictured on the front pages of newspapers across the country escorting his daughter to a majority black school to which she would be bused. Holton's bold directives on race relations and the example he set in his personal life helped the Old Dominion through its vital racial adjustment of the 20th century. But his actions were too liberal for Virginia Republicans, and he lost control of the party to its right wing by the time he left office.

After the Holton administration, Virginia politics disintegrated into a chaotic and formless period throughout the 1970s and into the 1980s. In 1973 Mills Godwin became the first man since the Civil War to serve a second term as governor of Virginia, but he returned as a Republican, and his second term was utterly undistinguished. By 1980 the Republican party held the governorship, one U.S. Senate seat, and 9 of the 10 congressional seats, yet it seemed due more to a reaction to the Democrats' leftward national bent rather than any specific attributes of Old Dominion Republicans. The Virginians on Capitol Hill were almost monolithically conservative, true to the Byrdian tradition, and unreflective of the growing progressivism of other Southern delegations. Moderates and the very few liberals who were elected had great difficulty surviving more than one term. The new generation of conservatives was different from the old in one respect: they had little clout, lacking the seniority, stature, and party identification to wield power exercised in the heyday of Harry Byrd, Sr. Perhaps the most curious election of all was that of Senator John Warner. Warner became the candidate after Richard D. Obenshain, the father of the GOP's superb modern organization, was tragically killed in the crash of a light plane during a campaign trip. Warner was a Virginia native and former Secretary of the Navy (under Richard Nixon) but was better known for his wives, heiress Constance Mellon, who reportedly settled $7 million on him, and actress Elizabeth Taylor, whose glamor clearly made the difference in his fourth-of-a-percentage point victory in 1978 over Democrat Andrew P. Miller. (Warner and Taylor were divorced in 1982.) In office, Warner maintained traditional conservatism, but proved to be a harder worker and advocate for nuclear defense than many critics expected. His election was a strong indicator of how much "media politics" had come to affect elections, even in the Old Dominion.

Democratic Lt. Gov. Charles Robb's 1981 gubernatorial victory reestablished Virginia as a two-party state. Robb and his Republican opponent, Attorney General Marshall Coleman, were two peas in a pod: both young, moderate conservatives, both former combat Marines and graduates of the University of Virginia Law School. The campaign was marked by nasty personal exchanges and intensive television advertising. Nationally, the outcome was heralded as evidence that a fiscally conservative but socially liberal Democrat could do well in the 1980s. The final results demonstrated the importance of the black vote in modern Virginia. Blacks worried that Republicans would set them back, and they turned out en masse, giving Robb such overwhelming victories as 97 percent in Richmond. In 1982 Virginia blacks teamed up, however, with the state's Republicans to force the Democratic-controlled state legislature to accept a new legislative-districting plan likely to result in some increase in blacks' existing representation in Richmond— only four blacks in the 100-member House and one in the 40-member Senate (despite a 19 percent black level in Virginia's population). The U.S. Justice Department and federal courts intervened on the blacks' behalf, rejecting the Democrats' earlier districting plans for alleged racial discrimination. Republicans also seemed likely to gain from the new plan because they would have more districts severed from pockets of inner-city votes.

In 1982, Virginia's seesaw politics continued unabated. Three-term Republican Rep. Paul S. Trible, Jr., of Tidewater, won the Senate seat of the retiring Harry Byrd. But 1982 was not a year of clear conservative victories in Virginia, as moderate-to-liberal Democrats did well in House races.

While Virginia politics drifted, the economy boomed. Only a handful of states have enjoyed a comparable economic diversification in the postwar period. Though farm jobs dropped and cotton disappeared almost entirely, agriculture remained vital. Total farm income, from the truck farms of the Eastern Shore to the tobacco in the south, reached some $1.6 billion in 1980. Manufacturing boomed, providing broad job opportunities for the younger generation. Since 1969 Virginia has pursued an active foreign recruitment program and was one of the first states to establish an overseas office in Europe. The state has attracted major plants from companies based in Sweden

(Volvo), France, Germany, and Switzerland. State officials told us that the critical element of Virginia's success is a long-standing Virginia tradition: opposing labor unions. Only seven states had a smaller share of nonfarm workers unionized in 1979; some 12.7 percent of Virginia's workers belonged to unions, compared with 23.6 percent nationally. Not surprisingly wages averaged about 17 percent below the national average.

There were many fortuitous factors in Virginia's economic rejuvenation. Chief among these was the state's location, not part of the "Bos-Wash" megalopolis but close enough to supply its markets with manufactured goods. As the Sunbelt became prime economic development territory, Virginia was in a superb trading position and capitalized on its fine harbor facilities in the Hampton Roads area. Nor did the state's economy suffer from the location of the nation's capital just across the Potomac River. Government offices, consulting and high-tech firms spread out in a great arc from Washington, and thousands of Virginians worked for the federal government, collecting its ever-more-impressive salaries and pensions. Virginia benefited as well from its usual long support of the military. The state ranked seventh nationally in defense contracts awarded in 1979, some $2.7 billion worth, and stood third in the nation in defense payroll receipts for another $2.7 billion.

Virginia's Separate Worlds

The contour of Virginia, Norfolk newspaperman Guy Friddell once wrote, "offers every scenery—seacoast, Tidewater, Piedmont, mountains—as if to say, beguilingly, stay, it's all here, all that earth can afford. . . . In the sweet, undulating role of Virginia, you catch the soft folds of the Blue Ridge mountains in the morning mist, the giddy, gaudy green Easter egg hills billowing around Albemarle, the lazy James embracing Richmond, the dark green tobacco fields somnolent in the Southside sun, and the long, pale green combers rolling in white thunder on Virginia Beach."

We begin our tour with the cradle of Virginia civilization, the Tidewater, that low, flat, sandy plain that stretches from the sea some hundred miles inland. This is a mostly rural region, with diverse agriculture, active fishing and oystering, and retirement homes. On the neck formed by the York and James Rivers lie Virginia's great historic treasures: Jamestown, Williamsburg, and the Yorktown battlefield. Across the bay to the east is the Old Dominion's Eastern Shore, a rich vegetable and fruit area, deeply rural in complexion, with special natural attractions, including the nature preserve at Assateague Island and the nearby seashore town of Chincoteague, where wild ponies make their famed swim each summer.

The southern reaches of the Tidewater, close by the North Carolina border, are the locus of Hampton Roads, the greatest natural seaport between New York and Rio de Janeiro, home to some 1.5 million people, more than a fifth of Virginia's population. Even before urbanization broke the homogeneity of Virginia's citizenry, the great Hampton Roads urban concentration and its people were quite un-Virginian. Except for a narrow strata of the blue-blood aristocracy that can trace familial roots back to the early days of the Old Dominion, these cities are filled largely with blue-collar working people and those birds of passage, the military. World War I, World War II, and the cold war years channeled a fantastic array of military facilities into Hampton Roads. The headquarters of the Navy's Atlantic fleet and some 22 other Navy commands are in Norfolk. The Newport News Shipbuilding and Drydock Company, one of the world's largest privately owned shipyards, has built ships ranging from tugs and passenger lines to aircraft carriers and Polaris submarines.

Of the individual cities that make up the Hampton Roads nexus, Norfolk (266,979) is the largest. This once-seedy, prostitution-infested Navy town began a massive reform campaign shortly after World War II, and it has paid impressive dividends. Norfolk was one of the nation's first cities to use federal urban renewal funds in the 1950s. Downtown development, a convention center, and highrise office buildings came in the 1960s. "Where painted ladies once raucously teased lonely seamen from the doorways of flophouses and tattoo parlors, secretaries now amble beneath a covered mall," observed newsman B. Drummond Ayres. The notability continues. Norfolk is home to the East Virginia Medical School, site of the nation's first in vitro fertilization clinic and the birth of America's first test-tube baby. In the early 1980s Norfolk revitalized its waterfront by hiring the firm of developer James Rouse—famed for his Baltimore "Harborplace" and Boston Faneuil Hall Marketplace—to build a festival marketplace. With luck, it would be a catalyst for redevelopment on Norfolk's vast sweeps of deserted downtown territory and would return nightlife for the first time in a generation.

Virginia's broad Southside area (pronounced "sothside") is the Old Dominion's brush with the Old South. It runs along the North Carolina border from Dismal Swamp (a long unrecognized ecological treasure where 75 varieties of birds nest) east to the mountains on the west and northward through the Piedmont to Richmond. Southside was the firmest bastion of the Byrd organization and still tends to vote Democratic. This is the Virginia where the plantation psychology was most entrenched, the poorest region of Virginia with the most black people,* the grittiest cities, the Virginia of the drowsy little county seats with their Confederate memorials, and the Virginia of Smithfield hams, tobacco, peanut fields, and soybeans. Manufacturing, primarily of the such low-wage varieties as textiles, apparel, and forest products, dots the region.

*A measure of social revolution has reached some of these erstwhile slave counties. Surry County, for example, has been hailed by a local black leader as "a code word for black progress and self-determination in Virginia." In 1970 the National Association for the Southern Poor set up an assembly there to mobilize blacks in a county where whites had all but abandoned the public school system. Surry also had no hospital and only one full-time physician. Blacks began to register in droves and eventually won four of five seats on the county board of supervisors. They created a new $4.5 million high school, with laboratories and advanced vocational education departments, a fully staffed $500,000 medical clinic, and a model county recreation center.

Virginia Beach, in the Hampton Roads orbit, grew by an astounding 52 percent in the 1970s (to 262,199) and one day may become the Old Dominion's largest city. A place of dull sprawl development, its population is young, affluent, and white.

At the far western reaches of Virginia's Southside, where the Piedmont gives way to the mountains, is the fast-growing city of Lynchburg. Lynchburg's population grew by 18 percent during the 1970s, to 66,743. It has such a diverse economy, including electronics, nuclear energy, pharmaceuticals, printing, and machinery manufacture, that it was a shock to the town in 1982 when the national recession brought record unemployment. It is also the base of the Rev. Jerry Falwell, the fundamentalist minister and founder of the Moral Majority. Falwell, the son of a well-to-do local businessman and one-time sheriff, took over the Thomas Road Baptist Church in 1956, when it had 35 members, and met in a former Donald Duck Bottling Company building. By the 1980s, the church claimed a congregation of 17,000 members and owned and operated a "Christian" academy, a home for alcoholics, a summer camp, a Bible institute, a seminary and Liberty Baptist College—an accredited institution where drinking, smoking, reading blacklisted books, and viewing blacklisted television programs were all prohibited.

Falwell, through the extraordinary force of his personality and appeal to many Americans' disorientation with modern life and fear of loss of national moral values, also became a factor in state and national political life. Exposure set the scene. Falwell claimed that every Sunday the services of his church were beamed via television to nearly 400 stations around the world, reaching an estimated 25 million viewers and making him the country's second most often watched television personality, after Johnny Carson. The Old Time Gospel Hour was, in 1980, the largest religious broadcasting operation in the nation, with an annual budget of $57 million. The church did help defeat the Equal Rights Amendment and other liberal legislation before the Virginia General Assembly. But the fundamentalists were strongly rebuked by the legislature in 1980 when they proposed a review and overhaul of the Virginia constitution's statutes on religious freedom, authored by Thomas Jefferson. Falwell's Moral Majority took credit for conservative electoral victories in many states in 1980, but by 1982 its political power appeared to fade. Various New Right factions disagreed over the intricacies of abortion legislation, and their candidates won few elections.

Virginia's center of gravity, its capital region at Richmond, has been prosperous for a good many years. All signs are that it will stay that way. Richmond considers itself the tobacco capital of the world, but manufactures everything from chemicals to furniture. Many blue chip corporations (Reynolds Metals, DuPont, the Ethyl Corporation, etc.) located facilities for research or manufacturing, or both, at Richmond. Federal and state government, banking, transportation, and trade and medical centers (the latter specializing in heart transplants and cancer research) round out the economy. This diversity has blessed Richmond with an unemployment rate usually several points below the national average. The Richmond metro area grew an impressive 58 percent in population between 1950 and 1970. Much of the population and economic growth has occurred in the suburban hinterlands of Henrico, Hanover, and Chesterfield counties, conservative (and oftentimes racist) areas that had strong growth rates in the 1970s while Richmond lost 12 percent of its population. Between 1929 and the 1960s, Richmond had not a single new office building. Hundreds of millions of dollars in public and private investment have since been poured into downtown, resulting in hand-some new office buildings along Main Street (Virginia's banking-finance center), a new coliseum, a new city hall, a $70 million federal reserve bank, and, for the first time, a number of major downtown apartment buildings. A revitalized downtown entertainment area, Shockoe Slip, has grown from tastefully redone antebellum warehouses, giving Richmond its first taste of top-notch restaurants and watering spots, absent entirely until 1968, when liquor-by-the-drink first became legal.

Richmond's postwar economic success also resulted in an historic "opening up" of the city's power structure, long centered in the city's West End. The social power became divorced from the political and economic power, a change of no little importance in the Southland. This did not mean that Richmond took major power shifts lightly, however. In 1977 the city council chose Richmond's first black mayor, Henry L. Marsh, III, a civil rights lawyer and cool-headed administrator and politician. While the Generals Robert E. Lee, Stonewall Jackson, and J. E. B. Stuart did not jump from the saddles of the stately equestrian statues that line Richmond's famous Monument Avenue (one of the prettiest streets in the nation), the change of power was not without its ugly tensions. Two years after Marsh's election, the black-con-trolled city council fired the city's highly regarded white city manager, a move that critics, including the newspapers, said was blatantly racially moti-vated. The manager's replacement, the first black city manager of any major Southern city, performed competently, and tensions appeared to ease. Marsh was on his way to becoming a national leader among mayors when in 1982, Roy A. West, a newly elected black city councilman, teamed up with four white council members to depose Marsh and elect himself mayor. West proclaimed that he would not be a figurehead for the white community, but the move was regarded as a successful attempt by Main Street business owners to regain control of the city's political leadership. The early 1980s were not a total loss for blacks in Richmond, however. After prolonged opposition by the white business community, the city and the Marriott Corporation also broke ground in 1982 for a hotel and convention center in a predominantly black center-city area. In 1982, Richmond Renaissance, a downtown redevel-opment corporation was created with nearly $4 million in private and city funds. Its board of directors had 30 blacks and 30 whites, and its executive committee of 12 was also equally divided by race.

West of Richmond is Charlottesville, home of Thomas Jefferson's Univer-sity of Virginia, famed for its preppy social life and nationally ranked basket-ball team, but also justly recognized for its high academic standards and honor code. Its law school ranks among the top in the nation and has trained many politicians for Virginia and other states. Because of the university's presence, Charlottesville has also become a center of high-technology industries.

One looks hopefully to the northern Virginia suburbs of Washington, D.C., and finds that despite high incomes, high educational levels, low unemployment, and such historic treasures as Mount Vernon and the city of Alexandria, they are a mess, an example of pell-mell development gone wrong, the devastation of a region of great national beauty. The office and housing boom began with the construction of the monstrous Pentagon building for the Defense Department and continued as the federal government decentralized offices into the suburbs. (The theory at the time was to make the offices less vulnerable to nuclear attack, but urbanologists have also claimed that high-ranking federal bureaucrats wanted the offices close to their homes.) The greatest and most tasteless accumulation of office buildings was in Rosslyn, just across the Potomac from Washington. Between 1962 and 1980, Rosslyn was transformed from a melange of one-story buildings, motels, gas stations, light industry, and pawn shops into 31 haphazardly placed office buildings, four hotels, two apartment buildings, and one subway stop, all within four square blocks! No amount of reasoning could persuade either Virginia officials or the construction industry that placing these architecturally mediocre monsters across from the nation's capital (some of such a height that they virtually gave the finger to Washington's carefully devised height limitations) was a national disgrace. The lobbyist-packed highrises were not Northern Virginia's only contribution to national affairs. The area also became the capital of that modern-day phenomenon, "direct mail" fundraising. The prime practitioner was conservative Richard Viguerie, who combined Madison Avenue writing techniques and millions of names to raise tens of millions of dollars for groups opposing abortion, gun control, and sex education, and boosting prayer in the public schools, the death penalty, and high rates of defense spending. A left-wing counterpart arose nearby: Craver, Mathews, Smith and Co., manipulating six million names for liberal causes. And in 1982, the Gannett Company launched its national daily, *U.S.A. Today*, from its Rosslyn offices.

Northern Virginia has become more heterogenous. Arlington, like many of the nation's close-in suburbs, became 100 percent urban and lost population during the 1970s. It also became home to many Latin Americans and such a settlement center for Vietnamese refugees that one Arlington commercial strip called Clarendon became known as "Little Saigon." Fairfax County, a suburban "Camelot" where the average income was $33,000 per year, grew 31 percent during the 1970s. The best-known area of Fairfax, and the one with the highest status, is McLean, site of multi-million dollar rolling estates where many Washington notables, including the Kennedys, reside.

At the outer reaches of the Northern Virginia suburbs are Prince William, Fauquier, and Loudon counties, once rural innocents, later the site of high society hunts, and now increasingly packed with dull subdivisions. Prince William (144,703), historically a quiet rural agricultural community where the biggest events ever were the two Battles of Bull Run in the Civil War, grew by 121 percent during the 1960s and another 30 percent in the 1970s. Loudon, site of the architecturally distinguished Dulles Airport, has more than doubled since 1960. Near Dulles is Reston, a model American "new town" of the sixties with a pleasant architecture of townhouses and tracts of common green space—a model more and more developers would later adopt as the standard suburban detached home became financially impractical. But the grander dream of Reston as a self-contained home-office-retailing-cultural center never quite came off; instead, it turned into a commuter town, albeit a very attractive one. In all these counties west of Washington, one finds concern for the blight of sprawl and active movements favoring the preservation of agricultural land.

Far Western Virginia is a world to itself, a territory of mountains and valleys and salubrious climate, quite distinct from the Tidewater and the Piedmont. The eastern flank of the region is the majestic Blue Ridge. On the western slope of the Blue Ridge lies the Great Valley, a long fertile furrow in the mountains running to the Tennessee border to the south. The broad northern section is the Valley of Virginia, the most famous section of which is the fabled Shenandoah Valley. Agriculture, tourism, and manufacturing provide a diversified economy in the Great Valley. The only city of any size is Roanoke (100,427), created by the Norfolk and Western Railway in the 1880s. Today Roanoke is a manufacturing center with strong civic leadership that won it an All-America City award in 1981.

Virginia's Southwestern Highlands, locale of the famous "Fighting Ninth" congressional district due to its strong two-party tradition, is the commonwealth's brush with Appalachia. The poorly educated, poorly housed people draw their main income from the region's rich and lately prospering coal fields. The Southwestern Highlands end at the Cumberland Gap, that dramatic notch in the mountains through which the restless progeny of the Old Dominion passed two centuries ago to begin to people the American continent.

WEST VIRGINIA

Still Struggling

MORE THAN TWENTY YEARS have passed since John F. Kennedy's presidential primary campaign brought such bright promises for chronically depressed West Virginia.* In the meantime, hundreds of millions of federal aid dollars have poured in. The coal miners and their friends staged a great black lung revolt, winning concessions from the state legislature, the federal government, and the coal companies themselves. The decadent United Mine Workers have gone through wrenching upheavals, and reform-minded political leaders such as Governor John D. (Jay) Rockefeller IV have emerged. But despite these signs of a quickening of the democratic spirit in the body politic, West Virginia's liabilities—physical, economic, political, and human—remained, two decades after Kennedy, heavy and discouraging in the extreme.

For each outward sign of improvement in the lives of West Virginians, each indicator that the state is in better shape, one could find a caveat. Federal and state programs had built thousands of miles of roads, and it was easier to get around most of the state than it used to be. But some interstate links remained uncompleted by the early 1980s; moreover, the new roads needed expensive maintenance, which the state seemed unwilling or unable to provide. The West Virginia economy did begin to improve in the 1970s, as the nation began to use more coal. But then in the early '80s came a virtual depression in the coal industry, bringing with it record unemployment and proving again that coal is the unquestioned king of West Virginia. Diversification of the economy, the justification for federal subsidization of roads, sewers, and other basic needs, remained elusive. Taxes on coal extracted from West Virginia soil finally began to bring some of the benefits of the state's wealth to its residents, but the mines remained in the control of outsiders. Miners continued to be injured, both in large-scale disasters and in individual accidents. And when the demand for coal went down, West Virginia was forced to borrow from

*The reason Kennedy entered West Virginia was not to corral its 25 delegate votes—in fact the primary was nonbinding. Rather, he wanted to demonstrate by defeating Hubert Humphrey of Minnesota that the people of a heavily Protestant, heavily unionized Border State would vote for a Roman Catholic for president. Ironically, the religious issue was not particularly well posed because West Virginia had no large minority of Catholics with whom the Protestants might have found themselves in conflict. Kennedy also had much more money. His political operatives, accustomed to the rough and tumble of Massachusetts politics, performed better than Humphrey's issue-oriented Minnesotans. Such details were lost on the public, however, which saw Kennedy win despite the supposed barrier of his Roman Catholicism. The general interpretation: religion was no longer a central issue, this man could be a viable presidential candidate.

the federal government to pay unemployment benefits, and there were fears that state employees would be fired and institutions built up during the affluent '70s closed.

The 1980 Census did reveal reversal of the dramatic 1950s and '60s population losses, the most severe any state has ever experienced in American history. West Virginia grew in the 1970s by 11.8 percent—about the national average—to 1,949,644 people. But the greatest population growth occurred in the Harper's Ferry area, where professionals settled and commuted to Washington, D.C., only 60 miles away, and retirees from big cities moved for cheaper and safer living. Thus West Virginia was becoming even more dependent on the federal government through a combination of professional salaries and retirement benefits. Black lung benefits undoubtedly made life easier for retired miners but were also an indicator of the continuing importance of federal distribution to the state.

West Virginia Roots

West Virginia has a little-known history previous to coal. These western mountains were a frontier territory of Virginia from the 1670s, when the first exploration occurred, clear down to the Civil War and separation from the mother state. The fur trade, part of an effort for diversification by wealthy Virginia tobacco planters, accounted for much of the early interest in the area. Later Virginia saw these western lands as a valuable buffer between the French and the Indians and encouraged Germans and Scotch-Irish to settle there. West Virginia's decision to break off from Virginia and become a separate state was quite predictable when one considered the historic evolution of the region. Mountainous in territory, with only a handful of slave-holding areas, the section had long complained of unfair taxes, unequal representation in the legislature, and the refusal of Virginia to build the internal improvements—turnpikes, canals, and railroads—that were needed. The mountains had stronger economic ties with the Ohio-Mississippi river system than with Virginia. They felt great loyalty to the federal government, which helped in suppression of hostile Indians and construction of the National Road. Thus the delegates from the west lined up strongly against Virginia's move into the Confederacy, voted against secession, and paved the way for passage of a statehood bill for West Virginia, which President Lincoln signed in 1863.

West Virginia was lucky enough to come through the Civil War without a single major battle having been fought on its soil. But the cruel divisions that afflicted the other Border states, between neighboring hollows and even within families, were present here too. In all some 36,000 West Virginians served with the Union Army, about 12,000 with the Confederate. And the Radical Republicans showed so little compassion for Southern sympathizers immediately after the war, seeking first to disenfranchise them, that the Democrats had returned to power by the early 1870s.

Coal mining got underway on a serious scale in the latter part of the 19th century as company towns, with their paternalistic and exploitive way of life, sprang up like weeds across the mountains. In 1870 only 600,000 tons of coal were mined in the state; by 1912 the figure was up to 67 million tons; in the early 1980s the annual figure was around 125 million tons. West Virginia developed other industries—farming, lumbering, chemical production, tourism. But for better, and often worse, coal became and remained the economic lifeblood of the state. West Virginia has always had to pay a gruesome price for its coal riches, however, and the development of the industry, its colonial politics, the struggle of its workers to organize into unions, and the health, safety, and environmental perils of mining overwhelm everything else that has happened in the state in modern times.

Next to coal, one has to cite geography—some say "Afghanistanism"—for West Virginia's enduring problems. With few exceptions, level land is simply not to be found. Most of the landscape is uneven and ragged, filled with jumps, gulleys, quick falls, and rises, a configuration that reaches its most extreme form in some of the southern coal counties. The historic consequences have been minimal agriculture, poor communications, fierce sectionalism, and severely constrained industry.

West Virginia's southern coal counties, with their machine-controlled vote, have been of vital importance in primaries and general elections in every decade, even up to the present day. In 1972, Jay Rockefeller's first run for the governorship was doomed by the southern county politicians, who were influenced by coal operators concerned about Rockefeller's stand against strip mining. Only after Rockefeller made his peace with the southern counties did he win. Southern West Virginia, nonetheless, is a far more civilized place now than during the decades of the gruesome mine wars of the early 20th century.

The Coal Wars

The struggle to unionize dates back to the 1830s; it is a history replete with hard-won advances, periodic reversals, and an incredible amount of bloodshed, especially after the United Mine Workers of America was formed in 1890 and undertook its dogged pursuit of the right to organize. The early mine operators were a hardbitten lot willing to use any means—legal and more often illegal—to keep the unions out and maintain their feudal proprietorship of the ill-paid miners who lived in the company towns and died by the hundreds in unsafe mines. The coal operators used court injunctions, martial law, suzerainty over county government, elaborate spy systems, coercion, intimidation, and blacklisting to keep out the union. Yet another device was to import blacks and unwitting foreigners as scabs. And then there were the political bosses of Logan and Mingo counties. The most famous boss of those days was Sheriff Don Chafin of Logan County. During his reign there were few roads in the county, and the principal means of ingress and egress were the railroads. Chafin kept out union organizers by posting one or more of his

deputy-gunmen at every railroad station to ask every stranger his business—
and to make sure those with unsatisfactory replies departed post haste.

The first great coal strike took place in 1912–13 at coal mines in the narrow
gorges of Cabin Creek and Paint Creek in the Kanawha Valley, not far from
Charleston. Some 7,500 coal-begrimed miners were involved; during the
course of the strike they would be evicted from their homes and forced into
tent colonies along the highways. In one great pitched battle, 12 miners and
4 mine guards were killed. Unionization did not achieve permanent status
until the first 100 days of President Roosevelt's New Deal in 1933 when labor's
right to bargain collectively, together with a ban on yellow dog contracts, was
written into legislation approved by Congress. Membership in West Virginia
unions promptly soared to more than 100,000 and continued to rise through
the 1930s. By the 1940s labor had formed an alliance with the statehouse
machine of former Senator and Governor Matthew Neely and was regarded
as the most powerful single influence in West Virginia politics.

Even at the peak of its political power, however, the UMW exhibited what
the late Miles Stanley, head of the West Virginia Labor Federation, AFL-
CIO, described to us as "a rather narrow, parochial kind of interest," concentrated on such issues as workmen's and unemployment compensation. The
merger of the AFL and CIO in 1957 brought a national union leadership more
attuned to broad issues of public policy. But the UMW was not part of it.
Until his retirement in 1960, the UMW *was* John L. Lewis, a figure splendidly
described by native West Virginian James Humphreys as "the enigmatic man
who spoke with the authority and cadence of an Old Testament prophet, the
Republican who was a favorite of Coolidge and was offered the Vice-Presi-
dency under his close friend, Herbert Hoover, the labor militant who built
the CIO largely with socialist and communist organizers and brazenly called
strikes in the country's coal fields during World War II, [and who] did it all
by his own hand and without the interference of internal dissent or loyal
opposition." Lewis and his hand-picked successor, W.A. (Tony) Boyle, became suspiciously cozy with management. In negotiating sessions during the
1960s, Boyle did get smartly increased wages for miners, but the union had
a vested interest in uninterrupted production since it received a per-ton
royalty, and it failed to ask for significant new safety regulations in this
exceedingly high-risk industry. To top it all off, Boyle and his cohorts granted
themselves royal salaries, fat expense accounts, and sumptuous pensions.

The *ancien regime* began to topple on November 20, 1968, when a massive
explosion shook a mine of the Consolidation Coal Company at Farmington,
West Virginia, and Boyle appeared at the burning portal to tell reporters that
such is the way of coal mining, and that Consolidation had a fine safety record.
To extinguish the fire and save the salable coal, the company, with the
permission of the UMW and the state and federal governments, sealed the
mine with the bodies of 78 miners still inside. At this moment an unconventional former college professor who had become a West Virginia congressman, Ken Hechler, broke with state tradition to demand that Congress pass
mine-safety legislation. The miners quickly created ad hoc organizations

dedicated to passing the safety laws the union should have encouraged all along. They also demanded compensation for victims of black lung, the popular name for pneumoconiosis, a gradual form of lung debilitation that results from prolonged inhaling of coal dust particles. In February 1969, a wildcat strike began, spreading in five days to encompass almost all of West Virginia's miners. They marched on the State Capitol and succeeded in getting the industry-approved workmen's compensation law rewritten to make it much easier for victims of black lung to qualify for disability benefits. Spurred by that stunning West Virginia victory, the miners' Black Lung Association pressed, through Ken Hechler and others in Washington, for a major new Federal Health and Safety Act, passed in 1969 with little or no help from the UMW leadership. Tacked on to the legislation was a supposedly temporary program to pay federal benefits to black lung victims—thus relieving the states and the coal industry of the burden, which would cost the federal government billions in subsequent years.

The United Mine Workers, meanwhile, entered a horrifying period of internal battles discussed at greater length in our Pennsylvania chapter—from the unseating of Boyle and his conviction of murdering his challenger, Joseph Yablonski, through the rule of West Virginian miner Arnold Miller, a leader of Miners for Democracy, the administration of successor Sam Church and yet another "reform" takeover in 1982.

Underground mining remains one of the most dangerous forms of employment. There have been 121,000 deaths in U.S. coal mining since 1870 and 1.7 million lost-time injuries since 1930. Each year the national news covers a coal mine disaster or two in West Virginia, but even more men and women die a few at a time in less spectacular accidents. According to Dr. Loren Kerr, an expert on occupational disease, the deaths of more than 4,000 coal miners each year can be attributed to black lung disease. Mining companies continue to be tempted to increase production and reduce costs even if that means such hazardous practices as raising dust levels above legally defined limits and not providing adequate ventilation or water spraying. The companies have continually urged cutbacks in federal and state mine inspection. This view has some appeal in a society worried about overregulation, but so do the words of coal miner Willie Anderson: "The only thing keeping the rock off your back when you're two miles underground," he told West Virginia writer Paul J. Nyden, "is government regulations."

Deep mining first blighted the West Virginia landscape by digging out the hillsides and dumping huge quantities of slate and other refuse into the hollows to form mountains of gray slag, which often caught on fire. But the environmental concern has now moved to strip mining, which is less labor intensive and also safer; in the early 1980s it accounted for about 20 percent of West Virginia's more than 120 million tons of annual coal production. The enemies of stripping lost a battle for a total ban in a major fight in the West Virginia legislature in 1971, and the issue was settled definitely in 1972 when Jay Rockefeller lost his first campaign for governor largely on his support of the ban. West Virginia has been considered stricter on enforcement of its strip mine laws than Kentucky, however, a reason offered for Kentucky assuming the number one position in coal production.

Geography of a Squid

The geographic outline of West Virginia, John Gunther suggested, is rather like that of a squid. It is the only state with two panhandles. The northern Panhandle cuts up like an arrow between Pennsylvania and Ohio, coming to a point northwest of Pittsburgh; it is heavily industrialized with great steel and chemical plants. The eastern Panhandle is placid and rural by contrast; it consists of four counties that "overhand" Virginia and are only part of West Virginia because, during the Civil War, they included the Baltimore and Ohio Railroad line and thus controlled the westerly approaches to Washington. The most famous town is legendary and picturesque Harper's Ferry, where the Civil War was made inevitable by John Brown's insurrection in October of 1859.

Economically, West Virginia can be considered as a state of four broad regions. There is the northern Panhandle and the counties just below it, fairly indistinguishable from nearby Pennsylvania and Ohio, a land of some coal mining, substantial industry, and urbanization. The chief cities are Wheeling (pop. 43,070), a grimy steel town with one of the finest municipal parks in the U.S., and Morgantown (27,205). This region did not grow as rapidly in the 1970s as other sections of the state. By the early 1980s there were indications that the relatively high wages of the northern Panhandle's unionized, heavy industries were causing deep troubles. The proud steel workers of Weirton launched an ambitious, if up-hill, battle to buy their steel mill when its owners, National Steel Corporation, announced it planned to phase out the Weirton division.

Eastern West Virginia contains both the panhandle of that name and a long string of rural counties where farming and cattle or sheep grazing are an important business. Agriculture is somewhat threatened, however, by the arrival of so many Washingtonians and retirees in recent years. Jefferson County, which contains Harpers Ferry, grew 42.4 percent in the 1970s—more than in the previous 120 years together—to 30,302 people. What makes this life possible for the Washingtonians is the train between Washington and Harpers Ferry, which the commuters must defend so constantly that they have formed an organization, Friends of the Railroad.

A third region is southern West Virginia, location of the dozens of sad coal towns of which we have already written. Finally, there is the western part of the state, which includes the state capital at Charleston (63,968), the industrialized Kanawha Valley, and then a number of cities facing the Ohio River. The two largest of these, Huntington (63,684) and Parkersburg (39,967), have a distinctively Midwestern flavor. Huntington's spunky *Herald Dispatch* had the courage to report in 1982 that a passel of woes—declining population, eroding tax base, and reduced retail sales against competition of a suburban mall—had all been exacerbated by "a lack of strong leadership, compounded by complacency and provincialism."

Charleston is alive and stimulated because it is West Virginia's seat of government and the financial center of the state. The rich supply of natural resources in the Great Kanawha Valley, including brine, sulphur, coal, and gas, have made it possible for Charleston to become one of the world's great chemical centers, although some companies have shifted to places with more plentiful gas supplies in recent years. Pollution has long been a problem here and has only partially been ameliorated by controls. One bright point has been vigorous downtown development, made possible in part because a huge, potentially competitive suburban mall was blocked with help of the Carter administration. Another Charleston plus has been the evolution of the *Gazette*, its leading paper, away from the conservative and property-oriented stance it had in the early 1950s, toward a progressive and sometimes crusading force.

West Virginia Politics: State and National

West Virginia has had two-party politics since the Civil War, but in a pattern called "cyclically competitive"—infrequent shifts that go all the way to one party or the other. From 1863 to 1871, and later from 1896 to 1932, the Republican party dominated the scene. The Democrats, on the other hand, controlled the state's politics, from 1871 to 1896 and again almost solidly from the advent of the New Deal forward.

Prior to 1940, the Democratic party was controlled by the so-called Bourbon faction—conservative, with its roots in Southern, rural, former slaveholding counties. With the growth of the United Mine Workers and the liberal ideology the union espoused in the early years, conflict was inevitable. Senator Matthew Neely, a crafty veteran who had been in Congress almost continuously since 1913, returned home in 1940 to run for governor. Neely won UMW and other middle-of-the-road Democratic support and established a kind of dynasty, with his selected successors following him to the governor's chair until 1956. This so-called Statehouse faction dominated the state's politics through a combination of state employees (mainly highway and liquor store operators), politically favored business, and special interest groups (including the UMW). It finally crumbled in the 1960s with several of its leaders in jail.

Governors with a deep sense of the people's needs have been a rarity in West Virginia politics, one reason (in addition to the candidate's famous name) that so much interest attended the election of John D. Rockefeller IV. Rockefeller's entry into West Virginia public life bore a striking resemblance to the impact on Arkansas of his late uncle, Governor Winthrop Rockefeller —Yankee transplant, farmer, and businessman. It was in 1964 that Jay Rockefeller, then 27 years of age, strolled into Emmons, a community of some 200 impoverished souls strung out along a hollow a few miles southwest of

Charleston. From Emmons, it was four miles over a rutted dirt road to the nearest store, and most of the people were jobless and on welfare. As a poverty worker there over the next two years, Rockefeller got an insight into poor people's lives that rich men rarely acquire. In 1966, having become a Democrat, Rockefeller won election to the West Virginia House of Delegates from Kanawha County (Charleston). Elected secretary of state in 1968, Rockefeller turned his attention to election reform, proposing laws aimed particularly at the southern counties known for the worst fraud and corruption. In 1970, after an extensive study he privately financed, Rockefeller proposed abolition of strip mining "by law, completely and forever," a position that cost him the governorship against Republican Arch Moore in 1972.

Anyone who thought a single defeat would drive Jay Rockefeller from his adopted state was to find himself mistaken. Rockefeller accepted the presidency of West Virginia Wesleyan College, bided his time for four years, and then was elected governor in 1976. In 1980, facing his old opponent, Arch Moore, Rockefeller won again but spent a reported $12 million, most of it on campaign commercials that appeared as far away as the Washington, D.C., and Pittsburgh media markets. This kind of spending produced bumper stickers reading "Make him spend it all, Arch" and endless speculation over whether Rockefeller's real goal was enough name recognition to run for president. By most accounts, Rockefeller proved an above average West Virginia governor. His extraordinary wealth provided welcome relief from the financial rough-and-tumble that often pervades the West Virginia governor's office. Yet it was also difficult to point to important Rockefeller accomplishments. He promoted road construction, but voters turned down a huge bond measure, and his promises to increase the number of industrial jobs proved difficult to fulfill. Compared with his uncles—Nelson, in New York, and Winthrop, in Arkansas—Jay's record seemed a trifle undramatic. But as he himself noted, the free-spending days of the '60s were gone.

West Virginia's governorship was one of the weakest in the country until 1970 when the governor was given more control over the budget and allowed to serve two terms. Six other offices are still elected statewide and independent of the governor, but they no longer have their own budget power.

Considering the general climate of state politics, West Virginia state government is not much better—or worse—than one might expect. The only area of exceptional program or management, as far as we could discover, has been welfare. All county governments were removed from welfare responsibilities, record keeping was tied to a central computer operation in Charleston, and processing of new applicants has been speedy.

West Virginia has had powerful men in the U.S. Senate for a long time. The patriarch of West Virginia politics has been Senator Jennings Randolph, an octogenarian who was in Congress on March 4, 1933, to hear Franklin Roosevelt say, "This nation asks for action, and action now." It was a time for the expenditure of vast amounts of money to pull the country out of the Depression, and Randolph voted for all the historic New Deal measures. From his freshman term in Congress through his many years as chairman of the Public Works Committee (after 1977, Environment and Public Works), Randolph fought for roads for his mountainous state, created the interstate highway system, and defended the highway trust fund, fighting with all his might to prevent tapping of the fund for mass transit. Over the years liberals came to criticize Randolph's highway building and to ask why he did not take a greater interest in mine safety. With the Republican takeover of the Senate in 1980 he lost his powerful public works chairmanship and found himself watching the Reagan administration try to dismantle many of the programs he had voted for. But Randolph remained the prototype of the New Deal liberal, hewing still to the idea that problems are solved by extracting money from the Treasury, and he fought hard—sometimes successfully—to save his most precious programs.

West Virginia's other Senator, Robert C. Byrd, the successor to Montana's Mike Mansfield as majority leader and minority leader after the Democrats lost control in 1980, is an even more fascinating character. Byrd's story is quintessentially West Virginian. He was born in North Carolina in 1918, but his mother died that year. As his carpenter father had no interest in raising him, he was sent to live with his aunt and uncle in Stotesbury, a dreary southern West Virginia mining town. He was the high school class valedictorian, but since there was no money to send him to college he worked at various jobs before becoming a butcher. In 1946, Byrd decided to run for the state legislature, and the first reporter ever to interview him—Thomas Stafford, then with the newspaper in nearby Beckley—wrote: "He was somewhat pontifical," but also "the most ambitious fellow I ever met. He has never wasted a moment in his life. . . . To be corny about it, he is the Horatio Alger of West Virginia." Byrd served in the West Virginia house and senate, going to college in his spare time, before running for the U.S. House in 1952, where he served three rather undistinguished terms before moving on to the Senate in 1958. After eight years of night classes, he earned a law degree from American University in 1963.

The keys to Byrd's success were his willingness to serve his constituents and his fellow senators. Driving himself relentlessly, denying himself any real social life, his most colorful features his fiddle playing and red vest, Byrd labored year-in and year-out to line up dozens of federal projects for his state. On Capitol Hill, he displayed a keen sense of power, cultivating early in his Senate career then-Majority Leader Lyndon Johnson and especially the patriarch of the powerful Southerners, Richard Russell of Georgia. As his transition to higher and higher political positions required, Byrd moved from the right to the center of American politics.

It would be fair to say that no burning sense of the American purpose impelled Robert Byrd to claw his way up from the bleak coal camps of West Virginia to the inner circle of the United States Senate. He seems to have entered politics in the first instance because it was the only way out of the poverty of his youth; later he delighted in telling his own story in terms of how a poor orphan boy could rise to the seats of the mighty. Byrd achieved all the outward signs of power, but according to other senators, remained insecure. His popularity as leader of the Democrats, for instance, was directly dependent on his willingness to schedule votes so that senators could make plans and perform such other household tasks vital to their images and reelections. After more than 20 years in Washington, Byrd lacked true friends in the Senate. He seemed, after Democrats lost control of the Senate in the 1980 elections, to function somewhat better as a minority rather than majority leader. Yet to socially and politically conscious Washington, he remained forever something of an outsider. The *Washington Post* was not beyond printing the meanest, most contemptuous remarks muttered about Byrd (off the record, of course) by fellow senators. If such treatment seemed both snobbish and cold-hearted, considering how long and hard Byrd had labored to climb to his high position, it was nevertheless somehow appropriate for a politician from a state that has struggled so hard, but still has so far to go.

NORTH CAROLINA

The Newest Megastate

THE HARD WORKING STATE of North Carolina has never loomed large in the national consciousness. Since colonial times, it has been called "a vale of humility between two mountains of conceit"—its haughty neighbors to the north and south, Virginia and South Carolina. Thus it came as no little surprise when the 1980 Census revealed that North Carolina had grown, suddenly vaulting past Massachusetts and Indiana in population size to become our 10th-largest state—a "megastate."

The Tar Heel state's relative obscurity is not difficult to fathom. Here is a state known not for glamorous families or dazzling cities but for its three large industries: tobacco, textiles, and furniture. Although North Carolina likes to think of itself as the South's most liberal state, its politics are inconsistent enough to be considered paradoxical. And in a sense, one could say its rise to megastate proportions was somewhat accidental. The states of Massachusetts and Indiana, a bit larger in 1970, grew only marginally in the '70s while North Carolina, plugging ahead at a 15.5 percent rate, reached a 1980 total of 5,874,429 people and its sudden Big Ten status. Many Americans may not realize how large North Carolina's territory is. From the lighthouse at Cape Hatteras to the Smokies, for instance, the distance is more than 500 miles —about the same as the distance from New York to Raleigh.

From colonial days onward, North Carolina was rarely notable. Unlike Virginia and South Carolina it lacked a first-class port (Wilmington, the state's best, was not established till the 1730s). There was a pathetically small planter aristocracy and, for quite a while, very few settlers. The Roanoke Island settlement financed by Sir Walter Raleigh in the 1580s vanished with no trace. Unlike many other Southern states, North Carolina never went through an early golden age. When Virginia was producing such luminaries as Washington, Jefferson, Madison, and Marshall, North Carolina was a land of fiercely independent small farmers, many of them Scotch-Irish, and few slaves. North Carolina, unlike Kentucky and Tennessee, did not enjoy flourishing growth during the age of Jackson and Clay. Rather, it was exporting people west. Three presidents were born in North Carolina—Jackson (though South Carolina also claims him), Polk, and Andrew Johnson—but all launched their political careers from Tennessee. North Carolinians fought lustily (and sometimes against each other) in the War for Independence and the War Between the States, yet in comparison to other places, there were no great political struggles or upheavals, no sharp shifts in the pace of eco-

3 4 8

nomic development. If Thomas Jefferson was right in saying that people needed a revolution every 20 years, North Carolina is long overdue.

The state's steady, even growth was, nevertheless, one of the reasons V.O. Key was able to report in *Southern Politics* (1949) that North Carolina "enjoys a reputation for progressive outlook and action in many phases of life, including industrial development, education and race relations." John Gunther, after his brief stop in the state for *Inside U.S.A.*, fairly gushed in saying, "That North Carolina is by a good deal the most liberal southern state will, I imagine, be agreed to by almost everybody."

V.O. Key more judiciously added that North Carolinians themselves are the first to point out that their state does not entirely deserve its progressive reputation. And in reality this is a state of paradoxes: behind every fact indicating its progressiveness lurks another suggesting quite the opposite.

North Carolina has an aggressive, enlightened press exemplified by such papers as the *Raleigh News* and *Observer*, serving the eastern portion of the state, and the *Charlotte Observer*, part of the Knight-Ridder chain and winner of the 1981 Pulitzer Prize for its series on "Brown Lung: A Case of Deadly Neglect." The press has contributed much to the state's "good government" reputation, but seek real consistency or some strong intellectual tradition in the state's politics and you will encounter major difficulty. The same state that first refused to ratify the Equal Rights Amendment in 1973 (and repeated that vote in 1982) pioneered in reducing criminal penalties for possession of marijuana in 1977. The same state that has prided itself on such progressive Democratic governors as Terry Sanford and James Hunt has also sent to the U.S. Senate two of the most conservative men to enter those portals in modern times: Republicans Jesse Helms and John East.

The paradoxes extend to economic matters as well. Here is a state that has long bragged about its ability to attract industry. In all the Southland, only mighty Texas exceeds it in factory output. North Carolina has a larger percentage of its work force (34.5 percent) employed in manufacturing than any other state in the country, even such industrial giants as Michigan, Ohio, and Illinois. But North Carolina industrial workers' earnings have long been dead last among the 50 states. Not surprisingly, only 6.5 percent of North Carolina's work force belong to unions, the lowest share among the 50 states.

North Carolina is proud, and in many respects justly so, of its system of public education, but in the early 1980s the state still lagged seriously in the number of school years its people complete: nearly 25 percent of North Carolina's adult population had not finished high school, and only 13.4 percent of adults had completed college compared to 16.3 percent nationwide. North Carolina's greatest educational achievement was its 16-campus university system, but into the 1980s the system was maintaining some campuses that were predominantly white and others predominantly black. In 1982 a divided U.S. Court of Appeals approved a U.S. Department of Education settlement that promised to add new programs to the black campuses, but did not require dismantling of duplicate programs at nearby white campuses. Civil rights activists who noted that the plan was developed by the conservative Reagan administration vowed to take the case to higher courts.

Several cases came to the fore in the 1970s in which black rights activists were pursued with suspicious fervor by law enforcement officials. Then, after conviction on questionable charges, they were sentenced to astonishingly long prison terms. Most famous was the "Wilmington 10" case in which 10 civil rights activists, 9 black men and 1 white woman, were convicted in connection with the firebombing of a grocery store. The white woman was later freed on parole, but the black men were sentenced to 20- to 29-year prison terms. Many people inside and outside North Carolina considered the men political prisoners. But the state courts rejected requests for a new trial, and Gov. James Hunt, considered a progressive, long refused to become involved.

This is also a state where the Ku Klux Klan must still be reckoned with, in occasional violence, if not politics. In the 1960s North Carolina was the home of one of the largest and most virulent Ku Klux Klans in the United States. Membership is reported to have fallen from 6,000 dues-paying members in 1960 to the hundreds by the late 1970s, but even then the Klan broke up an anti-Klan rally staged by the Communist Workers party at a public housing project in Greensboro. Klan members, aided by a group of Nazis, burst into the rally, killing five communists, including two doctors and an honors graduate of Duke University. The following year a Greensboro jury acquitted six Klan members of murder charges stemming from the incident.

Persons convicted of crimes in North Carolina are likely to go to jail. The state ranks first in America in numbers of prisoners jailed per 100,000 population, double the incarceration rate for New York State. In 1981, 77 percent of North Carolina's prison admissions were for crimes that did not involve violence or physical harm to others. Yet if North Carolina judges' inclination to incarcerate has had any effect on the state's crime rate, it has been a peculiar one. The crime rates for robbery, larceny, car thefts, and rape are among the lowest in the nation, while those for assault and murder are among the top 15 states.

North Carolina's new "megastate" status has created another set of paradoxes. The state may now boast the tenth-largest number of people in the country, yet one searches in vain for most of those characteristics of cultural and economic leadership often exhibited by other megastates—and indeed by some smaller states, such as Massachusetts and Minnesota. The state's economy has not diversified far beyond textiles, tobacco, and furniture. North Carolina has the headquarters of only eight *Fortune* 500 companies, fewer than any megastate except Florida. And except for the R.J. Reynolds Tobacco Company, and Nucor, a steel manufacturing firm, North Carolina's big companies are all in textiles: Burlington, Blue Bell, Akzona, Cone Mills, and Fieldcrest. Despite a well-publicized campaign to attract high-technology, North Carolina is still not among the top 13 states in the number of high-tech firms. This lack of diversification—unique among the megastates—is illustrated by the fact that even in 1980, one-fourth of all the nation's textile industry could be found in North Carolina. Nearly half of all the state's factory workers were employed in an amazingly high total of textile mills (1,200) and apparel plants (550). The notoriously low wages in the textile industry kept North Carolina's 1980 per capita income at 41st rank among the states. So much of the wealth that is produced in North Carolina goes to out-of-state owners and stockholders that the sum of all incomes in the state is exceptionally low, given its population ranking. The 1980 U.S. Trust Co. of New York survey of millionaires showed that North Carolina had only 10,938 millionaires, 19th among the states.

North Carolina is also more nativist than the other megastates. It was settled principally overland from Virginia and South Carolina, mostly by Scotch and Scotch-Irish farmers, and their stock still dominates. Less than 1 percent of the state's people were born in foreign lands, a proportion far below other large states. North Carolina's 1.3 million blacks in 1980 made up 22.4 percent of the population and were the state's only numerically significant minority group. We have heard reports that foreign businessmen still worry that they would not be accepted in this Southern state and avoid settling there even if they open plants in the state.

North Carolina, although a megastate, has no really major metropolitan center. The urbanized area around Charlotte, the largest city (pop. 637,218), is not as populous as Nashville, Tennessee. North Carolina's population is scattered first and foremost about the seemingly infinite number of smaller textile mill and furniture factory towns, second around the state's five cities, with more than 100,000 people—Charlotte, Greensboro, Winston-Salem, Raleigh, and Durham—and last in rural areas. North Carolina has industrialized without really urbanizing. Fitting that pattern, mobile homes abound: next to Florida and California, North Carolina has the most of any state. And they are not so much the homes of retirees or itinerants as shelter for the people who work in North Carolina's low-paying factories, often unable to afford a "site-built" home.

An Economic History of the Tar Heel State

Up until the Civil War, North Carolina was unrelievedly agricultural and mostly poor. In 1860 it had fewer slaves than any other Confederate state except Tennessee, and fewer big plantations. In the early years of the 1880s, the golden age of Kentucky and Tennessee, North Carolina became known as the Rip Van Winkle state; its population increased only sluggishly, as thousands of North Carolinians made their way west over the mountains. At the outbreak of the Civil War, this state of small farmers had no city of even 10,000 population.

North Carolina held out against secession until the guns began blazing over Fort Sumter and Virginia had seceded. And even though North Carolina soldiers made up one-quarter of the Confederate dead, the land was not as ravaged as Virginia's, nor did emancipation destroy the wealth of the state—as it did in South Carolina. Unlike many of its neighbors, North Carolina was poised to reach for what many said would be the South's salvation: industrialization.

The most important industry in North Carolina, from the Revolution to the Civil War, was the production of turpentine; it was distilled from pine sap and was, except for foodstuffs, the state's only export.* Then, in postbellum North Carolina, cotton textile mills began their years of heady expansion all across the state's productive midstate Piedmont region. From 1880 to 1900, the state saw an average of six new cotton mills built each year.

Why this concentration of textiles in the Carolina Piedmont? Inexpensive water power, tapping the fast-falling waters of such rivers as the Yadkin and Catawba and their tributaries, led the list. Another reason, clearly, was cheap labor. Just consider the average textile wages in 1900: $216 for men, $157 for women, $103 for children—*per year*. The chief raw material, cotton, was indigenous to the Southland. Finally, for reasons hard to divine, it was North Carolina entrepreneurs who had the gumption to gather the capital and launch the industry on a grand scale.

The tobacco industry offered perhaps the most colorful entrepreneurial story of all, in the person of James B. "Buck" Duke. In 1884, at the age of 27, he bought one of the first cigarette-making machines and undertook a frontal assault on the big companies of the day. With shrewd promotion and advertising and lower costs, Duke soon dominated the national market. In 1890 he set up the American Tobacco Company, combining under his control manufacturers of 90 percent of the cigarettes in the United States. Then Duke set out to outsell or to absorb the major manufacturers of pipe and chewing tobacco, snuff, and cigars. All the time, he promoted cigarette smoking, to his great enrichment. In 1911 the Supreme Court ordered Duke's tobacco trust dissolved, and it was broken into four companies: American Tobacco (now American Brands), R.J. Reynolds, P. Lorillard, and Liggett Myers. They still dominate the industry, and all have a major share of their operations in North Carolina. In 1980, North Carolina still grew 43 percent of the nation's tobacco, nearly twice as much as Kentucky, the next highest producer. The state was also responsible for producing more than half the nation's cigarettes: from just one of its 12 plants, the R.J. Reynolds Company spewed out 400 million cigarettes daily, enough to fill 12 railroad cars.

There's little mystery as to why North Carolina became America's top tobacco state: the product grew there most luxuriantly, particularly in the state's eastern regions. Similarly, raw material was responsible for its third great industry, furniture. Magnificent varieties of hardwoods flourished on the moist slopes of the Smokies and the hills of the western Piedmont. The

*The nickname "Tar Heel State" is not derived from this industry, however. It stems from an incident of the Revolutionary War when Cornwallis' soldiers crossed a North Carolina river into which tar had been poured, emerging with the substance stuck to their heels.

furniture industry grew up around the small towns of the western Piedmont, such as High Point.

Yet while North Carolina has more than fulfilled the 19th-century dream of industrialization to rescue the Southland from its dependence on the land, the state's low personal income figures prove it has not produced the bounteous society once hoped for. The North Carolina Fund pinpointed the problem in a 1967 report that still rings true: "We have seen North Carolina shift from a poor agricultural state to a poor industrial state. We have experienced industrialization without development."

Of the great Carolina industries, only tobacco pays above the national hourly average. Textiles are unquestionably the chief culprit in North Carolina's low-wage dilemma. They pay the lowest wages of all major U.S. industries; not surprisingly, they are also the least unionized. Unions have made sporadic attempts to organize North Carolina mills; there was even a Communist-led strike in Gastonia in 1929. But a massive drive in the late 1950s ended in disaster for the union, and until the Textile Workers Union managed to organize seven J.P. Stevens plants at Roanoke Rapids in 1974, virtually none of the state's textile mills and precious few furniture factories were organized. In 1980, after a bitter, 17-year battle, the Amalgamated Clothing Workers of America (with which the Textile Workers had merged in 1976) won the right to represent about 3,500 textile workers at 12 J.P. Stevens plants. The union was ratified after a campaign in which maverick organizer Ray Rogers used such unorthodox tactics as threatening to take union pension fund money out of any bank that did business with Stevens and using consumer groups to boycott Stevens products. The AFL-CIO's Industrial Union Department and the International Brotherhood of Teamsters have both made major efforts in the state. But even in the early 1980s, the unions were still losing more certification elections than they were winning. Why? There is the fierce independence, even orneriness, of Carolina working people, combined with a surplus of labor. But the primary reason for North Carolina's low rate of unionization is surely business hostility. And geography plays a role: few textile jobs are in the major North Carolina cities. Rather, they are spread through all the small, one-industry towns, where the textile makers, with their huge sums of capital and absolute control over workers' jobs, can still have things pretty much their own way.

Consider Cannon Mills, which produces half the nation's towels and a fifth of its sheets. In the Piedmont town of Kannapolis, some 16,000 people, nearly one-third of the residents, work for the Cannon Mills. Many live in the 1,600 company-owned homes. For a half century up to his death, in 1971, the company was run autocratically by Charles Cannon, who with his family held title to a huge portion of the unincorporated town of Kannapolis. Cannon even allowed his stock to be taken off the New York Stock Exchange rather than reveal information as the Exchange rules required. "Mr. Charlie," as he was known, would not even have considered a union at Cannon Mills. And more than 10 years after his death, no serious unionization drive had yet been launched against Cannon. The company itself fell into California hands.

Unionizing textile workers has become the stuff of folklore and even the subject of an Academy Award–winning film, *Norma Rae*. The Amalgamated Clothing Workers has been determined to organize in North Carolina and keeps trying in the face of adversity. Yet a gnawing doubt remains: would textiles, now subject to such heavy (and usually inexpensive) foreign competition, pay a great deal more even if they were unionized?

Unhappiness over low wages has sparked a state government campaign for economic diversification ever since the administration of Governor Luther Hodges, Sr., in the 1950s. Hodges, who was later to become U.S. Secretary of Commerce, spent much of his administration (1954–61) promoting North Carolina around the nation and to the Common Market countries and selling the state on the idea of diversification. Perhaps his most lasting contribution was the creation of the Research Triangle Park, near Durham, Chapel Hill, and Raleigh. The location provided access to the state's three major universities: Duke, the University of North Carolina, and North Carolina State. Land was leased or sold to corporations and government agencies for research facilities, and by the 1980s the park was booming. Some 41 corporations and government agencies were operating research facilities and manufacturing high-technology products. Tenants included IBM, General Electric, Monsanto, and the Burroughs Wellcome companies, as well as the U.S. Environmental Protection Agency and Forest Service. By the early 1980s more than 20,000 people were employed at Research Triangle Park, mostly in jobs paying far above the state's average wage, and high-tech employment in the state totalled 50,000 workers. But even in high-tech endeavors North Carolina had problems developing a top-notch image. A California high-technology company executive told us that engineers were still reluctant to move to North Carolina, preferring the "freer" social atmosphere of the Western states. Those attitudes were apparently confirmed by the fact that North Carolina seemed to attract more high-tech production facilities, with a lower wage scale for that industry, than research and development activities.

By 1980 the long-term diversification effort was showing some dividends. Textiles, which accounted for 51 percent of North Carolina's factory employment in 1955, were down to only 30 percent (with apparel another 11 percent). The textiles-furniture-tobacco trio, 63 percent of the state's manufacturing jobs in 1955, was down to 53 percent. What kind of firms were coming in to take up the slack? Plants making rubber and plastic products, chemicals, electrical and nonelectrical machinery. Most investments came in the Piedmont, from Raleigh to the foothills of the Smokies, and nearly 60 percent of the jobs, true to North Carolina form, appeared in rural areas.

North Carolina state officials have sometimes been criticized for blatantly promoting North Carolina's low wages and lack of unionization. But the state's economic development program seems to deserve the progressive label on two scores, the first in education. Starting under Gov. Terry Sanford, the state set up industrial education centers, gradually expanding them into a system of community and technical colleges designed to be within an hour's drive of any location in the state. The state's technical and community colleges, in addition to regular curriculums, customized industrial training packages for industries moving into or expanding within the state—at no cost to the firm. One out of every eight North Carolinians, some 700,000 people, were enrolled in some type of vocational training in 1980. The second area that earns the progressive label is, surprisingly, taxes. North Carolina has not aped the policy of so many states (including neighboring South Carolina) in offering massive tax concessions to prospective firms and was the last state to adopt an industrial revenue bond program. Business taxes are, of course, quite low, but favors for the "big fish" do not unfairly affect small, indigenous businesses.

The Underdeveloped East

By the early 1980s the big news about North Carolina's diversification program was that it had finally begun to show returns in the underdeveloped eastern portion of the state, which has the largest black population (33 percent) and is the most reliant on the tobacco economy.

The litany of the problems of the East is strikingly similar to that of the South Carolina Lowcountry, south Georgia, or southside Virginia. The residents are largely poor. The cities of eastern North Carolina are small; the largest are Wilmington (44,000), the state's largest port, and Fayetteville (50,057). The latter is almost a tributary of the Army's giant Fort Bragg, home of the 82nd Airborne.

To the extent that North Carolina ever had a plantation culture, it was in the East. The residual black population percentages would be even higher if so many had not left during the 1950s and '60s for the ghettos of Washington, Baltimore, Philadelphia, Newark, and New York. In parts of eastern North Carolina, entire high school graduating classes left, looking for jobs. So many left each summer that in the 1960s the Seaboard Coast Line Number 76 train became known as the "Chickenbone Special," because the young travelers usually carried a picnic lunch of fried chicken. Outmigration stopped in the 1970s as jobs in the Northern cities began to dry up, and stories of poor conditions "up there" convinced young black North Carolinians they were better off in the state of their birth. Many have, however, moved into North Carolina's own cities.

Until quite lately, the East had few industries, mostly low-wage "cut and sew" shops, hiring mainly women, often blacks whose husbands were trying to eke out a living on tobacco farms. Yet state figures for 1980 showed that nearly one-third of all North Carolina's new jobs that year were in the East and that the region attracted 40 percent of all new industrial development. One can hope that industrialization will lessen the regional importance of tobacco, a crop running into increasing troubles.

Even in its heyday, tobacco offered little better than a marginal living standard for sharecroppers, not much better for many of the landowning farmers, and created no great fortunes even for tobacco warehousemen. The right to grow tobacco is regulated by the government through a system of allotments strictly limiting the acreage and pounds of tobacco that can be grown. Allotments were originally assigned to growers in the 1930s; they have been passed along from father to son like a sacred birthright—or sold. Since 1933, the federal government has issued about 620,000 allotments. By the 1980s, fewer than half were owned by tobacco farmers; the remainder are owned by doctors, lawyers, churches, banks, industrial workers, and in many cases, widows, who lease them to farmers at prices exceeding $1,000 per acre. Among the owners: Mrs. Jesse Helms. This may help explain why Sen. Helms and others have fought so hard to preserve government tobacco price supports. But by 1982 Senators Helms and East were willing to support President Reagan's doubling of the federal tax on cigarettes even if North Carolinians felt betrayed. Antismoking campaigns had succeeded in reducing the percentage of Americans who smoked cigarettes to its lowest level since 1898, and as Helms explained, he would offend too many of his colleagues if he did not support the tax. At the same time, there were grumblings from the younger growers that the archaic system of leasing allotments was feudalistic, and even charges that the system of price supports had made the American product too expensive for international markets.

The Outer Banks, that string of sandy islets separating Albemarle and Pamlico Sounds from the ocean, represents the easternmost extremity of North Carolina. The waters here are treacherous, and among sailors the name of Cape Hatteras (the tip of the elbow that sticks out from the Banks into the Atlantic) is still feared: here, it is said, more than 700 shipwrecks have occurred.

The Banks were also the site of the Wright brothers' first flight at Kitty Hawk, and close by is Roanoke Island, where Sir Walter Raleigh tried to start a colony in 1587. One of the leaders returned to England for more provisions, and when he came back three years later he found no trace of the colonists except for the word "Croatoan," the name of a local Indian tribe, carved on a tree. No one knows what became of this Lost Colony.

For years the Outer Banks were so isolated from the rest of the state that the Bankers, as its residents are called, have retained 17th-century speech patterns and vocabulary. The Outer Banks have been kept relatively free of the kind of high-rise development that has marred Virginia Beach, to the north, and Myrtle Beach, to the south. Much of the beach is protected by the National Seashore designation, and the coast has also been protected by North Carolina's 1974 Coastal Zone Management Act and, some say, its lengthy distance from an interstate highway. But the Outer Banks still grew faster in the 1970s than any other section of North Carolina, and residents became embroiled in debates over future development. Favoring growth were the summer gentry, who began selling their old cedar homes to condominium developers and young, permanent residents who found the housing supply scarce and expensive. Opposing them were the recently arrived retirees who saw the arrival of three-story, condominium complexes, built in factories and shipped in, as a desecration of the natural scenic area to which they had moved.

The Piedmont

North Carolina's urban growth has not centered on one city, as in Georgia, but rather concentrated in the cities and suburbs of what is known as the Piedmont crescent. Roughly following Interstate 85 from northeast to south-west—and thus forming the eastern anchor of the vital growth line of the new South, which stretches through the South Carolina Piedmont cities and on to Atlanta and finally Birmingham—they are (with the 1980 metropolitan population figures): Raleigh-Durham (530,673), Greensboro-Winston-Salem-High Point (827,385), and Charlotte-Gastonia (637,218). These cities have developed and grown less as a function of their geography (none straddles a major river) than as headquarters of major economic interests. Greensboro is the headquarters of Burlington Industries; Winston-Salem, of R.J. Reynolds Tobacco and Hanes Hosiery; Durham, of the Duke tobacco interests; Raleigh, of state government; and Charlotte, of numerous banking and insurance interests.

There is little to distinguish the Piedmont cities from one another; even their physical layouts tend to be similar. Each emanates from a downtown that has some gleaming new skyscrapers (Durham is an exception), but diminished retail trade. Each has a black quadrant, roughly pie-shaped and spreading from downtown to the city limits, and a well-to-do white quadrant. To a Northerner, the racial patterns seem unusual. Blacks rather rarely move out into white neighborhoods; instead they push farther out, toward or beyond the city limits, into neighborhoods that have always been black or into new subdivisions that have been built for blacks—often by black developers.

Charlotte (314,447) is a city of branch offices, banks, insurance companies, and trucking firms. Every Monday morning, some 30,000 salesmen pour out of Charlotte to cover the mid-South. The city seems constantly to have its eye on Atlanta, and though it will never eclipse that colossus of the South, it will surely remain North Carolina's largest (it grew 30.2 percent in the '70s). Some of its greatest problems lie in physical growth that heeds neither land-use planning nor public transportation needs. Some of the good news in recent years has been the tasteful renewal of some inner-city neighborhoods and the creation of Spirit Square, a delightfully conceived multipurpose arts center near city center. Charlotte is headquarters of the North Carolina National Bank and its holding company, NCNB Corp., the largest banking concern in the Southeast. Benefiting from state law, which permits banks to build branches anywhere in North Carolina, and renowned for its competitiveness, NCNB has pursued a bold acquisition and merger policy—sometimes walking the tightrope of legality. Yet NCNB has not limited itself to profit-seeking; its community development corporation, a wholly owned nonprofit subsidiary, has helped refurbish the declining Fourth Ward of Charlotte and developed more than 225 housing units in Charlotte and Greesnboro. But what Charlotte is most known for nationally is the 1970 Charlotte-Mecklenburg County desegregation case in which a federal judge ordered extensive busing of school children across the city-county line. Parents were initially furious, but after a few years, the plan was working better than expected—surely far better than in many Northern cities—and tempers cooled.

Winston-Salem (131,885), where the mountains begin to rise from the hilly western Piedmont, is the headquarters of Reynolds Tobacco and the Wachovia National Bank, the state's largest until the early 1970s when Charlotte's North Carolina National eclipsed it. In addition to cigarettes and textiles, furniture and electronics are made here. In the 1950s, the Reynolds family financed the transfer of Wake Forest University from its namesake town near Raleigh, building a university almost singlehandedly, as James B. Duke had done many years before in Durham.

Winston-Salem has had an unusual commitment to the arts since its 18th-century settlers of the Moravian sect handcopied hymns, collected 10,000 music manuscripts, and earned the city the reputation of being a "hotbed of Haydn." Winston-Salem formed America's first city arts council in 1949; by the late 1970s that council was overseeing an ambitious effort to use arts as a catalyst to bring people back downtown. Several downtown buildings were renovated into a performing arts center, an arts and crafts school for children and adults, a park and amphitheater, which opened in 1982. Federal money helped finance the project, but the lion's share came from Winston-Salem's well-heeled private sector, led by an indefatigable proponent of the arts, R. Philip Hanes, Jr., of the Hanes hosiery family.

An integral part of the arts strategy was the North Carolina School of the Arts, which is connected with the University of North Carolina and attracts highly talented theater, dance, and music students from throughout the state and across the nation. When it was proposed, rural legislators called it a "toe-dancing school," but Governor Sanford was able to ram it through by horsetrading road projects and appointments. Admission to the school is by audition only; visiting the school, you can literally feel the striving, the search for artistic perfection as the young artists train. Graduates land jobs with top performing U.S. and European arts institutions. And there appears to be a clear economic dividend: North Carolina is finding that the state's cultural reputation—from annual European tours of the School of Arts' orchestra, for instance—helps draw foreign investment and makes the state more attractive to high-level executives. North Carolina also supports a symphony orchestra and an art museum. This Tar Heel vigor in the arts must be marked down as yet another paradox in a blue-collar state that one would expect to have little interest in sophisticated dance, drama, and music.

Near Winston-Salem are Greensboro (155,624), a headquarters town (in addition to Burlington, textile firms such as Cone, Blue Bell, and Glen Raven) and a cigarette and electronics manufacturing center, and High Point (64,107), the furniture capital.

Durham (100,831) is the Piedmont's grittiest city, headquarters for Chesterfield cigarettes and site of Duke University, one of the two or three most distinguished private universities in the South, with excellent medical and law schools. Duke is Durham's largest employer. Under the presidency of former Governor Sanford, Duke became a center for political thought and analysis. Enormous controversy was generated by an attempt to build the Nixon presidential library there. Duke's largely unrecognized role in politics and government, however, has been its education of many congressional and White House aides. Durham's proximity to Washington seems to lead many Duke graduates into government service.

Durham overall has the air of a factory town and is notable for its 47 percent black population, the highest figure of any of North Carolina's large cities. The most attractive high-rise building on Durham's skyline is the North Carolina Mutual Building, headquarters of an insurance company owned and operated by blacks and in business since 1898.

Raleigh (149,771) is dominated by state government and North Carolina State University. It benefits, as Durham does, from the nearby presence of the Research Triangle Park. Development pressures played an unusual role in mayoral elections in the 1970s. In 1973, the city, which is quite conservative and only 27 percent black, elected a black mayor. The victor, Clarence Lightner, owner of a funeral home and veteran of the city council, was elected by a coalition of blacks and white neighborhood groups seeking controlled growth. Four years later, a similar antidevelopment position catapulted political neophyte Isabella Cannon, a Scottish immigrant, widow, and retired library administrator, to the mayor's office, but she was followed by a developer, Smedes York.

Though not one of the Piedmont's larger cities, Chapel Hill (32,421), home of the University of North Carolina, is surely one of the nicest. Most of its permanent residents (12 percent of whom are black) are connected with the university, giving the city an affluent, white-collar, intellectual air. The university itself—the first state university in the nation, opened in 1795—is probably the most distinguished public institution of higher learning south of the Mason-Dixon line. In addition to a variety of excellent departments, particularly in the liberal arts, English, and health education, UNC is renowned for its excellent basketball teams. The entire state, in fact, is basketball crazy, much like Indiana.

Tiny Afton Township, in predominantly black and poor Warren County near the Virginia border, proved in 1982 that North Carolinians can rise to protest. Blacks and whites together—led by the Rev. Leon White, a veteran civil rights activist, and the Rev. Joseph Lowery, head of the Southern Christian Leadership Conference—were arrested by the hundreds for protesting against the state's selection of Afton as North Carolina's first dumping ground for PCB (polychlorinated biphenyl). When the activists were arrested, they were lying down, arm in arm, in front of state trucks hauling dirt laced with the toxic chemical to the dump site.

North Carolina's Mountains: The Gem of Appalachia

Announcing his retirement from the Senate in 1973, Sam J. Ervin, Jr., said that he intended to do a little fishing, sit around home in Morganton, and watch "the indescribable glory of the sun setting behind Hawksbill Mountain." As it happens, Hawksbill Mountain, just west of Morganton and about 50 miles west of Charlotte and Winston-Salem, is part of the Blue Ridge that rises from the hilly Piedmont and signals the beginnings of North Carolina's mountain country. The great wave of Western migration following the Revolutionary War went over the mountains, into Tennessee and Kentucky. The mountains did begin to fill up during this period, but their greatest growth awaited the industrial boom before and after the turn of the century, when furniture factories and, to a lesser extent, textile mills located there.

The Smokies of North Carolina are the highest mountains east of the Mississippi. They are also among this nation's most hauntingly beautiful: it is as if deep green velvet were draped loosely over the earth, rising and falling in curving folds, sometimes in bright relief under the sun, oftentimes barely discernible through the smoky haze that gave these mountains their name. There is also profound fascination in their weird, almost exotic shapes— ridgelines straight out of a fairytale. These hills are, in truth, the gem of the Appalachians; geologically, they are also some of the oldest mountains in North America. As far back as we know, this land was peopled by the Cherokee Indians. This remarkable tribe, which spread south into South Carolina, Georgia, and Alabama, adapted well to the white man's ways, and under the great chief Sequoyah, even developed its own alphabet and literature. But in the 1830s, mindful that whites wanted the Indians' land, the federal government dispatched General Winfield Scott to drive them west. Nearly one-quarter of the Cherokees died on the Trail of Tears to the arid lands they had been granted; it was perhaps the lowest moment of Jacksonian democracy. A little more than a thousand Cherokees had remained behind; today some 8,700 of their descendants live in western North Carolina.*

Up through the 1940s, western North Carolina was one of the most isolated sections of Eastern America. Then came tourism, industrialization, and the growth of mountain-based educational institutions. Now that the wall of isolation has been broken, thoughtful people of the region speak with deep concern of the head-over-heels tourist development, soaring land prices, bull-dozing of mountains to make way for condominiums, ski resorts, and golf courses, and the arrival of the plastic civilization of hamburger and fried chicken stands, gas stations, and all the rest. The once-exquisite Magee Valley, west of Asheville, is now full of snake farms and other such tourist attractions.

*There are actually far more Indians in eastern North Carolina, most of them Lumbees in and around Robeson County, south of Fayetteville, who may or may not be descendants of the Lost Colony of Roanoke. Altogether, North Carolina had nearly 65,000 Indians in 1980, the largest number east of the Mississippi.

"It's a mess," one local leader said, "and unfortunately the zoning can't be made retroactive."

The leading city in the west is Asheville (53,281), basically an industrial town. Asheville did have its own little golden age around the turn of the century, when its cool climate and beautiful scenery made it a fashionable resort for well-to-do Southerners.

Up in the mountains, in the village of Montreat, near Asheville, is the home of evangelist Billy Graham. From his comfortable house notched in the Smokies, Graham has gone forth to preach to huge crowds almost all over the world. Graham's fame was due initially to his vibrant, emotion-charged preaching style, but he also developed a closeness to presidents, from Truman to Nixon. In the days before the Moral Majority and other evangelical groups became involved in politics, he was something of an ambassador to presidents from that segment of American Christianity. Graham's strongest imprecations over the years have been directed at freer sexuality and godlessness; he was silent for years on the evils of racial segregation and never said a word against the American bombing in southeast Asia. Graham was unable to issue more than a mild rebuke to his friend Richard Nixon after Watergate, but the affair has reportedly made him cautious about further political involvement. In the early 1980s Graham shocked some conservative Christians by speaking out in favor of arms limitations and by visiting the Soviet Union.

Graham is not the first celebrity to come from Asheville, however. The novelist Thomas Wolfe was born in Asheville in 1900. In his prose, family friends have written, Wolfe "captured as did no one else the essence of his region's countryside and town, mountaineers and middle class, terror and tomfoolery."

Tar Heel Politics—and State Government

That we have come this far without mentioning, except in passing, politics or the state government, has been no accident. What has shaped North Carolina—what has determined how people live, where they work—is not so much government or politics as the face of the land and the raw economic power of the big textile, tobacco, and furniture companies, the utilities, the big banks, and the northern industries establishing branch plants.

What really matters in North Carolina politics is the governorship, and that in itself is another paradox, for the governor has less formal power than in any other state. Until 1978, the governor was prohibited from seeking a second consecutive term; the governor has no veto and must share administrative powers with a tribe of nine other elected officials. Withal, it is surprising that North Carolina governors have been able to accomplish much of anything, and, in fact, only a few have. The good reputation of the series of governors who held office for the 50 years from 1904 to 1954 was derived mainly from the fact that they were personally honest and conducted reasonably efficient regimes, free of gross corruption.

North Carolina has had three particularly outstanding post-war governors: Luther Hodges, Terry Sanford, and James Hunt. Hodges, as we have written, was the central figure in moving the state toward economic diversification. Sanford, his successor, was the moving force behind North Carolina's excellent public secondary and technical education system; he also took a deep interest in American federalism, authored an excellent book, *Storm Over the States*, and launched the Southern Growth Policies Board, a group studying the South's problems and prospects (and how to avoid, it was often claimed, the errors of the North). Hunt has promoted economic diversification, education, and a "balanced growth" plan for the state. He won voter approval for the second term for the governor and then won a second term himself (1980–1984). A former Ford Foundation economics adviser in Nepal, Hunt wore a liberal label before his election to the governorship in 1976, much of it because of his progressive stand on civil rights. He appointed many blacks to high positions in the state government but moderated on other positions, strongly backing the state university system in a quarrel with the federal government over the desegregation of its white campuses and refusing to pardon the Wilmington 10 activists, although he shortened their terms. Hodges, Sanford, and Hunt all enjoyed national reputations as leaders among governors.

Up to the 1970s, Republicans practically never won statewide elections in North Carolina. In 1968 Richard Nixon had become the first Republican presidential candidate to win since 1928, when the dominant Democrats opposed Catholic Al Smith. In 1972 North Carolinians elected a Republican senator and governor and voted for Nixon again. Republican victories signaled a decline in the power of the local courthouse politicians, who had been deemed capable of delivering their counties' votes, in favor of media campaigning. The Democrats recouped some of their losses in 1974, but North Carolina by the '80s was the closest to being a true two-party state it ever has been. The legislature has remained Democratic. The biggest change in the legislature came in the early 1970s when it moved into a splendid marble and glass legislative building designed by Edward Durell Stone; the new facilities diverted a lot of the important decision making from sessions in smoke-filled Raleigh hotel rooms, but business interests still have usually gotten what they want from the North Carolina legislature.

North Carolina has rarely had a strong impact in national politics. The grand exception in the early 1980s was Senator Jesse Alexander Helms, one of the U.S. Senate's most conservative members and a beacon of "New Right" politics. First elected in 1972, Helms was at first considered an extremist outsider by the Senate "club." But he mastered the parliamentary rules of the Senate by diligent study. He learned tactics to stall bills he opposed or add amendments to others, usually against school busing or in favor of school prayer.

In 1980, when the Senate shifted to Republican control, Helms became chairman of the Senate Agricultural Committee, and began to wield real power over such programs as tobacco supports, which he vigorously supported, and food stamps, which he just as strongly opposed. Helms' greatest power, however, lay in his drive to take the Republican party and national debate further to the right. He was never afraid to be the Senate's lone "nay" vote. A fierce hawk, pushing for ever-greater defense budgets, Helms was the force behind the so-called human rights bill, which would have statutorily established the beginning of human life at conception, thus making all abortion murder. Another Helms bill, which passed the Senate in early 1982, called for strict curtailment of school busing to achieve desegregation. Helms also favored returning the nation to the gold standard. But Helms and his socially conservative followers had a hard time agreeing on the fine points of legislation on such issues as abortion. Helms' ideological fanaticism and his legislative tactics won him few friends in the Senate. He grossly damaged his relations with his colleagues when he led an acrimonious two-week filibuster before Christmas 1982 against an increase in the federal gas tax.

However antediluvian Helms' agenda seemed to many, his political operation was strictly up to date. He created his political base as chief editorial commentator for WRAL-TV in Raleigh, delivering nightly editorials of a vividly conservative hue. In the Senate, he created a new type of political machine through his National Congressional Club, a direct-mail fundraising group that became the nation's largest political action committee, contributing millions of dollars to conservative candidates and assuring this North Carolina senator his own, independent political base—even if much of the money was spent on nasty, negative media campaigns against opponents. Hunt was expected to seek Helms' Senate seat in a 1984 contest of the political Titans.

In 1980 Helms and his campaign organizations were responsible for electing one of their own, John East, a little known college professor, to the other North Carolina Senate seat. East, who suffered from polio and has been confined since early adulthood to a wheel chair, used a media blitz during the last weeks of his campaign to eke out a narrow victory against his Democratic incumbent Robert Morgan. North Carolina's 11 congressmen (no woman has ever represented the state) have rarely risen to much prominence.

But it is fitting to close our portrait of North Carolina with its most statesmanlike politician, Senator Sam J. Ervin, Jr., who retired in 1974 after a brief period in the national limelight while he presided over the Watergate hearings. At the beginning of 1973, Sam Ervin was no more of a household word than was the Watergate office and apartment complex. Six months later, after the hearings brought Watergate and Ervin into just about every living room in America, college students began wearing Uncle Sam Ervin T-shirts, and Midwestern tourists cooed as they saw "him" shamble through the Capitol. People remembered with fondness his country yams and his habit of quoting the Bible, the Constitution, and random bits of poetry.

But beneath the fustian there was steel. When President Nixon, invoking executive privilege, announced he would forbid all his aides from testifying before Ervin's committee, Senator Sam responded that he would recommend sending federal marshals out to arrest the aides. Nixon backed down, and the committee exposed the crimes of the Committee to Reelect the President, and even the malfeasance of the president himself, to the nation.

Ervin's performance surprised many liberals who remembered him for his opposition to civil rights, the Equal Rights Amendment, and unions and for voting down the line with Johnson and Nixon on Vietnam. But Ervin could not be stuffed into a neat ideological pigeonhole. He had served on the committee that recommended the censure of Joe McCarthy, crusaded against what he considered the overweening power of the executive branch, and probed into Army spying on civilians and into abuses of government data banks. Ervin did not take up these causes because he sympathized with the people being spied on or because he favored high government spending. But, as the *Almanac of American Politics* summarized his career, "It is a measure of Sam Ervin's devotion to the Constitution that he has spent many of his years in the Senate defending the rights of people whose ideas he does not share."

TENNESSEE

Frontiers Old and New

IN THE FIRST HALF CENTURY or so of its existence, Tennessee epitomized the frontier society and some of the best and worst of early American traditions: Jacksonian Democracy, the exile of Indians, and the first glimmerings of manifest destiny. Since the 1930s, it has been the principal state of the Tennessee Valley Authority, America's first and only experiment in coordinated development of a region; and since the 1940s, the home of the Oak Ridge National Laboratory and its controversial research in nuclear energy. In the postwar era, Tennessee has given us national leaders such as Estes Kefauver and Howard Baker, Jr., the court case that revolutionized the legislatures of America, a fine example of metropolitan government, a poor people's labor union solidified by the martyrdom of Martin Luther King, Jr., and music from the hearts of the people (country music centered in Nashville, the blues from Memphis). Into the 1980s, Tennessee was constantly in the news as important national political battles took place over the Tennessee-Tombigbee Waterway, the Tellico Dam, and the Clinch River nuclear breeder reactor.

These events of national importance emerged from a state that has rarely accomplished anything notably progressive or innovative in the management of its own society. Tennessee, in fact, has been traditionally hard put to develop a single sense of itself.

For many years, highway signs read: "Welcome to the Three Great States of Tennessee." The reference was to the three Grand Divisions—East, Middle, and West Tennessee—which are officially recognized in the state constitution and represent lesson one of any Tennessee primer. Geographically, the Grand Divisions are about the only way to make sense out of a long, rectangular state (sometimes likened to a license plate), which seems to have been flung violently onto the map without regard to natural boundaries. Historically, they explain fairly coherently the early settlement pattern from the eastern highlands to the Mississippi lowlands. Politically, they divided in the Civil War (East for the Union, Middle and West for the Confederacy). Economically, they divided in the antebellum days (independent yeomen in the East, slaveowners in the Middle and especially West Tennessee).

Years of Glory

Tennessee's first glimmerings were as a western mountain offshoot of North Carolina. Many of the early settlers were fleeing the oppressive colonial government to the east, and a varied lot they were: hunters and traders, adventurers and land speculators, missionaries, outlaws, and outcasts. But timid they were not; one could not afford to be that and face log cabin life and precipitous mountain trails and the ever present danger of Indian ambush. Out of the crucible of frontier life and Indian wars and the American Revolution, which coincided with the first wave of serious settlement of the territory, there emerged a tough folk stream, a society of sturdy self-reliance, hair-trigger passions, and fervent evangelism.

At King's Mountain, S.C., in October 1780, for example, a ragtag regiment of Tennessee soldiers in Buckskin met and decimated the splendidly uniformed and trained soldiers of the King in a battle that Thomas Jefferson later called "the joyful annunciation of that turn of the tide of success which terminated the Revolutionary War with the seal of our independence."

The American leader in that battle was John Sevier, a veteran Indian fighter, described by an early Tennessee historian as "fluent, colloquial, and gallant. . . . Of books he knew little. Men, he had studied well and accurately." In 1784 the settlers of the Tennessee country bristled at a "land grab" by the North Carolina legislature and formed the would-be State of Franklin, with Sevier their governor. "Franklin" lasted only three years, but when Tennessee was actually admitted to the Union in 1796, Sevier was made governor.

The brawling frontier was not conducive to organized religion, and one cleric called Tennessee "a Sink of Iniquity, a Black Pit of Irreligion." Then, in the early 19th century came the "Great Revival" of camp meetings, which, according to one history, "swept the state like a wind-driven grass fire and thousands of converts came singing and shouting to the mourners' bench."

In the political realm the egalitarianism of the frontier—its peculiar contribution to American life—was most perfectly embodied in Andrew Jackson, seventh president of the United States. Variously a congressman, senator, and Tennessee judge, Jackson won national fame as the victor in the Battle of New Orleans in 1814–15. Americans revered him as a rough-hewn military leader of indomitable will and courage, as an embodiment of hardy frontier individualism, because he spoke for the common man. Martin Van Buren, Jackson's successor in the White House, said later that the people "were his blood relations, the only blood relations he had."

Jackson had his share of faults. Given to fierce hatreds as well as loyalties, he once killed a fellow Nashville attorney in a duel after an alleged slander of his beloved wife, Rachel. As president, Jackson personally ordered the army to evict the Cherokee Indians from their ancestral homelands in the southern Appalachians; the result was the long trek to Oklahoma, "The Trail of Tears," in which 4,000 of the 15,000 Cherokee perished—one of the greatest blots on our national history. Nevertheless, Jackson made an immense contribution to the vitality of American democracy. Thwarted in his run for the

White House in 1824, he won overwhelmingly in 1828 and 1832. Aristocrats gasped when he admitted the unwashed masses to the White House on his inaugural day and attacked him for instituting a spoils system in government. The moneyed powers of the East bristled at his attacks on the Bank of the United States. But when Southern interests raised the issue of nullification over the tariff, it was Jackson who embodied national power and prevented dissolution of the young Union. The concept of "Jacksonian Democracy" was to dominate American politics until Jackson's death and to form a major ideological base of the modern Democratic party.

Tennessee was the most important state of the mid-South in the decades following Jackson's inauguration. Wealth came by virtue of cotton, wheat, and the steamboat, and Nashville became the permanent capital in 1843. Thousands of restless Tennesseans pushed westward and into the Ohio country, Arkansas, Alabama, Mississippi, and especially Texas. It was Sam Houston— the greatest of Jackson's frontier captains and a former Tennessee congressman and governor—who led the Texas armed forces in their victorious struggle for independence from Mexico. Davy Crockett, Tennessee politician and congressman, later surrounded by fabulous myth about his prowess as a bear and 'coon hunter, marksman, wit, lover, and mighty drinker, was in the band of Texans annihilated by Santa Anna at the Alamo. Houston became the first president of the then-independent Republic of Texas, and as governor ended his public life in a lonely struggle against secession in 1861. His achievements seem even greater than those of the second Tennessean who became president, Jackson-follower James K. Polk (1845–49). But it was during Polk's administration that Texas joined the Union, as did California, thus completing the territorial expansion of the United States across the continent to the Pacific. From being the frontier itself, Tennessee in a remarkably short span of time had become the seedbed of the ever westward-moving American frontier.

The Civil War Century: From Secession to Crumpism

But then Tennessee's geographic position, which had made it such a prominent frontier state, made it an exposed border state and the scene of particularly bloody battles in the Civil War. Slavery divided Tennesseans, and while they finally and reluctantly voted for secession, several East Tennessee counties tried to withdraw from the state and cast their lot with the North.

Back and forth, the war raged across Tennessee soil, some 300 to 700 engagements in all. In 1862 a little church just across the border from Corinth, Miss., lent its name to one of the goriest clashes of the entire war, the Battle of Shiloh. It was to prove a vital turning point for the Union side in the West. No less bloody were Murfreesboro and Chickamauga, when "the pale river of death ran blood." Later, at fog-shrouded Lookout Mountain, "the Battle above the Clouds," the entire Mississippi Valley was assured to the Union.

In 1862 President Lincoln appointed Andrew Johnson—a former Tennessee congressman and governor, later to be vice president and then president —as military governor of the state. In 1865 when Johnson left for Washington, he was replaced as governor by the acid-tongued Knoxville editor and preacher William G. (Parson) Brownlow, whose Radical Republican's urge for vengeance was soon matched on the other side by the violence-prone Ku Klux Klan, formed by Confederate veterans at Pulaski, Tennessee.

There followed thousands of fights and ambushes between Union and Confederate veterans, between communities and even families torn asunder by the passions of the great conflict. And whether Northern or Southern in loyalty, the returning soldiers found a scene of incredible devastation. As they returned to power, the Democrats abolished the public school system and anti-Klan laws. Illiteracy was a terrible problem; even after an 1873 law that laid the basis for a modern school system, it was decades before the legislature appropriated enough money to make it a reality. Tennessee agriculture remained overwhelmingly centered on cotton, and the evils of a one-crop economy were compounded by the sharecropper and crop-lien system— slavery's unattractive successor. There was much talk of industrialization, centered in cities such a Chattanooga, where the floats in an 1878 parade proclaimed, "Cotton Was King," "Iron is King Now," and "Coal is Prime Minister." But the pace of industrialization and economic diversification was slow indeed. Even in 1929, just before the Depression, Tennesseans' per capita income was only $377 a year—barely more than half the national average.

Tennessee politics seemed particularly barren. A patchwork state constitution, ratified in 1870, lasted 83 years and became America's oldest unamended state constitution. Under it, Tennessee languished under rarely interrupted one-party rule for almost a century. For decades, the dead-end issue of Prohibition, popular in one of the most Baptist and Protestant of all American states, seemed to be the biggest question in public life.

In the place of substantive new public policies, Tennessee politicians did expose the voters to some lively antics. One of the most colorful political campaigns of American history was waged in 1886 between two brothers, Democrat Robert L. Taylor and Republican Alfred A. Taylor, running for governor. Traveling together through the state, they often shared the same bed and filled the air with oratory, wit, fiddle music, and occasional debate of issues in dozens of joint appearances. Yet, for the most part it was private Tennessee citizens, not the elected leaders, who made the greatest contributions in the years from the Civil War to World War II. Tennessee still reveres the memory of Alvin C. York, the hunter and blacksmith who came out of the Cumberland mountains to become—in the words of General John J. Pershing—the outstanding citizen-soldier of World War I.

Suffragette Sue Shelton White, another kind of volunteer, played a key role in making Tennessee the state that provided the decisive vote to graft the 19th Amendment, granting women the right to vote, onto the Constitution. In a very different realm, it was a 24-year-old school teacher at Dayton, Tennessee, who lent his name to one of the most important tests of freedom of expression in 20th-century America. The state had passed a law outlawing in the public schools "any theory that denies the story of the Divine as taught in the Bible, . . . teach[ing] instead that man has descended from a lower order of animals." John T. Scopes disobeyed the law, setting the stage for the famed "monkey trial" of 1925. The confrontation of William Jennings Bryan, the "Great Commoner," acting as a special prosecutor in the waning days of his life, pitted against Scopes' defender, Clarence Darrow of the American Civil Liberties Union, became one of the great news events of its day. The jury—"unanimously hot for Genesis," as H.L. Mencken caustically reported from the scene—quickly convicted Scopes, but the conviction was later set aside on a technicality.

The dominant power of Tennessee politics up to World War II was Edward H. Crump, the Democratic boss of Memphis, who provided a quarter century of unparalleled vituperation and political manipulation as he excoriated his political enemies, hand picked senators, congressmen, governors, and legislatures, and used them to implement his own plans for the promotion and development of Memphis. Crump's only real competition in this era was Colonel Luke Lea, commander of the 117th field artillery, regarded by many as a hero second only to York and a major power in Tennessee political life until 1930. In the city itself, Crump provided honest and efficient government by means of a controlled black vote and social terrorism leveled against any and all white opponents.

Fundamentally, prewar Tennessee suffered under what one critic described as an "established pattern of poverty-plenty, segregation-white supremacy, disfranchisement-oligarchy."

Postwar Politics: The Fresh Winds Blow

The first signal of change to come was the famed "G.I. Revolt" of 1946, in McGinn County, East Tennessee. The returning veterans, having battled tryanny abroad, determined not to countenance the vicious, corrupt Democratic politicians who had gouged the local populace and used physical violence and vote fraud to maintain their power. With rifles and dynamite—"as nearly justifiable," John Gunther commented, "as political violence can ever be"—they overthrew the local bosses and restored a semblance of democracy under the Republican banner.

Crump's downfall and collapse as the dictator of Tennessee politics came two years later, in 1948, with the election of returning veteran Gordon Browning, as governor, and liberal Democratic Congressman Estes Kefauver, of Chattanooga, to the Senate. Crump likened Kefauver to a pet coon who "had a foot in the Communist camp." Replied Kefauver; "I may be a coon, but I am not Mr. Crump's pet. The coon has rings on its tail but not in his nose. The coon is all-American. Davy Crockett, Sam Houston, all of our great men wore the familiar, ring-tailed coonskin cap." And so Kefauver, to the delight of Tennesseans, donned a coonskip cap and won the election, becoming as one of his admirers once said, a "self-made lowbrow." He was on his way to building a coalition of liberals, intellectuals, blue-collar workers, and blacks, which would play a substantial role in the postwar era. Outside Tennessee, Kefauver's homespun style was sometimes ridiculed. But it was a legitimate reincarnation of Jacksonian Democracy. Combined with the benefit of a Yale legal degree, it enabled Kefauver to project himself into the presidential arena, to mount his successful investigation of organized crime, and to tackle monopolistic practices in the drug and power industries before his tragic death at age 60, in 1963, just as he was gaining a high degree of seniority.

The 1952 primary saw the defeat of the last big-time politician of the Crump regime, Senator Kenneth Douglas McKellar, who had become the state's first popularly elected senator in 1917 and then spent 36 generally unproductive years in Washington. Through the inexorable workings of the seniority system, "Kay Dee" McKellar rose to immense power as chairman of the Appropriations Committee and President Pro Tempore of the Senate and second in line for the Presidency—a situation, John Gunther wrote in *Inside, U.S.A.*, "that made political philosophers whistle."

The man who defeated McKellar was Albert Gore, and from the 1950s into the 1960s the young Democratic triumvirate of Kefauver, Gore, and Gov. Frank G. Clement rode so high that each man was considered a presidential possibility. The nation got a view of the three Tennesseans at the 1956 Democratic Convention when Clement gave the keynote address, Gore hoped lightning would strike to make him the vice presidential candidate, and Kefauver did end up on the ticket with Adlai Stevenson.

America may never again produce Clement's equal in Bible-thumping politics. Gospel music and quotations from a Bible clutched in his hand were constant features of Clement campaign rallies, likened to the colorful Chautauqua crusades of earlier times. In his keynote speech to the 1956 Democratic convention, Clement assailed the "sordid record" of the Eisenhower-Nixon administration: "the vice-hatchet man slinging slander and spreading half-truths while the top man peers down the green fairways of indifference!" But the speech was more remembered for its painfully overdone "How long, O Lord, how long" line. It prompted the *New York Times*' late Red Smith to write one of the classic newspaper leads of our time: "The young governor of Tennessee, Frank G. Clement, slew the Republican party with the jawbone of an ass here last night. . . ."

Even in Tennessee, Clement was becoming an anachronism. Tennesseans were moving to cities and becoming more sophisticated, the Republicans were undergoing a renaissance, the momentous legislative redistricting case, *Baker* v. *Carr*, was brewing, and the black vote increased and became truly independent. Within a few years Tennessee politics changed practically beyond recognition.

Baker v. *Carr* arose because Tennessee ignored its own constitutional requirement of legislative reapportionment every 10 years, leaving legislative district lines untouched from 1901 onward. Sixty years later, the rural, Democratic counties of Middle and West Tennessee were vastly over-represented while the metropolitan counties had barely half the seats they were entitled to by population. The state supreme court would grant no relief. Going to federal court, the plaintiffs could prove that Tennessee had callously disregarded its own law, that relief was impossible in the state legislature or courts, and that only federal intervention could break the logjam. The Supreme Court so found in its landmark 1962 decision, entering the dreaded "political thicket" because the 14th Amendment guarantees of equal protection of the laws could not otherwise be realized. Within a few short years, the composition of virtually every state legislature in the Union changed.

Tennessee's road toward two-partyism opened in 1952, when Dwight Eisenhower narrowly carried Tennessee over Adlai Stevenson. The Republicans had long occupied a beachhead in East Tennessee, Union territory in the Civil War. Yet on a statewide basis the Republican high command had a legendary "working relationship" with the dominant Democratic factions that exchanged patronage and a few favors for not mounting significant opposition. Eisenhower won, as Senator Baker told us, because Middle and Western Tennesseans were finally willing to cast aside Civil War biases and consider the candidates. Since Ike's initial breakthrough, Republican presidential nominees have carried Tennessee in all elections save 1964 and 1976. In 1966, Baker won his Senate seat, and in 1970 Tennessee became the first state south of the Mason-Dixon line to have a Republican governor (its first in half a century) and two U.S. Senators. The second Republican senator, Bill Brock, lost his seat after one term, to Democrat James Sasser, but the governor's seat has see-sawed, and the Republicans have made enormous gains in the state legislature, although remaining in minority status almost continuously. Congressional seats have also swung back and forth.

Critics charge that the GOP has made its inroads by appealing to the wealthy, the aspirers, and the prejudiced. The core of the statewide organization was not an expansion of the moderate old East Tennessee party, but West and Middle Tennessee followers of Barry Goldwater who streamed into the party in the early '60s. The conservative New Guard brought the hard sell, the grassroots drive, and business-style organization, its vote grounded most heavily in Memphis and its suburbs—an area acutely displeased with the national Democratic party's advocacy for blacks.

The most popular Republican in the state, however, remained Howard Baker, Jr., a true son of the East Tennessee hills and a man who has melded moderate economic conservatism with a generally liberal stand on race and women's rights. Lamar Alexander, elected governor in 1978, and reelected in 1982, was a thoughtful Republican moderate and a leader on federalism reform within the National Governors Association.

Tennessee's Democrats made a gradual comeback in the 1970s and early '80s but suffered a monumental embarrassment when their governor, Ray Blanton, a few days before leaving office in early 1979 granted clemency to 52 convicts, including a political friend's son, who had been convicted of murder. The Democrats were forced to ask Alexander to take the oath of office a few days early. There were charges that Blanton had been selling paroles, but he and several aides were initially convicted of the more mundane crime of extortion and conspiracy in selling liquor licenses.

Tennesseans in Washington

In 1980, when the Republicans took control of the Senate, high honor came to Tennessee with the selection of its senior senator, Howard Baker, Jr., as majority leader—a pinnacle of power never achieved, ironically, by Baker's father-in-law, Senator Everett McKinley Dirksen of Illinois.

The Watergate hearings of 1973 and his theme question of "What did the President know, and when did he know it?" made Baker a national figure. But throughout his Senate career, starting in 1967, Baker demonstrated skills as a mediator and team player, a man who could conceptualize problems and find the more workable solutions for them. He became one of those senators whose voting record reflects his own carefully crafted positions rather than a moderate or conservative image; in many people's eyes the only blemish on Baker's record was his support of the monstrously expensive Clinch River breeder reactor, predicted to produce 4,500 jobs in Tennessee. Baker was not a pioneer in public policy, but showed a remarkable ability to get controversial issues —including key initiatives, from the Reagan budget to extension of the Voting Rights Act,—through the Senate. Baker announced he would not run for reelection in 1984, stimulating speculation that he might seek the presidency.

Tennessee's other senate seat was won in 1976 by Democrat James Sasser, who, in his first term, emphasized the stamping out of fraud and abuse. Sasser took the seat by defeating Brock, the candy heir, who had made little mark in one term as a senator but, went on to great success as the national Republican party chairman. Brock, in turn, in 1970 had defeated Democrat Albert Gore, a spunky liberal who exposed the Dixon-Yates private power contract of the Eisenhower years, refused to take the Southern position on school desegregation, stood up for TVA and the public power cause, and fought the Vietnam War at every turn.

The Gore name was not gone from Washington for long. Albert Gore, Jr., then 28, won a House seat from rural Middle Tennessee in 1976. Harvard graduate, Vietnam War vet (unlike so many college graduates of that era), young Gore easily became the most activist and interesting member of the Tennessee delegation, using his committee slots to conduct hearings on oil-pricing fraud, to push alternative fuels and solar energy, to investigate health issues and abandoned hazardous chemical waste dumps, and to expose a cartel of uranium producers and exporters. Gore developed his own homespun populism, using town hall meetings and abjuring polls to keep track of the public pulse, demonstrating that the national population shift toward the South and rural areas does not mean an automatic political shift toward conservatism.

Tennessee Economy and Government

Tennessee has every reason to prosper. The state has immense reserves of coal, millions of acres of productive forests, and a mighty river system, offering ample water for industry and cheap barge transportation. TVA's vast system of dams and steam plants offered—at least until recently—some of America's most rock-bottom energy prices. Tennessee's balanced economy is a regional rarity: diversified agriculture, the greatest mix of industries in the Southeast, and contrasting specialties, ranging from banking to insurance to tourism to country music. Factories added since World War II have ranged from chemicals, nylons, tires, leather, and glass to electronic equipment, machinery, aluminum, furniture, and trucks. Such blue chip firms as DuPont, Ford, and Alcoa have flooded in, and at Smyrna, a little town in the Nashville orbit, the Nissan Motor Company in the early 1980s opened its first U.S. factory, bringing along the Japanese robots and participatory management techniques.

There are some flies in the ointment. Tennesseeans' per capita income has risen briskly, but by 1980 there were still only six states with lower levels. Average factory wages are low, dragged down by notoriously low-paying garment and textile plants, even though Tennessee has tolerated labor unions somewhat more than have its Southeast neighbors. The state is surely not immune to recessions, though there's often one saving grace: many Tennesseans have continued to live on their small farms and can hunker down until the economy improves.

Businesses are courted in Tennessee with high quality worker training programs in which the industrialists, rather than educators, are in control. But business, because of the strong populist tradition, has to pay rather hefty taxes: 41 percent of Tennessee's state-local taxes, one of the nation's highest tax shares for businesses. Also unfairly burdened are Tennessee's poor people because of the state's high reliance on the sales tax. A broad-based income tax, which would introduce more equity and relieve both situations, has been furiously opposed, but, we were told, is gaining support.

Full racial justice and harmony are an elusive goal in Tennessee. Tennessee's black people remain the distinctive exception to the state's otherwise unvaried complexion of intermarried strands of Scotch, Irish, English, German, Dutch, and French stock. Interestingly, while the number of blacks has climbed steadily over the years, even greater growth among whites has steadily reduced the black share, from an 1880 peak of 26 percent to 15.8 percent (725,949) in 1980. The traces of the plantation system are still to be found in the heavy concentrations of black folk in rural counties of West (and to some degree Middle) Tennessee, although most black Tennesseans now live in cities, especially Memphis.

Tennessee rarely resorted to outright intimidation of blacks to prevent them from voting, but for decades the poll tax served as a severe depressant on black political participation. And legal segregation—in schools, trains, buses, restaurants and hotels, even marriage relations—afflicted Tennessee blacks throughout the Civil War century. Only a few localities had ended Jim Crow voluntarily when the federal government, in the postwar era, finally stopped the practice. Not until 1952, and then as a result of litigation, were blacks finally admitted to the University of Tennessee at Knoxville or voluntarily to Vanderbilt and other private universities.

School segregation problems have bedevilled the state, ever since racial agitators touched off violence at the little East Tennessee city of Clinton as it tried to integrate peacefully in 1956. By the '70s the big cities were in a terrible furor as the federal courts tried large-scale busing to achieve integration. Even in the early 1980s black Tennesseans suffered from housing segregation. But the most vicious tensions of all seemed to exist at the 19th- century Bushy Mountain State Penitentiary at Petros, dank and overcrowded and described by a Nashville lawyer as "walking into the mouth of hell." Here James Earl Ray, convicted killer of Martin Luther King, Jr., was stabbed by black prisoners before being moved to protective custody in Nashville. To some of the white inmates, Ray was considered a folk hero. The prisoners divided into racial gangs; at night guards could hear the sound of rival gangs using anything metal—guitar strings to carbide jewelers' chains—trying to cut themselves out of their cells.

East Tennessee, the TVA, Knoxville, and Chattanooga

East Tennessee is a land of high mountains, heavily forested foothills, and narrow valleys, an area as remote from major cities as this continent has known. The settlers built their log cabins deep in the ridges when Tennessee was not yet named; some of those enclaves remained virtually untouched by civilization for a century and more. Indeed, to this day strains of Elizabethan English and ballads carried from the Old World can still be heard in these mysteriously distant hills. East Tennesseans were traditionally the most stubbornly individualistic and reserved of peoples, often labeled hillbillies and the butt of malicious jokes and stories. But mostly they were unknown, described by an early 20th-century scholar as "ghettoed in the midst of a civilization that is as aloof from them as if it existed . . . on another planet." The mountaineers' isolation began to fade with the founding of the Great Smoky Mountains Park, the TVA's resettlement of bottomland farmers, World War II and Oak Ridge with its nuclear laboratories and scientific community, and finally radio and television. But some old folkways linger on: dulcimers of cherry wood are still fashioned by hand, sorghum and molasses are still produced by ancestral methods, and as recently as 1970, we heard of East Tennessee mountaineers who totally disbelieved the news of man's space flights to the moon.

The Tennessee Valley Authority, America's great experiment in coordinated development of a natural region, was born to controversy in the first blush of the New Deal as private business charged that it would lean the nation toward socialism. Ironically, it was not a mid-South senator but rather the prairie populist Senator William George Norris, of Nebraska, a bitter enemy of monopolies and vested private interests whose vision first embraced what the Tennessee Valley might be. When FDR became president, Norris convinced him to set up the TVA with the broadest conceivable charter—an authority that would not only produce low-cost electricity but be responsible for flood control, soil conservation, reforestation, industrial diversification, improved navigation and demonstration farming with cheap fertilizer. Since private industry often sought to strangle TVA, its political road was often rough. As TVA got bigger, it lost some of its innovative quality and became, critics said, "one more big aggrandizing utility," building huge coal-fired plants, resisting air pollution measures, and despoiling the environment through its strip-mining. It embarked on the nation's largest nuclear power construction program, an idea it gave up even more reluctantly than most private utilities when Three Mile Island raised doubts about the safety and fiscal practicality of nuclear plants. TVA did enjoy a renewed flurry of originality in the late 1970s, when David S. Freeman, the chairman appointed by President Carter, questioned the authority's backing of the Clinch River nuclear breeder reactor and the controversial Tellico Dam (of snail darter fame) and tried to return TVA to its original role of comprehensive developer. During the same era, however, TVA consumers were more concerned about fast rising power rates, a phenomenon new to them and due, they charged, to TVA's costly expansions. For outsiders the situation evoked crocodile tears at best; in the mid 1960s TVA customers paid about a penny a kilowatt hour, less than half the national rate; by 1981 they were paying 4.61 cents—yet still only 79 percent of the national average. Even many of its critics, however, had come to acknowledge TVA's great early basic accomplishments: damming the 1,000 mile turbulent river and bringing fertilizer to a desolated and hopeless land and electricity to homes still mired in the kerosene era. "TVA took over the valley when it was down to bedrock," Harry M. Caudill has written, "and it wasn't a decade after TVA started that the valley of the Tennessee was the showplace of the nation."

East Tennessee has the Great Smokies, snow-covered in winter, offering spectacular shows of flowering shrubs and trees in springtime and changing leaves in autumn, then the Great Valley of East Tennessee, running clear from Virginia to Alabama and housing most of the region's people and industries, and finally (moving westward) the Cumberland Mountains, spotted with fertile farmlands, rich in coal deposits. Oak Ridge surely offers a premier study of the sudden intrusion of an advanced scientific-technological community into a pristine, isolated agrarian society. It began with the secret World War II project to build the atomic bomb. Government agents were looking for a place to produce uranium 235 and finally settled on a crest known as Black Oak Ridge—a territory of sparse settlement and plenty of rainfall and TVA-produced power. The terrain of ridges and valleys, they thought, would provide natural buffers between several plants "if anything went wrong." In 1945, with the dropping of the atomic bomb over Japan, the secret of what had been happening at Oak Ridge became known to the world. In 1949 came the historic day when Oak Ridge was "opened" to the world. The Oak Ridge National Laboratory has since remained one of the world's largest and most important nuclear research facilities. After anthropologist Margaret Mead visited Oak Ridge and castigated the scientists for not getting involved with their mountain neighbors, the two worlds did begin to relate better than they had.

By the early 1980s the focus of the nuclear research had switched to the fast breeder reactor, to be built on the Clinch River some 30 miles from Knoxville. Proponents said the fast breeder reactor was the only means by which the U.S. could guarantee itself an unlimited supply of domestic nuclear fuel; opponents said it was not only one of the most outrageously expensive projects in the annals of the American republic but also a dangerous, complex project that could well end in abject failure. Politics—that is, Senator Baker's clout—kept it alive in times of soaring national budget deficits.

Knoxville, East Tennessee's lead city (pop. 183,139), has had unhappy experiences with outside commentators: John Gunther, in *Inside U.S.A.*, called it "the ugliest city I ever saw in America," an appellation that still rankles in this Tennessee River town of old red brick factories and office buildings. But Gunther's jab helped jolt Knoxville into renovation of the center city, with a handsome mall and shopping area and plans for a new coliseum. The University of Tennessee, which has its headquarters there, shucked its old reputation as a football college and scored advances in physical plant and intellectual quality. The town sought to be East Tennessee's economic nerve center, reducing its old industrial focus on textiles and iron. And in 1982, in an act of *chutzpah* that startled Tennessee and the nation alike, it staged a World's Fair based on an energy theme, drawing exhibits from many nations and crowds well beyond expectations. Over the postwar years, however, the downtown banks and mercantile interests proved themselves too lethargic to make the center city the focus of Knoxville's really important growth. That began some 10 miles to the west, where West Town Mall, an ultramodern, multimillion-dollar office building and shopping center complex was built.

Chattanooga (pop. 169,565) got its first big boost from ex-Union soldiers and industrialists who hoped to make the town a Pittsburgh of the South. It remains, first and last, a heavy industry town with labor unions unusually strong for the South. Yet to its consternation, Chattanooga failed to share in the Sunbelt expansionism of the '60s and '70s. Race problems have plagued the town: a fierce controversy over school busing, a 1971 riot that brought death for one black and scores of injuries, firebombing of several businesses after an all-white jury in 1980 acquitted two Ku Klux Klan members in the shotgun wounding of four black women. Increasingly in the early '80s, however, business and political leaders seemed intent on city facelifting and economic diversification to give Chattanooga a better image—and a better competitive stance.

Middle Tennessee and Nashville

Middle Tennessee, with its Nashville, has progressed handsomely as the governmental and financial center of a progressing state, far removed from Gunther's description as "mint-julep, big-plantation, old-Southern aristocracy" territory. This Grand Division of the state is hemmed in by the looping Tennessee River on both its eastern and western flanks. Most of it is gently rolling Bluegrass country; Tennessee has more Bluegrass territory than Kentucky and produces some of America's finest blooded horses. This is also prime tobacco country. The region has attracted considerable light, clean industry in recent years; its income levels exceed those of East or West Tennessee.

Nashville enjoys a string of assets, making it one of the Border South's most vibrant and promising cities. It is Tennessee's state capital and a sufficiently important center of higher education, the arts, trade, and finance that the slogans "Athens of the South" and "Wall Street of the South" cannot be dismissed as mere hyperbole. The inner city has been revamping its tired old physical plant through sweeping urban renewal. There is a rich historic tradition: one can visit, for example, Andrew Jackson's lovely home, the Hermitage, restored and furnished almost exactly as it was when Old Hickory lived there. Then there is the cash-register throb of the "Nashville sound."

Nashville's metropolitan government, formed in 1963 when Nashville merged with surrounding Davidson County, has won deserved acclaim. What existed before was a classic example of fiscal and legal imbalance in urban America: a city government bearing practically full responsibility for facilities used by all metropolitan citizens, including airport, library, hospitals, and parks, combined with expensive duplication of services and constant buck-passing between city and county. Consolidation might not have succeeded had Nashville not begun such aggressive annexations that thousands of suburbanities found themselves paying city taxes without accompanying municipal services. Consolidation did not, as proponents promised, provide less expensive government. But it did slow down the growth in taxes and save money in combined administration of the schools and the sewer and water districts. The Metro government was able to set aside hundreds of acres for parks and open space outside the old city borders before the subdividers and developers acquired all the vacant land. Tax equities were achieved by separate inner-city and outlying taxing districts, depending on the extent of services rendered. And what seemed like a rather unwieldy 40-person council, with 35 members elected from separate districts, actually provided sensitivity of representation, including several seats for center-city blacks, in the big combined jurisdiction (pop. 455,651).

Traditionally a trade and finance center of the Middle South, Nashville developed a number of extremely wealthy families who fostered insurance companies of national renown (National Life and others) and big banks that lent money in a generally capital-scarce region. "This is an old son-in-law town in which concentrations of wealth, power, and influence have come down through families," a chamber of commerce official told us. By the early 1980s, the major Nashville banks and insurance companies were said to control over $11 billion in capital, operating internationally as well as regionally. But the sense of local control departed when NLT Inc., the holding company that owned National Life, the Grand Ole Opry, and radio station WSM, was bought by American General Corporation of Houston.

Nashville boasts a huge printing industry and a whole nexus of religious-oriented activities creating a so-called Protestant Vatican. Here are headquarters of the big, powerful Southern Baptist Convention and its Board of Publications, the Board of Education of the Methodist Church and the Methodist Publishing House, the central offices of the Gideons, and the archives and library of the Disciples of Christ. The ultrafundamentalist and often intolerant Church of Christ treats Nashville as its little Jerusalem. Yet even if the famed Southern Bible Belt seam centered in Nashville, the conservative Protestant churches have not controlled the community mores. Nashville is actually the most progressive of Tennessee cities. It has a large contingent of enlightened, progressive businessmen. The religious community is not as monolithically conservative as it might appear: there are, for example, strong liberal elements among the Methodists and socially attuned Roman Catholic and Episcopal dioceses. Then there is the influence of the state labor movement, which has its headquarters in Nashville. To all of this one must add two other vital factors: Nashville's feudin' newspapers and its large university community.

Nashville's two dailies, the *Tennessean* and the *Banner*, have saved Nashville from the monotony of a single viewpoint, which deadens so many cities' public debate. The two papers were long bastions of personal journalism, the *Tennessean* owned by the Evans family and the *Banner* by the Stahlmans. The Stahlmans were supporters of old Boss Crump and Southern Conservatism; the Evans family detested Crump and fought for liberal ideas. The Evans family hired John Siegenthaler, a man out of a liberal Catholic background and Kennedy connections, as the *Tennessean*'s editor and made him publisher in 1972.* That same year, the *Banner* was sold to the Gannett chain, but in 1979 Gannett staged a remarkable switch by selling the *Banner* to a local group and then turning around to purchase the more widely circulated *Tennessean*. Nashville's century-old tradition in higher education embraces Vanderbilt, the Southland's first institution with an academic standard comparable to that of the better northern universities; Fisk, a premier university of black learning; and Meharry Medical College, America's only privately sponsored, predominantly black medical school, indispensable trainer of half of America's black physicians and dentists and a pioneer in community medicine.

Finally we come to Nashville's most renowned export: country music. For all the publicity attending "Nashville Sound," country music is not central to the city's economy. Many top country and western performers are found there, along with "Record Row" and its publishing houses, talent agencies,

*In 1982, when Gannett launched its national newspaper, *U.S.A. Today*, Siegenthaler was chosen as editor.

and recording studios. But many of the firms are owned by huge New York or Los Angeles-based companies. What country music has done for Nashville, J. Dewey Daane, vice chairman of the Tennessee Valley Bancorporation, told us, is "to give it a name and an identity."

"Country" emerged as a music form in the 1920s, straight from the heart of the Southern mountains, out of the soul of the common people and their travail and loves and everyday life, from roots of English ballads brought by early settlers, out of the mountaineers' hoedowns, jigs, reels, and hearthside myths. Gospel airs played a large role in early country music—"hillbilly music," as people called it then; in fact, Nashville's funky and famous Ryman Auditorium, so long the home of the Grand Ole Opry, was built in the 1890s as the Union Gospel Tabernacle. Many of the thousands who have gone to Nashville to hear the Opry have participated in all-night singings of Gospel hymns too. To the country music airs drifting out of the hills were added French Cajun moods from Louisiana; out of Memphis and New Orleans came the spiritual and blues and rhythm influence of the American Negro. Yet until recently, country music generally pretended to be the exclusive property of Southern whites, and the white working classes at that: rooted in rural conservatism ("You've got to have smelled mule manure before you can sing hillbilly," said Hank Williams, a revered early country star), blatantly patriotic, distrustful of wealthy city folks and intellectuals, fundamentalist but loving sweet Jesus and tolerant (as one observer put it) of "homegrown vices like boozing and philandering when accompanied by a footnote that they don't come free."

Critics lamented the "urbanization" of country music, but still the deep-gut appeal came through in many country stars. Johnny Cash still reflected legitimately the hard times he knew growing up in an Arkansas cotton patch. As Roy Acuff, veteran and king of the Opry, said, "Each of us had a type of cry in our voice." That cry still came through loud and clear in Loretta Lynn, married at 13 and a grandmother at 28, telling the absolute truth when she sang about her Kentucky roots: *Well, I was born a coal miner's daughter/In a cabin on a hill in Butcher Holler.* Loretta never made it beyond the eighth grade, but up in that bleak hollow she acquired a warmth and strength radiating through every word she sang.

Country music has unquestionably broadened. In 1967, Charlie Pride, part African, part Caucasian, part Indian, and former cotton picker from Sledge, Mississippi, gave his first Opry performance and in the 1970s became one of the biggest stars. In 1970, the Country Music Association gave Kris Kristofferson, the long-haired, pot-smoking hippie and former Rhodes Scholar, the Song of the Year award. During the '70s and into the '80s, country music became so popular with the American middle class that the Grand Ole Opry found its most famous performers lured away by lucrative movie and concert tour offers.

A visitor in search of the soul of the Border South could do no better than spend a Saturday night at the Grand Ole Opry. There are the excited crowds, likely to have heard Opry on the radio for years (it has been a Saturday show since Nashville's WSM broadcast the first program in 1925). Many will have traveled hundreds of miles one way to see the performers—who know how to please, stepping out in everything from iridescent blues and purples to subdued Western. The only disappointment is that the Opry is no longer at the downtown Ryman Auditorium with its churchlike wooden pews, thick with the aroma of sweat and Juicy Fruit and tobacco renewed for hundreds of Saturday nights. Since 1974 the Opry has had a new "home" as part of a new amusement park six miles from the Nashville Airport, the Disneyland of country music called "Opryland, U.S.A." The whole park is clean as a whistle and militantly red-white-and-blue Main Street America. It implicitly rejects country's themes of hard times, beer joints, prisons, and human frailty. Perhaps it is a metaphor for the fans' economic well-being of these later years. But the lyrics remain vintage Grand Old Opry: cheatin' women, disappointment, and travail.

West Tennessee and Memphis

Finally, we come to West Tennessee, bordered on the east by the northerly flowing Tennessee, on the west by the great Mississippi. Essentially a flat alluvial plain, spotted with rich valleys and black bottoms, this is Tennessee's most productive agricultural area, once overwhelmingly dedicated to King Cotton, now strong into soybeans and winter wheat. This region is in many ways an extension of Mississippi's Delta region, of which the great river port of Memphis is the real capital. Like the Delta, West Tennessee has a big black population: about one-third of the total. And in a style typical of the Deep South, it has a lot of apparel plants with heavier industries intruding in later years. Outside of Memphis, the only city of any size is Jackson, with some 49,000 people. West Tennessee harbors some egregious rural poverty and a large black ghetto population in Memphis. The terrible conditions in rural West Tennessee early in the 1930s inspired Myles Horton, a local boy-turned-disciple of the radical reformer Reinhold Niebuhr, to start the Highlander Center, which organized laborers and started the "citizenship schools," which helped blacks throughout the South pass literacy tests and gain voting power. Highlander lives on, under younger leaders who have taken up more complex issues such as land ownership and payment of taxes by absentee coal company landlords.

Standing on the Chickasaw Bluffs by the Father of Waters, heavily parked and verdant, one sees how Memphis remains a great port city, the true capital of the Mississippi Delta region and a great land area extending over West Tennessee and eastern Arkansas. Memphis' quintessential Southernhood was etched by the generations of folk from the Delta and other Dixie farmlands who made it their capital and city of migration. Yet Southern as it is, Memphis also has a hint of the West: the atmosphere of those vast glazed skies, the bustle, the raw energy.

For a while in the 1970s, Memphis almost lost its soul: the great Peabody

Hotel, sold and shuttered until civic leaders rightly determined it must be refurbished and returned to life, which it was. So Delta writer David L. Cohn's description of the Peabody—"the Paris Ritz, the Cairo Shepheard's, the London Savoy" of the Mississippi Delta—is once again true. "The Mississippi Delta begins in the lobby of the Peabody Hotel in Memphis and ends on Catfish Row in Vicksburg," Cohn wrote in some of the most memorable lines of Southern literature, continuing: "If you stand near its fountain in the middle of the lobby, where ducks waddle and turtles drowse, ultimately you will see everybody who is anybody in the Delta and many who are on the make." In Memphis, Cohn wrote, "the stern [Delta] business man shows the world his other soulside. . . . Here he goes in search of frail women, human, all too human, who live in houses with shades perpetually drawn, or he stumbles perhaps with a sudden gasp of delight upon some peripatetic beauty strolling sloe-eyed and lost in the soft darkness of the hotel mezzanine. Sin, a hydra-headed monster at home, becomes in Memphis a white dove cooing in the shade of tall cathedral columns." Sin or not, the ducks returned with the reopening; we have watched them at 5 in the afternoon perform a grand retreat, marching down from the fountain, across a red carpet to the elevators and their upstairs "quarters." And the Peabody lobby remains one of the world's most gracefully designed.

Memphis has not abandoned its agrarian base; it is still a cotton center and America's largest hardwood market. But its principal modern role is as the distribution center for a territory from the Mississippi Delta to the "bootheel" of Missouri. Here is home base of a dazzling entrepreneurial success, Federal Express, not to mention Holiday Inn, that incredibly successful chain of repetitious motels whose ubiqutious, eye-abusing signs now present themselves in every state and around the globe. By the early 1980s Holiday Inn had finally become well known enough to dare testing less conspicuous signs. Memphis industry has diversified into such areas as chemicals, pharmaceuticals, and electronic equipment.

Modern Memphis has a lively world of "high" culture, sparked by a fine art gallery and school, symphony and opera, and several local theater groups. Far better known nationally are the offbeat cultural activities in this city anxious to mimic Nashville as a major music and recording center. The "Memphis Sound" blends the blues—literally invented on Beale Street by the revered W.C. Handy—with black soul and rock and roll. Memphis was home of the fabulously successful Elvis Presley, first white singer to adopt the rhythm and blues style that emerged from the postwar black ghetto. The Presley image began to disintegrate after his death in 1977 when his heavy use of drugs was revealed. But the executors of his estate have opened to the public "Graceland," the mansion named for his mother, and fans line up to visit the house with its gold leaf piano, and an incredible room filled with chairs whose arms are shaped like alligators—a testament to the poor taste that vast sums of money can buy. The closest successor to Presley's mantle, Memphis-based Jerry Lee Lewis, has also suffered a host of personal problems.

Boss Crump's fabled machine fell from power in 1959. As his Democratic party fragmented, the Republicans, long a fringe black organization, changed to a conservative white organization, and Memphis became a two-party town. In 1968, the five-commissioner model that had been a mainstay of Crump power was replaced by a strong mayoral form of government, with a city council large enough to include a real cross-section of the community. The very process of gathering support for the new mayor-council government was healthy because business, the two parties, blacks, the newspapers, religious leaders, and women's groups had to work together for the first time in living memory. But just as Memphis was taking these forward steps, the cataclysm of the assassination of Martin Luther King, Jr., intruded on the scene.

In retrospect, a racial conflagration may have been well-nigh inevitable. Here was a city that had accepted repeated tides of immigrants—displaced white tenant farmers and black plantation hands. In the 1890s Memphis had registered so many public lynchings that it acquired an international reputation for white barbarity. In Crump's Memphis, epitome of the urban plantation, all but a handful of blacks were consigned to the most menial or unskilled work. What better fit that description than garbage collection? And even the garbage collectors were segregated by race. When black workers were sent home with two hours' pay and white men were kept for a full day's work in early 1968, 1,375 workers, affiliated with the small and officially unrecognized Local 1733 of the American Federation of State, County, and Municipal Employees walked off their jobs. The racist mayor of the time, Henry Loeb, stonily refused recognition of the union. Then came the marches through the streets to which King lent his presence and prestige. And at 6:01 P.M. on April 4, a bullet severed his spinal cord as he stood on the balcony of the Lorraine Motel. Whether King's convicted killer, James Earl Ray, was a paid agent or a race-crazed man acting alone, we may never know. Twelve days after King's death Memphis did recognize Local 1733, inspiring similar successful bids for recognition in other cities.

But Memphis failed to follow Dallas' model (after JFK's assassination) of installing an outstanding mayor to bind up the wounds. Loeb was succeeded by Wyeth Chandler, smart administrator, small of vision, and deeply prejudiced on matters racial. Chandler continued to win reelection (finally resigning in 1982 to accept a judgeship) even though by 1980 the black percentage climbed to 46.7 percent of the city's 646,356 people. Beginning in 1974, the black portions of Memphis did elect a black member of Congress, Harold E. Ford, member of a family that owns a funeral home; some analysts have said they are trying to develop Crump-like power. Broad-scale busing to desegregate the schools came with remarkable calm in January 1973. But the price of desegregation was a mushrooming of church-sponsored private schools for whites. By the early 1980s the public schools were about three-quarters black, and the school board, with the reluctant support of some blacks, began to cut back busing and reestablish neighborhood schools in an effort to win broader-based support of the school system.

Impressive labor solidarity developed in the Memphis of the '70s, although police and firefighters were organized separately from other city employees.

In 1978, the police and firefighters went on strike for six days before a new contract was signed. The same police force that had inflicted violence on the sanitation, clerical, and other public workers in demonstrations a decade earlier was now asking Memphis' other public and private labor unions for support. The effort to improve the lot of the working man and woman became truly biracial.

Memphis paid a price, however, for its social chaos, progressing so slowly economically that some called it "the dark spot in the Sunbelt." Bank deposits and investment decisions flowed to Nashville, whose metropolitan area grew 21.6 percent in the '70s while the Memphis area grew only 9.4 percent. The effects of Memphis' slow pace were felt throughout the Mississippi Delta, whose black youth were forced to go to faraway Texas cities to seek jobs. In 1980, however, a Memphis Jobs Conference began, mixing top local business leaders with neighborhood folk to lay strategy for the city's economic future. (The meetings, amazingly, were among the most "salt and pepper"—totally integrated—that we have seen anywhere in America.) William Morris, mayor of Shelby County, which encompasses Memphis, was trying to bridge the city's racial chasm, improve downtown design, and compensate for Chandler's civic indolence. The Cotton Row historic district and buildings throughout the inner city, largely deserted until the mid-'70s, were being taken over by young professionals for both homes and offices. After years of destructive renewal and frustrated redevelopment plans, the historic old Beale Street appeared ready to be reborn as an entertainment-restaurant center. And Mud Island, a new $62 million river park linked to center city by a monorail, opened to the public. It featured an ingenious five-block-long scale model of the Mississippi's course all the way from Cairo, Ill., to New Orleans, "flowing" with 1.2 million gallons of water.

And in the beleaguered inner-city Greenlaw area we found the Marist Sister Elizabeth Bonia talking enthusiastically about courting local resources to give poor black people a real stake in their own community. Since her mid-1970s arrival (fresh from assignment in a Jamaican leper colony), Sister Elizabeth had helped train neighborhood youths in building skills, opened congregate homes for the elderly, set up block clubs to teach every skill from sewing draperies to refinishing furniture, and screened low-income families for a "sweat equity" housing project in which the families received credit for each hour they put in on their own or someone else's house. Volunteer time and funds she sought in the greater Memphis community, too. Even Memphis' sometimes hard-hearted establishment was not able to resist her appeals: a model of inspired self-help and caring so different from Memphis' familiar national image of discrimination and confrontation.

KENTUCKY

Diverse, Genteel, and Violent

HORSES, COAL, BOURBON WHISKEY, BORDERLAND, a state of Ohio River ports sharing the industry of the Midwest and the fields of tobacco beckoning Southward, a land marked both by Bluegrass gentility and mountaineer feudin' and destitution—Kentucky has always meant many things to America.

In the 18th and 19th centuries, Kentucky was the Golden West of its time, and its Henry Clay was one of the great American statesmen. What is striking about modern Kentucky is how low the state's profile has become. The agrarian stamp on Kentucky society is still distinguishable; fewer Kentuckians live in metropolitan areas than in most states—just 21 percent in Greater Louisville and 7 percent in the Kentucky suburbs of Cincinnati, Ohio. Kentucky has attracted less industry than has either Mississippi or Arkansas; and only one small city, Lexington, has boomed. Kentucky's population grew 13.7 percent in the 1970s, to 3,661,433, slightly higher than the national average of 11.4 percent. The statewide figures hid the fact that the strongest growth was in Appalachian Eastern Kentucky, where a coal boom brought back Kentuckians who were forced to leave a generation ago when there was no work. Indeed, East Kentuckians continued to return home in the 1980—even when the coal boom had gone bust. The jobs in Detroit and other Northern cities had given way; all many had left was a small piece of Kentucky, or perhaps old familial roots there.

Kentucky is a curiously advanced and retarded, rich and poor, exquisite and environmentally ravaged state. The contrasts are everywhere to be seen. Handsome thoroughbreds graze on the luxuriant fields of the Bluegrass while not far to the east life at subsistence levels is eked out in the poverty-stricken hollows of Appalachia. Coal, manufacturing, distilling, horse raising, and tourism all produce great wealth in Kentucky, but the state's per capita income was only $7,613 in 1980, 46th among the states and down from its position of 41st in the early 1970s. Indications were that the relative shortage of professional and other while-collar employment would mean very little increase for the foreseeable future.

Kentucky politics, according to Michael Barone in *The Almanac of American Politics*, are "caught in some kind of time warp" with political divisions still based on splits caused by the Civil War. Kentucky's vivid politics, concerned more with style than substance, were long believed to be a fruit of the state's isolation, its poverty, and its low levels of education. Television has supposedly broadened people's horizons while a measure of affluence has cut down the importance of patronage jobs. But the governorship of Kentucky

Fried Chicken magnate John Y. Brown, Jr., a man showered with publicity for his own business acumen and his ex-Miss America–TV sportscaster wife, Phyllis George, suggested that Kentucky's traditional personality politics had only been intensified by the new media politics.

Kentucky has a fantastic history and tradition. In the 1760s and '70s, as Daniel Boone and the other early explorer-settlers penetrated the barrier of the Appalachians, there was an American myth that Kentucky was the "Eden of the West." Through the last years of the 18th century and the first of the 19th, Kentucky was the booming Golden West, the California of its day. In 1792, when its divorce from Virginia was final and Congress admitted it as the first state west of the Alleghenies, the territory held 74,000 people. By 1820 that figure had swelled to 564,000—larger than 5 of the original 13 states— representing almost 6 percent of the population of the United States, a figure the state never again equaled. (In 1980 the figure was 1.6 percent.)

From the early 19th century up to and through the Civil War, Kentucky played a vital role in national affairs. The state's leading national figure from the early 1800s to his death in 1852 was Henry Clay, who served as United States Senator, Speaker of the House, Secretary of State, and several times actual or potential candidate for the presidency. Clay fought for internal improvements to build the young nation and through his early leadership of the Whigs contributed to the development of the nation's two-party system. Most important of all, he moved heaven and earth to compromise on the issue of slavery that threatened to tear the fledgling nation apart. Clay might have been able to win the presidency, as Andrew Jackson did, had he not become so identified with the moneyed upper class of his time.

Legion were the Kentuckians, great and obscure, whose adventuring spirit took them to Ohio, to the Indiana, Illinois, and Missouri territories, and on to the far West, while Kentucky itself was still green behind the ears. Even Daniel Boone paddled on to a new home in Missouri. And as Americans were later to discover, two births of profound significance took place, less than a year apart, on Kentucky frontier farms. Abraham Lincoln was born to Tom Lincoln and his young wife, Nancy Hanks, in a simple log cabin on Sinking Spring farm, on the waters of the Nolin River, in 1809. Jefferson Davis, the tenth child of Samuel Davis, an emigrant from Georgia, was born in a fertile valley of the Pennyroyal section. While the future Union and Confederate presidents were still small boys, the Lincolns moved to Indiana and eventually to Illinois, the Davises downriver to the rich cotton lands of Mississippi.

The Civil War not only brought Kentucky's golden era to an abrupt halt but left a bitter legacy of violence, which persists there to this day. It is difficult to think of another state in which pro- and antislavery sentiment, loyalty to the Union, and affection for the South were so exquisitely balanced. Here was a state settled chiefly by Southerners, yet a place where the fabric of society, and the economic situation of the people, was much closer to that of the North. Kentucky was to become both a hotbed of abolitionist sentiment and a chief market place for slaves to be used in the new cotton states to the south. When the war began, Kentucky officially declared its neutrality. But the

Confederacy blockaded the Mississippi River with a mile-long chain and seized the Cumberland Gap, a site considered the Gibraltar of the West. When the Confederates refused to withdraw, the Kentucky legislature voted to align the state with the Union.

In terms of physical devastation, Kentucky suffered relatively little in the Civil War. But the state was to pay a gruesome price for this fratricidal conflict. Young hotheads of the Bluegrass and Purchase areas, understanding little of the fundamental issues, marched off to join the Confederacy. Mountain boys from eastern Kentucky, used to physical hardships, bored with the monotony of life in the intermontane fastness, tended to sign up for the Union Army. The overwhelming fact was the division of every area between Southern and Northern allegiance. Cousins divided and so, quite often, did fathers, sons, and brothers. As the casualty reports came back from the bloody battlefields of Virginia, and as raids and brigandage began to spread across the Kentucky countryside, differences hardened into bitter hatreds. The ill-regulated Kentucky Home Guards included many men willing to settle old grudges and open new feuds under the guise of public authority.

The recorded costs of the war were grave enough: 76,000 Kentuckians sent to fight on the Union side, 26,000 to the Confederacy, Kentuckians killing each other from Shiloh to Sherman's last march. Ten thousand died in battle, another 20,000 of disease and exposure. Approximately half the Kentuckians who reached manhood between 1850 and 1860 were either destroyed or disabled by war. Memories of the conflict would lead to generations of bloodshed, of assassination, of family feuds. The storied battles of the Kentucky McCoys and West Virginia Hatfields had their origin in the Civil War. There were less familiar but equally bloody struggles between other families. Such feuds, moreover, could not be dismissed as the excesses of illiterate backwoods families. Lawyers, judges, sheriffs, and merchants fought so bitterly that even their casual associates were often slain in revenge. According to one account, some 2,800 persons in the Kentucky Mountains died from vendettas that resulted only in an occasional conviction.

The questions of prosecution, conviction and sentencing—and pardoning —became political issues, and the murder and mayhem infected Kentucky. Political candidates and elected officials were killed by members of the losing parties. In the early 1900s tobacco farmers warred and burned each other's crops and barns over who was responsible for low prices. In the early 1930s, Kentucky society seemed on the verge of anarchy as gunfire cracked across the coal fields of Harlan and Perry Counties in the decisive struggle of the United Mine Workers to organize the coal mines there. Even in recent times Kentucky politics have been so intense that brothers have been known to kill brothers, and shootings have occurred over school board elections.

Despite the history of violence, Kentuckians love politics so much that they have elections every year, choosing national officials in even years, state and local officials in the odd. In this nonstop political theater, there is never a dark night—and scarcely enough respite between elections for Kentucky officeholders to get down to the serious business of governing.

Personalities, oratory, spoils, and skulduggery have been more important to Kentucky politics than strong and independent political parties, but a word should be said about partisan balances. Democrats have held most of the power in Kentucky since the Civil War, but the Republicans have been a strong second party. Kentuckians have frequently voted Republican for president. But while Republicans won virtually all U.S. Senate elections from the 1940s to the late '60s, and occasionally the governorship, in elections for the legislature and most state offices, Democrats carry the day. Relatively speaking this is a fairly conservative state—but not on race issues (Kentucky is 7 percent black). Blacks have long enjoyed unhampered access to the ballot box, and in 1968 George Wallace got only 18 percent of the Kentucky vote, compared to 34 percent in neighboring Tennessee.

Kentucky has continued to cling to the county as the essential unit of government, and each governor has his man or small committee—a local county "ring"—who relates to him. The administration man or his crowd is expected to "deliver" the county on election day in exchange for control of patronage positions. This power to dispense jobs and government business is particularly awesome in the poorer counties. Clan plays a stunning role in Kentucky county life. Sons, daughters, wives, cousins, and nephews show up on public payrolls by the score. There have been a number of reforms over the years, but patronage still reigns. One suspects that an honest and thorough application of the merit system might do wonders for state government.

When you ask "who runs Kentucky?" the answer is never "the people." Some political personality of the moment may be named, but soon the talk gets back to "the interests" that have bought governors and legislatures and directed the vital affairs here from time immemorial. Around the turn of the century, writer Thomas Clark noted, the vital powers included the railroad companies, of which the Louisville and Nashville Railroad exercised the most clout; the tobacco trusts, whose excesses were soon to trigger the Black Patch War; the whiskey distillers; the Jockey Club, symbolizing the racing interests; schoolbook and insurance companies; and the then-rising coal companies. The power structure is more variegated than in the past and less coordinated, but the intent to manipulate public policy for private ends remains unchanged. The coal, horse, and whiskey people are still influential, and one cannot ignore the burley tobacco interests, who have virtually all members of the congressional delegation championing their interests in Washington. Tobacco's political clout is magnified by the fact that the weed is grown in every county of the state. The Kentucky Education Association has grown into a huge and powerful lobby that gets candidates for governor to grovel for support.

The *Louisville Courier-Journal*, considered a power factor, presents a curious case. Its national recognition, including Pulitzer prizes, has been little less than overwhelming. It was the first daily in the country to hire a full-time ombudsman to monitor the paper's fairness and accuracy. Yet the paper has failed spectacularly to convince Kentuckians to approve many of its proposals. Many Kentuckians believe the *C-J* is judgmental and does not cover local news as well as the state's many weeklies.

Modern Successors to Henry Clay

A cavalcade of personalities has followed the oratorical model of Henry Clay in Kentucky politics. Kentucky's most famous politician of modern times was Alben W. Barkley, a native of Paducah on the state's western tip and a genial, witty, durable, and gallant campaigner. Barkley's fiery keynote speech to the Democratic national convention in 1948 brought a semblance of unity to a badly divided party and led directly to Barkley's nomination and subsequent election as vice president. Few American politicians have been held in such affection as Barkley during his years as "the Veep" under Harry Truman. History shows that the reform forces that Barkley first symbolized—chiefly the farmers and other rural folk of western and central Kentucky—were never to win control of the state government. Barkley did help his people through the Works Progress Administration, which he also used against his political foes. But his memory has been somewhat sullied by his apparent failure to pay income tax on thousands of dollars in speaking fees.

With every thought of serious grass-roots revolt safely behind it, Kentucky was free to play personal and factional politics with a vengeance from the 1930s up to recent times. Two of the most famous protagonists were Democrats Albert B. "Happy" Chandler and Earle C. Clements. Their rivalry stemmed from childhood, and it produced the bitterest primary feuds of modern times, dividing families and leaving wounds that remain to this day. Chandler drew on support from the wing of the Democratic party that favored backing the U.S. money supply with silver, Clements drew from the gold wing. Both men served as senator and governor, but their political leadership went far beyond mere officeholding. "Earle," in the words of veteran Kentucky newsman Hugh Morris, "didn't care who was governor as long as he could run him. Happy didn't care who ran things as long as he could be governor; in fact he was out of the state half the time he held the office."

Voting machines seem to have taken care of one of the more pernicious and persistent features of Kentucky politics, described by writer John Fenton as "taking certain liberties with the vote of the not-so-sovereign electorate." But ballot box skulduggery was also responsible for the political-personal tragedy of one of the grandest personalities of 20th-century Kentucky politics, Edward F. Prichard, Jr. A precocious child who showed an early passion for politics, Prichard excelled at Harvard Law School, was clerk to Justice Felix Frankfurter, and a confidant of Franklin D. Roosevelt before he returned to Kentucky to set up his own law firm and run for governor. But then, in 1948, he stuffed 254 ballots into boxes in Bourbon County. "In a stroke," *Courier-Journal* writer John Ed Pearce has noted, his "brilliant future became nightmare." Why Prichard committed this act has never been determined, but some speculated it may have been the result of a wager or a dare that

Washington had not made him too good for Bourbon County politics. His conviction, achieved on legally challengeable grounds, might have been reversed by the U.S. Supreme Court. But the Justices refused to hear the case because no less than four of them had been Prichard's friends and disqualified themselves. Prichard spent five months in federal prison before a pardon from President Truman. Years of agonizingly slow public rehabilitation followed, but gradually Kentucky governors turned to Prichard for political and governmental counsel, depending on his keen analytical mind. He had a tremendous influence on improvements in higher education, raising teacher salaries, and in the passage of Kentucky's first civil rights legislation in the 20th century. He also counseled many national leaders he counted as personal friends.

We last visited with Prichard in 1978 after diabetes had wracked his once formidable physique, his eyesight was gone, and his failed kidneys had forced him to twice-weekly dialysis. His spirit and his intellectual gifts were unimpaired. State governments, Prichard told us, are failing to realize their full potential for progressive leadership because of the inordinate influence of special interests armed with campaign contributions. Especially in the South, he detected "a real conspiracy between governments and industries to keep unions out"; one result, he said, were heavily regressive state taxes, which perpetuate poverty conditions. "However selfish and shortsighted" trade unions sometimes are, Prichard said, "year in and year out, they have been and are a progressive force in this country, and their relative weakness in the South is a serious problem."

Kentucky's most respected official of the 20th century has been John Sherman Cooper, a man who seemed to occupy the Olympian heights of probity, intelligence, compassion, and disinterested public service during the 20 years that he represented Kentucky in the U.S. Senate. Cooper, of course, was no stranger to the fractious world of Kentucky politics; a mountain man and native of the southeastern Kentucky town of Somerset, he was descended from a settler who came through the Cumberland Gap in 1790. He never let his Yale college education and Harvard law degree stand in the way of competing with the local boys to win election as a county judge and state representative in his early years. Cooper rose to be the ranking Republican on the Senate Public Works Committee and helped gain bipartisan backing for a number of important environmental laws.

Cooper's successor, Walter (Dee) Huddleston, a moderately liberal Democrat, spent most of his time promoting the Kentucky interests of tobacco, coal, and liquor, but also tried unsuccessfully to write a charter defining the scope of American intelligence services. Huddleston's junior colleague, Democrat Wendell Ford, was also devoted to the coal industry and concentrated on working out compromises in committee, rather than in more public postures.

In terms of substantive influence on domestic legislation, no Kentuckian has played a greater role since World War II than Carl Dewey Perkins, congressman from a poor Appalachian district in the eastern part of the state and (starting in 1967) chairman of the House Education and Labor Committee. The shape (and very existence) of federal aid-to-education programs, of antipoverty efforts, and a host of bills ranging from school lunches to "black lung" benefits to the Coal Mine Health and Safety Act were due in no small part to the intense efforts of Carl Perkins. A scrupulously honest and hardworking leader, Perkins won from his Kentucky mountaineer constituents a loyalty with few parallels in American politics.

Rep. William H. Natcher, from the rural, central part of the state around Owensboro, became a power on the House Appropriations Committee. As chairman of its Subcommittee on the District of Columbia, he fought tooth and nail to prevent construction of Washington's long-sought subway system until the complete local freeway network had advanced "beyond recall." (One side effect: by the time building of the Washington subway finally got under way, costs had escalated wildly.)

Few of Kentucky's governors have been brilliant, luminary leaders. If they know how to use it, however, they can wield great power with relative independence from the legislature. It is up to the governor to call the legislators into special sessions; the governor functions under a constitution that makes it virtually impossible to override a veto; moreover, the governor's powers of appointment are immense. Kentucky governors are limited, however, to one four-year term, as are all other state officials, due to a 19th-century spoils system scandal. The reelection bar, even if it forces good people to leave office, also forces out those who may be benefiting personally in office—as some Kentucky governors unquestionably have. The four-year limit obliges governors to put through all salient and controversial elements of their programs (if they have any) during the first year or two in office, before they become political eunuchs. In the meantime, they control in fact, if not in law, thousands of patronage jobs.

Surely the most famous Kentucky governor of modern times has been John Y. Brown, Jr. Brown did not actually create Kentucky Fried Chicken, but bought the recipe from Colonel Harlan Sanders and made his fortune promoting it and opening new outlets. After selling his fried chicken business, marrying Phyllis George, and then winning the governorship in 1979, Brown began promoting Kentucky the same way. He hacked at state payrolls and other expenses while courting national business firms. Even his critics conceded that Brown's business and job creation campaigns were somewhat successful and that he had managed to rid the state of its old patronage system of "personal service contracts." But the overall impression that Brown and George made was one of overambitious, tasteless self-promoters who knew little about governing. Small business owners said Brown romanced the large enterprises while they suffered, a charge that was confirmed when he expanded the use of tax-free industrial revenue bonds beyond manufacturing to include retailing. K-Mart used the money borrowed at cheap rates through the bond program to open a new store in Grayson, Ky., and within six weeks two small competitors were put out of business. Thoughtful Kentuckians were horrified when he suggested that a public hospital for Louisville's indigent be turned over to a for-profit company. Brown had no doubts about his own abilities. As he told the *Wall Street Journal*, "Most governors don't have the background to manage. I do."

One of the people Brown beat in his well-financed, highly publicized 1979 primary was Thelma Stovall, then lieutenant governor and a thorn in the side of Kentucky governors for 20 years. Stovall, first elected secretary of state in 1959, took advantage of the times the governors were out of state to right actions she considered wrong. Over the years she pardoned a prisoner who had been sentenced to life for stealing $28, killed the legislature's attempt to rescind its earlier ratification of the Equal Rights Amendment, and in 1979, when Governor Julian Carroll was traveling instead of providing leadership on tax issues, called the legislature into special session and convinced the legislators that relief was needed. Kentucky's "good old boy" politicians shuddered at Stovall's tactics, but the fact was she often outperformed them in seriousness and dedication to the people of the state.

A Tour of Kentucky

Modern, expansive, industrial Kentucky may be located by tracing a line on a map going from Ashland, in the northeast, through center-state a ways south of Lexington and Louisville, and then along the Western Kentucky Parkway all the way out to Paducah, northernmost city of the Jackson Purchase. From there north to the Ohio River lies a "frontier" of concentrated population and industrial growth. All along the river the atmosphere reminds one more of the nation's industrial heartland than classic pastoral Kentucky. Ashland (pop. 27,064) is the home of Ashland Oil, the nation's 35th-largest industrial corporation and the only Kentucky business among the *Fortune* 500. The Covington-Newport area is the home of suburbanites, factory workers, and their families but known to "tired businessmen," labor leaders, and others for its nightclubs, gambling, and touches of flesh. Along the Ohio's flank west of Louisville is Owensboro (54,450), the largest city in the dozen-odd counties of the western Kentucky coal fields.

Two smaller Kentucky regions also merit attention. The Pennyrile, or Pennyroyal, (named after a prevalent wild mint) encompasses the major chunk of central Kentucky. Much of it consists of rural backwater counties, where the soil is generally of middling quality and the farming less than robust. Here one finds Kentucky's interesting limestone belt (site of Mammoth Cave) and lots of water impoundments. To the north the Pennyrile overlaps with the western coal fields and includes Fort Knox, home of the famed U.S. Bullion Depository. There is one real growth center in the modern Pennyrile, Bowling Green (pop. 40,450). Kentucky's extreme western extension is the Jackson Purchase, or Mississippi Delta region, which extended the state's boundaries in the early 19th century. The Purchase strikes one as a piece of Mississippi or Arkansas, located accidentally in Kentucky. The largest town is Paducah (pop. 29,315), a placid city at the confluence of the Tennessee and Ohio rivers. Politically, the Purchase lands are a piece of the Old South. They were once big slaveholding territories.

The jewel of Kentucky's kingdoms is the Bluegrass, some thousand square miles of spring-fed and gently rolling land unmatched anywhere on earth for the nurturing of fine livestock. Here one finds the 300-odd horse farms (with names such as Castleton, Spendthrift, Pebblebrook, Calumet), nurturing grounds of some 200,000 thoroughbreds, standard-breds, and show animals who graze on placid meadows divided by miles of white plank fences—as perfect an example as one can find anywhere of man's manicuring of nature. Great chunks of the Bluegrass, of course, are given over to more mundane forms of agriculture and to the expansion of Lexington, the central city of the region. Yet the horse farms, for the most part, have remained unmolested, and steps are being taken to protect their future—as well they should be, considering the importance of the horse to Kentucky's history (many of the state's most illustrious earliest citizens, including Henry Clay, were avid horse breeders), economy (close to 12,000 Kentuckians make their living off the horse industry), and image (surely a more felicitious symbol than bourbon, tobacco, or coal).

Horse raising has, of course, become an incredibly expensive business. Since the Gilded Age following the Civil War, when fabulously wealthy Eastern business moguls began to buy up Bluegrass horse farms and race their prime specimens, the indigenous Kentucky aristocracy has generally taken a back seat in the horse world. Many of the wealthy outsiders have gravitated to Kentucky, however, and intermarried with Kentuckians. The horses themselves now sell for incredibly large amounts of money.

The Bluegrass orbit includes not only gracious countryside, but old and interesting cities such as Frankfort (25,973), the first state capital west of the Alleghenies, Versailles (6,472), and Paris (7,935), the county seat of Bourbon County, where some historians would have it that the first bourbon was distilled by Jack Spears in 1790. The major interest inevitably turns to Lexington, a town both intensely old and new. It was named for the Battle of Lexington, only a few weeks after that event, and following permanent settlement in 1779 became the chief commercial and cultural capital of the old frontier. Over the years, Lexington prospered as a farm center, the site of great tobacco auctions, and of course as a focal point of the horse industry. Today Lexington has an immense variety of activities, including large veterans' and public health facilities, the sprawling buildings of the University of Kentucky, large manufacturing plans and high-technology firms, Kentucky's leading economic research organization (Spindletop Research), the national headquarters of the Council of State Governments, and the homes of many Kentucky coal operators. All of this has created some serious growing pains. The combined population of the city and surrounding Fayette County, which was 78,899 in 1940, soared to 204,165 by 1980. Highways and subdivisions gobbled up some of the green space around Lexington, including some of its treasured horse farms, before restrictive zoning and development rules were adopted. Fayette County also decreed an urban service area of some 75 square miles beyond which it would not extend police, fire, or sewer services. The Lexington area in the early '70s also merged city and county government.

In contrast, Kentucky's lead city of Louisville, more than a century past its days as a brawling frontier riverfront town, is a comfortable, low-key place, generally a follower rather than a leader among America's urban centers. In most areas Louisville seems to slip into total lethargy, though every so often the town bestirs itself and lunges forward with political innovation or a new spurt of building. Louisville enjoyed a fabulous boom as the supersalesman to the postplantation South after the Civil War. But after 1900, except for the boomtimes of the '20s, the economy languished for a half century. Only the arrival of some big out-of-state firms prevented severe unemployment in the postwar years. In the '60s some local entrepreneurs such as John Y. Brown, Jr., and Stanley Yarmuth, a Passaic, N.J., native who started in Louisville as a used-car salesman and later controlled the Life Insurance Company of Kentucky, started a new spurt of entrepreneurism in Kentucky. By the late '60s the two biggest Kentucky financial establishments, Citizens Fidelity Bank Trust and First National Bank–Kentucky Trust Company, finally caught the spirit and built new downtown offices. Louisville did not seem as entrepreneurially dynamic in the 1970s although one company, Humana, owner of a chain of for-profit hospitals, prospered and made plans for a dramatic and controversial new downtown headquarters designed by New York architect Michael Graves. But by the late 1970s, Louisville had gained a reputation as the "strike capital of the world," and industrialists closed plants and opened few new ones. During the '70s, the Louisville metropolitan area grew only 4.5 percent, to 906,240.

The growth that did take place was concentrated in suburban Bullitt and Oldham Counties, and to a lesser degree in nearby Clark and Floyd Counties across the Indiana border. Louisville itself lost 17.5 percent of its population, dropping to 298,451, and even surrounding Jefferson County declined 1.5 percent, to 684,793. Years after, Lexington, Louisville, and surrounding Jefferson County tried to effect a governmental merger in a 1982 referendum. They failed by a hair's breadth margin. The mayor and county judge (who's actually chief elected officer of the county) supported the initiative, but it was opposed by blacks fearful of seeing their inner-city strength diluted, by city police and firemen jealous of their pension rights, and by "redneck" areas of the county. The well, indeed, was poisoned by school busing, which the U.S. courts forced on both the city and county schools after they merged in 1975. Nasty racial incidents followed.

The busing problems spoiled Louisville's reputation for relatively smooth relations between its whites and blacks, who made up 28 percent of the population in 1980. Although blacks were household slaves in antebellum Louisville, the record shows a relatively enlightened public policy afterward. Public education created a quite literate Negro populace within a few decades of the Civil War. Rigid segregation in schools and all sorts of public accommodations continued right down to the 1940s, but blacks were free to vote and there was a flourishing culture of black-owned stores, hotels, restaurants, theaters, and newspaper publishing houses. Louisville sent a black representative to the state legislature in 1934, elected its first black alderman in 1945, and chose its first black state senator—a personally delightful and politically astute woman named Georgia Davis—in 1967. Following the Supreme Court's 1954 school desegregation decision, Kentucky Gov. Lawrence Wetherby broke ranks with most other Southern and Border States governors by announcing that Kentucky would obey the law. Thanks to some sound planning by school boards and administrators in Louisville and Lexington (centers of a major portion of the black population) Kentucky did just that. All this relative liberalism seemed to take place within certain limits, however. Louisville never looked kindly upon the activities of social activists Carl and Anne Braden, who directed the Southern Conference Educational Fund, which had the avowed aim of helping "the powerless people of the South, white and black, organize themselves for new forms of joint political action that can bring them the power to control their own government, their economic resources, and the conditions of their lives." There were also race riots in 1967.

Black support helped in the electoral victories of Mayor Harvey Sloane, who served from 1973 to 1977 and was reelected in 1981. Sloane came to the mayor's office with one of the most unusual and sensitive backgrounds of any American mayor. Born in Virginia in the late 1930s, he graduated from Yale and Cleveland's Western Reserve School of Medicine. Rebelling against his family, he became a hobo for a while, sleeping in boxcars, getting to know different kinds of people around the United States. Sometimes relying on family wealth, Sloane found time to work on an oil rig in the Gulf of Mexico, to pick celery with migrant Mexicans in California and strawberries with Indians in Oregon, to be a construction worker in western Canada, and to work in Malaysia and Vietnam before running a health program in the mid-1960s in Appalachian Kentucky. Sloane settled down in Louisville in 1966 because, he said, "It enjoys the benefits of a large city while still having a small-town atmosphere. Its problems are solvable; it's not a Newark or a Cleveland, and America's future depends upon the future of its cities." Sloane established and ran for six years a federally funded neighborhood health center before entering the race for mayor. He was first dismissed by one alderman as a "loppy liberal" but came down strong for law and order and supported the strengthening of individual city neighborhoods. (Sloane lived in Old Louisville, a near-downtown neighborhood that has experienced a rebirth.) It was probably a sign of the times, however, that when we talked with Sloane in 1982, the man who had once been described as "Kennedyesque" for his emphasis on social programs told us he was spending most of his time on economic development, making presentations to corporations, and developing partnerships with the private sector—virtually anything, in fact, to create jobs.

Louisville has a proud literary and intellectual history, rooted in the early 19th century and enhanced by the broadminded and intelligent Germans who poured in during the 1840s. The University of Louisville, formed in antebellum days, was the first municipally owned university in the United States. But these institutions can hardly compete with the one great event that puts Louisville in the national news—the Kentucky Derby, run at doughty old Churchill Downs on the hallowed first Saturday of every May, just as it has been every year since 1875. The event is quintessential Kentuckiana—who could doubt it as the hawkers offer mint juleps and the strains of "My Old Kentucky Home" are played as the horses hit the track? But it is also quintessential Americana and inspires sportswriters to come up with lines such as "Unless you go to Kentucky and with your own eyes behold the Derby, you ain't been nowhere and you ain't never seen nothin'."

The Extraordinary "Other World" of Eastern Kentucky

Finally, we come to Eastern Kentucky, a region so little known to Americans a generation ago that John Gunther devoted barely a paragraph to it. By the 1960s, however, the region had become a national symbol of poverty, environmental degradation, and gaps in the affluent American society. East Kentucky emerged in the public consciousness in the late 1950s and early '60s following two crippling floods and John Kennedy's 1960 primary campaign in neighboring West Virginia—and through the publication in 1962 of Harry M. Caudill's *Night Comes to the Cumberlands,* an extraordinarily poignant and compelling account of the woes of an American region. Reporters, sociologists, social planners, federal bureaucrats, and on one occasion, even President Lyndon Johnson descended upon this problem child of state and union, observing and prescribing solutions for everything from its dire poverty and isolation to its coal-mine-ravaged landscape. The plight of East Kentucky was to lead directly to establishment of the Appalachian Regional Commission and to contribute significantly to Washington's decision to launch the Great Society's "war on poverty."

What makes East Kentucky the way it is? The answer lies in the peculiar convergence of people, land, and resources in this ragged backwoods of Eastern America. The first settlers who came through the Cumberland Gap found a land of sharp hillsides and small valleys, intricately compartmentalized. The whole was covered with great virgin hardwood forests; the waters were flashing clean; from streams and woodlands came fish and game plentiful for a settler's needs. Properly cultivated, some have suggested, this might have been as pleasing and prosperous a province as Switzerland.

Yet from the very start, "civilization" devastated the Cumberland Plateau. The frontiersmen viewed the wilderness as a place to be conquered, not to be preserved. They used farming methods that would seriously erode and deplete the soil before their grandchildren reached maturity. They hunted the once copious game virtually to the point of extinction of many species. Late in the 19th century came the great logging boom. The idea of reseeding never seemed to occur to the loggers. With the natural cover decimated, floods became an ever more serious problem. Then the coal barons completed the destruction, turning East Kentucky into a ravaged land.

Caudill, now a professor of history at the University of Louisville, suggests that the uncultured, rough people who settled East Kentucky, and then lived on there in splendid isolation, simply lacked the skills or intelligence to nurture their land and protect it from outside domination. One generally looked in vain, among those who came to occupy the hills, for men of letters or distinguished familial lines, skilled tradesmen or craftsmen or merchants. Rather, it was the castoffs of 18th-century society, English and Scotch-Irish, who had been street orphans or debtors or prisoners in Britain, despised by the motherland and sold into forms of indentured servanthood, who chose the frontier and spread "along every creek bed and up every hidden valley." No wonder the Appalachian frontiersman hated the crown and came to despise in America any manifestation of government.

Caudill believes the living conditions got worse as the isolation and depression of mountain life, the lawlessness and lack of opportunity drove out the most talented and promising sons and daughters of the region, those who might have built independent and self-reliant institutions on their own home soil. We sought to test Caudill's theory with William Hambley, a physician and mayor of Pikeville for over 20 years. Yes, said Hambley, there were instances of genetic disasters, although traveling salesmen, he suggested, had given cross breeding a healthy thrust. The greater problem, as Hambley saw it, was cultural confinement. Not all agree that only the ignorant and weak remain. Many East Kentuckians who left in the 1950s and '60s for the Northern cities demonstrated their love for the region by visiting frequently. In the 1970s, after a coal boom, so many expatriates returned that Appalachian Kentucky grew 22.8 percent during the decade. As one young Vietnam veteran told writer John Fetterman in the early 1970s, "Being here is being somebody. You don't have to buy your spot to be buried in. I want my children to always come see this place. It's beautiful and the people are that way. I can remember Grandma. She was so gentle, the wild birds would eat out of her hands."

By 1981 the federal government had spent $15 billion to "save" East Kentucky and the rest of Appalachia. Whether the Appalachian Regional Commission and other antipoverty efforts had reached their goals was a debatable issue. Infant mortality had dropped dramatically, albeit with great variations from county to county. Per capita income had risen from 78 percent of the national average in 1965 to 84 percent, yet averaged only 71 percent in an agglomeration of 85 hardcore central Appalachian highlands counties spread through eastern Kentucky, West Virginia, southwestern Virginia, and eastern Tennessee. The percentage of the population below the federal poverty line had dropped only 1 percent, from 12 to 11. Two-thirds of the money had gone for highway construction, but many of the roads were lightly traveled, which raised serious questions about the priorities of the federal spending.

Many social critics charged that the heavy federal spending had created a welfare culture in which the Appalachian people could no longer take care of themselves. To that, however, others replied that many people in Appalachia were too old or poorly educated to take care of themselves in any modern sense; to cut off the federal dole, went that argument, would return them to a life of utter misery.

The biggest disappointment about the development efforts, however, has been the failure to diversify the Appalachian economy away from its dependence on coal. Nature endowed Kentucky with 30 to 35 billion tons of recoverable coal, and both underground and surface mining have been important to the state for many generations. Coal has also been Kentucky's curse. At the turn of the century, clever outside interests used the infamous broad-form deed to dupe the unsuspecting and backward people to gain control of the mineral riches beneath the soil of East Kentucky. For a fee averaging 50 cents an acre, the highlander—who generally knew neither how to read nor write —would convey title to "all coal, oil, gas, stone, salt, and salt water, iron, ores and minerals and metallic substances whatsoever." By the time the deed-signing splurge was finished, the ownership of 94 percent of the mineral wealth of East Kentucky was sold to corporations with headquarters in such faraway places as London, Philadelphia, Pittsburgh, New York, and Baltimore. Deep-coal mining did, however, bring steady employment from the 1920s straight down to the years following World War II. With the mechanization of the mines, the number of miners decreased, although those who held on to their unionized jobs became what Harry Caudill called "a favored class, a sort of blue-collar royalty amid a population of industrial serfs."

In the mid '6os, when the world became aware of Appalachia, coal mining was at a low point and thousands had left to seek work elsewhere. In the early 1970s, the Norfolk and Western Railway, one of the largest landowners in Appalachia, built at a cost of nearly $1 million per mile a 24-mile branch line from West Virginia to Martin County, Kentucky. Shortly after the rail line went into full service, the OPEC oil embargo led to coal price hikes and increased levels of mining activity. Thousands of people returned to East Kentucky, not only to apply for the hard-to-get, high-paying ($30,000 per year and more) mining jobs, but to provide services that the newly affluent wanted. Kentucky now competes with West Virginia as the state that produces the most coal (about a fifth of the national total). It also has the dubious distinction of being the largest producer of surface-mined coal in the United States. Stripping is less dangerous to human life than deep coal mining, but environmentally it often causes worse damage. Bulldozers uncover the seams in great and unsightly gashes around the mountainside; sometimes the strippers scoop off the whole top of a mountain, where the seam lies that high.

With the boom, unemployment fell, per capita income rose, and bank deposits went up in East Kentucky. A coal severance tax forced the mining companies to leave a little of the wealth in the counties. But most of the profits still left the state, and power was still held by the same courthouse crowd. The *New York Times* Magazine reported in 1981 that for all its new wealth, Martin County, Kentucky, still had no sewer system, no garbage collection, no four-lane roads, no hospital, no movie theater, minimal police and fire protection, and housing so poor that only 700 of the 4,400 units could be classified as "sound." And as if to prove prosperity is but a fleeting phenomenon in these hills, the early 1980s cutbacks in such heavy industries as steel, plus slowed growth in electricity use, forced coal production to decline precipitously. Kentucky coal counties registered double-digit unemployment rates while some officials said the "real" unemployment, if one included discouraged workers, might be as high as 50 percent.

Of the efforts to diversify East Kentucky's economic base, perhaps the most energetic has been the Kentucky Highlands Investment Corporation, a federally backed organization supplying capital, loans, and business advice to small, low-technology, labor-intensive businesses such as manufacturers of kayaks, sleeping bags, coal truck beds, and stuffed animals. This effort to encourage indigenous economic muscle has suffered from the necessity of recruiting entrepreneurs from other states. Many local officials believe that as long as coal remains so dominant, industrialists and entrepreneurs, who do not want to live near coal production, will avoid the region.

Like it or not, coal is still king of East Kentucky. If coal demand is down, unemployment is the number one problem, and if production is high, environmental issues are at the top of the agenda. Harry Caudill has maintained that a rain such as the one that caused the huge flood of 1927 "would devastate the entire region." U.S. Interior Department officials say that the larger mining companies are doing a fairly good job of reclamation. But whether the land will truly be able to support agriculture or even buildings is very uncertain, and the history of colonial treatment of Appalachia is so firm that it is impossible for one to be optimistic about the area's long-term outlook.

This is not to say that East Kentucky is totally bereft of local attempts to improve living conditions and maintain the communities. Back in 1899, two "fotched-on" women started the Hindman Settlement School, which supplemented the local schools by teaching youngsters everything from the three "R's" to home nursing, sewing, weaving, and basketry. Mary Breckenridge, the daughter of a famous Kentucky patrician family, decided, in 1925, after the death of her own two children, to devote the rest of her life to the medical and nursing care of children in the remote backwoods areas of Leslie County. In a more contemporary vein are Tom and Pat Gish. Tom grew up the son of a foreman in a coal camp 10 miles from Whitesburg, studied journalism at the University of Kentucky, and was a United Press Correspondent in Frankfort from 1947 to 1957 before returning with his wife, Pat, also a journalist, to Whitesburg to buy the *Mountain Eagle*, a 50-year old weekly with the wonderful motto, "It Screams." The Gishes set about gathering news in the modern objective style and found themselves fighting "the issues of freedom of the press and freedom of speech we thought had been settled a long time ago." The *Mountain Eagle* plunged into controversial issues, publishing pictures of destructive strip-mining operations, revealing environmental desecrations, and questioning powerful antipoverty officials and Appalachian Regional Commission programs. The Gishes learned the tough financial life of running a weekly newspaper—Pat had to take an antipoverty job to make ends meet for their family of five children—but the paper persevered in investigative reporting that is rare in Appalachia. The Gishes are fierce defenders of the mountain people's right to self-determination.

Appalachia's greatest asset, amidst its poverty and environmental degradation, is its culture. Writer Jesse Stuart, who years ago celebrated the life of the East Kentucky people, observed that Appalachia "is the only region of this country with a real culture. It came to us from the British Isles—the music, the dances, the humor, the writers—but now it's ours, and I think we'll keep it." Appalachian folk songs and arts and crafts have achieved a certain chic throughout the nation and the world, but there is also the danger that the real thing will be lost. Fortunately, the record of that culture is being preserved at Berea College, in the Cumberland foothills, which now has the largest collection of literature on Appalachian life, history, music, and crafts ever assembled.

Berea College was founded in 1855 by native Kentuckians drawn together by their abolitionist sympathies to form a church school in which poor whites and Negroes could study together. Since 1892 Berea has not charged admission but rather required its students to participate in a work program. An even smaller institution, Alice Lloyd Junior College, at Pippa Passes, has had remarkable success in pioneering the concept of Appalachian youth in service to their communities. Founded in 1923, Alice Lloyd—like Berea—has imbued its students over the years with the idea that they have an obligation to return and serve in Appalachia once they have garnered their professional degrees in such fields as law, medicine, or teaching.

With institutions like these and the dedication of strong individuals, it is hard to believe that the future of East Kentucky's people is totally bleak. Yet the cry goes up, how long will it be before the mountain people can overcome the fear, ignorance, poverty, and colonialism that have so long afflicted them, and the hills where they live?

THE
DEEP SOUTH
STATES

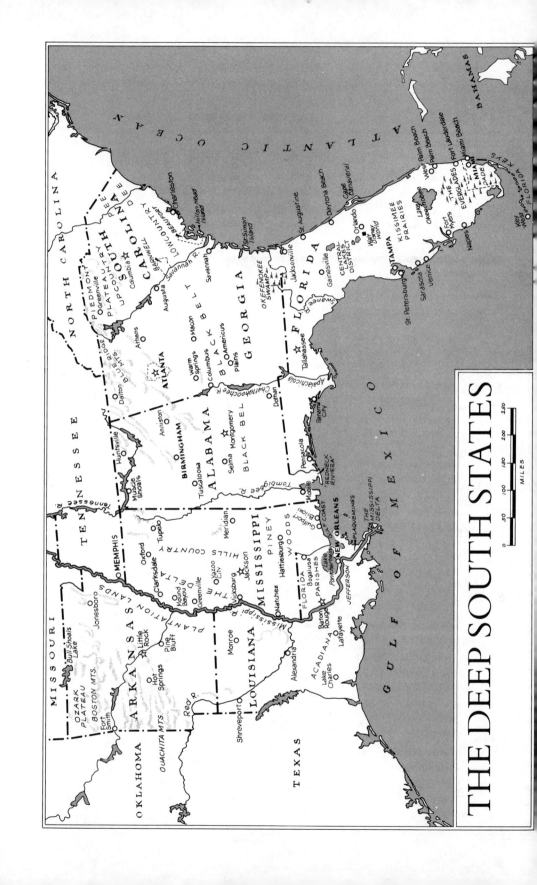

THE DEEP SOUTH STATES

GEORGIA

Empire State of the South

"I USED TO GET UP at four in the morning to pick peanuts. . . . My house had no running water. . . . But I made it to the U.S. Naval Academy and became a nuclear physicist. . . . Now I want to be your president so that I can give you a government that's honest and that's filled with love, competence and compassion." Thus Georgia's Governor Jimmy Carter appealed to a nation in his campaign for the presidency.

After only one term (1977–81), the Carter presidency would sink in one of the strongest rejections the American people have ever served upon a politician. Carter's defeat at the hands of Ronald Reagan was a sad event for his home state, which was proud to have sent the first man from the Deep South to the White House since the Civil War. But the upward striving that Carter represented continues just as surely as it has since the end of World War II when Governor Ellis Arnall proclaimed "Let's Get off Tobacco Road."

Even at the end of World War II, however, Georgia was better off than most Southern states. Georgia has the greatest land area of any state east of the Mississippi and a geography of fantastic diversity. To the north, there are the hills and mountains; then there is a broad swatch of rolling plateau and the state's famous red clays; finally, to the southeast lies a 150-mile shelf of coastal flatland that lay beneath the sea in prehistoric times. Georgia has been known for generations as the Empire State of the South, and the real reason —still true today—can be summed up in one word: Atlanta. Simply because of its strategic location, Atlanta became the major distribution point for the South's agrarian economy.

Still the postwar changes in Georgia have been phenomenal. In the 1940s, Georgia had a work force of about one million people, and one out of three worked on a farm. Today Georgia is a major manufacturing state in textiles, apparel, wood products, including paper (69 percent of Georgia's land is covered by forests), transportation equipment, chemicals, food processing, carpeting, airplanes, and mobile homes. Georgia has less than a third as many farms as it did a generation ago, but they are producing more than ever. Cotton and peaches have declined in importance, but Georgia leads all 50 states in poultry production. The other big farm moneymakers are its Carter-famous peanuts, cattle, and hogs. And the federal military establishment pumps billions into Georgia each year. Tourism declined slightly after the halcyon years of the Carter presidency but still nets huge sums each year. The result of all this development is that Georgia's per capita income, which was only 50 percent of the national average back in 1929 and 68 percent in 1950, had climbed to 97 percent in 1980.

Georgia's accomplishments are not only economic. The state has also made enormous strides in race relations. It has attracted back thousands of talented blacks who felt forced a generation or two ago to seek a life in the North. Jimmy Carter's best assurance for a place in history comes from his 1971 inaugural address: "I say to you quite frankly that the time for racial discrimination is over. Our people have already made this major and difficult decision. No poor, rural weak or black person should ever have to bear the additional burden of being deprived of the opportunity for an education, a job, or simple justice." Carter later hung the portrait of Martin Luther King, Jr., in the state capitol, still a courageous deed in the Georgia of the early 1970s.

Atlanta became one of the most vibrant cities of the latter 20th century, at once a symbol and the heartbeat of the new Southern economy. In the present day, according to Southern economist Philip Hammer, Atlanta's position is based on more than its location (though that is still vital). "It is based rather," according to Hammer, "upon a new set of essential functions in an increasingly complex industrial structure—the 'central work' functions of business, industry, finance and government that cannot be duplicated anywhere else. No other city in the region occupies or duplicates Atlanta's role as the spark plug, catalyst, generator, service center, financier, clearing house, trading point, policy maker and pace setter for the region's new economy." Hammer might have added that no other Southern city comes close to Atlanta as a center of intellectual ferment, black leadership, and the civil rights movement. Singly, no one of these factors might mean too much; taken together, they effect a kind of critical mass that makes Atlanta the premier city of the South and a force to be reckoned with nationally.

No matter what measure one draws from the statistical handbag, Atlanta's preeminence is illustrated. The rail lines of the South still converge there, but so do the interstate routes and the air routes at Atlanta's big new Hartsfield International Airport, opened in 1980. (Atlanta has become the world's busiest airport in number of planes taking off and second only to Chicago's O'Hare in volume of passengers.) There was an old joke in railroading days about Southerners agreeing that whether they went to heaven or hell, they would have to pass through Atlanta; now it has been revamped with a new punch line in which a Southerner, asked whether he will go "down" or "up" after death, replies, "I don't know, but whichever, I'll have to change planes in Atlanta." On this side of the Great Divide, all Southern capitalists turn now to Atlanta for money; its banks are among the most aggressive in the entire United States, and it is no longer necessary to run to New York for big financing. Atlantans like to point out that 431 of the *Fortune* 500 industrial firms have offices in Atlanta. The city is also the nerve center of federal government offices in the South. Retailing, professional services, light manufacturing, and construction have all boomed in postwar Atlanta. The downtown skyline has been entirely remade in the past years, and will be remade again in the next decades. In the 1970s, Atlanta became a media center through the entrepreneurship of Ted Turner, owner of the independent superstation WTBS-TV and founder of Cable News Network, launched to provide 24-hour news service to cable subscribers across America.

All the advances of this "Cinderella city" are now taken for granted by many. But they were not a foregone conclusion in 1945. George Sessions Perry wrote then in the *Saturday Evening Post* that Atlanta's chief claims to fame were (1) the "now defunct" Ku Klux Klan, (2) Coca-Cola, (3) grand-slamming Bobby Jones, and (4) Margaret Mitchell's *Gone with the Wind*. Atlanta, Perry wrote, "is a hot-bread, boiled-greens, fried-chicken-and-cream-gravy town," and "her downtown business district is less attractive than Birmingham's."

The years that followed would produce in Atlanta a generation of aggressive economic hustlers and personalities with the dynamism of architect-developer John Portman, the man responsible for some of postwar America's most architecturally adventuresome buildings. Atlanta's deeper problems were not, of course, to be dealt with in a twinkling. The city proper lost 70,000 people in the '70s, dropping to a total population of 425,022 while the suburbs gained. In the early 1980s, it went through the excruciating agony of the murder of 28 black children. Yet Atlanta also began to attract back talented blacks who went North years ago. In 1981, Rand McNally's *Places Rated Almanac* rated the Atlanta area as overall the best place to live in America.

The 1980 Census found 5,464,265 people in Georgia, a ranking of 13th among the states. About 2 million people live in the Atlanta area, and an additional 1.3 million in five other metropolitan areas (Savannah, Albany, Macon, Columbus, Augusta, and suburban Chattanooga, Tennessee) plus the counties around the medium-sized cities of Athens, Rome, and Valdosta. Economically and culturally, these cities and suburbs are "where the action is" in modern Georgia.

But one should not forget rural small-town Georgia, where the lifestyles and attitudes of the Old South hold on more tenaciously. Thirty-nine percent of Georgians still live in these areas, which one observer has summed up as "static Georgia" as opposed to "dynamic Georgia" of the larger cities and suburbs. Politically, rural Georgia divides into three regions: north Georgia, an Appalachian territory with few blacks; the black belt, which cuts across central and southwestern Georgia, including many counties with a black majority; and, finally, south Georgia, where whites form a heavier majority than in the black belt.

Politics of Turmoil

Georgia's politics have been chaotic and exciting ever since the early 1960s. The first big sign of change came in 1964 when the state that had *never* failed to go Democratic voted for Barry Goldwater for president. Two-party-ism developed for an unsavory reason: white Georgians' disgust with the Kennedy-Johnson administration's support of the civil rights movement. But other changes crested rapidly in the same era. The county unit system, Georgia's "rotten borough system in excelsis," was discarded as a way of nominating statewide officials. Federal "one-man, one-vote" court orders forced Georgia's legislature to end the rural dominance that had allowed just over a fifth of the state's voters to elect a majority in both the state senate and house. Following the federal Voting Rights Act, blacks began to vote in massive numbers, not only in the cities, but also in the black belt and south Georgia.

The three-tiered social structure of old Georgia has not disappeared: first, "wool hat," "pore white trash" Georgians, racist and fundamentalist in religion; second, the affluent whites of Atlanta and other cities who never sought integration but did feel some *noblesse oblige* toward blacks; and finally, the blacks themselves. The geographic strengths of the groups have changed, however. Many of the wool hats have moved to the cities and poorer suburbs, bringing their attitudes, but not necessarily their party affiliation, with them. The townsmen of north Georgia, always somewhat lukewarm about racist rabble-rousing, have begun to vote more like the other rural conservatives. And the growing black vote has tempered the conservative domination of black belt politics—not to mention its impact in the cities.

Indeed, increasing black populations have kept the cities Democratic, while many affluent whites have moved to comfortable suburbs and become Republicans. The development of the modern Republican party in Georgia was interrupted, however, by Jimmy Carter's presidential candidacy. When a Georgian sought the White House, all the old Georgia loyalty came out. Carter won 67 percent of the vote in 1976 and even in 1980, when he lost nationally, he still got 56 percent in Georgia, his biggest margin.

Georgia's voting in state and local elections—as opposed to those for president—is a much more complex matter and requires a flashback to earlier times. Georgia politics in the 1930s and '40s, V.O. Key wrote, was under the "rule of the rustics," a hegemony that had its roots in rural revolt against the Northern financiers and Georgia big-city interests who had tried to build an industrialized "New South," championed by Atlanta editor Henry Grady after the Civil War. The "New South" movement, however, ignored the interests of Georgia's plain dirt farmers, making a political counterattack inevitable.

First of the rustic leaders was Thomas E. Watson, who entered politics as an agrarian reformer and in the early 1900s served terms in the legislature and Congress, where he first proposed the idea of rural free delivery of mail. After Georgia's ruling aristocratic Bourbon Democrats used gerrymandering and fraud to oust him from office, and he lost Populist campaigns for the presidency, Watson began to hurl invectives at Catholics, blacks, Jews, and Socialists and became a champion of the Ku Klux Klan. The white primary was one of his monuments; he saw it as a way to prevent the selling and manipulation of black votes by the Bourbons. Another monument was the county unit system, a kind of miniaturized electoral college, which Watson thought would curb what he regarded as the corrupt influence of big-city politicians. As long as Georgia was predominantly rural, the system was reasonably related to the popular vote. But corrupt bosses did arise, and the growth of the cities and suburbs made the system, in the words of political scientist Joseph Bernd, "an increasingly grotesque caricature of a democratic representational system." By 1960, the 556,326 people then living in Fulton County (Atlanta) had the same unit vote strength as those of three small rural counties with 6,980 inhabitants among them—a disparity of almost 100-1.

The greatest beneficiary of the county system was Georgia's prime 20th-century demagogue, Eugene Talmadge. He was so effective in galvanizing support of the rustics that he won four terms as governor. Georgia politics from the '20s to '40s divided fairly simply into pro-Talmadge and anti-Talmadge groups. Old Gene often boasted that he did not want to carry any cities, and he once pastured a cow on the lawn of the governor's mansion because Mrs. Talmadge was dissatisfied with the milk being delivered to her door in big, slick Atlanta. Talmadge also appealed to the "forgotten" rural white voters by defending segregation and lambasting the corporations. But while the rustics gave him his votes, Talmadge voted against New Deal measures and often got his financial support from Atlanta bankers and corporation executives who learned that he was "safe." As Key noted, "Talmadge, like many professed champions of the forgotten man, in the showdown turned up on the side of the fellows who did the forgetting."

Occasionally, Talmadge or his candidate would be defeated. One rebel who succeeded most spectacularly was Ellis Arnall, who had been a Talmadge loyalist as a young state legislator but then rose up to win the governorship as the anti-Talmadge candidate in 1942. Arnall made historic strides in modernizing the climate of Georgia, including a leadership role in ending the poll tax and lowering the voting age to 18.

Ole Gene celebrated his Last Hurrah in 1946 in a campaign that stressed white supremacy and won him a victory based on unit votes—even though the moderate candidate backed by Arnall actually got more popular votes. But Talmadge died before inauguration day, and there ensued Georgia's famous "two governors" controversy. Herman Talmadge, then a young man of 33 anxious to don his daddy's mantle, lost out in his effort to be declared the governor, but he returned two years later to win a clear-cut victory and stayed on as governor until 1955.

Herman Talmadge, unlike his father, used the governorship to make Georgia into a modern, progressive state. He imposed a statewide 3 percent sales tax and used the money to spend more on education than had been spent in all the years since the start of the state's public school system in 1871. New industries were attracted—some 13,000 miles of new roads helped to get Georgia "out of the mud"—and big advances made in mental health and agricultural research. But while he proved his prowess as an executive, Talmadge never lost sight of the race issue as a way to ensure his political future.

The opening shot against Georgia's *ancien regime* was fired by the U.S. Supreme Court's 1962 "one-man, one-vote" decision, *Baker* v. *Carr*. On the very day the *Baker* decision was handed down, a new challenge to the county unit vote scheme was filed in Atlanta, and two months later, the federal court there declared that Georgia must henceforth nominate candidates on a direct vote basis. The governor elected in 1962, the first one nominated by direct vote since 1908, was Carl E. Sanders, a young state senator who symbolized the business-minded moderation of a new day in Georgia.

The growth of black voting in Georgia started earlier, and was more gradual, than in states such as Mississippi or Alabama, where blacks were almost totally repressed politically before the Voting Rights Act of 1965 opened the floodgates. By the same token, while the late 1950s and early '60s brought sporadic racial outbursts to Georgia—some beatings, church bombings, even killings—they lacked the magnitude of violence in Alabama or Mississippi. Georgia did not like the civil rights movement a bit more than Alabamians or Mississippians, reporter Jack Nelson has said, but Georgia did have "perhaps a touch more old South gentility, an aspiring national city whose leaders were determined to shake the Georgia cracker image and two governors, elected at strategic moments in time, who were under obligation to many of their supporters to practice moderation—Ernest Vandiver in 1958, and Sanders four years after that."*

The percentage of Georgia's voting age blacks registered to vote climbed from a mere 2 percent in 1940 to 44 percent by 1964. With federal legislation, black registration began to roll in rural areas as well, reaching 64 percent in 1972. Blacks elected their first state senator, Atlantan Leroy Johnson, in 1962; in the wake of federally ordered reapportionment, they elected another 10 black legislators by 1966 and 25 by 1982.

During his first session, in 1963, Johnson told us, white legislators refused to talk, shake hands, or eat lunch with him. A key turning point occurred in the education committee. When the author of a bill was trying to get it out of committee, the supporters, Johnson said, "saw a vote, not a Negro, walking through the door. I said I had two bills pending I wanted to get out of committee. It was the ancient *quid pro quo* of legislative politics. I made my deal, and then my vote got the stalled bill out of committee."

The last gasp of virulent legislative racism occurred in 1966 when the house, by a vote of 184 to 12, barred Julian Bond from taking his seat because he had endorsed a rather headstrong antiwar statement by the Student Nonviolent Coordinating Committee (SNCC). The pacifism of Bond's statement was alleged to undermine the Selective Service Act and thus aid enemies of the United States. But there was little likelihood that such a *cause celebre* would have been made if Bond had not been a black man. The U.S. Supreme Court ruled that Bond's First Amendment rights had been violated, and he was seated. Today the Georgia legislature has a strong black caucus. Julian Bond was the man who organized it, calling it his "most significant contribution."

---

*Vandiver, faced in 1961 with the stern choice of closing the University of Georgia or permitting token integration, opted for the token integration. One of the first two blacks to integrate the University of Georgia was a harrassed and worried looking girl who wanted to study journalism, Charlayne Hunter (later Gault), who became the first Harlem bureau chief of the *New York Times* and later joined the MacNeil-Lehrer Report on public television.

The story of black people's advance in Georgia must be interupted, however, by the phenomenon of Lester Maddox, the feisty little politician who
in the early '60s won high visibility brandishing ax handles—and, on one
occasion, a pistol—to scare away black customers from his flourishing Atlanta
chicken restaurant. Maddox's election as governor in 1966 confounded not
only Georgia's blacks—Martin Luther King, Jr., said it made him "ashamed
to be a Georgian"—but also moderate white leaders such as Atlanta's Mayor
Ivan Allen, Jr., who said when Maddox won, "The seal of the great State of
Georgia lies tarnished."

Elected governor in 1970, Jimmy Carter, then a state senator, made 1,800
speeches and met 600,000 Georgians in the process of four years of campaigning. Some said there was an implied racism to Carter's campaign against
former Gov. Carl Sanders; be that as it may, white Georgians accepted the
prematurely graying, soft-spoken man with a toothy smile a bit like the
Kennedys', as a fresh face, a man just enough like themselves to deserve
election. Even severe critics of Carter consider him to have been a good
governor of Georgia. Blacks who had given him only 7 percent of the runoff
primary vote forgave him soon after his famed inaugural speech. Steven Brill,
author of a 1976 *Harper's* article that charged Carter with overrating his
commitments to racial and social progress, nevertheless noted that Carter's
"regime had none of the phony, corrupt populism that has marked the Wallace years in neighboring Alabama. He fought for tough consumer laws and
banking regulation, and opened the government to blacks and women. He
developed new programs in health care, education, and corrections. . . . He
constantly traveled the state listening to citizen complaints, and he was the
kind of down-to-earth officeholder who could strike up a conversation with
a prison inmate mowing his lawn, find out that lawyers were bilking prisoners
with fake promises of parole, and do something about it." The most common
criticism of Carter was that his proposals were hurt by poor relations with the
legislature, a problem that was to reappear with grim consequences later in
his relations with Congress.

After his social progressivism, Carter is most remembered for his streamlining of state government from a confusing welter of 253 separate boards,
agencies, and commissions into 22 superagencies. No one ever verified
Carter's campaign statements that the reorganization and his "zero-based
budgeting" had saved the state $50 million per year, but they were an honest,
strong effort at reform.

Despite Georgia's economic advances, its per capita outlays for local
schools, higher education, and welfare have continued to lag well below the
national averages. There has been an exception in health and hospitals, for
which Georgia registered one of the nation's highest per capita expenditures.
The University of Georgia, at Athens, is an adequate but undistinguished
institution traditionally known as the place for future Georgia leaders to get
their educations. But despite embellishments such as Dean Rusk as a professor
of international law, the university's most outstanding department is still
agriculture. The academic level of Georgia Tech is substantially higher.

(Among private universities are well-endowed Emory in Atlanta and the various colleges of the black-operated Atlanta University Center.)

Carter's successor was George Busbee, an Albany lawyer who had been majority leader of the state house. During his first administration, Georgia law was changed so that the governor could succeed himself, and Busbee was reelected in 1978. Busbee became chairman of the National Governors Association and negotiated coolly and skillfully with the Reagan Administration, saving the states billions of dollars in Medicaid payments. The Democratic domination of the governor's office since Reconstruction continued under Busbee's successor, Joe Frank Harris, a rural veteran of the state assembly who pledged not to raise taxes and won the 1982 nomination over the objections of the Carter-Busbee urban, "New South" wing of the party.

Georgians in Washington

The presidency of Jimmy Carter remains the strongest image of Georgians in Washington: the darkhorse candidate who sought the White House after deciding he was equal to the parade of presidential candidates passing through the Georgia governor's mansion; the "outsider" candidate's amazing organizational and political success; and finally, the confusion and defeat that marked his term in office. However history judges Carter's record on the economy, Iran, and Middle East peace negotiations, Carter may be remembered in a positive light for drawing up an urban policy for the nation's troubled cities and forcing the Western states to begin thinking about new ways to finance water projects. In the selection of presidential aides, Carter's White House was Georgian to a fault.

Georgia has sent some "giants" to the U.S. Senate in this century. Walter F. George (1922–56) was one of the senators who withstood President Roosevelt's purge of conservatives in 1938; during the Eisenhower administration he became a tower of strength for bipartisan foreign policy. The death of Richard Brevard Russell, in 1971, symbolized the beginning of the end of the long Southern dominance of Congress, one of the most remarkable eras in American congressional history. If Russell had not come from Georgia, "where the race issue was so heated," Harry Truman wrote in his *Memoirs*, "he may very well have been President of the United States." But if the best of the old South —gentility, noble bearing, a deep sense of honor—were at the core of Richard Russell, so was the worst: an inflexibile, everlasting opposition to the cause of equal rights for the black man. Russell was the cunning field general of the Southern senators who met in his office to plan their fights against every bill to aid blacks, from the anti-lynching bills of the 1940s to the climactic civil rights statutes of the 1960s.

Herman Talmadge in the early '70s emerged as chairman of the Agriculture Committee. A close associate, quoted in a Ralph Nader congressional study, called him "a master at keeping his feet on the shifting sands of time." Indeed, the same man who in 1964 had been the featured speaker at a barbecue in honor of Samuel Green, grand dragon of the Ku Klux Klan, eventually received an honorary degree from predominantly black Morehouse College. But no one could have predicted that Talmadge would become an alcoholic (he has since recovered), decide to divorce his wife, Betty, or that she would learn of it on television news. Betty Talmadge retaliated by testifying before the Senate Ethics Committee that Talmadge kept thousands of dollars in unaccounted funds in an overcoat. The Senate denounced him for his financial conduct; in the 1980 election he was beaten by Mack Mattingly, an Indiana-born IBM executive and former Republican party chairman—the first Republican senator elected by popular vote in Georgia history, the first Republican senator since Reconstruction, and a GOP candidate who received an unprecedented third of the black vote.

Georgia has maintained real power in the Senate in the person of Sam Nunn, the conservative Democratic nephew of the late House veteran Carl Vinson. Nunn, first elected at age 34 in 1972, became an arms specialist on the Armed Services Committee to whom both Democrats and Republicans turn. Nunn convinced Carter to increase military spending on the grounds that a massive Soviet military preparation was underway; Senate watchers mark him as a likely future Armed Services chairman, as was Russell in times past. The most outstanding Georgian member of the House in this century was Carl Vinson, who actually served for 50 years from 1915 to 1965, and made his mark as chairman of the Armed Services Committee and "father of the modern Navy." The other standout was Andrew Young, the first black from the South since Reconstruction to be elected to Congress; Young became in 1977 Carter's ambassador to the United Nations, a position he left after he acted on his own in diplomatic negotiations one time too many. He later became mayor of Atlanta. In the early 1980s, the most active among the 10-member congressional delegation were Elliott Levitas, of Atlanta, who has run a one-man campaign to give Congress power over bureaucratically established rules and regulations; Wyche Fowler, a strong environmentalist who took over Andy Young's seat in Atlanta; and Newt Gingrich, a suburan Atlanta Republican who has urged the House Republican leadership toward confrontation rather than compromise with the Democrats.

Atlanta: Rise—and Fall?

"Bumptious, fractious, energetic, upstart: Atlanta was that always," *Atlanta Magazine* has described the city's history. It all started in the 1830s, when the Georgia legislature decided to build a rail line connecting the sea with the opening American interior and chose the place in the forest where Atlanta now stands as the terminus. Ten years later, a New York teacher visiting Atlanta wrote in his journal that "the people here bow and shake hands with everybody they meet, as there are so many coming in all the time that they cannot remember with whom they are acquainted." A little of the same remains today, as people from all over the country pour into Atlanta, national corporations move their people in and out, and the kaleidoscope of contact of a vital urban center revolves before one's very eyes. The constant flow of people in and out of Atlanta made it from the start a more urbane and tolerant place than most of the South but also a touch more predatory; in antebellum days, the city was known for its "pushy people" (a phrase from *Gone with the Wind.*) Margaret Mitchell also wrote of Atlanta: "It's brash and I like it." No genteel, familied aristocracy ever ruled in Atlanta; from the start, highest status went to its business entrepreneurs, the men who could attract capital. The moneyed group, and its sons and sons' sons, became the establishment and directed the political life too. But they never became a "closed corporation."

The success story of modern Atlanta is all the more appealing because the city, like its region, was in a state of de facto depression from 1864, when Sherman burned it on his march to the sea, until World War II. Not until the 1940s did Georgia property tax assessments return to the levels they had on the eve of the Civil War. Atlanta did reestablish itself as a transportation center after Sherman, but before World War II, Coca-Cola, founded in 1866, was the *only* pool of indigenous capital.* Not that Atlantans were not trying through all 75 years of depression. Henry Woodfin Grady came to Atlanta from Rome shortly after the Civil War and as editor of the *Constitution* preached his doctrine of a New South, where diversified industries would cast off the shackles of a one-crop economy. In 1925, Ivan Allen, Sr., launched the first "Forward Atlanta" program to proclaim the city's advantages in location, climate, labor supply, and natural resources. Even *Atlanta Magazine*, published by the chamber of commerce, has admitted that "the antiunion and ethnic thrust" of Forward Atlanta's advertisements are jolting to view today. But the campaign did help to create 762 new businesses and 20,000 jobs in the space of four years.

Atlanta's snail-like progress in the 75 years after Appomattox may have been a blessing in disguise. It never developed manufacturing, thus avoiding the overcrowding, smokestacks, and tenements of dynamic industrial cities. Not only did it become a gateway to the West, but the flow of trade and migration down the eastern flank of the Appalachians from the central Atlantic states led naturally to the city. And since Atlanta's altitude is higher than that of any large American cities, except Denver and Phoenix, it has one of the more salubrious climates in the Southern states.

One of the seeds of future prosperity was planted in the 1930s when William B. Hartsfield, a young alderman who had flown with the barnstormers in the

---

*The world's most popular soft drink was invented by a pharmacist and Confederate veteran named John S. Pemberton, who in 1886 made the first batch of coke—what he expected to be a hangover cure—in a three-legged iron pot in his Atlanta back yard. Ownership soon passed to another local pharmacist-entrepreneur, Asa Griggs Candler, who paid only $2,300 for his interest. When Candler finally sold out in 1916 to become mayor of Atlanta, he was worth $50 million. Though a relatively small Atlanta employer (2,500 in the early 1980s), Coca-Cola has 1,500 franchises around the world, grossing close to $6 billion a year, a literal money tree for many Atlantans and their civic causes.

early days of aviation, set out to make Atlanta the chief regional airport of the New York-to-Miami lighted air route. Birmingham, at the tip of the mountains, was the more natural site for the airport in that era when mountain-top beams were being used to mark the mail routes. But Atlanta "outgreeted" the low-ranking federal aviation official who made the recommendations and won the designation. Hartsfield was elected mayor in 1937 and served almost continuously until 1961. Though not a businessman, he forged the close business-political alliance that would characterize postwar Atlanta.

Despite its growth in the first postwar years, Atlanta was suffering a net loss of jobs in the late 1950s, and the second Forward Atlanta program was born. Its inventor was Ivan Allen, Jr., an inveterate Atlanta booster like his father. But there was more than boosterism to the second Forward Atlanta; Allen insisted that while the city sang its own praises, it would have to add expressways and mass transit, build a stadium, and preserve its public schools in the new era of integration. Adopting the new Forward Atlanta program, which he had formulated as president of the chamber of commerce in 1960, Allen ran for mayor and won election as Hartsfield's successor in 1961.

The '60s, a period of national prosperity, emerged as Atlanta's decade for incredible growth. A quarter million new jobs were created (for a new total of more than 600,000); 247 new office buildings and 353 warehouses went up. The movers and shakers and entrepreneurs and hustling bankers transformed the formerly humdrum business center of Atlanta into a shimmering, high-rise vision of the New South. Aggressive banking had a lot to do with the growth. The chief catalyst was Mills Lane, who made Citizens and Southern National Bank (where you could always reach him in person—no secretary to dodge) into one of the nation's most innovative and competitive consumer banks. By the end of the '60s, Atlanta was not only the leading money market of the South, but competitive with almost any other banking center in the country. Its banks, rather than participating in deals formulated in New York, were creating their own syndications (such as the one that loaned Delta Airlines $200 million in 1970) and inviting banks from New York and other cities to join the action.

But when the history of Atlanta's growth era is written, the central role will go not to a man who started as a real estate developer or financier, but rather to architect John C. Portman, Jr. An Atlanta native, Portman graduated from Georgia Tech in 1950, worked for three years for the local branch of a New York architectural firm, and then went into business for himself. His biggest project of the early years was the Merchandise Mart, on Peachtree Street— the wholesaling nerve center of the Southeast. As Portman was building the mart, he and his partner at the time, Trammell Crow of Dallas, started acquiring land around it on the theory that "We can't just allow anything to happen here." Other men with that kind of vision might have approached the city's business or political leadership, but Portman and Crow operated independently, trying to prove that each step-by-step addition to what they now called the Peachtree Center would have to justify itself as a business matter. "We're not building things to sell," Portman said. "We don't take rapid depreciation. We're trying to build sound, solid developments of lasting value."

Some 45 acres were acquired for the Peachtree Center, to include office towers, a hotel, gardens, galleries, restaurants, museums and theatres, and residential apartments. Portman's rule was that these coordinate urban units all be within seven and a half minutes walking time of each other—"the distance people will walk without thinking about wheels," he told us. He selected two horizontal connections between the buildings of the complex: one at 22 stories, by means of pedestrian passageways; the other at "the people or mall level."

The jewel of the Peachtree Center became Portman's Regency Hyatt House Hotel, its vast sunlit open central court, surrounded by 22 stories of rooms, dramatized (as if that were necessary) by glass-bubble elevators, festooned with lights, and a 70-foot fountain. Portman planned it as the antithesis of what he called "the typical hotel, where you go into a lobby with a fairly low ceiling and you get into a closed elevator and go to your room by way of a narrow corridor." It became the forerunner of swarms of other Portman hotels around the country, too stagy and flamboyant for some critics but beloved of business travelers.

There was also a profound tragedy in the Portman approach: blatant disregard of the city street in favor of blank walls and automobile-oriented entrances, the construction of cold and forbidding "megastructures" that had the effect of confining workers and visitors to "safe" interior spaces and blighting much of the territory about them. A block or two from the Peachtree Center and other humongous structures that came to line Peachtree Street one found a scene of urban devastation, from empty lots to ugly old warehouses. Real estate prices shot up so fast that nothing short of another multihundred-million-dollar megastructure was conceivable. There were precious few of the small and colorful shops, restaurants, galleries, and gathering points for people that give a city character. A business group, Central Atlanta Progress, strove mightily under leader Dan Sweat to introduce inner-city housing and to create "a high-grade So-Ho" in the 36-block Fairlie-Popular area flanking Peachtree Street from Five Points (the historic heart of Atlanta now synonymous with high finance) to the Peachtree Center. The tragedy was that a somewhat slower, less ambitious, less monumental approach to center city office and hotel building would have left much more of old Atlanta's texture in place, without the need to start again from scratch.

Atlanta has never developed a master plan like James Oglethorpe's for Savannah, and it has shown pitifully small regard for historic preservation—the standard excuse being that Sherman burned down everything of merit. But along Peachtree itself, one finds the vital spine of the city as it has evolved —running for 20 miles north and northeasterly from Five Points. Here are Rich's department store and the pre-mall retail jugular of the South, from specialty shops to fading junk stores. Soon after the flashing brilliance of Peachtree Center come shabby boarding houses and schlock stores, then miles of the pedestrian office structures which rule the South. At 15th Street, one sees the gleaming Atlanta Memorial Arts Center, built in the 1960s in memory of the 122 Atlanta art patrons who died in a 1962 air crash in Paris. Upper Peachtree is a melange of new hosteleries and older, sedate residences, of shopping centers and luxury apartment towers, of movie houses and auto lots. Finally the street reaches a point where the Indians had a crossroads, and there was a single peachtree (from whence this long street's name). The northernmost reaches of Atlanta, also along Peachtree's path, harbor posh residential sections where many of the "power structure" live in mansions at the end of long, gated driveways—the starkest conceivable contrast to grim Atlanta slums such as Buttermilk Bottom and Vine City.

During the boom years in the '60s, Atanta's national and international image was also enhanced by its position as the fountainhead of civil rights activity for the entire Southern United States. Dr. Martin Luther King, Jr.'s, Southern Christian Leadership Conference operated out of headquarters on Atlanta's "sweet Auburn," sparking the battles of Montgomery and Birmingham and Selma and countless little towns that never made a headline in the North, but transformed the life of black people all across the South. Even in the '80s, SCLC remained a leader in such causes as renewal of the Voting Rights Act, while the Voter Education Project kept careful track of black voting and officeholding progress across the Southland, especially in remote, rural counties still resistant to civil rights goals. Also based in Atlanta were other groups such as the Federation of Southern Cooperatives and the Emergency Land Fund which addressed the continuing problems of black owners of small farms and low-income rural families.

In the midst of Atlanta's black neighborhoods, one discovers the brick buildings of the Atlanta University Center, the largest center for black people's education in the world. There are four undergraduate colleges (Clark, Morehouse, Morris Brown, and Spellman), the Interdenominational Theological Seminary, and a graduate center, Atlanta University. Founded in the years after the Civil War, these institutions harbored such eminent black intellectuals as W.E.B. DuBois. They have produced thousands of black leaders in education, government, business, and religion. Nowhere has their contribution been greater than in Atlanta itself, where they formed the elite of the nation's best educated and uniquely self-assured black community. Martin Luther King, Jr., was the most prominent example of that, but there have been (and are) many others, including the leaders of the black Atlanta business community and political figures.

Though black economic power has emerged in the last decades in such cities as Detroit, Philadelphia, and Los Angeles, Atlanta pioneered black capitalism in America and still has an extraordinarily large pool of black capital and corporate wealth, centered in the banks, insurance companies, and stores—all owned and operated by blacks—along Auburn Avenue (now slightly seedy but long called "the richest Negro street in the world") and nearby Hunter Street. The depth of black roots in Georgia was expressed to us by former Mayor Maynard Jackson: "My roots are here," he said. "My mother was born two miles from here. I'm a fifth-generation Georgian. It may be deeper than that, but they didn't keep our records before 1865." And most important for the tenor of black and white relations, and the pride of the black community, Jackson said, is the memory of Martin Luther King, Jr. "He's buried here. His legacy is still living here. It still influences decisions here."*

Blacks became a vital force in Atlanta politics following World War II and abolition of the white primary and in time formed a working alliance with leading white moderates such as Mayor Ivan Allen, Jr. Allen was later able to recall how, step by step, his own attitudes on race changed (he had once favored segregation), and he was able to bring the Atlanta business community along with him toward full integration. Allen walked the streets of the ghetto years before Northern mayors got the idea and when rioting broke out in 1966 kept damage to a minimum by going to the scene and personally seeking to calm passions. (Seeds of racial understanding—and thus the path to a smooth transition—were also planted by Ralph McGill, editor and later publisher of the *Atlanta Constitution*, who deserved to be called, as he was by many, "the conscience of the South.")

In 1972, Atlanta made Southern political/racial history by electing Andrew J. Young, an erstwhile aide to Martin Luther King, Jr., as Georgia's—and the South's—first black congressman since Reconstruction. In 1973, when Maynard Jackson became Atlanta's first black mayor, many businessmen complained they had difficulty dealing with Jackson. But the fact was that Atlanta's skyline continued to burgeon as businesses such as Georgia Power, Coca-Cola, Georgia Pacific, and Southern Bell put up new headquarters. Central Atlanta boomed with new business support firms; construction proceeded on a vastly expanded airport; and the city moved ahead with the Southland's new subway/rapid rail system.

There were new concerns, however, about Atlanta neighborhoods, which had paid a heavy price (in freeway destruction) for much of center city's progress. Jackson won partly by opposing a new freeway pushed by downtown business interests, thus garnering the support of the new League of Neighborhoods. The successful anti-highway drive proved to be only the first step in the rise of neighborhood power; under a new city charter, 24 neighborhood "units" had the right to register their wishes and see them fed directly into the comprehensive plan and budget of the city.

*One of the most momentous occasions of Atlanta's history was the warm April day of 1968 when the fallen King's body was borne through the city streets on a wagon drawn by mules—symbols of the black man's sad heritage in the South. For the first time in history, every man on the Atlanta police department was on duty at the same time that day. But the real reason that order and reverence were maintained, while 20 burning cities elsewhere in America became King's funeral pyre, was that the black people of Atlanta wanted it to be peaceful, and that the white leadership (except for Lester Maddox, who kept the state capitol an armed garrison) showed they really cared. King's memory is kept alive by the continued residence of his family and the downtown Martin Luther King Center, where his civil rights work is carried forward.

Crime became a deep, nagging problem. By 1972, Atlanta had the highest homicide rate in the country, and even though the number of homicides had declined slightly in the early 1980s, the image remained due to the tragic murders of 28 young black people between 1979 and 1981. A black man, Wayne Williams, was convicted of two of them. One reason the young blacks may have been such easy prey was their level of poverty: police tried luring children into cars with a promise of $10, and according to Mayor Jackson, every child accepted the offer. Despite Atlanta's economic progress, 25 percent of city residents remained below the federal poverty line. The public schools had become almost totally black. While the city's population declined, the suburbs boomed. DeKalb County, the biggest and the wealthiest, ended the 1970s with 483,024 people, while some of the more distant suburban areas more than doubled their populations. Atlanta lost so many middle-class whites that by 1980 the population was 66.5 percent black; in the suburban areas, the black percentage was only 13.4 percent. Businesses, especially young, growing computer companies, were locating in the suburban office parks often close to the white work force, the superhighways, and the airport.

From the early '70s onward, it was apparent that Atlanta was not continuing the heady growth of the '60s. In 1974, a giddy real estate bubble burst, as speculators and bankers were left holding millions of square feet of office space and raw farmland far from downtown. In 1978, *Fortune* ran a headline "Atlanta Sobers Up," accompanied by a story noting that Atlanta had lost the economic characteristics that had made it so attractive to business in the '60s: a large supply of cheap labor due to the massive migration from rural Georgia and the unusually cohesive and pro-development business community.

Into this situation former Congressman and U.N. Ambassador Andrew Young came home to run for mayor in 1981. The business community put its solid backing behind Sidney Marcus, a liberal Jewish state legislator, but, as pollster Claibourne Darden noted after the election, Atlanta's electorate had become 56.3 percent black, making the prospect of electing any white remote. Atlantans split almost exactly along racial lines to elect Young. After the election, Young offered an olive branch to the business community and mounted a campaign against street crimes in the central business district. Young announced plans to turn Atlanta into an "international city" and used his contacts with African and Middle East nations to attract business to Atlanta—a forerunner of the "municipal international policies" that might be in store for many U.S. cities in the '80s and '90s. Young also surprised black leaders and pleased business leaders by fighting for an increase in the local sales tax, a measure designed to ameliorate skyrocketing property taxes which opponents claimed would hit poor people hardest. The voters eventually approved it. He also found himself opposing the neighborhood movement when he came out in favor of building the Carter presidential library and a sunken four-lane parkway to it in Inman Park, a neighborhood a couple miles from downtown Atlanta. But Young did not lose his civil rights fervor or position of leadership among blacks nationally. In 1982, while leading 400 black civil rights leaders and members of Congress at a prayer breakfast, he wept in a demonstration of the helplessness and hopelessness he felt over the bitter reversals blacks were experiencing under the Reagan administration.

Second-Tier Cities: From Savannah to Rome

After Atlanta, the story of urban Georgia turns quickly to coastal Savannah (pop. 141,634), the place where Georgia began. The founder was General James Oglethorpe, who arrived with his band of 125 English settlers in 1773. Before then, the white man's touch with Georgia had been limited to brief Spanish explorations, starting with Hernando de Soto's search for gold in 1540. The English planned Savannah to be the capital of their last and poorest New World colony, a military buffer between the thriving Carolinas and the Spanish in Florida, and a repository of the unfortunate souls of England's debtors prisons, whose cause Oglethorpe had made his own.

Oglethorpe went up the Savannah River some 10 miles from the sea, found "a healthy situation" for a town, on high land where the river formed a half moon, and there, he reported to his English trustees, "I have laid out the town." No one knows for sure what the genesis was of Oglethorpe's town plan. But the plan was so felicitous that Philadelphia's urban planner Edmund Bacon has called it "exalted . . . one of the finest diagrams for city organization and growth in existence."

Oglethorpe's plan was deceptively simple: a series of modular units, called "wards," each with public buildings and some 40 residential lots, with a public square at the center, laid out neatly across the landscape one beside the next. The public squares were the secret genius of the plan, because each became a quiet oasis at the front doorstep, or almost so, of every house—the equivalent of the green in a New England village. The plan succeeded so brilliantly because it allowed order and diversity to flourish together.

Nineteenth-century Savannah grew and prospered with King Cotton, as millions of tons each year passed through the factoring houses along the riverfront, there to be loaded on ships. By 1819, Savannah was the 16th-largest city in America. In December 1864, Union General William T. Sherman arrived in Savannah but decided to spare it from the torch and pillaging he had visited on Atlanta and countless other towns along his destructive march.

The golden age of Savannah came to an abrupt halt in 1895, when cotton prices collapsed, and the city had little to fall back on. A sleepy, indifferent ruling class controlled the life of Savannah, and little heed was paid to the life of the destitute blacks who inhabited a ring of dilapidated wooden structures, some dating back to the days of slavery.

Industries began to move in, most notably a mill of the Union Camp Corporation that was enticed in 1935 through city promises to protect it from property taxes and antipollution lawsuits. Eventually, the mill became the biggest paper-bag producer in the world (35 million a day), with 5,000 workers on its payroll. But it polluted the Savannah River, its rotten egg stench befouling the city. Another industrial recruit was American Cyanimid, which dumped about a million pounds of acid wastes into the river each day, cutting back the oyster beds, the shrimp, and the fish populations. Another culprit was the city of Savannah itself, which dumped the raw sewage of 150,000 people into the Savannah River. The good news: through state and federal regulatory efforts, virtually all the pollution was cleaned up in the 1970s.

After World War II suburban subdivisions prospered, a multimillion-dollar suburban shopping mall went up, and only decay and piecemeal demolition seemed to await the old center city. Then, in 1955, the seeds of a grand renewal were sown, sparked by a lost battle to save the city's historic old vegetable and fish market. Mrs. Anna C. Hunter and other Savannah *grande dames* formed the Historic Savannah Foundation, which began to buy up the old homes and then resell them quickly under protective covenants that required the new owners to restore the exteriors in harmony with each building's architectural heritage. The foundation did relatively little for Savannah's blacks or its lower-class whites; some were forced out of their neighborhoods and homes by the restoration process. In the 1970s, Leopold Adler II, an investment banker, descendant of an old Savannah family and former president of the foundation, turned his attention to the adjacent but seriously deteriorated "Victorian District"—a 45-block area of wood-frame, gingerbread homes where slumlords had packed in low-income black tenant families. Unable to convince aristocratic Historic Savannah to participate in his plan, Adler and his friends formed the nonprofit Savannah Landmark Rehabilitation Project to buy half the homes in the Victorian District, rehabilitate them, and rent them out to low-income people. With liberal use of federal subsidies, the project began to create a stable community of blacks and whites of all income levels living together in an historic neighborhood.

Garish neon signs proclaim that Columbus (pop. 169,441), some 90 miles southwest of Atlanta, is an Army town, and indeed it is: nearby is Fort Benning, one of the biggest Army bases anywhere, a place called "the university of the Army" because it houses schools for infantry, airborne, rangers, and officer candidates. Benning makes Columbus one of the "marryingest" places in America, as girls from small towns all over Georgia and Alabama float in, in hopes of catching a young officer or noncom. Benning also made Columbus an international dateline with the celebrated 1971 trial of 1st Lt. William L. Calley, Jr., on charges of murdering 102 Vietnamese civilians in a hamlet called Mylai. The Vietnam War took a heavy toll of casualties in fighting men from Columbus families, but this remained one of the most militaristic of American cities to the end.

Beneath the military gloss, Columbus remains a low-wage Southern textile mill town, with all the problems of same. By the early '80s, however, two of the six state representatives were black, one from a predominantly white area. Columbus' governmental merger with Muscogee County is one of the purest examples of city-county consolidation in the country. And military-mill town Columbus has discovered its past, restoring the Springer Opera House and turning an old Iron Works into a convention center.

Centrally located Macon, Georgia's third-largest city (pop. 116,860), gained some notoriety in the late '60s and early '70s when a firebrand mayor, Ronnie Thompson, suggested on the police radio during racial tensions that a submachine gun should have been test-fired "in the neighborhoods." Macon started out as a cotton town, boomed on textiles, and has a number of thriving diversified industries. Robins Air Force Base remains important, however.

One of Georgia's fastest-growing cities is Albany, in South Georgia, a town that had only 19,055 people in 1940, but 112,662 in its metropolitan area by the time of the 1980 Census. Long a peanut and pecan farming center, Albany has been drawing the excess farm folk to work in its many thriving new industries. The city operates its own electric and gas systems, a touch of socialism that industries happily overlook because it helps to keep taxes down. The startling array of plants drawn to Albany since 1970 include the likes of Kroger (a national food chain), Miller Brewing, Merck (pharmaceuticals), Proctor and Gamble (paper products), and Firestone (tires).

While Albany, an obscure town by national standards, was growing, the Savannah River city of Augusta, founded by Oglethorpe and kept famous by the annual Masters tournament of the Augusta National Golf Club, was in a state of serious decline. White people have fled this once proud "Garden City of the South," where six men lost their lives in 1970 in one of the worst race riots of modern Southern history. Early in the 1970s, blacks moved into the majority in Augusta; by 1980, the city had only 47,532 people—23,000 less than in 1960. In the meantime, nearby unincorporated areas, fed by military installations and burgeoning industries, more than doubled their populations.

Note might be taken of two smaller Georgia cities with special qualities to recommend them. Athens (pop. 42,549) has prospered because it is home of the University of Georgia; the town also harbors some of the most beautiful estates in the South. And in northwestern Georgia, Rome (29,654) has been saved from periodic floods, courtesy of the army engineers and their dikes, and a long-term decline of the downtown has been turned around. The flavor of Rome is very much that of the Appalachian hill people.

Rural Georgia

The rural counties of northern Georgia bear striking similarity to the other Appalachian hill areas of the South. Farms are small, in many places a kind of hillbilly culture (complete with moonshining) prevails, and poverty used to be endemic. The region has had pockets of Republicanism ever since the Civil War. Atlantans (and some Chattanoogans) have flocked into north Georgia for sports, the spring-to-autumn scenery, and vacation homes. The little north Georgia city of Dalton (pop. 20,743) is the tufted textile capital of America. Textiles, and food processing, are important in Gainesville (15,280), the backbone of Georgia's big poultry industry. In fact, a quite high percentage of north Georgia's working population now has jobs in manufacturing plants. Wages are below national averages, but the industries have helped to push per capita income far ahead of black belt and southern Georgia.

North Georgia is a prime example of how multi-county planning and development districts—an idea born in Georgia in the 1950s and since spread across the country—can do for an entire region of a state what no single county could do for itself. The Georgia Mountains Planning and Development District, set up in the mid-1960s, helped its 13 counties and 39 municipalities get millions of dollars in federal funds for parks, water, sewer facilities, roads, health clinics, and like projects—until the 1980s, when shrinkage of federal aid flows prompted serious rethinking of how rural areas can promote themselves from their own resources alone.

In middle Georgia, one comes on the black belt, once plantation land, the stronghold of first slavery and then the tenant farmer system. Tenant farming as it once was has largely disappeared, but 40 percent of farmers still rent part of their land. Driving through the black belt, one sees many abandoned houses, from shacks to plantations. A high proportion of the blacks—and many of those who used to be called the "white trash," too—have moved to nearby towns or the big Georgia cities. And the black belt supplied the lion's share of the 600,000 blacks who left Georgia altogether between 1940 and 1970.

Today the era of lynchings (491 Georgia blacks were lynched between 1882 and 1952) is over, along with the worst kind of police brutality and "accidental" jail killings so well documented by the U.S. Commission on Civil Rights in its early years. But still, the poverty lingers on. The thought of the black belt conjures up many visions of what was best and what was worst of Georgia's traditions, and of the painful, inexorable progress now being made toward a more equitable society.

Within the black belt lies Warm Springs, the town Franklin D. Roosevelt made famous. FDR had a home there, and died there; and Warm Springs may have played a greater role in history than its residents ever dreamed. Roosevelt biographers agree that his friendships with Warm Springs people, together with his observations of the crushing rural poverty of the area, were touchstones of many of the social reform measures of the New Deal.

Hancock County, an economically barren spot 85 miles southeast of Atlanta in Georgia's red clay country, became in 1968 the first biracial county in the Deep South, or in all of America for that matter, to come under black political control. Despite a black population of more than 80 percent, Hancock had been a die-hard bastion of white supremacy. The blacks, many of whom lived in tenant shacks on shabby farms, were rigorously consigned to separate but unequal facilities, and the county seat newspaper, the *Sparta Ishmaelite*, reserved its back page for "Colored News." But the white minority control began to disintegrate when blacks, in the wake of the 1965 Voting Rights Act, started registering in impressive numbers. In 1966 they sent the first members of their race ever to fill posts in the dowdy Faulknerian edifice called the county courthouse. By 1968, their control was complete.

The man who galvanized Hancock's blacks into political action was John L. McCown, a South Carolina native and itinerant civil rights worker. McCown brought millions of foundation and federal antipoverty dollars into

Hancock, but the dreams of prosperity for Hancock's blacks ended sadly in 1976 when an inebriated McCown died piloting his airplane, one of the many luxury items he had purchased with misused funds. More moderate blacks eventually took the reigns of power in Hancock and worked with the white establishment. But for all the wrong McCown did, one Hancock black told writer Phil Gailey, "he undid our chains and straightened our backs. You can't take that away from him."

South and southeast of the black belt, and stretching to the sea, lies the region called simply south Georgia. The physical image is of millions and millions of slash pines, which mature in 25 to 30 years in the hot climate, twice as fast as in the Pacific Northwest. All across the region, one sees giant smoke stacks of the pulp and paper mills. Most are new enough to have modern antipollution equipment. Georgia is the largest timber-producing state in the Southeast, harvesting some 54,000 acres per year at a value of $6.4 billion.

South Georgia harbors the vast and intriguing Okefenokee Swamp, the bog the Indians called "the land of the trembling earth." In the swamp, one finds great moss-bedecked cypresses, pines, hollies, and magnolias; the rich variety of fauna runs from bears and bobcats to threatening cottonmouth moccasins and the biggest alligators on the continent.

Georgia's window to the Atlantic is less than 100 miles long, running from Savannah, on the north, to the little fishing city of Brunswick, on the south. But the coastline is a priceless asset of still largely inviolate marshlands and what the first explorers called the "Golden Isles of Guale": Wassaw, St. Catherines, Blackbeard, Sapelo, St. Simons, Sea Isle, Jekyll, and Cumberland. Coastal attractions such as the wild, lush wilderness island of Cumberland (made a national seashore in 1972) are prime Georgia tourist territory. For a while in the 1970s, attention shifted inland toward the small dusty town of Plains, home of the Carter family (Miss Lillian, brother Billy, and President Jimmy). Things have calmed down in Plains, although President Carter returned there after leaving Washington.

The next "big town" to Plains is Americus, generally despised by the White House press corps from Carter days but worth viewing for a project most power-minded national reporters missed. Here in the 1940s a farmer-preacher named Clarence Jordan started Koinonia Farms, an integrated Christian community. The program was expanded by Habitat through Humanity, an organization started by Millard Fuller, a former Alabama millionaire-lawyer and protégé of Jordan. Habitat uses volunteer labor, gifts, and interest-free loans from individuals to build simple houses for the poor, and the program has expanded throughout the world. Most of Habitat's money still comes from individual contributors and churches in Northern states; sad to report, Southern Baptist churches have shown little interest. For all its progress in law, the so widely heralded New South still has far to go in matters of the spirit.

SOUTH CAROLINA

Fossil No More

SHOULD ANYONE DOUBT that historic experience can decisively shape and mold an American state, from its earliest times of European settlement even unto the present day, let him consider the case of South Carolina: a state that was the center, almost the embodiment, of the American South, when Mississippi was still Indian territory. In the 19th century, its leaders virtually created the South as a self-conscious region, and they led it out of the Union. Bleak years of poverty, pervasive Confederate nostalgia, and general intellectual stagnation came between the Civil War and World War II. It was then that South Carolina was truly a "fossilized" society. But in the 1960s, it was South Carolina that showed the South the way toward racial integration with dignity. During that decade and the one that followed, the state became a national showcase in attracting industrial development, both domestic and foreign, and in educating its work force to meet the new demands of high-skill employment.

So it is that from the peculiarly aristocratic nature of the early planter class and the intellectual life of old Charles Town, to the era of John C. Calhoun and the professed paternalistic care of slaves, to Fort Sumter, Reconstruction, the Upcountry textile culture, and the unique political roles of men such as James F. Byrnes, J. Strom Thurmond, and Ernest F. Hollings, the themes of a unique civilization ring down the corridors of history. Violence has raged, from the bloody suppression of early slave rebellions to countless lynchings in the middle years to the 1968 massacre at South Carolina State College at Orangeburg in which the state police, called to quell an unruly campus demonstration, shot point blank into a group of students, killing three and injuring 27 others. But those have been the exceptions to the rule. Primarily South Carolina has practiced a softer kind of coercion—most often, less from raw hatred between black and white people than in the interest of the hegemony of the ruling class. South Carolinians, Joseph B. Cummings, Jr., once wrote, are a lot like Orientals, worshipping their ancestors and eating rice, "but above all, they save face." Even segregationists, Cummings continued, were offended by extreme activities such as bus dumping, preferring to run things "with a surface grace, but with enormous emphasis on control —like a plantation or a cotton mill."

As it entered the 1980s, in its fourth century of history, South Carolina still carried a long list of disadvantages compared with other states. Its land, cultivated continuously for centuries, was still trying to regain its fertility. Despite an immense increase in industrial investment, manufacturing remained heavily weighted toward textiles, one of America's lowest paid industries and a major reason South Carolina factory wages ranked a miserable 47th among the states. Per capita income was only three-quarters of the national average (though this was an extraordinary improvement over the 38 percent of the national average in 1929). Health and nutrition problems continued to be among the most serious in the United States, accounting for one of the shortest life expectancies. Poverty was still rampant, particularly among blacks, who made up 30 percent of the population, the highest proportion of any state except Mississippi. Welfare payments ranked only above Mississippi. A deficient educational system was responsible for a high rate of functional illiteracy. South Carolinians ranked first in aggravated assaults and still tried to solve social problems by "locking them up"; only North Carolina had more people in prison for the size of its population.

But a new generation of politicians has been more interested in solving social and economic problems than refighting the Civil War. To its ancient value of courtesy, South Carolina has added concern about the underprivileged, including some increases in state social programs, which could make poorer people more participatory citizens. By the 1970s and early '80s, racism seldom succeeded as a political strategy. Had V.O. Key been writing his *Southern Politics* again, he would no longer have been able to make the assertion regarding South Carolina he did in the 1940s: "Whenever the going gets rough, when a glimmer of informed political self-interest begins to well up from the masses, the issue of white supremacy may be raised to whip them back into line." The Voting Rights Act of 1965 did enfranchise hundreds of thousands of black voters. Even Strom Thurmond, erstwhile Dixiecrat candidate for the presidency, found it necessary to extend constituent services to blacks.

The newly enfranchised black voters renewed the strength of the Democratic party vis-à-vis the rising Republicans. But despite a black population of almost 950,000, the state in 1982 had yet to elect a black to Congress. Persistent, too, was that ancient scourge: abysmally low voter turnout. In 1980 only 43 percent of South Carolina's eligible voters participated, the lowest rate among the states.

The Heritage Forms

Large portions of the Deep South states were rough-hewn frontier country into the early 19th century. Not so South Carolina, and especially not its Charles Town and the surrounding coastal Lowcountry, first settled by the English in 1670. Dependent from the start on slave labor, great plantations cultivating a single crop—first rice or indigo, then cotton—thrived from the earliest years. As Richard Hofstadter wrote in *America at 1750*, "South Carolina in its heyday enjoyed a prosperity that surpassed anything seen in the other colonies. . . . By comparison with Charles Town's elite, old Boston's upper crust looked poor and flimsy, and the hedonistic life of the South

Carolina capital put the other seaboard towns in the shade."

New Englander Josiah Quincy probably exaggerated when he said that South Carolina was "divided into opulent and lordly planters, poor and spiritless peasants and vile slaves." But a society of vivid class contrasts was certainly what the first South Carolinians had in mind. The English philosopher John Locke was commissioned to draw up laws for the Lords Proprietors appointed by King Charles II, and his "Grand Model" provided for three orders of nobility: barons, caciques, and landgraves, each with large landed estates. The Church of England would be the established religion. The proprietor system was abolished in 1707, but the idea of a titled nobility living at ease upon the labor of others persisted among the planters who appointed overseers for their plantations and lived in comfort in Charles Town. Many of the early settlers came from Barbados, bringing with them the West Indian slave plantation concept. Not even the later addition of Huguenots, Swiss, and Germans would seriously alter the aristocratic English and Barbadian tradition. "South Carolina," Hofstadter noted, "developed the most lordly and most leisured ruling class in America."

South Carolina's earliest settlement was confined to a thin coastal strip, some 15 to 20 miles deep, filled with waterways and great swamps ideal—with adequate slave labor—for the growing of rice. Between that tidewater region and the fall line, the essential geographic dividing line between Lowcountry and Upcountry South Carolina, German and Scotch-Irish began farming in the 1720s and '30s. Then, in the 1750s, waves of Scotch-Irish settlers from the northern colonies began to fill the rolling hills and ragged woods of the Piedmont Plateau. They were a fiercely Calvinistic lot, small farmers who rarely owned slaves and disdained the effete Lowcountry culture.

The differences between the Upcountry and Lowcountry and these two cultures created a conflict that would endure into the 20th century. By the late 1700s, Upcountry whites outnumbered Lowcountry whites. The Lowcountrymen, who had controlled the colony from the start, realized they would have to make some kind of compromise if they wanted to preserve the unity of South Carolina. They compromised to the extent of moving the capital from Charleston to Columbia, on the border of the fall line. But the state constitution of 1790 rigged the scheme of representation to assure continued Lowcountry control of the legislature, which—in the words of writer Jack Bass—"operated as a ruling committee of the landed gentry and provided in South Carolina an aristocratic republic."

South Carolina played an important role in the winning of American independence and sent distinguished delegates to the Continental Congress and the Constitutional Convention. But obsession with the slavery issue soon eclipsed that proud heritage. In the late 1700s, white immigration created a white majority, and slavery seemed to be waning. But in 1793 the Yankee Eli Whitney invented the cotton gin, and the cultivation of cotton—with slavery following in its wake—spread into the Upcountry. The slave trade was reopened in 1804, and by 1820 South Carolina again had a black majority population (and would until the 1920s). "The lust for the new money crop and the greed it generated," Bass wrote, "produced a closed society in which defense of slavery could not be questioned." Those who tried—such as the courageous Grimke Sisters, Sarah and Angelina, members of an aristocratic Charleston family—were forced into exile after they joined the Abolitionist movement. South Carolina's John C. Calhoun wrote as early as 1837: "Many in the South once believed that it [slavery] was a moral and political evil. That folly and delusion are gone."

Bellicosity, nullification, finally secession, these were the chief contributions of South Carolina to the young American republic. Calhoun was one of the so-called War Hawks in Congress who urged declaration of the War of 1812, and later 1,100 South Carolinian volunteers happily went off to fight against Mexico in 1846. The Citadel, South Carolina's military college at Charleston, was founded in 1824 in response to the danger of slave uprisings; later a detachment of volunteers from its cadet ranks manned the Charleston batteries that fired the first shots of the Civil War. The tariff begun in the 1810s seemed to South Carolinians a particular injustice to their regional interests; in 1830 the state made a formal declaration of States Rights principles, enacting an ordinance nullifying the act of Congress that imposed tariffs. Calhoun resigned as vice president under Andrew Jackson to enter the Senate and fight for nullification; the state mobilized for war, and conflict was barely averted through a compromise on the tariff. But the burning issue of a state's right to nullify federal acts or secede from the Union remained unresolved, and it was on December 20, 1860, that a convention in Charleston adopted the Ordinance of Secession—the first state to take that fatal step. A Charleston newspaper headline the next day read: "Union Dissolved," reflecting South Carolina's lofty self-importance. But the other Southern states soon followed suit. Then came the volley of shots against the federal *Star of the West,* as it tried to bring reinforcements to Fort Sumter in Charleston Harbor on January 9, 1861. In the great war that ensued, South Carolina would lose a quarter of the 63,000 men it sent into battle. When General William Tecumseh Sherman's troops arrived in Columbia in 1865, they devastated the city with no compunctions, for they remembered which state had first broken the bonds of Union and begun the conflict.* In fact, Sherman's troops cut a path of destruction 50 to 60 miles wide across the state, leaving a trail of destruction and vandalism and a legacy of bitterness in the hearts of South Carolinians that lingers to this day.

In the view of many South Carolinians, it was Reconstruction, an era of "organized hell, . . . villainy, anarchy, misrule, and robbery," which harmed the state the most. Modern historians confirm many of the abuses of the 1868–1876 Reconstruction period but point out that "the conditions imposed by the North were not satanic." There was widespread graft and corruption,

---

*Sherman's famous march had taken him from Atlanta to Savannah, and then to Columbia, skipping regal old Charleston. South Carolinians believe (true or not) that Sherman spared Charleston because he had a mistress there.

but the 1868 constitution was perhaps the best in the state's history. The Reconstruction legislature, the only one in the South with a majority of black members, established South Carolina's first public school system. Such an embellishment would have been irrelevant for the antebellum planter aristocracy, which sent its own young to private academies and considered education of the masses, especially blacks, more a threat than a blessing.

Physically and spiritually, it took South Carolina close to a century to recover from the ruination of war. The plantation system was expunged; the landowners had no capital and the laborers no land. Sharecropping became prevalent. The state's preeminent position in rice was lost to states farther west. Tobacco was renewed as a crop of some importance in the northeastern section, and corn and livestock were important. But basically South Carolina subsisted on cotton, the crop best suited to sharecropping and tenancy. In 1880 owners and tenants were about equal in number, but by 1935 the boll weevil and the harsh realities of the cotton economy had driven the number of farm owners down to 11,000—compared to 103,000 tenants. Millions of acres of land were so exhausted that they were no longer fit for cultivation.

Textiles expanded from the 1880s onward, providing some 89,000 jobs by 1939. Employment, however, was restricted almost entirely to whites, and much of the production took place in company towns in the Piedmont, a locale of both cheap water power and a docile labor force. High profits for the owners, crumbs for the workers, a dependence on cotton, and a strict color line—it was the plantation system reincarnate. (When the mills were built, Key observed, "often a first act of the new mill owner was to build a church, put the pastor on his payroll, and reap the profits of a theology propagating the doctrine that the meek shall inherit the earth.")

The burden of the past rested just as heavily on the political system. Reconstruction was ended and native white rule restored in the 1876 elections that brought to power Bourbon Democrats dedicated to white supremacy, parsimonious government, and the encouragement of manufacturing. The impoverished whites of the Upcountry, however, were not long content with rule of the old planter class. An agricultural depression hit in the 1880s, and South Carolina found its own Populist hero in Benjamin R. Tillman, a colorful stump speaker who attacked the "aristocratic oligarchy" that had dominated since the Lords Proprietors. Elected governor in 1890, Tillman tried to help the poor farmers, then reeling from rock-bottom cotton prices, by advancing agricultural and vocational education. But his electoral appeal also rested on violent racism. The Bourbons had permitted a number of blacks— whose votes they often controlled—to continue voting; in 1890 there were still several black legislators and one black congressman. Tillman would have none of that, and he proceeded to disenfranchise the black man. An 1895 constitutional convention instituted a poll tax and literacy test; from then until the 1940s, all South Carolina elections would be decided in a lily-white Democratic primary.

The South Carolina aristocracy despised Tillman as a mouthpiece of the hoi polloi, but the masses saw him as a latter-day Jacksonian hero. Free silver was a burning issue of the day; campaigning for the Senate, Tillman opposed President Grover Cleveland on the issue and promised to jab the president with his pitchfork. From then on, he was "Pitchfork Ben." He won the election and stayed in the Senate until his death, in 1918. But in his later years, he sold out to the Bourbons on issue after issue. "The fire-eating radical," V.O. Key wrote, "became a conservative of the conservatives, yet he was still a Democrat and a Negro-baiter."

Using the usual racial hyperbole to get elected governor in the 1930s, Olin D. Johnston made a greater effort than any recent predecessor to do something for "the rag tags, lintheads, and poor farmers." Later he went to the Senate, where he espoused such a liberal line (except on civil rights) that blacks, as they began to vote, gave him their support. These old-style South Carolina politics were not, however, as simple as they might seem. Strom Thurmond was a New Dealer in his early days and was opposed for governor in 1946 by conservatives who hinted darkly that he might be getting CIO money. Not long after Thurmond took office, he tried to get a mob convicted for lynching a hapless black and supported a successful campaign to repeal the poll tax. In the 1950 Senate primary in which Johnston and Thurmond clashed, Johnston, "the great liberal," attacked Thurmond for appointing a highly qualified black to the state board of medical examiners. Thurmond, Johnston said, should have appointed a good Confederate descendant in the place of that "big black buck nigger." But years later when the civil rights bill was being debated, Johnston made only obligatory remarks while Thurmond attacked the measure from stem to stern. Listening through a crack in the cloakroom door, Johnston was heard ruminating mostly to himself, "Listen to ole Strom. Just listen to him. He really believes that stuff."

If the reader considers these crosscurrents confusing, consider the plight of the poor South Carolina voter. For more than 250 years, Jack Bass noted, preoccuption with race "not only subordinated other political issues, but for most of the period stunted the growth of the state economically, culturally, and intellectually and forced thousands of the most ambitious natives of the state to seek their fortunes elsewhere."

Contemporary Palmetto State Politics

Because of the white primary and other restrictions, an infinitesimal number of black people were registered to vote in South Carolina until the 1940s. Even when the Supreme Court in 1944 found the white primary unconstitutional, the South Carolina Democrats managed by subterfuge to exclude blacks for four more years by reducing the Democratic party to the status of a private club and requiring members to uphold white supremacy. Then, in 1947, Federal Judge J. Waities Waring, of Charleston, wrote a decision that would forever alter the nature of South Carolina politics: "South Carolina is now the only state which now conducts a primary election solely for whites. . . . I cannot see where the skies will fall if South Carolina is put in the same class with [all] other states."*

South Carolina's whites did not resort to crude intimidation to stop black registration, handling the issue in a comparatively low-keyed and polite way. The crucial racial event was the peaceful reception—arranged behind the scenes by then-Gov. Ernest F. (Fritz) Hollings and other leaders—which welcomed black Harvey Gannt when he registered at Clemson College in 1963. From then on, it was clear that Palmetto leaders would not aid and abet the rabid segregationists. The leadership control mechanisms did not always work. In 1970, when the courts ordered massive school desegregation, including cross-district busing, a mob of angry whites in Lamar overturned school buses bringing black children to a previously all-white school. But the incident was an isolated one, and South Carolinians showed their disapproval in that year's governorship election when they rejected Republican Rep. Albert Watson, who had incited the Lamar citizenry against desegregation, in favor of John West, a progressive Democrat.

Gradually black voting began to make its mark. By 1982 blacks held 22 out of 124 seats in the state general assembly, but the 46-member state senate was still lily white. Many white members owed their seats to black votes and since the mid-1960s had acted on black demands such as a statewide food stamp program and a compulsory school attendance law. Blacks became a vital factor in any close election. A virtually unanimous black vote for Fritz Hollings assured his first U.S. Senate election, in 1966. There were 100,000 black votes that year; Hollings won by only 11,000. South Carolina Republicans, conversely, have shown little sincere interest in black needs.

The Republicans have, however, enjoyed a remarkable South Carolina renaissance, all the more amazing when one remembers that between 1900 and 1944, the Republicans never got more than 7.01 percent of South Carolina's presidential vote and slipped to as low as 1.4 percent in 1936 and 1.9 percent in 1940.

The decline of Democratic allegiance can be traced to 1948 and the amazingly durable figure J. Strom Thurmond. Thurmond reacted angrily to Hubert Humphrey's impassioned civil rights speech at the Democratic National Convention that year and not long afterward agreed to become presidential candidate of a new States Rights party. His message to the nation: "We believe that there are not enough troops in the Army to force Southern people to admit the Negroes into our theaters, swimming pools, and homes." Thurmond swept his own state with 72 percent of the vote—partly because he was listed there as the Democratic presidential candidate. But change beyond race was brewing among a managerial class of South Carolinians, some Yankee

---

*South Carolinians did not take kindly to Waring's admonition on voting rights, nor his early criticism of the "separate but equal" doctrine used to justify school segregation. Waring's life was threatened, and he was socially ostracized in Charleston, where his family had lived for eight generations. He resigned from the bench and left the state; at his funeral in Charleston in 1968, fewer than a dozen white persons were present, but there was a motorcade of more than 200 blacks.

transplants, many suburban in residence and attitude. As the national Democratic party became more and more identified with black people's interests, the combination of the race issue and conservative economics turned the new industrial class toward the GOP.

In 1952, the Republican cause in South Carolina—and across the South—was given an immense boost forward when the revered Gov. James F. Byrnes invited Dwight D. Eisenhower to speak at the State House and endorsed him for the presidency. In 1964, Strom Thurmond switched to what he called "the Goldwater Republican party," charging the national Democrats with leading the country toward socialistic dictatorship. Goldwater took 59 percent of the total state presidential vote that year, and South Carolina has voted Republican for president ever since, with the exception of 1976, when it gave 56 percent of its vote to fellow Southerner Jimmy Carter.

The Thurmond-led Republicans have done reasonably well at the very "top of the ticket"—for president, governor, and the U.S. House. But their performance at the grass roots level has been far less impressive. Even after the Nixon-Thurmond landslide of 1972, only 15 percent of the seats in the state legislature were held by Republicans. In 1982, the figure was only 16 percent.

A few personal and national political notes about Strom Thurmond are in order. Born in 1902, he seemed 80 years later to have the physique of a man half his age—perhaps because of his passion for exercise and abstemious personal habits, never touching alcohol or cigarettes. Thurmond cherished his image as a states' rights scrapper and made a record-breaking filibuster speech (24 hours, 18 minutes) against a civil rights bill in 1957. In more than 50 years of public life, he had only been defeated once (in 1950); he was the only man ever to win election to the Senate on a write-in vote (in 1954); and he is the only modern American politician to have run for office on four tickets—as a Democrat, a States' Righter, an independent, and a Republican. Some predicted it would be political suicide when in 1968 he married Nancy Moore, Miss South Carolina of 1966 and a woman 40 years his junior. But Thurmond made great political hay out of the four cherubic infants who followed in due course. America probably also has Thurmond to thank that Richard Nixon won the Republican presidential nomination and many Southern states in 1968. It was not backing won without a price: tacitly, at least, Nixon agreed in a famous Atlanta hotel-room meeting to ease up on civil rights enforcement, pick a nonliberal (it turned out to be Spiro Agnew) as his vice presidential running mate, and appoint "strict constructionists" to the Supreme Court. Following the Republican Senate takeover of 1980, Thurmond became not only president pro tem but also chairman of the Judiciary Committee.

It's hard to compete with Thurmond as a political personality, but Charlestonian Ernest Hollings, U.S. Senator since 1966, has had enormous impact in race relations, in economic development, and in attacking the problems of the poor and hungry. As a state legislator in the '50s, he helped pass a sales tax that started to pull South Carolina's public schools out of a deep trough of inadequacy. As governor in the late '50s and early '60s, he launched the massive industrialization campaign that would pay enormous dividends in the

'70s and '80s. While casting many conservative votes in his early Senate years (some said to protect his political flank from attack from the right), Hollings became an early advocate for expanded food stamp programs and more federal money to provide medical care and housing for the poor. He made several famous "hunger tours" of the state, resulting in the 1970 book *The Case Against Hunger*. He also supported big defense budgets (he was a graduate of the Citadel). He became highest-ranking Democrat on the Senate Budget Committee in 1980, and began mounting a 1984 presidential campaign calling for a national unity brand of economic recovery program involving a halt to tax cuts and a freeze on spending—whether for the military *or* social programs.

Thurmond and Hollings were but the latest of many South Carolinians to exert extraordinary national influence for so small a state. Consider Jimmy Byrnes. When Byrnes died, in 1972, at the age of 92, the obituaries could report he had probably served in more high U.S. government positions than any other man: U.S. House (seven terms, starting in 1911), U.S. Senate (two terms, becoming a key troubleshooter for his friend Franklin Roosevelt), U.S. Supreme Court, World War II Director of Economic Stabilization (a position Byrnes said "conferred on me greater authority than a President had ever previously delegated"), Secretary of State for two years, and a trusted adviser to President Truman (helping Truman formulate the fateful decision to drop the atomic bomb on Japan). Byrnes was disappointed, however, to be passed over for the vice presidential nomination in 1940 and again in 1944. He eventually fell out with President Truman, took issue with the national Democrats on the issue of civil rights and the "welfare state," and became a very embittered man. He said he personally liked blacks but ended up as a diehard segregationist in his four years as governor of South Carolina (1951–55). If that seemed incongruous to national observers who had accepted "Jimmy" Byrnes as an urban man of moderate persuasions, they did not know that Byrnes in his early days had been a close friend of "Pitchfork Ben" Tillman.

For a picture of the old autocratic southern committee chairman, one need look no further than the late L. Mendel Rivers, a Charleston congressman who spent the last five years of his life (he died in 1971) as chairman of the House Armed Services Committee, raising armies and launching navies and spending billions for bases, arms, and troops. Rivers ignored what many would have said was his constitutional duty: to cast a critical and suspicious eye on Pentagon requests; rather, he was an unabashed proponent of virtually any request the military made. He loaded so many military installations into his native Charleston that his predecessor as Armed Services chairman, Charles Vinson of Georgia, once said, "You put anything else down there in your district, Mendel, it's gonna sink." (Charleston could not wait for Rivers' death to honor him: in 1965 a bust of the florid old politician, mounted on a seven-foot granite shaft, was dedicated on Rivers Avenue, near the Navy Yard, and dozens of generals, admirals, astronauts, congressmen, and Cabinet members flew in—at taxpayer expense—to honor him.)

There were cheers in the nation's capital when another great oak of the

South Carolina delegation—John L. McMillan, a 74-year-old curmudgeon who had been in Congress since 1938—fell before a primary challenge in 1972. McMillan had been the chairman of the House District Committee for 24 years, quashing every home rule effort and doing his best to run the city of Washington like a South Carolina plantation. John Jenrette, the progressive young state legislator who beat McMillan, lost to a Republican in the general election but then made it to Congress in 1974 to start a Washington career that would end in disgrace. He was convicted in the famous "Abscam" scandal of 1980 for taking bribes from FBI agents dressed as Arab sheiks. Jenrette claimed he was an alcoholic and that the agents had gotten him drunk. Jenrette's eye-catching wife, Rita, sat by his side at his Abscam trial, lashing out like a black widow at her husband's detractors. But later she divorced him, posed nude for *Playboy* magazine, and pursued a show business career that included promotional television appearances in which she confessed to making love on the Capitol steps.

State Government and the Economy

In the annals of American state government there is scarcely a parallel to the decades of power exercised by Edgar A. Brown and Solomon Blatt, denizens of the little Lowcountry county of Barnwell and leaders of South Carolina's fabled "Barnwell Ring." Edgar Brown was first elected to the legislature in 1920, there to remain until his retirement, in 1972 at the age of 84, having spent 30 years as Senate president pro tem and chairman of the finance committee. Brown's power was so great that V.O. Key suggested half seriously that South Carolina go to a cabinet system of government and make Brown prime minister. Solomon Blatt was elected to the house in 1932 and served as house speaker (with one four-year break) from 1937 until his retirement from the speakership, in 1972. A decade later, at 86, Blatt still served in the legislature as house speaker emeritus.

Brown and Blatt stood for balanced budgets and rural control. They were extraordinarily responsive to South Carolina's big powers: the planters, textiles, utilities, and banks. While these men held sway, progressive governors saw their proposals run aground on the shoals of legislative opposition.

South Carolina legislators—and legislative leaders—have become far more progressive. There has been great moderation in the fierce parsimony that long placed South Carolina dead last, or close to it, in virtually every area of state spending. Search 50 states, however, and you will find no other in which the legislature holds such preeminent power compared to the governor. The governor is only one of a committee of five that draws up the state budget. The state board of education and the immensely powerful highway commission are elected by the legislative delegations from the 16 judicial courts. All state judges are elected by the legislature—usually from the ranks of its own alumni. The governor has but two advantages: a veto over legislation, and since a 1980 referendum, the right to run for a second successive term.

Figures of no small stature have filled the Palmetto governor's chair during recent decades, among them Democrats Hollings, Robert McNair, John West, and Richard Riley, and Republican James Edwards, the orthodontist President Reagan made Secretary of Energy (even while trying to abolish the department). West, inaugurated in 1971, promised a "color blind" administration; then when state agencies dragged their feet on affirmative action employment, he threatened to ask federal agencies to force compliance. Democrat Riley proved to be a progressive and unusually thoughtful governor. He suffered from an arthritic condition in early manhood that left him with a deceptively frail appearance, yet this was the man who candidly told Jimmy Carter, "Mr. President, you are not leading this nation. You are just managing the government." After Three Mile Island, Riley broke with South Carolina's 30-year romance with anything nuclear by announcing that his state was no longer willing to be the dumping ground for 85 percent of U.S. nuclear waste. South Carolina's big nuclear role began in 1950, when the Atomic Energy Commission announced its big Savannah River plant in Aiken and Barnwell counties. Plutonium and tritium—two of the key elements of atomic and hydrogen bombs—are reprocessed in South Carolina, and nearly 40 percent of the state's electricity is nuclear-generated. Riley's position forced major rethinking, both by the federal government and other states, about nuclear waste disposal issues.

South Carolina government has played a central role in transforming the economy, in a single generation, from cotton and old-style textiles to diversified industry. Vital change began in the World War II era with diversification of textiles into synthetics, as such firms as du Pont and Celanese moved in and the southerly flow of New England textile plants intensified.* Then, under Hollings, the state development board was transformed from a group of cronies to a scientifically oriented, business-minded agency that worked hand-in-hand with industrial prospects. From marketing and labor surveys to jet tours of potential sites and capital hunts, there was virtually nothing the board wouldn't do for a prospective industry. The state even created "special schools" to train a new industry's workers for it, *at state expense,* under simulated plant conditions. The diversification turned out to be vital when in the 1970s, textile jobs began moving to even cheaper labor overseas.

The hard sell to industrialists included such points as South Carolina's mild climate, reasonable energy costs, and proximity both to Northeastern and growing Sunbelt markets. There were also ethically questionable enticements: low wage levels, low levels of unionization, and the most generous tax abatements imaginable (the latter at the cost of potential revenues to improve the state's educational and social climate). There's no doubt the effort succeeded: South Carolina attracted nearly $4 billion in industrial investment in the 1960s, $10 billion in the 1970s, and a record $2 billion in 1980 alone. In 1979

*The old-fashioned textile mills, characterized by rows of sweating, lint-covered workers attending clanking machinery, have gradually given way to modern, automated plants turning out synthetics, blends, stretch knit goods, and carpets.

and 1980, nearly 1,400 industrial plants were opened or expanded. Investments covered not only textiles but such diversified fields as tool and die work, electronic design and assembly, chemical technology and precision metal-working. Blue chip companies opening facilities in South Carolina included General Electric, du Pont, Westinghouse, Union Carbide, Dow Chemical, Kimberly-Clark, Allis-Chalmers, and Lockheed. South Carolina also became a premier state in attracting foreign investment, partly a result of frequent overseas recruitment missions and permanent development board offices in Brussels, Tokyo, and Hong Kong. West German, French, British, Japanese, Dutch, and Swiss companies were all attracted. Local payoffs were sometimes breathtaking: Greenville, for example, attracted 13 major industrial plants between 1976 and 1980, increasing the community's tax base by 250 percent. But employment expansion in the state was overwhelmingly blue collar; in 1980, South Carolina had headquarters of only four *Fortune* 500 companies. With minimal unionization (6.7 percent—the lowest U.S. level except neighboring North Carolina) there was little prospect that South Carolina income levels would soon, if ever, reach the national average.

Lowcountry, Upcountry

South Carolina's greatest fascination, for native and outsider alike, rests in that land of semitropical swamps: the Lowcountry. Its peoples, character, and economy may be shifting with great military and foreign investments, yet it was only four decades ago that the South Carolina volume of the Federal Writers' Project could portray its citizen:

> The Lowcountryman may live in Charleston, a city that competes with the New Jerusalem in his dreams; or he may live in a drafty Georgian country house with a three-tiered piazza, hidden beneath live oaks and magnolias that drip curtains of gray moss above blazing azaleas, wisteria, and camellia japonicas; or he may live in a cabin near a swamp infested by swarms of malaria-bearing mosquitoes, and look out with dull eyes over acres he must till for an absentee landlord. But wherever he is, his attitude is keyed to leisure, he thinks in terms of ease, and has a philosophical contempt for long ordered hours of daily work.

The peoples and character of the Lowcountry have begun to experience deep change under the onslaught of great military installations and momentous foreign investments (the 700-worker steel plant built by West Germany's Korf Industries at Georgetown, for example). Yet the 281-mile coastline still offers seemingly endless miles of white sandy beaches, and all the leisure one might want. Some of the coastal resort areas have been subjected to neon strippery and rank commercialization, particularly near Myrtle Beach on the 50-mile stretch south of the North Carolina border. At the far southern end of the state is the beautiful Hilton Head Island, near Savannah, a verdant subtropical 12-mile strip of land that is actually the largest island south of Long

Island, N.Y. The vacation-retirement homes, low-rise condominiums, hotels, and inviting "Harbor Town," with its circular yacht basin, have become the jewel of the Intracoastal Waterway, and the entire Sea Island Plantation, a model for second-home development.

The American experience has yielded few more dramatic contrasts, however, than the opulence of Hilton Head and the abject poverty and deprivation of the surrounding coastal regions of Beaufort and Jasper counties. Even in the late 1960s, poor black residents of these counties could still be found suffering from severe hunger and malnutrition, from rickets, scurvy, and even pellagra. The area's woes were thrust into bold relief through the testimony of Donald Gatch, a courageous local physician, and Senator Hollings' investigations of hunger and malnutrition among the natives. The 1970s brought significant improvement. The Beaufort-Jasper Comprehensive Health Services became a model in delivering health care to those too poor or ill to visit a clinic and was visited by officials of several Third World countries trying to improve their health care.

While the Lowcountry is sure to intrigue a visitor the most, the vital economic thrust of modern South Carolina is in the Piedmont's 14 Upcountry counties. Much development is concentrated around Greenville and Spartanburg, fairly small cities (pop. 58,242 and 43,968, respectively) in a metropolitan area of 568,758. The cities are linked by a 30-mile stretch of Interstate 85 with all manner of modern, diversified industry along its flanks; this area received over $1 billion in industrial development between 1960 and 1981. Suburban shopping centers, new housing subdivisions, and construction abound, although Greenville, in 1981, launched an elaborate government-business revitalization effort including new office buildings, a convention center and a hotel wrapping around the Commons, a large enclosed public plaza. Greenville likes to call itself "the buckle of the Bible Belt" and is indeed the home of fundamentalist Bob Jones University, where the students are forbidden to smoke, drink, dance, hold hands, kiss, or even go out on dates without chaperones. Many Bob Jones male graduates go on to become missionaries, although some have begun to move out into more adventurous fields such as Christian filmmaking. Women students are encouraged to become wives. The Jones family, which runs the university, does not allow interracial dating on the grounds that it is "a biblically based injunction, coming from the word of God." Based on its racial policies, the Internal Revenue Service denied Bob Jones tax exempt status, a situation that took on national political significance in 1982, when the Reagan administration first said it opposed the IRS position and then, facing a hornet's nest of public protest, retreated. Greenville has had some outstanding mayors, including Republican Cooper White, Jr., who tried to mobilize public support for the schools during court-ordered desegregation, and Democrat Max Heller, a Jewish immigrant who escaped Hitler's Europe. The city would have had a U.S. Supreme Court Justice if the Senate had accepted President Nixon's appointee, Judge Clement Haynsworth.

The capital city of Columbia (pop. 99,296), in the dead center of the state between the Lowcountry and the Piedmont, is a city of striking contrasts:

between broad attractive streets and despicable slums, between historic old structures in tree-shaded settings and blocks of small service shops, between a struggling but modernizing center city and booming suburban areas. The metropolitan area grew 22 percent in the 1970s, while central city population dropped 12 percent. The metro area is in robust health in terms of growth in personal income, retail sales, construction, and industrial payrolls. To the extent that South Carolina has a center of banking, education, and government, Columbia is it. The city is also home to the 31,000-student University of South Carolina. Since the early 1970s, Columbia's business community has led an ambitious effort to redevelop the old inner city, an effort encouraged by the imaginative mayor Kirk Finlay, who proved something of a genius in leveraging government and private funds for recycling old buildings and new development.

Charleston: Motherstone of the South

Charleston is the quintessential city of the Old South and even to this day perhaps the most proud and self-possessed in the United States. Charlestonians' hubris is stunning, though in its more urbane citizens the pride is often laced with a touch of humor. Attorney Gedney Howe put it this way: "Charleston is the spiritual center of the South. Even an Atlantan will tell you that. Everybody in the South agrees Charleston is the best. It's a bunch of bull, but everybody agrees on it."

Right or wrong, Southerners seem to regard Charleston as a kind of holy place, and when they come to visit it (as countless thousands do each year), it is with a reverence that implies the Holy Grail of their Southernhood is somehow enshrined there in every memory, from the golden era of trade and leisured planter aristocracy to the events in Charleston Harbor in 1861.

The long-dormant Charleston economy returned to life as Navy Yard employment ballooned during World War II, an introduction to what later became the L. Mendel Rivers Military-Industrial Boom. Indeed, Rivers claimed credit for 90 percent of the additions: a Polaris submarine base, a Sixth Fleet ammunition and supply depot, a mine warfare center, an Air Force base, a Marine Corps air station, and the Parris Island recruit depot—the latter two both to the south in Beaufort County—an Army supply depot, and two Navy hospitals. After Rivers became Armed Services chairman, plants of Lockheed, J.P. Stevens, McDonnell-Douglas, Avco, and General Electric arrived. The esthetic consequences of all that Rivers wrought are unpleasant. North Charleston, home for most of the military personnel, became a disordered mess of trailer parks and cheap tract housing and beer joints cheek by jowl with expensive homes and chemical, paper, metal processing, petroleum, and fertilizer plants. But the economic growth cannot be ignored: Charleston's metropolitan area has been expanding rapidly (to 430,301 in 1980), of which Charleston itself (69,510) has become a small part.

Like Manhattan, Charleston is waterbound by two rivers and a harbor; the revealing ancient geography lesson of Charleston children holds that "Charleston is the place where the Ashley and Cooper rivers meet to form the Atlantic Ocean." And fabled old Charleston, the home of its aristocracy, is crowded into an area at the very tip of the peninsula: only 412 acres, running from around Cumberland Street to the Battery. Along the labyrinthian streets one discovers one architectural treasure after another, including more than 70 buildings that predate the Revolution, over 200 built before the War of 1812, and more than 850 constructed in the days before the Civil War. Architectural styles extend from early Georgian to late Victorian. The Historic Charleston Foundation has saved countless buildings from destruction and restored them. But the question of what and how to preserve is not without vivid controversy, illustrated in the 1970s when some preservationist factions opposed construction of the new Charleston Center, to include a hotel, a shopping center, and a conference complex. The project enjoyed, however, support of the Historic Charleston Foundation and the city's preservation-minded young mayor (and native son), Joseph P. Riley, Jr., who pointed out that the convention center would also create permanent employment for Charleston's many jobless blacks. Objections notwithstanding, the project went ahead.

There was also substantial local skepticism in 1977 when Italian composer Gian Carlo Menotti and the Countess Alicia Paolozzi decided to create in Charleston an American clone of Italy's Spoleto Festival. The yearly festival has brought to Charleston American premieres of operas, Broadway-bound plays, jazz concerts, and film retrospectives, as well as encouraging the performing arts among groups all over the Southeast U.S. Some Charlestonians complain of "too many tourists" and are horrified by the opening of the King Street Garden and Gun Club, a disco where gay and biracial couples mingle with city fathers and the children of the local aristocracy.

Old Charlestonians constitute an encapsulated old society with barriers to entrance as formidable as Boston's. In 1762 their forebears formed the St. Cecilia Society, which still thrives and remains, as former Mayor J. Palmer Gaillard, Jr., told us, "the gauge." Charleston was also one of America's first settlements to receive Jews, and they have added to its cosmopolitanism.

Charleston blacks—present for three centuries since their arrival as chattel, today 46 percent of the city's population—inspired DuBose Heyward's classic novel and folk opera, *Porgy and Bess.* In a 1946 food and tobacco workers' strike, Charleston blacks picked as their theme song the great hymn "We Shall Overcome," borrowed from a white Baptist hymnbook and destined to become the theme song of the civil rights movement. But their economic deprivation remains disturbingly real to this day.

Despite its conservatism, Charleston has always had an undercurrent of tolerance, a quality attorney Gedney Howe attributed to the Anglican and cavalier society of the early days. If it were not for that tolerant character, Howe told us, his defense of Charleston blacks accused of rape would have hurt his law practice. "Charleston may differ on what I stand for," he added, but "they're not going to try to throttle it."

ALABAMA

The Cradle Gets "Rocked"

"THIS IS STILL WALLACE COUNTRY," yelled joyful Alabamians on election night 1982. For the fourth time in 20 years, Alabamians had elected their bantam-sized, demagogue–folk-hero leader to the governorship. This time there was a difference, however, for George Corley Wallace owed much of his election to black voters.

The election shocked historians and civil rights activists who remembered Wallace's "stand at the school house door" and his blatant political appeals to the seething emotions of whites resentful of federally imposed integration. In the 1982 Democratic primary, most of Alabama's black officials had opposed Wallace, and Coretta Scott King came back to her native state to campaign for a more liberal opponent. But to the horror of Alabama's modern black establishment, a majority of black conservative rural preachers supported Wallace and denounced Mrs. King as an "outside agitator." Wallace defended Mrs. King's right to campaign, but in the same press conference announced that "one or both of Mrs. King's elderly parents, who live in Marion, Ala., plan to vote for me." Wallace won the primary with a third of the black vote and then the general election in which he was genuinely the *liberal* candidate against Emory Folmar, the ferociously conservative, law-and-order mayor of Montgomery.

To both black and white Alabamians, the election of Wallace to his fourth, nonconsecutive term was not so strange. Since race was no longer a viable political issue, Wallace turned back to the rhetoric of his populist roots. With Alabama's unemployment rate second only to Michigan, Wallace could make political hay by defending "the little man" against the big interests and Republicanism. Blacks on the street told reporters that they remembered the Wallace years as good ones when jobs were more plentiful, schools were built, and textbooks were free for the first time. Many blacks seemed to take their preachers' advice to forgive Wallace his racial sins, and others said they no longer feared him.

What then of Wallace's handicaps and admitted pain stemming from the assassination attempt on his life, and his deafness? "I got paralyzed in the legs, but I promise you I won't get paralyzed in the head," he was asserting. We wondered and spent an October evening in Dothan, Alabama, watching Wallace campaign before the Democratic faithful. When Wallace arrived to be wheeled around the room, and old friends came up to say hello, he looked pained and unhealthy. But the ensuing rally would have made a Hollywood director proud. First a black preacher prayed: "We boldly approach the throne of God asking for the election of Governor Wallace and all Democrats." Former Georgia Senator Herman Talmadge was brought out to note that when he and Wallace were in office, peanut prices were much higher and interest rates lower. Finally, Wallace himself was wheeled up the ramp to the microphone and suddenly the inveterate politican was in total charge again. Since Reagan came to power, Wallace said, "the rich have gotten richer and the poor have gotten poorer."

Clearly George Wallace could still campaign, perhaps better than ever. But could he govern? Alabamians perhaps didn't care; surely the record showed that Wallace had built his entire career on campaigning, not governing. Indeed, he had during his previous governorships so botched the job of governing that Alabama became a virtual fiefdom of the federal courts. It had always been on the stump that Wallace thrived: between 1958 and 1982 he toted up 10 major campaigns, including one gubernatorial campaign for his first wife Lurleen and four for president—a record unmatched in American political history. Years ago, one newspaper editor said of Wallace: "When there's no campaign in sight, he gets to looking wan and sickly." After the attempt on his life, campaigning apparently took Wallace's mind off the pain. "I have to run to live," he said.

But what of the sad condition of Alabama's economy in the early 1980s— unemployment in excess of 13 percent, low incomes, few growing industries? Wallace promised that his famous name would bring jobs to the state. But apprehensive Alabama business leaders worried that industrial locators would wonder why Alabama had put the notorious Wallace back in office.

The 1980s metamorphosis of George Wallace—if it were really that—was but a mild echo of convulsive change that came to Alabama since the 1960s. Here it was, in the "Cradle of the Confederacy," that a century of seething resentments triggered the second American Reconstruction. Official Alabama was set against it: the Stars and Bars still flew over the gleaming white State Capitol at Montgomery (with the United States flag relegated to a shorter flagpole on the grounds); the words "White Supremacy—For the Right" adorned the ruling Democratic party's ballot symbol. By their bitter reaction to the Montgomery bus boycott, by Bull Connor's police dogs in Birmingham, by the nightsticks and whips beating civil rights marchers, by the bridge in Selma, white Alabamians showed their abhorrence for the changes sweeping the South and the nation. Most men and women of moderation sealed their mouths; some fled the state.

Even in the late 1960s, as other Southern states began to readjust to the new realities, Alabama seemed to remain hopelessly obdurate. "Here, as in no other state," Pat Watters of the Southern Regional Council wrote in the *The South and the Nation*, "large numbers of young whites, high school age and over, still spouted unquestioningly the old catechisms of racism and Southern aristocracy. Before 1964 Mississippi had been more totalitarian, but in the late 1960s Alabama was the last bastion of Southern totalitarianism."

Yet if that were true, it was not from lack of valiant effort by civil rights forces. Next to Mississippi, for example, no state had been more outrageously resistant to black suffrage. (There were, for example, two counties with four-fifths black population and not a single black registered.) It was not accidental that Martin Luther King in 1965 decided to focus voting rights demonstrations in Selma, where the year before only 96 blacks of the 795 who sought to register were accepted. Sheriff James G. Clark responded to the demonstrations with mass arrests, driving captured protestors along with cattle prods. At the start of King's famed march to Montgomery, he and his followers were set upon by state troopers wielding whips, clubs, and tear gas, and 40 were severely injured. Two weeks later they set out again under a protective federal court order; their numbers swelled to 25,000 strong, they walked into the heart of Montgomery—and into American history—on March 25. Within weeks, the landmark Voting Rights Act of 1965 was law.

Grudgingly but inexorably, change came to Alabama in the 1970s. Jim Crow died a long-overdue death as schools, restaurants, hotels, and businesses were integrated; blacks came into the political process in record numbers (their registration jumping from 14 percent of eligible blacks in 1960 to 58 percent in 1980, and the number of black elected officials from zero to 247); young moderates of both races were running for office and winning; the feisty populism that was Alabama's proud heritage flourished again; the surge of Klan-inspired terrorism that had sullied Alabama for decades receded dramatically. Black political muscle was being flexed by the Alabama Democratic Conference, which claimed it could deliver up to 80 percent of Alabama's 300,000 black voters. And so it was that white candidates—many of whom built careers by haranguing against the "bloc vote," their racist code-word—had begun to court openly Alabama's biggest bloc of all.

But a stranger stumbling onto Alabama might well have the same reaction as Alice traveling through Wonderland: "curiouser and curiouser." In tough, violent Birmingham (nicknamed "Bombingham" during the turbulent 1960s), race relations improved so dramatically that a black was elected mayor in 1979, but bitter white backlash just two years later returned the city to racial polarization. And though in the orderly United States of America, the assumption by the early '80s was that blacks were physically safe in their daily lives, in the city of Mobile in 1981, three whites were charged with murder after the body of a bookish black teenager was found dangling from a tree in what the NAACP labeled a lynching. Even more serious was a rising white backlash. In the late 1970s, the Ku Klux Klan even showed some life, particularly in northern Alabama and in small towns throughout the state with proportionately few blacks.

Of Alabama's dramatic stories of the last generation, perhaps the most compelling was the titanic conflict between Wallace and his one-time friend and law school classmate, U.S. District Judge Frank M. Johnson, Jr. There was no state in the Union in which the federal courts intruded so deeply into the governmental process—and none in which the interference was more justified.

The lion's share of the vital federal court decisions was the work of Johnson, a hereditary Republican and racially tolerant son of Winston County in the northern Alabama hills. Johnson became the nation's youngest federal judge when President Eisenhower appointed him, at age 37, in 1955. Three years later, Johnson outwitted and overruled state judge Wallace, who had impounded voter registration records and threatened to jail investigators from the U.S. Civil Rights Commission. And thus began the symbiotic saga of this political odd couple: Johnson, issuing orders to govern Alabama as cases alleging negligence were brought before him, and Wallace, fighting him tooth and nail, rallying voters to his populist-segregationist cause by railing against "thugs and federal judges."

Just a partial list of Johnson's decisions illustrates why he was widely regarded as "the real governor of Alabama." It was he who extended for the first time the principle of the Supreme Court's 1954 school desegregation decision to a nonschool area—the Montgomery bus system—thus ending the Rev. Martin Luther King, Jr.'s, boycott and speeding integration of all public facilities. Johnson cleared the way for the historic civil rights march from Selma to Montgomery and in its tragic aftermath presided over the trial of the three Ku Klux Klansmen convicted by an all-white jury of murdering Viola Liuzzo. He issued landmark decisions affirming the rights of students to express their views and to hear the view of others in campus appearances. He also (either singly or as part of a judicial panel) abolished Alabama's poll tax; ordered school desegregation; forced one-man, one-vote legislative redistricting; applied the Equal Protection Clause of the U.S. Constitution to cases of discrimination against women; overhauled and equalized property tax assessments; required integration of jails, public parks, libraries, museums and juries; mandated a racially proportional state police force; and virtually took over administration of mental health and penal institutions, forcing an end to scandalous mistreatment of inmates. Though Johnson was threatened and vilified (Wallace complained such judicial activists were deserving of "political barbed-wire enemas") and his mother's home bombed, other Alabamians saw him more as savior than interloper. "Of course it's terrible that a federal judge has to do the state's work," then-Attorney General Bill Baxley observed in 1976. "But in terms of protecting people's constitutional rights, Judge Johnson has been doing the state's work for 20 years—because no one in the State Capitol has been willing to."

An intense, trim man known for running a taut courtroom and handing down thoroughly researched and scrupulously fair decisions, Johnson should have been a shoo-in for the Supreme Court. But President Nixon reportedly backed off from naming him in 1969 when outraged Southerners in Congress got wind of his plans. President Carter in 1977 persuaded Johnson to become FBI director, but illness forced withdrawal of the nomination; in 1979, Carter elevated Johnson to the Fifth U.S. Circuit Court of Appeals.

Alabama's Political Roots

Despite Alabama's reputation as a citadel of monolithic Southern reaction, Populism long has flourished here and the state has been sending progressives to Congress for more than 50 years. The roots of this interesting duality in attitudes lie in the two types of Anglo-Saxon pioneers who came flooding in during the early 1800s, after the United States had secured the territory and an end had come to centuries of full Indian culture and 250 years of scattered Spanish and French settlement.

Into southern Alabama came settlers from Georgia and South Carolina, establishing a plantation economy with a distinctly conservative political orientation. King Cotton's realm was the Black Belt, a 13,000-square-mile strip of sticky black soil spanning south-central Alabama; from it came nearly a quarter of the nation's cotton production by the years before the Civil War. In 1820, there had been only 41,879 Negro slaves in Alabama; by 1860, the figure had swollen to 435,080—45 percent of Alabama's population. While the plantation owners led lives of legendary opulence, marked by fox-hunting and lavish balls, the blacks lived in what one English lady visiting a plantation near Montgomery in 1835 described as "small, dingy, untidy houses . . . something between a haunt of monkeys and a dwelling of human beings."*

Hilly, hardscrabble northern Alabama was settled by yeomen from Tennessee, North Carolina, and Virginia who followed Appalachian paths to a more promising frontier. The life awaiting them in Alabama was not exactly idyllic. Tracts for cultivation were laboriously carved out from the forests; housing was in rough log cabins; malnutrition was common. The planter aristocracy looked down on them as "hillbillies" and "po' white trash." Few slaves were held here; even today, blacks are a rarity in these hills (only 69 were found, for example, in Winston County in 1980).

The slaveholding interests of the Black Belt barely won the day in the 1860 convention that decided for secession from the Union—but they did triumph, and the Confederate States of America were organized in the halls of the Alabama Capitol at Montgomery in February 1861. Yet when the Confederates sought conscripts in northern Alabama, those sturdy hillsmen drove them out with their squirrel rifles and joined the Union Army.

Alabama's post–Civil War history was typical of the South: slow recovery from physical devastation (the wartime property losses, including the value of slaves, was estimated at $500,000,000); congressionally imposed Reconstruction (marked by both abuses and unusually progressive reforms); and after 1874 the return to power of the wealthy landholding whites, popularly known as the Bourbons. One of the tools the Bourbons used to regain power was the Ku Klux Klan, which waged a campaign of violence and intimidation against carpetbaggers, scalawags, and, of course, the Negro.

---

*Floodtides of black migration to the North notwithstanding, the Black Belt has not changed its racial balance much. Ten Black Belt counties in 1980 had heavy black majorities (as high as 84.2 percent in Macon County, just east of Montgomery).

The Bourbons ruled as rank agrarian reactionaries, installing many conservative ex-Confederate officers in high government positions and cutting taxes needed for developing the state's primitive school system. Alabama proved fertile ground for late 19th-century Populism, which first took root in the northern counties. Populists hoped to build a general coalition of the dispossessed of both races, but Black Belters used outright fraud—and their controlled black vote—to defeat Populist candidates. By 1901, the Bourbons were able to write a new state constitution containing what Alabama historian Malcolm McMillan has called "the most restrictive and complicated suffrage article ever adopted by any state." To vote, a person had (1) to be 21 years old —and male; (2) to have never been convicted of any crime from a list of some 30 crimes, which began with wife-beating; (3) to prove his literacy by interpreting a section of the U.S. Constitution, or, alternatively, to be a property holder; and (4) to pay a $1.50 yearly poll tax, which if unpaid over a period of time, would be due cumulatively. Whites were given an extra chance by the notorious "fighting grandfather clause," under which any male could register if one of his ancestors had fought in any American war—including, of course, the Conferate side in the Civil War.

In 1900, a total of 78,311 Negroes had been registered in 14 Black Belt counties; three years later, the total fell to only 1,081. Popular participation in elections plunged. Even in the 1920–46 period, only 19 percent of adult Alabamians would vote in Democratic primaries; not until 1970 did the participation rate finally creep above 50 percent.

For six decades, until the federal courts finally blew the whistle in the mid-60s, the Black Belt and allied counties of southern Alabama blocked constitutionally mandated reapportionment and held an effective veto power over every progressive impulse in state government. Curiously enough, however, Alabama did (after 1902) turn to primary elections rather than nominations by courthouse "gangs" and thus wound up with progressive governors from time to time.

For robust showmanship and deep-gut populism, the best among them was James E. Folsom. Called "Big Jim," he was six feet, eight inches tall, weighed 255 pounds, and wore a size 16 shoe. Also known as "Kissin' Jim" (for his penchant for scattering kisses along the campaign trail), Folsom burst onto the Alabama scene in the 1940s with a foot-tappin' country band in tow.* Taking on the special-interest "Big Mules," who controlled the state capitol, Folsom later said that he had been "the first and last governor the little man, the young people, and the blacks ever had in Alabama." He battled for

---

*Attorney Charles Morgan, Jr., told us how as a boy he listened to Folsom's pitch to the rural folk in '46. "He told them how their state government was run by the industrial interests of Birmingham and the North and East, and the Black Belt plantation owners. In the classic populist tradition of the South, he waged political war against the rich city folk. Folsom spoke of the dreams of the little man, of the worker and the farmer, and they listened. He told them he remembered lying in bed in the morning at sun-up at his family's farm, when the dew was on the ground, and breathing that 'clean, fresh, green breeze that comes across the fields.' And when he got to Montgomery, Folsom said, he was going to be that 'clean, fresh green breeze' blowing."

reapportionment and for repealing the poll tax; he wanted pensions for the old folks; he fought for (and got) state permission to spend funds accumulated during World War II to pave thousands of miles of farm-to-market roads; and he won higher pay for teachers on the theory that "We don't want our children penalized for being born in Alabama." For his time, Folsom was remarkably advanced on race relations: he sabotaged the Ku Klux Klan by pushing through an anti-mask law; he tried to expand black voter registration and sipped scotch on the veranda of the governor's mansion with Harlem Congressman Adam Clayton Powell. In an era when a black man accused of rape would be sent to the electric chair, Folsom regularly commuted such sentences during his terms as governor (1947–51, 1955–59).

In the tense and angry mood following the 1954 Supreme Court school desegregation decision, Folsom's racial attitudes were simply too tolerant for Alabama. When the legislature in 1955 declared the Court's decision "null, void, and of no effect" in Alabama, Folsom termed the resolution "hogwash" and likened it to "an old hound dog bayin' at the moon." Scandals caused by his coterie of small-time crooks hurt him politically; so did his alcoholism. In 1962 Folsom went on television the night before the gubernatorial primary gloriously drunk (or drugged, as he claimed) unable even to remember the names of his children when he tried to introduce them. He never won another election—losing primaries through 1982.

George Wallace: Compulsive Campaigner

George Wallace, the man who beat Jim Folsom in that 1962 primary, came from a poor cotton-chopping county, Barbour, in southeastern Alabama, where blacks were a majority and segregation was the way of life. He did not start out as a rip-roaring racist politician; indeed, he was a lieutenant of Jim Folsom in the legislature. But in his first run for governor, in 1958, Wallace suffered a jolting defeat at the hands of arch-segregationist John Patterson, who courted Ku Klux Klan support and made Wallace look like a racial moderate in comparison. Afterward, Wallace reportedly said that Patterson "outniggered me, and I'll never be outniggered again." Other versions quoted Wallace as saying he would not be "outsegged"; he denied having said it either way. The fact is, however, that the 1962 race inaugurated two decades during which George Wallace would slake his thirst for public adulation at the trough of Alabama's racially troubled waters.

In his inaugural address, Wallace issued his clarion call to the Anglo-Southland, "In the name of the greatest people that have ever trod this earth, I draw the line in the dust and toss the gauntlet before the feet of tyranny and I say: Segregation now—segregation tomorrow—segregation forever."

Only five months later, Wallace made his promised stand in the school-house door, barring two blacks from enrolling at the University of Alabama in Tuscaloosa. His own National Guard was quickly federalized by President Kennedy, and the students registered a few hours later. Within four years,

300 black students were attending the university without incident. And Wallace had not long been governor before the first black children were enrolled in white Alabama schools, even though at one point he sent state troopers to encircle a Tuskegee school and prevent desegregation.

The scenario at Tuscaloosa had been carried on national television, and with increasing out-of-state forays, Wallace soon became a national figure. Wallace entered the 1964 presidential primaries in Wisconsin, Indiana and Maryland and might well have stayed in the race on third-party ticket if Barry Goldwater, newly revered in Dixie for his vote against the Civil Rights Act, had not been the GOP nominee. Goldwater swept Alabama with 70 percent of the vote.

"Wallace's brief flash on the national scene clearly established him," Montgomery newspaperman Ray Jenkins wrote, "as the first Southern politician since Huey Long of Louisiana to assemble a national following." To white Alabamians, who had seen one of their own frighten the national Democratic establishment, it was a heady experience. When the legislature rejected a state constitutional amendment to permit Wallace to run for a second successive term in 1966, he ran his wife, Lurleen, and thus remained governor in all but signature. She beat nine opponents, including two former governors, without a runoff—a clear sign that Alabamians wanted Wallace to run for the presidency in 1968. He ran, deserting the Democrats to form his own American Independent party and trumpet his whole panoply of populist issues and, of course, his racial stand. Wallace's success in getting his name on the ballot of all 50 states was one of the organizational miracles of modern politics. As small campaign contributions cascaded in from all over the country, and his standing in the early autumn national polls surged over 20 percent, it became clear that Wallace's challenge was far more serious than Strom Thurmond's Dixiecrat movement 20 years before. But the herculean efforts that organized labor expended to cut his blue-collar vote, and people's awareness that Wallace really had no chance of election, sharply diminished his actual vote in the North. Wallace finally carried only five states, all from the Deep South—Alabama, Mississippi, Louisiana, Georgia, and Arkansas. Even so, he counted the campaign a solid success. "I think my movement defeated Hubert Humphrey, which was something the majority of the people of my region wanted done," Wallace said.

Wallace's 1968 campaign was the high-water mark of Southern-based, third-party politics in the 20th century, with a tantalizing twist: What would have happened if Nixon had received (as almost happened) just under a majority of electoral votes, so that George Wallace would have held the power (through his 46 electors) to choose the next president? How would Wallace have instructed his electors? "The chances are the votes probably would have gone to Mr. Nixon, because we were violently opposed to Mr. Humphrey's philosophy and ideology," Wallace told us later, acknowledging he would have demanded such preconcessions from Nixon as reiteration of campaign promises against school busing and a pledge to halt—or at least soften—civil rights enforcement. Just as Rutherford B. Hayes had wheedled the electoral votes he needed to become president in 1876 by promising the South to terminate Reconstruction, the net of Wallace's demands would have been to end the "second Reconstruction"—the civil rights advancement of the 1960s.

Lurleen Wallace died of cancer in May 1968, obliging Wallace, seeking to unseat interim Gov. Albert Brewer in 1970, to campaign from outside the Governor's Mansion, privately telling people (after running behind in the first primary), "If I don't win, them niggers are going to control this state." In the end, Wallace won by a narrow margin. But his inaugural address, shorn of the fiery defiance of 1963, even included a line saying that "Alabama belongs to all of us—black and white, young and old, rich and poor alike."

Just before his inaugural, Wallace remarried. His bride was Cornelia Ellis Snively, a poised and attractive 31-year-old divorcee, a niece of Jim Folsom— and a smart politician in her own right. By the time of the 1972 presidential campaign, Cornelia had been able to get Wallace a bit more fashionably dressed and to improve his television style. Wallace abandoned his American Independent party to run as a Democrat, plunging into 15 primary battles, and in his first big one, Florida, coining *the* political slogan of 1972: "Send Them a Message." Millions of voters did seem upset with the power elites who had sent their sons off to fight unwinnable wars, raised their taxes, meddled with their neighborhood schools, and never seemed to listen to plain folks. Wallace defeated Humphrey and Edmund Muskie and the whole pack of Democratic hopefuls in Florida, severely shaking the Democratic establishment. After that he went on to win five more primaries, two of them—Maryland and Michigan —in the North.

Fear rode with Wallace on his campaign forays and a large bulletproof rostrum was used almost everywhere he spoke. Yet after a speech at a Laurel, Maryland, shopping center on May 15, 1972, Wallace decided to mix with the crowd. A "loner" named Arthur Bremer fired a volley of pistol shots. Wallace fell, one bullet penetrating his spine. He survived, only to be confined to a wheelchair for the rest of his life.

Wallace's brush with death—coinciding with some of his greatest primary triumphs—gave him the respectability he had so longed for. The president and would-be presidents and party chairmen came to his bedside; fourteen months later, even Edward Kennedy came to Alabama to present him a "Spirit of America" award. Restored to a semblance of health and the Alabama Constitution now permitting, Wallace rolled to yet another gubernatorial victory in 1974 and by early 1975 led the Gallup poll as the Democrats' choice for their 1976 presidential nomination. But Wallace hadn't glanced next door to Georgia, where another governor had similar lofty ambitions. Jimmy Carter swamped Wallace in the Florida primary by nearly 90,000 votes, and Wallace won not a single primary, his dream of a Southerner sitting in the White House coming true for "Jimmy Who?"

Barred from seeking a third consecutive term, in 1978, Wallace passed up a golden opportunity for election to a U.S. Senate seat (perhaps in part due to a messy divorce from Cornelia that January). His "retirement" stuck through the 1980 presidential campaign but came unglued in 1982 when Wallace took to the gubernatorial campaign trail again with his new wife, Lisa, 30 years his junior, at his side. The incumbent, Forrest (Fob) James, Jr., who had angered some interest groups, kept a vow not to seek a second term.

Wallace won fairly easily in 1982 even though the sum and substance of Wallace's earlier gubernatorial record was thin in the extreme. "Governor Wallace just never has paid any attention to doing the work a governor is supposed to do," Mabel Sanders Amos, former Alabama secretary of state, once observed. "He's never shown the slightest interest in carrying out the duties of his office once he's elected. He's actually the governor in name only." When Wallace took office in 1963, Alabama ranked at or near the bottom among the 50 states in almost everything—welfare, income, health, workmen's and unemployment compensation, prisons, schools, mental health, taxation. Under the regimes of George and Lurleen, those rankings barely budged. Some even went down: by 1975, the education budget had quadrupled to $1.6 billion, but Alabama dropped from 45th to 48th place in per capita school spending. And the improvements made were modest: for example, a program of regional mental health centers begun by Lurleen.

Alabama's taxes did remain less per capita (or in relation to personal income) than any state, except Arkansas, but at the heavy price of seriously below-par state services. And those taxes collected often benefited the Big Mules, not Wallace's little folks. The state sales tax—applicable even to groceries—was increased from 3 percent to 4 percent; localities could add up to 3 percent more. Several other taxes that fall heavily on low-income people were enacted or increased during the Wallace years; at the same time, personal and corporate income taxes had a 5 percent cap and accounted for a minuscule share of state revenue. Property taxes were among the nation's lowest, but it took Judge Johnson to remedy the grossly inequitable assessment system under which major corporations were paying as little as 17 cents an acre on their timberlands. On balance, it seems fair to say that whatever progress Alabama did make in the Wallace years was due to the orders of one federal judge, the largesse of the federal government, and the "pointy-headed bureaucrats" Wallace loved to assail.

There is far more to a state than its executive branch, and the Alabama judiciary improved greatly during the '70s under Chief Justice Howell Heflin, who later went to the U.S. Senate. The legislature—such a shoddy operation that the Citizens Conference on State Legislatures in the early '70s ranked it last among the states—benefited greatly from the court-ordered reapportionment that broke the backs of the "Big Mules" in Montgomery. Blacks and Republicans did not register the expected gains (there were only 17 black and 11 Republican members by 1981), but barefoot boys no longer passed up and down the aisles selling peanuts, members were less frequently seen relieving the monotony with nips of booze, and the general quality of legislators and committee operations did pick up. The governor continued to carry heavy sway, and the state's most powerful lobby, the Alabama Education Association, remained enormously influential. For the first time, in the 1980s, responsible business leadership seemed willing to help Alabama state government rather than simply manipulate it. Copying a successful Louisiana model, an Alabama Public Affairs Research Council was set up and began issuing objective reports on serious issues facing the state.

Saints and Sinners: Alabamians in Washington

George Wallace may have failed to get a lease on the White House, but his brand of politics did have a profound impact on Alabama's congressional delegation. Pre-Wallace, the contingent tended toward a neat balance between progressive Democrats from north Alabama and conservatives from the south. But by 1980, the entire delegation had a distinctly conservative, in several cases deeply conservative, hue. Gone were the likes of Carl Elliott, author of the first student loan legislation in Congress; Kenneth Roberts, who preceded Ralph Nader by several years in investigating auto safety standards; Albert Rains, one of Congress' outstanding legislators in housing; Robert Jones, TVA defender from north Alabama; and finally even a Republican who proved too moderate on race for his constituency to stomach, John Buchanan of Birmingham. A first sign of returning moderation came in 1982 when Benjamin Edrich, a liberal lawyer from Birmingham, was elected to the House. Both Mobile and Montgomery continued to be represented by conservative Republicans, however.

Father time finally caught up with Alabama's pair of long-tenured senators, Lister Hill and John J. Sparkman, men of a different era and a different mold. When Hill retired in 1968 (after 45 years in Congress) and Sparkman in 1978 (after 42 years) they, too, were replaced by men more aligned with the Wallace philosophy. Sparkman was responsible for virtually all the housing legislation passed by Congress in the postwar period. He served as Adlai Stevenson's vice presidential running mate in 1952 but over the years drifted to the right and defended himself against Alabama's Negrophobia by voting against every civil rights bill that came along.

Hill probably did more for the average Alabamian than anyone—Hugo Black perhaps excepted—the state ever sent to Washington. Son of a distinguished surgeon (the first American successfully to suture the human heart), Hill's consuming interest was health legislation. The Hill-Burton Act of 1946 helped to build more than 9,500 general hospitals (more than half of them in the rural South) and public health centers. Given the Old South's dismal health history, it was a momentous contribution.* With Senator George Norris of Nebraska, Hill was one of the two fathers of the TVA, which

---

*As Hill once told us, "Before we got those hospitals built here in Alabama, if someone had appendicitis, he might have been driven in a horse and buggy or old surrey or old Model T Ford over a rough muddy road to a local town to wait for a train to come through that could carry him—probably with a change of trains along the way—to one of the few big cities for his operation."

rescued northernmost Alabama from its ancient poverty and made it the state's most prosperous region.

Succeeding Lister Hill was James B. Allen, a lumbering, gentle giant of a man who had been Wallace's lieutenant governor. Possessed of keen intelligence, shrewd judgment, and unquestioned integrity, Jim Allen accomplished what few senators ever even attempt: mastery of Senate rules. This parliamentary skill enabled him to tie the Senate in knots in service of conservative ends—a tactic not universally loved but greatly admired. Allen's sudden death in May 1978—the same year Sparkman retired voluntarily—touched off a political free-for-all for the two Senate seats. One finally fell to Howell Heflin, the studious former Alabama Supreme Court Chief justice and, incidentally, nephew of the legendary "Cotton Tom" Heflin, a segregationist senator of the '20s. ("Cotton Tom" was the man who warned rural Alabamians in 1928 that if Al Smith won, "the Pope will sail up Mobile Bay in a submarine.") The other seat went to a feisty young moderate, Donald Stewart. But Stewart, running for a full term in 1980, was dumped in the Democratic primary by none other than "Kissin' Jim" Folsom's son. Even Jim Folsom, Jr., couldn't survive that November against Jeremiah Denton, who in the Reagan landslide became Alabama's first Republican senator in a century. A genuine Navy war hero, Denton spent seven years as a prisoner of war in Vietnam (and in a Viet propaganda film tipped off American authorities about what was going on by blinking T-O-R-T-U-R-E in Morse code). Denton brought home—and then to Washington—a rigid conservatism and morality. One of his first pieces of legislaton sought $30 million promoting teen-age chastity. Ultra-rightism was so dominant in Alabama by the end of the '70s that a former Republican, Charles Graddick, was elected attorney general after a tough law-and-order campaign in which he allegedly promised a return to electrocutions so that criminals would know in advance he would "fry 'em till their eyes pop out and smoke comes out their ears."

All these latter-day figures take on pygmy proportions in contrast to the one towering Alabama figure of the 20th century: Hugo Lafayette Black. A north Alabama native, Black early exhibited true Southern Populist concern for ordinary folks. As a senator to the left of President Roosevelt in the 1930s, Black battled for FDR's New Deal programs and was the sponsor of Fair Labor Standards Act. Roosevelt appointed him to the Supreme Court in 1937, where he would sit for 34 years, long finding himself in a minority on such issues as free speech, legislative apportionment, and the right of defendants to counsel. But eventually the majority turned in Black's direction. No other Supreme Court justice lived to see so many of his dissents become law. Black's absolutist faith in the Bill of Rights, and in particular the First Amendment, underlay his belief "that the ultimate happiness and security of a nation lies in its ability to explore, to change, to grow and ceaselessly adapt itself to new knowledge born of inquiry free from any kind of governmental control over the mind and spirit of man. Loyalty comes from love of good government, not fear of a bad one."

In Alabama, many viewed Black as a pariah, a traitor to the white Southern cause, even though discovery of his one-time membership in the Klan had caused controversy at the time of his appointment. Through most of the 1950s and '60s, he was never invited back to Alabama to address any group—a bitter exile that did not end until the last years of his life.

People and Economy of a Blue-Collar State

Alabama is for Alabamians; it is an inbred society virtually unleavened by "outlanders." The overall population of the state has inched forward over the last 40 years—to 3,890,061 in 1980—but only because natural increase has balanced a massive tide of black out-migration. The percentage of blacks declined from 34.7 percent of Alabama's people in 1940 to 25.6 percent in 1980.

From antebellum days to the mid 20th century, cotton dominated agricultural life from the Gulf to the Tennessee Valley; as Ray Jenkins noted, in late summer the fleecy cotton fields looked "like snow in August." But if Alabama embodied and romanticized cotton as the very essence of its Dixiehood, it ignored the fact that sharecroppers and tenant farmers tilled the fields in a condition not far removed from serfdom. Today, that cotton culture has almost vanished—the victim of the boll weevil, unreliable weather, sharply fluctuating prices, and competition from the huge, irrigated farms of Texas and California. By 1980, only 325,000 Alabama acres were planted in cotton, compared with 3,500,000 acres in 1930. Even in the Black Belt most of the flat meadows had been transformed into grazing lands for beef and dairy cattle. Soybeans were the big new crop: worth $237.2 million in 1980 (on 2.25 million acres), more than double the value of the cotton crop. But Alabama is no longer predominantly a crop state; in recent years, livestock and poultry have been a $1 billion-a-year business, accounting for three-quarters of farmers' cash receipts, the highest proportion in the Deep South. As "King Cotton" died, so too did the rural way of life in Alabama. In 1940, 70 percent of the people lived in rural areas; in 1980, only 38 percent. And while there were 232,000 farms on the eve of Pearl Harbor, there were only 57,500 in 1978.

As agricultural employment faded, factories began taking up the slack. A state planning and industrial board set up in 1955 under Governor Folsom (and legislation sponsored by George Wallace) undertook publicly subsidized industrial-development financing in a big way, and soon paper, textile, chemical, and food-processing plants were flowering as cotton once had. The industrial heavies were iron, steel, and aluminum mills benefiting from the cheap power of the Tennessee Valley. Oil and gas finds in southern Alabama added a lucrative new element to the state's economy. Alabama came to have one of the highest percentages of blue-collar workers (and lowest white-collar) in the country. In 1980 Alabamians still earned only 78 percent of the national average income. Yet that sad statistic was a far cry from the 1940s, when the figure was a bare 50 percent.

Some Alabamians see economic salvation in improved transportation.

There are already more than 1,000 miles of navigable rivers, and Alabamians in Congress have fought incessantly for a 463-mile canal linking the Tennessee River in the north with the Tombigbee River in the south, thus opening a through waterway to the Gulf. Seventy-percent completed in the early 1980s, its cost estimates spiraled yearly to hit more than $3 billion, causing near apoplexy among opponents of federal waste and gross pork barrelism. A far more promising direction for economic strategy would be toward the areas in which Alabama appears fearfully deficient in the '80s: high-technology, emerging service industries, and superior educational facilities to upgrade the work force. Pointing out that Alabama shared the Great Lakes States' over-reliance on such heavy material, capital-intensive industries as steel, chemicals, and plastics, one economist said: "Alabama is the Midwest of the South. It must diversify or die."

Touring the "Heart of Dixie"

If Alabama, as its license plates proudly proclaim, is truly "The Heart of Dixie," then that heart throbs with many different beats. From the industrialized Tennessee Valley towns south to Frenchified Mobile, there is the Alabama of the storied Old South (Talledega, Opelika, Scottsboro) and that of more brutal recent memory (Selma, Montgomery, Birmingham). In between are hundreds of scattered hamlets, many named for the once-surrounding great plantations or the families that owned them.

Huntsville (pop. 142,513) became one of the luckiest towns in America in 1941 when its young congressman, John Sparkman, delivered a plum: selection of Huntsville as the site of a new chemical warfare plant, which became known as the Redstone Arsenal. After World War II, the Army launched its rocketry program at Redstone. And in 1958, with the founding of the National Aeronautics and Space Administration, came Wehrner von Braun and the Marshall Space Flight Center, where the mighty Saturn rocket, which boosted men to the moon, would be developed. As some $400 million a year in NASA and Pentagon funds poured into the Huntsville area, the boom was astounding; the city's population jumped tenfold in three decades. Although NASA's presence has dwindled in recent years, the Redstone Arsenal still is the Army's largest missile facility. Perhaps because Huntsville was an abolitionist, pro-Union stronghold, integration was largely accomplished *before* the 1964 Civil Rights Act forced the rest of Alabama to take the first step.

Westward along the Tennessee lie Decatur (pop. 42,022) and such towns as Florence, Tuscumbia, Sheffield, and Muscle Shoals, winners industrially from TVA's cheap power. To these cities have been drawn such diverse concerns as 3M, Goodyear, Ford, and Reynolds Metals. Outside this thriving valley and the major cities, few areas of Alabama have been so economically fortunate. One exception is Dothan, just above the Florida border, which for years added an average of two new industries a year, saw its population spurt forward to 48,750, and enjoyed good schools and cosmopolitan culture. In the coccyx of the Appalachans, to the east, are found Gadsden (47,565), a heavily unionized iron-and-steel town hard hit by recession, unemployment, and out-migration in the 1970s; and Anniston (29,523), which saw its successful "New South" image shattered in 1961 when a screaming mob of whites attacked and burned a Freedom Riders' bus. City leaders of both races quickly set up a community relations service, and Jim Crow practices were ended peacefully. Also helping to bridge the racial gap was the Committee on Unified Leadership (COUL), which enables civic leaders to thrash out problems and brainstorm solutions. COUL's work—and that of the resident Alabama Shakespeare Festival, since 1977 designated the official state theater—won for Anniston an All-America City award from the National Municipal League.

Academia in Alabama is centered in Tuscaloosa (75,143), home of the University of Alabama; Auburn (28,4781), home of the land-grant university of the same name; and Tuskegee (12,716), where Booker T. Washington founded his institute for freed slaves. Long a citadel of Old South attitudes, the 'Bama campus erupted in a rage of riot and cross-burning when Autherine Lucy attempted to register in 1956. Dr. Frank A. Rose subsequently became university president. Backed by his trustees, Rose defied the vilest verbal abuse and innumerable Klan threats to build the university into an oasis of academic freedom and independent thought while winning national fame for its football teams coached by the late, great "Bear" Bryant. A young liberal, David Mathews, became president in 1969 and was later tapped by Gerald Ford to be Secretary of Health, Education and Welfare. The Tuskegee Institute, begun in a dilapidated shanty in 1881, quickly became a beacon of black education and black pride. Though blacks have rejected Booker T. Washington's doctrine that the Negro should learn a trade and be content with manual labor, Tuskegee is the nerve center of black politics in Alabama. Gradually overcoming bars to voting and blatant gerrymandering of their four-fifths-black county by the white legislature, Tuskegee blacks by 1968 elected Lucis Amerson as the first black sheriff in the South, sent the first two blacks to the state legislature, and in 1972 elected their first black mayor, Johnny Ford.

Mobile, the state's second-largest city (pop. 200,452), is an Alabama anomaly: subtropical, aristocratic, substantially Catholic, Creole, and cosmopolitan, yet uncompromisingly conservative. No Democratic presidential candidate has carried Mobile since 1960, and it elected a Republican congressman (Jack Edwards, who became vice chairman of the House GOP caucus) in 1964. The French first settled Mobile, 31 miles up Mobile Bay from the Gulf of Mexico, in 1702, and it was here, not in upstart New Orleans, that the Mardi Gras tradition began. Mobile's diversified economy ranges from a booming port to shipbuilding to paper products; the 1970s also brought extensive new oil and natural gas finds nearby. Wide-ranging restoration of antebellum buildings and a bayside park featuring the battleship Alabama draw an increasing tourist trade. But racism has died hard in this most southerly of Alabama cities. Federal courts were forced to order a stiff school busing plan; there were serious disorders and a rash of firebombings. Blacks, though 36 percent of the population, have never elected one of their number to the three-member city commission. They went to court to demand a subdistricting plan that would give them a better chance, but the U.S. Supreme Court rebuffed them in 1980. South of Mobile, along the bay and on the Gulf toward Pensacola, Fla., is a little known treasure the Alabamians call "the redneck riviera"; the beaches are some of the most beautiful we have seen in all America.

Montgomery (pop. 178,157) is dominated by state government and the Maxwell Air Force Base. But the spirit of freedom that kindled the civil rights movement insures Montgomery its place in history. It was a telephone call to the new pastor of the Dexter Avenue Baptist Church, the Rev. Martin Luther King, Jr., on December 1, 1955—just hours after Rosa Parks had refused to yield her bus seat to whites—that initiated the events leading King to national and historic prominence, the Nobel Peace Prize, and ultimate martyrdom.

Montgomery blacks suffered deep humiliation under the old segregated order. Bus drivers (all white) forced blacks to suffer epithets like "black ape," "black cow," and "dirty nigger." Blacks were always forced to the back of the bus. Mrs. Parks' refusal to put up with these indignities any longer kindled a legal, social, and economic protest that was to change American society far beyond the segregated South. King and his colleagues preached nonviolent protest and spearheaded the first direct action: a black boycott of Montgomery buses. For a year, through official harassments, arrests, bombings, and court cases, the boycott rolled on in an amazing show of black solidarity, capped by victory. In 1961, Freedom Riders were attacked by a white mob, and Attorney General Robert Kennedy had to send in 600 U.S. marshals to maintain order. Since then—despite the resignation of the mayor and police chief in 1977 at the height of a cover-up scandal following the shooting death of a black man by a white policeman—Montgomery has been remarkably free of racial violence and is a relatively well-integrated, peaceful city. Enormous signs proclaim I-85, slicing through its center, as the "MARTIN LUTHER KING, JR., EXPRESSWAY."

Birmingham: In Metamorphosis

Birmingham—Alabama's premier city, the "Pittsburgh of the South"—was founded in the free-wheeling capitalistic years following the Civil War, when the region's coal, iron, and limestone deposits made it a natural for the manufacture of steel. This aspect of Birmingham came to be symbolized by the largest iron figure ever cast, a 55-foot-high statue of Vulcan, the Roman god of the forge, perched atop Red Mountain, overlooking the industrially polluted Jones Valley. It also became the "Johannesburg of America"; this aspect of the city was symbolized by "Bull" Connor's police dogs, clubs, and firehoses routing civil rights demonstrators. Doubly plagued, Birmingham displayed none of the softer features of the Old South; even in the 1970s, the spurt of Sunbelt growth passed it by.

By 1982, Birmingham was clearly in deep trouble. Its metropolitan area, true, had reached 847,360 people (284,413 in the city), and the choking pall of air pollution had been largely dissipated under the dictates of the federal Clean Air Act. But U.S. Steel, which once had employed 25,000 workers (and for years fended off new industry to keep a lock on the labor market), shut down the last hearth at its mammoth Fairfield works. Unemployment shot to almost 15 percent; surface and air transportation were abysmal; tourist "draws" were utterly absent; racial polarization had returned. The suburbs cared little for the city; in 1981, suburban white legislators blocked state aid to bail out Birmingham's bankrupt bus system, largely patronized by blacks, so that it actually closed operations for several months.

Clear down to the 1960s, Birmingham lacked much of a natural aristocracy or humanitarian leadership. Many of the leading families were only three generations out of the coal mines. Society was split between the the poor and blue-collar classes on one hand, and the well-off (steel executives and their ilk living "over the mountain" in Mountain Brook, one of the snazziest suburbs of America) on the other. Lacking much of a white-collar middle class, culture, or independence of thought, Birmingham fell into the racial phobia of the rest of Alabama; city ordinances forbade integrated gatherings, and even union meetings were broken up by police.* No stranger to violence, the city erupted after the Supreme Court's desegregation decisions: between 1956 and 1961, there were 20 *reported* cases of racial bombings and beatings, even one castration. The U.S. Civil Rights Commission marveled over "the climate of fear and the conspiracy of silence that exists in Birmingham." Business leaders feared bombings or other reprisals if they were publicly identified as advocates or even negotiators in a process that could lead to desegregation; they stayed in their homes "over the mountain," depriving Birmingham of either their financial or moral support.

In 1957, the brutal Eugene "Bull" Connor was elected police commissioner and closed his eyes to (some say even encouraged) white terrorism. In 1963 —what blacks later would call "The Year of Birmingham"—the embattled city was a grisly scene of dogs set upon humans, of George Wallace vowing no compromise on segregation, of massive marches led by the likes of Ralph Abernathy, Andrew Young, Dick Gregory, and King (who penned the eloquent "Letter from Birmingham City Jail"), of tear gas and thousands of arrests, and finally, the bombing of the Sixteenth Street Baptist Church, killing four little black girls. It took federal troops and the National Guard to restore order.† In the midst of the storm of social chaos was an eye of

---

*Despite fierce early resistance to unionization, more than 250,000 Alabamians eventually became union members, the highest rate of organization in the Deep South. Labor has been in the forefront of racial moderation, but the state AFL-CIO president, Barney Weeks, has been a strong Wallace man.

†Bill Baxley was a 22-year-old law student in Tuscaloosa at the time. Sickened by the incident, he was powerless to do anything until six years later, when he won an upset victory to become attorney general. The church-bombing case was among the first he tackled, in 1977 winning a first-degree murder conviction and a life sentence for a former Klansman in the killings.

political moderation: a petition drive forced a special election to toss out Connor and his two fellow city commissioners and to establish a mayor-council form of government. The strategy worked, but Connor literally dug in; it took court orders to oust him from office. Racial peace, albeit an uneasy one, was restored, and integration proceeded. Thanks in part to the Voting Rights Act of 1965, blacks were able to elect one of their own, Arthur D. Shores, to the council in 1968; Richard Arrington joined him three years later and became mayor in 1979, by which time Birmingham had become a black-majority city.

Birmingham's business community for the first time committed itself openly and deeply to resolving the city's problems. The impetus came out of Operation New Birmingham (ONB); the vehicle was the Community Affairs Council, a broad-based biracial group of civic leaders that started meeting weekly to thrash out often-emotional issues behind closed doors. Slowly, gains were made: blacks came to sit on most city boards and commissions and to serve in increasing numbers on the police force; they were also attending once-white schools without busing, and jobs were opening up to them.

But politics were still polarized. Although Arrington helped form the 1975 biracial coalition that elected as mayor an outstanding moderate white, David Vann (once a law clerk to Hugo Black), four years later he turned against Vann to run himself. Arrington's victory was along strictly racial lines in a city divided by an alleged police brutality incident. In 1981, the city council campaign for five open seats was bitterly racial—Arrington backing an all-black slate against an all-white slate endorsed by the Fraternal Order of Police. White backlash and an astounding 60 percent voter turnout combined to elect four whites and one black, giving Birmingham, a 55.6 percent black city, seven whites on its nine-member council. Many liberals were angered at Arrington's role in the polarization. "Black racism isn't any prettier than white racism," observed one.

Birmingham's economy did diversify in the '70s, when 10,000 manufacturing jobs were lost, while 100,000 jobs were gained in government, transportation, other service industries, and above all in medical research and education. The sprawling University of Alabama-Birmingham campus and its outstanding medical center became the area's biggest employer, with a full-time staff of some 8,400. Attention turned to improving Birmingham's dreary physical image—split down the middle by a swath of railroad tracks, afflicted by urban rot. The ONB enlisted the Birmingham League of Architects to donate 5,000 hours of design time. Among the results: a six-square-block, $60 million civic center, including a 2,900-seat symphony hall and a 1,000-seat theater, as well as a large exhibition hall and coliseum. A large regional postal facility also came to Birmingham, as did Southern Bell Telephone's $40 million six-state headquarters. A pale shadow of what's been developing in Atlanta, New Orleans, and Miami? Perhaps. But Birmingham was at least a far more hopeful place than it had been 20, even 10 years before—a faint statement of optimism that applies to Alabama as a whole, the perplexing Cradle of Confederacy.

MISSISSIPPI

Hope At Last

LEGITIMIZED, CALLOUSLY CRUEL, and violent racism pervaded Mississippi
with a virulence matched by no other state. It did not begin to abate until the
1960s, and then only under the onslaught of those hated outsiders, the freedom
riders and civil rights activists, who worked for and with the long-downtrod-
den blacks of Mississippi to break the prototype of the closed society. Some
paid with their lives. But in the end, they overcame, as the moral cause they
championed brought to bear the cumulative weight of federal civil rights
enforcement. Finally the heavy application of national power created a climate in which the tender shoots of reason and decency could flourish. By
creating a milieu in which fruitful change could occur, the Mississippi experience raised deep questions about the old adage that laws cannot create morality.

Racism is the greatest, but not the only burden Mississippi has had to bear.
Ever since the Civil War, this once-rich cotton state has suffered from high
levels of poverty and an economic system that has been slow to modernize.
H.L. Mencken in the 1930s ranked all the states by their wealth and culture,
health and civic affairs; Mississippi ranked last, and by any fair rating of the
'80s would again. The 1970s brought enough economic progress to stop some
of the outward movement of young people and to register a population gain
of 13.7 percent (2.3 percent above the national average), pushing the state total
to 2,520,638. But evidence of the state's poverty and development problems still
abound. Mississippi's per capita income in 1980 was easily America's lowest,
and the differential between this state and others, after dropping for several
years, had begun to increase again. Social Security, welfare, and other transfer
payments were the principal source of income in 34 counties and the second
most importance source of income in the state. W.F. (Bill) Minor, the veteran
and courageous Mississippi journalist and editor, warned that the economic
recession and the federal cutbacks in the early 1980s made Mississippi's road
ahead "bleaker now than anytime since the Great Depression cut deeply into
the thin loins of the state back in the 1930s."

In race relations, Governor William Winter could truthfully say, "Compared to where we were in the mid-1960s, we've come a thousand light years."
Formal segregation had ended in the '60s; blacks no longer needed to worry
about their physical safety when they registered or voted; Mississippi had by
far the largest number of black elected officials of any state (436 in 1981), and
some 10 percent of the 175 state legislators were black in the early 1980s. But
there was still subtle discrimination and such isolated setbacks as a Ku Klux

Klan revival in the north Mississippi city of Tupelo (horrifying to a town that escaped racial violence in the '60s). Black Mississippians testified in the early 1980s that the extension of the federal Voting Rights Act was most desperately needed in their communities if their political gains were to be protected and improved upon.

Against that backdrop, legislation passed by the Mississippi legislature in a special session in December 1982 was probably what the exeptionally progressive and courageous governor of the time—William Winter—called it: "the most significant thing any legislature has ever done for this state." For the first time in Mississippi history, the legislators voted (as 49 states had before) to mandate free, public statewide kindergartens. They also increased Mississippi's generally miserable teachers' salaries by 10 percent, and for the first time provided enough funds and enforcement powers to make the compulsory school attendance law one likely to be respected. All this would be financed by a half-percent increase in the sales tax and a one-percent increase in individual and corporate income taxes for those earning over $10,000. Approval of the education/funding package did not come easily. Earlier in 1982 the legislators had rejected Winter's recommendations—even after the governor, in impassioned terms, told them that if they were not satisfied with 50th place in per capita income, or if they were tired of seeing their children having to go to Houston or Tulsa or some other place they never heard of to get good jobs, or if they were "concerned about Mississippi's slipping further behind rest of the South," then they should "do something about it" and vote for the reforms. The legislators, one journalist told a *Fortune* correspondent, thought "kindergartens would just be day-care centers for black kids" and did not want to offend their campaign contributors in oil and gas companies by raising the state severance tax above 6 percent. After that setback Winter spent much of the year traveling from one corner of the state to another, seeking to convince Mississippians that improved education was the indispensable key to fighting poverty, modernizing the state's economy, and placing the state in a competitive position for the future. That education was a prime failing scarcely could be denied: in 1982 an estimated 3,000 Mississippi children simply failed to show up for the first grade, and the high school drop-out rate was 42 percent, compared to 10 percent nationwide.

Seeds of the Legacy

The white man's domination of his black brother—first as chattel, then as sharecropper in an overwhelmingly rural society—has been the leitmotif of Mississippi history. Until the 1930s, blacks were in a majority (the legacy of plantation days); even in 1980, their 35 percent representation was the highest of any American state.

The transcendent event of Mississippi history was the Civil War, which cost plantation owners 437,000 slaves, then valued at $218 million. Mississippi's Jefferson Davis became president of the Confederacy. The human toll of the war was immense; Mississippi sent 78,000 men into the fight—more than its total male population between the ages of 18 and 45—but only 28,000 of them returned. In his book *The Past that Would Not Die*, Walter Lord provided a graphic picture of the devastation in which Mississippi lay when the war ended: Jackson, Meridian, and other cities lay in ashes, and "Mississippi seemed but a forest of chimneys." Nearly everyone's personal wealth was wiped out. Before the war, Mississippi had been the country's fifth-wealthiest state; afterward, it was last (to remain so for more than a century).

The Mississippi story for the remainder of the 1900s closely paralleled that of its sister Southern states: an original period of pure anarchy after Appomattox; imposition of the infamous Black Code (an effort to reenslave the black man in fact if not in law); the angry reaction of Congress in nullifying the Confederate-dominated state government and imposing Reconstruction, under which blacks controlled much of the political structure; the recapture of the government by white Bourbons in 1875, accompanied by the refusal of a strife-weary national government to intervene; and finally, around 1890, imposition of the Jim Crow laws and the almost total disenfranchisement of all blacks.

The unique elements of the Mississippi story in those years were the ferocity with which these things took place, the lack of moderate voices, the uninhibited violence, and the utter and abject poverty. Race mixing was feared, the white woman glorified. The *Jackson Daily News* announced in November 1865, "We must keep the ex-slave in a position of inferiority. We must pass such laws as will make him *feel* his inferiority." William Faulkner echoed the same thing years later when he had the Mississippian say, "We got to make him a nigger first. He's got to admit he's a nigger."

Mississippi labored meanwhile under unbreakable, wretched poverty. High tariffs and discriminatory freight rates stifled all efforts at economic recovery. The government in Washington came forward with no 19th-century Marshall Plan; between 1865 and 1875 the federal government spent $21 million on public works in Massachusetts and New York but only a paltry $185,000 in Mississippi and Arkansas. Per capita wealth was only 26 percent of what it was in the Northern states. The Mississippi state government economized brutally, perpetuating illiteracy by spending only $2 a head on schoolchildren (compared to $20 in Massachusetts).

A constitutional convention, called in 1890, legalized the methods of all-white, Democratic party control so totally through the poll tax and convoluted residency and literacy laws that Sen. Theodore Bilbo could boast half a century later that the document then produced was one "that damn few white men and no niggers at all can explain." But it was so successful in disenfranchising black people that the "Mississippi Plan," as it came to be known, was rapidly adopted by most Southern states.

At the same time, innumerable Jim Crow laws were put on the Mississippi statute books; eventually they applied to every kind of public accommodation, transportation, and even cemeteries. It was a virtual caste system. To shake hands with a black, to call him "Mr." or "Mrs." was to break the code. And when the black man refused to act in total deference to whites, he was in danger of being killed. According to statistics compiled by the Tuskegee Institute, 538 blacks were lynched in Mississippi between 1883 and 1959, the most of any state.

Race aside, the essential Mississippi conflict was between the Delta and the Hills, between the planters and the "rednecks." The planters were concentrated in the rich alluvial Delta plain that stretches along two-thirds of the state's western border, beside the Mississippi River; essentially conservative and devoted to agricultural and corporate interests, they were Mississippi's version of an aristocracy. The Hills, most of the remainder of Mississippi, were less fertile and peopled by hardscrabble farmers of minimal literacy who hoped that state government—through decent public roads, free textbooks, and the like—could do something to alleviate their miserable lot.

The first man to break up the closed circle of planter leadership was the "Great White Chief" of the Hillsmen, James K. Vardaman, a classic Southern populist demagogue who burst on the scene in 1903, winning the governorship and then a Senate seat. He was for the common man, against the corporations, and for better schools in the Hills, which the Delta would subsidize. And he appealed to race hatreds with cynicism and ugly rhetoric. The Negro, he said, was a "veneered savage" who, "like the mule, has neither pride of ancestry nor hope of posterity." "Why squander money on his education," Vardaman said, "when the only effect is to spoil a good field hand and make him an insolent cook? . . . The way to control the nigger is to whip him when he does not obey without it."

Bilbo succeeded Vardaman as Mississippi's prime demagogue, serving twice as governor and as U.S. Senator from 1934 until his death, in 1947. Bilbo was probably the most reprehensible politician America ever knew, personally venal, well described by the son of a political enemy as "a pert little monster, glib and shameless." Bilboian oratory—filled with obscenities—set him apart. He once described an opponent as "a cross between a hyena and a mongrel, begotten in a nigger graveyard at midnight, suckled by a sow, and educated by a fool." (Bilbo got a pistol whipping in return for that sally.) A sign of modern times, however, is that the bronze statue of Bilbo that stood in the rotunda of the State Capitol at Jackson for many years was packed away in a capitol renovation in the early 1980s.

An even more rabid racist—if that were possible—was Bilbo's contemporary, Congressman John Rankin. Palmer Weber, a former Southern labor organizer, told us, "If a black man got on an elevator with Rankin, the blood would come up in his face. I saw it actually happen myself, in the House Office Building elevator. He couldn't stand the sight." On the day that Estes Kefauver, then a congressman from Chattanooga, voted for the federal anti-poll tax bill, John Rankin ran across the House floor and jumped on Kefauver's back like a little dog, shouting, "Traitor! Traitor! Traitor!"

Under the spell of blatant racism and demagoguery, furiously resistant to new ideas or change, tied to a slowly declining one-crop economy, Mississippi stagnated until the 1960s. The 1920s brought the revival of the Ku Klux Klan, the boll weevil, and disastrous floods. The 1930s brought the Great Depression, tumbling cotton prices, and wages for blacks sinking to ten cents an hour. Some industries began to appear in the 1940s, helped along by World War II and a new set of laws passed to help industry, but even in 1950, 43 percent of the people still made their living from farming. For every person moving into Mississippi, 10 were leaving. The outflow of black Mississippians —many riding the Jim Crow cars of the Illinois Central line straight north to Chicago—had begun as a trickle around the time of World War I. By the 1940s, it had reached a mighty flood: in that single decade, 326,000 black people left Mississippi. But whites were leaving, too: 108,000 in the same decade. Three-quarters of college graduates saw no future in Mississippi and departed.

From the School Decision Through the '60s

Surveying Mississippi in 1950, Walter Lord noted a peculiar air of isolation. No major presidential candidate had been there since Henry Clay. The one bookstore in Jackson sold religious titles only. "The tendency to conform," Lord wrote, "was enormous. Far more than elsewhere, men wore the same necktie (dark), drove the same cars (cream colored), lived for the same football games (Ole Miss-LSU), and above all belonged to the same party (Democratic). The more postwar America changed, the more Mississippi retreated into its own self-contained little world. . . . Confederate flags hung from porches across Mississippi, and in case anyone needed reminding, there was always the reproachful gaze of the noble stone soldier who stood atop the Confederate monument in every courthouse square."

But Mississippi's days in its Confederate time capsule were numbered, as civil rights lawyers "up North" prepared their frontal attack on the public school system, to achieve victory in the Supreme Court in 1954 with *Brown v. Board of Education*. Mississippi's rigidly segregated schools proved the fiction of "separate but equal." In 1950 they spent a low $78.70 a year for each white pupil but $23.83, *less than a third as much*, for each black pupil.

Mississippi's reaction to the *Brown* decision was predictable and swift. "A black day of tragedy," the *Jackson Clarion-Ledger* said. For if applied, Mississippi knew, the decision would be a blow to the solar plexus of the segregated society. According to the state's ancient folklore, race mixing in the classroom would lead to interracial marriage, and mongrelization of the races, and a destruction of the supreme white race. Wrote Mississippi circuit court judge (and later state supreme court justice) Tom P. Brady in his book *Black Monday*, "The negroid man, like the modern lizard, evolved not"; by contrast, "The loveliest and purest of God's creatures, the nearest thing to an angelic being that treads this terrestial ball, is a well-bred, cultured Southern white woman or her blue-eyed, golden-haired little girl."

The first Citizens Council was organized in summer 1954, and by the next year the movement had ballooned to some 60,000 members, all Mississippi community leaders intent on preventing any black inroads into "the Southern way of life." It was a coterie that could apply frightful pressure on dissenters. Blacks who instituted desegregation suits or petitioned for school integration or even registered to vote often lost their jobs. The Councils played on Mississippian prejudice, saying that "the racial revolution seeking to wreck America's entire social system" was part of a "hideous" scheme, cooked up in the Soviet Union, "to mongrelize the races." It was not until 1964 that the federal courts actually forced the first trickle of black entrances into Mississippi's white public schools, not until 1970 that compete school desegregation was accomplished. Several thousand whites panicked and "went rushing," as Bill Minor described it, "into makeshift, 'instant' private schools which proliferated across the landscape, in creek-bank Baptist churches, long abandoned school buildings, empty factories and in private homes."

Segregation's last golden moment came in autumn 1962, when impatient federal courts told the University of Mississippi at Oxford ("Ole Miss") to stop its stalling and enroll black applicant James Meredith. The Ole Miss versus Kentucky football game in Jackson that weekend embodied it all: Ole Miss students displaying the world's largest Confederate flag, "Go Mississippi" flashed in huge letters on the score screen, and then the 46,000 students and friends calling in unison: "We want Ross! We want Ross!" The call was to Governor Ross Barnett, a Citizens Council member and staunch segregationist. Barnett moved from his box to a microphone on the floodlit field, raising his fist to shout in a hoarse voice: "I love Mississippi. I love her people. I honor her customs." The crowd was delirious with pleasure; in that last moment before the wall of segregation began its fall, the concepts of Mississippi and white supremacy and embattled resistance were all one.

The next afternoon, federal agents whisked James Meredith onto the Ole Miss campus and to a tightly guarded dormitory. That night, there was a pitched battle between 400 federal marshals and a screaming mob of 2,500 students and segregationist sympathizers before the Ole Miss Lyceum; inside were Deputy Attorney General Nicholas deB. Katzenbach and other federal officials, receiving moment-by-moment instructions from the command post set up in the White House in Washington. Obscenities, then bricks, sticks, and burning missiles poured in on the beleaguered marshals, who responded with tear gas; sporadic gunfire broke out; two people were killed; the Mississippi National Guard was federalized and called in; and finally regular Army troops arrived to raise the siege. Early Monday morning, Meredith was officially registered and started classes; protected by federal officers, he would remain until his graduation on a peaceful, sunlit morning of August 1963—a world apart from the night of Mississippi's Last Stand.

In 1982 Ole Miss felt compelled by all the national interest in the 20th anniversary of its integration to put on a week-long symposium evaluating the last 20 years of race relations. But the enrollment facts were still shockingly low. In 1981, of an undergraduate enrollment of 7,353, only 554 or 7.5 percent were black. Lesser state institutions did have a higher percentage of blacks; it was suggested to us that blacks avoided Ole Miss because the tuition was higher, the entrance requirements more rigorous than most blacks' could achieve after their poor schools, and the atmosphere unwelcoming.

The 1960s were unquestionably the decade of Mississippi's *real* Reconstruction. In 1961 came the Freedom Riders, in 1962 the Ole Miss crisis, in 1963 the cowardly sniper murder of Medgar Evers, who led the Mississippi NAACP, which was then and is still today the state's most influential black organization. When President Kennedy was assassinated, there was cheering in some of the schools (the white ones, of course). Official lawlessness was still often the rule, led by the group Walter Lord described as "Mississippi's collection of tough, fiercely independent sheriffs, deputies, and town cops. . . . There were dozens of communities where beet-faced deputies, bulging with holsters and cartridge belts, happily wallowed in defiance"—forever railing, of course, against "outside interference" in Mississippi's affairs.

Decent white Mississippians might have been shocked by police excesses and the continuing trail of officially condoned intimidation and violence, but they knew little of it. Most of the state's newspapers were propaganda sheets for the closed society. The few newspaper editors who dissented pursued a dangerous course. One of them, Oliver Emmerich in McComb, told us the story of how he was approached one day on the street by a man he had never met before. The man asked Emmerich a question about his relations with Northern newspapermen and then, without warning, smashed the 68-year-old Emmerich in the face, knocking him to the sidewalk.

If that was the fate that awaited the intrepid white moderate, the lot of blacks who sought to assert their rights was immeasurably worse. The most famous of all these cases was that of Fannie Lou Hamer, the wife of a Mississippi sharecropper, fired and later beaten for her voter registration activities. She told her story on national television as one of the blacks trying to gain seats as members of the Mississippi Freedom Democratic Party delegation at the 1964 Democratic National Convention. In the midst of that despair, President Johnson signed the monumental Civil Rights Act of 1964 into law. Its broad-ranging provisions for fair employment and free access to public accommodations and the powers it gave the Justice Department to enforce equal rights would have an immense impact in Mississippi. At the very moment it went into effect, groups of Northern college students—most of them white—were arriving in Mississippi to participate in the "Freedom Summer" of 1964. They paid their own way, lived with black Mississippi families, helped with voter registration, established community centers, set up schools for illiterates. They knew the dangers when they came to Mississippi, and some paid the highest price. In Longdale, a little community near Philadelphia, Mississippi, a black church was burned. Three of the young civil rights workers—one of them black, two white—went to investigate, were arrested, released, and then abducted and murdered. The church was rebuilt, and this plaque is attached to its wall:

OUT OF ONE BLOOD GOD HATH MADE ALL MEN
To the Memory of
MICHAEL SCHWERNER
JAMES CHANEY
ANDREW GOODMAN
Whose concern for others, and more particularly those
of this community, led to their early martyrdom. Their
death quickened men's consciences and more firmly
established justice, liberty and brotherhood in our land.

Despite the barbarity of Mississippi's response to the Freedom Summer—there were 80 beatings, 30 homes dynamited, countless cross burnings, bullets fired into autos and homes—the state was on the brink of a fantastic change in customs and mores. Three days after the 1964 Civil Rights Act became law, several black leaders registered without incident at Jackson's Heidelburg Hotel. Quickly, the color line was broken in hotels, restaurants, theaters, parks, and public places. Early in 1965 Mississippi's leading industrialists, concerned over threats of boycotts of goods made in Mississippi, broke with the Citizens Councils and began to speak out against racial lawlessness. The Klan and other never-say-die racists continued sporadic bombings, but without the umbrella of official protection that they had enjoyed before.

The last barrier to fall was disenfranchisement of the Mississippi black. Workers of the Southern Regional Council's Voter Education Project and other civil rights groups repeatedly risked their lives in an effort to register Mississippi blacks in the early 1960s, but local officials countered would-be registrants with false arrests, dogs, and loss of jobs. The answer was ultimately found in the Voting Rights Act of 1965, which brought federal examiners into Mississippi. Finally blacks began to register in large numbers. But, even then, there was a heavy price to pay. Six months after the law was signed by President Johnson, Vernon Dahmer, an NAACP leader in Hattiesburg, spoke on the local radio as the chairman of a new black registration campaign. Before dawn the next morning, his home and grocery store were firebombed. Grievously burned, Dahmer staggered from his flaming home and fired shotgun blasts at a fleeing car. On his deathbed, Dahmer said, "I've been trying to get people to register to vote. People who don't vote are deadbeats on the state. . . . What happened to us can happen to anyone, white or black."

In the summer of 1966, Mississippi was again astir with a vivid confrontation. James Meredith made his famous walk into the state to defy the pall of fear so many blacks still felt there; after he was wounded by a shotgun blast from a white man. Dr. Martin Luther King, Jr., and more militant apostles of "black power" came too. A massacre at the hands of white extremists was probably avoided when the governor reluctantly provided state police protection.

Since the mid-'60s, black leaders have exhorted the black masses to take full advantage of the right to vote, for which so many of their brothers sacrificed so much. The effort was complicated by the frightfully low educational levels of so many Mississippi blacks, but still the results were little short of astonishing. In 1980, 72.2 percent of eligible blacks in Mississippi were registered to vote, the second-highest percentage in the country (Missouri was first), according to the Washington-based Joint Center for Political Studies.

Mississippi Politics: A Time of Thaw

Breaking awayfrom its former "tantamount-to-election" style Democratic politics, Mississippi has developed some of America's most unusual political dynamics, the fruit of both blacks entering the electoral process and the rise of the Republicans.

The first compelling black politician to emerge after blacks' latter-day emancipation was Charles Evers, elected mayor of tiny Fayette, in southeast Mississippi, in 1969, a job he held until another black beat him in the 1981 primary. Even before his election, Evers was nationally famous as the brother of the slain Medgar, whose job as field secretary for the NAACP Charles took over in 1963. A big, articulate man with a compelling presence, Evers was perennially a puzzle to politicians and reporters trying to figure out whether his highly unconventional positions reflected advanced thinking or simply personal egotism. Evers unquestionably improved the lives of black people in Fayette, providing an example of entrepreneurship through his own shopping center, developing a comprehensive health program, and bringing numerous industries to town. He seemed to run Fayette as a kind of benign plantation. Guns and name calling were taboo. "If you come down here and call me a nigger, I'll arrest you for disturbing the nigger's peace," he told us. "If I call you a honkey, I'll be arrested for disturbing the honkey's peace."

The Evers image was diminished by his 1971 autobiography, *Evers*, revealing a personal history ranging from supplying GIs with prostitutes while in Manila with the Army to trying his hand at bootlegging while Mississippi was still officially "dry." Evers, who was running for governor that year, said, "I want the people to know that I told them first." He got only 22 percent of the vote in that race, but his presence did force Democrat William Waller, the eventual winner, to campaign for black support. Evers' penchant for nonconformity hit a zenith when he endorsed George Wallace for vice president, saying that Wallace had changed and that he would rather have "a George Wallace a heartbeat away than have an untried, smooth-mouth liberal who still doesn't realize that racism and poverty are every American's problems." In 1978, running as an independent for the U.S. Senate, Evers opposed school busing, saying, "I led the fight for busing in Mississippi but it isn't working. I wanted it so we could have quality education. But there is no quality education. They've bused every black kid out of our neighborhoods 15 and 10 and 30 miles away to predominantly white neighborhoods. . . . They closed down the black schools. We didn't want that. We lost our identity." Evers did get 23 percent of the vote, taking enough away from the Democratic candidate to elect Mississippi's first Republican senator of the 20th century, Thad Cochran. Eventually, Evers had a predictable and bitter falling out with Mississippi NAACP president and Democratic co-chairman Aaron Henry, even endorsing Reagan for president in 1980.

However history finally records the Charles Evers story, he was surely the first legitimate folk hero Mississippi blacks have had (or been allowed to have) in living memory. And his willingness to question liberal positions demonstrated an independence seen in few black politicians.

Mississippi has voted about the most conservative line imaginable in most presidential elections: 87.2 percent for the Dixiecrat ticket of Strom Thurmond and Mississippi's own Fielding Wright in 1948, 87 percent for Barry Goldwater in 1964, 63.5 percent for George Wallace in 1968, 78 percent for Richard Nixon in 1972. Fellow Southerner Jimmy Carter brought Mississippi narrowly into the Democrat column in 1976, but Ronald Reagan brought it back to the GOP in 1980.

Until the 1960s, the white official Mississippi Democratic party spoke not only for white Mississippi but for the state's blacks, whose population count swelled its representation in Congress and at Democratic national conventions. It was a morally indefensible position, and with the organization of the Mississippi Freedom Democratic Party in 1964, it came under legal challenge at the Democratic National Convention. Eventually, there was a compromise on that year's delegation from Mississippi and a permanent party policy to refuse seating, in all future Democratic conventions, to delegations where the party process deprived citizens of the right to vote by reason of their race or color. Thus was laid the groundwork for the entire national Democratic reform movement of the late 1960s and early 1970s—the most fundamental challenge to closed caucus, unit rule, unrepresentative party operations in the 20th century. Throughout the 1970s, Mississippi blacks regularly defected to independent candidates, and the regular and Freedom Democrats did not achieve an alliance that worked until the 1980s. During the late 1970s, some Mississippians said the Republicans had "the only" effective political machine in the state, with computerized mailing lists and all the accoutrements of a modern state party, a statement that would have been considered laughable not long before. For most of the prior century, the Republican machinery had been of zero influence, despite a long-standing feud between its "Black and Tans" and the "Lily Whites." In 1960, the Black and Tans gave up the ghost and the Mississippi GOP became lily white. The new Mississippi Republican party attracted socially conservative whites fleeing the Democratic party, as well as country clubbers and technocrats who have become important in Mississippi's economic modernization. Not until the early '70s did it even give lip service to attracting black support.

Beginning in 1964 with election of a single congressman, the Mississippi

Republicans began to make electoral gains on the coattails of popular GOP presidential candidates. In 1972, on the Nixon coattails, two Republicans won: Trent Lott and Thad Cochran, both destined for major roles. Lott was elected House minority whip in 1981, becoming the first Deep South Republican ever to rise that high in the party leadership. Cochran, meanwhile, went on to become Mississippi's first 20th-century Republican senator by replacing James O. Eastland, who decided not to run in 1978. In 1981, Cochran became chairman of the powerful Appropriations Subcommittee on Agriculture, a key post for heavily rural Mississippi.

Eastland had been a symbol of that one area in which Mississippi was second to none—congressional seniority. He went to the Senate in 1942; when he retired, he was the senior Democrat, president pro tempore, and chairman of the Judiciary Committee, where his name had long been synonymous with the fight to preserve racial segregation. Eastland owned a 5,400 acre plantation in Sunflower County in the Delta, where his plantation blacks lived in miserable shacks and generally desperate poverty but were not forced off the land when farm mechanization made their jobs obsolete. Eastland's attitude toward blacks as full citizens never varied far from his 1947 assessment: "The mental level of these people renders them incapable of suffrage."

James Eastland was not a raw, crude character like Theodore Bilbo, whose supporter and protégé he once had been in the Mississippi legislature. But Eastland used his Judiciary Committee chairmanship to kill civil rights bills whenever he could—127 bills, he claimed at one point in the 1960s—and to expedite or stall confirmation of presidential appointees, depending on their philosophy. Yet in his last years, liberal colleagues on Eastland's Judiciary Committee said he conducted committee business fairly. And some Mississippi state officials told us Eastland helped them, always behind the scenes, on programs that would help impoverished blacks.

Eastland left behind in the Senate his voting twin, John C. Stennis. The two voted alike almost 100 percent of the time: for fiscal conservatism, against civil rights, for tax breaks for business, for high military expenditures. John Stennis, however, has had a very different public image. Quiet and introspective by nature, he was considered the very epitome of Southern gentility, of decorum and dignity and unimpeached integrity. Stennis' primary Senate interest was in the military; for years he was chairman of the Armed Services Committee, ably representing the Pentagon's side in seeking ever-greater appropriations. His personal sense of honor stopped him from putting pressure on the military to spend more money in Mississippi, but the Pentagon money-allocators, knowing which side their bread was buttered on, sharply increased their outlays to Mississippi anyway. In 1982, at the age of 81, Stennis was reelected with 64 percent of the vote.

Jamie Whitten, Mississippi congressman from 1941 onward, became a formidable House power as chairman of the Appropriations Subcommittee on Agriculture, called by some "the permanent Secretary of Agriculture," a man with more influence over the gargantuan Agriculture Department than the ever-changing presidents or agriculture secretaries.

By the early 1980s, Mississippi had still not shaken its habit of electing Democratic governors, though starting with William Waller in 1971 they were consistently moderates. Cliff Finch, elected in 1975, won by putting together an unprecedented combination of poor blacks and hill country whites (known as "blacknecks" and "rednecks"). Finch made history by inviting black comedian Dick Gregory, who had been jailed in Mississippi in the 1960s, to his inauguration, making him an honorary colonel. Finch appointed many blacks to state positions, but his governorship was marred by increasingly erratic behavior, including a strange run for president in 1980 and a truly bizarre four-day meltdown before he left office in 1980 when, according to Bill Minor, "Mississippi was governed by a wild man hopped up on pills, totally out of touch with reality, issuing incredible edicts and orders like the Mad Hatter."

Finch's successor was William Winter, a highly intelligent, socially concerned, progressive Democratic politician. Winter had lost gubernatorial primaries in 1967 and 1975, but by 1979 three factors were going for him: Mississippi had moderated, his primary opponent was a woman (and some Mississippians still believed a woman governor worse than a liberal); and finally, Mississippi had developed a technocratic and professional class, often Republican voting, but attracted to Winter's background as a respected Jackson lawyer.

The Mississippi legislature's 1982 vote to upgrade the schools suggested the body might be ready to discard some of its horrifying reputation. But, despite the election of 17 blacks (15 of them after a 1979 court-ordered reapportionment), one woman, and a number of well-educated young whites, the body remained in the hands of an "ole boys club" which gave ground with the most profound reluctance.

Mississippi's tax system is deeply regressive, rooted in its retail sales tax— the first in the nation when enacted in 1932 and still America's most all-inclusive, extending to medicine, groceries, and even food stamps. A sales tax is inherently regressive, but in a poor state such as Mississippi, where so many people must expend every dollar in their meager incomes on the essentials of life, the burden can be extreme. The Old Guard fiscal leadership in the legislature, according to Bill Minor, resists any change in the sales tax—"a vestige of the philosophy that the sales tax is the 'one tax which blacks pay.' "

Mississippi Economy: From Cotton Upwards

Up through the 1930s, Mississippi was like one great cotton plantation. But the old system was becoming increasingly untenable as World War II approached. Cotton production, while increasingly concentrated and productive, required less and less labor. The tractor began to replace the tenant farmer with his balky mule pulling a broken-down plough through the cotton fields. The clanking mechanical pickers arrived in the '40s, each one throwing scores of untrained, unlettered field hands into a labor market offering virtually no other opportunities. "Our state," editor Oliver Emmerich of McComb told us, "was like an underdeveloped Latin country." Except for cotton, about the only resource Mississippi had was its great timber stands. But outside industries had swept the state clean of pine, leaving cutover lands and sediment-clogged streams and scarcely enough trees to provide seeds for natural regrowth; not until the '60s and '70s would lumber be a big factor in the economy again. "Our politicians spent their time attacking Wall Street and industry," Emmerich said. "How did that help the poor farmers in the fields?"

The year 1936 was to prove an historic one for Mississippi, for it was then that the legislature authorized the state's first industrial recruitment program. "Reflecting the long agrarian history of the state," historian Thomas D. Clark wrote, "the new law paid its respects to the past and courted the future in its title, 'Balance Agriculture With Industry.' " The "BAWI" advertising program was to prove a resounding success. One can see it today in the landscape dotted with light manufacturing plants. And figures prove the point. In 1939, the value added by manufacturing in Mississippi was $73 million; by 1978, it was over $6 billion a year. In 1940, manufacturing employment was only 59,000; by the '80s, it was close to 200,000. In 1966, for the first time, there were more Mississippians working in factories than on the land—proof that agriculture had indeed been "balanced" with industry. And thousands more made their living in services, trade, finance, and government.

Given the staggering loss of people Mississippi experienced between 1940 and 1970, even with BAWI, one can only imagine what might have evolved without the program: perhaps a Mississippi resembling a semideserted colony, inhabited just by plantation owners, their few remaining field hands, and perhaps workers for the tourist industry along the Gulf Coast. Nevertheless, Mississippi paid a price for BAWI. Industrial recruiters grabbed any factory they could, no questions asked, to land a smokestack for a job-hungry town. One of the first plants snared was a rubber factory in Natchez, which quickly added a new aroma to that historic old city. The unsubtle advertising pitch was for "willing and able labor," so that most of the plants that came were low-skill, low-wage outfits, many fleeing the pressures of Northern labor unions and minimum wage laws. Garment and hosiery plants, paying rock-bottom wages to largely female work forces, came in special abundance. BAWI plants sometimes seemed anxious to bow to the local mores on race, making off-the-record agreements to hire only whites or predominantly white labor forces. Local taxrolls were shortchanged by agreements, sanctioned by state law, to waive *all* local property taxes for 10 years for a new industry. Local bond issues were used to finance the entire cost of industrial buildings. There were some cases in which unscrupulous operatiors befuddled the locals by moving in only long enough to enjoy the tax free period in taxpayer-supported buildings, then disappearing from the scene.

By the early 1960s, Mississippi's leaders decided they could shift their sights from the raw number of new jobs to the quality of those jobs. State research efforts turned to getting industries offering higher pay, demanding higher skills, and utilizing higher technology. Symbolic of this development was the creation, in 1964, of the Mississippi Research and Development Center, which tried to use sophisticated systems analysis to determine which industries would match which counties best, and how to gear up to attract them. It was a remarkable leap into modern economic analysis by the most economically backward of all states. But the major reasons for growth through the '70s were probably still low wages and lack of unions, combined with growing oil and gas production, timber industry, and services in the urban areas.

A Whiff of Urbanism: Jackson . . .

We turn now to the towns and regions, and the nascent phenomenon of Mississippi urbanism. Rural plantation life absorbed the great bulk of Mississippi's population through most of its history. In 1900, Vicksburg and Meridian could boast only 14,000 inhabitants, and Natchez 12,000; Jackson, the present metropolis, was a village of 7,800. A million and a half people lived in Mississippi, but one had to look to the land to find them.

When John Gunther passed through Jackson in the 1940s, he saw "a curious town" with "a handful of impeccably shining skyscrapers, rising straight out of a muck of Negro hovels and poor-white slums." The legislature had designated the location as a state capital in 1821, but it had taken Jackson a long time to reach its World War II population level of 75,000. And not until recent years has Jackson reached the size (city population 202,895, metropolitan area 320,425) to make it a really important urban center, a place with the substantial pool of skilled labor, cultural-educational amenities, and financial institutions that major high-wage industries pick for their major installations. But the 1970s growth figures indicated clear success—from 82,000 jobs to 128,000 in the single decade.

Jackson has become one of the most attractive cities of the South: green, open, and pleasant, a surprise to outsiders who expect a city matching Mississippi's image of old. In a beauty contest with Baton Rouge or Montgomery, the capitals of its neighbors, Jackson would win hands down. But its defects include remnants of the slums that Gunther saw, places now filled with a constant influx of impoverished, ill-educated Delta blacks. There are several marginal, honky-tonk neon arteries. But because it is so new, Jackson also has stretches of suburban developments with a decent enough style and eye-pleasing greenery. Jackson's downtown has suffered, like those in so many other cities, as retailing moved out to shopping centers. Perhaps the greatest downtown tragedy into the 1980s was the deteriorated, shuttered state of Jackson's historic King Edward Hotel, which had been burned by Sherman's troops in 1863 and served as a hub for Mississippi politics in the 1920s and as a center of bootlegging during Prohibition.

Jackson has made great strides in race relations since the 1960s, when daily racist fulminations in the *Jackson Clarion-Ledger* and *Daily News* poisoned the atmosphere and the city was such a fountainhead of Citizens Council strength that the public swimming pools were closed rather than bow to the integration order of a federal court. (The pools were closed so long that they were beyond rehabilitation, with 8-inch pine trees growing through their bottoms.) Yet even in 1982, a black-owned and edited local weekly, the *Jackson Advocate*, was fired into by men with carbine rifles—the same ex-Ku Klux Klansmen who had been arrested four years earlier for raids on another newspaper, the feisty *Capital Reporter*, edited by Bill Minor. (The *Capital Reporter*, which eventually folded in 1981, was also victimized by a cross burning that set fire to electrical wiring in its office.)

It is true that Jackson bankers led the way in Mississippi employment integration by hiring black tellers and clerks in the 1960s, and that some local firms, including MPI (a large woodworking plant), took an early role in black hirings. In 1969, the segregationist hold on City Hall was broken with the election as mayor of Russell Davis, a native of Maryland who broke with precedent by promising "to work with the responsible Negro leadership of this community." Davis' administration became the first to put blacks in appointive city policymaking jobs. But even though the city was 47 percent black by 1980, it had never elected a black to the city council or as mayor, and the Justice Department had to insist, under the Voting Rights Act, that it establish single-member council districts.

Racial tensions were exacerbated in 1970, following the nationally publicized killings of two young blacks and wounding of 12 others during a student demonstration at the all-black Jackson State College. But only 16 months later, television viewers around the nation heard Walter Cronkite—in the midst of dynamited school buses in Pontiac, Michigan—praise Jackson schools as the nation's model for peaceful integration. Jackson's power structure had finally found the spirit of cooperation when they realized that the city's racist image had caused an alarming downturn in economic growth, and David Scott, the president of Allis-Chalmers, said he would not bring a divisional headquarters to the city unless the school situation—piecemeal integration, segregation academies, and the expectation of forced busing—were stabilized. By 1980, *New York Times* city watcher John Herbers was able to report that "Jackson is now the most integrated—in schools, neighborhoods and politics—of the Southern state capitals."

Jackson has for some time been the center of Mississippi's recognized business-media power structure. The most powerful banks are the First National and the Deposit Guaranty National. For decades, the media scene was dominated by the Hederman publishing family, which controlled the *Jackson Clarion-Ledger* and *Daily News*. The Hedermans were abstemious Baptists, fundamentalists, and for many decades hard-core segregationists. After 1970, however, the Hedermans entered the modern world and even signed full-page newspaper ads supporting Jackson's public schools and their busing plans. The papers had become quite mainstream and respectable by the time they were sold to the Gannett chain in 1982.

Gannett installed native Mississippian and former Washington newsman Charles Overby as executive editor. Overby's editorials could not be more different from the Mississippi of old. In 1982, he suggested that Senator Bilbo's statue be kept in its box after a capitol renovation, and as part of a 10-page special section on Ole Miss 20 years after integration, wrote of his own teenage memories of driving past the Governor's Mansion in a gesture of support for Ross Barnett—and how "wrong, wrong, wrong" he and the Mississippi establishment had been.

We cannot leave Jackson without mentioning WLBT, Mississippi's dominant commercial television station, whose racist policies in the 1960s forced the national issue of broadcaster sensitivity to community wishes. In 1964, after a meticulous, week-long, minute-by-minute record of the picture and sound of commercial television offerings in Jackson, the United Church of Christ's New York-based office of communication and civil rights leaders filed a petition with the Federal Communications Commission, asking it to deny license renewal. WLBT-TV was accused of permitting racial slurs to be spoken on the air, as well as excluding black community news and civil rights news reports from the NBC network. The FCC, customarily solicitous of existing station ownerships, refused to take the license away from its Southern white owners. But Warren Burger, then a federal Court of Appeals judge, overruled the FCC shortly before he became Chief Justice. The license was then operated for many years by a nonprofit organization that leased the license, made money, and won many awards for investigative reporting. In 1979, the FCC finally awarded the license to a black-controlled group headed by Aaron Henry, one of the original challengers.

The Gulf Coast and Miscellany

Mississippi's 70-mile Gulf Coast—literally a "strip city" between New Orleans and Mobile—is also fast growing. Between them, the coastal cities of Gulfport, Biloxi, Pascagoula, and their satellites and immediate hinterland had 309,933 people in 1980.

The Gulf Coast has always been a place apart from the rest of Mississippi —interlaced with French Catholics à la Southern Louisiana, less hung up on the race problem because it has had fewer blacks (only 18.5 percent by latest count), oriented to tourism and fishing and port life, and a place where travelers, including those from the moralistic dry counties, could always get a drink in a bone-dry state.

For more than a century, the coast was a favored summer playground of Old South gentility and, in winter, a favorite vacation spot of Midwesterners. The outlanders built stately Gulf-front mansions, circled with moss-covered oaks and magnolia trees and provided a clientle for luxurious resort hotels.

All of that began to change with World War II and its aftermath. A new industrial flavor was supplied by the shipbuilding industry at Pascagoula and new refineries and petrochemical plants. Large banana terminals and other port facilities were transferred from New Orleans. Veterans' hospitals and big military bases provided substantial local employment. And at one point in the 1960s, 4,000 people were employed at a $250 million NASA test center for moon rockets in Hancock County, close to New Orleans.

The postwar era brought a tourist boom of a new character. Much of the coast became a neoned strip of motels and boisterous nightclubs. Especially in Biloxi, gambling was wide open for intermittent periods; occasionally, the state stepped in to clean out the slot machines and dice, roulette, and blackjack games, but when Jackson's control relaxed, they always reappeared. The old summer mansions and hotels became relics of another age.

On August 17, 1969, Hurricane Camille—described by some as the most powerful hurricane in American history—roared ashore from the Gulf of Mexico, cutting a path of destruction in which 144 people met their death and more than $1 billion of property damage was inflicted. Gulfport, Biloxi, and Pass Christian seemed to lie in ruins, with doubtful future prospects. But, like a phoenix rising from the ashes, the Gulf Coast rebounded with incredible rapidity: so rapidly, alas, that plastic resort-sameness replaced much of its historic individuality.

After Jackson, the Gulf Coast, and the Memphis bedroom suburbs in its northwest corner, Mississippi has few population concentrations that would be considered very urban elsewhere in the United States. There are a number of towns worth noting because they are centers of their respective geographic regions. Meridian (pop. 46,577), in the dirt-poor Hills country of east-central Mississippi, is the largest of all but not growing. It makes most of its money from the region's cattle and timber, plus a sprinkling of industries. Columbus (27,383), noted for its antebellum homes, and fast-growing Tupelo (23,905) are centers of northeastern Mississippi; Tupelo in particular has broken away from hardscrabble small farms and ruined land to capitalize on TVA power and mount an impressive bootstrap campaign of industrial expansion. The chief cities of the big Piney Woods section of southern and southeastern Mississippi are Hattiesburg (40,829) and Laurel (21,897). Some of these little cities have made interesting contributions to American culture. Tupelo, for instance, was the birthplace of Elvis Presley. Laurel, on the other hand, was the native city of Leontyne Price. The cost of her musical instruction was defrayed by one of the old white families, a member of which was present when she made her debut at the Metropolitan Opera in New York.

The Mississippi redoubt of an encapsulated Old South is Natchez (22,015), on the Mississippi's banks in southwestern Mississippi. Natchez's golden era was in the decades before the Civil War, when the great fortunes were made from the buying and exporting of cotton, and thousands of slaves lived on vast plantations. In these days of brutal super highways, one road anyone with a love for the land and history will enjoy is the Natchez Trace Parkway: a quiet, two-lane road that the U.S. Park Service has built along the Trace (Old French for "a line of footprints") linking Natchez with Nashville. Before the age of the steamboat, it was easy enough for men from Kentucky and other regions of the then Western frontier to float their farm products downriver to Natchez and New Orleans. But sailing or rowing upstream was too laborious, and by 1800 a thousand each year were walking the Trace to Nashville on their return trips. Until the 1820s and the era of the steamboat, the Natchez

Trace was one of the great frontier roads of the American Republic. Later it fell into disuse, only to be "restored" in modern times.

There is new oil and manufacturing money in Natchez in the mid-1980s, but the upper crust remains the families who made their fortunes in antebellum days. Many of them live in exquisitely preserved mansions with romantic names such as D'Evereux, Rosalie, Monteigne, Mount Repose, Dunleith, and Green Leaves. Upstream from Natchez is Vicksburg (25,434), where each American state that participated in the Civil War has built a monument to its dead. The fall of this "Gibraltar of the Confederacy" on July 4, 1863, sealed the doom of the Southern cause, and Vicksburg has lived in the tortured glory of the war ever since, although it does have a port, oil, and new industries.

The Delta: A Phantasmagoria

The classic social definition of Mississippi's Delta (writer David Cohn's words, of which more in our Tennessee chapter) is that it "begins in the lobby of the Peabody Hotel in Memphis and ends on Catfish Row in Vicksburg." The geologic definition differs slightly: the Mississippi-Yazoo Delta is a flat alluvial plain of incredibly rich black earth—its depth as great as 35 feet—laid down through countless eons by the inundations of the Mississippi River. Its greatest length is 200 miles; its greatest width, 85 miles. Today the Mississippi's floods are held back by powerful levees.

The Delta has to be seen to be believed. It is as level as the mind could imagine, its wide flat fields, steaming with fertility, stretching on in seeming infinity. There are occasional plantation houses of the grand Southern style, contraposed to squat shack towns where the field hands still live. Nowhere in America do the lifestyles of the privileged and the less fortunate contrast so vividly. Modern Delta farming is subject to the vicissitudes of national and international markets, flooding, and Mississippi rains, which at even "normal" levels can ruin a crop; but essentially a Delta planter with a modicum of intelligence and any substantial amount of acreage has it made. The land is very productive, and multi-thousand-acre farms are not uncommon.

There are some planter families whose Delta roots go back five or six generations; others are descended from some smart foreman a generation or two back who got hold of a piece of land and scratched his way to affluence. And planter families lead a good life. They give lavish parties at home or the country club, charter air-conditioned buses to take their friends to the football games in Memphis, jet off to New York for Broadway shows, or to Europe, or to places in the sun for long winter sojourns.

Politically, the planters are a conservative lot, though they were rarely given to the Vardaman or Bilbo brand of racist extremism. The height of Delta moderation and cosmopolitanism is reached in Greenville (pop. 40,613), an old port and cotton processing center. The U.S. Commission on Civil Rights noted with some wonder that in the mid-1960s, when officially condoned lawlessness gripped most of Mississippi, the leaders of Greenville insisted on scrupulous and even-handed application of the law and saw to it that their city, unlike any other in the state, arrested and prosecuted the cross-burners of the Ku Klux Klan.

An indicator of Greenville's openness was that its business community tolerated—and patronized—the *Delta Democrat-Times*, the liberal newspaper founded in 1936 by Hodding Carter II. Over the years the Carters got their share of threats for their willingness to print the news straight and advocate racial harmony, but unlike other Mississippi editors experienced no beatings or bombs. Hodding Carter II wrote outspoken civil rights editorials years before the question was of wide-scale concern even in the North, winning the Pulitzer Prize in 1946 and continuing to report the civil rights struggle of the 1960s as no other paper in Mississippi. He died in 1972 and was succeeded by his son Hodding III, who later won national fame and plaudits as the State Department press secretary in the administration of Jimmy Carter. Afterward, Hodding III decided not to return to Mississippi. (He had divorced his wife and married Patricia Derian, Mississippi's Democratic national committeewoman, who directed the Carter administration's controversial human rights policy). No little consternation and disappointment were noted among progressive Mississippians when the Carter family in 1980 sold the *Delta Democrat-Times* for a reported $16 million to Freedom Newspapers of Santa Ana, California, an ultra-conservative chain that appeared to stand for the diametric opposite of what the Carters had always represented.

So many writers have made Greenville their home—the long list includes the Carters, the Percys (William Alexander and Walker), Shelby Foote, and novelist Ellen Douglas—that the city has sometimes been called the Concord of the South. The rest of Mississippi has had its share of illustrious literary figures: Faulkner, of course, and Willie Morris (whose writings made his native Yazoo City familiar to many), playwright Tennessee Williams, and the novelists Eudora Welty and Richard Wright. But Greenville is the only place where so many have congregated. It was the region that sent the only Mississippi moderate in many a decade, Frank L. Smith of Greenwood, to the U.S. House for five terms. In 1982, however, Deltans balked at a full step into a biracial society. Black state Rep. Robert Clark won the Deomcratic nomination for the U.S. House and support of virtually all Mississippi's major Democratic politicians, including John Stennis. But Clark, in the general election, lost narrowly to Republican Webb Franklin, whose TV ads picture him in front of a Confederate monument pledging to maintain "tradition."

Cheek by jowl with the planters and the plainer white folk of the Delta live the blacks—60 percent of the area's population. David Cohn wrote in the 1940s:

> The Negro's identification with the life of the Delta is fundamental and complete. . . . It was he who brought order out of a primeval wilderness, felling the trees, digging the ditches and draining the swamps. The vast rampart on the levees upon whose existence the life of the Delta depends sprang from the sweat and

brawn of the Negro. Wherever one looks in this land, whatever one sees that is the work of man, was erected by the toiling, straining bodies of the blacks.

Delta blacks have little to show for those generations of toil. For most, the bitter fact is that there are simply no farm jobs available anymore. Lost to the tides of mechanization is the historic sight of thousands of black hoe hands in spring and summer and the rows of men, women, and children moving through the fields at picking time in the fall. Between 1960 and 1971, the number of full-time farmers and farm workers dropped from 81,000 to 39,000. In the 1970s, the Delta was Mississippi's only area to lose population.

Where did the displaced blacks go? Some stayed on the land, living on Mississippi's lowest-in-the-nation welfare dole. Through the 1960s, most went North, on that famous Illinois Central line to Chicago. Then in the 1970s, as the Southern economy picked up, some headed for Jackson, but many still had to go farther afield to Texas and Oklahoma.

It takes a stranger driving through the Delta only an hour or two to see the human misery, and one wonders how the sophisticated planters view it all. "Many local wealthy people live on the incredible fiction that they don't have poverty all around them," Hodding Carter III said. "It's an elaborate edifice you have to maintain if want to live with yourself."

The problems involved in assuring decent living conditions and education and health care for the Delta's black people stagger the imagination. The least one can say is that before the 1960s the problem was a hidden national shame. Since then, it has become known, and, with many false starts, the arduous work of lasting change has begun. After the Freedom Summer of 1964, most of the out-of-state civil rights activists disappeared from the scene. But "deep in the morass of broken Negro hopes," as one writer put it, there remained a handful of young activists sent South by the National Council of Churches to act as spiritual advisers in that famous 1964 summer. They formed the Delta Ministry, a permanent Christian ministry in Greenville. The goal: to help blacks with their problems of illiteracy and to teach new skills to people who had never known any livelihood except hoeing and chopping cotton. The Delta Ministry initiated Mississippi's first Head Start programs and pressed for federal funds to alleviate hunger. The ministry also helped form several organizations run by Charles Bannerman, a particularly aggressive black leader who brought millions of dollars in federal antipoverty and national foundation grants to the Delta. Bannerman's Mississippi Action for Community Education, a membership organization of 25,000 persons, built subsidized housing projects and encouraged unincorporated areas to become municipalities so that they could qualify for state and federal aid. A related organization, the Delta Foundation, made loans to small farmers and business owners, helped black lawyers and doctors start their practices and, under its subsidiary Delta Enterprises, opened a series of manufacturing businesses.

To become president of Delta Enterprises in the early '80s, Bannerman persuaded the Cummins Engine company to loan him Carl Banyard, a black

Mississippian who had left in the '60s to go to a Vermont prep school, Yale College, and Harvard Business School. One evening at Greenville's Doe's Eat Place, a shacklike restaurant where the Delta's jet-set planters come to eat $20, two-pound minimum steaks on mismatched china, Banyard explained to us his love of Mississippi and the frustrations of even the most skilled economic development specialist to operate in the state. Despite the discrimination which he and his ancestors had experienced, Banyard said he loved Mississippi's personal friendliness which transcended racial lines. He had aggressively marketed Delta Enterprises' products, from blue jeans to railroad spikes, to bring some rare non-commodity, out-of-state income to the Delta. But the age-old strategy of encouraging low-skilled labor intensive businesses in high unemployment areas, Banyard said, was "bankrupt" due to the low margins in those businesses and the competition from overseas. Yet as long as Mississippi's educational levels remained so low, he added, economic development specialists did not have the raw material—educated people—necessary for the success of their programs.

In the northern Delta lies Mound Bayou, a virtually all-black town founded by former slaves in 1887—ironically, on land that once belonged to Jefferson Davis. Black power reigned in Mound Bayou when it was an impossible dream in the rest of Mississippi, but the town and its hinterland were all too typical of the grinding poverty of Mississippi black life. Within a 20 year period, however, Mound Bayou (pop. 2,917) was to emerge twice in the American consciousness as the symbol of rural, black poverty in America.

In the late 1960s and early '70s, Mound Bayou became the center of experimentation in delivering health care to poor black people. Dr. Jack Geiger, of Boston's Tufts University Medical School, picked Mound Bayou as the location of the Tufts Delta Health Center because surrounding Bolivar County was one of the poorest in America, and because the all-black community would provide insulation from potential harrassment by Mississippi whites. Grants were obtained from the federal Office of Economic Opportunity, including one of $800,000 to build a new health center, and medical specialists—black and white—were dispatched to the Delta to inaugurate a humanly touching and socially revolutionary chapter in American health care. For many patients, the visit to the Tufts Delta Health Center was the very first contact of their lives with any kind of medical care. Realizing that the real health enemy was malnutrition, aggravated by life in broken-windowed shacks infested by rats and roaches and often by contaminated drinking water from wells, the center encouraged people to start their own vegetable plots and install sanitary vault privies. A single medical team would see whichever member of a family might come to the center. The goal was a medical systems approach, in which every relevant factor—from home interpersonal relationships to nutrition and sanitation to specific ailments—could be treated. Tufts ran into relationship problems with Mound Bayou Community Hospital, a more conventional health facility staffed by Meharry Medical College of Nashville. So eventually it pulled out, albeit having established an important model for health care centers in all poor communities.

Beginning in 1969, Mound Bayou's Mayor Earl Lucas began chasing after other kinds of federal money to rebuild homes, pave roads, install a water system, build a 19-acre park with an indoor swimming pool, and pay city workers. A half-million dollars in federal funds also paid for a city hall with an entrance decorated with wood carvings of black heroes such as Muhammad Ali, Hank Aaron, Martin Luther King, Jr.—and Mayor Lucas.

Even friendly observers questioned whether the federal money was being spent wisely, or even honestly. In 1981, less than a year after Ronald Reagan became president, the federal funds had dried up to the point that Mound Bayou faced bankruptcy, the police unpaid, a federally built housing project burned because no fireman was on hand to take the call, even city hall telephones turned off for nonpayment. As a national symbol of black pride and the civil rights movement, Mound Bayou was able to attract donations that kept it afloat for a time.

Over the long run, however, Mound Bayou and all that had happened there raised the most basic questions about the relationship between the federal government and localities and about the advantages of accepting federal largesse. One could argue that until the late 1960s, Mound Bayou had been, in its own, shanty-style, dirt-road way, self-sufficient. But in its isolation, it had suffered crippling poverty and a frightening infant mortality rate. Simply to cut off outside aid, with no further effort to help Mound Bayou's blacks find a path toward more legitimate self-sufficiency, seemed a path both heartless and, in the long run, ill-advised. But Mississippi's white establishment seemed quite content to go that route. Indeed, the newly conservative *Delta Democrat-Times* suggested the city of Mound Bayou simply go out of existence, its impoverished residents presumably becoming quiescent and invisible. It was a suggestion even a James Vardaman or Theodore Bilbo would have found quite acceptable.

ARKANSAS

Up from Provincialism

DOWN THROUGH HISTORY, touched less by the ways of industrialized society than any of its neighbors, a place obdurately independent and hopelessly provincial, came the state of Arkansas. It was an island set apart, a civilization primitive and poor. "Whar's this road go to?" the *Arkansas Traveler* asked. "I've been livin' here fer years, 'n' I ain't seen it go no place," the squatter replied.

Then two governors changed it all. The first was named Orval Faubus, an Ozark original, who in 1957 tried to defy the U.S. Supreme Court's order to integrate the Little Rock public schools by ordering the Arkansas National Guard to bar the entry of black students. The incident gave Little Rock and Arkansas a name in history they have sought ever since to live down. The second was Winthrop Rockefeller, reared in the drawing rooms of New York, hardened in the oil fields of Texas. In four short years (1966–70), he began to free Arkansas from its age-old poverty of racism and underdevelopment.

Arkansas, 53,104 square miles, is tucked away in the lower valley of the Mississippi, just southeast of the center of the continent. The WPA Writers' Project of the 1930s defined it as "between the South of the piazza and the West of the pony." Its eastern border is the Mississippi River, opposite Tennessee and Mississippi; here is the flat, immensely fertile Delta country, which is part and parcel of the Old South. Gazing at the fields across the distant, level horizon, one can conjure up the past vision of blacks stooping under a hot sun to pick the cotton of great landowners; these days, machines do the picking, and cotton is crowded by other crops, including rice. The counties along the Mississippi border are all at least 40 percent black.

Southern Arkansas has low hills and swamp and vast stands of pine supporting a strong timber industry. Some of the area is reminiscent of neighboring Oklahoma and Texas with great ranch spreads and oil wells. The Ouachita Mountains are about halfway up the western border; to the northwest are the ancient Ozarks, shared with Oklahoma and Missouri. Until the 1970s, these mountains were one of the few frontier areas left in America, where the physical and cultural isolation preserved the centuries-old lifestyles, including vestiges of Elizabethan speech and the ballads of the people's English and Scotch-Irish forebears. Spotted through the Ozarks were isolated hamlets where men still turned the soil with a horse- or mule-drawn plow. The '70s, however, brought to northern Arkansas those twin phenomena of mobile retirees and footloose industry, accompanied by an unfamiliar population growth.

Through it all, bisecting Arkansas neatly from west to east, lies the valley of the Arkansas River—now navigable thanks to federal largesse, so that Fort Smith, Little Rock, and Pine Bluff have become true port cities. Regional contrasts in Arkansas may be seen in the ancestry of the people. The white plantation owners of eastern Arkansas came principally from Kentucky, Tennessee, and Mississippi, and this area has rarely sent progressives to Congress or the state legislature. Western and hill Arkansas, by contrast, was first settled by people from Missouri and mountainous areas of the South. This was the home of U.S. Senator J.W. Fulbright and former U.S. Representative Brooks Hays, the victim of a purge in 1958 after he had tried to mediate in the Little Rock school controversy.

Along the division between the two great regions, and sharing some characteristics with both, are the capital city of Little Rock (pop. 158,461) and its industrial neighbor, North Little Rock (64,419). Another 170,614 people live outside the central cities, in surrounding Pulaski County and neighboring Saline County. Little Rock is not only the seat of government, but the center of economic activity, home of the only two newspapers of statewide circulation and site of Arkansas' most widely heard radio and television stations. The *Arkansas Gazette* is a liberal queen among Southern newspapers, still reflecting the progressive attitudes that in 1957 produced the bitter enmity of Governor Orval Faubus as he opposed the U.S. Supreme Court's decision in favor of school desegregation. The rival *Arkansas Democrat* is more conservative.

Befitting its location, Little Rock is much less Southern than its famous uproar over school integration would indicate. People are as likely to wear western boots and talk of flying to Dallas or Houston for shopping or business as they are to speak with Southern accents. Little Rock's manner is nicely low-key, and downtown has experienced both quality historic preservation (the train station turned into a restaurant is especially pleasant) and new bank-owned skyscrapers. There has been a succession of progressive municipal administrations, with the first black elected to the city council in 1969 and a black city manager by 1980.

Little Rock's famous schools became both a model of integration and a prime example of the difficulties in trying to keep a school system integrated. By the early 1980s, the Little Rock schools had actually been able to reclaim some students who had gone to private schools; a group called Parents for Public Schools encouraged this. At Central High School, where all the trouble started, 65 percent of the students were going on to college. But the Little Rock school system had become 66 percent black overall, and in grades one through three, 85 percent of the pupils were black. As the percentage of whites in the city schools declined, voters proved increasingly reluctant to approve bond issues. In 1982 a school board composed of six whites and one black reduced busing in an attempt to keep the school system from becoming totally black; the chamber of commerce, meanwhile, launched a campaign to encourage public school enrollment. Black parents charged that resegregation would occur, but the federal appeals court in St. Louis denied their appeal. The real way to integrate the schools, civil rights advocates said, was to combine them with the suburban Pulaski County system, which remained 80 percent white.

Pulaski County had its share of political excitement in the 1970s. In 1974, ACORN, originally an acronym for Arkansas Community Organizations for Reform Now, a protest organization of working-class people, was formed in Pulaski by Wade Rathke, founder of the National Welfare Rights Organization. Rathke, who had discovered that welfare mothers were not a viable political constituency, managed to lead his people to capture nearly half the seats in Pulaski County's legislative body. By the early 1980s, ACORN had established chapters in 28 states and was known as the Association of Community Organizations for Reform Now. ACORN members "squatted" in vacant government-owned housing to protest the nation's lack of commitment to shelter poor people and constantly pressured the Democratic party to encourage participation of poor people in caucuses and conventions. At the other end of the political spectrum, the Pulaski County Sheriff, Tommy Robinson, was sent to jail in Memphis in 1982 for defying the orders of a black federal judge (a man whom he had intemperately called a "token" and an "affirmative action" appointment). The dispute was over improvement of jail conditions; after being locked up, the sheriff voiced the same complaints about the Memphis jails that he had often heard: denial of visitation, lack of religious practices, poor food, and subjection to a humiliating body search.

Politically, the Little Rock metropolitan area is in no position to dominate Arkansas. Little Rock's metropolitan population (393,494, up 21.7 percent in the '70s) still accounts for only 17.2 percent of the statewide population. The only two large cities besides Little Rock are Pine Bluff (56,636), in southeast Arkansas, and Fort Smith (71,626), on the Arkansas River at the Oklahoma border. Fort Smith advertises itself as "the gateway to the Ozarks" and has the most Western flavor of any Arkansas city. Pine Bluff boasts a handsome civic center designed by native son Edward Durrell Stone. The Army's nearby Pine Bluff Arsenal for years produced and housed the nation's total supply of deadly antipersonnel biological warfare weapons.

Arkansas still has one of the highest rural population shares among the 50 states. Among the distinctive smaller towns is the one-time health spa of Eureka Springs (pop. 1,989), whose Victorian architecture has attracted both retirees and professionals tired of the hustle and bustle of larger cities. Several newcomers to Eureka Springs have tried to help other Ozark towns preserve their social and architectural identities even as they welcome growth.

Capsule History: 1541 to 1954

Arkansas was discovered by de Soto in his vain search for gold in 1541–42, was first opened up to the French missionaries and traders in the 1660s, became a possession of the U.S. with the Louisiana Purchase in 1803, and broke off from Missouri to become a territory in its own right in 1819.

A measure of adversity has surrounded Arkansas' development since the earliest years. When it was admitted to the Union as the 25th state in 1836, it had barely the minimum requirement of 50,000 people—due mostly to the immense, often impassable swamp that then covered most of eastern Arkansas. Arkansas would just as soon have ignored the Civil War; though the state joined the Confederacy, it was said to have contributed thousands to Union armies as well. There were few major battles on Arkansas soil. Reconstruction came to Arkansas as surely as every other state, embodied in a Republican carpetbag regime and bringing enfranchisement for blacks, founding of the University of Arkansas, and the state's first system of free public education. These years were better in many respects than what was to follow—decades of control by conservative Democrats, who proceeded to put the blacks back in "their place" and to allow business low taxation and little regulation. At the same time, Arkansas' dependence on a single crop, cotton, became greater than ever before, and the demoralizing system of sharecropping entrapped great numbers of whites and blacks alike.

Until the entry of rebellious young war veterans into Arkansas politics in the 1940s, Bourbon conservatism was rarely challenged. The white and black peasantry of the Delta lived under an almost feudal social structure and in dire poverty. The blacks were, of course, excluded from voting, and of the whites, the *Arkansas Gazette* reported as late as 1948 that "Plantation owners in the Delta counties usually control the votes of their tenants, who cast their ballots in boxes set up in the owners' commissaries." The hillsmen were more independent but, if anything, poorer. Viewing the scene at the end of World War II, John Gunther identified the powers in Arkansas as the Delta plantation owners, the Baptist Church, timber interests, and the Arkansas Power and Light Company, the latter absentee-owned.

Because the conservatives controlled Arkansas so completely, politics clear into the 1940s were characterized by a fluid factionalism in which virtually no serious issues were discussed, with all attention centered instead—in V.O. Key's words—on "the petty argument and personal loyalty of the moment." Just such a factional fight within the Democratic party led to the removal of J.W. Fulbright as president of the University of Arkansas. Fulbright then ran in 1944 for the U.S. Senate, beginning his long road to chairmanship of the Senate Foreign Relations Committee and international distinction.

Back in Arkansas, there were few thoughts of national prominence in the 1940s. The schools were among the nation's worst, and charges of election irregularity tantamount to direct fraud arose repeatedly. "Arkansas' first problem," Key determined after talking with many informed citizens of the state, was "the establishment of the essential mechanisms of democratic government."

The first politician who seemed willing to try was young war veteran Sid McMath, whose political career began as a district prosecutor in the gambling resort town of Hot Springs, where he broke up a corrupt, entrenched political machine. McMath's "GI movement" went on to win a number of other offices and to elect McMath governor in 1948. There was hope that he would be a thoroughgoing reformer. But McMath, tripped up by charges of highway department graft in his second term, was resoundingly defeated in 1952.

Orval Faubus and the Schools

More than a quarter-century after the worldwide infamy of the confrontation at Little Rock, it is easy to forget how powerful a tool the fight against school integration was for Southern politicians of that era. Most accounts show that Orval Faubus was not even a segregationist. Yet he found the issue so mightily compelling to voters of those years that he could and did build a political career on it.

Faubus came not out of the "hard seg" plantation lowlands of Arkansas but rather from a little place called Greasy Creek, near Huntsville in Madison County, up in the Ozark territory of northwestern Arkansas. He was the first of seven children of Sam Faubus, a hardscrabble farmer. The early Faubus record hardly suggested incipient greatness. There was a catch-as-catch-can education, a spell out on the road as a seasonal migrant worker, election back home as clerk of the circuit court, four years in World War II, return home, and down payment on the local newpaper. But, as Robert Sherrill would later write, "Faubus has the kind of stubbornness that serves impoverished, untutored hillbillies as the great evolutionary gene needed to pull them out of the mud and onto the sunlit shore of civilization."

Governor Sid McMath read some of Faubus' high-minded liberal editorials and invited the young man into his administration. Faubus rapidly made contacts and, when McMath was defeated, went back home until he ran for governor in 1954.

Faubus had not raised the race issue in that campaign, nor for 13 months after taking office. Then he seized on race as a way to perpetuate himself in power, to win more than the informal limit of two two-year terms to which governors had been held for a half century. Immense advantage accrued to Faubus through long incumbency (eventually 12 years). Real power in Arkansas then lay in the hands of some 187 boards and commissions: only continuous power of appointment over five or more years gave the executive actual control over these multitudinous agencies, which regulated everything from highway contracts to banks, trucking tariffs to the university system. Once controlled, the boards were rich sources of patronage jobs, special favors, and indirectly, the money needed for campaigns—and, as one hears it, for politicians' own pockets. Faubus earned only $10,000 a year as governor, but when he finally left office, he built a home valued at over $1 million. Never a man to be cornered, Faubus explained that his good fortune came from his Scotch blood, which enabled him, he said, to husband his resources and use them wisely. But Faubus' close political friend, W.R. ("Witt") Stephens, chairman of the board of the Arkansas-Louisiana Gas Company, admitted to us that "Faubus got his support from people like me and a lot of other people who would chip in and pay the expense." Business was well repaid. Faubus' personal power over the legislature was great, and massive bond issues and other bills that the legislators scarcely understood would be rushed through either the Senate or the House with the cry, "Governor's bill! Call the roll!"

Faubus is said to have called his staff together in August 1957 and announced he would run for a third term, selecting in advance the issue of Central High, which was then preparing—after two years of careful planning—to desegregate in accordance with the Supreme Court's *Brown* decision. Thus, before school opened, Faubus warned bloodshed and violence might result if "forcible integration" were carried out. He called out 270 Arkansas National Guardsmen and ordered them to bar entry of the nine black students scheduled for entry. It was the only way, said Faubus, "to restore or maintain order," and he spoke darkly, conjuring up a fictional specter of "caravans" of unruly whites on their way to Little Rock to cause trouble. On September 3, as former *Arkansas Gazette* editor Harry Ashmore described it, "Little Rock arose to gaze upon the incredible spectacle of an empty high school surrounded by National Guard troops called out by Governor Faubus to protect life and property against a mob that never materialized."

Many people had warned Faubus of the dangers of physically resisting orders of the federal courts—a step no governor had taken since the Civil War. Among them were Winthrop Rockefeller, then head of the state industrial development effort. Rockefeller insisted, though Faubus denied it, that Faubus told him, "I'm sorry, but I'm already committed. I'm going to run for a third term, and if I don't do this, Jim Johnson and Bruce Bennett [two segregationist politicians] will tear me to shreads."

As it had to be, President Eisenhower federalized the Arkansas Guard, ordered in paratroopers, and insisted on implementation of the federal court order. At Central High, a band of nine black children, brave inheritors of a legacy of incredible hardship, marched through crowds of furious, swearing, shouting white supremacists and curiosity-seekers.* The school was integrated. But Arkansas' name was darkened both at home and abroad.

The manufactured crisis at Little Rock was to be repeated at Ole Miss, the "schoolhouse door" at the University of Alabama, and a hundred other Southern places in word if not in deed. (Always, governors threatened to "go to jail" if need be; of course, none ever did.) Yet another consequence, of course, was that years after Little Rock, everyone knew that the federal government, pushed too far, would act.

Faubus' immediate objective—to establish himself as governor—was completely achieved by his demagoguery at Little Rock. Four times again, be-

---

*Of the nine black students 25 years later, the only one remaining in Little Rock was Elizabeth Eckford, the girl who had become separated from the group on the first day and faced the screaming mobs and National Guard troops alone; she was still fighting the memory under a doctor's care. The most prominent was Ernest Green, who was assistant labor secretary in the Carter administration. Another was in Canada, married to a zoologist and working in protest groups; one in Brussels, managing a telecommunications firm; another, north of San Francisco, directing the mental health department in a hospital.

tween 1958 and 1964, he would run for reelection, and each time he won by generally handsome margins. Finally, in 1966, Faubus decided to retire from the governorship. After moving into a sumptuous home, and then out of it, divorce and re-marriage to a woman 20 years his junior, living in a trailer while publishing weekly newspapers and acting as president of Dogpatch, U.S.A., an Ozarks, amusement park, Faubus ran for governor again in 1970, losing to clean cut "country lawyer" Dale Bumpers. Faubus resurfaced once again in the early 1980s as head of the veterans affairs department in the administration of Governor Frank White.

Winthrop Rockefeller and Beyond

The name Rockefeller stands for everything that Arkansas is not: Eastern, wealthy, cosmopolitan, liberal. Why did Rockefeller move there in the first place? In childhood, he showed insecurity and shyness and somehow became the black sheep of that celebrated generation of grandchildren of John D.: Abby, John, Nelson, Laurence, Winthrop, and David Rockefeller. Winthrop was the huskiest of his generation—six feet, three inches, and 200 pounds by his early twenties. While his industrious brothers and sister received educations in the aristocratic tradition, built families, and began the Rockefellers' massive philanthropic and political push of the postwar years, Winthrop dropped out of Yale, worked as a roustabout for Humble Oil in the Texas oilfields at 75 cents an hour, halfheartedly tried a few years of conventional business in New York, flourished as a junior Army officer, and became a postwar playboy whose first marriage, to "Bobo" Sears, a one-time model and bit actress, resulted in a $6 million divorce settlement—the largest ever awarded as of that date. Shaken seriously by the divorce proceedings, Rockefeller accepted the suggestion of a wartime friend from Little Rock to move to Arkansas. In 1953, he purchased a largely undeveloped site atop Petit Jean Mountain, 68 miles northwest of Little Rock, and made his big move.

Winrock Farms grew to include several subdivisions, operating a total of 50,000 acres, to raise Santa Gertrudis cattle and grow rice, soybeans, and grain. A minor army transformed the dusty top of Petit Jean Mountain—described by Rockefeller's farm manager, G. W. Adkisson, as "the sorriest land you ever saw"—into one of the fanciest farms ever inhabited by man. We visited Rockefeller there in 1969, viewing with amazement how he had built roads, silos, and barns, an airfield (used by his four private planes, including a jet), a system to pump water up 850 feet to the stone-and-glass mansion atop the mountain and the nearby swimming pool, permanent guest and servant houses, a greenhouse. six artificial lakes, even an antique car museum.

Rockfeller soon became an exemplary Arkansan, contributing heavily to the magnificent new art center in Little Rock and stumping the state to raise the $1 million to build it, giving $1.25 million to construct a new public school near Petit Jean Mountain, donating $250,000 for college scholarships for outstanding Arkansas students, financing or contributing to numerous civic projects, especially in black communities, and making possible a number of mental health clinics. But Rockefeller's most important contribution began in 1955 when newly inaugurated Governor Faubus decided to create an Arkansas Industrial Development Corporation and asked Rockefeller to head it. On an understanding of no political interference in the job, Rockefeller accepted. Under his guidance, AIDC became the country's classiest state development authority. It was the start of a veritable economic rebirth for Arkansas, which for decades had vied with Mississippi on various economic scales as the poorest place in all the U.S.A. Rockefeller brought two unique assets: his name and an ability to recruit top-notch personnel from all over the U.S., occasionally dipping into his own pocket to supplement salaries (a policy he would later continue as governor).

Not every AIDC effort was what its sponsors hoped for; many of the first plants were apparel factories that paid low wages, often recruiting only women workers. But gradually the effort gained sophistication. By the time Rockefeller resigned his AIDC chairmanship to run for governor in 1964, more than 600 new industrial plants and 90,000 new jobs had been located in Arkansas, many in rural areas that had previously subsisted on farming alone. Young Arkansans began to remain in the state, and the population, which had been declining precipitously in the early 1950s, began to stabilize. The industrial recruitment effort was retarded, however, by the very action Rockefeller tried so hard to prevent: Faubus' intervention in the Little Rock schools. "Not until 1963 or 1964 could we get new industries into Little Rock again," Rockefeller told us later.

By 1959, Rockefeller had seen enough of Faubus and the ways of Arkansas to decide that the state must have a two-party system. But in the Arkansas Republican party, he discovered a minuscule, patronage-geared organization that had never turned out a majority for a Republican presidential candidate and not once in the 20th century elected a governor, U.S. senator, or representative. Rockefeller applied the typical family solution: an input of money (eventually millions) plus leadership. By 1964, he was ready to take on Orval Faubus. So that year the towns and hamlets of rustic Arkansas witnessed a scene unique in American politics: the urbane quarter-billionaire, globe-trotting businessman, and patron of the arts touring the byways (accompanied by a hillbilly band or folk singers for the expected entertainment, of course) and appealing for the votes of men in oldtime overalls and women in cotton dresses—some of the plainest people in all America.

Faubus, the master politician, won the '64 election, but two years later, when Faubus finally stepped down of his own accord, the Democrats ended up nominating Jim Johnson, founder of the Arkansas White Citizens Councils. Johnson's intemperate segregationist image drove thousands of independents and moderate Democrats into Rockefeller's arms, and by this point the newly born GOP organization was showing some muscle. So it was that Arkansas elected its first Republican governor since 1873, with some 54 percent of the vote cast. Two years later, with another quite mediocre opponent, Rockefeller again ran strongest in the city areas and got a strong black vote, which that year provided his margin of victory.

Election as governor brought Rockefeller immense satisfaction. He turned in a highly creditable performance, pointing the way, in field after field, to the first broad reform of Arkansas government in the 20th century. A department of administration was set up to coordinate disparate executive departments. The legislature was persuaded to pass the first meaningful minimum wage law in Arkansas history, to raise teachers' salaries, and to enact the Arkansas Freedom of Information Law, which required public bodies to allow public access to meetings. By executive order, Rockefeller created a code of ethics for government executives. That ancient hypocrisy, the law forbidding liquor by the drink in public establishments, was finally repealed. Machinery was set in motion to effect a rewriting of the museum-piece 1874 constitution. Rockefeller ordered and got a complete shutdown of illegal gambling operations at Hot Springs. Unprecedented numbers of blacks were appointed to important government jobs, together with the first black state troopers and the first blacks ever on local draft boards. Some, but not all, of Rockefeller's prison reform legislation was passed, and new industry continued to pour into Arkansas—at an average rate, Rockefeller claimed, of a new 50-worker plant every 36 hours.

In his dealings with the Democratic legislature, however, Winthrop Rockefeller experienced the same difficulties his brother Nelson had in New York. The legislature balked at his tax reform and tax increases, his push for higher salaries for government officials and university faculty, and some of the people he wanted to name to state boards, including blacks. But Rockefeller was never willing to engage in the kind of cajoling and favor swapping that most governors must endure to get their programs approved. Privately, he was contemptuous of the legislators. Nor were his liaison problems limited to the legislature. He was often a strangely inaccessible figure, sometimes inexplicably absent from the seat of government, often ducking uncomfortable appointments, troubled by a drinking problem that became public knowledge.

Outside of economic development, Rockefeller affected Arkansas most importantly in race relations and penal reform. "The day Arkansas changed," Leroy Donald of the *Arkansas Gazette* observed, "was the day after Martin Luther King, Jr.'s, assassination when Rockefeller stood on the capitol steps singing, 'We Shall Overcome.' " WR's joining the mourning blacks that day (despite security warnings that rednecks or gambling interests might do him violence) and his consistent efforts to advance blacks in state government were not isolated events, nor primarily political in motivation. "You've got to remember the tradition of the Rockefeller family in race relations," Rockefeller told us, pointing out that the vast majority of blacks over 35 in Arkansas with a college degree had attended colleges assisted by Rockefeller family funds. "It's a tradition that has never wavered over four generations," he insisted. At a time when many Southern Republicans were playing not-very-subtle racist politics, the Rockefeller stance stood out as a great exception and promise of a new day in Southern politics.

When defeat came to WR in the 1970 governor's race, it was overwhelming. He received only 32.4 percent of the vote against Democrat Dale Bumpers. In defeat, Rockefeller was crushed. But just two weeks before his gubernatorial term expired, he made his final point by commuting the sentences of all 15 men on death row in Arkansas, urging his fellow governors to follow suit. No other American governor had ever taken such a step. In the two years after his retirement, Rockefeller mellowed, reduced his drinking, spent much time working among the trees and plants at Winrock, and grew a Hemingwayesque beard, which made him the most liberated celebrity at the 1972 Republican national convention.

When Winthrop Rockefeller died, the *Arkansas Gazette* received calls from scores of people, asking in their thick Arkansas drawls, "Are we going to get to keep him here in Arkansas?" The answer was yes: Rockefeller's ashes were to be interred in a sanctuary near Winrock Farm. For so many years, Rockefeller had been trying to prove to his fellow Arkansans that he was really one of them. And now their concern, that he not be carried away for burial in some distant place like New York, was to be the final, conclusive proof that WR was an outlander no more. Nor did the Rockefeller presence and influence end with Winthrop's death. In his will, he created a massive trust—expected to have capitalization of several hundred million dollars when the estate was finally settled—which he hoped would be used chiefly for Arkansas charities. But he did not restrict the trustees, asking rather in his will that they "be innovative and venturesome" and "not feel that they need be conservative in the use of principal." Rockfeller's son and family continued to live at Winrock Farm, which also functioned as an agricultural research station.

In his farewell address as governor, Winthrop Rockefeller said that Arkansas, when he came, was "like a beautiful antebellum home, the doors and windows bolted, as though to deny the coming of Change; the curtains drawn in fear, somehow of discovering what Change might bring with it. . . . But now the fresh winds of new and exciting change are blowing. . . . I am proud and happy to have been a part in helping to open the doors and windows, bolted too long, to allow those fresh winds to penetrate our homes, and yes, even our minds." For once the vaunted Rockefeller hyperbole seemed quite well justified. We believe it justifiable to say WR had exerted a greater—and more beneficial—influence on a single state than any figure of his generation.

Succeeding Rockefeller, Bumpers continued Arkansas on a moderate course, acknowledging to us once that a figure of his moderation probably couldn't have won election without the Rockefeller interregnum. In 1971, the legislature approved Bumpers' plan for reorganizing the state government, based on a study financed by the Rockefeller Brothers Fund. A cabinet-style government was created, with some 60 boards, commissions, and agencies put under 13 "superdepartments"—most of them directly responsible to the governor. Bumpers was able to make the tax system substantially more progressive, and he expanded health care for poor and rural areas. In 1974, he moved to the Senate (after defeating J. William Fulbright in a primary) and was succeeded in the governor's chair by David Pryor, a progressive congressman.

Pryor, in turn, won conservative Sen. John McClellan's seat after the latter died, and Arkansas elected as governor in 1978 Bill Clinton, a 32-year-old lawyer, graduate of Georgetown University and Yale Law School and an Oxford University Rhodes Scholar. Arkansas seemed to view Clinton as a kind of "local boy made good" who embodied intellectual and educational accomplishment. Clinton rode into office with a long agenda emphasizing energy conservation and quickly won national attention as a bright and able young operator who might have presidential potential. But though he courted a populist image, Clinton seemed to have forgotten some of the folksiness that Arkansans expect of their politicians. He hired a staff that included out-of-state intellectuals who were sometime arrogant, raised auto license fees, and then suffered the Arkansans' anger over the placement of thousands of Cuban refugees at Fort Chaffee after the 1980 boatlift. In 1980, he was narrowly defeated by Republican businessman Frank White, whose victory seemed to signal renewal of Arkansas' deeply imbedded social conservatism.

In 1981, the legislature passed a bill, which White signed, requiring that if evolution were taught in the public schools, it must be accompanied by the teaching of creationism, which religious fundamentalists termed "creation science." But the American Civil Liberties Union challenged the case, and after a trial that reminded many of the Scopes trial in 1925, Federal Judge William Overton ruled it unconstitutional, saying that the law was "a religious crusade" and could not be conducted through the public schools.

The flurry over creationism shocked out-of-state sophisticates, but the 1982 gubernatorial campaign demonstrated anew the strength of traditional religious and moral thinking in Arkansas politics. Clinton, seeking to regain the governorship, blamed White for a heavy increase in utility rates, a populist pitch that appealed to the voters. But Clinton still found it necessary to promise *not* to oppose teaching of "creationism" in the schools, *not* to commute so many death sentences in his new term, and *not* to oppose gun control. His wife, a lawyer, also began calling herself "Mrs. Bill Clinton." He won with 55 percent of the vote.

No one could deny that Arkansas advanced light years in the post-Faubus era, with economic vitality, gradual healing of old racial wounds, and a new openness to ideas. Still, in 1980 less than 40 percent of its population had graduated from high school. Per capita expenditures for social services and schools were still some of the lowest. And despite the pride in new factories moving in, Arkansas remained one of the poorest states, its per capita income 48th in the country, trailing only Mississippi and South Carolina.

Arkansans in Washington

Arkansas' congressional delegation in the early 1980s blended conservatism and liberalism in a manner appropriate for a state embodying the transition from South to West. Senator Dale Bumpers had proven his independence from other Southern Democrats by battling the traditional committee structure, supporting gas rationing, tangling with oil companies, opposing nuclear projects such as the Clinch River breeder reactor, and supporting the SALT II arms limitation treaty. The junior senator, David Pryor, also a Democrat, had previously made a mark in Washington as a congressman who supported civil rights legislation and pursued his critical inquiry into nursing homes even when denied committee investigation funds. In the Senate, Pryor continually raised questions about "reckless spending" in federal procurement.

Both parties looked to the Arkansas House delegation for leadership. Bill Alexander, a Democrat from eastern Arkansas, was elected chief deputy whip, the fifth-ranking position in the Democratic leadership. Ed Bethune, representing Little Rock, was elected chairman of his 1978 incoming congressional class and proved that a Rockefeller protégé and moderate Republican could be outspokenly partisan when the need arose.

But for an expression of raw Arkansas power in Washington, one must harken back to the early 1970s when J.W. Fulbright headed the Senate Foreign Relations Committee; John McClellan, the Senate Appropriations Committee; and Wilbur Mills, the House Ways and Means Committee.

A perennial question about Arkansas politics was why America's most provincial state could tolerate such an urbane and even intellectually arrogant man as Fulbright in the U.S. Senate. Part of the answer may simply be pork barrel—Fulbright shared with others on the delegation credit for such plums as the $1.2 billion Arkansas River navigation project, a big Strategic Air Command base, missile installations, and half a dozen federal hydroelectric projects. A second explanation was that no matter how daring his oratory on subjects such as the Vietnam War, Fulbright voted against virtually every civil rights measure before Congress during his tenure and for maintaining the tax privileges of the oil and gas industry. One influential leader of the Arkansas gas industry related that he had told Fulbright before the 1968 campaign, "Senator, I'm gunna help you financially and be for you. Because the people of Arkansas have very few luxuries. And you're a luxury to us. We're just gunna keep you." But over the years the Arkansans' affection for Fulbright obviously waned; finally, Bumpers defeated him nearly 2 to 1 in the 1974 primary. Fulbright remained in Washington as an international lawyer.

John McClellan wielded immense power as head of the Senate Appropriations Committee from 1972 to his death in 1977. He also garnered endless headlines by heading investigations that looked into abuses by labor bosses (including the Teamsters' Jimmy Hoffa), military contractors, and alleged instigators of the big city riots of the 1960s. McClellan said that he "never resented" being called a conservative, because he "did not become a Senator to transfer the United States into a socialistic, paternalistic state." He was a major opponent of expanded federal budgets, except when projects for his state (like the Arkansas River navigation channel) were proposed.

Among the most powerful of all Americans in the late 1960s and early '70s was Congressman Wilbur Daigh Mills, from Kensett, a little town of 1,444 people set down where the Ozark foothills meet the Delta. The reasons for Mills' power were twofold. First, the House of Representatives originates, under the Constitution, all tax legislation; the committee from which it must come is the Ways and Means Committee, which Mills chaired. Second, Mills was a masterful legislative craftsman, with a grasp of the tax code unmatched by any other member of Congress (he could cite section after section almost by heart). Mills was also Capitol Hill's chief expert on trade legislation, on welfare, and on Social Security, all subjects falling under the purview of his committee. But Wilbur Mills' image of total devotion to his work came to an abrupt halt one night in August of 1974 when a strip teaser from Argentina known as Fanne Fox leaped from Mills' car to take a swim in Washington's Tidal Basin as U.S. Park Police looked on. Mills won reelection with a slogan "Never Drink Champagne with a Foreigner." But after Mills appeared on a strip show stage with the "Tidal Basin Bombshell," he was stripped of his chairmanship as well as other perquisites by the Democratic leadership. Mills entered Bethesda Naval Hospital for treatment of his avowed drinking problem and quietly finished his term. Like Fulbright, Mills did not go home to Arkansas, preferring to remain in the nation's capital campaigning against alcoholism and working as a lawyer.

LOUISIANA

An Evocation

THE VERY THOUGHT of Louisiana is evocative. Like a boat on a misty bayou, moving past cypress hung with Spanish moss, there is an air of mystery in so much of the state. Some of it is in the soul of the river; one stands on a levee and watches the Missouri and the Ohio and the Arkansas and all the rest that make up the mighty Mississippi, the very guts of a continent, the course over thousands of miles now finished. And with the flow of ships and people through New Orleans and its port, it is as if one is looking at a great funnel of the shifting earth, only faintly grasping its complexity.

In the people there is mystery too. Rural Cajuns live in a world apart, in "parishes"* with names like Evangeline and Acadia, still speaking French, trapping muskrat, and fishing for crawfish as they have since leaving Canada two centuries ago.

No one should take the Cajuns lightly, for they seem to absorb everybody long in contact with them—a "dominant gene" among ethnic groups, one might say. Then there are the Creoles, that delicate blend of Latin bloodstreams, a bit harder to identify, though they continue to represent a special kind of aristocracy in New Orleans and other towns of substance. In defining Creoles—white and tan-skinned alike—one proceeds with care. It seems certain that there was an early French-Spanish aristocracy of Louisiana that adopted this name. In their proud way, the Creoles resisted the cultural intrusions of the *Americains* who flooded into New Orleans after the Louisiana purchase. Historian Joseph G. Tregle, Jr., has recorded that "in the 1820s and 1830s 'Creole' was generally used in Louisiana to designate any person native to the state, be he white, black, or colored, French, Spanish or Anglo-American." Moreover, a mixture of races most certainly occurred; there were the famous Quadroon Balls of the late 18th and early 19th centuries that led to all manner of alliances, including arrangements by mulatto mistresses for their daughters to make *liaisons sans marriage* with young white men. The children were well educated and universally regarded as free men and women, not slaves—a race of *les gens de couleur libres* that would have been anathema anywhere else in Dixie. The distinctions are important even now. In 1978, Ernest "Dutch" Morial made national news by winning election as the first black mayor of Louisiana, but the Louisiana papers carefully noted

*The parishes are the equivalent of counties in other states; the term was originally used for the ecclesiastical units into which the Spanish governor divided Louisiana in the late 17th century.

that the light skinned man was a Creole. However relaxed personal relationships may have been, Louisiana legally continued to regard even a touch of black ancestry as something that should be noted. A 1970 state law required anyone whose ancestry is at least one-thirty-second black to be designated black on a birth certificate; the law was challenged in 1982 by a Lake Charles woman, Susie Guillory Phipps, who was raised white and shocked to learn in the 1970s that she had been classified black.

In New Orleans, one discovers a soft blend of social structures long ingrained, of Mardi Gras, provincialism, worldliness, colorful folkways, Dixieland, and the French Quarter; taken together, as Huey Long once said of himself, they must be considered *sui generis*. And what gentle spirit brings the finest cuisine of the American continent to New Orleans, with its superb blend of French recipes, Spanish seasoning, and American Indian herbs? In these softer graces of human life, Louisiana excels.

Yet there is another side to Louisiana. There is nothing soft about the oil and gas fields, the refineries, and petrochemical plants that line the banks of the Mississippi from Baton Rouge to New Orleans and have caused once-inviolate marshlands to be slashed to pieces. There is nothing sophisticated about the poverty that has beset Louisiana's poor whites and blacks, nor has there been anything genteel about some of its rancorous, corruption-ridden politics. There was never much sophistication about the Plaquemines Parish of the late Leander Perez and sons, run as a feudal island until the early 1980s with the black man so long subjugated.

Even if imperiled by "progress," many of the wondrous landscapes of Louisiana live on. All of Louisiana, in fact, lies within the Gulf Coastal Plain. Except for the northwestern part of the state, with its pine and hardwood forests, Louisiana is lowlands, water, and the River. A great part of southern Louisiana is a jungle of swamps and those devious waterways that pierce them, the bayous. And entirely within Louisiana lie the Mississippi's expansive delta and its great spreading mouth.

No other state is so flat; only Florida, perhaps, is so humid, and moist, and hurricane-prone. The hurricanes that hit Louisiana, some studies show, are now occurring more frequently than in past centuries. Yet, in contrast to that violence, one must speak of the life-giving qualities of the swamps and marshlands, which include half a million acres of wildlife preserves, homes for myriad varieties of birds, from the heron to the marsh wren, the laughing gull to the sandpiper, and North America's greatest wintering area for ducks and wild geese.

Each year, the silty load of the Mississippi creates some thousand new acres at the river's mouth. It provides the immense challenge of controlling the river's flow to prevent the fearsome floods the river generates along its course and the companion waterways of the valley. Now, in our time, a complex of levees and pumping stations extends over all of southern Louisiana. Large areas (including the city of New Orleans) are actually under sea level, as the Father of Waters rolls along behind its levees.

Cultures and History

The historic roots of Louisiana go back not to the westward push of Anglo-Saxons across the continent in the 1800s but rather to the 16th- and 17th-century struggles of Spain and France for New World ascendancy. The story began in the early 1500s, when Spanish explorers discovered the Mississippi River; it ended with the Louisiana Purchase of 1803, when President Jefferson obtained for $15 million a vast stretch of interior America, including one-third of the present continental United States, from Napoleon Bonaparte.

The southernmost portion of the purchase was declared the Territory of Orleans in 1804; eight years later, Congress added more land in the Southeast (known as the Florida Parishes), and the whole became the state of Louisiana on April 30, 1812. Less than three years later, in the waning days of the War of 1812, the English invaded Louisiana, and General Andrew Jackson led an army of volunteers from Kentucky, Tennessee, and Mississippi, plus a ragtag assortment of Louisianans including Creoles, Choctaw Indians, and free blacks, in defeating the invaders at the Battle of New Orleans.

This new American state was like none other, one with close to a full century of settled life as a Spanish and French colony behind it. New Orleans had been founded in 1718, when Houston was just a speck on Buffalo Bayou. Louisiana came into the Union trailing the French judicial system, the Code Napoleon, which underlies Louisiana law to this day. For many years, debate in the legislature could be in either French or English. State laws were published in both languages down to 1898.

Louisiana grew and thrived up to the Civil War. The first steamboat went into operation in 1812, and New Orleans became a great port city; the produce of the vast reaches of the Mississippi Valley was brought down river and deposited on its levees, then shipped on to the East and Europe. By 1840, she was America's fourth-largest city. This was also the golden age of Louisiana's sugar plantations, which expanded rapidly along the rivers and bayous, drawing their wealth from the rich river-bottom soil and slave labor. The planters dominated all aspects of Louisiana life, economic, political, and cultural.

But the seeds of another Louisiana were being planted in the uplands. The Red River was freed of the driftwood that had obstructed it for centuries, and hardy settlers poured in from the Carolinas, Georgia, Alabama, and Tennessee. Small farmers and Jacksonian Democrats, they quickly lined up against the planter interests. So it was that "redneck" Louisiana was born.

The planter interests propelled Louisiana into the Confederacy, but a Union fleet in 1862 captured New Orleans, so that until the end of the war Louisiana had two governments, one federally controlled at New Orleans, the other Confederate at Shreveport. Few states suffered as long and tumultuous a period of Reconstruction. The economy lay in ruins, carpetbaggers poured in, radical Republicans plundered the state and disenfranchised Confederate veterans. The whites, in turn, formed vigilante groups, including a White League that terrorized blacks. In one bloody riot at Colfax, 3 whites and 120 blacks were killed.

The 1877 withdrawal of federal troops brought bleak years for blacks, indeed for any political cause save that of the conservative Bourbon white Democrats. In 1898, the Bourbons instituted stiff property and educational requirements for voting but waived them for anyone who had voted before 1867, or his descendants, thus neatly disenfranchising most blacks. In the immediately preceding election, there had been 164,088 white and 130,344 black registrants; by the next presidential election, only 5,320 blacks were registered. Whites likewise lost interest in elections; the turnout declined from 63 percent of men of voting age in 1896 to 21 percent in 1900 and 14 percent in 1920.

The oligarchy that ruled Louisiana all those years was one of the most powerful and heartless in the annals of the Republic. Virtually nothing was done to cope with overwhelming problems of illiteracy and crushing poverty that left most Louisianans with inadequate food, shelter, and clothing well past the year 1900. It was 1898 when the state made its first serious efforts to guarantee free public education and 1916 before a compulsory education law was passed. The 1940 Census would show that 15 percent of the white men of Louisiana over 25 had not completed a *single year's* schooling.

Admittedly, the state's rulers faced gruesome problems. Each year the boiling springtime crests of the Mississippi threatened to inundate great portions of lowland Louisiana. Each year hundreds of Louisianans died from yellow fever, a disease not arrested until 1905 (when mosquitoes were identified as the carrying agents). Louisiana's oligarchy was all-embracing: from the New Orleans political machine and the New Orleans mercantile, financial, and shipping interests to the cotton planters of the Red River and the Mississippi, the lumber industry, railroads, utilities, and finally oil interests.

Unlike other Southern states, Louisiana never had Populist leaders who could loosen the rule of the power-brokers, even slightly. The oligarchy proved phenomenally skillful in playing off the Protestant North against the Catholic South. Louisiana became a classic case of arrested political development.

Longian Politics

When change came, it was volcanic. Its agent was Huey Pierce Long, born in 1893 in a small north central Louisiana town, the eighth of nine children of a hardscrabble farmer. Ethnically, Long's roots ranged from French to Scotch. Ethically, he did much that was questionable. Personally, he was rude and vulgar. He bullied friend and foe alike and ended up with virtually dictatorial powers—more power than any governor in U.S. history. The strength of Long's appeal to poor people reached its heights during the Great Depression, when he achieved a national following and considered running against President Roosevelt, whom he considered too closely aligned with established interests. All that came to an end with his assassination in the state capitol by the son-in-law of a political enemy. But up to that fateful moment in 1935, it was literally true in Louisiana: "L'Etat, c'est Huey."

Politically, Long was from start to finish what he presented himself to be: the champion of the little people against the entrenched interests. "Where," he asked impoverished Louisianans as he ran for governor in 1927, "are the schools that you have waited for your children to have, that have never come? Where are the roads and the highways that you sent your money to build, but are no nearer now than ever before? Where are the institutions to care for the sick and the disabled?"

What set Long apart from other Southern Populist demagogues was that he kept faith with the people. He did not, as one account puts it, "follow the customary practice of wearing a wool hat when he harangued the mob and a panama planter when he made his political deals with the Bourbons." Instead, he delivered on his promises to the people, letting his antagonists— the oil companies and other vested interests—pay the bill through greater taxation. Free schoolbooks were offered all children. A great program of highways and free bridges was undertaken. New hospitals rose. A rebuilt Louisiana became a kind of temple to Huey Long.

In the process, Long destroyed the integrity of government in Louisiana. He would brook no opposition. Mayors, judges, or parish officials who fought him were ripped from office or suffered profound economic coercion. Complete fealty was demanded of state legislators. Long's Robin Hood morality put untold millions of dollars in state money into the hands of his political heirs and followers. Eventually a number of his camp followers went to prison, and Louisiana politics took on a semblance of bifactionalism (always within the Democratic party, of course). On one side were the Longs, offering venal but people-oriented programs, on the other anti-Longs, providing relatively honest, unimaginative government in the mold of the gentlemanly do-nothing governors who preceded Huey. A prominent "anti-Long," Jimmie ("You Are My Sunshine") Davis, elected governor in 1944 and again in 1960, fitted the mold well enough by doing little when he was in office except to defend segregation to the last gasp and make movies and record albums.

Huey's most colorful successor was none other than his own brother, Earl K. Long, a man who in 1928 almost bit off the ear of a political enemy as they fought in a cramped elevator. Earl exhibited streaks of apparent insanity in his last years of life, apparently due to a series of small strokes. He did permit pervasive corruption in his administration as governor, but the late journalist Margaret Dixon, one of his close friends and supporters, was probably right when she told us, "Earl was more sinned against than sinning. He simply lacked any inhibitions." He had, in office, fought for welfare programs, equalized teachers' salaries and upgraded them tremendously, and put the tax screws on "the Standard Oil crowd."

Neither Huey nor Earl Long ever descended to "nigger-baiting"—then so popular—in their campaigns. Huey's strategem was apparently to pose as a segregationist, make a few disparaging comments about blacks, and then institute broad programs of social reform, which did more to uplift Louisiana blacks, in their day-to-day life, than anything done for them since the Civil War. Biographer T. Harry Williams quotes Huey as saying, "A lot of guys would have been murdered politically for what I've been able to do quietly for the niggers." Long did not regard words like "nigra" and "nigger" offensive, Williams said, and "he was completely without prejudice in his personal relations." Earl Long got along well with blacks, too; they represented his margin of victory in his 1956 campaign for governor. The last Longite to hold the governorship was John J. McKeithen, a former Long legislative leader who took office in the 1960s. (Of McKeithen, a man given to effusive, arm-waving flights of oratory, an astute observer told us, "He learned to lie from Earl Long, but Earl didn't teach him how to govern.")

One of the best descriptions of this political culture came from A.J. Liebling, who called Louisiana "the westernmost of the Arab states" and observed that its politics "is of an intensity and complexity that are matched, in my experience, only in the Republic of Lebanon. Louisiana is part of the Hellenistic—Mediterranean littoral—sensual, seductive, speculative, devious." Race, religion, corruption, and the flamboyance of the candidates all have more to do with elections than basic issues of public policy. Afficionados of the ethnic-regional oddities of Louisiana politics always look to see if an election has produced a definite cleavage between the fundamentalist north, which thinks and votes like most of the Deep South upcountry and piney-woods areas, and the more Catholic and languid Cajun- and Creole-dominated parishes of southern Louisiana, which bear such colorful names as Lafourche, Terrebonne, Calcasieu, and Plaquemines.

The geographic division actually has to be refined farther. One division, used by the Public Affairs Research Council of Louisiana, splits the state four ways: north Louisiana (the entire upper half of the state), Acadiana (the bayou-dotted French Catholic parishes covering all of southwestern and south central Louisiana), the Florida parishes (so called because they were once part of West Florida and were settled by Americans, not French), and finally the New Orleans area (which includes not only that ethnically variegated and worldly city but its vividly conservative outlying areas, including suburban Jefferson, St. Bernard, and Plaquemines Parish).

All these ethnic and geographical differentiations have been much more important to Louisiana voters than party affiliation, which has been overwhelmingly Democratic for generations. Over the years, for instance, there were many battles to see which presidential candidate would get the prized Democratic party symbol—the Rooster—over his slate of electors. As Leander Perez explained in 1968, generations of French-speaking South Louisianans had been taught *tapez le coq* (stamp the rooster)—without even looking to see whose name appeared below! In 1948, the Dixiecrats staged a coup in the Democratic state committee, getting the Rooster put above the electors for Strom Thurmond rather than Harry Truman. Thurmond proceeded to carry the state with ease.

The Republicans' record in Louisiana congressional elections had been the worst of *any party* in *any state* in the 20th century until in 1972 a new congressional district composed primarily of New Orleans' archconservative suburb, Jefferson Parish, sent Republican David Treen to Congress. Treen was the first Louisiana Republican congressman since 1888. In 1979, he became the first Republican governor of Louisiana since 1877. Two other Louisiana districts went Republican in the 1970s, but Treen's district reverted to Democratic hands, and the other five congressional districts remained Democratic. One is well advised to keep the Republican advances in perspective. In 1980, Louisiana Republicans registered only 7 percent of the voters, while 87 percent remained Democrats. The sentimental partisanship was reflected in the 1983–84 state legislature, where all 39 members of the state senate and 95 of 105 house members were Democrats. And even after Treen was elected governor, it was generally agreed that the most important political figure in state politics remained Edwin Edwards, the former Democratic governor. (Edwards himself, however, had made something of a breakthrough in Louisiana's ethnogeographic politics; elected in 1972, he became the first governor in 28 years who did not hail from northern Louisiana, and the first Roman Catholic governor of the 20th century.)

Treen, however, did make a name for himself by championing Louisiana's environmental protection and its economic diversification. To the shock of the oil community, he introduced a coastal wetlands environmental levy (a tax on petroleum products transported through coastal wetlands) to raise more funds for highways, bridges, and schools. The legislature rejected it. Treen also stepped up enforcement of environmental laws as Louisiana faced increasing environmental perils ranging from problems in New Orleans' drinking water to the dumping of hazardous chemicals.

Race seemed to be responsible for both the Republican party's rise and its problems. Louisiana blacks were totally isolated from decision making until the white primary was outlawed by the Supreme Court in 1944. After the Louisiana Democratic party in 1951 dropped its "whites only" rule for primaries, black registration rose quickly, especially in New Orleans and the French Catholic parishes—not because the French Catholics were avid integrationists, but because the Catholic Church stood squarely for blacks' equality in society. In some areas of northern Louisiana, by contrast, it took federal voting registrars in the '60s to get blacks registered.

In 1964, as Southern resentment boiled to a head over national Democrats' friendliness to civil rights legislation, Barry Goldwater took Louisiana with 57 percent of the vote. In 1968, George Wallace swept the state; in 1972, Richard Nixon carried every region. Race mixed with inherent conservatism seemed dominant in every vote. Louisianans did vote for fellow Southerner and Democrat Jimmy Carter in 1976 but returned to the Republican column with the Reagan election of 1980.

The Louisiana Democratic establishment has done everything conceivable, however, to deter state and local Republican inroads. A unique 1975 Louisiana law provides, for instance, that all candidates of both parties run against each other in the primary; if one candidate gets 50 percent of the vote, he or she automatically wins the general election. Thus Republicans rarely get a "second shot" at a Democratic nominee. Another Republican albatross: the party has done nothing to attract blacks in a state in which they account for 29 percent of the population.

Blacks have registered overwhelmingly as Democrats and made some gains in state legislative seats and local offices. Happily fading are memories of the "hard-seg" days of the 1950s, when the legislature, spurred on by the (white) Citizens Council movement, tried to purge blacks from voter registration rolls. But it was not until 1972 that the legislature repealed the old Jim Crow laws—already declared unconstitutional by the courts—which banned inter-racial marriage, dancing, or even socializing, and required segregated seating on buses and trains, separate rest rooms for blacks and whites, separate water fountains and waiting rooms. Immense credit in strangling Jim Crow went to the New Orleans–based U.S. Fifth Circuit Court of Appeals, which as Pat Watters wrote, "may have been the most important court in the country except the Supreme Court itself" during the crucial civil rights battles.

Political Theater and Governance

Politics have long been Louisiana's principal major form of entertainment. North-South, Protestant-Catholic, Cajun-black-white—the divisions all con-tribute to imaginative loops of political posturing. And then there is oil money. As Liebling once quoted a Louisianan, "the state slithers around in it." It seems that newly rich oilmen find political investments either a grand form of sport or a way to achieve personal status; in any event, they seem a major reason Louisiana races so often attract so many candidates, all of them well financed. The popular entertainment politicians offer does not end on election day. When it was reported that Governor Edwards had been gam-bling and carousing in Las Vegas in 1974, he called a news conference to say it was all true, to expose his losses, and to vow to visit Las Vegas again the first chance he got. The relaxed southern Louisianans were unfazed, and even the newspapers of the northern Baptist Belt commended Edwards for not being a hypocrite. (Edwards, one of the slipperiest politicians we ever encoun-tered, is the man who also entertained his constituents by straightfacedly insisting he hadn't known for two or three years afterward that his wife, Elaine, accepted a $10,000 gift from Korean influence peddler/businessman Tongsun Park.)

One problem in all this is that Louisiana governors take more joy in politics than in the nitty-gritty of governing. All Louisiana governors seem to make the fatal error of surrounding themselves with back-room politicians rather than expert staff. To this day, governors dominate the state's news pages in the style of a British monarch—even though, in a 1974 constitutional revision, the governor's inordinate power to control the legislature, even appointing legislators to executive branch positions, was curtailed.

The aroma of wrongdoing that surrounds Louisiana government seems never to dispel. Why so much corruption? One answer may lie in the unique fusion of Gallic and Anglo-Saxon cultures, another in a prevalent assumption (ever since Bourbon rule) that "someone is making money off the state, and it might as well be me." As recently as 1982, a federal grand jury indicted the Louisiana Senate president, his law partner, and three others on charges of participating in a $6 million bank fraud scheme. The more ordinary form of corruption has been shakedown of state contractors, a milieu in which someone's palm needs to be greased to do anything. And then there is Louisiana's thriving Mafia, no newcomer to the scene. By some accounts, the New Orleans "family" was organized by Sicilian immigrants in 1876 and thus has the distinction of being the first in America.

Unsavory influence peddling, if not outright corruption, continues to thrive in local government. Exhibit A-1 must be the archaic, bizarre property tax assessment practices in the state's 64 parishes. Under law, the parish assessors are supposed to assess all property at its fair market value, reporting the total assessment to the state tax commission, which is supposed to police the assessors. But since they are elected, the assessors curry political favor with voters by setting low assessments on their property; people they do not like are given high assessments. Not surprisingly, the assessor is often the most powerful of parish politicians. The state government has been trying to bring this into check, but abuses still occur.

Whatever the ethical problems in state and parish, Louisiana—thanks largely to the legacy of the Longs—does not have a parsimonious, indifferent government. Judging effort against taxable wealth, Louisiana makes a greater effort than the average state to finance health, hospitals, welfare, and education. Welfare payments (in dramatic contrast to the parsimony of neighboring Texas or Mississippi) are higher than the state's economic position would seem to justify. Louisiana unemployment compensation and workmen's compensation benefits are so high, they may in fact deter economic development. Louisiana has long been the South's strongest union state. Victor Bussie, the remarkable state AFL-CIO chief, started his career in the mid-1950s by getting the legislature to repeal a right-to-work statute then on the books. In 1976, a new business lobbying coalition, the Louisiana Association of Business and Industry, successfully reinstated right-to-work, to Bussie's deep disappointment. Yet Bussie had every right to be proud of his record on other issues. He ran the Louisiana AFL-CIO in a democratic mode distinctly lacking in many state labor councils. And his stands on race issues were so advanced he sometimes lost members. The AFL-CIO fought the closing of the schools in the big integration fight of the early 1960s, and Bussie once told us the tale of terror of the bombing of his house by the Ku Klux Klan.

Compared to most Southern states, Louisiana's state tax structure depends only lightly on the sales tax and is thus less onerous for lower-income people. Since the times of Huey Long, oil companies—and indirectly their customers nationwide—have been forced to contribute heavily to the financing of state government. By the early 1980s, according to an analysis by the Public Affairs Research Council of Louisiana (PAR), about 40 percent of Louisiana's revenues came directly from oil and gas. Federal deregulation of oil prices in 1979 plus general increases in price and production had led to spectacular increases in state revenues. Awash in oil revenues, the state set up a trust fund to hold some of the revenue as a permanent state resource, reduced the personal income tax, repealed the state's occupational license tax, and created new tax exemptions. State expenditures increased 44 percent between 1979 and 1981, as state and school employee salaries were raised and programs expanded. Some mean curves appeared on Easy Street, however, as in 1981 both the production and the price of oil fell, and the Supreme Court ruled that Louisiana could not charge taxes on gas that merely crossed the state. PAR predicted that state government financing would be a thorny problem throughout the 1980s. For one thing, said PAR, Louisiana would have to learn how to tighten the belt of its civil service. Louisiana ranks 10th among the states in number of state employees compared to number of residents, has no centralized personnel policies, offers generous annual and sick leave and comp-time policies, and has a pension liability approaching $3 billion for future generations of taxpayers to pay.

The creation of the Public Affairs Research Council, author of this pessimistic analysis, stemmed from the bitter fight between the Longs and Standard Oil of New Jersey. Cecil Morgan, a distinguished New Orleans lawyer who for years was counsel for Standard Oil and later became president of the National Municipal League, reasoned that the only way business could bring an objective approach to Louisiana's problems was to form a nonpartisan, nonpolitical research organization. Standard Oil took a back seat and enlisted chieftans of all kinds of organizations—farm, labor, big business, small business, and political factions—to form the organization in 1951. Even the AFL-CIO lent support. In time, whatever big business taint PAR had faded as, in its policy positions, it bucked the special interests of some of its own corporate members. Into the 1980s, PAR had issued frequent reports on Louisiana issues, from local finance to reapportionment to school transportation, providing in what had been one of the most governmentally backward of states an objective information and analysis service from which any in the union would benefit.

Louisiana in Washington

For unadulterated power on the Potomac, few Louisianans have ever equaled Russell Billiu Long, son of Huey, senator starting in 1948, and chairman of the Senate Finance Committee from 1965 to 1980. Even under Republican Senate control, Long remained senior Democrat on that committee and perhaps the most knowledgeable senator on American taxes, welfare, Social Security and Medicare, revenue sharing, foreign trade, and the national debt ceiling. Long has occasionally displayed Populist-liberal strands, reminiscent of his father. But mostly, Long's special-interest side dominated, opposing structural reform of the income tax, fighting for oil and gas interests—a seeming gross conflict of interest when, in Long's own words, "most of my income is from oil and gas." During the Nixon administration, Long was instrumental in defeating the Family Assistance Plan, which would have as much as *tripled* the income of many poor rural Southerners. The Louisiana sugar industry and shipbuilders, by contrast, have basked in his favor. Overshadowed by Long but no slouch is Louisiana's junior senator, Bennett Johnston, Jr., a power on the Senate Energy Committee. On occasion, Johnston has even been willing to break with established oil industry stands.

On the House side, Russell's cousin, Gillis, has served with unusual distinction, sitting on both the powerful House Rules Committee and the Joint Economic Committee (where he specialized in international economics). The dean of the Louisiana delegation in the early 1980s was also one of the youngest members, Cajun Country Democrat John Breaux, first elected in 1972 at age 28. In 1981, after Breaux agreed to accept President Reagan's spending cuts in exchange for costly price supports on sugar, a reporter asked if his vote could be purchased. No, Breaux replied, "it can be rented." Democrat Jerry Huckaby, from the rural north, played a major role in decreasing Alaskan wilderness land from 80 million to 50 million acres and opening it up for (what else?) oil and gas exploration and drilling.

By far the most universally liked and perhaps the most liberal of the Louisiana delegation of the early '80s was Lindy Boggs, of New Orleans. Mrs. Boggs was elected to the House after her husband Hale, then House Majority Leader, was killed when the small plane in which he was riding disappeared in Alaska in 1972. Mrs. Boggs had long been her husband's close adviser on matters political as well as personal, and she came to the House with the status of a freshman but the friendships and respect of a senior member. She has served on the House Appropriations Committee and was chairman of the 1976 Democratic National Convention. One New Orleans friend of the family described "Lindy," as she is called, as "a woman of unimpeachable personal integrity, of true gentility and nobleness of spirit." The loss of her husband was a real tragedy for Louisiana and the nation. A likely future Speaker, he had shown remarkable capacity for growth, taking progressive stands (including, eventually, civil rights legislation) of immense risk for a Louisiana congressman.

Other Louisiana powers in Washington have included F. Edward Hebert, chairman of House Armed Services until 1974, a superhawk, and often patsy of the military, and Otto E. Passman, whose Appropriations subcommittee chairmanship let him wield extraordinary power over U.S. foreign aid programs until 1976, when he was indicted for extorting ship contracts from foreign governments. Passman was acquitted by a home-town jury, but was retired by the voters. Congress has had a grayer image without Passman, who used to appear on the House floor, resplendent in a white suit, looking for all the world like central casting's conception of an affluent delta planter.

The Senate lost one of its patriarchs with the 1972 death of Allen J. Ellender, in earlier years floor leader for Huey Long in the Louisiana legislature and key figure in saving the Kingfish from impeachment. Ellender used his power as Senate Appropriations Public Works Subcommittee chairman to funnel huge sums of money into projects for a coastal state historically plagued by floods and rising tides. Mainly through his efforts, Louisiana moved from one-fourth to only one-eighth swamp.

Economy and Education: Promises Partially Fulfilled

Nature blessed Louisiana with magnificent resources: oil and gas, sulphur and salt in fabulous quantities; fertile alluvial soils; forests that cover more than half her surface; great waterways; and plentiful supplies of water for people and industries. Had Louisiana not exploited those resources, she might be a poor Mississippi today. But since the 1920s, the state's per capita income has soared from 29 to 89 percent of the national average, although unemployment has been chronically high.

Part of Louisiana's problem seems to be that its economy has never really diversified beyond natural resources. Oil and gas have paid the bills for relatively generous social programs, but they have also made it easy for Louisiana to be lackadaisical about needed economic diversification and education for a modern technological society. No other Southern state has had such sluggish growth. The economic dynamism of neighboring Texas, of cities such as Atlanta and Houston, is simply not present. One could well argue that more moderate growth can be preferable to the cultural mediocrity and wasteful practices that so often attend a boomtime economy. But below-national-average incomes and joblessness are no joke. Part of the problem is that so much of the wealth of Louisiana ends up in out-of-state banks; for projects of $100 million, a New Orleans official told us, the financing must come from out-of-state. Of the considerable capital that remains in the state, the investment tends toward time-honored shipbuilding, oil, and gas. There seems to be a lassitude, a let-well-enough-be attitude on the part of banker and industrialist alike—perhaps some of the Mediterranean and the planter philosophy throwing a shadow all the way to the last quarter of the 20th century.

Louisiana lies athwart the ocean end of America's most extensive river system, giving her ready access to all ports of the Mississippi Valley and the sea lanes of the world. There are literally thousands of miles of related waterways within her borders, including that inglorious ditch, the Gulf Intracoastal Canal, which runs from Florida to Texas. The port of New Orleans is Louisiana's economic aorta, its wharves handling immense quantities of wheat, iron, steel, coal, rice, soybeans, fish, bananas, rubber, plywood, oil, and chemicals. Sadly an eight-part 1982 series by the *New Orleans Times-Picayune* found the fabled queen of Gulf ports had lost its rank as second-busiest in the nation to Houston. General cargo had fallen from 7.1 million tons in 1970 to 6.9 million tons in 1981 as Houston and other smaller Gulf ports offered services and fees tailored to various industries' specific needs and as the Louisiana Dock Board offered a somewhat lackadaisical attitude toward modernization and marketing.

Louisiana seems literally to float on a sea of oil and natural gas. Between the huge reserves in northwestern Louisiana (centered around Shreveport), across almost all of southern Louisiana, and far out into the Gulf of Mexico, more oil and gas is produced than in any other state, save Texas. People flood to where that energy is produced: in the 1970s, for example, Louisiana's overall population grew a respectable 15.3 percent, to 4,203,972 people, but the growth rate in the oil and gas producing areas was over 25 percent.

Sometime in the next century, when the last oil and gas wells in America sputter dry, the era of offshore drilling and the saga of the men who spend so much of their working lives on the weird looking platforms astride the open seas may become part of America's history and folklore, like the gold rushes or early lumber camps of the Upper Midwest. There are thousands of offshore platforms; on a clear day one can get the impression of small cities springing up across the watery horizon. And considering the number of wells drilled, the occurence of "blowout," causing heavy pollution in the Gulf, is very rare. Thankfully, most oil companies have given up the practice of throwing garbage and refuse into the Gulf waters. The water now sparkles around most of the platforms, and great schools of fish are attracted by plankton growing on the undersea pipes. The most serious environmental hazard for the Gulf and Louisiana's rivers and marshes is the incessant barrage of minor oil leaks and spills—each none too serious in itself, the cumulative effect potentially devastating.

Oil and gas also dominate Louisiana manufacturing; the state is the third-largest petrochemical manufacturer (after Texas and New Jersey). In 1981 more than 4,000 oil and gas companies were doing business in Louisiana, although the largest share of production was in the hands of such multinational firms as Exxon, Standard of California, and Gulf. Some 151,000 Louisianans earned their livings in the oil and gas industry, supporting an estimated 600,000 people.

The news was less rosy on other economic fronts. Louisiana's agricultural and animal produce and the factories associated therewith—wood, sugar cane, cotton, soybeans, rice, livestock—were being increasingly automated and employing fewer people. New Orleans was finding it hard to keep up with the dynamism of other Southern cities, and many young people with college degrees found it necessary to leave the state to find a job. Tourism is a predictably large industry. To this day, some Louisianians make their living gathering and cutting the long Spanish moss that drapes the cypresses and live oaks of the marshes. Others hunt for alligators; still others (especially Cajuns operating in the swamps) bring in muskrat, raccoon, oppossum, and nutria pelts. Louisiana provides a major share of America's supply of shrimp, oysters, crabs, trout, flounder, snapper, and—of course—more frog's legs than any other state.*

Louisiana's future will likely remain forever limited until the educational system is drastically improved. The state's notoriously high illiteracy rate is fading, but educational quality lags badly. Interest in addressing the problem came, finally, not from organized parents but from the Louisiana Association of Business and Industry, which made education a top priority because out-of-state firms regarded Louisiana's work force as ill educated and the schools too poor for the children of their executives. The business group has urged more strenuous accreditation tests for teachers and in-service training—only to find the educational establishment stoutly resisting. The problem, a lobbyist told us, is just plain lethargy, an unwillingness to change the old, slow Louisiana way of doing things.

To be fair, the record should show that Louisiana by the early 1980s had begun to spend huge amounts of money on vocational education. Nor is Louisiana a wasteland in higher education: New Orleans' Tulane and Loyola, for example, have long had national reputations, and Louisiana State University has improved dramatically, especially in agriculture, since it received its first real money in the 1930s, under Huey Long.

New Orleans: Character, Power, Landmarks

"This is a fantastically strange town," Mrs. Helen Mervis, a prominent civic leader, observed when we talked in New Orleans. "I love it: many things that make it difficult to live in also make it easy to live in. There's a kind of ambivalence one has to have to live in New Orleans. We have great tolerance for many things good and bad, including corruption. It's a tolerance that goes in so many directions. It creates a kind of hedonistic environment. And never forget," she added, "that New Orleans is a Carnival city—so much revolves around the Mardi Gras." And indeed, talking about New Orleans one can suddenly be plunged into a discussion of anything from the amazing levees and pumps that keep the city from sinking into the ooze of deltaic Louisiana

---

*One Louisiana industry that is no more deserves a footnote in American cultural history: Hadacol, the murky mixture of vitamins and minerals purveyed by one of the most flamboyant politicians Louisiana ever produced, state senator Dudley J. LeBlanc, of Abbeville. Back in the 1940s, no Southerner's home medicine chest was complete without its bottle of Hadacol. Bob Hope, Mickey Rooney, Chico Marx, George Burns, and Gracie Allen were recruited for a national caravan to advertise Hadacol. The ill-smelling, ill-tasting nostrum was promoted for the treatment of cancer, tuberculosis, heart trouble, diabetes, paralysis, gallstones, epilepsy, migraine headaches, blood diseases, stomach ulcers, rheumatism, arthritis, high (or low) blood pressure, and cataracts. Perhaps the fact that Hadacol contained 12 percent alcohol has something to do with its popularity. Millions of dollars worth were sold before 1951, when the Federal Trade Commission stepped in, charging LeBlanc Corporation with "false, misleading, and deceptive advertising." The next day the company went bankrupt, but Dudley LeBlanc had already sold out his interest for $10 million.

to defining the difference between New Orleans jazz and Dixieland jazz.*

One comes upon New Orleans, Walker Percy once wrote, "in the unlikeliest of places, by penetrating the depths of the Bible Belt, running the gauntlet of Klan territory, the pine barrens of south Mississippi, Bogalusa and the Florida parishes of Louisiana." Embroidering on that theme, Percy added that New Orleans has "the ideological flavor of a Latin enclave in a Southern Scotch-Irish mainland."

Once there, the visitor has to be fascinated by the gumbo-melange of New Orleans society. People of French, Spanish, African, Italian, Irish, German, English, and European Jewish ancestry—they are all there. It is perhaps the only American city where Catholics are very much of the hierarchy and always have been. The blacks are now the majority, making up 55 percent of the city's population (557,482 in 1980). Their New Orleans heritage runs from the fearful slave market of antebellum days to the wondrous invention of jazz and, in our time, newborn freedoms circumscribed by poverty, occasional terror, and seeing one of their own elected as mayor.

Raising money for culture or charity has traditionally been quite difficult in New Orleans; one reason given is that the Christian elite spend too much of their spare cash on the floats and costumed balls of Mardi Gras. Often Jews take the civic lead.

Mardi Gras is the epitome of what makes New Orleans one of the great fun cities of the world. Walker Percy has defended it as "an organic, viable folk festival, perhaps the only one in the United States." Carnival time begins on Twelfth Night, January 6, and ends on Shrove Tuesday, or Mardi Gras (literally Fat Tuesday), the day before Ash Wednesday and the season of penitence. Sixty-some "krewes"—private social groups or eating clubs—sponsor the parades and balls, and at its best the bacchanal on the streets is a kaleidoscope of colorful and boisterous sights and sounds, of the festive floats with their sequined and beplumed revelers lurching along. Half the float-riders and spectators are inebriated, and under cover of costume mask, inhibitions are freed for fanny pinching or other amusements.†

---

*According to jazz connoisseur Charles Suhor, true New Orleans jazz in the style of the city's early musicians is characterized by a buoyant, uncluttered rhythmic pulse, sensitive ensemble work, and relatively simple, nonvirtuoso solos. He defined Dixieland jazz as "a slick, smooth offspring of New Orleans jazz, with faster tempos, more 'schooled' instrumental tone and longer solos." There have been two great jazz revivals, one in the late 1940s, another since the '60s, centered in New Orleans' Preservation Hall and Dixieland Hall. Jazz is taught in some classrooms, and there are some vital neighborhood troupes. Not yet obsolete are the authentic marching brass bands, renowned for their slow funeral dirges on the way to a graveside and then the soul-freeing refrains of jubilant music on the return. The late and incomparable Louis Armstrong, whose life began in New Orleans in 1900, made it abundantly clear that he had played too many New Orleans funerals to fear death.

†This kind of drinking while driving is absolutely legal in Louisiana. In 1982, Mothers Against Drunken Driving, a national organization, promoted a law that would have banned open containers in vehicles, but after a 2 and 1/2 hour debate, the state house of representatives killed this threat to a "way of life." It is common practice for Louisianans to stop at a drive-through bar on the way home from work and pick up a "to-go" cup.

Things begin to get snooty in the private masked balls of the oldest and most socially prominent krewes: Comus (1857), Rex (1872), Momus (1872), and Proteus (1882). These presumably secret societies, almost exclusively male and white, dominate the city's social hierarchy. The greatest social compliment a member of New Orleans society can receive is to be made king or queen of one of the carnival societies. The elitist of the elite among the krewes is Comus; a half step below Comus is Rex, which was organized over a century ago in the excitement of a New Orleans visit by Russian Grand Duke Alexis Romanoff Alexandrovitch. Rex is basically a businessmen's club and does have some Jewish members. We were somewhat pleased to learn from our New Orleans sources that the most spectacular parades and balls are now put on by *nouveau riche* Krewes such as Endymion, which has even invited a few prominent blacks to join, and Bacchus. Both Krewes open up their balls to anyone who can pay $50 to attend.

For the most part, blacks are *personae non gratae* in the white man's Carnival celebrations, though there are said to be some 185 black "social and pleasure Mardi Gras" organizations with their own elaborate social pecking orders. The most ultra are the Illinois Social and Pleasure Club and its offshoot, the Young Men's Illinois Club. What whites see the most of, however, is the black parade headed by King Zulu, sponsored by the Zulu Social Aid and Pleasure Club. Zulu first appeared in 1916, his court in grass skirts and blackfaced with white mouths and eyes. As merry as he was, Zulu was expected to lose his way, get drunk, fall off his float, and pass out cold in the street. The civil rights revolution led some to see an unhappy symbolism in all this, and the whitened eyes and mouths disappeared. But now Zulu parades down Canal Street, like the white revelers, remaining firmly planted on his float. "That King Zulu rides again, and hopefully forever," said one local writer, "is a tribute to [local blacks'] ability to separate Mardi Gras from the racial agonies of our times."

Carnival has had its troubles. In the 1960s, merchants (who view Carnival as much a money-making activity as a social institution) were up in arms over the presence of assorted longhairs, hippies, and college straights who, if they had no money, panhandled, slept in the parks, and turned the streets into public urinals (the city provides none). The Mardi Gras of 1970 was nicknamed the "Carnival of Crime" after a flying brick hit trumpeter Al Hirt. In 1979, Mayor Dutch Morial canceled the big parades rather than give in to the striking police, who had bet that the city would do anything to keep Mardi Gras on the calendar.

Come Ash Wednesday, what else is there to New Orleans? First of all there is the port. As the late Hale Boggs told us, "It was one of the most unlikely spots on earth to build a city—literally on a swamp, mostly below sea level, with floods and hurricanes and every pestilence known to man. But the port did it; that's why President Jefferson effected the Louisiana Purchase. He wanted the Mississippi, the greatest river system on earth, to belong to the United States."

As wet as the city's earthly berth may be, when the first Frenchmen came up the river to find a town site, it was probably the driest place in sight. The city they founded, on a great crescent of the Mississippi, is almost an island. It is bounded on the south by the Mississippi, on the north by the waters of Lake Pontchartrain, a body of water half the size of Rhode Island and prime recreation grounds for New Orleans residents before it became polluted.* (The Mississippi, by contrast, is too swift and treacherous, and has long been too polluted for recreation.)

New Orleans' famous cemeteries, with their aboveground crypts, are one byproduct of the city's watery location. In aerial photograph, they resemble a neatly designed city; like cities, the cemeteries can accept successive waves of inhabitants because with each new burial, older bones can be pushed to the back of the vaults, spilling down a shaft. Next to cremation, it may be the most efficient burial system ever invented.

The jewel of the New Orleans milieu, of course, is the area of the original town laid out by the French—the *Vieux Carre*, or French Quarter. The Quarter's myriad attractions range from the marvelous architecture, including the decorative ironwork of French and Spanish design, to Bourbon Street's jazz and flesh locales, from Royal Street's choice shops and galleries to the landscaped oasis of Jackson Square. In the Quarter, one finds illustrious and venerable restaurants such as Antoine's and Brennan's and Galatoire's, or if one likes, there is the lure of strong roast Louisiana coffee and hot fresh doughnuts at the French market by the levee.

The *Vieux Carre* is packed with buildings of historic import; just at Jackson Square, for instance, one finds St. Louis Cathedral (which dates back to 1794), the Pontalba Buildings, thought to be America's oldest apartments, resplendent behind iron balconies from France, and the Cabildo, headquarters of the Spanish administration of the city, where the formal transfer of the Louisiana Territory to the United States took place in 1803. The character of the *Vieux Carre* was nearly destroyed after World War II when no less than Robert Moses, the great freeway builder in New York, proposed that an elevated expressway be constructed along the riverfront. A battle raged between preservationists and developers from 1946 to 1969 when the U.S. Transportation Department finally canceled the road—a decision, as documented in *The Second Battle of New Orleans* that was the turning point in favor of preservationists in their battles against highway development throughout the country.

If Tennessee Williams' impoverished Blanche DuBois were to arrive in New Orleans in the 1980s, she would no longer be able to utter that famed line, "They told me to take a streetcar named Desire, transfer to one called Cemetery, and ride six blocks and get off at Elysian Fields." New Orleans replaced its streetcars with buses in 1948, just a year after *A Streetcar Named Desire* was produced. (Desire is, however, in a museum, and one streetcar line, the St. Charles, still runs to New Orleans' other famed neighborhood, the Garden District, with its spacious Greek Revival and Georgian-style homes.)

---

*The South's most spectacular highway is the Lake Pontchartrain Causeway, which runs across open water for 23 miles. In the center section, a motorist has the sensation of being at sea, because he cannot see land. The causeway was opened in 1956, with a second parallel road in 1969.

Nor would Blanche likely find the working-class Stanley Kowalski and his wife, Stella, living in the French Quarter; such exorbitant prices are now attached to its preserved architecture that only the affluent need apply.

New Orleans has been subject to constant comparisons with brash and bustling Houston, only 330 miles distant. On lifestyle, New Orleans consistently wins; on economic vigor, Houston. In recent years, however, New Orleans has gone on a suspiciously Houstonesque "megastructure" building spree. Shell's lofty New Orleans structure, for example, bears a striking resemblance to One Shell Plaza in Houston, an unhappy analogy for a city that likes to think of itself as graceful and feminine. New Orleans also set out to *outdo* Houston—or any city, for that matter—with a gigantic domed stadium called the Louisiana Superdome, built on 13 acres of what had been city blight near the downtown business-hotel district and the French Quarter. The name superdome was conceived as a direct affront to Houston and its Astrodome; Mayor Moon Landrieu, promoter *extraordinaire* of the project, boasted to visitors that "we could fit that thing [the Astrodome] inside the Superdome with no sweat." It is, in fact, the biggest indoor stadium in the world. It also costs the state treasury several million dollars a year, the result of an obligation taken on in the 1960s—plus gigantic cost overruns in construction. The Superdome represents a substantial investment by Louisiana's people in their premier, but aging city.

A serious question facing New Orleans has been economic diversification. Unlike many other older cities, New Orleans is not a major league banking and business services center, and Mayor Dutch Morial encouraged those sectors to become more aggressive. Morial also created the 7,000-acre Almonaster-Michoud Industrial District in East New Orleans, with the intention of attracting manufacturing, high-technology and port-related jobs.

In the 1970s and into the '80s, New Orleans enjoyed dynamic and progressive political leadership under Mayors Moon Landrieu and Dutch Morial. Progressives with a nose for city development, both were light years removed from the old regular Democrats, known as the Choctaws, who used to steal votes and make and unmake mayors with impunity. In 1946, middle-class reform elements delivered the mayorality to de Lesseps Story "Chep" Morrison, scion of a distinguished family just back from the war. *Time* called Morrison a "symbol of the bright new day which has come to the city of charming ruins." He cracked down on gambling and prostitution, cleared slums, erected a new civic center, and helped build the International Trade Mart, which was instrumental in propelling New Orleans from 16th to 2nd place among U.S. ports. This progressive image cracked in 1960 when Morrison and other members of the New Orleans establishment stood silent during the integration of the public schools, as both white and black children who participated were spat upon and fathers had their jobs threatened.

In 1969, sluggish old New Orleans elected Moon Landrieu, an outspoken liberal and the man who had thought he was "gazing into my political grave" when as a state legislator he stood tall, but virtually alone, to cast the sole vote against race-baiting bills during the 1960 school ruckus. Landrieu came not from the genteel old establishment, but from a Catholic family that struggled to live off the neighborhood grocery store. His election came with the blessing of concerned New Orleans leaders; he also benefited from the first black vote big enough to decide a New Orleans election.

Landrieu got the city council to enact an ordinance to prohibit discimination in public accommodations and appointed blacks to boards and commissions at every level of government. He changed the look of the French Quarter by supporting controversial renovation of the historic French Market and construction of a handsome river promenade, appropriately named the Moon Walk. He became an expert in obtaining federal urban aid, lobbied courageously in Washington for cities of all population ranks, and was named President Carter's second Housing and Urban Development secretary.

Viable black political organizations had appeared in the '60s, mobilizing the blacks into ghetto precincts, harnessing the organizing power of the substantial black middle class. Then, in 1971, single-member district reapportionment made it possible to elect five state representatives from the city, and Ernest "Dutch" Morial, a young attorney who had been the first black graduate of Louisiana State University, was elected to a city judgeship. Population change and black political advancement were so swift in the 1970s that by 1977 the now-majority black city elected Morial mayor. Beneath the New Orleans glitter, however, Morial inherited immense problems of poverty, crime, police brutality, decaying infrastructure, and local government finance. Some studies in the early 1980s listed New Orleans as the poorest of America's large cities; Morial took us for an auto tour of the city one day, and we could see the evidence, in destitute black housing projects and decayed neighborhoods. And the school system, close to 90 percent black, lost taxpayer support while its poorly funded programs suffered a high dropout rate.

The business community worried constantly about the city's high crime rate and its effect on tourism, while the city's poor blacks worried—with no little justification—about police brutality. Even in the early 1980s fewer than one-fourth of New Orleans police officers were black. The U.S. Justice Department received more complaints of police brutality from New Orleans than any other city, even much larger Houston, Los Angeles, or Chicago. If a policeman was killed, residents of ghettos and public housing projects such as Fisher and Desire could expect nighttime raids and broken down doors.* Morial claimed credit for reducing crime and for settling out of court a lengthy police department racial discrimination suit. Under the agreement, the police department was to hire and promote blacks until they constituted 50 percent of all ranks.

---

*Desire achieved its own fame in 1970 when the Black Panthers moved into a house, sandbagged their fortress, and terrorized local police. Some nasty incidents prompted the New Orleans police to restore order in a night of chaos, gunfire, and firebombs that ended with one black youth dead and 21 others injured. The fact that Desire exists at all is a commentary on the city: it squats near the river, isolated by railroad tracks and canals, and is the kind of place where children swim in sewers, garbage and trash pile up without collection, and drug traffic, muggings, and rape are so prevalent that adults are afraid to leave their homes.

New Orleans also faced one of America's most difficult municipal finance dilemmas. While most localities complained that they were too dependent on the property tax, New Orleans did not even have much of that. The 1974 Louisiana constitution included a homeowner's exemption for the first $50,-000 in property value (increased to $75,000 as inflation raised housing prices). The result: 79 percent of New Orleans homeowners paid no property tax. The core of city revenues came from sales taxes and state and federal government aid; the state legislature refused to permit a city payroll tax. New Orleans was obliged to start cutting its work force in the late '70s, only to see its problems worsen in the '80s as the Reagan administration began to strangle federal urban aid programs. The city's maintenance and capital improvement programs were among those cut most deeply—a dangerous business in a city as old and water-logged as New Orleans.

By 1982, Morial easily won reelection—even after Moon Landrieu endorsed his conservative white opponent (Landrieu and Morial were about the same age and intensely competitive). It seemed a remarkably true demonstration of black power when a greater percentage of blacks turned out than whites— possibly a first ever in the American South.

Beyond New Orleans

The visitor to New Orleans can drive westward along Lake Pontchartrain's lovely city shoreline, enjoying the vista of parklands, sailing marinas, and middle-class homes. Suddenly a canal appears, and a bridge, and the environment changes instantly to honky tonk modern strip development, the world of fast food and garish gas stations. You have arrived in Jefferson Parish, probably the most parasitic suburb in the entire United States. The median family income in Jefferson, one discovers, is at least a third higher than in New Orleans. But the parish's education system is horrendously over-crowded, its general government services poor, and for parks and play-grounds—well, New Orleans is close by. "But," says a New Orleans civic leader, "they don't pay a cent of taxes to us. They don't want to pay no taxes and ain't going to pay no taxes. And what's worse, they don't pay any taxes out here either." Jefferson Parish has some nice residential subdivisions and a fairly modern form of government, but also memories of Mafia control and at one time Mafia-owned casinos.

The big white noose around New Orleans swings from Jefferson (83 percent white) on the west and south to St. Bernard (94 percent white) on the east; St. Tammany's Parish, which grew an incredible 73.9 percent in the 1970s, is 86 percent white. St. Bernard melds geographically and politically into Plaquemines Parish, that spongy, hurricane-swept finger of swamp and marsh and bayou that extends a hundred miles from the New Orleans area down to the three ocean passes of the Mississippi.

"Timeless Plaquemines," one Louisianan has written of that strange parish, a place where "the land, the sea, the sky combine to create a feeling of remoteness." Practically, Plaquemines is also a place of immense wealth—rich from lush oil deposits and from sulphur taken from one of the world's largest sulphur cones. And politically, America's closest approximation to a full-blown dictatorship was exercised there for 40 years by Leander H. Perez, the man who fought his state, his nation, the Navy, big corporations, and even his church in the cause of segregation of the races. A heart attack felled Perez in 1969, and his funeral brought tears to the eyes of George Wallace and thousands of other mourners at final rites in the Catholic Church. Perez had once been excommunicated for telling the Archbishop of New Orleans to "go to hell" in a fight over integrating parochial schools in the parish. Leander's sons continued the family reign, into the 1980s, with Chalin serving as president of the parish commission council and Leander, Jr., as district attorney. The political shenanigans didn't end. In the early 1980s, Leander, Jr., appointed a grand jury to investigate political corruption in Plaquemines; the jury proceeded to indict Chalin on five counts, including malfeasance in office, and was about to indict Leander, Jr., himself when he had the grand jury dissolved on the grounds that his political enemies had tampered with it. In 1983, in the first council elections since the federal courts intervened in 1967, Plaquemines elected a woman and a black. Chalin, who had been stripped of his chief's powers by renegade commissioners, chose not to run. But Luke A. Petrovich, a Perez protégé and parish councilman who defected, still contended, "Anyone who thinks they're finished is being very, very naïve."

Seventy miles north of New Orleans lies the little paper mill city of Bogalusa, which became famous in the 1960s as the town of more race conflicts per capita than practically any other in America. The big difference between Bogalusa and other race-crazed towns was that the local blacks responded. They formed the secret Deacons for Defense and Justice. The Deacons armed themselves, just like their Klan enemies, and when black or white civil rights workers were threatened, a chain telephone alarm system let them spring to instant action. The very existence of the Deacons probably accounted, at least in part, for the general subsidence of Klan activity in Bogalusa. In 1969, an amazingly peaceful integration of the city's schools was effected.

Louisiana's second-largest city is thriving Shreveport (pop. 205,815), a place where rigidly conservative voting for state and federal offices is combined with generally progressive, civic-minded city government. Far to the north, Shreveport lacks the Gallic flavor of southern Louisiana; instead, it is predominantly white Protestant. There are minorities of Italian-, Greek-, and Mexican-descended peoples, plus a big black population that dates back to the days when thousands of slaves labored on the great cotton plantations along the Red River. Antebellum Shreveport was one of the great cotton centers of the Western world; as one account puts it, "the very streets and sidewalks were piled and cluttered with bales."

Today King Cotton is but a ghost of his former self, and 20th-century Shreveport has made most of its money (and its millionaires) from the rich oil and gas fields of Caddo Parish and neighboring Bossier Parish. Now oil, like cotton before it, is starting a gradual decline because exploration and production have shifted so heavily to the Gulf Coast. Diversified industries have been taking up the slack in local employment. Signifying its ties with neighboring states, Shreveport calls itself the center of the "Ark-La-Tex" trading area.

As cities go, Shreveport is one of the most attractive in the South. Unlike Baton Rouge, it never let its central business district go to pot, and a covey of striking office buildings and hotels have been added. An impressive big convention center is adjacent to a modern civic theater. With its renowned Little Theatre, Shreveport Symphony, et al., Shreveport makes a greater effort in the fine arts than any other Southern city its size.

When one travels to Baton Rouge and takes the elevator up to to the top of the towering State Capitol, clashing views meet the eye. Directly below is a splendidly landscaped park and a lake, to the east pleasant residential areas, to the south the stingily designed streets of the town's business district, and still farther south, the LSU campus. Close by on the west, the Mississippi River passes, vast and powerful. And with what is the Father of Waters adorned? An infested forest of oil storage tanks and stacks and distilling equipment, covering the ground northward almost as far as the eye can see, belching a continual haze of brown-black smoke into the skies. This is the beginning of the "petrochemical Gold Coast." Pollution controls have begun to cut down the vile smoke, but the 70-mile stretch from Baton Rouge to New Orleans has been dubbed "the cancer corridor." The oil boom caused Baton Rouge to grow 32 percent in the 1970s to 219,486, and its port (almost nonexistent in 1950) became the nation's fourth-largest. Baton Rouge is also home to Southern University, the nation's largest predominantly black university.

The real fascination of Baton Rouge is the Capitol itself, the place where Huey Long met the assassin's bullet almost 50 years ago. A.J. Liebling caught the spirit of the heroic statue of Huey that stands above his grave on the Capitol grounds: "The face, impudent, porcine and juvenile, is turned toward the building he put up—all 34 stories of it—in slightly more than a year, mostly with federal money. The bronze double-breasted jacket, tight over the plump belly, has already attained the dignity of a period costume, like Lincoln's frock coat." But there is some currency about that statue, too; it turns out that Russell Long posed for it. Inside the Capitol, in the corridor where Huey died, in the senate and house chambers and lobbyists' corners, the sense of *All The King's Men,* and the ghost of Earl, too, and all the sweat-soaked profundities of Louisiana politics, come rushing in. But the Louisiana legislature has made immense advances in such areas as professional staff.

Due west and slightly south of Baton Rouge, in the heart of Acadiana, lie the cities of Lafayette (pop. 81,961) and Lake Charles (75,051), both prospering as modern oil centers. The postwar years have been good ones for this area. An emphasis on the common French heritage has fostered cultural unity and helped to draw tourists. Wondrous to relate, French—either in purer form or patois—remains the dominant language of Lafayette and many smaller towns. In fact, the government of Quebec, the center of French Canada, now has a permanent office in Lafayette, from which it encourages revival of the French language and trading with the Cajuns. Today, thousands of school-children in the 22 Cajun counties are taught the purest French by young teachers dispatched by the government of France. The administrative end of the oil industry has brought tens of thousands of outsiders who have corrected some of the Cajun's economic lassitude and propensity for civic corruption.

After all is said and done with modern Louisiana, one lives still with a bittersweet nostalgia about this strangely different member of the family of American states. Susan Fenwick grasped it some years ago when she wrote in *New Orleans Magazine* of "the overwhelming feeling of longing for some-thing we had." She wrote of a faded marker of a battle in which the Confeder-ate forces had done themselves proud, and then of a freshly painted, unpreten-tious country church where "the plain people gather in their best" and "faith in God still works." And finally, a deserted plantation manor with a skewed sign: "Posted, Get Out, Stay Out." "Who were these men," the writer asked, "who carved out of a land with the labor of others a way of life that ended in a holocaust? In this peaceful isolation, there is nothing left but dreams of what might have been and thanks to God that it wasn't."

FLORIDA

State of Exiles

FROM NORTH AND SOUTH, from neighboring states and from distant places, they have come, each group claiming its piece of the fragile land: dirt poor farmers from the rural southern hinterland to work in factory jobs; military men and women to launch space flights and protect the nation's borders; refugees from Communist Cuba and the wretched poverty and political repression of Haiti; capitalists from Latin America, seeking safety for themselves and their money; drug dealers preying on the vast and wealthy North American market; and, the largest and most varied group of all, the retirees—wealthy WASPs who made fortunes in the Northeast industrial corridor, poor Jews who spent a working life sewing clothes in the garment district of New York City, middle-class farmers from the Midwest, and—most recently—blue-collar workers, their retirement in the sun made possible by Social Security and private pensions.

Florida's growth figures are barely comprehensible. In 1940, fewer than 2 million people lived in this state; in 1980, the count was 9,739,992. The 1970s alone produced a growth rate of 43.4 percent. Of the U.S.A.'s 25 fastest-growing metropolitan areas in the 1970s, 10 were in Florida. Two Florida communities were among the top 10 cities for sheer numbers of people added: Tampa–St. Petersburg increasing by 480,943 in the decade, the Fort Lauderdale–Hollywood area by 393,943.

This growth, and most particularly its velocity, has produced highly negative social conditions. The state has become almost as well known for its problems of crime, racial conflict, and environmental degradation as for its sunny beaches and glamorous resorts. The worst crime reports have emanated from South Florida, where Miami has nearly achieved the title of "Murder Capital U.S.A." Shocking newspaper stories of massive drug busts have been replaced by estimates that drug smuggling and selling have reached the proportions of a $7 to $12 billion industry, supplying much of Florida's investment capital. Florida officials candidly admit there is little they can do to control the problem. While Miami in 1980 ranked No. 1 among U.S. cities in its rate of violent and property crimes (related to population), six other Florida cities were among the top 11 nationally in crime: Gainesville, the West Palm Beach–Boca Raton area, Orlando, the Fort Lauderdale–Hollywood area, Daytona Beach, and Tallahassee.

As for the environmental problems of this fragile, ecologically sensitive state, they range from water shortages (from excessive land drainage) to the scars of pollution from phosphate strip mining to diminishment of the barrier islands as man greedily tries to consume the farthest land extremes of the continent.

How, one may ask, has this happened to the Promised Land? Geography plays a major part: the state would clearly not suffer from such a magnitude of crime and drug problems were it not the southernmost point of the United States, and its connecting point to Latin America. Smuggling and lawlessness are all-too-familiar visitors in border areas around the world.

But Florida's problems, we believe, go deeper. As immigrants from the North and South have flooded in, the state has lost, save in a few counties hard up against the Georgia and Alabama borders, whatever tenuous ties it had with its Deep South neighbors. Perhaps, in racial matters, that was good riddance. But what has developed on the Floridian peninsula is a deeply disjointed society, one that has yet to develop a coherent sense of itself and perhaps never will. Anglo factory workers, elderly fresh in from the Frostbelt, Latin Americans—all may call themselves Floridians. But many do not; they and all their Floridian neighbors know their roots are elsewhere and that they have a quite limited commitment to their new "home." Florida, in short, is not so much beneficiary as victim of its widely heralded growth. The Floridian experience proves that tumultuous, rapid growth is as destructive to a society and natural environment as the more feared processes of population decline and economic stagnation.

Florida is a demographic oddity. Consider these differences, recorded in the 1980 Census: 17.2 percent of Florida's population is over 65 (compared to just 11 percent nationally); another 11 percent of Floridians are between 55 and 64 and about to join the ranks of the "elderly." Less spectacular, on the surface, is that 8.8 percent of Floridians are of Spanish origin (compared to 6.5 percent nationally), while 13.7 percent are black (compared with 11.6 percent nationally). But these unusual concentrations of people are highly segregated. *Two-thirds* of the Hispanics live in just one area—in or around Miami. The elderly select their own ghettos: Jews in Miami Beach, Northeasterners on the East Coast, Midwesterners on the West Coast. Executives of multinational corporations with Florida offices choose Coral Gables, adjoining Miami, while the younger working-class migrants move mostly to cities in the northern and central sections (Orlando, et al.). Blacks are more dispersed, but in their largest numbers are to be found along the northern border and in the explosive Miami ghetto.

Middle-class people of working age, the very glue of American society, are numerically much less important in Florida. Socially cohesive issues are often missing or sublimated; by contrast, each minority—the elderly included—has its own political agenda. Social Security payments, revolution in Cuba, increasing the acceptability of Spanish, a strong defense of Israel, fighting economic and social discrimination if one is black, all these have been major issues in Florida campaigns. By contrast, it's much tougher in this state to get support for the public schools, for effective laws to protect the land, or for funds to build prisons—the 1982 legislature's increased spending on criminal justice notwithstanding. The prison issue illustrates the dangers of failed consensus: criminologists have pinpointed a decrepit, overcrowded prison system—one that turns minor offenders into hardened criminals—as a major cause of the high crime rate that so alarms Floridians.

This is not to say that Florida's political system and government are totally bereft of innovation. Florida's legislature has become one of the most progressive in the nation in the running of its own affairs; it was the first legislature to allow its sessions to be televised and to pass pioneering "sunshine" and "sunset" legislation. Several Florida statutes have indicated a growing (even if still insufficient) environmental consciousness. And the state has some of the country's finest newspapers, led by the Knight-Ridder *Miami Herald*, which provides fine coverage of Latin America as well as serious coverage of Miami, and the *St. Petersburg Times*, one of the country's outstanding middle-circulation papers and long a liberal voice in a very conservative town. Florida newspapers won eight Pulitzer Prizes in the 1960s and '70s, more than any other state.

Despite all its developmental errors and social problems, Florida continues to draw vast numbers of people. Parts of the state are undeniably the warmest within U.S. borders during the winter months, and 38 million tourists annually find worthwhile attractions both summer and winter. There's also considerable evidence that neither the native Floridians nor the newcomers are truly horrified by what some see as the deterioration of the state. Floridian John Rothchild, writing in *Rolling Stone*, has noted that county commissioners, even in conservative out-of-the-way areas of Florida, have testified as character witnesses for drug smugglers. Drug smuggling, he suggests, is merely an extension of the questionable business dealings that have pervaded Florida since the days of land speculation. And the environmental degradation, he continued, has had no effect on the growth rates.

The worst mistake that one can make about Florida is to dismiss it. In many ways it holds the keys to America's future. America will inevitably become older and more Hispanic, as the baby boom generation ages and the swelling populations of poor countries in Latin American spill across U.S. borders. The political agendas now important in Florida may be repeated, especially across America's Sunbelt states.

Geography and Ecology

Before the synthetic civilization came, there was only natural Florida—that remarkable peninsula extending more than 300 miles south of the major continental land mass, a great green mat, often broken by lakes and swamps, floating in a deep blue sea. The farther south one looked, the more remarkable it was. From north to south, this was the view: first, the low-rolling, pine-covered hills of the north and the panhandle, close kin to the red clay hills of neighboring Georgia and Alabama, a land of magnolias and the languid Suwannee River, live oaks and Spanish moss. Then came the central lakes district, later to become the heartland of Florida's great citrus industry. After this, the Kissimmee Prairies, covered with grass and patches of palmetto, where the great cattle ranges would later be developed. These lands drain into Lake Okeechobee, one of the largest lakes on the North American continent and certainly the largest of the 30,000-odd that dot the Floridian landscape.

Okeechobee has no single outlet, but rather flows southerly toward the ocean as the land tilts ever so slightly down to the south through that remarkable sea of grass known as the Everglades. (The dominant sawgrass is hardly grass at all, growing 10 feet tall with edges set like teeth.) The Everglades stretch for over 5,000 square miles, the muddy waters draining imperceptibly below, the level area broken only by occasional "hammocks," where the underlying limestone protrudes to the surface and trees have grown.

As the ocean is reached, along some of the keys and the coast of southwestern Florida, the mangrove forests appear, constantly building land out of water until hurricanes occur to demolish their work. The Florida Keys are a fantastic coral-built achipelago stretching 200 miles south and southwesterly from Miami, a unique geologic occurrence in North America. Finally, one should mention the long, sandy, buffer spits or islands lying just off the Atlantic Coast and part of the Gulf Coast. Not only did they provide most of the fabled Florida beach front, but behind their banks a safe Inland Waterway could be created.

Florida's record of stewardship of this land is mixed. The state has one of the most impressive state park systems in the nation. The fabulous and gigantic Everglades National Park grew from land first acquired by the Florida Federation of Women's Clubs in 1915. But the drive to remake nature into a synthetic environment has been costly to the ecology; as one observer noted (even before the last 2 million people arrived), Florida's "500-mile-long peninsula has been cut and channeled, bulldozed and bulkheaded, scraped and scissored to a point where the principal life resources have been threatened." Even if that view is prematurely apocalyptic, the dangers are very real. In 1972, the legislature did pass a water and land management act hailed by Gov. Reubin Askew as "a giant step toward controlling our growth." That law and companion statutes set up a mechanism that started with local land-use control, then with an ascending staircase of planning controls to regions, and then the state government itself—by which new developments (housing, airports, incursions on the seacoast, for example) could be controlled and certain lands declared environmentally endangered. There were major shortcomings in the system, however: the regulatory power of the state government extended to only 10 or 20 percent of the largest development projects, for instance, and local land use plans, of drastically varying quality, were not reviewed above the regional level, and then often quite haphazardly. To protect environmentally valuable but endangered lands such as barrier islands, the state was obliged to embark on an ambitious program of land purchase. But owners often resisted, and the legislature refused to authorize use of eminent domain to assure saving the lands for posterity. In general, land developments from the early '70s onward were more sensitive to natural systems, with higher quality housing and access to transportation than in the exploitive '50s and

'6os. The state also paid more attention to protection of water resources. The problems lay in the sheer burden of 10 million inhabitants and the legislature's unwillingness to force environmental accountability on all local governments.

Discovery and Development

Except to the Seminole Indians, the land called Florida was unknown until the Spanish conquistador Don Juan Ponce de Leon came upon it in April of 1513 while following a commission from the king of Spain to "explore and colonize Bimini." The Spanish were quickly exposed to the perils of what they would later learn was the North American mainland: even before they could land, a tropical squall came up and almost wrecked their ships on a promontory that would later become known as Cape Canaveral. Ponce de Leon on April 2, 1513, selecting for this region the name *Florida* because—as the royal chronicler later wrote—"it has a very beautiful view of many cool woodlands, and it was level and uniform; and because, moreover, they discovered it in the time of the Feast of Flowers [Easter season]." A day later, Ponce and his men landed at what would become St. Augustine, looking for the fountain of youth (as did so many after them); in 1565, there was indeed a permanent settlement at St. Augustine, and the serious peopling of the continent had begun.

Between Ponce's discovery and formal U.S. proprietorship, 308 years were to pass. But the Spanish were continually harrassed by competing French and English colonists, and when they finally relinquished the land in 1821, there was little to show for their efforts except the small towns of St. Augustine and Pensacola. Most of the Spanish flavor one finds in Florida today—Tampa, with its Ybor City and Spanish restaurants, Miami with the big Cuban colony —dates from comparatively modern times. Florida's early years under U.S. rule—the winning of statehood in 1845, Indian wars, involvement on the Confederate side in the Civil War, Reconstruction—have been well depicted as a "faint duplication" of life elsewhere in America in those times.

The real history of modern Florida awaited the 1880s and the arrival of the first big promoters: hotel and railmen Henry M. Flagler and Henry B. Plant. Shocked by the primitive hotel accommodations Florida had to offer, Flagler in 1885 began to build the fabulously opulent Hotel Ponce de Leon in St. Augustine. Stung by Flagler's success, his west Florida rival, Plant, spent more than $3 million building the Tampa Bay Hotel, opened in 1891. But Flagler, who had already made millions as a partner of John D. Rockefeller, was not to be outdone. Thousands of affluent East Coast residents began to travel to Florida on the posh all-Pullman train he put into service. First, St. Augustine was the southernmost point; then Flagler decided on a southerly extension to Palm Beach, which he literally "made" with its sumptuous new hotel, the Breakers. Soon the private railway cars of the ultra-rich could be seen on the Palm Beach sidings, and large private homes called "cottages" were erected near the Breakers.

In those days, Miami was just a frontier village with a few sand trails and makeshift wooden shacks, but one of its first genteel Northern settlers, a young widow named Julia Tuttle, had a vision of its future. After a savage frost in the winter of 1894–95, which destroyed the citrus crop of middle Florida, Mrs. Tuttle was able to send Flagler sprigs of unharmed orange blossom to prove that Miami was south of the frost line. Within a year's time, the railroad was extended to Miami, and out of the "tangled mass of vine, brush, trees and rocks" Mrs. Tuttle had once described to a friend, there began to grow a great city—starting, of course, with a Flagler hotel.

But this was the era of Manifest Destiny, and Flagler dreamed of an even greater city, at the very tip of the continent, Key West. And true enough, from 1904 to 1912, work went on to construct the Overseas Railroad across the subtropical keys. Huge engineering obstacles, mosquitoes, blazing summers, and three hurricanes had to be endured, and 700 men were washed away by storms. But in 1912 an 82-year-old Flagler rode the first train, all the way down from Jacksonville, over the bridges and viaducts and the sea, and into Key West. Florida's eastern coast had been conquered, and the frontier was no more. (A raging hurricane in 1935 swept away main sections of the Key West line and a whole train with its passengers, but Flagler's roadbed was used to extend U.S. 1 across the Keys on the Overseas Highway.)

Soon the great Florida land boom of the '20s was on. Hundreds of thousands of land speculators poured in—2.5 million people in the year 1925 alone —and prices zoomed to many times real value. But in the spring of 1926, the bubble broke; banks began to fail; paper millionaires became paupers overnight. And in the autumn of that year, hundreds died as one of the worst hurricanes of recorded history tore apart the flimsy boom-time buildings.

But Florida seemed to prosper through all adversities. Half a million permanent new residents were noted in the 1920s, and despite the Great Depression, another 430,000 people found their way to Florida by the eve of World War II. The war slowed development, but by 1950 the great boom of all Florida history—the one that continues, little abated, to this day—was underway. Lavish hotels began to spring up everywhere; air travel made it easy for Northerners to spend quick vacations in Florida; the retirement communities boomed; air conditioning arrived in a serious way; and by the 1960s NASA's $2 billion expenditures were lining Floridian pockets.

By the early 1980s, Florida had established a highly diversified economy. If you counted gross dollars earned and people hired, tourism still led other industries. Indeed, incredible numbers of people even traveled to Florida during the gruesomely hot and humid summers. Agriculture was booming, too: on its relatively few but huge farms Florida was growing more citrus than any other state and running a respectable second to California in winter vegetables. Sugar cane, beef, and fishing also brought in formidable incomes. Manufacturing continued to invade this state where it was once virtually unknown: by 1980, some 466,500 people worked in Florida factories, in every field from food processing to chemicals, paper and pulp to printing, cigars to aerospace equipment and computers. There was a large mining industry in phosphates. Starting in the mid 1970s, Florida also became a major banking center, for reasons both legitimate and nefarious.

Floridians' per capita income crept up from 74 percent of the national average in 1928 to 94 percent in 1980. But much of the rise could be attributed to the tremendous wealth of a narrow cross section of upper-income people. Florida workers get substantially less pay than the national average, partly because tourism and agriculture yield such low wages. An indicator of the position of organized labor is that Florida was the first state to enact a right-to-work law (1944); despite pockets of strength, labor has never been a major force in the state. Average income is also depressed by the poorer retirees.

The opulence of Florida's communities for wealthy retirees and executives is matched by the squalor and poverty of the migrant worker camps. It came home to us most clearly when one morning we toured the Kennedy Space Center facilities, where billions were being poured into the moon shots, and that same afternoon we saw a sick farm laborer's child, flies swarming around its little body, lying on a bed at the Old Top Labor Camp near Winter Haven. One of the terrors of migrant life are the crew leaders, who have power of life or death over each migrant's job and have been assailed by a spokesman for migrants as "thieves, con men, fraud artists and alcoholics—any one or combination." Into the '80s groups of farm laborers were discovered working under conditions of virtual peonage. This life of deprivation was hidden to most Americans until a weekend of 1960 when Edward R. Murrow, on CBS stations across the country, proclaimed a Harvest of Shame—precursor to the poverty wars of the 1960s. With a dusty road and battered trucks and milling people behind him, Murrow intoned, "This scene is not taking place in the Congo. The hawkers you hear are chanting the going piece rate at the various fields. This is Belle Glade, Florida. This is the way the humans who harvest the food for the best-fed people in the world get hired."

Conditions have changed little since Murrow's day, except that there are fewer native-born Americans in the camps. The alien laborers—from Mexico, Jamaica and other Caribbean islands—lack U.S. citizenship and are even more subject to terrorization by crew leaders.

Politics and Government in the Retirement State

Florida was so implacably Democratic in past times that it was not until 1970, reacting to stinging defeats their party had suffered in the '60s, that Florida Democrats coalesced into a unified state organization. Modern Florida Republicanism made its first inroads in urban counties receiving the big migration from the North. With Eisenhower leading the ticket, this urban base was expanded on for solid Republican victories in 1952 and 1956, and again with Nixon heading the ticket in 1960 and later in 1968 and 1972. Floridians broke with their new Republican tradition to vote for Jimmy Carter in 1976, but angry over the handling of the Cuban boatlift in 1980, returned to the Republicans to vote for Ronald Reagan.

Florida still elects many more Democrats to office than Republicans. The increased numbers of blue-collar retirees with their fondness for New Deal programs—along with the state's black population—indicate continued Democratic strength. Campaigning in Florida has become an expensive process of using the media to influence a constantly changing population. But Floridians vote at about the same rate as the nation as a whole—a surprising feat in a growing state and a testament to the voting proclivities of senior citizens.

Florida's old-style Democrats offered a mix of fiscal conservatism, antigovernmentalism, opposition to any kind of welfare, nationalistic patriotism, and mild racism. A typical conservative was Spessard Holland, governor in the 1940s and senator from 1947 to 1971—a states' righter, a citrus and big-business man, a chief sponsor of legislation giving the states title to tidelands, but also a leading opponent of the poll tax, which he helped abolish in Florida in 1937 and for the U.S. through constitutional amendment in the 1960s. From 1937 to 1951 Florida also had a liberal senator, Claude Pepper. Pepper was defeated by Democrat George Smathers, who accused him of "softness" on Communism.* Miami and its suburbs, however, sent Pepper to the House in 1962, where he became *the* national spokesman for the elderly and their political lobbies. Still going strong in the early '80s (he was born in 1900), Pepper defended Social Security as though it were the Holy Grail and in 1983 broadened his scope by becoming chairman of the House Rules Committee.

Pepper overshadowed Florida's congressional delegation in the early 1980s. Democrat Charles Bennett, of Jacksonville, first elected in 1948, had won the reputation of "Mr. Ethics" for his early advocacy of ethical codes in both federal employment and the U.S. House. Republican C.W. Bill Young, of St. Petersburg, upset the foreign policy establishment by insisting the U.S. should better control spending the money it gives to such international bodies as the World Bank. Democrat Sam Gibbons, of Tampa, continually fought for the cause of free trade. Miami's Dante Fascell became the House Foreign Affairs Committee's expert on Latin America. Between the military installations, Social Security, immigration problems, and health care for the aged, Florida is one of the states most dependent on the federal government, and its members of Congress find it necessary to spend an enormous amount of time protecting the state's interests. They ought to have the requisite clout: by the early '80s population growth had swelled Florida's House delegation to 19 seats—compared to 6 in the 1940s.

Florida's U.S. Sen. Lawton Chiles literally invented the walking tour as a campaign tool in 1970, spurning large newspaper and television advertising but reaping bushels of free publicity as he walked over 1,000 miles from one end of Florida to another, meeting some 45,000 common citizens. In Wash-

---

*This was the same campaign in which Smathers reportedly told an audience of yokels, "Are you aware that Claude Pepper is known all over Washington as a shameless extrovert? Not only that, but this man is reliably reported to practice nepotism with his sister-in-law, and he has a sister who was once a thespian in wicked New York. Worst of all, it is an established fact that Mr. Pepper, before his marriage, practiced celibacy."

ington, Democrat Chiles maintained the image of a religious populist whose greatest legislative victory was passage of the 1976 federal "sunshine" law, requiring federal agencies to open their decision-making meetings to the public. Florida made political history in 1980 by sending Republican Paula Hawkins to the Senate, the first woman elected to that august body on her own reputation alone. Hawkins had made her political mark as a consumer-minded member of the Florida Public Service Commission. Her election did not thrill the women's movement, however, since as a Utah-born Mormon, she voted conservatively and opposed federal financing of abortions.

Florida's mercurial, buffoonish Republican governor of the late 1960s was Claude R. Kirk, Jr., who delighted the press with many pranks, including showing up at his inaugural ball with a beauteous blonde he introduced only as "Madam X"—a German-born Brazilian divorcee he later married. But during his term, the state adopted a new constitution to replace an antiquated 1885 version, and the legislature enacted the most far-reaching reorganization of the executive branch since the Civil War. Succeeding Kirk in 1971 was Democrat Reubin O'D. Askew, who turned out to be one of the most accomplished state chief executives of the '70s. Askew not only ran on a platform advocating a corporate income tax, but got first the legislature and then the people in a statewide vote (70 percent in favor) to authorize it. In 1976, after the state senate repeatedly refused to require financial disclosure of state officers and candidates, Askew organized the only successful campaign in the state's history to amend the constitution by initiative. In 1978, when heavily bankrolled gambling interests tried to pass an initiative authorizing casino gambling in Miami Beach, Askew warned of the grave dangers in crime and corruption and persuaded a majority of Floridians to vote down the proposal.

Even with the corporate income tax, Florida's taxation system is grossly inequitable, and the services it funds are inadequate for a society with so many dependent people. Florida is prohibited by its own constitution from levying taxes on personal income. Its 5 percent sales tax is often advertised as a way to put the bite on tourists, but the fact is it also penalizes low-income families and relieves richer people of the major tax burden that even a flat-rate income tax would effect. Florida also lacks any state inheritance tax. There is a homestead property exemption that makes it extremely difficult to raise taxes in poorer sections of the state. With a will, Florida could raise substantially more taxes without great pain. The present system is parasitic because it encourages retirees to bring with them the wealth generated in other states.

Florida's geographic distribution of government services became more equitable in the wake of "one-man, one-vote" districting in the '60s. Few states had a more egregiously malapportioned legislature. The infamous "Pork Chop Gang"—a name brilliantly conceived by *Tampa Tribune* editor James Clendinen—emerged in 1953 when 22 rural senators, mostly from the counties along the Georgia and Alabama borders and central Florida, banded together to block reapportionment. Not only did they succeed, but they blocked urban renewal and managed to get a grossly disproportionate share of state monies spent in their jurisdictions. In addition, the Pork Choppers were closely tied to special interests: banks, private utilities, truckers, the liquor industry, timber and paper mills, small loan companies, and the like. Court-ordered reapportionment broke their hold. Then came election of the first house speaker ever chosen from Dade County, Richard Pettigrew, a progressive in the Askew-Chiles mold, who was instrumental in the passage of Askew's legislative program. The Florida house has developed into a well-run legislative body while the senate has been likened to an "appellate court" that decides which of the house's initiatives it will allow to become law; in the early 1980s, a coalition of conservative Democrats and Republicans, under the leadership of Dempsey Barron of Panama City, controlled the Senate to a degree approaching that of the old Pork Chop Gang. Both houses have reapportioned themselves into single-member districts, assuring more seats for blacks and Hispanics.

Miami, the Beach, the Cubans

The habitable area of Miami and its surrounding cities is confined to a narrow strip of high-lying land bordered by the Everglades on the west and Biscayne Bay on the east. Aside from Miami Beach, the major attractions of Biscayne Bay are beautiful Virginia Key and the self-proclaimed island paradise of Key Biscayne. The latter literally swarms with pleasure craft of every description and has man-made Dodge Island the world's leading passenger port, often filled with big cruising ships headed for Nassau, San Juan, and St. Thomas. Right beside the docks is Miami's verdant Bayfront Park, remembered as the spot where Franklin Roosevelt barely escaped assassination in 1933.

Back from downtown and the bay, the city of Miami proper stretches toward the Everglades in a monotony of white stucco checkerboard blocks. Through the heart of this, headed due west on its way toward Tampa, is the Tamiami Trail, Route 41; within the city limits it is S.W. 8th Street, which with nearby West Flagler Street as "Colle Ocho" forms the spine of Little Havana, where Cuban refugees in 1959 began the speediest and most incredible transformation of any American city.

Until 1959 and the day Fidel Castro stepped off the Sierra Maestra and came to power in Cuba, thus triggering the Great Migration of his dissenting countrymen, the total image of Miami and its satellite communities was one of sun, sand, sex, and sin. The outside world's real interest centered on Miami Beach, that narrow Babylon-by-the-Atlantic with hundreds of hotels, including some of the most luxurious in the world, and a wintertime population of 1,000,000 people. Miami was a minor city until the wild boom-and-bust real estate speculation of the 1920s; governmentally, the only interesting event occurred, ironically enough, also in 1959 when the people of Dade County enacted a fairly strong metropolitan government.

Dade County's Spanish-speaking population in 1959 was only 22,000. By 1980, there were 581,030 Hispanics—the Census Bureau does not distinguish among them by place of origin—making up 35 percent of the county population and some 55.9 percent of the city of Miami itself. In less than a quarter century, the old resort had been transformed into a bustling center of business and international finance, a place wracked with drug smuggling, racial and ethnic conflict, the burden of coping with a constant stream of Caribbean refugees, and monstrous murder and property crime rates. The city was flush with money from international trade and smuggling, but officials worried constantly about the image thus created for tourism, still the single largest legal business.

The Cubans who arrived immediately after the revolution were the cream of Cuban society. Over 12 percent had been to college, almost two-thirds lived in Havana rather than small towns and villages, and they included a disproportionately high percentage of doctors, lawyers, teachers, and other professional people. Among those educated Cubans, the period of menial labor in Miami was short-lived; soon they had licenses to practice their professions. The entrepreneurial middle class, meanwhile, opened cigar factories, boatyards, restaurants, gas stations, bakeries, cinemas, night clubs, auto dealerships, and every other business one can imagine. The Cuban labor pool suddenly propelled Miami to third place in the U.S. (after New York and California) in garment manufacturing.

Then, in a development of immense import, a number of Cubans began an export trade with Latin America, often using as contacts relatives who had settled in various countries there after the Cuban revolution. As the Cuban Americans traveled around Latin America, other businessmen began to grasp the value of banking in Miami: interest rates often half those demanded in their own countries, financial and personal safety (at a time when Latin America was experiencing increased political tensions), and business negotiations conducted in an atmosphere of North American efficiency and Latin ambiance. So many business decisions came to be made in Miami that in 1979 Ecuadorian President Jaime Roldos proclaimed at a hemispheric conference that Miami had become the "Capital of Latin America." By the early 1980s, Miami had become so capital rich that more than 100 international institutions, including the likes of Chase International, Bank of America, Lloyd's, Bank of Tokyo, and Banco do Brasil, had rushed in to open offices there.

The drug trade behind many of the big deposits in Miami banks was hard to ignore, however. According to the U.S. Drug Enforcement Administration, 70 percent of the country's marijuana and cocaine and 90 percent of its Quaaludes come through the Miami wholesale pipeline, a business far exceeding Miami's tourism grosses of $4 billion per year. That Florida should become a drug smuggling center was an accident of geography; Colombia, the source of much of the marijuana smoked in the United States, is only a few hundred miles from Florida. Drugs came in through the hard-to-patrol 3,000-mile coastline, the Port of Miami, and Miami International Airport. A common ploy was to station a "mother ship," usually an old freighter, outside U.S. waters and then send speedboats and pleasure craft out to pick up the drugs; the boat owner would receive $50,000 for one night's work while those who loaded the drugs got $10,000 apiece. The illegal substances were then distributed throughout the country, and the cash filtered into Miami—often in the form of the dirty, crumpled, smelly bills the pushers had "earned" on the streets. The Federal Reserve System began to understand what was happening when it realized that while all other regions of the country ran short of cash, Miami always had a surplus ($5 billion in 1980). Bankers asked about their tolerance of handling such transactions responded that it was impossible to tell the difference between drug money and the assets of Latin American industrialists who bring their money to Miami because they are worried about revolutions in their own countries.

The drug sellers have added a slice of never-never land to Miami, even compared to the grossest tourist excesses of yesteryear. Stories abound of young men buying Mercedes Benz cars for $37,000 carried in shopping bags, as well as buying gold chains, condominiums, planes, emeralds, $5,000 hats, and $600 bottles of wine. There can be little question of the drug trade's partial responsibility for Miami's rising tide of violent crime—feuds, retribution killings, occasionally even the slaying of innocent bystanders. A much publicized Reagan administration crackdown, including the dispatching of federal agents from other parts of the country, and backed up by military planes and ships, hampered the Florida Connection in 1982. But federal officials candidly admitted they were only diverting drug trafficking to other states, while local observers noted that the drug money was so important to the local economy that if the effort were *too* successful there would be a considerable amount of behind-the-scenes screaming from established powers.

In 1980, 125,000 additional Cuban refugees were processed into Miami, and 92,000 settled there. The latest wave included not only the freedom-loving Cubans who had flooded into the Peruvian Embassy in Havana but hordes of mental patients, criminals, and assorted prisoners whom Castro was eager to expel from his country. The stateside problems of the Marielitos (as they were named after the Cuban bay from which they embarked) began with botched handling of their arrival by the Carter administration. Established Cuban leaders did their best to find employment and homes for the new arrivals, but it was obvious this group would have a far more difficult time of integration into U.S. life than the exiles of '59. Some older Cubans even regretted or resented their coming. For the first time, Miami developed a ghetto of poor Cubans. Two years after their arrival, half the people arrested for violent crimes in Miami were said to be Marielitos. Their arrival was the straw that broke the camel's back in terms of hospitality on the part of Dade County's Anglos. Already there had been some "Anglo flight" northward in the county as the Hispanic community expanded. Non-Hispanics resented the instrusion of Spanish language and culture, and young Anglos believed they could not find jobs without speaking Spanish. Dade County voters, with Anglos still in the majority in 1980, repealed the 1973 ordinance that made the county officially bilingual—a clear indication of Anglo resentment. (Dade County voters had earlier revealed their distaste for pluralism by repealing a gay rights ordinance following a campaign led by singer Anita Bryant.)

Aid extended to the Marielitos was particularly resented by Miami's blacks, who had never benefited from the Latin boom. Miami is not a very happy city for blacks. They first arrived in large numbers in the 1920s to work as domestics in the big hotels; since Miami lacked an industrial base, they remained tied to low-paying service jobs. Talented or lucky young blacks often went North to get educations, rarely to return. In 1980, in a black population of 280,000, there were only 32 doctors, 18 dentists, and 57 lawyers—about half the number of professionals in the comparable black community in Cleveland. Urban renewal and Interstate 95 destroyed a massive amount of low-priced housing that was never replaced, and in the public housing projects of Liberty City, fewer than 20 percent of the apartments were air conditioned. When Cubans began to own businesses in Miami, they usually hired refugees from their own country and often disqualified blacks for not speaking Spanish.

The fearsomely destructive riots that broke out in Liberty City on May 17, 1980 had nothing to do, however, with the Hispanic community. They were triggered rather by a classic Deep South occurrence—the refusal of an all-white jury in Tampa to find four Dade County policemen guilty in the death of a black insurance salesman. The chaos that followed left 18 people, including one policeman, dead. It was the worst U.S. racial disturbance since the 1960s, in a major sense even worse than the '60s because alienated black youths were now launching savage attacks on almost any Anglo who crossed their path. No significant effort was made to help the black community establish the economic base it so desperately needed, and in late December 1982, following the fatal shooting of a young black in a video arcade by a Hispanic policeman, rioting broke out in the Overtown neighborhood near the Orange Bowl.

Not surprisingly, Miami politics were deeply affected by the advent of the Hispanics. For several years, the Cubans did not take out citizenship; indeed, the Cuban colony seethed with plots and vainglorious schemes to reconquer the homeland and drive Castro from power. Eventually it became clear, however, that the Bay of Pigs had ended that option. By the 1970s many Cubans, especially the younger generation, had begun to think of themselves as Americans. Miami elected its first Hispanic mayor in 1973, Puerto Rican Maurice Ferre, and despite the dominance of the Cubans, he remained in office into the 1980s, elected by a coalition of Anglos, blacks, and Hispanics who believed that a Cuban mayor would heighten social tensions. By 1980, the elections of Mayor Ferre and two Cuban commissioners had placed Miami's government in Hispanic control.

Black political power seemed limited to one seat on the city commission. And blacks had their own refugee situation to contend with—thousands of Haitians fleeing the regime of President-for-life Jean Claude Duvalier. The "black boat people" often traveled the 900 mile journey from Haiti to Florida in small boats, some drowning along the way, or even as they approached the U.S. shore. Once they reached the U.S., the question was whether they were fleeing political repression (making them officially eligible for refugee status) or simply trying to better themselves economically (legal grounds for deportation). Some national black leaders charged that the U.S. government applied stricter standards to the Haitians than Anglos or Asians seeking political refugee status. But few Floridians were thrilled about the Haitan influx; Miami blacks themselves seemed torn between sympathy for fellow blacks and concern about increasing the size of a black labor pool already plagued by heavy unemployment.

Was the internationalization of Miami a positive development? Many Anglos and tourists viewed newly Hispanic Miami with alarm; Cubans and other Latin Americans believed they had brought spirit to a soulless place, working hard to create a new life in a new land. Mayor Ferre displayed a degree of cultural arrogance when he told a reporter, "We consider this a Latin city." But Ferre was also accurate when he pointed out to us that "had it not been for the Cubans moving in here, Miami would be a limp, sick, anemic place." Miami's decline as a resort had been apparent since the 1950s; wealthy Americans had started traveling farther south, to Caribbean islands, and downtown Miami had deteriorated badly. "Hispanization" changed all that; Miami was almost alone among "older" U.S. cities that did not lose population in the '70s. By the early '80s, Miami was enjoying full-scale renovation of its main retail core and adding huge new buildings, including a 50-story World Trade Center designed by I.M Pei, a cultural center by Philip Johnson, and a Dade County administration building by Hugh Stubbins. An elevated rapid rail transit system and an "open 24-hours-per day" zone promised to continue that vitality. In 1982, a public-private committee announced plans to revitalize the Miami River, little used since the 1960s. Miami, we might add, is flanked on the south by the exclusive, independent, and quite lovely city of Coral Gables and the once-independent town of Coconut Grove, a Bohemian-flavored enclave of winding streets and estate homes.

For a taste of what Miami might have been like without the international focus, one need only travel across Biscayne Bay to that old queen of resorts, Miami Beach. The Beach may well have celebrated its last great fling in 1968 when it hosted the Republican national convention and in 1972 when both national parties convened there. The '70s brought bankruptcies and reorganizations of the major hotels, including the gaudy, opulent Fontainbleau, billed as "the World's Greatest Resort Hotel." The Fontainbleau reopened under new management, and the Army Corps of Engineers extended the eroded beach 300 feet into the sea. The wealthy tourists were reluctant to return, however, and Miami Beach resorted to bringing in budget tours from Great Britain. The people who retire to Miami Beach today are less wealthy than in the past, and even some of the New York Jews, who viewed it as a retirement haven, have left as Hispanics have moved in. There has been enough developer interest in building condominiums to necessitate an historic preservation movement to save the Art Deco apartment buildings of the South Beach area, said to be the purest and largest such collection in the country. There is real poverty, especially among some of the elderly Jewish retirees. Yet on occasion the old magic is to be viewed—as on a summer afternoon, for example, one drives across the Bay toward the Beach, seeing the huge cumulus clouds and thunderheads blown in by the trade winds and the line of gleaming white hotels below.

Up the Gold Coast, to the Panhandle

The Florida Gold Coast, from Miami to Palm Beach, has become a multi-million-person megalopolis of seeming wall-to-wall condominiums marching up the Atlantic coastline. Traveling north the first major landmark one sees is Fort Lauderdale, which grew to national fame as the destination point for tens of thousands of college students who came to sun, frolic, and sometimes riot on its beaches. Beneath that hoopla is the fact that Lauderdale has flowered into one of the most magnificent resort and retirement cities in America. It does have its faults, especially the Galt Ocean Mile, where oceanside hotels and condominiums are packed together in tasteless fashion akin to Miami Beach. But there is also a superb six-mile stretch of public beach, acquired by farsighted city commissioners and closed forever to the developers. Moreover, starting at the center city and spreading out some 35 miles are 300 navigable canals and waterways that help to make this the yachting capital of America. The yachting crowd that made Fort Lauderdale in the postwar years, Stephen Birmingham observes, was so heavily from the industrial Midwest that Lauderdale "could have been kiddingly likened to a Cleveland-by-the-Sea."

All the yachts, forever in need of repairs or refurbishing, help sustain a thriving marine industry in Fort Lauderdale. Just to the south is Port Everglades, the deepest harbor between Norfolk and New Orleans and now port of call for many Caribbean cruise ships. Cast in much the same mold as Fort Lauderdale, but lacking its special character, are Hollywood, on its southern flank, and Pompano Beach, to the north, all sharing in the region's scarcely credible population growth as Northern vacationers and retirees pour in and everyone else goes to work servicing them. Virtually every town of Broward County experienced dual flows of migration in the '70s: from Northerners moving southward, from Dade County Anglos moving north. The population grew a spectacular 63.5 percent, to 1,014,043. Boca Raton (Spanish for "rat's mouth"), a few miles farther up the Gold Coast, had 447 inhabitants in 1930, less than 1,000 in 1950, and 49,505 by 1980.

The northern anchor of the Gold Coast lies in the vicinity of that most aristocratic of all American resorts, Palm Beach. It is actually an island, 14 miles long and no more than 2 miles wide, occupied by only 9,729 persons year-round but several times that during the high winter season. It was just a narrow sandspit, much of it swamp, when the inimitable Henry Flagler came upon it in 1890 and decided this would be the place to build his ultimate resort hotel. Flagler's hotel, the Royal Poinciana, was the largest wooden structure in the world and must have been quite a sight to see; it is gone now, but his second hotel, the Breakers, still stands, truly one of the most magnificent hotels in the world.

Palm Beach is not quite as ostentatious as in the old days when as many as 80 private railroad cars would arrive there for the winter. But wealth incomprehensible to an average man still winters here, and so do some names of European royalty that always make us flinch when we read of Palm Beach as the acme of the American Dream. Palm Beach divides itself quite strictly into WASP and Jewish communities; each has its own country club, with initiation fees at the Jewish Palm Beach Country Club at $40,000, and admittance only if you have a proven record of philanthropy. People who have visited Palm Beach have noted that it is incorrect to ask "What do you do?" since many people do nothing, at least for a living. The sweat of many brows made this place, however: the property on the diminutive island was valued at $12 billion in the early 1980s.

The gerontocracy rules Palm Beach. The average age at the Palm Beach Country Club is said to be 72.5 years. After the death of Marjorie Merriweather Post, the grande dame of Palm Beach society, Mrs. Rose Kennedy became the most famous of all Palm Beach home owners. But Palm Beach is not as immutable as many would like to have it. The American progressive income tax has made it hard for anyone but foreigners to afford the huge, old mansions, and there has been an influx of condominiums lining the beaches. There are constant fears of kidnapping; if police receive a "code red" signal, all three bridges to the mainland go up, and squad cars cut the coastal road.

Across Lake Worth lies West Palm Beach, the city Flagler built "for my help." Almost a quarter of West Palm Beach's 62,530 people are black, many descendants of Flagler's servant class. It used to be that a black caught on Palm Beach at night without a good excuse would face a beating or a night in jail. But West Palm Beach has a lot of other thoughts on its mind, including the making of money from its own resorts, agriculture, and the payrolls of advanced technological firms located nearby (Pratt Whitney, Minneapolis Honeywell, RCA, etc.). The city is also home of that extraordinary "newspaper," the *National Enquirer*.

North of the neon-lined Gold Coast, Florida's flank to the Atlantic is less densely populated, but the growth figures are barely credible. St. Lucie County, surrounding Fort Pierce, for example, grew 71.5 percent in the 1970s. The only Atlantic Coast county exhibiting apparent "normalcy" in that decade was Brevard, which grew a mere 18.7 percent, to 272,959. But it deserved a rest, for Brevard County is the home of Cape Canaveral, and during the early years of space exploration it was the fastest-growing county in all America—from 23,653 in 1950 to 111,435 in 1960 and 230,006 in 1970.

A delightful old lighthouse has been flashing warnings to ships at sea for over a century out at the tip of Cape Canaveral. From time immemorial, this had been a place of scrub oak and grassy dunes, mangrove swamps and quiet, sunny isolation. That era ended forever when the government in 1948 determined it would turn the flat, sandy land carved into irregular pieces by the Indian and Banana rivers into a base for launching long-range guided missiles. The first missile launch took place in 1950, and thus began a series of launchings that would make Cape Canaveral one of the most famous spots on earth, from the earliest Explorer missile to counter the Soviet's Sputnik to such unmanned satellites and space probes as Echo, Tiros, Telstar, and Early Bird, to the Redstone missile carrying Alan Shepard, Jr., America's first man in space, to the Saturn V carrying Neil A. Armstrong and his crew to a moon landing on July 30, 1969, and on April 12, 1981, the first reusable space shuttle.

The burgeoning Brevard population was due not only to NASA's own personnel, but workers for the multitude of contractors laboring on various stages of the rockets—companies such as Boeing, North American Rockwell, Bendix, RCA, McDonnell Douglas, IBM, General Electric, and Martin Marietta. Eventually, however, the Cape found itself forced to share the glory of the space age with NASA's Manned Spacecraft Center in Houston, which directed most phases of manned spacecraft planning and direction. The Cape was reduced to playing the role of a glorious launching pad.

In a national paroxysm of memorialitis after President Kennedy's assassination, Cape Canaveral was summarily renamed Cape Kennedy, thus expunging from the maps a name dating from the earliest Spanish explorations. But local residents of all political persuasions decided they wanted the Cape's old name back. In 1973, while the Kennedy Space Center retained its new name, the federal government ordered that the Cape would again have the name it is believed Ponce de Leon himself assigned it—Cape Canaveral.

The largest city in the world, in terms of area—827 square miles—is Jacksonville (pop. 540,898), the famed "Gateway" to Florida in the heyday of the passenger railroads. Jacksonville is an oddity, isolated in the northeast corner of the state, a place tourists fly over rather than view from train or car. It serves the back country of northern Florida and not much more. It is dominated by the conservative attitude of nearby southern Georgia. It has grown less than any other area of Florida.

Bad times visited Jacksonville in the '60s as whites moved out, the schools were disaccredited, and city officials indicted for shady insurance dealings. Citizen leadership prompted founding of a local government study commission, which proposed merging Jacksonville with surrounding Duval County in a consolidated metropolitan government. The measure carried, 2-to-1, in a 1967 referendum. In a twinkling, Jacksonville grew from 30 square miles to her present size. Under Mayor Hans Tanzler, a raw-boned, six-foot, five-inch dynamo, the city moved on race relations (once among the worst in the state), improved fire and police protection and ambulance service, and cleaned up the horribly polluted St. Johns River, which bisects the city. Rebuilding of the moldering downtown, which had actually begun a few years before, proceeded apace, so that both banks of the river came to gleam with new buildings. Aided by ownership of the local electric utility, Jacksonville had the lowest taxes of any major U.S. city. But the tax benefits alone did not lure business, Tanzler's successor, Jake Godbold, told us. The city finally decided to concentrate on the arts and riverfront development to create a city of real drawing power.

Until his death, in 1981, the most powerful man in Jacksonville and arguably in Florida was Edward W. Ball, head of the billion-dollar Alfred I. duPont estate, long an archconservative force in Florida politics. "Mr. Ball," as even longtime friends called him, had the good fortune to be the brother of a schoolteacher who married Alfred I. duPont and came into control of $30 million in duPont money. In time this snowballed into what *Fortune* called "one of the great private treasures in America," an estate with $1 billion or more in Florida timberland, the Florida East Coast Railway, a telephone company, and 30 banks. Once described by a *Miami Herald* writer as "arch-conservative, segregationist, antilabor, antibureaucrat, anti–big government," Ball was a potent force in Florida politics, the leading figure in getting Florida to adopt a sales tax instead of any kind of income tax. Indeed, his commitment to keeping wealth in the hands of a few lives on in the state's regressive tax structure.

Whatever feeling of the Old South is left in Florida, in the look of the land, in race relations and politics, may be found in northern Florida, from Jacksonville west and across the panhandle. Here are miles and miles of Dixie-style piney woods and a great pulp farming industry, tobacco and peanut farms, and still those languorous rivers of yore. But like the rest of the South, this region is changing.

Take the case of Gainesville (pop. 81,371), home of the University of Florida. The old Southern trappings are there. Visit in the springtime, for instance, and you will find dogwoods, redbud trees, and azaleas in bloom and new leaves pushing out the moss-laden oaks that shade the residential streets. But the university has shaken off its reputation for mediocrity. And who would have expected Gainesville to proclaim itself the "solar capital of the world" or to be home to Hazel Henderson, the British-born leftist economist/environmentalist and aspirer to the mantle of Margaret Mead?

Tallahassee, Florida's charming old capital city, renowned for its parklike hills lined with giant oaks and antebellum mansions, has also hummed in recent years with huge condominium and recreational projects and thousands of new hotel rooms—and the familiar problems of urban sprawl. Tallahassee's metro area, including Leon and Wakulla counties, grew 45.9 percent in the 1970s, to 159,542. Tallahassee's Capitol Center, consisting of the state capitol and several other big government buildings, has a class many states fail to match. Tallahassee is also home to Florida A&M University, a remnant of the old system of segregated higher education for blacks, which managed to develop a nationally renowned business school even as it faced declining enrollments after major state schools were opened up to blacks.

Moving out across the panhandle, the Old South flavor is leavened with more cosmopolitanism, perhaps because it has miles and miles of beautiful white sand and with it the tourist trade. There is also a large military component (Navy at the big airbase at Pensacola, Air Force at Fort Walton Beach), heavy lumbering, and small farming.

Pensacola, so far west it seems within a stone's throw of Alabama, is another one of those Florida cities with a long Spanish history but little to show for it. In fact, there is no special Spanish flavor to the city at all. The Naval Air Station has been the mainstay of Pensacola's economy since 1914, permitting slow, steady growth to a 1980 metropolitan area total of 289,782.

Central Florida: Orlando, Disney World, et al.

Central Florida is preeminently citrus Florida, mile after mile of orange and sometimes tangerine and grapefruit orchards, the world's greatest concentration of those fruits. Its largest city is Orlando, grown from a late-19th-century trading post on a cow range to a booming metropolis of some 128,394 people with 572,305 more in its immediate hinterland. Citrus and the prosperity of a well-to-do retirement center gave Orlando its initial thrust; military bases, electronics, aerospace, the proximity to Cape Canaveral 65 miles distant, and Disney World 16 miles away have continued to propel it forward.

Physically, Orlando is far more attractive than many of the more celebrated coastal areas, the city proper and the land for miles around dotted with blue lakes contrasting with the evergreen foliage in gently rolling countryside. High buildings, including the Florida headquarters of several large insurance firms, have given focus to the sprawling city proper. Among the technologically oriented companies that have fueled the local economy are Martin Marietta's aerospace division, General Electric, Xerox, and Control Data.

On a huge drained swamp to the west rises perhaps the greatest American monument ever to the gods of fun and escape: Walt Disney World. The great Disney himself, before his death in 1966, personally set in motion plans for this project. Disney World is in the genre of the original California Disneyland, complete with fairyland castles (Cinderella's castle is 18 stories high with gold turrets), the plaster mountains (Space Mountain is 30 stories high), the animated animals, the monorails, the boat rides. But Walt Disney World (27,400 acres) is vastly larger than Disneyland (230 acres) and it is far more than an amusement park. It has several hotels (American, Asian, Polynesian, Venetian), three golf courses, bridle trails, picnic grounds, lagoons and a big lake, beaches and campgrounds on a 2,500-acre Vacation Kingdom, a 100-acre Magic Kingdom with six fantasylands, ranging from Frontierland to Tomorrowland.

An early environmentalist, Disney ordered his planners to preserve as much of Disney World in its natural state as possible. Cars must be parked while visitors ride around in vehicles powered by steam or compressed natural gas. Waste from hotels and restaurants is collected through underground pneumatic tubes, baled, and burned in an incinerator that emits almost no smoke. Disney did not repeat the mistake he had made at Disneyland, where the small amusement park is surrounded by parasitic non-Disney enterprises. Frontmen bought up thousands of acres on all sides to protect the main project. The Disney operatives also won many concessions from the dazzled Florida legislature, including powers for Disney's chartered town, Buena Vista, which exceed those of any county commission in the state.

From the day that Disney World opened, it was clear that Orlando and Orange County's conservative free-enterprise-minded politicians could not handle such massive growth. Massive traffic jams, housing shortages, crime, and higher taxes for longtime residents became part of the Orlando way of life. The county's history began to be measured in B.D. and A.D., indicating Before and After Disney. Since they could not locate near the Disney property, enterpreneurs located amusement parks some miles distant. The amusement parks, combined with electronics, transportation, and construction ballooned the county work force while the number of people coming annually to Disney World reached 13 million by the early 1980s. A total of 20 million was expected after Disney opened in 1982 the late Walt's ultimate vision, an Experimental Prototype Community of Tomorrow (EPCOT), a futuristic toytown for adults depicting man's evolution and the world of tomorrow in spectacular pavillions and squeaky-clean glory. Central Florida was, in fact, rapidly gaining ground as a tourist destination while south Florida, the traditional fun-in-the-sun capital, suffered from headlines about crime and racial strife. South Florida remained, however, the larger generator of tourism revenue.

A superabundance of economic growth failed to solve Orlando's social ills; in fact, it seemed to produce more. In the early 1970s, the Orlando black community—some 40,000 people—had developed strong leadership and begun to work well with the city's white establishment. So it came as a great shock in 1980 when West Orlando blacks rioted, following the disturbances in Miami and Tampa. The amusement park economy provided only bottom-rung "bed maker" type jobs, and few blacks had sufficient education to find employment in the electronics firms. Only one black served on the Orlando city commission, none on the school board, and blacks complained about police brutality and poor quality housing.

If Disney World was the ultimate in calculated and programmed amusement for the millions, Cypress Gardens—at Winter Haven, about 60 miles southwest on the way to Tampa—was Florida's best indigenous specimen of how one used publicity, cheesecake, and pure nerve to make something worth millions out of virtually nothing. In this case, the nothing was a tangled muck swamp that the engineers had given up on draining in the 1930s; the something is Cypress Gardens, one of the most fabulously successful tourist attractions in the U.S.A. and the creation of a single master promoter, Dick Pope. Pope and his imitators are the type who make it possible to state seriously: *Florida is the state man made.* He got Cypress Gardens built with WPA men working at one dollar a day to create walkways and floral displays around a grove of cypress trees growing out of a lake. Pope's real genius was in publicity. As soon as the gardens opened, mountains of pictures of speedboats on the lake and pretty girls posing beside cypress and flowers, and purple prose about the "inconceivably beautiful gardens" were flowing to the nation's newspapers —which, lacking anything better for their space, printed without charge. Hundreds of newsreels featured Pope and his gardens, with every excuse from the crowning of some kind of queen (he once crowned seven queens in a day) to water-skiing extravaganzas. Then there were numerous movies filmed at the gardens, television shows, and celebrity guests by the hundreds. When we met Pope in 1969, a bouncy, extroverted enthusiast in a rainbow-colored sports jacket, he summed up a lot of the Florida psyche in eight words: "If it ain't fun, the hell with it." He and his family continued to operate Cypress Gardens under that maxim into the 1980s.

Down the Sun Coast, on to Key West

The big population center on Florida's western flank centers on Tampa and St. Petersburg, the northern anchor of the so-called Sun Coast, which covers some 120 miles on the Gulf of Mexico, down through Bradenton and Sarasota to Fort Myers. The area grew 44.2 percent in the 1970s, adding no less than 480,943 people in one decade.

Tampa, western Florida's biggest town, is essentially an industrial and distribution center, quite unlike most Florida cities. There are big, masculine industries such as beer brewing, steel, and cigar making. The port of Tampa is one of the most important in the Southeastern U.S. and the world's largest export point for phosphate, which is mined only 40 miles away. Tampa is not particularly a magnet for retirees; its growth has been due to its attractiveness to business—the absence of a city or state income tax or strong labor unions.

Fortune began to smile on Tampa in the 1880s with the discovery of big phosphate reserves nearby, the arrival of Henry Plant's South Florida Railroad in 1884, and the appearance of Vincente Martinez Ybor's cigar factory, which moved lock, stock, and barrel from Key West and brought a dash of Spanish-Cuban culture, which endures to this day. Tampa shared in the real-estate boom of the 1920s, got in on the floor of the citrus industry as a shipping and processing point, boomed as a shipbuilding center in World War II, and has since added a multitude of small industries to supplement beer, cigars, and the port. Florida's biggest shrimp fleet harbors at Tampa, and just south of town is MacDill, one of the country's largest Air Force bases.

Probably due to its industrial Democratic heritage, Tampa became Florida's first urban renewal city, leading to a great facelifting for the old waterfront, where railroad lines and old warehouses were torn out to make room for a $4.5 million convention center, a splendid new library, and a hotel. The central business district has been rejuvenated with new high-rise office buildings and hotels; Ybor City, which still has America's largest cigar factory, has been revived as a center of Spanish culture. Tampa practiced strict racial segregation to the 1950s, but then local politics moderated and Tampa accepted the various federal antipoverty programs. The city's leaders displayed a free-enterprise outlook when President Reagan announced that federal urban aid would be cut in the early 1980s. The costs of growth—water and sewer system construction, transportation facilities—could be passed on to developers, local officials told Rochelle Stanfield of *National Journal*, but the community was unlikely to volunteer higher taxes to help the poor.

Basking in the sun on the seaward side of Tampa Bay lies St. Petersburg, removed from Tampa by just a few miles of open water but its diametric opposite by almost any standard. Tampa is a rich ethnic stew; St. Petersburg has people from everywhere in the U.S.A., but is predominantly white, middle-class America. The *Tampa Tribune*, property of the Richmond, Virginia, papers, is generally conservative; the *St. Petersburg Times*, owned by publisher Nelson Poynter until his death in 1978, is liberal and sometimes downright crusading.

St. Petersburg's role as a retirement-vacation center has been secure since the 1880s, when the *Journal of the American Medical Association* said the climate made it the healthiest place in the world to live. How that judgment could have been made only a decade after nearby Tampa was ravaged by yellow fever remains something of a mystery—but then, the city has always been expert in the art of self-promotion. In 1918, St. Petersburg became the first city in the world to hire a press agent. In the 1960s, the city tried to downpedal its reputation as a geriatric heaven, emphasizing instead the glowing opportunities for investment, family vacation, and business relocation by removing a number of the fabled green benches where the old folks may congregate to exchange reminiscences and snooze in the sun. There is still so much to attract the senior citizens, however—shuffleboard courts, afternoon band concerts in Williams Park, and quick, cheap blood pressure tests in local drug stores— that some people continue to refer to St. Pete as "God's Waiting Room" and "The Last Resort."

Depending on their economic status, St. Pete's elderly are to be found in stately old hotels, $100,000 retirement homes in posh sections, dingy downtown rooming houses, or seemingly endless rows of little white cottages surrounded by palm trees and tropical flowers. The big middle-class elderly vote was an early foundation of the Republican revival, which brought GOP control of most local government positions and, in the 1954 election, Florida's first Republican Congressman of the 20th century.

One activity in which the Tampa Bay area seems to have an edge on the rest of Florida is baseball spring training. St. Petersburg has the St. Louis Cardinals and New York Mets, Tampa the Cincinnati Reds, Clearwater the Phillies, Dunedin the Toronto Blue Jays, and nearby Sarasota the Chicago White Sox.

Sarasota used to have another form of winter training: the circus. Now the great Ringling Bros., Barnum and Bailey has migrated a few miles south to the town of Venice, where animals, trainers, clowns, acrobats, and all the rest go through their paces each winter before heading north in March. In matters of arts and culture Sarasota seems to lead all Florida.

Despite all the mind-numbing growth statistics we have recited in this chapter, the most incredible is reserved for Fort Myers, farther down the West Coast on the Caloosahatchee River. This is where Midwesterners bought land at $20 per month for many years and have now arrived to live on it. In the 1970s, more than 100,000 people arrived in the Fort Myers–Cape Coral area, a growth rate of *95.1 percent*, the highest for any metropolitan area in the nation. Retirement here must be a dream come true for many of the blue-collar Midwesterners, providing they can stomach the sprawl development of hamburger stands and gas stations. Nor is this area just for middle-income folk: in 1982, we discovered a luxury mobile home park selling units in the $70,000 to $90,000 range. It was, of course, an "adults only" park—children not welcome. If the model of a graying America is being written in these southern reaches, a certain oppressiveness and selfishness must be reported. Cape Coral, for example, has ordinances prohibiting parking a pickup truck in the driveway overnight, leaving a garage door open, or letting the lawn grow above a certain height. Although Lee County has triple the national average of people over 60, the number of school children increased by 50 percent in a decade as "service" families moved in to provide for the elderly —only to find those same elderly extremely reluctant to approve new bond issues for school construction.

Fort Myers has an extraordinary daily newspaper, the Gannett-owned *News-Press*. In 1978, the paper spent eight months studying Fort Myers' black community, home of almost 12,000 people. Whites in Fort Myers, the *News-Press* reported, still saw blacks in terms of one street, Anderson, an unsightly maze of bars, vacant lots, and dilapidated housing. Whites had yet to recognize the reality of black wage earners, church-goers, taxpayers, and family raisers.

Collier County, directly to the south, had only 85,791 people in 1980, most of them concentrated around the posh retirement community of Naples. But the county grew an amazing 125 percent in the '70s, and it was not hard to divine where Florida's next great growth splurge might occur. After Naples, all that remains of the southwest coast are swamplands, including the Ten Thousand Islands (of mangrove) and Everglades National Park.

Then, across Florida Bay, lie the Keys, dotted with resort areas of every stripe. The fever pitch of recreation-area development has threatened to engulf the Keys; in 1972, a dredge-and-fill moratorium was imposed to prevent ecological disaster along the dazzling coral reefs. Key Largo, on the northern end of the Keys, offers visitors the country's first continental underseas park (Pennelamp Coral Reef State Park) and the luxurious accommodations of the Ocean Reef Club, a combination hotel, yachtsmen's haven, and vacation-retirement home development, where the pains of recession are never felt.

Set at the Keys' southern tip is the old city of Key West (pop. 24,292). Key West's real days of glory were around 1880, when with 9,890 people this was the largest city in Florida. Prosperity came from being the world's largest cigar manufacturing center and from profits of the "salvage" crews, which used to "rescue" ships wrecked on the reefs and shoals surrounding the Keys. Eventually, both these sources of income dried up: the salvaging by government decree, cigar producing by Ybor's move to Tampa. But Key West kept the ethnic mix of its early years: many Cubans, "Conchs" who trace their ancestry back to Cockney English settlers in the Bahamas, Yankee sailing men, Virginia merchants, and a number of native Bahamians.

A big factor in putting Key West back on the map after World War II—outside of the Overseas Highway, a prerequisite to meaningful tourism—was the publicity stemming from President Harry Truman's frequent visits to his "little White House" there. Since the 1960s, Key West's location and reputation for tolerance have made it a destination first for hippies, then gays, and wealthy urbanites seeking vacation homes. But only a few remain for very long. Key West's population dropped in both the '60s and '70s. As one local fellow told us, "Key West is for people who have made it or are never going to."

THE
GREAT PLAINS
STATES

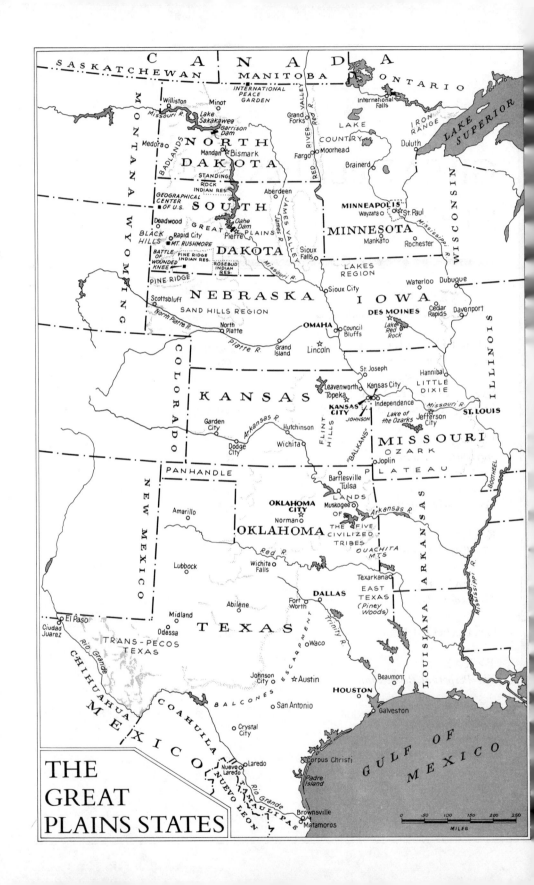

THE
GREAT
PLAINS STATES

MINNESOTA

The Successful Society Challenged

Search america from sea to sea and you will not find a state that has offered as close a model to the ideal of the successful society as Minnesota. The state has, of course, its failings. Yet in all, it is a one in which people can take justifiable pride. Minnesota leaders, from Harold Stassen and Hubert Humphrey to Walter Mondale and David Durenberger, have played a prominent role in national life, far out of proportion to their state's modest 2 percent of the national population. The Minnesota political structure remains open, issue-oriented, responsive. Questioning of how things are done—up to a very high level—is not only tolerated but encouraged. The state government has been a national leader in services delivered to people, and the quality of delivery has generally been so high that Minnesota citizens and corporations have been willing to pay a rather high tax bill. Few states have exceeded Minnesota in the quality and extent of the education offered in the schools and colleges; none appears to provide health care of comparable quality.

Through the 1970s, Minnesota enjoyed years of strong and steady economic growth—a trend reversed by the deep recession of the early 1980s, with uncertain prospects for the future. The mainstays were the brainpower industries that emerged in the electronic age, along with the familiar mainstays of farming, milling, and mining. (The greatest concern of the early '80s was that the decimation of the national steel industry would bring the state's Iron Range, always more a colony of Cleveland than an integral part of Minnesota, down with it.) Minnesota's greatest strength remained the clear focus of economic, political, and cultural leadership in her Twin Cities of Minneapolis and St. Paul, whose great locally controlled industries stoutly resisted the siren call of the national conglomerates to create an extraordinarily durable and strong decision-making center on questions affecting the state future.

Again and again, national "quality of life" studies star Minnesota. The state's well-advertised sub-arctic winters and summer heat waves notwithstanding, young people rarely choose to leave for lack of opportunity. And again, one is driven to the question, what *does* this state have going for it? Perhaps the simplest answer is the most convincing: Minnesotans appear, in fact as well as theory, to control their own destiny. No single industrial cabal, no bank group, no patronage-hungry courthouse, no single liberal or conservative interest group or labor union controls the state. Ask Minnesotans who "runs" their state, and you get a blank stare in response. The special interest groups lobby in the legislature: railroads, private power companies, labor and business groups, religious organizations, for instance. But none is consistently successful, and the crucial decisions of a public nature are made through the political process with few invisible powers lurking behind the throne. In sum, Minnesota is a deceptively simple example of how a democratic society should work.

Admirers of the Minnesota success story should not be too quick to compare other states unfavorably with it, however. Minnesota's situation has been eased by its longtime affluence and the homogeneity of its population. In 1980 Minnesota was still only 2.09 percent black and Hispanic and 0.9 percent Indian, and the state had not had to devote substantial resources to achieve racial integration or cope with racial strife. Despite its homogeneity, Minnesota had a hard time achieving consensus on the controversial social issues that erupted in the 1970s. The divisive issue of abortion tore at the fabric of both the Democratic Farmer-Labor and the Republican party. This most pro-government of states quickly rescinded its medicaid payments for abortions for poor women as soon as the U.S. Supreme Court made that possible. While Minnesota gays elected more of their number as delegates to the 1980 Democratic National Convention than counterparts in any other state, St. Paul voters in 1978 trooped to the polls to *invalidate* a gay rights ordinance. Environmentalists' efforts to curb the use of snowmobiles and motorboats in the northern Boundary Waters Canoe Area led to an agonizing statewide debate that ended only when the U.S. Congress banned motorboats on 60 percent of the lakes.

The acrimony surrounding these issues seemed unusual for Minnesota, but not if one had read *Main Street,* Sinclair Lewis' 1920 novel of small-town Minnesota life, to which the conflicts resembled a real-life sequel.* The novel's heroine, Carol Kennicott, a young bride, vows to fight for liberal reforms in the mythical Gopher Prairie. But more importantly she raises her children to develop their thoughts, "not take Gopher Prairie's version of them." Pointing to her daughter's head, Carol asks her conservative doctor husband, "Do you see that object on the pillow? Do you know what it is? It's a bomb to blow up smugness. If you Tories were wise, you wouldn't arrest anarchists; you'd arrest all these children while they're asleep in their cribs. Think what that baby will see and meddle with before she dies in the year 2000! She may see an industrial union of the whole world, she may see aeroplanes going to Mars." After interviewing many Minnesotans, we cannot help but believe that millions of Minnesota children must have come under the same mixture of liberal and conservative influences over the last 60 years. A certain smugness, insularity, desire to keep "other" kinds of folk at arm's length is to be felt. But the insurrectionary forces that combatted the *Main Street* psyche have proven powerful indeed. The result is an intelligent, dynamic, politically active society.

---

*Other famous literary figures from Minnesota have included F. Scott Fitzgerald and Ole Edvard Rolvaag, father of the DFL governor of the 1920s, Karl Rolvaag. The elder Rolvaag's *Giants in the Earth* was one of the most powerful novels ever written about pioneer life on the Plains.

Ethnic Roots and Party Politics

Trace Minnesota ethnic and political history, and the mystery surrounding the state character begins to dissipate. Here is a state in which government has traditionally been seen as an instrument for achieving public good, not an oppressive or patronage-ridden mechanism. From the first years, Minnesota's dominant ethnic strain was Northern (American Yankee, Scandinavian, German), and her leading religions Protestant. Achieving statehood in 1858, Minnesota was the first to offer troops to the Union side. Republicanism became the natural order of the day; until the New Deal, Minnesota never once voted for a Democratic presidential candidate, and Republicans won 30 of 35 elections for governor.

Minnesota's Republicanism, however, was remarkably progressive. In the wake of the Civil War, a massive inflow of literate, liberal Swedes and Norwegians naturally allied themselves with the Yankee Protestant element of the Republican party that was opposed to slavery and liquor. Numerically, the combinations of Yankees and Scandinavians easily outvoted the Democratic party, supported by German Catholics, the Irish, and after 1890, East European immigrants brought in to man the forestry and mining industries of the north.

Most importantly, the Republicans found ways to bend government to meet the needs and problems of laborers and particularly the Scandinavian wheat farmers, who were often caught in a price squeeze and blamed their plight on warehouse and commission merchants and the railroads. Discontented farmers and laborers responded to movements designed to help them, but the Republicans took the steam out of the radicals by enacting a state-enforced system of grading and inspection, regulation of railroads, freight and elevators, and the first mandatory statewide primary. The Republicans also prosecuted the Northern Securities Company, a giant scheme to monopolize control of the railroads engineered by Pierpont Morgan, Edward H. Harriman, and others. One result of this responsiveness of an established political party was that Minnesota abjured the initiative and referendum and other Populist-era devices used by people to check governments they did not trust; this left responsibility squarely in the hands of the regularly elected legislature, and Minnesota's is still one of the most powerful and sensitive to public demand in the country today. (In 1980—at the very peak of nationwide disillusionment with politicians and of voters "taking things into their own hands"—Minnesotans had an opportunity to vote on a proposed initiative and referendum system in their state. The measure did not pass.)

The fathers of modern Minnesota politics are Harold E. Stassen, whose emergence in the 1930s put the state's Republicans on a clear moderate track, and Hubert H. Humphrey, who was to merge the hitherto-anemic Democrats with the fiery Farmer-Labor party born in the populist struggles of the 'teens against greedy packing plants and other corporate powers. Stassen is generally remembered by most Americans as the quixotic, perenially unsuccessful candidate for president of the United States, governor of Pennsylvania, or mayor of Philadelphia; his downfall, born of over-weaning ambition, must be considered a poignant personal-political tragedy. But in the Minnesota of 1938, this big, sandy-haired, hard-thinking man of just 31 years was a godsend for his Republican party—and state government. As governor, Stassen cleaned up the mess left by an inept Farmer-Labor governor and instituted comprehensive civil service. This fundamental reform has transformed the nature of Minnesota politics, making it a highly honorable profession in which citizens participate as willingly as in a United Fund drive or PTA; there simply are no "bosses," and virtually no one goes into Minnesota politics out of a patronage motive. By taking politics out of the back room and engaging thousands of men and women in political activity—among them Warren Burger, future Chief Justice of the United States—Stassen made the government process in Minnesota a superior instrument of the people's will. Stassen and his moderate-liberal Republican successors in the governorship held sway for 16 years (1939–55) and made significant advances in welfare, conservation, and mental health.

In 1944, a young political science professor at Macalester College named Hubert H. Humphrey took the lead in persuading the Democrats and the Farmer-Laborites to merge, arguing that as long as they stayed divided, the Republicans would be assured of victory. This merger joined into a single party the urban German, Irish, and Polish Catholics who had been the mainstay of the old Democratic party and the rural Scandinavian Lutherans whose support had been the backbone of the Farmer-Labor party; it also combined conservative Democrats with left-wing elements, although the less radical, anti-Communist faction won control under Humphrey, who was elected to the U.S. Senate in 1948 after serving two terms as mayor of Minneapolis.

In the succeeding years, the DFL offered a series of "stars" for public office, all either students or faculty associates of Humphrey at the University of Minnesota or other academic institutions. Many rose to national prominence: Governor Orville Freeman, who later served as Secretary of Agriculture during the entire Kennedy-Johnson period in Washington; Eugene McCarthy, a representative from 1949 to 1959 and then senator until 1971; Donald M. Fraser, representative from 1963 until 1978 and then mayor of Minneapolis; and Walter F. Mondale, Minnesota attorney general, U.S. senator from 1964 until 1976, and vice president under Jimmy Carter.

None of Humphrey's protégés, however, came close to competing with "the happy warrior" in governmental accomplishment as senator and as vice president under Lyndon Johnson during the passage of the Great Society legislation. Humphrey first rose to national attention in 1948 with an impassioned civil rights speech before the Democratic National Convention; though he never became majority leader of the U.S. Senate, he guided the landmark Civil Rights Act of 1964 to passage and was the father of such monumental legislative enactments as Medicare for the aged under Social Security, the Peace Corps, the Arms Control and Disarmament Agency, many parts of the National Defense Education Act, the Food for Peace program, and the Wilderness Act.

Humphrey's election as vice president elevated him to the heights of national prestige. But from there it was mostly downhill: the challenge from his old Senate colleague McCarthy to President Johnson and Humphrey over the Vietnam War (which Humphrey defended, partly from conviction, partly because of his tie to Johnson), the tumultuous Democratic National Convention in Chicago and eventual defeat for the Humphrey-Muskie ticket nationally, though it won Minnesota with ease. Reelected to McCarthy's old Senate seat in 1970, Humphrey could not resist a 1972 try for the presidency even when his brand of big government liberalism was going out of style. Humphrey lost the nomination to South Dakota Sen. George McGovern. In 1976, Humphrey even considered one more try for the presidency but settled for another reelection to the Senate, which Minnesotans awarded him despite confirmation that he was suffering from cancer. It is a testimony to Humphrey's career that his long illness, and death in January 1978, were marked by laudatory declarations from liberals and staunch conservatives alike, and not just in Minnesota, but from one end of America to another. There was even a measure of reevaluation of Humphrey by members of the '60s generation who had, sadly, known him not as a civil rights warrior but as an apologist for the detested conflict in Southeast Asia.

The death of Humphrey, the DFL's founder and perennial unifier, revealed the party's deep schisms. By coincidence, both Senate seats and the governorship were held by DFLers, and on election day 1978 the Republicans seized control of all three posts. The DFL's divisions were thrown into boldest relief in the contest for Humphrey's old seat. The party had become divided between ultra liberals (pro-environment, pro-gun control, freedom of choice on abortion, and pro-gay rights); moderates (old-time DFLers, still the source of most statewide candidates); and on the right, "pro-lifers," also known as anti-abortionists, including Catholics and conservative rural folk. These forces were at each other's throats in the 1978 primary, creating such deep Democratic wounds that the party could not recuperate and watched with horror as Republicans Dave Durenberger and Rudy Boschwitz fell heir to the old Humphrey and McCarthy Senate seats while Republican U.S. Rep. Albert Quie was elected governor. It was the first time since the 1960s that the Republicans had registered strongly in a Minnesota election. Sadly for the Republicans, it was not to be a particularly long-lived recovery. Quie soon committed a form of political hari-kari, plunging Minnesota into a form of supply-side economics (including income tax indexing) just before the economically disastrous recession of the early '80s. So rapidly did his stature slip that he did not even try to win reelection in 1982. The DFL was able to recover sufficiently to carry Minnesota for the Carter-Mondale ticket in 1980 and retain both legislative houses in the 1980 and 1982 elections, returning a Democrat (Rudy Perpich) to the governor's chair in 1982.

By the '80s Republicans had a party machinery firmly in conservative hands —a great change from the days when Minnesota Republicans were among the first and few to line up for Nelson Rockefeller for president, or when Quie, as a congressman, had been one of the Republicans' most prominent education and antipoverty advocates. The power of the Republican conservatives, however, continued to be held in check by Minnesota's essential liberalism and by socially progressive Republican corporate executives, important to the GOP in several roles, including fund-raising. The most important long-term outcome of the watershed 1978 election might eventually prove to be Durenberger's election to the Senate. Equipped with a razor-sharp mind, Durenberger quickly made a name for himself as a thoughtful Senate moderate, willing to buck a Republican president on matters of principle. One of his specialties was federal system reform, an issue on which he became the most insightful and original figure in Congress. Even in the strong Democratic year of 1982, Durenberger was able to win reelection to a full term. The man he defeated, 35-year-old Mark Dayton, was heir to the Dayton-Hudson department store fortune and son-in-law of John D. Rockefeller III. Dayton forked out more than $7 million of family money in his unsuccessful effort to buy himself a Senate seat—a U.S. Record.

The Economy: Adaptive, Diversified

While Minnesota's liberal traditions are based on a sound economy, it might not have been so. The state was hit hard by the Great Depression and might well have become an economic backwater after World War II, having depleted its natural resources of timber and iron ore to a staggering degree. Geographically, it was at the far end of the Midwestern "manufacturing belt." Milling virtually disappeared as a major Minnesota industry after 1950, moving eastward toward the point of consumption.

Yet instead of declining, the Minnesota economy moved forward with vigor. For natural resources, the state substituted intelligence-devouring activities and industry. Finance, insurance, and services boomed. National and international markets and connections were built by Honeywell, manufacturers of computers, thermostats, and aerospace components; Minnesota Mining and Manufacturing (3M), which had started with the world's worst sandpaper but then developed Scotch Tape, photo duplicating equipment, and myriad related products; and Control Data, in the electronics field. At the same time, the traditional industries began to adapt to changing economic conditions. With high-grade iron ore deposits exhausted, Minnesota scientists found a way to convert low-grade ore-bearing rock (known as taconite) into high-grade concentrates. The great agribusiness firms (General Mills, Pillsbury, Cargill, Peavey, etc.) kept their home offices in the Twin Cities, diversifying from milling into other consumer foods and even unrelated products.

Considering its geographic location and relatively small population (4,075,970 in 1980, up 7 percent in a decade), Minnesota is the home of a phenomenal number of major industries. Some companies listed on the New York Stock Exchange have their headquarters in Minnesota. The state is home to Northwest Airlines and, despite the move of Burlington Northern to Seattle, still a great railhead for all commerce with the Great Plains and

Pacific Northwest. Minneapolis is headquarters of one of the country's most aggressive retailers, Dayton-Hudson, and of Investors Diversified Services, one of the world's largest mutual fund conglomerates. Two bank holding companies in the Twin Cities (Northwest Bank Corporation and First Bank Systems) hold sway over most of the banks in Minnesota and North Dakota, a substantial share of the banks in South Dakota, and even the largest bank in Des Moines, Iowa.*

There are theories aplenty to explain Minnesota's vigorous economic base, ranging from the ethnic mix and the Yankee's early bent for advanced education to the benefits of having the population, business, and intellectual power of the state concentrated in the single Twin Cities area. A relevant factor was Minnesota's history of small economic units—farmers and small businesses—without a single dominant industrial interest, and with extremely little out-of-state ownership. Pride in maintaining that local ownership led town leaders in the postwar era to prevent the control of Minnesota corporations from drifting into the hands of other states and cities. There are men in Minneapolis trust companies, one hears, who make their living figuring out ways to keep companies under local ownership so that Minneapolis won't become a branch office town like Louisville or Milwaukee. The result, civic leader Wheelock Whitney (the unsuccessful 1982 Republican gubernatorial nominee) told us, is that "when we want to do something like getting the Tyrone Guthrie Theatre here [one of the nation's first and best regional theaters] or to boost our United Fund, or any project for civic improvement and betterment, we don't have to wire back to some home office to see what a company is willing to do. The money and the resources and the people are here."

Among Twin Cities leaders, we sense a deep orientation to change—and a determination not to be engulfed by that change, but rather to make it work constructively. The leaders of the prestigious national and international firms in Minneapolis and St. Paul live on the edge of "two worlds"—the small-scale 19th-century America that begins with the Great Plains, but also the sophisticated Eastern world of high finance and complex organization. By moving in both worlds, they maintain a human, unpretentious quality (many answer their own phones) even while adapting their economy to professional management and organization.

The most astounding exemplar of this dual character is William Norris, the man who founded Control Data on a shoestring in 1957 and a quarter century later could see his giant computer firm and its subsidiaries grossing $3.8 billion in yearly revenues. Norris spent a hardscrabble youth on a Nebraska cattle and hog farm in the drought and Depression '30s. Yet he brought to business remarkable acumen and sophistication. In one daring move, he launched an antitrust suit against arch competitor IBM and ended up enriching Control Data's coffers by a cool $1 billion. Control Data became known for its em-

*The bank holdings have frequently led to charges of economic exploitation by Minnesota, especially in North Dakota, a state also dependent on Minnesota to ship and process its grain crop.

ployee paternalism, generosity, and especially its support of new ideas. Following 1968 riots in the heart of black Northside Minneapolis, the corporation opened a major manufacturing plant there, employing minority workers to make computer parts essential to Control Data's worldwide operations. And that proved to be just the start of the civic experimentation of William Norris/Control Data. Soon came a child development center using computer teaching techniques, prototype solar energy greenhouses, earth-sheltered housing for energy conservation, and "business and technology centers" to act as a kind of incubator for start-up entrepreneurs in St. Paul, Toledo (Ohio), and other cities.

Norris insisted that "small innovative enterprises can play an important role in renewing blighted inner cities, improving the environment, developing energy alternatives, and conserving resources." Control Data spun off a new, independent corporation to work on inner-city renovation projects—"City Ventures" and a similar group, "Rural Ventures"—to prove there can be a strong and promising future for small, family-run farms in America, providing they have access to sophisticated audiovisual and computer-accessed information systems. It would be years before these enterprises, running so strongly against the grain of modern U.S. practices, could be judged successes or failures. Critics quickly noted that behind every project lay a marketing strategy for Control Data equipment and/or information systems. City Venture depended heavily on government grants and hit the rocks in Minneapolis in 1981 amidst charges of Control Data arrogance toward the affected poor neighborhoods, manipulation, and lack of knowledge. Always at the cutting edge, however, Norris and his colleagues early in the '80s were proposing that most of the American computer industry form a research and development cooperative, outside of government, to compete with the Japanese. In Minnesota, they pressed hard to get other corporations and foundations to *invest in*—not just contribute to—a seed capital fund for start-up businesses.

Minnesota corporate concern with the society at large was by no means limited to Control Data. For 35 years, Dayton-Hudson has been giving 5 percent of its pretax profits—the maximum portion of corporate income tax that is deductible—to community causes, in social action or the arts. In the mid '70s, a "5% Club" was formed, soon garnering over 50 Minnesota corporations into its fold—a level of corporate commitment to the community virtually unparalleled in the U.S. The Minnesota Project on Corporate Responsibility, with top CEOs participating, met regularly to discuss how major firms could contribute—not just in philanthropic giving, but through public-private partnerships, in creating jobs for the hard-to-employ, and in motivating a broad range of corporate personnel to participate in community projects. Often such projects were coordinated with the extraordinarily broad and innovative community outreach efforts of such foundations as McKnight and the Minneapolis Foundation. In 1977, a group of corporations, including Dayton-Hudson, 3M, and General Mills, formed a Minnesota Business Partnership to involve chief executives and senior managers as partners with state government on issues of broad import to Minnesota, not just business' particular special interests. A number of reports on Minnesota's competitive interstate position on economic development issues emerged. Elsewhere such an effort might be laughed off as a crude subterfuge for increased business influence. Not so in Minnesota. There is, for instance, a traditional requirement of major civic service as part of one's qualification to succession to the top of a Twin Cities–headquartered corporation.

But no one should pretend that Minnesota's corporations, however civic minded, are consistently angelic in their behavior. In 1974, in the wake of the Watergate scandal, Minnesotans were shocked to learn that 3M executives had maintained a half-million-dollar illegal political slush fund.

About two decades ago, manufacturing replaced farming as the major source of Minnesota's income, and the state now ranks 20th in the value of her annual industrial output. Agribusiness, however, remains an important industry; actual farm employment plus food processing, marketing, and farm supply industries account for almost 30 percent of Minnesota jobs. Two-thirds of the state's agricultural income actually comes from livestock. The big crop is corn; wheat, once virtually the only crop grown in the state, slipped behind corn during the 1930s, and Minnesota now ranks 9th among wheat producers. The Scandinavian farmers have a great predilection for co-ops, which are active in everything from wheat to gasoline. The richest, most productive Minnesota farmland is in the southern part of the state, a rich prairie land. But farm products from across the upper Midwest pours through the Twin Cities. Among the business goliaths spawned by farming are Land O' Lakes, the dairy co-op, and Farmers Union Central Exchange at St. Paul.

Minnesota's agribusinesses also include the mysterious Cargill Corporation, the Minneapolis grain merchant, one of America's largest privately held corporations. Cargill's annual sales equal those of Pillsbury and General Mills *combined,* but as Dan Morgan noted in his excellent account of the grain companies, *Merchants of Grain,* the Cargill and MacMillan families control their diversified worldwide empire from their French-style chateau and office building in a secluded park in suburban Wayzata. As traders of grain rather than producers and millers, they have accepted little responsibility in Minnesota affairs.

Well over half America's iron ore supply originated for years in the massive Mesabi Iron Range of northern Minnesota—high-grade ore until it ran out in the immediate postwar years, since then low-grade taconite converted into concentrated pellets ready for the blast furnace. A massive environmental battle was won in 1980 when Reserve Mining Company finally succumbed to environmentalist pressure and stopped dumping some 67,000 tons of taconite tailings a day into Lake Superior, the cleanest and youngest of the Great Lakes. But the hardy Irish and Italian and Scandinavian miners of the Mesabi Range faced another peril: sharply reduced demand for Great Lakes ores as Midwestern steel production eroded rapidly in the face of competition from abroad. The recession of 1981–82 hit Hibbing, Virginia, Calumet, Mountain

Iron, and other towns of the Iron Range with particular ferocity, throwing some 14,000 people out of work; in some mining communities, unemployment was as high as 90 percent.

Duluth, 150 miles north of Minneapolis and the state's third-largest city (pop. 92,811), became the westernmost port of the Atlantic Ocean with completion of the St. Lawrence Seaway in 1959. Perched on hills almost as steep as San Francisco's and overlooking a beautiful natural harbor, Duluth has one of the most attractive settings of American cities. Its old homes, architecturally distinguished and well preserved, are a joy to behold. But Superior Street, the main artery, has declined and not recovered despite some new hotel and convention center construction. A feisty battle was underway at the start of the '80s over whether a huge new shopping mall for the region would be built directly off Superior, or rather—as Sears, Roebuck and others oblivious to Duluth's future insisted—in suburban Hermantown.

Duluth is an important gateway to Minnesota's often remote and wild northern reaches, studded with hills, forests, and many of the 15,000-plus lakes of the "land of sky blue waters." More than 9 million people, including 4 million out-of-staters, vacation in Minnesota yearly, and the tourist industry was a major protagonist in the dispute over the Boundary Waters Canoe Areas.

The passion of Minnesotans for outdoor life is hard to grasp. Nearly everyone seems to have a "cabin" on a lake—humble or pretentious, according to income. During September and October it is often as difficult to find a Minnesota businessman at his office (especially on a Friday afternoon or Monday morning) as a Parisian in Paris in August. Why? That is duck season, a hallowed time when wives resign themselves to temporary widowhood, as again many must for the two weeks of deer season in November. But the outdoor passion extends far beyond the stalking of dumb animals; it is an exuberant love of the outdoors that may fill Minnesotans' brains with the extra oxygen that aids and abets a vital society.

Power and Progress: The Amazing Twin Cities and the State Government

Almost everything of note in modern Minnesota is concentrated in the Twin Cities orbit: the state capitol, the state university, the state fair, all trade and finance, the major media and cultural facilities, sports and transportation—a center as important to Minnesota as Paris is to France.

St. Paul (pop. 270,320), the smaller and more easterly of the two, is the state capital, major port, grain terminal, stockyards city, important in railroading, publishing, and insurance. St. Paul's population is heavily German and Irish Catholic laboring people, and while all this would be expected to make her world outlook and politics more careful and conservative, being second in size to Minneapolis has actually obliged St. Paul to be quicker and smarter and take more risks. Symbolic of this was George Latimer, the bearded erstwhile labor lawyer who served as the city's engaging and incredibly energetic mayor of the late 1970s and early '80s. Latimer put St. Paul at the forefront of the most advanced urban experiments, including a district heating system and energy park of energy-efficient light industry and housing. Resorting freely to federal subsidy programs, he also pulled St. Paul out of its building doldrums with a multihundred-million-dollar downtown construction program, which included a $75 million Town Square project featuring office towers, retailing, a hotel, and a spectacular four-level, glass-enclosed greenhouse public park. For St. Paul's long depressed Lowertown area, there was a $100 million redevelopment project headed by a famed Chinese-American city planner, Weiming Lu. His labor background and liberal views on such issues as abortion and gay rights notwithstanding, Latimer became something of a hero to the business community—and St. Paul at large.

Minneapolis (pop. 370,951) is a flat prairie town that got her start as a miller of the West's wheat. She is larger and traditionally more sophisticated than St. Paul, a more important banking and finance center, and generally more Scandinavian in population—though she also has many Germans. A historic wave of building has hit Minneapolis since the mid '50s, when the move of General Mills to a suburban headquarters and the opening of Southdale, an early enclosed suburban shopping mall, stirred a businessmen's Downtown Council to form and move into action. The results may be seen today in such developments as the pioneering pedestrian-transit Nicollet Mall, by designer Lawrence Halprin (opened in 1967, expanded in 1981), a flamboyant Federal Reserve Bank Building, by Gunnar Birkerts, restored old industrial buildings, renowned museums, and the 57-story Investors Diversified Services (IDS) Tower, by Philip Johnson—the tallest structure between Chicago and the Pacific, featuring a multistoried Crystal Court, where one finds the convergence of Minneapolis' system of 20 skywalks to protect mortals against the ferocity of Minnesota winters. Yet as wondrous as these glittering attractions all are, architectural critics note that Minneapolis and St. Paul also have a goodly share of unimaginative building, acres of depressing parking lots in the heart of downtown, and indeed no sense of the coherent identity of a Boston, Chicago, or San Francisco. Neither city offers any night life to speak of; both, in fact, are essentially private, middle-class cities. As Paul Goldberger wrote in the New York Times in 1981, "Minneapolis and St. Paul are clean, neat and safe—low in urban horrors, but low also in that raw, admittedly vulgar energy that powers great cities."

Raw poverty and ugly slums are fairly rare in the Twin Cities, but there are social problems aplenty—among some poor whites, among blacks in the inner cities, among Indochinese refugees (who poured in at a heavy rate in the late '70s and early '80s), and finally among native American Indians, who have their greatest urban concentration in America in the Twin Cities. One finds the heaviest Indian concentration on and near Minneapolis' Franklin Avenue, a neighborhood that belies the Twin Cities' squeaky-clean, progressive image. Here one finds a startling array of social pathologies: massive unemployment, alcoholism, vagrancy, knifings, rapes, and chronic welfare dependency. During the winter of 1981 we were shown a spot between a garage and fence just off the avenue; there was a doghouse in which three Indians actually sought shelter. But Franklin Avenue is also home to the American Indian Business Development Corporation, the country's only organization devoted to economic development for city Indians, which in 1981 started building a major shopping center to create a point of pride and profit for urban native peoples.

The city of Minneapolis has had four unusual mayors in the postwar period: Hubert Humphrey, Arthur Naftalin, Charles S. Stenvig, and Donald Fraser. All have been obliged to rule by little more than moral authority, since the careful Yankees and Scandinavians who wrote the state laws (collected as the "city charter" back in the 1920s), were suspicious of the bossism they saw in other cities and gave almost all the power to the city council. All were considered liberal and intellectual save for Stenvig, a policeman elected to two terms when Minneapolitans tired of '60s liberalism and concessions to the city's tiny (7.6 percent) black minority. Stenvig appealed to the fears of low-income white folk, but his law-and-order rhetoric had no lasting impact on Minneapolis politics. In 1979, the city chose ultraliberal ex-Congressman Fraser as mayor.

The Cowles family's *Minneapolis Tribune* and *Star* deserved major credit for the moderate-to-liberal political climate of Minnesota through the 1970s. Early on, the papers moved to an internationalist point of view, contradicting the area's traditional Scandinavian and German isolationism. Over the years, they supported substantial school and university budgets, opposed the demagoguery of Sen. Joseph McCarthy from neighboring Wisconsin, and championed such causes as civil rights, freedom of speech, gay rights, freedom of choice on abortion, and the environmentalists' position on the Boundary Waters Canoe Area. This is not to say Minnesotans always heeded the papers' counsel; their effort to approve charter reform giving the mayor of Minneapolis more power was rejected, for instance. We have heard conservative and suburban Minnesotans excoriate the papers' liberalism as ferociously as die-hard segregationist Southerners used to attack the *Atlanta Constitution*. Yet what the two papers did for promotion and development of the Upper Midwest (a term they invented) and the Twin Cities area was of immense importance. In 1982, the evening *Star* was folded into the more profitable morning *Tribune*, going the way of so many U.S. afternoon papers. A few months later the financially pressed *Tribune* pink-slipped 75 staffers, including 28 newsroom employees—prompting Charles W. Bailey, the highly respected editor, to quit in protest. Publisher John Cowles, Jr., the founder's son, was dismissed by the board of directors, and Minneapolitans hoped for a return to the journalistic and management standards that had made the paper one of the nations 10 best. Some also foresaw circulation wars for the metropolitan market with St. Paul's two Knight-Ridder papers, the *Pioneer Press* and *Dispatch*.

The fierce onetime rivalry between the Twin Cities has faded dramatically, partly because suburbanites, who play such a prominent role in metropolitan life, find it a bore. Sports have also done much to draw the two cities together. When business leaders realized they could only get a major league baseball team by classifying the two cities together, they did just that. The American League Minnesota Twins were organized in 1961, followed by football and hockey teams.

Twin Cities unity is often achieved on governmental fronts by timely intervention of the area's Citizens League, a voluntary organization of citizen task forces that have addressed every issue from sewer lines to hospital costs, from crime and justice to land use issues. The Citizens League is the godfather of the Minneapolis–St. Paul Metropolitan Council, to which the state legislature in 1967 awarded a tax base of its own, gubernatorially appointed members, and control over metropolitanwide agencies that handle sewers, transportation, airports, and parks. Short of a full-fledged metropolitan government, this may be the country's best model of metropolitanwide coordination of services and area-wide decision making. In 1976, the Council gained the power to write the nation's first mandatory land use planning law for an entire metropolitan region—again, the result of Citizens League agitation and timely state legislative action.

The Citizens League, never willing to rest on its laurels, was still stirring the pot in 1980 with a remarkable report lauding the idea of open competition between private and public organizations to carry out government services. Any monopoly institution, it was argued, inevitably becomes top heavy and bureaucratized and thus insensitive; people have begun to react, demanding choices and sometimes a right to "do for themselves" through self-help strategies in medicine, education, social services, and housing; therefore, citizens should have a right to "exit" to other service deliverers.* The pioneering development of such thought and attitudes—in the state of Hubert Humphrey Democratic liberalism, indeed by many of his erstwhile supporters— seems proof positive of the Twin Cities' remarkable innovative capacity.

A few ritzy Twin Cities suburbs—Wayzata, Edina, and others—are famed, but in fact there are 189 suburban jurisdictions in all, filled with folk who headed outward from the city for housing and open space (not because of racism—that isn't the Twin Cities' problem) and created a big-lot, auto-dependent, sprawl pattern stoutly resistant to conventional mass transit. To start nipping at the edges of that problem, carpooling and especially vanpooling have been pushed with unusual vigor.

Minnesota state government charges some of the nation's highest corporate and income taxes. Property taxes, by contrast, were driven down spectacularly in the '70s—from around 2 percent of market value to less than 1 percent —through DFL programs shifting the tax burden onto state revenues. Grous-

---

*The Twin Cities' live example of such choice in action is the rapid growth there of health maintenance organizations, which have competed successfully with standard fee-for-service medicine by offering prepayment packages that stress preventive health care and typically cost the consumer 10 to 40 percent less than comparable private insurance coverage.

ing over the sales and income levies, while perennial, rarely reaches crisis levels: partly because of the generally high quality of state services, partly because there is no patronage system to arouse citizens' ire as it siphons off tax money for political satraps. Good government does not, however, protect against hard times. By the early '80s revenues plunged so drastically that the legislature had to endure the pain of raising the state sales tax, the fierce anti-tax mood of the times notwithstanding. It seemed that the Minnesota economy was less recession-proof than had long been hoped and believed, and that the press of hard fiscal realities might force significant retreat from the carefully built standards of high services and high taxes.

Yet should full-scale retrenchment continue, much could be lost. Along with other Americans, for example, Minnesotans by the '80s were becoming concerned with the quality and costs of education. Yet over the years, scarcely any state government had shone more brightly than Minnesota on education. An advanced state foundation program went far toward equalizing school dollars between rich and poor counties, and Minnesota achieved the nation's lowest high school dropout rate. Minnesota ranked only 21st in income and 23rd in population nationally, but she developed the fourth-largest public university system in America. One need not denigrate the fine private education tradition of the state—at such institutions as Carleton, St. Olaf, or Macalester, which welcomed Hubert Humphrey as a visiting professor after his defeat for the presidency in 1968—to celebrate its public institutions, most particularly the University of Minnesota, with its nationally recognized faculties in political science, engineering, physics, mining, agriculture, medicine, and dentistry.

In addition, the University of Minnesota is the mother institution of one of the nation's outstanding medical schools, which now cooperates with its old rival, the famed Mayo Clinic at Rochester. This is a university whose Institute of Technology, under a forceful dean, Roger Staehle, offers pioneering programs in control systems, heat transfer, biomedical engineering, and microelectronics. And finally, this university's Hubert H. Humphrey Institute of Public Affairs (created out of the school of public affairs and in 1980 made a free-standing academic unit of the university), could well set the pace for imaginative public affairs training and advanced thought through the '80s. No less a figure than Harlan Cleveland, former ambassador to NATO, former president of the University of Hawaii, and one of America's most imaginative public affairs thinkers, agreed to become the Humphrey Institute's dean. In short order, the Humphrey Institute had declared its intention to operate across all disciplines and professions of the university—to combat "specialized achievement, the chief bottleneck of our society." And with the aid of such figures as Ted Kolderie, the distinguished former head of the Citizens League, it was preparing a mid-career program for politicians, administrators, and journalists that would be "a mind-stretching inquiry into the nature, techniques, purposes, and ethics of leadership" in the late-20th-century city, state, nation, and international order. Should one dismiss that as overweening intellectual ambition? In many states, yes. But not, we suspect, in Minnesota.

NORTH DAKOTA

Still the Lone Prairie

NEAR THE LITTLE TOWN OF RUGBY, some 54 miles from the Canadian border in north central North Dakota, a stone cairn marks the geographic center of the North American continent. From Rugby, one would have to travel some 1,500 miles to reach the Gulf of Mexico, the Arctic Archipelago, the Atlantic, or the Pacific. Similarly, and more importantly for North Dakotans, from Rugby or any other point in North Dakota, one has to travel several hundred miles to reach a major city. (The nearest are Minneapolis, Denver, and Winnipeg, Canada.) North Dakota seems, and is, far from cities and coasts.

For hundreds of miles from this central point on the continent, the prairie lands of America—so vast, untreed, and unpeopled that the first explorers called them the Great American desert—stretch relentlessly to distant horizons. Predictably, the people who inhabit such vast and lonely lands are a sturdy, tenacious lot, honest, thrifty, and proud.

North Dakotans have been anything but dull conformists, however; North Dakota has been celebrated as one of the most radical states of the Union. The record shows she has rebelled against manipulative outside interests ever since the Populists revolted against absentee ownership in the 1890s and the Nonpartisan League arose to fight the grain merchants early in the century. To this date, North Dakota has the only state-owned bank in the United States, although her leaders still chafe under the ownership of most of the larger, private banks in the state by massive Minneapolis-based bank holding companies. The North Dakota citizenry, fearful of the destruction of small towns, schools, and churches by monstrous corporate farms, has rejected corporate farming except for families. North Dakota's most famed politician, gravel-voiced governor and later Senator William ("Wild Bill") Langer, was at once a warmhearted Populist and a man of picaresque ethics who flirted with the edges of the law but whose only conviction was successfully appealed. It was North Dakota's Senator Gerald P. Nye who roused national attention with a sharply critical investigation of the munitions makers in the early 1930s; in 1936 it was North Dakota Congressman William Lemke whom Father Coughlin was backing in an agrarian-isolationist campaign for the presidency.

A few other facts set the North Dakota stage: With its cool, sunny climate, North Dakota is classic small-grain country, producing a hard, flinty high-protein wheat ideal for making bread; in all the U.S.A., North Dakota usually ranks second only to Kansas in overall wheat production; it is first in durum wheat, barley, flaxseed, and sunflower seed. Vast wheat farms make the state's average farm acreage—close to 1,100 acres—several times the national average. Farm cooperatives are nowhere so strong as in North Dakota, and it is the banner state for the liberally inclined Farmers Union (actually larger here, in contrast to the national norm, than the Farm Bureau). The Farmers Union, avowedly Democratic, favors government-controlled markets and price supports to undergird family farming. The heart of its North Dakota strength is the vigorous structure of farmer cooperatives—for selling grain, buying oil and gas, lumber, sometimes even hardwares and groceries—active in every county of the state. Many of the co-op grain elevators have a Farmers Union dues check-off procedure.

North Dakota may still be the most agricultural state, but much of the public debate of recent years has concerned the growing importance of oil and coal. Oil was discovered in the Williston Basin near the Montana border in the early 1950s, and annual production has topped 40 million barrels. Beneath the state's western reaches lie 28,000 square miles of lignite coal deposits, one of the nation's richest energy stores. Most of the region has already been leased for coal production, and 13 mine-mouth power plants—harbingers of more to come—have opened, followed by construction of the nation's first coal gasification plant. They are plugged into a major power grid and ship most of their electricity out of state. The energy boom has raised concern about threats to the natural landscape posed by widespread strip mining.

Energy development created enough jobs to reverse the long North Dakota population decline triggered by the Great Depression, although even the 1980 population of 652,717 was less than the state had in 1930. Fears of "boom town" development created a remarkable French-North Dakota tie: the federal Energy Department provided money to five small towns in Mercer County to experiment with a French economic development model under which all local county officials sit on a single board that enables them, on more equal terms, to confront the private mining and electricity interests over such issues as location of facilities and construction of employee housing. The towns, bearing such colorful names as Zap and Pick City, have so far experienced little of the fearful physical and social dislocation registered in such boom towns as Gillette and Rock Spring, Wyoming.

People, Land, and Weather

To think of North Dakota as one vast, undifferentiated prairie would be a mistake; rather it has at least three distinct geographical regions. Along the Minnesota border, to the east, lies the relatively humid Red River Valley, an ancient lake bed with rich chernozem soils that produce wheat, potatoes, oats, barley, flax, corn, soybeans, sugar beets, sunflowers, and legumes. In the valley are Fargo, a North Dakota-Minnesota regional trade center that is the state's largest city (61,308) and Grand Forks (43,765), home of the University of North Dakota. West of the valley, stretching to the Missouri River at the state's mid-point, lie thousands of square miles of drift prairie, softly undulating fields of wheat, a much dryer and largely treeless land. Still farther west and running to the Montana border is the high, dry ranch land known as the Slope, a semi-arid belt of short grasses, buffalo berries, deep valleys, and flat-topped steep buttes and hills. Here wheat farming gradually gives way to grazing, rainfall is very low, and the population very sparse.

Astride the Missouri River, at the border between the drift prairie and the Slope, lie the state's second- and fourth-ranking cities, the state capital, Bismarck (44,485), and Minot (32,843), some hundred miles northward. Traversing the continent with his now legendary dog, Charley, John Steinbeck was struck by the change of worlds on the Missouri River—between Bismarck and the neighboring town of Mandan (15,513): "On the Bismarck side it is the Eastern landscape, Eastern grass, with the look and smell of Eastern America. Across the Missouri on the Mandan side, it is pure West, with brown grass and water scorings and small outcrops. The two sides of the river might as well be a thousand miles apart."

As one moves westward, North Dakotans change gradually from the valley's relatively reserved, conservative, formal, church-going residents to the western Slope's often hard-drinking, poker-playing, free-and-easy lot who dress in Western-style clothes. The ethnicity of these regions is still largely that of the first inhabitants brought in by the railroads that settled North Dakota. The Northern Pacific brought mostly Germans and Russians; they settled mainly in southern North Dakota, leaving an isolationist, conservative, and Republican legacy. The Great Northern, by contrast, went across the northern part of the state and recruited mostly Scandinavians to ride westward on its line; today one still finds liberal and strong Farmers Union territory in areas around Grand Forks, Minot, and Williston, and, indeed, across most of the northern counties.

North Dakota is a young state; she received her first settlers just over a century ago and in 1870 numbered less than 2,500 souls. Then, during the 1870s, as the Northern Pacific Railroad was extended across the territory, land speculators ("boomers") and homesteaders flooded in. No other state received so many of its settlers directly from the old country; Bismarck received its name in a promotional bid by the railroad to attract settlers from Germany. One-way tickets were offered from "Bremen to Bismarck." By 1880, the area had 37,000 people attracted to the vast, virgin prairie; by 1890 (a year after statehood was achieved), 191,000. The homesteading continued until after the turn of the century; both sets of co-author Hagstrom's grandparents came from Sweden and Minnesota (of Norwegian descent) to homestead within 35 miles of Bismarck after 1905.

But it was not an entirely hospitable land to which the settlers came. Precariously set in the heart of the great central plains, without mountains or trees to break the fast-moving winds of the central continent, North Dakotans found themselves exposed to cruelly cold winters and searingly hot summers. North Dakota still holds the Western Hemisphere record for absolute range of temperature in the same year: in 1936, it was 60 degrees below zero at Parshall on February 15 and 121 degrees above at Steele on July 6. The *average* temperature in January in North Dakota is a chill seven degrees! Former CBS news commentator Eric Sevareid has written of his childhood home at Velva, N.D.: "It was a trial of the human spirit just to live there, and a triumph of faith and fortitude for those who stayed on through the terrible blasting of the summer winds, the merciless suns, through the frozen darkness of the winters when the deathly mourn of the coyote seemed at times to be the only signal of life."

North Dakota's dazzling skies exact their price on the arid land, too. Before the white man came, the thick matting of grasses and their roots on the open prairie retained a measure of moisture and protected the soil from the winds. But the first generation of farmers lacked foresight; they failed to diversify their crops, concentrating on the single great moneymaker: wheat. In the 1930s, nature brought both severe drought and high winds, along with low grain prices. Bankruptcies were common, some 86,000 persons fled North Dakota, and only the state's ban on corporate farming kept the land in the hands of individuals.

Fifty years later, long since recovered from the trauma of the "dirty '30s," North Dakota's agriculture seemed stable indeed. Crop rotation, irrigation, and conservation have made the land viable again and as protected against drought as man can make it. Rising land and machinery prices have made North Dakota farming highly capital-intensive; many young farmers say that low grain prices make the threat of bankruptcy greater than in the old days, when farmers depended on the sweat of the brow. But in reality, the cost of land has made farming a "closed" industry, with entry limited to those youth whose families are already in it. North Dakota has also sent many young people to college and "exported" them to professional jobs in Minneapolis, Denver, and Seattle. Except among the Indians, there is little poverty in North Dakota today.

North Dakota's prosperity is dependent on federal government agricultural programs and export policies. REA power rates are another form of federal assistance. But the greatest of all federal projects, a vast diversion of Missouri River waters for irrigation, has run into deep trouble. In one of the huge water conservation, flood control, irrigation, power projects of modern times, the Army Corps of Engineers has dammed the great Missouri all the way from Wolf Point, Montana, to the South Dakota–Nebraska border; the entire river valley is flooded for that entire distance, excepting a 70-mile stretch in North Dakota. The Garrison Diversion Project was supposed to diversify North Dakota agriculture, but part way through the construction of a 150-mile canal, environmentalists and the Canadian government objected to the salts and unwanted fish in the Souris River water that flows into Canada. Court suits over its completion appear endless. Informal newspaper polls show that a substantial majority of North Dakotans still favor Garrison Diversion, and the state's politicians continue to promote it. Even those who would benefit directly from irrigation speak wistfully, however, of the price the great dam has already exacted: the flooding of some 300,000 acres of choice river bottom land, the loss of many homes and the death of three towns (though others were built). Had the dam been proposed in the 1970s rather than the more callous era of the 1940s, one can imagine the furor that might have been raised by conservationists and Indian rights groups since much of the flooded land was part of the Fort Berthold Indian Reservation. An 1851 treaty had guaranteed the land to the Indians in perpetuity, but some of the Indian leaders were ordered to Washington to sign, unwillingly, the agreement to take their land. A photo still exists showing the officials gathered; in it one sees George Gillette, chairman of the Fort Berthold Indian Tribal Business Council, openly weeping.

A Tourist Diversion

North Dakota is not normally considered a tourist state; it lacks the woods and lake resorts that can hold tourists for a week or two. But it can provide attractions with a special flavor of the Old West: the western Badlands, an area of roughly sculptured hills in subtle hues that includes the Theodore Roosevelt National Park, filled with buffalo herds and prairie dogs; on the Canadian border, the joint North Dakota–Manitoba sponsored International Peace Garden; near Washburn, the place where Lewis and Clark encamped for the winter of 1804–1805 on their trek to the Pacific Northwest; on the Standing Rock Indian Reservation, the burial place of Sitting Bull until his remains were removed to South Dakota. On a relatively modern note, there is, in Strasburg, the birthplace of that king of "champagne music" and famous North Dakota native, Lawrence Welk.* In Fargo and other cities, the popularity of legalized gambling since its approval by the legislature in 1981 has put conservative North Dakotans into culture shock. Gambling got through the legislature because most of the revenue goes to charitable causes; one of the beneficiaries is Prairie Public Television. Hotels, motels, and restaurants where the blackjack, bingo, pull tabs, sports pools, and raffles are played have reported increased business, including special weekly bus junkets from Winnipeg and Minneapolis.

The state has spent little public money on tourism, but Harold Schafer, a native who founded the Gold Seal Company (wax, Snowy Bleach, Mr. Bubble), has invested more than $1 million restoring the old cowtown of Medora near the Badlands and T.R. Park. Founded by a French adventurer, the Marquis de Mores, as what he hoped would be the keystone of a vast meat-packing empire, Medora was christened by the cracking of a champagne bottle over a tent peg in 1883. But de Mores' financial schemes went sour, and Medora won its real claim to fame as headquarters for Teddy Roosevelt and his Roughriders. Both T.R. and de Mores would surely appreciate Schafer, who was raised on a North Dakota farm, lives in Medora, and keeps his

---

*North Dakota is also the birthplace of quite a different musical performer, singer-composer Peggy Lee, who was born Norma Egstrom at Jamestown. Her musical legacy may well overwhelm Welk's, but North Dakotans have found it difficult to appreciate her sexy blues style.

headquarters in Bismarck. But all of Gold Seal's production facilities are outside of North Dakota, closer to major markets.

Politics: From NPL to Normalcy

As fans of the award-winning late-1970s movie *Northern Lights* know, what made North Dakota politics erratic and radical for so many decades was the Nonpartisan League, a farm revolt of 1915 born out of the yeoman's conviction that farmers were being victimized by big-city money, by the railroads, and by the grain combines. A legendary incident occurred that year when a group of farmers went to the state capitol to protest their lot, only to be told by a big-town legislator, named Treadwell Twichell, to "go home and slop the hogs." Two years after its founding, the NPL controlled all major state offices in North Dakota and promptly enacted one of the most socialistic programs in American history, including the state bank, the state mill and elevator, a state workmen's compensation bureau, and insurance programs.

The League's heyday ran to 1921, but in that year three of its main officeholders, including the governor of the moment, were recalled by the people. The NPL would never again exert such complete control, but it did remain a potent political force through World War II, sending Langer to the Senate and Lemke and Usher Burdick to the House. From its birth until the 1950s, the NPL operated as a splinter group within the Republican party—apparently, as John Gunther learned, because Democrats were as rare as ocelots. But in the wake of World War II, a group of young veterans, many with ties to the Farmers Union, started a six-year battle, eventually successful, to tie the NPL with the liberal national Democratic party.

The Democrats soon forgot about the special NPL identity, and the shift has made North Dakota politics a lot duller but probably more responsible. For the first time, the state now has a visible two-party system. The Democrats held the governorship from 1961 to 1980. William L. Guy, governor from 1961 through 1972, modernized the state government and was a great ambassador for the remote state. North Dakota's recent and current senators in Washington have lacked the fervor of Bill Langer and Usher Burdick. From 1945 to 1980, the state was represented in the Senate by Republican Milton Young. Langer's old seat is now occupied by Usher's son, Democrat Quentin Burdick. Neither Young nor the younger Burdick made the most of his Senate seat; both men regularly turned back money available to them for staff and rarely initiated legislation. Young was succeeded by another Republican moderate, former Rep. Mark Andrews.

Though dead and gone, the Nonpartisan League has left an indelible mark on North Dakota. The state bank, state mill, and state elevator continue to this day, though out-of-state critics say the bank is not nearly as creative in today's economy as it was when it saved farmers from bankruptcy. Another holdover is the continued, frequent use of iniative and referendum. Since 1918 there has not been an election year without referred and/or initiated measures on the ballot. The petition device was used frequently in the 1960s and '70s by Robert McCarney. A cigar-chomping, former Bismarck auto dealer who learned his politics as Bill Langer's chauffeur and has fought a rough and tumble (and some say unprincipled) battle against taxes, McCarney was for the little people and against government extravagance. He considers himself a Republican, but the Republicans want none of him. McCarney referred tax increases passed by the legislatures to the voters and sponsored successful initiatives to cut the sales tax and the state individual income tax. In 1980 the initiative goals were reversed when a liberal coalition (including the Farmers Union, the AFL-CIO, the statewide Association of Rural Electric Coopera- tives, and the North Dakota Education Association) sponsored an initiative campaign. It was to impose a 6½ percent oil extraction tax on top of the existing 5 percent oil and gas production tax with the revenues earmarked for increased state aid to public schools and for filling gaps created by reductions in the individual income and property taxes mandated by the measure. The people approved this form of taxation, and the legislature went on a spending spree, reducing income taxes further—only to end up with state financial problems.

The real successor to Langer—and the state's most exciting officeholder in generations—is Byron Dorgan, state tax commissioner for over 11 years before his 1980 election to the House. In the kind of populist act that North Dakotans love, Dorgan forced out-of-state corporations to pay state income taxes they had avoided and then organized other states to do the same. Dorgan's progres- sive instincts, however, are economic, rather than social; he compromised with North Dakota's many religious fundamentalists by promising to vote for a constitutional amendment banning abortion.

North Dakota's populist tradition and the closeness of North Dakota soci- ety are also illustrated through the state's voter registration system, under which voters simply go to the polls on election day, give their name, age, and residence, and unless challenged (a fairly rare occurrence) just take a ballot and mark it. No other state is quite so liberal about not requiring advance registration, and North Dakotans are quite happy with their system.

SOUTH DAKOTA

State of Reluctant Change

IN THE LANGUAGE OF THE SIOUX, "Dakota" can be translated roughly as "league of friends." North and South Dakota are set neatly on top of one another and share a common border some 360 miles long. Most Americans think of them as a bloc. If Republican senators had not been greedily intent on adding four instead of two senators of their party to the Union in the 1880s, the Dakota Territory would probably have been admitted as one state.

But the states were admitted separately, and not only do they view the world differently, but they have little indeed to do with each other. As John Gunther summarized the situation in the late 1940s:

> Nothing is more remarkable in the United States than the difference between the Dakotas. North Dakota is one of the most radical states of the Union, and South Dakota one of the most conservative. . . . South thinks North is inhabited mostly by Bolsheviks; North thinks that South is a preserve for all people to the right of Hoover. South looks down across the river to Iowa and southward to Nebraska; it never looks North at all, if it can help it. . . .

But there are continuing similarities between the Dakotas. Each is still so young, comparatively, that the sweat and blood of the frontier heritage is not yet dry. Except for West Virginia, they have the highest percentage of people living in small villages and farms among all the states. The agrarian mentality still dominates, because almost three-quarters of the people either live on farms or grew up there. No other states—not even fertile Iowa—even approach the Dakotas in the percentage of people who earn their principal living from the land. It's been noted that South Dakota supports twice as many sheep as people. As for total population, both states declined by 2 percent during the 1960s, but in the 1970s South Dakota grew by 3.7 percent and North Dakota by 5.7 percent. The 1980 Census found 690,768 people in South Dakota and 652,717 in North Dakota.

The Dakotas are also geographic twins: fertile and humid river valleys to the east (Red River in North Dakota, James and Big Sioux rivers in South Dakota); then steadily increasing aridity on vast butte-dotted plains and marginal ranchlands that reach to western borders, interrupted by the central flow of the Missouri River and the Badlands. But the agriculture is different— South Dakota produces a lot more corn and livestock and substantially less wheat.

From time immemorial, Sioux Indians have populated the territory now within South Dakota. Today, 1 of every 20 people in the state is a Sioux, although the Indians tend to be sadly removed from the mainstream of South Dakota life. The white population has a rural cosmopolitanism: substantial numbers of Anglo-Saxons, Norwegians, Germans, Swedes, Russo-Germans, Danes, Czechs, and Dutch. As in North Dakota, the greatest influx came during the several decades beginning with the 1870s, and the state has yet to match the population peak of 692,849, which the census-takers recorded in 1930. There was a tremendous outflow of young people in their productive years, balanced only in part by natural increase due to the excess of births over deaths.

The gross population figures also obscure the major population trends within South Dakota: a continued flight from the land and the small villages, a modest growth of the medium-sized towns, and continued domination by the eastern quarter of the state in cities ranging from Sioux Falls (the state's largest, with 81,343 people) to Yankton (12,011).

West of the Missouri River is mainly a great expanse of bleak plains and grazing land with few inhabitants; as one eastern South Dakotan told us, disparagingly, "West of the river we have a lot of ranchers living like feudal lords." The west does have its tourist attractions in the Badlands and Black Hills; it also has most of the Indian reservations in the state and Rapid City (46,492), second-largest in South Dakota and site of the worst floods in American history on June 9, 1972.

The Political Tides

South Dakota's radical political experience came during the 1890s, the first decade of statehood. As Walter Prescott Webb later described the period, the isolated farmers of the lonely Plains, "far from markets, burned by drought, beaten by hail, withered by hot winds, frozen by blizzards, eaten out by grasshoppers, exploited by capitalists, and cozened by politicians," organized into the Populist party and listed their demands: railroads and grain elevator regulation to stop manipulation by outside interests, free silver to loosen the hold of the bankers, and initiative and referendum as a curb on government. In fusion with the Democrats, the Populists actually elected their man to the governorship in 1896 and 1898. Working with the national Progressive movement, the Populists seized control of the South Dakota Republican party and pushed through measures such as a direct primary, railway controls, and limitations on campaign spending and lobbying.

The key figure of early South Dakota politics was the self-professed "Theodore Roosevelt Republican" and careful reformer Peter Norbeck, who was elected governor in 1916 after attacking as socialistic the left-wing Nonpartisan League, which was making its successful bid for power in North Dakota at the same time. Norbeck's way of dealing with NPL demands was to push successfully for adoption of reforms on the NPL model whenever the NPLers became too strident.

Thus, South Dakota adopted workmen's compensation, child labor legislation, and state-sponsored enterprises, including a rural credit system, hail insurance, a coal mine, and a cement plant (the latter still in operation in Rapid City). But radical control of the state government was averted. During the Depression, several of the socialistic programs failed or put a serious strain on the state treasury. The result was a conservative reaction against new government programs, which has given South Dakota one of the most Republican and conservative governments in the nation. Fear of change has been the hallmark of South Dakota life ever since World War II: first, because the people's rural, isolated prairie existence is the dominant fact of life, and second, because they remember the 1930s. In this state, which just in the last years has finished burying its pioneers, the virtues are still sturdy self-reliance and individualism.

Charts of party strength in South Dakota show a pattern of normal Republican dominance, broken by a few short eras of Democratic breakthroughs— in the early New Deal Days, in the late 1950s (in reaction to the Eisenhower-Benson farm policies), and a wave that started in the late 1960s. And while party affiliation was declining nationally, in 1980 South Dakota's 447,508 voters just about evenly divided themselves between the Democratic and Republican parties while only 39,000 people (9 percent of the electorate) identified themselves as independents or members of smaller parties. The power structure of South Dakota and the Republican party are often so closely entwined as to be virtually indistinguishable. Major power lies in the two great Minneapolis bank holding companies, which control a substantial percentage of South Dakota bank deposits; in groups such as the South Dakota Wheat Growers Association and the ultraconservative South Dakota Stockgrowers Association; in private utilities such as Northern States Power; and in the gold mining interests represented by the Homestake Mine. Where continuing Democratic strength is to be found in the state, its base is usually among the farmers, especially the Scandinavians; the Farmers Union (stronger here than the Farm Bureau) is a major support for the Democrats; so are rural co-ops and rural electrification interests.

The inevitable question about South Dakota politics, however, is how a state could send both Karl F. Mundt and George S. McGovern to Congress. Mundt, who was honored with four terms in the U.S. Senate before suffering a stroke in 1969 and finally retiring in 1972, focused his stump assaults on godless, atheistic communism and its evils; he was noted nationally for presiding over the 1948 House Un-American Activities Committee hearings, which uncovered the "pumpkin papers" and led to the conviction of Alger Hiss, and for voting against senate censure of McCarthy, saying, "Joe is one of the best friends I have in the Senate."

Part of the answer to the Mundt-McGovern question lies, of course, in South Dakota's history of agrarian protest. McGovern, an erstwhile college professor, won a seat in Congress in 1956 by opposing Eisenhower's farm policies, defending the family farm, high price supports, increased bargaining power for farmers, rural electrification, and liberal farm credit. After his election to the Senate in 1962, McGovern broadened his interests from agriculture to foreign affairs and began a "peace appeal," which included outspoken criticism of the Vietnam War. McGovern proposed cutting billions of dollars from the defense budget on the grounds that America already had a strategic "overkill" capacity and could better spend its wealth for education, job training, urban programs, conservation, and agriculture. McGovern found some real response in South Dakota, where he has been an active Methodist, and where rejection of unnecessary foreign commitments was part of the Plains States' traditional Populist-isolationist movement. But most South Dakotans were astonished when McGovern announced his runs for the presidency in 1968 (as a stand-in for the assassinated Robert F. Kennedy) and in 1972.

Organizational hard work was the essential ingredient in McGovern's upward climb—first in almost singlehandedly resuscitating the South Dakota Democratic party after World War II, then in winning the 1972 Democratic nomination. But as a national campaigner, he declined from the moment he won the 1972 nomination at the Democratic convention in Miami Beach and picked Missouri Senator Thomas Eagleton as running mate. It was revealed soon after that Eagleton had earlier been hospitalized for depression and undergone electroshock treatments, and McGovern removed him from the ticket to prevent mental health from becoming the central issue of the fall campaign. The situation appeared to the American people as though the White Knight of truth had been guilty of duplicity and expediency, both weak-kneed and cruel at the same time. McGovern lost every state but Massachusetts; even his own South Dakota voted against him. Unlike William Jennings Bryan, that other Populist thwarted in search of the presidency, McGovern did not influence public issues. But he did have his national legacy: the rules opening up the party convention to minority groups and women. Most of this was accomplished while McGovern was chairman of the party reform commission after the 1968 convention. His young followers developed campaign skills they used to put liberal candidates in office for years afterward. Among the most prominent were McGovern's campaign manager, Gary Hart, who became a U.S. Senator from Colorado, and Patrick Caddell, the pollster who went on to play an influential role in the Carter administration.*

McGovern nearly moved to England after his presidential defeat but instead recovered and trotted out his seniority and agricultural performance to win reelection in 1974. In 1980, however, McGovern's liberal luck ran out when virulent ad campaigns by anti-abortionists and conservatives characterized him as a "baby killer" and "big spender" and put Republican Rep. James Abdnor in the Senate.

*A legacy of a slightly different order was left by Republican Francis Case, who represented South Dakota in the House and Senate from 1937 to 1962. Case, wrote Lyndon Johnson's Senate aide Harry McPherson, was the prototype of the eager little school boy grown up, "pale, square, and deadly dull. When he died, this little man, so tidy and severe, left a monument which archaeologists a millennium from now may find to be proof of our productive genius, or madness or both—the Interstate Highway System."

South Dakota's other senators of recent years have been more noted for style than political accomplishment: James Abourezk, son of an immigrant Lebanese back-peddler who championed Arab and American Indian causes for a term in Mundt's old seat, and his successor, Republican Larry Pressler, a former Rhodes Scholar with a Harvard graduate degree who went to the Senate at the tender age of 37 and—strangely for a South Dakotan—proved to be an insatiable publicity hound (including a generally ignored presidential campaign in 1980). In 1982, after losing one of their two House seats, South Dakotans stuck with populist Democrat Thomas A. Daschle, a strong veterans and agriculture advocate.

South Dakota's state government is located at Pierre (pronounced "Peer"), a drab prairie town of 11,973 souls settled between mustard-colored buttes along the Missouri River. Centrality is apparently Pierre's main virtue; if you take an official South Dakota map and fold it so that the eastern and western borders are lined up evenly, the center crease will barely miss Pierre. The capital's isolation also has its effect on the state government. As University of South Dakota political scientist Alan Clem has written, "The nerves of state government are thickly insulated by the vastness of the prairie from popular pressures, and as a result the response of state government to many needs and wishes has often been relatively slow. State and local programs and budgets reflect yesterday's and today's problems, seldom tomorrow's." Even in 1982, when the federal minimum wage was $3.35 an hour, the South Dakota Legislature thought it safe to raise the state minimum to no more than $2.80; in the same session, it voted to continue for another year the cap on unemployment benefits at $129 per *month*. Yet the state's economic climate—no personal income tax, no corporate tax, but right-to-work and average hourly wages far below the national average—has lured many firms from high-tax states. Citibank of New York moved its credit card operations to Sioux Falls in 1982, lured by the state's helpful repeal of usury laws; eventually it expected to expand to 2,000 employes in South Dakota (the proportional equivalent of 51,000 new jobs in New York State). From 1969 to 1982, some 60 businesses moved all or part of their operations across the Minnesota border, bringing 10,000 jobs with them. Among them were plants of Control Data, 3M, Litton Industries; and OK Hardware. Minnesota Governor Rudy Perpich could hardly believe it: "South Dakota is 50th in everything—quality of life, services, you name it. . . . My slogan is 'when you wake up in South Dakota, you're still in South Dakota.'"

The early 1980s administration of Governor William J. Janklow was marked by a provincialism rare even for South Dakota. After California refused to extradite an Indian activist who had been arrested in South Dakota in a demonstration, Janklow told 93 South Dakota criminal defendants they could avoid prosecution if they moved to California. In a break with Western state tradition, Janklow also reached agreement to sell South Dakota's water for use in a Wyoming-based coal slurry pipeline, thus provoking court suits from environmentalists, Sioux Indians, and states downstream. The sale was expected to generate some $1.4 billion in revenues to South Dakota over 50 years, and the legislature earmarked proceeds for a development fund to help the Coyote State meet its own water needs through low-interest loans to underwrite water projects. Janklow rolled up a record 71 percent of the vote in winning reelection in 1982.

Agriculture, Great Dams, Tourism

More than 90 percent of South Dakota's land surface is farmland, and agriculture—now a billion-dollar-a-year business—dominates the economy, sustaining both the farms and the cities. The combination of vast grazing lands in the western part of the state and heavy on-farm feeding of corn and other grains in the eastern sections make South Dakota primarily a livestock-producing state. Almost 7 out of every 10 dollars in farm income are derived from livestock, in sharp contrast to North Dakota, where wheat and other grains dominate. South Dakota is second only to North Dakota in spring wheat, however, and produces more rye than any other state. But all the federal farm programs have failed to stop the inexorable trend to bigger and bigger farms. In 1930, South Dakota had 83,000 farms; today, about 41,500; and the average farm size has risen from 439 to 1,095 acres.

The nationwide economic recovery of the World War II years coincided with a cycle of relatively heavy rainfall in the Plains, and South Dakota has not since experienced a serious depression. As in North Dakota, the damming of the Missouri River played an important role in the state's postwar development. South Dakota's equivalent of the Garrison Dam and Diversion Project is the Oahe Project. Harnessing the Missouri, the federal government decided, would eliminate forever the flooding that ravaged the state in the 1930s, bring electrification, improve recreation, and above all provide water to irrigate the dryland farms. As in North Dakota, the grand plans to irrigate vast stretches of the prairie came a cropper. Environmentalists asked such compellingly logical questions as why 110,000 acres, almost all already in wheat and cattle production, should be condemned to irrigate only 190,000 other acres. A local protest group, United Family Farmers, cleverly elected their members to a local board originally set up to promote Oahe. Over the protest of South Dakota's political establishment, they forced the Bureau of Reclamation and Army Corps of Engineers to halt the project. Its legacy today: a long, unused ditch.

Industrialization has proceeded at a snail's pace in South Dakota, but the state grosses millions from tourism. One great attraction is the barren wasteland known as the Badlands in the southwest, aptly called by General Custer "a part of hell with the fires burnt out." The kinder pine forests of the Black Hills are the site of a renowned Passion Play. What they are best known for, however, is Mt. Rushmore, the mountain on which sculptor Gutzon Borglum carved 60-foot high heads of Washington, Jefferson, Lincoln, and Theodore Roosevelt. Only a few miles away sculptor Korczak Ziolkowski for years sought to outdo Borglum with a statue of Crazy Horse and his mount, which would be a stupendous 641 feet long and 563 feet high, hacked out of a mountainside. Ziolkowski got his inspiration in 1939 when Sioux Chief Henry Standing Bear wrote asking him "to caress a mountain so that the white man will know that the red man had great heroes, too." His work far from complete, the great bearded Ziolkowski died in 1982.

Occasionally, the traveler can still get exposed to the Wild West in South Dakota. Deadwood, near the Wyoming border, is the final resting ground for both Wild Bill Hickock and Calamity Jane, but only in 1980 did the town shut down its oldest businesses: Pam's, Dixie's, and the "white door" whorehouses. Forty Deadwood residents mounted a parade protesting the loss of Deadwood's eccentric heritage, but (at least by official report) the brothels remained closed.

The Unhappy Plight of the Sioux

One out of every 25 South Dakotans is a Sioux Indian living on or registered with one of the five reservations that cover hundreds of thousands of acres from the Missouri River Valley westward, the greatest concentration of Indians in any Great Plains state today. There is no more tragic aspect of South Dakota's life.

Once a resourceful, proud, nomadic people who could send 10,000 warriors into battle, the Sioux were forced onto reservations and had to become ranchers and farmers on barely arable land. A Messiah craze appeared among the Sioux in 1890, when one of their number reported a vision in which he had seen the buffalo restored and the white man evicted. Before the resultant disturbances were ended, the great Sioux chief, Sitting Bull, had been killed and several hundred Sioux men, women, and children intercepted by U.S. Cavalry and brutally slain at a creek called Wounded Knee. The Sioux still remember that massacre, the last great clash of the Indian wars, with bitterness. Wounded Knee's symbolic significance was the reason the militant American Indian Movement seized the settlement's church and trading post in 1973 to dramatize their unhappiness with an elected tribal government they contended was dictatorial and corrupt. AIM held Wounded Knee for weeks, an occupation highly successful in media terms (constant national newspaper, Vietnam battle-style television coverage). The publicity convinced Washington to conduct an independent audit of the tribal council's finances—a far cry from the days when the U.S. Cavalry might have stormed the village. Later, two FBI agents were killed by AIM militants. But however unhappy the Sioux were, a majority voted against AIM co-founder Russell Means in a race for tribal chairman and reelected his enemy Richard Wilson, who has remained in that office for many years. The terrible social problems that have been characteristic of reservation life remain. The unemployment rate is staggeringly high, and many people live in log cabins or mobile homes or houses so small that the yard becomes a kind of attic for every waste, from discarded furniture to junked cars.

The conditions in the Sioux nation are not due to a lack of federal assistance. Indeed, the federal government has created a welfare state with a large bureaucracy that doles out enough money to keep people alive. At the core of the problems is the century-long clash of cultural values between the defeated Indian and dominant white culture. This not only pits Indians against whites, but against each other. For many years the federal government encouraged Indians to assimilate into the white culture, and the most fortunate Indians (except for a lucky few who succeeded as ranchers) were the employees of the Bureau of Indian Affairs, many of whom were mixed-bloods who had picked up white people's ways from their parents. Yet assimilation never took hold among many Sioux, who resisted losing their own identity and doubted quite correctly that the white world would accept them anyway.

In the early 1970s, even the federal government made "self-determination" an official policy, and Indian schools were told to stop emphasizing the "superiority" of the white man's ways and to teach Indian pride. But cultural neglect and poverty still rule the reservation, and sometimes the cultural development occurs under the saddest of circumstances. One place the Sioux are learning about their culture is in prison. As a result of AIM's activism—through the courts and a 1975 protest march that included Harry Belafonte and Marlon Brando—the South Dakota Penitentiary now provides Indian religious, educational, and social programs. For many of the Indians in prison, whose past life consisted more of alcohol, violence, and poverty than either Indian or white "culture," the experience of literally passing the peace pipe and entering a sweat lodge (a small tentlike "sauna") has proven to be a spiritual, even life-changing event. But when these people get out of prison, they still have trouble getting jobs. Another very different group of young Sioux have managed to combine cultural awareness and graduate education in law and other professional fields.

The hottest issue for the Sioux is no longer poverty and discrimination, but control of the Black Hills and the mining of uranium from what the Sioux consider sacred lands. In 1980, after 24 years of legal battles, the U.S. Supreme Court ruled that 100 square miles of the Black Hills had been improperly taken from the Sioux; the eight Sioux tribes were awarded $122 million in compensation. Even before the 1980 decision, the Ogalala Sioux had split off from the other tribes, contending that they would be satisfied only by restoration of the land. In April 1981, followers of the Dakota AIM, including Means, set up a Black Hills camp that they named Yellow Thunder after a young Indian who a decade earlier had been made to dance naked by young whites and later was killed. Means' hardline positions, plus his sometimes violent activism, led to charges by South Dakota ranchers and conservatives that he was a socialist or communist. But Means disproved these labels in a speech at a July 1980 Black Hills International Survival Gathering of several thousand people from all over the world. Means' speech was reprinted by *Mother Jones* magazine, which found his words so inflammatorily anti-leftist the editors had to assure their left-wing readership that they did not agree with all he said. Yet the speech contained some of the fieriest and most provocative language ever to come out of South Dakota. A few excerpts:

I do not really believe that capitalism itself is really responsible for the situation in which American Indians have been declared a national sacrifice. No, it is the European tradition; European culture itself is responsible. Marxism is just the latest continuation of this tradition, not a solution to it. . . . There is another way. There is the traditional Lakota way and the ways of the other American Indian peoples. It is the way that knows that humans do not have the right to degrade Mother Earth, that there are forces beyond anything the European mind has conceived, that humans must be in harmony with *all* relations or the relations will eventually eliminate the disharmony. A lopsided emphasis on humans by humans—the Europeans' arrogance of acting as though they were beyond the nature of all related things—can only result in a total disharmony and a readjustment which cuts arrogant humans down to size, gives them a taste of that reality beyond their grasp or control and restores harmony. . . . Distilled to its basic terms, European faith —including the new faith in science—equals a belief that man is God. Europe has always sought a Messiah, whether that be the man Jesus Christ or the man Karl Marx or the man Albert Einstein. American Indians know this to be totally absurd. Humans are the weakest of creatures. . . . Humans are able to survive only through the exercise of rationality since they lack the abilities of other creatures to gain food through the use of fang and claw. But rationality is a curse since it can cause humans to forget the natural order of things in ways other creatures do not. A wolf never forgets his or her place in the natural order. American Indians can. Europeans almost always do. We pray our thanks to the deer, our relations, for allowing us their flesh to eat; Europeans simply take the flesh for granted and consider the deer inferior. . . . It's only a matter of time until what Europeans call "a major catastrophe of global proportions" will occur. It is the role of the American Indian peoples, the role of all natural beings, to survive. A part of our survival is to resist. We resist not to overthrow a government or to take political power, but because it is natural to resist extermination, to survive. We don't want power over white institutions; we want white institutions to disappear. *That's* revolution.

American Indians are still in touch with these realities—the prophecies, the traditions of our ancestors. We learn from the elders, from nature, from the powers. And when the catastrophe is over, we American Indian peoples will still be here to inhabit the hemisphere. I don't care if it's only a handful living high in the Andes. American Indian people will survive; harmony will be reestablished. *That's* revolution.

IOWA

Agristate Extraordinary

IOWA, LUSHLY FERTILE, agristate extraordinary, landlocked, American Gothic, birthplace of Herbert Hoover and Henry Wallace, home of the former's Presidential Library, is the quintessence of America. But Iowa has also entertained a lengthy love affair with the Soviet Union. The Iowa-Soviet connection started in 1959 when Soviet Premier Nikita S. Khruschev, accompanied by an army of diplomats, journalists, and translators, descended on the farm of the late Roswell Garst, near Coon Rapids, to learn something of American agriculture. "It was the funniest damn thing you ever saw," Garst recalled to us several years later. "Khruschev came for symbolic reasons, to show the Russian people his interest in agriculture. He was a real man. He knew how to laugh and yell. So we laughed and yelled back and forth for three or four hours. I enjoyed him, frankly."

Khruschev's visit was hailed as the most "international" event ever to take place on a farm, but it pales in comparison with the relationship that has evolved in the intervening years between Iowa agriculture and foreign buyers, including the Soviet Union. The pervasive technological revolution that has boosted farm yields beyond the dreams of earlier decades has led to vast surpluses the American market could never absorb; about 25 percent of Iowa's food production goes to international markets, resulting in over $2 billion per year in sales. The Soviet Union's need to import food played no small role in Iowa's agricultural prosperity and has turned conservative Iowa farmers into regular readers of international news and advocates of free trade. In the early 1980s, after the Carter and Reagan administrations had limited food exports to the Soviet Union in response to the invasion of Afghanistan and repression in Poland, the Iowa farmers' patriotism turned to deep unhappiness over U.S. government policy. After it was clear that the Soviet Union had simply turned to other countries to buy their grain, and U.S. wheat and corn prices were depressed, we found Roswell Garst's son, Steve, proclaiming the policy a failure. "It was our government's attempt to use food production as the basis of war," Garst told us, "but it probably hurt us worse than the Russians because it hurt us economically." The effect of the embargo, Garst argued, was not only harmful to farmers; it reduced America's trade balance, created a grain glut in the port cities of Galveston and Houston and added inflationary pressures because the government was politically bound to assume part of the farmers' losses. Garst, whose holdings cover thousands of acres, raises 4,000 head of cattle each year and runs a large corn and seed business; he may make more sophisticated arguments than most Iowans, but his views provide a glimpse of the internationalism that pervades present-day Iowa.

Corn, Cattle, and Industry

If there was to be such an explosion of agricultural abundance anywhere on the American continent, it is not surprising that it occurred in Iowa. With only 1.6 percent of the land area of the United States, Iowa has 25 percent of its Grade A topsoil, a legacy of four glacial sweeps across her surface, the last only 10,000 years ago. A native of rockier places, Robert Frost once said of the rich Iowa earth, "It looks good enough to eat without putting it through vegetables."

Iowa is the very heart of the Corn Belt, which stretches from Nebraska and South Dakota clear through to Central Ohio, but only one other state, Illinois, comes close to Iowa's production.* Together with soybeans, alfalfa, and other grains, the crop income of the state's farmers is second only to California. The corn is fed through those convenient creatures, cattle, hogs, and sheep, to create the highest livestock income in the country. Iowa also remains the banner state of the Union for hog production, the third-largest cattle state (behind only Texas and Nebraska), and high in dairy cows, chickens, and sheep. Some 95 percent of the land area of Iowa is under cultivation. No state has a higher standard of living in its rural areas, although the number of people who live on farms has dropped since mechanization, (from 200,000 to about 100,000) and the struggle to maintain a middle-class way of life is intense, especially when international markets are unstable. In most years the value of an average Iowa farmer's land, machinery, buildings, and livestock is more than double the national average. Most Iowa farming is still diversified—a job that takes up to 70 hours a week (11 hours six days a week and 4 on Sunday). But for the man who loves the land and the outdoors and being with his family any time of the day, it's a great life.Some critics have contended that Iowa farmers, as dedicated as they are to their way of life, are less than the best stewards of the soil. Iowa loses more topsoil through erosion than any other state, and many farmers have adopted an "I'll treat my land as I see fit" attitude and been slow to address the problem. By the early 1980s, about half the farmland in the state was tilled without the plow—a recommendation by agricultural experts to help stop erosion. Environmentalists raised concerns about the heavy use of pesticides in this "no-till" agriculture, leaving some farmers wondering which method would be better for their land.

Iowa's largest farm organization is the Farm Bureau, which boasts of 146,000 family memberships and a highly developed buying, lobbying, and

---

*"The Corn Belt," according to J. Russell Smith (quoted by John Gunther), "is a gift of the gods —the rain god, the sun god, the ice god, and the gods of geology." More scientifically, it is land with at least the following: a mean summer temperature of at least 70 degrees, frequent summer showers, and a growing season of 140 or more days.

insurance operation that makes it a major force in the state's life. By general consensus, the Farm Bureau is the most potent influence in the legislature, active on policy issues affecting education, highways, property, and income taxes. The Farm Bureau has remained powerful even though the number of farmers has declined and farmers have lost direct electoral power through reapportionments to correct rural over-representation. In fact, the Farm Bureau membership has increased even as the number of farmers has dropped, suggesting there might be some validity to charges that the Farm Bureau's conservative views often represent the many bankers, agribusinessmen, machinery dealers, and other small town-merchants who belong. Whatever its membership, the Farm Bureau is big business in Iowa. About 50 percent of Iowa Farm Bureau members now have insurance policies with the Bureau, a program that started at the request of its members because regular insurance firms disdained the farmer's business. The Bureau likewise entered the cooperative farm supply business.

In direct contrast to the Farm Bureau's comfortable downtown Des Moines office building and its comfortable relationship with the business community is the National Farmers Organization (NFO), founded in 1955 in the small hamlet of Corning in southwest Iowa and still located there. NFO's approach is simple: because the farmer is the only unorganized man in the highly organized economy of the nation, he is at the mercy of the buyers who set the prices for his goods. Therefore, farmers must organize by boycotting production of selected commodities, or by withholding commodities from the market, until a vacuum occurs in the normal supply and buyers are forced to bid up the price. In NFO's early days, its members sometimes resorted to slaughtering animals and dumping milk to protest low prices and gain nationwide sympathy—though the tactics sometimes backfired. The NFO's history has had its ups and downs, but by the early 1980s, the national membership was marketing—and bargaining on the price of—close to $2 billion in meat, grain, and milk.

The picture of Iowa as one vast breadbasket, the agristate *par excellence,* is only half accurate. True, about three-quarters of the state's people survive economically on industries related to agriculture—either farming itself or food processing or making tractors and other field machines. No state is so consciously aware of its tie to the land, which has always been and remains its greatest resource. Scratch an Iowa factory worker, and one is almost sure to find the son or grandson of a farmer. But the breadbasket image is partially false: many people have left the land, and the daily life of the vast majority of Iowans is remote from farm chores, crops, and livestock. Underlying all that corn, for example, geologists have discovered vast coal deposits extending over at least a third of the state's area. Since World War II, Iowa has developed a diversified industrial base to balance agriculture. Just how dependent Iowa still is on agriculture, however, was illustrated by the farm machinery plant shutdowns and high unemployment rates in the early 1980s when hard-pressed farmers around the country could not afford to buy new equipment. The smaller farm population and low-key industrial growth were reflected in a weak population growth rate of 5.7 percent in the 1970s, bringing the Iowa population to 2,913,808.

A review of its major cities shows how much Iowa has veered away from the pastoral. Des Moines, the capital and the largest city (pop. 191,003, metropolitan area 338,048), is a major insurance, banking, and printing center and is advanced industrially. The once-prosperous city of Dubuque (pop. 93,745), looking across the Mississippi at Wisconsin and Illinois, achieved the dubious distinction of recording the nation's highest unemployment rate—23 percent —in January 1982. That was after Deere & Co., the city's major employer, laid off almost half its force but *before* the Dubuque Packing Co., the city's No. 2 employer, announced it would close the following October. Top business, labor and government leaders quickly galvinized into the Economic Action Coalition and were able to stave off the shutdown; they then turned to strategy for general economic recovery.

Cedar Rapids and Davenport are also major farm machinery producers, and even smaller cities harbor important manufacturing enterprises. Clinton, for example, has steel and chemical companies, while Fort Madison is the home of Schaeffer Pen. The bucolic setting of the Amana colonies is also the manufacturing point for Amana refrigeration equipment, and the little town of Forest City produced two dozen millionaires (some on paper) during the Winnebago camper boom. Even Sioux City, famed for its stockyards, was thrown into a tizzy when its largest employer, Zenith, moved its stereo and television set manufacturing business to Mexico and Taiwan, where labor costs were lower.

There is still, however, the small-town Iowa world of carefree marching bands, the setting for Meredith Wilson's *Music Man;* if one is in Cedar Falls or Algona or Clarina or Mason City or a score of other Iowa towns on the right day of the year, one will hear the spirit poured forth in band concerts of unparalleled excellence. The essential rural flavor of Iowa is also reflected in such events as springtime tulip festivals, the famed Iowa State Fair each August, rodeos, and settler and thresher reunions.

Politics and the Presidential Caucuses

Iowa is by instinct and normal voting pattern Republican, although it has become a closely divided state in recent years. Iowa Republicanism is a clear reflection of the Protestant hard-work ethic of its countless county seats and little towns. History helps explain why: though the state was first peopled by Southerners, coming by way of Kentucky and Missouri, they were followed in the 1840s by settlers from New England, northern New York, and the northern sections of Ohio, Indiana, and Illinois—a Yankee Protestant element that is still dominant. The state also received many Germans (some Protestant, others Catholic), along with Scandinavian, Dutch, and Czech immigrants. But it never had the strong Populist impulses of the cash grain and heavily Scandinavian Plains States such as Minnesota and the Dakotas. The small towns have rarely deviated from straight Republicanism, although the farm areas have veered occasionally to the Democrats for more than a generation now, both in state and federal elections. The farmers' most celebrated rebellion was in 1948, when they helped reelect Harry Truman because of their fear that Thomas Dewey and the Republicans might take away their federal farm programs.

The larger cities, by contrast, tend to have more Roman Catholics and certainly vote more Democratic than most rural areas. If one draws a pie shape on the Iowa map, with the western anchor set at Des Moines and separate lines going to the northeast and southeast corners, only 35 to 40 percent of the state's geographic area is included. But the triangle contains the vast majority of Iowa's major cities: Des Moines, Cedar Rapids, Davenport, Dubuque, Waterloo, Clinton, Ottumwa, Fort Madison, and the like, most of which have grown at the expense of the towns and farmlands. If one puts a couple of jogs on the lines of the triangle, the principal state universities are included as well. This triangle is where the principal liberal and Democratic voting strength of Iowa is located. It is also the area of population growth, while the rest of the state declines. Its growth explains why Iowa is becoming increasingly marginal in its politics, relegating to the status of historical oddity the statement of a great turn-of-the-century Republican Senator, Jonathan Dolliver; "When Iowa goes Democratic, Hell will go Methodist."

Iowa's Republican normalcy failed to take account, however, of Harold E. Hughes, an ex-truck driver, ex-alcoholic Democrat who had Indian features, spoke bluntly, and ignited a revolution in Iowa politics and government when he was elected governor in 1962. Hughes brought to Iowa politics a rare combination of deeply held convictions and exceptional natural intelligence that made him one of the most charismatic, effective reformers the Plains States produced in many years. Hughes gained his greatest fame for successfully overturning Iowa's hypocritical law forbidding liquor by the drink and establishing straight population-based apportionment for the state legislature. But in retrospect, Hughes said he was more proud of other achievements: elimination of capital punishment, establishment of the first pre-release farm for prisoners, major advances in the treatment of alcoholism and mental illness, law enforcement modernization, and industrial development.

In his one term in the U.S. Senate (1969–1975), Hughes chaired a special subcommittee on alcoholism and narcotics. Some Washington regulars accused him of being practically a one-issue senator with his constant attention to "the problem," but a *Washington Post* writer noted that "Washington has trouble with politicians who have passion. They upset the pace." Hughes also fought hard for many of the Democratic party's reforms that opened up the party's apparatus to minorities and women. Many Democratic reformers and the reporters who covered Hughes hoped that he would run for president, but after a brief, unannounced campaign in 1972, he withdrew. In 1973, Hughes announced he was leaving the Senate to devote the rest of his life to another side of his fascinating character: his openly expressed religious faith, at once mystic and evangelistic. Hughes had already served as father confessor to alcoholics, including some prominent politicians; as a lay religious worker, he counseled, among others, Charles Colson, the Nixon aide who was imprisoned for his role in the Watergate scandal.

The elections to the U.S. Senate of Dick Clark in 1972 and John Culver in 1974 proved that other Democrats could be elected to high office in Iowa. But the defeat of both after single terms sent shivers down the spines of liberals in Iowa and across the country. The liberals did not count on the political clout of the New Right, which opposed both Clark's and Culver's liberal views on foreign policy and federally funded abortions and awarded their opponents financial and volunteer help. Clark's successor, former Lieutenant Governor Roger Jepson, was generally considered a lightweight outside the Republican mainstream; Culver's successor, former Rep. Charles E. Grassley, is known as an ornery rural conservative devoted to budget cutting and returning weekly to his farm. One interpretation of the Clark and Culver defeats was provided by Robert Ray, the man who succeeded Hughes as governor. It had fallen to Ray to cope with the state government's financial gaps after the social programs were adopted under Hughes. Ray, a thoughtful, low-keyed man, worked for more taxes and introduced cost-cutting reorganization and a number of innovations, including a program to assist the rail industry in modernizing necessary branch lines. But by the early 1980s, Ray told us, the people's mood had switched from viewing government spending as "responsive" to wanting government to "get out of their lives." Neither Clark nor Culver, both uncompromising liberals, could survive in that new climate.

Nor was the new conservative climate comfortable for Ray, a widely respected stalwart of the shrinking moderate wing of the GOP. By 1982 Ray was the nation's senior governor, with 14 years' service; he had been an effective chairman of the National Governor's Conference and was still enormously popular at home. Only 53, he chose to "retire." The GOP fielded its young, rigidly conservative lieutenant governor, Terry E. Branstad; the Democrats, former U.S. Attorney Roxanne Conlin, a down-the-line liberal. She jumped to an early lead and seemed well on the way to becoming Iowa's first woman governor when she released a balance sheet showing that she and her husband were millionaires—and, thanks to judicious use of tax shelters, had paid no state income tax the year before. That would have been bad enough for any candidate, but nigh onto unforgivable for a Democrat who had been stumping the state castigating Republicans as "the party of privilege" and denouncing tax shelters. The press pounced, flooding newspapers and airwaves with stories about the tax flap in an unrelenting deluge of indignation, led by the enormously influential *Des Moines Register*. Branstad ended up winning with 53 percent of the vote—while Democrats were grabbing control of the legislature and three other major state offices.

Iowa's most conspicuous congressman from the 1950s to the 1970s was H.R. Gross, a cantankerous man of diminutive stature and booming voice who waged an unrelenting, personal war against bloated federal budgets, junketing by high colleagues, and hanky-panky in high places. The bright side of Gross was that his caustic remarks often enlivened dull House debates and forced legislators to be well prepared for debate. Oddly enough, Gross, the Iowa Gothic champion of olden values, may have been one of the first "media candidates" in American history. Many Iowans remember Gross as the voice of doom on Des Moines radio station WHO in his newscasting days before he went to Congress in 1948; the man who introduced Gross and acted his commercials was—yes, Ronald Reagan.

Iowa's presidential caucuses, the earliest in the country, held on an inevitably cold day in January, have escalated the importance of Iowa in presidential politics. Swarms of reporters and TV crews descend upon Iowa to find out whom the Iowans have chosen and why. The Iowa caucuses are supplanting the New Hampshire primary as the first official event of the presidential election year, and the country is probably the better for it, given Iowa's more balanced political climate (and no *Manchester Union Leader*). Winning the Iowa caucuses was the first big break in Jimmy Carter's presidential career; as columnist Jack W. Germond wrote in 1976, Carter achieved "instant legitimacy" by winning the Iowa caucuses. Four years later, Carter trounced Sen. Edward M. Kennedy, heading toward renomination in what would eventually prove an ill-starred renomination bid. George Bush defeated Reagan— a lead that soon evaporated but did help elevate Bush to the vice presidency. For Iowans and other rural Americans, the caucuses perform the additional function of guaranteeing that presidential candidates will address agricultural and rural issues.

Des Moines and Its Great Newspaper

> It was hot that August afternoon in Des Moines, blisteringly hot. The waitress saw me sweltering. "Never mind," she said, "this is the kind of weather that's good for corn."

Thus John Gunther reported on Agristate's capital some years ago, suggesting that, like the rest of Iowa, Des Moines' real preoccupation is with the soil. Even now, one hears from some that Des Moines is "a kind of county seat at the state level." Its chief business is state government, bringing the rest of Iowa to its doorstep, and its factory and office workers are likely to have dads and moms or grandparents back in the small towns or on the farm.

But Des Moines for many decades has also been an important printing, banking, and especially insurance center; it has even been labeled the "Hartford of the West," although its insurance holdings (substantial firms such as the century-old Equitable Life of Iowa, Bankers Life, Central Life, etc.) pale in comparison to those in Hartford or Los Angeles. In modern times, Des Moines has acquired significant amounts of manufacturing.

Surprisingly, Des Moines ranks high among U.S. cities in per capita income, with some amazing concentrations of wealth. But the money was first accumulated by men who specialized in minimizing their risks in banking and insurance, not in maximizing income. As a result, the city has actually suffered from a shortage of risk capital, in contrast to Minneapolis, which has spawned many new products and ideas. The principal manufacturing plants are owned by outsiders, not Des Moines interests. Des Moines' downtown never declined as badly as that of many American cities in the 1950s and 1960s, and the city has long benefited from the unusual amount of cooperation between its political leaders and the business community. In the mid-1960s, city leaders, afraid that offices and major retailers would all filter to the suburbs, persuaded a single store, J.C. Penney Co., to build a new outlet in center city to maintain confidence. In recent years, the city has built a civic center and several parking ramps, while the business community has responded by refurbishing old hotels, building one new one, and constructing office buildings. These plans were developed under an unusually talented young mayor, Thomas Urban, in the late 1960s and carried out by his successor, Richard Olson, a youthful insurance executive who helped cement business-political relations.

At the urging of Governor Ray, Des Moines made a name for itself as an attractive destination for Indochinese refugees. Ray urged Iowans to open their hearts to people forced to leave Indochina after the U.S. withdrawal, and the state made one of the strongest efforts in the nation to resettle the refugees with proper housing, health care, and most importantly, jobs. Ray stated proudly that almost no refugees were on welfare and that the state had been able to absorb the refugees without increasing its low unemployment rate. But the nationwide praise Iowa won for its efforts did not appease the anger of Des Moines' 12 percent black community, which at first helped resettle the refugees and then grew tired of suffering high unemployment while special attention was paid to the new arrivals. "We were amazed at how quickly we were able to get them jobs," black leader Arzania Williams, who had helped with resettlement, told the *Wall Street Journal*. "The employers took them much quicker than they would the black male."

Highly significant voices for moderation and reason in Iowa were for decades the illustrious *Des Moines Register* and *Tribune*, part of the Cowles family publishing empire, which includes the Minneapolis papers. But while the *Register* (with its comprehensive domestic and foreign news coverage) succeeded, its afternoon sister, the *Tribune* (which concentrated on metropolitan news) could not. From a circulation peak of 147,000 in 1947, it slumped to 70,000 in 1982 and shut down that fall, ending a 75-year publishing history. To Michael Gartner, president of the parent company, the issue was economic: "Either we have two mediocre newspapers or one good one." While many readers were disappointed, some public figures who had felt the papers' editorial stings were relieved. "I've been surprised," remarked Tom Whitney, chairman of the Polk County Board of Supervisors, "by the number of people who said, 'Thank God. Now they only get one shot a day at us.'"

The morning *Register* enjoys a unique position among American newspapers in that it is truly a state rather than a city newspaper; on Sunday, when its circulation is over 400,000 (reaching two out of three Iowa households), less than 24 percent of the copies are actually delivered in Des Moines. Sunday

Register delivery is available to any farm or home in any of Iowa's 99 counties. The paper is justifiably famed for the high quality of its reporting and its independence in endorsing candidates, factors which go far to explain why Iowa is not strictly the conservative rural bastion many outsiders imagine it to be.

Nor is the *Register*'s influence felt in politics alone. Thousands of athletes feel it every summer in the *Register*'s Annual Great Bicycle Ride Across Iowa (RAGBRAI, pronounced to rhyme with "frenchfry"). What started as somewhat of a gag by a *Register* staffer in 1973 had ten years later become a slap-happy sporting event with 7,000 entrants, aged to 80, pedaling a meandering 500-odd-mile course from the Missouri to the Mississippi. After suffering through the grueling course of RAGBRAI VII, *Washington Post* managing editor Howard Simons found himself amazed that "a perfectly good, flat state" like Iowa had been metamorphosed "into a series of grueling, back-to-back hills" for the single event.

NEBRASKA

Periodically Populist

On November 2, 1982, the conservative political establishment that had ruled Nebraska for 40 years went to bed in a state of shock. On a single election day, Nebraskans had voted to ban further corporate farming and had thrown out their conventional Republican governor in favor of a 39-year-old divorced Democrat who had protested the Vietnam War. Indeed, as a member of the city of Lincoln's Commission on Human Rights he had strayed so far from conservative Nebraskan norms as to vote for placing a gay rights ordinance on the ballot.

To the outside world, none of these actions may have seemed exceptional. A number of farm states have banned corporate farming. Moreover, Bob Kerrey, the new governor, was hardly a radical. He had served in Vietnam, losing part of a leg and receiving a Medal of Honor, before he came home and demonstrated against a nationally controversial war. Far from taking any anti-capitalist stands, he made his living as a restaurant entrepreneur.

Nor was the Nebraskans' decision to break with their deeply ingrained conservatism without precedent. Populism periodically sweeps this state when the people become disillusioned with conventional politics and politicians. But Nebraskans, located so squarely in the middle of the country, so far from the fast-changing coasts and cities, so protective of their traditional economic and social values, sometimes wait decades to resurrect their populism. The 1982 elections were the first real expression of populist outrage since the great populist Senator George Norris' last election victory in 1936. Kerrey's victory came precisely 40 years after Nebraskans decided to retire Norris. It was a sure sign that the Cornhuskers were truly provoked.

Slow to anger they had been. In virtually every year from World War II onward, more and more family farmers had been squeezed out, even while insurance companies and other corporations increased their agricultural holdings. And while some corporations were good farm neighbors, others were not—using irrigation, for example, to convert ranchland to cropland, thus lowering the water tables and the productivity of other people's land. Eventually a broad array of groups came to support a prohibition on corporate farming—among them the National Farmers Union, the Grange, the National Farmers Organization, Women Involved in Farm Economics, the American Agricultural Movement, and allies in the Catholic Church and organized labor. For close to a decade, the legislature refused to act. But in 1982, with low farm prices spurring the fear of brankruptcy and sale of land to outsiders, the Farmers Union and some of its allies garnered enough signatures to put an anti-corporate state constitutional amendment on the ballot. The conservative Farm Bureau remained neutral, leaving the stock growers and livestock feeders (who feared a corporate ban would make it tougher to build feed lots) as the only agricultural interests in opposition.

That grassroots effort might never have succeeded, however, had it not been for an egregious case of overkill by a major corporate farm interest, the life insurance industry. The Prudential Life Insurance Company, owner and manager of more than 33,000 Nebraska farm acres, poured $250,000 into a media campaign so grandiose that television stations ended up offering the other side free time to avoid being prosecuted for violating the Federal communications Commission's fairness doctrine. When campaign finance reports (required by state law) revealed the corporate kitty had reached $400,000, Nebraskans bristled, deciding the threat of outside control was simply too great. The measure passed, 57 to 43 percent. It did not affect land already in corporate hands and allowed farm incorporations by family members within the fourth kindred. But as a state constitutional amendment, the Nebraska ban became the strongest in the nation.

Kerrey's election as governor was an independent event—incumbent Republican Governor Charles Thone, like Kerrey, favored the corporate ban. Yet there was immense significance in Kerrey's victory—and Thone's defeat. Thone, a former congressman, was a run-of-the-mill Republican. Harried by the recession and Kerrey's aggressiveness, he turned to negative campaign tactics, boasting that he was "what Nebraska is all about" and seeking to paint Kerrey as unpatriotic, ultraliberal, and too "cute" for staid Nebraskans. The strategy backfired.

"A Place to Come from, a Place to Die"

That Nebraska was ripe for some political excitement and innovation there could be little doubt. After losing people from the 1930s through the 1950s, the population finally began to creep up in the 1960s, and in the 1970s there was an increase of 84,673 people (for a new total of 1,570,000). The change was not only numerical: Nebraska's percentage of people over 65, one of the highest in the country, began to decline.

But why, one asks, had Nebraska been so conservative, so long?

The best answer to the riddle we found was in a dry report by Nebraska political scientist James Maynard: "Life in Nebraska was extremely rugged, both physically and emotionally, up to the 1950s, and the parental stock . . . have met and survived some of the most basic laws of nature."

In other words, a sheer rule of survival of the fittest had been at work; those who made it through drought, plague, blizzard, and storm without quitting are the Nebraskans of today. The weak bodies have left; the rugged individualists, or their children, remain. If there is validity in this, then it is easier to understand the Nebraska character.

The state was settled, one native pointed out to us, by boomers—people with great expectations. The agricultural depressions, he said, scared out the optimists and builders and retained the conservators—those who buy property and hold it (an especially German trait). Combine that with a dash of embittered agrarianism springing from the old feeling of exploitation by Eastern bankers and outside milling interests, add the fact that Nebraskans have inbred and received few outside population infusions for two generations, and the components of the Nebraskan personality begin to emerge. Economically this means: Don't overextend yourself, keep taxes down, be cautious. Politically it means: I've always done for myself, so should other folks; government should stay away from giveaways.

Even during its most conservative periods, Nebraska gave birth to leaders, but they often found their talents valued elsewhere. President Gerald Ford was born in Omaha but grew up in Michigan, where he began his political career. President Kennedy's special counsel Theodore C. Sorensen was a Nebraska native, and Kennedy once said, "I've hired more people from Nebraska than voted for me." Sorensen had damning words for the state when he returned to Nebraska in 1961 from the cockpit of national power to address the hundredth anniversary of the birth of George Norris. Nebraska, whose pioneers had vowed that every child should go to the common school, had such a low commitment to education, Sorensen told the assembled, that Nebraska had been "left behind, old, outmoded, a place to come from or a place to die." (It took until 1967 for Nebraska to pass a modern program of general state aid to local schools. Only New Hampshire was more behind the times.)

Until their retirements in the 1970s, Nebraska was represented in the Senate by two Republicans, Roman Hruska and Carl Curtis, who had national reputations as nay-sayers to every new idea. Many an observer of Capitol Hill smiled with quiet satisfaction in 1972 when columnist Jack Anderson had the temerity to go into Lincoln and tell an audience of Nebraskans that Hruska and Curtis were "dolts" and "the two worst members of the United States Senate." Curtis is best remembered for defending Richard Nixon after the release of the tape transcripts, though Curtis did have a little-publicized moderate side as the sponsor of progressive criminal justice reform legislation. History has taken note of Hruska as the first senator ever to advocate a quota for "mediocre" men on the Supreme Court. When asked on television in 1970 about charges that President Nixon's nominee G. Harrold Carswell was "mediocre," Hruska replied, "There are a lot of mediocre judges and people and lawyers. They are entitled to a little representation, aren't they? We can't have all Brandeises, Frankfurters and Cardozos." The remark gave wavering senators a perfect excuse to oppose the nomination.

Nebraska elected two Democrats to succeed Curtis and Hruska—former Omaha Mayor Edward Zorinsky and former Governor J. James Exon. But how Democratic? Zorinsky was a nominal Republican mayor (officially nonpartisan) who seized the Democratic nomination when the Republicans chose someone else; at times he flirted with the idea of crossing the aisle to join the Republicans. Exon captured the governorship in 1970 from a liberal Republican governor, Norbert T. Tiemann, who had provided Nebraska with progressive leadership rare in the postwar era.

The state's House delegation has not been much more exciting, although Tiemman's top planning official, Douglas Bereuter, elected from the district encompassing Lincoln, took a rare Nebraska interest in land-planning issues. The only Democrat to serve Nebraska in the U.S. House since 1948 was John Cavanaugh (1977–81), an Irish Catholic from Omaha, Nebraska's sole center of working-class Catholic and black populations.

All these latter-day politicians pale in comparison with the giant political characters whom Nebraska offered the nation after statehood in 1867. Three times the presidential nominee of his party, Williams Jennings Bryan was the friend of farmers plagued by drought, depression, and creditors; his free-silver banner united the Democrats and Populists. Of him the poet Vachel Lindsay wrote, "He was Nebraska's 'shout of joy'. . . . a gigantic troubadour, speaking like a siege gun, smashing Plymouth Rock with his boulders from the West. . . ."

And for 40 years, until his ultimate defeat in 1942, Nebraska voters sent to Washington one of the most gifted legislators of all time, William George Norris. Norris led the successful fight against the autocratic rule of House Speaker Joe Cannon (a battle that would win him a place in John Kennedy's *Profiles in Courage*). He fought for direct election of senators, fathered the Tennessee Valley Authority, wrote the Lame Duck amendment to the federal constitution, and showed the courage of his convictions by voting against the nation's entry into World War I. Norris said the accomplishment he most wanted to be remembered for was the Rural Electrification Administration he fathered; his reason was that electricity would free women of the slavery of farm work. And of Nebraska, said Norris, "I am a part of its soil, and its soil is a part of me."

The Unicameral and Public Power

Sadly, the two great Nebraska reforms instituted with Senator Norris' backing, the unicameral nonpartisan legislature and public power, do not refute the conservative Nebraska image.

The unicameral legislature was proposed in the early 1930s when Nebraska was in the grip of drought and depression. Frugal Nebraskans had just finished paying for the construction of their magnificent skyscraper Capitol in Lincoln on a pay-as-you-go basis over 10 years, and the unicameral system appealed mightily as a way to cut down on state government expenses.

Nor has the unicameral legislature thwarted the special interests as Norris hoped it would. The most significant element of the system is not its unicameralism, but the fact that the 49 "senators" are elected on a nonpartisan basis. Thus there are no party leaders to set priorities and put a quiet kibosh on bad bills; in effect, each man is his own party, and logrolling is rampant. The relationship between lobbyists and senators is a warm one. Many ex-legislators become lobbyists, and lobbyists win legislative seats.

One must recognize several positive features of Nebraska's unicameral system, even though they all seem more procedural than substantive: bills cannot be stalled by petty bickering between two chambers, for instance; committee work is not duplicated; almost all bills introduced get a public hearing. An interesting experiment would be for some state to try a *partisan,* unicameral legislature.

Public power, the second Nebraska reform pointed to as evidence of progressive spirit, has been going strong since the 1930s and until the late 1970s gave Nebraska some of the lowest power rates in the nation. No one now suggests going back to private power. But the fact is that public power evolved not because of distrust of private power interests or a desire for cheap power for all the people. Rather, the drought-plagued farmers sitting in the legislature at the depth of the Depression voted for public power so that they could get the federal government to finance irrigation of their fields; the vehicle that would accomplish that goal—large reservoirs that would also have hydroelectric generating capacity—was in many ways incidental. Once the public power system was established, Nebraskans saw no need for an oversight commission and gave management little direction. The result: by the 1970s, rates were creeping up despite the lack of a profit motive and the use of tax-exempt bond financing. Management had taken on a "chamber-of-commerce" growth attitude (despite indications of falling demand) and was discussing joint national projects with private utilities even though farmers protested the construction of additional power lines over their fields.

"The Agribusiness Economy" and the Cities

Set astride the 98th Meridian like its Plains neighbors, the Dakotas to the North and Kansas to the South, Nebraska has the familiar pattern of a cyclically moist east and a permanently semi-arid west. Coursing from west to east across Nebraska and joining the Missouri near Omaha is the Platte River, its valley a fertile, irrigated strip in which corn, sugar beets, potatoes, and beans can be grown even in the driest regions. So much of Nebraska is in agricultural use, in fact, that the Nature Conservancy, a private conservation group, has purchased a 54,000-acre, 22-mile stretch of untilled land near Norden so that future generations may comprehend the vast prairies that once covered the mid-section of America.

"Agribusiness" indeed is what Nebraska chiefly lives on; some 14 million acres are under cultivation in addition to the great ranches, some as large as 120,000 acres, where Angus and Herefords graze over the Sandhills and produce three-quarters of the state's farm income. Nebraska's interior ranchers and farmers sport business acumen that puts them light years ahead of their small-town cousins in business. The greatest threats to agriculture in Nebraska may come from the exhaustion of water supplies and increasing costs of the fertilizer and chemicals on which the industry is based. Next to Nebraska's thick rug of alluvial soil, water is doubtless the state's most important asset. It is a fantastic resource—547 trillion gallons, or enough to cover the entire state to a depth of 34 feet if pumped up—as long as it is properly managed. Some 6.7 million acres of Nebraska farmland are now irrigated. There is no immediate crisis, but Governor Kerrey in 1982 began trying to achieve a consensus that would make state water planning possible.

Nebraska factory jobs, chiefly related to agriculture, have been growing, and in the 1960s outstripped farm employment for the first time. On a broad scale, however, Nebraska has been unsuccessful in attracting the quality and quantity of industries to hold its rural and small-city population. Strategic Air Command headquarters, the place from which the command would go forth if the United States were to launch an airborne nuclear attack, is located at Offutt Air Force Base, south of Omaha.

Seventy percent of the people now live in the eastern third of the state, mostly in Omaha and Lincoln, the cities developed by the Union Pacific and Burlington railroads, respectively. Omaha, according to the 1980 Census, had 311,681 people, with a quarter million more in the suburbs—a huge metropolis by Plains standards. The famed packing plants have fallen on evil days, but in the 1960s the city began a rebirth by selling the City Hall to the Woodmen of the World Life Insurance Company, replacing it with a handsome sky-scraper, downtown's first significant building in decades. Significant numbers of Irish and Czech Catholics and blacks live on Omaha's south side. Many are descendants of railway workers. Omaha was the scene of racial violence in the late 1960s and again in the 1980s. Its mayor in the early '80s, Mike Boyle, was a fiscally conservative Democrat out of the ethnic Irish Catholic network, which dominates Omaha politics. He pressed for revival of the downtown business district and seemed likely to be a force for Democratic politics in Nebraska for some time.

Sixty miles west of Omaha lies Lincoln (pop. 171,932), a pleasant, green, Protestant-dominated town once lambasted by Willa Cather for insularity and smugness, but due to the state government and university, the most liberal voting community in Nebraska. Its landmark is the limestone shaft of the state capitol, rising 437 feet above the plains and nicknamed, inevitably, "the penis of the prairies." Under the leadership of its unusually sharp mayor, Helen Boosalis, Lincoln won a National Municipal League All-America city award in 1977–78. The judges cited it for the unusual amount of cooperation between neighborhood groups, City Hall, and the metropolitan region in the city's redevelopment scheme.

The big action in Lincoln—as far as most Nebraskans are concerned—is football. The sport approaches an obsession in this state. The stadium of the "Big Red" at the University in Lincoln has 76,000 seats, more than Yankee Stadium. Ever since the 1920s, when the Cornhuskers turned out to be the only team able to vanquish Knute Rockne and his Four Horsemen, football has been what Nebraskans had in common. Judging from responses to a 1982 newspaper poll, allegiance to the University of Nebraska football team is the only reservation that Nebraskans in the state's western panhandle would have about seceding from Nebraska to join lower-tax Wyoming. As *Life* noted, "Omaha lawyers and ranchers from Chadron recite a shared litany of the team's past glories. School boys and farm wives know every word to *Dear Old Nebraska U.*"

To charitable donors, the best-known settlement in Nebraska is Boys Town, started on a farm 10 miles from Omaha in 1917 by Msgr. Edward J. Flanagan as a nonsectarian home for homeless, neglected, and under-privileged boys. Like many other Nebraska institutions, Boys Town con-tinued on the same track for many years after conditions in the rest of the world had changed. Until 1974, the "city of little men" was unbelievably regimented; the inhabitants ate according to a series of bells, mail was cen-sored, and "scrip" money was used. In 1972, the Omaha Sun Newspapers disclosed that Boys Town had accumulated $209 million from investments and solicitations. Fund raising was suspended for a year, and part of the endowment has been devoted to satellite homes around the country so that boys no longer have to travel to remote Nebraska to be helped.

One ought not leave Nebraska without noting the array of performers who have left Nebraska's prairies for glittering careers. Marlon Brando and the late Henry Fonda both got their starts in Brando's mother's playhouse in Omaha. That symbol of sophisticated elegance, dancer Fred Astaire, was born in Nebraska. But to many Americans, Nebraska is most important as the home state of the kings of talk show television—Dick Cavett, darling of elite audi-ences, and Johnny Carson, the comedian of the masses whose ability to draw 13.5 million viewers at bedtime earns him $3 million per year. The National Broadcasting Company agreed to pay Carson that fantastic sum after he threatened to retire in 1979, and the stock of the Radio Corporation of America (NBC's parent) began plummeting. Stockholders had discovered that Car-son's single show was responsible for 17 percent of NBC's earnings—not bad for a prairie son who started out doing magic tricks in small Nebraska towns.

KANSAS

The Eclipsed State

"WHEN ANYTHING IS GOING TO HAPPEN in this country, it happens first in Kansas," William Allen White, fabled editor of the *Emporia Gazette*, once wrote. Kansas, he said, is "hardly a state but a kind of prophecy."

On went the list of Kansas firsts: scene of fiery abolitionist crusades of the 1850s led by John Brown, who was executed after his abortive attack on Harper's Ferry; birthplace of the prohibitionist movement in America; seedbed of the Populist party and embittered agrarian dissent; early and strong adherent to Bull Moose Progressivism.

White wrote between the world wars. Today Kansas, home to 2,363,679 people in 1980, 31 percent more than in 1940, is scarcely the place where things happen "first." Indeed, nowhere on the American continent can the eclipse of a region or state as a vital force—a focal point of creative change or exemplar of national life—be felt so strongly and poignantly as in Kansas. If the Plains States became an economic and political backwater in the postwar years (a case not difficult to document), then the slide into obscurity is all the more tragic for Kansas, simply because she stood for so much and gave so much to the nation in her earlier years.

William Allen White's Kansas

As time goes on, White appears more and more as the pivotal figure of Kansas history, the man in whom her strange voices of protest and conservatism, ruralism and wise worldliness, all seemed to have been concentrated—and whose death diminished his home state.

It was only 14 years before William Allen White's birth, in 1868, that the Kansas-Nebraska Act repealed the Missouri Compromise and opened the way for proslavers and freestaters to fight it out for possession of the new land. In the "Bleeding Kansas" of 1854–57 was held the dress rehearsal for the Civil War; the state's admittance to the Union as a free state in 1861 marked an historic victory for a determined contingent of New England abolitionists whose fierce piety would dominate Kansas culture for years to come.

In describing the peopling of Kansas, White emphasized the Yankee nature of the blood flowing in Kansas veins, derived from the first wave of New England settlers in the 1850s and later a wave of Union veterans and their wives seeking free homesteads. Kansas, White noted, adopted prohibition and advertised it to keep out "the beer drinking, liberty-loving immigrants from northern Europe which Kansas needed so badly to enrich her blood." But contrary to White, New Englanders were never numerically dominant; in 1860, there were only 4,208 Kansans of New England birth compared to a total of 78,539 born in other states. Francis H. Heller, of the University of Kansas, points out that it took three tries to produce a state constitution, largely because the proslavery and antislavery forces were so evenly matched. "Leavenworth and Atchison," Heller notes, "are to this day as Southern in atmosphere and outlook as if the Mason and Dixon line were at the Nebraska border."

Most of White's childhood was actually spent in the little frontier town of El Dorado, Kansas, some 60 miles from Emporia; visits by Indians, shootings, lynchings, cowboys, open gambling, and wide-open saloons were all part of life in the town. As a boy, White also witnessed prairie fires, tornadoes, terrible droughts, and infestations of grasshoppers; and he watched thousands of "mover" wagons carrying settlers toward the open prairie lands of western Kansas. White's childhood and early professional years embraced some of Kansas' historic reforms: state regulation of the freight and passenger rates of the rapacious railroads, an eight-hour labor law, compulsory education, outlawing of child labor, control of oil and gas companies, "blue sky" legislation to control investment companies, banking regulation, and pioneering in women's suffrage.

At the age of 27 White purchased the *Emporia Gazette*; just a year later he wrote the editorial that would make him famous, "What's the Matter with Kansas?" As White saw it then, Kansas' trouble was a surfeit of free silver, Democrats, and hell-raising Populists; under their domination, he said, Kansas had become "poorer and ornerier and meaner than a spavined, distempered mule." In time though, White freely acknowledged his error in condemning the radicals of the 1890s and decided Kansas suffered from too much conservatism. "Being what I was, a child of the governing class, I was blinded by my birthright," White wrote.

In the first decades of the century, White became a confidant of and publicist for President Theodore Roosevelt and the Progressive Movement. He backed American entrance into the League of Nations and ran for governor on an anti-Ku Klux Klan platform when the Klan reared its head in Kansas. In the 1930s, he helped launch Herbert Hoover's and Alf Landon's presidential campaigns; while remaining true to the GOP at election time, he did support many New Deal laws to tame monopoly capitalism. Just before World War II, he was an active opponent of isolationism. The Republican party had no more influential and tenacious spokesman for moderation, liberalism, internationalism, and adaptation to changing times.

And yet it was White's special sensitivity to human qualities that gave him the power he had. In 1921, when White's daughter, Mary, only 17, died after a horseback riding accident, the editorial White wrote for the *Gazette*, picked up and printed throughout the land, established his national role as a sensitive interpreter of life. After commenting on Mary White's simple life, her pure, intense, girlish enthusiasms, her fight to get a restroom for the black girls at her high school, her father concluded,

> For her pallbearers only her friends were chosen: her Latin teacher, W.L. Holtz; her High School principal, Rice Brown; her doctor, Frank Foncannon; her friend, W.W. Finney; her pal at the *Gazette* office, Walter Hughes; and her brother Bill. It would have made her happy to know that her friend, Charley O'Brien, the traffic cop, had been transferred from Sixth and Commercial to the corner near the church to direct her friends who came to bid her good-bye.
>
> A rift in the clouds in a gray day threw a shaft of sunlight upon her coffin as her nervous, energetic little body sank to its last sleep. But the soul of her, the glowing, gorgeous, fervent soul of her, surely was flaming in eager joy upon some other dawn.

Increasing steadily in influence in Kansas and the nation at large, White lived on for two more decades. In 1944, a *Chicago Sun* reporter would send his report of White's own funeral: "In the cemetery, in the dying sun, under the dead trees, William Allen White was only a tired editor gone home to greet his little girl."

Kansas in the Shadows

By the sheer force of his personality and writing, White had kept Kansas' name alive—if no longer as a driving political force, at least an an exemplar of the best of American life. Since his passing, the Sunflower State seems to have slipped into the shadows. Occasionally a Kansan name appears in newspaper headlines across the country—Alf Landon reaching another birthday, his daughter, Nancy Kassebaum, winning election to the U.S. Senate in 1978, or Senator Robert Dole speaking out for the Republican cause.* Kansas also makes news whenever the state considers revising its constitutional ban on sales of liquor "in open saloons"—and then rejects the idea, sending Kansans back to their hypocritical private clubs. But as a general rule, people or events in Kansas are rarely of enough importance to be reported outside the state's borders. Kansas seems to have become an extraordinarily ordinary place, unnoticed by most Americans.

Kansans, quite understandably, may take exception to our analysis. After reading an early draft of this chapter, Francis Heller, of the University of

---

*Despite Kansas' general national eclipse of recent decades, a special niche in the hearts of his countrymen has been carved out in his twilight years by Alf M. Landon. Unfairly characterized by Democrats and many in the media as a colorless, standpat Midwesterner during and after his disastrous race against F.D.R. in 1936, Landon did, in fact, initiate the long process of reshaping the Republican party from its Depression-era neanderthalism into a broadened vehicle that could deal in rational terms with the emerging phenomena of big government, conservation, farm relief, and social security.

Kansas, wrote: "I think you have very accurately perceived the stagnant mood of the public scene in Kansas today. *I wish you were wrong.*" Perhaps, Heller suggested, Kansas ought to be declared "a national monument, the best source of quality human talent—most of it for export." The University of Kansas has produced an unusual number of Rhodes Scholars, Heller noted, but today those scholars are "scattered from Boston to Australia." Perhaps, Heller concluded, "Kansas is not the eclipsed state, but the exporting state. Somehow that sounds less depressing."

When one speaks of famous Kansas exports, the name of Dwight David Eisenhower must head the list. Eisenhower spent his boyhood in Abilene, that little Kansas city that had once been the great receiving station for the massive cattle drives from Texas. His military career removed him from the Kansas scene, though he did come back for rather frequent visits. But in Eisenhower's selection for the Republican presidential nomination in 1952 an important role was played by three Kansans: Roy Roberts, famed editor of the *Kansas City Star*; former Senate and Republican National Committeeman Harry Darby; and Senator Frank Carlson. This Kansas group recruited Eisenhower to run for president and conceived the strategy of demanding openly approved rules in an open convention and challenging the rigged Southern delegations supporting Senator Robert A. Taft. Later, Eisenhower chose Abilene as the place for his Presidential Library and final resting place, to which he came in 1969. But he had lived so many places and had been away from Kansas so many decades that no one thought of him primarily as a Kansas president. There was no "Kansas gang" in the White House when he was president, and it will be recalled that Eisenhower chose Gettysburg, Pennsylvania, rather than Abilene, as his home for the last two decades of his life.

Since an aging Arthur Capper—a battler for social reform and father of the co-op banking system—stepped down in 1948, Kansas has sent few powerful leaders to Congress. In the postwar years, Senators Frank Carlson, Andrew F. Schoepel, and James Pearson were hard-working and thoughtful, but low-key senators. Robert Dole, who took over Carlson's old seat in 1969, is a tough ambitious partisan who singlehandedly fought his way up in national politics to become the Republican vice presidential nominee in 1976 and, for a short time, a presidential candidate in 1980. As chairman of the Republican National Committee during the Watergate period of the early '70s, Dole developed a reputation as a highly articulate, self-appointed defender of the Nixon administration. Dole's wise-cracking, strident image softened in the early 1980s when Republicans took control of the Senate for the first time in nearly 20 years. Suddenly one of the three most powerful members as chairman of the Finance Committee at a time of economic turmoil, Dole almost overnight grew in maturity and stature as he helped achieve the compromise to assure extension of the Voting Rights Act, resisted cuts in the food stamp program, and wrote and nurtured the 1982 bill raising taxes over the opposition of many of his Republican colleagues. Part of Dole's apparent concern for the less fortunate stemmed from his own memories of the disabling wounds he suffered in World War II and his difficult recovery, but he also believed that if the Republicans were going to be a majority party, they would have to reach out to broader constituencies.

With few exceptions, obscurity has been the fate of Kansas' other politicians and its state government. Its U.S. House delegation had the disadvantage of often being 100 percent Republican in an era when the Democrats controlled Congress. Kansas state government, actually controlled by Populist governors for a period in the turbulent 1890s, has settled down to complete typicality in modern times. Take any measure of government policy and performance—from taxation to services, highways to education—and Kansas will rank about midway in the 50 states. The outstanding governor from the 1940s onward was John A. Anderson, Jr. (1961–65), a thoughtful moderate who began major strides in reform of the state prison system and a sweeping program to consolidate school districts.

Kansas' political history is inextricably bound up with its newspapers. For decades, no influence could rival that of the *Kansas City Star*, edited and printed in Missouri but carried wherever the rails went, and farther, into Kansas. (John Gunther had this to say about Kansas City, Missouri, home of the *Star:* "This great and extraordinary city, while not the capital of its own state, is in effect the capital of another, a situation without parallel in the country.") No paper now published or distributed in the state of Kansas has either the distinction or influence of papers like the old *Star* under its 300-pound domineering editor Roy Roberts, who died in 1967, or White's *Emporia Gazette*, John P. Harris' *Hutchinson News*, or Ed Howe's *Atchison Globe*. Real power in Kansas today, close observers of the legislature relate, is with the banks, the power companies, and still to a substantial degree, the railroads. Among the farm groups, only the Farm Bureau can exert substantial influence, but even it triumphs only when its stands coincide with those of the economic interests named above.

The Economy: From Dust Bowl to Vegetable Bowl and Industry

The strange irony of modern Kansas is that while its national role has diminished, the life of its people has improved immeasurably since the dust bowl and Depression days of the 1930s. In those lean years, the dust storms howled so unremittingly across the High Plains that many lost their faith in the land. Thousands fled the state. The situation was the worst in the High Plains of western Kansas, but serious enough in the Flint Hills region of center state (an area of rolling hills with heavy grass cover) and in traditionally more moist and fertile eastern Kansas. But today, even on the High Plains, an agriculture of abundance has emerged through irrigation, soil conservation, and new farming techniques. To be sure, High Plains weather still brings hazards; hail and disease and drought such as the one in 1980 wipe out hundreds of acres of crops. As in other agricultural states, Kansas has witnessed severe declines in family farming with inflationary pressures and poor markets forcing many farmers to sell out to big-scale corporate operations or land developers. Some 1,000 farms were lost between 1975 and 1981 alone. Depending on the year, Kansas remains America's No. 1 or No. 2 wheat producer. In raw dollar terms it is not wheat, but livestock that produces a majority of the Kansas agricultural dollar. Thanks to federally aided construction of farmponds and irrigation by subterranean water, Kansas also grows cucumbers, tomatoes, carrots, beans, even lettuce and cantaloupes on the High Plains that were once the very heart of the dustbowl. But there may be a dark cloud on the horizon: not rain, not a grasshopper plague like that of the '30s, but depletion of the great Ogallala Aquifer.

Not normally included in government crop reports is one that thrives happily in Kansas, when allowed: *Cannibis sativa*, better known as marijuana. The weed flourishes across the Plains States, but nowhere in such profusion as in Kansas, where it was once planted intentionally by farmers who sold its strong fibers to rope manufacturers. The Kansas name is "loco weed," for its giddy effect on farm animals.

Not all Kansas' wealth comes from its fields. Wichita, Kansas' only serious metropolis (pop. 279,272, metropolitan area 411,313), busily produces jet parts and general aviation craft, processes grain and livestock, mills flour, and even refines some oil. Wichita was once an important point on the Chisholm Trail over which Texas longhorns were driven north to the railheads of Kansas, and its stockyards still process thousands of head of cattle a year. Wichita's most prominent modern industry, however, is aerospace; Cessna, Beach, Gates, Learjet, and Boeing are all in Wichita and produce a substantial portion of the nation's private and commuter airplanes. Wichita is a well-managed town governmentally but has suffered from ongoing racial discord.

Kansas City, Kansas (pop. 161,087), the state's second-largest city, inevitably lives under the shadow of its big brother across the river, Kansas City, Missouri. Kansas City, Kansas, which used to live off the railroads and packing houses, has maintained its strong industrial base by building the first industrial park in the West and attracting food-processing, electronics, and automobile assembly plants.

The Department of Defense spends about $1.2 billion in Kansas each year at military installations, including two that date back to the Indian wars of the 19th century: Fort Riley, the home of the First Infantry Division, and Fort Leavenworth, which houses the world's largest tactical school for advanced military training and is better known for its federal military and civilian prisons.

Kansas also has significant oil and gas production, an asset of no small value in today's world: studies of the late 1970s showed the state produced, in aggregate, 134 percent of its energy needs, compared to only 21 percent in Nebraska, or 9 percent in Missouri. And through decontrol of oil prices, state government revenues were expected to climb $900 million during the '80s.

Economically, Kansas' Achilles heel has been its southeast corner, known as the "Kansas Balkans" because of its variegated East European ethnic base and divisive, sometimes radical, politics. The area also has a history of labor discord in its coal, lead, and zinc mines. In the last 25 years, a 10-country development group named Mid-America, Inc. has been so successful in attracting industries that the unemployment rate is usually far below the national average, even if wage levels lag.*

A lot of tourist dollars are dropped by travelers on their way to or from Kansas' western neighbor, Colorado; as they race across the prairies, a few even pause to look at Holcomb, site of the mass murder of the Clutter family made famous by Truman Capote's *In Cold Blood*. The more usual sights include the Eisenhower Center at Abilene, Dodge City of Old West fame, the Agricultural Hall of Fame near Kansas City, the Wichita Art Museum, and recreational lands around federal reservoirs and lakes. If the tourists take the time to look carefully as they drive across the Flint Hills region of eastern Kansas, they will catch a glimpse of what the prairie was like before men tilled most of it for fields of corn and wheat. This area contains what is possibly the largest area of essentially untouched prairie anywhere on the continent, with rolling hills and flats and broad vistas, the original tall bluestem grass, the magnificent wildflowers from spring into the autumn.

The Amazing Menningers

With logic that is hard to question, many Kansans regard the Menninger Foundation in Topeka as their state's most important institution. The internationally known psychiatric treatment center has been run with an amazingly practical and inventive bent by Drs. Karl and Will Menninger and their sons ever since its doors first opened in 1919.

Clinical services have always been the backbone of Menninger programs, and more than 100,000 patients have registered since the sanitarium opened. Since the foundation can handle only about 500 adults and children as hospital patients and another 12,000 on an outpatient basis per year, its directors have focused on preventive psychiatry, or put in a broader context, fostering the mental health of society. The Menningers have led the way for psychiatric involvement in industry, in poor neighborhoods, in rehabilitation of criminal offenders, and more recently in developing model group homes for neglected children and finding unsubsidized jobs for disabled individuals.

We asked Menninger psychiatrists if there has been an increase in the rate of mental illness in America since World War II. Their reply was that in

---

*The Balkans city of Pittsburg plays an important, little known part in American life: it is the home of "Pittsburg Personal Census Service Branch," where the U.S. Census Bureau keeps more than a billion Census listings—one for every household and its inhabitants in the nine Census counts from 1900 through 1980. Just by giving the name of the head of household, the Census year, and state, a person can obtain a certificate attesting to his age at the time of the Census, his place of birth, race, and sometimes even his occupation—legal proof, often unobtainable elsewhere, for inheritance and insurance claims, passports, Social Security and Medicare benefits, and naturalization.

terms of classic psychoses and neuroses, apparently not. But there has been a dramatic rise in the indexes of American divorces, crime, juvenile delinquency, illegitimate births, and drug use. "The very processes of living in America today seem increasingly stressful," the foundation's J. Cotter Hirschberg, M.D., told us. But Hirschberg is also concerned about our affluent society's tendency "to seek instant relief for whatever ails us by popping a pill, by running to the doctor for the slightest complaint with a request for a prescription." As an alternative, Menninger psychiatrists are now promoting the development of better "coping" strategies to relieve or manage stress, including biofeedback training, which enables people to control or prevent disorders such as hypertension, anxiety, and migraine headaches and to reduce the symptoms of asthmatic and arthritic patients. "Just as we are finding that our national gluttony in energy is going to force us to change the way we live, we also will find future availability of health care and the skyrocketing health costs will force us to take some individual responsibility to change our lifestyles to avoid illness," Hirschberg said. Coming from the prestigious Menninger Foundation, those were important and timely words for both the mental health profession and society.

MISSOURI

Microcosm, U.S.A.

"Missouri is all America in one place," wrote Irving Dilliard when he was editorial page editor of the *St. Louis Post-Dispatch* some years ago. "In May, Missouri is Virginia and billowing apple orchards pink-white for blossomtime. In late June, it is the beginning of the Great Plains and waving, golden-ripe wheat of Kansas, Nebraska and Dakotas. In August, Missouri is Illinois' blazing cornland prairie. It is rocky New England farmlands, bright with larkspur and hollyhocks along rail fences. It is sun-baked mine fields of Oklahoma, New Mexico and Arizona. It is broad patches of cotton and beet pickers with their bulging bags from Alabama, Mississippi and Louisiana."

Today, Missouri, because it has no people-packed "suncoasts," is perhaps less typical of the whole U.S.A. But aside from that, Missouri is still about the best microcosm there is of our country. Part of the reason lies in Missouri's unique geographic position. Its borders are abutted by such wildly contradicting ecologies and cultures as those of Nebraska and Tennessee, Kansas and Kentucky, Illinois and Oklahoma, Iowa and Arkansas. The state in the midst of those eight is bound to be something of a potpourri of America.

Then there are the two great cities—St. Louis, last metropolis of the East, and Kansas City, the first of the West—the two set on Missouri's longitudinal extremes, making her, as William Seward, Secretary of State in the cabinets of Abraham Lincoln and Andrew Johnson, envisioned, "the middle man, the mediator, the common center between the Pacific and the Atlantic."

And to the equation one must add Missouri's two great arteries of water, providing her with 1,937 miles of navigable waterway and access to the entire heartland and the Gulf of Mexico. From the northwest comes the muddy, turbulent Missouri River, now finishing its course over a thousand miles of prairie as it cuts eastward through Missouri toward St. Louis in its inexorable surge to the Mississippi. From the North comes the "Father of Waters" itself (ironically, with less water flow than the Missouri it absorbs), forming Missouri's eastern border before it dips into the Deep South.

Missouri as a microcosm of the United States is well illustrated by her regions, her clear cut geology, the ancestry of her people, and her politics.

Rich farmland not unlike that of neighboring Iowa covers the third of Missouri that lies north of the Missouri River; its soil is ideal for field crops, cattle feeding, and hogs. Some of the first settlers in the counties between the Missouri and Mississippi rivers in central and northeastern Missouri had come upriver from the South. Slaveholding was widespread among these people; they sympathized with the South in the Civil War; and for more than a century their region has been known as "Little Dixie." North and northwest of Little Dixie are a number of Iowa border counties settled by sturdy yeomen from Ohio, Iowa, and Kansas. South of the river one finds poorer, hillier land.

The most famous region is the Ozark Mountains (rather, hills, since the highest is only 1,772 feet above sea level). This is a picturesque, and in places remote, land of 10,000 natural springs, first peopled by the suspicious backwooders of Kentucky, eastern Tennessee, and West Virginia. They scorned the slaveholding ways of their fellow Southerners in Little Dixie, sided with the Union in the war, and developed a culture of hillbilly ballads and rich mountain lore. Poverty sometimes reaches extremes in the Ozarks, one of America's most economically depressed areas. For several decades, "civilization" has intruded into parts of the Ozarks through scenery-despoiling billboards and curio and trinket shop tourism. And in recent times the Ozarks have become one of Middle America's greatest recreation areas, where huge man-made lakes and pristine streams appeal to tourists from Chicago to New Orleans.

Finally, we must mention the seven counties of the Missouri "Bootheel," which digs in between Tennessee and Arkansas on the state's southeastern extremity. These counties are dead ringers for the Old South—on flat delta cotton-growing land, with high percentages of blacks and traditionally Democratic Deep South voting habits. The bootheel was actually a wheat-growing area and Northern oriented until 1924, when the boll weevil ruined the cotton crop in adjoining states and encouraged the invasion of Southern cotton growers, who brought thousands of black sharecroppers with them.

Not regions in the broad geographic sense, but nevertheless vital factors in the microcosm that Missouri is, are the metropolitan areas of St. Louis and Kansas City, which account for 65.9 percent of the 4,917,444 people living in Missouri. They reflect almost every urban problem and prospect known across America.

The roots of Missourians and the state's history have produced an independent "show me" spirit and cussed streak that surfaces again and again. "I come from a state that raises corn and cotton and cockleburs and Democrats," a now forgotten congressman, William Vandiver, declared in 1889. "Frothy eloquence neither convinces nor satisfies me. I am from Missouri. You have got to show me."

The origins of the "show me" spirit appear to come from the major share of the modern Missouri bloodstream, which descends from the Southerners who came before the Civil War; they were not a conforming lot, but rather independent backwoodsmen or restless younger sons of plantation owners seeking *lebensraum*. And in this century, Missouri experienced rather little of the southern and eastern European migration stream that prompted Anglo-Saxons to forget their differences and make common cause in other states.

Finally, consider the legacy of the War Between the States. The conflict tore Missouri cruelly asunder. Some 30,000 of her youth fought in gray uniform, about 109,000 in blue. Exactly 1,160, or 11 percent of the engagements of the war, took place on Missouri soil. And the conflict was not just formal and military, but internal too; the passions of the war set family against family, county against county. There were murders, bushwhacking, and general guerrilla warfare. When the war was ended, the enemy had not retreated to some distant other region of America but was still immediate: if not at one's own supper table, then over the hill in the next county. In rural Missouri, with its more static population, the enmities of the war would eclipse every other political issue and influence elections for more than 100 years. In that atmosphere of suspicion and latent hostility, no easy consensus of people could emerge; rather, questioning, conflict, and perversity prevailed.

The "show me" spirit has produced some remarkable national leaders. One thinks fondly back to 1948 and that grinning, delighted face of President Harry S Truman, on his way back to Washington after thwarting every prognosticator to defeat Thomas E. Dewey. Of the momentous decisions, foreign and domestic, that Truman made as president to set the nation on its course in the postwar years, no recital is required here. But it is good to recall the words of Washington Cathedral Dean Francis B. Sayre at Truman's memorial service in 1972. "There were no wrinkles in his honesty," Sayre said; he was a man "earthy, plain, of sturdy soul and tempered true."

But also consider other, less known Missourians:

•St. Louisian Clark M. Clifford, brought into public life by Harry Truman, was influential for years behind the scenes in formulating American foreign and defense policy before he rose to national prominence as President Johnson's Secretary of Defense in 1968. He later overcame his image as the embodiment of the military-industrial establishment to pressure Johnson to announce an end to the bombing of North Vietnam and begin disengagement.

•Thomas H. Benton, who represented Missouri in the Senate during her first 30 years of statehood, from 1820 to 1850, went to Congress as a Southerner, became a spokesman of the Western frontier people, and finally lost his seat when his stalwart stand against slavery destroyed his base of support at home.

•Stuart Symington, who was born of an aristocratic Maryland family but moved to Missouri early in his adult life and became a U.S. Senator, was transformed late in his career from Vietnam hawk to dove. Some said it was out of conviction; others, because he was in the race of his life against John Danforth. Symington did run a half-credible race for the Democratic presidential nomination in 1960.

•Thomas F. Eagleton was first elected to the Senate in 1968 and was George McGovern's vice-presidential running mate until it was revealed that he had been hospitalized on three occasions in the early 1960s for nervous exhaustion and fatigue and had twice undergone electric shock treatments for depression. Eagleton left the national ticket but continued to be elected to the Senate. He offered Missourians, as one reporter noted, "intense social conscience, revved-up personal drive, and a first-rate extroverted wit."

•John C. Danforth, Ralston Purina heir, lawyer, ordained Episcopal priest, state attorney general before he became one of the richest men in the U.S. Senate, was known for his mesmerizing speeches (some said sermons). Danforth exercised his Missouri skepticism on extensions of federal welfare and health programs and the SALT treaty; first elected in 1976, he has been described by political analyst Michael Barone as one of the "cerebral, cautious young Republicans" on the rise in the Senate.

•Richard Bolling, from Kansas City, was an antimachine man and brilliant thinker whose frontal assaults on the House's antediluvian rules and procedures seemed to close him off from the leadership rung to Speaker from his earliest years in the House. Yet Bolling later rose to be chairman of the powerful Rules Committee and continued until retirement in 1982 his probing questions of where the House—and nation—were headed. He was succeeded by Alan Wheat, a young black Democratic state legislator who won 59 percent of the vote in a district that was two-thirds white.

•Richard A. Gephardt, a former St. Louis Alderman elected to the House in 1976, proved to be one of the thoughtful young independent Democrats whose vote could not be taken for granted by labor and other liberal causes. By the early 1980s, Gephardt had become a growing influence on the House Ways and Means Committee, showing no little mastery of fiscal policy.

The excellence that has sometimes distinguished members of Missouri's congressional delegation is rarely reflected in the capitol at Jefferson City. In fact, Missouri has traditionally had a low-tax, low-service state government, despite significant budget increases in recent years. History records that Missouri missed the Populist sweep of the late 19th century altogether, largely because the Democratic party of Missouri came out for free silver (while staying conservative on other subjects). And Missouri has never had a liberal Democratic experience in state government.

In the 1970s, however, the rural domination of Missouri politics ended. Most candidates for important statewide offices now come from St. Louis or Kansas City or their suburbs. Even more importantly, political analyst Dana Spitzer told us, the money to finance Missouri political campaigns comes from the cities. This increased urban influence was reflected in increased expenditures for school aid, mental health, and welfare begun in the late 1960s under the last rural governor, Warren E. Hearnes, and continued under the administrations of Republican Christopher S. ("Kit") Bond and Democrat Joseph Teasdale.

Bond's ups and downs demonstrate the increasingly complex issues that affect modern Missouri politics. Initially elected in 1972 with some help from Richard Nixon's coattails and a weak Democratic opponent who had ties to the unsavory Steamfitters Union, he emerged as a GOP star among governors; in 1976, caught in political crossfire over construction of the Meramec Dam (which he favored, but environmentalists opposed) and faced with Teasdale's promise to reduce utility rates, Bond was defeated. By 1980, however, it was obvious Teasdale had been sold a false bill of goods on utility cost reduction and was regarded as incompetent. Bond, aided by the Reagan landslide, was returned to office.

County vs. City and the Missouri Economy

A great gulf is apparent between the people of the large cities and all the rest of Missouri, as though they lived in different worlds. Spiritually, this may be true; economically, it is not, as the rural areas of the state have become more and more industrialized (even while, ironically, such giant agribusiness corporations as Ralston Purina and Monsanto in St. Louis tie the city to the countryside). Missouri is unique in having two federal reserve banks, one in St. Louis, the other in Kansas City; along with the great commercial banks of those cities, they watch and foster a variegated and highly interdependent economy. But Missouri's growth—measured by such yardsticks as increases in income, per capita income, and the number of jobs added—has fallen somewhat short of national averages.

Led by aerospace and automobiles, manufacturing dominates Missouri's economy. Agriculture, dominated by livestock, is the state's second-largest income producer. Tourism comes in third.

One reason for the distant feeling, at least on the part of city people toward their country cousins, may be the location of the state capital in smallish Jefferson City (33,619), arbitrarily located halfway between the two metropolitan centers on the Missouri River. The location is so undesirable that a law had to be passed *requiring* state officials to live there. Among the other second-string cities of note are Springfield, the largest shopping center for Ozark farmers; Independence, beginning of the Santa Fe Trail and home of Harry Truman; St. Joseph, a Missouri River town north of Kansas City and the birthplace of Walter Cronkite, to which he sometimes repairs to gauge the national mood; Columbia, home of the University of Missouri and its celebrated journalism school; and legendary Hannibal, home for Samuel Clemens during his boyhood and setting for many incidents from *Huckleberry Finn* and other Mark Twain novels.

St. Louis: City and County

"I have found a situation where I intend establishing a settlement, which in the future, shall become one of the most beautiful cities in the world." These first words about St. Louis were written by the French fur trader Pierre Laclede in 1763. Over two hundred years later, it must be recorded that St. Louis' golden age ended with the Louisiana Purchase Exposition in 1904, and that the city has spent the rest of the 20th century engaged in one attempt or another to recapture its past glory.

Since 1965, St. Louis' skyline has been dominated by the city's great and delicate Arch of shimmering stainless steel, towering 630 feet at the spot along the Mississippi where Laclede had decided on a settlement. Even the most callous observer, standing at ground zero below the Arch and looking upward past its flanks, brushed diagonally by the sun, to the clear, cutting lines of great arms that soar to a delicate, perfect juncture at an apex far above, must be awed by what has been wrought. As one walks through the city streets, whether past new office buildings and vacant land or slums, there is always the glance toward the levee and the Arch; suddenly, each part of the urban scene is somehow enhanced by its lordly neighbor.

The Arch symbolizes St. Louis, the gateway, the central point on the Mississippi from which trapper, explorer, sodbuster, and railroader launched their adventures into the virgin West. During its first century and a half, St. Louis was initially a great port of call for steamers and then a great railroad and manufacturing center. In the 1860s, James Eads made engineering history by building his graceful triple-span steel-arch bridge across the turbulent waters of the Mississippi at St. Louis, a job the experts had said couldn't be done. (The bridge still stands, near the Arch.)

However proud its history or however elegant the Arch, central city St. Louis is in desperate straits today and competes with Newark and Detroit for the title of most-distressed American city. Frightfully confined in 19th century borders, St. Louis has lost her economic heart to her suburbs. The 1980 Census showed that the St. Louis metropolitan area had 2.4 million people, while the city of St. Louis had only 453,085 people; even worse, the city lost 27.2 percent of its population in the 1970s, a higher percentage than any other city in the country.

St. Louis' decline apparently started with Prohibition, which forced the great brewing industry to close down. Corruption afflicted the city government, and the land along the river that Laclede had first sighted became a grimy, smoky no-man's land of decaying warehouses and tenements, many deserted.

The first flicker of renewal appeared in 1933, in the depth of the Great Depression, with a proposal to establish on the water's edge a memorial to Thomas Jefferson and the Louisiana Purchase. World War II ground that development to a halt. Enter the central figure of St. Louis' postwar history, Raymond R. Tucker, a professor of chemical engineering at Washington University who developed the civil ordinances that began a cleanup of St. Louis' polluted air. As mayor, Tucker achieved an agreement on the memorial, lobbied the state legislature for new taxes, promoted bond issues and urban renewal, built recreation centers, hospitals, and major freeways, and cleared 50 blocks of the Archway area for construction of offices, apartments, and hotels. Important backing for Tucker's proposals came from Civic Progress, a powerful businessmen's group consisting of chief executive officers of the large locally domiciled companies—McDonnell Douglas, Monsanto, Anheuser-Busch, Ralston Purina, and the like—plus the heads of Washington and St. Louis universities, the mayor of St. Louis, and the executive of St. Louis County. "What Civic Progress doesn't endorse, doesn't go," said one local observer.

In the early 1960s, news dispatches out of the city talked of a "New Spirit of St. Louis." But despite the myriad initiatives of the Tucker years, St. Louis continued to lose population, jobs, and confidence. The ultimate insult came in 1978 when *New York Times* writer Robert Reinhold reported that the city was literally being carted away; so many dwellings were being torn down that, after Chicago, St. Louis had become the leading brick exporter of America, its architectural heritage used to decorate houses in other cities.

The most frightening failure of renewal, however, was the Pruitt-Igoe housing project, once touted by *Architectural Forum* as a national model of how to solve poor people's housing problems. Built in 1954, Pruitt-Igoe consisted of 33 characterless, forbidding high-rises. The original idea, as with most public housing, was to provide temporary shelter for upwardly mobile whites and some blacks, but by the late 1950s the hard-pressed welfare department began to admit more welfare recipients and black emigres from deepest Dixie. Eventually, Pruitt-Igoe became all black, and in the words of the *Globe-Democrat*, "a terrified city, a matriarchal society of too many unwed or deserted mothers and uncontrollable children, a community on the dole with an estimated two-thirds receiving some sort of welfare assistance, most surviving on welfare handouts." Designed for 10,000 people, the population reached 12,000 to 20,000. By 1970, the acres of broken windows, the hallway stench of mixed garbage, urine, and debris, gangs, narcotics pushers, and robberies, murders, rapes, and assaults had become such a disaster that the city and the federal government decided to dynamite the place and move out the tenants who had not already fled. Pruitt-Igoe was the most monumental failure of public housing ever constructed in America.

Surprisingly, by the early 1980s St. Louis was once again regarded as the national leader in urban housing; this time, however, the emphasis was on the reverse: stabilization of neighborhoods and sponsorship of "gut" repair of discarded houses and apartment buildings. Thousands of units were reclaimed as the city went to extraordinary lengths to provide incentives for private development. Some $30 million in federal community development funds were poured into pump-priming for private housing development. The city also used a unique Missouri law to give private developers the power of eminent domain.

Despite some improvements in the neighborhoods, the overall picture of St. Louis remained clouded by the city's inability to create jobs. In 1978 and 1979, St. Louis actually reversed its decline to gain 5,500 manufacturing jobs. But in a decision that even *Business Week* called "shocking," General Motors announced that it was closing its 10,000-employee St. Louis assembly plant to relocate in rural Wentzville, Mo., 40 miles away. "Everything we could do in five years to attract jobs has been wiped out overnight," said April L. Young, the city's director of economic development. Indeed, between early 1980 and early 1982 the number of auto industry workers fell from 28,442 to 8,930.

To a degree, such corporate-inflicted blows—with their devastating impact on the tax base—are offset by St. Louis' favorable location as a transportation hub. The city remains the Mississippi River's northernmost ice-free port; on it converge five interstate highways and a dozen major rail lines. And then there is the seemingly incongruous office building boom in center city; it has continued, even accelerated, in recent years, while the rest of the economy has seemed to crumble. Again, this center city rebuilding has been aided by the eminent domain law plus a 25-year tax abatement. At Laclede's Landing, after only a few years, a collection of vacant and ragtag warehouses has become an office community by day and the city's hottest tourist spot by night, complemented by old river steamers, some of them now restaurants, tied up on the adjacent Mississippi River levee. By 1980 Tom Purcell, president of Laclede's Landing Redevelopment Corp., could boast, "This is an area that has had no money since the Spanish-American War, but in four years we've financed 600,000 square feet of redevelopment." Indeed, by 1982 a heated battle was underway centering on the Gateway Mall, planned to stretch from the Gateway Arch into the heart of downtown, the question not being whether a major development would occur, but precisely how (and under whose control). In the meantime, even in the depths of national recession, the city had undertaken a $1.2 million cleanup and beautification campaign and was enjoying an influx of new speciality shops, restaurants, and service establishments.

St. Louis continues to pride itself on a variety of outstanding institutions and individuals. "Decay may not be good for business, but it often makes for land-office literature," noted Stephen Darst, a former reporter for the *St. Louis Review*. Among the writers who marked some segment of their lives in St. Louis were Tennessee Williams, Mark Twain, Thomas Wolfe, Fannie Hurst, William Burroughs, and T.S. Eliot. Masters and Johnson, whose inventive and daring sexual research at Washington University became the basis for *Human Sexual Response* and other books, carried on their research and writing in St. Louis into the early '80s. In addition, the medical complex centered around Barnes Hospital and Washington University Medical School became renowned for research in cancer and other areas. Among those who have contributed to Washington University's reputation as one of the nation's outstanding institutions are environmentalist Barry Commoner, novelist Stanley Elkins, and Pulitzer Prize poet Howard Nemerov. Yet in the corporate realm, at least, there may be a perverse side to great eminence and global scope. McDonnell Douglas, Monsanto, Anheuser-Busch, and Ralston Purina, for example, have worldwide interests and bring to St. Louis an educated community of engineers and scientists on the cutting edge of modern technology. By the same token, however, a person making million-dollar decisions regarding operations in the Mideast, Europe, or the Orient is not likely to be too interested in what is (and is not) happening in downtown St. Louis. We have heard similar lamentations in many U.S. cities, where the greater the corporation, the less may be its local sensitivity or effectiveness.

For better or worse, St. Louis has enjoyed strong labor leadership. One of the country's most remarkable leaders was Harold J. Gibbons, president of the St. Louis-based Teamsters Local 688. He was accused by Senate investigators of labor racketering, but others remember him as an urban affairs scholar and fighter for civil rights. On the seedy side, it would be difficult to match the record of St. Louis' Steamfitters Union. Between 1947 and the late '60s it assessed its 5,000 members a dollar *a day* and thus dispensed $18 million in cold cash to favored politicians. The union's high ride ended in an internal squabble and five bullet holes in the body of its president.

Despite strong ethnic constituencies and a black population that reached 45.6 percent in 1980, St. Louis has enjoyed remarkable freedom from major racial disturbance. Peculiarities of the city's political system suggest why. There is a big board of aldermen (28 members), each alderman with a single ward to which he is close; there have been black aldermen for many decades so that blacks have not had quite the feeling of political powerlessness present in many major cities. St. Louis blacks have also had "their" congressman: William L. Clay, who initially made his mark by serving 113 days in jail for participating in a 1963 demonstration to get a local bank to hire black tellers.

On St. Louis' black North Side, a stone's throw from the empty fields where the Pruitt-Igoe housing project once stood, one finds the home turf of Jeff-Vander-Lou, one of America's outstanding community development groups. Jeff-Vander-Lou advanced from fighting absentee landlords in the '60s to owning and managing its own housing, delivering government social services under contract, and providing job referrals in the '70s. Macler Shepard, Jeff-Vander-Lou's charismatic president, told us the real need for poor neighborhoods is to gain some control over the millions of dollars in wages and welfare that flow into a neighborhood—but are never "dammed up" to recirculate there because the neighborhood lacks its own enterprises.

While the city of St. Louis frets over problems of race, crime, short budgets, and a low tax base, surrounding St. Louis County enjoys one of the most efficient governments in the United States and has more jobs than the city. Ironically, the city and county were one entity until 1876, when the conservative Dutchmen who ran St. Louis asked for and got a divorce. Today the wealth of the county is precisely what the city needs to solve its problems, but the suburban voters have overwhelmingly rejected unification proposals. In 1982, however, Monsanto chief executive John Hanley sparked Civic Progress into exploring new avenues of city-county cooperation, perhaps even a re-entry of the city to the county—an adventuresome route that major corporations, in easier times, would probably never have contemplated. Quite to the contrary, since the '50s a number of big corporations had located in the "second downtown"—Clayton in St. Louis County—doubtless both to avoid the problems of the city and to be closer to their own homes. While St. Louis County does have some early postwar subdivisions verging on slumhood, it is predominantly a comfortable, middle-class place. Confronted with evidence that it had intentionally contributed to school segregation, St. Louis County agreed in 1983 to participate with the city in rare interdistrict school busing. City students were to be bused to the suburbs while city magnet schools would attract suburban children.

"Ev'rthin's Up to Date in Kansas City"

St. Louis and Kansas City are in the same state, both happen to be situated on rivers, and both have less affluent satellite cities across the water (East St. Louis, Illinois, and Kansas City, Kansas* But the essential similarity stops there. Where St. Louis is cosmopolitan and perhaps even haughty with her Archway and cultural adornments, Kansas City conveys an infectious Midwestern warmth and pretends to be little more than the overgrown cowtown she is. Where St. Louis looks East and South, Kansas City looks West. Where St. Louis is the home town of many great corporations, Kansas City is principally a branch town. Where St. Louis is hemmed in to the same 60 square miles of land she lived in 85 years ago, Kansas City has steadily annexed a number of fairly affluent suburbs and is now 215.6 square miles in size. As a result, while St. Louis' city population is declining, Kansas City's is growing —by 1980 448,159, up from 399,178 in 1940. Whether that's good news for Kansas City depends on one's perspective. In one sense, it means less-concentrated inner-city problems than St. Louis has and is, indeed, a welcome relief. In another, it means a city with no true center or focus and no palpable identity or spirit.

And even as a branch town, Kansas City does quite nicely for itself in economics. From steel to auto assembly to electronics, there are few branches of U.S. industry unrepresented. TWA brings in big payrolls through its international aircraft overhaul facilities, located at the massive Kansas City International Airport, opened in 1972. And the city is recognized as a major financial capital for industry and agriculture in the six-state (Missouri, Kansas, Oklahoma, Iowa, Nebraska, Arkansas) region of mid-America.

For entertainment value, Kansas City politics these days can scarcely hold a candle to the earlier decades of this century when boss Tom Pendergast ruled. And he ruled absolutely. Virtually everyone had to pay protection money to the machine. Revenue poured in from a 12-block red-light district, wide open gambling joints, and narcotics sales. Pendergast further lined his politics with a "legitimate" business: cement. Massive government buildings, still standing, were built with Pendergast cement, and Kansas Citians still remind one that Brush Creek, winding for several miles through the city, is literally paved with the stuff.

Pendergast put most U.S. city machine bosses to shame by managing to control, for several years, Missouri state politics as well. His method was to turn out astronomical Kansas City margins—including some 60,000 "ghost" ballots—for his handpicked candidates. When rural voters showed signs of discomfort with Pendergast dominance, he won them back by supporting a

*Much of Kansas City's elite, it should be noted, lives in Johnson County, Kansas, one of the country's wealthiest communities and a factor (because it attracts so many of the area's Republicans) in making Kansas City—and thus Missouri—more Democratic than it might otherwise be. Kansas City author Richard Rhodes was quoted (by the *Chicago Tribune*) as saying of Johnson County, "The 1950s dream is still alive in that county. The perfect lawn, two cars in the driveway, a new casserole recipe on the table. Incredible! Of course, some of the kids take drugs."

friendly small-town veteran, Harry S Truman, for county judge. Truman apparently never shared in the machine's spoils, but he did give it a respectable "front" and as a U.S. Senator directed public works projects (using, of course, much cement) back to Missouri.

The indignation of an aroused citizenry through newspapers and a housewives' crusade finally ousted the Pendergast machine. The boss himself ended up in Leavenworth. Since the early '40s, reform politics—and quite high-grade, professional government—have been the order of the day.

Kansas City race relations, generally placid in recent years, received a jolt in 1979 when a black captured the Democratic mayoral nomination. White voters then turned out in record numbers to elect Richard L. Berkley, the first Republican mayor since the 1920s. Even phenomenal black voter turnouts—in the 61 to 70 percent range—weren't enough to overcome the city's 73 percent white majority. As Bruce Watkins, the black undertaker defeated in the 1979 election, told a reporter, "We've got a head full of rights and an empty belly."

Strangers are apt to think of Kansas City as a flat place; actually it is an attractive town of trees and rolling hills (some very steep). Its principal buildings are on high land a few blocks from the Missouri River. The downtown, afflicted by the familiar seediness and decline of older central cities, has struggled to get back on its feet. Among its notable structures are the Hotel Muehlebach, favored by Harry Truman and recently refurbished by the Radisson chain. A mile and a half south of downtown lies Crown Center, the gigantic Hallmark Card-financed office, condominium, and shopping complex completed in the '70s. The Hall family's imprint on Kansas City began with Joyce C. Hall, the Nebraskan who came to town in 1910 to sell imported picture postcards and ended up developing the world's greatest greeting card company. Critics differ on whether Crown Center's major impact was to help the city by stemming corporate flight to the suburbs or to harm it by attracting tenants away from downtown.*

Finally, when you think of Kansas City you have to think of its Country Club Plaza, built in 1923 and thus the first totally planned shopping center in America. The plaza has a Spanish motif, which hardly seems appropriate to Kansas City. But the effect is pleasing; indeed, of the thousands of shopping centers that have sprung up across America in recent decades, none is more architecturally fine than this first in Kansas City. It suggests that Kansas City is about as "up to date" as it needs to be. Not a state often found at the cutting edge of things new, flashy, and exciting in the latter 20th century, a lot of what Missouri offers, even if "old," nevertheless often turns out be best.

*On July 17, 1981, the Crown Center's fancy Hyatt Hotel, only a year old, was the scene of a horrendous building disaster. Two aerial skywalks collapsed, crashing tons of steel and concrete on the lobby packed with 1,500 people, including many elderly, attending a tea dance. The death toll was 114. A design change was ruled responsible for the collapse. The financial settlements indicated that developers around the country might be more careful in the future. By 1983, the victims and their families had been awarded over $50 million, and Hallmark Cards agreed to make $6.5 million in charitable contributions in Kansas City as a "healing gesture."

OKLAHOMA!

OKLAHOMA PRESENTS a blustering, macho image of cowboys and Indians and oil wells pumping easy wealth from the ground. Its reality, however, is of an extraordinarily youthful and fragile society, at the mercy of the outside world's whims in pricing its three basic commodities—oil, gas, and wheat—and management decisions controlling its many branch plants.

Here is a state so young that it has recently buried the last of its founding patriarchs, including E.K. Gaylord, who arrived in Oklahoma City in 1902 whilst Oklahoma was still a territory, prospered for decades as publisher of the *Daily Oklahoman* and *Times,* and celebrated his 101st birthday before his death in 1974. Indeed, less than a century ago it was the announced policy of the U.S. Government that the land now Oklahoma be pure and simple "Indian Territory," free of white men altogether and for all time. That was not to be, of course, and the "run" that brought Oklahoma its first white settlement in 1889 ranks among the most celebrated events of American frontier history. Statehood did not come until 1907, and even to this day Oklahoma remains in large part an open frontier society, where status is based on recent accomplishment rather than lineage or history.

From the beginning Oklahoma's economic base has been insecure. Its agriculture has often been ravaged by the vagaries of prairie weather, most notably in the 1930s when the "Okies" of the Dust Bowl became the subjects of great Depression-era photographers and John Steinbeck's *Grapes of Wrath* —the years when topsoil and black blizzards choked cattle and crops, and some 350,000 farmers fled the state. Oklahoma's greatest wealth, however, was discovered in oil, which brought with it the buccaneer culture of wildcatting and speculating. Industrialization began in the late 1950s, yet it has always been oil that makes Oklahoma booms and busts. In the 1970s, oil boosted Oklahoma to affluence without precedent in its history. But the volatility of oil as an economic base was demonstrated anew in 1982 with the failure of Oklahoma City's Penn Square Bank, involved in a series of questionable oil and gas deals. In the early 1980s, Oklahoma's unemployment rate remained one of the lowest in the nation, and the economy appeared one of the healthiest. But Dale Mitchell, president of the Citizens National Bank and Trust Company of Oklahoma City, warned us that a strong percentage of the money raised by get-rich-quick tax shelters of the 1970s had not been invested in stable "asset-building" companies but in fly-by-night firms that spent too much money on promotion, office buildings, inflated salaries, and even jewelry. Such spending, Mitchell noted, permeates a community with prosperity but creates a big setback when it disappears. An even more sobering future looms: a time not too many decades distant when Oklahoma's black gold will be exhausted forever.

Oklahoma's political reputation is conservative Democrat, but its dependence on outside markets for its minerals and farm products has fostered colorful streaks of populism and independence. In this atmosphere, it produced humorist Will Rogers, who never shied away from poking fun at politicians of all stripes, and has elected a spicy assortment of lawmakers, ranging from rambunctious old "Alfalfa Bill" Murray and that amiable pirate Robert S. Kerr, to the dimunitive man who became speaker of the U.S. House, Carl Albert, and the super-serious chairman of the House Budget Committee, James Jones.

Oklahoma law has been marked by a social conservatism rooted in the beliefs of the Baptist Church. Into the 1980s, Oklahoma maintained an antique statute forbidding liquor by the drink. The law did not keep mixed drinks from flowing like water in the Wild West atmosphere of Oklahoma, but it did produce an elaborate subterfuge of private clubs, daily violations of the law, and occasional raids that embarrassed prominent people. One night in Oklahoma City, we were served drinks on the presentation of our out-of-state drivers' licenses (tantamount to club membership) while an Oklahoman was refused—until he produced his business card stating he worked for the state legislature.

"As Long As the Grass Grows and the Waters Run"

But the Indians were first. Even the name Oklahoma is Indian, from the Choctaw words *okla* (people) and *homma* (red). It was coined by Allen Wright, a Choctaw chief, in 1866. Nomadic Indians remained Oklahoma's only permanent inhabitants, disturbed only rarely by trappers or traders, for two centuries and more after 1541 when deSoto and Coronado both ventured through, finding not gold but great reaches of tall prairie grass and full rivers. In 1803 the land passed into U.S. control as part of the Louisiana Purchase. Soon America's Old South states put pressure on the federal government to relocate the "Five Civilized Tribes"—Cherokee, Seminole, Choctaw, Creek, and Chickasaw—who still disturbed the peace within their borders through occasional uprisings, not to mention occupying land the white men coveted. Oklahoma was a great and unknown no-man's land, and the red men could be safely dispatched there. And so it was that the tribes were obliged to agree to their "removal" to what would be an inviolate "Indian Territory": a land the U.S. Government solemnly promised would be theirs and theirs alone "as long as the grass grows and the waters run."

The "Trail of Tears" by which the Five Tribes were herded westward from the Old South remains a dark blot in American history. When Army troops

came in to round up the people, many were totally unprepared; it is recorded
that women left meals cooking over fireplaces, men dropped their plows,
children forgot their toys as they were hurried away from their ancestral
homes. Hunger, cold, tuberculosis, pneumonia, all took a ferocious toll along
the way, and of the Cherokees, 4,000 out of 15,000 perished before they
reached Oklahoma. But the Five Civilized Tribes, already a largely literate
and Christian group, soon reestablished themselves into quite successful communities in their newly ceded territory in eastern Oklahoma.

The tide of white aggrandizement was not to be so easily satisfied. Stage-
lines, then railroads, and finally the Chisholm Trail began to criss-cross the
territory. The nations found themselves involved in the Civil War, a conflict
in which they suffered much and gained nothing. White settlers began to sift
westward and squat on Indian lands. The railroads sent out parties to destroy
the buffalo, thus destroying the livelihood of the Plains Indians. In response
to violent disputes and sporadic raids by Indian hotheads, the U.S. Army in
the 1860s and '70s carried on a bloody "pacification" campaign strikingly
similar in some of its basic aspects to the Vietnam War a century later,
including near massacres of entire villages in which rebellious Indians were
thought to be taking shelter among the more peaceable.

The Five Civilized Tribes perfected sophisticated "nation" governments,
ran excellent schools having a number of white teachers, and published newspapers. When land-hungry whites suggested the Civilized Tribes were holding more land than they really occupied or needed, the Indians reacted with
strong initial hostility—seeing, understandably, the first step down another
Trail of Tears. Educators, churchmen, and other groups across the United
States opposed any expropriation of surplus Indian lands in Oklahoma. But
the pressure of white settlers for fresh land increased constantly. By the 1880s
large camps of "Boomers" were settling around the fringes of Oklahoma,
waiting for a chance to enter and homestead. Finally, the Creeks offered in
1889 to sell land they owned in central Oklahoma, and the federal government
quickly agreed on a price. President Benjamin Harrison announced that on
April 22, 1889, a big chunk of territory in central Oklahoma—the "Unassigned
Lands"—would be opened for white settlement.

Oklahoma histories glow with excitement when they talk of that day.
Thousands of hardy young settlers and their families surrounded the Unassigned Lands. Federal troops formed a fence between the homeseekers and
the land, but even so some settlers ventured out earlier, thus giving birth to
the nickname "Sooner." Most, however, waited behind the lines, and then at
noon on April 22 a cannon was fired and the legal Boomers went rushing
across the lines. On foot they came, or on race horses, or driving two-wheeled
racing sulkies or farm wagons or high bicycles—or jumping off the steps of
a special Santa Fe Railway train. Quickly the flagged stakes, marking out
homesteads or plots, formed their patterns. That morning the Unassigned
Lands had an official population of zero; that night it was some 20,000. Among
the cities that sprouted from the prairie in a single day were Oklahoma City,
Guthrie, Norman, and Stillwater.

The 1889 Run broke the dike; soon the Indians were obliged to surrender more and more of the territory once held inviolate. Three more runs between 1889 and 1895 opened up 10 million additional acres. The Indian nations struggled for several years to remain independent of the Oklahoma Territory, but gradually they lost virtually all of their land. Then came the final glimpse of Camelot for the Indians—a proposal by the Five Civilized Tribes, in 1905, for a new Indian state of the Union, in eastern Oklahoma, to be called the "State of Sequoyah." But Congress spurned the idea, authorizing a single state of the Oklahoma and Indian Territories in 1906. On November 16, 1907, Oklahoma became the 46th state of the Union; the only four still younger are Arizona, New Mexico, Alaska, and Hawaii.

Today Oklahoma's Five Civilized Tribes, stripped of most powers except ceremonial, continue with their own councils, chiefs, structures, and cultures in eastern Oklahoma. Out in the state's western reaches there are still many Plains Indians, including Cheyennes, Apaches, and Arapahoes. Oklahoma in 1980 had 169,464 Indians—more than any other state except California, yet because of the expanding white population over the years, only 5.6 percent of the state's population.

History was made in the 1960s when for the first time there was a joint meeting of the chiefs of both the Five Tribes and the Plains Indians. In terms of living standards, the Civilized Tribes are said to be more fortunate than most native Americans. And there have been reports of Indians near Oklahoma City who have become millionaires overnight because their gas holdings have been exploited. But all this is relative. Ten percent of Indians in Oklahoma were still on welfare in the early 1980s. True unemployment among Indians, it was estimated, might be as high as 60 percent.

The White Man's Oklahoma

For the white man, Oklahoma since the 1960s has been one of the most hospitable states in the nation. Thousands of young Americans, many straight off farms that were becoming mechanized and often without the highest skills, have found jobs and homes in Oklahoma. Some were the descendants of people who left during the Depression. The economic growth in the 1970s was so strong that Oklahoma added 465,803 new people (reaching 3,025,266 in all). All those newcomers found wages slightly below the national average, but also a lower cost of living. Over the years, Oklahoma had remained slightly poorer than Texas but several degrees better off than the Deep South states to the east, and had materially improved its position vis-à-vis its northern neighbors, the Plains States. Agriculture—especially when one took into account food processing and other related "agribusiness"—remained the single largest element in the economy. But the number of farmers and farms had continued to drop while the average size grew from 194 to 479 acres. Oklahoma in the early '80s was among the leading five states in wheat production and also ranked high in cattle.

Oklahoma's oil history began with the first wildcatting, in 1880, and the first producing well, in 1897. The big pools started coming in a decade later, and with them the problems of ruthless exploitation of a natural resource. No attempt was made at conservation, and the life of every important field was shortened by waste of millions of barrels of oil and billions of cubic feet of gas. The courts gave landowners total discretion over the use of the oil and gas and even ruled that the owner "may crowd the adjoining farms so as to enable him to draw the oil and gas from them. What then can the neighbor do? . . . Nothing; only go and do likewise." Among the landowners profiting handsomely from the sale of oil leases on their land were the Osage Indians, made the world's richest race of people per capita by 1921 oil leases that were still earning them $76 million in royalties in 1981.

Hard times came in the 1930s when the opening of the East Texas oil fields and the Depression drove the price of Oklahoma crude down to as low as 10 cents a barrel. Even though Governor Murray sent in the National Guard to close down the oil fields, there was a widespread traffic in "hot oil" smuggled out of the state. Since then, the Oklahoma Corporation Commission has administered an effective proration program. The decline of Oklahoma petroleum reserves forced the state's two big homegrown oil companies—Phillips Petroleum and Kerr-McGee—to survey the world for additional sources. Kerr-McGee, founded by the late Senator Kerr and a partner in 1929, eventually became a pioneer in seismic exploration work and drilling far off the Louisiana coast and moved heavily (and profitably) into petrochemical manufacturing, uranium mining, and enrichment. Kerr-McGee's nuclear operations have undergone intense scrutiny since 1974 when Karen Silkwood, a Kerr-McGee employee and union activist, was killed in an automobile accident while on her way to meet a *New York Times* reporter to talk about safety in a plant near Oklahoma City. There were immediate allegations that Kerr-McGee or its agents had been involved in the death. A federal court jury found Kerr-McGee guilty of her contamination by highly radioactive plutonium and awarded her family $10.5 million in punitive damages. The award was overturned by an appeals court, and the Silkwood family took the case to the U.S. Supreme Court.

Phillips was a Nebraska-born barber who made his way to Bartlesville in 1904, telling a brother, "I think people are going to buy quite a passel of these gasoline buggies, and they need gasoline to make 'em go. It may be this thing has a future." When he died, in 1950, Phillips Petroleum was worth $660 million and operating in more than half the states. Neither Kerr-McGee nor Phillips has ever been shy in flexing its political muscle. One incredible success: bankrolling (and winning) 1930s referenda to permit drilling of the fabulously rich oil field underlying residential areas of Oklahoma City and even the State Capitol grounds. We will not soon forget the surprise, on a first visit to Oklahoma City, of seeing an oil well (painted gold for its special location) pumping close to the Capitol's front entrance, and bearing the sign of one of Oklahoma's oil companies.

When world oil prices rose in the 1970s, Oklahoma boomed. Oil fields long considered uneconomic suddenly became worth exploring. Explorers, wild-catters, and drillers swarmed into small towns such as Elk City and Hammon in southwest Oklahoma's Anadarko Basin. Some farmers became overnight millionaires (known locally as "oileys") and stopped worrying about wheat and cotton prices. The oil boom also fueled a construction boom. "It's almost like a reverse 'Grapes of Wrath,' " Danny George, assistant city manager of Elk City, told a visiting reporter.

Industrialization, even in remote rural Oklahoma, was an equally amazing economic miracle to many "Okies"—the nickname Governor Dewey Bart-lett, pushing economic development in the '60s, declared was an acronym for "Oklahoma, Key to Industrial Expansion." Hundreds of small communities used general revenue bonds to build plants to which they lured small factories. The U.S. Economic Development Administration and the Ozarks Regional Commission helped out in the most depressed areas. Bartlett became what General Electric board chairman Gerald L. Phillippe called an "aggressive bearcat of a governor," and annual new investments in the state did more than double, and then triple previous levels. Bartlett was criticized, however, for the "giveaway" gimmick of excusing new businesses from property taxes for 30 years, an issue used to defeat him in the 1970 campaign. In the 1970s industrialization appeared to be continuing of its own accord in computers, metal fabricating, and aerospace. Some of these plants were technically owned by a tax-exempt state agency, the Oklahoma Industries Authority, until popu-list Attorney General Jan Eric Cartwright issued an opinion that such owner-ship arrangements to avoid taxation were contrary to the state constitution, a lengthy document written in the era of Grange and Populist radicalism. Directors of the authority had also used the tax schemes for their personal benefit, Cartwright charged. General Motors and other companies that faced millions of dollars in tax obligations argued that they had made a deal with the state of Oklahoma; Cartwright was unfazed, however, asking if no one on GM's huge staff of attorneys could read the state constitution and figure out the tax breaks were illegal. The Supreme Court agreed with the attorney general, to the horror of insiders such as Edward L. Gaylord, son of the founder of the *Daily Oklahoman*. Into the 1980s Gaylord served as president and editor of the newspaper *and* chairman of the Oklahoma Industries Au-thority, an arrangement once common in the Old West but now seen in many other states as a conflict of interest.

The Political Scoreboard

"Sooners" have packed more political feudin' and a-fussin' into their brief history since the first Run than many older states can account for in longer, more placid existences. Oklahoma politics are informal, youthful, and person-ality-oriented. In 1982 we watched Governor George Nigh, dressed in cow-boy boots, blue jeans, and a deep-cut purple silk shirt bearing a decal "Keep Me," rally his reelection troops with a plan to fill Oklahoma City's shopping centers so that rural shoppers would return home with word of the campaign's tremendous momentum in the city.

Oklahoma has been willing to elect its talented youth, even if they are unusually liberal, such as Cleta Detherage, of Norman, who in 1982 at the age of 31 was chairman of the Oklahoma house budget and appropriations committee. But Oklahoma also reveres its old hands. One man, Lloyd Rader, was state welfare director for three decades and controlled a $1.2 billion budget, which was not scrutinized by the state legislature until 1982. Even critics had agreed that Rader had pushed the state forward, beyond its neighbors, in social services. But when he became old, there was tremendous resistance to replacing him or modernizing the governmental system. Oklahomans pay very low taxes, Detherage noted, but the constant national publicity about high taxation has made them think their taxes should be reduced, too. By 1982 the state was raking in more money from its oil and gas severance tax than from any other source—even its personal income tax. The cloud on the horizon was that production declines in future years would force more austerity—or self-taxation.

Oklahoma's biggest recent progress has concerned its prison system. In 1970, state corrections director Arnold Pontesso resigned, charging, "We cage people like animals in a zoo. We not only pay our real zookeepers more than our people working in prisons, we provide bigger and better cages in real zoos." Federal court orders to expand and improve the prisons followed, and by the early 1980s Oklahoma became the first state to see all its adult correctional facilities accredited by the American Correctional Association. Serious problems remained in the juvenile facilities, however, where there were allegations of brutality and the mixing of criminal offenders with youths whose most serious offense had been running away, or in the case of teenage girls (if one can still believe this in the 1980s), sexual promiscuity.

Except for a few "freak" elections, Oklahoma was blindly Democratic until the 1960s, a spinoff of the state's Southern location, its surfeit of down-and-outers, and the fact that Democrats early got a stranglehold on the most posts, including the county rings, that held sway until scandal felled them in the 1970s. Republicans managed their first major breakthrough by electing wheat farmer Henry L. Bellmon as governor in 1962, the result of a statewide organization Bellmon had built as well as the heavy Republican vote that had developed in such cities as Tulsa. Bellmon went on to serve in the U.S. Senate (1968–80), where he confounded other Southwestern Republicans by voting to hold the line on defense spending and farm programs while favoring civil rights legislation. The election of Tulsa oilman Dewey F. Bartlett, the Republicans' second governor (1966–70), was a particular surprise because he was a Roman Catholic and a Princeton graduate—hardly the right credentials in a hard-shell Baptist, distinctly non-Eastern state. Anti-Catholic sentiment was thought to have had a lot to do with the overwhelming Oklahoma defeats suffered by Al Smith in 1928 and John F. Kennedy in 1960.

The innate and growing conservatism of Oklahomans has been best reflected on the presidential level, where Republicans have reigned supreme since 1952, except for 1964, when Oklahomans rejected Barry Goldwater in favor of Lyndon Johnson. Not even Southerner Jimmy Carter returned Oklahoma to the Democratic column.

The most colorful Oklahoma politico of all time was doubtless William ("Alfalfa Bill") Murray, who wore out three gavels chairing the 1907 state constitutional convention. Murray had been a successful courtroom attorney, showing sharp native intelligence, but when he ran for governor against a wealthy oilman in the hard-times year of 1930, he cultivated a common-man image, letting his long mustache go untrimmed and ragged and the trousers of his old brown suit bag at the knees. "I'm not an extremist. I believe firmly in our capitalistic plan—if capitalism can be forced to restrain its ungodly greed and serve the needs of humanity," Murray declared. In office, Murray was in fact no radical. But colorful he remained throughout. John Gunther recalled that an unsuspecting visitor to the gubernatorial offices, sitting in a chair carefully placed three feet from Murray's desk, might try to hitch himself closer—only to discover that the chair was nailed to the floor and hear Murray shout, "What the hell do you want?" He often went barefoot and kept his socks in his desk.

Robert S. Kerr made it from the Oklahoma log cabin where he was born to become a multimillionaire oilman, the state's first native-born governor, and—along with Lyndon B. Johnson—one of the two most effective power-brokers in the U.S. Senate. Kerr was a great bear of a man (six feet, three inches and 220 to 275 pounds), jovial, exuberant, a formidable opponent. A fervent Baptist and Sunday School teacher, he was depicted to us by Dean A. McGee, his oil industry partner, as "a man of complete integrity, big-hearted, highly intellectual, a great doer, a real Christian gentleman who lived his religion." Others have not been so charitable, suggesting Kerr used his Senate position to defend and profit personally from the 27½ percent oil depletion allowance and other legislation of direct aid to Kerr-McGee with its far-flung interests in petroleum, natural gas, beryllium, boron, helium, potash, and uranium. *Time*'s Capitol Hill correspondent Neil MacNeil reported Kerr had been "one of the most ruthless politicians ever to enter the Senate, . . . exacting a price for every favor he gave, even from the President."

Carl A. Albert, Speaker of the House of Representatives (1971–77), was from "Little Dixie," the poorest part of southeastern Oklahoma, the son of a tenant farmer and sometime coal miner. He didn't live in a house with electricity or running water until he was 16 and wore bib overalls to school. Later he went on to the University of Oklahoma, won a Rhodes scholarship, and after World War II won term after term in Congress, breaking the Oklahoma mold by refusing big campaign contributions from anyone, including oil and labor interests. Albert's district was just across the Red River from the one in Texas that the late Sam Rayburn used to represent, and the two men became close friends in something akin to a father-son relationship. As Speaker, Albert performed admirably during the Watergate crisis and sought to advance congressional reform; criticism came from those who said he was too much of a consensus politician, not a forceful enough leader.

In recent years Oklahoma has sent conservatives of both parties to Washington, but all with an independent streak. Tops in power was Tulsa Congressman James R. Jones, who became chairman of the House Budget Committee in 1981, trying to move the Democratic party away from its big-spending ways. Jones found it difficult, however, to steer a middle course between the Democratic liberals and "Boll Weevil" Democrats supporting President Reagan's budget. Senator and former Governor David L. Boren, Yale graduate and former Rhodes Scholar, was the most active Democratic supporter of President Reagan's tax cuts but also retained a Populist streak, railing on the Senate floor against high interest rates. Oklahoma's junior senator, Republican Don Nickles, could give pause to anyone who equated the baby boom generation with social liberalism: born in 1948, he won election in 1980 as the favorite of the Moral Majority and as founder of a hawkish organization called the Oklahoma Coalition for Peace Through Strength.*

That it was dangerous in Oklahoma politics to turn too far to the left had been learned by Fred Harris, Democratic senator during the '60s, member of the Kerner Commission on racial disorders (which cited "white racism"), and Democratic national chairman for a year. After he shifted from hawk to dove on the Vietnam War, Harris realized he had moved far beyond the Oklahoma pale. He declined, at age 40, to seek reelection to the Senate, moving to Albuquerque, N.M., to teach and write. He ran a short-lived, deficit-plagued "New Populist" campign for the Presidency in 1976.

Oklahomans have some reason to be skeptical about politics and politicians. In the 1920s there were gutter fights over impeachment of governors. The era of cronyism and patronage in virtually all state government jobs, of unsavory highway and election scandals, lasted well into the postwar period. A general cleanup of government was effected by J. Howard Edmondson, a controversial but courageous governor of the late '50s and early '60s. But in 1975 former Governor David Hall was sentenced to three years in prison on four counts of bribery and extortion.

And in 1981 *two-thirds* of Oklahoma's county commissioners—more than 120 persons—pleaded guilty or were found guilty in what turned out to be the largest kickback scandal in U.S. history. For all anyone knew, the kickbacks may have been going on for decades since the "good ol' boys" had held an iron lock on the county governments since statehood was achieved in 1907. The beginning of the end came when Dorothy Griffin, a lumber-yard owner in Farris, got into trouble with the Internal Revenue Service and 'fessed up to federal investigators that she had written more than $1 million in phony invoices for nonexistent transactions between suppliers and county commissioners. "I'm just a dumb old country woman standing out here in my bare

---

*The *oldest* member of the Oklahoma congressional delegation in the early 1980s was the state's only Republican House member, Mickey Edwards, of Oklahoma City, born in 1937. Edwards was chairman of the American Conservative Union, but also displayed the Oklahoma penchant for independence, wooing organized labor and, after Three Mile Island, expressing a loss of faith in nuclear power.

feet," Mrs. Griffin told the press, "but I do know that you don't do wrong and get by." Another supplier admitted he had paid more than 8,000 kickbacks in 28 years. The scandal resulted in the reform of state purchasing laws although the county commissioners did retain power over road building.

Geographic Oklahoma and the Waterway

Oklahoma is basically a big rectangle—305 miles from east to west, 210 miles from north to south—with an odd 165-mile-long panhandle protruding over Texas from its northwest corner. This shape has been likened to a butcher's cleaver, with the panhandle representing the handle and the line of the Red River, which defines the southern boundary, like an irregular cutting edge. The 98th meridian, where the grassy lowlands of the Mississippi Valley fade into the high and dry Great Plains, slices down through the state a few miles west of Oklahoma City. Annual rainfall ranges up to 50–56 inches in the southeastern corner, a land with bayous and huge water cypress trees like Louisiana's. As far west as Oklahoma City, moist winds blowing up from the Gulf of Mexico deposit enough rainfall for crops of cotton, soybeans, and grains. But in the westernmost reaches, only dry farming of winter wheat and cattle grazing are practicable. On the High Plains at the tip of the Panhandle, precipitation dips to an arid 16 inches a year. This was Dust Bowl territory in the '30s; since then, prosperity has returned due to increased rainfall, massive pumping of underground water, and soil conservation practices.

Southeastern Oklahoma went into deep recession in the 1920s and did not truly recover even as the state flowed with oil money in the 1970s. Despite some better-off farms and income from oil, recreation, and paper milling, travelers through the region still see dilapidated houses and islands of hillbilly poverty. Northeastern Oklahoma, by contrast, has the big and bustling city of Tulsa and an abundance of power-producing natural resources: natural gas, coal, and hydroelectric power from the Arkansas River.

Eastern Oklahoma includes parts of the low-lying Ozark and Ouachita mountain systems, both regions of natural beauty, especially the Ozarks with their hardwoods and flamboyant autumns. But the truly exciting attraction is water. Within little more than a generation, eastern Oklahoma has been transformed from the marginal scrubland to an aquatic paradise. Oklahoma itself built Lake O'The Cherokees, with its 1,300-mile shoreline, but mostly the federal government is to thank for such huge lakes and reservoirs as the Eufaula, Fort Gibson, Tenkiller Ferry, and Thunderbird. They provide hydroelectric power, flood control, irrigation, and municipal water supplies, and of course abundant new playgrounds for boaters, water-skiers, and fishermen. Eastern Oklahoma acquired a ratio of water to land higher than Minnesota's. By the '80s bone dry western Oklahoma was eying the watery bonanza. But eastern Oklahoma was intensely protective of its treasure, and it was not hard to discern a red hot Sooner political issue for the rest of the century.

There have been times when Oklahoma had more water than it liked. Will

Rogers once wrote: "When the Arkansas, Red River, Salt Fork, Verdigris, Caney, Cat Creek, Possum Creek, Dog Creek, and Skunk Branch all are up after a rain, we got more seacoast than Australia." It was the gruesome flooding of the Arkansas that prompted Kerr—risen to the power of chairmanship of the Senate Public Works Rivers and Harbors Subcommittee—to undertake the battle for the Arkansas River navigation and flood-control project. This modest little piece of home state pork barrel eventually cost U.S. taxpayers a staggering $1.2 billion, more than the Panama Canal and the St. Lawrence Seaway combined. The result: a navigable 446-mile channel, running all the way from the Arkansas' mouth on the Mississippi to the Tulsa suburb of Catoosa. The big ditch, up to 300 feet wide and at least 9 feet deep, includes 17 locks and dams to facilitate the movement of ships and barges over the 420-foot elevation differential. Instead of a dangerous, meandering stream, the Arkansas was transformed into a series of placid lakes and canals. Ten of the dams provide hydroelectric power (three billion kilowatt-hours of electricity per year). And seven upstream reservoirs provided the flood protection for which Oklahoma longed.

Urban Oklahoma and the Press

Burgeoning Oklahoma City and Tulsa dominate urban Oklahoma and compete to see which can grow the fastest and bestest. Oklahoma City had the population edge in 1980: 404,213, compared to Tulsa's 360,919. Both metropolitan areas grew mightily in the 1970s: Oklahoma City, 19 percent; Tulsa, 25 percent. Houston's long lead notwithstanding, Tulsa still proclaims itself "Oil Capital of the World." The headquarters of Cities Service and hundreds of small oil companies are there. Phillips is located in Bartlesville, only 40 miles distant. Oklahoma City, on the other hand, has added a long list of blue-chip industrial firms through an aggressive chamber of commerce factory recruiting job.

Oklahoma City is remembered as the city that popped up out of the prairie between noon and sunset on April 22, 1889. Before that, Oklahoma historian George Shirk recorded, the location "was just a dusty depot on the sunscorched prairie. A stop for Santa Fe trains. No trees. The entire water supply came from a single well, about where Broadway and Main Street meet today." After the famous run, Oklahoma City became a big country cattle town and state capital and prospered as a major city on the Santa Fe main line. It got in on the big and fast money when oil hit in the 1930s.

A touch of the exploitive, get-rich-quick psychology of the world of oil derricks still lingers in Oklahoma City. But there are some new, softer themes. In 1971 voters elected Mrs. Patience Sewell Latting as their mayor—the first woman to head an American city of more than 200,000 people. Mrs. Latting proved to have staying power and was still in office more than 10 years later.

In the 1960s, Oklahoma City began to rebuild its downtown almost from scratch: a new civic and convention center, new office buildings, and a refurbishing of the famed Skirvin Plaza hotel with its hand-tooled leather ceiling. The Skirvin was once the home of the late, famed Washington hostess Perle Mesta, whose father owned it. A downtown subterranean tunnel filled with restaurants and boutiques linked 16 buildings, allowing office workers to move between buildings and meet friends for lunch without going outside into the broiling heat that marks Oklahoma City much of the year. Oklahoma City's tunnel is one of the few examples of architectural innovation and adaptation that truly works in the American Southwest. Latting and a group of civic leaders visited Tivoli Gardens in Copenhagen and built their own version in Oklahoma City, connecting it with the 1930 Courthouse and Town Hall. Famed city planner and developer Edmund Bacon has proclaimed Oklahoma City "just a jewel of a little city—going back to its central focus." A visitor could only wish that downtown would grow, creating a critical mass of activity and lessening the office sprawl over the plains.

Tulsa made a start in 1879 as a post office on the pony express route through Indian Territory and as late as 1905 was called Tulsey Town, an unkempt frontier settlement where—in the words of one settler—"we had to dodge roaming hogs, goats, and cows when crossing, and sometimes wild animals would venture into the middle of town." But in 1906 the big break came with the discovery of the high-grade Glenn Oil Pool nearby. Tulsa's canny town fathers persuaded hundreds of oil companies to set up their headquarters in town. Today, Tulsa prospers not only as a prime site of petroleum technology and research but as an aviation-aerospace center (including major operations of American Airlines, McDonnell Douglas and Rockwell International) and through telecommunications and data processing (no other city in the world processes more credit card slips). At one point in 1981 it had the lowest unemployment rate of any U.S. metropolitan area.

Tulsa became the focal point of conservative Republican politics in the Sooner State. The county went overwhelmingly for Barry Goldwater in 1964, gave Nixon and Wallace a combined 77 percent in 1968, and Ronald Reagan 66.2 percent in 1980. The conservative temper of Tulsa is fostered by two rightward-oriented newspapers, the *Tulsa Tribune* and *Tulsa World.* The former is edited by an urbane newsman and syndicated columnist, Jenkin Lloyd Jones.

Tulsa's tail was twisted twice in recent years by the *New York Times,* which suggested in articles by William Stevens and John Herbers that this "robust, conservative town, an upholder of Western individualism," preaching "do-it-yourself values straight off the frontier," was in fact not nearly as independent of the federal government as it let on. In fact, the *Times* ascertained, relying partly on data from University of Tulsa economists, that as much as a quarter of Tulsa-area local government budgets could be traced to the federal treasury, including major grants for big urban renewal projects and $100 million a year in Tulsa County, mostly on behalf of the poor and elderly. The revelations failed to inhibit Tulsa's young Republican mayor, James Inhofe, from urging the Reagan administration to hack away heavily at federal aid to cities, including many (in contrast to Tulsa) coping with heavy unemployment and huge numbers of poor people.

Tulsa is home base for the famed fundamentalist evangelist Oral Roberts, whose televised religious services and faith healings became known across the continent. Roberts' evangelical empire, built with millions of dollars sent by T.V. watchers, includes Oral Roberts University, complete with a modernistic 200-foot "prayer tower" (Tulsa's biggest tourist attraction) and a 60-story "Christian" medical center, built over the objections of the local medical authorities who said the city had enough hospital beds. That Roberts should prevail over any local objections is a common event. Roberts, a country boy from Pontooc County, Oklahoma, came to Tulsa in the late 1940s with $25 in his pocket and a slogan—"Expect a miracle"—and became a pillar of the Tulsa community, a bank and chamber-of-commerce director. More traditional church leaders and businessmen might have been expected to question Roberts' rather brassy approach. In the medical center, for example, a glass elevator in the manner of a Hyatt Hotel takes visitors to the second floor. The building towers above a man-made "river of life" and a pair of enormous bronze hands. The visitor may pick up a headphone to hear a recorded message from Mrs. Roberts extolling her husband's work. But Roberts' charisma has won over the Tulsa establishment, and the newspapers have supported his projects on the basis of freedom of religion and choice. "Wholesomeness" is the way of life at Roberts University. Church attendance for students is compulsory, they must wear shirts, ties, or dresses to all classes, and they are prohibited from "(a) profanity, (b) smoking, (c) gambling, (d) cheating, (e) drinking alcoholic beverages of any kind, and (f) immorality."

Tulsa takes justifiable pride in an arts tradition that goes back to the early oil days. The city's outstanding institution is the Thomas Gilcrease Institute of American History and Art; its collection of Western American art by Russell, Remington, and lesser known names was started by a part-Indian oil man and is now a city-owned museum. The Philbrook Art Center has also acquired a large Indian collection; and it has many lesser works by famed European and American painters. The grounds of the Philbrook are an extraordinary sight in themselves—a terraced Italian garden on the edge of the prairies. Early Tulsans were determined to bring high culture, and we were told current residents still get more excited about a visiting European or American show than their own treasure trove of Indian and Western art. Tulsa's early prosperity coincided with the Art Deco period in architecture, and many fine examples of the "zigzag" school of the '20s, the "streamlined" '30s, and the chunky classicism of the Depression and New Deal eras still grace downtown Tulsa.

The city's main thoroughfare was largely replaced by the Main Street mall, which limited traffic and increased retail business by 60 percent. In the 1970s the Williams Companies, a diversified energy conglomerate, began a 225-acre mixed-use project, including a Tulsa Performing Arts Center (for which conservative Tulsans twice turned down bonds until private businesses coughed up a larger share of the cost) complete with music hall, playhouse, and two theaters. Built nearby were The Green, a two-and-one-half acre park, a 400-room hotel, a 3-level shopping center, the 52-story Bank of Oklahoma Tower, and the headquarters of the Williams Companies.

Oklahoma's small-city and rural complexion is emphasized by the lack of large cities other than Oklahoma City and Tulsa. Lawton, in southwestern Oklahoma, was the last of the state's cities to be born overnight. That was in 1901; then in 1903 nearby Fort Sill became the U.S. Army's principal artillery school, and Lawton has lived and prospered under the shadow of that gigantic military reservation ever since. The 1980 population was 80,054. Next in population is Norman (68,020), set close to Oklahoma City and home of the University of Oklahoma. Enid (50,363) is a big wheat and oil center in the northwestern part of the state.

Muskogee (pop. 40,011), in the heart of eastern Oklahoma's one-time Indian Territory, is by Oklahoma standards an old town (1872); it achieved new prosperity because of its strategic location on the Arkansas River Waterway. The town's image is set indelibly by Merle Haggard's *Okie from Muskogee*. When the song was No. 1 on the charts in 1970, it seemed out of sync with the draft card burnings, pot smoking, and long hair of the times. Who would have dreamed the song would still be played more than a dozen years later and that Muskogee and its healthy respect for traditional values would be back in vogue:

> And I'm proud to be an Okie from Muskogee;
> A place where even squares can have a ball.
> We still wave Ol' Glory down at the Court House,
> White lightning's still the biggest thrill of all.
> In Muskogee, Oklahoma, U.S.A.*

*From the song *Okie from Muskogee*, written by Merle Haggard and Roy Edward Burris. Copyright 1969 Blue Book Music, Bakersfield, Calif. Used by permission. All rights reserved.

TEXAS

The Perpetual Boom State?

BIG, BRAWLING TEXAS, always the braggart in the family of American states, inspires love and hate.

There is, first of all, the early history of the Alamo—the tradition of fiercely independent Americans who migrated to a huge land north of the Rio Grande and built themselves a "civilization." Texas has preserved American individualism and its economic partner, entrepreneurship, in gloriously pure form. In Texas, the self-made man still commands more respect than anyone else. Old wealth is unlikely to go back more than a few generations. What American was not fascinated—if only disapprovingly—by such fabulous characters as Lyndon Johnson, John Connally, the incredibly wealthy Hunt Brothers, the Klebergs (owners of the King Ranch), or David Hannah, Jr., who in 1982 launched the first privately financed rocket, hopefully beginning an era of private enterprise in space. Many Texans distrusted George Bush even after he had become vice president because of his wealthy Eastern roots. But Bush *had* proven he was a Texan by making a fortune in the oil business. *Dallas*, the evening soap opera about that ultimate Texan oil and ranching family, the Ewings, has attracted an audience of multimillions around the world.*

Respect in Texas for entrepreneurship runs deeper than the stories of its few fabulously wealthy and powerful men would imply. To the man (and once in a while the woman) with a business idea and the guts to try it out, Texas offers the most hospitable climate in the Union: low taxes, minimal governmental regulation, and heavy discouragement of such "socialistic" institutions as labor unions. Even an occasional failure is tolerated as the mark of a truly adventurous entrepreneur. One result: Texas has one of America's highest rates of new business formation and thus stunningly high numbers of new jobs. In the 1970s Texas' unemployment rate was among the lowest in the nation, even while the state grew 27.1 percent in population, to 14,228,383 and a rank of third-largest in the nation, exchanging places with Pennsylvania. Census studies following 1980 showed more Americans selecting Texas as a new home than any other state. In the 1982–1983 recession, Texas suffered

---

*The appeal of *Dallas* knows no borders. We were on a visit to the Santa Katarina Monastery in the Sinai Peninsula, one of the remotest spots on earth, when an Egyptian wearing an American cowboy hat walked up and asked, "Could you tell me who shot J.R.?" As we stood speechless, his friends rushed up, shouting "Don't tell him. We watch *Dallas* every week on TV in Cairo and haven't had that episode yet!"

a sharp increase in unemployment and a serious downturn in its oil industry and high-technology firms, and the collapse of one of its famed corporations, Braniff Airways. But compared to most other states, Texas still enjoyed a robust economy and low taxes.

However many and gratifying its pluses, there is also some truth in Texas' global image as a vainglorious, illiberal place where money and power are worshipped without shame. Over the decades, Texans themselves permitted and abetted a distortion of the Texas tradition: a bigger-and-bestest-of-every-thing braggadocio that evinced sometimes wonder, sometimes scorn from afar. As historian Joe B. Frantz (a Texan) noted some years ago,

> Whether you thought that Texans were pleasant buffoons, a bit tiresome but still good for some extravagant yaks, or petted Texans the way you might a cavorting Eskimo husky; whether you were impressed with the private airplanes, the Olympic-sized swimming pools, 40-foot fireplaces, or ranch females built with all the solidity of an Anheuser-Busch draft horse, or whether, like my thrifty Illinois father, you always felt a bit superior to those Scripture-quoting Texans who spouted waste-not, want-not slogans while cotton wore out their black land, rivers carried their farms to the Gulf, their farm machinery rusted and ruined for want of simple upkeep, their Negroes rusted and ruined on a diet of cornbread, syrup, and grease, their Mexicans' insides exploded on corn, hot chilis, and amoebic dysentry, and their bankers refused to rehabilitate acres that cried for comeback—regardless of how the non-Texan viewed the Texan, he gloried in some aspects of him, commercialized and exploited him where he could, and steadily built the myth. . . .

To this day, the prevalent Texas attitude seems to be that free enterprise capitalism can hardly do wrong. If the free market system fails to provide for the elderly or handicapped, if it excludes minorities or women or discriminates occasionally against the "little man," most Texans believe the state should do little to fill the gap. That is said to be the role of churches, charities, and individual families. And if they can't help or won't help, so be it. Welfare is thought to sap people of their desire to work, no matter how badly off they may be. In the early 1980s, Texas' weekly welfare payment for a family of four was a deeply sub-poverty level of $34. Only Mississippi paid less.

Yet it is not hard to glimpse rank hypocrisy in Texans' preachments against a government dole. One of the greatest Texas fortunes, built by the Brown and Root construction company, sprang in no little measure from government business, a process only the naïve would believe was free from political favoritism. Lyndon Johnson's wealth was tied to government-granted broadcast licenses while he served in Congress. H. Ross Perot made his initial fortune by computerizing the federal government's medical insurance systems, becoming, one critic said, "the first welfare billionaire." Federal subsidies and meat import restrictions have propped up Texas agriproducers time and again. There are few historic parallels to the cozy relationship the oil and gas industries have long enjoyed with the federal government, generations of

Texas congressmen having spent their careers protecting the oil depletion allowance and other tax breaks.* And one can legitimately ask, how much of Texas' incredible economic growth can be traced to its swashbuckling free enterprise ways, how much to sheer geologic luck?

As much as even outsiders can rejoice with Texans in the happy turn of their fortunes, the record shows lingering meanness in Texas public life. Texas did join the Confederacy; it did practice raw racial discrimination for decades. Prosperity has dulled some of the rougher edges of Texas social conflict. But into the 1980s, Texas continued its notorious practice of tolerating small school districts, thus allowing affluent sections of a city to provide high quality schools for their children while poor whites, blacks, and Chicanos were obliged to tax themselves at a higher rate to provide even a minimal education. A dark leaf in modern Texas history was the state's effort (until forbidden by the U.S. Supreme Court in 1982) to deny public school education to the children of illegal aliens—the very group Texas employers had been coaxing across the border for cheap labor for generations.

The contrasts in modern Texas are overwhelming: in great cities, incredibly conspicuous displays of consumption, while unpaved streets or bitter desperation, or both, fester in nearby barrios and ghettoes; in many cities, posh residential sections, the most lavish housing and gardens, while rural south Texas harbors plain, wretched poverty overwhelmingly reminiscent of the Old South of the '30s and '40s. Texans are unquestionably correct when they argue that many Northern states went overboard in their commitments to the poor, or in succumbing to expensive demands of public employee unions. But Texas is no longer a struggling undeveloped province of the nation; it has immense wealth and power; it is America's third-largest state; it deserves to be judged just as critically as New York or California. All too often, the Texas Establishment exults on the one hand about a phenomenal growth rate and future prospects but then pleads poverty when questions of social equity are raised. But even if Texas, somewhat surprisingly, ranks only 10th among the states in its millionaires (according to the 1980 U.S. Trust Company survey), its per capita income has come up to 100 percent of the national average—actually more than 100 percent because the Texas cost of living is less than in the Northern states. Yet Texas' per capita outlays for virtually any kind of social service are near the bottom on any list of states.

Some of the severest criticism of Texas comes from Lone Star natives who have moved away. Eugene Keilin, a Texas-born, Harvard-educated lawyer who has helped New York investment banker Felix Rohatyn bail New York and other declining Northeastern and Midwestern cities out of their financial troubles, said he was shocked by how little feeling his Texas friends and

---

*Two of the biggest wielders of oil and gas power were Lyndon Johnson and Sam Rayburn. For two decades Rayburn was a zealous guardian of the gates to the tax-writing House Ways and Means Committee. Johnson, his onetime Senate aide Harry McPherson has written, did not have any particular love for the oil and gas industry, but dutifully hewed the line. Thus considered "sound on oil and gas," he could survive politically in Texas, his civil rights stand notwithstanding.

relatives had for people in other parts of the country and how much pride they took in the state's oil and gas. We asked James Howell, a Texas native who is vice president of the First National Bank of Boston (and forever goading New Englanders about their shortcomings), how Texas had changed since he left in the 1950s. "It's noisy" from the new oil and gas wealth, Howell replied. "The fastest-growing educational institution on the face of the earth today is Texas A & M University, where I went. But when you can pay a football coach $3 million, it says something about either a deplorable academic situation or misplaced priorities."

Not all successful Texans flaunt big money to cover a lack of self-confidence. New breeds of Texans have also emerged: George Bush and his crowd, the Northerners who went South, became Texans, and gave new life to the Republican party; people such as Reagan Chief of Staff James Baker, a native-Texan, who went to Princeton, returned home, and has been described by the *Washington Post* as comfortable in country-club clothes one weekend and cowboy boots the next; and finally, thousands of lesser known Texas scientists and businessmen who deal daily, with class and competence, in the national economy. Texas has changed in many other ways, too. The federal Voting Rights Act has forced Texas to recognize its blacks and Hispanics and to reconstruct the state political system, and minorities have now occasionally won political office. Eighty percent of Texans live in cities, and it is the only state to claim three of the eleven largest metropolises in the country: Houston, Dallas, and San Antonio. Texans, however, do seem fixated on the old, rural life. Texas writers, Larry McMurtry (author of *The Last Picture Show*) wrote in the *Texas Observer* in 1981, "have been too ready to fall back on the country idyll rather than attempting novels, poems and dramas. The result is a limited, shallow, self-repetitive literature which so far has failed completely to do justice to the complexities of life in the state."

Whatever its problems, Texans take a pride in their state little short of contagious to new residents. Alfred Watkins, a University of Texas political science professor denied tenure (probably because of his liberal to radical political views), told us he could not help but have fond memories of the state as he recalled how easy it was to present his ideas to members of the legislature. "If you have something to contribute, they'll take it," he said. Despite all the injustices that Texas Anglos served upon blacks and Hispanics over the generations, the minorities have always been included in the Texas tradition. Barbara Jordan, the former Houston congresswoman who won national plaudits for her oratory during the Watergate hearings, cut her own deal with the Texas Democratic establishment. Texas Chicanos have been known to oppose the federal appointment of a fellow Chicano from another state because a Texas Anglo was competing for the same job. State Rep. Gonzalo Barrientos told us he strongly disliked the growing California custom of referring to minorities as "Third World peoples." "I am a Texan," he said proudly.

Texas' modern history traces back to 1821, when Stephen Austin—with permission of the Mexican government, then sovereign over the territory—

established the first permanent Anglo-American settlement, at San Felipe de Austin on the Brazos River. Some 25,000 to 30,000 Anglos came to Texas over the next 15 years. Some brought slaves, and the Deep South traditions were established on Texas soil. From 1824 to 1835, Texas was joined with its southern neighbor, Coahuila, as one state of the federal Mexican Republic. When Santa Anna abolished the federal republic in 1835 in favor of a dictatorship, the Anglo Texans proclaimed a provisional government. Santa Anna sent troops into Texas. On March 6, 1836, 187 Texans—Anglo, Latin, and black—died defending the Alamo in San Antonio. Among the dead were Indian-fighter James Bowie and Davy Crockett. In the Battle of San Jacinto, near today's Houston, Santa Anna was defeated by a Texan army under General Sam Houston.

The independent Republic of Texas lasted for nine years, from 1836 to 1845. The experiment in boisterous, frontier democracy was without parallel in the settlement of the continent; unquestionably, it gave birth to the unique sense of themselves that Texans exhibit to this day. Texas was recognized as an independent republic by the United States, Great Britain, France, Holland, and several German states. It even had its own army and navy, postal services, and currency. No wonder Texans so dislike orders from Washington! The young republic's location made statehood almost inevitable, however, and after lengthy opposition by Northern states over the slavery issue, Texas was admitted to the Union in 1845. Texan statehood prompted war between the United States and Mexico, which led to the establishment of the Rio Grande River as the international border. During the early years of statehood, the heaviest stream of settlers came from the nearby Southern states. This, Joe Frantz has written, was "for reasons of propinquity. But other participants came from Indiana, New York, Massachusetts, and from beyond—England, Ireland, Denmark, France, German states, and Africa. Truly they were a United Nations' force dedicated to building a social and political climate in which men could go their separate, non-conforming ways without fear." This view suggests that the Texas tradition belongs to many more than the privileged WASP elite who occupy the heights of the Texas power structure and have monopolized attention for so many decades.

It is well worth remembering, when considering matters Texan, that old Sam Houston bravely warned his state against abandoning the Union, even though his stubborn slave-owning fellow pioneers removed him from the governorship for such apostasy and joined the Confederacy anyway. And a century later, it was another Texan, Lyndon B. Johnson, who dared to go against Southern prejudice—and not just as president, but as early as 1956, when he refused to sign the Southern Manifesto against the Supreme Court's school desegregation decision. Johnson went on to guide the pioneering Civil Rights Acts of 1957 and 1960 through the Senate and, of course, as president, to fight for passage of the landmark Civil Rights Act of 1964 and the Voting Rights Act a year later. Even if one might say the cause of black Americans' rights was ripe for fulfillment in history, and even if black America contributed mightily through its own nonviolent but determined stand, it took the leadership of a strong president to write those penultimate civil rights statutes into American law, and Johnson did not flinch before the task. It was a contribution paralleling Sam Houston's.

Sadly, history must also judge Johnson for leading the country deeper into the morass of the Vietnam War. And if in civil rights Johnson harkened back to Sam Houston, on Vietnam it was the Alamo. Ronnie Dugger, editor of the *Texas Observer* and Johnson biographer, has sketched that case quite convincingly. "In the scene that is central to the Alamo story," Dugger wrote in *The Politician*, "the commander drew a line in the dust with his sword and told all the men who would stay and fight to the death with him to step across the line. The one who did not, the arch-coward of Texas history, skulked away one night before the massacre and survived in immortal disgrace, an object lesson for generations of Texas school children, including Lyndon B. Johnson." The story of the Alamo, Dugger continued, "structured into the President's character, became one cause of Vietnam. The Alamo became Khe Sanh, San Jacinto the Tet offensive, and victory defeat." Thus in the very birthing moment of his state was planted the seed that would bring ruin to the presidency of Lyndon Johnson.

Texas Oil, Texas Wealth

The first great Texas oil strike was made in an inconspicuous mound of earth called Spindletop, near Beaumont on the Gulf Coast, in January 1901. The 1,060-foot hole punctured in the earth hit a "salt dome" in which oil was under such pressure that it shot up in a great, black fountain that covered the surrounding countryside with 25,000 to 100,000 barrels in a day. Oilmen and promoters swarmed onto the Gulf Coast, great firms such as Texaco and Gulf were born, and Texas became the center of the American petroleum industry.

But as late as 1930 most of Texas was drifting along as a rural, agrarian, poor state. Almost 60 percent of its 5.8 million people lived on farms or in little towns, making their living principally from cattle and cotton. Then, 170 miles north of of Spindletop, in the peanut and sweet potato patches of Rusk County, a determined old "wildcatter," 71-year-old C.M. "Dad" Joiner, who had sunk his last dollars into a makeshift drilling rig, finally hit oil at 3,600 feet. The strike opened up the vast East Texas field—the greatest field ever located in the United States until the Alaska North Slope strike in the 1960s. This was followed later by major discoveries on the West Texas plains.

Thousands of Texans became proficient in the skills of exploring and drilling for oil and hundreds became millionaires in their own right; the great pools of petroleum generated equally great pools of risk capital, a gigantic petrochemical industry formed, and Texas became one of the great manufacturing states in chemicals, electronics, aircraft, and metals. Military bases sprouted during World War II, and in the postwar years Texas became the country's second-largest defense contractor (after California). Dallas and Houston, the big financial, legal, and headquarters cities, grew into great

American metropolises, continuing their growth into the 1980s at a stunning rate. It is a widely dispersed urban population, however, covering 26 metropolitan areas (more than any other state), from Texarkana in the northeast to El Paso in the west, from Amarillo in the north to Brownsville in the south.

Search for a reason for Texas' explosive new wealth and you will find it not in the state's own ingenuity as much as in the spiraling world price of oil. In 1980, almost a billion barrels of oil were produced at a value of over $21 billion; gas production of 7.5 million cubic feet was valued at $11 billion. Texas' actual petroleum production went down slightly in the '70s. Looking afar, the major oil companies were engaged in aggressive global searches for new oil and gas sources. Yet in the '70s the value of oil increased five times and gas ten times, creating capital that fueled the state's extraordinary industrial expansion. The petrochemical industry born during World War II continued to grow, centered in Houston, Beaumont, and along the whole Gulf Coast in a complex informally called the "spaghetti bowl"—a reference to the thousands of miles of pipelines running from one factory to the next. But the oil towns of Midland and Odessa in distant West Texas prospered in the '70s, too. The dangerous side of continued dependence on oil became apparent in the early 1980s when lower world prices and declining production led directly to Texas' highest unemployment rates since the 1930s and a shrinking of the oil and gas severance tax receipts, which accounted for 30 percent of state revenues and had kept other taxes down. Over the long term, Texans also have to face the reality of dwindling reserves.

Texas agriculture has its own set of superlatives. For years the state has been America's foremost cattle raiser (13.2 million head in 1980), but the practice begun in the days of the great cattle drives of shipping the animals to the Midwest for feeding and eventual slaughter has given way to Texan feedlots (now more even than Iowa, mostly in the Panhandle) and, increasingly, Texan slaughterhouses. However, real cowboys still drive cattle in West Texas, and the huge cattle ranches still exist, most now complete with their own planes and airstrips. Many of the largest ranches, of course, have extensive energy deposits. The farm picture is rounded out by sheep and goats (more than any other state), usually the nation's biggest crops of cotton, watermelon, spinach, and pecans, and vast annual shipments of every fruit, from grapefruit to canteloupe, and every vegetable, from onions to carrots.

But to think of Texas only in terms of oil, gas, cattle, and farm products is to flounder in dated romanticism. Energy and agribusiness remain the wellsprings of the economy, but manufacturing now accounts for the largest single share of personal income. Petrochemicals lead the way, but Texas manufacturing has diversified into everything from textile plants to electronics. With its heady growth, Houston became one of the hottest steel markets in the world, and U.S. Steel and Armco have plants there. Texas construction firms led by Brown and Root undertake some of the world's largest projects. By 1982, 26 Texas companies made the *Fortune* 500 list and another 44 were on the *Second* 500, with more companies headed that direction. Five of the nation's 50 largest banks, were also in Texas. Not only was the state rich, but it really could finance much of its growth at home.

Politics, Texas Style: Establishment Power Unparalleled

Texas political life has been directed by a single moneyed establishment. In no other state has the control been so direct and unambiguous. The establishment has its roots in the banks and law firms of Dallas, Houston, and, to a lesser degree, Austin. Its untold billions of wealth are in oil, insurance, high finance, construction, broadcasting, real estate, electronics, and the manufacture of weaponry. Its spokesmen are the great metropolitan dailies of Texas —papers such as the *Dallas Morning News,* the *Houston Chronicle,* and the *Fort Worth Star-Telegram,* and in turn, the great bulk of the state's television stations. Lyndon Johnson was very much a part of this establishment. But Allan Shivers, the conservative governor and a man whose political endorsement was sought even into the 1980s, was its first great postwar leader. And John Connally—at least until he deviated into Republican byways—was its epitome.

Connally's story is quintessentially Texan. He grew up as one of seven children of a dirt-poor butcher, farmer, and later bus driver. Yet in his adulthood there were in all America few politicians who could compete with him for cool, suave manner, good looks, and height, a man never ill at ease. San Antonio lawyer John Peace, who met Connally at the University of Texas (then *de rigeur* training ground for aspiring Texas politicians), recalled even then a quality about the man that made others "want him to be chairman of the board. Connally did more to make Johnson than anyone else in the U.S." Peace insisted to us, that most of the Johnson forces were originally Connally people whose "first loyalty and tie was to Connally" (a group including Jake Pickle and Frank Ikard, both later to be congressmen; Ikard, subsequently became the oil industry's chief Washington lobbyist).

Finishing law school in 1938, Connally started almost immediately as an aide to freshman Congressman Johnson; later he received decorations for Navy service during World War II. In 1948, Connally operated in the thick of the events that led to the appearance of a miraculous uncounted vote box from Jim Wells County, which suddenly turned a narrow Johnson loss into an 87-vote victory and election to the U.S. Senate.

Connally began to build his own personal fortune and to solidify his ties with the Texas establishment in 1951 when he became an attorney for Sid Richardson, who had amassed a fortune of some $2 billion in oil, making him one of the richest men on earth. After Richardson's death, Connally earned $750,000 as an executor of his estate. The Richardson tie brought Connally into contact with the Murchison clan, which had major interests in railroads, steel, insurance, and oil. In 1965, he purchased the essential symbol of status and seriousness for any successful Texas businessman or politician: the ranch, in this case the 14,500-acre Tortuga Ranch in South Texas. The price was about $300,000. Connally remained a chief Johnson political operative, lining up financial backing among his oil industry friends and working for Johnson's unsuccessful bids for the presidential nomination in 1956 and 1960. When Johnson became vice president in 1960, Connally was appointed Secretary of the Navy. But within a year he was back in Texas, running for governor.

That campaign, in a sense, made Texas the state it is today. Connally, ironically, was accused of being "Lyndon's Boy"; in reality, Johnson, entertaining great disdain for state government, had counseled Connally to stay in Washington, where, as LBJ saw it, the real action was. But Connally and his old political-business colleagues, then in their mid-40s, detected a drift in the Texas economy and politics, a failure to be really competitive with the East and California in education or business growth. They were determined to make Texas a Class A state—not to go, one Texan told us, "the route of Mississippi, Alabama, and Louisiana." Connally and his friends were determined to protect Texas' one-party system, to freeze out the Republicans, and to save the state from the left wing of the Democratic party (militant unionists, liberals, and minority group leaders). Connally's gubernatorial bid, a classic power play by the establishment, was successful through then-record spending plus monolithic backing of the state press.

Connally took office in January 1963, and in November of that year President Kennedy scheduled his ill-starred trip to the state to try and calm the fierce internecine war between the liberal wing, led by Senator Ralph Yarborough, and the conservative wing, already known as the Connally wing. In the presidential motorcade going into Dallas, Connally had a coveted seat in Kennedy's limousine and was almost killed by a bullet. After Dallas, Connally was politically invincible and coasted to easy second- and third-term victories in 1964 and 1966. He proved a master of articulation of Texas' long-term needs in fields ranging from constitutional revision to higher education. Labor and the minorities got the back of Connally's hand.

By the time Johnson left the presidency and Connally the governorship, the establishment had created the new Texas it wanted: an aggressive state, oriented to the space-age and a far cry from the Old South syndrome. Connally was responsible for major new funding to expand the University of Texas into one of the nation's top teaching and research institutes. And the federal largesse was pouring in: a 242 percent increase in prime defense contracts in five years, for example, and location of the NASA Manned Spacecraft Center at Houston.

The pinnacle of John Connally's power may have come in 1972, after he had shocked the Texas political world by serving a year and a half as Secretary of the Treasury in Richard Nixon's Cabinet. In one of his greatest articles, David Broder described a presidential visit to Connally's South Texas ranch:

The flagstone ranch house was ablaze with light. The magnificent live oaks in the yard were hung with pots of orange mums, swaying in the evening breeze; more flowers floated in the pool; and the sweet scent of the prairie grass mingled with the odors of the steaming barbecue.

The guests arrived Texas-style, setting their executive jets down on the Picosa Ranch airstrip, with the great red Santa Gertrudis cattle watching.

The guest list, Broder wrote, was a "directory" of the members of Texas' moneyed establishment, from Allan Shivers to H.L. Hunt's son Nelson, and various other lawyers, ranchers, land speculators, broadcasters, publishers, and editors known for their steadfast allegiance to the establishment. After supper, Broder noted, President Nixon assured the guests America would never be defeated in Southeast Asia and "praised their friend and hero John Connally, who saved the state government from a serious liberal challenge in 1962 and gave them six more years of freedom from corporate income taxes or real utility regulation."

In 1972, Connally chaired Democrats for Nixon; the next year he became a Republican himself. But the developing Texas Republican party viewed him as a "Johnny-come-lately"; other wealthy, big-name Texas Democrats failed to follow Connally into the GOP; and Connally's two attempts to win the Republican presidential nomination were rather abysmal failures. Connally remained, however, an important political fund raiser and behind-the-scenes mover and shaker.

Back in the 1930s, when initial fortunes were just being made out of the East Texas oil fields and the ruling structure was largely unformed, maintaining the Texas establishment was fairly easy. Today the moneyed structure involves several times the number of people and has had to accommodate new elements such as the computer industry, university leaders, and occasionally transplanted Northerners and foreign interests. But the endless chains of inter- and intra-city, family and club, formal and informal relationships seem capable of incorporating and co-opting the new forces.

The establishment does have its Achilles heel: ethics. Even in theory, it recognizes no line between private interest and public responsibility. If a fledgling establishment politician lacks prior wealth, for example, steps are taken to see that he stays a poor boy no longer, often by selling him stock in an up-and-coming local corporation, the investment made by a loan from an establishment bank with the securities themselves the sole collateral. Then there are campaign contributions. Liberal candidates scratch for minimal funds while, as reporter Morton Mintz has written, contributions from businessmen "seem to fall like confetti" into the coffers of the establishment candidates.

Within the dominant Democratic party, however, lie conservative vs. liberal, establishment vs. populist conflicts with deep roots. When depressions hit Texas in the 1880s and '90s, Populists and Greenbacks turned the farmer's ire on the railroads that transported his crops, the financial houses that held his mortgages, and the trusts that fixed prices on his supplies. James Stephen Hogg, elected governor in 1890, ran on a platform attacking business abuses and asking for trust and railroad regulation. Hogg's ally, Thomas Campbell, won the governorship in 1906 and succeeded in strengthening antitrust legislation and instituting control of lobbies. More commonly, however, Texas elected governors who were pliable to the special business interests.

Republicans elected a governor during post–Civil War Reconstruction, then faded into insignificance. A poll tax law discouraged blacks and Populists from voting. Only the Democrats held a primary, on which all the interest centered (blacks were effectively excluded). Enough colorful personalities arose to entertain Texans for decades, while their state government largely marked time. Governor James or "Farmer Jim" Ferguson, a stemwinder and champion of rural voters, had the courage to oppose both Prohibition and the Ku Klux Klan. But the legislature caught Ferguson with his hand in the till and impeached him in 1917. Ferguson hit on the strategem (then original) of running his wife instead. The slogan was: "Two Governors for the Price of One." "Ma" Ferguson ran five times and won twice.

A similar appeal to the rustics launched the political career of Wilbert Lee ("Pappy") O'Daniel, already known through the hillbilly band he directed on a daily radio program advertising "Hillbilly" flour. Promising to give everyone over 65 a $30-a-month pension, abolish the poll tax, and defend the Ten Commandments, O'Daniel twice won the governorship and in a 1941 special election for the U.S. Senate defeated a young New Deal congressman, Lyndon Johnson, by only 1,311 votes. In Washington, O'Daniel talked the language of the country people but voted like a *Chicago Tribune* Republican.

By World War II, the Texas Republican party had disintegrated to a few old Yankee families sharing judgeships and customs agent positions when Republicans held national power. But in 1952, younger and more aggressive Republicans tried to get delegates favoring General Eisenhower elected to that year's GOP National Convention. The party's Old Guard so strongly favored Senator Robert A. Taft that party chieftain Henry Zweifel was quoted as saying, "I'd rather lose with Taft than win with Eisenhower." The party regulars' attempt to disqualify the Eisenhower delegates caused a national furor, and their eventual seating gave "Ike" a psychological advantage that helped him win the nomination. That fall, conservative Texas Democrats were so disillusioned with their party that Governor Shivers endorsed Eisenhower over Adlai Stevenson. Ike carried the state. And ever since, the "Shivercrat" wing of the Democratic party has bolted to Republicans in presidential elections, carrying the state for the GOP candidate in all years save 1960 (Kennedy, with Johnson for vice president), 1964 (Johnson himself heading the ticket), and 1976 (Jimmy Carter, fellow Southerner).

But most "Shivercrats" remained officially Democrats, voting for conservatives in state and local primaries and dashing the hopes of the liberal Democrats, organized labor, and minorities to become major forces in their own party. The only liberal victorious statewide was Ralph Yarborough, thrice elected to the U.S. Senate before losing to conservative Lloyd Bentsen in the

1970 primary.* Into the 1980s, liberals hoped the growing respectability of the Republican party would encourage conservatives to go that route—and allow the "real Democrats," as they put it, to take over the Democratic party. But the liberals continued to suffer from two terrible disabilities: lack of money (they are constantly, overwhelmingly outspent by the business-oil establishment) and lack of voice (scarcely a major newspaper or television station friendly to their cause). The liberals, however, did pave the way for the first Republican statewide victory since Reconstruction by withholding their votes from the conservative Democratic opponent to Republican Senate contender John G. Tower in 1961, thus making Tower's election possible.

The Tower precedent notwithstanding, the Texas Democrats were shaken in 1978 when William P. Clements became Texas' first modern-day Republican governor in 100 years. Clements, a self-made, utterly self-confident, and sometimes abrasive Dallas millionaire who founded the world's largest oilfield equipment company, won by promising to cut Texas' state government and spending a record $7 million on the campaign. Both Tower and Clements won by only 1 percent, however, illustrating how fragile was the Republican toehold in Texas. And in 1982, Clements lost, dashing the Republicans' claim that Texas had truly become a two-party state. Clements himself was partly to blame; he spent $12 million, which horrified even Texans and underscored his image as the candidate of Big Oil. The Republicans were also confounded when the Democrats nominated a conservative, Attorney General Mark White. White proved there were still enough rich Democrats to provide him a $7 million campaign chest, and he combined the money with organizational support from labor unions and populist criticism of increased utility rates, which he blamed on Clements' appointees.

White actually received fewer votes than a string of attractive and articulate younger liberals who were swept into second-tier, statewide offices: former U.S. Rep. Jim Mattox, of Dallas, as attorney general; former *Texas Observer* editor and outspoken populist Jim Hightower as agriculture commissioner; long-time liberal activist Ann Richards as state treasurer; and Gary Mauro, a former aide to George McGovern, as land commissioner. These victories constituted the liberal Democratic activists' greatest breakthrough in a generation and sparked their hopes of seizing the governorship in time. But liberal progress has been thwarted so often before that one could not help but remain skeptical.

Why, one may wonder, is the Texas establishment still so Democratic, more than 100 years after Reconstruction, especially since the Republican's opposition to government regulation of business and support of an aggressive

*As the only liberal Texas ever sent to the Senate, Yarborough played an important role in the Senate passage of several important pieces of legislation: broad minimum wage expansion in 1966, chief sponsorship of the landmark Occupational Safety and Health Act of 1970, GI benefits for post-Korea veterans, federal funding for bilingual education, and approval of the Padre Island National Seashore and Guadalupe Mountain National Park. Sadly, Yarborough always feared that other liberal candidates would cut into his own support and did not make use of his position to liberalize the Texas Democratic party.

national defense so precisely match the attitudes of many powerful Texans? Charles (Chase) Untermeyer, a Republican state legislator from Houston who became a White House aide to Vice President Bush, suggests the conservative Democrats and Republicans are divided by one great obstacle: the pork barrel. Conservative Democrats are anxious to tap it whenever they can; Republicans are more opposed to government spending of any kind, he maintained. Many businessmen prefer the "pliability" of Democratic congressmen and legislators, Untermeyer said, recalling that many times, as a state representative, Houston businessmen told him they agreed with his ideology and then asked him to use the government to help them out.

And then there are the factors of sheer personality, perhaps best embodied in Robert Strauss, erstwhile Democratic national chairman, U.S. special trade representative, Carter campaign manager in 1980, and through it all friend of John Connally (whose protégé he was in UT days). A Dallas lawyer, Strauss made his fortune in shrewd real-estate and radio-station investments, raised funds for Connally's first gubernatorial campaign, became treasurer of the Democratic National Committee and almost erased its gargantuan post-1968 debt, moved on to the national party chairmanship—all the while making and keeping friends in every political camp. Strauss became renowned for his hearty, jocular, colorful, profane, persuasive nature; he was at once a prototypical big-talking Texan and the master salesman of American politics.

Texas in Washington: Persistent Power

With the death in 1961 of fabled Speaker of the House Sam Rayburn, and more particularly the ending seven years later of the Johnson presidency, there was some thought that Texan power on the Potomac would henceforth be but a shadow of its former self. It would not prove altogether so. John Connally, as we have noted, wielded no little influence during the Nixon administration. Jim Wright of Fort Worth—a man first elected as a liberal, but who later proclaimed himself a centrist—was elected House majority leader in 1976 and made no bones about either his love of oratory, especially in partisan tangling with Republicans, or his hope one day to be Speaker.

Time and the political tides finally swept away such potent Texas House committee chairmen as George Mahon, Appropriations; Olin Teague, Science and Astronautics; W. R. Poage, Agriculture; and Wright Patman, Banking and Currency. (Patman, an east Texas populist who excoriated banks and high interest rates, died in 1976, before he ever saw how incredibly high the rates *could* go.) Texas committee power did, however, persist into the '70s under such figures as Jack Brooks, a crotchety, smart operator and former Rayburn protégé who became chairman of Government Operations in 1975, from which pulpit he sought unsuccessfully to kill federal revenue sharing to states and cities. Failing on that, Brooks became revenue sharing's monitor.

Into the 1980s Texas' congressional delegation, like the state legislature, remained more than 75 percent Democratic. Even though the post-1980 Census redistricting added three House seats (to a total of 27), the legislature dumped so many Republicans into the five already Republican districts that the G.O.P. made no immediate gains. Democratic Rep. Phil Gramm gained national attention as the Reagan administration's most important ally in the House and the cosponsor (with Republican Delbert Latta, of Ohio) of budget substitutes slashing federal spending. Gramm led the "Boll Weevils," the Conservative Democratic Forum, a group that included fellow Texans Kent Hance and Charlie Stenholm. When Congress reconvened in 1983, the Democratic leadership stripped Gramm of his budget Committee position, and he returned home as a Republican to win a special election.

Texas has continued to send only one black to congress, Mickey Leland of Houston, who replaced Barbara Jordan upon her retirement in 1978. There were three "safe" Hispanic districts by 1983, one held by conservative E. Kika de la Garza of South Texas, chairman of the House Agriculture Committee and ally of big Anglo growers.

On the Senate side, Lloyd Bentsen chaired the Joint Economic Committee in 1979 and 1980 and was reelected in 1982. He established himself early as a champion of big business and supply-side economics and played a crucial role in reducing the capital gains tax—a step leading to substantial increases in investment in small but growing high-technology companies. Even more stature and power accrued to Republican John Tower, holder of LBJ's old Senate seat, who became a foremost Senate authority on military affairs and defense. Republican takeover of the Senate gave Tower chairmanship of the Armed Services Committee, even as the nation embarked, wisely or not, on the kind of momentous defense buildup he had long advocated.

In the early 1980s, for the second time in twenty years, Texans had their man in the vice presidency. But this time he was not the LBJ variety born-and-bred-in-Texas politician, but rather George Bush, a personification of the modern Texas Republican party. Bush's father, Prescott, was a senator from Connecticut (1952–63), and George Bush received a classic New England aristocratic education, prepping at Phillips Andover and graduating from Yale. But he passed up the opportunity to join his father's Wall Street banking firm to return to Texas, where he had been stationed during World War II, and to start with friends the Zapata Petroleum Co. (named after the old Marlon Brando movie *Viva Zapata.*) Bush's company soon found profitable wells near Midland; an offshoot company pioneered in seabed drilling equipment. Bush thus succeeded in that business which above all can offer an instant Texas pedigree. He first got involved in Texas politics as a precinct chairman, later as Harris County (Houston) Republican chairman. In 1964, as a Goldwater, hawkish, right-wing conservative, promising to vote against Lyndon Johnson's civil rights bill, Bush ran against Yarborough but lost— '64 being the year of LBJ and unhealthy for Republicans. Two years later, however, Bush came back to win a U.S. House seat from Houston's West Side, one of the most affluent areas of the state. There he represented many of the Northerners who had come to Texas to cash in on the oil boom and brought with them not just Republican but also more progressive ideals. Bush moved steadily toward a more moderate position, voting for the 1968 open housing bill and gaining a reputation among his colleagues as a thoughtful, reasonable man willing to hear both sides of an argument. He lost a 1970 Senate race but subsequently was appointed ambassador to the United Nations by President Nixon. His next post was chairman of the Republican National Committee, where he tried to remove the taint of Watergate from Republican candidates. President Ford named him envoy to the People's Republic of China, later to head the Central Intelligence Agency.

Bush began his own campaign for the presidency in 1977, cultivating the grass roots, winning the early Iowa caucuses, but finding few fans among the emerging New Right. Ronald Reagan chose him as a vice president sure to appeal to Eastern, liberal Republicans. Bush managed to swallow his primary campaign description of Reagan's "voodoo economics," spent his time giving the brand of vacuous speeches for which vice presidents are famed, performed smoothly in the wake of the attempted assassination of Reagan, and—like all vice presidents—waited.

Government (and Nongovernment)

Texas state government is shameful and antiquated. Texas places poorly in any of the tests one might impose on government: breadth of services provided, innovative programming, tax effort and fairness, strong executive control, an efficient civil service, regulation of business and freedom from outside influence, and efficiency in the legislature. The booming Texas economy produced a 1980 ranking of 18th in per capita income among the 50 states, but Texas' per person government expenditures ranked only 44th. The state's per capita expenditures for health and hospitals ranked only 30th among the states; for education, 31st; and for public welfare, 46th. Even highways—Texas has more miles of road than there are miles to the moon—surprisingly, ranked only 35th. Texas' inactive state government is matched by a regressive tax structure. About 35 percent of government income is provided by sales and property taxes, which place the greatest burden on middle- and low-income persons. Into the 1980s, Texas refused to institute a state income tax.

Texas state regulatory bodies have never earned a reputation for toughness in dealing with private interests, nor have they received very strong mandates from the legislature. Texas' industrial safety and water pollution standards were among the weakest in the country, compelling labor unions and environmentalists to ask the federal government to step in. An interesting special case, however, is that of the Texas Railroad Commission, originally set up to regulate oil shipments by railroad tank cars, but since the 1930s the body that sets production "allowables" on oil. Martial law had to be imposed before the commission's quotas on production were obeyed, but ever since the commission has wisely conserved a natural resource. The simultaneous effect, of course, has been to increase profit to the oilmen by keeping prices up through limited supply.

Critics say Texas' state board of education indirectly and unduly influences the content of textbooks across the U.S.A. with its proclamation that texts "shall promote citizenship and the understanding of the free-enterprise system, emphasize patriotism and respect for recognized authority," and "shall not encourage lifestyles deviating from generally accepted standards of society." Board policy into the 1980s allowed only *negative* testimony, which a determined band of Texas social conservatives used to discourage references (1) to protest activities and (2) to certain parts of the body. Since Texas public schools may use only state-approved books, and Texas is country's second-largest schoolbook market, publishers think twice about putting out a book that will fail its peculiar standards.

Court-enforced reapportionment brought many new urban legislators to the Texas House and Senate, and subdistricting brought blacks and Chicanos. Conservative Democrats, nevertheless, remained firmly in control. The blacks were well organized by Craig Washington, a Houston legislator, who bargained for committee chairmanships. The Mexican-Americans have never gotten organized or played the state capitol game as effectively.

The governor's powers are fearsomely circumscribed. Most of the actual governing is done by more than 200 boards with overlapping six-year terms, generally appointed by the governor. Real power often ends up in the hands of agency heads who stay for many years. It's often said that the lieutenant governor has more power than the governor. He presides over the senate, and with his counterpart, the house speaker, appoints all legislative committees and chairmen and assigns all bills to them.

The most controversial single element of Texas state government is its prison system. In the best frontier spirit, Texas takes pride in not coddling criminals. The Texas prison system is the nation's largest, with some 36,000 prisoners. Expenditures per inmate have been incredibly low—less than a third of the national average. One way Texas keeps costs down is by requiring prisoners to work on its farm lands (63,000 acres for growing corn and cotton and raisins, 16,000 head of cattle). Texas prison officials claim that the work details have avoided the idleness, drugs, gangs, and inmate violence that have plagued other state prison systems. Prison reform groups have charged for years that the Texas prisons were inhumane places, and a massive case, *Ruiz* v. *Estelle*, came to trial in 1978. The Texas system received surprisingly guarded praise from Bruce Jackson, a New York academic and analyst of prison culture in many states. "As a northern liberal Jew, the idea of forcing someone to work is repulsive to me," Jackson testified at the trial. But Jackson added that if his son were ever imprisoned, "I would much rather he be in Texas' prisons than New York's."

The trial, however, revealed brutalities that confirmed critics' worst fears: inmate trusties called "building tenders" who brutalized other prisoners, a system 230 percent over capacity by federal standards, with inmates sleeping three to a cell and in tents, one physician assigned to 17,000 prisoners, and inmates performing surgery on each other. One prisoner testified that he was told to feed silage into a threshing machine by hand, violating normal safety practices, lost both arms in the process, endured a lengthy wait for an ambulance, and was then raped by another prisoner at the hospital while awaiting treatment. Federal District Judge William Wayne Justice ordered the State Board of Corrections to halt the overcrowding and the use of inmates in supervisory positions, to provide adequate medical care, access to the courts, and due process of law. Texas responded by spending about $2 million in legal fees trying to preserve the system. In 1982, the U.S. Court of Appeals upheld most of the reforms but ruled that the state could house two inmates in a cell, a decision Governor Clements hailed as a victory. Any substantive reforms would require constant court supervision, given the popularity of hardline positions on crime and prisons in Texas political campaigns. The politicians have complained that the majority of Texans do not want reform in the system. Judge Justice's response: "The plain fact of the matter is that the majority is sometimes wrong."

In 1982 Texas had a new claim to fame on the criminal justice front: the first execution by injection, a newly legalized method witnesses claimed was painless, although they reported that convicted murderer Charlie Brooks, Jr., yawned, gasped, and wheezed while his stomach moved up and down during the administration of the drugs. The Texas state government expected to get a lot of practice with death by injection: the state department of corrections had 171 prisoners on death row.

Geographic Texas: From Gulf to Panhandle to Rio Grande

Alaska's unmatched size notwithstanding, Texas remains a huge and multisplendored state. It covers one-twelfth the land area of the coterminous U.S.A., a territory equaling New York, New Jersey, Pennsylvania, Ohio, Illinois, plus all of New England combined. East to west, Texas extends 773 miles, north to south an intimidating 801 miles. Just one of Texas' 254 counties (of course, no other state has so many) is larger than the entire state of Connecticut.

Texans inherited an empire so vast that colonizer Stephen F. Austin once called it "a wild, howling, interminable solitude." Even with the civilizing influence of 14 million people, getting one's bearings is still difficult. The basic division the geologists talk of is the Balcones Escarpment, a fault line that splits Texas into basic eastern and western regions. East of the escarpment lies the Gulf Coastal Plain—hot, low country (the center of Texas' oil and chemical industries), site of such big cities as Houston and Corpus Christi, the "Piney Woods" section covering the whole northeastern corner of the state (north of Houston, east of Dallas), and the fertile lower Rio Grande Valley, known for its winter gardens and citrus fruit.

Two plains regions lie west of the escarpment: the Central Plains, mostly rolling prairie, classic cattle, sheep, and goat country that was once the southernmost range of the buffalo, and farther west, the arid, level High Plains, which form a clear-cut belt all the way to the Canadian border. The entire Texas Panhandle lies within the High Plains region.

Finally, there is the desertlike triangle of westernmost Texas, actually south of New Mexico. This is Trans-Pecos Texas, a land of gaunt scenery, high mountains, mesquite, cacti, and lonely distances. Here one finds the Big Bend National Park, on the Rio Grande, the Guadalupe Mountains National Park, on the border with New Mexico, and, at Texas' westernmost extremity, the city of El Paso. At El Paso, the average annual rainfall is less than 8 inches; a measure of the contrast in Texas' regions is that Houston's average annual rainfall is over 45 inches (with humidity to match).

With that capsulated geography in mind, we may retrace our steps, taking in, along the way, a glimpse of Texas' multitudinous cities. We will leave only the three largest urban conglomerates—Houston, Dallas–Fort Worth, and San Antonio—for individual treatment later.

The Gulf Coast, with its 370-mile-long window to the sea, is Texas' most cosmopolitan region, heavily populated with Mexican-Americans toward the Rio Grande and mixtures of rural white Southerners, blacks, and Cajuns farther north toward Louisiana. The shallow gulf has created incredibly long sandbars, forming a series of long sand islands that protect most of the shore from direct ocean weather. Best known and farthest south is 117-mile-long Padre Island, a creation of the winds, tides, and storms and stretching from near the Mexican border to Corpus Christi. These same gulf shores are wintering grounds for millions of waterfowl and a strong magnet for fishermen, hunters, and sailboat enthusiasts—a place, in the words of Texas writer Lewis C. Fay, "of peace and the swoop of seagulls, and the soft purples of twilight plunging into east-dark sky."

Some of Texas' most important oil fields lie in an arc just inland from the Gulf, as do the low, damp lands in which a major portion of the U.S. rice crop is produced. Not to be overlooked is the huge King Ranch, the grazing land of some 45,000 head of cattle and more than 2,000 horses, including some of the nation's finest thoroughbred racing stock. The ranch developed the Santa Gertrudis brand of cattle, but oil, discovered in 1939, actually brings in several times more income. In the old paternalistic tradition, the many Mexican-Americans who work on the ranch are known as "kinenos." There is simply no ranching operation in all America in any way comparable to the King Ranch, which was founded back in the 1850s. The Kleberg family, which owns the ranch, is very secretive about its affairs.

The major gulf area cities begin to the northeast with Corpus Christi (pop. 231,999, up from a mere 27,741 in 1930), which booms with a magnificent yacht basin and marina in its downtown section plus oil in its backlands. Up the coast, Galveston (61,902) was Texas' principal port city before the opening of the Houston Ship Channel in 1917. Victorian buildings have survived on Strand Street, the "Wall Street of the Southwest" in the 19th century, despite the ravages of hurricanes such as the one in 1900 that killed 6,000 people and despite a period, from the 1920s to the 1950s, when it was known as the sin city of Texas. Private foundations poured over $200 million into Galveston between 1960 and 1980, saving many buildings and producing many plans for the city's future.

Beaumont (118,102) and Port Arthur (61,195) belong to the Houston industrial triangle. Politically, the Gulf Coast cities are the most liberally Democratic in Texas, a phenomenon explained by the high proportion of organized labor, a heavy black population, and many Roman Catholics. But these older cities have not shared in the industrial development and population growth of Houston and more northern Texas cities. There is a positively Mediterranean atmosphere to Port Arthur, where many Cajuns came to work in the refineries; in the 1970s, the city also performed a political miracle in forcing the multinational oil firms operating locally to cough up a fairer share of taxes.

The great oil strike of 1930 never altered the character of East Texas. It remains the "piney woods" it has always been, a touch of the Deep South, Texas' most tradition-bound region. The first settlers from the South, William Humphreys wrote in *The Ordways*, "came out of the canebrakes and the towering pines" into the "flat and featureless immensity" of the East Texas prairie and retreated to the familiar forest, "from there to farm the margins of the prairie like a timid bather testing the water with his toe." What they chose to farm was principally cotton, and many ended up importing slaves; thus was born the old-style plantation civilization of Texas. Just in the past generation, the ruined old East Texas cottonfields have been converted to tree farms and cattle ranches. Blacks are present in large numbers but have had a hard time gaining political power. Just north of Beaumont, some 84,550 acres of East Texas have been preserved in the Big Thicket National Preserve, the result of a political battle led by Houston's former populist congressman, Bob Eckhardt, fighting the big timber interests. This is the only area of America where the flora and fauna of the evergreen Appalachia meet tropical life— from orchids to sugar maple, palmetto to ferns, otters to armadillos, alligators to anteaters.

Starting just west of the piney woods, in a broad swatch coming down from Oklahoma and reaching almost to the gulf is a strip of dark, rich prairie soil some call the Blacklands. Five major Texas cities—Dallas, Fort Worth, Waco, Austin, and San Antonio—lie astride the region. Surely the loveliest and most livable of these is Austin, possessed of the state capitol, the University of Texas, and an increasingly large and prosperous base of "light and clean" high-technology industry sparking Texas' highest growth rates. Austin proper grew 36.3 percent in the 1970s, to 345,496; its environs, 78 percent.

The University of Texas has indeed made startling academic advances in a generation, not only at the mother campus at Austin but as a truly statewide institution with branch campuses at Houston, El Paso, Arlington, Odessa, Dallas, and San Antonio, including several medical schools. Stretching toward greatness is not financially difficult for UT since it holds deeds to 21 million acres of rich oil fields and has an endowment valued at $1.3 billion (not, at least yet, larger than Harvard's, but the greatest of any U.S. public university). Some of UT's procedures have raised eyebrows in academic circles. The school has hired several Nobel laureates and other famous academics away from competing schools, but the claim is often made that UT is less willing to hire bright young faculty and provide them the resources to develop into the great academic leaders of the future. UT expects its teachers to steer clear of politics and its students not to demonstrate, while the regents run the university with a large degree of direction from the governor.

Physically, the UT campus at Austin still manages a pleasing ambiance. The Spanish accent of the earlier architecture gives a strong flavor to the scene, despite such steel and concrete intrusions as the massive Lyndon Baines Johnson Library and School of Public Affairs, planned on a typically Johnsonian grandiose scale that dwarfs the libraries of prior presidents.

Austin's other great landmark is the 308-foot-high State Capitol, set in lovely tree-filled grounds and commanding a long view down Congress Avenue, the city's major thoroughfare. Of course, it is the largest capitol in any of the 50 states. But in other ways, Austin is un-Texan. It was the national center of the so-called outlaw country music scene popularized by Willie Nelson, and then the Texas center for punk rock. Austin has 130 neighborhood organizations—many intensely activist. Blacks, browns, and developers are all politically potent. It elected a "radical" mayor in the '70s. Gays are not just socially or politically active; they have restored old Sixth Street into a lively center of fern bars, restaurants galore, a shopping mall, and preppy shops. Recycling of old buildings is omnipresent in the downtown. And around UT are quantities of expensive condominiums purchased by rich Texans for their offspring—perish the thought that the darlings would have to live in ordinary dormitories. Austin has developed a slow-growth image, but local residents, pointing to the rate of population growth, say it does not amount to much of a policy.

Waco (pop. 101,261), midpoint between Austin and Dallas, is filled with so many lavishly built Baptist churches that some have nicknamed it the Baptists' Rome. It is home to Baylor, the well-known Southern Baptist university. Waco is also the unlikely home of Bernard Rapaport, who makes a living selling insurance to union members and a hobby of raising and giving funds to liberal causes on a national basis.

West of Fort Worth, Austin, et al., the Central Plains begin. The ride west from Austin leads through the famed Hill Country to the LBJ Ranch. Johnson inspired an outpouring of federal largesse that brought his beloved Hill Country, once subject to ruinous overgrazing and cotton growing, back to life. The luckiest place, perhaps, was Johnson City (pop. 872), a decaying, unpaved cowtown when LBJ went to Washington and a thriving tourist mecca when he returned. Just a few miles west of the LBJ ranch is the little city of Fredericksburg (6,412), a reminder of the strong German liberal, slavery-scorning heritage of many counties in this part of Texas.

Wichita Falls (pop. 94,201), near the Oklahoma border, is the home of Midwestern University, where John G. Tower was a professor of political science before being catapulted to the Senate in 1961. In 1979, a tornado took 46 lives and caused $600 million in property damage, but within a year

Wichita Falls had been rebuilt so well it won an All-America City award. Some 140 miles south is the fabled old cattle town of Abilene (98,315), living off an Air Force base, regional oil, agricultural activity, and some manufacturing. A few more miles south is San Angelo, heart of one of the world's greatest sheep- and goat-raising territories.

The High Plains are truly the endless lone prairie. Here Texas gets its taste of the "continental climate": frigid winters, hot summers, and the wind blowing and blowing and blowing. In winter, "blue northers" roar down the unbroken sweep of the Panhandle plains. Up to 1870, the Panhandle was shunned by white men as uninhabitable, a place where "a man might wander aimlessly until the blistering sun and the windblown dust finally felled him." Then came the buffalo hunters and, after them, the first ranchers and settlers, battling the winds and intermittent droughts. World War I demand for wheat stimulated farmers to plow under the native buffalo grass in favor of grain farming, leading to wind erosion and the wreckage of the Dust Bowl. Except in drought times, the High Plains now support not only wheat but a thriving cattle industry and huge cotton harvests. But for this they pay a considerable price: constant draining of the supplies of underground water, including the great Ogallala aquifer. The underground water, built up over centuries, is not being replenished; its level is dropping. A future retrenchment to dryland farming is likely.

Three big cities thrive on the High Plains: Amarillo, Lubbock, and Midland-Odessa. Amarillo (pop. 149,230) is the natural capital of a huge region extending over all the Panhandle and deep into Oklahoma and Kansas. Aside from its renowed attractions of high winds, oil, cattle, and wheat, the town actually has some civic attractions not expected on the prairies: a zoo and several good art galleries. Outside of town is the Pantex assembly plant, where America's nuclear weapons are assembled. In the early 1980s, the Catholic Bishop, Leroy Matthiesen, touched off an immense controversy by suggesting that Pantex workers quit their jobs rather than continuing work on weapons of mass destruction.

Lubbock (pop. 173,979) has probably grown faster since 1940 than any other agriculture-based city in America. Ten percent of the cotton grown in the U.S. is harvested within 50 miles, and the local economy is also boosted by Texas Technological University. There is lots of prosperity, but also poverty, especially among the Mexican-Americans.

Still farther to the south, on the harsh and desolate West Texas plain, are Midland and Odessa, begun 100 years ago as sidings on the line of the Texas and Pacific Railway line from Fort Worth to El Paso. In the 1940s and 1950s, they became the gold dust twins of the rapid and gas exploitation of the 90,000 square-mile Permian Basin. Midland (pop. 70,525) has been a city of millionaire owners, of white-collar workers and executives, working in big high-rise office buildings incongruously set on the plains. Odessa (90,027), by contrast, is a hard-hat town, filled with roughnecks, roustabouts, and engineers.

Looking westward 225 miles, over the ravished glories of Trans-Peco Texas, to the westernmost extremity of this gargantuan state, we find the city of El

Paso. Together with its sister city of Ciudad Juarez, directly across the Rio Grande, El Paso is surrounded by dramatic, towering mountains and forms part of the largest bilingual metropolis on an international boundary anywhere in the world. Spurred on by military installations and new industries, El Paso more than doubled its population in the '50s, added 16 percent in the '60s and 32 percent in the '70s, to a 1980 total of 425,259. U.S. citizens often ignore the huge population just south of the border but the fact of the matter is, neighboring Juarez had 700,000 people by 1980.

El Paso is at once at the cutting-edge of the U.S.A.'s rapidly evolving relations with Mexico and a place somewhat removed, a step backward from urban development in other Texas cities. In recent years it has thoughtlessly ripped out block after block of downtown structures, many historically significant, yet failed to provide adequate redevelopment. The city's people are 62.5 percent Mexican-American, many of them poor and uneducated, laboring in low-wage garment factories. El Paso is also the site of the U.S.A.'s largest electrolytic refinery (Phelps-Dodge), the largest custom smelter in the world (American Smelting and Refining Company), Fort Bliss (home of the U.S. Army Defense Center) and, nearby, the White Sands Missile Range.

El Paso and Juarez are the largest and most western of several sets of Texas-Mexican border towns with perplexing problems. The next-largest in population are Laredo (91,449) and Nuevo Laredo (265,000), then Brownsville (84,997) and Matamoros (250,000). The Mexican cities have grown enormously because the Mexican government, trying to curb heavy migration to Mexico City and other industrial centers, has urged jobless people in the rural interior to move to the border areas. The American cities, though among some of the poorest in the U.S., have grown rapidly due to a high birth rate, the influx of industrial workers, Midwestern retirees seeking some of the nation's cheapest retirement homes, and Mexican immigrants. All these sets of sister cities face intense conflict between the social and environmental standards appropriate for developing Mexico, and just across an imaginary line, the industrialized and environmentally conscious United States. El Paso, for example, has come under U.S. government pressure to improve its air quality, but it claims that some of that dirty air actually comes from Juarez. At the same time, the Mexicans have charged that smelter operators in El Paso turn off the air quality controls when the wind blows toward Mexico. Health officials report that Mexican nationals come to hospitals on the U.S. side for care they could not afford in their own country, and the U.S. cities also fear spread of disease from dogs, coyotes, skunks, and other animals that cross the Rio Grande. Solutions are complicated by the fact that decisions made at the state and local level in the United States are made in Mexico by the national government in Mexico City. Officials on both sides of the border told us they felt ignored by their faraway national capitals and often had to work things out as best they could in this hybrid, interdependent society.

The U.S. has become concerned about illegal immigration, but controlling the border is another question. It takes a visit to one of the border towns to realize just how easily the U.S. is entered. In Brownsville, for example, the border crossing is in the middle of downtown, and to check each automobile would create massive traffic tie-ups 24 hours a day. The checkpoint is so busy, city planner Florencio Peña noted with a smile, that downtown Brownsville should never suffer the abandonment that other central cities have experienced. The U.S. government issues more or less permanent visas to Mexican border area residents who can prove they have permanent ties to their home country, and thousands of Mexicans travel legally across the border each day to shop, work, visit relatives, and seek services unavailable in Mexico. Illegal immigration aside, local officials in the border area occasionally complain about the added expenses for health care, police, and schools (which they believe the federal government should pay). But it's hard to find a local government official favoring any policy that would seal the border in any way. The 1982 Mexican peso devaluation revealed how totally dependent the border is on policies made far away. Laredo, which had processed 26 percent of U.S.–Mexican trade, looked like a ghost town, while the U.S. Border Patrol reported massive increases in the number of illegal alien arrests.

Houston: Boom Town on the Bayou

"Houston," architectural critic Ada Louise Huxtable wrote a few years back, "is the city of the second half of the 20th century. Houston even requires a new definition of urbanity."

The city of which Huxtable was writing fascinates architectural and social critics with its dynamism and repels them with its physical and human chaos. Its growth has been fantastic. In the 1970s, Houston and its suburbs added 906,034 people, more than any other U.S. metropolitan area. Some of that growth was due to a broadening of the metro area, but one suburban county expanded by 160 percent, and the city of Houston alone grew 29.2 percent, adding 360,551 through population growth and annexations. The *Philadelphia Inquirer* determined that Houston passed Philadelphia to become America's fourth-largest city on August 5, 1981. Houston's superheated oil refining-manufacturing-management-shipping economy created over 670,000 jobs in the '70s.

Houston, alone among major U.S. cities, has had no zoning laws. Only freeways seem to hold the city together. Houston annexed so aggressively (until the U.S. Justice Department ruled it was diluting the minority vote) that it mushroomed into a 557-square-mile monster. The downtown has been described as "27 significant buildings surrounded by trivia": vacant lots, parking lots, and no-man's land. Houston's wealth has turned it into a skyscraper laboratory and attracted architects such as Philip Johnson, John Burgee, I.M. Pei, Cesar Pelli, and Kohn Pedersen Fox. The Galleria, a 20th-century interpretation of the famous 19th-century galleria in Milan, Italy, won the Urban Land Institute's excellence award for its exceptional achievement in mixing offices, department stores, a shopping mall, and an olympic-sized skating rink. Houston reveals some splendid embellishments, including the Houston Civic

Center with its convention hall and the celebrated Alley Theater, a pioneer in the regional theater movement, the building designed in a free-flowing, castlelike style of sandblasted concrete with nine great turreted towers. Houston, *The New York Times'* Paul Goldberger has written, "has an almost exhilarating sense of freedom—new things are tried here with an eagerness that would never be found in New York—but it is all at a price. What Houston has not managed to do is give itself a cohesive form."

The irony of it all is the location. Beset by fantastic heat and humidity, Houston was just a mosquito-infested, muddy tract of land near the sluggish Buffalo Bayou in 1836 before two New York real estate developers, the Allen brothers, paid a dollar an acre to buy it from the widow of the great Texas settler, John Austin. The late Marvin Hurley, executive vice president of the Houston Chamber of Commerce, cheerily observed that it was "the most inhospitable place to start a city that anyone could have found." Air conditioning takes the worst edge off that condition, and no one thinks of Houston as a sleepy bayou town anymore. Instead, Houston is spoken of as a remarkably open, young, informal, progressive city—a place that revels in the conspicuous consumption of its new wealth.

Houston's significant 20th-century development began with the Houston Ship Channel, opened in 1914, which snakes through some 50 miles of bayou, river, and Galveston Bay shallows to the Gulf of Mexico. The channel is deep and wide enough for large oceangoing ships, and the port of Houston, measured by tonnage, is exceeded only by New York and New Orleans. The deepwater port makes Houstonians advocates of national free trade policy, and many foreign countries have located consulates there.

Spindletop made Houston a big oil center, and the visitor need only glance at the names on the skyscrapers of downtown Houston to see who's there now: Gulf, Shell, Texaco, Conoco, Exxon, Tenneco, among others. The logic in all this is that Houston's service area, at least 600 miles in circumference, produces most of America's oil. Oil was a huge business before World War II, but then came the great petrochemical thrust of recent decades, mixing oil, gas, sulphur, and salt with other chemicals to produce a broad range of plastics and synthetic materials. The results were both a vast new wealth and vile pollution in the ship channel, the bottom lined with a putrid sludge, the surface frequently covered with floating grease, oil, debris, and colored chemicals. In the early 1970s came the government-ordered cleanup that industry would never have agreed to voluntarily. It was such a success that by the end of the '70s, dolphins had returned to the channel's lower reaches, and fish, including tarpon, were seen as close as five miles to the head. But between the chemical plants and Houston's armies of autos, air pollution was still a serious problem.

Oil and chemicals' dominance notwithstanding, Houston's economy is not of the single-track variety. It is what the economists call "vertically integrated": oil and gas are at the base, topped by succeeding layers of petrochemicals, metal fabrication, and food processing. U.S. Steel runs America's largest and most automated steel works here. Houston and its port, the country's number one wheat exporter, are also important in cattle and rice. To all of this one must add some of the nation's most advanced medical services, including the Texas Medical Center (where the Drs. Michael DeBakey and Denton Cooley pioneered heart transplant techniques), the Johnson Space Center, and finally the big law firms that end up negotiating, arbitrating and processing the million and one deals, from downtown buildings to oil leases and shipping arrangements, that keep Houston humming.

There is also a substantial Arab presence. "What New York has long been to Israel and Jews, Houston has become to the Saudis," the *Washington Post's* Dan Balz has reported. Saudi Arabia became Houston's number one trading partner through oil and construction contracts with Texas' Brown and Root and other engineering and architectural firms there.

"Growing, growing, growing, that's Houston," was the way publisher Jesse Jones, the renowned "Mr. Houston," used to sum up the city before his death in 1956. Some demographers have estimated that Houston may have hit its peak in 1978 and ended a period of explosive growth that was similar to the development of New York and Los Angeles earlier in this century. But large-scale plans for massive skyscrapers, shopping-office complexes, and new residences continued into the 1980s. On the drawing boards was a glittering skyscraper designed by Chicago architect Helmut Jahn in a style reminiscent of the Chrysler Building in New York. Its 82 stories, a focal point for the city, would top all other Texas buildings—indeed all but five in the world.

The Houston establishment has fueled the perpetual boom with a pro-business attitude that has made land, construction, and operating costs cheaper than in any other major world city. The establishment was in its prime when it began truly Texas-sized projects, such as the Astrodome, the world's first all-purpose air-conditioned domed stadium, $4\frac{1}{2}$ times the diameter of Rome's Colosseum.

In its commitment to unfettered free enterprise and individualism, Houston has created a horrendous urban mess. The city's streets and highways are the stuff of nightmares. As 1,000 new vehicles arrived in town each week, Houston became known as the pothole capital of the world. In 1978 it was estimated that 25 percent of the city's streets were unlighted and some 400 miles of streets unpaved. Traffic jams became so legendary that out-of-town travelers told seemingly fantastic, but true stories of arising several hours early to get to the airport on time. Finally, in the late '70s, Houstonians by referendum approved a sales tax to build a mass transit system expected to carry 250,000 passengers a day.

Establishment worries about intolerable congestion and pollution were mounting in the '70s. Then, in 1981, Houston voters sent a resounding signal that they wanted a reversal of course by electing as mayor, Kathy Whitmire, the 35-year-old city controller. Whitmire did not oppose growth per se but suggested it (and Houston) could be managed a lot better. Yet for Houston to elect a young, progressive, acknowledged feminist was nearly revolutionary. In 1982, the city passed its first limited land-use planning law.

Whitmire also faced grave police problems. She received election support from Houston's blacks (27.6 percent of the population), Hispanics (17.6 percent), and gays, who have become one of Houston's most organized political forces. All three groups clamored for reform of the police department, nationally notorious for its brutality. Houston's count of fatal shootings by police was twice the national average, and national black and Hispanic groups had taken several celebrated police brutality cases to the U.S. Justice Department. The police department in the early 1980s was still only 8 percent black and 8 percent Hispanic. Whitmire shook things up by hiring as police chief Lee P. Brown, the highly respected Atlanta public safety commissioner. The Houston Police Officers Association lobbied against Brown, but he was sworn in as Houston's first black chief of police in April 1982.

Minorities have had a love-hate relationship with Houston. Many rural blacks and Hispanics have moved there and found the greatest economic opportunity of their lives—even holding Houston's lowest rung jobs. Houston effectively froze minorities from political power until 1978 when the Justice Department, under the federal Voting Rights Act, ordered the City Council restructured into single member districts. The Texas House of Representatives, however, had adopted single-member districts in 1972. Perhaps the most eloquent of Houston's new council types was Ben Reyes, a Chicano who gave up a state legislature seat he had held for eight years to run for the council and to address dire conditions of poverty and decaying public facilities he alleged the Houston establishment had swept under the rug. Houston, Reyes argued, had grown topsy-turvy because a small group of developers and bankers "reaped tremendous profits at the expense of the masses." Firms such as Exxon and Shell, he said, got tax breaks to locate in Houston; industrial firms set their own real estate valuations for taxation at laughably low levels. So if the masses are asked to cough up more taxes while such big downtown firms as Exxon and Shell get tax breaks, Reyes told us, the response would be "Go to hell—we've been denied even a semblance of city services."

Houston's establishment was most shocked to discover the city was becoming a mecca for gays (former Mayor Jim McConn lamented, "What are we doing wrong?"). But gay activist leaders reported that Houston was much more tolerant—and sophisticated—than its frontier image suggested, and by the early 1980s, the gay population was estimated at 250,000. The electoral power of the Houston Gay Political Caucus was first demonstrated in the 1979 council elections when longtime councilman Frank Mann used vile and abusive language to depict homosexuals. The gays' telephone banks and door-to-door canvassing were credited with the election of his opponent, Eleanor Tinsley, who had endorsed homosexual rights and became one of the first two women elected to the Houston City Council.

Despite its general planning chaos, Houston has some very nice neighborhoods. A premier U.S. residential subdivision and the most prestigious Houston neighborhood is River Oaks, close to downtown. The irony is that River Oaks was planned very carefully by architects and planners hired by Will Hogg, son of the famed governor; its homeowners' association—composed of some of America's strongest opponents of restrictions on free enterprise—

goes to great lengths to make sure that deed restrictions are maintained.

Other interesting neighborhoods include the Montrose area, which comes closest to being Houston's Greenwich Village (improving itself through a *lack* of zoning in the '70s as a wild melange of residences, artsy shops, homes turned into restaurants, banks, and gas stations flourished without restrictive zoning codes to cope with); South MacGregor, a formerly Jewish and now proud middle-class black area; and Magnolia, Houston's oldest Mexican-American barrio, home to generations of industrial workers. But thousands of blacks and Mexican-Americans occupy the worst slum areas, such as Sunnyside, Third Ward, and Acres Homes. Here are found pockets of the classic Southern slum dwelling: the shotgun house. Minority politicians complain city negligence is responsible for flooding, sewer backups, unpaved streets, and the rusting refrigerators and abandoned autos that rot in front of dilapidated frame houses and provide nesting places for rats.

A few miles north of Houston there is even a planned community, the Woodlands, the only unqualified success story among those the federal government guaranteed in the early '70s. The success of the Woodlands was apparently due to Houston's good times and the patience of its developer, oil man George Mitchell. The Woodlands, with 12,000 residents in the early '80s, is expected to reach 160,000 by the turn of the century.

Houston has two powerful, separately owned and operated newspapers: the *Post* (A.M.) and *Chronicle* (A.M. and P.M.). The *Chronicle* is owned by Jesse Jones' legacy, the Houston Endowment, Inc., which has substantial interests in downtown office buildings, hotels, oil royalties, ranchland, and blue chip stocks. The *Post* is the domain of that attractive and forceful woman Oveta Culp Hobby, who served in the Eisenhower cabinet. Her son, William P. Hobby, Jr., served ably as executive editor of the *Post* before winning election as lieutenant governor in 1972. Because the lieutenant governor's job in Texas is only part-time (a unique situation among the megastates), Hobby was also able to assume the reins as the *Post*'s publisher.

Dallas–Fort Worth: The Metroplex

Dallas was the city born with a wooden spoon in its mouth. Its location was remote, it had no port or access to the sea, the farmland about it was not particularly fertile, and neighboring Fort Worth soon monopolized the Western cattle trade. Nor have oil or gas ever been found beneath Dallas. But cotton buoyed the city's early economy after the railroads were bribed or forced to divert their tracks through the town. When the East Texas oil field opened in the 1930s, Dallas quickly cashed in as banker for the operation. Hundreds of Dallasites became millionaires, and the huge capital reserves created were then available to finance more exploration for oil and diversification into such fields as insurance and electronics manufacture. Dallas also became a great gateway for Southwestern trade, leading the region in banks, distribution, and even fashion.

By dollar-and-cents measures, Dallas' wooden spoon has turned to gold. Dallas has three of Texas' five largest banks, the regional Federal Reserve Bank, and more than 200 insurance companies. Old-fashioned entrepreneurial daring had a lot to do with the growth of such postwar Dallas-based companies as Texas Instruments.

Dallas' real rival for power and prominence has not been nearby Fort Worth, but booming, bustling Houston, 240 miles distant. Dallas was bigger first, but Houston has outpaced it. Both cities are run by business oligarchies, but they could not be more different in their attitudes. In Dallas, a moneyed aristocracy has exercised its power for what it considered "sensible and orderly" growth and a highly professional city government; Houston contemplated the prospect of growth and decided to "let 'er rip" while city government was systematically undernourished and neglected, lacking recognizably professional management. Dallas' restraint must be understood in Texas terms, however: its aristocracy goes back only to the 1930s, and its "slow pace" of growth has been outranked nationally only by the likes of Houston.

Even if the space between them is sometimes cold and forbidding, Dallas has managed to concentrate its greatest new buildings downtown. Huge complexes such as One Dallas Center, the Plaza of the Americas, and Reunion have incorporated offices, hotels, and shopping in high-grade mixed-use development. Reunion, the most dramatic downtown project with its 30-story mirrored glass hotel and 50-story tower topped by a geodesic dome, even has a sports arena. Recently, Dallas has begun to develop something of a sense for historic preservation. Recycled old residences started the trend. Then the fabulously wealthy Hunt Brothers gave the fledgling historic preservation movement an unplanned boost by demolishing the landmark old Kress Building in 1981. The public was outraged, and lavish economic incentives were enacted to encourage developers to preserve buildings. In the early '80s, a big suburban developer was building expensive houses within walking distance of the central business district, and other developers were attempting market-rate apartment towers in Dallas' "central arts district," which was scheduled to have a new museum, symphony, library and other facilities.

This is not to say that downtown Dallas is one beautiful skyscraper after another. Rather, the inner city alternates between the great skyscrapers and tawdry beer joints and missions not far from Texas' fabled department store, Neiman-Marcus.

Dallas' suburbs have also seen large-scale development due to lower costs and massive freeways providing easy access. Residentially, North Dallas is the most fashionable part of the city. Within North Dallas are Highland Park and University Park, incorporated townships surrounded entirely by city territory. Both are almost exclusively white enclaves. University Park boasts the Fine Arts Center, the Museum of Fine Arts, the Dallas Theater Center, and Southern Methodist University. Between Highland Park and downtown is Turtle Creek, the site of the granddaddy of the apartment complexes that have sprung up all over Dallas. The city's slums are to the west and south. West Dallas, where frequent flooding occurs, is an industrial, low-income neighborhood with gigantic federal housing projects. Most of Dallas' blacks live in South Dallas, where conditions are little better.

Aside from the slums, Dallas' streets, bridges, and sewers are probably the soundest in the nation, according to the Urban Institute. The attention and money devoted to the maintenance of its physical plant reflects the priorities of Dallas' business community, which at least until the early 1980s dominated city politics as in no other city. From 1936 until the late '70s, the ultimate power rested with the Dallas Citizens' Council, an organization of 200 chief executive officers; an affiliate organization ran candidates for city council and the school board, and they almost always won and picked city managers who carried out the businessmen's priorities. The business candidates ignored the fact that Dallas was becoming 29 percent black and 12 percent Hispanic—and doing very little for those neighborhoods. In 1980, the U.S. Justice Department, under the Voting Rights Act, held up elections for 10 months until the city replaced its system of city-wide elections with districts which were designed to guarantee at least three minorities on the 11-member council. The plan indeed succeeded; one of the new councilmen was a Chicano previously a leader of the fiery "Brown Berets." New residents from the Northern states, attuned to a higher level of city services, also began to voice their concerns, and some older politicians expressed fears that Dallas would lose its appeal to business and white middle-class people. But in August 1982, Dallasites indicated they still had a strong faith in their city government by approving, with a "yes" vote of 59 percent or more, 11 bond issues totaling $247 million to finance everything from fire and flood and police protection to parks, a library, transit, the zoo, a farmers' market, and a concert hall.

Dallas has surely come a long way from the spirit of right-wing extremism rampant when President John F. Kennedy was assassinated there on November 22, 1963. Killer Lee Harvey Oswald's politics, with its Cuban-Soviet tinge, was diametrically opposed to Dallas' prevailing conservatism. But the deed of violence was performed in a city where violent rhetoric had come into vogue, where Lyndon Johnson and his wife were subjected to shouting, shoving, and spitting in the 1960 campaign, and United Nations Ambassador Adlai Stevenson had to bear similar abuse in October 1963. Right-wing extremism apparently became acceptable in Dallas because of the combined syndromes of new money (the tax collector was quickly viewed as the greatest threat) and the strong—almost overwhelming—conservative Baptist complexion of Dallas. In this pro-business milieu, bland Protestantism gave way to uninhibited superpatriotism. After the assassination, there was a tremendous backlash against right-wingism. Texas Instruments founder Erik Jonsson, who became mayor in February 1964, led the city toward a more moderate future, instituting along the way the "goals for Dallas" process, involving all races and economic groups—a model which cities across America would look to later.

One of the positive forces in the post-assassination period was the *Dallas Times-Herald*, having switched to a moderate course after its previous conservatism. By the early 1980s, Dallas had become one of the few cities in the nation with truly competing newspapers. The *Morning News*, once viciously

right-wing, had moved to reasonable conservatism and made a name for itself
in business reporting, even scooping national publications. The *Times-Herald*,
purchased in 1969 by the Los Angeles Times and Mirror Company, opened
regional bureaus and even one in Central America, becoming Texas' best
paper in the breadth of news coverage, but was finding the wooing of readers
and advertisers a tough job.

Nothing in Texas seems so immutable as the fact that Dallas and Fort
Worth (one third the size of Dallas) are different. Though a mere 33 miles
divide them, John Gunther wrote, there "is a chasm practically as definitive
as the Continental Divide." Dallas was forever written of as the place where
the East ends, Fort Worth as the place "where the West begins." Fort Worth,
is no longer "Cowtown, U.S.A." Swift and Co., the last big meat processor,
closed down its Fort Worth plant in 1971. What's left of the stockyards still
handles about 5,000 animals per week, but it is just one of dozens of small
regional stockyards around the country. Some sections of abandoned packing
houses have been converted into boutiques, restaurants, and a shopping mall.
But its Old West atmosphere remains one of its strongest selling points. When
tour companies bring Europeans to Texas, we were told, they spend more
time in Fort Worth's Old Texas atmosphere than in bustling, but relatively
characterless Dallas. Nationwide, Fort Worth's best known attraction is Billy
Bob's, a humongous old cattle barn near the stockyards that can accommodate
as many as 6,300 cowboys and bosomy T-shirted Texas girls at 43 bars and
many game arcades. The biggest attraction, however, is dancing to country
music, often played by name bands.

Fort Worth leaders became worried about the city's image after a 1982 Louis
Harris poll showed that most Americans had *no* image of Fort Worth. Yet
Fort Worth does have much to crow about. By 1983 several gigantic office
structures soared up to 40 stories above the prairie horizon—double the
height, and double the office space of New Year's Day 1980. This erstwhile
sleepy cowtown was headed toward 2,000 Class A hotel rooms. Main Street
had been bricked over, and there was an astounding abundance of historic
building recycling downtown, including Neiman-Marcus' first bar—called
the Red River Saloon. Its Amon Carter Museum is one of the nation's finest
in Western art. Fort Worth has a pronounced poverty and racial division (22
percent black and 12 percent Hispanic), but both business leaders and social
activists told us that all interests in the city have demonstrated a remarkable
willingness to listen to each other and solve problems.

The Census Bureau in 1973 designated Dallas and Fort Worth as a single
metropolitan statistical area, the "Metroplex," the nation's largest physically
and eighth- or ninth-largest in population by the early 1980s. In reality, time,
sprawl, and politics had already tied the two cities tightly together. The 33
miles between them had filled up with factories and suburbs called the "Mid
Cities," including Arlington (pop. 160,123), an infinity of subdivisions and
arterial roads with the distinction of being America's most heavily populated
place with no city center whatever. Dallas and Fort Worth were dragooned
into cooperation when the Civil Aeronautics Board told them to agree on a

common airport location or the decision would be made for them by the feds. The result was the region's symbol of unity, the Dallas-Fort Worth Regional Airport, opened in 1974 halfway between the two and the largest commercial airport in the world. Other symbols unifying the two cities include the Six Flags Over Texas amusement park, the Texas Stadium (home of the football Cowboys), and Arlington Stadium (home of the baseball Rangers).

Most of the Metroplex's population growth—up 25 percent in the '70s—is suburban. Dallas itself, ringed by suburbs, grew only 4.1 percent, to 904,078, and Fort Worth actually lost about 8,000 people, a 2.1 percent decline, to 385,141. But several surrounding counties almost doubled their population.

San Antonio: Old and Thriving

"San Antonio," Larry McMurtry has written, "is of Texas, and yet it transcends Texas in some way, as San Francisco transcends California, as New Orleans transcends Louisiana. Houston and Dallas express Texas—San Antonio speaks for itself." For this there is good reason: San Antonio was over 100 years old when Dallas and Houston were founded, and its original purpose was not profit, but politics and religion.

Even while the French were settling New Orleans, the Spanish advanced northward from Mexico and in 1718 founded San Antonio, making it the capital of their province of Texas. Franciscan friars came and erected a series of missions. Four of these—San Jose, Concepcion, Capistrano, and Espada—still stand, and together with the Alamo and the Spanish Governor's Palace, their wonderfully distinctive style is a reminder of empire, a tie to the past that the rest of Texas scarcely knows.

Soon after the Civil War, San Antonio became the first of the cowtowns of the legendary West, a base area for the cattle trails—Chisholm, Shawnee, Western—heading up to final destination points in Missouri, Kansas, and Nebraska. The railroad came in 1877, and the lusty business of the open range made San Antonio into a veritable cattle capital, filled with picturesque saloons and gaming tables where men whose herds ranged over millions of acres played recklessly for high stakes. Eventually, the cattle trade began to share the scene with pedestrian breweries, cement factories, milling, and oil. San Antonio became one of the great military cities of the United States. But still, that Spanish admixture and Latin population remained, together with a strong dose of German immigration that leavened the urban mix and created an atmosphere unduplicated anywhere in America.

From its early-20th-century heights as Texas' largest city and financial center, San Antonio lost ground rapidly to Houston and Dallas, exploiters of the East Texas oil fields. Decline was in the air; by the '60s the only bases of the city's once-thriving economy were local military installations and tourism.

HemisFair '68, designed to celebrate San Antonio's 250th birthday, signaled a resurgence and got the city to think of itself as major league once more. New thinking came none too soon, because huge population pressures were building. San Antonio grew 20.6 percent in the 1970s, to 785,419, rising from 15th-largest to 11th-largest among all U.S. cities (although the overall metropolitan area, just over 1 million, ranked only 36th in the nation).

Downtown San Antonio retains a delightful Spanish flavor. On a meandering course once known as "A-Drunken-Old-Man-Going-Home-At-Night," runs the San Antonio River, an intriguing and unique city waterfront. The river had once been little more than a neglected slough periodically overflowing nearby districts. But in the 1930s an ingenious flood control program, carried out by the WPA, at the instigation of Maury Maverick, Sr., San Antonio's great New Deal era congressman, resulted in rock retaining walls, picturesque footbridges and walkways, and landscaped banks. Today this four-mile "Paseo Del Rio" is lined with restaurants and shops, an open-air theater, and nightclubs, a place of life and joy that draws one irresistibly. The River Walk was extended in 1964, and a special side channel replete with the same ferns and magnolias extends to the lagoon where San Antonio's new convention center and Theater of Performing Arts stand. There are plans to extend it farther, to the San Antonio Museum of Art, created in the late 1970s in the old castlelike Lonestar Brewery. Gondolas run along these waterways, and if you stay in one of the hotels along the river, you can go to the theater or restaurant by boat.

The Alamo is still the epicenter of downtown San Antonio. Nearby is La Villita, a restored square block replica of 18th-century San Antonio, with stucco and roughhewn timbers. West of downtown is El Mercado, a large open-air Mexican-style market. Just south of downtown is the historic King William District, a not-quite-completely gentrified showplace neighborhood boasting San Antonio's most beautifully restored old mansions.

Beyond these attractions, San Antonio seems caught in early-20th-century dowdiness. From the HemisFair tower one sees relatively few buildings of postwar vintage; most major office structures date from the '20s and '30s, and parking lots abound. From the same tower vantage point, one looks west, past center city to the heavy Chicano areas, east to San Antonio's black areas, and south to a mixed bag of neighborhoods, plus a strong representation of the military-industrial complex. (Fort Sam Houston and four Air Force bases, South Texas Medical Center and the Southwest Research Center are located *within* San Antonio's city limits.)

What San Antonio has over Houston and Dallas in charm it loses in economics: its per capita income is almost 25 percent lower. The Anglo aristocracy, living in its north side bastions of Alamo Heights, Olmos Park and Terrell Hills is informal in the Southwestern manner but also cleverly self-centered. There are, for example, 15 separate school districts, all independent taxing units, allowing the wealthy to tax themselves at a much lower rate while providing their children a high-quality education; the poor Chicanos and blacks must pay higher rates on their low tax base to come up with even a minimum of educational facilities.

The great West Side barrio is one of the most striking slums of the continent. For block after block, the tiny shacks and hovels stretch on, many with outdoor privies and lacking water. Until the federal government's poverty programs started in the 1960s, the city of San Antonio largely ignored the barrios. But even in the early 1980s, many of the streets were not paved, and every year floods still led to several deaths.

While San Antonio's aristocrats were long willing to rely on their old fortunes, high-technology companies were streaming into San Antonio by the 1980s. A new San Antonio was growing up along Loop 410, which encircles the city, a world of industrial parks and typical new subdivisions.

The Anglo power structure of San Antonio had practiced informal Jim Crow into the 1960s and managed to retain political power well into the '70s. Most of the elections (all nonpartisan) were won by candidates of the Good Government League (GGL), a group of private citizens started as a reform group but later highly conservative. Vital change began in 1974 when Ernesto Cortez, Jr., trained in Saul Alinsky tactics at the Industrial Areas Foundation in Chicago, organized COPS (Communities Organized for Public Service)— a network of activist groups based in the city's West and South Side barrios. COPS received the blessing of Bishop (later Archbishop) Patricio Flores and received church monies at its start. Its main goals were to halt city subsidies for extension of services to new affluent subdivisions and to channel city and federal funds toward poor neighborhoods in dire need of improved drainage, streets, and schools. COPS initially used such Alinsky-style confrontation tactics as lining up members 10-deep at teller lines of the Frost Bank to exchange pennies for currency, then lining up again to have them changed back. Eventually, the city fathers got the message and listened when COPS wanted to make its point.

With its sometime ally, the boosterish Economic Development Foundation, COPS shattered San Antonio's established conservative order. The federal Justice Department helped out by invoking the Voting Rights Act to order single-member city council districts. The result, in 1977, was election of five Hispanics and one black to form a "majority of minorities." An even more vivid symbol of rising Hispanic power was the 1981 election of one of the new councilmen, Henry Cisneros, as the first Mexican-American mayor of a major American city. Cisneros was not the firebrand type of minority politician but a man who had transcended his barrio roots with a bachelor's degree from Texas A&M, graduate degrees from George Washington and Harvard universities, and a White House fellowship under Elliot Richardson during the Nixon administration. Cisneros had returned to Texas to teach urban planning at the University of Texas at San Antonio.

Cisneros actually ran on the GGL slate and won a good share of the non-Hispanic vote. But he disassociated himself from the conservative orthodoxy shortly after the election. Cisneros' high educational level and sophistication about business made him an almost instant national figure. Many viewed him as a "man of the '80s," a minority leader more interested in bringing high-technology to his community than engaging in political rhetoric. He produced a 242-page San Antonio high-tech economic development

plan, ranging from fiberoptics to laser technology, written entirely on his own
—a contribution we know of no other mayor making to his city. Cisneros'
ambition (aside from furthering his own career, likely one day for higher
office) was to propel long-disadvantaged barrio residents into technological
literacy and a brighter future than the dead-end jobs otherwise awaiting them.
He waged a successful battle to capture an engineering school at the University of Texas at San Antonio, sought out new companies, and resisted suggestions from COPS that he concentrate all his efforts on poor neighborhoods:
he would not, Cisneros said, "fall into the trap of giving mixed signals about
my city's attitude toward growth and development." A man of high intelligence, charm, and dedication, Cisneros nonetheless faced a continuous battle
to convince his impoverished Mexican-American constituency that he was
still one of them and working fast enough to improve their lot.

Mextex

The Census takers of 1980 found 2,985,643 Texans of Spanish origin, 21 percent
of the state's population and virtually all of Mexican heritage. Eighty percent
showed up as city dwellers, a radical break from the past. The shift is not yet
total, however. In the Rio Grande Valley of South Texas, the old story of
rural Hispanic poverty and farm work continues. These people have traditionally lived in the cruelest poverty: income but a fraction of Anglos', education minimal (with substantial illiteracy), all but the most menial jobs denied,
and hampered by language barrier. Outright discrimination—in schools, public places, restaurants, theaters—differed little from that practiced on blacks.
Only a very small minority managed to earn a decent income and to educate
their children through high school. None of that changed significantly until
World War II, the civil rights efforts of the '50s and '60s, and the development
of the Mexican vote into an independent, not-for-sale commodity in the 1950s
and 1960s. The Viva Kennedy clubs of 1960, of which San Antonio Mexican
leader (and later Congressman) Henry B. Gonzalez was national chairman,
marked a vital turning point.

For generations, the Valley counties were under the unshakable hold of
"heavies," or *patrons*—sheriffs and judges who often had close ties to the
Texas power structure of oil, gas, and banks. The *patron* would look after the
well-being of "his" Mexicans and obligingly pay their poll taxes. In return,
the Mexicans would simply wait for a signal on how they should vote.

The most famous *patrons* were the Parrs of Duval County, in South Texas'
dusty oil-cattle-sagebrush territory. Archie Parr was a cowhand who died rich
in lands and cattle. His son George expanded the usual benevolent ways of
the *patron* by maintaining an army of some 200 gun-toting *pistoleros*, who
masqueraded as deputy sheriffs and helped keep the electorate in line. Starting
in the 1920s, individual state candidates blessed by the Parrs usually received
close to 100 percent of the vote.

Mexican-Americans from Texas constitute a huge proportion of America's migrant farm workers. Year after year, the great waves of migration originate out of Texas in early spring, traveling as far north as the Dakotas by autumn, and then subside again, returning to the ancestral homes on the Rio Grande. Other migrants stay entirely within Texas, picking early crops in the Lower Rio Grande Valley and late crops on the High Plains. But the Texas Mexican-Americans also face competition from thousands of illegal immigrants from across the Rio Grande. The stories of the Mexicans' mishandling by "coyotes," the people smugglers, are legion. Yet both Texas Anglos and Mexican-Americans have deeply mixed feelings about illegal immigration. The Mexican-Americans would not mind at all increasing their numbers and potentially their political influence; but they also know that the immigrants depress wages for those who are already here. Anglo ranchers and business-men like to see the laborers come but want them to leave as soon as their work is done. From World War II until 1962, Mexicans came to the United States legally under the *bracero* program. Gonzalez was a leading force in getting Congress to discontinue the program, arguing that it made it easier for grow-ers to pay disgracefully low wages under terrible working conditions. The substitute however has been illegal immigration.

Texas farm worker movements have had a much harder political road than those in California. There was a great march to Austin in 1966 that resulted, eventually, in passage of a minimum wage law applying to farm workers.* Times were tough for union organizing in the late '70s, but the Texas Farm Workers Union remained active, and activists considered the populist Demo-cratic Agriculture Commissioner Jim Hightower an ally.

In the heated 1960s, Texas' Mexican-Americans divided politically into "liberal" and "militant" camps. The liberals' most prominent leader was Henry Gonzalez, who in 1956 had become the first Mexican-American to win election to the Texas legislature in 110 years, and in 1961 the first Mexican-American congressman in Texas history. But the radical and the young came to despise Gonzalez and his allies as obstacles in their road to revolution. This tension reached a high point in 1967 with the formulation of MAYO (Mexi-can-American Youth Organization), the brainchild of five young Mexican-American college students who were depressed by their race's slow progress in civil rights and disgusted with the policies of traditional leaders. After a number of staged confrontations with local power structures, in San Antonio

---

*The 1966 marchers included, among others, some wonderful brown- and leathery-faced old men, veterans of thousands of days working the fields of the Valley, carrying with them a dignity and purpose Texas had never expected to see in its *Mexicano*. But an incident along the way told worlds about the commanding establishment and its view of this great minority within Texas. Suddenly one day, a cavalcade of Lincolns swooped down on the line of march and out stepped several politicians led by then-Governor Connally. He would not be in Austin when they reached the state capitol, Connally told the marchers. And even if he were, said this man who later presented himself as a candidate for the presidency of the United States, "I still would not have met with you . . . because . . . marches throughout this nation . . . have resulted in riots and bloodshed." The marchers' sole demand, it is worth recalling, was a minimum wage of $1.25 an hour.

and elsewhere, the young Chicanos* (pioneers in the use of that term) switched their attention to the lower Rio Grande Valley in 1970, forming their own political party (La Raza Unida) and actually winning several elections in Mexican-American majority areas.

The center of La Raza Unida activity was the little town of Crystal City (pop. 8,334) in Zavala County, some 125 miles south of San Antonio. About 94 percent Mexican, Crystal City will be remembered as the place that startled Texas when it elected five Mexican-Americans to its city council in 1963, an unheard-of event up to that time. Economic power remained, however, with the Anglo businessmen who had proclaimed Crystal City "the spinach capital of the world" and erected a statue of Popeye in the town plaza.

In the late '60s, Crystal City became nationally famous as the charismatic, young José Angel Gutierrez, one of the founders of MAYO, attracted "war on poverty" money from the Ford Foundation, national churches, and the federal government. When Gutierrez switched to talking of "eliminating the gringo," Congressman Gonzalez accused the Ford Foundation of supporting "Brown Bilbos" and a "new racism" in Texas; Ford backed off. Gutierrez turned his attention to La Raza Unida, winning himself election to the Crystal City School Board and later as Zavala County judge. But the party failed to attract the vast majority of Chicanos and by 1978 was little more than a memory. Gutierrez resigned his judgeship in 1981 and headed for that great exile state of '60s radicals, Oregon, to teach at Cesar Chavez College in Mount Angel.

So the liberal Congressman Gonzalez proved the long distance runner, remaining in office into the 1980s. But like other militants down through history, Gutierrez' ideas made the establishment pay heed to a group it had coldly ignored before. Most of all, he left a legacy of voting and political participation, helping Texas' Mexican-Americans build a political base in the cities and rural areas so long ruled by conservative Anglos. Vital work on that front continued under the San Antonio-based Southwest Voter Registration and Education Project, started by the Ford Foundation in 1975. By 1980, from its modest offices above an old movie theater in downtown San Antonio, the Southwest project had conducted more than 300 voter registration drives throughout the Southwest and fought gerrymandering of districts that kept Chicanos out of office. Albeit from a narrow base, the number of Chicano-elected officials was rising rapidly.

From Willie Velasquez, director of the Southwest project, we heard, "I don't want to be part of an effort to pick the Mexican vote as if it were a crop every four years and to herd them toward a [Presidential] candidate. We need city councilmen in small towns to hire our people with masters' degrees, school board members to institute bilingual education, and county commis-

---

*The term has been traced to the Indians of Mexico, who pronounced *Mexicano* "Meh-chee-cano" and then shortened it to "chicano." The term is still disliked by some older Mexican-Americans, especially those of lighter skin and strong Spanish roots, but has gained widespread acceptance among the younger generations.

sioners to get roads paved." A passing acquaintance with Texas politics and establishment power suggested that would be a long, hard road. Yet by the same token, it was certain that a fuller brand of Lone Star state democracy, a more legitimate sharing of Texas' fabulous wealth, would come only from those who cared enough to organize from the grassroots up.

THE
MOUNTAIN
STATES

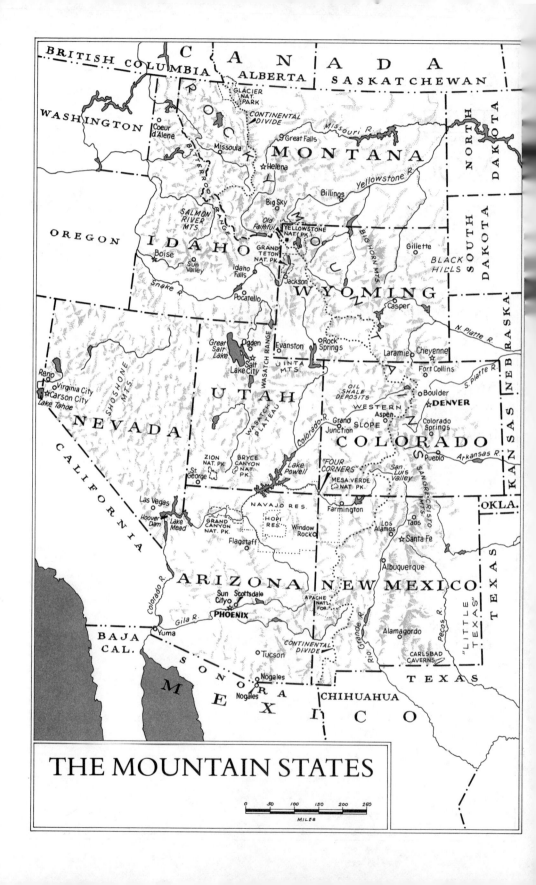

THE MOUNTAIN STATES

CANADA

ALBERTA

SASKATCHEWAN

WASHINGTON

Coeur d'Alene

Missoula

GLACIER NAT. PARK

CONTINENTAL DIVIDE

Missouri R.

Great Falls

MONTANA

NORTH DAKOTA

☆Helena

Big Sky

Billings

Yellowstone R.

SALMON RIVER MTS.

Old Faithful

YELLOWSTONE NAT. PK.

BIGHORN MTS.

Gillette

SOUTH DAKOTA

OREGON

Boise

Sun Valley

Idaho Falls

GRAND TETON NAT. PK.

BLACK HILLS

IDAHO

Snake R.

Pocatello

Jackson

WYOMING

Casper

N. Platte R.

NEBRASKA

Reno

Virginia City

Carson City

Lake Tahoe

Great Salt Lake

Ogden

Salt Lake City

Evanston

Rock Springs

Laramie

Cheyenne

☆

Fort Collins

S. Platte R.

NEVADA

SHOSHONE MTS.

WASATCH RANGE

UTAH

UINTA MTS.

OIL SHALE DEPOSITS

WESTERN SLOPE

Aspen

Boulder

♦DENVER

Colorado Springs

KANSAS

CALIFORNIA

WASATCH PLATEAU

Colorado R.

Grand Junction

COLORADO

ZION NAT. PK.

BRYCE CANYON NAT. PK.

Lake Powell

"FOUR CORNERS"

San Luis Valley

Pueblo

Arkansas R.

St. George

MESA VERDE NAT. PK.

SANGRE CRISTO MTS.

OKLA.

Las Vegas

Hoover Dam

Lake Mead

NAVAJO RES.

HOPI RES.

Window Rock

Farmington

Los Alamos

Taos

☆Santa Fe

GRAND CANYON NAT. PK.

Flagstaff

ARIZONA

NEW MEXICO

TEXAS

Colorado R.

Sun City

Scottsdale

☆

♦PHOENIX

APACHE NATL. FOR.

Albuquerque

"LITTLE TEXAS"

BAJA CAL.

Yuma

Gila R.

CONTINENTAL DIVIDE

Alamagordo

Pecos R.

CARLSBAD CAVERNS

Tucson

RIO GRANDE R.

SONORA

Nogales

TEXAS

M

E

Nogales

X

I

C

O

CHIHUAHUA

0 50 100 150 200 250

MILES

COLORADO

A Tragedy in the Making

MIDWAY ACROSS COLORADO, 1,000 miles of the American prairie ends. The great face of the American Rockies, the snowcapped spine of a continent, appears. The Midwest has ended; the mountains have begun.

The Rockies, as the *Denver Post*'s Bill Hosokawa has written, "dominate the Colorado scene as no mountains dominate any state." The mountains are the source of everything that makes Colorado unique—the entrancing scenery that attracts tourists and immigrants from all over the world, the world-class ski slopes with their quaint little villages, the fantastic mineral reserves whose extraction creates fortunes and threatens the environment, the water that must be moved many miles to make it possible for Denverites to survive and for crops to grow.

Traveling through the mountain West a generation ago, John Gunther paid homage to the scenery of Colorado, but after assessing life there he entitled his chapter, "—But Scenery Is Not Enough." So inbred were Coloradans, and so low the levels of state aid to education and rural health services, Gunther opined, that the state was guilty of "Olympian inertness."

Today, by contrast, Colorado throbs with new life and the influence of the hundreds of thousands who have moved there. Since Gunther's mid-'40s visit, Colorado's population has more than doubled, to 2.8 million, a rate of growth almost twice as great as that of the nation as a whole. The migration was started by thousands of ex-servicemen who had been trained in Colorado during World War II, fell in love with the scenery, and vowed to return. The ex-GIs were followed in the 1950s by government, defense, and scientific workers, in the 1960s by all kinds of young people, including hippies, looking for a pleasant place to live, and in the 1970s by the energy crowd, executives and blue-collar types alike. At some point the movement to Colorado began to take on a life of its own, and there are now stories of companies choosing a Colorado location to please their executives and to take advantage of the highly skilled labor pool.

Gunther's complaints about the levels of government services were long ago corrected. But Colorado's politics remain troubled. Behind the glitter of the energy boom and ski resorts and the pristine beauty of the national forests lurk massive problems that Coloradans as a society seem unwilling to address. Colorado's Front Range, a 160-mile-long megalopolis along the Eastern Front of the Rockies and home of 80 percent of Colorado's people, continues to sprawl farther and farther east and west. Yet neither the Denver region nor the state has established any effective land use planning system. The high altitude renders automobiles inefficient and increases their emissions by an estimated 60 to 100 percent and more, causing air pollution second only to Los Angeles. The air pollution problem is intensified by temperature inversions that keep the pollutants trapped in the bowl-shaped setting in which Denver has grown up. Yet Denver and its suburbs have been unwilling to take mass transit seriously. The Front Range cities could not possibly survive without water they receive from the mountains, and repeated studies have shown this water, by virtue of the various interstate compacts that govern its use, to be one of the world's most overcommitted resources. Yet Colorado developers and government officials talk of building yet more dams, even exploiting distant out-of-state sources, lest the state's growth rate be imperiled. Of the mineral-rich Western states, Colorado has some of the lowest minerals severance taxes and one of the poorest programs of state aid to energy-impacted areas. Colorado's substantial black and Chicano populations are isolated from the energy boom that is increasing the level of wealth in the state; few efforts are made to recruit even middle-class blacks and Chicanos into modern Colorado's greatest generator of wealth.

Compare Colorado to other fragile, resource-rich states—Oregon and Washington, for example, or even Wyoming and Montana—and its record in handling development comes up as a massive failure. Why is this? Perhaps because Colorado's situation is more complex: it has economic diversification, intense pressures for development, extraordinarily varied interests to be accommodated. But one could say the same of California, where the environmental record is far more distinguished. Rather, it seems that Coloradans have never become serious in deciding how they are going to accommodate their love of unfettered growth with their love of the outdoors, how they will accommodate the increasingly heterogeneous elements of their society.

The failure of environmental organizations to build strong and appropriate political coalitions illustrates the problem. Colorado has active chapters of just about every environmental organization in the United States, but they have relied so much on national laws that they have never developed the mainstream constituency needed to affect state policy and state legislative elections. In their zeal to keep undeveloped areas as pure as possible, the environmentalists have irresponsibly refused to play a role in shaping the energy development; likewise, they have ignored the issues of labor unions and minorities who could become their allies against conservative business interests run rampant. Democratic strength is formidable only in Denver. The Republicans are strong in suburbs, smaller cities, and rural areas, but Republican state legislators are often so conservative and unthinking that they simply ignore sensitive quality-of-life issues such as air and water pollution and seldom make the grade in statewide elections.

All these trends defy the "eco-freak" image that the national press gave Colorado for a short time in the early 1970s after it rejected hosting the 1976 Winter Olympic Games and elected a number of liberals, including the environmentalist Governor Richard D. Lamm, to office. Yet Lamm is a case in point of how difficult it is to be a centrist leader in Colorado. The fact that the state had actually elected as governor the silver-haired young environmentalist who had led the successful fights against the Olympics and for easier access to abortion services surprised many Coloradans and shocked others. But Lamm, once in office, found himself obliged—while maintaining a pure environmentalist attitude in many discussions—to accommodate himself and the state to development. He backed a number of federally supported water projects, for instance, saying environmentalists were "hopelessly naïve" in their opposition. All this enraged the environmentalists, who accused Lamm of using their issues to get elected and swore never to trust him again. Yet Lamm had equal if not greater problems with the Republican-controlled legislature, a body ferociously pro-development in its mindset and perennially on bad personal terms with the prickly independent Democratic governor.

"It is a never ending irony to me," said Lamm, "that I can be elected governor of this state, then reelected by a substantial margin, but can't get through the legislature the policies which almost everyone agrees are necessary to protect the state." Lamm said he found it "unbelievable" how political Colorado could "be so myopic, so ill-prepared" in the face of a crescendo of development, blithely ignoring the problem before it. Over the years, Lamm did win grudging respect—even from many Republicans—by such steps as appointment of a politically balanced blue-ribbon panel to study the Front Range's problems and future growth. Rex Jennings, head of the Denver Chamber of Commerce, even told us that Lamm's proposal for turning some of the state's energy wealth into a state development fund was worth consideration. But real cooperation was yet a step too far, and the politics of extreme growth versus extreme environmental protection continued.

After this dismal portrait of Colorado politics, we would be less than honest if we did not acknowledge that Colorado is still one of the most pleasant and agreeable of the states. The vistas are breathtaking, the air still dry and pure in many places, the jobs relatively plentiful, the educational system superior, the pace of life relaxed, and the people friendly. There is no stark degradation or shocking environmental disaster to be seen in the state. And yet this may be Colorado's worst problem. Its people may have been lulled into thinking there will be no crisis, that a solution can be found to all growth problems. But we see a gathering crisis of deeply disturbing proportions: the gradual decline in the quality of life, a steady loss of agricultural land, open space, wildlife habitat, landscape diversity, all accompanied by worsening traffic and deteriorating air quality. If this is the model of the "developed" Western state in America, then it will not be just one politician or another who appears a failure: a once-in-a-generation opportunity to build a resilient, conserving society in one of the most exquisite places on earth will have been forsaken.

Denver and the Front Range

Denver's destiny, George Sessions Perry wrote decades ago in the *Saturday Evening Post,* is to serve not only the state of Colorado but the entire Rocky

Mountain region "as doctor, lawyer, merchant, and [political] chief, as well as banker, butcher, teacher, and supplier of transportation, markets, entertainment, culture, and shelter for the transient." Denver's empire has since expanded. States as far east as the Dakotas and Nebraska look toward the federal government's regional offices in Denver. Western governors as distant as those of Washington and Alaska are organized through a regional association based in Denver. The Farmers Union has its national headquarters in the city. And geologists and energy magnates from western Canada to Mexico and even Brazil meet in Denver to exchange information and cut their billion-dollar deals.

Denver today is a better capital than ever before. The good climate has attracted lawyers, accountants, and executives of the highest skill. Denver's Stapleton Airport connects the region and has spawned a string of nearby hotels to which decision makers fly for one-day meetings. The classic Brown Palace Hotel remains the premier hotel and dining room of the city, but the variety of aspiring new hotels and fine restaurants is endless.

Until the 1980s, Denver's real disappointment as a modern regional capital was its newspapers. Both the *Denver Post* and the *Rocky Mountain News* suffered from unstable management in the 1970s, and neither paper undertook the hardnosed reporting or established the independent voice that was much needed in the early stages of the energy boom. Since Denver's papers are the only ones with large circulations in the intermountain West and are distributed widely, it was a true loss for the region. The *Post* was sold in 1980 to the Los Angeles Times and Mirror Company, ending a troubled period that began in 1970 with the retirement of editor-publisher Palmer Hoyt, who had transformed the paper into a progressive force after World War II, and the death in 1972 of Helen G. Bonfils, daughter of the co-founder. Bonfils fought for 12 years to keep the paper in local hands, and leaving no heirs, she placed the paper's stock in two foundations to benefit her dream of a performing arts center in Denver. The fact that Bonfils' lawyer, Donald Seawell, was president, publisher, and chairman of the board of the *Denver Post* and at the same time controlled the trusts and ran the Denver Center for the Performing Arts set up a conflict of interest between the cash needs of the paper and the cultural center; it was not resolved until the paper's sale. The *Rocky* also gained new leadership after the ouster of editor Michael Howard, a member of the Scripps Howard family, which owns the paper. A circulation battle ensued, complete with Howard's confessions to the *Post* that he had been addicted to cocaine and protected by the police. The news quality of both papers improved dramatically.*

Denver today is a much more powerful city than in the past, but there are

*Denver shows no signs, however, of developing a truly anti-establishment voice to replace the late Eugene Cervi, whose *Cervi's Rocky Mountain Journal* for years delighted in exposing every chicanery, real and imagined, it could detect among the vested interests. "What's good, thrilling, exciting about Colorado was produced by God—not the Denver Chamber of Commerce," Cervi once told us. "The mountains dwarf even men's ambitions and aspirations. There's less gut thinking here—the mountains dwarf you and make you feel small."

limits to what can be accomplished there. Since the federal government owns so much land in the West, many decisions made in Washington remain a determinative force. And Denver's capital shortages mean energy companies must go to New York to raise money for their capital-intensive operations.

With an early base in military contracting, Denver in two decades emerged as the most important scientific-technical center between Boston and California. By 1980 the city had 1,200 energy companies, though local wags pointed out that some of these had only an executive, a geologist, a secretary—and an unproven future. But some of these men (the energy business is notoriously male-dominated) would undoubtedly follow in the footsteps of such colorful figures as Marvin Davis, the Denver oil man who made so much money he bought the Twentieth Century Fox film company and the Aspen Skiing Corporation. Or the quieter Jerry Lewis, who founded Petro-Lewis and finally acquired a corporate headquarters able to compete with Manhattan's most elegant through its dazzling display of Western art.

The demand for office space has pushed Denver skyward. Downtown, sprouting what seemed like a new skyscraper each week into the early 1980s, unquestionably threw off its "overgrown cowtown" image (and not a little of its old charm in the process). The city's architectural gem of the new construction was Helen Bonfils' dream, the Denver Center for the Performing Arts. Outdoors-minded Denver was a full generation behind other regional capitals in building its cultural center, and it literally took Bonfils' will (plus public money) to do it. But outside architectural critics justly proclaimed the results "stunning," the new theaters "full of drama, full of a sense of technology's promise."

Denver's boom slowed down slightly in the early 1980s with the announcement that once again oil shale development would not go forward, but not before downtown was literally exploding with new skyscraper construction. Where low-scale development and natural Western friendliness once prevailed, Denver banks and corporations were throwing their great marble slabs up to the sky, creating high-rise canyons and oftentimes a repelling street-level atmosphere. With the roaring office space boom, Denver had a ghost-town aura after working hours. Then some hope intruded as Downtown Denver, the city's traditional trade association, recruited Richard Fleming, one of the nation's most determined "civic entrepreneurs," to form a new private-sector leadership forum, the Denver Partnership, which quickly dedicated itself to such values as quality urban design, historic preservation, downtown and close-in neighborhood housing. Downtown Denver itself reemerged as a "state of the art" management corporation with formal powers to control (through a mandatory assessment of merchants and city-ceded authority) the 50-square block district surrounding the new mile-long 16th Street pedestrian mall. An urban design team proposed how to make the new mall a more livable and attractive place; a new zoning code was designed to encourage such amenities as ground-level, pedestrian oriented retail space, and open plazas to let in the sunlight. Fresh initiative from the private sector seemed Denver's only hope: several times the city had reelected as mayor Bill

McNichols, a conservative, pro-growth Democrat who refused to take air pollution (or almost any other planning problem) very seriously.

The center of a massive growth wave, Denver proper saw its population drop 5.4 percent—to 491,396—during the 1970s. But a fair assessment could not attribute the loss to the Northeast-Midwest pattern of flight and disillusionment; rather, baby-boom generation youth were simply leaving their parents' homes and not finding places to live in the city. Denver's residential areas remained beautifully maintained, protected by the affluence of their homeowners and neighborhood-based officials who defended them at city hall. Denver's black and integrated areas (largely private homes) showed almost none of the signs of decay found in the Eastern ghettos; the Chicano areas were slightly less attractive. Denver has had a reputation for racial moderation that goes back to its settlements of Pullman porters and waiters and to the antidiscrimination regulations of the large federal presence. Sadly that reputation became somewhat tarnished by school busing controversies, violent clashes between blacks, Chicanos and Vietnamese refugees, and bilingual difficulties. We were told that a major reason Denver suburbanites resisted metropolitan government—considered essential to addressing Denver's air pollution problem—was that they feared it would become involved in the administration of Denver's schools. Denver has one of the best inner-city school systems in the country, but white people with children still tend to settle in the suburbs, and the percentages of black and Hispanic children have increased. Many blacks still come to Denver in the hope of a less abrasive environment than in the South; Colorado's black population increased 53 percent in the 1970s, to 101,702, the largest percentage increase in the West, and more than half live in Denver. Denver's population was 12.1 percent black and 18.7 percent Hispanic in 1980, and members of both groups have been elected to the Denver city council and the state legislature.

Continuous population growth has marked Denver's surrounding suburban counties—Jefferson to the west, Arapahoe to the south and east, Douglas to the south, and Adams to the north. To these areas flock Colorado's newcomers, an extremely well-educated breed drawn by scientific jobs and access to the mountains. Some come from the Northeast and Midwest, but most of the migrants grew up in conservative Plains states, such as Iowa, Missouri, Kansas, and Nebraska; a considerable number have tried California, found it too much to handle, and chosen Colorado as a happy medium. Those who are single may settle in Denver for a while. But they are likely to have little interest in urban life, and one looks in vain for much social sensitivity.

Denver is actually about midway down the long Front Range population belt, an urbanization that landscape architect Grady Clay has likened to Italy's thickly settled Po Valley. Northernmost on the Front Range is Fort Collins (pop. 64,632), home of Colorado State University, with its nationally recognized agricultural and veterinary schools. Then (proceeding southward) is Greeley (53,006), another college town and home of Monfort Beef, Colorado's biggest feedlot. In the foothills of the Rockies sits Boulder (76,685), home of the University of Colorado and one of the most pleasant university towns in

America.* Boulder, never a follower in matters political, was a center of the peace movement in the 1960s and in 1977 passed a stiff growth-control ordinance that limited developers to 450 new housing units a year, a 2 percent growth rate for the city. It was followed in 1980 by an ordinance seeking to curb mushrooming housing costs—a problem that Boulder, like the nation's other growth-control cities, was experiencing in acute form. In a way, Boulder illustrated the inherent frustration of local growth-control efforts without state support. When the city council, joined by downtown businessmen and local environmentalists, tried to block a new shopping center just outside Boulder's legal boundaries, the officials of the adjacent territory tartly reminded the Boulderites they were on foreign territory. If Colorado had statewide land use planning, of course, there would have been a court of higher appeal.

On the Front Range south of Denver lies Colorado Springs, a handsome city of 215,150 people known for Pikes Peak, the Garden of the Gods, the Broadmoor Hotel, and the U.S. Air Force Academy, but politically a seat of military and retiree conservatism. Colorado Springs is also site of the North American Air Defense Command (NORAD), an underground citadel that would receive the first warning of an air attack on the United States or Canada and would direct the air defense battle.

Farther south still is Pueblo, a city about as different from Colorado Springs as possible. Pueblo is heavily ethnic, increasingly Hispanic, predictably Democratic, a center of Mafia activity, and the strongest labor union town in Colorado. Pueblo's largest industry is the C F and I Steel Company, owned by the Rockefeller family until 1945 and now by the Crane Company of New York. The history of unionizing the steel plant is so rife with tragedy and death that such a distant figure as Governor Jay D. Rockefeller of West Virginia has been politically embarrassed by the one-time barbarities of his great-grandfather's firm. With automation decreasing the number of jobs in heavy industry, Pueblo has barely maintained a stable population of 101,686. The nearby coal-mining towns of Walsenburg and Trinidad lost population in the 1970s.

In contrast to the Front Range, neither eastern nor southern rural Colorado is a boom area in any sense. The sparsely populated farm lands of eastern Colorado are part and parcel of the Great Plains climatic zone. This is dry farming country of sparse rainfall, often afflicted by high winds, sometimes torn by an angry tornado. Three times, the land of eastern Colorado has almost been destroyed by poor farming practices and drought, and there are fears that poor soil conservation practices may be threatening the land again. Eastern Colorado is really a land of two cultures. North of the Arkansas River

---

*Colorado's colleges and universities are a little-recognized source of its population growth; many out-of-state students never return home. In addition to those already mentioned, other fine schools include the Colorado School of Mines at Golden, Colorado College in Colorado Springs, and the University of Denver, whose business and law schools have trained many leaders throughout the Rocky Mountain region.

it is virtually indistinguishable from Nebraska or western Kansas—strongly Republican and Protestant. South of the Arkansas one is in territory as Southwestern as Arizona or New Mexico. Catholicism and Democratic sentiment are predominant, and much of the population is Hispanic.

Mountainous south-central Colorado harbors one of the state's most fascinating areas: the beauteous San Luis Valley, where Colorado's first permanent settlement was established in 1851. Set at 7,500 feet altitude and some 100 miles in length, the mountain-lined valley is naturally arid but heavily irrigated. The large farms, reminiscent of those in California's Central Valley, raise vast quantities of potatoes, lettuce, cabbage, malting barley, spinach, and carrots. State and federal agencies have for years been trying to improve economic conditions in the valley, an extension in many ways of poor northern New Mexico. But in the 1970s the population in such counties as Las Animas, Costilla, and Conejos actually dropped, as young people looked elsewhere for opportunities.

The Western Slope

Western Colorado bows to the towering peaks along the Continental Divide, the ridgepole of a continent from which the waters flow north and west to the Pacific, east and south to the Gulf of Mexico. Coloradans are fond of quoting the startling height statistics: the Rocky Mountain summits rising more than 14,000 feet are all in Colorado; of the 81 peaks of such altitude on the North American continent, Colorado has 54. By virtue of these lofty mountains, Colorado's average elevation is 6,800 feet—highest of any state.

This is the land of summer snow banks in high ranges, of mountain plateaus and icy Alpine lakes, of small emerald valleys with cascading streams where early autumns turn the delicate aspen to bright gold, of stands of pine and spruce, of passes 12,000 feet above the sea. Proceeding farther west from the Divide one comes on the semi-arid uplands of the Colorado Plateau, some underlain by oil shale. Gaunt mountains give way to occasional green valleys, but most of the territory is stark, preparing one for the desertlike stretches of neighboring Utah.

For several generations Western Slope culture has been that of the classic Intermountain West: large cattle and sheep ranches (with much grazing on federal lands) and outdoors tourism, from camping to dude ranches to skiing to hunting.

Skiing is without question the great tourist industry success story of Colorado's postwar years. In 1945 there were just two ski areas in the state with a total capital investment of some $50,000; by the '80s Colorado had over 30 ski areas, with constant expansions. Close to a million and a half skiers visited the slopes each winter, many from out of state, seeking the soft powder snow that differentiates the Rockies from the Eastern U.S. or Europe. For many urban Americans, there seems to be an incomparable release in speeding down mountains and then enjoying the comradery of the skiing fraternity. Yet the social skeptic could well note that only an exceedingly affluent nation (one perhaps with some of its priorities misplaced) could afford to maintain, in these distant mountains, an industry of such high costs in every area from transportation and lodgings to equipment.

Many prominent skiers, including former President Gerald Ford, former Vice President Walter Mondale, and Ohio Senator John Glenn, head for Vail, 110 miles west of Denver, where an entire Swiss Alpine village was created in the early 1960s out of what its founder, Peter W. Seibert, called a "wasteland at the foot of a nameless mountain." One White House correspondent during the Ford presidency called Vail "Bavarian shake and bake." But its ski slopes cannot be faulted.

Colorado's premier ski resort remains Aspen, set among steep mountain slopes in the valley of the Roaring Fork River, 200 miles from Denver. Unlike Vail, Aspen has a history. It began as a booming silver-mining town but went into a long decline when silver was demonetized in 1893. Aspen's second birth was presaged by the arrival in 1945 of Walter Paepcke, chairman of the Container Corporation of America. Paepcke founded the Aspen Institute for Humanistic Studies, bringing men from American business management to two-week conferences to reexamine their basic beliefs and premises, to rediscover their humanism. Paepcke also took a lively interest in the development of Aspen as a ski resort. The skiing side of Aspen has expanded to include hundreds of miles of trails and the Snowmass development several miles away. There are also music and ballet festivals. The combination of skiing, culture, and the beautiful mountain setting made Aspen the favorite destination for the famous and the beautiful, for industrial and government leaders, and for a variety of free spirits. Aspen soon became a center of experimental lifestyles and politics based on affluence or youth or both (writer Hunter S. Thompson once ran for sheriff). As early as the 1950s, people began asking, "Has success spoiled Aspen?" It depends on what you consider important. Surely the ski facilities and restaurants have improved. And Aspen's beauty has pretty much been maintained. Aspen passed some of the nation's earliest laws regulating architectural design and billboards. Later, Aspenites worried about *any* growth and passed an ordinance that curbed condominium development. Antigrowth actions became so pervasive, in fact, that the Aspen Institute itself had to move most of its operations elsewhere because it wasn't allowed to expand. Housing prices soared, and the stories of young couples making their way in Aspen today are not those of ski-all-day, work-all-night maids and bartenders, but rather of lawyers married to each other who find it difficult to buy homes even with their pooled income. Ski bums were officially declared an "endangered species" by *Esquire* in 1979; the menial jobs in Aspen and other Colorado ski resorts have been taken up by Indochinese refugees who have no choice but to put up with low quality, cramped housing and low pay. The closest thing to the remnants of the old ski atmosphere may be found in nearby Crested Butte, where leaders must constantly fight to keep mining from ruining the town's ambience, or the even more remote but growing Telluride in southwestern Colorado.

Colorado's ghost towns are a vivid reminder that it was mining that first opened the Western Slope to settlement—and may once again dominate. Gold and silver production has been in the doldrums for many years, but substantial amounts of coal, uranium, zinc, lead, molybdenum, oil, and gas have continued to flow from Colorado. All of Colorado's past mining pales, however, before the prospect of "synfuels": synthetic oil and gas, cooked out of the immense reserves of shale encased in the federally owned Piceance Creek Basin (north of the Colorado River between Grand Junction and Rifle) and in Utah's nearby Uinta Basin. Various proposals for oil shale commercialization have involved digging monstrous pits in the earth and importing thousands of miners and refinery workers to complete the extraction and processing. One shudders to think how such development would transform western Colorado, but by the early '80s none of the grand plans had come to pass. The most serious scenario appeared to be the joint Exxon-Tosco Colony Oil Shale project on the banks of the Colorado, for which Exxon began to build a whole new city for its expected oil shale work force, Battlement Mesa. But in 1982, Exxon, the world's largest industrial corporation, announced that cost over-runs had become too high, and it was abandoning the project.

The prospect of big oil shale sparked lively interest in local government. Garfield and Rio Blanco County officials became so upset over the lack of state, federal, or oil company concern that they established special-use permits that force the energy companies to participate in planning for housing, education, school, and sanitation needs. One spunky mayor, Peggy Rector of Rangely (2,200), even enlisted the help of a Washington, D.C. law firm to force the developer of a coal mine, across the Utah border, to cover the costs of its impact on her town. With local officials like that, western Colorado might even have a future!

If energy development, especially of oil shale, were to proceed on a massive scale, it could renew Colorado's and the West's oldest political dilemma: water. In its oil scenario for the Western Slope, Exxon proposed building three 10-foot pipes to transfer (pumping uphill) 1.7 million acre-feet of water a year from the Oahe Reservoir in South Dakota, over 600 miles away. Others have suggested diverting Columbia River water from the Pacific Northwest to parched southern California so that Colorado could legally take more water from the overcommitted Colorado River. The Front Range needs more water for new homes, farmers still expect water for irrigation, and various energy development projects also depend on obtaining water rights. This combination could easily end the relative peace on water issues of recent decades, a period in which the Denver Water Board aggressively obtained rights to Western Slope water and federal money built transmountain projects—until, in any event, Congress tired of footing the bill for new water ventures. Such conflicts could make John Gunther's old analysis of Colorado's water situation once again ring true. "Water is blood in Colorado," Gunther wrote in *Inside U.S.A.* "Touch water, and you touch everything; about water the state is as sensitive as a carbuncle."

Coloradans in Washington

In the old days Colorado sent to Washington men such as House Interior Committee Chairman Wayne Aspinall or the late "Big Ed" Johnson, U.S. Senator and governor for 24 years, who prided themselves on championing special state needs first (water projects most of all). Ideological issues ran a distant second. But by the '70s, Colorado elected its national officeholders mostly on national issues. And the migratory population had no problem in electing candidates so fresh to the scene they would be considered carpetbaggers in other states. The well-educated, independent Coloradans pay little attention to party affiliation, apparently consider each candidate on his or her individual merits, and send a mix of Republicans and Democrats to Washington. In vivid contrast to times past, no seat can be considered safe.

Several youthful Colorado officeholders—all in their early '40s—have made their mark in Washington. Rep. Pat Schroeder, a Democrat from Denver, has opposed hawkish military acts from her seat on the House Armed Services Committee and taken up the feminist cause. Rep. Timothy Wirth, another Democrat, was considered a one-time anti-Watergate fluke when he won election in the Denver suburbs and Boulder in 1974 but held on to become a powerful congressional figure in the regulation of telecommunications.

The Colorado official receiving the most national attention in the early 1980s was Democratic Senator Gary Hart, who got his start in national politics as George McGovern's presidential campaign manager in 1972 but moved steadily away from his mentor's positions to develop a pragmatic liberalism. It paid off in 1980 when he was the only Mountain State Democratic senator to survive the year's Reagan-conservative tidal wave. Like a good liberal, Hart defended the Clean Air Act, but he walked a fine line on energy development issues. Hart took a seat on the Armed Services Committee, which seemed a natural for his base-laden state, but was generally recognized as the first senator in decades to study seriously the options for defense and challenge the Pentagon's pronouncements. In the initial stages of a bid for the 1984 Democratic presidential nomination, Hart contended that the Democratic party needs to go back to its Jeffersonian and Jacksonian principles of individual liberties and opposition to centralized power, in both government and business. Those ideas, he told us, need to be wed to New Deal and Great Society principles of social justice, but with less bureaucracy and regulation.

Conservatism may have to compete hard in Colorado these days, but it is still influential at the national level. The junior senator, William Armstrong, a radio station owner representing old-fashioned conservatism and the entrepreneurial side of Colorado thinking, achieved considerable power in the Senate's economic policymaking committees and carried the right wing's economic and tax-cutting banner. Colorado conservatives have also played important national roles outside the electoral sphere. In 1973 Joseph Coors, the ultraconservative president of the Adolph Coors beer company, of Golden, began bankrolling the Washington-based Heritage Foundation, which launched a campaign against school textbooks, federal support of day-care centers, welfare, and national health insurance. The Heritage Foundation was considered a radical fringe outfit until its 1,093-page "Mandate for Leadership" became a guidebook for policymakers. Reagan also found in Colorado his Environmental Protection Agency administrator Anne Gorsuch Burford and his controversial, conservative Interior Secretary James G. Watt, who was president of Mountain States Legal Foundation, a law center started by Coors that sued the federal government over environmental regulation.

The dilemma of the 1980s was whether Joe Coors and James Watt represented the future of Colorado—or whether it would be the likes of Dick Lamm (reelected by an impressive margin to a third term in 1982) and Gary Hart. Or would some amalgam, still invisible, appear to resolve the political and social paradoxes of this ever-growing state? The answers to these questions remained obscure. But one point was clear enough: the influx of hundreds of thousands of Americans into this fragile environment, each staking out his piece of turf with little regard for others or for the natural heritage, together with energy booms and halfhearted planning, carried within it the seeds of one of America's most profound tragedies.

WYOMING

The Lonesome Land

WYOMING IS A BARREN UPLAND, scrub and sage, a giant mesa broken by outthrusts of high, snowy peaks and low, grim buttes. It is a land of freerunning antelope, cowboys and their ponies, sheep and cattle—and treasure below the soil: vast deposits of oil and gas, lodes of uranium and trona, and enough coal to heat the continent for generations. Save for Alaska, Wyoming is the least-densely populated state of the union. Despite extraordinary population growth related to the energy boom—41.3 percent in the 1970s—Wyoming's 1980 population was only 469,557. It remains what the former Governor and Senator Milward Simpson called it: "the land of high altitude and low multitudes."

Wyoming life is tough. Its people are scattered over a space 78 times the size of Rhode Island, filling only one town, Casper, to more than a 50,000 count and leaving unpopulated stretches of 50 to even 100 miles from one ranchhouse to the next.* But the Wyomingite loves his sparkling open spaces; vast terrain exhilarates rather than depresses him; the trappings of culture may be far distant, but beside the door there is always the rifle and the fishing pole, and there is a deer to be shot over the hill or a fast-running trout to catch in a nearby stream. This is a singularly masculine society, and always has been. Nowhere is the stranger greeted more warmly; nowhere, however, is he expected to conform more completely to the values of the state society. Dissent is not smiled on here.

The pressing question for the future of Wyoming is how long this way of life can continue in the face of the energy boom and rapid population growth. Starting in 1970, Wyoming increased its coal production 20 percent *annually;* by 1981 it trailed only Kentucky and West Virginia with a yearly output of more than 100 million tons. Of all the Western states undergoing energy exploitation in the 1970s and '80s, no other has been so totally affected as Wyoming. And the boom is just beginning, for there is the first and foremost

---

*Wyoming's cities—Casper (pop. 51,016), the energy center, Cheyenne (47,283), the state capital, and Laramie (24,410), home of the state university—are unmemorable, compared to the colorful energy boom towns. Casper merits special note as the home city of KTWO-TV, respected as the most influential news medium in Wyoming and a crusader more outspoken than the state's newspapers. We found no other small-state television station—and few in large cities—which make a comparable effort in public affairs.

target of exploitation—the Overthrust Belt, the oil- and gas-rich geologic formation that stretches from Alaska to Mexico, a storehouse of mineral riches likely to attract capital and feverish activity for decades and decades to come.

Visit Wyoming and the physical and societal changes stemming from all this will not hit you in the eye: so vast are the expanses that oil and gas rigs —not to mention additional people—seem to fade into the infinite horizon. Energy boom towns, such as Rock Springs (19,458), Gillette (12,134), and Evanston (6,421), made famous by their social problems and frontier atmosphere, are really quite few in number. Their populations, though growing, are still those of small towns. But the key point to remember is that the thousands of construction workers, drillers, and their helpers make relatively high wages (averaging close to $15 per hour). With so few diversions in the boom towns, they spend their free time traversing the state, often with "a wife, a baby, and a gun rack in a four-wheel drive vehicle," as one state legislator described the status symbols of their lives. Sometimes they head south toward Denver, but more often toward Wyoming's Yellowstone and Grand Teton National Parks and the Big Horn Mountains. They also hunt and fish, legally and illegally. And they set—through their presence, their money, their demands—the political context for Wyoming for years ahead.

While many Wyomingites resist changes in their way of life, polls have shown that most believe the future of the state is under the ground. The land is barely able to support agriculture. Few are the places where the soil is rich enough, even if irrigated, for crops. Grass is so sparse that each steer or sheep needs acres of his own. There are 10 times as many cattle and sheep as human beings in Wyoming, and still the state's livestock industry fails to rank among the 10 largest by state. As for manufacturing, Wyoming's location is generally too distant, the costs of transportation too great. The state government and its planners pay lip service to diversification of the economy to avoid the "boom and bust" cycle of energy exploitation. But specific proposals, much less successes, are few. Tourism and military spending helped some in the postwar years, but until the energy boom of the 1970s, Wyoming's population was static or declining, its children moving elsewhere to look for work. Finally, Wyomingites accept their lot. "We know we're going to be the energy breadbasket of America," U.S. Senator Alan Simpson (Milward's son) told us.

New for Wyomingites is their insistence on a role in shaping energy development. This is a direct contradiction of Wyoming's history as one of America's classic colonial states. Forty-six percent of the land is owned by the federal government, and almost all mineral leases are owned and developed by national and multinational companies based in the East and in Texas. Most important of these is the Union Pacific Corp., which was given checkerboard sections at 20-mile stretches in exchange for putting the railway across the prairie in the 19th century. For many years the Union Pacific and Burlington Northern railroads have hauled millions of pounds of coal to out-of-state and foreign markets. From its infancy, and with scarcely a break until the 1960s, the Union Pacific and the energy companies, in combination with the cattle barons, ran the Wyoming government to their advantage. Then, in 1969, in a stinging rebuke for one of the most powerful lobbies ever organized, the Wyoming legislature passed a minerals severance tax.* By 1981–82, severance taxes accounted for 22.6 percent of state taxes, and the coal tax was at 17.5 percent of sale price, second only to Montana's 30 percent tax. Some money was kept aside for a long-term state endowment. The legislature also passed a landmark industrial-siting law, which gives a state council the power to judge the effects of projects on the environment and nearby communities— and to reject or modify construction plans if it sees fit.

Wyoming's energy income has unquestionably lightened the burden of rapid-fire development for affected cities. And it has probably made energy development more popular. The money goes to all localities, plus a bonus in discretionary aid to the boom towns. This unusually fair distribution was enacted, noted one state legislator, because Wyoming is so homogeneous that "everyone felt we were in this together." Contrary to popular impression, he added, the majority of Wyomingites do not live on isolated ranches, but in "small towns we call cities," most of which have 1,000 people or fewer. For these places, energy tax money has solved some but not all fiscal problems. Since the money isn't collected until mining begins, the municipalities still face the problem of "upfront costs" for new schools, hospitals, roads, and sewers. In several areas, energy companies have formed associations to make contributions to the communities or to buy or guarantee municipal bonds. But this is an expense the companies resent since they would prefer to prepay taxes, a practice that's illegal in Wyoming.

The boom towns themselves have not been able to avoid horrendous problems. National writers have descended on them frequently to report the litany of problems: transiency, housing shortages and high rents, wealth with few recreational opportunities, alcoholism, spouse and child abuse, crime in general. In Rock Springs conditions got so bad in the late 1970s that the police chief went on trial for murder.

Some boom town problems are not amenable to money solutions. Evanston, for example, has failed to solve the problem of job-hunting families parking their mobile homes, campers, cars, and school buses in a makeshift "squatters camp" on the open prairies outside town. The police gave up forcing the squatters out since they simply moved to another piece of open land; evictions, moreover, made the police look heartless to some members of

*A major share of the credit for the tax goes to Ernest Wilkerson, a refined, silver-haired, fastidious Casper attorney who mounted a populist campaign for governor with a call for a severance tax and the slogan "Wyoming's Wealth for Wyoming's People." This un-Wyoming-like candidate lost, but the winner, Governor Stanley Hathaway, picked up the idea, even some of the state's newspapers endorsed it, and it soon garnered widespread public support. One wonders whatever happened to lonely pioneers like Wilkerson. We checked and found he had moved to an apartment on Central Park South in Manhattan, from which he occasionally fires off letters of judgment to Wyoming editors.

the media and the community. And it is sometimes difficult to separate fact from fiction in the boom towns. Evanstonians love their Wild West image and tell visiting reporters of the "organized" prostitution in town; construction managers talk of taking their workers on bus trips to the delights of Elko, Nev. But longtime locals are less willing to talk about what is a much more prevalent problem: drug abuse. Marijuana and cocaine have become so common, acceptable, and uncontrollable that energy companies have had to institute lunch-box and body searches to discourage drug use on dangerous work sites.

The energy boom could also wreak havoc with Wyoming's fabled wildlife. Antelope now run around gas-processing plants and oil rigs, but Rod Dody, president of the Wyoming Wildlife Federation, told us that he believes the development plus poaching are leading to a cumulative and serious toll on wildlife. The frontier, buccaneering psyche holds so firmly—even in this sportsmen's paradise—that the Wildlife Federation has only a couple thousand members and is partially immobilized by its fear of being branded an environmentalist group. And though Wyomingites have opted for development in both principle and action, their deepened environmental sensitivity was apparent in the early 1980s when conservative ranchers opposed the plans of Reagan administration Interior Secretary (and Wyoming native) James Watt to allow oil and gas leasing in wilderness areas. Watt finally agreed to ban the leasing. Most Wyomingites accepted, however, a Reagan administration plan to base the MX missile in Wyoming after Mormon Utah successfully lobbied against putting it there; a "ranchers for peace" movement was stillborn.

History will certainly record that Wyoming in the 1970s and early 1980s was in one of its classic boom cycles, sure to be followed by a bust. It is an established pattern. Until the early 19th century, Wyoming was an uncharted wilderness, still the private hunting ground of the Crow, the Blackfoot, the Sioux, the Cheyenne. First came the trappers and scouts, then the transcontinental wagon trains whose ruts can still be seen across the prairie today. But before 1867 fewer than 1,000 people lived in the entire Wyoming Territory-to-be. Then came the great iron monster across the plains, the track-laying crews hammering out an epoch in rails and spikes. Cheyenne was established as the first Union Pacific terminal in Wyoming on July 4, 1867; four months later, the town's population had swelled from zero to 4,000, and Wyoming had its first boom town.

With the railroad came "changes bewildering to contemplate," as one newspaper put it. First came the burly Irish workingmen and then the Chinese contract workers, who completed some of the toughest construction work. Later when jobs became scarce, white Wyomingites killed 28 Chinese in a riot in Rock Springs and caused federal troops to be stationed in the town for 13 years to protect the Chinese. The railroad marked the decline of the buffalo, which were even shot from train windows, and it brought more settlers. The Indians, who attacked settlers, wagon trains, and railroad crews, received the vengeance of the U.S. Army in return.*

Finally, with the railroad came the cattle business. Appropriately, "don't fence me in" became the obsession of the new Wyoming cattle barons, who would stake out their right to a 160-acre homestead for ranch headquarters and a corral and then turn their cattle out to graze over thousands of government-owned acres of range, which was free in the early days. Thievery became such a problem that the Laramie County Stock Growers Association was founded for mutual self-protection and brand listing in 1873; it would grow into the Wyoming Stock Growers Association, the state's most powerful group for a century to follow.

The cattlemen wrote a bloody chapter in Wyoming history, through their fights with small homesteaders who put wire fences around their property, barring the cattle from water, and with sheepmen, who competed with them to graze their flocks on public land. Even today, Wyoming cattlemen like to take the law into their own hands and are constantly fighting with the federal government over protection of animals and the environment. The sheepmen claim that federally protected eagles kill thousands of their lambs, but their greatest anger is reserved for federal restrictions on poisons to kill coyotes.

Thousands of Wyomingites still make their living from livestock. But the ranches have grown bigger, the number of ranchers and cowboys fewer. For Wyoming that means a future of even greater reliance on extraction of raw materials as the preeminent creator of wealth—and probably more boom and bust cycles.

Governing a Colonial State

Life on Wyoming's wind-swept plateaus, where a man must be courageous and self-reliant if he hopes to survive, has fostered a fierce independence and individualism that survive to this day. Political bossism is unthinkable in such a setting, and while Wyoming usually votes Republican, it votes first and foremost for the man, not the party.

Energy issues and ferocious antifederal sentiment dominate Wyoming politics. The days are gone when the Wyoming Stock Growers Association cooperated with the Union Pacific Railway and the energy companies to keep taxes low through minimal government and minimal regulation of industry. Each element of that old political triumvirate retains significant political

*Wyoming today has only about 7,000 Indians. But in 1980, a United States Geological Survey employee inspecting oil leases on Wyoming's Wind River Reservation touched off an uproar by stopping a truck filled with oil that turned out to have been produced illegally (i.e., without the legally required royalty to the Indian tribe). The incident led to the conviction of an oil company president, and energy-producing tribes throughout the West began questioning whether companies were stealing from them either through production without permission or accounting trickery. The U.S.G.S. employee, Chuck Thomas, went into business as an Indian oil sleuth, and was inducted into the Blackfeet tribe, which named him Chief Night Rider.

power, but they sometimes compete among themselves. And they are rivaled now by the Wyoming Association of Municipalities and educational interests for legislators' attention. The state's lawmakers still meet only 40 days in odd-numbered and 20 days in budget session in even-numbered years, but they have a much stronger vision of themselves as Westerners and are much less controllable and predictable than in the old days. Just months after Wyoming voted overwhelmingly for Ronald Reagan and his antispending views, the 1981 Wyoming legislature voted to improve workers' compensation and the state employees' retirement program and, even more incredibly for masculine Wyoming, created a new division of state government to help battered women.* Furthermore, the legislators financed this increased spending by raising the minerals severance taxes.

Wyoming's irritation over seemingly heavyhanded federal control of nationally owned lands has harmed Democrats and helped Republicans seeking national office. In 1978, the congressional delegation became totally Republican. These men are conservative but not the social Neanderthals sometimes sent to Washington from such Western states as Idaho and Utah. Sen. Alan Simpson led the fight for environmental planning in the state legislature; as a member of the Senate Judiciary Committee he won praise for a balanced and thoughtful effort to revise U.S. immigration policy. Sen. Malcolm Wallop is a millionaire rancher who graduated from Yale and opposes federal bans on abortions. The state's lone representative, Richard Cheney, was Gerald Ford's White House chief of staff, and is a rising leader in the House.

Wyoming has also enjoyed a series of progressive governors who have brought the state into the modern age. First came Clifford P. Hansen, a Republican who, in 1962, won repeal of a law forbidding the use of state funds to match federal grants and later sat in the U.S. Senate; then, Stanley Hathaway, a Republican who fought for minerals severance taxes but could not win confirmation as Gerald Ford's Interior Secretary because environmentalists considered him too pro-business; and finally, Ed Herschler, a Democrat who emerged as the Western governors' spokesman to oppose a federal cap on energy severance taxes.

---

*Women's lot presents a much discussed footnote to Wyoming political history. The state led the nation in granting women the right to vote when it was a territory (in 1869) and subsequently a state (on admission to the union in 1890). But the legislators really had little interest in equality, according to the state's distinguished historian, T.A. Larson. The *Cheyenne Leader* commented at the time that suffrage might attract more women but called the act "nothing more than or less than a shrewd advertising dodge, a cunning device to obtain for Wyoming a widespread notoriety." Wyoming was also the first state to elect a woman as state legislator and as governor. In the early 1980s, three of Wyoming's top elected officials were women (secretary of state, treasurer, and superintendent of public instruction); sitting on a number of state boards and commissions with the governor and the state auditor, they held considerable power. At the same time, there were three women in the 40-member Wyoming Senate and 19 in the 62-member House. (The Equal Rights Amendment sailed through the legislature in 1973.) This acceptance of women in political life did not always carry down to the social level. In the boom towns, a social worker told us, there is still concern about the status of women. "This is the West," she said. "This is man's country."

Passing now into political memory is the one-time base Democrats had in the towns along the Union Pacific line, settled by thousands of eastern and southern Europeans who came to man the mines and refuel the trains. The population dispersed when the trains went to diesel in the 1950s. One immigrant miner's son, Teno Roncalio, was elected to Congress for five terms before he got tired of running such tight races and retired in 1978. Another successful Wyoming Democrat was U.S. Senator Gale McGee (1959–77). McGee's eventual defeat suggested Wyomingites had become more interested in controlling federal activities than in receiving federal water project money, which McGee had delivered. Some analysts believe Wyoming and other rapidly developing Western states may become fertile Democratic territory as industrialization increases and people become more concerned about preserving the environment. But such change remains a dream: energy companies are proving difficult to unionize (only 12 percent of Wyoming workers belong to unions), and environmentalist organizations (though no longer the causes they champion) are still considered foreign devils from the East or West Coasts.

Tourism and the Great Parks

For many Americans and foreigners, energy and stock raising and the politics of both are secondary to other attractions in Wyoming: the geysers of Yellowstone, the startling beauty of the Tetons, the grandeur of the Big Horn Mountains. Northern Wyoming is big dude-ranch territory and has also attracted a number of rich out-of-staters who have purchased or built their own ranches. One such family, the Rockefellers, defied local cattlemen in 1950 to turn a major tract of grazing land into Grand Teton National Park.

It was in Wyoming, as explorers gathered around a campfire one night in 1870, that the idea of Yellowstone, America's first and still largest and grandest national park, was conceived. Its marvelous geysers and brilliant pools and boiling springs are a mecca to millions. Grand Teton, only eight miles from Yellowstone's border, presents glacier-packed ragged peaks of the geologically young Tetons thrusting abruptly skyward from the floor of Jackson Hole, a ski resort in winter. One of the great ironies of distant and remote Wyoming is that these parks—Yellowstone in particular—are now so overwhelmed by tourists that friends of their flora and fauna and natural wonders fear for their future.

MONTANA

Roughhewn Ecostate

FAR-FLUNG AND REMOTE MONTANA, third-largest of all the American states, once the private satrapy of the Anaconda Copper Mining Company, in our time the embodiment of the most liberal and environmentally protective political culture of any Mountain state, is a place of infinite contrasts and contradictions.

The geography is one's first clue to the diversity that is Montana. The eastern reaches are high plains country, mile after mile of level or gently rolling wheatfield and grazing land, covering fully three-fifths of the state, sharing a common culture with the Dakotas and Wyoming. This is the Montana of dryland farming and great cattle spreads, interspersed with occasional buttes and the gorges cut by the Missouri and Yellowstone rivers. Close to the rivers, one finds spots of irrigation where a few cottonwood groves appear, and there are a few forested areas. Otherwise, the lonely expanse is broken only by an occasional grain elevator or water tower looming over a little town, or once in a while by an oil rig or a coal strip mine.

Western Montana is high Rocky Mountain and Continental Divide country, stretching from Glacier National Park at the Canadian border to Yellowstone on the Wyoming border. It is a terrain of snow-capped peaks and mountain streams, hillsides richly forested with fir and larch and pine, of mining gulches and cool lakes and green valleys. Two-fifths of the state, this western portion has some cattle, like the eastern part, but everything else is different. Preeminently, it is mining, lumber, and tourist territory.

The weather differs between sections as much as the landscape. Eastern Montana lies on the unprotected Great Plains of Canada and the United States, where the ranchers and wheat farmers bake in summer heats that have soared to 117 degrees. Then, in winter, they must steel themselves against fierce blizzards and sleet storms that have more than once killed thousands of cattle. Western Montana, by contrast, is protected from the Arctic winds by its mountains, and while the snow cover is deep, the prevailing Pacific weather patterns make the winters milder and even permit cherry orchards in some counties. There are exceptions to this, however; near Helena, in 1954, the temperature plunged to −70 degrees, the coldest ever recorded in the continental U.S.A.

Montana is so vast and disjointed, its cities and towns separated by such gulfs of space, that it was traditionally difficult to talk of any common Montanan culture. There is still no single leading Montana city, and the people of the state find themselves under the cultural and economic influence of such distant places as Minneapolis-St. Paul, Denver, and Seattle. Yet for many decades, Montanans have thought nothing of driving hundreds of miles for a high-school football game or a social occasion, a practice untrammeled by the transition from the days of cheap to high gasoline prices. The late historian K. Ross Toole has written of Montanans' "strong sense of belonging, stemming from their common adversities with nature, since the very beginning of the state." Those natural adversities, however, were a weak strand of commonality compared with the environmental consciousness that binds Montanans together today. Montana has a history of brutal exploitation of its natural resources—the kill-and-run fur trade days, uncontrolled timber cuts, sheep and beef overgrazing the land, the frenetic dig for copper. Until recent times, there were few voices being raised to question these practices.

A startling transformation in Montana politics—toward an antibusiness and environmentally protective atmosphere—began in the late 1960s and has since flowered. The initial change in tone, Toole believed, lay in the declining fortunes of the Anaconda Company rather than any indigenous Montana revolt. When Anaconda's market value fell from $1.4 billion in 1969 to $260 million in 1972, "it resulted in a legislature quite suddenly set free," Toole observed. And other forces of change were also afoot. To fulfill the growing national demand for electric power, energy companies began to express strong interest in mining the estimated 50 billion tons of strippable sulfur coal in southeastern Montana. The anticipation of widespread strip mining set up an automatic conflict between agricultural interests and energy development and led to the formation of the Northern Plains Resource Council, an umbrella lobbying group representing some 19 grassroots organizations around the state with some 1,600 members, mostly farmers and ranchers. This was also the era of national environmental consciousness, and the Montana Environmental Information Center, a more urban-oriented citizen lobbying group, with 1,400 members, was set up to concentrate on statewide environmental issues such as clean air and water. At the same time, a new Montana ethic seemed to evolve. As Toole explained to us, "There's a subliminal kind of idea in the Montanan's mind that what used to be our curse—the space and distance and freight rates and so forth—is somehow now going to turn to our blessing." Montanans have an idea, Toole believed, "that we have something of great value here—it's air, it's sky, it's mountains, it's prairies, it's space—we share this in common."

This new independence and spirit culminated in a new state constitution stressing populist, environmental, and consumer protection values. The constitution was approved in 1972, and extraordinary environmental statutes were passed in 1973. The Montana Strip Mine Reclamation Act emerged as the strongest in American history and became a model for other states. The Utility Siting Act gave state government strong power over the location of power plants, transmission lines, and rail spurs. The legislature imposed severance taxes on the minehead price of coal, metals, oil, and natural gas production when these substances are extracted from the ground, and the people of Montana voted by popular initiative to place 50 percent of the revenue in a Resource Indemnity Trust Fund. Never again, the Montanans decided, would outside companies be allowed to come into the state, take the minerals, and leave behind environmental degradation and ghost towns when the mineral was depleted. The severance taxes would be set aside as a permanent endowment for the state, to pay for environmental cleanup in case the companies did not live up to their promises of land reclamation and to try to diversify the state's economy away from its dependence on mineral extraction. The income from investing the severance taxes, it was reasoned, would subsidize state government and build new schools, roads, hospitals, and other facilities in the boom towns.

The success of this radical, populist effort to gain a measure of control over big energy companies won for Montanans respect and envy all over the country. But not without controversy. In the wake of Montana's 1975 decision to raise its coal severance tax to 30 percent, the very highest in the nation (Wyoming is next, at 17.5 percent), charges arose that the state was gouging cold, energy-poor Midwestern states already reeling from the decline of their heavy industries. The Northeast-Midwest Congressional Coalition declared that Montana and other Western states could become "a kind of United American Emirates." The coalition joined with the coal companies in asking the U.S. Supreme Court to declare that the high level of taxation was a violation of interstate commerce. The court refused, but it left the door open for Congress to put a cap on such taxes.

Arguing against any such limit, Montana's U.S. Sen. John Melcher noted that the high Montana coal severance tax added only $5 a year to the average Midwestern consumer's electric bill, a price he suggested was warranted because users were assured "of a stable supply of coal at a lower price than is available elsewhere, and the nation was assured the state of Montana will not become a 'welfare client' of the nation as a result of having been plundered by the more populous states with no return for the booty."

As Montanans saw it, the threat of colonial exploitation was neither abstract nor distant. Montana state Sen. Tom Towe, the man who introduced the 30 percent severance tax legislation, told us: "The copper kings who became fabulously wealthy did not leave their money to Montana. They endowed the Los Angeles Symphony Orchestra, the Stanford University Library, the Corcoran Gallery of Art in Washington, D.C., and built the University of Virginia Law School. The only thing I can find they left in Montana was $20,000 toward the construction of a theater inside the state prison. We are determined to leave future generations something more than unknown environmental problems and a depressed economy. If we don't, we have squandered our heritage."

Montana's environmental commitments were doubly impressive in light of the state's modest rates of economic and population growth. Montana's population grew by only 13.3 percent in the 1970s, less than half the rate of the other

Mountain states. Many wheat-growing communities of Montana were still losing population or remaining stable, as mechanization of agriculture continued. Professor Lauren McKinsey of Montana State University observed that Montana youths in many fields must still go out of state to find jobs, especially those that pay decently. Montana is so remote from major markets that manufacturing is largely impractical. Financial and management control of the mining industry remains in the hands of national and multinational corporations that lobby hard for cheaper mining conditions. But the environmental consciousness has become so embedded in the fabric of Montana life that in 1981, when the Republicans gained control of the legislature for the first time in 10 years, all proposals to gut the environmental laws and energy taxes went down to defeat.

Whenever Montanans are tempted to waver in their environmental commitment, or wonder if they may be too tough on mineral developers, all that proponents of the new order need do is remind them of what life was like under the Anaconda heel, pointing to the degraded cities of Butte and Anaconda as Example No. 1. In one of the most colorful and controversial chapters of *Inside U.S.A.*, John Gunther reported that the Anaconda Company had "a constrictorlike grip on much that goes on, and Montana is nearest to a 'colony' of any American state, Delaware alone possibly excepted." Actually Anaconda was already starting to relax its grip and to extricate itself from direct involvement in election campaigns by the time Gunther wrote his book (1947). But the story he told of one corporation's feudalistic control of every aspect of a state was true well into the 1930s and was to continue in a more subtle form into the 1960s. Secretive and often vindictive, Anaconda controlled almost all elections into the 1930s, dragging in the "cemetery vote" where necessary. A common saying was that Anaconda "has only lost one governorship since statehood." State legislators were often vassals of the company, and Gunther quoted one Anaconda lobbyist as saying, "Give me a case of Scotch, a case of gin, one blonde, and one brunette, and I can take any liberal!" To top it off, Anaconda owned most of the daily newspapers of Montana, stifling public debate and providing Montanans with a homogenized, sanitized view of their state and the world. Dissent was so frowned on that letters to the editors were never printed.

The reasons for Anaconda's one-time deep involvement in Montana politics went back to the titanic "War of the Copper Kings," manipulators (including one who literally bought his way into a U.S. Senate seat from Montana) who battled to control the incalculable wealth in the mine sites near Butte. The sheer havoc of that era goes far toward explaining why Anaconda, once it had the upper hand in Montana, determined to keep the press and political system under its thumb. Anaconda also had the cooperation of the Montana Power Company, which it had created and to which it was tied by interlocking directorates. Often, the two were referred to as "the Twins" or simply as "the Company," a close union reflected in their use of the same legal counsel.

W.H. Hoover, who took over the presidency of Anaconda in 1933, curbed the company's bludgeonlike activities. Hoover, for example, reduced Anaconda's 24-hour-per-day alcohol-filled "hospitality rooms" in Helena during the legislative session to three hours per day. The practice persisted, however, until 1971, when Anaconda and Montana Power finally gave up their legislative "watering holes" altogether, finding them no longer effective with the new sophisticated legislator. Anaconda finally sold its newspapers in 1959 to the Iowa-based Lee syndicate. (Today the Montana papers revel in freedom of the press. The Lee chain leaves each paper free to formulate its own editorial policy; they compete also with the *Great Falls Tribune*, the great holdout of independent journalism during the years of Anaconda domination and since 1965 a subsidiary of the Minneapolis Star and Tribune Company.)

As the years wore on, Anaconda had also been obliged to compete— especially with big oil and timber—for the attention and fealty of Montana legislators. Anaconda emerged as a worldwide firm whose international operations for a time completely outshone those in Montana and necessitated a less heavy-handed image back home. But a slow decline, including expropriation of Anaconda's holdings in Chile in the 1960s, resulted in its 1977 acquisition by the Atlantic Richfield Company (ARCO). In 1980, ARCO closed the smelter in the town of Anaconda near Butte, citing sagging world copper prices and claiming the smelter would have cost $400 million to meet federal and state pollution and safety regulations. (The announcement came at the end of a four-month strike, and there were allegations that ARCO was really trying to bust the unions.) ARCO did turn over Anaconda properties to the city and leave a $3 million "community adjustment" fund. But attracting new industry to this remote city, one of the world's ugliest, proved no easy task. "The Company's" smelter smokestack, the world's largest, remained the overwhelming physical presence. The closures and resulting unemployment were agonizing to Montanans; in one year, nearly 2,000 workers lost their jobs. Yet Montanans refused to panic, turning down proposals to relax environmental standards.

In 1983, almost one century after Marcus Daly discovered copper in the Butte gulches, ARCO announced it was closing the remaining copper mine at Butte. An ARCO spokesman said production might be resumed at some future, unspecified date but described the closing as "the end of an era as we know it." Thus the once supreme Anaconda left Montana to a range of energy companies now scrambling to exploit Montana's resources: Exxon, ASARCO, the Consolidated, Westmoreland, and Peabody coal companies, and Montana Power among them. But Anaconda remained a presence in a way its founders would never have expected. The mine at Butte has become a living wound on the Montana landscape—its inactive pit the trump card of the state's environmental movement, a symbol to even the least cause-minded Montanans of the physical and human degradation they do not want repeated in their state.

Gunther called Butte "the toughest, bawdiest town in America," but over the years the image of hard-drinking miners, prostitutes, and gambling have given way to ugliness and sad decline.* No one who has ever seen it is likely to forget it—the city set on a bare south slope, the massive open-pit Berkeley Mine, the skeletonlike frame remnants of the deep mines, shacks, and slag piles unnumbered, an aging center district palely reflecting some past glory, old and unemployed men walking the streets. Butte was once known as the richest hill on earth, but the population has declined from more than 80,000 at the turn of the century to 23,000 in 1980, and it has enormous unemployment and other social problems that a host of federal and state aid programs have only fractionally addressed. But Butte is still rich with ore, and when operations ceased, the open-pit copper mine was gobbling up parks and residential neighborhoods and edging closer to the business district, which many residents believe will be mined one day.

The real mineral action in Montana has shifted to coal, which lies in vast fields throughout the entire eastern third of the state, estimated to hold over 50 billion tons of strippable coal. Utility companies like the Montana deposits because the coal is exceptionally low in sulphur, which pollutes the air, and sodium, which coats burners. (The companies likewise detest the 30 percent severance tax, but easily pass it on to their consumers.) Vast stretches of eastern Montana crawl with mucking monsters that remove huge quantities of overburden at a single pass and mine hundreds of tons of coal in a day. By 1980, the number of tons mined per year had reached almost 30 million. Most of it left Montana, shipped in incredibly long 105-unit trains to the Great Lakes region or converted into electricity at the mine site and dispatched over high-tension lines to the Pacific Northwest. The eastern Montana county of Rosebud became a typical modern energy boom area: the small town of Forsyth saw its population double in just a few years. A community called Colstrip was expected to grow from three families to 8,000 persons—with the promise that its population would shrink again to 4,500 once Montana Power was through constructing four coal-fed generators there. The pros and cons

---

*Old-time and now fading Butte is unlikely to have another tribute comparable to a posthumously published piece by Jack Kerouac, famous for his On the Road, "The Great Western Bus Ride" (Esquire, March 1970): "I walked the sloping streets in super below-zero weather . . . and saw that everybody in Butte was drunk. It was Sunday night, I had hoped the saloons would stay open long enough for me to see them. They never even closed. In a great old-time saloon I had a giant beer. On the wall was a big electric signboard flashing gambling numbers. The bartender gave me the honor of selecting a number for him on the chance of beginner's luck. No soap. 'Arrived here 22 years ago and stayed. Montanans drink too much, fight too much, love too much.' What characters in there: old prospectors, gamblers, whores, miners, Indians, cowboys, tobacco-chewing businessmen! Groups of sullen Indians drank red rotgut in the john. Hundreds of men played cards in an atmosphere of smoke and spittoons. It was the end of my quest for an ideal bar. An old blackjack dealer tore my heart out, he reminded me so much of W.C. Fields and my father, fat, with a bulbous nose, great rugged pockmarked angelic face. . . . I also saw a 90-year-old man called Old John who coolly played cards till dawn with slitted eyes, and had been doing so since 1880 in Montana, . . . since the days of the winter cattle drive to Texas, and the days of Sitting Bull. . . . There were Greeks and Chinamen. The bus didn't leave Butte till dawn. I promised myself I'd come back. The bus roared down the slope and looking back I saw Butte on her fabled Gold Hill still lit like jewelry and sparkling on the mountainside in the blue northern dawn."

of these large-scale mining and generating projects caused agonizing debates, locally and statewide. Forsyth and Colstrip were able to ease the rapid ups and downs in population with millions of dollars in grants from the coal severance tax fund to build sewers, streets, and schools. Much less certain was the future of the land that was strip mined. Mining companies claimed that the land could be reclaimed for farming and ranching, but fewer than 1,000 acres had actually undergone reclamation work, and it would be many years before the land's true productivity could be known.

Much of the debate about energy development has involved American Indians, who have title to considerable mineral wealth on their reservations. For Northern Cheyennes, on their reservation near Lame Deer, the interests became broader. The Northern Cheyennes had a particular attachment to their land since they had fought successfully a century ago to defend it at the Battle of the Little Big Horn. In the '70s they went to court to preserve the area's "class one" pristine air quality, which was endangered even though the development was off the reservation. The court agreed, and the power plants at Colstrip had to be fitted accordingly. The Cheyennes have engaged in their own internal debate over whether to develop their minerals while the Crows, whose reservation abuts the Cheyennes', have negotiated a number of leases. The Flathead Tribe has taken the position that any disruption of the ecosystem would disturb their way of life. Indian activists have engaged in a wide-ranging debate over which path is the wisest. Some argued that exploiting the mineral wealth was a way out of poverty and dependence; others opposed development on religious grounds and noted that the history of exploitation by the white man is so great that Indians were wisest to preserve their land as a home and refuge.

Non-mining Montana

Montana has a long history of Indian-white conflict, which has become more complicated since the rise of the "red power" movement in the 1960s. Montana Indians, like those in other states, have striven to reassert jurisdiction over their reservations' original boundaries. Indian landowners have been encouraged to place land under tribal status and give up the right to sell it. This transfer has assured that the land will remain in Indian hands since individuals are unable to sell it for quick cash. But it has also terminated individual Indians' property tax obligations to local counties, even though they have retained the right to vote in local elections to approve tax increases that white landowners, mostly ranchers, are required to pay. Problems such as this led to the formation in the mid-1970s of the white "civil rights" group, Montanans Opposed to Discrimination (MOD), which joined forces with white ranchers in other states to urge the federal government to make payments to localities in compensation for Indian lands within their borders. On the surface, the demand seemed one more federal bailout proposal for a middle-class group.

But it was also a reminder that the cruelty and rapaciousness of the United States in its early dealings with its native peoples have come to haunt later generations.

In 1981, Montana's Gov. Ted Schwinden became the first governor to appoint, to his personal staff, an Indian aide to deal with state relations with Indians. It was a courageous act for a Western governor, since many Western politicians, even liberals, have found it too controversial to approach the Indian situation with overt sympathy.

Agriculture is still Montana's number one money maker. The state is the sixth-ranking wheat producer, but two-thirds of the farm income comes from livestock now. Lumbering grew by leaps and bounds in the Western mountains and created thousands of new jobs following World War II. But government remained the largest employer, and federal expenditures loom large in the state economy.

Though advertising itself as a beckoning "Big Sky" country, Montana is sufficiently off the tourist track that it receives fewer visitors and dollars than other Rocky Mountain states. Montana's pride and joy is Glacier National Park—actually part of the Waterton-Glacier International Peace Park on the Canadian border. South of Glacier lies the massive Bob Marshall Wilderness, some 950,000 acres of pure solitude where the mountain streams yield trout up to 23 inches in length and 9 pounds in weight. There are also the National Bison Range, established in 1908 to save the then almost extinct lords of the plains; ghost towns, the best of which is Virginia City; and on the state's western flank, the Bitterroot National Forest. One looks in vain for a glamorous resort comparable to Idaho's Sun Valley or Colorado's Aspen and Vail. The closest thing to it may be "Big Sky of Montana," the recreational complex started by the late newscaster and Montana native Chet Huntley next to the Spanish Peaks primitive area north of Yellowstone Park.

Butte strikes one as Montana's most colorful city, but several others are much larger and more important. Billings (66,798) is a bustling, modern plains city, an important livestock, trade, and transportation center. Great Falls (56,725), set on a great bend of the Missouri, best combines the worlds of west and east in Montana. Great Falls still pays reverence to Charles M. Russell, whose meticulously honest paintings of early Western life—the Indian, the cowboy, the open plains as they were—are classics of their genre. Helena (23,938), among the most remote and lightly populated of state capitals, sits amid low mountains, looking out over the flat and almost treeless Prickly Pear Valley. Appropriately, the capitol building has a copper dome. Missoula (33,388) is home of the University of Montana and as is so often the case among college towns, one of the state's more liberal communities. It is also, however, one of the more gruesome examples of tasteless sprawl development run amok in God's country.

Montana also offers occasional surprises. Since 1912 several colonies of Hutterites, a communal farming sect, have thrived near Lewiston and other cities. A community of Hmong, a Laotian tribe that helped the Central

Intelligence Agency in the early 1960s, have settled near Missoula. Montana has also attracted a substantial number of urban dropouts, some of whom have found farming a tougher life than they bargained for.

Big Sky Politics

Until the advent of environmentalism, Montana's politics could easily have been summed up as a personality split between two traditions: the conservative-exploitive and the liberal-welfarist. The conservative-exploitive tradition went back to the days of the Copper Kings and was firmly anchored in the Republican party of stockmen, businessmen, and oilmen. The liberal-welfarist strain in Montana history reads like that of an altogether different state. It began in the free silver-populist era just before the turn of the century and in Butte's labor camps. Butte has a long, stormy history of labor relations going back to the 1890s when the Butte Miners Union succeeded in playing the Copper Kings off against each other to gain recognition and a closed shop, decades ahead of most other U.S. unions. There followed a few years early in this century when a local editor could call Butte "the strongest union town on earth." Then came great disputes over whether the union should join the avowedly anticapitalist Industrial Workers of the World (IWW), followed by bloody revolts and establishment of an open shop. But in 1934, after a four-month strike, the Butte miners again obtained the closed shop.

Between 1900 and World War I, Montana's liberal-welfarists succeeded in passing progressive laws to prohibit child labor, gain initiative and referendum and the direct primary, assure an eight-hour work day, guarantee workmen compensation for their injuries, and regulate grain grading and marketing for protection of the wheat farmers. The Montana Democratic party became a combination of organized labor in the western mining and lumber counties and wheat farmers of the "Hi-Line" eastern counties with their Farmers Union co-op and Rural Electrification Administration. (Montana did not go the third-party farmer-labor route of North Dakota and Minnesota, largely because of the personal role of one extraordinary politician, Senator Burton K. Wheeler, an agrarian progressive of the Norris-La Follette-Borah stripe).

Not until the decline of Anaconda and the rise of the environmental movement in the early 1970s, however, did the progressives have much success at bucking "The Companies" at Helena. Only in 1971 did the legislature approve the first minimum wage legislation, and until the new constitution was passed in 1972, many taxes on mining companies and livestock operations were prohibited. The rise of environmentalism began as a liberal-welfarist notion, but as we have seen, attracted legitimately bipartisan support.

Montana has sent some exceptional men—and one woman—to Congress. The woman, Jeannette Rankin, was the first member of her sex ever to sit in Congress and the "original dove." Serving a term in 1917–18, she voted against United States entry into World War I; elected again for a single term in

1941–42, she was the only member of Congress to vote against the declaration in World War II. Other Montanans still remembered are Senator Thomas J. Walsh, who led the investigation that unearthed the Teapot Dome scandal in the 1920s, and Senator Lee Metcalf, who took straight-arrow aim on the nation's electric utilities and founded and led the liberal Democratic Study Group as a House member in the late 1950s. Montana's senators of the 1980s —moderate Democrats John Melcher and Max Baucus—have stood up to rightist lobbies, and Baucus has taken a pro-feminist lead position regarding freedom-of-choice on abortion. Into the 1980s Montana continued its rarely interrupted congressional tradition of sending a Democrat from the western district and a Republican from the east. In presidential politics, however, Montana usually votes Republican. Ronald Reagan won in 1980 with a not inconsiderable 59 percent of the vote.

Modern Montana governors are in a position to make weighty decisions on coal mining and environmental issues. Thomas L. Judge, a Democrat, is likely to go down in history as the governor who shepherded the environmental statutes through the legislature in the early 1970s; he was defeated and succeeded by another Democrat, Ted Schwinden, who defended Montana's coal severance tax as if it were the equivalent of the Holy Grail.

None of the current officeholders can compare, however, with the legendary Mike Mansfield, who represented Montana in the House and Senate for 34 continuous years and was Senate majority leader from 1961 to 1976, longer than any other Senator in American history. A tall, quiet, self-effacing man, Mansfield was born the son of Irish immigrant parents in the Hell's Kitchen section of Manhattan and was sent to Montana to live with relatives when he was three years old. Mansfield was a sailor, soldier, miner in the Butte mines, and professor of Far Eastern and Latin American history before running for Congress in 1942 and defeating none other than Jeannette Rankin. Mansfield's own legislative record was not as noteworthy as some other senators because he so often suggested that the credit go to others, but he was known as an implacable foe of the Vietnam War, played a powerful role in the 1964 Civil Rights Act, and was the chief author and strategist of the voting-rights amendment, which assured all young Americans the vote at 18. Mansfield was once described by *Washington Post* writer Spencer Rich as having "an almost oriental way of sliding things into place, fading into the background, and allowing others to take the lead when he agrees with what they are doing— and in that way, heading the Senate in the direction he wants." It turned out to be an oddly prophetic description, for within a few months of his retirement in 1976, President Carter appointed Mansfield U.S. Ambassador to Japan. Mansfield won so many friends in Japan that President Reagan reappointed him. The lengthy career of Mansfield, the internationalist and conservationist, man of reason and reflection, was a sign of the true potential of Montana, that raw, frontier society only now coming into its own.

IDAHO

Divided It Stands

IDAHO IS AN ODDLY SHAPED PIECE OF REAL ESTATE wedged between six other states of the Intermountain West. Its 83,557 square miles leave it only the 13th largest state, but still bigger than Maryland and Delaware and all of New England combined. As the crow flies, it is more than 500 miles from north to south, 300 miles across on the state's wide southern plain, but only 44 miles across the odd northwestern Idaho panhandle, which stretches up to the Canadian border. This geographic extremism is the handiwork of congressional mapmakers who in 1863 created an Idaho Territory bigger than Texas but promptly cropped away what is now Montana and Wyoming.

Northern and southern Idaho are broken into two separate and isolated entities by the fiercely mountainous backlands of central Idaho, that land where the Salmon River Mountains brood over some of the most remote and impassable territory of the continental United States, including its largest wilderness area. A single highway, completed in 1927, is still the only land connection.

Northern Idaho is the land of the forest gods, where the handsome stands of pine and fir and larch, of cedar, hemlock, and spruce, spread their cover over the mountainsides. Water is pure and abundant in the great rain forests and the rivers to which they give birth. The people make their living from lumbering and mining and the tourist trade; a few grow wheat. The political climate, born in the old mining camps, is much more liberal and more Democratic than the rest of Idaho. Economically, the panhandle is part of Spokane's vaunted "Inland Empire."

Southern Idaho is dominated by the arid prairie and sagebrush plains that run along each side of the Snake River, a 600-mile arc from the Snake's headwaters near Yellowstone National Park on the east to the Oregon border west of Boise. The Snake, major tributary of the still-greater Columbia, is literally southern Idaho's lifeline. Extensive irrigation from the Snake has kept the area from being pure desert and made possible the splendid farmlands that grow, among other things, the famous Idaho potatoes. (Idaho's agricultural industries employ a smaller percentage of Idaho workers than in past years, but total agricultural income amounts to a healthy $540 million annually.)

Two distinct cultures flourish along the Snake Valley. To the east, constituting the southeast quadrant of the state, is land settled by the early Mormons, the first great irrigators of Idaho's soil. Most of the people are still affiliated with the Church of Jesus Christ of the Latter-day Saints (statewide, the Mormons are about 25 percent). Economically, the major southeastern cities—Pocatello and Idaho Falls—are relatively self-sufficient. But in matters spiritual and cultural, all eyes look to Salt Lake City; there is in fact no area outside of Utah itself where the Mormon imprint is so deep.

Southwestern Idaho, likewise sustained in large part by the irrigated farming along the valley of the Snake, is site of the city of Boise, which, in turn, has the state capitol, Idaho's best climate, thriving light industry, and the income of a strong distribution center. Perhaps even more important for modern Idaho, Boise is headquarters city of some major national corporations: Boise Cascade, the lumber and paper conglomerate; Morrison-Knudsen, one of the largest construction-engineering firms in the country; J.R. Simplot, a multimillion-dollar potato and mining empire; Ore-Ida, the big corporate farmers; and Albertson's, a food store chain.

Thus in a state still predominantly agricultural, still close to its pioneer roots, an element of sophisticated finance and industry is introduced—and not the classic out-of-state exploiters of old, but home-grown capital-creating enterprises. Nowhere in the Intermountain West, not even Denver, does one find so much indigenous corporate control. Much of the corporate growth is pure good luck; Boise simply happened to be the home of several corporations that grew from little acorns into great oaks by dint of skillful management. But the fact that the corporations have chosen to stay headquartered in Boise after growing into national or multinational firms has had a snowball effect. Idaho's relative nearness to Northern California also made it attractive to computer companies searching for cheaper locations for their plants. By the early 1980s, Hewlett Packard's Boise plant employed 2,800 people, and Idaho officials vigorously recruited others. Idaho has surely benefited from its location, relatively close to California, where there are many companies looking for cheaper sites on which to expand. Industrial locators recommend Idaho because it has no inventory tax, a low corporate income tax, a 3 percent sales tax that cannot be increased without voter approval, poor labor union representation, and lower hospital costs, which keep company-paid insurance premiums lower. The state has a reputation for high labor productivity; Eugene Armstrong, executive vice president of Morrison-Knudsen, has estimated that the per capita production in the company's industrial operations is 18 to 19 percent higher than the national average.

These pro-industry conditions produced a per capita income of only $8,126, or 36th among the states, in 1980. But many out-of-staters seemed to ignore the low dollar wages and moved to Idaho anyway to take advantage of the availability of jobs and the outdoor lifestyle. Immigration, combined with an above-average birth rate, produced a formidable 32.4 percent population growth rate in the 1970s, leading to a total of 943,935. Boise's metropolitan area grew an amazing 54.2 percent, to 173,036 people. But growth rates of 25 and 30 percent were also common in small towns throughout the state, and Idaho was able to continue a pattern of evenly distributed population highly unusual for a Rocky Mountain state (compare it, for example, with the high percentages of Coloradans crowded into the Denver area, or Utahans around Salt Lake City). Many of the newcomers were young working-class families, some of whom had sold homes elsewhere before moving to Idaho to buy a larger and relatively cheaper piece of property. "We have a lot of mobile homes here," Joseph A. Scorcio of the Kootenai County Planning and Zoning Commission, told a visiting reporter. "There's a saying that what you see is five acres, a pickup truck, a mobile home, and a starving horse. And that's all there is."

More of Idaho's new residents come from California than any other single state. Some have Idaho roots, but left years ago only because it was impossible to find a job in Idaho; others were born elsewhere and moved to California for a few years or a generation before deciding that the Golden State had become too urbanized, too polluted, or too socially liberal. Once in Idaho, the newcomers usually conform to the natives' almost virulently anti-California attitude. Why the bad feelings? First, California is a colonial power in Idaho. Many Californians who have moved to Idaho have superior educations and have taken the best-paying jobs. The money Californians bring with them pushes up local housing and land prices. Idahoans also feel California's cultural dominance and fear the Californians will bring with them freeways, hamburger stands, tract houses, and liberal social values.

Idaho's not-so-old history places its latter-day divisions in perspective. This was, in fact, the last of the American states to be seen by Europeans. The sighting occurred on a fair day of August 1805 when Meriwether Lewis and William Clark crossed over the Continental Divide at a point later to become part of the Montana-Idaho border. Soon they would meet with Indians who had never before encountered a white man. Lewis' and Clark's reports of the wild, untamed country, and especially of fur-bearing animals—so many, they said, that they got in each other's way—were a sure signal for trappers to invade the territory, starting a vigorous, competitive trade that would reach its peak in the 1820s and '30s. Idaho's first permanent settlement was made in 1860, by Mormons in the southeast who actually thought they were settling in Utah. The Saints' geometric little towns with their communal irrigation projects would set one type of lifestyle for Idaho; quite another began, likewise in 1860, with Captain E.D. Pierce's discovery of placer gold in the clearwater country of the north. A mighty gold rush ensued, unique until then in American history because the tide of emigration came from the West (Oregon, Washington, and California) rather than the East. Silver ledges and gold-bearing quartz were discovered, and Idaho was on its way to becoming a principal mining state.

Territorial status came in 1863. The 1870s witnessed the Indian wars and now legendary struggle of the Nez Perce against confinement on a reservation. The 1870s brought, too, the great cattle grazing interests; and the 1880s, the railroads, which gave stability to the state's agricultural economy.

Even as the Idaho Territory passed into statehood in 1890, violence persisted over religion and valuable minerals. The state erupted with vengeful labor wars between unions and the silver mine owners of the Coeur d'Alene region, leading to dynamiting of mines, the summoning of federal troops to restore order, and in 1906 the assassination of former Governor Frank Steunenberg (who had called in the troops) by a bomb set to his garden gate by an ex-miner. The courtroom trial pitted Clarence E. Darrow for the defense against a youthful William E. Borah for the prosecution; both would make their reputations from the trial, Borah going on to win election six times as United States Senator from Idaho. Borah was the great exemplar of a vigorous tradition of liberal opposition to the established powers that defies Idaho's normal conservative reputation and goes back to the first years of statehood and the role of Progressive Republicans in the Grand Old party in the 1910s and 1920s.

Idaho's early government set a moderately progressive course. The 1890 constitution, for example, established state control over water rights, provided for an eight-hour work day on all public works, and prohibited child labor in the mines. But Idaho was still a state torn by conflict. Not only was it wracked by the labor wars, assaults on the Mormons, and conflicts between Masonic Republicans and Irish Catholic Democrats, but the distinct geographic regions engaged in a ferocious sectional rivalry. Modern Idahoans have had to make and keep a lot of truces to live in peace together.

In the years after World War II a period of moderate Republican rule gradually gave way to two very different and competing political strains: right-wing Republicanism and environmental protectionism. Two close losses illustrated the transition. In 1960, even while Republicanism swept most of the Mountain West, John Kennedy received a quite respectable 46 percent of Idaho's vote. Yet four years later, when Republican Barry Goldwater was going down to ignominious defeat in most regions, he got 49.1 percent here —almost a majority. That near-win heralded a strong surge of rigid Republican conservatism. There was not, in fact, a single Democratic congressman from Idaho from 1966 into the 1980s, and the Republicans sent to Washington grew increasingly conservative. In 1974 the Republicans threw out moderate and thoughtful Republican Congressman Orval Hansen in favor of George Hansen, a rightist described by *The Almanac of American Politics* as "one of the authentic zanies in the Congress." Senator James McClure, a favorite of ultraconservative groups such as the Americans for Constitutional Action, became chairman of the Senate Energy and Natural Resources Committee, which oversees the Interior Department. There he took pro-energy industry positions, promoted nuclear power, and favored development of federal lands rather than preservation.

From 1957 to 1980, Idahoans also sent to Washington the environmentally conscious, liberal Democratic senator, Frank Church. Church, articulate and a touch sanctimonious, entered the Senate in 1957 at the tender age of 32, and in the early 1960s supported the Wilderness Act, which the users of public land—the mining, grazing, and timber interests—predictably condemned as a lockup of vital resources. Overwhelmingly reelected in 1962—a victory he claimed proved "that Idaho people cared a great deal about the outdoors" and that "long dominant interests" could no longer use the public domain for private gain—Church led the fight for the National Wild Rivers System to keep streams natural, free flowing, unobstructed, and unpolluted. He also sponsored legislation to create the Sawtooth National Forest (in part to prevent molybdenum mining in the high, fragile White Cloud Mountains 25 miles northwest of Sun Valley) and in 1980 the 2.3 million-acre River of No Return Wilderness, the single largest wilderness preserve in the lower 48 states.*

Though these environmental laws offended many Idaho interests, Church managed to hang on to his Senate seat for four terms. He strengthened his political hand by supporting federally financed water projects and the federal nuclear power testing site near Idaho Falls. He even dared to use his seat on the Foreign Relations Committee (of which he eventually became chairman) to become one of the most outspoken Senate opponents of the Vietnam War. In 1980, however, right-wing groups set up an "Anybody but Church Committee" and attacked him for practically all his famed liberal positions, including support of the Panama Canal treaties and aid for New York City. By investigating the CIA, they charged, Church had weakened the nation's intelligence agency. In what became the classic liberal-conservative race of 1980, Idahoans unseated their prestigious senior senator in favor of U.S. Representative Steven D. Symms, who had been described by *Congressional Quarterly* as having "a reputation in the House for flamboyance—if not flakiness." (As a Representative, Symms had opposed gun control—he once appeared at a press conference armed with two revolvers—and food stamps, but defended sugar beet subsidies important to Idaho growers.)

What did Symms' victory say about Idaho? It unquestionably confirmed that many Idahoans hold conservative views on social and defense matters and often found themselves at odds with the federal government, which Church had come to symbolize. The vote was also a reminder of the power of the Mormon Church and the religious fundamentalism of the many newcomers who opposed abortion, gun control, and school busing (even though Idaho has relatively few minorities: 2,700 blacks, 10,000 Indians, 5,600 Asians, and 36,000 people of Spanish origin). But Symms' margin—only 4,000 votes—was too low to prove an across-the-board conservative mandate.

With the exceptions of Democratic Governors Cecil Andrus (1971–77) and his successor, John Evans, Idahoans have generally elected state officials who matched the views and political styles of Symms and Hansen. The Idaho Legislature had been in Republican control for many years, but the Republican label is hardly an indicator of the deep rural and religious-based conservatism that surfaces among many of Idaho's legislators. The legislature, however, distinguished itself in surprising fashion through its fair handling of the Proposition 13-style tax limit that Idaho voters passed in 1979. The Idaho

---

*Sun Valley, which attracts skiers from all over the world, is Idaho's international jewel. The resort was "manufactured" in 1936 by W. Averell Harriman, then chairman of the Union Pacific Railroad. Harriman had become intrigued with the popularity of ski resorts in Europe and thought that constructing an American equivalent might show that Union Pacific was doing something "constructive" during the Depression. Sun Valley never really made money for Union Pacific, but from the beginning it did attract movie and other stars. Its most famous resident was author Ernest Hemingway.

measure was a carbon copy of California's Prop 13, but since Idaho law prohibits constitutional amendments by initiative, it took the form of a statute, which the legislators had the pleasure of cleaning up. The tax-limit had come about because Idahoans found their property taxes increasing with the inflated value of their residential property. The legislators modified the more extreme elements of the initiative, leaving stiff but not draconian limits on property tax collections (a two-year freeze, after which 5 percent yearly increases were permitted). In inflationary times, that meant a sharp reduction in local government revenues. Down went the quality of local services such as police and fire; up went many service fees.

However controversial fiscal and social issues, the most vital questions facing Idaho public officials are environmental. Should the magnificent water supply, unique among the Mountain States, be further dammed up or allowed to run free? Should the high mountain wilderness, in an abundance unmatched in any state save Alaska, remain the last refuge on the continent where man himself has always been visitor, never master, or should more mining be allowed? Should the state's growing population be confined to settled areas, or should new roads be built to allow the newcomers to settle on wild land, as earlier generations did? Idaho tore through the 19th century and burst into the 20th determined to "open up the wilderness" and "bring the people in," but in the 1960s and 1970s a truely indigenous environmental protection movement grew up. Environmentalists contended that Church's defeat was not a sign that Idahoans had turned their back on the environment, that better indications of Idahoans' environmental views were the elections of Democratic Governors Andrus and Evans, both of whom campaigned on the environmental protection theme.

But we found that on environmental issues, Idahoans have difficulty making up their minds. Compared with the people of other Rocky Mountain states, Idahoans are most like Coloradans. They want it all: economic development, population growth, freedom from federal interference, no zoning, and an individual outdoor experience comparable to 50 years ago. We were told that the most popular political personality in the state was Andrus, who as Interior Secretary under President Carter was both architect of the legislation to protect a large chunk of Alaska as well as great compromiser between environmentalists and industry on off-shore drilling and surface mining. Since Idaho is 63 percent federally managed, the environmentalists have made great progress through federal protection in the last 20 years; but the mining and timber interests remain strong. The loss of 2,000 of the 4,000 jobs in the Silver Valley of northern Idaho in the early 1980s underscored the complex nature of Idaho's political and economic climate and the state's dependence on the larger world. Years of fires and pollution had denuded the hills around Kellogg, a sliver, lead, and zinc refining town, and the federal and state governments imposed much-needed emission-control orders. To avoid closure, both the federal and state governments agreed to relax the mandates they had imposed on the Bunker Hill mine and smelter, Idaho's second-largest employer. Nevertheless, Gulf Resources and Chemical Company, the parent corporation, closed Bunker Hill in 1982, blaming high labor costs and lowered world silver prices. An attempt by local investors to buy the smelter failed when the United Steelworkers refused to approve a local union vote to accept a 25 percent pay cut and loss of other benefits. But a more reasonable national union might not have saved the day: other silver mines in northern Idaho also closed, and silver industry analysts said prices were likely to remain low for a dozen years because industries were afraid of using silver after the market manipulations of the Texas-based Hunt Brothers (who also indirectly controlled Bunker Hill). Silver Valley's richest lodes had also been depleted, the analysts said. Thus Idaho, the refuge from the pressures and mores of modern life for so many newcomers, learned once again how deeply its fate is intertwined with forces beyond its control.

UTAH

The State the Saints Built

"WE BELIEVE ... THAT ZION will be built upon this [the American] continent," wrote Founder Joseph Smith in the Articles of Faith for that most persecuted, enduring, and successful of the revivalist-utopian religious movements of the 19th century, the Church of Jesus Christ of Latter-day Saints.

Not many years later, on a July afternoon of 1847, Brigham Young, master colonizer and successor to the martyred Smith as prophet-president of the Mormons, would rise from his carriage/sickbed at the mouth of a mountain canyon above the Salt Lake Valley and proclaim: "This is the place." Almost 1,400 miles across the trackless Great Plains from their last home, at Nauvoo, Illinois, Young had led an advance party of 143 men, three women, and two children in 72 covered wagons. Thousands of followers, pulling and pushing handcarts or riding in wagons, would follow in one of the epic folk movements of American history; hundreds never made it, dying of diseases, exposure, or starvation on the way.

The land upon which Zion was to be built lay arid and savage before the Mormons, but here, at least, the Saints hoped to escape the brutal persecution that had come down upon them in the East for their unique claims to divine authority, their clannishness and industry, and their practice of polygamy.

In truth, as the Old Testament had promised, the desert did bloom. For the first time since the early days of the Massachusetts Bay Colony, a pure theocracy—complete union of church and state—flourished in America. In the Old Testament patriarchal way, the Mormon leaders went about God's business of populating the world with chosen people. By the time Young died in 1877, there were 358 new communities in addition to Salt Lake City, with a combined population of about 140,000. Young played his own role in the population explosion, taking unto him 27 wives and siring 56 children.

The Mormons were wrong, of course, in thinking that they could continue their pure theocracy, or be allowed to continue the practice of polygamy, without incurring the wrath of the government of the United States. The great State of Deseret, which Young proclaimed to include all of what is now Utah and Nevada, most of Arizona, part of Idaho, Colorado, Oregon, New Mexico, and even a strip of coastal California, was eventually whittled down, by act of Congress, to what is now the state of Utah. With the Gold Rush came the first meaningful settlement of non-Mormons—"gentiles" in Utah— and the beginnings of bitter religious conflict within the state. Polygamy would be attacked as barbarous by the national political parties and prevent Utah's admission as a state, despite at least five attempts, until 1896—and even then, her first men in Washington would be challenged on the issue of multiple marriage and some denied their seats.

Yet the Latter-day Saints Church and the people of Utah would survive all this and continue to prosper. Today, Mormons still account for 72 percent of the population, overwhelming numbers that set the metes and bounds of Utah culture. The pervasiveness of the influence is underscored by the church's role in the economy of the state and the Mormon belief that religion should govern the individual's total life. Wallace Turner wrote in his excellent book *The Mormon Establishment:* "To be born a Mormon is to be born with a second nationality."

As America has grown more socially liberal, Utah has become, socially and culturally, a uniquely conservative state. Mormon doctrine—industriousness (the Beehive is fittingly the church and state symbol), patriarchal family life, and strict rules forbidding absolutely the use of tobacco, coffee, tea, and alcohol—has made the lives of most Utahans different from those of most modern Americans. Utah has the highest birth rate in the United States, 29.5 births per 1,000 people—a figure more than twice the national average, higher than Puerto Rico's, equal to Costa Rica's, and approaching India's. When a Utah congressman was convicted in 1976 of soliciting a female police decoy as a prostitute, he was quickly and easily driven from politics. On the race front, the church became nationally known for its exclusion of blacks from its priesthood—a necessary step before a Mormon can enter the temple to perform ceremonies assuring happiness through eternity. Yet it was not until 1978 that Church President Spencer W. Kimball received a "revelation" from God that black males of African descent were eligible for the priesthood. His decision ended the traditional Mormon belief, based on lines in Joseph Smith's translation of the Book of Abraham, that African Negroes were "cursed . . . as pertaining to the priesthood" because they were descended from Ham (the son of Noah), whose black wife Egyptus was descended from the broth-er-killer Cain. (U.S. civil rights groups had been clamoring for years for a change in the Mormon policy, but there was another source of pressure on the church: its missionary work in Latin America. A number of Brazilian converts to Mormonism found, on researching their lineage to arrange Latter-day-Saints proxy baptisms and marriages for their ancestors—a strong church practice, albeit one most puzzling to outsiders—that they had African ances-tors.)

Today Utah's political and religious traditions are at once stronger than ever and coming under the strongest challenges since the Church rejected multiple marriage in 1890.* At a time when several mainstream American churches have lost members, the Mormon Church has grown to 3 million

*Plural marriage is today outlawed by the Saints, and if any of their number is found "living in the doctrine," as they call it, he is promptly excommunicated. Yet surreptitiously, often unknown to neighbors and associates, the practice of plural marriage continues to this day. One of the major hideouts for polygamists is the lonely Strip Country of northern Arizona, isolated from both the church authorities at Salt Lake City and the civil authorities in Phoenix.

persons in the United States (doubled in two decades), and another 1.8 million persons worldwide. The Mormon Church has become one of the key conservative social forces in the country; at the direction of the Church hierarchy, its members join with other conservatives across the country to fight women's rights, liberalized abortion, and homosexual rights.

Utahans are also increasingly influential in Washington. When the Republicans achieved a Senate majority in 1980, Utah's two conservative Republican senators, Jake Garn and Orrin Hatch, became powerful men, heading committees that were previously the province of Senate liberals. Garn became chairman of the Banking, Housing and Urban Affairs Committee. Hatch took over the Labor and Human Resources Committee. The state's phenomenal 37.9 percent population growth in the 1970s (due to both the high birth rate and immigration) won the state a third member of the House of Representatives in the reapportionment after the 1980 Census. Mormon influence is strong behind the scenes in Washington also. Because their religion trains them to be hard working and adhere to a hierarchical line of command, Mormons have long been favored as political aides and FBI and CIA employees. There are so many Mormons in the Washington area that a $15 million marble temple topped by six gold spires was constructed in the woods of Kensington, Md., in 1974. So many young Mormons go to law school in Washington that the Utah bar has more graduates of the George Washington University's National Law Center than any other state bar association. Among the most prominent Mormons on the national scene have been hotel man and Republican donor J. Willard Marriott, newspaper columnist Jack Anderson and former Michigan Governor George Romney.

In fact, Mormonism seemed so "in" by the start of the 1980s that John Dart, the *Los Angeles Times*'s religion editor, could write that many Americans, disenchanted with years of social change, liberal government, and strong emphasis on individualism in U.S. life, were admiringly coming to view the Mormons as "super-Americans."

At the same time, there were unmistakable signs of severe internal tensions within the Mormon Church itself. It took, for example, a hardline position against the proposed Equal Rights Amendment to the Constitution, even going so far as to excommunicate a number of women members for publicly supporting it. The action served to underscore deep gulfs within the Church. A basic tenet of Mormonism is that a woman's place is in the home. But other basic beliefs—in large families, in tithing, in education—are so expensive to maintain that more than half the women in Utah held outside jobs by 1982 (double the number ten years before) and, ironically, the percentage of working women in Utah was *higher* than the national average, although they earned less. While new temples, chapels, and members were being added in unprecedented numbers, thousands had fallen away from strict observance of the faith as prescribed by Joseph Smith and those who succeeded him in authority. These "Jack Mormons" maintained their official church membership, or at least took no concrete action to disaffiliate themselves. But many strayed far from the rules prohibiting stimulants, many disregarded the requirement of a full tithe—a tenth of income—as contribution to the church, and many simply disregarded the church's rigorous requirements for meetings not only on Sundays but during the week as well. And in part, the church itself was probably spawning the "Jack Mormon" phenomenon. With its emphasis on education, it was turning out thousands of college graduates with keen and inquiring minds. To forbid those young Mormons to speculate fully about religion and ethical values and to expect their compliance was somewhat naïve. Many Mormons, moreover, were questioning whether the complex web of expected church activities had much relevance to the social problems of the modern world.

The church's leadership is unlikely to adopt modern social mores anytime soon. As in Joseph Smith's day, absolute authority lies with the upper hierarchy of the church, and especially the president-prophet, who alone is considered able to receive direct divine revelation regarding church policies. He is selected by and from the Council of the Twelve Apostles and is usually the man in their number senior in service. The apostles remain in office until they are gathered to their eternal reward. The result of this self-perpetuating seniority system has been to put power in the hands of aged men to an even greater degree than one sees in the Roman Catholic Church. The "prophet, seer and relevator" of the Saints at this writing was Spencer W. Kimball, born in 1895; next in line was Ezra Taft Benson, born in 1899, secretary of agriculture in the Eisenhower administration. How different from Joseph Smith, who was 24 when he founded the LDS Church and only 38 the day he was murdered in Illinois.

Church and State and Business

Of all our states, Utah has the closest relationship between organized religion, politics, and business. Non-Mormons have long been fascinated with the great theocratic corporation that is the Church of Jesus Christ of Latter-day Saints —an organization sometimes said to be, on a per capita basis, the richest church in the world. The assertion is not subject to proof or disproof, since the LDS authorities have never made more than the sketchiest public accounting of the church's income and expenditures. The fetish for secrecy probably stems from the early days of persecution when church leaders had to fear the federal marshals swooping down on them to look for extra wives. Among church holdings are the Beneficial Life Insurance Company, hotels, radio and television stations, the Deseret News Publishing Company, and the Zion Cooperative Mercantile Institution (the U.S.A.'s first department store), substantial commercial real estate in downtown Salt Lake City and many other cities, plus securities and livestock throughout the West. Contrary to popular belief in the Mountain West, Wallace Turner has observed that the men at the top of the church have *not* deliberately sought to gain control over a broad range of businesses. The church is not involved in mining. And instead of plowing corporate profits back into business in the past several decades, the

Mormons have been busy spending them to spread the Restored Gospel. By the time the Mormons complete their temple construction program in cities such as Lima, Seoul, Manila, Frankfurt, Johannesburg, Dallas, and Chicago, there will be 37 temples around the world—a massive capital drain. Indeed, there is good reason to believe that the church's financial practices, rather than stimulating the Utah economy, are depressing it. Channeling so much personal income into the church, for instance, removes growth and risk capital from plants, shops, stores, and partnerships.

As we have already noted, the Mormon Church frequently "advises" its members on political issues. Utah has elected few non-Mormons to high office. As Utah has become relatively more affluent and the national Democratic party increasingly liberal on social issues, Utah has become increasingly conservative and Republican. Any Democratic presidential candidate would have a hard time winning in Utah. In 1982 Republican Senator Orrin Hatch —despite an image of being a strident and humorless apostle of the New Right —easily repulsed a stiff reelection challenge from Democrat Ted Wilson, the Salt Lake City mayor and a fellow Mormon nearly as conservative as he. But it would be wrong to assume that Utahans always vote Republican—or follow the dictates of Church officials. In the Great Depression, Mormons defied the Church to vote for President Franklin Roosevelt and to end Prohibition. Utahans have also elected in succession two Democratic governors, Calvin Rampton and Scott Matheson, who would be considered conservative, pro-growth Democrats elsewhere but are relative liberals in Utah. Both Rampton (who served from 1965 until 1977) and Matheson, who succeeded him, were highly popular and widely regarded as among the most capable U.S. governors of their time. Both, among other achievements, rose to be chairmen of the National Governors Association and were respected spokesmen for the states on federalism issues.

Utah's state government is not as ultraconservative as one might think. The state has one of the country's best "mixes" among property, sales, and income taxes. Utah spends unusual sums on education, especially on colleges and universities, again a reflection of the Mormon belief that "the glory of God is intelligence." The Mormon Church, of course, also finances Brigham Young University. The Mormons have for decades been legendary for taking care of their own through their exceptional private welfare system. The "help thy neighbor help himself" system, set up in 1936, is financed by asking all Mormons to fast two meals a month and to give the equivalent cost (or more) in cash. Other Utahans who need to go on public relief, however, find their assistance well below the national average.

Great Salt Lake and Its City

The Great Salt Lake is the largest body of water between the Great Lakes and the Pacific. Not too many years ago, it was one of the prime tourist attractions of the West because of its bouyant waters, six times as salty as the ocean. (It was impossible to sink!) Then raw sewage from Salt Lake City and other towns, together with unfiltered industrial wastes, polluted this wondrous body of water. Cleanups have registered some success, but to this day foul odors from refineries still restrict bathing. Another assault came when a 50-mile rock causeway was built to carry the main line of the Southern Pacific Railroad, dividing the lake in half and drastically altering the mineral content and environment of the two halves. Both environmentalists and mining companies are fascinated with the Great Salt Lake—the former for its unique ecological system and its marshlands, where three million birds annually rest and nest, the latter for the profits it may produce. Magnesium and potash are already extracted; there is exploration for oil. And scientists talk of using the lake's elements to help produce solar energy.

Great Salt Lake's namesake city was founded four days after the Latter-day Saints arrived in the Great Salt Lake Valley in 1847, and Brigham Young walked to a spot of ground between two forks of a small mountain stream, put his cane to the ground, and declared "here will be the temple of our God!" Today Temple Square occupies 10 acres in the heart of Salt Lake City. The many spired temple, begun in 1853 and completed some 40 years later, soars above all else; no gentile may enter it, and indeed only those Mormons with "recommends" or permits from their ward bishops, indicating that they are faithful, active, and obedient members may go through its portals. Nearby is the great whale-shaped tabernacle, built in the 1860s, a meeting hall open to all from which the Sunday morning concerts of the Mormon Tabernacle Choir have been broadcast since 1929.

Salt Lake City's physical setting, perched directly beside the timeless mountains of the Wasatch Front, is one of the most spectacular in America. On a summer evening one sees these heights rising in a blue twilight with the flickering lights of the city below; snow-decked on a winter morning, they throw the Saints' Holy City into crystal-clear perspective. Within this setting the views of the lake, the high-set State Capitol, Temple Square, the downtown office structures, the broad streets (they are 132 feet wide, broad enough to turn a span of oxen as Brigham Young had commanded)—all suggest this is not just another provincial city. No distant board of directors makes the great decisions for Salt Lake City; this is no branch town. Its fate lies foremost in the hands of the General Authorities of the church, for whom it is mecca. One result is that Salt Lake City's retail core has not declined, as other cities have. Despite satellite shopping centers, Zion Cooperative Mercantile Institution (ZCMI) has constructed a new downtown mall, and its competitors have also invested millions in expansion. Across the street from ZCMI and directly opposite Temple Square sits the Crossroads Plaza, supposedly the largest covered downtown mall in the country, with some 120 shops. But the big news —and the big money—in recent years was Moslem, not Mormon. Saudi Arabian brothers Adnan and Essam Khasshogi took a liking to Salt Lake in 1975 and began pouring nearly $1 billion into various development projects, including a $450 million industrial park near the airport and a $410 million downtown complex, the Triad Center, boasting twin 40-story office towers, condominiums, and a hotel.

The chief negative is perhaps that Salt Lake, like so many other Western cities, is constantly threatened by automobile air pollution and faces a severe scarcity of water, practically all of which it must take from distant dams and diversion projects financed by the federal government. There are serious growth problems, too. During the 1970s the population of Salt Lake County soared by 61 percent, to 619,066, triggering not only severe sprawl development but also a severe overload on sewage treatment facilities. Nor have the city and its suburbs, the overriding power of the Mormon Church notwithstanding, been able to join in a form of sensible metropolitan governance or even close coordination between units of government.

In 1978, Salt Lake City and County voters turned down a proposal to combine city, county, and 25 special purpose districts into one government. An 11-member elected legislative council would have replaced 27 commissions and boards, although some city governments, schools boards, and special districts would have remained. Governors Rampton and Matheson, several Salt Lake City mayors including Jake Garn, the *Salt Lake Tribune*, the city's gentile newspaper, and good government groups strongly backed the idea, but many local officeholders did not. Opponents convinced the voters that unification would mean less local control and eventually lead to higher government costs.

Mormon conservatism and middle-class values lie heavily on the city, but Salt Lake has taken on an increasingly secular character in recent years. Culturally it is well known throughout the West for, of all things, three fine dance companies, which tour extensively. After long and tortured debates, the tourism industry has managed to achieve a compromise with the church on alcohol; miniature bottles may now be purchased from a state liquor store branches in most fine restaurants.

Utah's second-ranking cities—Ogden (pop. 64,407) and Provo (74,108)—lie 33 miles north and 42 miles south, respectively, of Salt Lake City. They are also on the Wasatch Front in the oasis pattern so typical of the West's urban areas. Ogden, where whiskey-drinking gentiles arrived with transcontinental railroad in 1869, may still be the least Mormon city in Utah. Provo, best known as the home of the singing Osmond family, is also the site of Brigham Young University. Another economic mainstay is the massive Geneva Steel Works, built by the government for World War II production and the catalyst for Utah's present-day industrial economy. The arrival of Big Steel symbolized a shift of Utah from its exclusive dependence on farming and mining, and to this day the employees of the Geneva Works revere the plant as a tool of economic upward mobility. When the Environmental Protection Agency tried to clean up the Geneva Works, U.S. Steel, pleading poverty, threatened to close the plant, and thousands of workers marched in protest.

Within an hour of Salt Lake's airport are also a dozen ski resorts, including the famed Alta, Snowbird, and Sundance, developed by Utah's most famous part-time resident, the actor-environmentalist Robert Redford.

Natural Utah

For generations it has seemed that Utah's great land bulk—primitive, wild, high mountains, canyonlands, and eternities of salt desert—have erected a physical wall to match the mental wall toward the outside world that the Saints often seem to have built for themselves. Utah's cities and agricultural land (only 5 percent of the state total) lie in a 10- to 25-mile-wide valley at the foot of the Wasatch Mountain rampart, stretching 150 miles north and south in the north central part of the state. In just the 85-mile strip from Provo north to Salt Lake City and on to Ogden reside three-fourths of the state's 1,461,037 people. The Wasatch peaks are adjoined on their east by the even-higher Uinta Mountains (up to 13,500 feet), likewise 150 miles in length, but unique in all the U.S.A. because they stretch east-west rather than north-south. Together these two snow-capped ranges furnish most of Utah's stream water and form the natural eastern boundary of Mormon country. To the west lies the equally formidable barrier of the Great Salt Lake and the thousands of miles of hostile salt flats. South of the high Uintas in eastern Utah one comes on the rugged uplands of the Colorado plateau, a region that then broadens to cover practically the whole breadth of the state to the Arizona border to the south.

These same vast open spaces lie at the core of modern challenges to the Mormon traditions. The flat-topped mountains and violently colored deep-gouged canyons of southern Utah—a virtual Hollywood backlot where hundreds of movie Westerns were shot—have become a bitter battleground with environmentalists pitted against the mining companies and the Mormon power structure. In all America there is no more brilliant sight than the crimson and buff pinnacles, spires, and walls of southern Utah's Bryce Canyon National Park, or any more breathtaking mountain grandeur than at nearby Zion, also a national park. A "golden circle" of eight national parks, all within 200 miles of each other, each year attracts hundreds of thousands of vacationers from all the world seeking rest and renewal from the great natural beauty untouched by man. But southern Utah also holds most of Utah's 23.4 billion tons of low-sulfur coal reserves, an energy storehouse viewed covetously by California utilities and even Japan. The development-environmental conflict first came to national attention in 1975 when it was reported that several utility companies were planning to build a 3,000-megawatt coal-fired electric plant on the Kaiparowits Plateau less than 100 miles from Bryce Canyon and Zion National Parks. The plant was scheduled to be the first of a string of five. Kaiparowits was eventually canceled, and environmentalists attempted to protect the area's vistas and some of the land from degradation with the passage of the federal Surface Mining Act of 1977. Economics, rather than protest, appears to be the strongest protector of these lands; decreased electricity demand in California due to higher rates led to the reconsideration of other plants. But the population and industrialization pressures are so intense in the Southwestern states that this debate is likely to continue for many years to come.

One project that has gone forward is the $8 billion-plus Intermountain Power Project near Lynndyl, in west central Utah. Environmentalists, utilities, state and federal officials agreed on this site after other, more aesthetically delicate places were rejected. Intermountain, which is expected to be the nation's biggest coal-fired power plant when it opens in 1986, will serve mostly Los Angeles.

Opposition to mining in Utah comes almost totally from the national environmental organizations. The Mormons' position is a curious one. Brigham Young preached that mining was an unreligious way of life; consequently control of Utah's vast wealth in precious metals, copper, and coal passed to gentiles. But the Mormons also believe that mining will lead to economic development. Southern Utahans are especially strong supporters of mining; many are the descendants of settlers who went there at Brigham Young's request to take civilization to an inhospitable land. They have always found it hard to make ends meet, and many believe coal mining may bring the only relatively high-paying jobs that would allow their children to remain close to home. A few southern Utah individuals have begun to worry that the highly publicized problems in other energy boom towns might follow rapid population growth in Utah, but most local leaders still find it difficult to believe that the same problems could surface in their towns. When the boom hits, the impact may be doubly severe because Utah has not made the preparation for development that some other states have. Despite Gov. Matheson's efforts, the legislature has refused to establish a coal severance tax (though severance taxes exist on other minerals) or a state power plant siting law.

Water has not receded as a burning regional issue. Orrin Hatch, chief Senate sponsor in 1982 of a constitutional amendment to require a balanced federal budget, didn't even blush when he simultaneously promoted a $1.5 billion project to pump Colorado River water more than 150 miles to Salt Lake City. The Central Utah Project, years fermenting in the federal pork barrel (where original cost estimates quadrupled), would include 140 miles of pipes, canals, and aqueducts; 10 new reservoirs; and 3 new electric power plants. Environmentalists claimed it also would wreak havoc on trout streams, wildlife habitats, and water supplies of the Ute Indians. President Jimmy Carter put the Central Utah Project at the top of his "hit list" of wasteful water projects in 1977, but Hatch and others rode out of the West to rescue it.

A major challenge to Mormon tradition has been how to maintain traditional church support for a strong national defense. Since World War II, the Utah welcome mat has been out for military bases. But in 1981, faced with the prospect of being made the recipient (with Nevada) of the massive MX mobile intercontinental ballistic missile system, the church hierarchy finally rebelled. It would be "ironic and a denial of the very essence" of church gospel to locate a mammoth weapons system—one potentially capable of destroying much of civilization—on the same land to which their fathers had come to build their Zion on the American continent, said the Church in an official statement. The Church did not oppose the missile system in principle, however. But no sooner had Washington abandoned the MX basing plan than another nuclear threat arose to shadow Utah's future: placement of the deep salt beds in the Paradox Basin, not far from Moab, high on the Energy Department's list of future nuclear waste dump sites.

By the early 1980s the 20,000 residents of the "virtually uninhabited" area of southern Utah, eastern Nevada, and northwestern Arizona were discovering the price of being so close to the atmospheric nuclear tests conducted from 1951 to 1963. Over the years thyroid cancer, Hodgkin's disease, leukemia, miscarriages, and births of retarded children became much more commonplace. A St. George, Utah, woman spent years gathering information and writing letters to the federal government (which denied all charges) before the case finally went to federal court in 1981, beginning a long judicial process likely to end in the Supreme Court.

Thus it was that this desert state, the distant point sought by Brigham Young 13 decades ago, was finding the protection of those great empty spaces that had so long isolated it falling away through the demands of modern military technology and a national voracious energy appetite. Drawn ever more into the national and international maelstrom, Utah's uniqueness would unquestionably come under greater and greater strain before the 20th century ended. But there was a saving factor: being so distinctive, so strong in its special convictions, Utah would be able to withstand the fearsome pressures from outside longer, and probably more successfully, than any other state of the American Union—ironically, that same Union in which it had experienced such difficulty gaining membership and acceptance in the first instance.

NEVADA

Gomorrah on the Desert

IN ITS NATURAL STATE the land now called Nevada is one of the most hostile places on earth for human settlement. The Great Sierra Mountains block the moisture-laden clouds rolling in from the Pacific. Lacking water, the land is a bleak, sun-scorched wilderness of mountain-rimmed basins and high plateaus. This Great American Desert is not only essentially treeless— the ubiquitous sagebrush is the dominant form of plant life—but vast stretches of its territory are the salt and alkaline remnants of dead lakes, a soil that not even irrigation could redeem. A handful of lakes do remain, and in the softness of early evening the raw, harsh desert peaks may take on warm pastel hues, bringing a kind of haunting beauty to a hostile land. But man must struggle to sustain his life systems in this driest of all the American states; in all the 109,889 square miles of Nevada (seventh-largest in the Union and equal to all of New England plus most of New York State), there are only three cities worthy of the name: Las Vegas, Reno, and Carson City. In the words of the Western writer Neil Morgan, "There is very little but rock and sand, alkaline-laden dry lakes, buttes and craggy mountains. The desolation of Nevada is awesome."

What then draws people? In the past century, it was the gold and silver in the hills. Cattle ranching has long eked out a bare existence. But today it is gambling. First in that spectacularly successful industry, catering ingeniously to Californian and transcontinental pleasure-seekers, Nevada for four decades has been growing by leaps and bounds. Its population grew 63.5 percent in the 1970s to 488,738—enough people to warrant a second congressional seat beginning in 1982. Since the end of World War II, no other state's population has expanded at a comparable rate. Today the mining of precious metals is reviving, cattlemen still ply their trade, and the Chamber of Commerce vigorously promotes Nevada's pro-industry tax position: no personal income taxes, no corporate income taxes, no inventory taxes, no rental company taxes, no franchise taxes, no bank or corporation taxes, a constitutional limit on property taxes, and a sales tax of only 3 to 3½ percent. All these tax advantages plus a right-to-work law that keeps wages down have managed to make Nevada the Western warehousing and product distribution center for companies such as J.C. Penney and Levi Strauss and to attract a few other industries.

But essentially Nevada remains a one-industry state. Some 32 percent of the people make their living directly off the gaming business (as it's called there), and another 25 percent of the labor force work in related businesses. The single most important revenue source for state government is the gross receipts tax, which licensed gambling establishments pay on their earnings—3 percent on the first $150,000, 4 percent on the next $250,000, and 5.75 percent on earnings over $400,000. Take away gambling—legal since 1931, the only American state in which it was until 1978, when New Jersey voters agreed to allow casinos in Atlantic City—and Nevada might well be one of the most desperately depressed regions of the hemisphere.

Chance and gamble have marked Nevada's history from the start. The first white men to try a permanent settlement were the Mormons, dispatched by Brigham Young in 1855. The Mormons persevered when the Paiute Indians raided their fields—today, for instance there are dozens of Mormon congregations in Las Vegas alone. But Nevada was not to be part of the great, ill-fated State of Deseret proclaimed by Young in 1859. For in the same year the Great Comstock Lode—the richest single treasure of gold and silver the world has ever seen—was discovered.

The little towns of Virginia City and Carson City became boom towns overnight—the latter so flush with success it was made the state capital when statehood came in 1864. In poured the miners, speculators, gamblers, prostitutes, dance-hall girls; not the least of the new residents was Mark Twain, who wrote truth and fiction for the *Territorial Enterprise* for two years before being chased out of town in the wake of editorial insults that involved him in a law-breaking duel.* Ever since, Virginia City has been a grist mill for Western writers. More than a billion dollars of gold and silver came out of the hundreds of miles of shafts, tunnels, drifts, and inclines of the Comstock Lode, helping to finance the Civil War and creating many millionaires and multimillionaires, most of whom took their wealth to San Francisco or other more desirable places than the Nevada desert.

Then (and one might say now) Nevada had few of the requisites of a viable state. But President Abraham Lincoln needed more states to ratify the 13th Amendment abolishing slavery, so Nevada was rushed into the Union by having its entire 16,000-word constitution telegraphed to Washington (at a cost of $3,416.77!) on October 26, 1864. For decades after statehood, Nevada was exploited and controlled politically by outsiders, principally San Franciscans, who took the wealth from the Comstock Lode and controlled the Southern Pacific Railroad, which as the state's most important private land-

*The latter-day Nevada press is notably duller and/or more conservative than Twain. The glaring exception to this rule is the *Las Vegas Sun*, the property of flamboyant Hank Greenspun, who was once described by the *New Yorker* as "an editor-publisher of the type popularly supposed to have gone out with derringer pistols and the Gold Rush." Greenspun focused attention on the unsavory business dealings of former Senator Pat McCarran, has campaigned for better schools, and fervidly defends individual liberties. The paper is so concerned about the dictatorial powers of the Internal Revenue Service that if a subscriber is audited, the paper will send a reporter with a tape recorder to the audit meeting and provide the subscriber with two hours of free legal advice.

owner ran Nevada politics. Free silver was the overriding preoccupation of Nevada's congressional delegation for many decades. By the turn of the century, the mines at Virginia City had been depleted—at least by the methods used then, and based on the prices of the times—the place became first the West's most illustrious ghost town (a "fragrant tomb," John Gunther called it in the '40s) and then something of a tourist trap.* In the early 1900s gold and silver strikes at the isolated mining camps of Goldfield and Tonopah brought some upturn in the state's economy; with this came a new complexion in ownership, since Nevadans held the controlling interest. They often battled among themselves over grazing lands. For many years, there were four times as many cattle and sheep in Nevada as people.

The Great Depression hit Nevada with unusual cruelty, and a desperate state government decided to legalize casino gambling. Thus begins our story of the present-day Gomorrah on the desert.

The Gaming Business and Its Culture

Casino gambling has been in and out of the door several times in Nevada. It sprouted naturally in the first mining camps, was illegal from 1864 to 1869, then legalized for 41 years, outlawed in 1910, then made legal again in 1931— partly to draw in out-of-state money, partly to make legitimate an ancient trade that had proven totally unsuppressible in any event.† Prewar gambling was reminiscent of the mining camp, operating in darkened halls, the dealers in shirtsleeves and green eyeshades. Today, of course, Nevada gambling operates out of plush palacelike casinos, built at a cost of millions, handling fantastic sums of money in each day of operations. It is a major national industry whose stocks are traded on the New York Stock Exchange. Wall Street employs analysts who specialize in understanding gambling stocks, and investment banking houses arrange the financing for their never-ending expansion and redecoration.

---

*In recent years Virginia City has become embroiled in one of the most ironic environmental controversies in the West. A firm called Houston Oils and Minerals decided it could make money on the lodes of gold and silver still remaining in the area and opened a sizeable open-pit mine in adjacent Gold Hill in 1978. The locals, used to their historic buildings, a tourism industry, and a peaceful way of life, became enraged when cracks began appearing in a highway, an historic mining road collapsed, and the municipal water supply was endangered. The mining continued, but the company had to offer $1 million to endow a county-administered foundation and agreed to a production royalty tied to the market price of silver. Mining companies believe northeastern Nevada could be a substantial silver producer once again and unquestionably America's number one area in gold. However extensive the operations become, it's clear that the West is not the land of "rape and run" it was before it had a nontransient population to defend it.

†Nevadans celebrated the official lifting of the gambling ban with a statewide carnival that lasted nearly a fortnight. But the man who introduced the gambling bill in the legislature—a bankhouse cowboy and nongambler named Phil M. Tobin—never got much credit, nor a penny of profits from the great bonanza he uncorked.

The turn from the suspect old green-shade days to modern big business began in the late 1930s when Harold Smith, later joined by his father, Raymond ("Pappy") Smith, an ex-carnival man, opened the honest, well lit, well-ventilated Harolds Club in Reno and promoted it by blanketing the highways of the West with the ubiquitous "Harolds Club or Bust" billboards. It was not long, however, before brash little Las Vegas, a town of only 8,422 souls in 1940, began to overtake Reno as the gaming center. This was largely a phenomenon of Vegas' strategic location closer to population-heavy Southern California, its warmer climate (not subject to Reno's mid-winter slowdown), and the advent of air conditioning. Las Vegas' downtown, a smaller version of Reno's, was soon overshadowed by the Strip—glittering miles of deluxe casino-hotels along U.S. 91. Opulent, garish decor, wildly flashing signs, lavish floorshows, massive casinos—these are the hallmarks of the temples of hedonism along the free-spending Strip. As a come-on to the gamblers, Las Vegas offers the best-performed and slickly staged nightclub entertainment in the world. After years of subsidizing these shows, the hotels have raised cover charges to try to make the entertainment a profit center, but it's hard when superstars are pulling down more than $200,000 per week for their performances. The top-paid included Frank Sinatra ($50,000 per show), country singers Dolly Parton and Kenny Rogers ($350,000 each per week), Willie Nelson ($250,000 per week) and variety show performers Cher, Ann-Margret, and Engelbert Humperdinck ($200,000 per week). Singer Wayne Newton ($175,000 per week) actually earned the most on the Las Vegas night club circuit in 1981, grossing about $6.3 million for 36 weeks of work.

One of the first of the deluxe casino hotels, the Flamingo, was opened in 1947 by "Bugsy" Siegel, a notorious underworld figure. Siegel's ganglandstyle assassination in his Los Angeles home in 1947 brought national attention to the gangsterism in Nevada gambling. Since the 1950s a state gaming commission has examined the backgrounds of casino operators and barred men who have still-active associations with gangster elements or out-of-state gambling interests. Sinatra was forced to give up his Nevada gambling license in 1963 because he had entertained the blacklisted Chicago hoodlum king, Sam Giancana, at the Cal-Neva Lodge at Lake Tahoe; in the early '80s, listing his friend Ronald Reagan as a reference, Sinatra persuaded a compliant Nevada Gaming Commission to let him have his lucrative gambling business back (after making it clear he'd withdraw his application if too-tough questions were asked at the hearing).

To hear gaming industry spokesmen and Nevada officials, one would conclude that gambling in the state is now as clean as a hound's tooth. Big corporate ownership, they say, has reduced illegal activity because investors worry about what would happen at the Securities and Exchange Commission if skimming or other illegal activities were detected. One reason Nevada officials encouraged Howard Hughes to buy casinos during his bizarre four-year stay in Las Vegas (1966–1970) was the belief that he and his Mormon aides would clean house.* Hughes did fire some unsavory managers, but Hughes aides also told the *Wall Street Journal* that some men with long-time mobster connections were retained because they knew so much about the business that they were indispensable. The fact is that both illegal activities and ties to national syndicate figures continue to turn up. When New Jersey's Casino Control Commission ruled in 1980 that two Las Vegas casino executives were unqualified to hold casino licenses in Atlantic City due to mobster connections, it was clear that Nevada's gaming commission had access to most of the same information and had not acted to keep its house clean. Some law enforcement officials say that the maze of corporate ownership may make it easier to hide underworld owners. In the last analysis, total integrity may simply be incompatible with the type of business gambling is. There is every reason to believe Nevada spokesmen when they say that the slots are honest (inspectors check to make sure they aren't plugged to prevent a jackpot), that a dealer second-carding or bottom-carding at a Twenty-one table will be caught, that roulette wheels aren't wired, that the dice aren't weighted. Enforcement in this area is vigorous, and major establishments at Las Vegas, Reno, and Lake Tahoe have all been forced to close down after cheating was confirmed, until they got new owners. The real problems come in counting of the house's take (where skimming is so tempting), in hoodlum-type ownership, and in paralysis of regulatory machinery when an industry as wealthy and dominant as gaming is involved.

Gambling is not the only unusual industry in Nevada. Nevada has quickie marriage chapels (no waiting time required) and easy divorce laws (still six weeks' residency, though less important since other states relaxed their divorce laws). Both activities enrich Nevada hotels, guest ranches, justices of the peace, and lawyers. Open prostitution flourishes in 15 of Nevada's 17 counties, the exceptions being Clark County (Las Vegas) and Washoe County (Reno), where local ordinances still forbid it. Nevada is the only state with a scheduled airline—Mustang Air Service, which carries customers from Las Vegas, the point of origin, to lonely air strips, each with its own bawdy house immediately adjacent. The Mustang Ranch brothel itself, located near Virginia City, was purchased for nearly $20 million in 1980; its new owners promised to spruce up the mobile homes filled with girls to make the establishment even more hospitable.

So what kind of society has Nevada created in this fast-buck atmosphere? We turn to the words of Neil Morgan: "The most insidious influence of Las

---

*Hughes' Nevada buying spree began a few weeks after his arrival when the Desert Inn told him he would have to leave to make room for a group of "high rollers" expected in town. Hughes' purchase of the hotel from a Mafia-connected syndicate was the first of many. He also bought the feeder airline, Air West, and Harolds Club in Reno. Through his extensive holdings and the fantastic wealth held in reserve, there was no question that Hughes was the most powerful man in Nevada when he departed just as mysteriously as he arrived. Long after his death in 1976, Hughes' ghost still lingers over Nevada. As of this writing, his Summa Corporation is still running the businesses while potential heirs fight over the estate.

Vegas is its destruction of wonder: the wonder of sex, the wonder of chance, and the wonder of oneself. Everything is settled fast in Las Vegas. Like the lava outcroppings in the desert, Nevada has become a molten overflow of the American passion for excess. It is a long way from Plymouth Rock."[*]

One can admire the Nevadans for creating something out of nothing. In many ways, Nevada has the earmarks of a wealthy state today. Its 1980 per capita income of $10,458 ranked seventh among the 50 states, and the state had so ingeniously structured her tax system that the great burden fell on tourists, not resident Nevadans. But one can also look at the social statistics. Nevada has the worst alcoholism rate in the country, a suicide rate more than double the national average, and almost as miserable a standing in robberies, murder, and manslaughter, as well as unfortunate patterns of child abuse, infant mortality, and life expectancy. Many people who move to Nevada are basically unhappy and dissatisfied with American life for many different reasons, hoping to find contentment among the lights and glitter of Las Vegas, according to one state planning official. The *Nevada Public Affairs Review,* published by the University of Nevada at Reno, concluded that "at several critical junctures, most obviously with the 1931 legislative decision to legalize casino gambling, Nevada implicitly accepted far more than its share of social problems in exchange for economic survival and hopes for prosperity."

But even the supposedly recession-proof gaming industry felt the economic squeeze of the '80s. Long accustomed to annual 15 percent to 20 percent growth rates in casino business, Nevada experienced gambling growth of just 8.3 percent in 1980 and 5.6 percent in 1981. By the end of 1982, Las Vegas was reeling as unemployment hit 12.4 percent, the Royal Americana Hotel closed, the Dunes Hotel was sold, and the Riviera Hotel was deeply in debt. Part of the problem was some 1,500 miles away in New Jersey, where the blossoming casino business in Atlantic City was diverting untold thousands of gamblers who once winged to Vegas.

One could more easily, in a live-and-let-live spirit, dismiss the Nevada deviation from national norms if some of this state's policies and activities didn't so directly affect other Americans. It was the remarkably lax regulatory policy of Clark County—not requiring, for example, automatic fire sprinklers in high-rise buildings—that led to death of 84 people, mostly out-of-staters, in the MGM Grand Hotel fire in November 1980. (After the fact, the county did move to require the sprinklers in such buildings.) Then there is the question of where the water and electricity comes from to service Gomorrah-on-the-Desert. The gambling culture would in fact be impossible without water made available to Las Vegas and Reno by federally financed water projects, in which the national taxpayer bears the lion's part of the cost. As

[*]The Las Vegas strip has not repelled all observers. In 1972, architects Robert Venturi, Denise Scott Brown, and Steven Izenour shocked the elitist architectural establishment when they published *Learning from Las Vegas.* Beginning their study with a studio course on the strip at the Yale School of Art and Architecture, the authors stated: "We believe a careful documentation of its physical form is as important to architects and urbanists today as were the studies of medieval Europe and ancient Rome and Greece to earlier generations."

for energy, Las Vegas has the highest rate of electricity usage in the U.S.—twice the national average—to feed its appetite for air conditioning and neon lights. Yet the state itself has little coal, not enough water to keep a nuclear power plant cool, and only minuscule amounts of its own natural gas and oil. By the early 1980s, in what could surely prove to be an environmental travesty, Nevada was hoping to obtain still more electricity for its high-growth plans by mining coal and burning it in plants near the spectacularly beautiful national parks, including Grand Canyon, Bryce Canyon, and Zion. (The only other possible source would be Hoover Dam, the man-made wonder on the Colorado River 30 miles from Las Vegas. Nevada's power needs were so small when the federally funded dam was completed in 1936 that the 50-year lease, which expires in 1986, sent most of the power to Arizona and California.)

Finally, the gambling industry and its developers have been responsible for the environmental degradation of Lake Tahoe, the nation's largest alpine lake. Twenty-two miles long and up to ten in width, in spots as deep as 1,600 feet, Lake Tahoe has evoked much praise, and Mark Twain once wrote that "so singularly clear was the water that where it was only 20 or 30 feet deep the bottom was so perfectly distinct that the boat seemed to be floating on air! Yes, where it was even 80 feet deep." But Nevada's senators have kept it from becoming a national park, and the state's politicians and developers, until what seemed a promising change of course to adopt a long-range conservation plan in 1982, frustrated the efforts of a bistate planning agency with California. (The lake lies across the two states' border.) High on these once pristine, inviolate shores flash miles of gaudy neon beckoning the avaricious. Meanwhile, the massive land development in the Tahoe Basin releases vast amounts of minerals and fertilizers to flow into the lake, tourists' automobiles have brought air pollution, and wildlife habitats have been destroyed. All this, to our minds, is the most appalling assault on God-given natural beauty on the American continent.

Nevada-style Politics

With so few resources and so much outside domination, Nevada has moved fitfully toward an independent political character. So short is the state's history that not until 1932 was a Nevada-born man (Pat McCarran) sent to the U.S. Senate. For generations, Nevada politics were dominated by the desire for economic development. Since the federal government owns 86.4 percent of the state's land area, Nevada's relations with Washington were always a key element. Over the years, Nevada senators used their seniority and clout to develop a host of federal policies that helped Nevada interests: land management for the benefit of grazing and mining interests, water projects to allow the desert to blossom into cities, federal defense programs that brought Nevada a big payroll, and nuclear research that resulted in detonations at the Nevada Test Site, some 75 miles northwest of Las Vegas. Nevadans in Washington also opposed federal investigations in the gambling industry and, whenever necessary, campaigned to keep up the silver content of coins.

Not suprisingly, Nevada gambling and politics are interwined, the former investing heavily in the latter. A Justice Department Strike Force closed in during the early '80s and claimed a prominent political victim: Senator Howard Cannon. Teamsters President Roy Williams and four associates were indicted on charges of conspiring to bribe Cannon, then Senate Commerce Committee chairman, with a piece of cut-rate Las Vegas real estate in return for thwarting a trucking deregulation bill. Cannon himself was not indicted but fell victim, after a quarter century in the Senate, to an out-of-the-blue Republican challenger, Jacob (Chic) Hecht. Williams and his cohorts were convicted.

In 1979, Nevada became the leader among Western states in the "Sagebrush Rebellion," which showed that the old ownership-largesse relationship with Washington had broken down. The Nevada legislature passed, and Republican Governor Robert List signed, a measure declaring state sovereignty over 49 million acres of Nevada territory owned by the federal Bureau of Land Management (BLM). The issue could not be decided without court action, which threatened to be lengthy, but the bill struck a chord in 13 other Western states with heavy federal land ownership; like-minded legislators throughout the West introduced similar bills and formed their own organization. What had happened? As the environmental movement gained power in the 1970s, federal laws were changed, and the BLM and other government land agencies broadened federal land policies to take into consideration issues such as rehabilitation of rangelands, recreation needs, and wilderness designation. Ranchers and miners, used to the BLM as "their" agency—environmentalists called it the *Bureau of Livestock and Mining*—were offended and perhaps economically threatened when they received orders to cut down on the size of herds grazing on federal property and to restrict drilling for minerals. The Nevada legislators saw Eastern environmental extremist bureaucrats running roughshod over the state's livelihood. "It's impossible for a landlord who's 3,000 miles away to manage" Western lands, Nevada legislator Dean A. Rhoads, president of the rebellious legislators' group, told us. But others noted that Westerners had dominated the congressional committees that crafted the new laws. The real conflict, in many ways, was between the Old West of ranchers and miners and the New West of urban-based people with a stake in keeping public lands open and unspoiled for hunting, fishing, and hiking. Arizona's Governor Bruce Babbitt charged that the Sagebrush Rebellion was a "landgrab in thin disguise." The states would never be able to manage so much land, Babbitt said, and would sell it off to ranchers who would overgraze it and restrict access for hunters, fishermen, and sportsmen. But even Babbitt agreed that the Western states had suffered from too little state sovereignty over these large federal holdings. The pro-development policies of President Reagan's Interior Secretary James Watt took some of the sting out of the Sagebrush Rebellion, but the legislators promised to press their cause.

Nevadans demonstrated their independence once again in 1981 when virtually every interest group in the state except the chamber of commerce and real estate speculators opposed basing the MX missile system on Nevada's vast open stretches. The system, as approved by President Carter in 1979, would have designated the Great Basin of Nevada and Utah as the locale of 200 intercontinental ballistic missiles—to be moved continually over tracks connecting 4,600 "shelters" in a "shell game" that was supposed to keep the Soviets guessing on where to aim their nuclear warheads.

In the words of Air Force Brigadier General Guy Hecker, the program would have been "man's largest project, larger than the Great Wall, larger than the Pyramids, larger than the Alaska pipeline, or the Panama Canal." But so massive and fearsome were the proportions of the MX that it galvanized an extraordinary coalition in opposition—from cattlemen to environmentalists, from the Mormon Church to American Indians to taxpayer groups.

The Sagebrush Rebellion and MX symbolized a scrappy defense of self-interests at once close to old Nevada politics and new in the alliances formed. Dean Rhoads told us that for too long Nevada has been "America's dumping ground." Nor was the state making out on federal aid as well as some of its neighbors; a *National Journal* survey study showed it alone among the Mountain States in sending more money to Washington than it gets back. Nevada also had a memorably sad experience as a result of the serious health problems that came in the wake of federal nuclear testing. Perhaps by the early 1980s Nevada had finally reached a critical mass of population and affluence that enabled it to say no to at least some terrible plans—even if they meant growth. National recessions were affecting Nevada politics, too. In 1982, caught in a recessionary gale that turned a state budget surplus turn into a deficit and set off a nasty tax wrangle, List became the first incumbent governor ousted by Nevada voters in 56 years.

Throughout the MX debate, one Nevada political tradition remained true to form: the importance of a strong personality. It fell to U.S. Senator Paul Laxalt, a conservative, pro-defense Republican, to convince President Reagan not to build the MX system in Nevada and neighboring Utah, where opposition was even stronger. That Laxalt succeeded so totally should perhaps have been no surprise. He and Reagan had first met during the Goldwater presidential campaign of 1964 and become personal friends when they were governors of Nevada and California, respectively. Laxalt was chairman of Reagan's successful 1980 campaign for the White House and subsequently developed a distinct role as unofficial liaison between Capitol Hill and the Reagan White House.

Laxalt's politics are so conservative that even the reserved *Congressional Quarterly* said, "it is probably fair to call Laxalt an ideologue." He opposed busing, abortion, gun control, government regulation, and high taxation. He favored the death penalty, higher defense spending, and a maximum of individual and corporate freedom. Laxalt did exhibit a populist strain, however, expressing concern that large corporations were too dependent on federal regulation.

One of the curiosities about Laxalt was how a senator from a state where gambling and prostitution flourish could become a strong backer of the Family Protection Act, legislation seeking to restore "traditional morality" in America. The bill's 31 provisions ran the gamut from reestablishing prayer in the public schools to forbidding use of federal funds to promote homosexual or feminist values or even "the intermingling of the sexes in [school] sports activities."

How could Laxalt support such legislation when as governor he had once said of Nevada's prostitution—"You're never going to eliminate the girls. It's a very old profession and a very lucrative one in Vegas"? Could there be inconsistency, even hypocrisy? Perhaps, but we wouldn't be too harsh. Beneath its go-go atmosphere, Nevada is really very old-fashioned. Its product may be sin, but not any new-fangled, deviationist form of behavior. What Nevada offers is age-old, garden-variety sin.

NEW MEXICO

The Gentle Culture?

BEFORE JAMESTOWN OR PLYMOUTH ROCK, while most of what is today the United States slumbered through its last age of innocence, Spanish conquistadores pushed deep into New Mexico and mingled their blood with the native Indian to form what is romantically called La Raza, the New Breed, the Cosmic Race. And they began a line of governors that runs continuously —under four flags—from 1595 to the present day.

Nowhere on the American continent does history seem so deep or so immediate. Santa Fe became New Mexico's capital in 1609 or 1610 (the history books differ); its Palace of the Governors is the oldest public building in the United States. In the early 17th century, the ravages of the Inquisition were felt here. The Pueblos, whose own history goes back hundreds of years before the Spanish, drove their European masters out in 1680, a situation reversed by a bloodless Hispanic reconquest a dozen years later. With Mexico's independence in 1821, New Mexico became one of her provinces; by warfare, the United States won the territory as its own in 1846. During the Civil War, the Confederate flag even flew briefly over Santa Fe. Finally, in 1912, New Mexico achieved statehood, a young 47th among the 50 we now have.

New Mexico's population was almost entirely Indian and Hispanic until the 1880s, when Anglo-Saxon ranchers and merchants began to move in. Starting around the turn of the century the native ethnic base was further diluted by the arrival of large numbers of Texans in eastern New Mexico; the next decades also brought many migrants attracted by the dry, clean air as a way to solve their tubercular and other health problems. In the 1920s and 1930s, the brooding mountains and surrealistic timelessness of Santa Fe and Taos attracted the wealthy Mabel Dodge Luhan, writer D.H. Lawrence, and artist Georgia O'Keefe, whose celebrity led to New Mexico's international reputation as a place of magical beauty and artistic inspiration.*

Up to World War II, however, the dominant image New Mexico offered the world was still that of a sleepy land of *mañana* and *poco tiempo*. Then, at first secretly, came the great change. From the laboratories at Los Alamos emerged the first atomic bomb, to be detonated in the early morning hours

---

*In the early 1980s, Miss O'Keefe was still living her quite hermetic existence in an adobe house on a high bluff overlooking Chama River Valley at Abiquiu, where all her neighbors are Indian or Hispanic. She has been spending her summers in the New Mexico desert since 1929 and has lived there year-round since the 1940s, producing paintings that reflect a kind of mystic communion with the harsh desert landscape.

of July 16, 1945, on the desert north of Alamogordo. Perfecting, building, and storing nuclear weapons and working on other atomic research, a whole civilization of scientists and technicians was transplanted onto New Mexican soil. The atomic economy was only the beginning of an Anglo population influx that has lasted to this day. Hundreds of millions of dollars for defense and space research projects, much of it at Sandia Laboratories in Albuquerque, brought more scientists, servicemen, and their families. In the 1970s, as America's domestic natural resources rose in value, multinational energy companies increased their exploitation of New Mexico's vast stores of uranium, coal and gas, copper, and potash. (New Mexico produces nearly half the nation's output of uranium and is considered the uranium "capital" of the world.)

As Americans became more footloose, New Mexico's climate and *simpatico* atmosphere made it one of *the* destinations. In the summer of 1967, when such urban meccas as Haight Ashbury, the East Village, and Sunset Strip turned mean, Taos, Santa Fe, and Española became the targets for settlement by rural hippies. The young dropouts were followed in much greater numbers by retirees, the richest settling in Santa Fe, the more middle class in southern towns such as Carlsbad, Roswell, Las Cruces, Albuquerque, and Truth or Consequences (which took the name of the 1950s TV show to gain an identity). Eventually, electronic companies, with some prodding from state and local governments, began to recognize the twin labor advantages of locating plants in Albuquerque: management talent in retired military men and young engineers and cheap assembly plant workers in young Hispanics, mostly women, willing to work for low wages.

The cumulative impact of growth was to increase New Mexico's population by a startling 28.1 percent during the 1970s alone. So heavy had the Anglo influx been that the count of New Mexicans with Spanish surnames was just 37 percent of a total 1980 population of 1,302,894—down from 45 percent in a population of only 531,818 in 1940. Yet even in 1980, if one totaled the Spanish population with the Indian (8 percent) and black, one came up with 47 percent —the largest minority population in any of the 50 states. It is this colorful ethnic mix, coupled with the fast pace of modern development, that has made New Mexico one of the most politically fascinating of America's small population states in our times. (New Mexico ranked only 37th nationally in 1980, despite its growth.) The overwhelming, enduring question is how the political and economic interests of the Hispanics, the Indians, and the varied elements of the Anglo majority mesh and clash.

For years starting with the New Deal, New Mexico was classified as a normally "safe" Democratic state. All that changed during the '60s and '70s as the Anglo population expanded and the national Democratic party took on strong social liberal hues. New Mexico politics became increasingly Republican, and in *Congressional Quarterly*'s apt description, "increasingly 'Anglocized.'" The state legislature remained in Democratic control, but in the late '70s conservative Democratic ranchers in the state House formed an alliance with Republicans, which effectively terminated liberal Democratic statehouse rule. When the Republicans achieved a U.S. Senate majority in 1981, New Mexico's Republican Senator Pete Domenici gained a crucial position of power in Washington but employed it not in the familiar tradition of bringing home the bacon to his impoverished state, but rather to control federal spending as chairman of the Senate Budget Committee. Earlier, in 1976, New Mexico voters had unseated Senator Joseph Montoya, a "patron" who had secured millions in federal aid for the state. Montoya's replacement: astronaut Harrison Schmitt, who audaciously questioned just how Montoya had become a millionaire while in the Senate—an issue New Mexicans had previously considered secondary to Montoya's adeptness in delivering federal aid.

But it proved premature to decree a Republican era in the state. While electing Republicans to Congress, New Mexico through the '70s elected such Democratic governors as Jerry Apodaca and Bruce King. This was one of the few Rocky Mountain States to get along without a right-to-work law. (The realigned legislature passed one in 1980, but Gov. King was there to veto it.) And by 1982, the New Mexico Democratic party had moved from giving out gas money to potential voters on election day to computerized get-out-the-vote-drives. The results were stunning. Schmitt lost his Senate seat to Attorney General Jeff Bingaman, a moderate Harvard and Stanford Law School graduate. Former Attorney General Toney Anaya, a Hispanic known for his commitment to crime-fighting and environmental and consumer causes, was elected governor, and enough liberal Democrats were elected to the legislature to oust the ruling conservative coalition. Republican incumbents Manuel Lujan and Joe Skeen kept their U.S. House seats, but a new northern New Mexico district was won by Democrat Bill Richardson, a Hispanic from his mother's heritage and former Washington foreign relations adviser.

It was easy to see why New Mexico was still fertile territory for Democrats willing to challenge the free enterprise establishment. There remained gross economic inequalities in New Mexico. For while the economic boom had placed the state seventh nationally in per capita income growth during the '70s, actual income was still only 38th nationally, well below the other Rocky Mountain States. And what wealth there was in New Mexico was poorly distributed. Poverty remained rampant among Hispanics in northern New Mexico, who continued to vote Democratic in the hope of social and economic reform. Santa Fe continued to be a high-voting mecca for liberal, even radical intellectuals and bureaucrats. Before the 1982 elections, Paul Wieck, the *Albuquerque Journal*'s veteran Washington correspondent, noted that grassroots New Mexico politics remained overwhelmingly Democratic. The Republican party, Wieck wrote, still lacked a base of loyal support among wage earners, students or run-of-the-mill blue-collar workers. Only businessmen (large and small) appeared irrecoverably Republican, he noted. One top Republican strategist even admitted to Wieck that "Republicans make the mistake of living and breathing in the business community."

New Mexico's volatile Anglo immigrants tend toward fiscal conservatism, but they seem to love to split their tickets. They can easily be aroused on such environmental issues as uranium development. (Thousands of New Mexicans, for instance, joined organizations opposed to dumping nuclear wastes in the southeastern part of the state.)

New Mexicans' state government was long reputed to be high-tax, high-corruption, lobby-ridden, and inefficient. Much of that has now changed. Civil service has replaced the worst of the old spoils system. Today state employees are no longer forced to give a percentage of their salaries to the party in power. Especially for such a small state, the legislature seems to be highly professionally staffed—even though powerful lobbies, such as out-of-state energy companies, seem to wield unusual influence with legislators. As an example, after the Three Mile Island accident in Pennsylvania plunged the nuclear power industry into the doldrums, the legislature reduced the severance tax on uranium. But the tax cut did not keep companies from closing down operations, and in retrospect the cut could only be viewed as a gift to a favored industry. In the early 1980s, mineral taxes accounted for an astounding 23 percent of state tax revenues, however, and have made New Mexico permanently wealthy. Each year some of the money is placed in permanent endowments and only the interest may be spent. These funds totaled $693 million by 1983. New Mexico is one of the most creative states in using its mineral-generated wealth to stimulate the state economy, backing municipal bonds and depositing money in banks in the state, for example. Income taxes are low, but the state's tax structure is not particularly progressive since it places heavy reliance on the sales tax.

Distributing water rights is the most crucial of all state policy decisions. Of all 50 states, none has as small a portion of its land surface in lakes and rivers as New Mexico: a minuscule .002 percent. Farming, mining, and growing cities all compete for the scarce resource. Into the 1980s, New Mexico's water had been divided up for over 25 years by one man, Stephen E. Reynolds, the state engineer. Reynolds' job was technically a political appointment, but his knowledge of New Mexico water law and his political connections were so strong that no governor dared replace him. Most of the Anglo power structure respected Reynolds—though they might disagree with him on specific projects—but the environmentalists in the state considered his approaches out of date, and Hispanic farmers with small holdings long complained that the conservation districts he pushed led only to such high maintenance expenses that they lost their lands in the name of a "progress" that translates into agribusiness, tourism, retiree housing, and Anglo control.

The overarching question for New Mexico state government in the last years of the 20th century may well be its competence—given the less-than-ideal governmental structure handed down from earlier times—to handle such burning questions as population growth, development, and the division of tax burdens. An example of structural problems is that the governor not only has severely limited powers but cannot serve consecutive terms—an invitation to weak leadership and constantly shifting policy directions. Moreover, actual delivery of services to the people is jeopardized by a creaky form of board- and special-commission government easily manipulated by lobbies.

Of Race and Character

Beautiful scenery and the arts aside, New Mexico is best known across the nation for racial liberalism, sophistication, and respect for different cultures, including the primitive. Is that reputation deserved? An answer must begin with an understanding of how New Mexicans view themselves. Six population groups appear significant: Spanish-American, Pueblo Indian, Navajo Indian, Mormon, Texan, and Anglo. For the most part, however, New Mexicans use "Anglo" as a catch-all encompassing Anglo-Saxons, Jews, Chinese, or anybody else without some native New Mexican (Indian or Spanish) blood. The terms for persons of Spanish origin are a story in themselves. The descendants of the old land-grant families that ruled New Mexico before the 1880s have preferred either Spanish-American or Hispanic and have detested the term Mexican-American, since it connotes lower-class status and coming from Mexico, which is factually incorrect. Since American ethnic groups achieved new levels of consciousness in the 1960s, some younger Hispanics have called themselves Chicanos. To make this even more confusing, it's important to remember that "of Spanish origin" is not a racial classification; Hispanics may be Caucasian, Indian, even black (though rarely in New Mexico), or some combination thereof. When the 1980 Census takers asked New Mexicans to "self identify," 37 percent said they were of Spanish origin, while 75 percent—both Anglos and Hispanics—said they were white.

New Mexicans do see themselves as more tolerant, less self-aggrandizing than their Texan or Arizonan neighbors, and they have a strong tradition of civil liberties written into their state constitution. Adopted in 1910, it declares in no uncertain terms that "The right of any citizen of the state to vote, hold office, or sit upon juries shall never be restricted, abridged or impaired, on account of religion, race, language or color, inability to speak, read or write the English or Spanish language." Does Hispanic representation in government match that ideal? Studies have indicated that New Mexico has elected more Hispanics to the U.S. Senate, House, governorship, legislative and local offices than virtually any other state. (An exception: Hispanics have received few judgeships.) The downside, of course, is that New Mexico's progressive claims stop abruptly when it comes to economics and distribution of wealth.

Spanish-speaking New Mexicans are a proud, dignified people, accustomed to roles of leadership. The San Antonio-based Southwest Voter Registration and Education Project found in 1982 that registered Hispanics in New Mexico voted in the same percentages as Anglos, the only state in which that was true. When forced to leave the state to find jobs, they have often become prominent Hispanic leaders, carrying with them a political poise and self-confidence so notably lacking among large portions of Mexican-Americans. For instance, California's first Hispanic congressman, Ed Roybal, is a native of New Mexico. The New Mexicans may be compared with West Indian blacks, a people possessed of the similar chance to develop leadership skills, which allowed them to rise rapidly to the ranks of American leadership.

On Feb. 2, 1980, New Mexico's reputation as a decent and humane state and a gentle culture was severely damaged by a riot at the penitentiary near Santa Fe. Fourteen guards were held hostage, seven of them beaten, while hundreds of prisoners looted and burned the institution. Thirty-three inmates were killed by fellow prisoners in the most gruesome ways possible, including beheadings, and as many as 200 were severely beaten and raped. More people died during the rioting than in any other prison riot in U.S. history. No one has ever ascertained quite what caused the prisoners to reach the levels of brutality that they exhibited, but several analyses have shown that the riot was spawned by frustration. At the time, the pen was housing 1,157 male inmates in space that a federal court had ruled should house only 900 men. Nearly 400 prisoners were idle. The guard force consisted mostly of recent high school graduates, paid little and given scarcely any training. But the most damning evidence about the "Land of Enchantment" came in the public and political reaction after the riot. At Governor King's urging, the state legislature passed a $107 million prison construction package. The plan improved the prison industries program, but legislators refused to pay for a community corrections program, which would have placed the less serious offenders outside the prison walls and provided counseling. Nor did the state revise its lengthy sentences, which are said to make prisoners so desperate and bitter that they see no reason not to riot. We visited the pen a year and a half after the riot and found the sleeping facilities repaired and the medical facilities modernized. But we could not help but focus on the construction of many new mesh fences *inside* the prison to keep the men from moving too far should they riot again. Continued stabbings and murders of prisoners and guards may have justified the new fences, of course. But one had to wonder: what hope was there that these convicts would receive any psychological aid or job training to help them avoid a quick relapse into crime when they were freed—as almost all of them would be in time? Michael Serrill, editor of *Corrections*, the magazine on prisons, told us, "There is no indigenous prison reform movement in New Mexico." The failure of both the Hispanic or Anglo peoples of the state to respond more adequately to the prison situation displayed a blindness and insensitivity wholly inconsonant with New Mexico's treasured self-image.

Land of Enchantment

Few state nicknames are more aptly chosen than New Mexico's "Land of Enchantment." True, much of the landscape is harsh, unredeemed desert, and across the eastern reaches there are endless miles where the wind sweeps unchecked across the bunch grass. But by the same token, there are deep, picturesque canyons and vividly hued mesas, buttes, and rock terraces. Their reds and yellows, when the sun strikes them in favorable perspectives, are otherworldly and as hauntingly beautiful as any scene on the North American continent. And at night, in John Gunther's words, there is "the purple desert flowing endlessly under lonely stars."

In the north, the mountains ascend to heights of more than 13,000 feet, yet few pass timberline or reach the level of eternal snow. These are the southernmost of the Rockies, somehow softer and mellower than their younger, more jagged neighbors to the north. This is Rio Grande Valley country, named in honor of that shallow but famous river, so thoroughly damned up and diverted for agriculture that its flow is no more than waist-high most of the year. The Rio Grande runs centrally on a north-south course from the Colorado River, in the north, to Mexico, in the south.

In huge, rural Rio Arriba County, ranging northwesterly from a few miles north of Santa Fe to the Colorado border, New Mexico life continues much as it was in the early days of statehood and even before. Anthropologists observe that the area's peculiar political-economic system developed out of the isolation from centers of civilization in Spain and New Mexico. The village agricultural economy was based on large family groups; devout Catholicism was the core of all institutional activity; and politics was controlled by a *patron*, a large landowner or person of prestige and sense of obligation who had ties to the larger world. These family and political alliances, rather than strict numerical voting, dictated choices at the polls. It was this unique brand of rural machine politics that was responsible for the delightful story of the night when the Associated Press, trying to smoke out returns from Spanish-American precincts in the mountainous north, set up special election wires. "How many votes you got up there?" an AP reporter asked at one point. Back came the reply, in a Spanish accent: "How many you need?"

Old-fashioned vote stealing seems to be on the decline since the advent of voting machines. But by the early 1980s Rio Arriba (pop. 29,282) had been controlled for over 25 years by one *patron*, Emilio Naranjo, chairman of the county Democratic party, county manager, member of the state senate, and former sheriff. On election days, Naranjo delivered enough votes to tip a close statewide race for the Democrats. That he could still deliver so reliably was mute testimony to the ongoing poverty of Rio Arriba, a place where a patronage job, money to buy food, or help from a deputy sheriff to start a car to get to work on a cold winter morning could make the difference between destitution and survival. Naranjo's people lived worlds apart from some of the Spanish-Americans at the upper echelons of New Mexico life.

In their poverty, Rio Arribans continue to nurse bitter resentments about the fashion in which the old "Santa Fe Ring" of Anglo and upper-class Hispanic politicians succeeded in taking from them—by taxation, fraud, theft, and in some cases legal purchase—the vast land grants made by the Spanish crown in colonial times and guaranteed by the Treaty of Guadalupe Hidalgo at the end of the Mexican-American War. Land disputes often lead to violence in northern New Mexico. In 1967, Reies Lopez Tijerina, a Texan native of Mexican extraction and onetime Pentecostal minister, led poor Hispanic peasants to take physical claim to part of the Carson National Forest and a year later raided the Rio Arriba county courthouse. Tijerina later went to federal prison, but his radicalism inspired continuing Hispanic activism on land issues.

Traveling southward, we come to the Rio Grande area most celebrated and most visited; stretching from Taos down to Albuquerque in center state, a valley floor some 40 miles wide and 160 miles long guarded by the Sangre de Cristo Mountains on the east, the Jemez on the west, and the Sandia Peaks near Albuquerque on the south. The early Spanish chose well in locating their capital at Santa Fe—within the valley of the Rio Grande, but high, northerly, and on a 6,947 foot plateau much cooler and less arid than the valley's lower reaches. Santa Fe's delightfully unplanned narrow, winding streets, high walls shielding Spanish gardens, and ancient adobe buildings of a terra cotta tone, seem part and parcel of the natural landscape. The architectural integrity is jealously guarded by a group known as the Old Santa Fe Association, which started in 1926; historic preservation is such an old cause in Santa Fe that its original supporters opposed the incursion of *Victorian* architecture.

The culture, the air, the mountains all continue to draw an exceptionally cosmopolitan assemblage of people to Santa Fe. Novelist John Nichols wrote a trilogy capturing the spirit and conflicts of late 20th-century New Mexico. Santa Fe is home to many artists' studios, but more importantly is the sales center for artists throughout the Southwest. The true cultural gem of the city is its opera. Set in dramatic mountain terrain ten miles north of the city, the Santa Fe Opera Company was virtually the singlehanded creation of one man, general director John Crosby, a New Yorker who lived part of the year in Santa Fe. Santa Fe also sponsors a music festival, and in the summer of 1981 a professional theater finally opened, prompting *Time* to describe Santa Fe as the "Salzburg of the Southwest." The opera has given many singers an early career break, and the theater offered three talented young men the chance to develop their own theater. We attended an opening night at the theater and were told that the Santa Fe name is so magical that the theater's young founders had been able to stage galas in New York and San Francisco to raise funds to start it. Yet only a couple of miles from the theater we saw Hispanics living in conditions of poor nutrition and sanitation reminiscent of Old Mexico and even West Africa.

Santa Fe County grew 37.6 percent in the 1970s, to a population of 75,360, causing many residents to worry that even more drastic population growth and environmental problems might be coming. Physically, there did seem to be some de facto protection in Santa Fe's growth controls, water shortage, and high costs—factors suggesting that at least the old city would not be altered too drastically. (So strong, indeed, is the tradition that even subdivisions outside the historic district are often built in adobe style.) The mix of people who have given Santa Fe and nearby Taos their special character could more easily be altered, however. Until the recent past, Santa Fe's retirees tended to be more intellectual and active than the aging sun-seekers in Florida and Arizona; as George Chieger, a retired auto executive from Detroit, told us, he and his wife chose Santa Fe for its four seasons. But Santa Fe is attracting more and more fabulously wealthy people, movie stars, and foreigners seeking a safe haven for their money. This big-moneyed atmosphere makes it tougher and tougher for artists and other talented young people to survive in Santa

Fe. So far, they continue to come, regarding the Santa Fe of our time, like the Paris of the 1920s, as a Moveable Feast.

Up the valley from Santa Fe lies the town of Taos (pop. 3,369), whose valley view D.H. Lawrence called the most beautiful in the world. Taos has been an art colony since the turn of the century and the home of the Pueblo Indians for many centuries. The multistoried Taos Pueblo, surviving from the golden age of Pueblo culture some 800 to 1,000 years ago, is world renowned. It is the northernmost of 18 Indian pueblos (villages) spread down the length of the Rio Grande Valley, their ancestral settlements and way of life as close to the primitive as one will find among any American Indians today.

Set in the Sangre de Cristo Mountains, some 25 miles east of Taos, is Blue Lake, part of the 48,000-acre watershed where the Taos Pueblo Indians have been in residence since the 14th century; they consider it the source of all life. The federal government took control of this land in 1906 to be part of the Carson National Forest, but after a long battle Congress returned the watershed to them in perpetuity. Most of the Pueblos live on in grinding poverty, though some groups have collective wealth from uranium or other minerals. Most of the older Pueblos have remained so conservative that they refused to participate in the white man's elections. The young people are encouraged to follow the old ways, but by the 1970s, the tradition had reportedly broken to the point that a majority of upcoming generations were seeking a life and work in the outside world.

Forty-five miles west and north of Santa Fe in the Jemez Mountains sits the atomic city of Los Alamos, in World War II a forbidden enclave behind a 12-foot barbed-wire fence, but now something of a sad company town of 11,000 people associated with a national laboratory whose principal mission has come and gone.

Albuquerque is New Mexico's only really metropolitan city. It was founded in 1706 and named after the Duke of Albuquerque, Viceroy of Spain. In the first 234 years of its history, the city grew to 35,499 souls; in the next 40 years (from 1940 to 1980), the metropolitan area added more than *ten times* that amount, reaching a new total of 331,767 in the city and another 122,737 in the outlying areas. The city is heavily dependent on federally stimulated nuclear and space contracts. But the electronics industry, the energy boom, and footloose Social Security recipients appear to be making the economic base more independent. Albuquerque has also benefited indirectly from the improved education in rural New Mexico. This is so, noted Alex Mercure, an erstwhile antipoverty worker who later became an assistant secretary of agriculture under President Carter and state director of economic development under Governor Anaya, because so many young New Mexicans have been forced to look there for jobs. The Albuquerque metropolitan area is now home to more than one-third of New Mexico's population, making it the political power center of the state. But Albuquerque lacks the political distinctiveness of the rest of the state, and as Mercure notes, "votes like the rest of the nation."

Sadly, we must report that although much of the old Spanish town has been retained, the newer sections of Albuquerque lack any architectural distinction. The city, indeed, echoes the familiar urban tale: decaying downtown and inner-city neighborhoods, urban renewal (and removal), the heart of retail activity moving to shopping centers (one called Winrock, developed by Winthrop Rockefeller), housing sprawl, and finally automobile-induced air pollution. With Santa Fe's marvelous example of distinction through preservation so nearby, Albuquerque's unappealing sprawl poses a troubling national question: Can the best of the old ways of urban life be retained only in small enclaves closely watched by the wealthy? Is there no way to encourage foresight and planning for distinction in dynamic cities?

The only latter-day break from Albuquerque's go-go spirit of sprawl growth was the election, for one four-year term as mayor, of David Rusk, son of former Secretary of State Dean Rusk. Rusk came to Albuquerque as a career Labor Department bureaucrat and tried to attack Albuquerque's destructive growth patterns with an activist brand of mayoral politics almost unknown in the West. Rusk favored rebuilding the old downtown, while developers wanted the city's capital improvement program to emphasize new development on the fringe. To the amazement of Albuquerque's establishment, he cordoned off six blocks of decaying downtown on Saturday nights and set up ethnic fairs—and tens of thousands came. Rusk got high marks for innovation, even from his conservative city council. But he was always under suspicion of using Albuquerque to run for higher office and was soundly defeated for reelection in 1981.

Albuquerque's most significant contribution to urban America may well be a program called Crimestoppers. Crimes are reenacted on the television news, and rewards are given to those who provide the tips that lead to indictments or arrest. Operating closely with the police department, but controlled by a citizen board, Crimestoppers solved 1,450 felony cases between 1976 and 1981. Contrary to what television crime drama would have you believe, says founder-policeman Greg MacAlesee, most felonies are solved not through investigations, but from information supplied by neighbors and witnesses. Crimestoppers has spread in various forms to over 80 cities.

South of Albuquerque, one speaks of the Lower Valley of the Rio Grande, or Rio Abajo; here the river courses into hotter and lower territory, near the region the Spanish called Jornada del Muerto (Journey of Death), the territory where, fittingly, the first atomic bomb was detonated. Finishing its course through New Mexico, the Rio Grande veers eastward and forms the Texas border with Mexico.

While most of New Mexico's people, life, and history have always been along the central north-south strip of the Rio Grande, there are other distinct regions both in the east and west. In northwestern New Mexico one discovers the bleak Four Corners territory left to the Navajos on their reservation atop the Colorado Plateau. Nearby lies the fertile valley of the San Juan, celebrated for apples, peaches, and oil. In the lands south of the Navajo Reservation and west of the Rio Grande rise the gaunt Mexican Highlands, the locale of ghost mining towns and modern-day underground riches. Finally, one comes on the spacious level country of "Little Texas," which occupies most of eastern New Mexico. The geography and spirit are of the Great Plains, as in the neighboring sections of Texas and Oklahoma. Its conservative ranchers were equally Baptist and Democratic for many years, but they have become disenchanted with federal "interference" in land matters. Many were backers of the Sagebrush Rebellion of the early 1980s, and as they also gained oil wealth moved increasingly to the Republican column. Aside from wheat and cattle, Little Texas is heavy with oil rigs. Near Roswell one finds the ranch of Robert O. Anderson, chairman of the Atlantic Richfield Company, a humanitarian among corporate leaders and New Mexico's richest and most powerful resident. Even on the Plains, New Mexico offers some enchantment: the limestone cave formations at Carlsbad are so spectacular they were declared a national park.

Land of the Navajo

It was not much more than a century ago that the federal government finally despaired of making everyday frugal farmers out of the wild and adventurous Navajo Indians whom it had corralled during Civil War years and marched to detention in eastern New Mexico. These were the Dineh, the People, the Navajo; the archeologists tell us they are descended directly from nomads who migrated to North America across the Bering Strait when it was a land bridge. Their language group is called Athabascan, like the Indians of Alaska. Probably not too long before the Spaniards arrived, the People had migrated southward to the starkly beautiful desert land of what is now known as the Southwest's Four Corners area. From the Spanish they learned the use of horses and how to raise sheep and goats. And so, for centuries, they lived in isolated mud huts (called hogans), many miles from the next neighbor, each family carving out a large stretch of the high, arid land to graze its sheep and, so enemies charged, stealing from the Spanish and the Pueblos.

The government sought to change this lifestyle when it became tired of the Navajos' freewheeling raids, slave business, and theft of horses by the hundreds. An 1864-military expedition under the command of Kit Carson slaughtered all the Navajo sheep, destroyed their fields, and herded the Navajo families on a bitterly remembered "Long Walk" to Bosque Redondo in eastern New Mexico, where a four-year experiment in "civilizing" failed miserably. The captivity did, however, force the Navajos to form a central tribal council and sign a peace treaty that they have never broken. Under the pact, several thousand were allowed to return, with a few sheep and goats, to the high desert country of the Four Corners region, a land so gaunt and inhospitable that no white man could then dream of its being put to productive use.

The story of what then happened is not without irony. Instead of dying off, as many in Washington privately hoped, the Navajo multiplied and multiplied from the band of a few thousand that returned to Four Corners in 1868; today they number 160,000 and continue to grow in population.

As for the land no one wanted, it contains today some of the world's most scenic attractions and a fabulous concentration of national parks and monuments, either entirely enclosed or on its borders: Lake Powell and the Grand Canyon of the Colorado, Monument Valley, Mesa Verde National Park, the Petrified Forest, and many others. In sheer land bulk holding, the Navajo are as fortunate as one could hope for: their reservation, some 23,500 square miles in area, encompassing parts of Arizona, New Mexico, and Utah, is as large as the states of Massachusetts, Connecticut, and New Hampshire combined.

The stern red-rock land was not as worthless as the American government thought, for gas and oil, coal and uranium have brought the Navajos millions of dollars in royalties, and deposits worth billions more remain in the ground. Neither the mineral royalties nor the federal government's payments to tribes and individuals have been invested in long-term projects, however, and the Navajos have continued to live in conditions as appalling as any on the continent. Infant mortality, tuberculosis, hepatitis, and deaths associated with unsanitary conditions have all been far above the national average. A not untypical home is a wretched hovel located beside an unsightly drainage ditch, an abandoned and gutted automobile hulk in front.

Until the last two decades, the Navajos' plight was little known because of their complete isolation, like a separate, remote, inaccessible country within U.S. borders. Earnest change began with World War II, when so many Navajo youth went off to war. After the war, the population increased so rapidly that available grazing land was not enough to support the Navajo, and Congress passed a program for schools, hospitals, roads, and irrigation facilities. By the 1980s only some 5 percent of the Navajo made their living from sheep-grazing. The rest had turned to service jobs, manufacturing, irrigated farming, tourism—and the jobless rolls. The Tribal Council has recruited many businesses, a few of which have flourished and many of which have failed.

Renewed interest in the Navajos' mineral wealth has raised both new hopes that conditions might permanently be improved and intense controversy over whether this development could be the key to true self-determination and self-sufficiency or finally destroy both Navajo land and culture. The chief promoter of full exploration of Navajo-owned minerals and industrialization of the reservation was Peter MacDonald, elected as tribal chairman from 1970 to 1982. MacDonald succeeded as no other tribal chairman in the country in gaining control over tribal resources and becoming a politician and businessman in the mainstream American sense. After gaining a college education and working as an electrical engineer for Hughes Aircraft in California, he returned to the reservation in 1963 to become head of the Great Society–funded Office of Navajo Economic Opportunity. MacDonald's distribution of federal antipoverty money reached nearly every poor family on the reservation and created his political base. In many speeches, MacDonald also denounced the white man, the Bureau of Indian Affairs, and the energy companies. He started the Council of Energy Resource Tribes, an OPEC-like organization pledged to help Indians develop their energy resources and receive a high price.

For a time many people, including members of other Indian tribes, believed that MacDonald was the best Indian leader in modern times—the one man who had a plan to achieve self-determination and handle the white world's business dealings. But *Mother Jones* magazine, one of the few publications that regularly covers Indian affairs, albeit from a leftist perspective, charged in 1982 after several months of research that "MacDonald's brand of development has created a classic Third World colony look on the reservation: visible signs of wealth and status in bureaucratic Window Rock, Ariz., surrounded by a sea of rural poverty and helplessness." While Navajo per capita income remained static at about $2,900 a year, MacDonald earned $55,000 per year and was charged with being "a dictator."

On election day 1982, the Navajos threw out MacDonald in favor of Peterson Zah, 45, who without a law degree had founded and successfully directed the reservation's legal aid program. Zah pledged to involve the tribal council and villages in important decisions, hire Navajos instead of the outside consultants and lawyers to whom MacDonald had paid millions of dollars, and develop the reservation's resources "with all due respect for Mother Earth."

Zah and the tribal council immediately began reviewing all the tribal energy leases. Zah seemed to be saying, however, that his first concern was not money but the tribe's self-reliance, indeed its very cultural survival. A journeyman carpenter, he had built two homes for his family and declared Navajo-built homes a better housing approach than factory-made house trailers. "I like the concept of building things. We have to build a strong Navajo nation," declared this new leader. His road toward self-reliance seemed sure to encounter the impatience of tribesmen who had become accustomed to handouts. Yet it seemed totally in accord with ancient Navajo tradition.

ARIZONA

Oasis Civilization

FOR 300 DAYS OF EACH YEAR, the sun beats down mercilessly on the shimmering desert. The landscape is interspersed with gaunt mountain peaks; the saguaro cacti hold up their arms; scattered mesquite strives for life. Along the desert floor the lizard, scorpion, tarantula, and Gila monster hold sway. Strange geological formations break the monotony of parched yellow sand; there are deep gorges, multicolored buttes and vistas, and in the state's northern reaches, cooler forests and the grand canyon of the Colorado. Repulsed by the harsh southern desert, where on summer days the temperature in the shade may soar to 120 degrees, a government surveyor reported to Congress in 1858: "The region is altogether valueless. After entering it, there is nothing to do but leave."

Yet paradoxically, in this "land where time stands still," a thriving oasis population has sprung into being. Today there are 2.7 million people in Arizona—more than four times as many as there were at the end of World War II and almost a million more than in 1970. Three-quarters of them now live in two great oases: Maricopa County (Phoenix), with 55 percent of the Arizona population, and Pima County (Tucson), with another 19.5 percent. Phoenix and Tucson each grew by more than 50 percent in the 1970s, but even more astounding is the number of people who moved to Phoenix: 540,607 in a single decade. Only the Texas go-go cities of Houston and Dallas–Ft. Worth attracted more people.

To approach Phoenix by air is to see in a glance both Arizona's growth and its typically late-20th-century lifestyle. Suddenly, in the midst of the rugged, brown desert terrain, great splotches of green appear. All around the city there are verdant squares of irrigated farmland. And then one sees mile after mile of grassy suburban sprawl—many of the lawns harboring swimming pools that blink like blue dots into the sky. Finally, in an unordered profusion along a single great palm-lined central "draw"—Central Avenue—are scores of sleek glass and concrete high-rise buildings, the commercial heart of what may be America's least-planned city.

Americans have come to the oases on the desert first for the good life of year-round sun, and second for jobs. From a largely extractive economy (its big "C's" were once cattle, copper, cotton, climate, and citrus) Arizona has been transformed into a manufacturing state. The booming economy has also attracted a much less heralded wave of legal and illegal Mexican immigrants

726

fleeing their overpopulated, underdeveloped country in search of any kind of job at any wage level.

How can the desert sustain such life? The answers, as we shall see, are twofold: water (through one of the largest diversion and storage projects on the continent) and air conditioning. Before air conditioning arrived in the early 1950s, the scorching summer months used to send the wealthy scurrying to the mountains and leave the less fortunate stay-behinds to wrap themselves in wet sheets to survive the nights.

The population influx also transformed Arizona from a safe Democratic state to a predominantly Republican one. Beginning in the early 1950s the overwhelmingly white, middle-to-upper class, well-educated, high-income, confident, aggressive, individualistic Arizonan society led the way in creating a conservative, free enterprise Republicanism that has proven to be the model for political attitudes and voting patterns in other growing and diversifying Southern and Western states. In Arizona these Republicans have held a majority of powerful positions. The symbol and chief architect of such politics was, of course, U.S. Senator Barry Goldwater, who carried these Arizona themes to the national Republican party.

Before we proceed to the human history that led up to this extraordinary modern state, let us turn our eyes to natural Arizona, a landscape familiar to millions of Americans through that most handsome of state pictorial magazines, *Arizona Highways*. Of natural Arizona, Josef Muench, one of the magazine's most illustrious photographers, once wrote, "It is because in Arizona the arresting framework, the very skeleton of the earth, is exposed that the scenery is so compelling and meaningful. Its bone structure is superb."

On Arizona's northern roof lies the great expanse of the Colorado River Plateau, a high, rugged tableland gashed by huge canyons, the greatest of which was carved by the Colorado River itself. At the northeastern extremity lies the Four Corners juncture with Utah, Colorado and New Mexico, the only point in the Union where so many states touch each other. This is the land of the Navajos and the Hopi, of the Painted Desert, Petrified Forest, mysterious and remote Monument Valley, the gigantic Hoover and Glen Canyon dams, and finally Grand Canyon National Park, called by one of its first white visitors, John Wesley Powell, "the most sublime spectacle on earth." Tourists who take the time to hike down to the canyon floor experience the grand tableau of two billion years of exposed geologic history that the Colorado has laid bare. But even in this most breathtaking and spectacular natural phenomenon on the North American continent, there has been continual conflict between environmental values and the pressures of modern life. The electricity-producing Glen Canyon Dam, at the head of the canyon, is, from the environmentalist perspective, "the dam which never should have been built." Environmentalists charge both that it has altered the nature of the Colorado River and the ecology of the canyon and that further increases in the power generation of the dam could also increase the fluctuations in the river, making it more difficult for wildlife to survive and for river runners to enjoy themselves. The river runners themselves have become controversial as their numbers increased to 12,000 per year and they left garbage on the river's bank. Environmentalists have tried to get the motorboats, which carry 80 percent of the runners, banned.

Few regions of the continental U.S.A. are as remote from civilization as the Strip Country of Arizona, a northwestern triangle of some 8,500 square miles bounded by the Colorado River and Utah and Nevada borders. The scale of the harsh plateau, peaks, and gorges is so immense that man seems dwarfed here; in fact there are only some 2,000 souls in the entire region. In one little hamlet, Colorado City, the remoteness protects a substantial community of Mormons still actively practicing polygamy in violation of all their church ordinances and civil statutes.

Separating northern Arizona from the southern desert area is a fairly narrow belt of high mountains, many heavily timbered in soft ponderosa pine. Transversing the state diagonally, from northwest to southeast, this belt escapes the extreme aridity of most of Arizona, its meadows and high forests showing a more fertile face to the world. Set at the foot of the lofty San Francisco Peak, is Flagstaff (pop. 34,743), the principal town north of Phoenix, a trading center for cattle and sheep ranchers, lumbermen, and Indians, and the jumping off point for the Grand Canyon and other scenic wonders of the region. So much could be said of the fascinating sights, natural and man-made, in the Flagstaff orbit: spectacular Oak Creek Canyon with its red-rock formations; Walnut Canyon with its prehistoric cliff dwellings; ghostly Meteor Crater; picturesque Sedona; the ghost mining town of Jerome; and the first territorial capital—Prescott, where Barry Goldwater has begun each of his campaigns for public office, even the presidency.

The great desert beckons us, commencing where the mountain belt ends and marching into Mexico. But should we really dismiss it as "desert"? True, writes John Steinbeck in *Travels with Charley*, it is a "mysterious wasteland, a sun-punished place." But he quickly adds, "It is a mystery, something concealed and waiting." Steinbeck reminds us too of the hidden desert: the "secrets of survival" in the oil armor of the dusty sage, protecting its inward small moistness, the hard dry outer skins of animals defying dessication, the secret burrows and outcroppings where rodents and reptiles go to escape the sun's unremitting glare. And of the life of the desert night when "a world of creatures awakens and takes up its intricate pattern."

One would think of the desert as indestructible, but even here the ecological battle is fought. Along the rivers, the federal Bureau of Reclamation and the Army Corps of Engineers have removed huge swatches of water-consuming mesquite shrubs and salt cedar trees in an apparently futile attempt to control floods and to save water. But the largest-scale threat to desert life is plant-rustling. The problem of Arizonans simply driving out on the desert and taking the beautiful cactus specimens for themselves is not new. Arizona was forced to pass the nation's first Native Plant Law in 1929, but the fines and jail sentences have proven only partially successful in protecting the 45,000 square miles of cactus-producing land.

The line of human history up to recent times bears just the faintest relation to the civilization that exists in Arizona today. A quick and colorful review of the state's history in the *Monitor,* a local telephone company magazine, noted, "Arizona has been the home of hairy aborigines who stoned to death the giant sloth and the mammoth 20,000 years ago; of nomads who huddled in natural caves hunting with spears and bows; of prehistoric Indians who engineered extensive irrigation systems and built canals, developing a civilization far beyond most of their contemporaries; of pastoral Indians who ranged over Arizona, building pueblos, planting corn and cotton." Spanish conquistadores arrived, searching for gold, but the terrain was so forbidding that, unlike neighboring New Mexico, little early Spanish civilization flourished on the land that is now Arizona. Spain held the land, however, until Mexico won its independence in 1822; Mexico in turn relinquished the territory to the United States at the end of the Mexican War in 1848. A handful of gold and silver prospectors, fur traders, and brave early homesteaders (many of them Mormons from nearby Utah) then began to filter onto the land, and territorial status was won in 1863. But the Indians, especially the Navajo and the fierce Apaches, resisted the white man's incursions with cunning, and it was not until 1886, with the surrender of the Apaches' great chieftain, Geronimo, that orderly settlement could proceed. About the same time, the railroad came, and Arizona's great copper deposits were discovered.

Arizona was admitted to the Union in 1912—the last of the coterminous 48 states. But even before statehood, the area began to depend on federally sponsored diversion projects to bring it the water needed for growth. Settlers discovered early that, with irrigation, the desert can produce abundant crops. In the Salt River Valley, where Phoenix began in the 1860s as a hay camp to supply forage for cavalry troops, the settlers began to utilize the canals constructed by the Hohokan Indians some 600 years before to bring the water onto the land. As a sort of prelude to statehood a year later, former President Theodore Roosevelt in 1911 came to Arizona to dedicate the nation's first federal reclamation project: a great dam, on the Salt River, to provide better irrigation for Phoenix. With successive water projects, this made possible the Arizona civilization as we know it today.

Until World War II, Arizona depended on copper (it was still the greatest copper mining state, accounting for 60 percent of U.S. and 12 percent of world production until severe recession and foreign competition forced mine shutdowns in the early '80s). Other early economic mainstays were irrigated farming and the climate, which attracted wealthy Easterners and those seeking relief from tuberculosis, arthritis, and asthma. It was not until World War II that Arizona's earnest growth—first in military bases (the dry desert and clear skies were especially suited for the training of fliers), then in research and industry—would begin. Arizona's phenomenal postwar population increase began with servicemen who had been stationed there during World War II, liked it, and returned with their families. In more recent years, studies by the state government have identified the chief motivations of new settlers as health, climate, transfer, and opportunity. The greatest growth has been in manufacturing, and within manufacturing, electronics has been the real boom industry. Companies such as Motorola, Sperry-Rand, General Electric, Honeywell and Hughes Aircraft (for years the state's largest employer) found they could easily draw skilled workers to the Arizona environment—and at the same time take advantage of the state's relatively low wage scales and aversion to unionization. (Arizona passed one of the nation's first right-to-work laws, and unions there remain politically powerless compared to those in other states.) By 1983, fully 38 percent of Arizona's economy was in high-tech—five times the national average.

Immigrants to Arizona now come from all parts of the country, including not only the snowy Northern climes but other Southwestern states. Like Idaho, Arizona attracts its share of Californians who find the life on the coast too hectic or congested. Contrary to popular opinion, Arizona has not become an old folks' haven; the state actually has a relatively low median age (28 years) and one of the highest birth rates in the U.S. The population boom shows few signs of abating, and the overall population grew by 53 percent in the 1970s, a growth rate exceeded only by Nevada and Florida among the 50 states.

A chief attraction of Arizona is its openness in both business and politics. Rags-to-riches stories dominate the development of the real-estate and electronics industries, just as they did in minerals and ranching in the old days. In the postwar years, Arizona's business and political culture have been governed not by a few old wealthy families trying to maintain the status quo, but by succeeding generations of entrepreneurial immigrants who see to it that the state's politicians provide a maximum amount of aid (federal water projects and pro-business state laws) and a minimum of regulation. As Goldwater once told us, the new generations of entrepreneurs have "the same spirit of men like my grandfather. Now it's just a new set of pioneers."

Arizona's fast-buck, anti-regulatory atmosphere eventually led to problems, however. The Mafia moved into Arizona in the 1960s, first using Tucson as a retirement haven for leaders such as the notorious Joe Bonanno, the New York underworld kingpin labeled by *Time* as "one of the bloodiest killers in Cosa Nostra's history." Bonanno and others soon discovered how easy it was to operate in Arizona. Illegal activity and occasional violence have been present ever since. Arizonans were shocked out of their live-and-let-live attitude in June, 1976, with the contract murder of Don Bolles, an *Arizona Republic* investigative reporter. According to court testimony, a contract had also been made on the life of Bruce Babbitt, the state attorney general, whose subsequent cleanup of crime was a strong factor in his election as governor. A six-month investigation of Arizona corruption by 40 reporters and editors from 27 news organizations around the country showed that proximity to narcotics warehouses in Mexico was a prime Mafia attraction, but that the Mafia had also funneled its profits into land, buildings, parking lots, and housing developments through dummy corporations, which lax state laws allowed to exist. The report charged that various members of the Arizona political, business, and legal hierarchy had condoned and nurtured the growing presence of mobsters. The *Arizona Republic*, the *Washington Post*, and the

Chicago Tribune chose not to publish the report even though they had participated in the investigation because the paper's management said that the allegations about prominent Arizonans were hearsay. Babbitt told us, however, that "the essential allegation was right. The old-time establishment weren't the crooks. But their negative and patronizing sense of government allowed it all to happen."

Life in Arizona is not so comfortable for the Mafia anymore. The state toughened its law enforcement and adopted a statewide grand jury system with more power than the old county-by-county prosecution authority. Credit for the passage of the statewide grand jury bill must go to the late Eugene Pulliam, publisher of the *Arizona Republic,* an ultraconservative who in his last years came to believe that he had been sold out by many politicians. In an editorial published on April 27, 1975, Pulliam charged that those who opposed the statewide grand jury were as much as supporting and condoning organized crime. The bill passed the next day.

The darker side of Arizona business life has also included a number of famous swindles, which have affected many more individuals than the Mafia ever has. Arizona has gone a long way to clean up those schemes. The real-estate industry, paranoid about its national image, helped clean up land scams. A new state securities division was established, but small-scale franchise gold and silver schemes continued to plague the state.

Political Metamorphoses; and the Stories of Barry and Mo

Arizona politics is a story of metamorphoses. The state entered the Union during the heyday of the Progressive movement, with an advanced constitution that guaranteed women the right to vote, provided for workmen's compensation, and banned trusts and monopolies. The constitution, however, proved to be no match for the copper interests, which proceeded to buy and control the legislatures with monotonous regularity. John Gunther reported that Phelps Dodge in particular extended itself in politics with a pervasive, autocratic control in much the same manner as Anaconda Copper in Montana.* During the 1920s, Arizona seemed to have become a legitimate two-party state. But in the '30s and '40s it veered toward one-partyism of the conservative, rural-dominated Democratic variety, not dissimilar from the

---

*In Arizona, the Queen of the Copper Camps was Bisbee, in the southeast corner of the state. Bisbee's days of copper glory lasted more or less until 1975 when Phelps Dodge closed the mine it had operated since before World War I. Bisbee became the exception to the rule of Arizona's population growth, dropping 14 percent of its people, to 7,154. Bisbee's nickname also changed from "Little San Francisco" to "the Cleveland of Arizona." The sale of miners' housing for as little as $1,000 per house attracted two types of people: retirees and hippies. They immediately disliked each other. When a woman offended retirees' mores by suckling her infant in the Copper Queen Hotel and was subsequently ejected, her friends began a breast feed-in that lasted for weeks.

model of neighboring Texas; the difference was that while in Texas oil was the power behind the throne, in Arizona it was copper. With the legislature apportioned to favor rural areas, this condition would extend into the postwar years, maintaining the rural-conservative copper base even as the cities ballooned in population. When the Republicans finally came to power, the cities, not the countryside, would be their bastion, and in 1950 Howard Pyle, the first successful Republican gubernatorial candidate of modern times, attacked the Democratic party for being the vassal of Arizona's immense copper and other corporate interests.

The most remarkable political character out of this Democratic era was Carl Hayden, who served in Congress longer than any other man in American history, fighting doggedly for Arizona interests over most of this century. Hayden took his seat as a member of the House of Representatives in 1912, five days after Arizona gained statehood. He served in Washington until 1969, the last 42 of those years in the Senate. What had Hayden wrought in Washington? Arizona writer Ray Thomson answered the question: "Highways, dams and reservoirs, irrigation projects, a desert that bloomed beyond anyone's imagination; all these and more stand as monuments to his dedication, hard work, and love of Arizona." Hayden's touch is still being felt on the Arizona landscape. His crowning achievement after decades of effort, the multibillion-dollar Colorado River–Central Arizona Project, remained controversial and under construction into the 1980s. Hayden also had a national legacy. He sponsored the 19th Amendment to the Constitution to guarantee women the right to vote, was father of the bill to establish the Grand Canyon National Park, and was coauthor of the legislation that led to the great interstate highway system.

Not even Hayden, however, won national prominence to compare with that of Barry Morris Goldwater, father of the Arizona Republican party and the state's postwar conservative political metamorphosis. Surprisingly, Goldwater actually had some Democratic roots. He was the department-store heir grandson of Michel Goldwater, an early Arizona settler who stemmed from a Jewish family of Russian background.* Goldwater's uncle had helped form the Democratic party in the Territory. After the war, the young Goldwater felt the state needed a two-party system because a "one-party system put up dogs for office." Goldwater and his friends made a start by taking over the Republican state convention in 1948. The following year he teamed up with businessman Harry Rosenzweig and other would-be reformers in a bipartisan Phoenix Charter Government Committee. Goldwater was elected to the Council and in 1950 ran the gubernatorial campaign for his friend Howard Pyle, a radio commentator, who won by 3,000 votes in a historic reversal of Arizona's decades-old one-partyism. Two years later Goldwater, preaching

---

*Goldwater himself was raised as an Episcopalian by his Christian mother. "I'm proud of my Jewish father and grandfather," Goldwater has said, adding, "I've never been discriminated against because I am part Jewish"—a credit, we might add, to the openness of Arizona frontier society.

a conservative gospel and riding Eisenhower's coattails, was elected to the U.S. Senate, and Republican John J Rhodes broke the Democratic monopoly on seats in the U.S. House. Since the watershed elections of the early 1950s, the Republicans have generally held sway, controlling one or both of the Senate seats, the legislature, and the powerful Arizona Corporation Commission. But U.S. Sen. Dennis DeConcini, elected in 1976, maintained the Hayden tradition as an independent, thoughtful Democrat.

What turned Arizona to the GOP? First of all, it was the new population —heavily Midwestern, often Republican by heritage, an independent kind of people making a new start and repelled by the closed, fiefdom-ridden old Democratic party. Retirees, technicians, and engineers in the new industries also tended to be Republican. A second factor was the purchase in 1948 of the Phoenix-based *Arizona Republic* and *Gazette* by Pulliam—a rock-ribbed Republican power in Indiana—who was determined to build a two-party state. A final and essential factor in the Republican rise was the quality of its major candidates: men like Goldwater, Pyle, and Rhodes, men of integrity and ability compared to the mediocre Democratic leaders of that time.

It was in his first Senate campaign, in 1952, that Goldwater's special brand of politics surfaced. "What kind of Republican are you, anyway?" he was asked at a rally. Goldwater's reply was just as accurate in describing his stand 12 years later when he ran for president, or today: "Well, I am not a me-too Republican. . . . I am a Republican opposed to the superstate and to gigantic, bureaucratic, centralized authority." Add to this Goldwater's belief in bold military action in the defense of American foreign ventures, and his moral crusade, proclaimed in 1964, against violence in the streets and the degeneration of traditional American values (Goldwater was the first national figure to make this a major issue), and one has the philosophy of Goldwater fairly well encapsulated.

The nation was not ready for these ideas when Goldwater ran for the presidency in 1964. His defeat was crushing; he ran 23 percentage points behind President Johnson and carried only five states, all in the Deep South, except for Arizona. His defense of "extremism in the defense of liberty" drove millions of moderate-to-liberal Republicans out of the party, many of them for good. But historians will surely record that Goldwater's positions skewed the Republican course substantially to the right, exposed the weakness of the once-vaunted Eastern establishment in party ranks, and laid the groundwork for the nomination of Ronald Reagan for president 16 years later.

These political shifts will be Goldwater's legacy—not the legislative output of a man like Carl Hayden. Goldwater's name has not been attached to major legislation, and he has lived up to his viewpoint: "I have little interest in streamlining government or in making it more efficient," he once wrote, "for I mean to reduce its size. My aim is not to pass laws, but to repeal them."

Many old-time conservatives thought that the Reagan presidency would be a time of glory for Goldwater, but it was not to be. Shortly after the election, Reagan paid tribute to Goldwater at a Washington dinner given by GOP senators. "If he hadn't walked that lonely road, some of us wouldn't be here tonight," Reagan said, but the new president did not make Goldwater part of his inner circle. Part of the reason was Goldwater's age and ill health and his disinclination toward active governing, but Republican insiders also noted Goldwater had backed Gerald Ford for the 1976 Republican nomination.

Age did not tone down Goldwater's refreshing willingness to publicly state his honest political opinions, a habit that occasionally offended fellow conservatives. In the early stages of the Watergate scandal, while Nixon was still president, Goldwater called the situation "one of the most scandalous and stupid in the history of the country." In 1981, after the New Right religious groups had opposed the nomination of fellow Arizonan Sandra Day O'Connor to the Supreme Court on the basis of her stance on the single issue of abortion, Goldwater said that he was "sick and tired of the political preachers across this country telling me as a citizen that if I want to be a moral person, I must believe in 'A,' 'B,' 'C,' and 'D.' Just who do they think they are?" The Moral Majority and other New Right organizations, Goldwater continued, were undermining the basic American principles of separation of church and state, and the Rev. Jerry Falwell, head of the Moral Majority, deserved a "kick in the ass" for his opposition to O'Connor. (O'Connor did become the first woman on the high court, and a study of her opinions during her first seven months on the job showed her to be a solid conservative.)

No member of the U.S. Congress would differ more in ideology from Goldwater than Arizona's second-most-prominent politician, Rep. Morris Udall of Tucson. Udall became one of the premier environmentalists in the House, the father of both the federal strip mine law and the bill that restricted development on 104 million acres of Alaska lands. He also sponsored unsuccessful bills to provide federal aid for local land use planning. In 1976, Udall was the leading liberal alternative to the primary candidacy of Jimmy Carter for president, although he never won a primary. How can a Morris Udall win in the same state that launched Barry Goldwater's Republicanism? The answers are heritage and hard work. The Udall family is part of what the congressman himself calls the "dirt aristocracy" of Arizona's pioneer days; his father was a Supreme Court justice and his mother a local Democratic activist. Morris Udall was first elected to his congressional seat in 1961 when his brother Stewart, a congressman since 1955, resigned to become President Kennedy's Secretary of the Interior—and gained the reputation of a modern prophet in awakening the country to the dangers of despoiling the environment. Tucson has always been more traditional, liberal, and Democratic than Phoenix and has had a larger Mexican-American population. Over the years, however, Udall's traditional Democratic base has been eroded by the massive influx of affluent retirees and middle-income employees of the area's new high-technology industries. "Every time there's a blizzard in Buffalo or Detroit, we get 5,000 more conservative retirees in the district," an aide to Udall once joked. The newcomers don't have the natives' respect for the Udall name, and he has had to campaign harder and harder to stay in office. But Udall has demonstrated remarkable resilience; despite the disclosure that he was suffering from Parkinson's disease and the Reagan landslide, Udall won reelection with ease in both 1980 and 1982.

Udall's national environmental reputation was severely tested by his dog-ged support of the Central Arizona Project (CAP). With the annual precipita-tion in Phoenix and Tucson usually no more than a scant 10 inches, compared to 25 inches in the most heavily populated areas of the United States, Arizona has searched constantly for water and the federal money to pay for damming, storing, and moving it. Beginning in 1927, the subsiding water table caused cracks as deep as 400 feet and some running for miles to open in the Arizona earth; by 1983, there were more than 100 such fissures. Arizona struggled with neighboring states for a good portion of this century over its share of the water flow from the Colorado River and was finally guaranteed, by edict of the Supreme Court in 1963, an annual 2.8 million acre-feet of Colorado River water. This decision put into motion the forces that finally passed the CAP in 1968. When completed, it will consist of a 400-mile system of aqueducts and dams to divert a yearly 1.2 million acre-feet of the Colorado River's allotment from Lake Havasu, behind Parker Dam, on the Colorado River, to the Phoenix and Tucson areas. The cost of this gigantic system, together with power generation to pump the water, was authorized at $892 million in 1968 and had escalated to $2.2 billion by 1981. Ninety percent of the water will be used for agriculture, but it will be an insurance policy for the oasis cities. As the environmental movement grew, questions about the project arose from all sides. Common Cause in 1977 showed that five of the seven members of the State Water Commission had potential conflicts of interest, including owner-ship of land, businesses, and banks that would be affected by the project. *Fortune* magazine questioned the federal outlays and pointed out that, despite the aridity and the difficulty of obtaining water, Arizona water is so cheap to consumers that the state ranks eighth-highest in water use per capita. Even Udall came to question the wisdom of the CAP.

With the completion of the Central Arizona Project virtually guaranteed, there still were continuing fears of a day of reckoning when Arizona's boom-ing agriculture and its booming cities would shrivel. In 1980 the legislature made a dramatic breakthrough by passing a far-reaching law to manage groundwater. The overall goal was to stop the lowering of the water table, which had been going on for many years, by gradually reducing the ground-water pumping to the same amount of water as is recharged. The law estab-lished a statewide management and conservation program, provided civil and criminal penalties for violations, and required statewide registration of wells and strict conservation measures in Phoenix, Tucson, Prescott, and Pinal County. By the year 2020, the pumping and recharging should be in balance. The bill took years to put together and required delicate negotiations among farmers, miners, and urbanites. Carter Administration Interior Secretary Cecil Andrus' threat to hold up the Central Arizona Project if the state did not update its 1948 law was also a major impetus. "The history books will be kind to this 34th legislature," Governor Bruce Babbitt said of the assembled. "It has succeeded where its predecessors have failed for more than 40 years. This is the most far-reaching water management system in the United States.

We have assured that Arizona will have water resources for a bright and expanding future."

By all accounts, Babbitt was given credit for cajoling and pushing the accord through the state legislature. The young governor, then 42, was also recognized as a new type of politician in the state. Babbitt's roots were totally Arizonan—he was born into a pioneer family that settled near Flagstaff in the 1880s to operate Indian trading posts—but he spent his formative years exposing himself to other places. Babbitt left Arizona and spent the 1960s excelling as an undergraduate at Notre Dame and earning a master's degree in geophysics in England and a law degree at Harvard. On a geology trip to Bolivia, he was deeply affected by the human deprivation he witnessed, and he joined the 1963 civil rights march in Selma, Alabama, before spending two years in Washington as assistant to the director of VISTA, the federal volunteer program. Back home, Babbitt was elected attorney general in 1974 and quickly became the "Mr. Clean" of a state wracked by white-collar crime. He was thrust into the governorship in 1978 by the resignation of one incumbent and the death of his successor.

Babbitt called himself a liberal, although many traditional, national liberals would not identify with him. His positions seemed to be as progressive as Arizona could bear. He vetoed a "Sagebrush Rebellion" bill approved by the legislature on the grounds that the federally owned land being sought would only fall into the hands of selfish private interests. (But a "Sagebrush Rebellion" proposition appeared on the 1982 statewide ballot and was passed.) He left unchallenged Arizona's religion of the desirability of growth, but he did seek to influence growth through the new water law and advocated energy and water-efficient "urban villages" he hoped to see constructed on state-owned lands near Phoenix and Tucson. He was the first Arizona Anglo politician to align himself with the growing Mexican-American community, learned to speak Spanish, and encouraged Chicanos to improve their anemic voter turn-out. Among the nation's governors, he has often seemed the pre-eminent figure in urging a new version of responsible states' rights and reform of the nation's congested and overcentralized intergovernmental system. Both Babbitt's intellect and his pragmatic centralism seemed to position him for a future presidential run—a prospect he told us he would welcome "if lightning strikes."

Babbitt's political strength and the 1980 water law raised the question: was Arizona entering another political metamorphosis? Most probably not. The basic political premise of Arizona set in the 1950s remained strong: that private sector economic development with as little regulation as possible will bring prosperity and happiness to the citizenry. Almost everyone in Arizona—natives and newcomers—believed their lives had improved extraordinarily and that business development had been the fountainhead from which that higher standard of living flowed. Newcomers found space, sun, and the jobs that make it possible to enjoy Arizona's outdoor life. Some natives argued that population growth had destroyed their quiet way of life, but most of them made money on the growth. Even with Babbitt in the state house, Arizona's government performance indicated that change is slow. Arizona law still severely restricted increases in state spending, and high school students were still required to take a course touting the benefits of free enterprise. State government indifference left county governments to carry a staggering load for care of indigents. Arizona was the only state in the country to refuse to participate in Medicaid, although it did accept a federal block grant experiment in 1981 and was beginning—finally—to provide something more for its poor and minorities than federal aid pass-throughs.

Nevertheless, important changes were afoot in Arizona government and politics by the early '80s. Babbitt did shake up the regulatory agencies of Arizona state government, charging they had "gone mushy" and been infected by the idea that public officials "were supposed to sleep at their desks and not disturb those who should be regulated." Arizona's voters, on average a group with remarkably high educational levels, showed signs of becoming more sophisticated, independent, and less ideological. A key indicator was Goldwater's reelection by only 1 percent in 1980. In earlier elections, analyzed Pat Murphy, editor of the *Arizona Republic*, "Goldwater's state was small, and he was large." Arizonans no longer automatically support conservative candidates, and they view with some cynicism the standard campaign pitches of cutting taxes and curbing government spending, Murphy told us. The state's greatest political asset, he added, was its emerging crop of bright, young, well-educated politicians, both Democratic and Republican.

As we visited Arizona's oasis culture, we wondered what kind of policies this younger breed would develop. Would concerns about air pollution overtake pro-growth attitudes? Would labor unions ever organize more than 14 percent of the state's workers and bring issues of wages and working conditions to the political forefront? Would Arizona ever establish severance taxes on its minerals? How would the growing Mexican-American population be accommodated? As central as those questions might seem to the Arizonan future, however, a candidate's position on them might be less important in the '80s than such personal qualities as honesty, candor, directness, and leadership ability. "Those qualities mean a lot to Arizona voters," Murphy noted. "Goldwater has those qualities. That's why he was so strong."

Phoenicians, Tucsonians, Indians, Mexicans

Within a universe of four categories—Phoenicians, Tucsonians, Indians, and Mexicans—you have captured most Arizonans (some twice). In numbers, the sprawling urban cultures encompass the vast majority of the state's people.

The founders of Phoenix probably never dreamed how strongly the city's development would resemble its namesake, the mythical bird that rose from its own ashes. The name was chosen because the site of the 1868 settlement near the Salt River contained old Indian canals and civilization. Phoenix was a minor settlement until 1911 and completion of the Roosevelt Dam. In 1940 the Census still found only 65,414 people there. Forty years later, the Phoenix metropolitan area had grown to 1,508,030 people. The city of Phoenix spiraled from 20th- to 9th-largest in the country in the single decade of the 1970s, though by 1980 the metropolitan area still ranked only 26th.

If Phoenix has any sacred value, it is growth. It reveres builders such as Walter Bimson, who came in the late 1930s and by able management and endless promotion schemes built the Valley National Bank into such a powerful force that it became one of the West's largest banks. "Phoenix is a developer's city, the pivot of the Southwest's growth machine, a builder's dream come true," wrote Los Angeles freelance writer Bob Gottlieb in *The Nation*. Arizona has attracted corporate headquarters such as the Greyhound Corporation, Southwest Forest Industries, and Krueger, all on the *Fortune* 1,000 list. But the true core of its economy and spirit is smaller, growing companies whose entrepreneurial founders dream of one day making *Fortune*'s list.

Despite the growth, Phoenix has maintained what *Washington Post* correspondent Daniel J. Balz has called "the feel and flavor of a small town. Its downtown is quiet by day, desolate by night. Its pace is noticeably slower than in many other larger cities. Even its country music station seems weeks behind those elsewhere." Phoenix Mayor Margaret Hance has said she is proud of being accused of having the biggest small town in America. "It means the openness and friendliness has not disappeared," in her words.

Phoenix has unquestionably offered hospitality and opportunity to hundreds of thousands of newcomers, but it's also easy to argue that, despite Hance's claims, Phoenix has become a large city that is not handling its new status very well. Few would maintain that Phoenix's rapid growth has brought grace or quality; instead, a seemingly boundless "spread city" (growing from just 17 square miles in 1950 to more than 330 in 1983) creeps out onto the desert and toward or onto the gaunt, forbidding Camelback, Superstition, and Four Peaks, which rim the center as grim reminders of the barren nothingness that preceded man's canals and hectic building. Unlike rival Tucson, Phoenix has failed to retain any of the special Southwestern flavor of its birth (although it does have some spectacular museums, notably the Heard, whose collections include Barry Goldwater's Kachina dolls). Phoenix does not even have a freeway system, much less adequate mass transit. Early in the 1960s, land prices skyrocketed in the downtown, and the developers (who are in total control of the city's physical development) began building in other locations. One savings and loan executive has maintained that this sprawl "is in many ways a positive thing. People can live in lower density communities with less social friction, and urban facilities can be regionalized." Mayor Hance has maintained that the city must keep on annexing to avoid even more "leapfrog" development on open land, but so far her promises of "in-fill" development on pieces of property within the city limits have not come to fruition.

There is little opposition to these hell-bent-for-election growth patterns. "Part of the problem," Vernon Swaback, architect and planner of the Frank Lloyd Wright Foundation, told *National Geographic*, "is that most newcomers never had it so good in terms of clean air, climate and mobility. The idyllic

circumstances create complacency. Based on present trends, the future promises an environmental breakdown. We're on a collision course with very
little interest being paid to warning signs along the way."

Visual aesthetics may be too much to ask in this frontier society, but
Phoenicians deserve severe criticism for despoiling the air for which Arizona
was once famed. Even though Arizona was one of the first states with an
auto-emissions laws, air pollution has become so bad in Phoenix that the
Council on Environmental Quality ranked it tenth from the bottom in air
quality, and physicians no longer advise people with asthma and respiratory
problems to relocate there.

Fortunately the city's annexation policies have captured the tax base better
than in the North, where suburban boundaries have cut the central cities off
from regional wealth. The reward has been high quality bond ratings, making
it cheaper for the city to borrow money to extend city services farther and
farther out. But there are still plenty of problems of social instability in
Phoenix. The city has one of the highest divorce rates of all major U.S. cities,
an FBI crime rate index above the national average, and drug problems among
the youth. There is also plenty of inequality. There are 16 independent school
districts within the city, and quality varies widely depending on the tax base.
Heavily Hispanic, black, and Indian South Phoenix has been termed a "40
square mile poverty pocket" with its old farm shacks, junkyards, sagebrush,
vacant lots, and recently built low-income housing. Phoenix paid little attention to the poor side of town until federal programs were established. Then
it pumped federal aid into police, fire, street maintenance, jobs, housing, and
community development, all without raising local taxes. In a study entitled
"Phoenix: the New Federal City," Arizona State University researchers concluded that by limiting social spending to federal grant programs, "Phoenix
was able to have it both ways: building a city administration on a federal
foundation while claiming a parochial orientation to crime control and maintenance of a Southwest life style." Just how uncaring Phoenicians were
became evident in 1981 when the Reagan administration cut federal social and
urban spending. Mayor Hance told *Fortune* that she would minimize the
effects on basic services such as police, fire, and street lighting by cutting
programs to aid the poor. "The poor are a federal, not a local, responsibility,"
Hance declared. "If Washington cannot afford those programs, we certainly
can't. Local people do not feel that welfare programs should be financed by
local taxes."

The power behind-the-scenes is held by Phoenix 40, an organization of 40
top executives of corporations and firms who meet about once a month. They
operate in a very low-profile manner, and much of their persuasion is conducted by telephone. In the late 1970s Phoenix 40 started Valley Leadership
to bring young men and women into the fold and train them to lead in the
same, conservative fashion. Another group, called Urban Focus, with a more
diverse membership of interested citizens and professionals, was trying to
challenge the heavy-handed business leadership with philosophical positions
on urbanization and mass transit. But the city establishment lost a major battle

in 1982 when Phoenix voters narrowly approved scrapping the city's historic system of electing members of the city council at large in favor of an election-by-district system. The mayor and the city's power structure (including the Phoenix 40) argued in vain that, in the words of the *Phoenix Gazette*, "the ward system would produce ugly brawls of untethered ward heelers." Unlike other Southern and Western cities, where single-member districts were sought to empower minorities, in Phoenix the 15-percent Hispanic community was not the impetus behind the movement. Instead, it came from the many newcomers from the Northern states.

Notwithstanding Phoenix's steady growth by annexation, the suburbs that surround it in the so-called Valley of the Sun now have almost as large a population. The most illustrious of these is Scottsdale, a dusty crossroads filling station at the end of World War II, but now Arizona's third-largest city (pop. 88,412) and the location of many of the Phoenix area's leading winter resorts (especially at Camelback Mountain) and winter homes for the wealthy.

Near Scottsdale are two architectural learning centers that defy Arizona's reputation as an architectural and urban planning wasteland. The most prominent is Taliesin West, where followers of Frank Lloyd Wright continue his architectural tradition. Wright's work may be seen in Arizona in the delicately sculpted circular auditorium on the Arizona State University campus at Tempe. Not too far away, Paolo Soleri, once a Wright protégé, is building his controversial city, Arcosanti. Soleri's theory is based on miniaturization —that man can, with thrift and organization, confine his waste and keep to a minimum the damage he does to the world. Soleri was widely hailed in the 1960s, but his subsequent lack of financial progress brought criticism that he was nothing more than a charismatic charlatan taking advantage of the students who came to work for him. But the work went on. "On a windy cliffside," *Phoenix* magazine reported, "is a mass of earthstone pillbox buildings, half domes, and cubes which seem to creep and crawl across the terrain in surrealistic fashion."

We would be remiss, of course, not to mention the prominent developments for retirees, starting with Del Webb's classic Sun City and its thousands of low, white-roofed, pastel-tinted houses built around a continuous golf course and a 33-acre artificial lake. Others with names like Leisure World, Carefree, and Dreamland Village have followed. As the number of older Americans increases, there seems to be no limit to this market. Most of these retirement havens have a reputation for political conservatism, except, of course, when it comes to government aid for the elderly.

Most visitors to Arizona have preferred Tucson for its more traditional, liberal, and flavorful character. It lies some 125 miles farther to the south (Mexico is just 66 miles down the road), but the city is cooler than Phoenix because its elevation is 1,500 feet higher. Life in Tucson is slower and less urban, and one feels closer to Arizona's frontier. Tucson has a rich sense of history, which stems from the many flags, from Spanish and Mexican to Confederate to U.S., under which it has lived. What strikes a visitor to Tucson most immediately and forcefully is the architecture; in place of Phoenix's bland modernity, Tucson has preserved the best of the old Spanish adobe style, the pale yellows blending marvelously into the desert sands. As the nation's largest city to rely on underground wells, Tucson lacks the great green splotches of irrigated land.

But, as we noted in our story of Mo Udall, Tucson is also changing. The population, 531,263, is much smaller than Phoenix, but the growth rate is about the same. The Santa Catalina Mountains and the cactus and scraggly scrub brush in Brear Creek Canyon have been bulldozed for real-estate development. To the University of Arizona/Hughes Aircraft/military/tourism economy has been added the electronics industry, led by companies fleeing California's Silicon Valley and its skyrocketing housing prices. Growth control advocates won a majority of Tucson's City Council seats in 1975, but their reign was short lived. Tucson's debate over growth continues to be the most vigorous and best-argued in the state.

After California and Oklahoma, Arizona has the third-highest Indian population in the United States—152,857 in 1980. Indians are also Arizona's most rural people; only 28,000 live in Phoenix and Tucson combined; most of the rest have chosen to stay on the reservations, or have returned after an unhappy and unprofitable try at city life. Arizona Indians are land- and resource-rich but dollar-poor. Some 20 million acres—more than a quarter of the entire state—are set aside for their reservations; among these is the great Navajo Reservation, which spills over into New Mexico and is so large that other Indians say it functions almost like a state.

Thirteen tribes of Indians live in Arizona, each with a distinct culture. Among the most fascinating are the Hopi, who practice communal farming and live on high mesas in the midst of the Navajo Reservation near Four Corners. Unlike the nomadic Navajo, the Hopi are a stationary people, many living in homes built centuries ago. The Hopi are thought to be the oldest extant tribe in the U.S.—literally the first "Americans." Their village of Oraibi is the oldest continuously inhabited town in the country. "The wisdom and reasoning" of the Hopi, Goldwater related, "is scarcely to be believed"; the young people are sought assiduously by electronics firms for complex wiring tasks. The Hopis have maintained a testy relationship with their numerous Navajo neighbors, sharing with them, since 1882, 1.8 million acres that surround the 600,000-acre Hopi reservation. Tribal differences between the Hopi farmer-hunter culture and the Navajo sheep-grazing culture caused such continual problems that Congress finally divided the land and began moving people to their respective tribal areas in 1981.

Energy development has brought several tribes into conflict—amongst themselves and, in turn, with the energy companies. The Hopi have been deeply split between those who control the tribal council and a group of so-called traditional leaders who reject proposals for working more closely with the white man and exploiting their coal. Peabody Coal Company of St. Louis, a subsidiary of Kennecot Copper, has strip-mined a small portion of the reservation for coal to feed the generating plants that are part of the huge new Western power grid supplying current to the West Coast.

While many Arizona Indians still resist white civilization, overall contact with white society has unquestionably increased in recent years. The Pima-Maricopa Tribe, whose reservation is only 12 miles from the center of Phoenix, has become surrounded by so many houses, shopping centers, and factories that a tribal consultant described it as "one of the largest undeveloped individual tracts of urban land still remaining in the United States." Tribal leaders hope to replace the reservation's barley, alfalfa, and cotton fields with industrial development and better jobs, although some Pimas still worry about losing tribal identity—and being outwitted by white developers as so many of their ancestors were.

Arizona Indians have never been a potent political force; until 1948, indeed, they were legally barred from voting because of their "guardianship" status. But in Apache County, where Navajos are in the majority, they do control the county commission and determine the tax rates for the white land holders. The whites are bitter about this, as might be expected, since the Indians do not have to pay taxes on their land.

Arizona's Mexican-American population has risen in one generation from the most docile and acquiescent in the Southwest to one of the most politically skillful. In 1983, 12 persons of Spanish origin served in the 90-member Arizona legislature, or about 13 percent of the body, close to the Hispanics' 16 percent of the Arizona population. In the late 1970s, Alfredo Gutierrez, then in his late 20s, served as majority leader of the Arizona Senate. Arizona in 1974 elected its first Mexican-American governor, Raul Castro, a significant political accomplishment even though a touch of scandal led him to resign. Many Mexican-Americans now sit on city councils and county commissions and can be expected to run for higher office in the future.

As recently as the 1960s the situation of the Mexican-Americans in Arizona was not only materially, but politically tragic. For generations they have been the chore boys of Arizona, performing grueling stoop labor in the fields and manning the copper mines. Mexican-American men were lynched, women raped, children forbidden to use swimming pools, and land was stolen by conniving Anglo settlers. "The Mexican-American has been the black man of the Southwest," Ronnie Lopez, an executive assistant to Babbitt, told us. Language and cultural differences created the basic bars against political participation, and whatever interest remained was overwhelmed by the Anglos' strong will to keep control. The Mexican-Americans all too often seemed satisfied with crumbs from Anglo patrons—paving a local street, arranging a welfare check, for example.

What awakened the Mexican-Americans politically? Probably more than anything else, their growing urbanization made political organization possible. Contrary to popular impression, farm workers make up only a small percentage of the Mexican-American population; 70 percent of Arizona's Mexican-Americans live in Phoenix and Tucson. But national cultural movements also played a role. The political liberation movements of the 1960s gave credibility to the Chicano consciousness; for the first time respectability was won by that fusion of Spanish and Indian blood that is the heritage of most of Arizona's Mexican-Americans. (In neighboring New Mexico there are many pure Castilians who never suffered from the same degree of cultural indignity.) At the same time, the first generation of college-educated, professionally trained young Chicanos emerged. The Ford Foundation provided important initial funding for community development corporations such as Phoenix's Chicanos Por La Causa, which worked to improve housing, educational, and economic conditions, but even more importantly offered young Chicanos an institutional setting from which to lead their communities. Gutierrez, Lopez, and Rick Hernandez, who later became a White House aide to President Carter, all got their start in Chicanos Por La Causa.

Whatever their political gains, Chicanos in Arizona still have a long way to go to achieve equality with whites. On the Chicano side of town, paved streets, adequate sewers, health care, and decent and safe housing are still rallying cries. Spanish-speaking childrens' school drop-out rates are still 60 percent higher than whites'.

To understand the depth of Arizona's relationship with Mexico one really has to visit the border and see how people move back and forth on a daily basis, working and shopping. The Arizona city of Nogales grew by 75 percent during the 1970s, to 15,683, but its Mexican counterpart of the same name was believed to house 120,000 to 150,000 people in the early 1980s. Most of the Mexican fresh vegetables that enter the United States come through Nogales, and a few years back when Florida growers charged that the Mexican imports constituted cheap, unfair competition, Arizonans sided with Mexicans in U.S. government proceedings. In the U.S. and Mexican cities of Nogales, some 50 companies operate "twin plants" or "maquiladoras" in which U.S.–produced components are imported without duty into Mexico, assembled by a vast supply of cheap labor, and then sent back to the United States with duty paid only on the cost of assembly.

Mexican immigration, both legal and illegal, poses the biggest long-term question about the future of Arizona society. In recent years, race relations have improved greatly. Governor Babbitt said in his first inaugural speech that "my policies will recognize that diversity and variety, a pluralistic culture, enriches us all, and that no group should be pressured, however subtly, by prevailing norms to abandon its heritage." But Arizona is still so heavily Anglo that we doubt that the Anglos have really considered the ramifications of a pluralistic culture. Babbitt told us America's past experiences with assimilation would not provide keys to Arizona's sociological future. The new immigrants, Babbitt said, "are tied to their motherland and their mother country by an umbilical cord across a common border, and there's going to be more coming through that umbilical cord than there is melting at the other end. We'll have ethnic pluralism; the melting pot isn't going to happen here."

THE
PACIFIC
STATES

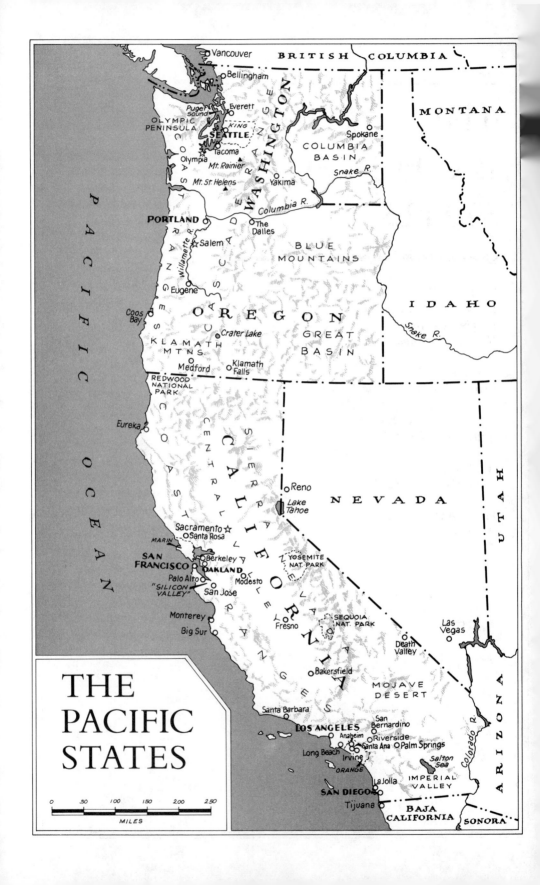

THE
PACIFIC
STATES

0   50   100   150   200   250
MILES

CALIFORNIA

I. The Great Nation State

> But in California the lights went on all at once, in a blaze, and they have never been dimmed.
>
> —Carey McWilliams, *California: The Great Exception*

VIEWED FROM AFAR, California is a mysterious, shimmering entity on our continental edge, forever arresting our attention as in bursts of Delphic prescience it hints at what we shall be. Closer up, the power and the wealth (and the pollution) are palpable. There has never been a state even faintly resembling California. Here live over 24 million people, seven times the population in all the first 13 states in 1790, since 1964 more populous than New York, and home now to one of every ten Americans. Were this an independent country, it would exceed more than 100 other nations in population and 92 in land area. Its gross national product—close to $350 billion—would be greater than those of all nations save the United States and 6 others. The People's Republic of China, with its billion people, produces less. Agriculturally, it would be among the world's leading nations. Of all the United States, California is the one that could most easily exist alone.

Sometimes California does seem almost independent. Located so far from the nation's traditional power centers in the East and with a population so huge it creates its own markets for products and ideas, California alone has been able to challenge New York as the center of economic decision making and Massachusetts as the Athens of America. California has become a colonial power, with an empire stretching through the Mountain states, across the South, into Mexico, and westward to Hawaii and across the Pacific. Yet in another sense, California is very much a part of—and dependent on—the United States. The government in Washington (and taxpayers everywhere) invest fantastic wealth in California's multitudinous defense industries. Half of California's 101 million acres are owned by the federal government. On the economic front, California is home to the nation's largest commercial financial institution, the Bank of America, and second to none in venture capital activity. But California industrialists still must fly to New York to arrange major mergers and to sell corporate stocks and bonds, just as California's municipalities still sell their bonds on the New York markets. Without U.S. markets—and the mighty flow of immigrants the other states have provided —California would be a pale shadow of what it is today.

The third-largest state in land area, after Alaska and Texas, California is so huge geographically—800 miles from corner to corner—that people have sometimes despaired of running it as a single entity. Two of the largest cities, Los Angeles and San Diego, are 360 and 470 air miles, respectively, from the state capital at Sacramento, a separation greater than that in any other state. The legislature actually voted in 1859 (nine years after statehood) to split into north and south states, a proposal frustrated only by the failure of Congress to approve it. The two-state idea continues to be raised when the northern end of the state becomes frustrated with the southern, and vice versa, especially over water issues. But there are strong bonds of unity. The expressways between Northern and Southern California are packed with traffic, and the San Francisco–Los Angeles air corridor is one of the world's most heavily traveled. Even the University of California, with all its campuses, offers unity.

But what, one asks, lies at the heart of this particular vortex of human energy and desire called California? Theories abound: futurism, sun and leisure culture in a beneficent climate, a lemminglike rush to the precipice of the next great earthquake. What does seem constant, as the late Carey McWilliams (the foremost interpreter of modern California) observed, is rapid revolutionary change: "Just as the energies released by the discovery of gold put California into orbit with one mighty blast-off, so it has been kept spinning, faster and faster, by a succession of subsequent, providentially timed discoveries and 'explosions' of one kind or another: the green-gold of lettuce and other produce crops; . . . the black gold of oil; motion pictures, tourism, the aerospace industry. . . . California has raced through the familiar evolutionary cycle—pastoral, agricultural, industrial, post-industrial. . . ."

The pace of technological change is matched by the societal. In the 1960s and early '70s, California was the state of movement: new houses, new cars, new mates. California had become an unstratified society made up of communities of strangers, and the sense of impermanence was overwhelming. In no state was there such a dramatic introduction to the age of the student revolt and campus violence (dating from Berkeley in 1964). By the late '70s and early '80s, a higher cost of living and the aging of the baby boom generation had reduced Californians' mobility. After the voters in 1978 passed Proposition 13, the largest property-tax cut in the nation's history, the spirit of economy and cutback and diminished expectations seemed to rule the day. Largely immune to the effects of most post–World War II recessions, California suffered seriously in the deep national economic downturn of the early 80s' and worried more and more about its sustained leadership and competitive edge in high technology. The state in its 1982 gubernatorial election narrowly rejected its leading black politician, Los Angeles Mayor Tom Bradley, in favor of state Attorney General George Deukmejian, a rather conservative Republican who boasted of having authored 190 anti-crime bills during a 16-year state legislative career. A degree of political schizophrenia was evidenced the same year as Californians simultaneously endorsed a bilateral nuclear freeze agreement with the Soviet Union and yet rejected a domestic disarmament proposal—a ballot initiative to require registration and restrict sales of America's chief weapon of murder and mayhem: the handgun.

And in a country swept up by self-doubt, California seems to doubt the most. After World War II and up to the early 1960s, public opinion polls showed that people were still excited about California and believed in its golden future as an article of faith. In growing measure since 1960, this faith has been replaced by creeping negativism, more doubt about the state's future, and discontent with taxes. All of this translated into the Proposition 13 syndrome, such a deep threat to public outlays that many feared for the future of the great public institutions—universities, schools, parks, freeway systems, water systems, together with assiduous government attention to social services and protection of the great California coastline and other environmental treasures—that had made California the magnificently great civilization it was.

California gained 4 million residents from natural increase and immigration in the 1970s. But the profile of Californian society was shifting fairly rapidly: proportionately fewer Anglo whites (though they remained the majority), many more Hispanics and Orientals. Economically, California had become less accessible to the Midwesterners who used to flood into the Golden State in search of factory jobs and an easier life in the sun. A combination of high demand, strict building permit controls, and—some said—the effects of environmental protection had made housing extraordinarily expensive in California. A single-family home came to cost *several times* in California what it would cost in a Midwestern or Southeastern state, thus clearly out of the reach of the average wage earner. There were thousands of California "refugees" seeking a simpler (and sometimes more affordable) life in various states including New Mexico, Idaho, Arizona, and especially Oregon and Washington.

Though still seen as the Promised Land by many, California became more competitive than ever before. Only the very talented and hard-working engineer, lawyer, or other professional could command the salary to buy middle-class amenities and participate in all the special things California has to offer. And retiring to California became too costly for the average elderly person. Yet simultaneously, California had become the new Ellis Island of America, attracting during the 1970s alone several million Mexicans, other Latin Americans, and refugees from Asia and the Phillipines. By 1980 almost one in five Californians was Hispanic—more than when California was ceded to the United States by Mexico in 1848. By some projections, Hispanics would constitute over 28 percent of Californians by 2000. Asian population seemed likely to rise from 6.7 percent to about 10 percent. Floodtides of immigration cause inevitable social tensions with longtime Californians, both black and white, who see their state being "taken over."

The Grand Tradition: Hiram Johnson to Earl Warren

California politics have weak party organization, dominant personalities, wide use of referenda and initiatives, and maximum feasible nonpartisanship, all a reaction to the era of heavy-handed control by the railroad barons from 1870 to 1910. The control was so complete it has been called "absolute dictatorship." As the state's largest private landowner (thanks to the gift of alternate sections of land along the right of way made by the government), the Southern Pacific Railroad exercised monopolistic control of the principal means of transportation. It used every means, bribery the most prevalent, to control California politics for the purpose of enriching the corporate coffers.

The agent of reform was Hiram Warren Johnson, a fiery attorney. Twice elected governor, in 1910 and 1914, Johnson then went on to the U.S. Senate, where he lived out the remainder of his turbulent days (to 1945). "Get the Southern Pacific Railroad out of politics!" Johnson bellowed in his 1910 campaign. When he won, he quickly secured passage of an arsenal of bills intended to cripple political machines and old-style patronage politics. Initiative, referendum, and recall were enacted, as well as nonpartisan election of judges, a cross-filing system for primaries that permitted office-seekers of one party to run in the primary election of the other, county home rule, and civil service throughout the state government. Other bills made the railroad commission into an effective regulatory body, controlled utilities and their rates, prohibited child labor, instituted workmen's compensation, and began many flood and conservation projects. It was the golden era of Progressive reform and determined the character of California politics up to the present day. California, as much as it has a historic memory, will never forget Hiram Johnson.

The not unfair criticism leveled against Johnson the reformer is that he threw out the baby of normal two-party operation with the bath water of corruption. A politics of chaos ensued; the wonder is that a large share of able and moderate politicians, both Republican and Democratic, were nevertheless able to mold in California one of the best state governments in history, remarkably honest and responsive during decades of convulsive growth.

By the 1920s, Progressivism had spent itself, and a succession of regular Republican governors kept things on an even keel in Sacramento. The Depression, however, hit California especially hard, with high unemployment and severe strikes. Tens of thousands were on relief, and crops rotted in the fields for lack of a market. In 1934, Upton Sinclair, the famous novelist and former Socialist nominee for governor, captured the Democratic gubernatorial nomination and shocked California with his EPIC platform—End Poverty in California. Applying simple Marxist theory, Sinclair advocated turning over to workers some of the means of production—in this instance, the farms and factories of California idled by the Depression. The other elements of Sinclair's platform—graduated income taxes, state support of the jobless, and a $50-a-month pension for the aged and widowed—hardly sound revolutionary today. The propertied California "establishment" was horrified beyond description and spared no effort (or money) to stop Sinclair. Actually a mild-mannered vegetarian with a searing belief in social justice, Sinclair was charged with being "an anarchist, a free-lover, an agent of Moscow, a Communist, and anti-Christ." Eventually he was defeated by 259,000 votes, but only after giving the capitalist class the fright of its life.

Sinclair's EPIC was not the only strange idea to hit California in the mid-1930s; its successors ranged from Technocracy (to let the country be run by engineers and technicians) to the "Ham and Eggs" movement of generous pensions for all over 50. In retrospect, though, the turmoil of the '30s was simply prelude to the Age of Warren.

Earl Warren is the watershed figure of modern-day California politics, the man who took the nonpartisanship of Hiram Johnson (whom he revered) and gave it its ultimate expression; in a wider sense, he is the man who prepared California to become the nation it is today. No politician of modern times has been so popular. Warren is the only man ever elected to three terms as governor of California (in 1942, 1946, and 1950) and the only gubernatorial candidate to win the nominations of both parties (in 1946, before cross-filing was abolished). In 1953, he resigned to accept President Eisenhower's appointment as Chief Justice of the United States.

To the world, Earl Warren offered a wholesome, pleasant exterior: a big, six-foot, 215-pound man exuding good-willed Americanism. His basic instincts—political, judicial, moral—proved superb for the times. About the only incident of a long state career for which Warren is still criticized in California is his consenting to the wartime incarceration of 110,000 Japanese-Americans—some 70,000 of them U.S. citizens—in concentration camps.

Warren showed amazing capacity for growth. For his start in politics, he owed much to the hotly partisan Old Guard Republican faction headed by the Knowland family, which ran the *Oakland Tribune*. He not only cross-filed when he ran for state office but seemed to choose his cabinet and other chief officers on the basis of capabilities rather than party.

Warren's nonpartisanship drove doctrinaire Democrats and reactionary Republicans to apoplexy, but it never failed at the ballot box. It even drew the grudging admiration of President Truman, who once said of Warren, "He's a Democrat—and doesn't know it." The specific list of Warren's accomplishments in California would seem to bear out Truman's assessment. Among them were major advances in state welfare programs, including increased old-age pensions and workmen's compensation, mental hospital and prison reforms, a state crime commission, and enthusiastic backing of the massive Central Valley water project. Warren did not shrink from fights with some of California's toughest lobbies, including oil and private power.

During World War II, as aircraft and other defense industries burgeoned in California and filled the state coffers with tax revenues, Warren refused the temptation to enact tax cuts and instead siphoned off virtually all the excess receipts into reserve funds. At the end of the war, there was then a huge melon of accumulated surpluses that could go into long-neglected schools, colleges, prisons, hospitals, and water projects. Rarely has a politician showed such foresight. Without Warren's hoarding of the pot of gold in the 1940s, California might well have been unable to make the quantum jump in services indispensable to accommodating its fantastic postwar population inflow.

In 1953, Warren went to the Supreme Court, and within less than a year persuaded his fellow Justices to agree to a unanimous decision on school desegregation. As the years went on, the "Warren Court" altered the basic thrust of American law—and history—in the fields of civil rights and liberties, the rights of the accused, and legislative apportionment. Thousands of Americans divided into camps of strong approval or bitter diapproval of Earl Warren.

Parties and Personalities

California has its Republican and Democratic parties. The Republican party has become noted for its successful promotion of conservative economics through the governorship and presidency of Ronald Reagan and its triumph over the party's more liberal, Eastern wing. The California Democratic party has not achieved an influence within the national party commensurate with the state's size. But in the media-dominated world of California, it is the individual candidate who matters. Here are a few of the personalities who have crowded the klieg-lit stage of California politics in recent times.

Richard M. Nixon. Nixon's name must lead the list, for he was the first Californian since Herbert Hoover to win the presidency. Nixon's personality and national record will be well known to the reader. His relationship to California was a curious one. He never held a state or local government office. As a successful candidate for the U.S. House (1946, 1948) and Senate (1950), Nixon was known mainly for the skilled (and with historic perspective, one must say reprehensible) way that he attributed Communist or other radical tendencies to his liberal Democratic opponents. After his eight years as Eisenhower's vice president and his defeat for president in 1960, Nixon returned to his native state, ran a race for governor in which he charged incumbent Edmund G. (Pat) Brown with bungling and being less than hard on Communists, and lost by almost 300,000 votes. There followed Nixon's famous outburst at his "last press conference," his departure for a lucrative law practice in New York City, and Ronald Reagan's eclipse of him as the controlling Republican politician of California. Following his 1968 presidential election, Nixon shifted his voting residence back from New York to the "Western White House" at San Clemente, the home to which he returned when he resigned from the presidency on August 9, 1974. But except, perhaps, in Orange County, there was never any special feeling in California about Nixon as a native son, and the state did not welcome the resigned and disgraced president back with open arms. In 1979 Nixon left again for New York, later moving to suburban New Jersey.

Ronald Reagan. California began a new trend in American politics when it took a veteran movie actor who had not a day's experience in electoral office, elected him governor, and launched him toward the presidency. Other states would later elect such nonpolitical personalities as astronauts (Ohio's John

Glenn) and semi-distinguished men married to famous women (Kentucky's John Y. Brown and Virginia's John Warner), but California did it first. Being rejected for battle service during World War II due to poor eyesight, according to several biographers, made Reagan strongly patriotic, while his substitute reserve service as an officer in a wartime film unit made him suspicious of government bureaucracy. Reagan's interest in public affairs dated from his early acting years, but his political bent then was definitely liberal Democrat. After the war, he was a president of the Screen Actors Guild and a cofounder with Melvyn Douglas of the state chapter of the Americans for Democratic Action. Reagan's tenure as spokesman for the screen actors coincided with the McCarthy era investigations in Hollywood, and it was during this period that Reagan moved to the right. About the same time his career (mostly Grade B movies with some exceptions, such as "Kings Row") began to flounder; it was not long before he landed a job as host for television's "General Electric Theatre" and became a conservative evangelizer for GE at banquets around the U.S.A. It was in this role that Reagan came to the attention of Los Angeles millionaires Henry Salvatori, Holmes Tuttle, and others who decided Reagan could enunciate the conservatives' cause better than any other figure on the political horizon. Reagan became California co-chairman for Barry Goldwater in 1964. From there it took only two years and a careful cram course in state government, arranged by Spencer-Roberts and Associates of Los Angeles, for Reagan to become the preeminent citizen politician and then governor of the nation state. Reagan was considered the dark horse candidate of the right wing until his extraordinarily strong race against President Ford in 1976. By 1980 the Republican party was ready to give him the nomination. In what seemed to many one of the great watershed elections of modern U.S. history, rejecting the liberal Democratic tradition prevalent ever since the New Deal, Reagan won an overwhelming victory over Jimmy Carter for the presidency.

Joel Kotkin and Paul Grabowicz contended in *California, Inc.* that Reagan's original political following—his so-called kitchen cabinet of mostly Los Angeles millionaires—was "essentially nonideological. . . . obsessed by the maintenance of the free enterprise system and their privileged place in it." Reagan sold his supporters' message with superb articulation, demonstrated an innate sense of political appeal and timing, and carefully seized on such events of the time as the Watts racial riots and the Berkeley student revolt to win the political loyalty of middle-class Californians. And he showed immense resilience. Four years after his initial election California was arguably worse off in the areas he had complained of—runaway taxes, soaring welfare costs, escalating crime, and violence on the campuses. The incumbent should have been in trouble, but he was not. For each evil, Reagan found an appropriate villain. Taxes and high budgets were the fault of inflation and spendthrift legislators. High welfare costs were to be blamed on welfare cheaters, permissive social workers, and federal regulations that hamstrung California's cost-cutting programs. Crime was the fault of judges, cop haters, bombers, and Democratic legislators who resisted Reagan's law enforcement programs.

Campus unrest was the fault of undisciplined students, rascally professors, and outside agitators. But the voter could count on Reagan to stand between him and the unruly ones, to stop the outrage short of the patio gate. The natural political charm and telegenic appeal of the man, an aura of modesty even while being tough, sounding liberal even while taking terribly illiberal positions, set Reagan apart from other conservative leaders. The engaging smile, the soft-spoken aura of utter reasonableness, and occasional put-upon-ness, all transmitted uncritically by television, made Reagan a unique commodity among American politicians. When he became president, the same contradictions between promises and performances would be raised—and the same personal qualities would encourage the American people to trust him and like him long after opponents had thought the problems would overwhelm him.

What was Reagan's actual record, behind the image, in California? He appointed some top-drawer men (yet also some real mediocrities) to the judiciary, and though philosophically opposed to payroll tax withholding for income taxes, allowed it to go into effect in 1972. He attempted welfare reform. Oftentimes, Reagan and the Democratic legislature were in such disagreement that new programs were postponed and the highly professional California bureaucracy carried on without major gubernatorial involvement. But just as he would as president, Reagan created the feeling in California that he favored the wealthy over the poor (after his reelection in 1970, it came out that he had used tax shelters to avoid all California income tax that year) and deliberately scorned and alienated minorities to create his political majority. A prime example of Reagan's attitude toward the unfortunate in society was his 1970 veto of the federal grant for the California Rural Legal Assistance Agency. CRLA had begun in 1966 after Cesar Chavez and his farm workers' union focused attention on the problems of the rural poor. Tens of thousands of indigent Californians were able to turn to CRLA offices for help. But local power structures and especially big farmers (a key Reagan constituency) were enraged. Reagan exhorted the Nixon administration in Washington to kill the whole program but failed as CRLA was repeatedly exonerated and praised for its work. As president, Reagan again sought to cripple legal aid—this time with more success.

The broadest criticism leveled at Reagan as governor was that he failed to come to grips with California's long-term problems of smog and water pollution, transit and parks, open space and land use. A similar judgment of inaction in the face of looming problems would doubtless be levelled at his presidency. Yet in another sense, Reagan in both California and Washington was utterly relevant to his times, recognizing that the burgeoning governments of postwar America were growing too rapidly, and acting more imperiously, than the citizenry in the long run would tolerate, and that the American political culture required far greater dependence on the private sector.

Edmund G. ("Jerry") Brown, Jr. It is hard to imagine a greater contrast between two governors than that between Reagan and his successor, Jerry Brown (1975–83). While Reagan was elderly, Brown represented youth. While

Reagan revered America's industrial and social past, Brown tried to be at the cutting edge of change. The difference was not, however, between classic conservative and liberal, for it became Brown's lot to institute economies, to consider the implications of an "age of limits," and to forge the gap between the old America and the new frontiers of high technology and social thinking. Some of Brown's futuristic ideas proved so futuristic that some called him "Governor Moonbeam." Yet for years he was unquestionably the most creative thinking public official in the nation.

To understand the significance of Brown's originality, it's necessary to compare him with his father, Edmund G. ("Pat") Brown, who had knocked down two Republican heavies to win two terms as governor—William F. Knowland in 1958 and Nixon in 1962—before being defeated by Reagan in 1966. A progressive in the Johnson-Warren mold, Pat Brown was a moderate governor noted not for glamor, but for good administration. In hindsight, Pat Brown emerges as the last of the California governors that could operate on the principle that unlimited growth in itself was a desirable end. While he was in office, the great $1.7 billion California Water Plan was passed. Some 1,000 miles of freeway, now seen as a mixed blessing, were constructed. In terms of Brown's times, these were great achievements. His years in office also saw the first major overhaul of the executive branch in 30 years, abolition of the troublesome cross-filing system in primaries, and creation of California's first fair employment practices commission. A master plan for higher education made it possible for young people to "move up" in the system, according to their talents, and the universities were showered with financial support. Equalization of state aid to school districts was inaugurated, and the state began to invest more in aid for the needy and the mentally ill.

Like his father, Jerry Brown was elected as a Democrat, but there the similarities stopped. The young bachelor Brown (he was born in 1938) refused to move into the huge governor's mansion Reagan had built, rode in a Plymouth instead of a chauffeured limousine, and occasionally retreated to a Zen Buddhist monastery to meditate (he had studied in a Jesuit seminary before entering Yale Law School). But despite this seemingly ascetic lifestyle, he also broke with politicians' conventional discretion to travel to Africa with his companion, rock singer Linda Ronstadt. Intellectually, Brown symbolized his generation's dissatisfaction with big institutions and megasolutions. He set up the nation's first Office of Appropriate Technology to explore and test such concepts as environmental and climatically designed buildings, including wind power and solar heating, bioconversion (using waste to produce energy) and home organic farming to increase people's self-sufficiency. He launched California onto an energy conservation path unequalled by any other state, consistently opposed nuclear power, maintained the nation's toughest air and water pollution standards and laws against toxic wastes, and created the Agricultural Labor Relations Board, which leaned to the left in its regulation of farm-labor relations. He made precedent-shattering appointments of women, blacks, Hispanics, and Asians, who received 50 percent of his 6,000-plus executive appointments and 40 percent of those he made to the courts.

The "old boy networks" of white males were closed out. Hundreds of laypersons were placed on California's 41 consumer boards, breaking the monopoly control of groups—from doctors to engineers—who've often used the state's regulatory boards for their professions' interests rather than the public interest. Brown ended up with five women in his ten-member cabinet—not to mention his highly controversial appointment of a liberal female lawyer, Rose Elizabeth Bird, as California's chief justice. In the last weeks of Brown's governorship, we asked him the rationale of his appointments approach. His reply: "to make government a mirror image of what society is" in a state with millions of working women and fast-rising numbers of minorities and the foreign born. His appointees' skills, Brown admitted, often weren't the highest. But the alternative was to leave a "dying" white male coalition in power. "I came down on the side of opening a window to the future."

Brown authored a state urban policy to revitalize inner cities and discourage wasteful sprawl—a first in any Sunbelt state. He inaugurated an energy and resources fund, financed from tidelands oil revenues, to foster California fisheries, reforestation, soil conservation, wetlands, and coastal protection. He cajoled government pension funds to invest more (up to $900 million a year) in California housing and economic enterprises, rather than distant investments irrelevant to the state's economic future. Enamored of high technology, which he believed must be a linchpin of both California and national economic growth strategies, he created an industrial innovation commission (including many successful high-tech entrepreneurs), which recommended "a new governing coalition between business, labor, academia and government" to foster growth industries and dominate international markets in such cutting-edge areas as semiconductors, computers, telecommunications, robotics, and biotechnology. Brown argued that radically improved scientific education in schools and colleges, combined with ambitious workers retraining, was imperative for state and national economic survival. He gave energy and direction to a highly innovative California Conservation Corps for young people. Belatedly, he tried to tame soaring health costs through a "czar" to prenegotiate economical doctor and hospital rates, on a competitive basis, for patients of the state-subsidized "MediCal" system.

Even Brown admirers agree his style was often arrogant and showboaty, that his flip-flops on such issues as Proposition 13 (first against, then for) gave him an image of opportunism and political craftiness. Until his last years in office, his relations with the legislature were horrendous. His administrative record was seriously flawed in such fields as mental health; he delayed dangerously in spraying insecticides to control the Mediterranean fruit fly—a dire threat to California's bounteous agriculture. His ambition seemed overweaning as he ran twice for president (in 1976 and 1980). Gradually his base of political support disintegrated, and he was soundly trounced by San Diego Mayor "Pete" Wilson when he sought a U.S. Senate seat in 1982.

But for challenging old ways of operation, for introducing new ideas, Brown was unparalleled. Whether his political demise (at the young age of 44) proved temporary or permanent, American government agendas to the end of the century were likely to reflect copies and adaptations of his pioneering programs.

Jess Unruh. Born the son of an illiterate and impoverished Kansas sharecropper, Unruh grew up in Texas, hitchhiked to California at 18 with five dollars in his pocket, and became the speaker of the Assembly at 39. In the 1950s, Unruh uttered two harsh dicta still remembered: "Money is the mother's milk of politics," and, speaking of lobbyists, "If you can't take their money, drink their booze, screw their women, and look them in the eye and vote against them, you don't belong here." But during the 1960s, Unruh decided to discard his "Big Daddy" image, lost 100 pounds, and turned his attention to shaping the Assembly into the most professional, best-staffed legislative house in the United States. He also became a national authority and lecturer on state legislatures and governments. Unruh was a longtime Kennedy supporter and stood only a few feet from Robert Kennedy when he was shot by Sirhan Sirhan at the Ambassador Hotel in 1968; afterward Unruh went back to more activist and participatory politics and ran a populist-style "give-em-hell" campaign against Reagan for governor in 1970. If the California press had not prematurely discounted Unruh's viability as a candidate (he lacked money for media), he might have come much closer to beating Reagan. Later, Unruh returned to Sacramento as state treasurer, forever a fountain of wisdom on California government (and of good quotes), but in power not a shadow of his former self.

Willie Brown. In the late 1960s, Unruh took aside a young black assemblyman who had just delivered a brilliant speech, and said, "It's a good thing you aren't white. Because if you were, you'd own the place." In 1980, Willie Brown became speaker of the assembly. If anyone overcame even greater odds than Unruh to achieve high political office, it was Brown.

Born in Mineola, Texas, eight miles east of Dallas, in 1934, Brown endured debasing discrimination until he graduated from high school and left for San Francisco to join his uncle, Itsie Collins, a gambler and big wheel in the Fillmore District. Young Willie dreamed of going to college; Texas had so poorly educated him, however, that he scored near the bottom in his admission test for San Francisco State. But the school accepted Brown as one of 100 below-par students in an experimental program. Brown took his studies seriously, became a lawyer representing whores, petty criminals, and civil rights defendants. He entered politics under the wing of San Francisco's liberal Burton brothers, winning election to the assembly in 1964. His early years there were marked by actions considered radical at the time, such as marching for free speech in Berkeley and for civil rights in Selma, Alabama. Brown even declared the Watts riots to have been "selective burning" of symbols of oppression. In the legislature itself, he boycotted the annual budget vote because, he said, it neglected the poor and blacks. By the end of the '60s, however, Brown started to participate in budget negotiations, to mute his rhetoric, and to compromise ideology for the sake of gaining power. In 1971, he became chairman of the ways and means committee, built up the committee's staff, and ran strict committee hearings that began at the unheard of hour —for legislators—of 8 A.M.

In 1981 Brown scored a brilliant political coup. Democratic Speaker Leo McCarthy and his even-more-liberal opponent, Howard Berman, were locked in a tight, bitter struggle for speakership of the incoming Assembly. Conservatives of both parties sought a compromise candidate who would be both trustworthy and flexible; Brown, in secret meetings, offered them multiple concessions. So Brown got solid Republican support and half the Democratic votes and became Speaker. Brown's personal evolution also took him from love beads to $1,200 suits and Porsches, which he financed by earning $200,000 per year moonlighting as an attorney. He was a political ally of Governor Jerry Brown, but in personal style the radiant, energized antithesis of the ascetic governor (whom he called "the lesser Brown"). "My car is my life," he explained. "My body would reject a Plymouth." Flashes of liberalism and radicalism remained when he fought to repeal laws against oral sex and sodomy, awarding his opponents in the legislature bogus contracts to star in a movie *Carnal Ignorance.*

Alan Cranston. A journalist and real estate executive in a family business, Cranston began his political career as a founder of the California Democratic Council, an important liberal action group in the 1950s and '60s. After serving eight years as state controller, Cranston won a Senate seat in 1968. Representing California on the Potomac, Cranston proved a classic liberal on most social issues and a vigorous opponent of nuclear proliferation. More than the younger neo-liberals of the Jerry Brown mold, he favored government intervention in the economy, including an effort to shore up traditional industries —not just promote high technology. But Cranston also protected California's economic interests. He was responsible for the passage of the $250 million loan guarantee to Lockheed when it got into trouble in the early 1970s; he also saw to it that California (and other states) were exempted from paying the windfall profits tax on their oil holdings. Cranston kept good relations with conservatives and struck compromises with other senators, talents that helped him win the position of Senate Democratic whip in 1976. A health enthusiast and world-class runner for his age, Cranston began a presidential campaign at the age of 68 in 1982.

"Pete" Wilson, winning California's other Senate seat in 1982, became the first experienced politician to hold it in many years. Former San Francisco State College President S.I. "Sam" Hayakawa, who had won a conservative following for putting down a student strike in 1968, held the seat from 1977 to 1982. Hayakawa had beaten another one-termer, John V. Tunney, a congressman and son of the ex-heavyweight boxing champion Gene Tunney; Tunney, in turn, had taken the seat from one-term Sen. George Murphy, the first of the California actors to break into big-time politics.

California's big House delegation increased along with the state's population from 30 in the 1950s to 45 after 1982, more than 10 percent of the membership. But considering its size, the delegation has much less power than one might expect. It is often close to evenly split between Democrats and Republicans. Yet if the delegation rarely works together to achieve a single goal, it is also true that California is so rich and diverse its interests are rarely of the single-track type of smaller states—where unity is more prevalent.

From the '70s into the '80s, the most powerful and influential California House member was Democrat Phillip Burton of San Francisco. Starting with his initial election in 1964, Burton opposed the Vietnam War, successfully advocated the abolition of the House Un-American Activities Committee, became (as a member of the Education and Labor Committee) an expert on welfare legislation, and contributed heavily to reforming the House into a more open institution. As chairman of the Democratic Study Group, Burton raised campaign funds and hoped to become Democratic majority leader. His fellow House members rejected him, however, in favor of Thomas P. O'Neill of Massachusetts, mostly because of uneasiness over Burton's mercurial personality. Burton's California power remained formidable indeed. The Democratic-controlled legislature rubber-stamped a California congressional redistricting plan for the '80s written by Burton—a plan so egregiously partisan that Republicans took it to statewide referendum and killed it. Burton, *Congressional Quarterly* has said, is a "San Francisco version of Lyndon Johnson."

Some of the other members have stood out on occasion. Among Democrats, Henry Waxman, of Los Angeles, proved powerful when he used his chairmanship of the House Energy and Commerce Committee's Health Subcommittee to block President Reagan's efforts to slash Medicaid and other health programs. Leon Panetta, of Carmel Valley, a member of the Budget Committee, was also a key strategist for Democrats in their budget fights with Reagan. Ron Dellums, of Oakland, has waged an increasingly lonely battle to bring radical and socialist views, as well as the needs of his fellow black constituents, before Congress. Norman Mineta, the former mayor of San Jose, has chalked up good committee assignments (Budget, Public Works and Transportation, Select Intelligence), and his fellow House members have often mentioned him as a potential future House leader. Augustus F. Hawkins, the senior member of the congressional Black Caucus, went to Washington in 1962 after serving in the state assembly since 1935; in Congress he concentrated on the nitty gritty of job creation and eschewed radical black rhetoric. He coauthored the 1978 Humphrey-Hawkins full employment bill, a conceptual last gasp of the New Deal that would have required the government to become an employer of last resort; the bill was passed, but with only its goal and no enforcement teeth in place.

California's Republicans have rarely stood out in the House, and in 1982 lost some of their most famed members, including the conservative and personable John Rousselot, erstwhile John Birch Society member, who lost to a Hispanic Democrat in a sharply redistricted section of Los Angeles County, and Paul "Pete" McCloskey, of Menlo Park, a liberal Republican who was an early critic of the Vietnam War and ran a short-lived campaign against President Nixon in 1972 for the party nomination. McCloskey sacrificed reelection to the House when he ran unsuccessfully for the Republican Senate nomination. He represented "Silicon Valley," the nation's largest concentration of high-technology companies and favored their interests, such as reduction in the capital gains tax. (McCloskey was replaced by another liberal Republican Ed Zschau, the first high-tech executive to be elected to Congress.)

Everything happens so fast in California that former officeholders fade fast from memory. But a few should be noted. One of the most powerful men in modern California was William F. Knowland, "the Lone Moose" who published the family-owned *Oakland Tribune* and served in the U.S. Senate (1945–59), where he took inflexibly conservative positions and succeeded Robert Taft as Senate Republican leader. In 1958, Knowland almost caused the ruination of the California GOP when he returned to California determined to run for governor in a thinly disguised move to position himself for the 1960 Republican presidential nomination. Governor Goodwin Knight had to be persuaded to run for Knowland's Senate seat instead. This game of musical chairs offended the voters, who sent both men down to crashing defeat. Returning to Oakland as publisher, Knowland took a conciliatory position on black-white relations there before committing suicide in 1974.

Innovative Politics

Hiram Johnson invented and Earl Warren institutionalized multitudinous devices to make California's politics unique among the states. Yet California was still busy in the early 1980s on innovations the rest of the country may pick up later. Some prime examples of the old and new:

Initiative and Referendum. California has one of the nation's best legislatures, but one the people trust the least. Since 1911, when initiative and referendum were written into the state constitution, hundreds upon hundreds of constitutional changes and new statutes have been placed on the ballot for the people's verdict, not to mention referendums on laws already passed by the legislature. Initiatives can go on the ballot by vote of the legislature or by popular petition of a set percentage of the state's voters. In Johnson's day, it took about 30,000 signatures to put an initiative on the ballot; by the early 1980s, more than 345,000 were required, and signature gathering had become a big business costing close to $1 per head.

The focus of initiatives on the ballot has changed over time. In the first decades, many proposals dealt with moral and economic problems such as prohibition, prize fighting, compulsory vaccination, and the eight-hour day. In the 1920s, several dealt with public education (in an attempt to get the state to shoulder more of its cost). The voters also forced the state to adopt an executive budget, still hailed by many as the initiative's greatest accomplishment. The 1930s saw the focus turn to the various pension plans; "Ham & Eggs" alone made it to the ballot five times between 1938 and 1948. The biggest battle of the 1950s was over "right to work" (which was defeated); of the '60s, an effort to repeal fair housing legislation (passed but overruled by the state supreme court). Yet of all California initiatives over the years, none had national repercussions faintly resembling Proposition 13 in 1978. It slashed California property taxes 60 percent and gave credibility and ammunition to the great state-local tax revolt of the times.

Recall. Also enacted by Johnson and his followers in 1911, recall has been used frequently in local elections. There have been aborted recall movements against governors, none ever coming to a vote, and repealed efforts to use the device to oust Chief Justice Bird, target of California conservatives' bitterest resentment.

Local Nonpartisanship. The state constitution requires nonpartisan elections for all county and municipal offices. The result is quite simple: no local partisan "machines" in the style known to the East and Midwest; rarely, if ever, a serious election fraud; an entrenched civil service often indifferent to elected officials and new policies they may try to effect.

Presidential Primaries. Popular election of national convention delegates was another one of Hiram Johnson's ideas and early enactments. But in its first seven decades of use, the California presidential primary has rarely played a crucial role in a nomination fight. The major problem is the date, the first Tuesday in June, after primaries have already been held in many other states. If California placed its primary earlier in the year, as has been proposed several times, it seems inevitable it would begin to achieve the potency appropriate for the most populous state of the nation.

There have been four important postwar primaries, however: Adlai Stevenson's decisive victory over Estes Kefauver in the 1956 Democratic contest; Barry Goldwater's knockout punch to Nelson Rockefeller in the Republican primary of 1964; Robert Kennedy's 1968 victory over Hubert Humphrey (the victory Kennedy was celebrating when felled by an assassin's bullets in Los Angeles); and, finally, Ronald Reagan's two-to-one victory over President Ford in 1976, establishing the Reagan momentum that would finally push him to his 1980 nomination.

Campaign Management Firms. California is the state where the first professional campaign management firms appeared and where the largest national firms are still located. Granddaddy of the profession was the San Francisco firm of Whitaker and Baxter, begun in 1933 as a professional (and later matrimonial) alliance of Clem Whitaker, a young reporter and public relations man, and Leone Baxter, manager of the Redding Chamber of Commerce. Their idea was simple, but revolutionary: a public relations firm specializing in politics. California provided especially fertile ground because (a) each ballot was crowded with initiatives and referenda, many so important to certain groups that they would spend into the millions to ensure their passage or defeat, and (b) professional assistance for candidates was needed to fill the vacuum created by the lack of adequate party organizations. In all, W and B won 70 of its 75 campaigns between 1933 and 1955. In classic PR style, a single, preferably emotional issue would be found as the central theme of a campaign, and then driven home again and again. "The average American," Whitaker once said, "doesn't want to be educated; he doesn't want to improve his mind; he doesn't even want to work, consciously, at becoming a good citizen."

Another firm, Spencer-Roberts and Associates, later pioneered in the use of "scientific" political techniques such as polling and systems approaches to political campaigning. William Roberts did not agree with Whitaker's old disdain for the people: "I think they make wonderful decisions based on the knowledge they have. I don't say that they are ignorant and stupid and can be led around by the nose. . . . I'm opposed to putting a lot of rules and restrictions on campaigning. I think I ought to have the right to lie to you if I think it'll help me win. I think you have the right to detect my lie and vote no when you go in the polling booth."

As early as 1971, Roberts said that the traditional party apparatuses in California and increasingly across the country were "almost irrelevant to winning" contemporary elections. He worried, though, that the campaign consultants would become the people who decide which candidates are best. Within the decade his prediction was born out, and even more amazing, political polling became an element of public policy itself. President Carter hired Cambridge, Mass.-based Patrick Caddell to advise him on policy; when Ronald Reagan became president, he switched the job to the California-based Decision Making Information, a Spencer-Roberts offshoot that had pioneered in the use of advanced computer techniques.

As campaign costs soared in California, so did the need for professional campaign management; firms sprouted left and right, some fly-by-night, some formidable and permanent. By the 1980s, campaign consulting had become a national business—the largest firms in California competing with outfits in Washington, New York, Boston, and other cities. These campaign practices were severely criticized by some political scientists. Wrote Larry J. Sabato in *The Rise of Political Consultants:* "Political professionals and their techniques have helped homogenize American politics, added significantly to campaign costs, lengthened campaigns, and narrowed the focus of elections. Consultants have emphasized personality and gimmickry over issues, often exploiting emotional and negative themes rather than encouraging rational discussion. They have sought candidates who fit their technologies more than the requirements of office and have given an extra boost to candidates who are more skilled at electioneering than governing."

The political consultants replied that they were replacing already atrophied party structures. The parties and oldtime bosses, they noted, maintained a closed candidate selection process and kept issues they opposed from receiving a proper airing. Whatever the pros and cons, this California-bred campaign business had become the national norm.

A challenge to the mainstream political consulting firms, came from the right-wing direct mail firm of state Senator H.L. (Bill) Richardson, of Arcadia, in Los Angeles County. In 1974, during an ill-fated run against Senator Alan Cranston, Richardson learned the techniques of national conservative direct mail czar Richard Viguerie and, after the election, began applying them to California. Richardson has used his expertise (making money all the while) to generate mail campaigns in favor of death penalty legislation and against gun control, to raise money for the Republican party, and to help favored candidates. Richardson's highly negative and successful 1980 campaign against the venerable Democratic state Senator Albert Rodda, of Sacramento, Jonathan Kirsch has written, "has made over California politics in his own image—bloodthirsty, rancorous, colorful but also brutal."

"Holl-i-ticking." The elevation of Reagan-the-actor to the presidency brought the entertainment industry a respectability and prominence previously unknown in the United States (or in any other country, for that matter). It was already common, however, for Hollywood film executives and stars to play important roles in financing campaigns and, in more recent times, to endorse candidates. On the Republican side, Bob Hope, Jimmy Stewart, Buddy Ebsen, and the late John Wayne were among the Hollywood personalities who opened their checkbooks and lined up support. The Democrats may have profited even more. In the days of the big Hollywood studios, many of the moguls were Jewish and donated to the Democrats. Other celebrities aiding the Democrats included Shirley MacLaine, Henry Fonda, and Dean Martin. (Frank Sinatra was on that list in the early Kennedy era but later switched to the Republicans and Reagan.) More than cash contributions, however, the stars have contributed celebrity appearances, especially rock concert political benefits. Actor-director Warren Beatty literally invented such events during the 1972 George McGovern presidential campaign, according to Colorado Senator Gary Hart, co-manager of the McGovern campaign. In the 1970s, after Congress limited individuals' donations to $1,000 per candidate, the rock concerts rose in import since many thousands of dollars could be raised in one evening. A concert by the Allman Brothers band in 1976 was credited with saving Jimmy Carter's presidential campaign when it was almost out of money. Republican politicians also raked in cash, through the activities of such performers as Pat and Debby Boone, Shaun Cassidy, the Osmonds, and Wayne Newton.

A number of performers have donated their money, talent, and names to special causes, such as the anti-nuclear movement. Hollywood's biggest political controversy since the McCarthy-era witchhunts came in the early 1980s when liberal actor Ed Asner, star of TV's "Lou Grant," was elected president of the Screen Actors Guild and received a broader audience for his personal views, especially his denunciation of U.S. involvement in El Salvador. Asner's TV series was canceled, and there was an unsuccessful move to oust him from his Guild position. Actress Jane Fonda's money allowed her husband, Tom Hayden, one of the founders of the 1960s radical student group Students for a Democratic Society, to start his own political movement in California in the 1970s, the Campaign for Economic Democracy, and to win an astonishingly expensive 1982 state assembly race.

Governing Nation-State

The combination of its size, its wealth, its distance from Washington, and its progressive traditions have all made the California state government perhaps the most exciting and innovative in the U.S. California's state constitution is weak, lengthy, and has been frequently amended, but it includes the executive budget, which permits the governor, through his department of finance (the state equivalent of the federal Office of Management and Budget) to guide the operation of state government. The governor's authority is enhanced by a line item veto authority, permitting him to reduce the dollar amount for any item in an appropriation bill—a power U.S. presidents would dearly love to have. Two-thirds of the budget, however, is locked in by constitutional provisions or statutes, beyond gubernatorial control.

Since the days of Jesse Unruh's speakership in the 1960s, California has had the best paid, best staffed, full-time legislature in the country. The lion's share of credit for this goes to Unruh, with important help from Robert T. Monagan, Republican assembly leader when Unruh was speaker and his successor in 1969–70. When Reagan proved to be a budget-minded governor with little interest in new programs, the legislature became the programmatic, innovative branch of state government. By the 1980s, however, it was time to ask whether the reforms were worth the bill. Legislators were making $28,000 plus fringe benefits, while critics such as *Los Angeles Times* political correspondent Bill Boyarsky charged that full-time legislators, as opposed to the citizen legislators of old, had turned out to be "mediocrities." The legislative staff had ballooned to 1,700 employees and the legislature's total budget to $106 million, even as Proposition 13 had caused cuts in health and welfare. The issue was not a minor one, nor restricted to California, since at the urging of a reform movement led by legislative consultant Larry Margolis, Unruh's right-hand man in the '60s, many other legislatures had developed some variation of the California model of higher salaries and staffs.

Highly professional legislative staffs have made legislators less dependent on lobbyists for basic information, but whether the higher legislative salaries and increased staff have made them more independent in their voting is open to question. Direct bribes and similar skullduggery, by most accounts, are now unacceptable to the California legislature. Long past are the days of the '40s when lobbyist Arthur H. ("Artie") Samish could boast: "I'm the governor of the legislature. To hell with the governor of the state. If you get a long enough ladder and put it up against the Capitol dome, you can take a picture of me unscrewing the gold cupola." (For that indiscretion in a magazine interview, Samish ended up being barred "forever" from lobbying in the California legislature.)

Sacramento was one of the first state capitals to develop the "new breed" of lobbyists, men and women with governmental expertise who rely on argument rather than the old techniques of friendships, dinners, and tricky legislative tactics. In 1975, in the wake of Watergate, California voters passed an initiative creating the nation's toughest political reform laws, prohibiting lawmakers from taking more than $10 per month from a lobbyist, even in food and drink, and creating the Fair Political Practices Commission to monitor enforcement of the law. But huge, legal campaign contributions by corporations and professionals continued, intensifying the trend of powerful economic interests to receive preferred treatment in Sacramento.

The "Third House" of lobbyists still flourishes in Sacramento, but the "heavyweights" have changed over time. The power of such individual corporations as Pacific Gas and Electric Co., Standard Oil of California, and Bank of America has given way to political action committees organized by professionals and business groups. If size of campaign contributions is any indicator of lobbying power (and it usually is), the top lobbyists in California in the early 1980s were the California Medical Association, California State Employees Association, California Association of Realtors, United of California (a business coalition), California Gun Owners Association, California Dental Association, the Teamsters Union, Bankers for Responsible Government, the AFL-CIO (through its political action committee), the Agricultural Council of California, and the Farm Bureau. The single most effective lobbyist was believed to be James D. Garibaldi, an ex-legislator who represented horse racing, the liquor industry, and other business interests. A man so much of the old school that he is known as the "last of the lobbyists" is Donald Kent BrOwn (he insists on that peculiar capitalization), who represents, among others, the companies owned by the late Howard Hughes.

From the late 1940s through the early 1970s, California pioneered in innovative government on a scale virtually unprecedented among state governments (New York perhaps excepted). Its multibillion-dollar State Water Plan, inaugurated under Pat Brown, was long cited as one example, though there may have been serious ecological damage as a result of it. A California career executive assignment system, inaugurated in 1963, provided at least a measure of the flexibility in assignment of top careerists often cited as a grave shortcoming in state civil service systems. In the mid 1960s, California pioneered in community health center development. The argument was that the mentally disturbed could be happier and better treated in their own communities, while money could be saved by reducing the number of people in institutions. The budgets for community mental health were later cut, even as mental patients were deinstitutionalized, resulting in ghettos of mentally ill in major cities. In the 1950s and '60s, California led in progressive prison legislation, including family visitation for prisoners and job placement. But the succeeding decade, in which the "baby boom" generation was at the height of its crime-prone age—teens and early '20s—brought crime waves, demands for more imprisonment of criminals, and less sympathetic attitudes toward criminals. The California system still ranked as one of the better in the country, but life could be a living hell for a California convict, and the situation in the prisons became particularly complicated in the '70s by the growth of Hispanic prison gangs. Blacks, both in gangs and in reform movements, had already organized in the '60s.

The increasingly impatient public reaction to crime was manifested in the death penalty issue. Early in 1972, in what appeared to be more evidence of progressivism in state government, the California Supreme Court decreed that the death penalty "may no longer be exacted" because of conflict with the California constitution. The state's voters, however, quickly restored it by initiative.

The natural environment is a big issue in California, and Californians rank among its most determined exploiters, desecrators, and protectors. Like its citizens, the state government has a spotty record, which began in despoliation, turned to the possibilities of conservation, and tries to save for future generations much of the magnificent heritage of natural California.

Smog, now a severe national problem, first evidenced its ugly presence in the Los Angeles Basin, later to appear in alarming measure in cities such as San Jose, Oakland, and Fresno. For almost three decades, air pollution bills have been winning approval in Sacramento, well ahead of the national government. One shred of good news of the early '80s was that Southern California's air pollution levels, compared to a decade before, had improved measurably. California also faces severe water pollution problems, in part through agricultral and industrial chemicals that contaminate soils and underground water supplies.

Of California's 100 million acres, the federal government owns about half —largely as national forests, parks, and military bases. Private holdings total 50 million acres. Only a small percentage of the land area is occupied by cities, but they are often in the choicest locations, and their environs have been in peril ever since the great postwar housing surge began to push subdivisions out across exquisite fields and orchards.

Some notable conservation victories have included bond issues for purchase of new parklands, defeat of a freeway through virgin redwood forests in the north, and a halt to the filling in of San Francisco Bay. A scenic roads program got its start in the early 1960s when conservationists became upset by the state highway department's plan to "improve" the twisty, picturesque old Route 1 along the Big Sur coastline into a four- or eight-lane highway, which would have despoiled one of the most exciting, magnificent highway stretches anywhere in the world. A cooperative effort by state and local government to select and then protect scenic corridors was started and led to the federal scenic roads program.

Aesthetics, however, have not been the main point of California's gargantuan postwar freeway development. More than 5,400 miles of freeways have been built since the Pasadena Freeway, California's first in 1940. The state highway department has extraordinary powers of eminent domain and gets its huge budget from a 1937 constitutional amendment that dedicates highway user taxes (gasoline, oil, vehicle registrations) exclusively for highway building or improvement. Despite the fact that they plowed through open land or neighborhoods, the freeways for years generated scant opposition, and many were welcomed. In the late 1950s, however, came the now famous revolt of San Franciscans against the unsightly Embarcadero Freeway, the prelude to many other battles—some won by the highway lobby, some by opponents.

Governor Jerry Brown viewed highway building as an energy-inefficient extravagance in an "era of limits" and brought highway construction to a virtual halt. The major elements of the freeway system have been built, however.

California has spawned more conservation groups than any other state, the most famous of all being the Sierra Club, founded by the naturalist John Muir in 1892 to "explore, enjoy and preserve the Sierra Nevada and other scenic resources of the U.S." The club still has a lot of hikers, but its principal visibility has come through its great fights to preserve the natural environment through both lobbying and lawsuits.

In 1971, the Sierra Club and other environmental groups were in the forefront of a fight to pass legislation to provide orderly planning and growth along the coastline. The idea was lobbied to death in Sacramento by oil companies, utilities concerned about their power plant sites, and owners of major seashore land developments. But the environmentalists turned the proposal into an initiative, which the voters approved. The measure removed control of the coast from cities and counties and gave it to the newly created California Coastal Commission. A decade later, the commission had proven itself to be the toughest, most hardline government environmental agency in the United States. No new subdivisions had been built on coastal farmlands, very few marshlands had been filled or diked, Highway One had been preserved as a scenic, two-lane highway, and few high-rise buildings and no power plants had been allowed along the beach. The commission also increased public access to the beaches and encouraged housing for low- and moderate-income families near the shore. All this did not proceed, of course, without heavy opposition from landowners and developers, who charged that property rights were infringed and that regulations were nitpicking. Middle-class homeowners also charged that the commission's standards made it expensive to build or remodel houses. Oil companies objected to the commission's powers to regulate off-shore drilling (the commission, remembering the oil blowout near Santa Barbara in 1969, was very strict) and sought in the early 1980s to have the Reagan administration in Washington overturn it. The cities and counties also objected to their inability to control the destiny of land in their political jurisdictions. The localities were given the opportunity to develop their own coastal management plans. By the early 1980s, less than half had done so, but the pressure for more local control continued to mount.

Many things Californian evoke superlatives; no institution merits them more than the University of California. Despite its many tribulations, UC remains the most successful institution of higher education that the United States, and perhaps the world, has ever known. From humble beginnings as an academy in an Oakland dance hall in 1853, it has developed into a "multiversity" of more than 138,000 students and a staff of 70,000 working and studying in nine distinct campuses. The university has an annual budget of well over $1.5 billion, offers in excess of 10,000 courses, operates four nuclear laboratories and more than 100 research and experimental stations located in all counties of the state but one. It had 14 Nobel prize laureates on its faculty at last count.

The benefit that has accrued to California's people through their fantastic investment in UC is almost beyond estimation. Without the university's distinction in agricultural research, the physical sciences, technology, and water conservation, California would be, economically a weak shadow of what it is today. And foremost among the American states, California has given its young people an opportunity to take advantage of higher public education. Under the master plan for higher education, adopted in 1960, every California youngster interested in continuing his education beyond high school has an opportunity to do so under a three-tiered program. At the base are community colleges, an idea California pioneered (for itself, and the rest of America) at Pasadena City College over 70 years ago. In 1981–82 there were 107 such campuses, almost all commuter schools in students' home areas, with 1,252,323 students. Among other achievements, the community colleges have turned out many technicians for California industries, in fields as disparate as computer programming and medical technology. Next up the rung are state colleges (more recently called state universities)—in the early '80s, 19 in number with an enrollment of 319,565 students. Their four-year program, leading to a bachelor's degree, is open to any California high school graduate who places in the upper third of his class, plus successful community college graduates. The emphasis is on undergraduate instruction, and some of the state colleges—notably, San Jose State, San Diego State, and Long Beach State—compare well in program and teaching to the best state universities of the country.

The University of California, at the top of the pyramid, accepts only the top 12.5 percent of California high school graduates, plus a limited number of out-of-state students, who must meet even tougher standards. Academically, the university intended to be, and is, an elitist institution. It also has three exclusive and jealously guarded functions with California public higher education: to act as the state's primary agency for research; to grant doctorates; to train students for such professions as medicine, dentistry, pharmacy, law, and architecture.

UC's tight admission requirements came under increasing criticism in the late 1960s because blacks and Chicanos, while 19 percent of California high school enrollees, made up only 2 percent of UC's student body. A "special action" admission provision was enacted for culturally and economically deprived applicants who, admissions officers believe, could, with proper motivation and counseling, perform satisfactorily at the university level. Up to 6 percent of the students may be so admitted.

The nine UC campuses are a fascinating study in diversity. UCLA, in the posh Los Angeles suburb of Westwood, did not grant a doctorate before 1938 but now ranks among the nation's top universities; it is strong in community involvement, athletics, and several academic disciplines. San Diego has one of the best natural science facilities in the U.S. (Scripps Institution of Oceanography and others), plus a unique system of "cluster colleges": science-oriented Revelle; academically and socially freer John Muir; and a controversial Third College, where a majority of the student body are members of minority groups. Santa Barbara is known, as always, as the fun-in-the-sun campus, although recently it has improved its academic reputation. San Francisco has no undergraduates, just the prestigious UC Medical Center. Santa Cruz, opened in 1965, tried to conquer academic impersonality by division into physically separated colleges of 800 students each. Davis, just outside Sacramento, has conducted much of the agricultural research enriching large-scale agribusiness, but its "back-to-nature" students also study and experiment with nonchemical farming, conservation, and development of renewable resources. Riverside, outside Los Angeles, was a pioneer in citrus research and has capitalized on being one of the world's smoggiest places by developing a center for smog research. Irvine, on land donated by the ranch of the same name in booming Orange County, is strong in physical and social sciences, especially computers and information services.

But Berkeley, mother of all the others, is still the brightest light of the UC system. Academically, it may be most famous for its work in physics, biochemistry, and English, but scores of its faculty, in widely divergent disciplines, stand at the top of their fields. Berkeley, whose in-state tuition is $800 per year, has often vied with private and expensive Harvard for the title of most balanced and distinguished university in the country. Heaven for a UC professor, it is said, is to have six or seven graduate students interested in his field of concentration so that he can do his research using their imagination and talents, even while he is training them. The result is that UC does more research and turns out more doctorates than any other institution of higher learning in America. Much of the work is vital, economically, to the state of California. For decades, the UC board of regents had no blacks or Hispanics. Instead, persons reflecting corporate interests such as the Hearst Corporation and Bank of America (both with economic interests ranging far beyond their immediate fields of publishing and banking) held seats over long periods of time. Beneath the lofty, distant regents is the huge bureaucracy needed to administer the gigantic UC empire. And then there is the faculty, preoccupied with prestige and award-winning research, often oblivious to the interests and intellectual development of all save the brightest and most aggressive students.

All these factors contributed to the ill-defined but powerful Free Speech Movement of 1964-65, which ushered in the era of protest on American campuses. The students were protesting what seemed to them the impersonality and dehumanization of the university through its bureaucracy, the premium placed on research over teaching, the factorylike approach to producing people for industry, and above all else, the lack of any real student role in shaping the goals and values of the university. Compared with the protests that would emerge around the Vietnam War, the recognition of the plight of blacks and Chicanos, those supporting the Free Speech Movement—entirely student-based, generally nonviolent—seem mild and innocent in retrospect. But the California public was angered and frustrated by the apparent uprising that public tax dollars were supporting. The faculty did not want to give up its privileges, and the board of regents, concerned about public reaction, was not anxious to see fundamental reforms. Then came 1966 and Reagan's first gubernatorial campaign, as he railed against "a minority of malcontents, beatniks, and filthy-speech advocates." Students must "obey the rules or get out," Reagan said repeatedly.

The early Reagan years predictably plunged the university into political turmoil. The new governor sought a 25 percent cut in the UC budget, asked tuition for the first time in UC history, and got the regents to dismiss UC president Clark Kerr, who was sympathetic to student viewpoints. Reagan even suggested—he later said "figuratively"—that a "bloodbath" might be needed to quell campus demonstrations, while students and faculty accused Reagan of trying to "repeal the Renaissance."

All of this did not, as Reagan's enemies predicted, plunge the university into fiscal chaos, with massive faculty departures and thousands of rejected students. But there was a feeling that some of the cutting edge of UC's greatness had been lost. It has surely never again been the "sacred cow" it was between 1929 and 1958, when the legislature gave president Robert Gordon Sproul nearly anything he wanted, or in the happy early days of Clark Kerr's presidency. Surprisingly, the intellectual and socially liberal Governor Jerry Brown continued the cuts in the university budget. Brown's criticism was not that the institution had become too liberal, but that it was not giving back to California as much as its entrenched bureaucracy was taking. "The problem with the university is that it's out to lunch," Brown's chief of staff, Gray Davis, was reported as saying in *California, Inc.* "A decade ago the university had a blank check, and there was no greater claim on the government's coffers. They want everyone to be studying Greek and Latin. Well, today you've got to do better than that."

The UC cutbacks turned out, however, to be just an inkling of what awaited California state government in general. In wave after wave flowing from the passage of Proposition 13 into the 1980s, the impact of the draconian tax cut sold to Californians by master anti-tax salesman Howard Jarvis swept over Golden State government. (Proposition 13 was not the start and end of the revenue limitations: among those subsequently voted by the people were an indexing of the state income tax and near abolition of the state inheritance tax.) By temporary good fortune in the late '70s, the state had a large accumulated surplus it could siphon back to county and city governments to let them absorb the heavy cuts they suffered in local property tax revenue. There was much moaning and groaning about the loss of local home rule in becoming heavily dependent on Sacramento, but in fact most local budgets did not—initially—decline too seriously. And many local governments discovered a thousand and one ingenious ways to make ends meet in harder times, ranging from concerted management productivity efforts to dramatically increased user fees for many types of municipal services.

By 1982, however, the surplus (at one point as high as $7 billion) was exhausted, and California faced a grim day of fiscal reality—made all the worse by the national recession, which hit California with severe unemployment and hundreds of plant closings. The state that thought such nasty occurrences were supposed to happen only in the economically decadent East had a rude surprise. The $25.2 billion budget approved in 1982 was, for the first time since 1943, actually lower than the previous year's budget. Among the heavy losers were local governments and school districts, suddenly cut off from much of their post-Proposition 13 aid. No cost-of-living increases were allowed for welfare recipients or state employees, and the state's $5 billion health-care program, Medi-Cal, received a major cost-saving overhaul that included denying recipients freedom of choice in arranging medical care. Republican George Deukmejian won the governorship in 1982, promising no new taxes. But in early 1983, the state had to borrow $428 million from banks to pay its bills, and Deukmejian agreed to raise the sales tax if the economic climate did not improve and increase state revenues. Democrats controlled the legislature by solid majorities, as well as all other statewide offices (starting with Lt. Gov. Leo McCarthy, the former assembly speaker). The Golden State seemed to face harsh times—a situation made even graver by broad concern about a precipitous decline in the quality of education delivered by its once proud public schools. This seemed a product not only of Proposition 13–era funding cutbacks but also lax standards, students picking "lifestyle" courses in place of traditional academics, and a smug educational establishment willing to accept larger class sizes if teacher pay could be increased constantly. Decline in high school students' achievement tests imperiled California's prospects for success in a highly competitive, technology-oriented national and international economy.

"I think the state will slide gradually back to what it was in my boyhood during and just after World War II," Bill Boyarsky of the *Los Angeles Times* told us. "There were pretty good public schools in those years, but the buildings needed painting and classes had 45 to 50 kids. The roads were narrow, and all needed repair. We had public parks, but the grass was not cut or watered much. But more than a decline in physical facilities, the state will retrench from the strong commitment it made to the poor in the '50s and '60s."

The problem, as Boyarsky saw it, was that "the great public institutions of California were created because of the support of the white middle class. We vacationed in those parks and demanded more camp sites. We went to the public library, and our branch was sort of a community center in those pre-television days. There were damn few people I knew in the class of '56 at Berkeley who had not gone exclusively to public schools. But now the white middle class no longer strongly supports these public institutions."

Yet one could not help but wonder whether progressive, clean-government-minded California would remain satisfied with mediocre services and an inferior economic future. Through its initiative-driven tax-cutting spree, noted John Shannon of the U.S. Advisory Commission on Intergovernmental Relations, California had moved toward a far less progressive tax system, one typical of Old South states—"light on income and property taxes and heavy on sales taxes." The "real question," Shannon said, is "whether Californians, with their high tastes for public goods and services, can subsist on an Alabama-type revenue system."

Latter-day California remains capable, however, of innovation and creativity. There was, for example, Jerry Brown's California Conservation Corps, a revival of the Depression-era Civilian Conservation Corps. Brown's trump card was to make B.T. Collins, his deputy legislative lobbyist and, later, chief of staff, the CCC's director. Collins, a profane, tough-as-nails 40-year-old ex-Green beret who had the misfortune of losing his right leg and arm after a grenade he was throwing exploded prematurely in Vietnam in 1967, made five rules for the young recruits: "No booze. No dope. No violence. No destruction of property. No refusal to work." Seventy-two percent dropped out before a full year—half voluntarily, half fired—but there was also a long waiting list of applicants willing to try out the organization's motto of "hard work, low pay, miserable conditions." CCCers told us delightedly of back-breaking feats: of clearing streams of old logs so that the salmon and steelhead can swim upstream to spawn once again, of tree plantings on 45-degree slopes in freezing weather, of trailblazing in remote wilderness, of stripping trees to kill the larvae of the dangerous Medfly.

On a more dramatic scale, however, were Brown's energy and utilities policies, including the death blow he helped administer in 1978 to the long-planned San Diego Gas and Electric Co.'s Sundesert plant. As an alternative, Brown encouraged research in such now-exotic renewable resources as geothermal, agricultural waste products, wind and sun, with a slight bow to increased use of coal as a bridge to California's energy future.

The centerpiece of the Brown energy plan, however, was conservation. From 1975 onward, the California Public Utilities Commission, staffed with conservation-minded Brown appointees, imposed conservation requirements on utilities. The PUC goaded the utilities, for example, into an ambitious program of zero-interest weatherization loans to home and apartment-house owners and sharply higher rates for big consumers at "peak load" times—a program aimed at radical reduction of the state's residential gas and electricity needs, thus eliminating the need for new nuclear or conventional power plants. (Pioneering research proving the practicability of this breakthrough idea—conservation in lieu of new power plants—was first undertaken by the Berkeley-based Environmental Defense Fund.) The utilities resisted (at least initially), but in fact California, a state possessed of wealth beyond comprehension, had also become the premier state of the Union in forging a national path to a more economic, practical, affordable "soft" energy future.

Geographic California

"Of the states subsequent to the original thirteen, California is the only one with a genuine natural boundary," James Bryce observed in *The American*

Commonwealth. Westward lies the irridescent Pacific; to the south, the Colorado River and the Mexican desert; to the east, the high, snowy peaks of the Sierra Nevadas; to the north, more mountains and the forests of Oregon. Superimposed on the East Coast, the outline of California would run from New York City on the north to within a few miles of Jacksonville, Florida, on the south. It is a land of startling contrasts: dense forests, sun-scorched deserts, alpine mountains, fruitful valleys. The most cited contrast is between 14,494-foot Mt. Whitney, highest peak south of Alaska, and Death Valley, just 60 miles to the southeast, dipping 282 feet below sea level, the lowest point of the Western Hemisphere and the hottest and driest in the U.S. Rainfall along the moist northern coast averages 35 inches a year and has gone to a record 190 inches at Honeydew; at Bagdad, a weather station in the Mojave Desert, two years have been known to pass without a drop of precipitation.

Much of coastal California is sunny and balmy, the kind of lotus land that has drawn millions. But nature can play cruel tricks. Californians live in uneasy knowledge, and some in intense terror, of the San Andreas fault, which runs practically the entire length of the state, the longest and most exposed fracture anywhere in the world's crust. It has been in motion 65 million years, with slippage between the two sides of about one and one-half inches per year. What concerns geologists is that the two abutting edges of the fault near San Francisco and Los Angeles are frozen together. Incredible amounts of restrained energy are thus built up; eventually, they demand release. More than 15 severe earthquakes have struck California in the past century. In 1857, an earthquake in the Tehachapis, north of Los Angeles, caused a 30-foot jump in the fault's western edge. The great 1906 earthquake in San Francisco caused a 30-foot movement. Buildings collapsed, streets sank, fires ravaged the heart of the city, and close to 700 people died. In February 1971, Californians got another grim reminder: a tremor officially described as "moderate" occurred near Los Angeles' San Fernando Valley on the line of the San Gabriel fault, which is part of the San Andreas network. The quake took 64 lives, caused damage that cost over $1 billion to repair, triggered more than 1,000 landslides, and released methane gas from the ocean floor near Malibu Point. This is mere child's play in comparison to the potential destruction of a really serious quake, like that of 1906. The "Palmdale bulge," more than 150 miles long and up to 10 inches high, has led some fault watchers to anticipate another major earthquake along the San Andreas "soon." A legislative committee report estimated a major quake before 2006.

Scientists discount the hypothesis that all of California west of the San Andreas might slip into the ocean in a great superquake. But Curt Gentry, in his book *The Late, Great State of California,* made just that assumption and called his book "nonfiction."

Earthquake is not the only threat to naturally pleasant California. The Southern coastal region is caught in a cycle of wind, fire, floods, and mud-slides. Over the low hills near the ocean grows a low, dry undergrowth known as chaparral, along with pine forests a few miles farther inland. At the end of a long, dry summer, the prevailing wind patterns from the ocean may change and the Santa Ana winds, crackling dry and powerful, come sweeping in from the desert. The slightest spark on the chaparral and a conflagration ensues.

Fire is not alone in the cycle. In winter, especially after bad fires have destroyed the ground cover, torrential downpours on the desertlike land may cause mudslides that come down the canyons to envelop houses, causing incalculable damage. Hundreds of homes built precariously on cliffs of flood-prone areas in Southern California have been destroyed.

For all of California's sweetness and artificiality, the primordial cycles of fire and rain and earthquake continue, nature keeping man in his place.

Befitting California's nation size, its geography may be reviewed in three distinct parts.

First, there is the California that remains fairly close to its original condition. Here one speaks of the mountain and big timber country of the North Coast and lordly Sierra Nevada, the forbidding southern desert, and the great Central Valley.

Second, there is the man-made civilization around the shores of San Francisco Bay.

Finally, there is the California Southland, a megalopolis stretching from San Diego to Santa Barbara, with Los Angeles its linchpin.

Natural California

The rugged, lonely coastline stretching northward from San Francisco is a land of rolling fog, breakers smashing against high bluffs, and moist, deep forests. The most renowned of these hold the stately redwoods, which soar to 200 or 300 feet and endure—where lumbermen spare them—for a lifespan of 400 to 800 years. Few human experiences compare to standing within a grove of these ancient redwoods, where the light is a dim cathedral luminescence broken by occasional sun beams filtering through to the forest floor.

In 1920, when California logging began, there were two million acres of redwoods in a strip extending from the Big Sur Country south of San Francisco to the Oregon border. Today, fewer than 270,000 acres of virgin redwoods still stand. A great conservationist battle, led by the Save-the-Redwoods League and the Sierra Club, led to establishment of the Redwoods National Park in 1968. With an expansion in 1978—a move lumbermen opposed bitterly, claiming it would exacerbate unemployment and economic hardship—another 108,000 acres of the most handsome virgin redwood stands were saved. The redwoods fights were just the first chapter in a battle to preserve Northern California's lush treasures, including wilderness areas, the state's few wild rivers, the lush Napa Valley vineyards, and some of the best open land in California. Although desecration still occurred, lumber companies and developers were always aware that one of California's environmental groups would be right behind with a lawsuit or bill to correct the situation.

The biggest city on the entire North Coast is Eureka (pop. 24,153), with the world's largest redwood mills and a superb natural harbor. For the most part, the North Coast has only small lumbering and fishing villages, some with a distinctly New England flavor reflecting their first settlers. The area is still inbred and rugged, a '60s and '70s influx of ecologically minded outsiders notwithstanding. Humboldt County, where many settled, happens coincidentally to be California's premier marijuana growing area; "Humboldt Sinsemilla" is said to have splendid quality.

Ranging southward 430 miles from Mount Lassen are the magnificent Sierra Nevada Mountains, the great granite spine that cracks California from the rest of the continent. The Sierra Nevada played an inextricable role in California history, for at their feet settlers found gold, touching off the great Gold Rush of 1849 and the state's first great population boom. (Beyond an architectural influence, by contrast, the much older Spanish mission civilization of early California has played a minimal role in the development of the California we know today.) It was the Sierras that inspired the poet's words chiseled on the State Capitol at Sacramento: "Bring me men to match my mountains." As Neil Morgan has written, "The Sierra Nevada tends to unite Californians in some sense of community. In its alpine fastness, one cannot escape the feel of history. Here lies an unyielding, unchanging California in contrast to the one below."

The jewel of the Sierras is Yosemite National Park, created in 1890 by a Congress influenced by the writings of John Muir, the great naturalist who spent many years of his life in these mountains that he named the "range of light." The breathtaking Yosemite Valley, with its El Capitan, Half Dome, Bridalveil, and Yosemite Falls, is thought by many to be the most beautiful valley on this continent. But the park—farsightedly created to encompass 1,189 square miles—also contains the great sequoia groves, with trees that began their growth as much as 1,500 years before the birth of Christ, and remote highlands filled with alpine meadows, pine stands, rushing streams, and waterfalls. Most of this territory is still accessible only on foot or horseback.

Not until the 1920s was the first automobile road built into Yosemite. What the automobile did to the Yosemite Valley is a sad story. By 1981, Yosemite attracted 2.6 million tourists in 935,821 private fume-spewing vehicles that added to the smog problem created by the thousands of campfires they built. A tram was built up to Mariposa Grove, and a shuttle bus system was set. But plans to eliminate cars over a 10 to 15 year period had not been instituted.

The next most popular spot in the Sierra Nevada is cold, radiant Lake Tahoe on the border with Nevada. California has tried to keep "its side" of the lake fairly pure, but only bi-state cooperation could make the effort truly effective, and Nevada has continued to allow cheap gambling casinos and other developments that pollute the lake.

Mount Whitney, the highest spot in the continental 48 states, has also been threatened by too many Americans bringing along bottles, cans, wrappers, and other reminders of the world below that too often get left along the trail. But not far from Mount Whitney environmentalists had a great victory in the

1970s when the exquisite Mineral King Valley, ringed by majestic snowy peaks with eight vast, natural snow bowls, was declared a part of Sequoia National Park and preserved from a planned ski development.

The topographic map of the Western U.S.A., honeycombed with mountains and outthrusts, reveals no level area to compare with California's Great Central Valley. Its dimensions, covering a sixth of California's land area, are hard to grasp; as Neil Morgan points out, the Appalachian mountain range of the East could easily fit into the valley, the fields are flat and monotonous; the dusty little farm towns click off every few miles with scarcely a distinguishing mark. Great irrigation canals flow soundlessly through the fields, adding mugginess to the hot air. Only occasionally do tall windbreaks of cottonwoods or eucalyptus break the dull infinity of straight crop lines. For Californian and visitor alike, there seems little reason to tarry.

But this great mechanized farm plant is a wonder all in itself. Chiefly because of it, California leads America in the value of farm products—more than $13.2 billion in 1981. No other California business—not even aerospace— is of comparable magnitude. Within the valley grows every species of temperate-zone or subtropical fruit, vegetable, and field crop known to man, tobacco alone excepted. The astonishing variety, concentrated in various parts of the valley according to soil type and precise climatic conditions, includes grapes, olives, plums, figs, peaches, oranges and lemons, alfalfa, Irish potatoes, sweet-potatoes, walnuts, almonds, tomatoes, corn, sugarbeets, prunes, rice, strawberries, clover, asparagus, celery, lettuce, beans, onions, apricots, pomegranates, avocados, guavas, artichokes, cherries, honeydew melons, cantaloupes, cauliflower, spinach, dry beans, garlic, wheat, hops, barley, apples, and grapefruit—and this is only a partial list. The valley is also a major producer of beef and dairy cattle, concentrated in its dry borders. The state is second to Florida in citrus, second to Texas in cotton, the preeminent or exclusive producer of a wide variety of exotic fruits and nuts, and ranks high in livestock.

California's great vineyards—in the Napa and Sonoma valleys, and now more and more in the Salinas Valley near Monterey—produce 90 percent of the nation's wine output, a $4.4 billion-a-year business. The wine industry has grown enormously in importance since wine has become more popular in the United States; annual consumption increased from nine-tenths of a gallon to 2.21 gallons per adult just since 1960. Wine-tasting expeditions to the Napa and Sonoma wineries are a most delectable adventure.

Technically, the Central Valley is two: the valley of the Sacramento River to the north, of the San Joaquin to the south. Both valleys are served by waters flowing down from the Sierra through the most intricate and extensive irrigation system man has ever built. A major portion of the labyrinth of dams, pumping stations, and canals has been financed by federal dollars through the Central Valley Project, first approved as a state project in the 1930s. Among other things, the CVP transfers water from the mountainous upper reach of the Sacramento River Valley to the drier San Joaquin Valley, where the combination of water and high temperatures makes possible a phenomenal growing season of nine to ten months.*

Without the massive technical assistance it has received from the University of California—in development of hybrid strains, fertilizers, mechanical harvesters, pesticides, scientific irrigation, and feeding and extension courses—the state's farm industry would never have attained the heights it now occupies. The university's citrus experiment station at the Riverside campus, for instance, literally saved California's orange trees, afflicted by a rare virus, from obliteration in the 1940s; a disease-resistant variety was discovered and grafted onto trees throughout the state. In the early 1960s, a university scientist announced he had developed a hormone to double the annual production from an acre of grapes. University scientists invented a lettuce picker with pressure sensors to feel if a head is ready to pick and automatic knives to cut the stem. Pneumatic tree-shakers have been developed to harvest nuts and olives. Men lofted in the cages of scissor-extended booms pick citrus by wielding suction tubes. The university's scientists have worked to breed grapes, melons, asparagus, and other fruits that can be machine harvested; among the most celebrated of these is a new, squarish variety of tomato, developed through computer-controlled genetic breeding, which can be picked without damage by a harvesting machine developed at the university. One reason California made such dramatic inroads on Southern cotton production was that it was able to pick nine-tenths of its crop. At Davis, there is a three-year course in wine-making—in effect, a free trade school for the California wine industry. University scientists help farmers carry on biological and chemical warfare against more than 100 varieties of insects plus fungi and viruses. Many beneficial and harmless insects, birds, and other wildlife died in the process, resulting in a "web of death" documented by Rachel Carson in *Silent Spring,* followed by increased regulations of chemicals and pesticides. The farmers contended, however, that their economic interests were hurt, and when real threats occurred, such as the Medfly crisis, the farm interests still tended to prevail.

Since the days of the gigantic Spanish and Mexican landholdings, most of which fell into Anglo hands after 1848, California has been preeminently a state of big farms. In recent decades, the ownership trends have been toward larger, corporate farms of 500 acres or more, and "hobby" farms of 1 to 49 acres, with the medium-sized 50-to-500-acre, family-owned farms decreasing. After falling for decades, the number of farms actually increased from 54,000 to 57,000 between 1969 and 1978. In the early 1980s, California farm land was valued at $1,186 per acre. Most of the corporate operations were probably family farms that had incorporated to limit their tax liability. Some of the big

---

*The Central Valley Project should not be confused with the subsequently developed California Water Plan to transfer water from the north as far as Los Angeles and San Diego. It should be borne in mind that producing an average acre of crops on desert land requires five acre-feet of water; even with California's huge population, nine-tenths of the water used in the state is still for agriculture.

corporations found that they lacked expertise in tending the land and did not like the fluctuations in farm prices or the rising cost of farm labor.

California's big farm landholding interests have for decades been favored by subsidization by state and federal governments alike, and critics in California delighted in calling J.G. Boswell, of Fresno, "the number one welfare recipient," because he received such large farm subsidy payments. A principal reason the state of California moved so rapidly into vast water projects for irrigation was that the big Central Valley landholders would be ineligible to receive water under federally sponsored irrigation projects, which have a 160-acre limitation for a single owner (a provision thrown out in the case of the Imperial Valley, as we shall see). The landowners made sure that California enacted no such restriction on its own projects. Over the years, critics such as Ralph Nader have charged that these huge, publicly financed, environmentally questionable projects benefit only a few landowners. The water projects have become even more complicated as environmental restrictions have been added. In the early 1980s when the Peripheral Canal was proposed to connect the Sacramento River with the California Aqueduct, both the Sierra Club and the Farm Bureau supported it at various times, and both ended up opposing the final initiative: the Sierra Club, for environmental reasons; the Farm Bureau, because it had too many environmental restrictions. Californians seemed doomed to endless battles over the desire to continue agriculture and housing in water-short areas and the environmental and public subsidy questions of constructing more gargantuan dams and canals.

By contrast, the farm workers who till the fields in the Central Valley have had to engage in an enormous struggle to win the right to unionize and to achieve even a modicum of dignity and material benefit. But the story of the development of the United Farm Workers of America under the charismatic Cesar Chavez is one of the great sagas of 20th-century America.

Mechanization has sharply cut back the number of farm workers required, but California farmers still need, as Richard G. Lillard wrote in *Eden in Jeopardy,* men and women to "chop, trim, thin, girdle, top, stoop, bend, feel, dig, pound, cut, pull, walk, climb, reach up and out, lift, carry, amid heat, dust, cold, rain, mud, insects, from dawn to sundown." In the years after World War II, the Mexican and Filipino-Americans and Mexican nationals working the fields were earning an average of less than $1,400 a year, far below the federal poverty level. Such amenities as overtime pay, paid holidays, vacation, sick leaves, and pensions were virtually unknown. Indiscriminate grower use of highly toxic pesticides led to illness among many farm workers and their children. Workers also found themselves at the mercy of the labor contractors, and the middlemen between them and the growers. The only housing available was often in dirt-floored, tin and tarpaper shanties. No people ever more clearly needed a savior, a Moses to lead them from the wilderness. In 1965, such a man appeared. His name was Cesar Chavez.

The son of impoverished migrant workers, educated only through the seventh grade, Chavez became a self-educated man and in 1961, after several years with a Los Angeles group learning Saul Alinsky-type organizing tactics, moved to Delano with his wife and eight children to work in the vineyards at $1.25 per hour and to start the long process of organization. In 1962, he organized the National Farm Workers Association and in a battered old station wagon started driving hundreds of miles through the Central Valley, talking with farm workers. Years later, one of his fervent followers recalled Chavez at that time: "Here was Cesar, burning with a patient fire, poor like us, dark like us, talking quietly, moving people to talk about their problems, suggesting, always suggesting—never more than that—solutions that seemed attainable. We didn't know it until we met him, but he was the leader we had been waiting for."

When an AFL-CIO union called a farmworkers' strike near Delano in 1965 and obdurate owners started evicting families, Chavez offered the NFWA's help. The growers were surely not prepared for the strikers' almost total nonviolence nor Chavez's ability to organize broad outside support from minority groups, clergymen, labor unions, students, and liberal political leaders. These allies gathered contributions, sent food, joined picket lines. The growers were one of the most establishment groups in California, closely tied to the banks, oil companies, and the University of California, but Chavez had just the right touch of charisma and drama to transform *La Huelga* (the strike) into *La Causa*.

At no point was the strike in the fields particularly effective; the labor pool of impoverished migrants the growers could draw on was simply too great. Thus came the boycott of the grapes produced by Joseph Guimarra's 5,000-acre vineyards, which spread to a national boycott of all California table grapes after Guimarra started shipping its grapes in the cartons of its competitors. The national grape boycott obliged all Americans, in effect, to take a stand for or against La Huelga. Governor Reagan called the strike and boycott "immoral" and "attempted blackmail," and Richard Nixon publicly condemned it and gleefully ate grapes at a public rally in California. But the boycott was supported by millions, and having lost millions of dollars in income, Guimarra and the other big growers capitulated—not only recognizing Chavez's union but signing a three-year contract with significant wage increases. At the signing with Guimarra, Chavez said simply, "This is the beginning of a new day."

By 1980, unionized farm laborers were earning $4.50 to $6 an hour, with many union contracts providing benefits farmworkers had never dreamed of: health care, paid holidays, and pensions. But keeping a farm labor movement and union going had proven to be a tough job. The Teamsters Union (acting in cooperation with growers) grabbed away most of the grapepicking contracts (there being no requirement of worker votes). But the legislature established the California Agricultural Labor Relations Act, which required worker votes, and Chavez signed a peace treaty with the Teamsters in 1976. Soon came charges, however, that Chavez was having a hard time making the transition from leading a movement to running a union and that he refused to tolerate dissent or share authority. Open dissension broke out in the union; Chavez began to avoid reporters when he felt mistreated. But when we visited him at his modest compound, Nuestra Señora de la Paz, near Keene, we found him still living modestly and certainly not engaging in the materialistic excesses of many other labor leaders. A continually fascinating point about Chavez is that he remained a labor leader, rather than the Chicano politician into which many people wanted to make him. Though willing to help Hispanic immigrants already in the U.S., for instance, he opposed liberal immigration policies that would flood the farm labor market. Organizing farmworkers remained devilishly difficult business: the UFW came, for example, to represent more than 100,000 workers, but it had only 30,000 dues-paying members working year-round. And grower abuses continued, with frequent reports of their hiring undocumented foreign laborers and the illegal use of child labor in the fields.

A concluding note on Central Valley cities. The largest is Sacramento (pop. 275,741), the state capital, which saw its first great spurt of growth in the Gold Rush days around Sutter's Fort. With government, agribusiness, an inland port, and a vigorous injection of defense space industries, Sacramento reached a 1980 metropolitan area population of 1,014,002. Palms, verdant lawns, and colorful flowerbeds surround the glistening "wedding-cake" Capitol (exquisitely restored, at great cost, in recent years), and the center city has a handsome retailing mall and a colorful quarter in "Old Sacramento," the commercial district during the gold rush. The city has more than its share of dreary, boxlike government buildings packed with civil servants and computers to manage a complex nation-state—plus one fascinating new one, the ultimate energy-efficient office building conceived and built during the days of (who else?) Jerry Brown. Sacramento's leading newspaper, the McClatchy-owned *Bee*, has long been considered a leading voice of California liberalism. It offers balanced coverage, an ombudsman to handle the public's complaints, and—in a rarity among papers—a weekly column on feminist activities.

In the Sacramento orbit is the extraordinarily progressive little university city of Davis (pop. 36,640), foremost in the U.S.A. on a broad range of energy conservation policies—from a peak hour energy conservation pact with Pacific Gas & Electric to mandatory southward orientation of new homes—which save its citizens and government hundreds of thousands of dollars each year. Davis is also a state leader in contracting out municipal services and insuring itself for workers compensation, liability, and property insurance—all demonstrating that smart "progressivism" may equal frugality and affordability in the cutback era of the '80's.

Miles to the south, approximately halfway between San Francisco and Los Angeles, lies the city of Fresno (pop. 218,202, metro area 515,013), one of the most important centers of agribusiness in the nation. Fresno has a particularly attractive downtown mall, conceived by Victor Gruen Associates with an eye to undergirding, not replacing the Main Street U.S.A. shops that line it. At the midpoint of the valley lies Stockton (149,779), which suffers from excessive unemployment, especially in the winter, when the canneries are out of operation, but can boast a bustling port. Far to the south, not far from Los Angeles, is Bakersfield (pop. 105,611, metro 403,089), a center of oil and gas production and hub of a prosperous farm area.

Life and Water in Desert California

A great swath of the Southland, covering practically a quarter of the entire Californian land surface, is harsh, unredeemed desert, a land of stark, treeless mountains, baked flatlands, and an infinity of rock and sand. Some 650,000 visitors a year make their way to the otherworldly wasteland of Death Valley, renowned for its great wind-riffled sand flows, the dried lake bottom of lacerated salt crystal, brilliantly hued canyons and mountains, and below-sea-level elevation. Wintertime temperatures are in a comfortably moderate range, but the valley maintains its reputation for extreme heat with frequent summer readings of 120 degrees and a record ground temperature of 190 degrees one July day in 1958.

A massive 140-mile-long trough, Death Valley is but a small part of the greater Mojave to which it belongs. This bleak desert, formed by truncated mountain ranges and high, arid plains, covers 25,000 square miles, an area equal to several Eastern states combined. Scattered mining towns, where borax (of 20-mule-team fame), iron ore, tungsten, gypsum, and salts are extracted, account for much of the sparse population. Thousands of acres have been appropriated by the military for bombing ranges and space-equipment test stations including Edwards Air Force Base, landing place for space shuttles.

The principal feature of the Colorado Desert, filling California's southernmost extremity, is the indefatigable old Colorado River and the man-made diversions from it, which have made possible a flourishing agriculture in the steaming desert land of the Imperial Valley. A principal source of water for Southern California is the Colorado River Aqueduct, which crosses the Colorado Desert from Parker Dam (several miles below Hoover Dam) to the metropolitan region, its passage facilitated by 42 tunnels through the mountains and 5 pumping stations. Once thought fit only for rabbits and rattlesnakes, the 3,000-square-mile Imperial Valley, which has an altitude lower than the Colorado, or indeed the ocean itself, started siphoning water from the river in 1901. The desert land began to bloom with crops until, in 1905, an unwise cut into the river, followed by roaring spring floods and desert cloudbursts, brought disaster. The Colorado deserted its normal channel, flooding the valley and creating the Salton Sea, some 24 miles long and now a familiar feature to air travelers. Only in 1907, at the expenditure of many millions of dollars and heroic efforts by Southern Pacific Railroad crews, were the rampaging flood waters finally turned back to their normal channel.

Thirty-four years later, work was completed on the federally sponsored All-American Canal to link, safely, the Colorado River with the Imperial

Valley. The canal, actually a concrete-lined river some 200 feet wide, carries 2 billion gallons of water each day to thousands of miles of feeder canals built by the Imperial Irrigation District. The valley soaks up twice as much water daily as all 119 Southern California cities and towns serviced by the Colorado River Aqueduct. Now one of the most productive farm areas of the country, hot, sun-baked Imperial Valley—sometimes called the Algiers of the U.S.A. —produces rich crops of melon, tomatoes, carrots, cotton, tangerines, asparagus, lettuce, and dates, some even in the dead of winter.

Imperial Valley power is concentrated in the prosperous growers who dominate the Imperial Immigration District. There is no more poignant case in America of government subsidy originally designed to help the "little man" —in this case, the small farmer—being channeled to the advantage of the quite rich and very rich. A 13-year-long battle to enforce the federal government's 1902 law, which seemed to limit, unequivocally, irrigation rights to farms of 160 acres, ended in defeat in 1980 when the U.S. Supreme Court ruled that the Imperial Valley had somehow been exempted from the law in a 1933 Interior Department decision. It had been the dream of a physician Ben Yellen, who moved to the Imperial Valley in the 1920s, to break up the land holdings so that the poor farmworkers he treated might have a chance to own land. Instead, the big owners continued to tap irrigation water for a minuscule percentage of the real cost.

The Imperial Valley's largest city, El Centro (23,996), claims to be the biggest settlement below sea level in this hemisphere; the lowest city of all in the valley, Calipatria (2,636), runs colored lights up a 184-foot flagpole at Christmastime. The top is precisely at sea level.

Miles to the northwest lies the resort of Palm Springs (32,271), set on the desert floor in the lee of precipitous, dramatic Mt. San Jacinto. Here conspicuous consumption reaches rare heights. Famous movie stars and big-business moguls, a generation of the proud self-made, congregate here, patronizing the expensive golf clubs and driving the most luxurious autos. The late President Eisenhower (modest in his material pleasures by Palm Springs standards) retired here, as did President Gerald Ford.

The well-to-do, however, must share the scene with Mexicans and blacks, who used to be crowded into an appalling slum called Section 14 until it was bulldozed for development. Palm Springs' social consciousness can be judged by the fact that no alternative housing was found for them, and when we tried to find out where they moved, no one seemed to know. A far more fortunate minority group is the Agua Caliente Indians. Fewer than 100 in number, the Indians own huge sections of Palm Springs land that they lease out to well-tanned palefaces. Some of America's wealthiest Indians live here, but others, unfortunate enough to hold undesirable tracts of land, are virtually penniless.

II. The Bay Area

San Francisco: City and Skyline

> San Francisco put on a show for me. I saw her across the bay, from the great road that bypasses Sausalito and enters the Golden Gate Bridge. The afternoon sun painted her white and gold—rising on her hills like a noble city in a happy dream. A city on hills has it over flat-land places. New York makes its own hills with craning buildings, but this gold-and-white acropolis rising wave on wave against the blue of the Pacific sky was a stunning thing, a painted thing like a picture of a medieval Italian city which can never have existed. . . .
>
> Over the green higher hills to the south, the evening fog rolled like herds of sheep coming to cote in the golden city. I've never seen her more lovely. When I was a child and we were going to the City, I couldn't sleep for several nights before, out of bursting excitement. She leaves a mark.
>
> —John Steinbeck, *Travels with Charley*

SAN FRANCISCO WINS hands down when American cities are ranked for their sophistication and enchantment. The Gallup Poll found that true in 1969 when it asked Americans what city they would most like to live in. A dozen years later, even after San Francisco had endured the murder of a mayor, the highest housing costs in the nation, and a crime rate that negated its mellow image, San Francisco still retained its following among Americans.

San Francisco's charm begins with the physical. We share with Steinbeck the memory of one of those first views of the city on a distant summer afternoon: the red-orange lines of that high, daring bridge, the sparkling bay to one side, the fog-banked ocean to the other, the rows of chalk-white buildings running uphill and down. Key to these wondrous images is geographic compactness (46.6 square miles), the water on three sides, the 40-odd hills, the constantly shifting panoramas of hillcrest, blue ocean and bridge, gargoyled houses and towers—a city fashioned to a human scale. In a single morning or afternoon, the walker can stroll from the downtown financial district to Union Square to Chinatown, check the North Beach, swing on to a cable car, and wind up at Fisherman's Wharf for a seafood delicacy, and then browse about Ghiradelli Square (a pleasing complex of shops, restaurants, fountains, and lights fashioned out of the buildings of an old chocolate and spice factory). Many remember San Francisco as the city where you could sit in the lounge at the Top of the Mark at day's end and see the city spread before you, the Bay Bridge arching gracefully across to the East Bay, ships to and from the Orient steaming under the Golden Gate, twilight azure giving way to a million night lights.

Such a city needs no massive urban facelifting to make it livable. Its people love it as it is. In the 1940s, Mrs. Freida Klussman singlehandedly organized a great petition drive to save those dangerous, silly, delightful cable cars—and won. (In the early '80s, the rickety old cars were undergoing a $58 million rehabilitation.) In 1958 a great "freeway revolt" stopped construction of ugly double-decked superhighway being built along the Embarcadero.

But inexorable physical change began to press in on San Francisco in the 1950s, threatening what some call "Manhattanization"—the brutalization of the uniquely delicate skyline with sterile, forbidding monuments of glass and steel twice as high as anything that preceded them and totally out of scale with the existing hills and city setting. San Fransiscans became alarmed at what Nicholas Von Hoffman called "the Bank of America's sinister black-and-brown tower, which rises up like an emblem of corporate insensitivity." The 52-story building was the tallest west of the Mississippi for a time, and its darkness contrasted unpleasantly with San Francisco's traditional pattern of white, slim structures. The city soon established rules to keep the color of buildings pastoral, but rapid construction of high-rise buildings continued. During the 1960s, 21 high-rise buildings sprouted in the heart of the city, and 14 structures of 30 stories or more rose between 1971 and 1978. Downtown office space quadrupled in 15 years, from 7.8 million square feet to 31 million square feet. Many San Francisco lovers said the result was to obstruct views of the bay, create wind tunnels with wall-to-wall high-rise corridors, and clog streets with ever more cars.

Some of this construction was doubtless inevitable if San Francisco was to remain a Class A business city and retain a tax base. The Transamerica Corporation's 835-foot, spire-mounted pyramidal office tower on Montgomery Street, the "Wall Street of the West," actually evolved into a city landmark. Mayor Dianne Feinstein told us (and, we are sure, many other visitors) not to worry, that building would not be allowed to ruin the essential character of San Francisco. But such fantastic arrays of new office structures were on the blueboards that one could easily envision such a forest of jagged building tops that the profile of San Francisco's precipitous hills would be irrevocably lost. A San Francisco Chamber of Commerce study showed the new buildings increased retail sales and generated twice as much municipal revenue as expenses. Historic preservation groups have worried, however, that increased armies of office workers will fatally overload the city's subway, bus, and highway systems; they also noted that many of the 165,000 new jobs added between 1965 and 1980 went to commuters who do not pay city taxes. Some fear that a continuing influx of white-collar professionals will put even more stress on an already tight housing market. By the '60s city regulations required that all new buildings be approved by the planning commission and take into account pedestrian space, historic preservation, provision for housing, and energy conservation. The Feinstein administration invented a rule unique in America: developers of all major office buildings must either construct, or put up funds toward, moderate-income housing within the city. But the tougher step of restricting the heights on new structures, pushed by preservationists, went on the ballot three times in the '70s and lost each time.

The diversity of this city of light and color has inspired such adjectives as Mediterranean, Renaissance, *joie de vivre*, elegant, witty. San Francisco has a lovely sense of the absurd, preserved in the artful foolishness of old Victorian houses and the ding-dong cable cars, sure cures for depression. It is also like an elegant woman, with an indefinable mystique all its own. As Herbert Gold wrote, it "is still the great city of America where a walker can experience nostalgia for the place while he is still there—a little, even a lot, like the *nostalgie de Paris.*"

Among other things, San Francisco also has the best little restaurants, in every ethnic variety imaginable, of any American city except, of course, New York. Its stores, both big and small, are often a joy and a delight. But what makes all this possible is the variety of people in San Francisco and the tolerant way in which they have interacted. Figuring out how this came about always verges on speculation, but writers Howard Becker and Irving Horowitz have suggested it is because San Francisco has a Latin heritage and has always been a seaport that tolerates the vice sailors seek out. Explosive growth at the time of the Gold Rush inhibited conventional social controls. Ethnic minorities, especially the Chinese, were ceded the right to engage in activities such as prostitution and gambling. An image of wickedness and high living helped draw tourists, and some minor downtown streets were even named for famous madames of the Gold Rush era. Instead of a socially repressive working class, San Franciscans had as their union leaders Harry Bridges' libertarian and intellectually strong Longshoremen. And finally, the high complement of single people living in San Francisco worried little about what public deviance might do to children.*

The tradition of San Francisco's pioneering in the new and open lifestyle of the postwar era began, some think, with the arrival on the North Beach of Jack Kerouac and his unbarbered street saints in the 1950s. The bohemian-beatniks first encamped on the North Beach, but rising rents, throngs of tourists, and some degree of police harassment eventually triggered a move to the Haight-Ashbury district. The colony at first went largely unnoticed because its members preferred to sedate themselves on nothing more unconventional than alcohol and marijuana, their preoccupation was with art, and most lived as couples or alone. The lifestyle was free, joyous, and, in its own way, talking sensitively to America. But all this changed drastically in 1964 "with the popular acceptance of mescaline, LSD and other hallucinogens and the advent of the Ginsberg-Leary-Kesey nomadic, passive, communal electric and acid-oriented life style," according to a *Trans-action* study. Rock groups

---

*The spirit of tolerance in San Francisco goes beyond mere acquiescence. Since large numbers of mentally ill people all over the country have been deinstitutionalized, a disproportionate number have migrated to San Francisco, straining the public medical system. The city's special feeling for "public inebriates" has led to the nation's only Wino Park complete with campsite and extra-wide benches for sleeping.

began to prepare what would soon be known as the "San Francisco sound."

In 1966 a Trips Festival was hosted at Longshoreman's Hall by Ken Kesey. The attendance figure was 15,000, and the word "hippie" was born. A year later, the new community staged a Human Be-In for 20,000 on the polo fields of Golden Gate Park; the movement of the hippie flower people was now a familiar one in the national media. The publicity may have been its undoing, for thousands of young people from California and across the country poured in; soon the Haight was so crowded that a new kind of living unit—the crash pad—emerged. Hundreds suffered frightening hallucinogenic drug reactions, and in the unsanitary, crowded environment, infectious diseases abounded—influenza, streptococcal pharyngitis, hepatitis, and venereal disease. A free medical center, set up with volunteer doctors and helpers, opened up in Haight-Ashbury and fought valiantly to help kids coming off bad trips and to stem the disease rate. The police did move in with a tactical squad in 1967 when the flower children's dream community of Haight-Ashbury turned into a nightmare of LSD and speed use.

Out of this same tolerance for deviationist lifestyles and self-expression was growing a homosexual or gay political movement that stemmed from gay settlement after many were forced out of the armed services during World War II. During the years when homosexual men and women faced "queer bashings" at the hands of police and, at the least, social ostracism in other places around the country, San Francisco, long known for its liberal heterosexual mores, came to tolerate them. Eventually, San Francisco became the American gay mecca. With tolerance or even acceptance, gays sought legitimization through political recognition.* The specific agenda included freedom from discrimination in housing and employment, an end to the occasional police raids on gay bars and other gay establishments, and nondiscriminatory treatment at venereal disease centers. San Francisco politicians started courting the gay vote in the 1960s. In 1975, after the city switched from at-large to district elections, Harvey Milk, the openly gay owner of a camera shop in the Castro District, the most heavily gay neighborhood, was elected to the board of supervisors, San Francisco's city council.

But Milk's fellow councilman—and soon arch political enemy—was Dan White, a one-time cop and fireman who served as the spokesman for the socially conservative, white ethnic neighborhoods that had once been a real power in the city's politics but now felt themselves being eclipsed. In 1978 White resigned in a fit of anger, and then asked Mayor George Moscone for his seat back, a favor Moscone refused. Infuriated, White walked into Moscone's office, shot and killed him, and walked down the hall and did the same

---

*Gays who were liberal or radical in advocating their own rights sometimes turned out to be less than understanding of others. A San Francisco paper quoted a gay real estate speculator in a ghetto area as saying, "I'm down here because the property is cheap. I can maximize my investment here. The architecture is lovely. Why the hell should this gem of a city be given over to welfare blacks? Put them in Idaho, or at least in Oakland."

to Milk. The tolerant city-by-the-sea immediately went into public mourning, as Moscone's successor, Dianne Feinstein, called for peace and tranquility.* Later, when a jury bought the defense argument that White had "diminished mental capacity" and found him guilty only of voluntary manslaughter, mass gay demonstrations and rioting ensued. Another gay, Harry Britt, was appointed to Milk's seat.

Dan White's terrible deeds were the acts of one deranged or evil man, but it was also true that the working class, family-oriented people who elected him were losing power and position as San Francisco evolved into America's model postindustrial city. In its postwar development, San Francisco had lost much of its old manufacturing base as companies moved to roomier, one-level suburban factories easier for truck access. San Francisco also decided not to containerize its port and lost the shipment of heavy goods to Oakland while San Francisco's harbor contented itself with tourism and some fishing. San Francisco did not decline, however. On the contrary, its beauty and sophisticated image allowed it to capitalize on its base of corporate headquarters, banking, and federal regional offices. San Francisco became the West Coast center of highly specialized service industries: law, accounting, banking, insurance, and the like (though Los Angeles was a strong competitor). All this combined to turn it into a city for the rich and poor, less attractive to the blue-collar class. Highly paid professionals moving in decided to buy houses by themselves, or with spouses or lovers. Gay men and women, whether highly paid or not, pooled their incomes with lovers and friends to rent or buy houses. Eventually, San Francisco became known as America's premier city of "gentrification," a term borrowed from the British. Housing became ever scarcer and more expensive. Many lower-middle-income people were offered high prices for their homes and happily left for the wider, family-oriented spaces of the suburbs, while renters were often forced out. With the average housing price at more than $120,000, the highest of any city in the continental U.S. in 1980, it was clear that the only people who could afford to settle in San Francisco were the wealthy, the singles and couples who doubled up in tight quarters—plus people poor enough to qualify for the limited supply of publicly assisted housing.

A remarkable demographic profile came out of all this by 1980. The city population dropped 5.1 percent, to 678,974, with whites off 23 percent, and blacks down 10 percent in the 1970s. Asians increased by more than 50 percent, mostly because Southeast Asian refugees found comfort and support in tightly packed Chinatown; upwardly mobile Chinese were moving into the suburban mainstream. In 1980 the city was officially 58 percent white, 12.7 percent black, 21.7 percent Asian, and 12.2 percent Hispanic. Almost surely the

---

*It was a particularly hard time for San Francisco. Only a month earlier had come the deaths by suicide and poisoning of 900 followers of the Rev. Jim Jones and his People's Temple in Guyana. Before leading his followers to Guyana, Jones had cultivated strong ties to both black and white San Francisco leaders. Moscone had even appointed him to the city housing authority.

real Hispanic figure was somewhat higher, with illegal aliens hiding from the Census takers. The largest Hispanic group was not of Mexican origin, as one might expect, but Nicaraguan, followed by El Salvadoran, then Mexican. Thirty-four percent of San Franciscans were single, and estimates of the gay population (one question the Census had yet to pose) ranged from 10 to 30 percent. Only 41 percent of the city's 101,782 married couples had children. The net result: this city of nearly 700,000 people had only about 57,000 children in the public schools and a few thousand more in private schools.

Where all this might well be leading politically was speculated on by the *California Journal* when it suggested that San Francisco in the '80s might well choose as mayor "a moderate, nominal Democrat, perhaps Asian male, homosexual, who runs on a platform of human rights, lower taxes, and reduced city payrolls."

San Francisco Potpourri

San Francisco has its Social Establishment, a modern gentility descended in large measure from the rough-hewn capitalists of the Gold Rush and railroad-building eras; there are even a select few whose families came *before* 1849. High-society life revolves around institutions and events such as the "Monday lunch" in the St. Francis Hotel's Mural Room; the opening of the San Francisco Opera; traditional old clubs such as the Pacific Union, the Burlingame, and the Bohemian (a redoubt of some of America's most powerful white males and their white male guests, including ex-presidents, with a yearly camp on the Russian River); and the still by-invitation-only Debutante Cotillion. The disdain with which the San Francisco blue-bloods regard the upstart society of the California Southland has no bounds. In fact, there is a marked provincialism to San Francisco and a closed character to its old society and highest business positions that explains why many Californians are much less enthusiastic about the city than Eastern and foreign visitors. An ambitious young person can "make it" much faster in the go-go world of Southern California, which may be one reason so many more of them have chosen to live there.

In almost narcissistic measure, San Francisco prides itself on the brilliance of its arts—ballet, opera (second only to the Metropolitan Opera in New York), Symphony Orchestra, and American Conservatory Theatre. But Los Angeles certainly has done much more than San Francisco in recent times, especially in theater. Even some of San Francisco's own have accused it of being too self-contented. Herbert Gold once speculated that "maybe San Francisco majors in the minors," and the visitor will notice an extraordinary amount of affection for posters, unusual post cards, and whatever offbeat music might be popular at the time. In the early 1980s, it was a punk group called the Dead Kennedys. Yet while San Francisco has become more expensive, it has encouraged a counterculture of poets, writers and filmmakers, and one gets the impression that even corporate types enjoy the offbeat people to a degree that could be compared only with New Yorkers. Bookstores abound, as do small presses such as City Lights. In the '60s, the Bay Area was at the cutting edge of the underground newspaper movement, which printed everything from radical anti–Vietnam War editorials to details on how to achieve a sexually liberated lifestyle. In the 1970s, San Francisco's *Advocate*, the national gay newspaper, proved to have more staying power. But San Franciscans have never had to wait very long before their own newspapers, the *Chronicle* and the *Examiner*, cover the latest in lifestyles. One distinct disappointment about life in the Bay Area has been the lack of serious political or economic coverage equal to that of newspapers in New York, Los Angeles, Chicago, or Miami, though the papers have begun to improve in the 1980s. Columnist Herb Caen remains the journalistic personality of the city. On an offbeat note, San Francisco does have *Mother Jones*, winner of the National Magazine award. *Mother Jones*, which is worker-managed, is published by the Foundation for National Progress, which also founded the New School for Democratic Management, a business training ground for counterculturalists tired of red ink. The *Mother Jones* crowd, together with a radical foundation movement started by young heirs who wish to counter the conservative philanthropic policies of their own parents, forms the core of a leftist intellectual community that seems committed to decentralized economic power and new forms of entrepreneurship in America.

San Francisco, it has been said, has two establishments—a Big Establishment peopled by industrialists and financiers whose interests run beyond the Bay Area to the nation and the world, and a Small Establishment of those whose activities are almost exclusively city-, or at most, Bay Area–oriented. Among the latter are the multitudinous ethnic group leaders and, of course, the politicians.

As for the Big Establishment, San Francisco is not quite the great shipping, financial, and headquarters city its leaders would have one believe, and it has continually lost ground in recent years to ever-growing Los Angeles. By 1980 Los Angeles had 13 headquarters offices of Fortune 500 corporations while San Francisco had only 4. Even some consulates, seeking the bigger business action, moved to Los Angeles. Nevertheless, San Francisco—by the standards of any other American city—must be considered a financial giant. Here is the home office of the Bank of America, in most years the nation's largest nongovernmental bank, with assets of $121 billion and more than 1,000 branches in the state of California, plus many overseas. (Founder Amadeo Peter Giannini, the son of an Italian immigrant laborer, rose to the pinnacle of American banking in the great Horatio Alger story of the 20th century. Among the bank's inventions: Bank Americard.) Other great San Francisco banks include Wells Fargo (assets $23.2 billion, father of "Master Charge") and Crocker-Citizens National (assets $22.5 billion), which though controlled by Midland Bank of London remains California's fourth-largest bank. The Southern Pacific Railroad (now the diversified Southern Pacific Company, still California's largest private landowner, with 2 million acres from 19th-century railway land grants) and the huge truck common carrier, Consolidated Freightways, are in San Francisco. The city also has California's biggest industrial corporation, Standard Oil of California, and it is the headquarters of Pacific Gas Electric Co., the largest investor-owned energy utility in the U.S., with yearly revenues of $6.2 billion.*

Generally speaking, these corporate giants, their attention riveted on state, national, and overseas operations, have not played major roles in local political life. Those most interested in local power have been the real-estate, tourism, and construction interests, who in cooperation with labor unions, have favored the city's heavy downtown growth, including huge public projects such as the George Moscone Convention Center, which opened in 1981. But business heavyweights and management teams from such firms as TransAmerica, Crown Zellerbach, Pacific Telephone, Bank of America, and the Wells Fargo and Crocker banks stepped in to serve on a mayor's advisory committee vital to the city's fiscal survival in the tax-decimating Proposition 13 era. The group was co-chaired by investment banker Richard Blum, who in the process got to know and eventually married Mayor Dianne Feinstein in an epitome of the "public-private partnerships" of the era. City hall was in dire need of help. The city, fiscal administrator Rudy Nothenberg told us, had been "a totally unmanaged conglomeration of principalities and duchies." The financial advisers centralized insurance coverage, revamped management of temporarily idle funds, modernized the accounting system, and set up training programs for top executives, middle management, and supervisors. The team even promoted successful personnel reforms in one of America's most entrenched civil service systems. In all, the city managed to survive reasonably well on a budget $75 million less—in constant dollars—than it had before Proposition 13.

Another success of latter-day San Francisco—this one totally nongovernmental—has been the volunteer San Francisco Community Boards' neighborhood-based justice system, which handles problems the police and court systems are often helpless to deal with: personal disputes and fights, petty theft or vandalism, wife and child abuse, conflicts over parking places, barking dogs, loud stereos, and work-place harassment. Neighborhood residents are trained as hearing panelists, and case referral comes from word of mouth in the neighborhoods, call-in responses to Community Board publicity, or occasionally from the police. The parties first present their stories to the panel and then turn their chairs around and talk directly to each other—a venting of frustrations and direct communication that formal court proceedings simply don't permit. Community boards, according to founder and director Raymond Shonholtz, are a modern substitute for "those natural dispute resolvers,

*PG & E might be said to need every million of those billions to pay for some of its problems, including the Diablo Canyon nuclear power plant, begun in the mid-1960s south of San Luis Obispo with the expectation of being completed two years later at a cost of $450 million. Thirteen years and $2.3 billion later, the facility, which turned out to be close to an active earthquake fault, was still awaiting licensing by the Nuclear Regulatory Commission. Diablo Canyon's opposition cast included the full anti-nuclear panoply, including the Abalone Alliance, the California League of Women Voters, the Sierra Club, and a cast of the prominent indignants led by Jerry Brown, Jane Fonda and husband Tom Hayden, and rock-singer Jackson Brown.

those ministers, priests, rabbis, high-school principals, mom-and-pop grocery store folks that you once knew well because you lived in the community so long." Among the people who have turned to the boards have been gays in conflict with Hispanics, a bar owner and the local teenagers harassing him, and fearful local residents arguing against organizers of a proposed halfway house for mentally ill senior citizens. One goal is to nip in the bud tensions that might otherwise lead to serious crime.

In state and national politics, San Francisco is a liberal bastion and strongly Democratic. The two Burton brothers—Congressman Phil Burton and his brother, former Congressman John Burton—have long been the acknowledged leaders of the Democratic left wing, one of the nation's few radical political families successful in urban politics. Municipal politics are officially nonpartisan and harder and harder for the outsider to follow as old ethnic groups such as the Irish and the Italians give way to young professionals, gays, and the growing variety of Asians and Latin Americans even while downtown business interests and private and public sectors unions remain strong. The last of the old-style mayors was Joseph Alioto, the son of an immigrant Sicilian fisherman who made his fortune as an aggressive attorney before plunging into politics in the late '60s. Alioto was accused by *Look* magazine of having Mafia alliances, but he eventually won a libel suit against the publication. George Moscone, his successor, was a strong liberal who opened up dialogue with the business establishment; Feinstein, succeeding Moscone, proved a forceful personality and able mediator between civic camps. San Francisco's eccentric politics seem never-ending. In 1983, the White Panther Party, a self-described communist organization, collected enough signatures to force a recall election on Feinstein's mayoralty. The White Panthers charged that the board of supervisors' pioneering ban of most pistols, which Feinstein supported, would interfere with the people's right to protect themselves from the police. The gay community was upset with Feinstein's veto of a "domestic partners" bill, which would have allowed unmarried city employees to extend health and other benefits to their live-in partners. The recall also produced editorials suggesting a toughening of recall requirements.

In the 1980s, *the* places to live in San Francisco remained Nob Hill and Pacific Heights, the latter with row houses that are enormous by Eastern standards. The Mission District, which has gone from Italian to Irish to Hispanic, had begun to attract Anglo professionals. The Castro celebrated the gay lifestyle. Conditions remained deplorable for blacks crowded into Hunters Point, a depressed and isolated shantytown of "temporary" World War II housing on the southeastern edge of the city. In the other predominantly black area, the Fillmore, blacks were showing some fears that gentrification might push them out. North Beach was still considered "Little Italy," although the Chinese had transcended the traditional Broadway boundary. Another Asian community had formed near Golden Gate Park.

Chinatown—America's greatest Oriental population concentration and oldest ghetto—lies squeezed into 42 square blocks of land between elegant Nob Hill and Montgomery Street. Tourists throng Grant Avenue, the main drag, packed with colorful curio shops, banks, and savings and loan associations, tile fronts, bright signs, and vivid tones of gold and turquoise, yellow and red. There are close to 100 restaurants and numerous food import stores selling everything from quail eggs, squid, and shark fins to bamboo shoots, dry fungus, rice, and tea. Daily Chinese newspapers flourish, along with Chinese movies, Chinese radio stations, and Chinatown's own telephone exchange (in a pagoda on Washington Street).

The old-time image of the coolie, the shuffling Chinese houseboy, and the corrupt opium den having dissipated, the Chinese have become regarded as hard-working, frugal, and the most uncompromising ingredient of the melting pot. For the thousands of Chinese who have moved out into the greater society, landing good jobs and living in comfortable communities, the middle-class stereotype is true. For most of Chinatown's people, it is highly misleading. By any normal standards, Chinatown is a slum—perhaps the most glamorous slum in America, but still a slum. Young Chinese-American planners who have tried to upgrade conditions in Chinatown have found it a frustrating process indeed, with government funds never enough, and a conservative Chinese power structure that is distrustful of outsiders and willing to exploit many of its own in sweatshops. The problems with Chinese youth gangs have actually been relatively few, but are shocking to San Franciscans who remember the traditionally docile Chinese youth of past generations. All of these problems have been aggravated by a heavy influx of new Chinese and other Asian immigrants and refugees for whom the Chinatown ghetto offers protection. But if previous generations are an example, Chinatown will continue to be an ultimate success story—with the successes being counted in other neighborhoods, in suburbs, in high-tech engineering firms, and today finally in leadership positions in American corporations and politics.

In San Francisco's Orbit

San Francisco proper accounts for only 13 percent of the 5.2 million people scattered through the San Francisco Bay's nine counties, including countless suburban towns plus big cities such as Oakland and San Jose.

The air over San Francisco is constantly cleansed by strong offshore winds, but around the interior, bay smog often builds to alarming levels—rivaling that of Los Angeles. Land use problems are also acute: except in recessions, subdivisions and highways gobble up thousands of acres of farmland and green space each year. There is a nine-county Association of Bay Area Governments, but despite its noblest efforts, no sound regional development plan has been enacted to deal with such disparate but related problems as waste disposal, air- and water-pollution control, mass transit, and open space.

Substantial progress has been made, however, in the protection and preservation of San Francisco Bay, a priceless asset well described by writer Judson Gooding as "an immense, extraordinarily lovely series of inland seas stretching 50 miles from north to south, and extending inland to the great Sac-

ramento delta where the waters from 16 rivers flow down from the Sierras."
Over a century, diking and filling by developers has reduced the water area
of the bay by more than a third, from 680 to 400 square miles. In the 1960s,
a citizens group formed the Save San Francisco Bay Association, through
whose efforts the San Francisco Bay Conservation and Development Commission was created and given authority over any project within a hundred
feet of the shoreline. A process of negotiation and environmental mediation
developed between the commission and potential developers, but proposals
that could harm the bay (such as the proposed Peripheral Canal) are constant,
and bay savers feel they must be constantly vigilant.

The Bay Area's grand but not totally successful experiment of the last
decades has been the San Francisco Bay Area Rapid Transit District (BART).
Construction began in 1964, with rave reviews about the first major U.S.
subway system since 1906. Opened in 1972, after many delays, BART was
hailed as the United States' most advanced modern transit system, in both its
space-age technological aspects and its aesthetic aspects. (The cars can acceler-
ate, for example, from zero to a top speed of 80 miles per hour in 45 seconds.)
But while the cars are a world away from the screeching underground horrors
of the New York system, they—and indeed the entire system—were egregiously "overengineered" and full of technical bugs that caused breakdowns,
slow service, and the realization, when a fireman was killed in 1979, that the
modern interiors were potential torches. Over time, most of the technological
kinks were worked out. Financing was another matter. The system, originally
financed by a $792 million bond issue, ended up costing $1.7 billion. Of the
$105 million operating budget, fares and advertising financed about $45.4
million while a special half-cent sales tax levied in BART's three counties (San
Francisco, Contra Costa, and Alameda) provided a $60 million subsidy.

BART's ridership has proven disappointing partly, it is said, because its
beautiful stations are so far apart, because it is oriented to longer-distance
commuting, and because the lines fail (except for a stretch under busy Market
Street) to service much of the city itself. The latter problem has been partly
relieved by San Francisco's construction of its own intown MUNI subway
system with "light rail" (i.e., trolley-type) cars instead of the heavy BART
variety. But BART, even if it has failed to decrease auto traffic as originally
hoped and promised, has helped to knit the Bay Area together. Indeed, some
critics say it has furthered the "Manhattanization" of San Francisco by encouraging construction of office buildings and more and more commuter
traffic. It also seems to have boosted nearby retailing. Macy's store one block
from the Powell Street Station, for example, has the highest gross income per
square foot in the company's empire.

What San Francisco represents among cities, Marin County—just to the
north, over the Golden Gate—represents among suburbs. Expensive and
environmentally conscious, it grew only 6.9 percent in the 1970s, to 222,952.
Its geography is varied and a pleasure to the eye—a place where mountains,
ocean, and bay meet, known for canyons, loamy farmland, lagoons, and
streams. Here are some of San Franciscans' favorite relaxing spots, including

Stinson beach and beautiful Point Reyes, where Congress created a national seashore in 1962. Many towns have strong personalities: one thinks of elegant Tiburon or Riviera-like Sausalito, with its delightful harbor location and artists and hippies on houseboats. Mill Valley has a rural quaintness and houses that reflect upper-class taste. But along with the old, cozy communities, Marin has dull, flat, newer subdivisions low on both planning and architectural quality.

Primarily, Marin is a commuter county for San Francisco's well-heeled, a place that has changed, like most of the North Coast from rural backwardness to a sophistication and urbanity. San Rafael (pop. 44,700) is the closest thing to a city in Marin County, and its newspaper, the *Independent-Journal*, is superior to any San Francisco paper. Marin County residents became enraged by the county's reputation as a center of divorce and silly, materialistic superficiality (especially after a national television special showed housewives in Marin going in for a rubdown with peacock feathers!) That reputation began, however, with a book entitled *The Serial*, written by local resident Cyra McFadden, and we have yet to meet anyone from Marin who did not in some small way encourage the stereotype. Marin also faces the difficult problem of spending the income from a $300 million foundation (the nation's 11th-largest) left to the "needy" of Marin by Mrs. Beryl Buck in 1975.

In Sonoma County, north of Marin, is the resolute little city of Santa Rosa (pop. 83,205), where Luther Burbank once carried on his great plant breeding experiments. Many of its Main Street buildings destroyed in a 1969 earthquake, Santa Rosa coalesced business and citizen leadership to build a successful regional shopping center and semi-pedestrian mall in the downtown. An intensive citizens' committee educational campaign also persuaded several neighborhoods to drop their often fierce initial hostility and accept scattered-site low-income housing. For these achievements Santa Rosa won a 1982–83 All-America City award.

The two counties of "the Peninsula"—directly south of San Francisco—are San Mateo and Santa Clara. They live in large degree off a heavy concentration of aerospace industries. San Mateo (588,164) boomed in the 1960s from the population flow of San Francisco to the north, the employment at San Francisco International Airport on the bay side, and the research overflow from Stanford University, just beyond its border to the south. Many of the towns are rich, flowery bowers of gardened California at its most attractive; by contrast, the county has huge ticky-tacky row housing developments climbing up over its hills. As an example of the desecration, developers went in for "mountain cropping"—converting what could otherwise be interesting hillside building locations into ordinary flatland to cram in more houses more cheaply. The major cities are San Mateo (77,561), Redwood City (54,965), and Daly City (78,519).

Santa Clara County, at the foot of the bay, is the home of the famed "Silicon Valley," the nation's preeminent center of high-technology industries and the kind of explosive growth that might be expected to follow. Santa Clara's population rose from 290,547 in 1950 to 1,295,071 in 1980, a 21 percent rate in the 1970s alone. In place of a tranquil valley of prune and cherry and apricot orchards, ablaze with blossoms each spring, developers moved in with what environmentalist critics called "greed, corruption, and incredible shortsightedness" to create an infinity of tasteless housing subdivisions. We took a rush-hour flight over Santa Clara Valley with county supervisor Dan McCorquodale, and it confirmed every fear and suspicion about unfettered sprawl development we ever had. Below were miles and miles of subdivisions built with the acquiescence of local government in league with powerful property owners who apparently never gave a thought to building centers of denser housing or trying to locate housing in any way convenient to people's places of work. And then there were the roads—freeways crammed with thousands upon thousands of cars, resembling little ants captured on an endless treadmill, which is exactly how the occupants feel, McCorquodale told us: like they're "part of something they have no control over." Industrial parks, more than 150 shopping centers, gas stations, taco stands, gaudy signs, traffic congestion, and air pollution complete the scene.

The center of Santa Clara's growth has been the city of San Jose, a quiet farm capital of 95,280 souls in 1950; in 1980, a sprawling city of 636,550. Both the San Jose city and Santa Clara County governments have tried to control growth in recent years, and the pace has slowed some—partly because the county has begun to fill up. But the most appealing ideas—"infill" development on available empty lots, perhaps even building housing over the electronics firms' monstrous parking lots—have proceeded slowly if at all.

An interesting note about Santa Clara and San Jose politics is the control by women. Janet Gray Hayes served several years as mayor of San Jose into the early 1980s, and 7 of San Jose's 10-member city council and 3 of the county supervisors were women. The strongly feminist city government ironically found itself the subject of a 1981 strike over the emerging issue of equalizing pay for positions that have traditionally been held by women.

The intellectual anchor of the Silicon Valley is Stanford University, located in Palo Alto (55,225), a pleasant university city that had the foresight to annex and protect as green space thousands of acres of the wooded foothills on its western flank. Palo Alto also has a satellite, East Palo Alto (pop. approximately 8,000), a teeming black ghetto that militants once tried to rename "Nairobi." Stanford, founded by one of the railroad tycoons of the 1880s who hoped it would become the Harvard of the West, has indeed risen to a position of prominence, along with CalTech, in a state where public higher education is so preeminent. The collaborative history between Stanford, business, and science goes back to the 1910s. But the major breakthrough came after World War II, when Stanford helped to spark and then became a centerpiece of the scientific and military industrial complex spreading across the Southern Peninsula, ranking with Route 128-Cambridge as one of the most important in America, in time to become known as "Silicon Valley." By the 1980s, according to studies by economist Michael Kieschnick, 52.7 percent of California's venture capital (which was 35 percent of the nation's total) was flowing to Santa Clara County's high-technology firms, which were constantly expanding internally and, as their engineers spun off new companies, creating a new generation of American fortunes. Not until the national recession reached a deep trough in 1982–83 did many of the go-go young electronics firms feel the bite of hard economic times. The high-tech companies pride themselves on developing a new style of management at once paternalistic (campuslike office parks complete with gyms and picnic areas) and breaking fresh ground in the decentralization of management decision making and profit sharing. Liberal critics have charged, however, that such innovations often involve mostly professional engineers, not production workers, and that the companies are vigorously anti-union.

Stanford has helped high-tech scientists stay up to date in their fields, and in return the university has raked in huge contributions, which it fed into its liberal arts and engineering divisions. Stanford's academic standing, many believe, is equaled only by Harvard and Berkeley, even though its prominence in national affairs is muted because of its graduates' preference to stay in California. When Ronald Reagan became president, however, Stanford's Hoover Institution on War, Revolution and Peace, in the past regarded as a bastion of rightist orthodoxy, saw many of its ideas (and scholars) employed by the national government and received a new dose of respectability and fame.

In contrast to the beehive of activity along the bay side, the ocean side of the San Francisco Peninsula is quiet and low-keyed, a place where gentle mountainsides go down to beaches and the settlement is still remarkably light. The weathered beach-resort community of Santa Cruz (41,483) combines one of the highest percentages of retirees in the country with a new-lifestyle campus of the University of California, a political combination that led to the election of a majority of radicals on the city council in the early 1980s.

Just below Santa Cruz is Monterey Bay and the famed town of Monterey (27,558), steeped in ancient Spanish and Mexican history. This is the town that John Steinbeck loved and made popular in novels such as *Cannery Row, Sweet Thursday,* and *Tortilla Flat.* Cannery Row no longer gathers innocent sardines into their tin coffins; the reason is that gross overfishing upset nature's balance and swept Monterey Bay, where annual crops of 250,000 tons had once been brought in, clean of sardines by the late 1960s. But the Row has had a revival as an artist colony and spot for atmospheric restaurants and bistros. More flavor is added by Monterey's annual jazz festival, one of the West's great events. There are few more beautiful ocean stretches than Seventeen Mile Drive with its incomparable golf courses, poetic cypress trees, the sea, cliffs, sand dunes, and sea otters barking on the rocks. Quaint little Carmel-by-the-Sea (4,707), packed with rich retirees, scene of an annual Bach Festival, is called by some a tourist trap (artificial artiness, high prices).

A few miles inland lies Salinas (80,479), a great vegetable capital and center of the 100-mile-long Salinas Valley, birthplace of John Steinbeck, a city that has striven bravely in recent years to recover from plant shutdowns, revitalize its central business district, support the arts, and become a pioneer in paper, glass, and metal recycling.

South of Monterey is Big Sur country, a wild and sparsely inhabited stretch of the coast visited by wise tourists and a semi-permanent home for a number of escapees from the plastic civilizations of urban California. California Route 1, an old two-lane highway, blessedly unimproved, winds along the coastline, offering incomparable views. Here the land drops precipitously from towering cliffs and mountains down to the raging sea, one of America's most awesome and exhilarating sights.

Across the bay from San Francisco lies Alameda County, dominated by Oakland (339,288) and Berkeley (103,328), both old and established cities afflicted by thorny problems of race and poverty complicated by the presence of thousands of students. The East Bay also has a boom county, Contra Costa, whose population rose from 100,450 in 1940 to 657,252 by the 1980 Census count. Environmentalist William Bronson has charged that Contra Costa "has undergone perhaps the worst-planned growth in the state," by relinquishing its shoreline and most of its land with a view over water to industry and permitting its rich agricultural land to be taken over by crowded and undistinguished tract housing. The presence of so many refineries and petrochemical plants has raised concerns about cancer and birth defects in Contra Costa.

With completion of the transcontinental railway in 1869, Oakland became the great Western terminus. The city boomed, especially in the two decades following the 1906 earthquake and fire that almost demolished San Francisco. Excellent urban parks and transit systems were developed. And Oakland remained the principal metropolis for commerce and culture on the East Bay through the late 1930s because San Francisco could only be reached by a nostalgic but rather inefficient ferry system. But then the Bay Bridge was completed. It became easy for any East Bay people, even those from Contra Costa County, to reach San Francisco by automobile. The airplane began to eclipse the trains, and Oakland became a semi-ghost town, and sometimes has suffered from unemployment *twice* the national average.

But Oakland also has continuing strengths and a spirit that other go-go California cities have never had occasion to develop. There is a modern city art museum of extraordinary quality. The economic strong points include the prosperous and progressive Port of Oakland (second only to New York in containerized cargoes and a constant humiliation to San Francisco, which did not containerize), an international airport, University of California payrolls, the Alameda Naval Air Station and Oakland Army Terminal, nuts and bolts manufacturing, and major rail and trucking facilities. A new age for downtown Oakland was predicted when BART made the trip to downtown San Francisco only 15 minutes, and in the early 1980s it appeared that might finally come to be. The *Oakland Tribune* and the locally owned Kaiser Aluminum and Clorox Company invested $1 million in a new Hyatt Regency that would be part of the $23 million Oakland City Center commercial and retail project. A federal urban development action grant provided the final needed monies to go ahead. In Oakland's Chinatown, the Trans Pacific Centre, a four block complex of offices, restaurants, shops, and hotels worth over $250 million was being built by high-rolling Hong Kong developers, the Carrian Group.

Vital signs of Oakland's spirit have been its vigorous attempts to keep its major league football and baseball teams. Even in the 1970s, when Oakland was going through some of its toughest days, the Raiders football team and the "A's" baseball team were frequent champions and kept the city's fragile pride alive. But there have been continual attempts by the owners of both teams to move them to other cities where they might make more money. When Oakland A's owner Charlie Finley was determined to sell the club, it was purchased by San Francisco's Levi-Strauss Corp., thus avoiding the loss of the team to another city. But few stories of civic devotion can compare with Oakland's efforts to stop owner Al Davis from moving the Raiders to Los Angeles. In 1982 after Davis made a deal to move the team, the city used eminent domain powers to take possession of the team, a legally unprecedented act that the federal courts initially upheld.

None of this new age of activism would be possible without a new generation of talented leadership, which to everyone's amazement is some of the most racially integrated in the nation. The city has had a substantial number of blacks ever since they first came a century ago as railroad construction workers or porters. With World War II came a major influx of blacks to work in the shipyards and in defense industries such as Kaiser Steel. The black percentage rose steadily, with the familiar flight of whites to the suburbs, until the 1980 Census showed blacks a large minority (47 percent) of the population. Oakland's black community became nationally famous as the original spawning ground of the Black Panthers—founded, as the story goes, over expresso coffee one day in early October 1966 by Bobby G. Seale (who became chairman) and Huey P. Newton (minister of defense).

By the 1980s the Panthers had passed largely into history, but black leadership in Oakland surely had not. Prominent black leaders included the mayor, Lionel Wilson, the first Democrat to hold the office since 1948; Robert C. Maynard, distinguished editor and publisher of what had once been the Knowland family's Oakland Tribune; J. David Boswick, superintendent of the city schools; the Rev. J. Alfred Smith, chairman of the new Bay Area Black United Fund and a member of the board of education; and Thomas Berkeley, one of two black members of the Port of Oakland Commission and its former president. The city council had three blacks, two Asians, and two whites, and the city was putting itself on the line for new ideas—city-raised bond funds to lower house mortgage payments for moderate-income people, for example —that other cities could well emulate.

Oakland's representative in Congress is also black, avowedly socialist Ronald V. Dellums, but he comes from the neighboring city of Berkeley, once known as "the Athens of the West," and a place as academic and white collar as Oakland is blue collar. Dellums sat on the Berkeley City Council during the controversial student activism of the '60s. There is still something of a sense in the streets of Berkeley (especially Telegraph Avenue) that this is where the Free Speech Movement started; with the overwhelming presence of the University of California campus, there probably always will be. Acknowledged radicals took over the city council in 1971, and the city has become noted for all kinds of progressive measures, from school integration to attempts to keep economic control in local hands, from bans on handgun sales or smoking in public places to traffic barriers to discourage speeding on residential streets. In 1981 moderates recaptured a majority of council seats, but the council still prided itself on being the "only city government in America with a foreign policy"—leftist, of course.

III. The Southland

Los Angeles: Capital of Mass Culture

THE DAY ENTERS ITS WANING HOURS, and the visitor from the East disembarks from a transcontinental jet, rents an automobile, and starts motoring up the San Diego Freeway toward the Santa Monica Freeway and then central Los Angeles. The setting sun, its image grossly enlarged by the particulates in the polluted air, hangs like a huge movie prop. The visitor accelerates his car to Southern California speed. He looks around to see sleek, confident, people in the vehicles about him. Most are tanned, many blond, and one imagines so many of them to be in a frenetic race for success, their cars bespeaking their personalities. Gazing on the endless acres of boxy little houses on individual lots, catching glimpses of the hills, one might bemoan the irrevocable loss of delicately flowered, precious, natural California. Yet one also senses the wealth, the driving power, of California's Southland. Behind the wheel of the automobile, one feels a strong exhilaration. *This* is Los Angeles, this is the excess, the myth, dream, heights, and lurking tragedy all rolled into one. It is frightening to be here; one would not want *not* to be here.

Los Angeles, the vortex of civilization where mankind devours every habitable place and then sprawls farther and farther out into the desert, the place of movie stars and aerospace, possibly the most diverse economy to be found anywhere, has become the world's model for urban and social development in the late 20th century. From the 1940 construction of the Pasadena Freeway onward, Los Angeles pioneered the super-road, annihilated the sidewalk, and slaughtered public transportation. In time, young cities such as Houston, Phoenix, and Denver would burgeon on the Los Angeles model (often with huge subdivisions, commercial strips, and shopping centers built by Los Angeles-based developers). Suburbias from Cleveland to Long Island to Seattle showed Southern California roots. Even Europe experienced creeping "Californiazation." As far away as Jerusalem, we have visited suburbs where residents were fighting strict local zoning controls, trying to build California-style homes on mountainsides and roads to make it easier to accommodate private autos. Urban "experts" the world over have condemned California's sprawl as wasteful and dehumanizing, and who is to say they are wrong? But to people around the world, the image of Southern California has become synonymous with individual liberty, unprecedented personal mobility, affluence, and "the good life." That image will not soon be banished.

America has always been a nation of immigrants, but in Southern California the arrival of newcomers has been constant. California was always the last possible stop before the Pacific Ocean. It attracted Americans forsaking their earlier lives for the new existence here. Some came for fame, others for relaxation in the sun, others—like the Okies in Depression times—hoping this El Dorado would assuage their poverty. Thousands came alone or in twos, oftentimes adding children but without the context of the traditional "extended" family bridging three or more generations. Divorces seemed as ordinary as the common cold. No more fluid society ever existed, nor one in which impermanence, rootlessness, lack of belonging loomed so powerfully. This was a culture that literally bred materialism and hedonism. Liberated sexuality and the body-conscious society flourished first and foremost in Southern California, in Hollywood's purveyance of the single female sex symbol, then in the beach-and-auto society of unfettered, bronzed young bodies, the golden California girls and their swains. As the center of the most far-reaching communications media yet invented, motion pictures and television, Southern California's way of life was almost inevitably conveyed to the nation and the world.

The drawing power of Southern Californian ideas was in part because their promises of a better life were within the reach of the masses—a small, single-family house with a "patio," an automobile for personal liberty, smooth roads, movies for cheap entertainment. Thornton Bradshaw, an Eastern aristocrat who became president of the Atlantic Richfield Oil Company and was instrumental in moving its headquarters to Los Angeles, told the authors of *California, Inc.* that he viewed Southern California's mass culture as "sound—and a very hopeful harbinger of the future. The United States for a long time consisted of fairly rigid groups characterized by the farmer, the small businessman, the New York intellectual, the Jews, the Hamtramck Polish. . . . We're developing a common culture. We are no longer these groups bound together. We are individuals. . . . This kind of breaking out, that's what California and the West represent."

As Los Angeles entered the 1980s, however, there were some signs that the underpinnings of the mobile go-go society were under severe stress. The city of Los Angeles itself actually *lost* population in several years, as baby boom children left home and the city experienced racial and cultural conflicts. When Los Angeles did add population, it was most often real immigrants: Mexican nationals, arriving legally and illegally, Central and South Americans, Yugoslavs, Koreans, Filipinos, and refugees from Asia. Of Los Angeles County's 7.5 million people in 1980, over two million (27 percent) were of Hispanic origin; blacks made up 12.6 percent of the population; and Asians,

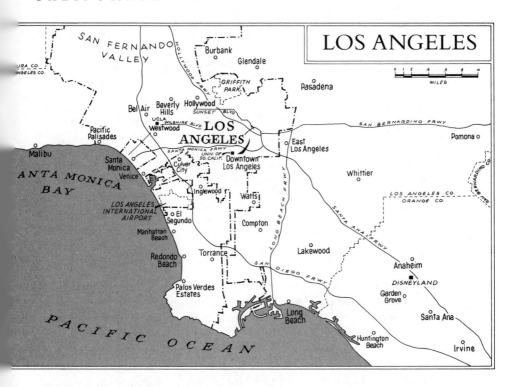

5.8 percent. That many Angelenos expressed wonderment at these new presences demonstrated how Protestant/Midwestern had been the Southern California dream. And suddenly more Southern Californians seemed not so mobile as they once were. Groups sprang up to protest the effects of freeways on neighborhoods. Housing prices skyrocketed to astronomical levels, and Americans considering a move to Southern California from elsewhere in the U.S. started having many second thoughts.

But it had not become a static society. Population growth continued on the edges of Los Angeles County, in San Bernardino, Riverside, Ventura, and Santa Barbara, in Orange County and in San Diego. As a center of business, Los Angeles was stronger than ever. If the message Southern California broadcast was growing more complex, it was often still in advance of what was happening in other parts of the nation and the world.

Growth for Growth's Sake

Some say that America's Sunbelt was born a century ago when Los Angeles speculators and land hustlers lured Easterners with advertisements proclaiming "Land Boom!" "Jobs! Golden Opportunity for All!" Surely the population boom the early promoters sought came in proportions beyond their earliest dreams. By 1980 some 13 million people lived in this narrow coastal strip some 210 miles long from Santa Barbara in the north to San Diego in the south. Up and down the coast there were numerous cities of more than 50,000 people that would qualify as metropolitan areas elsewhere but here fade into never-ending suburbia. Consider the growth figures of Southern California since 1940 shown in the table below.

COUNTY	1940	1970	1980	% CHANGE '40–'80
Los Angeles	2,785,643	7,041,980	7,477,503	168
Orange	130,760	1,421,233	1,932,709	1,378
San Bernardino	289,348	682,233	895,016	209
San Diego	161,108	1,357,854	1,861,846	1,055
Riverside	105,524	456,916	663,166	528
Ventura	69,685	378,497	529,176	660
Santa Barbara	70,555	264,324	298,694	323
Regional total	3,612,623	11,603,037	13,658,108	278
Percentage of U.S. Population	2.7	5.7	6.0	

California's growth curve has occasionally been cut back, but all predictions that California is "filled up" have been proven wrong. Even in the '70s most of the Southland's major areas added a half million people each, and such growth was largely unplanned. Only the privileged classes have generally occupied creative and earth-respecting developments. For the mass market, land developers cavalierly snapped up land parcels of opportunity (especially near freeways), staked out rectangular blocks because they are the easiest to plot, and then built tight-pressed little houses, superficially smart but often of flimsy construction, each with just enough space for the inevitable patio. Some of this housing, in locations such as Santa Monica and the southern end of the San Fernando Valley, has been torn down for higher density apartment buildings and condominiums. In the tract developments the visitor quickly discovers what California Tomorrow, an environmental group, calls "slurbs": endless rows of pastel-colored boxlike homes, occasional industrial parks, low-lying shopping centers filled with stereotyped branches of big chains, and strips of neon-beckoning, honky-tonk gas stations, hot dog stands, and pizza parlors. The future of suburban America was writ here first.

As housing prices reached for the moon in the coastal counties, people by the late 1970s were pouring a thousand a week into San Bernardino and Riverside counties, those huge stretches of territory reaching miles and miles to the east of Los Angeles. Many settled in the fertile valleys; some pressed deep into the Mojave Desert. Some were retirees; many more were willing to endure brutal daily auto commutes, for 50, 60, even 100 miles to jobs in Los Angeles or Orange Counties, so they could preserve their American dream of owning a home in the sun. Both counties reported an astounding increase in people building their homes—or planting their mobile homes—directly on the desert. Hemet, tucked up against gaunt mountains in Riverside County, is reputed to be America's largest community of mobile homes.

Virtually all Southern Californians own automobiles; even the public housing projects have parking lots where some of the oldest, most polluting vehicles end up. Those who can't afford cars, or don't drive, are simply out of luck. The pedestrian is *persona non grata* in Southern California; several areas (such as residential Beverly Hills) have dispensed with sidewalks altogether. The Southern California motorist, by contrast, was able, to pioneer such activities as drive-in movies, drive-in restaurants, drive-in banks, and yes, drive-in churches. A simple glance from a plane—showing how central Los Angeles has become a concrete and asphalt jungle of freeways, feeder streets, gas stations, and interminable parking lots, and how shopping center parking lots the size of a football field dominate suburbia—confirms that the automobile, heralded as a device to conquer space, has come to fill it. The freeways, slicing cruelly across mountains, elevated for mile after mile across the basin areas like a labyrinth of Chinese walls, became the only sure geographic reference points of this far-flung region. These are good roads, exceptionally well marked, but their construction slaughtered many a neighborhood—the prime reason that heated opposition to new ones welled up in the '70s.

The inevitable question raised by Los Angeles' auto and freeway snarl is, why not mass transit? The irony is that the region once had a magnificent interurban rail system, the Pacific Electric. The PE's big red cars ran outward from downtown Los Angeles to reach the mountains and the ocean, doing much to develop such far-flung communities as Pasadena, Hollywood, Long Beach, Santa Ana, and San Bernardino. By 1930, with 1,200 miles of track, it was America's longest city rail system; in 1945 it was still carrying 109 million passengers yearly. But then competition from the automobile, and PE's own failure to improve its equipment and lines, led to rapid decline. The last big red car ran in 1963.

The automobile seemed certain to maintain its dominance in Los Angeles far into the 21st century. But auto *exclusivity*, a foregone conclusion in 1970, was brought into deep question in the '70s by OPEC, skyrocketing oil prices, and the belated flowering of downtown Los Angeles and the Wilshire corridor into some of America's most heavily populated territory. Los Angeles began to rebuild its dilapidated bus system; ridership rose to 1 million riders a day; and the lines along Wilshire Boulevard became some of the most heavily used in the nation. Downtown Los Angeles was growing so rapidly that corporations became desperately concerned about how they could get their workers to, and then through, downtown. Plans moved ahead for a Wilshire corridor subway and some form of rail line from Los Angeles to Long Beach. A Los Angeles downtown people-mover was in the works when Ronald Reagan became president and stopped its federal funding. By 1980 Angelenos' perennial hostility to mass transit was weakening: the county voters approved a half-cent sales tax for rapid rail and reduced transit fares from 85 cents to 50 cents. Private firms announced their intent to go forward on some major transit projects—with or without federal subsidies.

Along with traffic migraines, Angelenos faced the problem of smog. There are still days when the wind flows in briskly from the Pacific, across the Los Angeles basin, and up into the surrounding hills. And if, on such a day, there has also been a rain to cleanse the air, the ring of hills stands out with startling clarity, and suddenly the "city of angels" seems worthy of its name. Unfortunately, the occurrence is rare. A typical summer morning commuter is more likely to see gray air, yellow as the morning progresses, and finally brown. Up through the 1950s, automobile-loving Angelenos could assume that the smoke pall over their city came from factories. But then scientific research burst the bubble, fixing the fault on auto emissions, and California, followed later by the federal government, began to impose emission controls. Few areas of government regulation would prove more controversial. By the early '80s some major improvements were reported, even though Los Angeles still had America's most serious ozone problem.

With sparse annual rainfall, Southern California is technically a desert and has no natural way to support the water needs of its millions. The Los Angeles region has been able to grow into the formidable megalopolis it is today only through massive amounts of water being "imported" or "stolen" from remote spots in California's lightly populated northwestern mountains, plus the dammed up waters carried southward under the $1.75 billion California Water Plan, and Colorado River water conveyed by massive aqueducts.

Fully 85 percent of California's water goes, however, for agricultural irrigation involving highly subsidized dams and aqueducts. By the 1980s ever more urban Californians were asking why they should vote for farmers' subsidized water. That doubt, and fear of the $3.1 billion pricetag in times of austerity, lay behind California voters' rejection, in June 1982, of the Peripheral Canal and other elements of a far-reaching proposal to move water in the state's huge Central Valley from the wetter north to the more arid south.

All Around L.A.

Through the 1950s all that the motorists whizzing by on the elevated freeways could see of downtown Los Angeles were a few civic center buildings, chiefly the City Hall (then L.A.'s only claim to a skyline), rows of down-at-the-heels stores, a handful of oil company offices, and banks, newspaper offices, cheap bars, and dowdy hotels. Fashionable Los Angeles had long since passed downtown by in a westward rush along the elegant Wilshire Corridor, and the old core was populated principally by low-income Mexican-Americans, blacks, and assorted retirees.

But in the early 1960s a great reversal took place as the ultimate "spread city" decided to build itself a true downtown in 1,000 acres of choice real estate wedged between four freeways. The momentum has never since been lost, with one wave after another of gigantic new skyscraper office buildings, hotels, and retail office space complexes. Hundreds of thousands of square feet of new office space were added, with 13 million more valued at a staggering $36 billion and expected to house 100,000 additional downtown workers by the latter 1980s. In 1981 the city council granted approval to the biggest project yet: California Plaza, a five-square-block, $1.2 billion complex of office buildings, condominiums, theaters, shops, and an art museum that was to complete a 15-year redevelopment effort in the Bunker Hill area near the 1960s vintage Los Angeles Music Center.

However massive, Los Angeles' downtown was somehow still not a great city. Planning in the gargantuan expansion was weak or nonexistent. The arrival of some 19,000 permanent middle-to-upper class "gentrifiers" notwithstanding, the area lacked the downtown coffee shops, good restaurants, and bookstores and theaters that make up the fabric of a pleasing, around-the-clock city. And few were the critics who saw much of distinction in the new architecture. Megastructures lined up one beside the other, but to what total effect? One of the few remaining downtown architectural gems in 1982 was the Los Angeles Central Library, a Spanish-Byzantine-Art Moderne building from the 1930s, which the city was interested in tearing down.

Once one has accounted for the limited area of "downtown," the geographic ordering of Los Angeles becomes a nightmarish puzzle. The city itself, 469 square miles in a county of 4,068 square miles, has a crazy-quilt pattern starting high in the San Fernando Valley, jumping over the Santa Monica Mountains, running through downtown, and then plunging down an 18-mile-long corridor, just a half-mile wide, so that the city limits can reach the harbor at San Pedro without interruption (much like the corridor that linked ancient Athens and Piraeus). Enclaves are carved into every edge of the city, and in fact independent cities such as San Fernando (17,731) and Beverly Hills (32,367) are completely surrounded by it.

Los Angeles County, on the other hand, is shaped normally enough, with the ocean on its western and southwestern flanks (offering miles of still magnificent beaches), the desert over the hills to the east (in the direction of San Bernardino and Riverside), an unobstructed opening to Orange County on the southern flank, and the massive San Gabriel Mountains rising to the north. Some 700 square miles are urbanized and built up, but forests and federal lands take up more than 1,000 acres.

Perhaps Los Angeles' ultimate urban sprawl can be visualized by imagining downtown L.A. as the center of a great clock, and the great chunks of land as hour segments with 12 o'clock due north, 6 o'clock south, etc. We can start clockwise at 9 o'clock.*

Nine to ten o'clock. The dominant feature is Wilshire Boulevard, immensely elongated (15 miles in all) but still the most elegant street in the California Southland and indeed one of the world's most sumptuous. Sleek high-rise apartment and office buildings line mile after mile of Wilshire, where beanfields still abounded in the 1920s; the Wilshire Corridor also has Los Angeles' finest stores, the excellent County Museum of Art, the strongly Jewish Fairfax Avenue neighborhood recently strengthened by the arrival of Russian immigrants, and such adornments as Beverly Hills and Century City (elegant office buildings, apartments, and hotels) along its way or nearby. Beverly Hills

---

*For the "state of the art" in urban guidebooks, the reader is referred to Richard Saul Wurman's highly inventive *LA/Access* (1982).

remains one of America's most prestigious communities, physically spotless, wealthy, disdainful of cooperating with the rest of the Los Angeles community, and heavily Jewish.

Farther out on Wilshire at well-to-do Westwood Village is the campus of the University of California at Los Angeles, rivaling Berkeley to the north (of which it was once just the "Southern campus") in prestige and weight in California affairs.

The whole outer flank of this belt is dominated by the Santa Monica Mountains, 92 square miles of extremely rugged territory (as big as Pittsburgh and San Francisco put together), intruded into the heart of a heavily urbanized area. Where they meet the sea, one finds famous Malibu Beach. Geologically, the mountains are less than hospitable, with earthquake faults, steep grades, and fire-prone chaparral. Yet some Angelenos insist on their mountain homes, feeling they can lead a distinctive way of life in their own little canyons or on the remote hilltops.

Ten to eleven o'clock. Close-in, there's Hollywood, out farther, the San Fernando Valley, in between, more of the Santa Monica Mountains. Sunset Boulevard, hugging the southern exposure of the mountains, meanders through this section and then veers south and west to reach the sea. Called the Sunset Strip, it was once a glittery street of restaurants and nightclubs that loaned its name to a 1950s private eye TV show. It has become a jumble of office buildings housing famous entertainment companies.

Out beyond the Santa Monicas is the San Fernando Valley, mostly farmland in the 1930s, subsequently transformed into a vast slurb covering 235 square miles (the size of Chicago) and is home to a million people, including an awesome number of teenagers. Its center is deadly flat; surrounding mountains seal it off from the ocean and the rest of Los Angeles like an immense football stadium. The valley is not a bedroom community, however; its commercial and industrial base provide jobs for most of its residents. The Valley became known in the '70s for conservatism (Proposition 13 was born among the Valley's homeowner-taxpayer groups) and ferocious, eventually successful opposition to school busing to achieve integration.

Eleven to twelve o'clock. Close in, there is the Los Angeles Dodgers' Stadium; then one comes on multisplendored Griffith Park (America's largest municipal park). Further out are the cities of Glendale (pop. 139,060), site of gaudy Forest Lawn Memorial Park, and Burbank (84,625), home of NBC's California studios and famous since TV's *Laugh-In* for its very middle-classness.

Twelve to one o'clock. This segment starts with a jumble of freeways, then encompasses the eastern portion of Glendale and moves out to the mountains until 35 miles from downtown one comes upon the dusty town of Palmdale (12,277), a center of aerospace construction (Lockheed, Rockwell International) and homes.

One to two o'clock. Here the dominant feature is Pasadena (119,374), long a household word in the U.S.A. for its dazzling New Year's Day Tournament of Roses. Pasadena embellishments include the California Institute of Technology campus and scientific, pharmaceutical, and cosmetic plants. CalTech, one of the nation's most prestigious scientific schools, has developed whole new technologies and industries and numbers many Nobel prize winners among its graduates and faculty. Pasadena is about 20 percent black and 18 percent Hispanic; its population mix and culture give it a legitimate urban texture glaringly absent in many Southland cities. Out beyond Pasadena is the famed Mt. Wilson Observatory and the huge Devil and Bear Canyon Primitive Areas, again underscoring L.A. County's fantastic diversity.

Two to three o'clock. Now our orientation moves to the east of downtown L.A., and for the next 180 degrees we must deal mostly with characterless suburbia. First in this segment is the San Gabriel Valley. In the 1970s, the town of San Gabriel became a mecca for second-generation, middle-class Hispanics who had "made it." By 1980 San Gabriel was 38 percent Hispanic, and was one of the few places in California where Hispanics had significant political power on the school board and in city offices.

Farther out on the San Bernardino Freeway, over the hills, out of the L.A. Basin, and into the desert is the city of San Bernardino (118,057), where the economic base is military, aerospace, and agriculture.

Three to five o'clock. Now we come to East Los Angeles and the Mexican-Americans—so many of them, in fact, that only Mexico City has more. But first we must note that a stretch of Olympic Boulevard became a bustling Koreatown during the '70s. Beyond east L.A. lies the suburban dullsville of Whittier (68,872) and Pomona (92,742), site of the Los Angeles County Fair, and Riverside (170,876), site of an agriculturally inclined UC campus and victim of air pollution almost as serious as L.A.'s.

The sprawling Mexican barrio (or ghetto) of East Los Angeles, some 40 percent of its territory in the city of L.A. and the remainder in unincorporated areas of the adjoining county, is the focal point of L.A. County's 2.06 million Mexican-Americans. The classic conditions to fill a people with clotted rage are to be seen in East L.A.—insensitive school boards, abhorrent housing, inadequate health care, few decent job opportunities, police harassment. Since the 1960s, a number of organizations to improve the lot of the Mexican-Americans have risen here. One of the best known was The East Los Angeles Community Union (Telacu), started by the United Auto Workers and the Ford Foundation. Telacu, a community development corporation, received much federal money but also made sure its top people lived well. In 1982—sparked by a sensational *Los Angeles Times* expose—it found itself under investigation for misuse of $46 million in government funds. More tightly interwoven into the community was UNO (United Neighborhoods Organization), closely tied to Catholic Church parishes and employing the protest techniques of the late Chicago organizer, Saul Alinsky. UNO causes have ranged from fighting discriminatory auto insurance policies to pressing for improved schools. It has also sponsored many voter registration drives, though politics remains the area in which Los Angeles Chicanos have made the least progress. In the early 1980s, Chicanos had yet to elect one of their own to the Los Angeles city council, and political analysts continually wondered when this "sleeping giant" of a constituency would awaken and transform the face of local politics.

Five to seven o'clock. This section, defining a broad arc of land running south from downtown, encompasses L.A.'s black ghettos, big bland suburban cities, and then, at the ocean's edge, the thriving submetropolis of Long Beach and posh Palos Verdes Estates.

The 1980 Census showed that 944,009 blacks lived in Los Angeles County, 523,446 of them in the city proper. For four days in 1965, the nation became critically aware of one small black section of south central L.A. known as Watts. Watts' spread-out, palm-lined streets are in such vivid contrast to the stark tenements of South Side Chicago, Harlem, and Bedford-Stuyvesant that no one would ever have imagined the spark of black riots, later to spread to Newark, Detroit, and elsewhere, would be ignited in this area. But what looked good in comparison to other ghettos was hardly adequate in comparison to the "good life" of Southern California—and especially to the opulent flashy world of Hollywood reported regularly to Watts on television. The commission appointed by Governor Pat Brown later reported that only 14 percent of the people in Watts had automobiles, and the closest employment agency was an hour and a half away on three separate bus lines. The schools were substandard, and 40 percent of the girls were dropping out of high school due to pregnancy. The area had no hospital—the nearest public hospital was two hours away by bus. The toll of the riot: 34 killed (mostly blacks), 1,034 injured, close to $40 million in damage, some 4,000 arrested in one-square-mile, burned-over area.

In the years following, there were a number of extraordinary efforts to improve the situation, such as the Watts Labor Community Action Committee, a United Auto Workers-sponsored organization that put together union, foundation, and government money to operate grocery stores and gas stations, to offer vocational training, build parks, and construct low-cost housing. But most of the private business operations set up in Watts did not survive, and living conditions were in some ways worse in 1980 than in 1965. Blacks who were well educated and had good jobs moved out, even beyond heavily black communities such as Inglewood and Compton. Outside Los Angeles proper, the largest numbers of blacks by 1980 were in such cities as Compton (60,812 of 82,602 people), Inglewood (54,010 of 94,245), and Pasadena (24,594 of 119,374), but there were small numbers of blacks in all jurisdictions.

As Hispanic and Asian immigrants poured in during the '70s, many blacks believed that employers preferred the immigrants, who often agreed to work longer hours for lower pay. While higher income blacks were leaving Watts, Hispanics were moving in, keeping the competition for housing intense.

The bulk of southern Los Angeles County is filled with instant cities of the 1940s and '50s, many of which have become slums or close to it: Gardena (45,165), Torrance (131,497), Carson (81,221), and Lakewood (74,654). The scene is overwhelmingly one of little frame houses built quickly for aircraft and shipbuilding workers on monotonous straight-line streets.

Moving still farther south in the 5-to-6 o'clock segment, we finally reach Long Beach (361,334) and the oceanside. The booming port, and especially the great oozy oil field underlying its city, port, and harbor, make Long Beach one of the U.S.A.'s richest cities. With the tidelands oil royalties, which it shares with the state, Long Beach has spent millions on recreational development in the harbor area (including the Queen Mary's permanent berth) and billed itself as a major convention center. Oil rigs still mar the landscape and contribute to depressing stretches of waterfront, but in the harbor they have been camouflaged to look like high-rise buildings surrounded by waterfalls and trees. For employment, Long Beachers look to Douglas Aircraft and the harbor.

Seven to eight o'clock. Here we pass through the western extremities of the black ghetto, encounter Inglewood (94,245), another one of those long, sprawling suburban cities, the Los Angeles International Airport, and finally the ocean and a string of middle-class beach communities beside it.

Eight to nine o'clock. In this final segment, we move westerly through nondescript commercial and residential sections of the city and the University of Southern California campus, through Culver City (38,139) of M-G-M fame, and finally to the coastal region, rich in aerospace firms, and two of the most fascinating communities of Southern California—artsy Venice and Santa Monica.

No section of Los Angeles was so *in* in the 1970s as Venice, which in the 1960s had begun an effort to reclaim its fabled canals and return to the prosperity of its 19th-century founding years. Venice's atmosphere attracted so many types of people—older Jews, hippies, artists, blacks, Chicanos, and old-time Bible Belters, poor young artists and antique dealers—that it became tagged the Greenwich Village of Southern California. If you have ever wondered where the idea of adult people roller skating down the street came from, it was Venice's boardwalk. The '70s also brought to Venice the phenomenon of real-estate speculation as tacky little houses went for over $100,000.

Nearby Santa Monica (88,314), settled by Midwesterners and home of the Rand Corporation, shattered its conservative, middle-class image in the late 1970s when it replaced Berkeley as the center of radical electoral politics in California. The vital issue: rent control in a community in which some 80 percent of the residents are renters, extreme housing demand pressure was felt from nearby Los Angeles, and the average 1982 condominium price was $210,000. Among the local activists—making conservative Santa Monica businessmen apoplectic—were those symbols of the radical left in the '60s, actress Jane Fonda and her husband state Assemblyman Tom Hayden.

In 1981 the radicals won a majority of city council seats, and Ruth Yanatta Goldway, 35, was elected mayor. Her husband, Derek Shearer, a radical economic theorist, was appointed city planning director. The radical council quickly took a hard line on growth, placing a moratorium on new construction and then forcing developers to make concessions such as building parks, day-care centers, and low-income rental housing before they could proceed. John Alshuler, a national expert on community energy conservation, was brought in as city manager. What was fascinating about the radicals in what some dubbed "the People's Republic of Santa Monica" or "Gucci Leninism" was not just their election in a prosperous city but their commitment to localism. Shearer, for example, favored "local democratic planning" by residents of their own economic future instead of what he called the "royalist" national-scale planning ideas of such national Democratic activists as investment banker Felix Rohatyn and economist Lester Thurow. And on that radical note we are back at 9 o'clock, and the Santa Monica-Wilshire axis from which we started.

Power in L.A.

Less than a century ago, Los Angeles was just emerging from its drowsy, Arcadian era of citrus groves, exotic shrubbery, and resort life. Oil was discovered in 1890, and the first movies were filmed soon after the turn of the century. After World War I, as the movies made Hollywood an entertainment and scandal center of the world, the aircraft business grew toward major-industry status, and the first large residential subdivisions appeared. In World War II, the big aircraft plants hummed day and night. Millions of dollars poured into California's new steel mills and shipyards as Southern California, for the first time, became a vital part of the U.S. economy.

The postwar story is one of superlatives. Los Angeles County became not only the Southwestern United States' economic center, but an industrial, financial, and commercial complex of world import. In 1965 L.A. surpassed San Francisco as the financial center of the West by forging ahead in three critical measures: total loans, deposits, and savings. Both Los Angeles and Long Beach have magnificent, side-by-side, and highly competitive sea harbors behind nine miles of breakwater, and together with Southern California's several fine airports, serve as the West Coast's major gateways for trade to and from the Pacific Rim countries. The combination of aircraft, computing and communications equipment, motor vehicles, cosmetics, and much more enables the Los Angeles metropolitan area to lead all others in the nation. Through aerospace (Lockheed, Douglas, Northrup, Hughes, North American, *et al.*), California became the leading defense contracting state. Complementary defense installations (the Air Force's Space Technology Laboratory, the Pacific Missile Range, Vandenberg Air Force Base with its rocket-launching capabilities) also gravitated to California. And then there were the fabled think tanks, led by the Rand Corporation, set close by the glistening Pacific at Santa Monica. Though Rand in later years learned how to diversify into nonaerospace/military work, its copy of the top-secret Pentagon Papers study of the Vietnam War was the one released to the press by Daniel Ellsberg.

Los Angeles and the rest of Southern California have also developed a healthy business and consumer electronics sector, second only to Northern California's Silicon Valley and competitive with New England. Los Angeles' position as a world center of finance and industry has also stimulated the demand to make it a world-class center for such advanced services as health care, accounting, and law.

The single industry for which Los Angeles is globally known, however, is entertainment. From the 1920s onward, "Hollywood" meant movie making, Los Angeles' great seminal industry and its most unique contribution to American culture. The glory days for movie making were in the 1940s when a handful of titanic studios such as Metro-Goldwyn-Mayer, Paramount, 20th Century Fox, Warner Brothers, and Columbia made a total of 400 movies *each year*. Television soon intervened, movie attendance plummeted, conglomerates bought up studios, and there were dire predictions that "Hollywood" (always a euphemism for the studios and lots scattered from Burbank to Culver City) was finished. But, as is the case with Broadway, the obituaries proved premature. Conglomerate takeovers only continued, in new form, the perennial tension between the creative artists and the front office. Filmmakers eventually found ways to co-opt television, making movies for American TV and releasing them overseas in theaters. Young independent producers began to achieve successes with more avant-garde films. Sound stages were booked solidly throughout the 1970s, and one-third of the nation's total employment in motion picture production and distribution remained in Los Angeles.

Los Angeles' climb into a first-rate cultural center was immensely abetted by the arrival in the 1940s of talented European refugees, some but not all Jews fleeing the Hitlerian onslaught, including such figures as Bertolt Brecht, Igor Stravinsky, Arnold Schoenberg, Arthur Rubinstein, and Jascha Heifetz. Collectively, the exiles made Los Angeles into a music center second only to New York in this hemisphere and stimulated the growth of bookshops, art dealers, and the like. Then Los Angeles' old and leading families for the first time became determined to make their city a High Culture capital; in 1974 the massive Los Angeles Music Center rose like an acropolis on a downtown hill, becoming home to the Los Angeles Philharmonic (considered one of the country's greatest symphony orchestras), a regional theater, a light opera, and a choral society. In 1965 the County Art Museum opened on Wilshire Boulevard. Few of these projects would have been possible without the extraordinary fund-raising activities of Dorothy (Mrs. Norman) Chandler, the mother of the *Los Angeles Times* publisher and wife of his predecessor. Los Angeles also teems with amateur musicians and artists, community orchestras and chamber-music societies, as well as many lesser playhouses where movie actors often perform on stage.

Culture is not the only area in which Los Angeles has grown up. Today its dominant newspaper, the *Los Angeles Times,* competes closely with the

New York Times and *Washington Post* for the honor of being considered the finest in the U.S.A. The national-level quality of the *Times*' reporting—especially coverage of the Southwestern states, Mexico, the Western regional economy—is sadly missed by many national business and political leaders, who unwisely ignore it because of its West Coast location. Until 1960, when Otis Chandler succeeded his father, Norman, as publisher, the paper was a fat mediocrity—highly provincial, slanted in coverage, uncrusading, the safe and sound voice of California Republicanism and the WASP community of Los Angeles. Otis Chandler and his editors decided to go first class, with spectacular results in content, style, and editorial direction. Slowly at first, then more rapidly, the *Times* broke loose from its old conservative editorial moorings. Formerly, it had called itself a Republican newspaper; that was changed to "independent Republican," and finally just to "independent." If the *Times* has an Achilles heel, it is its skimpy treatment of the growing Los Angeles Hispanic community on the grounds that they do not read newspapers. When the *Times* has acquired other newspapers, it has usually imposed its own quality standards. Examples: the *Dallas Times-Herald*, Long Island's *Newsday*, and the *Denver Post*.

There is scarcely any American city where the question of who holds the power in town evokes such unsatisfactory answers as in Los Angeles. The city seems to be so diffuse that no one knows what's going on, let alone controls it; certainly there is no "establishment" comparable to Chicago or San Francisco. Only a few "old families" qualify; few fortunes are more than a generation old. Otis Chandler's own name automatically goes on any tentative list of Los Angeles leaders, but he told us, "There is no power structure here—only people who think they are." Several Los Angeles businessmen, such as Holmes Tuttle, an owner of Ford-Lincoln distributorships, and self-made oil millionaire Henry Salvatori, are the people who bankrolled Ronald Reagan's campaigns until he finally reached the White House. Not all Southern California money is so conservative, however. Here, for instance, is one of America's great pools of Jewish wealth, channeled both to liberal and pro-Israeli causes.

Afflicted by a political boss system and the machinations of power-hungry corporations, Angelenos at the turn of the century rose up in a great municipal reform movement that resulted in the recall of the mayor, who was involved in sugar company stock speculation. It was the first use of the recall method in U.S. history. Post–World War II Los Angeles politics were blandly pro-business until the 1961 election of Sam Yorty, a former congressman who capitalized on his neopopulist image as a gutsy politician for the little guy "against" the bosses and the politicians. Not a small part of Yorty's appeal was racist (anti-black) and emotional (anti-Catholic in opposing Kennedy for president in 1960). In 1969 Yorty was forced into a runoff against Tom Bradley, a quiet, bright city councilman, former policeman, and Los Angeles' most prominent black politician. Yorty won 53 percent of the vote by suggesting that Bradley was linked to radicals. But in a 1973 rematch, Bradley won by putting together a coalition of minorities, West

Side liberals, and homeowners angry over Yorty's pro-developer bias.

Bradley quickly established a business-dominated Economic Advisory Council with such broad influence that Donald Hanauer, executive vice-president of the L.A. Area Chamber of Commerce, said that "business was made a managing partner in running the city." Bradley's Los Angeles became an international symbol of racial stability, progress, and public-private cooperation, a reputation that was enhanced by the strong role he played in bringing the 1984 Summer Olympics to the city. But he always took care to make no waves, to raise no controversial issue, disappointing many blacks and liberals. He refused to give his endorsement to a school busing plan, and during his administration, the city—to the amazement of civil rights activists—appealed all the way to the U.S. Supreme Court an order to integrate the police and fire departments. Critics said his public housing program was in a shambles. Personally, however, Bradley remained so popular that there was never any real question he would receive the Democratic gubernatorial nomination when he sought it in 1982. And when, after leading in practically all pre-election polls, he barely lost the general election to George Deukmejian, it seemed likely Californians' vestigial racism, not Bradley's lack of qualification, cost him the governorship.

Both Los Angeles City and County (the latter fallen under conservative control) came on hard fiscal times in the wake of Proposition 13. The city, wracked by spiraling police and pension costs, cut its work force deeply and allowed street resurfacing to slip to a once-every-130 years schedule. "And we already have every user fee you can think of," chief administrative officer Keith Comrie told us. "We charge for building and safety and planning permits, for swimming pools, golf courses, the zoo, you name it. But how do you come up with a fee for police?" The message was equally grim in the county offices, where heavy cuts were made in health, welfare, and criminal justice programs. Said L.A. County Executive Harry Hufford: "People want less government, but always say cut the budget elsewhere. But the parks are jammed on weekends. Hospital clinics are full. Welfare loads are going up. Inner-city schools are crowded. People call for law and order, but the jails are already overcrowded. The buses are a disgrace. These are the issues. We'll provide the government people are willing to pay for."

With low-income Hispanics and Asians and blacks becoming an ever greater part of Los Angeles, the question for this erstwhile Lotus Land was becoming not only who would pay, but how.

Setting Records in Orange County

"In the beginning and in the end, there is the real estate." Thus Michael A. Hiltzik of the *L.A. Times* accurately summed up the driving force of Orange County, California. Assembled into ranches from Spanish land grants, this southern coastal plain still grows some oranges and raises some cattle. But since the freeways came, the real money has been in subdividing. For many years, Orange was the fastest-growing big county in the United States, increasing its population more than 1,000 percent from a 1940 count of 130,760 to 1,931,570 in 1980. The population explosion peaked in the '60s when more than 700,000 people moved in; soaring land and housing prices slowed the growth in the '70s, but the population still grew by more than 500,000.

The story of the Irvine Ranch, the greatest of all Orange County landholdings, reads like the quintessential American historical saga—the assembly of some 110,000 acres by Scottish immigrant James Irvine, the defense of that land at gunpoint, the land's passage to James II, who created a charitable foundation to hold the land, and the spunky headstrong fight of Joan Irvine Smith, the last of the family, to take control of the ranch away from the foundation whose officers she charged with deliberate mismanagement of the company and conflicts of interest. Smith lobbied hard for 1969 changes in federal tax law that eventually required the foundation to sell its 54 percent interest in the company in 1977; the purchaser was Detroit shopping center developer A. Alfred Taubman, and the price for 77,000 acres, 95 percent undeveloped, was a cool $337.4 million.

Partly due to Smith's pressures, the Irvine Company had already begun developing the land. The company was persuaded to donate 1,000 acres to the University of California for a campus. Only 80,000 people lived in Irvine Company developments by the early 1980s, but the company's policies had generally shaped most of the transportation, commercial, and residential patterns of southern Orange County. As the Irvine Company's ambitions and desire for profit grew, the developments became denser and less environmentally sensitive, according to both architectural critics and residents.

Orange County's growth has brought closer its goal of independence from Los Angeles. In the early 1970s, the first tall office buildings sprouted in Newport Center (an Irvine development); by 1980 the county actually developed a skyline! Industrialists, especially aerospace and high-tech entrepreneurs, loved Orange County's open land and pro-business attitudes and opened many plants there. More than 500,000 jobs were created in Orange County in the 1970s. By 1981 more than 90 percent of the income earned by Orange County residents was earned within the county. All these developments turned Orange County into what sociologists call a nearly independent "outer city," comparable to New York's Long Island. This feeling was enhanced by the movement of the California Angels baseball team and the Los Angeles Rams to Anaheim; the county fathers determined, however, that no place was truly independent until it was "culturally" independent and made plans for a $60 million performing arts complex in Costa Mesa.

Orange County is not simply endless suburbia with factories and office buildings. It has Mission San Juan Capistrano, from which the swallows depart every St. John's Day (October 23) to return on St. Joseph's Day (March 19). It has 40 miles of magnificent beach and choice surfside communities, of which one of our favorites on this entire continent is Laguna Beach; it is the home of world-famed Disneyland, the Crystal Cathedral (from which the Rev. Robert Schuller broadcasts his "Hour of Power"), oil wells, and remnants of the orange groves which gave the county its name. Orange County was the birthplace (at Yorba Linda) of Richard Nixon, who also selected San Clemente, on the seacoast, as his Western White House.

In his heyday, Nixon could not have found greater political acceptance than he got in the overwhelmingly white, middle-class, rightward leaning precincts of Orange County. To reach Orange County, they used to say in Los Angeles, "You go down the freeway and turn right." One reason for the county's conservatism was the domination for 35 years (until his demise in 1970) of Raymond Cyrus Hoiles, publisher of the *Santa Ana* (now Orange County) *Register*. Hoiles wanted to abolish both the public schools, because he thought their financing a form of compulsory taxation, and child labor laws ("Give him a pick and shovel and let him get started").

As Orange County has grown, its population and its politics have become less homogenous. The white population percentage dropped from 92 percent in 1970 to 86 percent in 1980; blacks still made up only 1.3 percent of the population and Asians only 4.4 percent. Hispanics' share of the population had increased to almost 15 percent. This vast suburb has never developed a metropolitan heart, but it has five cities of more than 100,000 souls: Anaheim (221,847), Santa Ana (203,713), Huntington Beach (170,505), Garden Grove (122,841), and Fullerton (102,034). Santa Ana was 54 percent minority in the 1980 Census—heavily Hispanic, but also black and Asian with refugees from Vietnam, Cambodia, and Laos (of whom more than 25 percent spoke no English). Neighborhood organizations galvanized to prevent deterioration, and such self-help groups as the Loa Family Community offered emergency translation, temporary housing, and language and vocational training. The Santa Ana police department, was once so right-wing the John Birch Society tried to form a cell within it. In the early '70s gang violence spread from the barrios into the downtown area, and two police officers were murdered. But a progressive police chief sparked creation of a community-oriented policing program in close cooperation with citizens in both Hispanic and Anglo neighborhoods—a signal advance helping win Santa Ana an All-America City award.

Incipient moderation hit Orange County in the '70s; in '78 the county even voted for Jerry Brown for governor. Democrats briefly held a registration edge. Why the shift? Engineers, it was said, began to recognize that recessions hit them, too, so that unemployment benefits and federal aid were important. Nor was unfettered free enterprise about to solve the county's housing crisis. As the number of jobs grew and housing prices soared beyond the means of factory workers, the county adopted in 1979 an inclusionary zoning provision requiring one-fourth of all units in new developments to be in the low to moderate price range. The move was timely indeed: firms had come to complain that they could no longer move to or expand in Orange County because workers could not find affordable housing.

Much of Orange's conservative image remains true, however. The last time the county voted for a Democratic presidential candidate was 1936. It's hard for Democrats to counter such forces as the 1,000 member Leisure World chapter of the National Federation of Republican Women, which once stuffed and mailed 11,000 pieces of campaign literature in one day for a county supervisor candidate.

The Flower of Santa Barbara

Before continuing our southward tour of Southern California, we must take a detour 100 miles up the coast from Los Angeles to exquisitely gardened Santa Barbara, a city set in a crescent-shaped valley between the honey-colored Santa Ynez Mountains and the Pacific. Santa Barbara is so imbued with quiet gentility and tradition that its real soul sister is San Francisco, not the flashy new urban creations of the Southland. No California city is so close, in architecture and lifestyle, to the ancient Spanish. Here is the Queen of the Missions, where the altar candle flame the Padres lighted in 1786 has never been snuffed out.

Nor is there any California city so Eastern. As the *Los Angeles Times* commented: "Color it Boston, little Back Bay West with blooming begonias, a New England style blueblood community with two social registers, a court house which looks like a Moorish palace and the third-oldest polo playing club in America." Even more than yachting, the proper Santa Barbaran's chosen pastime is riding polo ponies over the brown, rolling hills that sweep to canyon crests over the surf.

Santa Barbara more than anywhere else in California has tried to stay out of the pro-growth society. Despite local resistance, however, offshore oil drilling proceeded, and on January 28, 1969, a horrible dream came true. Union Oil workmen drilling offshore cut a hole into a high-pressure deposit of oil and gas. Oil spread across the blue water at the rate of almost 1,000 gallons an hour for 11 days; 40 miles of beach front were covered with acrid, tarlike slime, and thousands of birds lay dying, unable to raise their oil-soaked wings. There was remarkably little long-term damage, but the Santa Barbara situation led Congress to place restrictions on offshore drilling. Santa Barbara has proven a good rallying point for environmentalists ever since and indeed may be more so in the future: by 1983 a consensus was forming among oilmen that the fields off Santa Barbara's wide beach and sunbaked harbor could well hold more than a billion barrels, the most important U.S. oil find since Alaska's North Slope in 1968.

Santa Barbara's environmental consciousness has resulted in restrictive planning policies. After large population gains in the 1950s and '60s, the city grew a mere 6.2 percent in the '70s, to a total of 74,542. But the small cities of Santa Maria and Lompoc have encouraged manufacturing, and the county's overall population increased 13 percent, to 298,660. More than half the land remains in agriculture, much of it in large "ranchos" owned by the descendants of California's settling families. A bit of this way of life comes to an end each year, as one generation dies, and a combination of taxes, housing demand, and estate battles turns multi-thousand-acre ranchos into 100-acre ranchettes.

San Diego: California's Second City?

One hundred twenty-five miles south of Los Angeles, at the southwestern extremity of the continental U.S.A., lies one of the world's great natural harbors, set off by shining hills and mesas, and, in winter, snowcapped mountains. Seaward lies the steep-sided, wind-swept promontory of Point Loma, that last point of land for the hundreds of thousands of sailors who have ridden out and back with the fleets for more than a century.

San Diego's role in California history was vital, for it was on a parched, sun-bleached hill overlooking its harbor that Father Junipero Serra stood in 1769 to proclaim the founding of the first permanent Christian settlement of California. Through the mission years, Mexican rule and afterwards, little changed; the city's age-old rival, Los Angeles, started ahead and stayed ahead in population, wealth, and power. Set at California's far corner, with mountains to block off transcontinental travel, San Diego had little but tourism plus the growing commerce generated by the Navy (a constant caller since 1846).

The pace quickened with World War I and the coming of the early aviation companies (Convair and Ryan Aeronautical) in the '20s and '30s. World War II brought San Diego into a military-aircraft boom-bust cycle that the city has tried ever since to break, with greater success each decade. In the 1970 Census, fast-growing San Diego replaced San Francisco as California's second-most-populous city, a position it held even more firmly in 1980 after its population had jumped another 25.5 percent, to 875,504. The metropolitan area of San Diego County has only 1,861,846 people, however, smaller than San Francisco's 3.3 million, not to mention Los Angeles' 7.5 million.

San Diego in the 1980s comes the closest to the Southern California that many Americans remember nostalgically. The mild climate and the natural beauty of San Diego Bay and the nearby mountains have not been marred by pollution and the hurried, angry, and intense atmosphere of Los Angeles. San Diego has been described as "terminally laid back," and in 1982 the producers of a TV situation comedy rejected San Diego as a location because it was not "sexy" enough. San Diegans objected, but in reality they like the wholesome outdoor atmosphere of their civilization with its tourist and resident beaches, hang gliding, and charming little towns. Roving retirees, having rejected most places in California, still come to San Diego (providing they are rich enough to afford its sky-high housing prices). San Diego is also a favorite of engineers and their families, as well as active military personnel who often stay on when they retire. The old-fashioned atmosphere is also reflected in the racial demographics. San Diego County is only 5 percent black, and though cheek-by-jowl with Mexico, just 15 percent Hispanic. Much Mexican immigration—legal and illegal—pours through San Diego, but the newcomers tend to proceed farther north for low-skilled, entry-level jobs.

Engineers' affinity for San Diego has encouraged high-tech companies seeking low employee turnover to locate there, to the joy of city fathers looking for just that kind of clean, modern industry. Aerospace and electronics account for about half of manufacturing, followed by metal fabricating, printing and publishing (most notably since 1982, Harcourt Brace Jovanovich), seafood canning, and shipbuilding. The military, in the form of the U.S. Navy's largest operational complex plus the Camp Pendleton Marine Corps base, contributes heavily to the economy. San Diego has also become a national center in oceanography, a development preordained by the founding, in 1912, of the Scripps Institute of Oceanography at La Jolla (the affluent gem of a town a few miles north on the coast). The Salk Institute and the University of California San Diego Medical School are important in health research.

Tourism is more than a footnote in San Diego County. The attractions besides the climate include the celebrated San Diego Zoo at Balboa Park, historic missions, Sea World, and the town of Coronado, linked to the city by the graceful arch of the Coronado Bridge, high enough for any war vessel to pass beneath. That great, lumbering, white Victorian wonder, the Hotel del Coronado, adds flavor rare in this century (even harp music accompanying Sunday brunch). The more socially inquisitive tourist may wish to visit Chicano Park beneath the San Diego side of the bridge. When the bridge was built, in 1969, its interchange with Interstate 5 was located in the heart of Barrio Logan, the waterfront Chicano neighborhood. The city had plans for a highway patrol headquarters beneath the bridge, but in a display of radical action that was as rare for San Diego Chicanos as it was common for that period of protest, Barrio Logan residents occupied the site for 12 days and stopped construction, cleaned up the area, planted trees and bushes, and took control of the land. The city gave in, the park became the focal point of the neighborhood, and the bridge's pillars have been painted in Latin murals. Since the number of pillars seems endless, there is always new art to see.

The wealth of San Diego retirees and engineers, complemented by the predictably military orientation of those who sup at the Navy/aerospace table, has made San Diego County predictably conservative political territory. But the *San Diego Union,* flagship of the Copley newspaper chain, has abandoned the rigid Republican conservatism and militarism of its earlier years and become a newspaper of excellence.

San Diego's real power brokers, by all accounts, are not so much politicians as leading moguls of the business-financial community. But some of the anti-planning, profit-for-growth crowd came a cropper of the law in the '70s, and the dangers of unfettered growth were thrown into bold relief as once-beautiful Harbor Drive became a heavily traveled airport service road, and what amounted to a second city core sprang up along a freeway corridor more than five minutes distant from the decaying downtown. In 1971 San Diegans elected as mayor Pete Wilson, a 38-year-old state assemblyman who had distinguished himself in pressing for environmental protection legislation. Under Wilson, San Diego led other cities in controlling sprawl by requiring developers to pay for extensions of such services as streets, gutters, and sewers, by encouraging "infill" development of center city lots and expediting permits for selective construction sites. Wilson had a tougher time trying to redevelop what San Diegans called "centre city," fallen into some seediness with its retail heart sapped by too much suburban development. New office buildings and hotels rose in the '70s and early '80s to meet market demand. But a massive retail department store and theater-restaurant project, Horton Plaza, proceeded at a snail's pace as its chief private participant, developer Ernest W. Hahn, seemed in the eyes of some critics to be more anxious to complete his competitive outlying shopping centers. There was hope, however, that all would be in place by the mid-'80s, reviving big-time downtown retailing—in part to cater to a Mexican clientele. Wilson resigned in 1983, having won his U.S. Senate seat on a strongly conservative platform.

Out of San Diego's downtown development schemes came America's first light rail transit line in decades—the "Tijuana Trolley," opened in 1981. The idea originated with State Senator James Mills, a transit buff who authored legislation setting aside San Diego gas taxes for mass transit. It was built without federal funds and time-consuming federal approvals and regulations, on schedule and on budget ($86 million), with two miles in town (starting at the historic old Santa Fe depot), then switching to a pre-existent railbed for 14 more miles to the border at Tijuana. Tourists, shoppers, and commuters flocked to ride the sturdy German-made cars. By 1982 there was a cloud on the horizon: Mexico's sick economy and sick peso, raising questions about how dependent San Diego should be on Mexican shopping. But the trolley might long be remembered in California history as a return to *popular* public transit in America's preeminent auto state, local financing in place of federal funding, a city strategizing for its own economic future, and finally a link by increasingly Hispanic California to the great Spanish-speaking neighbor on its southern flank.

OREGON

Fearing Growth, Seeking Growth

OREGON IN THE 1960s AND '70s reveled in its image as a lush paradise, sparsely populated by individualists who made no secret of their desire to protect the state from the "Californification" they feared was creeping northward. With its tough environmental and land-use laws—the strongest in the nation—Oregon sought to keep a lid on its population influx and protect its lifestyle from the hazards of too much development. Tom McCall, then its popular governor, summed it up neatly in a speech to conventioneers in Portland during the early '70s: "Welcome to Oregon. While you're here, I want you to enjoy yourselves. Travel, visit, drink in the great beauty of our state. But for God's sake, don't move here."

By 1982, however, with unemployment nudging 12 percent and Oregon's corporate climate ranked 36th in the continental U.S., Governor Victor Atiyeh proclaimed a different message: "Oregon is open for business." The disturbing early '80s downturn in the national economy had made the extreme vulnerability of an economy based on Oregon's natural resources painfully clear. The state's timber companies were reeling from the national recession just as much as the auto plants of Detroit. Oregon's powerbrokers were increasingly preoccupied with the issue of economic development. There was even talk, considered blasphemy in some circles, of easing up on Oregon's environmental restrictions, if that were required to attract business and jobs. But any significant environmental retreat was unlikely. Oregon voters had expressed strong support for land-use laws in two statewide referenda of the '70s and did so again in 1982—ample evidence of great pride in their state and a fervent desire to protect its natural heritage.

Oregon's population grew rapidly in the 1970s. The 1980 Census showed a population of 2,632,663, a formidable 25.9 percent increase over the 1970 total. The newcomers were mostly young—the median age of Oregonians was only 30 in 1980—and they overwhelmingly supported the state's commitment to protecting its natural heritage, often to a greater degree than did the natives. Many were professional people seeking a pleasant place to locate; the state in fact developed a glut of doctors and lawyers. Some were students who stayed in Oregon after they completed school; others were "granolas" yearning for simple, alternate lifestyles. Many were "burnouts" from the East, Midwest, and California. They tended to be the type of people who insulated their homes and experimented with solar power to preserve energy, recycled their garbage, gardened without chemicals. And they luxuriated in the fine backpacking, river-rafting, skiing, and camping that are within easy reach of all

Oregon cities, not to mention the lack of social conflict and the freedom of the Oregonian way of life. Would this immigrant stream continue through the difficult times of the '80s? No one could say, but if anything, Oregon's deep economic troubles seemed to have the potential of returning the state to stable growth by scaring away all but the most employable immigrants. By 1983, some desperately unemployed Oregon immigrants were even reported returning to their families in California.

Conventional wisdom has it that Oregon's prim and conservative manners spring from a strong, early infusion of New England stock. Place names like Portland and Salem and the profusion of church spires and tidy white houses in the Willamette Valley all seem evidence of this. In 1845 a toss of the coin decided the name of a 640-acre tract along Willamette River, near its junction with the Columbia: Amos Lovejoy, of Massachusetts, wanted the town called Boston, while Francis Pettygrove, of Maine, held out for Portland. Pettygrove won the toss. The state has always had a fairly homogeneous, overwhelmingly white and Protestant population; Roman Catholics still make up only 12 percent of the state, about half the national average. But the New England roots may have been exaggerated. As they had done in Kansas, New Englanders set their mark on Oregon in public education. Literacy and educational levels in Oregon remain high to this day. But one looks in vain for flashes of brilliance: great writers, musicians, or artists of the type one would expect a Boston to foster. Instead, Oregon leads the Pacific Coast states in its interest in genealogy; to be descended from one of the early pioneers is a real mark of distinction.

The most decisive factor in molding Oregon's character may have been less the regional origin of its people than the predilections of its settlers, from whatever region. During the heyday of the Oregon Trail, a choice of immense future consequences was made by the pioneers at a juncture near the Snake River in southeastern Idaho. Wagon trains of farmers and merchants chose the northern extension of the trail, over the Cascades into Oregon's Willamette Valley; the gold seekers and other, more adventurous, types picked the southern spur, over the Sierra Nevada toward Sutter's Mill and the El Dorado known as California.

The 20th century has brought new waves of immigrants, altering the old patterns to some degree. During both the world wars and the 1930s, an influx of conservative border-state Southerners moved into southern Oregon. The thousands of workers who moved to Oregon during World War II were a polyglot bunch, certainly less conservative and predictable than the denizens of old, Republican, rural Oregon.

The 1980 Census found only about 37,000 black and 66,000 Hispanic Oregonians. A major development of the '70s was the influx of Asian immigrants, mostly Vietnamese, ethnic Chinese, Cambodians, and Laotians. Oregon ranked fourth in the nation for resettlement of Asian refugees, most of whom settled in Portland. The Census counted 35,000 Asians and Pacific islanders.

The Natural Environment—and Its Protection

On a December day in 1843, John C. Fremont and his party ascended to an altitude of 7,000 feet amid snows and howling winds in south central Oregon. Suddenly, they looked down 3,000 feet on a lake margined with grass and surprisingly green trees. Down they went, from winter into summer. Fremont named the two points Winter Rim and Summer Lake. The episode aptly illustrates the geologic diversity of Oregon, one of the most beautiful of our states. Here is a land of frosty, high mountain peaks, of an incomparable coastline with high bluffs and sandy beaches, of broad and productive river valleys, of upland plains cut by deep gorges of rushing rivers, heavily timbered ranges, and gaunt desert.

Measuring some 280 miles from north to south, and 380 miles from east to west, Oregon's western third is set off by the imposing barrier of the Cascade Mountains, a chain crowned by volcanic peaks, of which the greatest and most illustrious is perpetually snow-clad Mount Hood, clearly visible from the city of Portland.

Between the Cascades and the Coast Range lies the Willamette Valley, the heartland of Oregon, stretching 180 miles south of Portland; within it is Oregon's breadbasket and some of its great timber stands. The state's three large cities—Portland, Salem, and Eugene—are here; in fact, no Oregon city of more than 30,000 people is located outside the valley.

About halfway down the state, the Willamette Valley stops, and one is in rough territory of mountains, timber stands, and farm valleys between the Cascades and Coastal Range down to the California border. Close by, in the Cascades, is Oregon's great natural wonder: Crater Lake, with its deep, blue waters resting in the cone of a massive, collapsed volcano.

Over the relatively modest barrier of the Coastal Range, one comes on coastal Oregon, a strip averaging 25 miles in width running along the Pacific Coast. High rainfall produces luxuriant vegetation, and the area is prime farm, fishing, and foresting territory. But the real fascination is with that coastline, which has been described as the most scenic marine border in the world. Oregon has been busily at work eliminating all private beaches, so that the state will own the whole coastline, and each section will be open to the public (with planned access points, parking, and trails to the beach every three miles). Slashes of pure white beach with the surf foaming over, high promontories, battered headlands, secret coves and little inlets, gaunt rock shapes in the water, sea lion herds, lighthouses, dramatic waterfalls—such are the images of this long stretch of land's end by the Pacific.

Before departing coastal Oregon, note should be taken of Astoria, set just inside the mouth of the Columbia (with predictably breathtaking river views) in the extreme northwest corner of the state. Astoria (pop. 9,998) advertises itself as the "oldest American city West of the Mississippi," known to white men since 1792 and founded by Jacob Astor's fur traders in 1811. It is also remarkable as a heavily ethnic city in an otherwise homogeneous state. Finnish immigrants started migrating to Astoria shortly after the Civil War, and in Finland the town is known as the Finnish capital of America. Astorians make their living from the sea, from which they have been drawing magnificent catches of salmon and tuna for 75 years.

Oregonians take justifiable pride in the job they have done in protecting their environment. Oregon was fortunate, first of all, not to have been logged-over during the preconservation era; by the time the axes fell in Oregon, some bitter lessons had been learned in the Upper Midwest, and advanced ideas about the danger of erosion and the need for reforestation had developed. Few states developed a park program comparable to Oregon's: there are presently well over 200 state parks, and close to 4,000 campsites and 6,000 picnic sites scattered from border to border, with a special concentration along the seashore. But it was not until the late '60s, with the McCall administration, that Oregon began making a name for itself on the environmental front. The earliest successes came in correcting water pollution. Soon after taking office in 1967, McCall oversaw passage of a strict set of water quality standards and publication of an enforcement plan covering every stream and every city and industry on each Oregon waterway. The Willamette River, once considered one of the nation's dirtiest, was cleansed of 90 percent of its municipal and industrial waste by the time McCall left office eight years later.

The big step came in 1973, with the passage of Oregon Senate Bill 100. The legislation was meant to protect the state's farm and forest land through zoning and tax measures; in time it came to embody Oregon's unique and deeply felt approach to growth and planning. The agency created to implement the law, the Land Conservation and Development Commission, was empowered to review land-use plans from Oregon's 278 localities and either to accept or reject them on the basis of whether they complied with 19 state land-use goals. The localities were required to draw urban growth boundaries based on population projections 20 years into the future. Beyond those boundaries generally lie farm and forest zones. In this fashion, vast stretches of Oregon acres were put under "exclusive farm use" designation.

The commission operated from its inception under a cloud of criticism from industry and labor leaders, who complained that businesses were reluctant to locate in Oregon because the land-use restrictions make land too expensive and because they feared becoming involved in the kind of prolonged political haggling and litigation often associated with individual localities' plans. Singled out for vilification by those opposing the planning goals was Portland lawyer Henry Richmond and his public interest organization, "1000 Friends of Oregon," which monitored implementation of Senate Bill 100 and sued localities whose planning decisions didn't comply with the goals. But when the land-use act was subjected, for a second time in the '70s, to referendum attack, many builders and developers decided, surprisingly, to defend the statute. The law, they had discovered, not only stipulated where development might *not* occur (outside urban growth boundaries), but it cut away ambiguities about their right to develop *within* those boundaries. But even Gov. Victor Atiyeh, who came to office at the end of the 70's and was one of those Republicans most friendly to it, worried about over-zealous enforcement that might create "the misperception that we are not interested in trying to create jobs in Oregon." Even so, there was no sign that Oregonians would quickly or willingly abandon the most thorough, operative statewide approach to land use in the United States. It was, in short, a passport to the future they wanted for themselves and their descendants on Oregon soil.

There remained tremendous, perhaps growing public support for the large body of companion Oregon environmental laws. Among them were the controversial 1971 "bottle bill" prohibiting the use of nonreturnable beverage bottles and cans, the country's toughest standards for siting nuclear power plants, and a ban (in vivid contrast to neighboring Washington) on the storage of nuclear waste in the state.

Politics: "Oregon System" and a State of Independents

Throughout its history, Oregon has received more national political notice than its size seems to warrant: from Oregon's status as a pawn in the free slave-state dispute of the 1850s, its central role in the disputed 1876 Hayes-Tilden election, its drive of reform around the turn of the century, which won Oregon the title of "political experiment station of the nation," to decisive votes in a number of crucial presidential primaries from the 1940s onward.

After the Civil War, Oregon's Republicans appropriated to themselves a "monopoly on respectability" that was pleasing and appropriate to the staid, middle-class state. But the corruption that marked the "Gilded Age" across the nation became a special problem in Oregon in the 1880s and '90s, when powerful moneyed interests took control of political organizations and nominating conventions and filled the legislative halls.

The venal, established order came under attack in the 1890s from the Populist movement, feeding on farmers' dislike of the monopolistic out-of-state control of the economy in which bankers, railroads, and land speculators rigged interest rates, farm prices, and land sales to their private gain. Eventually though reluctantly, the major party leaders agreed to the first great reform: initiative and referendum (approved by a phenomenal 11–1 ratio in a statewide vote in 1902). This, in turn, opened the door to the great reforms of the "Oregon system," by which common Oregon citizens appropriated to themselves, for a number of years, the final decision on virtually all momentous issues.

The power of the established and graft-ridden political parties was broken, never again to be reasserted; also diminished in great measure was the influence of the special interests. In six elections, starting with 1904, Oregon voters expressed their will on 107 specific constitutional or statutory proposals. They instituted direct primary elections in the state and approved a presidential primary law, prohibited railway passes (a favorite method of corrupting government officials), authorized municipal home rule and local direct legislation by the people, controlled freight rates, placed taxes on public utilities, formed an industrial accident commission, limited the working day for women to 10 hours, and put a corrupt practices act on the books. Political scientist Frederic C. Howe in 1911 described Oregon as "the most complete democracy in the world," where "every . . . community is being trained to a knowledge of politics." Woodrow Wilson, then-governor of New Jersey, said Oregon's new laws seemed "to point the direction which we must also take." To this day, it is the rare public policy question affecting broad masses of people that does not end up on the Oregon ballot.

Oregon was once called the "Vermont of the West" for its staunch Republican voting habits. The Republicans' long-term registration edge in the state disappeared by the mid-1950s, paving the way for a Democratic party revival led by such urban-oriented liberals as Richard Neuberger, who was elected to the Senate in 1954, and Senator Wayne Morse, the fiery Republican, then-Independent, who finally became a Democrat in 1956.

Unlike Oregon's old-time Democrats, many of whom were agrarian and Southern conservative, Neuberger and company were modern, urban oriented liberals. In 1958 their movement was strong enough to win Democratic control of both houses of the legislature for the first time in the century. But Oregon's Republicans effected a strong comeback through the appealing personalities of their major candidates, all of whom represented a moderate and sometimes downright liberal Republicanism that was close to the winning Oregon mainstream. The first of the new breed was Mark Hatfield, who was elected secretary of state in 1956, governor in 1958, and senator in 1966. McCall, another liberal Republican, succeeded him as governor. In 1968, the Democratic rout was completed with the defeat of Senator Morse by Bob Packwood, a state legislator of moderate-to-liberal persuasion. And while the Republican right wing occasionally rises up in wrath, the basic facts about Oregon Republicanism are that it is moderate and dominant in the state.

Oregon voters rank consistently among the highest in the percentage turning out for elections. Their quadrennial presidential preference primary, in which all "generally advocated" candidates appear on the ballot (they may remove their names only by filing affidavits saying they do not intend to be candidates for the presidency), has been copied by several states as the best way to flush out likely contenders. As more and more states have gone the presidential primary route, however, Oregon's impact has diminished. The most decisive Oregon primary was that of 1948, when Thomas E. Dewey and Harold E. Stassen clashed in a broadcast debate over outlawing the Communist party (Stassen for, Dewey against)—following which Dewey won the primary, eliminated Stassen as an effective opponent, and went on to win the Republican nomination but lose to President Harry Truman in November. The 1968 Democratic primary made history of another sort: it resulted in the first ballot box defeat ever for a member of that illustrious political clan, the sons of Joseph P. Kennedy. Eugene McCarthy defeated Robert Kennedy in the Democratic preference vote—in part, surely, because Oregon had fewer of the blacks and poor who had provided Kennedy's margin in other states. That outcome aside, somehow the memory flickers back to the young candidate walking barefoot along the magnificent Oregon beach, touching nature a last time before the tinsel world of California, a few days later, would swallow him up and kill him.

Oregon state politics during the '60s and early '70s were dominated by the two strongest and, by general agreement, best governors of recent decades: Hatfield (1959–67) and McCall (1967–75), both men of unusual intellect, independence, and commitment. Hatfield pioneered in economic development, civil rights, and education. McCall, a television newscaster before entering politics, left in addition to his impressive record on the environment the most sweeping reorganization of state agencies in this century. Articulate and always comfortable in the spotlight, McCall became a national figure during his term and, in the view of many Oregonians, put the state on the map. In 1982, fighting the third of the initiative efforts to overturn the land-use planning law, McCall acknowledged it would be his last battle: "You all know that I have terminal cancer, and I have a lot of it. But what many of you might not know is that stress induces its spread and induces its activity. Stress may even bring it on. Yet stress is the fuel of the activist. This activist loves Oregon more than he loves life. I know I can't have both very long, but the tradeoff is all right with me." Three months later, McCall was gone, but Oregon's land-use protections remained inviolate.

Following McCall as governor in 1975 was Democratic State Treasurer Robert Straub, who studiously implemented McCall's policies but failed to make much personal impact. Aided by the anti-big-government climate that followed approval of California's Proposition 13, Republican Victor Atiyeh beat Straub in 1978 after destroying McCall's comeback attempt in the Republican primary. But Atiyeh, whose general political philosophy was "If it ain't broke, don't fix it," had the misfortune to take over the statehouse just as the Oregon economy began to disintegrate. His administration was marked by repeated, gruesome fiscal crises. But Atiyeh ended up scoring an overwhelming reelection victory after a much-publicized correspondence with President Reagan in which Atiyeh said he was "greatly distrubed and saddened" by the president's economic policies. Oregonians, one finds again, like their politicians prickly independent.

Oregon's legislature never gained status as a great and independent policymaking body, if for no other reason than because the people are always looking over its shoulder and correcting or adding to its work in referendum and initiative votes. It has always been split sharply along urban-rural lines, and the reapportionment that followed the 1980 Census channeled some power from the cities to the more conservative areas of the state, including heavily Republican suburbs such as Beaverton, Gresham, Hillsboro, and Lake Oswego. The most powerful Oregon interest groups have always been the public utilities, the lumber companies, and, although Oregon is a weak state as unions go, organized labor. A review of Oregon powers would be incomplete without mention of the *Portland Oregonian*, the state's most widely read paper and still a force to be reckoned with—even if no longer *the* great oracle and arbiter of state politics it was in earlier times. The most outstanding downstate papers are the *Eugene Register-Guard* and *Salem Statesman-Journal.*

In Washington, Oregonians in the early '80s held more power than they had in many decades, the result of the Republican sweep of 1980 that gave the GOP control of the Senate and put two strong committee chairmanships in the hands of their Senators: Appropriations for Hatfield and Commerce, Science and Transportation for Packwood.

Before the light of latter-day memory dims, however, the life and personality of Wayne Morse deserve a final flashback. Ornery and self-righteous, he was also a man of immense courage and brilliance who never doubted that he spoke for the little man. In his prime, Morse was a fearsome force, able to deliver a 22-hour filibuster speech in an attempt to defeat an oil tidelands bill, fight against exempting natural gas producers from federal regulation, or violently oppose the Landrum-Griffin labor reform bill. In 1964 Morse and Senator Ernest Gruening of Alaska were the only two senators to oppose the Gulf of Tonkin resolution authorizing President Johnson's escalation of the Vietnam War. Morse's fatal flaw was arrogant pride. As biographer A. Robert Smith noted, Morse "hacked a bloody swashbuckling trail through both the Republican and Democratic parties, beheading old friends and allies faster than he could recruit replacements." At one point, Morse even descended to a roaring feud with Neuberger, his colleague and former close friend.

The Morse tradition makes it easier to understand the remarkable independence, even unto defying his party and president, of Mark Hatfield. A man of deep religious conviction, Hatfield views wars and armaments as the greatest scourge of the modern world. In 1970 he cosponsored with George McGovern an amendment to end the Vietnam War; he was the major congressional opponent of the neutron bomb and always voted against U.S. arms sales—even using the prestige of his Appropriations chairmanship to try to curb Pentagon spending. During the Nixon years, Hatfield denounced the administration's "Southern strategy" and the provocative speeches of Vice President Agnew; he charged that his party was practicing "the politics of revulsion." Hatfield's actual voting record on domestic issues was, however, relatively mainstream Republican.

Packwood, who succeeded Morse, made the most impact with his strong support of both abortion rights and Israel and his proposal to provide tuition tax credits to parents of children in private schools. In a repeat of the Morse-Neuberger feud of the 1950s, the ambitious, occasionally calculating Packwood and the low-key, sometimes aloof Hatfield were said to have little use for each other. Packwood nettled the Reagan White House on a wide range of issues, from the ERA to sale of sophisticated arms to Saudi Arabia, and the Reaganites helped engineer his removal as head of fund-dispensing Republican Senatorial Campaign Committee. Then Packwood complained that Reagan's policies were driving women, blacks, Hispanics, and Jews away from the Republican Party in droves and started a national crusade for what he called "the soul of my party."

On the House side, Oregon has not had a strong voice since the 1980 defeat of Al Ullman, erstwhile chairman of the Ways and Means Committee, and Edith Green, the high-ranking liberal Democrat on the Education and Labor Committee who in her latter congressional years showed remarkable prescience by breaking with organized labor and opposing federal dictation to state and local governments on education aid and poverty programs.

Timber!

One of the most awesome sights of the primordial American continent must have been the great stands of virgin timber in the Pacific Northwest—spread from the oceanside to the flanks of the Cascades, rolling blankets of Douglas fir, some as high as 280 feet, interspersed with hemlock and cedar; on the eastern slope, millions of ponderosa pine, aspen, and cottonwood—timber enough to build millions of ships or house hundreds of millions of people.

Northwest boosters say their region is the best in the world for growing quality softwood timber. While the region has been diversifying rapidly over the past two decades, lumber remains central to both the Oregon and Washington economies. Almost half of the country's entire production is located on the Pacific Coast. Until 1937, Washington ranked as the nation's top producer of forest products. Since then, it has been Oregon. Northwestern lumbermen never inflicted on the forests the unspeakable damage that was perpetrated in the northern Great Lakes states—perhaps because the federal government early on got control of so much Northwestern timber, perhaps because the loggers themselves foresaw the damage that might be done. But billions of board feet of lumber cannot be extracted from the forests each year without profound effect. Every day great trucks thunder out of the forests carrying massive logs headed for sawmill or pulp plant. Light years seem to separate the axes of the early loggers from today's mechanization—devices such as the automatic chipper that can move out in the forest and then literally consume the whole tree, moving logs up its central belt, stripping them of bark and branches, then cutting them into convenient small pieces from which to make pulp. Douglas fir, 80 percent of the forest stand, cannot be cut selectively from a forest but must be harvested in big patches (usually 50 to 100 acres) that make a lot of Western forest lands look like huge checkerboards from the air. During the '60s and '70s the U.S. Forest Service came under criticism from conservationists for excessive clear-cutting and other land-destructive practices.

By the early '80s, however, timber and the environment issues had given way to profound concern about the health of the timber industry—and Oregon's very heavy dependence on it. High interest rates nationwide and a moribund housing industry left a quarter of the state's woodworkers idle. With more than 40 percent of the state's manufacturing employment still tied to wood, the loss of lumber money had been felt keenly in Oregon's rather overdeveloped retail and service industries. Unemployment in Oregon by the spring of 1982 topped 12 percent, among the highest levels in the U.S.A.

Nor did the crisis seem a temporary one. There was deep apprehension in Oregon that the early '80s rash of mill closures would be permanent and the jobs gone for good. The state's big timber companies were looking increasingly to the South, where labor is cheaper and the trees grow faster. Georgia Pacific, for example, had moved its headquarters from Portland to Atlanta, and other big timber firms having long associations with the Northwest—Weyerhaeuser, Crown Zellerbach, and Boise Cascade—also were involved deeply in the South. Middle-class Americans were being forced by high costs to abandon building big free-standing homes and to turn increasingly to multifamily and ever-smaller housing units (including all-metal mobile homes), thus raising doubts whether the timber industry would ever again witness demand for the fantastic amount of lumber harvested in the post–World War II decades.

Demand of another kind might be in log exports. Oregon was doing a brisk business in selling logs to Pacific rim countries. This was a point of no little controversy, however, since Oregonians would prefer to see their state export finished lumber, so their sawmills can keep busy. Meanwhile, the federal government was setting more and more land aside for wilderness and park lands, a process that has always aroused fervent opposition in the lumber industry.

But Oregon was at least beginning to move away from its traditional resource-based economy. Though still highly dependent on timber and agriculture—wheat, tree fruits, and nuts are traditionally the major farm products —Oregon in the '60s and '70s saw a boom in such industries as metals and machinery, finance, women's sportswear, and electronics. It was electronics, the "clean" industry, that Oregonians especially hoped to see expand to compensate for some of the jobs certain to be lost in timber. The state embarked on an expensive economic development campaign to lure more high-technology firms such as Tektronix, the biggest employer in the Portland area.

Whether Oregon could attract the high-tech industry it wanted was not at all certain. A strong base in higher education—the starting point and base, or both, of most hi-tech concentrations—was simply lacking in Oregon. In times of fiscal crisis, the state's universities and colleges, already an unexceptional group, were suffering deep cuts. Some saw hope in the Oregon Graduate Center, a private, nonprofit research and accredited higher-education facility in Beaverton with departments in computer science and engineering, chemical and biochemical science, applied physics, electronics, and environmental science. Oregon high-techers did keep in close contact with Cal Tech and other California institutions, but whether the California connection was close enough to foster a major spin-off area in Oregon was debatable. And there was another, potentially quite serious roadblock: the business climate. High-tech leaders complained that Oregon offered a hostile climate for business—high hourly wages and workers' compensation costs second only to Michigan, for example. The voters' continual rejection of a sales tax (it lost 8–1 the last time it was considered) resulted in the second-highest personal income tax and the ninth-highest corporate tax in the nation, both clear deterrents to high-tech firms. Industry also complained that Oregon's land-use laws caused a shortage of large industrial sites.

On the plus side, Oregon continued to offer a highly desirable quality of life (vital to drawing scientists and executives), relatively cheap housing, and a labor force only moderately unionized. Some said that the answer to economic troubles lay not in attracting high-tech companies that may only draw highly skilled workers from other states. Economic development funds, in the view of many Oregonians, would be better spent in research and development, perhaps to find more uses for wood products or to improve the state's crumbling infrastructure and modernize the port facilities at Portland. Among American states, Oregon has the most to gain through trade with the Japanese, who are interested in its wheat, aluminum, cattle, and timber.

Clouding Oregon's chances for a return to economic prosperity has been the specter of the Washington Public Power Supply System. "Whoops," as the supply system is appropriately called, has tied ratepayers throughout the Northwest to a massive nuclear power program plagued by inept planning and massive cost overruns. Although Northwest power in the early '80s was still cheap relative to that of other regions, the shadow of the Whoops consortium and its five plants—two of which were effectively mothballed—could become dark enough to scare away industry. A common sentiment in the state was expressed by Ron Buel, then-editor of Portland's *Willamette Week*: "We've really mortgaged our future."

The Prospect of Portland

If any West Coast city could historically have been said to have a monopoly on propriety and an anxiousness to "keep things as they are," it was Portland, a town of quiet old wealth, discreet culture, and cautious politics. Although that is far less true than in times past, the attractions that drew folk to Portland, and perhaps made them happy with life as it was, have not changed. The city is a lovely one, set in the green valley of the Willamette just below its juncture with the Columbia, a place of 7,000 acres of parkland, including not only beautiful gardens but also wilderness areas and miles of rustic trails and an almost magical view of Mt. Hood, to the east. Often the mist settles in a band below Hood's summit, leaving the top "floating" on the horizon. In the moist coastal climate zone, vegetation flourishes, and each June since 1909 there has been the famous Rose Festival.

The 1980 Census found 366,383 people in Portland, a slight drop from 1970. But the suburbs had grown rapidly. Washington County, to the west of the city, blossomed with subdivisions throughout the '70s and offered perhaps the clearest evidence in Oregon of California-style sprawl; it was up by 55.4 percent in population and a startling 84.6 percent in housing units during the decade. With a 1980 metropolitan area of about a million people, Portland and its suburbs accounted for nearly 40 percent of Oregon's total population.

Portland and the urban parts of its three counties in 1978 approved America's first directly elected regional government by giving the Metropolitan Service District, which previously managed garbage disposal and the zoo, statutory authority over such vital matters as land use, water, and even the dispersal of low-income housing units. Elected as the first executive of Metro, as the regional entity was called, was former consultant and state legislator Rick Gustafson; he served along with 12 part-time councilors elected from districts. Conceptually, the Metro idea was a major breakthrough in U.S. concepts of regional governance. But it lacked the breadth of power and political consensus of the older (albeit unelected) Metropolitan Council in Minneapolis–St. Paul. Additionally, it suffered a major setback when the voters denied it a permanent tax base.

The creation of Metro did little to affect the individual county commissions and the municipal government of Portland itself, which continued to function under a comfortable, honest, but quite inefficient form of government. For years, Portland suffered with a weak mayoral system and a general inability to implement long-term plans and reallocate resources. This began to change in 1972 with the election as mayor of Neil Goldschmidt, a brilliant, humorous, aggressive legal-services attorney who became a city council member. When we first interviewed Goldschmidt in his cubby-hole legal services office in north Portland in 1969, he told us Portland needed a political upheaval to shake off its complacency. A half decade later, he himself had accomplished that revolution. The youngest mayor (32) of any major American city when he was elected, Goldschmidt emphasized careful economic and physical planning, together with a major role for neighborhood groups in guiding the growth and development of their areas. During his administration, Portland grew from a quiet, overgrown town to a highly innovative city.

A jewel of the new development was Portland's transit mall, a $15 million project, financed almost entirely by the federal Urban Mass Transit Administration and encompassing 10 blocks of the city's two busiest downtown streets. Most of the mall, which was completed in 1978, was off limits to cars, and buses carried passengers around the downtown area for free. Wide brick sidewalks were installed, along with controversial outdoor sculpture and elegant passenger shelters, the latter including television screens that show constantly updated bus schedules. Within a few years of completion, bus passenger trips to the downtown area increased by about a third, and there was a marked upturn in the retailing fortunes of the downtown, which had been losing valuable patronage to suburban malls. Portland also instituted an extraordinarily tough policy to discourage downtown commuter parking, including a denial of a building owner's right to demolish his structure and put a parking lot in its place. (Unfortunately, few cities followed the Portland example.)

In his final years as mayor, Goldschmidt added support to development of Portland's energy plan, perhaps the best conceived in the entire nation. With city hall's encouragement, a broadly representative energy steering committee—people from business, labor, neighborhoods, environmentalist groups, banking, and utility companies—worked for eight months to fashion an energy conservation blueprint that would permit a 30 percent cutback in city-wide energy use (and thus $162 million in annual dollar savings) by the mid-1980s. Portland was one of the first cities to develop the concept of the municipal energy balance sheet—pinpointing the amount the city's residents, businesses, and government spent to buy energy each year, and then calculating how much of that could be saved through conservation. Thus, instead of flowing to outside energy suppliers, the funds could be retained to create jobs and keep the city competitive economically.

The most controversial element of the Portland energy plan required that any Portland homeowner who by 1984 hadn't weatherized his house to energy "cost efficiency" simply wouldn't be allowed to resell the house until the improvements were made. Similarly stiff requirements were posed for apartment-house owners and businesses. There was also a major land-use component, encouraging more dense building (attached and multifamily units) and concentrated developments of housing, retailing, and offices, all accessible by mass transit and shorter auto trips. Other U.S. cities did not rush to duplicate the Portland plan (though such places as Minneapolis–St. Paul, Seattle, and California's Davis, Berkeley, and Palo Alto all approximated it). What had been posited, however, was the blueprint for what might be, for American cities, a transition to an age of significant energy conservation, with efficiency and grace, and without severe social discord.

Goldschmidt left Portland in 1979 to become President Carter's transportation secretary. A year later, the mayoralty went to his long-time adversary on the city council, conservative Democrat Frank Ivancie, a negative-minded individual. Portland returned, more or less, to business as usual.

Portland is Oregon's economic capital, locale of the big banks, law firms, and corporate headquarters of the giant lumber companies. It is also a great port city and home of many electronic component companies, textile firms (notably specialty woolen mills), big aluminum factories (drawing on the supply of hydroelectricity), logging-lumbering equipment plants, lumber mills, and chemical plants. The Port of Portland is a major exporter of heavy cargoes such as wheat, lumber, and wool, bringing in, by contrast, petroleum and ores. Big docks and terminals line the Willamette River.

Running on a north-northwesterly course right through the heart of the city, the Willamette creates distinct east and west bank communities that are frequently at loggerheads about planning and financing of city projects. The west side has the gleaming high-rise structures and quaint renovations of a revitalized downtown, most of Portland's immense, rambling parklands, and well-to-do West Hills, which encompass several handsome residential sections with stunning hilltop views. The east side of the river contains a great polyglot of neighborhoods, from poor black to wealthy white Protestant, as well as, several of Oregon's relatively few Catholic communities. Although its residents frequently complain of an attitude that "Portland ends on the west bank of the Willamette," they were scheduled to receive by 1985 a 15-mile light rail line to carry commuters downtown from the east suburbs. The $309 million project was being financed mostly by federal money freed by the cancellation of a freeway project, demonstrating strict limits to Oregonians' love affair with the automobile.

Postwar city planners had permitted an ugly freeway to slice right along the downtown waterfront, decisively separating water and city. Recent years have seen some handsome recreational development along the west bank, however. So desirable had inner-city and waterfront housing locations become that in 1981 an enterprising local team of brothers of Japanese ancestry, Sam and Bill Naito, were able to open and fill a huge middle-income townhouse rental project in a grimy industrial section sandwiched between the city's old railroad station and the Willamette's banks. The same Naito brothers earlier resuscitated a building of the grand-old-arcade type in the downtown and then led in restoration of Portland's Old Town Section.

After Portland, Eugene and Salem (the state capital) are the only two Oregon cities of more than 50,000 souls. Eugene, located 110 miles south of Portland in the upper Willamette Valley, went from 50,977 inhabitants in 1960 to 105,624 in 1980. Eugene's growth spurt may have run its course, however. Home of the University of Oregon, its student population has been steadily dropping, and it has been hit hard by shutdowns in the timber industry. Salem (pop. 89,233), one of America's most pleasant and relaxed state capitals, is just 45 miles south of Portland. It lives off the state payrolls, a prosperous fruit- and vegetable-canning industry, and some timber.

The low-slung marble State Capitol, built in the 1930s after a predecessor was destroyed by fire, is eye-arresting, but we find hard to say beautiful. Atop the cupola stands an imposing statue of "the pioneer," the work of Ulric Ellerhusen. If the pioneer could see, he might be discouraged by a recent development between Salem and Portland: wall-to-wall subdivisions across that once-inviolate valley of the Willamette.

WASHINGTON

Evergreen and Puzzling

WASHINGTON is a puzzling state. We think of it as cool, pristine, and evergreen. Yet the civilization around Puget Sound is industrial, cosmopolitan, intense, wracked by economic boom and bust. There are little towns in Washington as staid and conservative as anything the Midwest can offer, but the same state has a strain of feisty radical politics unrivaled in the American West. In population, Washington ranks 20th nationally and trails only California west of the Rockies, with 4,130,163 residents in 1980.

The 1970s vaulted Washington into the national consciousness as one of the best places in America to live. Until the early 1980's recession reversed the trend (and caused net outmigration), the state's newborn popularity was reflected in a growth rate of no less than 21 percent in the single decade. Search for an explanation and one is hard put to improve on U.S. Senator Slade Gorton's comment about Washington's largest city: "In the 1970s Seattle became what one might call the San Francisco of the last quarter of the Twentieth Century, rather than a quaint and interesting place about which people nodded politely." Gorton himself, in fact, was somewhat typical of the state's fresh image: an "outsider" who initially came to Seattle from a prestigious Boston law firm (his family was the Gortons of Gloucester fish products) —a lover of the outdoors and thin rail of a man who goes jogging every morning and once bicycled with his family across the continent, a Republican, and a liberal on environmental matters but rather unsympathetic to unions. Gorton won election to the Senate in 1980 by defeating no less a Washington State institution than Sen. Warren Magnuson, member of Congress for 44 years, powerful committee chairman, and bread-and-butter Democrat with working-class roots.

As Washington filled up with ever more immigrants, there were many who agonized about its future. Was it destined to be a junior-sized California, careening into its second century with waves of exploitive growth that carelessly devour landscape and fledgling traditions? Or was there to be found here, in the geographically remote northwestern extremity of the coterminous U.S.A., a civilization more happily balancing man and nature, cultural innovation and social stability—an ecotopia, as some have called it? The ingredients for all possible outcomes have been and remain visible in modern Washington. Washington seems forever to be in a state of becoming.

Washington's modern history goes back to 1792, the year that Captain George Vancouver sailed into an exquisite estuary he named Puget Sound. Vancouver also sighted and gave names to landmarks such as Mount Baker and Mount Rainier. Next came the era of the great trading companies. Between 1834 and 1837 some 405,000 pelts—mostly beaver—were received by the Hudson's Bay Company's post at Fort Vancouver. In 1845 the provisional government of Oregon turned away a train of 80 overland wagons because they bore one black, free-born George Bush; the party then made its way to a site near what is now Olympia, and Washington had its first permanent American settlement. In 1851 the settlers north of the Columbia started a clamor for separate territorial status from Oregon, a request Congress granted two years later.

The next decades brought explosive growth. Thousands of Midwesterners, plus an influential leavening of New Englanders, came to homestead and to found and run the new cities of Seattle, Tacoma, Spokane, Walla Walla, Vancouver, and Olympia. In 1857 there was a gold rush on the Fraser River; in the 1860s the young territory sent men to fight for the Union; the first railroads arrived; and in 1889, having grown to 350,000 souls, Washington gained statehood. The economy was dominated by lumber, and the woods soon filled with Swedes and Norwegians whose lifeblood was logging—indeed many came by way of timber-stripped Wisconsin and Minnesota. The Alaskan Gold Rush of 1897 brought a ton of gold on a single ship arriving at the Seattle docks, and by 1910 more than a million people inhabited the state. The Scandinavian element remained strong and with it an affinity for the Populist-Farmer-Labor politics of the Upper Midwest. Washington remains one of the most Protestant of American states, and it is no accident that the two most famous of its United States senators were named Warren Grant Magnuson and Henry Martin Luther Jackson.

Depressions in Washington's mercurial economy and the wretched living conditions in company-owned towns, where loggers were fed poorly and forced to live in barracks that had vermin-infested bunks, fed the fires of radical unionism around the turn of the century. From the Populist movement, many Washington workers and their sympathizers fed into the Socialist party and then between 1905 and 1910 became the spearhead of the new Industrial Workers of the World—better known as the "Wobblies." In 1916 the Wobblies struck lumber mills in Everett. Infuriated Everett industrialists broke the strike and ran about 40 Wobblies out of town, forcing them to run a gauntlet where they were beaten as they departed. The Seattle IWW retaliated by sending a steamboat with 250 protesters to Everett, where they were met by gunfire from deputies; several died. In 1919 Seattle shipyard workers triggered a general strike that paralyzed that city for several days and aroused fears of a genuine revolution on American soil. A pitched battle broke out in Centralia between IWW members and American Legionnaires. After that, the IWW declined in strength, but a seed of radicalism, scarcely known elsewhere in America, had been planted.

The left-wing specter rose again in the depression of the 1930s, when the erratically led Unemployed Citizens' League of Seattle came close to seizing control of the state Democratic party and frightened businessmen and property owners. Several radically inclined men were sent to Congress. Fresh fuel for the radical fires came from "blowed-out, burned-out" Dust Bowl farmers who drifted in during the depression years, occupying miserable shanty towns on the edge of Seattle and other cities, scrounging farm jobs where they could and helping to build Grand Coulee Dam. Then came the bitter fight between backers of public and private power that bloodied Washington politics during the 1930s. It was out of this setting that James Farley could make his celebrated remark about "the 47 states and the soviet of Washington."

Washington Geography and Economy

At 8:23 on the morning of May 18, 1980, a volcanic eruption engulfed Mt. St. Helens, 100 miles southeast of Seattle, with the explosive equivalent of a 20 megaton nuclear blast. An accompanying earthquake registered 5.0 on the Richter scale. The high cone of the once-lovely Cascade Mountains peak disintegrated as a cubic mile of rock was thrown into the atmosphere. Fifty-nine persons were killed. As far distant as 17 miles, 150-foot Douglas firs were uprooted or snapped in pieces. A massive ash fall of some 4 billion tons turned the sky darker than a moonless night and was noticed as far away as Montana. No resident of the Pacific Northwest would soon forget that day. In the words of one Seattle psychiatrist, "We were suddenly brought face to face with something incomprehensible."

The violent disturbance of that May morning was the first volcanic eruption in the continental U.S. since a series of much milder eruptions of Lassen Peak in California from 1914 to 1917. But it was a vivid reminder that America's Pacific States sit on the great "rim of fire" encircling the entire Pacific Basin. In sheer beauty, these states seem to surpass all others on the continent, with rough, craggy, dramatic shorelines and their fantastically beautiful mountains. This is no settled Appalachian Range, but a region still in formation. It has a geology, in short, to match the very youth, uncertainty, power, and risks of America's farthest reaches.

The borders that Congress finally settled on for Washington State make it the West's smallest, roughly the shape of a rectangle with the northwestern corner nibbled away by the ocean. One finds within the state every topographic feature, from dense rain forests to arid interior uplands, from river basins to alpine heights. The Cascade Range provides not just beauty and geologic excitement, but in its north-to-south course divides Washington into two entirely different life zones.

Eastern Washington, embracing two-thirds of the state's land area, is continental in climate, light on forests, and locked by mountain ranges. Its people, a quarter of the state's population, are cautious by temperament. The region's big interests are wheat, fruit, and cattle, plus scattered industry (especially around Spokane, the lead city). Here too is the Columbia River basin, in large part flat, arid desert land.

West of the Cascades, a temperate, moist climate is assured by the Pacific Ocean breezes, warmed by the Japan Current. The rainfall averages 36 inches a year, though it goes as high as 142 inches in the great rain forests of the Olympic Peninsula—so thick that sunshine rarely reaches the ground and dark green ferns grow to the height of small trees (the wettest spot on the continent). By the time Pacific clouds reach the Cascades, however, they have lost most of their moisture. Eastern Washington is semi-arid, with 10 to 20 inches of rain in a year.

About three-quarters of the people live west of the Cascades, and there one must also look for the seat of political and economic power. One finds it along the shores of Puget Sound, bordered by cities and towns from Bellingham and Everett on the north to Seattle and then Tacoma and Olympia in the south. The state capitol at Olympia, in fact, sits on a height with a commanding view of the sound, perhaps the loveliest capitol site in America. Despite the rapid urbanization, there are still tree-lined and unspoiled stretches along Puget Sound's 1,800 miles of shoreline—reminiscent of the times, little more than a century ago, when a dense forest of Douglas fir, spruce, cedar, and hemlock swept down from the Cascades to the coast, unbroken except for Indian trails and occasional lowland valleys. The beauty of water, islands, and shores is enhanced by the view—whenever the mists clear sufficiently—of lordly Rainier, highest and most breathtaking of the great volcanic Cascade peaks to the east, and then the Olympic Mountains, high alpine sentinels of the Olympic Peninsula to the west.

Washington moved rapidly from its old wheat-timber-extractive economic base to a manufacturing economy from the 1940s onward. The Boeing Company, its plants set in a string from Kent, south of Seattle, to Everett in the north, came to dominate the economy of a large metropolitan region and a state as few other industrial firms in America have done. But since Boeing's fortunes were tied to two mercurial markets—the demand for civilian aircraft and that for military weaponry—a highly unsettling, roller-coaster tempo engulfed the state and regional economy. Following the aerospace decline of the early 1970s, which was called "the Boeing recession," Washington set out to diversify its economies. But the even deeper recession of the early 1980s dispelled any doubt that the aerospace industry and another sector, timber, still counted for a huge portion of the state's economy. By spring 1982, Washington's unemployment rate ranked third in the nation at 13 percent, exceeded only by Michigan and Alabama. With the nation's home construction industry in a depression, Washington's timber industry was in serious straits. Despite some lucrative new defense contracts, Boeing was again into a nosedive because of the ailing condition of commercial airlines, on which it had come to depend far more heavily than military business. (Even in depression, however, Boeing remained Washington's largest private employer with 73,628 persons on the job in 1982. Economists agree that 2.5 non-Boeing jobs are dependent on each job at the aerospace giant.)

Washingtonians prayed that the devastating unemployment of the early '80s recession would prove a short-term phenomenon. But the prospects were mixed at best. Skills of phenomenal clairvoyance were necessary to see what might happen to national and international economies—and thus to aircraft demand. As for the forest products industry, it was already involved in a great migration: from the Pacific Northwest to the South, especially as many private companies found they had logged over their Washington land holdings. One great exception was Weyerhaeuser, which excelled in forest genetics and tree farms before many other firms even began to think of restocking their lands. Weyerhaeuser was looking increasingly to the export market in the Pacific Rim countries of Japan, Korea, and China. Another sign of Washington's emerging international trade sector lay with Burlington Northern, Inc., which moved its headquarters from St. Paul, Minn., to Seattle in 1981. "Seattle, with its strong orientation toward international trade, is a good fit," said BN's president Richard M. Bressler. With vast coal reserves in the Powder River Basin of Montana and Wyoming, BN seemed likely to be a big player in the growing coal export game. Pacific Rim countries were also becoming ever-more-important customers for Washington and Montana wheat, shipped out of Puget Sound.

Bitter days came to Washington's fishing industry in the '70s and early '80s, with continued depletion of salmon population. Eruption of Mount St. Helens dealt a severe blow to salmon spawning. Long-standing friction between whites and Indians over salmon fishing rights boiled to a head, and the U.S. Supreme Court upheld a local federal district court ruling that Indians were entitled to 50 percent of the salmon catch off certain rivers that flow into Puget Sound. In addition, the great hydroelectric dams of the Columbia River were taking such a toll that some experts feared the great Chinook Salmon was headed for the endangered-species list. (There was evidence, however, that the salmon were returning to the Cowlitz and Toutle Rivers. And Cohos and Chinooks were taking firm hold in, of all places, the Great Lakes, where they had been planted as an experiment 15 years before.)

The Political Equations

Few are the Western states that grant their senators and congressmen such longevity in office as Washington. The practice has paid off handsomely— in federal largesse. Consider the most visible and stupendous evidence of this: the mighty hydroelectric power installations along the Columbia River. So sumptuously has the Columbia region been treated that there were years in the early 1960s, at the height of dam building, when federal outlays for regional development in eastern Washington alone ran well over $100 million —about 10 percent of the national public-works budget for an area with 0.4 percent of the national population.

Washington has also received far more than its share of national defense spending (in 1978, for example, $1.2 billion more in Pentagon outlays than its proportionate share of taxes for defense). The state's major defense installations include Fort Lewis, McChord Air Force Base, Fairchild Air Force Base, the Trident Submarine Base at Bangor, Puget Sound Naval Shipyard in Bremerton, and the Keyport Naval Underwater Weapons Station. The state also has two major Veterans Administration hospitals and numerous major defense contractors, including the Boeing Co., Todd Shipyards, Tacoma Boatbuilding Co., and Lockheed Shipbuilding. Joel Garreau, in his *Nine Nations of North America*, questioned Washingtonians (whom he has placed at the center of a northwestern American region called "Ecotopia") about their tolerance of Doomsday weapon production in a land that reveres quality of life. When we visited Washington in summer 1982, however, we found colorful demonstrations (including an amateur flotilla) trying to block one of the Trident submarines from docking.

Measured by committee chairmen, Washington seemed to reach the apex of its political clout in the nation's capital in the 1960s and '70s. At one point, Warren Magnuson was chairman of the Senate Appropriations Committee, Henry Jackson was chairman of the Senate Energy and Natural Resources Committee, and Rep. Tom Foley, representing eastern Washington, was chairman of the House Agriculture Committee. In the years before congressional reform, such clout might have swept all opposition before it. But it did not last; indeed the accumulated seniority sank precipitously in 1980 when Magnuson was defeated by Slade Gorton, the first Republican to represent Washington in the Senate in 28 years. Since the Republicans took control of the Senate in that election, Jackson also lost his chairmanship. Foley, however, advanced in the House to become the number three Democratic party leader, the majority whip.

Henry Jackson, by the early '80s, was approaching the twilight of his congressional career—and a vital career it had been. One of his longtime associates described him as "a living embodiment of the Puritan ethic, a man to whom work is virtue and pleasure is sin." He could take chief credit for many landmark bills, most memorably the wilderness bill in the early 1960s, the Redwoods National Park Act, the landmark 1969 National Environmental Protection Act, and the Alaskan Native Claims Act of 1970. For years—and especially in his strong run for the Democratic presidential nomination in 1976 —Jackson was the epitome of the old-style liberal, close to organized labor, strongly pro-Israel, and an unflinching advocate of a strong national security. (Eugene McCarthy once said of Jackson: "You can't have enough security for Henry. If he had his way, the sky would be black with supersonic planes, preferably Boeings, of course.")

As a result of its extended period of Democratic predominance and stability, Washington's congressional delegation bred its own successors. Foley, for instance, began his Washington, D.C., career as an aide to Jackson. Magnuson, however, was unrivaled in the number of political careers he spawned, creating a remarkably extensive personal network into the state's power structure. On the federal scene, an extended family of former aides, which might be called the House of Magnuson, counted among its number the chairmen of the Interstate Commerce Commission and the Federal Trade Commission and the heads of the Urban Mass Transit Administration and the National Oceanic and Atmospheric Administration. The House of Magnuson also filled the ranks of the state's major law firms, three of which had branch offices in Washington, D.C. Another Magnuson administrative assistant, Gerald Grinstein, built the law firm of Preston, Thorgrimson, Ellis, Holman and Fletcher into the most politically influential firm in the state. It maintained 17 lawyers in Washington, D.C., and counted the Port of Seattle and the Northern Tier Pipeline Co. among its clients.

With Magnuson out of power, such law firms have lost their easy access to the power of the Senate Appropriations Committee. But they have retained impressive client lists and built contacts with Magnuson's successors. So pervasive is the influence of Preston, Thorgrimson, and so forth, that it can be called a shadow government. "I don't ascribe any cosmic results to the fact that I beat Maggie," said Gorton. "I was a person who had a very good sense of timing who caught a person who had provided great services to the state of Washington at a time when he shouldn't have run."

If there has been a change in Washington State's politics since the 1960s, it's that the most Democratic of Western states has developed a thriving moderate Republican party, which has elected a U.S. senator, three congressmen, and two governors. Former Washington Gov. Dan Evans deserves primary credit for this. His protégés have included Gorton, and Representatives Joel Pritchard and Sid Morrison. The only fly in the ointment is that while the Evans movement achieved prominent successes in statewide races, a more traditional, very conservative Republican wing dominated state legislative races and delegations to Republican national conventions.

Daniel Jackson Evans broke into politics from the unlikeliest of all professions—civil engineering. A tall, shy man with a clean-cut, Dick Tracy look, he never quite lost the aura of the Eagle Scout he was in his boyhood. Evans made his political debut in 1956, at age 31, when he was elected to the state house, where he eventually became the Republican floor leader. Eight years later, he was elected governor. In that office, he showed himself to be one of those splendid human beings so sorely needed in leadership roles—a man of impeccable integrity and graciousness, a master of the intricacies of government and political maneuver, eager to involve everyday citizens, courageous and tenacious in pursuing his idealistic goals.

Evans' record had its flaws. He let the biennial state budget rise from some $2 billion to about $7 billion; he failed to achieve fundamental modernization of state government; and he failed to correct a regressive tax system through the income tax he backed openly and strongly but the voters twice rejected. In retrospect, however, Evans' achievements loom far larger than his shortcomings. He recruited highly talented managers, and he persuaded more than 100,000 Washingtonians to participate in an "Alternatives for Washington" program to chart the state's future. Washington will long appreciate him for the remarkable package of environmental laws—among them the nation's first comprehensive state department of ecology, the first broad-gauged energy siting council, one of the country's first and most extensive shoreline management programs—which he persuaded the legislature to pass in 1970. George Weeks, longtime aide to Michigan's Gov. William Milliken and a veteran governor watcher, placed Evans in a "Statehouse Hall of Fame"—the 10 most outstanding governors of the 20th century.* In our judgment he belongs there not only for his Washington State record, but because as chairman of the National Governors Conference (1973–74) he decided the state chief executives should become more assertive, participating in national decision making from the start rather than waiting for initiatives from Congress or the executive branch. This led to a vastly improved staffing arrangement for the governors in Washington, D.C. to far more serious meetings of the governors (a good-bye to the "Good Time Charlies"), and eventually the governors' capacity to bargain with the White House on fundamental federal system reform in the early 1980s. After three terms as governor, Evans withdrew from politics in 1976 and became president of Evergreen State College in Olympia.

Evans' successor, Dixy Lee Ray, was a classic "anti-politician"—sixtyish, roundish, scientist, academician—who lived in a trailer with her dogs, wore knee socks, and most importantly said just what was on her mind in the bluntest terms. She was not only generally anti-environmentalist but also outspokenly pro-nuclear power. In her 1976 race she met the public's post-Watergate demand for nonpolitical faces in politics. But in office, Ray fought with the press, the legislature, liberals, environmentalists, and even Canada, which she told to "mind your business and we'll mind ours" (when protests were heard in British Columbia about her plan to let supertankers into the Puget Sound area). She ended up being dumped unceremoniously in the 1980 Democratic primary.

In Ray's place the voters installed mild-mannered John Spellman, who had served as King County executive and supervised construction of Seattle's domed stadium, the Kingdome, built on schedule and without cost overruns. But as he entered the governorship, Washington was spiraling into its disastrously deep recession of the early '80s. Again and again, Spellman (a moderate) and the legislature (under conservative Republican control)† would cut heavily into expenditures and raise taxes—only to find in a short time that the economy was deteriorating even more rapidly than predicted, forcing them back to the drawing board and the political agony of more cuts and tax hikes. (Spellman, forced to rely on Democrats to get the job done, branded Republican ideologues "troglodytes" for their stubborn insistence on deeper budget cuts and no tax hikes. Voters responded by returning legislative control to the Democrats in 1982.) Part of the fiscal squeeze could be attributed to Reagan

---

*The other governors on Weeks' list were Robert M. La Follette (Republican of Wisconsin, 1901–6), Woodrow Wilson (Democrat of New Jersey, 1911–13), Alfred E. Smith (Democrat of New York, 1919–21 and 1923–29), Huey Long (Democrat of Louisiana, 1928–32), Earl Warren (Republican of California, 1943–53), Thomas E. Dewey (Republican of New York, 1943–54), Nelson A. Rockefeller (Republican of New York, 1959–73), Terry Sanford (Democrat of North Carolina, 1961–65), and Reubin Askew (Democrat of Florida, 1971–79). The list strikes us as exceptionally well crafted.

†Most frequently in the '60s and '70, Democrats controlled the legislature—though not a particularly progressive brand of Democrats, on the whole. Republican takeover of the legislature in 1980 followed conviction of both the Democratic House co-speaker and Senate majority leader for a gambling conspiracy.

administration cutbacks, even more to decisions since the mid '70s, both through ballot propositions and legislative action, to reduce taxes by $1.5 billion. Another reason was the inherent flaw of a state revenue structure built on the sales tax, directly tied to retail commerce that fluctuates wildly with twists in the economy, and without the stability of a state income tax—the problem Dan Evans, without success, had tried to fix. Perhaps most basically, Washingtonians were coming face to face with the grim possibility that they had accustomed themselves to a standard of living, to a set of government services, and to immense free time for a life of vibrant fun in the outdoors, simply unsustainable in the grim economic world of the '80s.

If Spellman did nothing else while governor, he was likely to be remembered as the man who blocked the Northern Tier Pipeline, a proposal to move Alaskan oil from Puget Sound to the Midwest via underground pipeline. After every other state and national licensing authority had given its approval, Spellman announced that the risk of oil spills in Puget Sound, to which the oil would have to be brought by tanker, was too high and that he would not approve siting the pipeline's western terminus at Port Angeles. The decision evoked anger in the Reagan administration and among Midwestern governors, including Spellman's fellow Republicans. But there was little doubt it rang true to Washington State's environmentally conscious voters.

Northwest Water and Power

The elemental power and force of the Columbia River and its tributaries is a source of continual wonder. In its circuitous 1,207-mile course, from headwaters in a mountain lake in remote British Columbia to the Pacific, 100 miles west of Portland, the river drops 2,650 feet, creating a third of the total hydroelectric capacity of the United States. The volume of its flow—1.9 million gallons a second—is second only to the Missouri-Mississippi system and 14 times as great as the Colorado, lifeline of the Southwest.

To no state is the Columbia more important than Washington, which it flows across or borders for 750 miles. From an entrance point in the northeast, the river courses in a huge bow around eastern Washington, then moves southerly to a juncture with the Snake River (which itself is 1,000 miles long), and finally forms the border with Oregon for its westerly plunge to the sea. At Portland, the Willamette, Oregon's great interior river, joins the Columbia. Both states depend heavily on the flow of cheap electricity from the great hydroelectric projects made possible by the dams.

As the major natural resource of the Northwest, the Columbia has dominated the region's and Washington's politics for decades. It is difficult today to imagine the virulent opposition to the first Columbia River dams, Bonneville and Grand Coulee, which were called white elephants when they were proposed in the 1930s. As a result of the white-hot battles between public and private power advocates in the '30s, Washington became largely a public power state while its then-Republican neighbor, Oregon, opted largely for private power.

The distinction between public and private power became blurred, however, when Congress passed the Pacific Northwest Electric Power Planning and Conservation Act in 1980. The single most important piece of legislation for the Northwest since the Bonneville Project Act of 1937, the law for the first time gave private power companies the right to tap the cheap hydropower from federally built dams to which public power districts had historically been given priority access. And the federal Bonneville Power Administration was directed to broaden its mission from a simple power marketing agency to promoting conservation and renewable energy resources such as solar, wind, and geothermal power. For the first time, the utilities would be second-guessed on how much energy the region would need, and the best ways (more power capacity or conservation) to get it. The vehicle to assure this was an independent citizens' electric power planning board (of which ex-Governor Evans was made chairman). In short order, it turned out that Bonneville and the private utilities had been dead wrong in claiming that unless nuclear power installations were planned and completed, the region would suffer severe energy deficits and brownouts.

Then came a black day for public power and Washington State: the unraveling of the state's attempt to build five nuclear reactors. To bring the massive reactors into being, the Washington legislature had established a consortium of public and private utilities called the Washington Public Power Supply System, whose acronym WPPSS was pronounced "Whoops." By 1982, WPPSS had become the biggest single borrower in the U.S. municipal bond market, and even more astoundingly, the largest public works project underway anywhere in the world. It had also become a synonym for cost overruns of almost incredible proportions (total price up from $4.1 billion to $23.8 billion) and a regional public debt of staggering proportions. Leery of WPPSS' huge debt and poor performance, the national bond rating services downgraded its bonds. Angry Washington citizens in 1981 approved an initiative requiring that the public vote on any major new energy project, including additional bond sales for WPPSS nuclear plants.* Two of the reactors were mothballed. Customers, enraged by doubling and tripling of their utility bills, were organizing and marching and withholding payment of rate increases WPPSS needed to service its gargantuan debt. A collapse of the system became a real possibility.

---

*The nuclear lobby—Wall Street brokers, contractors, construction unions, utilities, aluminum companies—poured an astounding $1.2 million into the campaign to beat the initiative, an all-time record in Washington State initiative campaigns. Proponents had a budget only a sixth as large, but got 58 percent of the vote. We heard that New York–based financial advisers and bond counsel bore heavy responsibility for the debacle of WPPSS in the first instance, victimizing in particular naïve public utility leaders by convincing them to agree to gargantuan indebtedness on the unproven assumption that the public's appetite for energy was infinite, its willingness to pay the bill without limits.

Because of WPPSS, some said the promise of Washington's basic resource —cheap electricity—had been squandered and lost forever. Without question, the state's energy picture had been dramatically altered. The creditworthiness of all Washington State governments was brought into question. "The WPPSS debt will slow down both economic and population growth," said Senator Gorton.

If WPPSS had mortgaged a significant share of Washington's energy future, some cities and local power agencies demonstrated considerably more foresight and wisdom. Most notable was Seattle, which in the mid-1970s set up a citizens' committee of businessmen, engineers, economists, and environmentalists to study the city's future energy needs. The recommendation: that Seattle City Light (the municipally owned public utility) *not* participate in WPPSS' last two nuclear plants (the ones that turned out to be such total disasters). Instead, the city embarked on an aggressive, remarkably comprehensive energy conservation plan designed to save 230 megawatts of electricity by 2000. The plan relied on strict energy-saving building codes, zero-interest loans to citizens to insulate their homes, emphasis on public transportation over private auto commuting, and investigation of such alternative energy sources as combining solar with hydropower. Adopted statewide, such an approach would have saved Washington the agony of WPPSS' ultimate excesses and assured a much brighter regional future.

Nuclear operations have been underway in Washington ever since World War II, when considerations of secrecy led to selection of Hanford, a desolate desert spot in the state's south central region, for the production of plutonium for atomic bombs. Triggered by federally sponsored research and development of nuclear weapons and domestic nuclear projects, the population of the Tri-Cities area adjacent to the Hanford Nuclear Reservation (Kennewick, Richland, and Pasco) ballooned from 400 in 1940 to 115,000 in 1980. Hanford never seemed to develop the others' fears of a great explosion or harmful radiation; the *Tri-City Herald* once ran the headline: "Plutonium only as dangerous as inhaled dust." But in fact, the area became the world's greatest nuclear garbage dump: "enough," Northwest specialist A. Robert Smith reported a few years ago, "to eliminate human life from much of the continent if it ever got loose in the air and water." Between 1958 and 1965, leaks were discovered in 10 waste storage tanks and radioactive materials were presumed to have leaked into the Columbia River. The tanks were re-sealed and their condition was presumably stabilized—yet for how long, no one knew.

Seattlescape and the Lesser Cities

For day after day, the dark, moist clouds may come scudding in over the Olympic Mountains, across Puget Sound, and onto Seattle, cutting visibility to a minimum and leaving one wondering just what the surrounding city is like. And then the cloud cover recedes, and the scrubbed Seattle air glows like that of few cities on earth. Everywhere, brilliant waters surround this isthmus city of half a million people: Puget Sound on the west, Lake Washington on the east, and a canal tying them together. In the distance, icy mountains stand sentinel on every side, Rainier the greatest among them. And then there are the hills of the city itself: shockingly precipitous, omnipresent, and offering, as in San Francisco, ever shifting city- and waterscapes. Of all American cities, there are few—perhaps none—more beautiful.

One is impressed by how verdant a city this is, the Pacific moisture forever nurturing the growth, and how overwhelmingly middle class it is. But a caution about typing Seattle's people: this placid city of trim homes also has a major (and politically potent) gay community; the second-highest alcoholism and suicide rates in the U.S. (after San Francisco); and the highest divorce rate of any American urban county, bar none. No one has yet explained these phenomena, except that the divorce rate could reflect the low Catholic population. Church membership in the Northwest as a whole is markedly below the national average.

No one goes far in a straight line in Seattle, for there is always a lake, an insurmountable hill, or a twist in the land to throw you off. Personally, we find the city one of the hardest in America to get around in, a cartographer's nightmare, but one of delightful variety.

Among Seattle's unusual sights are Lake Washington, with its varied shoreline of marinas and parks and many homes of architectural excellence, and smaller Lake Union, where some 6,000 to 7,000 people live permanently on houseboats. Lake Washington, threatened by a build-up of planktonic algae and loss of water clarity, was subjected in the 1950s and '60s to a vigorous and ultimately successful clean-up that required legislative approval of a 10-city form of limited metropolitan government and issuance of bonds for more than $140 million. Among other Seattle attractions are the University of Washington in its pleasant, wooded, tightly packed campus; the sequestered, sylvanlike setting of the Seattle Research Center, part of the nationally operative Battelle Memorial Institute for scientific research; and some jewels of parks, including the university arboretum. The city has neighborhoods of every income description up to the most patrician housing settlement, The Highlands.

Seattle has made two quite successful efforts to establish its place in the sun by means of fairs: first the Alaska-Yukon Pacific Exposition in 1909, and then the Seattle World's Fair of 1962. The modern-day fair was a key turning point in bringing Seattle out of its provincial shell, a departure from the complacency that seemed to overtake Seattle for many decades of the 20th century. Since most of the 1962 fair's buildings were constructed for permanent use, the city was left with a grand, cost-free (to the taxpayer) $90 million legacy: the Seattle Center, which became the cultural and recreation center of the city, including the illustrious Space Needle, theaters, art gallery, and science center.

Another vestige of the 1962 fair, Seattle's monorail, takes one from the Seattle Center to downtown Seattle in 95 seconds. It is a downtown that "progress" almost ruined in the 1960s—and with a little bad luck, might indeed decimate by the end of this century. Massive buildings, such as the bronze 50-story First National Bank Building with its cold, sloping ground-level approach, hostile to pedestrian and balanced cityscape alike, were erected. The business community pushed redevelopment strategies focused on expressways to move automobiles in and out of town, along with multileveled garages to accommodate them. Seattle's cherished 1907-vintage Pike Place Market, set on a downtown promontory of seedy wooden stores and rooming houses, with a roughness reminiscent of Seattle's beginnings, was slated for extinction in favor of seven layers of parking, a hotel, and apartments. But that scheme proved the straw that broke the camel's back. The farmers and fish dealers, the fruit sellers and butchers ought not to be evicted, said preservationists. They took the issue to the public in 1971, winning a great victory over the business establishment by passing an initiative to bar any development, except restoration, in a seven-square block tract including the market.

Another sign of change was the 1969 election as mayor of Wes Uhlman, a distinctly nonestablishment candidate who put together a coalition of labor, black, and youthful voters to win and then lent his aid to Seattleites challenging raze-and-rebuild urban renewal. Uhlman enthusiastically backed renewal of Pioneer Square, where in Seattle's early days a wild and colorful frontier life had flourished as hustlers, madams, and sharp speculators made or stole their fortunes and logs were rolled down steep Skid Road to a mill at the water's edge. A destructive 1889 fire had destroyed much of the area but then it was rebuilt in a distinctive array of arches, turrets, and rich architectural detail. In time the center of the city moved a few blocks northward and Skid Road—a name that would be corrupted into "Skid Row" elsewhere—became a center of cheap rooming houses for single men including winos and derelicts. By the 1960s, 80 percent of the area was vacant, dotted with missions, flophouses, thrift shops, and bars. The downtown business community eyed the area as a storage place for shoppers' and commuters' autos. But then some preservationist pioneers began to restore the splendid old architectural specimens for commercial space. Uhlman, according to an account by the Conservation Foundation's Phyllis Myers, lent his support to restoration because he genuinely liked the area. Still lusty and slightly ribald, its transients still welcome, Pioneer Square became an exciting array of good restaurants and bars, art galleries, book stores, craft shops, handsomely restored office space, and a landscaped cobblestone mall.

Pioneer Square was not an isolated oddity. Uhlman, a forward-looking city council, and a broad coalition of anti-freeway buffs, arts advocates, and assorted reformers and neighborhood leaders shifted Seattle's focus to urban conservation and the preservation of tightly knit neighborhoods. In the mid-1970s Seattle celebrated an important burial—of a short stretch of Interstate 5, the concrete canyon of 10 lines of traffic that slashes through center city. The freeway trench was bridged with a splendidly landscaped six-acre urban park, designed by Lawrence Halperin and Associates of San Francisco. The park, filled with trees and grass and flowers and cascading water, including a 32-foot high waterfall, all masking the roar of traffic a few feet below, became a drawing card for Seattleites of all ages. The whole project took ingenious planning and financing, eight years of close teamwork between city, county, state, and federal governments, and most particularly a human catalyst in the form of civic leader James R. Ellis, whose 1968 "Forward Thrust" bond improvement program for the city's future included $2.8 million for a small park beside the freeway.

Ellis' Forward Thrust, which he first proposed in 1965, scored many other successes, including funding for some 4,000 square miles of parkland and 50 miles of public waterfront, an arterial road improvement program designed to facilitate a regional bus system, Seattle's new aquarium and waterfront park, and the Kingdome Stadium. The bonds were financed at what would later look like a bargain basement rate of 5.9 percent. The voters did reject some of the proposed bonds, including those meant for a regional rapid rail transit system, which Ellis believed—and still maintained 15 years later— would someday be essential to handle the traffic crush of Seattle in its restricted "hourglass" physical configuration. The regional bus system, put under control of the regional "Metro" agency in 1972, has been one of America's most successful: it acquired superior equipment (including advanced "articulated," or double-section buses); it created a downtown "free" zone for bus transit; it got its workers to accept split shifts—an immense economy unknown in most transit agencies—and developed, with Seattle's First National Bank and other major employers, one of the United States' first systems of totally employer-financed free transit passes for workers.

By the mid-1970s Paul Schell, then community development director for the city, could show us how the Seattle Center, Pioneer Square, Pike Place Market, Freeway Park, the Seattle waterfront, a new domed stadium, and the downtown business district were all being tied together by walkways and bikeways, the monorail, and free downtown bus service. To all that was added, in 1982, a waterfront trolley line of delightfully rickety old cars from Melbourne, Australia—the dream of City Councilman George Benson, who beat seemingly insurmountable obstacles to make it a reality. The only big development disappointment of the '70s and early '80s was failure to bring to fruition the proposed Westlake Mall, a major retailing-entertainment complex in the heart of the city's old, declining downtown retailing core. But many positive developments were going forward—restoration at Rainier Square, for example, of the multi-splendored Olympic Hotel and the 1926-vintage 5th Avenue Theatre, the latter a 2,100-seat former vaudeville and movie house patterned after an ancient palace in Peking's Forbidden City.

Seattle's chief quandary as the '80s opened seemed to be too much development of one nature: great office and hotel structures. Downtown office space, less than 17 million square feet in 1975, topped 23 million in 1982 and was expected (at least before the early '80s recession intervened) to hit 42 million in the early 1990s. Hotel rooms were projected to rise from 4,000 in 1975 to 10,000 in 1995. As many as 48 massive new buildings—one 75 stories high— were projected for the central business district. The sensitive, restoration-type projects made Seattle popular with professionals and a magnet for new buildings. Real fears arose about the "Houstonization" or "San Franciscoization" of Seattle, destroying with megastructures the rolling beauty of the city's superb, precipitous downtown setting.

On the social front, a liberally inclined Seattle school board, concerned about growing white-black-Asian concentrations in many schools and the possibility of court-ordered desegregation, in 1978 instituted a mandatory busing plan together with "magnet schools" and other programs to soften the compulsory nature of the plan. Anti-busing forces then sponsored and passed a state initiative banning busing for racial purposes except under court order. Eventually the U.S. Supreme Court invalidated the initiative, but Seattle continued to face the problem of ever-growing percentages of black, Asian, Hispanic, and Indian enrollment—and white flight. The media front brought news of a different nature—protracted legal battles over a joint operating agreement between the financially ailing *Seattle Post-Intelligencer* and its rival, the afternoon *Seattle Times*. The stakes for Seattle: the future of independent news and editorial operations and thus vigor in public debate.

Elected Seattle's mayor in 1977 and again four years later, was ex-television commentator Charles Royer, who ran (at least initially) as champion of the neighborhoods and against excessive attention to the downtown. By the early '80s Royer's Seattle was plunged into severe fiscal crises requiring heavy layoffs—the bitter, seemingly inevitable fruit of the times. Despite the outrageously circumscribed home-rule powers granted Seattle by the state, one report could say of the liberal Royer: "In the last two years he has raised the sales tax, slapped a 40 percent surcharge on local business, cut police and fire service, laid off 5 percent of the work force, closed the consumer protection office, floated a bond issue to build 1,000 low-income apartments, taken over a Public Health Service hospital, and imposed fees on everything from parks to building inspections." A personable politician, Royer was elected president of the National League of Cities and considered a likely future Democratic candidate for the governorship or the U.S. Senate.

Seattleites have long made fun of eastern Washington's major city, Spokane, and not entirely without reason: until the 1970s Spokane was terribly ingrown and under control of reactionary business groups. But Spokane rapidly gained self-confidence as a result of its world's fair, Expo '74. At the start of the decade, center Spokane gave a warmed-over 1930s impression, except for one new parking garage; by 1980 there had been substantial new building, and the city had a handsomely redone waterfront park complex. Spokane remains the center of the Inland Empire, an interior economy that stretches into Idaho, Montana, and Canada and is based on agriculture, mining, and manufacturing. The city held even in population in the '70s (the 1980 figure was 171,300), while the outlying areas grew.

Tacoma, Washington's third-largest city (pop. 158,501), has sought valiantly to shake off a reputation as the dingiest, most polluted, divided, and politically perplexed city on the West Coast. The job has not been made easier by the fact that it is a great lumber center in that industry's years of travail. The city remains, however, the headquarters city of the giant Weyerhaeuser Co.; there has been a downtown renaissance of sorts, and Sea-Land Service Inc. in 1982 announced its shipping business would be moved from Seattle to Tacoma.

Two areas of strong growth have been the suburbs of Seattle and Clark County, just across the river from Portland, Oregon. While Seattle's population declined by 7 percent during the 1970s (to 493,846), King County (of which it is a part) grew 12 percent, to 775,903, and Snohomish County, directly to the north, expanded by 27.1 percent. The biggest city in Snohomish—though not its source of growth—is Everett, an overgrown old mill and fishing fleet town, enriched in recent times by Boeing. A little megalopolis —some call it Pugetopolis—has formed from Everett southward through Seattle to Tacoma near the foot of the sound, a stretch of some 60 miles. Clark County registered an amazing 49.6 percent increase during the decade— virtually all outside its lead city of Vancouver (pop. 42,834). All of this had involved, however, no little urban sprawl. We recall the description of Bellevue, on the eastern shore of Lake Washington, offered by a Seattleite just after the 1960s, when Bellevue expanded by an incredible 337 percent (from 12,809 to 61,102): "That place is an unmitigated disaster, where the tasteless tract architecture and the bad shopping centers have affected the quality of thought, too." (By the '70s Bellevue was down to a staid 21 percent growth rate and boasted a gargantuan enclosed shopping mall. But class it had not.)*

An invidious comparison to Oregon is hard to avoid: while that state has pioneered in land use planning, carefully defining urban growth boundaries, saving outlying lands for agriculture and open space, Washington politicians have been unwilling to take the political heat for applying such controls. So now their state pays a high price in urban sprawl. In the case of Clark County, where the new electronics manufacturing industry has fueled growth, the sprawl even threatens to urbanize the magnificent Columbia River Gorge.

*In sharp contrast to Bellevue is big, exurban Bainbridge Island, which hugs the western shore of Puget Sound. Still without a bridge to the mainland, it is filled with farms and lots of wilderness —and would prefer to stay that way.

ALASKA

The Great Land Awakens

THE MASTODONIC GREAT LAND of Alaska, which entered the union as our 49th state in 1959, is of such immense proportions that residents of the "Lower 48" have difficulty grasping it. It sweeps across four time zones, encompassing 586,412 square miles. The diversity is just as incredible as the size of this lonely, last frontier. Alaska has great plains, Arctic deserts, swamps, immense forests, the highest mountains of North America, glaciers, ice fields, broad valleys, fjords, 12 major river systems, active volcanoes, 3 million lakes, countless islands, and 50 percent more seacoast (33,904 miles) than all the continental United States. The coasts are washed by two oceans and three major seas. But the entire state has fewer people than Mobile, Alabama. The 1980 Census counted 401,851 Alaskans, reflecting a population growth of 33 percent in a decade. Of these, 60,000 were native peoples: Eskimos, Aleuts, and Indians.

Half of all Alaskans today—about 200,000 people—live in greater Anchorage. Another 60,000 live in Fairbanks. The remaining 140,000 reside in sparsely dispersed villages and small urban settlements. With .7 persons per square mile, the state remains one of the least populated places of the globe where man has ventured. And the climate and wilderness impinge upon normal ways of living in a thousand ways. Until the 1970s and a sudden gushing of oil revenues, long-distance telephoning in Alaska always required an operator's assistance and was expensive and complicated. Television was available in just a handful of locations: the first live programming from outside waited until 1969. To this day, and despite the highway built to the North Slope to accommodate the oil industry, relatively few towns or cities are connected by highway because of the immense difficulties of building roads over long distances, often with quaky permafrost beneath and with mountain ranges and glaciers as great obstacles. Those who insist on moving about Alaska are usually obliged to do so by airplane; here one finds, among the bush pilots, some of the world's most daring aviators. They not infrequently land on sand bars, glaciers, ice floes, beaches, lakes, or ball fields—always knowing this landing may be their last.

Roughly speaking, there are two types of white Alaskans: those who think the Great Land is God's Country and swear never to leave, and another group more interested in the fast buck. On the trail or in large cities, the first group is a friendly, outgoing lot, sharing, as it were, their common glory and adversity. The latter type—be they oilmen or divers, fishermen or lawyers—strive to make their fortune, great or small, and then retire to Hawaii, or back home, or anyplace where the winters are easier. There is no other state so essentially free of class distinctions, where a young person can rise so rapidly to the top in business or the professions. But the rigorous winters drive away even some of the most committed people in their prime years: there is a paucity of older community leaders who could provide balance and luster to the social structure.

One of the chief social ills of Alaska is alcoholism, which is tied in part to the raucous frontier environment and wide-open bars sporting names like Silver Dollar, Polar Bear, Gold Dusk, Elbow Room, and Red Dog—and atmospheres to match. Men outnumbering women may partially account for the alcoholism. "Cabin fever"—being closed indoors during the long, dark hours of the bitterly cold winter—may explain the alcoholism even more adequately. Drug abuse presents some problems, although personal use of marijuana in one's own home was legalized in 1975, making Alaska and Nepal the only two such places in the world.

A kind of weird unreality pervades many things Alaskan. Man and his doings nowhere seem so transient and insubstantial, like a flash of Northern Lights in the Arctic sky—there now, likely to be gone in a moment. And the Alaskan climate seems deliberately programmed to keep man at bay. Fort Yukon, in the interior, has reported temperatures as low as 75 degrees below zero, as high as 100 above. Soggy Port Walter, on the southeastern Panhandle, is deluged with 18 feet of water each year, but the wind-dried North Slope has only a few inches of precipitation a year. While Anchorage asserts it has warmer winters than northern New England, the fact is that in Fairbanks, the only city of the interior, brutal cold of 30 and sometimes more than 55 below zero drives people indoors for weeks on end. To step outside without proper clothing on the North Slope, when low temperatures and winds coincide, invites fatal exposure.

Geography

Alaska lies in three great climatic belts, separated by massive mountain ranges: from south to north, the Pacific Mountain area, the Central Plateau, and the North Slope. The corresponding climatic belts range from moist, relatively mild temperatures to arctic, fierce winter colds.

Pacific Mountain area. The Japan Current, sweeping northward and eastward beneath the curve of the Aleutians, around the Gulf of Alaska and then the Panhandle, maintains relatively mild temperatures here. The Panhandle, starting some 500 miles north of Seattle, has a moist climate and thick forests. Seaward, this stretch of land offers us the countless islands of the Alexander Archipelago—the remnants of ancient submerged mountains and one of the world's loveliest fjord areas. Towering forests of spruce and hemlock abound; naturally, this is the center of Alaska's pulp and timber industry.

About a sixth of Alaskans live in the Panhandle region, most of them around Juneau, the remainder scattered through little fishing and lumber towns such as picturesque Sitka (once capital and great center for the Russians, when they held Alaska), Ketchikan, and Skagway (still breathing some of the spirit of the Klondike Gold Rush). No state capital is so removed from the state's population and geographic center as Juneau—one reason there have been so many efforts to revoke its status in recent years. Towering mountains dominate the little storybook city, which is set on narrow, precipitous streets not far from huge glaciers, magnificent waterfalls, and great, untracked forests where one could easily tangle with a bear coming down to fish in the rivers at salmon-spawning time.

The Panhandle is effectively separated from the main body of Alaska by the spectacular St. Elias Mountains and the massive Malaspina Glacier. South Central Alaska, site of Anchorage and home for over half the state's people, fronts on the broad Bay of Alaska. Around that gulf, the most exciting modern development has been oil exploration on the Kenai Peninsula and in the waters of Cook Inlet. The strike of 1957, not to be confused with the far greater strike on the North Slope a decade later, did trigger $1 billion in oil company investments. The Alaska maritime belt, stretching from the Panhandle hundreds of miles westward to the Aleutians, is the home of Alaskan fisheries. The yearly value of the catch—in salmon, Alaska king crab, halibut, Dungeness crab, shrimp, and herring—reached an astounding $1.5 billion in the early 1980s. This temperate band includes Alaska's only significant farming area: the Matanuska Valley, northeast of Anchorage, where cabbages grow to bushel-size in the 20-hour-daylight period of June and July. In the 1970s Alaskan agriculture took a leap forward; the state even became a grain exporter. But imports still accounted for 90 percent of the state's food supply.

The westernmost edge of the Bay of Alaska is anchored by big Kodiak Island, site of the town of Kodiak, one of America's great fisheries, devastated by the great Alaskan earthquake of 1964 but since recovered. And finally, we come to the Aleutians, countless islands and islets carving a 1,400-mile arc into the Pacific, swept by wind and fog, shaken by earthquakes, and harboring 27 volcanic peaks, an eerie stretch of creation where the skies seem forever leaden with low-flying stratus clouds that screen out the sunshine except for some 25 days a year. The only ground fighting of World War II on North American soil took place on Japanese-held Attu Island, the westernmost of the chain.

Central Plateau. Now we pass northward, past icefalls, glaciers, ridges, and the high mountain peaks surrounding lordly Mount McKinley, to the Central Plateau. Rolling from the Canadian border to the Bering Sea, from the walls of McKinley to the northern barrier of the Brooks Range, the plateau is bigger than all of Texas. Through it flow the mighty Yukon River and its tributaries, dotted with native villages along their banks. Here one finds Alaska's most brutally cold winters and likewise its hottest summer temperatures.

Settlement of the Central Plateau is stunted, now and perhaps forevermore,

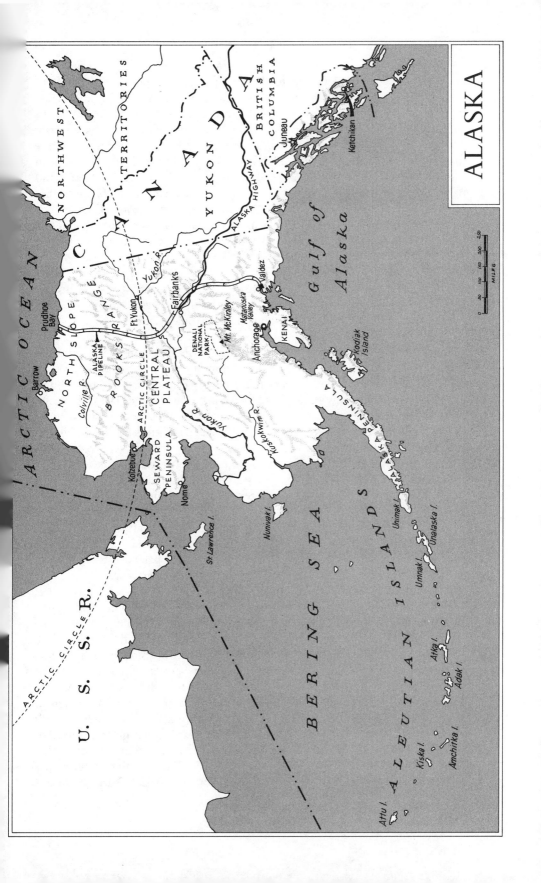

ALASKA

by permafrost—subsoil frozen to depths of 1,000 feet or more by eons of freezing temperatures. In summer the surface turns to a gooey sludge while the earth below remains frozen to rocklike solidity. Visit (as we have) towns such as Kotzebue or Bethel or Nome and you witness the startling contrast between Eskimo civilization as it has been lived for millennia and the white man's world of welfare checks. Nor is the geography similar to anything in the Lower 48. The tundra, a blanket of moss, sedges, lichens, bunch grass, and berry plants, soft and mushy in summer and frozen hard in winter, stretches off to an unpeopled horizon. Not a tree breaks the monotony. Dark clouds come scudding in low over the horizon. On a beach, one may see fish and seal skins drying on racks, and caribou hides too—and a modern snowmobile parked nearby.

North Slope. Between the Central Plateau and the North Slope is the Brooks Range—a region so vast its territory equals the size of Italy. No one who has ever witnessed the coming of spring to the Brooks Range, reports a *Time* magazine writer, is ever quite the same again: "After three months of frozen silence, the sun reappears as a long, slanting shaft that illuminates only the highest peaks. Each day the light descends, until finally even the darkest valley is bathed in warmth. The ice breaks, roaring like a cannon fire, and the ground explodes with color as wild flowers bloom. Big bears stagger out of hibernation. Rivers team with salmon, grayling, and char. Caribou march in long single files toward new feeding grounds. Glacial ice glitters like emeralds and sapphires. The world seems reborn."

From the Brooks Range, the plateauland of the North Slope sweeps over thousands of square miles to the Arctic Ocean. Summertime brings bright wildflowers across the tundra; in winter there is nothing but a hostile, white expanse of space. Winter snowfall is light, but once it touches the ground, it is not likely to melt until the following summer. The ocean ice pack recedes for no more than four or five months of a year. This is the land of the midnight sun, with two months of perpetual summertime light balanced by 72 days of complete winter darkness, starting November 15 of each year.

The discovery of oil on the North Slope did not come as a total surprise: early explorers mushing across the tundra had found places where oil seeped through the soil. In 1923, President Harding set aside a sizable portion of the Arctic as "Naval Petroleum Reserve Number Four." But the historic 1968 strike by Atlantic Richfield near Prudhoe Bay was of immense magnitude; some said it might eventually exceed 100 *billion* barrels. "Except maybe for parts of Siberia, it's the worst place in the world to drill for oil," an Alaska-based supervisor for Mobil Oil noted in the early '70s. "There's no sign of vegetation other than the tundra. No people, no trees. And in wintertime, it's always dark." He was not exaggerating. In blizzards, men go from place to place by pulling themselves along on cables between buildings; otherwise, with visibility often a foot or less, they may die. Exposed flesh freezes in a matter of seconds. Shelter is provided in tightly built prefabricated buildings that have thermopane windows and outer doors like the doors of big walk-in refrigerators. We traveled to the Atlantic Richfield half of the field one August day (when the Arctic weather was in the 30s and 40s) and found the whole atmosphere reminiscent of a space station. Employees fly from Anchorage by charter jet, working one week and taking the next off. After working 12-hour days (often in "spacesuits" to ward off the cold), they return to an operations center designed to cheer them with bright colors, gymnasiums, saunas, a library, and a movie theater. Well-prepared, hearty food is on hand (in such quantities that signs indicate the calorie content). Wages are stupendous—not uncommonly $40,000 per year for lower level jobs—and have even attracted a fair number of women. But the companies constantly fear that the boredom will lead to use of forbidden drugs and alcohol, and no rooms have locks. Back in Anchorage, some men have returned home to find their wives could not stand either the cold or the loneliness and have left with other men.

One of the great environmental battles of history, complicated as well by claims of Alaskan native groups, preceded the start of construction, in 1974, of the great oil pipeline—four feet wide, 800 miles long—from Prudhoe Bay to Valdez on the Bay of Alaska where the oil is shipped to the Lower 48 for refining. A highway had also to be built across the great empty spaces, for construction work and later maintenance. Finally an act of Congress was necessary to undo the legal obstacles and let the oil companies proceed with their multibillion-dollar project. The environmental effort has by almost all accounts been a remarkable success, although oil leaks have occurred occasionally. As we drove up to the Arctic Ocean, everything was pristine, and along the pipeline caribou cavorted.

Urban Alaska

Anchorage, the metropolis no one anticipated, made its start in 1914 as Ship Creek Landing, a tent city at the head of Cook Inlet for surveyors and workers on the Alaskan Railroad. Historians record the streets were two feet deep in dust, water sold for five cents a bucket, and the garbage was dumped on an outgoing tide every 24 hours. A year later, the town was moved up and away from the waterfront, and two special reserves were established: "Bohunk Village," for the workmen, mostly single men recruited in Southern Europe, and "South Anchorage," for the prostitutes. Even at the eve of World War II, the city had only 3,495 residents. Then came the impetus of military building during and after the war, as Alaska came to be recognized as what Brigadier General Billy Mitchell, the great evangelist of air power, called "the most central place in the world of aircraft." With the breaks of luck and no small amount of civic boosterism, the city expanded to 44,237 people in 1960 and 174,431 in 1980.

Anchorage is indubitably the epicenter of financial, political, and even governmental power in its state.* Alaska's powerful and mighty gather in such spots as the Captain Cook Hotel and superb seafood restaurants with spectacular sunset views toward the Cook Inlet and Mt. Susitna, the sleeping lady. The major oil companies helped downtown Anchorage by building offices there instead of in the suburbs, and there is a beautiful museum depicting Alaskan history. But it is not a city without problems. Anchorage has become a sprawl of subdivisions, shopping centers, and ugly, reflective glass-fronted office buildings, and roads, roads, roads. (Only .6 percent of trips are made by public transportation.) Center Anchorage, a panel of the Urban Land Institute warned in the late '70s, could follow the downward path of other U.S. cities through misguided development decisions and "benign neglect."

Fairbanks, Alaska's second-largest city (22,645), has received some massive economic injections—most recently from the oil pipeline boom of the '70s, which drew some 30,000 people through the city. But Fairbanks, at heart, is still a frontier town sitting on the edge of one of the world's great wildernesses. Away from the main drags, there are many ill-kept, unpaved roads. Frontiertype swinging-door saloons still abound. A civilizing touch is added by the University of Alaska campus, not far from town, but Fairbanks has another nemesis called the weather. In wintertime the thermometer may drop to 44 below zero for weeks, at night somewhere around 60 below. Cars clump around on "square" tires frozen in the fall with a flat side to the ground. An eerie "ice fog," not unlike heavy smog, forms out of ice crystals and settles on the ground, often not budging for days.

Juneau, Alaska's tiny capital (19,528) is located in the southeast, two time zones away from the bulk of the state's population. In 1974, voters approved an initiative to move the capital closer to the people. To allay complications sprouting from intercity jealousy, the initiative stipulated the new site would not be within 30 miles of either Anchorage or Fairbanks. A capital site selection committee then proposed three alternative sites, and in 1976 the voters chose Willow, a hamlet 37 miles north of Anchorage graced with a spectacular view of Mt. McKinley. The plans of a San Francisco architectural firm were accepted in 1977: Willow was to be in a style sensitive to Alaskan character —"contemporary log cabin," in short, with abundant personal access to government offices, housing, and recreation. But Alaskans apparently didn't appreciate what the cost would be. In 1906, the capital move from Sitka to Juneau had involved just three persons, seven filing cabinets, and a small boat. Now, it appeared, the cost would mount into the billions. In 1978 and 1982 capital construction bond issues went down in statewide votes. Some Alaskans also believed that high technology may have made the move nearer to population centers "immaterial." Residents throughout the state—even at the

*One should probably exert restraint in using any earthquake-related term in relation to Anchorage. So fearsome was the 1964 upheaval there—8.4 on the Richter Scale, the severest earthquake ever recorded on the North American continent—that there were, according to *Anchorage Daily Times* publisher Robert Atwood, serious suggestions to abandon whole sections of the city. The quake simply scythed the ground out from under one row of old cafés on the city's main street, for instance, forming a trough-shaped depression, or graben.

Arctic Circle—were able to keep up with the status of bills in the legislature by dialing a computer in Juneau; they made their wishes known to legislators through electronic mail and teleconference calls. Whether or not the capital was ever officially moved, however, Anchorage was expected to continue as the logical location for many state offices or their branches.

Economic Alaska, Native Alaska

Up to the 1970s Alaska labored under a weak, subsidized, high-cost economy. The state's great storehouse of resources and energy notwithstanding, 55 percent of Alaskans' personal income came from the federal government in 1950; 38 percent in 1968. Washington, moreover, owned or controlled 96 percent of Alaska's land area and kept most of it locked up. Perhaps the greatest problem was the cost of doing business in Alaska. Economists characterized the state's economy as "insular, nondiversified, service oriented, structurally fragmented. . . ." Indeed, Japan rather than the Lower 48 consumed 75 to 90 percent of Alaska's pre-oil exports: fish, lumber, natural minerals.

Oil began to change the picture dramatically. Indeed, based on $900 million raised for North Shore oil rights, the state began intensive capital investments from 1969 onward. News of the pipeline construction drew hordes of would-be workers from the Lower 48, seeking hard work and hard pay, and the lucky ones who actually landed jobs could easily gross from $950 to $1,500 a week. Crude oil began flowing through the pipeline in 1977; soon the state treasury was awash with money. Parallel to oil came North Shore natural gas, or at least its prospect: the problem was where and how to build a 5,000-mile pipeline to the U.S. Midwest. A route across Canada was chosen, and construction started from the southern end. But cost estimates, which began at $10 to $15 billion, rose so high that a poorly run consortium of oil and gas pipeline companies, after trying but failing to get government subsidy, put the project on ice.

Never in American history has a single bonanza enriched a state as oil did Alaska. In 1969 the state budget was $124 million; a dozen years later, it had ballooned to $1.8 billion. Between royalties and severance taxes, oil was financing no less than 90 percent of the state budget by 1981. While state and local governments in the Lower 48 were scraping up pennies to maintain essential services, Alaska in 1980 abolished its entire state income tax and had a 1981 accumulated surplus of $3 billion—a figure some said might rise to $100 billion by 2000. Under a "Special Fund" established in 1978, a general stock ownership plan was established to invest in major industrial projects with each Alaskan getting an annual dividend check. The legislature also granted local governments $1,000 per resident for social service and capital improvement projects and launched the state's own $5 billion hydropower project.

All of this looked like unseemly profiteering off the luck of oil and OPEC's international price gouging—as, indeed, it was. But there was another side. As early as 1975, Governor Jay Hammond was expressing concern over the expected oil boom and stating his belief in "preservation" and "slow growth" and the necessity to plan "past the pipeline" to long-term economic stability. Hammond set up a growth policy council and began to encourage creation or expansion of alternative businesses—all the way from Alaska "traditionals" such as fisheries and timber to plastics manufacturing, from barley farming to mining for copper, asbestos, lead, zinc, silver, and gold. At Hammond's urging, the legislature in 1976 set up a Permanent Fund to receive a share of annual oil revenues and look into fruitful long-term investments. And all along Hammond tried to dispel Alaska's Shangri-La image, reciting "sobering facts" about Alaska's unemployment rate (often the nation's highest), cost of living (also tops in the U.S.A.), and poverty conditions in native villages that made Appalachia look affluent. In the early 1980s, Hammond's ministrations took on more meaning when oil revenues plummeted, the state budget outlook suddenly darkened, unemployment soared, and the state hired a spokesman to tell people to stay away unless they came with enough money to live for a few months and to buy a plane ticket home if necessary. Alaskans stoutly defended their oil revenues as right and proper in a state with a history of boom-and-bust cycles. But so concerned were they about the national image of a greedy, oil-rich state handing out subsidies to all its citizens that they mounted a major public relations campaign in the Lower 48 to build sympathy for the state's multitudinous and lasting problems.

Alaska's native peoples—Eskimos (northern and western Alaska), Aleuts (of the Aleutians), and Indians (Athapascan dominating the Central Plateau, Tlingits on the Panhandle)—meanwhile discovered themselves. There are few parallels in history of an aboriginal people, occupying a vast portion of the earth for millennia with scarcely any intergroup contact, suddenly coalescing to define their common heritage, articulate their needs, and mount a program of militant action in common accord. But that is what happened in Alaska. Concerned about the disposition of 102 million acres of land the federal government had agreed to grant Alaska under statehood, as well as a later-aborted Atomic Energy Commission plan to detonate a nuclear device creating a harbor 30 miles from Point Hope, the first meeting of Northwest natives was called in November 1961 in Barrow. It was to be the forerunner of hundreds out of which emerged the 20-odd native groups, covering every native people and area of Alaska. Ever since they have been real factors in Alaskan public life.

Land was the central issue: Alaskan natives, unlike Indians in the Lower 48, had never entered into treaties defining their land rights. As the state began to appropriate lands under the statehood act, it ran into a buzzsaw of angry native protest. Natives began to file stupendous land claims, overlapping federally held public domain, state-selected land, and the billion-dollar North Slope oil lands. Years of wrangling culminated in the 1971 Alaska Native Claims Settlement Act, an incredibly generous settlement compared to all prior agreements with aboriginal peoples. The natives were given the right to select 40 million acres of land: the equivalent of 62,500 square miles, an area larger than that of 30 other U.S. states. The ultimate cash settlement would give them $965 million ($19,300 for each living native), roughly half from the federal treasury, half from oil royalties, payable over an 11-year period to 12 native corporations. Peoples scarcely able to balance a checkbook suddenly found themselves running massive corporations. The native corporations plunged into virtually every area of the Alaskan economy, from fish canning to banking, from hotels to reindeer herding, from construction engineering to timber and mineral exploration. One native corporation Sealaska, a timber and salmon producer, had made it onto *Fortune*'s list of the 1,000 largest U.S. corporations. But several of the native corporations hit rough economic seas. Willie Hensley, president of the Nana Development Corporation and the state's most prominent native leader, told us that to judge the native corporations on solely capitalistic criteria was not to recognize their total pupose. "Business and politics are not an end," Hensley said. "They are simply a means to the primary task of tribal renewal and survival."

Money and technology had also produced a startling change in native lifestyles. Previously subsistence-level Eskimos suddenly became corporate stockholders, whale hunting began to be pursued by outboard motor boats with CB radios and dog sleds were replaced by snowmobiles. In small native towns it was not uncommon to find elder natives setting out to kill a bear with a spear, while being recorded on home videotape by their grandchildren— even though the log houses in which they lived might have no sewerage or running water. Alaska natives still suffer from high rates of unemployment, alcoholism, and family breakups, which their leaders say are due to generations of pressure to assimilate into the white man's culture. But despite the continuing problems of native education and a need to renew ancient cultural traditions, Hensley said the native groups now have "all the elements for successful future survival"—land, capital, fairly experienced politicians, and managers.

Politics of the Great Land

As history marks the affairs of man, Alaska's arduous battle for statehood was won only yesterday. But the pace of subsequent events has been so rapid— the earthquake of 1964, the great native awakening, land claims settlement, oil riches beyond imagination—that the statehood struggle now seems like the affair of another age. Nine decades passed from that day in 1867 on which Senator Charles Sumner, supporting the purchase from Russia, dedicated the territory to future statehood (finally approved by Congress in July 1958). Ironically, just 22 years later some Alaskans questioned whether statehood was such a good idea after all.

Let the historic credit be given to E.L. (Bob) Bartlett, indefatigable statehood proponent, one of the state's first two senators and a figure so broadly acknowledged as the state's founding father that his statue now stands in the rotunda of the Capitol in Washington. Honor of another nature attends the other "first" senator, Democrat Ernest Gruening, Harvard Medical School graduate of 1912, editor of several distinguished national journals, appointed Alaska's governor by President Roosevelt in 1939, early advocate of population control, and a man who dared—as early as March 10, 1964—to declare the Vietnam War a "putrid mess" and to urge his fellow senators to support immediate U.S. withdrawal.

The most enduring of the statehood fighters was Democrat William Egan, who became the first governor after statehood in 1958, lost out to the colorful Republican Walter J. Hickel in 1966, but returned for another term in the 1970 elections. A small-town grocer by trade, Egan was considered honest beyond reproach, the kind of fair-minded and accessible governor Alaska needed after decades of cold, impersonal territorial rule.

Walter Hickel's appointment as Secretary of the Interior—the first Cabinet post for an Alaskan—was the source of great pride in the state, followed by dismay when President Nixon dismissed him in 1970. Hickel aroused environmentalists' ire by declaring, on entering the Cabinet, that it was wrong to put federal lands under "lock and key" for conservation. Later, when he had shut down federally controlled oil wells in the Santa Barbara Channel following the "blow" of an offshore rig there and showed his mettle by cracking down on industrial polluters, he was the conservationists' hero. The entire Hickel story, in fact, was pure Alaskan. The son of impoverished Kansas tenant farmers, he arrived on the dock at Seward in 1940 with 37 cents in his pocket. He got his first grubstake in the boxing ring, then moved into the construction business, hotels, and natural gas, amassing a fortune of some $5 million. As Interior Secretary he proved to be the most flamboyant figure to perch on Harold Ickes' old roost since the Old Curmudgeon occupied it himself. In the midst of the 1970 Kent State–Cambodian crisis he fired off a letter to the president (having failed to get an appointment) calling on Nixon to stop alienating American youth. The White House crew reacted with scarcely disguised fury, but Hickel ignored veiled signals he should resign. "President Nixon hired me. He will have to fire me," said Hickel. "If I go away, I'm going with an arrow in my heart and not a bullet in my back." So Nixon had to go through a personal confrontation and the first firing of a Cabinet member in 18 years.

Other Alaskans in Washington have received attention: the erratic Democrat Mike Gravel, who defeated an aging Senator Gruening in 1968 but himself was ousted in 1980 (Fairbanks banker Frank Murkowski, a Republican, got the seat), and Ted Stevens, first elected in 1970 and by the early '80s not only Senate Republican Whip but a power on the Appropriations Committee.

It was up to Stevens and Gravel (political opponents who eventually developed a deep hatred for each other) to lead the Alaskan opposition to what they claimed was an unjustifiable lock-up of oil, mineral, and timber resources in the Alaskan lands legislation that finally cleared Congress in 1980. On one side of the often vitriolic battle was a coalition of 51 environmental and wildlife protection groups, plus President Carter (who called it "the conservation decision of the century") and Interior Secretary Cecil Andrus; on the other, one found mining, timber, and oil companies, the Chamber of Commerce of the U.S., the National Rifle Association—and most Alaskans. The final legislation tripled the size of America's national park system by adding 43.6 million acres, establishing 53.6 million acres of wildlife refuge, adding 3.4 million acres to the national forest system, setting aside 1.2 million acres as wild and scenic rivers—and more. But it also had to be considered a masterpiece of legislative compromise, because it gave the conservationists less than they had wanted and did, in fact, open up to mining, logging, and oil exploration many areas that had hitherto been off limits.

It is difficult to overestimate the intensity of Alaskan emotion aroused by the federal government's effort to withhold so many million acres from development. The idea of President Carter, "East Coast liberals," and other outsiders barring exploitation of so much wealth was regarded as idiotic and catastrophic; most Alaskans, by contrast, thought they had a God-given right to do with their land as they pleased. So high ran the emotions that Alaskan voters in summer 1980 narrowly approved a ballot measure calling for "reexamination" of what had been so long and finally victoriously sought—statehood. So the legislature was obliged to establish a statehood commission, the first time since the Civil War that any state's people had asked to reexamine their relationship to the union. In 1982 the commission reported, charging that "the federal government has reneged on its solemn promises to the state in the Statehood Act," rallying Alaskans to action against any national effort to negate oil severance taxes. But secession, said the report, was simply not a realistic alternative for Alaska.

For two terms (1975–83) Alaska's internal politics were dominated by Jay Hammond. No state but Alaska could have elected him—a bearded bush pilot, big game hunter, poet, philosopher, lover of nature (and his native wife), but believer, too, in his state's untold economic potential. Hammond's successor in 1983 was Bill Sheffield, a Democrat and millionaire hotel-owner who had opposed moving the capital—an issue that brought out 70 percent of the voters: the highest turnout in the nation. Alaskans in 1982 also displayed a social consciousness rare in Western states by defeating a proposition to repeal the natives' hunting and fishing priority, and another that would have repealed state funding of abortions for poor women.

Yet whatever the political tides of the moment, it is nature, not man and his works, which fascinates one the most, and will forever set this part of America apart. The Great Land's immensity may be its final salvation. In the words of Robert Weeden, an Alaskan ecologist: "The world needs an embodiment of the frontier mythology, the sense of horizons unexplored, the mystery of uninhabited miles. It needs a place where wolves stalk the stand lines, because a land that can produce a wolf is healthy, robust, and perfect land."

HAWAII

American Idyll

SIX HOURS AFTER THE RISING SUN touches the tip of Mount Katahdin, in Maine, its warming rays filter through the Pacific sky to lighten the summits of fiery Mauna Loa and Mauna Kea, towering almost three miles above the "Big Island" of Hawaii, the 50th of the 50 states, a quarter of the way around the globe. Here is that most improbable of states, a beautiful semitropical archipelago set in the vast void of the Pacific, 2,400 miles from our West Coast.

There may be nowhere else on the globe such an idyllic place to live. "The loveliest fleet of islands that lies anchored in any ocean," Mark Twain wrote of them. "No alien land in all the world has any deep, strong charm for me but that one," he continued. "No other land could longingly and so beseechingly haunt me, sleeping and waking, through half a lifetime. . . ."

In Hawaii, every group is a minority. The people are a mix of the original native Hawaiian stock plus Caucasians, Japanese, Chinese, Korean, Filipino, and other minor strains, speaking 40 languages and dialects. This is the only one of the 50 states whose principal ethnic roots are Asian, not European. Amazingly, the Islands' polyglot of the world's peoples lives together in substantial peace and mutual respect. Not unrelated is all that lies behind the spirit called "Aloha"—a remarkable word that means hello, good-bye, love, affection, compassion, mercy, kindness, *and tolerance*—all at the same time.

We realize that such a view of Hawaii is highly romantic and idealized. As we shall see later, greedy tourist development threatens the natural beauty of this Pacific paradise. Crass commercialism endangers the Aloha spirit. Deep strains of racial exploitation run throughout modern Hawaiian history, and a counterreaction among descendants of the original native Hawaiian peoples has even led to a handful of vicious, unprovoked attacks on tourists in recent years.

But we deliberately chose to go the romantic route first. Why? Because the negatives are all aberrations, not the norm of Hawaii life. And because, in reaching out to these emerald isles of the distant Pacific to establish its 50th state, the United States did incorporate into the Union that one place under the Stars and Stripes where the realities of place and society so closely approximate what they *ought to be*. Hawaii may be an American idyll. But it is also, in many respects, an American ideal.

The birth of the Hawaiian Islands has been matchlessly chronicled in the

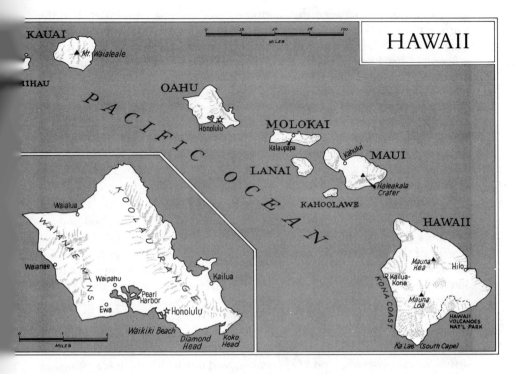

gospel according to Michener,* always a wonder to reread: How in the bosom of the boundless deep, countless millions of years before man first walked the earth, a massive fissure some 2,000 miles long suddenly appeared, exuding torrents of white-hot, liquid rock that exploded on contact with the heavy, wet burden of water, sending columns of released steam upward for nearly four miles to break loose on the surface of the sea and form a cloud. And for 40 million years, more or less, the dense, volcanic basalt built up, layer after layer; and one day, there was another molten eruption from the earth's core, except that now it reached the surface of the sea, and there was a tremendous explosion as liquid rock struck water and air together, and there was land. And then still more millions of years, the rise and fall of that and myriad other volcanic isles, and wind and water brought the first tenuous plant and animal life—perhaps the seeds of plants and trees, or a coconut washed up against a shore, or a bird from distant realms—and then interspersed ice ages, and finally, in the latter days of time the creation of the Hawaii we know—of lush valley and precipice, of volcanic peaks (some still active—Kilauea, for example, which began spewing rivers of fire again in 1983), of palm-fringed blue water, and flowers, and white surf, some islands already receding into the sea, others still growing.

On a map of the plateaus and trenches and seamounts of the Pacific Ocean

*Hawaii, James A. Michener (New York: Random House, 1959).

floor, one feature, between the Aleutians and Australia, stands out. It is the great wall of the Hawaiian Range, set in the very middle of the Pacific, the mountains within it rising as much as 18,000 feet off the ocean floor, but only a few ever reaching the surface. At the southeastern extremity of the range are the 20 islands of the state of Hawaii, 7 of them inhabited. The largest of these is the most southeasterly, Hawaii, the "Big Island," bearing the name of the entire chain. It has 4,030 square miles, more than twice the area of Delaware and Rhode Island combined. The most heavily populated island is Oahu, 200 miles to the northwest; on it is the city of Honolulu and 79 percent of the state's people, but it is only a seventh the size of the Big Island.

Oahu will necessarily dominate much of our account, but let us start with the "Neighbor Islands." The island of Hawaii not only covers 63 percent of the state's land area but is still growing through volcanic activity. There are few other places in the world where the elemental forces of earth building are so visible. Volcanic fumes leak out from a thousand orifices, and along great sweeps of the coastline one sees immense flows of hardened lava from recent outbreaks. Mauna Loa (13,677 feet above sea level) is one of the world's most active volcanos; it erupted in 1950 for 23 days and produced the greatest amount of lava noted in modern times. While most of the volcanic eruptions pose little immediate danger to human life, they have wiped out villages in recent times, and there are fears that the prosperous city of Hilo on Hawaii's east coast could one day be wiped out by rifts from Mauna Loa's flank. Hilo thrives as a sugar-loading port, county seat, and tourist center. It is a reflection of Honolulu's dominance that this little city of 37,017 souls is actually second-largest in the entire state.

In the prevailing pattern of the archipelago, the Big Island has a verdant, moist northeastern side where the trade winds deposit the burden of clouds blown in over thousands of miles of open sea. The southwestern flank, by contrast, is dry and hot. Sugar cane and cattle ranching are the traditional and still important farm industries, but Hawaii has long been America's leading orchid center and is unique in the U.S. for coffee growing along its eastern Kona coast. There is also a prosperous business in macadamia nut growing and harvesting the vast hardwood forests.

The Big Island's greatest economic advances of recent years, however, have sprung from tourism—grand resort complexes, starting with the 1960 opening of Laurance Rockefeller's Mauna Kea Beach Hotel (perhaps the most lavish on earth) and the first direct jet flights between Hilo and the West Coast in 1967. The 1980 population count of the Big Island was 92,053, just over 12 percent of Oahu's. This, incidentally, was the island believed to be first inhabited by the Polynesians, perhaps around 750 A.D. The first European sea captain to set foot on Hawaii, Captain James Cook, met his death at Hawaii's Kealakekua Bay in 1779. And the first American missionaries landed at Kona, which is the site of the first Christian church in the islands.

Between the Big Island and Oahu is Maui, the second-largest island in the chain, and its three small neighbors: Molokai, Lanai, and Kahoolawe. The county of Maui, which includes all four, noted a 1980 population of 70,847.

Maui is called the Valley Isle, for the simple reason that it consists of two volcanic mountains separated by a low isthmus. One of the peaks, West Maui, is ancient in geologic time, but not so Haleakala, the "House of the Sun," a 10,023-foot volcano that last erupted sometime around 1790 and remains the world's largest dormant volcano, with a 33-square-mile crater that could swallow Manhattan Island and all its skyscrapers. Maui also offers some 33 miles of beaches, some of black volcanic origin, others of golden sand, many among the most beautiful in all the Islands. Only the past decades have brought major tourist developments. Elmer Cravalho, the county boss for years up to his 1979 retirement, fought ferociously against high-rise resorts and jumbo jets and sought to protect native Mauians from being squeezed out of housing and other basics by an onrush of development.

Maui's neighbor, Molokai, with 261 square miles, is commonly depicted as the Friendly Isle because its inhabitants are thought of as the most affable of all Hawaiians. Until the mid-1960s, it was practically untouched by tourist development and retained a kind of idyllic peacefulness like the dreamy Hawaii of yesteryear. Much sought out now by tourists is the place all would have avoided like poison in times past—the leper colony at Kalaupapa, still home for a few victims of Hansen's disease, who have a state guarantee that they may remain as long as they live.

The island of Lanai, just west of Maui and south of Molokai, is the perfect company town. It is 100 percent owned by the Dole Pineapple Company, and virtually all its 2,119 people make their living cultivating the 15,000 acres and harvesting 120 million pineapples each year.

Last and clearly least in the Maui orbit is pitiful Kahoolawe. This is a 45-square-mile hump eight miles off Maui's west side that the U.S. Navy has been practice-bombing and strafing since 1945. Not a soul lives there. And yet it is a treasure trove for archeologists, laden with remnants of its Polynesian settlers a thousand years ago; to native Hawaiians, it is sacred land. Renewed nationalist efforts to press native claims and protect Hawaiian heritage focused on Kahoolawe and were partially successful: in 1981 the little island was listed on the National Register of Historic Places, and the Navy was forced to compromise by allowing scientific and educational visits.

All the Neighbor Islands we have spoken of so far are east of Oahu. There is one major island farther west, some 95 miles out toward Midway. It is Kauai, 551 square miles of lush and tropical beauty, so much the personification of the idyllic South Sea isle that Hollywood chose it as the location for *South Pacific* and other films of like theme.

Kauai was the first of the Hawaiian chain to emerge from the sea, and has been without volcanic activity longer than any of its neighbors. This has permitted the lavas to erode into rich black and red soil that is carved by constant rains into colorful canyons and deep valleys covered with wondrous plants and floral exuberance. Green-carpeted canefields, deserted white beaches lined with clusters of coconut palms, cliffs that plunge a thousand feet to the sea, swamps and abysmal crevices, areas of utter remoteness, and a central volcanic peak almost eternally surrounded by clouds—these are the hallmarks of Kauai, well named the Garden Island. Mount Waialeale has an astonishing average of more than 50 *feet* of rain every year, making it the wettest spot on earth. Only a few miles away, there is a place where less than one foot a year is recorded. The 39,082 people who live on Kauai make their living first from agriculture (sugar cane, pineapple, livestock), second from tourism, and third from the scientific-military installations.

Off the coast of Kauai lies Niihau, the "forbidden island," the private property of the Robinson family ever since King Kamehameha IV sold it to a familial ancestor for $10,000 in 1864. The Robinsons were Scots whose idea was to preserve on the island the gentle life of the native Hawaiians they found there. The 226 people on the 18-mile-long island still speak the old Hawaiian language; roughly two-thirds are still of absolutely pure Hawaiian stock. No visitors are ever permitted, and government officials who go ashore by longboat must leave before nightfall. The islanders live a primitive life of raising sheep and shorthorn cattle, keeping bees for honey, and hunting wild pigs, turkey, and peacocks. Movies, alcohol, and dogs are banned.

For many years after World War II, the Neighbor Islands declined in population as agricultural employment declined. Virtual ghost towns appeared; leaders despaired for the future. But with tourism and related activities, the Neighbor Island population rose an astounding 69 percent between 1970 and 1980 and seemed sure to rise as Oahu became more congested.

Oahu: Where the Action Is

Whatever the charm of the Neighbor Islands may be, the island of Oahu and its city of Honolulu are where the people are and where the action is. Intensive development started in this area because Honolulu and contiguous Pearl Harbor are the only safe deep-water ports in all the Islands.

By 1980, the population of Oahu reached 762,874, up a full 21 percent from the previous Census. Honolulu itself had 365,048 people. Many consider Oahu's development dangerously fast and helter-skelter, but the fact is that a fantastic amount of human activity has been crowded into this relatively small island (about 40 miles long and 20 miles wide), with the natural environment still largely intact.

A drive around Oahu quickly reveals a land heavily touched by civilization though still beautiful and varied in the extreme. In short time, one can come on smooth white beaches and rocky foam-swept coast, placid lagoons and an anomalous section of "interstate" highway, massive sugar cane and pineapple plantations and smaller farms that grow coconut palms and bananas and avocados, precipitous cliffs and raw jungle, California-style subdivisions and condominium apartments but also flower-bedecked villages on low stilts.

To the west is the Leeward Coast, calm, sultry, and lightly populated; to the northeast, the Windward Coast, approached from Honolulu through a very windy pass. But the intense activity of the Honolulu metropolitan concentration is still largely confined to Oahu's southern plain, anchored by Pearl

Harbor on the west and Koko Head (beyond Diamond Head) on the east. Even here, there are natural sights supreme. We recall the view from a friend's mountain home above Ewa, some 30 miles to the west of the city. Honolulu could be seen gleaming white in the distance, with the familiar bulk of Diamond Head just beyond it. Ranging from the city northward was the spiny ridge of the Koolau Range, dividing windward Oahu from Honolulu. A constant veil of clouds on the mountains mixed with sunshine splashing across the island's central valley of sugar cane and pineapple fields in their distinctive verdant mantles. More southerly, the three great fingers (lochs) of Pearl Harbor could be seen and, beyond that, the emerald green at ocean's edge leading into the cobalt blue of Pacific sky and water. Afternoon brought a rainstorm creating not just a single rainbow but a perfect reflection of itself from the valley floor to the heights. And in the night, Honolulu sparkled below and the stars mirrored their special vividness in the crystal ocean skies.

Pearl Harbor, a reservation of some 10,000 acres, combines not only the vivid history of December 7, 1941, but the present-day command of U.S. Naval operations to the western-most reaches of the Pacific. In Pearl's environs, the commander-in-chief of the Pacific (CINC-PAC) has directed the massive American military presence clear across to Asia, including the war zones in Vietnam and Korea.

Honolulu Harbor remains the funnel through which passes most of that vast array of goods that Hawaii cannot or will not make for itself. The harbor, still dominated by its colorful old Aloha Tower, is close by the downtown financial district. Here the economic powers of the Islands are housed in an odd combination of soaring modern skyscrapers and placid, squat older buildings so reminiscent of the small, tropical port of yesteryear. So confined is the space of the city, on a narrow corridor hard against the lower slope of the headlands, that national studies have nominated it as one of the nation's most promising (and necessary) sites for a rapid rail transit. But Mayor Eileen Anderson quashed planning for a system in 1981 on grounds that neither federal capital funding aid nor the requisite local subsidies were likely to be found. The decision seemed right in the short term, but was one ever-growing Honolulu might live to regret.

Close to the center of downtown Honolulu is the Iolani Palace, a wonderful old Victorian extravagance completed by the last of the Hawaiian kings, Kalakaua, in 1882. The old palace, all done up in the iron and grillwork considered so elegant in its time, fairly reeks with history. Queen Liliuokalani (1891–93) ruled from its chambers until her autocratic ways led to the over-throw of the monarchy. Sanford Ballard Dole, the son of a missionary who led the republican revolution in the Islands, ruled from the palace first as president of the independent republic of Hawaii (starting in 1893) and then as the first presidentially appointed governor of the new territory. Ceremonies to mark Hawaii's annexation to the United States were held on the front steps of the palace on August 12, 1898. For the next six decades, the territorial Senate met in the onetime royal dining room in the palace; the House, in what had been the throne room! The old palace was still the chief government building in 1959, when the last appointed governor, William F. Quinn, became the first popularly elected state governor. Not until a decade later, in 1969, did John A. Burns, Quinn's successor, sit for one last day as governor in the Iolani Palace and then move to the new State Capitol.

That new Capitol is one of the most exalted public buildings of our times. The strong but airy design by San Francisco architect John Carl Warnecke is rife with Hawaiian symbolism. Like an island, the building stands in a reflecting pool. Its great interior courtyard has openings both to sea and to mountains. And high above, that courtyard is open to the sky through a cone-shaped roof unmistakably patterned after a volcano. Just inside the roof opening, there is a band of deep blue. And up and through that great aperture, the skein of light Hawaiian clouds can be seen in constant motion.

Perched on the mountainside less than half a mile from the Capitol is the extinct old volcano, Punchbowl, with its tender burden: the graves of thousands of American servicemen from World War II, from Korea, and from the bitter Vietnam War.

Most of Hawaii's illustrious educational institutions lie within a one- to two-mile radius east of the Capitol. These include two famous old private preparatory schools (Punahoa and Iolani), McKinley High School (which counts among its graduates the first *two* U.S. Senators of Oriental origin, Hiram L. Fong and Daniel K. Inouye), and the University of Hawaii. The university, founded as a land-grant college in 1907, was still regarded as a third-grade farmers' and surfers' school when Hawaii achieved statehood. Then, under the presidency of Thomas H. Hamilton and his successor in 1969, former NATO Ambassador Harlan Cleveland, enrollment tripled. The school began to develop into a first-class regional university, building on its natural bases in geology, oceanography, and Oriental languages and literature. The campus is home for the East-West Institute established by Congress in the early 1960s.

The economic heart of Hawaii's big tourist industry and its most severe developmental and environmental problem is Waikiki Beach. Behind a narrow, mile-long strip of glittering sand stands an almost solid wall of huge, multistory hotels, jam-packed with tens of thousands of visitor rooms. The development began in modest measure with the first hotel in 1901, reached perhaps its esthetic height with the Moorish-style Royal Hawaiian in 1927, was revived by industrialist-developer Henry Kaiser in the 1950s, and after 1960 proceeded at a pace that left Hawaii gasping.

Viewing the Waikiki debacle, writer Horace Sutton described a "billion-dollar cement mistake" and pointed out that Honolulu never had an architectural review committee and never placed significant height limitation on Waikiki buildings. Much of the building was done by fast-moving operators who made a business of buying up small lots and building quickly on them. They created a tourist ghetto light years removed from the Aloha spirit.

Just east and south of Waikiki is the wonderful green tableland of Kapiolani Park, a favorite spot for swimming and watching the magnificent Hawaiian sunsets. Then comes the low-slung profile, a symbol of the Islands around the world: Diamond Head. Diamond Head crater is, we hope, extinct and a constant reminder to arriving and departing air travelers (who can see right down into its bowl) of the geologic origin of the Islands. The illustrious profile was endangered in 1967, when a group of developers proposed erecting high-rise apartment houses around its lower slopes. Forty-some citizen groups banded together in protest, led by the Outdoor Circle, a 54-year-old women's conservation organization whose long list of accomplishments included having purged Hawaii of all billboards. At a now historic meeting of the Honolulu City Council, crowded by 500 witnesses, the citizen voice was unmistakable: save Diamond Head's environs for parkland or single-family residences; at all costs, bar high rises. The council decided against the developers and for—it would seem—the people. It was after the Diamond Head victory that conservation and opposition to developer usurpation became the hot issues of Honolulu politics.

The Great Mixing Bowl

Hawaii's ethnic history is thought to go back to about the 8th century A.D., when Polynesians in long-distance canoes made their incredible voyages over hundreds of miles of open sea, to discover and settle the archipelago. When Captain Cook's ships first came upon the Islands in 1778, some 300,000 natives lived there. Seventy-five years later, after ample exposure to white man's culture and his diseases (starting with syphilis carried by men off Cook's *Resolution* and *Discovery*), only 71,000 natives survived. By one count in the mid-1960s, only 9,741 Hawaiians of pure native ancestry remained.

Nevertheless, the ethnic history of Hawaii is considered a model of successful mingling of the world's races—as one Hawaii politician put it to us, "the salvation light of civilization." An early 1980s state report broke down the Islands' population as:

RACE	%
Caucasian	26.3%
Japanese	23.3%
Hawaiian and part-Hawaiian	18.9%
Filipino	11.2%
Chinese	5.1%
Other races and mixtures	15.2%

Of this unique aggregate of peoples, a high portion are descended from foreign-born laborers brought to Hawaii during the 19th century to man the great sugar and pineapple plantations. In order of introduction, these were Chinese, Japanese, Portuguese, Puerto Rican, Korean, Spanish, and Filipino. At first the native Hawaiians and the early Anglos, known as *haoles*, considered them all "foreigners." But the weight of numbers—and thereby the future—rested with the newcomers.

Though native Hawaiians were always regarded with some respect, the *baoles* did dominate Hawaii, as a kind of preferred race, straight up to the attack on Pearl Harbor. Even by the 1980s, some forms of *baole* discrimination lingered on, however faintly. The Oahu Country Club, for example, remained snobbish about non-*baole* admissions, although the venerable Pacific Club shed that old nonsense some years before.

The significant racial problems of latter-day Oahu were of a different order, centering importantly on the ascendancy of the Japanese, a people risen from dark suspicion in the days immediately after Pearl Harbor to the heights of Hawaiian public life—and the resentment of some others—three decades later. At the start of World War II all Hawaiian Japanese were subject to slurs about their patriotism, and several hundred were placed in internment camps. The Japanese response was to demonstrate American patriotism beyond any shadow of doubt. The Japanese community led in the purchase of war bonds and gave freely to the blood bank. And as soon as Japanese military enlistments were permitted, the all-Japanese 100th Infantry Battalion and the 442nd Regimental Combat Team were formed. Off they went to Italy and France, to fight with great valor and suffer cruel losses.

The returning Japanese proved a resourceful group, many taking advantage of the GI Bill to get college and advanced degrees. Daniel K. Inouye, a member of the 442nd who left an arm behind in Italy, used the GI Bill to go through the University of Hawaii and George Washington University Law School and was elected to the U.S. Senate in 1962. Spark Matsunaga used his GI Bill to go through Harvard Law School and became first a congressman and then, in 1977, senator from Hawaii. George Ariyoshi became governor in 1975 and held that office into the 1980s. By the late '70s, according to a survey by the *Washington Post*'s Lou Cannon, not only Hawaii's U.S. Senators but also the attorney general, the leadership of both legislative houses, and a majority of Democratic state legislators (sometimes referred to as "The Diet" by members of other ethnic groups) were Japanese-American. So were 7 out of 10 school principals and most teachers in the state. Any Hawaiian in conflict with authority was likely to find it behind a Japanese face. Japanese-Americans had also done well in business, and Japanese directly from Nippon were flooding in as tourists. Major hotel and real-estate investments were made by such major Japanese firms as Mitsubishi, Tokyu, and Japan Airlines.

Among Hawaii's other non-*baole* ethnic groups, the Chinese became perhaps the wealthiest of all, many of their number dominant in the professions and as owners of banks, insurance companies, and large real-estate companies. Among the most successful were multimillionaire businessman Chin Ho and former U.S. Sen. Hiram Fong. Low on the totem pole were the Filipinos and Samoans. The Filipinos, the last big group to be imported to work on the plantations, remained the biggest group there, though younger Filipinos moved more fully into the general life of the Islands. The Samoans, fresh arrivals of the 1960s, took menial jobs to start with and mixed with Filipinos in the poorest areas of Honolulu. Filipino-Samoan sections were among the few identifiable ethnic neighborhoods in a city that used to be packed with assorted racial enclaves. In contrast to the mainland, most blacks are not ghettoized. Many of them are families of servicemen, in good quality housing.

The saddest and most perplexing story is that of those whose ancestors once had the Island to themselves, the surviving original Hawaiians. One hears again and again that the Hawaiian, by basic temperament, loves life and believes man is not made to work. He believes things are put here by the Almighty for us to enjoy. The idea of getting out and working and not enjoying life makes little sense—it is, in fact, an alien *baole* idea. As crime problems among younger Hawaiians—including wanton attacks on whites—mounted in the 1970s, Gard Kaeloha, president of the Hawaiian City Club of Honolulu, explained to a reporter: "Hawaiians readily intermarried with Americans, but never embraced the materialism in the American way of life as other groups did. Not liking what they saw, they went back to their little homes and lived off the sea and the land." But in time, he explained, rising taxes on land plots forced Hawaiians into urban areas where "the pressures of modern life promoted social breakdown." Thus Hawaiians began to account for a disproportionate share of the state's destitute families, school dropouts, and children arrested.

Native Hawaiian resentment was fired in the '70s by increasing economic problems and the rise of ethnicity in America, giving fresh credence to ancient resentments about overthrow of the native monarchy and subsequent U.S. annexation in the 1890s. Hawaiians began to demand a greater share of the state's wealth and political power. In 1979 the legislature created an Office of Hawaiian Affairs, to run all programs aimed at helping Hawaiians and to serve as an advocate for Hawaiian rights. The agency was unusual because only citizens with Hawaiian blood could vote to elect its special trustees. Adelaide Frenchy DeSoto, the chairman of the Office of Hawaiian Affairs, summed up the growing sentiment of Hawaiians when she said, "The urgency to revitalize our culture is a matter of life and death. Historically, Hawaiians have welcomed all peoples of the world, and we don't intend to stop now, but somewhere along the line we've been lost in the shuffle." Demands by militants for a return to Hawaiian independence were not given much chance of success—or even support—by the islanders. But Congress in 1975 recognized Hawaiians as among native Americans (like Indians, Eskimos, and Aleuts) and in 1980 established a Native Hawaiians Study Commission to survey lingering problems, including complex land claims and possible reparations. In 1978 the state made the melodic Hawaiian language co-official with English and the teaching of native history, language, and culture mandatory in public schools.

None of Hawaii's latter-day ethnic problems have been serious enough to vitiate the glowing words we heard in 1969 from George Chaplin, editor of the *Honolulu Advertiser.* "Hawaii's greatest strength," he said, "is its people. They have an innate friendliness—perhaps stemming from the Polynesian laissez-faire with a New England ethic laminated onto it. Then you add in Chinese, Japanese, Koreans, and Portuguese from the Azores, and you get a fascinating society. People are proud of their admixture and will tell you they're one-eighth Irish, one-eighth Chinese, etc. It's regarded as an asset rather than something to put behind you." Indeed, intermarriage has created so many Caucasian-Oriental-Polynesian mixes that one expert counted 60 separate strains. The process has been likened to Hawaiian flowers, since there are some hybrids that grow only on the Islands. In such a context, insurmountable racial divisions are hard to imagine.

The Economy: From Feudalism to Tourism

Hawaii's economy grew first on the sandalwood trade, then shifted to whaling, and still later centered around the output of the great sugar and pineapple plantations. With World War II, the federal military role became central; after that, tourism grew by leaps and bounds. For decades, Hawaiian economic power hinged on the feudalistic authority of the "Big Five," a tight-knit group of companies dominating sugar, pineapples and, through those basic industries, the entire economy of the Islands. The companies were held and managed by 30 or 40 families, frequently intermarried, with almost hereditary succession into board chairmanships and presidencies.* Through direct ownership or interlocking directorates, the Big Five were able to control many banks, public utilities, insurance firms, and hotels.

The same oligarchic relationships symbolized by the Big Five pervaded the ownership of land and have never ended. The old Hawaiian kings jealously guarded their ownership of land, and the Big Five and the big estates that seized it in the 19th century never let go either. Of all the land in Hawaii, according to late 1960s figures, the state government owned 38.7 percent; the federal government, 9.8 percent; small landowners, less than 5 percent. The remaining 47 percent was in the hands of only 72 big landowners. Only a quarter of Hawaii's housing units were occupied by people holding title to the land. In the legislature, far-sweeping bills to break up the estates and trusts have been consistently rejected.

The whole issue of leasehold land boiled up in the mid '70s, when the McCandless Estate proposed turning its properties in Oahu's verdant and rustic Waiahole and Waikane Valleys into residential subdivisions. Many of the tenants of small plots in the picturesque windward valley had farmed and

*The Big Five included such sturdy and enduring firms as C. Brewer and Co., founded by a New England sea captain in 1826 and later big in sugar, molasses, insurance, and ranching. Castle and Cooke was started in 1851 by missionaries Samuel Castle and Amos Cooke, who would doubtless have uttered a hearty huzzah if they could have seen how well their offspring was doing by 1981 —owner and operator of Hawaiian sugar and pineapple and macadamia nut plantations, the Philippines' largest coffee producer (among many foreign operations), owner of Bumble Bee Seafoods and Dole Pineapple. But conglomeratization and internationalization have taken a toll. Brewer is now owned by a Delaware-based conglomerate; Castle & Cooke has moved its headquarters to California, as has the biggest of the original five, Amfac (born in 1848 as H. Hackfeld & Co.). Theo H. Davies & Co. is owned by a Hong Kong firm. Only Alexander & Baldwin (a major sugar producer and operator of Matson shipping line) has remained Hawaii-based.

lived there for years. Appealing under Hawaii's state land-use law, the residents successfully blocked rezoning for the subdivision. Then, to make sure rising rents would not force out the farmers anyway, Governor Ariyoshi had the state purchase about 600 acres of land. "Before," Isaac Manalo, a Waiahole Valley resident with six children told us, "I thought the landlord had all the power in the world. Now I know he doesn't."

The Big Five's control of Hawaii's economy and life was twice eroded: first, when the ILWU (International Longshoremen's and Warehousemen's Union) staged, and won, great postwar strikes to organize the sugar and pineapple workers; second, when statehood and the great tourist explosion demanded the building of huge hotels and resort facilities. This was a task before which the Big Five, lacking the requisite managerial talent, flinched. So capital poured in from the outside, with the inevitable dilution of the old clubby patterns of local control. The Big Five did not die economically—far from it. They chose instead to export their skills in land management and agriculture to far-flung corners of the world, profiting immensely therefrom. But the oligopoly in Hawaii was gone forever.

All prior Hawaiian economic activity dimmed, in a sense, compared to the immense tourism boom that soared in the wake of statehood and introduction of direct jet service around 1960. In the next 20 years, Hawaii's population rose 52.5 percent, to the 1980 level of 965,000. Between the late '60s and early '70s one of the most dramatic building booms of American history hit Hawaii, with 30,000 new hotel rooms, 3 million square feet of office space, and some 100,000 housing units. Job opportunities expanded rapidly. Yet all the "progress" involved a price: soaring crime rates (though more of property violation than physical violence), rapidly rising taxes, exacerbation of the already sky-high cost of living, and environmental degradation. Many began to ask whether tourism was being allowed to proceed so rapidly that it could devour the very charms that draw visitors to the "Land of the Golden People" (a phrase coined by the Hawaii Visitors Bureau). The late George Walters, a talented Hawaiian planner, pointed out that the cane and pineapple fields beginning to vanish under spreading asphalt are part of Hawaii's uniqueness. "Why travel," he said, "if it means nothing more than whizzing around in a sealed tourist bus only to sink exhausted in front of a television set in a standard hotel room? We've got to stop paving everything. Modern life demands planning, but at the heart of the plans must be respect for the natural world, the essential mystery of man's fragile survival on this planet that the Orient knows so well."

To those who wanted to limit the tourist influx in an arbitrary way, however, men like Gov. John Burns had a strong counterargument. Addressing the legislature in 1968, Burns dwelt on his theme that "We are a free people . . . we are an open society. . . . We welcome all visitors to our Island home. . . . Provincialism must never get a foothold in these Islands." For modern-day Hawaiians "to be anything but generous and open to all who wish to come here," said Burns, would be to "forsake" the Hawaiian tradition set by its native people who "with supreme generosity risked all they possessed in welcoming Caucasians, Chinese, Japanese, Filipinos, Puerto Ricans, and others to their Islands."

Yet the issue Burns raised, of the right of the world's peoples to visit and enjoy the garden spots of the globe—and the concomitant danger to those places brought by the traffic—was to reappear again and again. Governor Ariyoshi in 1977 complained that the waves of immigration to Hawaii were so overwhelming that the U.S. Constitution should be amended to permit a state to limit the number of new residents it accepts. "Hawaii," said Ariyoshi, "cannot forever endure an accelerating welfare, educational, and housing burden imposed by inequitable and uncontrolled migration"—both from other states and foreign nations. "Uncontrolled urbanization may adversely and irreversibly affect Hawaii's natural beauty and environment," he said. "That degradation would be an irreparable loss." The proposed population limit amendment never received serious consideration. But in 1978 Hawaii expanded its first-in-the-nation land-use plan, enacted in 1961, with a specific state plan specifying growth, no-growth, and slow-growth areas.

Next to tourism, the U.S. military—with immense installations on Oahu and 62,000 personnel stationed in the Islands—is the largest factor of Hawaii's economy. Sugar and pineapple, onetime leaders of the Hawaiian economy, now rank third, with farm employment—a massive 46 percent of Hawaii's work force in 1930—down to less than 3 percent. A world-wide sugar glut of the early '80s caused Hawaiian sugar producers to post heavy losses, and the industry's future was imperiled. Hawaii does produce some other crops: cabbage, lettuce, celery, papayas, mangos, bananas, melons, beef, hogs, for example, and by popular reports immensely valuable quantities of marijuana. But four-fifths of Hawaii's land surface consists of scenic but unproductive mountains, lava flows and semibarren deserts, foreclosed to agriculture. Even fishing—for bigeye scad, jackmackerel, marlin, tuna, and other varieties—is disappointingly small.

Hawaii probably always will be dependent on the U.S. mainland for the vast bulk of its supplies—from basic foodstuffs to gas and oil, from medical supplies to cars and trucks. Under federal law, it all has to come on American bottoms, adding to the inflationary pressures. Shipping strikes can cripple the Islands' economy. Small businesses go under, unemployment rises, goods become scarce, and inflationary pressures are compounded. Against this background, the 1970s brought much talk—but less concrete action—to diversify the Hawaiian economy and foster less dependence on the outside. Ideas ranged from sophisticated aquaculture to flowers, forestry, magnesium, and a tuna cannery. On Kilauea, a pilot electric plant was built to tap the world's hottest geothermal well. Ocean thermal conversion—using the temperate differential between Hawaii's warm surface waters and cold water from adjacent ocean depths—was viewed as a way to reduce Hawaii's overwhelming dependence on imported fuel oil to power electric generators. But despite successful thermal conversion experiments, the Reagan administration in 1981 withdrew federal support for the effort, and there was doubt whether Hawaii —however great the need and promise—would quickly proceed on its own.

Jack Hall, Statehood, Jack Burns

If any person deserves to be called "the father of modern Hawaii," it is doubtless John A. Burns. In the years following World War II, this Montana-born ex-policeman (1) paved the way for acceptance of the Japanese into the Islands' Democratic party, formed ethnically balanced tickets, and master-minded the smashing of the ancient Republican regime; (2) as a Delegate to Congress, plotted the strategy by which Hawaii won its long-sought state-hood in 1959; and (3) three times won election as governor of his Hawaii. Among the secrets of Burns' phenomenal success were a plainness and direct-ness of speech that left no room for doubts, intense loyalty to friends, the classic skills of a consensus-type politician, and a dogged dedication to what it is he believed in, his orbit including the Roman Catholic Church (he attended Mass every morning), racial equality, tourism and more tourism, and Hawaii's role as the center of the Pacific.

As Hawaii emerged from martial law during World War II, it was still ruled by the Republican party, which had held unbroken control of the territorial legislature since 1903 and served largely as an agent of the Caucasian business community. The Democrats had all too often been patronage men waiting for a Democratic president for a few plums. Burns revolutionized all this by reading, quite accurately, the figures showing how many Orientals were becoming naturalized; of course their sons and daughters were Ameri-can citizens by birth. These were the rejected of the Republican regime; Burns determined to take them to the heart of a new Democratic effort. The constant theme of Burns' new Democratic party was the election ticket carefully balanced between Japanese, Filipinos, Hawaiians, Chinese, and *baoles*. But most important of all was the political role given to the Japanese, who yearned for recognition and represented close to a third of the entire voter pool. Labor was brought in to the same house, and in 1954 the Democrats won the territorial legislature for the first time. In 1956 the party finally elected Jack Burns as Hawaii's Delegate to Congress.

In Washington, the debate over Hawaiian statehood was moving into its third arduous decade. Hawaii had had ample opportunity to learn about second-class citizenship: taxation without representation, no protection against sudden abolition of all forms of self-government, presidential appoint-ment of a governor rather than his popular election, and the obvious inability to win from Congress one's fair share of federal money for roads, conserva-tion, or harbors projects. Most of the arguments raised in Congress against Hawaiian statehood were specious cover-ups for the gut issue of race. Opposi-tion was led by Southern Democrats who feared that two Hawaiian senators would weaken their ability to kill civil rights bills, or who looked with some horror on the idea of Oriental colleagues. After that, there was the issue of Communism, stemming from the power in Hawaii of the left-leaning Longshoremen's Union. Senator James Eastland said it was certain that the Islands were "tinctured with Communism." And in the House, conservative New York Republican John Pillion said that giving statehood to Hawaii would be inviting "four Soviet agents to take seats in Congress."*

The pro-statehood arguments, by contrast, were quite simple: It was unfair to keep levying federal taxes on the Islands without representation. The population of the Islands was greater than any other state on admission, except for Oklahoma. Hawaii's people were literate, had proven their patriotism in the crucible of war, and were ready for first-class citizenship. On the question of noncontiguity to the U.S. mainland, Hawaiians could point out that communications were instant and that when Pearl Harbor was attacked, the country had reacted as if Hawaii were indeed already a part of the Union. As the problem of which territory took precedence—Alaska or Hawaii—became an increasingly serious obstacle, Delegate Burns in 1958 opted for an unorthodox maneuver: to let Alaska, even though its population and statehood credentials were inferior to Hawaii's, go first. The ploy worked: Alaska won statehood in 1958, Hawaii the following March 13.

It must have been quite a day in Honolulu. Just after 9:57 A.M., Hawaii time, when the deciding "aye" vote was cast in the U.S. House, William F. Quinn, the territorial governor, went to a telephone booth adjoining the House chamber in Washington and placed a telephone call to Honolulu to relay the news. A two-day holiday was declared. The 52 air-raid sirens on Oahu began to wail. Church bells pealed. Auto horns blew. Ships in Honolulu Harbor sounded their whistles. Honolulu Mayor Neal Blaisdell began to ring the City Hall bell and, his eyes brimming with tears, lighted a 30-foot string of firecrackers. The bells began to ring at Kawaiahao Church, and in front of City hall, the Royal Hawaiian Band began to play "Hawaii Pono'i," the national anthem when Hawaii was an independent nation, now the state song. At the Iolani Palace, someone put an "Out of Business" sign on the door of the Hawaii Statehood Commission.

That fall, Burns was persuaded by fellow Democrats to run for governor. Giving up almost assured election to the U.S. Senate, he agreed—but lost out in the general election to Quinn, a popular Republican liberal. But Burns' day came in 1962 when he was able to coalesce all the ethnic and labor factions friendly to the Democratic party and to win a strong victory. He would remain governor until four months before his death, in 1975. The Democrats have been in clear control of Hawaii ever since Burns' first victory. The state has turned in some of the country's highest Democratic presidential percentages; with few exceptions, the heads of the four island governments, the city council on each island, the two houses of the state legislature, both U.S. Representatives, the governor, and both U.S. Senators have been Democratic. Indeed the Democrats' dominance has been so complete that they have felt free to engage in sometimes vicious factional politics, especially in battles between Governor Ariyoshi, Burns' former lieutenant governor and successor, and Frank Fasi, the mercurial, anti-establishment politician three times elected mayor of Honolulu.

*One wonders how a man or his family must feel when it becomes clear that on the one issue for which history remembers him, he was so abhorrently wrong.

But the Republicans have been unable to capitalize fully on the Democratic divisions. A tremendous Republican disability is its continuing image as the "Haole-Big Five" party, harking back to the socially restrictive plantation economy days. Many Hawaiians—and especially the electorally potent Japanese segment of the population—consider the GOP simply out of step with the labor and social revolution that has swept the Islands.

The groundwork for the rise of labor was set back in 1935 when a young seaman and union organizer named Jack Hall left the SS *Mariposa* in Honolulu Harbor to start organizing the territory's waterfront workers. Hall would never go back to sea again, but he would leave an indelible mark in Hawaiian history. Up to that point, unionism on the Islands had made scarcely any progress. No sooner had Jack Hall arrived than he started a weekly newspaper, *Voice of Labor*, to alleviate workers' fear and create a unified labor movement. In 1944 the International Longshoremen's and Warehousemen's Union (ILWU) made Hall its regional director; soon he had not only organized waterfront workers but was moving through the plantations "like one great canefield fire." By the late '40s Hawaii was wracked by sugar and pine and dock strikes, the ILWU was moving into Democratic politics, and charges were raised—often with solid evidence to back them up —that there were Communists or former Communists, Jack Hall included, in the Hawaiian labor movement. Hall took the Fifth Amendment before the House Un-American Activities Committee when asked if he had ever been a Communist, and in 1953 he was convicted under the Smith Act for conspiring to overthrow the U.S. government by violence and force. Even when Hall and six other Hawaiians saw their convictions reversed, the image of a dangerously radical and unsavory leader persisted and was encouraged by employers.

Yet, as time went on, Hall mellowed. Still a tough negotiator, he nevertheless showed a willingness to relieve some hard-pressed plantation owners of demands he made on the industry in general. Abandoning its bid for outright control of the Democratic party, the ILWU settled back to a more relaxed political game (and with no little success: between 1960 and 1972, for example, no major candidate it endorsed lost an election).

Jack Hall remained a formidable labor leader—once quoted as saying, "Anybody who plays me for anything else is going to get his pants clawed off." In 1969 when Hall finally left the Islands, he bequeathed his successors a virile union of 23,900 workers: 11,000 in sugar, 6,100 in pineapples, 1,600 longshoremen, 3,000 hotel worker, tour guides, and bus drivers, and 2,100 in general trades that ranged from newspapers and bakeries to scrap iron collectors and tuna canners and workers in cemeteries.

In Hawaii today, the ILWU is regarded as a solid part of the establishment. At an Aloha party held to mark Hall's departure, the business and political establishment of Hawaii turned out to honor him. The same day, the once violently conservative *Honolulu Advertiser* said in a full-page editorial that "more than any other man, Hall helped bring industrial democracy to these Islands as they moved from feudalism and paternalism to the sophisticated and broadly affluent society of today." Hall, a man once so hated by the Big Five business establishments that two attempts were made on his life, found it all a little hard to believe.

The Most Progressive State?

Finally, a word about the constitution and laws of the Aloha state. Under the very modern constitution that went into effect with statehood, the Islands have perhaps the most centralized government among all the 50 states. The only elected statewide officials are the governor and lieutenant governor (who run together as a team) and the members of the state board of education. In territorial days there had been 104 separate departments, boards, and commissions; in 1959 the new constitution pared the number down to 20, their heads appointed by and responsible to the governor.

The taxing and spending authority is heavily centralized in the state government, which spends 80 percent of all public funds. (Counties expend the other 20 percent; there are no city governments.) Hawaiians demand a lot of service from government—and they pay for it. Not only must they pay a heavy and steeply graduated personal and corporate income tax, but a general excise tax (including a 4 percent sales tax) that rakes in huge revenues and excludes virtually nothing—neither food nor hotel rooms nor business supplies. Hawaii's "tax effort"—combined state and local taxation in relation to personal income—ranks near the top among all states.

Perhaps the most dramatic illustration of centralization is the school system. Instead of the customary multiplicity of school boards and districts, Hawaii has a single, unitary statewide school district. All schools are under the same financing, the same board of education, the same superintendent of education. No child's opportunity to learn depends on whether he lives in a rich or poor community, since all schools are equally funded on a per capital basis. For the same reason, no sullen taxpayer or eroding local tax base can suddenly undermine one of the schools. There is a price to pay, of course: the loss of local control, since community school councils have advisory powers only.

Another Hawaiian breakthrough is its first-in-the-nation land-use plan, enacted in 1961; still another is the office of state ombudsman, also initiated in the '60s, to handle citizen complaints and try to prevent abuses by public officials and agencies. What makes the Hawaii ombudsman program so impressive is the independence and power given the office. The ombudsman is appointed by the legislature in joint session but then enjoys a six-year term and can be removed from office only by a two-thirds vote of the legislature, and then only for neglect of duty, misconduct, or disability. He can hold hearings, issue subpoenas, and cause fines to be imposed on those who resist his information-gathering activities.

Hawaii has also created an office of legislative auditor, with wide powers to probe the financing, performance, and planning of the state bureaucracy. He and the ombudsman are sometimes referred to around the capitol as "the third house." On a similar plane, the legislature also set up an office of consumer protection, which has wide powers to cope with unscrupulous types who prey on consumers.

A person injured by a crime in Hawaii—or while trying to prevent one—can claim injury compensation of up to $10,000 from the state. But there are limits to Hawaii's governmental generosity. In 1971 the legislature set up a one-year residency requirement for welfare recipients to discourage thousands of young people coming in search of a state-supported holiday on the Islands. Ariyoshi said the bill was needed to stop "welfare hippies . . . who have been flocking to our shores in search of the nearest social welfare office."

What are the forces within Hawaii's legislature propelling it to such liberal and controversial laws? One factor may have been legislative reapportionment, which shifted control from the conservative Neighbor Islands to more liberal Oahu. Related to this may be the liberal outlook of Japanese legislators. Having just "arrived," and with fewer vested positions to defend, the Japanese have decided to make their mark with a program that will make Hawaii a model of progressive legislation. Many *baole* and old Hawaiian and other Oriental groups are supporting a number of the new ideas, of course, but the fact remains that the basic impetus is Japanese. Thus it happens, in one of those odd quirks of history, that the very group so darkly depicted a few years ago as incapable of democratic self-government is building one of the most imaginative records of legislators anywhere in the Union. There could scarcely be a more exemplary state—interracial, governed with broad public consensus, and illustrating yet again the wellsprings of creative strength at the grassroots—with which to end our *Book of America*.

Index

Page numbers in **boldface** refer to main discussions of subjects mentioned on several pages.